Classroom Companion: Economics

The Classroom Companion series in Economics includes undergraduate and graduate textbooks alike. It welcomes fundamental textbooks aimed at introducing students to the core concepts, empirical methods, theories and tools of the field, as well as advanced textbooks written for students at the Master and PhD level seeking a deeper understanding of economic theory, mathematical tools and quantitative methods.

Michael Roos

Principles of Complexity Economics

Concepts, Methods and Applications

Springer

Michael Roos
Department of Management and Economics / Center for Environmental Management, Resources and Energy (CURE) / Chair of Macroeconomics
Ruhr University Bochum
Bochum, Nordrhein-Westfalen, Germany

ISSN 2662-2882 ISSN 2662-2890 (electronic)
Classroom Companion: Economics
ISBN 978-3-031-51435-7 ISBN 978-3-031-51436-4 (eBook)
https://doi.org/10.1007/978-3-031-51436-4

This Springer imprint is published by the registered company Springer Nature Switzerland AG
The registered company address is: Gewerbestrasse 11, 6330 Cham, Switzerland

Acknowledgments

Writing a textbook always requires the help of many people. My first thanks go to Nina Kämmerling and León Tewes, who helped me with the many figures and all the formal issues. Without their support, it would have taken me at least twice as long (or maybe I would not have finished at all). I would also like to thank Sandra Zdunek and Leon Kämmerling for their beautiful illustrations. Many people have provided comments and feedback. Special thanks go to Elias Schmitt, Daniel Pauls, Marion Steven, Lasse Gerrits, and Gerd Schuster, who provided detailed feedback on one or more chapters. I also benefited from many discussions with members of my team, especially Frederik Banning, Michelle Alfers, Florian Lewalder, Marvin Siegmann, Paola D'Orazio, Jessica Reale, Christian Stehr, Christina Timko, Matthias Reccius, and Jan-Hendrik Kamlage. Even when we did not explicitly discuss the book, I often took away many ideas from our conversations. I am very grateful to Margaret Neyenhuys who handles all the administration at my chair in a very professional manner. All the students in my courses "Complexity Economics and Agent-based Modeling," "Macroeconomics and Sustainability," and "Macroeconomics II" that I have taught in the past years helped me to clarify my ideas. Of course, I also received many comments and questions from colleagues at various conferences, seminars, and workshops. Thanks to all of them. I would also like to thank Yvonne Schwark-Reiber and Nico Chtouris from Springer for their very professional and friendly support. Of course, the most important thanks go to my family for their patience when I spent many hours at the computer.

About this Book

> The study of economics does not seem to require any specialised gifts of an unusually high order. Is it not, intellectually regarded, a very easy subject compared with the higher branches of philosophy and pure science? Yet good, or even competent, economists are the rarest of birds. An easy subject, at which very few excel! The paradox finds its explanation, perhaps, in that the master-economist must possess a rare combination of gifts. He must reach a high standard in several different directions and must combine talents not often found together. He must be mathematician, historian, statesman, philosopher – in some degree. He must understand symbols and speak words. He must contemplate the particular in terms of the general, and touch abstract and concrete in the same flight of thought. He must study the present in the light of the past for the purposes of the future. No part of man's nature or his institutions must lie entirely outside his regard. He must be purposeful and disinterested in a simultaneous mood; as aloof and incorruptible as an artist, yet sometimes as near the earth as a politician.
>
> John Maynard Keynes (1924), pp. 321/322

Why Reading This Book?

Do you know the feeling of being bored and frustrated by an economics textbook or lecture? The feeling that all those equations and the talk about equilibria are sterile and light years away from the colorful and fascinating world the economy is a part of. The economy is mind-boggling, but economists reduce it to neat little toy models, often expressed in simple graphs of linear functions intersecting at an equilibrium. What can this kind of economics tell us about disruptive innovation, decision-making in the face of fundamental uncertainty, or societal transformation? The answer is not much.

The world is changing all the time. Sometimes the change is slow and gradual, resulting in economic development or to a shift in norms, values, and institutions. But at other times, the change is abrupt, seems to come out of the blue, and has a profound impact on the lives of many people. Financial crises are such events, which can impoverish many people almost overnight. Moreover, the world is highly interconnected. What happens in one part of the world ripples out to many other places. Sometimes the causal chain between the event and its consequences is quite obvious, as when a cargo ship gets stuck in the Suez Canal and causes shortages in European and U.S. markets.[1] In other cases, the causal links are harder to see, such as how the 2022 record heat wave in China affected the global auto industry.[2] High interconnectedness with opaque causality makes systems difficult to understand, to predict, and to control or, in other words, complex. Complexity arises from the fact (or the perception) that everything is connected to everything else in intricate ways.

Many economists hope to understand the economy by reducing complexity. That's why they build mathematical models that focus on a few factors and mechanisms. But simple models reduce complexity only in our minds, not in reality. The economy will remain complex and difficult to understand, even if we have elegant models that isolate single causal relationships. We cannot reduce the complexity of reality. We can only find better or worse ways to cope with it. Complexity economics provides tools and approaches to adequately account for complexity in the economy.

Complexity economics is both new and very old. Many great economic thinkers such as Adam Smith, Thorstein Veblen, Alfred Marshall, John Maynard Keynes, Joseph Schumpeter, Friedrich August von Hayek, and Herbert Simon were well aware of complexity and were, in effect, complexity economists. Ideas such as the invisible hand, creative destruction, spontaneous order, bounded rationality, and increasing returns, which are well established in economics, are highly compatible with complexity economics and will be treated in this book. Although many of the concepts mentioned are well-accepted in mainstream economics, the complexity approach to economics differs significantly from how most mainstream economists do economic theory. Since the 1950s, it is mandatory in microeconomics to work with abstract deductive mathematical models based on maximization. Since the 1970s, macroeconomics and all other fields as well must be based on the same microeconomic principles. It is the explicit goal of mainstream economics to have a unified body of theory in all economic subfields that applies the same microeconomic principles and the same mathematical tools everywhere. The result is an abstract economic theory with a high degree of coherence and internal consistency.

Complexity economics is different as you will see in this book. It is more eclectic and holistic than current mainstream economics, both in terms of its methods and in terms of its perspectives. While much of mainstream economics takes a microscopic view zooming in on specific mechanisms, complexity economics has a strong interest in the big picture. From a macroscopic perspective, complexity economics tries to connect the dots and to find not only knowledge, but also meaning. The opening quote from John Maynard Keynes suggests that a good (complexity)

---

[1] See the story of the Ever Given that jammed the Suez Canal in 2021, https://www.wired.co.uk/article/ever-given-global-supply-chain.

[2] China was forced to ration electricity, which affected the production of semiconductors and batteries, see https://edition.cnn.com/2022/08/22/business/china-heat-wave-power-cuts-tesla-intl-hnk/index.html.

economist needs to master many different skills: mathematics, history, politics, and philosophy. This breadth of required approaches makes complexity economics fascinating, but also challenging. Keynes (1924) reports that Max Planck, the Nobel Prize-winning physicist who developed quantum theory, had thought of studying economics, but found it too difficult. As Keynes argues, Planck was not intimidated by the mathematics used in economics, but by "the amalgam of logic and intuition and the wide knowledge of facts, most of which are not precise, which is required for economic interpretation in its highest form" (Keynes 1924, p. 333). Keynes and his academic teacher Alfred Marshall developed a methodological agenda that is now considered old-fashioned by most mainstream economists. However, their methodology should not be seen as a sign of their inability to think rigorously by the standard of today's mainstream, but as an adequate way to deal with complexity. Far from being outdated, their approach is highly modern. Marchionatti (2003, p. 49) summarizes their agenda for analyzing complex economic systems as follows:

1. Mathematics is the correct approach only when it is coherent with the properties of the system to be analyzed.
2. The search for general results that hold for all times and every situation—exact generalizations to cover everything—is a "chimera."
3. The quasi-formal style of exposition is often the most appropriate one: it is intended to suggest "the whole bundle of associated ideas."
4. A mixture of intuition, judgments of value, and analytical ability (i.e., trained common sense) is required for dealing with complexity in economics; the ability to constantly amalgamate "logic and intuition and wide knowledge of facts" is the crucial factor in economic interpretation.

One of the main goals of this textbook is to introduce the reader to this approach and to help develop an intuition for complexity and the ability to make judgments. To achieve this, the book differs from most other economics textbooks. It does not aim to teach established truths and a single correct way of looking at the economic world. It is also organized not along economic topics, but around important concepts of complexity. This structure serves to emphasize the complexity perspective. The economic applications presented in the book are not intended to cover all of economics or to provide a complete overview of a subfield such as macroeconomics or microeconomics. Instead, they serve as examples to illustrate why the complexity perspective is relevant. What the reader will learn is a way of thinking that is critical and flexible, which involves both challenging established views and developing new ideas. To some extent, a maverick mindset is necessary to keep pace in our ever-changing world.

It may be unfamiliar to many readers that the book presents many insights and examples from other disciplines. Most economics textbooks do not discuss other fields, even if they are close to economics, such as sociology and political science. Mainstream economics cultivates a splendid isolation in teaching and research that is untenable from a complexity perspective. Complexity economics holds that we cannot understand the economy without considering its connections to other domains of the social world. This is why Keynes believed that the master economist must also be a historian, a statesman, and a philosopher.

But detours into other social sciences and humanities are not enough. Perhaps even more surprisingly, the book also takes the reader into physics, biology, chemistry, information science, and computer science. This very broad approach is the novel aspect of complexity in economics, going far beyond the insights of the great economists before the second half of the twentieth century. Complexity science emerged as a multidisciplinary science in the second half of the twentieth century, with strong origins in modern physics. Today, complexity is a topic in many sciences, and there is hope that complexity theory can provide a common language that facilitates the interdisciplinary exchange of ideas. Since the 1980s, the mission of the Santa Fe Institute in New Mexico has been to bring together open-minded researchers from different disciplines to explore complexity. One of the pioneers was Nobel laureate economist Kenneth Arrow, who in 1987 teamed up with Nobel laureate physicist Philip Anderson to organize a workshop in which economists and scientists discussed the economy as a complex system. W. Brian Arthur, one of those economists, coined the term complexity economics in 1999.

Modern complexity research is closely linked to the computer. Computational methods are common in many fields and have greatly expanded the toolkit of research methods. For this reason, simulation methods such as system dynamics and agent-based modeling are extensively discussed in this book. However, the book cannot provide an intensive technical introduction to these methods, which must be delegated to other textbooks. What the book can do is show how such approaches can be used to gain important insights.

Plan of the Book

Chapter 1 motivates why complexity economics is needed. It characterizes complexity economics as an economic theory of fundamental change and non-equilibrium phenomena. The opening chapter outlines some of the political, technological, scientific, and environmental changes that have occurred over the past 30 years and that will continue to shape our world for the next 30 years. Our world is undergoing fundamental transformations caused, among other things, by climate change and advances in information technology. Unlike mainstream economics, complexity economics views most societal challenges as wicked problems rather than tame problems. Dealing with these wicked problems and the great societal challenges of our time requires twenty-first century skills that can be acquired through the study of complexity economics.

Chapter 2 provides definitions and characterizations of complexity, complexity science, complex adaptive systems, complexity thinking, and the complexity worldview. It is important to define these terms properly to avoid the loose "complexity talk" that has become fashionable in some of the business literature and popular press. Some background on the historical origins of complexity economics is also given. The chapter concludes with some philosophical considerations, particularly on philosophy of science and methodology, and introduces the concepts of complexity that are discussed in later chapters.

Chapter 3 introduces different ways of measuring aspects of complexity. This book is based on the scientific view that measurement enforces precision and links theory to fact. Since complexity is a multidimensional concept, there is no single way to measure it. Many attempts to quantify complexity rely on Shannon entropy from information science, which is explained in detail. How Shannon entropy and other measures can be applied in economics is demonstrated with a number of examples.

Chapter 4 contrasts complexity economics and neoclassical economics. The current economic mainstream is dominated by neoclassical economics. To show that complexity economics is different, it is useful to define neoclassical economics and discuss its main properties. The chapter also presents topics where complexity economics has a clear advantage over neoclassical economics and shows the relationships with other economic schools of thought. Complexity economics emphasizes algorithmic thinking, which explains the heavy use of computational methods, which, along with other methods, are briefly introduced at the end of the chapter.

Chapter 5 explains why the economy is a complex adaptive system and presents a number of examples of a systems view of the economy. The chapter also introduces the concept of economic complexity, which is a useful method for working with high-dimensional economic data. This quantitative approach is complemented by a qualitative account of the history of the automobile as an example of structural economic and societal change caused by technological innovation. In addition, the chapter introduces the multilevel perspective framework from transition theory as a useful tool for thinking about long-term transformations.

Chapter 6 discusses nonlinearity as the first fundamental complexity concept. Many phenomena of interest to complexity science and complexity economics are related to nonlinearity. At the same time, nonlinearity is so pervasive in the natural and social world that it should be considered the normal case. The first part of the chapter provides an introduction to the mathematics of nonlinear dynamics, which serves as background for the rest of the book. In the second part, some exemplary economic models that use this kind of mathematics are presented.

Chapter 7 is about feedback, circular causality, and system dynamics modeling. Circular causality due to positive or negative feedback is a major cause of complexity. When the causality between variables is not linear but circular, we cannot separate causes and effects, which makes it difficult to predict what will happen in a system. System dynamics modeling is an excellent way to analyze the effects of feedback and circular causality. After a thorough discussion of causality, the chapter introduces the basics of system dynamics and presents a number of economic applications.

Chapter 8 focuses on self-organization, which explains the formation of structure without external control. Self-organization is found in physical, chemical, and biological systems. Examples from these disciplines are used to show that self-organization of agents does not require cognition or purposeful behavior. Self-organization is also found in social systems, but with the complication that it interacts with human-designed organization. Several examples of small-scale self-organization in social systems are presented before discussing large-scale self-organization. Hayek's concept of spontaneous order is introduced and compared with the complexity concept of self-organization. The chapter concludes with a detailed discussion of the concept of dissipative systems and dissipative structure, which originated in chemistry but is highly relevant to economics. In terms of methods, the chapter introduces cellular automata and agent-based models as highly relevant tools for complexity economics.

Chapter 9 deals with the difficult topic of emergence. Complexity science is sometimes called the science of emergence, meaning that a system can have properties that are not found in its parts. While self-organization describes the formation of structure at one level of the system, emergence always requires at least two levels. Complex systems are often organized on multiple levels that form a hierarchy. Economics knows the micro level of agents and the macro level of the system, but it can be useful to think of additional levels such as a meso level. From a complexity perspective, the common practice in economics of working with representative agents, which eliminates the difference between levels, is a major fallacy of composition. As an alternative to this practice, the chapter introduces emergent or agent-based macroeconomics.

Chapter 10 takes a long-term view of economic evolution. Evolutionary theory is another important part of complexity economics. It is particularly helpful in explaining the emergence of innovation and new knowledge. The chapter begins with an explanation of evolution in biology and then presents the more general computational view of evolution, of which both biological and economic evolution are instances. It argues why the economy is not like an evolutionary system, but is in fact an evolutionary system. For complexity economics, genetic or evolutionary algorithms are a useful technical tool, along with cultural algorithms, cladistics, and evolutionary systems modeling, all of which are explained. Chapter 10 also discusses the relationship of complexity economics to its sister discipline, evolutionary economics. The chapter concludes with some thoughts on diversity and resilience in systems.

Chapter 11 differs from the previous chapters in that it covers the more qualitative approach of economic history. Complexity economists are convinced that history matters, which means that the economy does not always converge to the same equilibrium regardless of initial conditions. The evolution of the economy is often path dependent, so that small events can lead the economy to one of several equilibria. If this is true, attention to historical detail is important in explaining economic phenomena observed in the present. The chapter also introduces the concepts of lock-in, critical junctures, and punctuated equilibrium. These concepts are illustrated with a narrative account of the history of the automobile. Finally, the chapter shows how some of these concepts can be formally modeled.

Chapter 12 identifies adaptation as the last major complexity concept. Unlike complex systems in physics and chemistry, the economy is a complex adaptive system, meaning that its parts—the economic agents—change their characteristics and behavior over time. To understand adaptation, it is necessary to discuss the behavior and learning of agents, i.e. to adopt a microeconomic perspective. Complexity economics rejects the standard rational choice approach of neoclassical economics in favor of the theoretically and empirically more plausible bounded rationality approach. In this respect, complexity economics overlaps with some branches of behavioral economics. An agent-based model of collective problem solving and social learning is presented to emphasize that behavior has not only an individual but also a social aspect. Moreover, the chapter briefly discusses the link between complexity economics and the recently emerged narrative economics, which highlights the importance of sense-making for economic agents.

Chapter 13 concludes the book by summarizing the top ten lessons for complexity thinking. The relevance of complexity thinking is demonstrated by comparing the neoclassical and complexity approaches to the analysis of climate change. Some thoughts on how complexity economics might contribute to a new economic order and policy follow.

For Whom the Book Is Relevant

Advanced undergraduate economics students are the primary audience for this textbook. The book assumes that the reader has a basic knowledge of economics as taught in standard Principles of Microeconomics and Principles of Macroeconomics courses. Some of the mathematical parts of the book are beyond this level, but this should not be an obstacle to learning the main lessons of the book. As said before, the main goal of the book is to teach a way of thinking rather than how to use formal methods. The book is about economic theory. Modeling skills are important, but the book focuses on motivating why models are useful rather than on how to model.

The book is also written for anyone who wants to know what complexity economics is all about. There are many other excellent introductions to complexity theory and complex systems, but no comprehensive introduction to how complexity thinking can be applied to economics. Most existing introductions, such as Bar-Yam (1997), Mitchell (2009), and Fieguth (2021), take a multidisciplinary approach and/or are rooted in the natural sciences, which sometimes makes it difficult for economists to apply the insights to economic issues. As the research literature in complexity economics has grown strongly in the last two decades, it is not easy for beginners to get an overview and to find a good starting point for their own work in complexity economics. Therefore, the book also aims to provide graduate students and experienced researchers with an overview of important strands in the research literature. In particular, graduate students looking for promising topics and tools can benefit from this book. There is a strong movement toward complexity in many scientific fields, so it is likely that the importance of complexity economics will increase in the future. Complexity economics is largely computational economics. It is hard to imagine that the relevance of computers and algorithms will not increase in the future. An economist who does not use computational methods is like a biologist who prefers the light microscope to the electron microscope.

Mainstream economists or scholars from other economic schools of thought who do not want to do their own research in complexity economics, but who want to understand how complexity economics differs from their own approach, may find the book helpful. Open-minded economists trained in neoclassical theory can learn why this theory is often criticized. Economists from non-mainstream schools, such as institutional economics, evolutionary economics, or ecological economics, can learn where complexity economics overlaps with their approaches. Complexity economics shares many assumptions with these schools, as well as their reservations about neoclassical economics. These economists will find that the differences between their approaches and complexity economics are more in style than in substance.

Finally, the book can make economics more accessible to researchers from other disciplines in the natural and social sciences. Both natural scientists and other social scientists are often taken aback when they first encounter the neoclassical approach. Waldrop (1992) reports on the reactions of physicists to the economists' presentations at the Santa Fe workshop in 1987:

"They were almost too good," says one young physicist, who remembers shaking his head in disbelief. "It seemed as though they were dazzling themselves with fancy mathematics, until they couldn't really see the forest for the trees. So much time was being spent on trying to absorb the mathematics that I thought they often weren't looking at what the models were for, and what they did, and whether the underlying assumptions were good. In a lot of cases, what was required was just some common sense. Maybe if they all had lower IQs, they had been making better models." (Waldrop 1992, p. 140).

"They kept pushing us and pushing us," says Arthur. "The physicists were shocked at the assumptions the economists were making—that the test was not a match against reality, but whether the assumptions were the common currency of the field. I can just see Phil Anderson, laid back with a smile on his face, saying, `You guys really *believe* that?'" (Waldrop 1992, p. 142)

From the perspective of physics, economic models look familiar, but often old-fashioned with rather simple mathematics. Despite economists' admiration or even envy of physics, mainstream economics has remained largely untouched by the developments in physics in the twentieth century. Many of these developments are related to complexity, which has also influenced other disciplines including sociology (Castellani and Hafferty 2009), political science (Cairney 2012), and other social sciences (Byrne and Callaghan 2022). This book shows complexity researchers in other fields that complexity has reached economics, too, and that an interdisciplinary exchange of ideas in a common language is possible.

How to Use It

The book could be used for a one- or two-semester introduction to complexity economics in a BSc or MSc program in economics. Two semesters may be necessary to cover all the material, especially if the theory is complemented by a more in-depth discussion of the methods presented. The theory alone, without practical exercises in agent-based modeling or system dynamics, can be taught in one semester.

Chapter 6 is mathematically more challenging than what is usually taught to undergraduate economics students. The mathematical methods presented there are not necessary for the following chapters, but the insight that nonlinearity is important is. If the nonlinear math in Chap. 6 is too difficult for undergraduate students, some key ideas about nonlinearity can be gleaned from the more accessible Chap. 7.

At present, complexity economics is rarely taught in mainstream economics programs. But economists with a pluralist mindset in these programs may be interested in adding a complexity perspective to their courses. In this case, Chaps. 2 and 4 would serve as a good introduction, and some of the later chapters could be chosen depending on the course. An intermediate microeconomics course might use Chap. 12, while a macroeconomics course might benefit from Chap. 9. Chapters 7 and 8 would be interesting for an environmental economics or ecological economics course, but also for public economics. Innovation economics courses could include Chap. 10.

References

Bar-Yam Y (1997) Dynamics of complex systems. Routledge, London & New York

Byrne D, Callaghan G (2022) Complexity theory and the social sciences. The state of the art. Routledge, London & New York

Cairney P (2012) Complexity theory in political science and public policy. Political Stud Rev, 10(3), 346–358.

Castellani B, Hafferty FW (2009) Sociology and complexity science: a new field of inquiry. Springer Science & Business Media, Berlin

Fieguth P (2021) An introduction to complex systems. Society, ecology, and nonlinear dynamics. Springer Nature, Cham

Keynes JM (1924) Alfred Marshall, 1842–1924. Econ J, 34(135), 311–372.

Marchionatti R (2003) Dealing with complexity: Marshall and Keynes on the nature of economic thinking. In: Arena R, Quéré M (eds.) The Economics of Alfred Marshall: Revisiting Marshall's Legacy, 32–52. Palgrave Macmillan.

Mitchell M (2009) Complexity – A guided tour. Oxford University Press, Oxford

Waldrop MM (1992) Complexity – The emerging science at the edge of order and chaos. Simon & Schuster, New York

Contents

1 **Understanding a Complex World** 1
1.1 Introduction 2
1.2 What Happened in the Past 30 Years? 5
1.2.1 Geopolitical Change 5
1.2.2 Globalization and Economic Crises 8
1.2.3 Advances in Information Technology 10
1.2.4 Advances in Biotechnology 12
1.2.5 Environmental Changes 14
1.2.6 Lessons from the Past 30 Years 20
1.3 A VUCA World 23
1.4 Wicked Problems and Social Messes 25
1.5 What Might Happen in the Future? 27
1.6 What Are Twenty-First Century Skills? 29
1.7 How Can Complexity Economics Help? 32
References 35

2 **What Is Complexity?** 39
2.1 Introduction 40
2.2 Complexity Sciences 42
2.3 Systems 44
2.4 Non-Complex Systems and the Degree of Complexity 48
2.5 Complex Systems 50
2.6 Complex Adaptive Systems 53
2.7 Complexity Thinking and the Complexity Worldview 55
2.8 Complexity Concepts 61
References 68

3 **Measurement of Complexity** 71
3.1 Introduction 72
3.2 Patterns 74
3.3 Complexity and Information 79
3.3.1 Information 81
3.3.2 Information Theory 81
3.3.3 Shannon Entropy 84

3.4 Complexity of Patterns 87
3.4.1 Entropy and Patterns 87
3.4.2 Permutation Entropy 90
3.4.3 Statistical Complexity 94
3.5 Complexity of Systems 97
3.5.1 Measurement of System Complexity 98
3.5.2 Structural Complexity 100
3.5.3 Functional Complexity 103
3.5.4 Cyclomatic Complexity 105
3.5.5 Organizational Complexity 107
3.5.6 Objective and Subjective Complexity 109
References 113

4 Complexity Economics 115
4.1 Introduction 116
4.2 What Is Economics All About? 117
4.3 Neoclassical Economics 119
4.3.1 A Market Model with Rational Expectations 120
4.3.2 The Ramsey–Cass–Koopmans Model 124
4.4 Complexity Economics 129
4.4.1 Complexity Economics and Neoclassical Economics 131
4.4.2 Complexity Economics and Other Schools of Thought 137
4.5 Methods of Complexity Economics 140
4.5.1 Nonlinear Dynamics and Chaos 140
4.5.2 System Dynamics 142
4.5.3 Agent-Based Modeling 143
4.5.4 Social Network Analysis 143
4.5.5 Scenario Analysis 144
References 145

5 The Economy as a Complex Adaptive System 147
5.1 Introduction 148
5.2 Systemic Views on the Economy 149
5.3 Economic Complexity 157
5.3.1 Combination of Specialized Knowledge 158
5.3.2 Measurement of Economic Complexity 160
5.3.3 Empirical Results 167
5.4 The Automobile and Dynamic Complexity 172
5.5 A Conceptual Framework for Socio-technical Transitions 179
5.6 Things to Remember 181
References 182

6 Nonlinearity 183
6.1 Introduction 184
6.2 Dynamical Systems 188

6.2.1 Differential Equations and Difference Equations 188
6.2.2 Dynamics of One-dimensional Continuous-time Systems 190
6.2.3 Dynamics of Two-dimensional Continuous-time Systems 194
6.2.4 Lotka–Volterra Population Models 203
6.2.5 Bifurcations 208
6.2.6 Catastrophes 213
6.2.7 Iterated Maps 215
6.2.8 Logistic Map and Chaos 217
6.2.9 Lyapunov Exponent 223
6.3 Business Cycles and Financial Instability 225
6.3.1 The Goodwin Model of Business Cycles 225
6.3.2 Great Moderation and Financial Crisis 228
6.3.3 Minsky's Financial Instability Hypothesis 229
6.3.4 Keen's Basic Minsky Model 230
6.3.5 Keen's Minsky Model with Money Creation 232
6.4 Nonlinear Expectation Formation and the Business Cycle 237
6.4.1 Modified Multiplier–Accelerator Model 237
6.4.2 Properties of the Model 238
6.5 Nonlinearity in Economics 241
6.5.1 Applications of Nonlinearity 241
6.5.2 Empirical Evidence 245
6.5.3 Nonlinearity and Economic Worldviews 246
References 249

7 Feedback, Circular Causality, and System Dynamics 253
7.1 Introduction 254
7.2 Unintended Consequences 256
7.3 Causality in the Social Sciences 262
7.3.1 Explanation by Reasons, Causes, and Processes 262
7.3.2 Types of Causes 266
7.3.3 Modeling Causal Mechanisms 271
7.3.4 Causality in Economics 273
7.4 Feedback and System Dynamics 275
7.4.1 Feedback 275
7.4.2 Causal Loop Diagrams 277
7.4.3 Modes of Dynamic Behavior 280
7.4.4 Stock-flow Diagrams 289
7.4.5 System Dynamics Models 293
7.5 Infection and Diffusion 297
7.5.1 The SIR Model 297
7.5.2 Sentiment and Narratives 301
7.5.3 The Bass Diffusion Model 304

7.6 Dynamic Decision-making and Oscillations . . . 307
7.6.1 Stock Management Control Problems . . . 308
7.6.2 The Beer Distribution Game and the Bullwhip Effect . . . 309
7.6.3 System Dynamics Model of the Beer Distribution Game . . . 314
7.7 Collapse . . . 319
7.7.1 Exploitation of Renewable Common-pool Resources . . . 320
7.7.2 Collapse of Civilizations . . . 327
7.8 Causal Complexity . . . 331
References . . . 335

8 Self-organization . . . 339
8.1 Introduction . . . 341
8.2 Cellular Automata and Agent-Based Models . . . 343
8.2.1 Cellular Automata . . . 343
8.2.2 Agent-Based Models . . . 345
8.3 Self-Organization in the Natural World . . . 348
8.3.1 General Characterization . . . 348
8.3.2 The Ising Model from Statistical Physics . . . 349
8.3.3 A Cellular Automaton of a Chemical Oscillator . . . 354
8.3.4 An Agent-Based Model of Flocking Birds . . . 356
8.4 Self-Organization in the Human World . . . 359
8.4.1 Spatial Patterns . . . 360
8.4.2 Temporal Patterns . . . 363
8.4.3 Functional Patterns . . . 364
8.5 Models of Self-Organization in the Social Sciences . . . 368
8.5.1 Simple Contagion . . . 368
8.5.2 Social Influence and Complex Contagion . . . 372
8.5.3 Segregation and Spatial Organization . . . 376
8.5.4 Self-organized Industrial Symbiosis . . . 379
8.6 Spontaneous Order . . . 384
8.6.1 Hayek on Spontaneous Order . . . 384
8.6.2 Hayek's Theory and Complexity Economics . . . 388
8.7 The Economy as a Dissipative Structure . . . 390
8.7.1 Thermodynamic Equilibrium and Entropy . . . 392
8.7.2 Dissipative Structures . . . 396
8.7.3 Dissipative Structures in Nature . . . 398
8.7.4 The Fourth Law of Thermodynamics . . . 401
8.7.5 Relevance for Economics . . . 407
References . . . 415

9 Emergence, Levels, and Hierarchy . . . 419
9.1 Introduction . . . 420
9.2 Levels and Hierarchies . . . 424

9.2.1 Hierarchies in the Social World 428
9.2.2 Levels in the Economy 429
9.2.3 Fallacy of Composition and Representative Agents 435
9.3 Emergence 441
9.3.1 Weak Emergence 443
9.3.2 Strong Emergence 448
9.4 Macrofoundations of Microeconomics 450
9.4.1 Downward Causation 451
9.4.2 The Emergence Paradigm in Sociology 452
9.4.3 Multiple Equilibria and Indeterminacy 456
9.5 Institutions in Economics 457
9.5.1 New Institutional Economics 458
9.5.2 Traditional Institutional Economics 459
9.5.3 A Model of the Emergence of Norms 463
9.6 Emergent Macroeconomics 468
9.6.1 The Flaws of Neoclassical Macroeconomics 469
9.6.2 The Generative View to Macroeconomics 471
9.6.3 Stylized Facts 473
9.6.4 An Agent-Based Business Cycle Model 475
9.6.5 Other Agent-Based Macro Models 485
References 490

10 Economic Evolution, Novelty, and Diversity 495
10.1 Introduction 497
10.2 Novelty 500
10.2.1 Some Theoretical Considerations on Novelty 500
10.2.2 A Short History of Technical Inventions 502
10.3 Evolution as Process and Theory 507
10.3.1 Theory of Evolution 508
10.3.2 Genetic Algorithms 512
10.3.3 Fitness Landscape 517
10.3.4 Virtual Creatures 521
10.3.5 Cultural Evolution 524
10.4 Coevolution of Behaviors and Social Institutions 529
10.5 The Economy as an Evolutionary System 534
10.5.1 Evolution as Computation 537
10.5.2 Economic Evolution 539
10.5.3 Evolutionary Economics and Complexity Economics 542
10.6 Evolution of Knowledge 543
10.6.1 Knowledge of an Individual Person 544
10.6.2 Knowledge of an Organization 547
10.7 Evolution of Social Technologies 549
10.7.1 Cladistic Classification 549
10.7.2 Evolutionary Systems Modeling 551

10.8 Diversity . . . 558
10.8.1 Kinds of Diversity . . . 558
10.8.2 Framework for Analyzing Diversity . . . 563
10.8.3 Diversity, Complexity, and Coping with External Stress . . . 567
References . . . 576

11 History and Path Dependence . . . 581
11.1 Introduction . . . 582
11.2 Historical and Ahistorical Economics . . . 585
11.2.1 Economic Thinking vs. Historical Thinking . . . 585
11.2.2 The Arrow of Time . . . 591
11.2.3 Historical Economics . . . 593
11.3 Path Dependence . . . 596
11.3.1 Negative Definition of Path Dependence and Ergodicity . . . 597
11.3.2 Positive Definition of Path Dependence . . . 600
11.3.3 Reasons for Path Dependence . . . 601
11.4 Lock-in . . . 610
11.4.1 Some Examples of Lock-in . . . 611
11.4.2 Responses to the Liebowitz–Margolis Critique . . . 614
11.4.3 Types and Causes of Systemic Lock-in . . . 616
11.5 Path Formation and Path Change . . . 619
11.5.1 Critical Junctures . . . 619
11.5.2 A Framework for Path Formation . . . 621
11.5.3 Punctuated Equilibrium and Path Changes . . . 622
11.6 The History of the Automobile in the Twentieth Century . . . 627
11.6.1 Was the Gasoline-Fueled ICE a Good Choice? . . . 627
11.6.2 Decisive Factors for the Choice of the ICE . . . 629
11.6.3 Positive Feedback and Path Stabilization . . . 632
11.7 Modeling Future Transitions of the Automobile . . . 633
11.7.1 Model . . . 634
11.7.2 Application to Sustainable Road Transport . . . 636
References . . . 641

12 Adaptation, Learning, and Behavior . . . 647
12.1 Introduction . . . 648
12.2 Modes of Behavior and Learning . . . 652
12.2.1 Modes of Behavior . . . 653
12.2.2 A Conceptual Model of Consumer Behavior . . . 655
12.2.3 Types of Learning . . . 659
12.3 Rational Behavior and Maximization . . . 660
12.3.1 What Makes Decisions Difficult . . . 660
12.3.2 Computational Complexity . . . 663

12.3.3 As-if and Approximation 666
12.3.4 Example of Intertemporal Utility Maximization 668
12.4 Behavior and Learning of Boundedly Rational Individuals 670
12.4.1 Heuristics and Biases 673
12.4.2 Fast and Frugal Heuristics 676
12.4.3 Learning 681
12.5 Cultural Adaptation and Imitation 685
12.6 Collaborative Problem-solving and Social Learning 690
12.6.1 Collaborative Problem-Solving 691
12.6.2 Social Learning 694
12.7 Sense-making and Narratives 698
References 705

13 Conclusion: What Does it all Mean? 709
13.1 Introduction 710
13.2 Ten Lessons for Complexity Thinking 710
13.3 Why Does it Matter? 716
13.4 The Complex Economy and Complexity Economics 723
References 728

Index 731

Understanding a Complex World

1

Contents

1.1 Introduction 2
1.2 What Happened in the Past 30 Years? 5
  1.2.1 Geopolitical Change 5
  1.2.2 Globalization and Economic Crises 8
  1.2.3 Advances in Information Technology 10
  1.2.4 Advances in Biotechnology 12
  1.2.5 Environmental Changes 14
  1.2.6 Lessons from the Past 30 Years 20
1.3 A VUCA World 23
1.4 Wicked Problems and Social Messes 25
1.5 What Might Happen in the Future? 27
1.6 What Are Twenty-First Century Skills? 29
1.7 How Can Complexity Economics Help? 32
References 35

Abstract

This chapter motivates why complexity economics is needed. It characterizes complexity economics as an economic theory of fundamental change and non-equilibrium phenomena. The opening chapter outlines some of the political, technological, scientific, and environmental changes that have occurred over the past 30 years and that will continue to shape our world for the next 30 years. Our world is undergoing fundamental transformations caused, among other things, by climate change and advances in information technology. Unlike mainstream economics, complexity economics views most societal challenges as wicked problems rather than tame problems. Dealing with these wicked problems and the great societal challenges of our time requires twenty-first century skills that can be acquired through the study of complexity economics.

M. Roos, *Principles of Complexity Economics*, Classroom Companion: Economics,
https://doi.org/10.1007/978-3-031-51436-4_1

Keywords

Twenty-first century skills · Change · VUCA · Wicked problems

Guiding Questions

- Why do we need complexity economics?
- What is the context in which complexity economics emerged?
- Why is transformation the hallmark of our time?
- What does "end of history" mean and has it actually been reached?
- What lessons can we learn from the history of the past 30 years?
- What does VUCA mean?
- How do wicked problems differ from tame problems?
- What is a singularity in mathematics and how does this relate to complexity?
- What are twenty-first century skills?

1.1 Introduction

Our world is complex and confusing. Every day we are confronted with occurrences that we do not really understand. We may be puzzled by how other people behave, we marvel at how a small seed can grow into a beautiful flower, or we wonder why our bodies develop allergies against certain foods. We are surrounded by technical equipment that we can use, but which we cannot fix if it does not function properly. And, of course, we often resign when we try to understand what is going on in the political and economic world.

In everyday language, *complexity* means that something has many different parts and is difficult to understand, analyze, or find an answer to. *Complex* is often used with the meaning of being very complicated or difficult. Complexity is hence related to our ignorance, lack of understanding, and also the feeling of being overwhelmed. We are confused, if we cannot discern the reason why something happened or if we cannot explain why something happened at all. Another source of confusion is when things develop in a different way to what we expected. This is related to the problem that we cannot predict what will happen in a certain situation or what the consequence of our own actions will be. And finally, confusion arises when we have the choice among too many options that we cannot evaluate properly.

Being exposed to phenomena that are difficult to understand is nothing new. The inability to understand the world always was a driver of human development, as humans seem to have an inherent desire to understand their world and feel a need for explanations. Before the advent of science, myths and religion provided explanations for many questions. In prehistoric times, religion and early science mixed, for example in ancient Egypt or Mesopotamia, where astronomers systematically watched the movements of stars and planets. Their ability to predict the position of celestial bodies was important for fixing religious festivals and structuring time. Puzzlement and the desire to know have been the engines of knowledge production. If complexity was only related to our subjective feeling of puzzlement, the situation today would not be much different from what it was for our ancestors. However, complexity also has objective characteristics that we can measure. The world actually *is* more complex today than it was in the past and it will become ever more complex in the future.

Ironically, although we have the most advanced scientific system today, our ignorance has also never been greater. While we published less than one million scientific papers per year before 1980, the number of publications in more than 34,000 active peer-reviewed journals exceeded seven million in 2014 (Fire and Guestrin 2019). According to UNESCO, the number of full-time researchers worldwide increased by 21% from 2007 to 2013 and by another 13.7% through 2018. The current number of researchers worldwide is about 8.8 million. From 2014 to 2018, global expenditure on science increased by 19% (Schneegans et al. 2021). The explosion of scientific output is amazing, but it also creates problems because it is hard for individual researchers to keep track of all the new research. In 2021, nearly 35,500 articles appeared in economics journals. 2155 dealt with economic growth, 1267 with monetary policy, and 1073 with inflation.[1] If you wanted to read all the articles published on monetary policy in 2021, you would have to read 3.5 articles a day. But there is also a deeper problem with the huge production of scientific results. After the tremendous scientific progress of the first half of the twentieth century, skepticism about science as a producer of knowledge emerged in the 1980s, because science produces at least as much ignorance as it does produce new knowledge. Whenever researchers discover something new, they also generate new questions and find out what they do not yet know. Every scientific study transforms *unknown unknowns* into *known unknowns*.

Scientific progress has created new methods that allow us to see more complexity and to create more complexity. The technological capabilities of the modern world, developed over the past 200 years, have transformed the planet in unprecedented ways. But technology has a Janus face. On the one hand, it makes it possible to sustain a global population of nearly 8 billion people, many of whom enjoy a level of wealth and well-being beyond that of kings and emperors of old. On the other hand, it is undeniable that modern technology has the power to destroy much of human life on Earth. The use of fossil fuels has caused dangerous climate change, but nuclear weapons remain the greatest threat. On January 24, 2023, the Science and Security Board of the Bulletin of Atomic Scientists moved the hands of its *Doomsday Clock* forward by 10–90 s to midnight. Even during the Cold War, it was never so close to midnight. Moreover, synthetic fertilizers, pesticides, and other chemical substances contribute to the mass extinction of species and harm human health.

[1] Numbers from Clarivate Web of Science (2021), retrieved on December 28, 2021. Category economics.

Remarkably, the technologies whose consequences threaten us today are based on physics and chemistry and were developed many generations ago. The large-scale use of fossil fuels originated in the eighteenth century, major breakthroughs in chemistry such as the Haber–Bosch process for the production of ammonia occurred in the late nineteenth and early twentieth centuries, and the atomic bomb was developed in the 1940s. It can be argued that today's most important innovations are based on information technology, biotechnology, and their combination. In this book, *Homo Deus: A Brief History of Tomorrow*, historian Yuval Noah Harari (2016) suggests that we now have the opportunity to create a superior human race, or homo deus, by combining powerful computer technology with our new ability to modify the genetic code. While Harari warns of the dangers of this enterprise, transhumanist thinkers believe that technologically enhanced humans or posthumans are a logical consequence of human progress. They welcome this development and see themselves in the tradition of the Enlightenment.

Given the fundamental advances in physics and also in biology with the discovery of DNA and its manipulation in the twentieth century, it is a natural question to ask which science will be the leading science in the twenty-first century. In a newspaper interview in 2000, the popular theoretical physicist Stephen Hawking did not favor either physics or biology, but predicted that the twenty-first century would be the century of complexity (Hawking 2000). Of course, Hawking did not mean that our century will be the century of mystery and incomprehension, but the century of *complexity theory* or *complexity science*.

This book introduces the basic concepts of complexity science and how they can be used in economics. While the complexity sciences have their origins in the 1940s and 1950s—especially in the mathematics of complexity, systems theory, and cybernetics—complexity theory began to influence economics in the late 1980s at the Santa Fe Institute (SFI), where researchers from many different disciplines met in order to explore the principles of complexity. The Nobel Prize-winning economist Kenneth Arrow was instrumental in bringing together ten economists and ten physicists at the SFI, where he initiated the influential 1987 meeting "The Economy as an Evolving, Complex System." Arrow was one of the researchers who brought general equilibrium theory to the forefront of economics. Together with Gérard Debreu he proved the existence of general equilibrium (also called Walrasian equilibrium) under fairly general conditions in the Arrow–Debreu model of competitive economies. Nevertheless, Arrow was fascinated by the idea of *non-equilibrium economics* and encouraged the economists working at the SFI to develop ideas on how to do economics without relying on the concept of equilibrium. In 1999, W. Brian Arthur, who was one of the pioneering economists working in the SFI research program on non-equilibrium economics, coined the term *complexity economics* (Arthur 1999).

Complexity economics and complexity theory can provide a fresh perspective on economic issues. Using the tools of complexity economics, such as agent-based models, system dynamics models, network models, or evolutionary models, we can address issues that are intractable in equilibrium models. But more importantly, complexity economics offers not only new tools for analysis but also a different worldview and a different framework for thinking about the economy. Complexity economics offers a new theory that can provide new insights and alternative interpretations of the available empirical evidence. It is therefore an alternative or complement to the *neoclassical economics* that currently dominates mainstream teaching and research. If you have been taught economics in a standard economics program anywhere in the world in the last few decades, chances are high that you have been trained in neoclassical economics, even if it was not called that.

This chapter provides some context from history and science theory that is important for assessing the potential and relevance of complexity economics. First, we look back 30 years in history and describe the major changes that have led to an increase in the complexity of the world. These developments are reflected in the increasing popularity of the management buzzword *VUCA* and the widespread recognition that most problems in planning and public policy are *wicked problems*. While we cannot know what will happen in the future, we can be sure that the world will change significantly. Students will need to acquire different skills than previous generations of students, so-called *twenty-first century skills*. The chapter concludes with a discussion of why complexity economics can help develop twenty-first century skills.

1.2 What Happened in the Past 30 Years?

When we reflect on the human life, it is natural for us to think about it in terms of generations. A familial generation usually counts about 30 years such that a normal life roughly spans three generations—childhood and youth, midlife, and old age. In many industrialized countries, 25–30 years is the average age of the mother at the birth of her first child.

The last 30 years have been a time of enormous political, technological, scientific, environmental, cultural, and economic change. Of course, the world has always been changing, but many social scientists believe that a fundamental shift began in the early 1990s. Some say that *postmodernity* began in 1991 and that we now live in an *information society* that has led to a significant acceleration of social change (e.g., sociologist Hartmut Rosa or anthropologist Thomas Hylland Eriksen). Postmodernity is the cultural condition of society after *modernity*. It is characterized by increased diversity and choice of lifestyles and identities, the merging of cultures, increased uncertainty, the emergence of hyperreality, disbelief in metanarratives, and a loss of trust in experts. To understand what all this means, it is helpful to outline the major events of the past 30 years.

1.2.1 Geopolitical Change

The new era began with the fall of the Iron Curtain and the Berlin Wall in 1989, which led to the dissolution of the Soviet Union in 1991 and the disintegration of the Eastern Bloc. The collapse of the communist Soviet Union and its allies ended the

Cold War, which, despite the constant threat of nuclear annihilation of the planet, was a period of relative geopolitical stability. Above all, it was an era of simplicity, for the world was divided into only three worlds. The First World was the capitalist West, led by the superpower USA, and included the members of NATO, Western-aligned countries such as Israel, Japan, or South Africa, and some neutral European countries such as Austria or Sweden. The Second World consisted of the superpower Soviet Union, its Warsaw Pact allies, and other communist countries such as China and Cuba. The poor countries of the Third World in Africa, Asia, and Latin America were not aligned with either the capitalist West or the communist East, but both blocs tried to gain influence over these countries and were involved in proxy wars, such as in Vietnam or Afghanistan. The collapse of the communist world was a great triumph for the Western world, not only politically but also intellectually. Many Western thinkers believed that history had vindicated them, and the political scientist Francis Fukuyama (1989, 1992) even declared the *end of history* in an essay and a famous book published in 1992. Fukuyama and others believed that Western liberal democracy and market capitalism had proven superior to any alternative political-economic system. It would be the only viable system in the long run, ending human history as a dialectical struggle between ideologies and systems. In this view, liberal democracy is the end point of humanity's ideological evolution.

At first, the 1990s seemed to support these beliefs. Russia radically transformed its economy with sweeping reforms, privatization, and market liberalization. In addition to the transition to capitalism, the countries of Central and Eastern Europe adopted Western-style democratic systems. Modern *globalization* entered a new phase after World War II, as political restructuring opened up many markets to Western companies, allowing them to take advantage of low production costs. Globalization was also aided by the creation of the World Trade Organization in 1995, which was established to facilitate international trade and impose new internationally agreed rules on trade between nations.

With the end of the Cold War, however, came a series of hot wars involving Western nations. In 1990, Iraq, a former ally of the Soviet Union, invaded Kuwait, sparking the first Gulf War in 1991, in which the USA led a coalition of 35 nations in driving Iraq out of Kuwait. While Iraqi dictator Saddam Hussein remained in power, the victorious coalition imposed severe economic sanctions on Iraq, which had serious repercussions. In Europe, the former Yugoslavia disintegrated as Croatia, Slovenia, Macedonia, and Bosnia and Herzegovina declared their independence. From 1991 to 2001, the region was plagued by a series of wars, ethnic conflicts, and insurgencies, including NATO airstrikes against Bosnian Serbs in the 1995 Bosnian War. Among many other wars and conflicts in the 1990s, the most notable was the Afghan Civil War of 1996–2001, during which the Taliban conquered about three-quarters of the new Islamic State of Afghanistan created in 1994. While the so-called Northern Alliance tried to defend the Islamic State of Afghanistan and was supported by Russia, Iran, Turkey, and the USA, among others, the Taliban established the Islamic Emirate of Afghanistan and received support from Pakistan, Saudi Arabia, the United Arab Emirates, and Qatar.

Another political turning point was the 9/11 terrorist attacks against the USA by 19 members of the militant Islamist organization al-Qaeda. The leader of al-Qaeda, Osama bin Laden, declared a holy war against the USA, to which US President George W. Bush responded by declaring a war on terror. Among the motives for the 9/11 attacks, bin Laden cited the sanctions against Iraq and the US military presence in Saudi Arabia, home to Islam's holiest sites. Whether or not al-Qaeda actually intended to provoke a US war against Islamic countries in order to unite them, the US response to the terrorist attacks led to the war in Afghanistan (2001–2021), the Second Gulf War against Iraq (2003–2011), the intervention of the US and its allies in the Syrian civil war (2014–present) against the militant group Islamic State, and many other conflicts in Africa and Asia. The result of these wars and the additional revolutions in many Arab countries, the so-called Arab Spring of 2010–2012, was a significant destabilization of many countries in North Africa and the Middle East.

Today's political world is more complex than that of the 1980s for other reasons as well. While Russia struggled economically in the 1990s and searched for its global role, it regained political power in the 2000s under Vladimir Putin. More and more often, Western countries and Russia found themselves in covert or overt conflict, such as after Russia's annexation of Crimea, its support for the Syrian government, or its alleged meddling in US and European elections or the Brexit referendum. The provisional endpoint of this development was Russia's invasion of Ukraine in February 2022. In the ensuing war, NATO supported Ukraine, while China more or less openly supported Russia.

Turkey and Iran emerged as regional powers, often at odds with the West, although Turkey remains a member of NATO. China rose from a poor country to a political and economic power challenging the global leadership of the USA in the twenty-first century. In Europe, the 1990s and 2000s were marked by the deepening and broadening of European integration. With the Maastricht Treaty in 1992, twelve countries established the European Union, which grew to 28 member states with the accession of Croatia in 2013. Shortly thereafter, in 2016, the UK decided to leave the EU again, which occurred in 2020. Currently, there are serious conflicts between the older EU countries and the four countries of the Visegrád Group, the Czech Republic, Hungary, Poland, and Slovakia. Hungary and Poland, in particular, have right-wing governments that often oppose EU laws and initiatives. But it is not only in these newly democratized countries that liberal democracy is under pressure. Even in old democracies like the UK, the USA, or France, populist or anti-liberal right-wing movements are strong. The election of Donald Trump who severely damaged the democratic discourse, because he made it acceptable to deny facts and contested the 2020 election result just to remain in power, shows the vulnerability of old democracies to populists. All these political developments since the 1990s seriously challenge Fukuyama's thesis of the *end of history* and the final victory of liberal democracy. History will continue, but it is unclear what the world will look like after the end of Russia's war on Ukraine and rising tensions between the West and China.

The fall of the Berlin Wall on November 9, which triggered the chain of revolutions in Eastern Europe, was not the only significant event of 1989. On June 4, 1989, the Chinese army crushed the Chinese democracy movement in the

Tiananmen Square massacre. The violent response to the protests marked the end of the Chinese liberalization process of the 1980s, strengthened the Communist Party, and suppressed further democratization in China to this day. Interestingly, the violent defense of communism in China may have contributed to the collapse of communist states in Europe. Communist Party leaders in the German Democratic Republic (GDR) applauded the Chinese leaders for restoring order and spoke of the "Chinese solution" to the democratization movement. For many GDR citizens, this was a sign that their communist leaders were unwilling to reform the system, triggering both mass flight and mass protest that ultimately brought down the communist regime. Despite voiced support, the GDR regime did not use force to end the protests, nor did the Soviet troops garrisoned in East Germany. Given that the opening of the East German border on November 9 occurred in a disorganized and chaotic manner, there may be a strong element of luck in the fact that European history took a different course than China's.

1.2.2 Globalization and Economic Crises

The economic development was in some ways similar to the political one. In the early 1990s, there was a strong belief that liberal democracy, market capitalism, and economic prosperity were interdependent and mutually reinforcing. Global real GDP per capita grew by about 85% between 1990 and 2018, from about 8200 to 15,200 international dollars (Maddison data, Bolt & Luiten van Zanden 2020). However, it is no longer so clear that democracy and market capitalism are necessary and sufficient conditions for long-term growth and that growth generally leads to democratization. First, China is no more democratic today than it was in 1990 and has a largely unfree economy according to the Heritage Index of Economic Freedom. Yet its GDP per capita has grown faster than that of the USA. China improved its GDP per capita by a factor of nearly 4.4, from $2900 in 1990 to $13,100 in 2018. The 1990s saw strong anti-globalization protests in Western countries. Some protesters feared the loss of jobs and the dismantling of social security systems in rich countries due to increased international competition. Others opposed the growing power of corporations and the national and international inequalities resulting from *turbo-capitalism* or *casino capitalism*.

Financial deregulation and the creation of global financial markets are part of globalization. During these years, several financial and economic crises occurred, such as the Asian financial crisis in 1997, the first Russian financial crisis in 1998, the Argentinean economic crisis in 1999–2002, the economic crisis in Turkey in 2000–2001, the global financial and economic crisis in 2007–2009, the European sovereign debt crisis in 2010–2014, and the second Russian financial crisis in 2014–2016. These crises caused much economic and social hardship in the affected countries. More than 10 years after the global financial crises, monetary policy remains unconventional. The EU debt crisis has crippled economic growth in many EU countries, and GDP per capita is no higher today than it was in 2007. In many Western countries, however, inequality has increased since 1990 (see

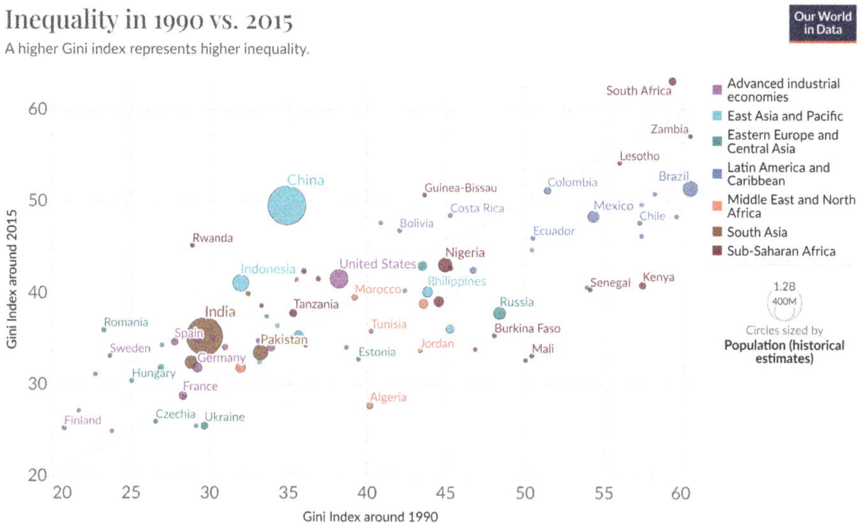

Fig. 1.1 Evolution of inequality. Source: Our World in Data (2023), based on data by Atkinson et al. (2017), Kanbur and Wang (2017), World Bank (2018). CC BY 4.0 (https://creativecommons.org/licenses/by/4.0/)

Fig. 1.1). There is evidence that economic crises and the austerity policies that often follow undermine public confidence in governments and the financial sector and lead to the rise of populism. More generally, political scientists and some economists, such as Dani Rodrik, attribute the rise of populism in many countries at least in part to the effects of globalization.

Several of the aforementioned characteristics of postmodernity can be linked to the economic development of the last 30 years. First, the economic crises created uncertainty and shattered confidence in smooth economic development. This experience of economic instability is associated with a loss of trust in experts, especially economists. In 2003, Nobel laureate Robert Lucas declared that the study of depressions was no longer a macroeconomic priority because the problem of depression prevention had been solved. Not only did many economists fail to predict the financial crisis of 2007/2008, they were not even able to imagine that such a crisis could happen. Moreover, many economists underestimated the impact of globalization and the offshoring of jobs on manufacturing regions in the USA and the UK. *Incredulity towards metanarratives* (Lyotard 1984) was the key element of postmodernism as described by the French philosopher Jean-François Lyotard in 1979. This means that the great stories that cultures told themselves in the era of modernity have lost credibility. A key element of modern metanarratives is the notion of history as a progression toward social enlightenment, progress, and emancipation. The Marxist meta-narrative was abandoned in 1991, but the liberal meta-narrative of social and economic progress is no longer universal either. Possible reasons for this disillusionment could be the increase in inequality in many Western countries since the 1980s, but also the increasingly obvious destructive effects of the Western lifestyle on the natural environment. As a consequence of the end of metanarratives, postmodern theorists like Lyotard see postmodernity as an age of multiple small narratives, fragmentation, and pluralism of worldviews.

1.2.3 Advances in Information Technology

The Internet, and mobile access to it through smartphones and other mobile devices, has changed our lives more than any other innovation in the past 30 years, and probably much longer. While the Internet began as a network of computers at universities and research institutes in the 1960s, it became available for personal and commercial use in 1989. The first web browser, *WordWideWeb*, was created in 1990, but the breakthrough that popularized the Internet was the *Mosaic* browser, released in 1993. Similarly, the first email was sent in 1971, but its mass use depended on the popularity of the Internet.

Today, it is estimated that between 4.3 and 5 billion people—at least 54% of the world's population—are active Internet users. Milestones in the Internet's popularity have been the creation of companies that are now among the world's largest corporations: Amazon in 1994, Google and Tencent in 1998, Alibaba in 1999, Baidu in 2000, Facebook in 2004, and YouTube in 2005. Another important step was Apple's launch of the iPhone, the first mass-market smartphone, in 2007.

The Internet has had a profound impact on almost everything we do. It has changed how we communicate, how we work, how we date, how we shop, how we spend our leisure time, how we get information about the world, and how we get educated. In 2021, about 320 billion emails were sent and received every day, with about 50% of them being spam. In 2021, according to a global survey, Internet users aged 16–64 spent 7 h a day on the Internet, including 2.5 h using social media and about 1.25 h playing video games. In 2020, users uploaded 500 h of new videos to YouTube every minute. In November 2021, the English version of Wikipedia contained 6.4 million articles with about 4 billion words, the equivalent of 33,201 GB or 3000 volumes of the Encyclopaedia Britannica. It is not only the sheer volume of information available that has a dramatic impact on how we perceive the world, but also the instant access from almost every corner of the planet. The Internet has expanded choice and reduced transaction costs. With a Spotify subscription, users have instant access to 70 million songs (June 2021) across a wide variety of genres. Amazon sells over 75 million products (March 2021). Including the Amazon Marketplace, users have access to 353 million products, many of which are delivered the next day, often on the same day the order is placed. By comparison, Macy's Herald Square in New York City, one of the world's largest department stores, offers about one million products on a typical day.

The flood of information and the huge opportunity of choice has been dubbed *information overload*, *infoxication*, or *information explosion*. Information overload means that the information available to us exceeds our ability to process it, thus impairing our ability to make good decisions. In addition, the Internet has made it possible to interact with any other Internet user in real time at almost no cost. While the expansion of social interaction is very attractive to many people, it has also created the phenomenon of *fear of missing out* (FOMO), which has been linked to psychological disorders such as depression and anxiety. A consequence of information technologies, but also of other technological developments in the past, is the acceleration of life, which many people find unhealthy and unnatural.

Along with the growth in connectivity and availability of information, there has been a tremendous increase in computing power. From 1990 to 2020, the number of transistors on microchips increased by a factor of about 20,000. In 1997, the computer Deep Blue became the first to beat an active world chess champion. In 2016, the computer program AlphaGo achieved a similar success in the more difficult game of Go. A year later, AlphaGo's development team reported that the software AlphaGo Zero was able to beat AlphaGo 100:0 after three days of self-learning without human data. Today, artificial intelligence is better than any human at chess and Go and performs similarly to humans at classifying images or recognizing handwriting. Humans are still better than AI at object, face, and speech recognition, and at performing manual tasks, but it's probably only a matter of time before computers and robots outperform humans in these areas as well. The first two-qubit quantum computer capable of performing computations has been created. In October 2019, Google Quantum AI reported that it had achieved *quantum supremacy*, which is practical proof that a quantum computer can solve a complex problem that a conventional computer cannot solve in a reasonable amount of time. Since then, governments and private companies have been investing heavily in the commercialization of quantum computers. Artificial intelligence reached a new level of public interest and applicability with the launch of ChatGPT, a chatbot developed by OpenAI, in November 2022. By January 2023, it had gained more than 100 million users, making it the fastest growing consumer application in history to date. Since it is listed as a co-author in several research papers (Stokel-Walker 2023) and its updated version GPT-4 was able to pass many educational exams (Varanasi 2023), it seems necessary to rethink education and research.

The combination of networked computers, massive computing power, new hardware, and powerful algorithms has created new realities. At first glance, one might think that the new information technology is being used to represent and simulate the real world. Representing real-world objects in a digital format is called *digitization*. Images and sounds can be stored and transmitted as digital signals. We can also store information about people on computers and use simulations to mimic how real-world processes evolve over time. Simulations can be used to learn how real systems behave and to analyze the effects of interventions. They are also useful for training purposes or for identifying optimal policies. Importantly, simulations are created to be valid representations of the real-world system. However, there are also digital representations of people—or digital twins—that are not necessarily exact clones of their real-life counterparts. Whatever we do on the Internet leaves a digital trail that is analyzed by algorithms of private companies and sometimes governments. Companies collect and analyze data to assess the preferences of potential customers, their creditworthiness, or the health status of employees or insurance applicants. Algorithms influence the jobs we get, the medical treatment we receive, the insurance we get, and whether we are convicted in court. Even former Google executive Eric Schmidt and Jared Cohen, CEO of Google's offshoot Jigsaw, openly admit that digital twins can be quite different from their real-world counterparts and can severely impact lives through discrimination and virtual honor killings (Schmidt and Cohen 2013).

Algorithms can inadvertently create biased representations of reality, but there are also efforts to augment reality with virtual elements—that is, to intentionally blend the real and virtual worlds. A step further, companies are designing virtual realities for entertainment that are intentionally different from the real world. Virtual reality can include environments and people that do not exist but appear to be real. The illusion of reality is already very high today and will become even higher in the future. French philosopher Jean Baudrillard published his book *Simulacra and Simulation* in 1981, in which he discussed hyperreality as a condition of technologically advanced postmodern societies (Baudrillard 1994). While a *simulation* either represents reality or mixes it with new virtual elements, a *simulacrum* is not a copy of something real, but a sign or image that has no relation to any reality. Simulacra create their own reality and can even shape the real world, for which the metaphor of the map forming the territory is used. Drastic examples of simulacra influencing reality are people who undergo plastic surgery to look like a virtual ideal. *Snapchat dysmorphia* is a term coined in 2018 for patients who ask plastic surgeons to transform them so that they look like the filtered images of themselves on Snapchat or Instagram. Valeria Lukyanova and Justin Jedlica became famous for plastic surgeries that transformed them into a human Barbie doll and a human Ken doll. Japanese model and YouTuber Vanilla Chamu spent more than $100,000 on more than 30 surgeries to look like a French doll.

1.2.4 Advances in Biotechnology

The past 30 years have also seen great advances in biological research. They have paved the way for new technologies and applications in health and nutrition that have the potential to improve the quality of life for many people in the twenty-first century. Major global problems related to human disease and the environmental impact of meat production could be solved with new biotechnologies. But advances in genetic engineering also make many people uncomfortable because of the power to systematically manipulate and create life. Let's look at some of the milestones in biotechnology research.

In 1990, the Human Genome Project was launched, a government-sponsored research project by 20 universities and research centers in seven countries to completely identify and map the human genome. The project was declared complete in 2003. Today, genome sequencing is commonplace. While the cost of sequencing the human genome was $95.26 million in 2001, it will cost only $454 in 2021 (see Fig. 1.2).

The first US patent for tissue-engineered meat for human consumption was granted in 1991. The first cultured beef burger patty was created in 2013 after

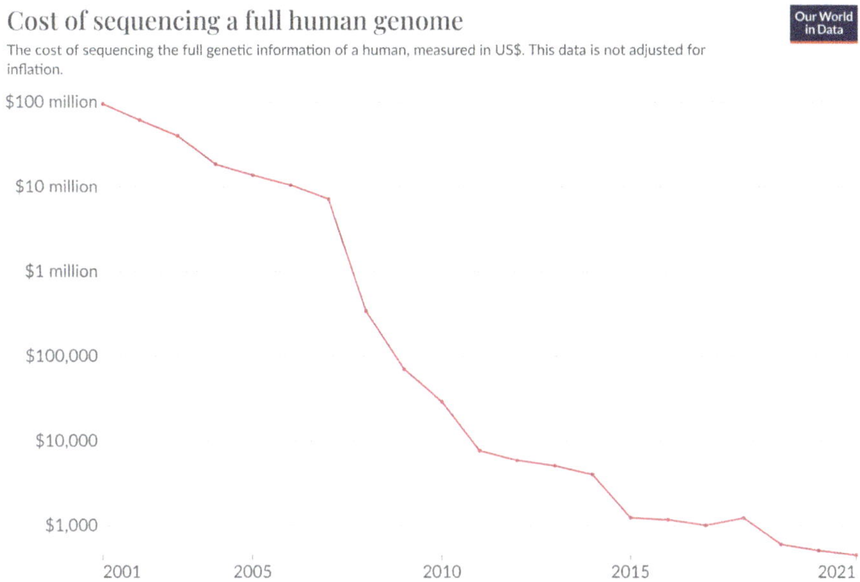

Fig. 1.2 Cost decrease of human genome sequencing. Source: Our World in Data (2022a), based on data by Wetterstrand (2022). CC BY 4.0 (https://creativecommons.org/licenses/by/4.0/)

2 years of production and a cost of $300,000. It took until 2020 for the first commercial pilot plants to open. The US company Eat Just first sold cultured meat to customers at a restaurant in Singapore in 2020.

A major event in genetic engineering was the approval for sale of Flavr Savr, the first genetically modified or transgenic tomato. It was developed by the US company Calgene to slow down the ripening process, giving the tomato a longer shelf life. Although it was a commercial failure, it ushered in the era of genetically modified foods. Today, genetically modified corn, soybeans, canola, and rice are both common and controversial. While there is scientific consensus that the crops themselves do not pose a risk to human health, there are concerns about their impact on ecosystems. They may affect natural plants in unexpected ways. In addition, an important genetic modification is to make the crops resistant to herbicides and pesticides, the overuse of which harms biodiversity.

The famous sheep Dolly became the first cloned mammal in 1997. Other large mammals cloned later included pigs, horses, and bulls. Perhaps more importantly, the cloning of adult animals led to advances in stem cell research. In 1998, human stem cells were isolated and cultured for the first time. Stem cell therapy has the potential to treat serious diseases such as leukemia, heart disease, and brain and spinal cord injuries.

In 2012, the first use of CRISPR/Cas gene editing was reported. The so-called genetic scissors are a revolutionary tool for manipulating biological systems. Science magazine called it the breakthrough of the year, and in 2020 Emmanuelle Charpentier and Jennifer Doudna were awarded the Nobel Prize in Chemistry for

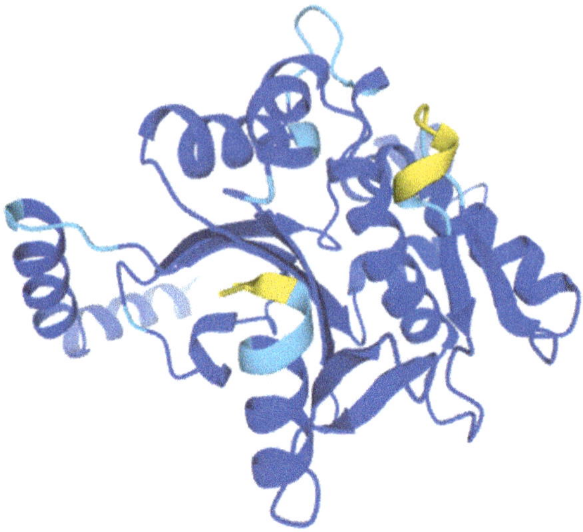

Fig. 1.3 3D structure of DmBCA protein from *Drosophila melanogaster* predicted by AlphaFold. Source: AlphaFold (2021), Wikimedia Commons

their research on CRISPR/Cas and genome editing. According to Nature (2021), "it is clear, however, that the discovery of these genetic scissors has been monumental, and the contributions to science and society in general will be realized for a long time to come."

Finally, there has been a significant process of protein engineering, in which useful proteins can be designed and produced either by so-called *rational protein design* or by *directed evolution*, which mimics the natural evolutionary process of selection. The mRNA vaccines developed in 2020 against SARS-CoV-2 are an application of RNA therapeutics using methods to induce protein synthesis in cells. The first studies documenting the successful transfection of designed mRNA into cells date back to 1989 and 1990. A major problem in protein research is the *problem of protein folding*. The chains of amino acids that make up proteins spontaneously fold into complex three-dimensional structures that are important for the biological functions of proteins (see Fig. 1.3). Predicting protein structure is an extremely challenging scientific task because of the combinatorial complexity involved. In 1994, the Critical Assessment of Protein Structure Prediction (CASP) was launched, a worldwide experiment or competition to test prediction methods. In 2018 and 2020, the AI software AlphaFold, developed by Google's subsidiary DeepMind, won the 13th and 14th CASP competitions, which is considered a major achievement in computational biology.

1.2.5 Environmental Changes

Global environmental policy began with the United Nations Earth Summit (United Nations Conference on the Human Environment) in Stockholm in 1972, the year the famous Club of Rome report Limits to Growth was published. However, the Stockholm Earth Summit was only a partial success because it was boycotted by the Soviet Union and many Eastern Bloc countries. Rich Western countries such as the USA, Britain, France, and Italy attended, but tried to dilute the impact of the conference for economic reasons. The new world order after the end of the Cold War was a new opportunity for international agreements on sustainable development, leading to the 1992 Earth Summit in Rio de Janeiro (United Nations Conference on Environment and Development). The Rio Earth Summit was considered a great success and resulted in three major legally binding international agreements: the Framework Convention on Climate Change, the Convention on Biological Diversity, and the UN Convention to Combat Desertification. The Climate Convention led to the 1997 Kyoto Protocol and later to the 2015 Paris Climate Agreement. So there was reason to be optimistic about the environment in the early 1990s.

Unfortunately, actual developments over the past 30 years have dashed these hopes. In 2009, a group of Earth system and environmental scientists published an influential article in the journal *Nature* on planetary boundaries, which define a safe operating space for humanity in what were originally nine environmental dimensions (Rockström et al. 2009). Crossing these boundaries could lead to catastrophic consequences for humanity due to abrupt, nonlinear responses of the Earth system to human activities. The original article reported that the three boundaries—climate crisis, nitrogen cycle, and biodiversity loss—had already been crossed in 2009. In 2023, six boundaries were transgressed (Richardson et al. 2023). So how have ecosystems changed since the early 1990s?

It is now widely accepted that human-induced climate change is in full swing. The global atmospheric concentration of CO_2 is projected to increase from 354 ppm in 1990 to 421 ppm in 2022, which is 50% above pre-industrial levels. As a result, the global temperature is about 1.1 °C higher than before the Industrial Revolution. About half of this increase has occurred since the early 1990s. We can see many consequences of climate change today. Figure 1.4 shows the loss of ice in the Arctic Ocean since 1978. Melting ice at the poles and disappearing glaciers have caused sea levels to rise by about 7 cm since 1990.

Another consequence of climate change is the increase in the number and size of wildfires in many countries. Figure 1.5 shows that the number of acres burned in a given year in the USA has increased in recent decades.

The state of the oceans has also deteriorated. Plastic pollution of the oceans has received a great deal of public attention. Figure 1.6 shows that the amount of macroplastics in the surface ocean has increased by a factor of six since 1990, and the increase in the amount of microplastics has been even greater.

But other developments are even more worrying. The oceans are absorbing CO_2 from the atmosphere, lowering their pH, a process called acidification. Since 1990, the average pH of seawater has dropped from 8.11 to about 8.05. Ocean acidification is often called the evil twin of global warming because it harms calcifying organisms such as corals, shellfish, algae, and mollusks, as well as fish larvae. All of these organisms form complex food webs, the disruption of which can lead to the collapse of marine ecosystems. There are other reasons for the collapse of marine ecosystems. A famous example is the collapse of the North Atlantic cod stock in 1992 due to overfishing (see Fig. 1.7) after 500 years of cod fishing. The proportion of global fish

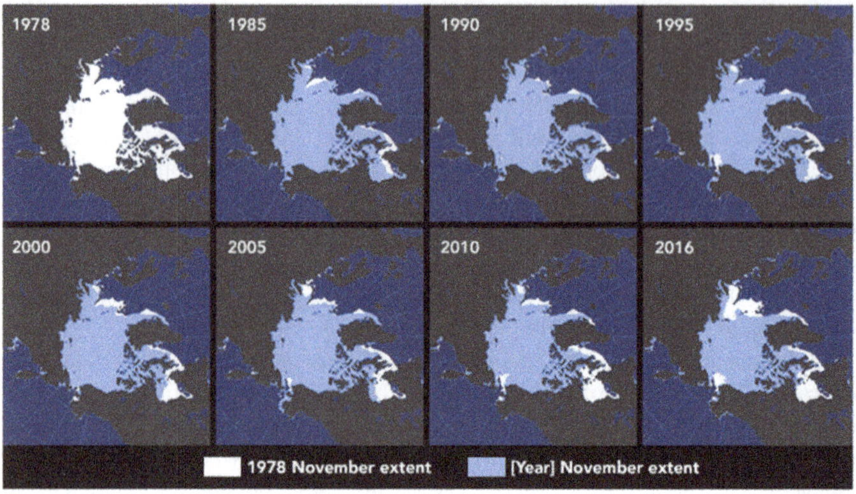

Fig. 1.4 Ice loss in the Arctic sea. Source: NASA Earth Observatory images by Joshua Stevens (2016), using data from the National Snow and Ice Data Center. Caption by Kathryn Hansen

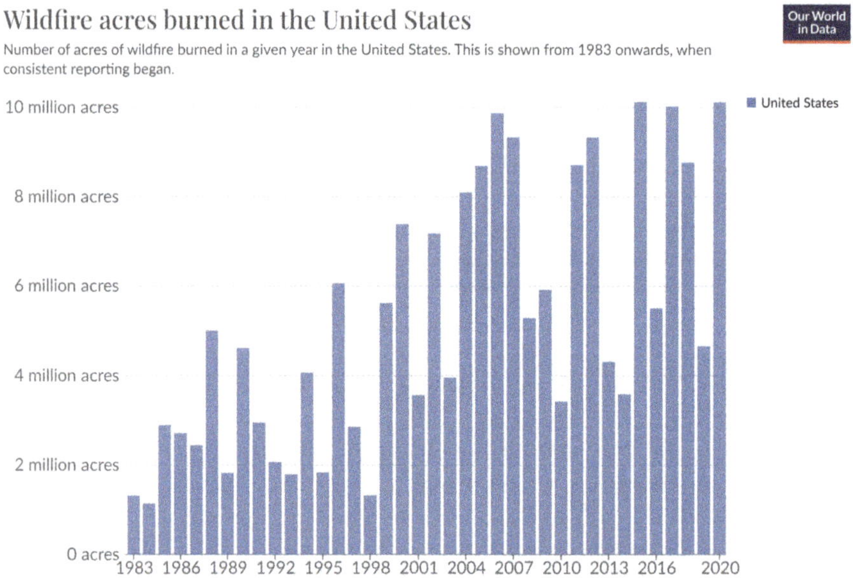

Fig. 1.5 Wildfires in the USA. Source: Our World in Data (2018), based on data by National Interagency Fire Center (2018). CC BY 4.0 (https://creativecommons.org/licenses/by/4.0/)

stocks that are overexploited by fishing has risen from about 20% in 1990 to about one-third today.

Marine life is also threatened by the use of synthetic fertilizers in industrial agriculture, which end up in the ocean and cause eutrophication. Eutrophication is

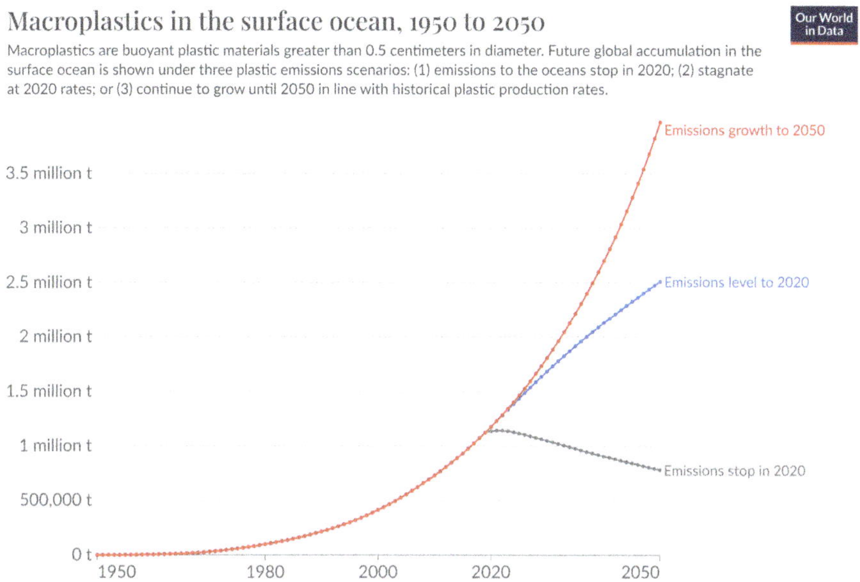

Fig. 1.6 Plastics in the ocean. Source: Our World in Data (2019), based on data by Lebreton et al. (2019). CC BY 4.0 (https://creativecommons.org/licenses/by/4.0/)

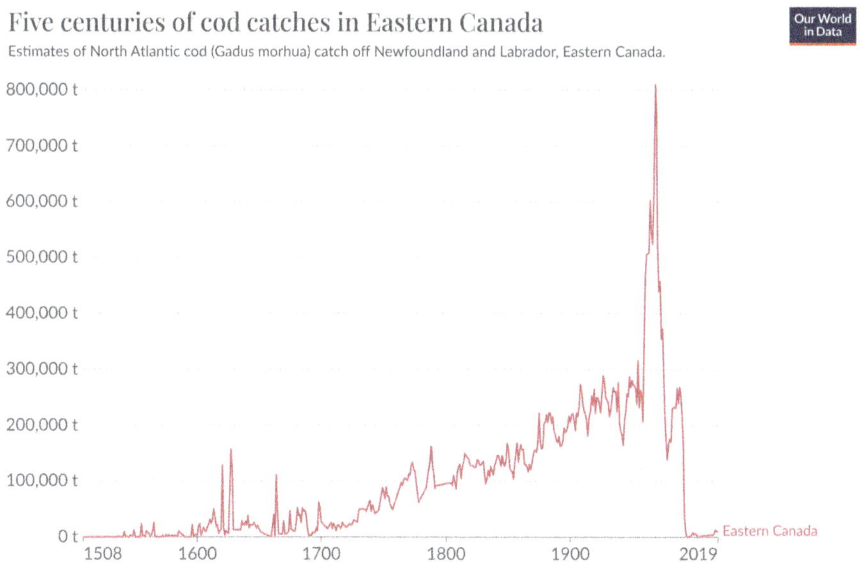

Fig. 1.7 Collapse of cod fishery in the North Atlantic. Source: Our World in Data (2021), based on data by Schijns et al. (2021). CC BY 4.0 (https://creativecommons.org/licenses/by/4.0/)

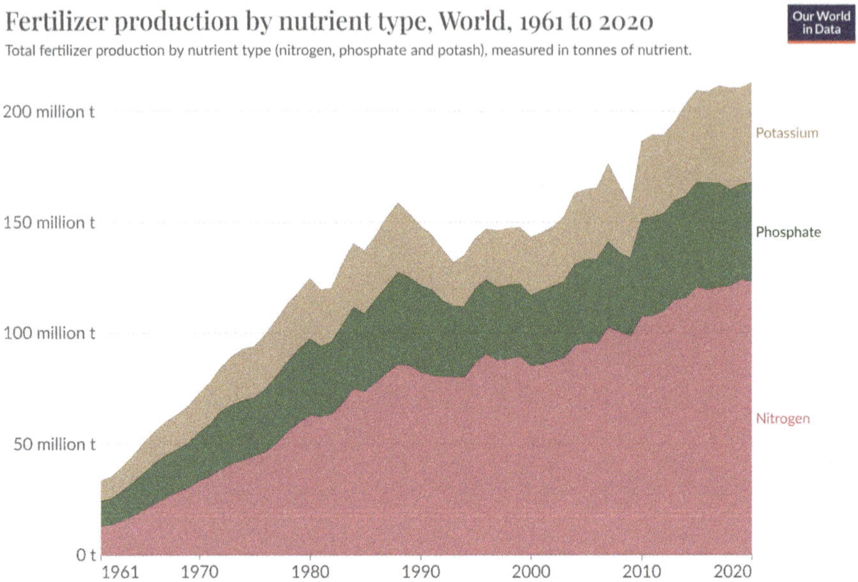

Fig. 1.8 Production of fertilizers. Source: Our World in Data (2022b), based on data by Food and Agriculture Organization of the United Nations (2022). CC BY 4.0 (https://creativecommons.org/licenses/by/4.0/)

the enrichment of water with nutrients, which first leads to algal blooms and later to oxygen depletion as bacteria break down the algae. This oxygen depletion creates marine dead zones where marine life cannot survive. The number and size of marine dead zones has doubled every decade since the 1970s. While a 2008 study in Science reported about 400 dead zones worldwide (Diaz and Rosenberg 2008), more than 500 coastal ecosystems are now affected by dead zones. Heavy use of fertilizers, especially phosphate and nitrogen fertilizers, continues to increase, as shown in Fig. 1.8.

Biodiversity loss is not just happening in the oceans. In February 2021, the UK government published a review of the economics of biodiversity led by Sir Partha Dasgupta—the so-called Dasgupta Review. The report found:

> Collectively, however, we have failed to manage our global portfolio of assets sustainably. Estimates show that between 1992 and 2014, produced capital per person doubled, and human capital per person increased by about 13% globally; but the stock of natural capital per person declined by nearly 40%. … Biodiversity is declining faster than at any time in human history. Current extinction rates, for example, are around 100–1,000 times higher than the baseline rate, and they are increasing. Such declines are undermining Nature's productivity, resilience and adaptability, and are in turn fuelling extreme risk and uncertainty for our economies and well-being. The devastating impacts of COVID-19 and other emerging infectious diseases – of which land-use change and species exploitation are major drivers – could prove to be just the tip of the iceberg if we continue on our current path. (Dasgupta 2021, p. 1)

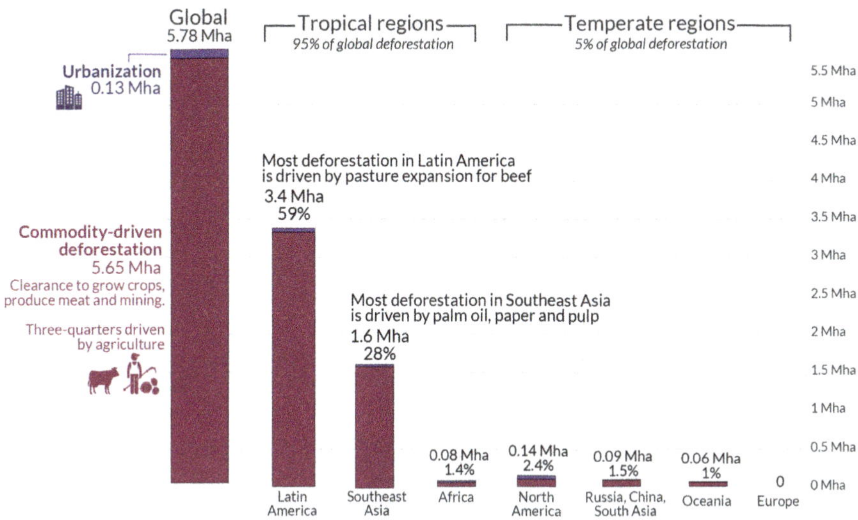

Fig. 1.9 Causes of global deforestation. Source: Ritchie (2021), based on data by Curtis et al. (2018). CC BY 4.0 (https://creativecommons.org/licenses/by/4.0/)

For Germany, the so-called Krefeld study (Sorg et al. 2013) from 2013 and a reanalysis from 2017 (Leather 2018) report a decline in insect biomass of about 80% from 1989 to 2016, which may be due to intensive agriculture. Agriculture and related land-use changes are also the main driver of global forest loss (Fig. 1.9).

A dramatic example of human-induced ecosystem collapse resulting from the complex interaction of land-use change, intensive agriculture, water mismanagement, and climate change is the disappearance of the Aral Sea since the 1960s. The Aral Sea was the fourth largest lake in the world and an important factor in the ecosystem and local economies of Central Asia. By 1997, it had shrunk to 90% of its original size. Figure 1.10 shows how it changed from 1989 to 2014. One of the reasons for the shrinkage was the irrigation of the desert to grow cotton, melons, rice, and cereals.

One of the human impacts of ecosystem collapse and associated biodiversity loss is the increase in outbreaks of zoonotic and vector-borne diseases such as COVID-19. Figure 1.11, taken from a recent study (Morand and Lajaunie 2021), shows a strong correlation between infectious disease outbreaks and deforestation from 1990 to 2016. But it is not only the loss of natural habitats that contributes to epidemics. There is also a link with the loss of biodiversity caused by reforestation and plantations of oil palm, for example.

Fig. 1.10 Shrinking of the Aral Sea from 1989 to 2014. Source: Wikimedia Commons, NASA Collage by Producercunningham (2014)

1.2.6 Lessons from the Past 30 Years

What can we learn from recent history? The past 30 years teach us three important lessons: (1) fundamental change is pervasive, (2) the world is more complex than ever before, and (3) we cannot separate economic issues from their political, technological, social, and environmental context.

Since 1990, our world has undergone fundamental political, technological, social, environmental, and economic changes. The changes have not been incremental in the sense that we now have more democracy, more computer power, more GDP, and less biodiversity. The changes have been qualitative and have transformed the world so that it is different today. We now have a multipolar world instead of a bipolar one, with many democracies threatened by post-truth populism. The Internet, smartphones, social media, and the algorithms associated with them have radically changed the way we live and created new realities. Some ecosystems have collapsed and are unlikely to recover within human time horizons. True, there have always been fundamental changes brought about by technological and social innovation. But what is different today is the pace of change. Disruptive innovations seem to

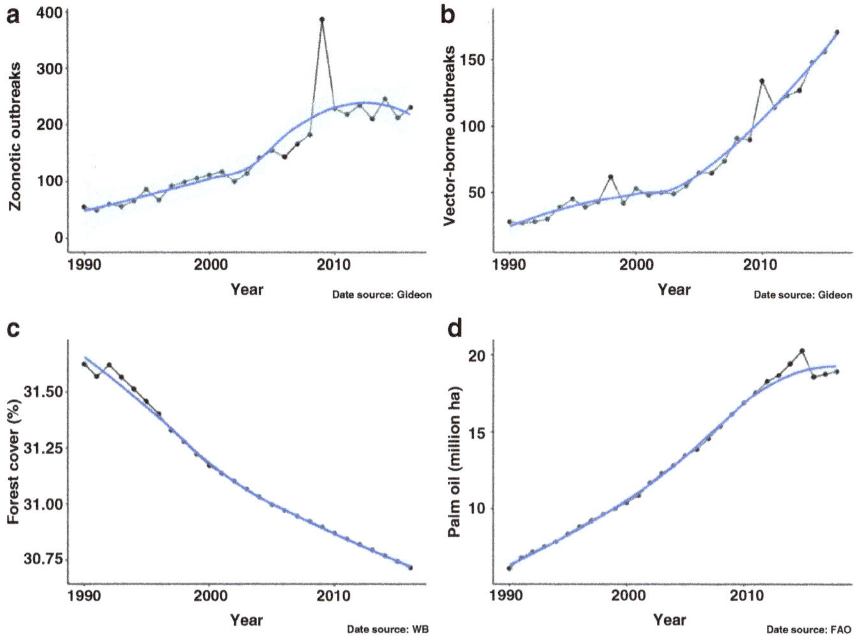

Fig. 1.11 Outbreaks of infectious diseases and deforestation. Source: Morand and Lajaunie (2021). CC BY 4.0 (https://creativecommons.org/licenses/by/4.0/)

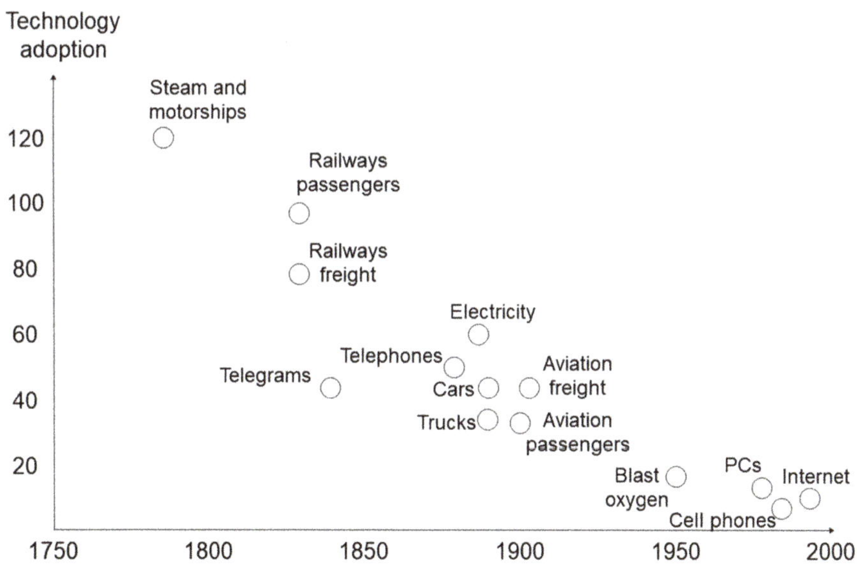

Fig. 1.12 Duration of adoption of new technologies. Source: Comin and Hobijn (2010), reproduced with kind permission of the American Economic Review (copyright owner American Economic Association)

occur more frequently than before, and the adoption of new technologies has also accelerated (see Fig. 1.12). Many technological changes are cumulative and synergistic, reinforcing each other and potentially leading to even faster and more radical change in the future. The symbiosis of computer technology and biotechnology is a prime candidate.

In what sense has complexity increased? As already mentioned, complexity has a subjective and an objective dimension. Especially the experienced acceleration of life in general, all kinds of events and crises, and information overload make it difficult to find the time to reflect on what is happening. Yet deep reflection is necessary to gain a sense of understanding. We will specify the objective dimension of complexity later in the book, but for now it is sufficient to say that the changes of the past 30 years have increased the interconnectedness of agents, the quantity and variety of lifestyles, worldviews, and products, the amount of information available, and the speed with which new information is generated. In addition, the organization of global society and the distribution of power among various private and public actors have changed. On the one hand, power is more widely distributed among different actors. On the other hand, many more individual actors have more technological and economic power to cause major crises. Today, eight states are known to have nuclear weapons, and Israel is believed to have them. Other states, such as Iran and Saudi Arabia, are believed to be pursuing nuclear weapons. In early 2022, Apple became the first company whose market value reached $3 trillion, which was more than the 2021 GDP of France, which ranked seventh in the list of countries by GDP. In November 2021, Elon Musk became the first person with an estimated net worth of more than $300 billion, which is equal to the 2021 GDP of Finland (44th among countries).

It should be obvious that all these important developments are also economic issues. They are both caused by economic forces and have economic consequences. The collapse of the communist bloc had economic causes, such as national debt, low productivity, and consumer dissatisfaction with the quality and availability of consumer goods. The various financial crises from the 1990s to the 2010s are clearly economic problems. Private capital and corporations fueled the success of the Internet and information technology, which created new business opportunities and disrupted old business models. Most environmental problems have economic roots, either in the overexploitation of natural resources or in the excessive pollution of the natural environment with waste from production and consumption. The economy is also affected by political, technological, social, and environmental changes because they change the environment in which economic activity takes place. Political changes have enabled globalization, which has created global financial networks and global supply chains. As the COVID-19 pandemic demonstrated, this global economy has become highly vulnerable to shocks. Climate change and biodiversity loss are causing significant economic losses. The economy and other social systems are interdependent. They feed back on each other and evolve together. Therefore, to understand the economy in the medium and long term, we need to take into account seemingly non-economic factors.

1.3 A VUCA World

The end of the Cold War was a challenge for the US military because it no longer faced a single powerful enemy, but rather multiple threats of different kinds. US forces were involved in formal wars such as the Gulf War against Iraq, but also in operations such as the Battle of Mogadishu in 1993 against Somali militias in the Somali Civil War, or NATO operations in the Bosnian War in 1995. In addition, the USA was the target of terrorist attacks even before September 11, 2001, with the bombing of the World Trade Center in 1993, the Oklahoma City bombing in 1995, and the bombings of the US embassies in Kenya and Tanzania in 1998. The Cold War situation was relatively stable and transparent, so game theory was a common tool for strategic analysis. In contrast, the new situation, with many more different actors with different agendas, was chaotic and thus required a different strategic approach. The US military coined the term VUCA to describe the chaotic new environment. VUCA stands for volatility, uncertainty, complexity, and ambiguity. In the 2000s, the concept of VUCA spread from the military to the world of business, planning, and political management. Today, it is a common foundation of strategic leadership approaches such as the Cynefin framework proposed by David Snowden. In the business strategy literature, the elements of VUCA are often vaguely defined, so the differences between them are not always clear. A useful characterization of the elements might be as follows.

Volatility describes the nature of changes, especially their magnitude. In statistics and finance, the standard deviation of a variable over time is a measure of fluctuations and thus of the dynamics of the variable. Describing an environment as VUCA means that the volatility of relevant variables is high; i.e., the environment is perceived as changing rapidly with large swings.

Uncertainty refers to a lack of knowledge and implies that it is difficult for decision-makers to predict the future. Uncertainty can relate to the occurrence of events, the evolution of processes, or the behavior of other agents. It may be difficult to assess the likelihood of events occurring or to predict what might happen. Surprise is a common consequence of uncertainty, when agents did not expect what actually happened. Because uncertainty is the result of imperfect or missing knowledge, it is a subjective concept that is tied to an individual's available knowledge and ability to generate knowledge. As with volatility, the use of VUCA suggests that there is more uncertainty today than in the past.

The main meaning of *complexity* in VUCA terminology is that the many interconnections in the environment make it difficult to identify the causes of observed effects. Interconnections between parts of a system can lead to nonlinear relationships between causes and effects, in the sense that small events can have large consequences, and large events sometimes have only small observable effects. For many people, such nonlinearity is counterintuitive and difficult to understand. Another feature of complexity is *context dependence*, which means that cause–effect relationships are not fixed over time. Accordingly, a system may respond differently to the same stimulus under seemingly identical conditions at two different points in time.

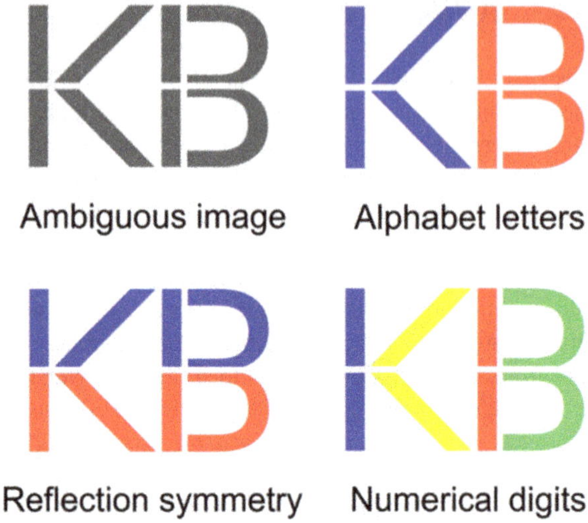

Fig. 1.13 Ambiguous image. Source: Wikimedia Commons, by Postic et al. (2017)

Ambiguity describes a situation that is open to different interpretations, as shown in Fig. 1.13. To an observer, information can have different meanings, and there is no way to determine a single correct meaning. In irregular warfare, soldiers may not be able to determine whether people they encounter are civilians or guerrillas. An economic example of ambiguity is the interpretation of rising asset prices, which can often reflect either an improvement in fundamental value or a speculative bubble. Decision-makers also experience ambiguity when there are several possible solutions to a problem or approaches to dealing with an issue, but they have no criteria for deciding which approach is best.

The concept of VUCA is used to describe current business conditions, particularly with the connotation that today's world is more volatile, uncertain, complex, and ambiguous than in the past. Reasons for the VUCA nature of business today include technological advances and short innovation cycles; the rapid and frequent appearance of new competitors, often seemingly out of the blue; new regulatory frameworks; and fluctuating demand from more diverse customers. The VUCA framework is not a single model or theory, but a heuristic used to derive action strategies. There is no general consensus on how the four terms relate to each other, but Mack and Khare (2016) suggest that volatility, uncertainty, and ambiguity are the consequences of complexity. While volatility is something that can be objectively measured, uncertainty and ambiguity are subjective characterizations that an observer ascribes to a situation. Complexity can also be seen as a subjective perception, but also as a result of objective properties of a system. The degree of complexity can be determined by the number of system elements, the relationships between the elements, and how these relationships change over time. The interactions between the elements of the system determine the possible states that the system can take. A system with more possible states can be considered more complex than a system with fewer states. More possible states obviously generate more uncertainty and possibly volatility when the system switches between multiple states. Whether an observer perceives a system as complex may depend on her ability to distinguish the system's elements and relationships and to identify the system's states.

High volatility, uncertainty, complexity, and ambiguity are challenges for decision-makers. This is easy to see in the example of how price movements affect an investor's decisions. Volatility creates time pressure because large changes can occur quickly. Decision-makers must react quickly to avoid losses or to take advantage of an opportunity, but they do not have the time for careful analysis. Uncertainty means that the decision-maker cannot predict how the situation will develop. Will it get better or worse? Will prices go up or down? The problem with complexity is that the decision-maker cannot see what effects the decisions will have. A decision may have direct effects that are easy to predict, but also side effects in the medium or long term that may overcompensate for the direct effects. Finally, ambiguity implies that several decision options appear equally favorable and that the decision-maker has no criteria to make a rational choice. It may not be clear whether a situation is a threat or an opportunity, so the potentially appropriate decisions may even be contradictory, such as investing less or more.

Economists and managers are taught to make rational decisions. Many people even equate economics with the science of rational decision-making or rational choice theory. Traditional management practices therefore focus on rational analysis, planning, and control, but the conditions under which rational decision-making is possible are not present in a VUCA world. When traditional management practices do not work, alternative strategies are needed, such as the so-called *Stacey matrix*, based on the work of Ralph Stacey, which is common in the strategic management literature (see Fig. 1.14). The Stacey Matrix has the two dimensions of *certainty* and *agreement* as crucial factors that determine the appropriate type of decision-making. While (un)certainty has been discussed before, agreement is a new factor that arises from uncertainty and ambiguity. In organizations, strategic decisions are typically made not by single individuals, but by teams whose members may disagree on the goals or on the evaluation of ambiguous situations. For example, a team may disagree about which is the greater error: missing an opportunity by not investing, or incurring a loss by misinvesting. Such questions are related to the values of the decision-makers involved. When there is a conflict among decision-makers about the right decision based on different values, decisions must be made through negotiation and consensus rather than by analyzing facts.

1.4 Wicked Problems and Social Messes

While the VUCA framework has become popular in the business world in the last 20 years, the related notion of *wicked problems* in planning and public policy is much older. In 1973, Horst Rittel and Melvin Webber considered a general theory of social planning and concluded that it was not possible to develop such a general theory because social problems are *wicked*, unlike *tame* technical problems. *Tame*

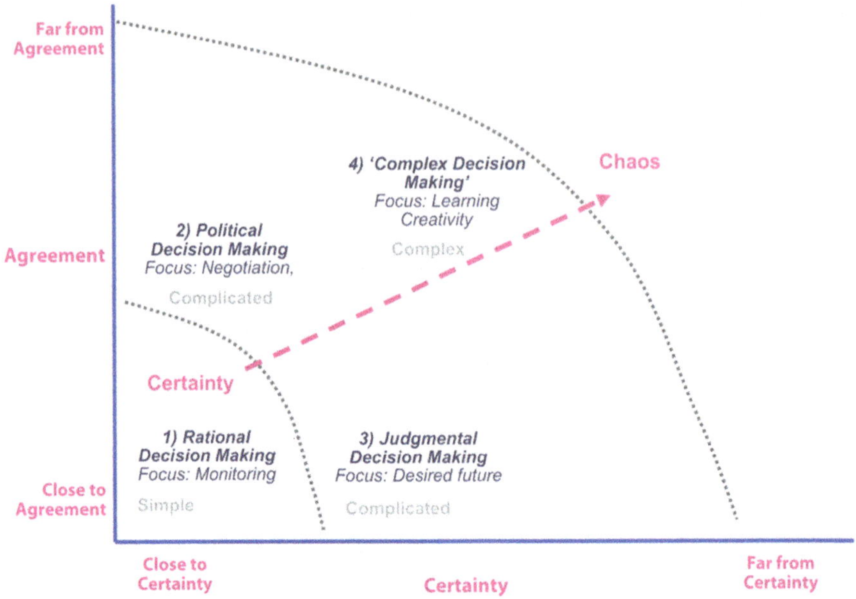

Fig. 1.14 Stacey matrix. Source: Lane and Down (2010), reproduced with kind permission of Emerald Publishing Limited

problems have an end called a *solution*. The problem can be described objectively, from which one or more solutions follow. Likewise, it is possible to determine ex post whether the problem has been solved or not. A solution to a tame problem can be applied to similar problems and to the same problem over time if it recurs. *Wicked problems* do not have these properties. They have no stopping rule, which means they have no final solution. In fact, there may be no solution at all, only relative improvements to the situation. Whether a situation is improved or not depends on the judgment of different stakeholders, who usually have opposing views. The different views of stakeholders imply that the problem cannot be unambiguously defined ex ante and that the problem definition depends on the proposed solution. Finally, each wicked problem is unique and novel, so any solution is a customized and one-time solution that cannot be applied to other problems or repeated over time.

Rittel and Webber (1973, p. 161) emphasize that there is no single and objective way to formulate wicked problems:

> The information needed to understand the problem depends on one's idea for solving it. That is to say: in order to describe a wicked-problem in sufficient detail, one has to develop an exhaustive inventory of all conceivable solutions ahead of time. The reason is that every question asking for additional information depends upon the understanding of the problem – and its resolution – at that time. Problem understanding and problem resolution are concomitant to each other. Therefore, in order to anticipate all questions (in order to anticipate all information required for resolution ahead of time), knowledge of all conceivable solutions is required.

Typical examples of wicked problems are poverty, crime, health problems, pandemics, environmental problems, and many others. In fact, all socially relevant problems are wicked problems. But even business problems, such as designing a new product, can be interpreted as wicked problems.

Head (2008) does not distinguish between tame and wicked problems, but instead introduces the degree of wickedness of a problem. For him, wickedness depends on three factors: (1) complexity, (2) uncertainty, and (3) value divergence. Truly wicked problems score high on all three dimensions. Complexity alone, which refers to the number of elements, subsystems, and interdependencies, is necessary but not sufficient for wicked problems, because complex problems are amenable to scientific analysis and technical control. Uncertainty refers to the unknown consequences of actions and changes in patterns and relationships. Value differences and the fragmentation of viewpoints and interests are the reason why wicked problems have no solution and are difficult to define ex ante. The normative dimension is the reason why wicked problems cannot be addressed by traditional scientific methods of problem-solving.

A similar concept is that of a mess, proposed by management scholar Russell Ackoff (1979). A *mess* is a system of interacting problems. Trying to solve one problem will have an effect on other problems; such a mess cannot be solved by tackling individual problems. Instead, managers and policy makers need a systems perspective that includes normative aspects. Like wicked problems, messes involve different stakeholders with different goals and perspectives on the problems. Like wicked problems, messes have no solutions because there is no single goal that a policy maker could pursue.

1.5 What Might Happen in the Future?

We cannot know what will happen in the next 30 years, but we can be sure that there will be major changes in society and the economy. Many changes are already underway, as the history of the last 30 years shows. Let's focus on two of them: climate change and the transformation brought about by information technologies.

Climate change will affect our lives whether or not we succeed in decarbonizing our economies. Halting climate change will require mitigation efforts that significantly change the way we produce, transport, and consume goods. Decarbonizing the economy will be a transformation comparable to the Industrial Revolution. Energy production will have to shift from fossil fuels to renewable sources, new technologies will have to be developed, companies will have to invest in new capital and reorganize production processes, governments will have to finance and build new infrastructure, and households will have to change their lifestyles. The less we do all of this, the more we will have to deal with and adapt to the impacts of climate change, which will also mean changes. Depending on how much the climate changes as a result of failed mitigation, life in many regions of the world will be severely affected by the direct consequences of climate change, such as droughts, water scarcity, heavy precipitation, floods, and all kinds of extreme weather. In addition, many regions may become uninhabitable due to heat or rising sea levels. These direct impacts, which will hit poor countries hardest, will also have indirect effects on rich countries, for example through climate-induced migration, international conflicts, or disrupted supply chains and export markets. Rising food prices due to climate impacts on food security could also affect poor people in rich countries. While we do not yet know what the impacts of climate change will be, it is clear that adaptation will be costly and difficult for all countries.

As with other societal problems, many people hope that there are technological solutions to the problem of climate change. New technologies such as *carbon capture and storage* could help mitigate climate change without having to change modern lifestyles too much. Similarly, there is hope that *climate engineering*, or *geoengineering*, could be a solution to avoid very bad outcomes if we are unable to stop climate change. Geoengineering refers to large-scale technological intervention in the Earth's climate system, primarily through solar radiation management. The idea is to reflect sunlight back into space to cool the atmosphere. In principle, this could be achieved by injecting aerosols into the stratosphere or by manipulating or creating clouds. While new technologies will continue to improve our lives, they will also have unwanted side effects, as all technologies do. The problem is that today's technologies are already extremely powerful, and societies are struggling to contain their unwanted destructive potential. Future technologies will undoubtedly have even greater potential to cause large-scale damage.

Predictions about technological progress are always highly controversial. This is also true for the notion of *technological singularity*, which refers to the hypothesis that technological change could become uncontrollable in the future, causing human civilization to change in unimaginable ways. The term *singularity* is used in mathematics, physics, and systems theory, and is closely related to complexity. In mathematics, a singularity is a point at which a function does not behave well; for example, it is not differentiable because the derivative is not defined. In general, a singularity describes a discontinuity where a small change can have arbitrarily large effects, leading to strange behavior. This idea is formalized in mathematical chaos theory and bifurcation theory. Because the state of a system changes radically and unpredictably at a singularity, the concept of singularity is closely related to the central ideas of complexity, which will be explained later in this book.

The great mathematician John von Neumann used the concept of singularity in the context of technological change. His colleague, the mathematician and physicist Stanislaw Ulam, recalled:

> One of the topics of conversation was the ever-accelerating progress of technology and the changes in the human way of life which give the appearance of approaching some essential singularity in the history of the race, beyond which human affairs as we know them could not continue (Ulam 1958, p. 5).

More specifically, the technological singularity is often thought to be the result of the emergence of *superintelligence* that surpasses any human intelligence. Advances in artificial intelligence may lead to self-learning systems that process information at an

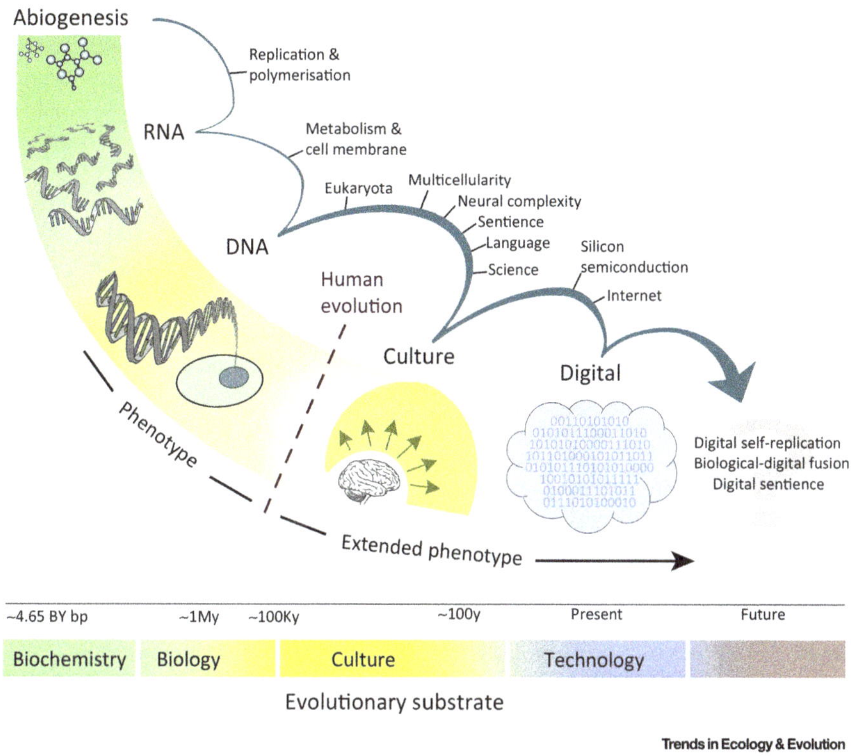

Fig. 1.15 Evolution. Source: Gillings et al. (2016), reproduced with kind permission of Elsevier

incredible rate and improve their own capabilities at an increasing rate. A first glimpse of such advances can be seen in the rapid evolution of ChatGPT and GPT-4. This process would lead to an *intelligence explosion*. Combined with advances in biotechnology, this superintelligence would be a next step in evolution, as shown in Fig. 1.15. While some thinkers, such as Ray Kurzweil, predict that this singularity will occur before 2050, others doubt that it will ever happen. But regardless of whether a singularity occurs in the next 30 years, it seems safe to predict that advances in information technologies will cause significant societal changes.

1.6 What Are Twenty-First Century Skills?

The perception that the twenty-first century will be very different from the twentieth century in terms of how we live and work is reflected in an educational debate about so-called *twenty-first century skills*. If the world has become more VUCA, then knowledge on relevant topics becomes obsolete very quickly or may even be unavailable. At the same time, in the information age, there is information overload.

Therefore, schools and universities should not see their primary role as teaching content knowledge. Students will not need much of the existing knowledge in their future lives because it will be outdated, but the knowledge they will need does not yet exist. Therefore, the focus of educational activities should shift from teaching knowledge about the world to helping students acquire skills that they will need in their future lives in the twenty-first century.

Several organizations have developed frameworks that could guide education reform. One well-known example was developed by the Partnership for 21st Century Learning (P21), a nonprofit organization founded by the US National Education Association, the US Department of Education, and several private companies, including Apple, Dell, and Microsoft. P21 has proposed a framework for US K-12 education that groups twenty-first century skills into three broad categories: (1) ICT literacy, (2) career and life skills, and (3) learning and innovation skills. ICT literacy includes the ability to use computers, to acquire information from digital sources, and to evaluate its relevance and reliability. Programming skills are also considered part of ICT skills. Vocational and life skills are skills that enable people to cope with the challenges of life and work. They include skills such as self-management and effective self-regulation of emotions, stress, and motivation. In a changing work environment, it is necessary for employees to be able to adapt to new conditions and to have a certain degree of flexibility and resilience in the face of external stressors. Career and life skills aim, at least in part, at character development, i.e., the development of values, behaviors, and attributes that make it possible to lead a fulfilling life in a social context. Awareness and acceptance of diversity, as well as tolerance for uncertainty and ambiguity, are important mental and moral attributes. In a world full of wicked problems, awareness of normative issues and the ethical skills to deal with value conflicts are also crucial. In terms of learning and innovation skills, P21 defines the four Cs of twenty-first century learning: *collaboration*, *communication*, *creativity*, and *critical thinking*.

Other organizations such as the OECD, the World Economic Forum, and the US National Research Council have proposed similar frameworks, all of which include character-building elements and versions of the Four Cs. The World Economic Forum sees the Four Cs as competencies needed to address complex challenges. Learning, solving complex problems, and innovating require cognitive skills related to identifying and filtering relevant information and existing knowledge. Often, however, problem solvers must also create new knowledge for new problems through innovative recombinations of existing knowledge. In many situations, however, it is not possible to fully understand a problem, so the decision-maker must be able to act with incomplete or preliminary knowledge, especially when time is of the essence. When a problem is not only complex but wicked, it is a helpful skill to recognize the limits of reasoning and to see when the main difficulties arise from normative conflict rather than limited understanding. In the context of complexity thinking, it is worth noting that the US Army War College has identified five strategic thinking competencies needed to deal with VUCA environments: *critical thinking*, *creative thinking*, *systems thinking*, *thinking in time*, and *ethical thinking*.

Critical thinking has a long tradition dating back to the ancient Greek philosopher Socrates. It describes a process of self-directed thinking with high intellectual standards that involves self-monitoring and self-correction. A critical thinker constantly monitors his or her thinking process for biases, prejudices, fallacies, or the effects of emotion and attempts to correct these distortions of rationality. The goal of critical thinking is to arrive at a position on an issue that can be the basis for good decisions. As a result of constant self-reflection, a critical thinker is aware of how his or her position was reached and can defend it on rational grounds. Critical thinking involves weighing arguments and evidence. All complex issues can and should be approached from multiple perspectives. Different perspectives illuminate different aspects of an issue, but never provide a complete picture. It is therefore important to identify the *relevant* aspects of a problem, which will always depend on the specific goals and objectives. Deciding what is relevant and what is not requires *judgment*.

Creative thinking aims to generate new ideas or find an unknown solution to a problem. It is often equated with *divergent thinking* as opposed to *convergent thinking*. The goal of convergent thinking is to find a correct solution to a problem, which assumes that there is a unique solution and a sequence of logical steps by which that solution can be found. Conventional neoclassical economics primarily trains convergent thinking by focusing on optimization problems. Normally, optimization problems have a unique (global) optimum that we can find by applying appropriate optimization techniques. Divergent thinking, on the other hand, is a spontaneous, unordered, and nonlinear thought process designed to generate many possible solutions to a problem, some of which may be novel. Novel solutions can emerge because creative thinking is an associative process that does not exclude ideas that may seem peripheral. Digressions and side paths are allowed, making it possible to discover unexpected connections between different ideas. Novelty is always the product of new combinations of previously unrelated ideas.

Systems thinking recognizes that systems are important and that complex problems cannot be understood by looking at individual parts of a system in isolation. The *analytical approach* attempts to reduce complexity by breaking systems down into their constituent parts to find out how they work. In contrast, the systems approach assumes that important insights are lost when parts of a system are considered in isolation because each part of a system is connected to other parts. These connections or relationships determine both the behavior of the system and the behavior of the individual parts. Thus, systems thinking always looks at things in relation to other things as part of a larger system.

Thinking in time means that all problem-solving and decision-making is embedded in a historical context. Wicked problems that are never solved have a history and a future. The assessment of the current situation and the available and acceptable ways to deal with the current situation depend on how the problem has been dealt with in the past. By comparing past situations that appear analogous, decision-makers can identify relationships between factors and connect events. Imagining possible futures, assessing their desirability, and considering how they might relate to current events and decisions is also important for strategy development.

Ethical thinking is important in VUCA situations for two reasons. First, it can help identify the reasons for the behavior of the stakeholders involved. Values, norms, and moral considerations are determinants of human behavior. Apparently irrational behavior can be explained when these determinants are taken into account. Second, moral factors also play a role in decision-makers' own behavior, either consciously or unconsciously. What looks like the conclusion of a rational thought process may in fact be driven by hidden normative assumptions. It is probably inevitable that normative assumptions will influence one's behavior. Ethical reasoning leads to awareness of this fact and enables decision-makers to evaluate their own behavior from a normative perspective, leading to more enlightened decisions.

As will become clear throughout this book, complexity economics is closely related to twenty-first century skills. The practice of complexity economics requires and trains critical thinking, creative thinking, systems thinking, thinking in time, and ethical thinking.

1.7 How Can Complexity Economics Help?

As we have seen, life in the twenty-first century is characterized by fundamental changes in multiple dimensions, which—of course—also affect the economy. We therefore need an *economic theory of change*. More precisely, we need a theory of structural change in the economy, or economic transformation, understood as a permanent and profound change in the economic system. Conventional neoclassical economics is not a theory of economic change. While it explains why firms and economies grow, it does not explain why and how new firms, products, and markets emerge and old ones disappear. Changing technologies and new ways of organizing the economy also lead to changes in individual behavior and lifestyles. Economic change also involves changes in values that lead to changes in consumer preferences. We have also seen that change is associated with uncertainty and ambiguity, for which neoclassical economics has no good tools. Neoclassical economics can deal with quantifiable *risk*, but not with *fundamental uncertainty*.

The notion that the economy is in constant flux and that change, not stasis, is the normal state of an economic system is at odds with equilibrium analysis as the main tool of economic research. Complexity economics is non-equilibrium economics and treats the economy as a *complex adaptive system* with rich nonlinear dynamics at different levels and time scales. A non-equilibrium view of the economy does not deny the existence of stable patterns or structures amenable to equilibrium analysis. However, complexity economics views such patterns as temporary and explains their emergence and dissolution. This disappearance of old patterns and the emergence of new ones is the meaning of structural change. Since the 1990s, many econometric methods have been developed that can deal with all kinds of structural change, demonstrating that structural change is indeed an important economic phenomenon. Complexity economics provides a theory that is helpful in understanding structural change.

A theory is a body of knowledge generated by systematic thought and structured empirical observation. It requires a precise language, well-defined concepts, and methods by which (tentative) claims to truth can be justified. All theories describe, explain, and predict observable phenomena in their domain, but the relative importance of description, explanation, and prediction may vary. Likewise, all theories aim to make general statements that are true not only for single, specific cases, but scientific disciplines and schools of thought differ in the degree of generality they aim for.

Complexity economics enriches economic theory with new concepts such as *emergence, self-organization, interaction, feedback, phase transition, adaptation, sense-making*, and others. These concepts are part of a new language that can be used to think and talk about the emergence and change of structure in the economy. This new language makes it possible for economists to communicate with other complexity researchers in the natural and social sciences who are also working on societal challenges whose scope transcends disciplinary boundaries. In addition to a new language, complexity economics adds new research methods to the toolbox of economists. These are mainly mathematical methods from nonlinear dynamics and chaos, as well as algorithmic mathematics, which includes computer simulation methods such as system-dynamic modeling, agent-based modeling, and network modeling. While there is an emphasis on formal research methods, complexity economics is also open to qualitative research approaches, such as narrative research, because it recognizes the value of pluralism and methodological triangulation. By its very nature, complexity research is interdisciplinary and pluralistic in terms of topics, approaches, and methods. It is ingrained in the complexity worldview that any one methodological approach can capture only a part of complex reality. As a result, biologist and philosopher of science Richard Levins (1966, p. 423) postulated that "our truth is the intersection of independent lies."

The research methods and concepts of complexity economics presented in this book are very useful for innovative research on important issues. But perhaps the greater value of complexity economics is that it embraces a complexity worldview, a particular way of looking at economic issues. The complexity worldview is closely linked to critical thinking and a deep awareness of the limits of our knowledge. Since our understanding of complex adaptive systems is always limited, the complexity worldview also entails doubts about the predictability and controllability of economic systems, which is obviously highly relevant for economic policy, management, and planning. One of the central goals of this textbook is to help you develop critical thinking skills and a complexity worldview.

Things to Remember

- Complexity economics is a theory of fundamental structural change in the economy. It is a nonequilibrium theory with a strong emphasis on dynamics. Some of the origins of complexity theory are complexity mathematics, systems theory, and cybernetics. Complexity theory began to influence economics in the 1980s, promoted by the Santa Fe Institute, a leading research institute in complexity science.

(continued)

- Our time is characterized by fundamental change and the acceleration of change. Changes are taking place in politics, international relations, science, technology, and nature. All of these developments are important to the economy because they are caused by economic forces and have economic consequences. We cannot separate economics from seemingly non-economic factors.
- In the early 1990s, some Western intellectuals believed that the end of the Cold War and the collapse of the Soviet Union marked the end of history. According to this view, Western liberal democracy and market capitalism had won the battle of political and economic systems. In the long run, liberal democracy would be the end point of humanity's ideological evolution. The history of the last 30 years does not support this view.
- Recent history since the 1990s has been characterized by economic globalization, but also by growing tensions in an increasingly multipolar world. China became a global power but did not democratize. A series of financial and economic crises hit the world economy, culminating in the global financial crisis of 2007–2008. The economic crises and their aftermath shook many people's confidence in the political system and mainstream economics, which had not anticipated the crises. Technological breakthroughs were made in information technology and biotechnology. At the same time, climate change and environmental degradation accelerated.
- The concept of VUCA describes the perception that the world has become more volatile, uncertain, complex, and ambiguous over the last 30 years. VUCA makes it difficult to make good decisions and find good solutions to problems.
- Societal problems are wicked problems or messes. They often lack clear solutions and are characterized by disagreement among stakeholders about problem interpretations, possible solutions, and desirable goals. Economic theory often deals with tame problems that have objective solutions. Value divergences do not play a role in tame problems.
- In mathematics, a singularity is a point at which a function does not behave well. Because the state of a system changes radically and unpredictably at a singularity, the concept of singularity is closely related to the central ideas of complexity. The notion of the technological singularity refers to the hypothesis that technological change could become uncontrollable in the future, causing human civilization to change in unimaginable ways.
- Future decision-makers need twenty-first-century skills that enable collaboration, communication, creativity, and critical thinking. Another twenty-first-century skill is systems thinking. The complexity worldview embraces pluralism and fosters both critical and systems thinking.

References

Ackoff RL (1979) The future of operational research is past. J Oper Res Soc 30:93–104. https://doi.org/10.2307/3009290

AlphaFold (2021). https://alphafold.ebi.ac.uk/entry/Q9VHJ5. Accessed 17 June 2023

Arthur WB (1999) Complexity and the economy. Science 284:107–109. https://doi.org/10.1126/science.284.5411.107

Atkinson AB, Hasell J, Morelli S, Roser M (2017) The chartbook of economic inequality. https://www.chartbookofeconomicinequality.com/. Accessed 19 Nov 2023

Baudrillard J (1994) Simulacra and simulation. University of Michigan Press, Ann Arbor

Bolt J, Luiten van Zanden J (2020) Maddison project database. https://www.rug.nl/ggdc/historicaldevelopment/maddison/releases/maddison-project-database-2020. Accessed 19 Nov 2023

Clarivate Web of Science. https://www.webofscience.com/wos/woscc/basic-search. Accessed 28 Dec 2021

Comin D, Hobijn B (2010) An exploration of technology diffusion. Am Econ Rev 100:2031–2059. https://doi.org/10.1257/aer.100.5.2031

Curtis PG, Slay CM, Harris NL, Tyukavina A, Hansen MC (2018) Classifying drivers of global forest loss. Science 361(6407):1108–1111. https://doi.org/10.1126/science.aau3445

Dasgupta P (2021) The economics of biodiversity: the Dasgupta review. HM Treasury, London

Diaz RJ, Rosenberg R (2008) Spreading dead zones and consequences for marine ecosystems. Science 321:926–929. https://doi.org/10.1126/science.1156401

Fire M, Guestrin C (2019) Over-optimization of academic publishing metrics: observing Goodhart's Law in action. GigaScience 8:giz053. https://doi.org/10.1093/gigascience/giz053

Food and Agriculture Organization of the United Nations (2022) Fertilizers by nutrient. http://www.fao.org/faostat/en/#data/RFN. Accessed 19 November 2023

Fukuyama F (1989) The end of history? The National Interest:3–18

Fukuyama F (1992) The end of history and the last man. Free Press, New York

Gillings MR, Hilbert M, Kemp DJ (2016) Information in the biosphere: biological and digital worlds. Trends Ecol Evol 31:180–189. https://doi.org/10.1016/j.tree.2015.12.013

Harari YN (2016) Homo deus: a brief history of tomorrow. Harvill Secker, London

Hawking S (2000) "'Unified theory' is getting closer, Hawking predicts". 23 January 2000. San Jose Mercury News

Head BW (2008) Wicked problems in public policy. Public Policy 3:101–118

Kanbur R, Wang Y (2017) The great Chinese inequality turnaround. ECINEQ Working Paper Series WP 2017–433

Lane DA, Down M (2010) The art of managing for the future: leadership of turbulence. Manag Decis 48:512–527. https://doi.org/10.1108/00251741011041328

Leather SR (2018) "Ecological armageddon"—more evidence for the drastic decline in insect numbers. Ann Appl Biol 172:1–3. https://doi.org/10.1111/aab.12410

Lebreton L, Egger M, Slat B (2019) A global ass budget for positively buoyant macroplastic debris in the ocean. Sci Rep 9:12922. https://doi.org/10.1038/s41598-019-49413-5

Levins R (1966) The strategy of model building in population biology. Am Sci 54:421–431

Lucas RE Jr (2003) Macroeconomic priorities. Am Econ Rev 93:1–14. https://doi.org/10.1257/000282803321455133

Lyotard J-F (1984) The postmodern condition: a report on knowledge. University of Minnesota Press, Minneapolis

Mack O, Khare A (2016) Perspectives on a VUCA world. In: Mack O, Khare A, Krämer A, Burgartz T (eds) Managing in a VUCA world. Springer, Cham, pp 3–19

Morand S, Lajaunie C (2021) Outbreaks of vector-borne and zoonotic diseases are associated with changes in forest cover and oil palm expansion at global scale. Front Vet Sci Sect Parasitol 8:661063. https://doi.org/10.3389/fvets.2021.661063

NASA Collage by Producercunningham (2014) A comparison of the Aral Sea in 1989 (left) and 2014 (right). Data is in public domain. https://commons.wikimedia.org/wiki/File:AralSea1989_2014.jpg. Accessed 16 Mar 2023

National Interagency Fire Center (2018) Wildfires and acres. https://www.nifc.gov/fire-information/statistics/wildfires. Accessed 19 Nov 2023

Nature (2021) A Nobel Prize for genetic scissors. Nat Mater 20:1–1. https://doi.org/10.1038/s41563-020-00895-z

Our World in Data (2018) Wildfire acres burned in the United States. https://ourworldindata.org/grapher/acres-burned-usa. Accessed 16 Mar 2023

Our World in Data (2019) Macroplastics in the surface ocean. https://ourworldindata.org/grapher/macroplastics-in-ocean. Accessed 16 Mar 2023

Our World in Data (2021) Five centuries of cod catches in Eastern Canada. https://ourworldindata.org/grapher/long-term-cod-catch. Accessed 16 Mar 2023

Our World in Data (2022a) Cost of sequencing a full human genome. https://ourworldindata.org/grapher/cost-of-sequencing-a-full-human-genome. Accessed 16 Mar 2023

Our World in Data (2022b) Fertilizer production by nutrient type, World, 1961 to 2019. https://ourworldindata.org/grapher/fertilizer-production-by-nutrient-type-npk. Accessed 16 Mar 2023

Our World in Data (2023) Inequality in 1990 vs. 2015. https://ourworldindata.org/grapher/gini-index-around-2015-1990-2015-countries-vs-gini-index-around-1990-1990-2015-countries. Accessed 19 Nov 2023

Postic G, Ghouzam Y, Chebrek R, Gelly J-C (2017) KB ambiguous image. https://commons.wikimedia.org/wiki/File:KB_ambiguous_image.png. Accessed 21 Apr 2023

Richardson K et al (2023) Earth beyond six of nine planetary boundaries. Science. Advances 9(37): eadh2458. https://doi.org/10.1126/sciadv.adh2458

Ritchie H (2021) Nearly all of global deforestation occurs in the tropics. https://ourworldindata.org/uploads/2021/02/Forest-loss-by-driver-1536x1124.png. Accessed 16 Mar 2023

Rittel HWJ, Webber MM (1973) Dilemmas in a general theory of planning. Policy Sci 4:155–169. https://doi.org/10.1007/BF01405730

Rockström J, Steffen W, Noone K et al (2009) Planetary boundaries: exploring the safe operating space for humanity. Ecol Soc 14(2):32. https://doi.org/10.5751/ES-03180-140232

Schijns R, Froese R, Hutchings JA, Pauly D (2021) Five centuries of cod catches in Eastern Canada. ICES J Mar Sci 78(8):2675–2683

Schmidt E, Cohen J (2013) The new digital age: transforming nations, businesses, and our lives. Knopf Doubleday Publishing Group

Schneegans S, Straza T, Lewis J (eds) (2021) UNESCO science report: the race against time for smarter development. UNESCO, Paris

Sorg M, Schwan H, Stenmans W, Müller A (2013) Ermittlung der Biomassen flugaktiver Insekten im Naturschutzgebiet Orbroicher Bruch mit Malaise Fallen in den Jahren 1989 und 2013. Entomologischen Verein Krefeld, Krefeld

Stevens J (2016) 1978–2016 November extent. https://eoimages.gsfc.nasa.gov/images/imagerecords/89000/89223/arctic_ssi_201611_multiples_lrg.png. Accessed 16 Mar 2023

Stokel-Walker C (2023) ChatGPT listed as author on research papers: many scientists disapprove. Nature 613:620–621. https://doi.org/10.1038/d41586-023-00107-z

Ulam S (1958) John von Neumann 1903-1957. Bull Am Math Soc 64:1–49. https://doi.org/10.1090/S0002-9904-1958-10189-5

Varanasi L (2023) OpenAI just announced GPT-4, an updated chatbot that can pass everything from a bar exam to AP Biology. Here's a list of difficult exams both AI versions have passed. In: Business Insider. https://www.businessinsider.com/list-here-are-the-exams-chatgpt-has-passed-so-far-2023-1. Accessed 12 May 2023

Wetterstrand KA (2022) DNA sequencing costs: data from the NHGRI genome sequencing program. https://www.genome.gov/about-genomics/fact-sheets/DNA-Sequencing-Costs-Data. Accessed 19 Nov 2023

World Bank (2018) Poverty and inequality platform. https://pip.worldbank.org/home. Accessed 19 Nov 2023

What Is Complexity?

2

Contents

2.1 Introduction 40
2.2 Complexity Sciences 42
2.3 Systems 44
2.4 Non-Complex Systems and the Degree of Complexity 48
2.5 Complex Systems 50
2.6 Complex Adaptive Systems 53
2.7 Complexity Thinking and the Complexity Worldview 55
2.8 Complexity Concepts 61
References 68

Abstract

The chapter provides definitions and characterizations of complexity, complexity science, complex adaptive systems, complexity thinking, and the complexity worldview. It is important to define these terms properly to avoid the loose "complexity talk" that has become fashionable in some of the business literature and popular press. In particular, the concept of complex adaptive systems is key to the rest of the book. Several definitions of complex adaptive systems are discussed, some of which overlap. Some background on the historical origins of complexity economics is also given. The chapter concludes with some philosophical considerations, particularly on philosophy of science and methodology, and introduces the concepts of complexity that are discussed in later chapters: nonlinearity, feedback, self-organization, emergence, evolution, history, and adaptation.

Keywords

Complex adaptive system · Complexity concepts · Complexity worldview · Philosophy of science · System

M. Roos, *Principles of Complexity Economics*, Classroom Companion: Economics,
https://doi.org/10.1007/978-3-031-51436-4_2

Guiding Questions

- How can we define complexity?
- What is the difference between hard complexity science and soft complexity science?
- What is a system?
- How can we define a complex system?
- What is a complex adaptive system?
- What are complexity thinking and the complexity worldview?
- What does "gray science for the stuff in between" mean?
- How does complexity thinking relate to Taoist philosophy?
- What are the seven key concepts of complexity science covered in this book?
- How does complexity thinking challenge the economic worldview?

2.1 Introduction

The Cambridge Dictionary defines complexity as the state of having many parts and being difficult to understand or find an answer to. While this definition has an intuitive meaning, it is fuzzy and needs clarification. In particular, we need to find out why something that is complex is difficult to understand. Furthermore, this definition does not capture the literal meaning of the Latin word complexus, which is the origin of complex. *Complexus* means interwoven, entwined, or braided. A complex object is made up of elements that have relationships with each other and derive their meaning from other elements, such as the fabric in Fig. 2.1, in which the threads of different colors form shapes and patterns. We cannot pull a single thread without destroying or damaging the entire fabric.

Complexity is related to patterns and their formation, transformation, and deformation in the sense of their dissolution. *Patterns* are visible or detectable regularities in data and thus represent order. *Order* implies the presence of symmetry, separation, and correlation, and disorder implies their absence. *Disorder* is sometimes equated with *randomness* and mixing. If a series of events has no discernible pattern, it is unpredictable. We would not call all patterns complex, because highly ordered patterns, such as the first in Fig. 2.2, are not difficult to understand. Likewise, random patterns like the one at right are simple. Traditional science has established tools to deal with order, such as classical mechanics, and randomness, such as statistical mechanics. Complexity, however, is often said to lie *between order and randomness*, such as the second pattern in Fig. 2.2. A complex pattern is a mixture of a generating law and random peculiarities that require individual descriptions. Another characterization is that complexity is on the *edge of chaos*; i.e., it is generated by a dynamic interplay between order and disorder that leads to bounded instability.

Fig. 2.1 Woven waistcoat from the eighteenth century. Source: LACMA (2009), Wikimedia Commons, public domain

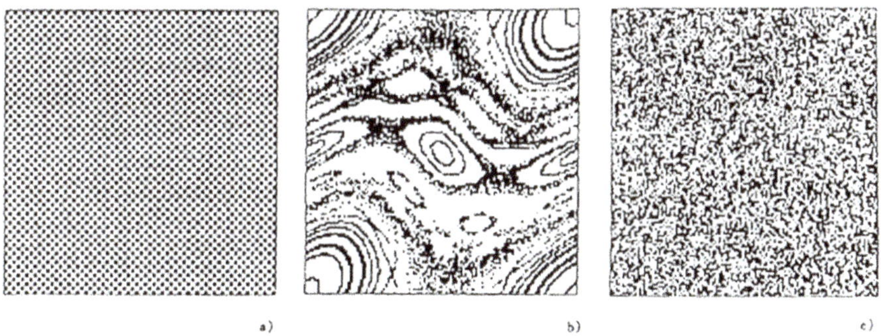

Fig. 2.2 Order, complex pattern, randomness. Source: Grassberger (1991), reproduced with kind permission of World Scientific Publishing Co, Inc.

As noted above, complexity is not only a property of patterns themselves, but also of the process that generates them. Complexity is also about the emergence of patterns, about how order emerges from disorder. Physicists speak of *symmetry breaking* when a disordered symmetric state is transformed into an ordered but less symmetric state. In particular, it is of interest to understand how complex patterns emerge without a designer's intended organization. We speak of pattern formation rather than pattern design.

Complexity is closely related to the concept of systems. In fact, complexity research is largely concerned with *complex systems* (CS) and *complex adaptive systems* (CAS). Before we characterize C(A)S, it is useful to define systems in general. Systems have structure and systems can create patterns.

In this chapter, we begin with a discussion of the complexity sciences and a brief historical overview over their origins. We then look at what a system is and move on to complex systems and complex adaptive systems. Next, we introduce the *complexity worldview*, which is a specific way of thinking about the world that differs significantly from the worldview of classical science. The discussion of the complexity worldview is somewhat philosophical and abstract, but nevertheless very important for an understanding of complexity. The chapter concludes with an introduction of the basic concepts of complexity that structure the book and are explained in detail in later chapters.

2.2 Complexity Sciences

The *complexity sciences* explore the principles of complexity, provide the methods to do so, and apply complexity concepts to practical problems in many different fields. The plural "complexity sciences" is used to indicate that the research field is multidisciplinary and has multiple origins. All complexity sciences share the conviction that a new scientific approach is needed that departs from the reductionist ideal of classical science, which attempts to reduce complexity by searching for simple laws beneath the messy surface of appearances. Depending on their origins and proximity to a particular discipline, complexity researchers differ in their approaches and the methods they use. There are five streams of complexity research that interact and cross-fertilize.[1]

Dynamical systems theory is the mathematics of nonlinear dynamics and chaos. The French mathematician Henri Poincaré developed important foundations such as the qualitative theory of differential equations and chaos theory. *Systems theory*, to which the Austrian Ludwig von Bertalanffy made important contributions, has strong ties to biology and the analysis of living systems. As a *general systems theory*, it claims to be applicable to all kinds of systems, both natural and man-made, and provides an important vocabulary for complexity research. *Complex systems theory* is the branch with strong roots in physics and chemistry, pioneered by Nobel laureates Philip Anderson and Ilya Prigogine. The fourth stream has its roots in Norbert Wiener's *cybernetics*, which is concerned with regulatory and purposeful

[1] We cannot give a complete summary here, but focus on a selection of important contributions, some of which are well known in economics. An excellent overview of the history of complexity science can be found in Castellani & Gerrits (2021), see here: https://www.art-sciencefactory.com/complexity-map_feb09.html Accessed October 26, 2023

systems. One definition is that it is concerned with control and communication in animals and machines. As such, it lends itself to applications in engineering, but also in the social and behavioral sciences. Other important early contributors to cybernetics were the English psychiatrist W. Ross Ashby and the American cultural anthropologist Margaret Mead. Because of its interest in the control of systems, cybernetics has influenced social systems theorists such as the sociologists Talcott Parsons and Niklas Luhmann and the economist Friedrich August von Hayek. The final stream of complexity research is *artificial intelligence*, the academic field that attempts to develop thinking machines and simulate the workings of the brain with computers. The Dartmouth Summer Research Project on Artificial Intelligence in 1956 is considered the founding event of artificial intelligence. It was organized by the computer scientist and cognitive scientist John McCarthy. Important contributions were made by Claude Shannon, the father of information theory; Herbert Simon, known in economics for his concept of *bounded rationality*; and the polymath John von Neumann, who contributed to mathematical economics and laid the foundations of game theory. Artificial intelligence has developed important computational tools for complexity research, such as *cellular automata* and *agent-based modeling*.

Richardson and Cilliers (2001) propose a classification of different schools of complexity research: *hard* or *reductionist complexity science*, *soft complexity science*, and *complexity thinking*. The differences between these schools are quite large and involve deep ontological and epistemological disagreements. Hard complexity science, also called restricted complexity science, bases its understanding of complexity on the observation that complicated macro-patterns can emerge from a few simple rules and simple behavior at the micro-level. This view is sometimes summarized in the phrase "much from little." As in physics, scholars of this school of thought aim to discover a small number of universal principles that underlie many observed complex phenomena. The universal principles may be applicable to complexity in general, transcending disciplinary boundaries. Hard complexity science thus ignores specific contexts and relies on mathematical and computational models. It favors quantitative research methods. Soft complexity science, also called complex complexity science, is the opposite of hard complexity science in the sense that it does not believe that complex phenomena can be reduced to simple rules. It also postulates that the social world is inherently different from the natural world. The reason for the difference is that the social world is constituted or constructed through language, symbols, and meaning. Soft complexity science emphasizes the subjective elements of complexity and the richness of social agents' internal representations of the external world. Scholars of this school tend to be skeptical about the usefulness of mathematics and emphasize the importance of context and subtext in understanding complexity. They favor qualitative and interpretive research methods.

Complexity thinking lies between hard and soft complexity science and is characterized by the belief that complexity implies limits to knowledge. According to Richardson and Cilliers (2001), an important "law" of complexity is that complex systems are *incompressible*, meaning that any description claiming completeness must be as complex as the system itself. Thus, even small details of a situation matter and can make a difference in understanding the system. Knowledge is context dependent and inherently limited and tentative. To gain approximate and applicable knowledge about a system, we must use alternative representations of the system, each of which allows us to see certain features while hiding others. Complexity thinking therefore advocates a pluralism of methods and does not favor either quantitative or qualitative research approaches. Instead, complexity thinkers prefer mixed methods approaches. Phelan (2001) argues that many authors, especially in the management literature, use the jargon of hard complexity science metaphorically to describe business problems. He criticizes such approaches based on resemblance thinking as pseudoscience. An example of similarity thinking is: "Mars is red, red is the color of blood, therefore Mars rules war and anger" (Phelan 2001, p. 126). We might call such pseudoscientific use of complexity metaphors *complexity talking*.

This textbook adopts an approach to complexity thinking that recognizes insights from both the hard reductionist school and the soft constructivist school. The quantitative methods and abstractions of hard complexity science are attractive to economists because they are compatible with the style of reasoning that has dominated the discipline since at least the mid-twentieth century. At the same time, it is undeniable that economics is a social science, and its most basic agents are human beings, not inanimate entities subject to natural laws but lacking cognition. Scholars of soft complexity are certainly right to argue that social systems are different from natural systems, although the dividing line is probably between inanimate and living systems. Furthermore, we can of course use the language of mathematics to gain insight into social systems, as long as we are aware of its limitations and complement it with natural language to capture relevant context.

2.3 Systems

A system is a unified whole composed of *parts* (or elements) that are connected by *relationships,* which form the system's *structure* (see Fig. 2.3). A system has a *boundary* that separates it from its *environment* and defines its identity. A system is an ordered whole or structured entity, as opposed to an aggregate of elements.

Systems may be isolated, closed, or open. In theory, *isolated systems* do not interact with their environment by exchanging energy and mass with it. In practice, there are no truly isolated systems, so they are only useful idealizations for mathematical modeling of certain natural phenomena. *Closed systems* exchange energy with their environment, but their boundary is impermeable to mass. Systems in physics, chemistry, and engineering, such as mechanical machines, can be treated as closed. All biological and human systems are *open systems*. The economy—or economic system—receives raw materials and energy from the natural system and returns waste and heat to the natural environment. Open systems take in matter, energy, and information from their environment as inputs and use them internally. The output of an open system is, on the one hand, waste products that the system does not need. On the other hand, systems can communicate with other systems and can also (partially) control their environment. For example, some plants produce

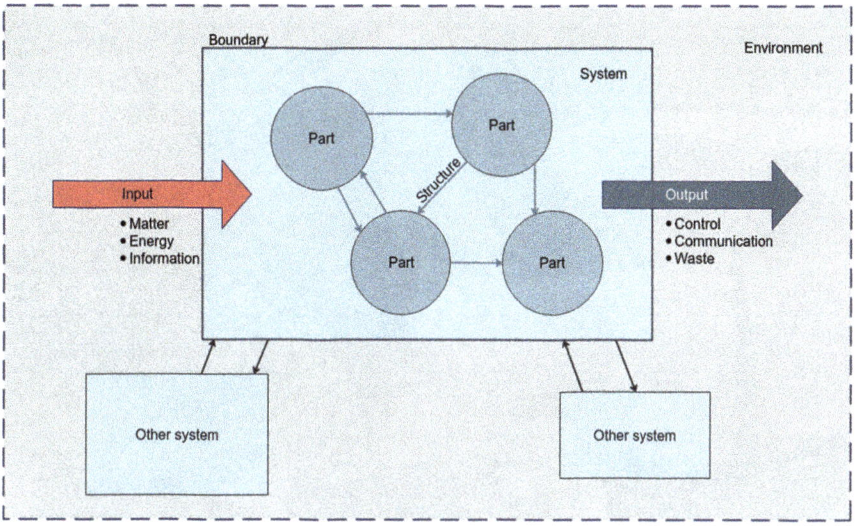

Fig. 2.3 System. Source: Author

chemicals to either repel insect herbivores or attract pollinators. In biology, the sum of all chemical processes that convert inputs into usable energy, system growth, and output is called *metabolism*.

The identity of a system—what the system *is*—derives from its function or purpose, which is recognizable to an observer. Systems can be natural or man-made. While man-made systems, such as machines, may have a purpose intended by those who design and operate them, other human systems, such as social systems, may not have been designed by anyone with a specific intent. They often function in ways other than intended. Therefore, cybernetics postulates that "the purpose of a system is what it does" (POSIWID). In this sense, *function* may be a better term for what a system does in pursuit of that purpose. Natural systems have specific functions; that is, they "do" certain things and not others. For example, a river has the function of carrying water to the sea. The parts of the system and the structure of the system, that is, the relationships between the parts, determine the function and identity of the system. Systems are unified wholes of essential elements that cannot be removed without destroying the system. A system loses its identity and can no longer fulfill its function when essential elements are removed. For example, a car without wheels or an engine ceases to be a car. This means that the parts of a system also have functions. They are functions within the system that contribute to the overall function of the whole system. Many systems consist of different parts that specialize in specific functions, such as the engine of a car. In other systems, some parts may be multifunctional. In these cases, if a specific part is removed, other parts can take over so that the functionality is maintained. The human brain is an example because there is no perfect correlation between spatial areas and functions.

Fig. 2.4 Old car as a planter. Source: Greyling (2017)

The discussion of the identity and function of systems suggests that systems do not have unique definitions, but are constructs of an observer. Systems have an objective physical basis, but their function or purpose depends on the context in which they are placed by the observer. The old car in Fig. 2.4 still has many of the essential parts of a car, such as the body, windshield, and steering wheel. The absence of the wheels and engine disqualifies the entity as a car because it can no longer drive. Self-propelled driving is the defining characteristic of a car, and both wheels and engine are necessary for this central function. However, the entity without wheels and engine can still be seen as a system, for example, as a habitat for plants and animals, or as decoration. Similarly, we can define the function of a river not as transporting water to the sea, but as providing an environment for aquatic organisms.

The ambiguity in defining certain systems also concerns the boundary and the *essential* parts. As argued earlier, wheels and an engine are essential for a system to be a car, but doors and headlights are not. In natural and technical systems, it is often relatively easy to define the boundary that separates the system from an environment and surrounds the parts of the system. A cell always has a membrane that forms its boundary, and a lake is bounded by the surrounding land and the water surface (see Fig. 2.5). For a lake, however, it can be difficult to determine exactly where the lake ends and a surrounding marsh begins.

It is much more difficult to define the essential parts and boundaries of social systems. Take a market as an example. In antitrust cases, it is often a difficult task to define the relevant market or industry in which an accused company may have a

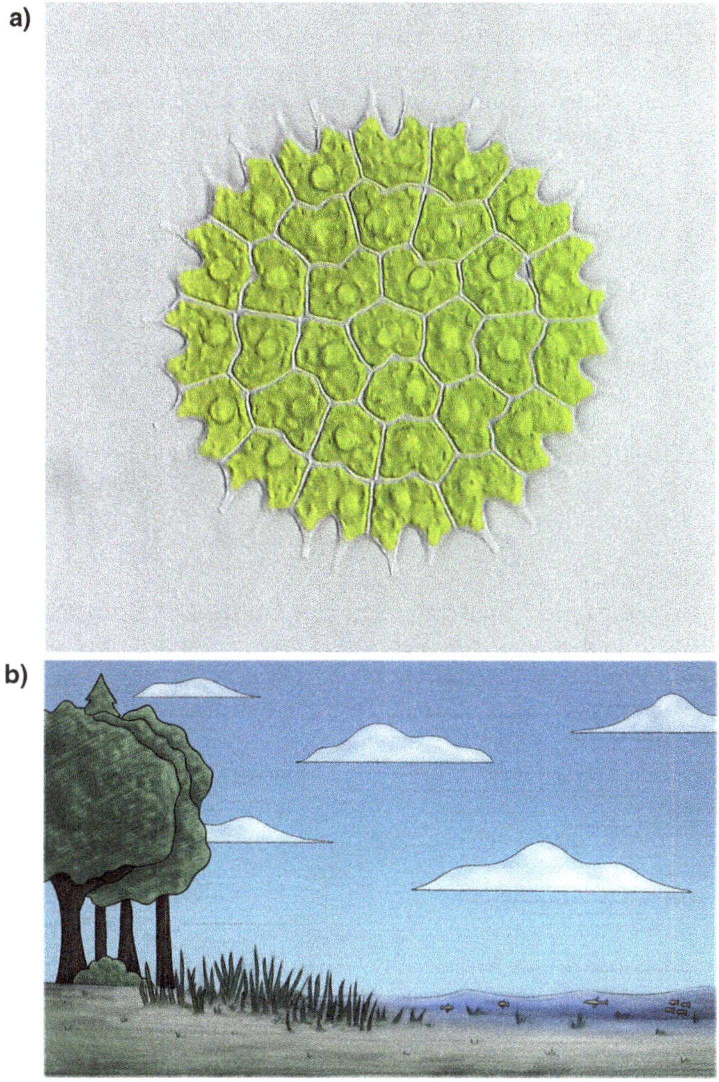

Fig. 2.5 System boundaries. (**a**) Boundaries of *Pediastrum* algae. Source: Andrei Savitsky (2017), Wikimedia Commons, CC BY 4.0 (https://creativecommons.org/licenses/by/4.0/). (**b**) Boundary of a lake. Source: Author

monopoly position. The judge must decide whether there are close substitutes for a product that could be included in the market, and what the geographic scope of the market is. Even a local market for bread can be difficult to define. A local baker may have some monopoly power in setting the price of his bread, but there is a constraint imposed by other bakeries not too far away, or by sellers of goods that could be substitutes for bread, such as crackers, cookies, cakes, oatmeal, or even other staples such as sweet potatoes, corn, or rice. Of course, we can define a narrow market for bread, but this market will be part of a larger market for staple foods.

An important difference between natural systems and human social systems is that natural systems have a single physical entity and a unique location in space. A human skin cell is a well-defined object of a particular human being. In contrast, a person can be part of many different social systems that are not defined by a physical entity and location in space. A person is typically part of a family, a group of friends, a company, a city, a nation, and a culture. These social systems overlap and are not defined by objective boundaries. Social systems are largely defined by the observer, depending on the reason why the observer is looking at the system.

While many things can be seen as systems, some entities are difficult to interpret as systems. For example, a heap of sand is not a system by the above definition, but an aggregate of grains of sand. A heap of sand is not a unified or structured whole that is destroyed when we remove some of its parts. If we take away half of the sand, the heap of sand will be smaller than before, but it will still be a heap of sand. Furthermore, there is no functional differentiation or diversity of parts, because all sand grains are the same.

2.4 Non-Complex Systems and the Degree of Complexity

If there are complex systems, there should also be systems that are not complex; otherwise the attribute complex would be redundant. Unfortunately, there is currently no simple and consensual definition of complex systems, if we expect a definition to provide clear criteria for separating complex systems from non-complex systems. It may not even be possible to define complex systems succinctly. It is common to characterize complex systems by their properties, but it is not always clear whether certain properties are necessary, sufficient, or both. One way to think about this is to understand the complexity of a system not as binary, i.e., complex or not complex, but as a matter of degree, i.e., more or less complex. Intuitively, systems are complex when they are difficult to describe, understand, predict, or control. Page (2011) defines complexity as DEEP: complexity cannot be easily described, explained, engineered, or predicted. These difficulties arise because complex systems have many interconnected parts. Difficulty depends on a reference, so complex systems are difficult relative to simple systems. So what are simple systems? Let's look at some examples.

A chair is a system because it meets the criteria of a system. It is a structured whole consisting of parts such as seat, legs, and back. These parts are physically connected and need to be arranged in an appropriate way to fulfill the function of a chair as seating furniture. A chair can exchange energy with its environment, e.g., in the form of heat, but in a passive way. We can consider a chair as a simple system because it is inanimate, is static, and does not "do" anything except exist. It is easy to describe its structure and function and to predict its behavior.

Many mechanical systems, such as the cograils and cogs in Fig. 2.6, are also simple. The parts interact and convert the input of force moving cograil X to the left

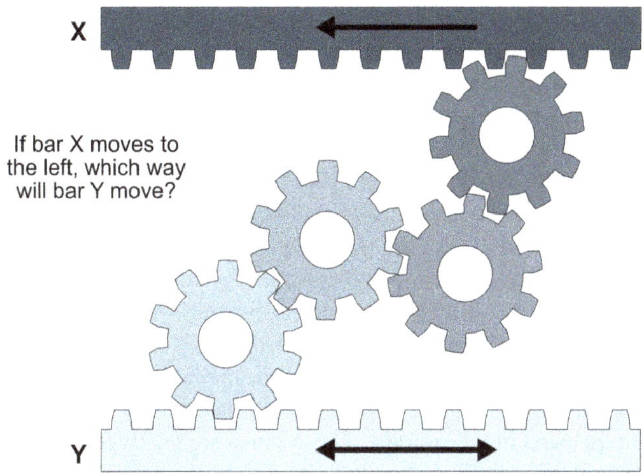

Fig. 2.6 Cograils and cogs as example of a simple mechanical system. Source: Author

into the output of moving cograil Y to the left. This behavior is perfectly predictable as long as the system is not constrained. The system has no eigendynamics, i.e., dynamics generated by the system itself.

Astronomical systems consisting of two celestial bodies may serve as another example of simple systems. These systems are central to classical mechanics. The so-called *two-body problem* consists in predicting the motion of the two parts of such a system interacting with each other due to gravitational forces. A simpler version is the *one-body* or *central-force problem*, in which one of the two entities is treated as an immobile object with a unidirectional action on the other object whose motion is to be predicted. Solving the two-body problem was a major scientific breakthrough. In fact, Kepler's laws of planetary motion, which describe the motion of a planet around a sun, are still very accurate approximations of planetary dynamics today. They were a fundamental demonstration of the power of scientific reasoning at the dawn of the modern era. Appropriate simplifying assumptions, such as treating the objects as point particles and ignoring other objects, allow the system to be described in mathematical terms and to use the powerful tools of geometry, (linear) algebra, and analysis. Two-body systems are simple in the sense that their dynamics can be described and predicted very precisely by relatively simple differential equations.

Remarkably, even the *three-body problem,* as a special case of the *n-body problem,* is not simple. While the problem of how three gravitationally interacting bodies move as a function of their initial positions and velocities can be described by a set of second-order differential equations, there is no general closed-form solution to the problem. In many cases, the gravitational interaction of three objects produces *chaotic dynamics* that can only be simulated with numerical methods.

Another example of the transition from a simple system to a more complex one is gases. Under moderate temperature and pressure, real gases can be well described as systems of very large numbers of moving point particles with no interparticle interaction or with interaction limited to perfectly elastic collisions of the point particles. Such a theoretical system is called an ideal gas. Using the ideal gas law, we can, for example, calculate the volume of a gas given its temperature, pressure, and amount of substance. However, the ideal gas model does not describe the state of real gases at low temperature and high pressure, where particle interactions become important. At moderate temperature and pressure, gas molecules can move freely in space, and their intermolecular repulsive and attractive forces do not matter because the distances between molecules are generally large. When a gas is compressed by high pressure, the attractive intermolecular forces become important and the gas can condense into a liquid or solid. The change between the basic states of matter—solid, liquid, gas, and plasma—is called a *phase transition*.

Note that the difficulty of describing and predicting the physical systems discussed—the motion of $n > 2$ bodies and the state of a gas—arises from the interactions of the parts of the systems. The systems are relatively simple if either the number of parts is very small, so that the interaction can be explicitly captured by a mathematical model, or the number is very large and the conditions are such that it is possible to ignore the interactions. Every economics student is confronted with a similar problem in the first year of microeconomics. When markets are discussed in introductory courses, students learn that two market structures are easy to analyze: monopoly with only one firm and perfect competition with a very large (or even infinite) number of firms. In both cases, interaction between firms does not matter, either because a monopolist can set the profit-maximizing price independently of other firms or because firms have no market power and must take the market price as given. Things get complicated in oligopolistic markets, where there are only a few firms that react to each other's actions. The only oligopolistic markets that are easy to analyze are duopolies with only two firms. But even in duopolies, complex phenomena can arise, especially when cost and demand functions are nonlinear, which will be discussed in Chap. 6.

2.5 Complex Systems

A classic description of *complex systems* was given by Herbert Simon (1962, p. 468):

> Roughly by a complex system I mean one made up of a large number of parts that interact in a nonsimple way. In such systems, the whole is more than the sum of the parts, not in an ultimate metaphysical sense, but in the important pragmatic sense that, given the properties of the parts and the laws of their interaction, it is not a trivial matter to infer the properties of the whole.

Prokopenko et al. (2009, p. 11) specify the description as follows:

> Complex Systems Science studies general phenomena of systems comprised of many simple elements interacting in a nontrivial fashion. Currently, fuzzy quantifiers like "many" and "nontrivial" are inevitable. "Many" implies a number large enough so that no individual

> component/feature predominates the dynamics of the system, but not so large that features are completely irrelevant. Interactions need to be "nontrivial" so that the degrees of freedom are suitably reduced, but not constraining to the point that the arising structure possesses no further degree of freedom. Crudely put, systems with a huge number of components interacting trivially are explained by statistical mechanics, and systems with precisely defined and constrained interactions are the concern of fields like chemistry and engineering. In so far as the domain of complex systems science overlaps these fields, it contributes insights when the classical assumptions are violated.

Another, slightly different definition is provided by Ladyman et al. (2013, p. 57):

> A complex system is an ensemble of many elements which are interacting in a disordered way, resulting in robust organisation and memory.

These definitions have some features in common, but also deviate slightly from each other, illustrating the previous claim that there is no unambiguous definition of complex systems at the moment. All definitions have in common that complex systems consist of "a large number of parts" or "many elements." What is relevant, however, is not the absolute number, but rather that the number of parts is somehow intermediate, i.e., not "too small" or "too large." When the number is small, such as in the case of a monopoly ($n = 1$), a duopoly ($n = 2$), or the two-body problem ($n = 2$), single elements dominate the system or their interaction can be fully captured. When the number becomes "very large" or "huge," their interaction may become trivial and the individual properties of the parts are irrelevant. The definitions also agree that the interaction must be "non-simple," "nontrivial," or "disordered." But as with "many," the meaning of "nontrivial interaction" is ambiguous and requires further specification.

Interaction occurs as an exchange of energy, matter, or information. There must be a direct interaction between the parts, not an indirect one through a third party or common cause. Direct interaction creates interdependence of the parts, which is critical for complex systems. Interdependence means that the behavior and state of a part cannot be predicted by looking at the part in isolation. A firm will behave very differently as a monopolist and as part of an oligopoly with multiple competitors. In an oligopoly, the behavior of each firm causes a response from all the other oligopolists, which does not occur in perfect competition, where each individual firm is too small to affect all the others. In this sense, the parts of a complex system are "interwoven," and we cannot eliminate or isolate individual parts without affecting their behavior and the behavior of the whole system. The characterization that interaction in complex systems is "disordered" seems different from "non-simple" but has a similar meaning. It means that each part must have some degree of freedom, even though it depends on other parts. The cogs in Fig. 2.6 clearly interact, and the motion of each cog depends directly on the motion of its neighbor to the right. But this interaction is simple in the sense that each cog causes the motion of its left neighbor, so the cogs have no degree of freedom to behave differently.

The definitions of Simon and Ladyman et al. link the non-simple interactions of the parts to the properties of the whole. In contrast to simple systems, the whole of complex systems is "more than the sum of the parts." Philip W. Anderson (1972), a Nobel laureate in physics, succinctly phrased this as "more is different." The technical term for "more is different" is *emergence*, which means that the system as a whole and the parts have different properties, such that the relationship between the whole and the parts is not just a matter of scaling. Again, this is best illustrated with examples from physics. The weight of a pile of sand is not an emergent property, because each grain of sand also has a weight. The weight of the pile of sand is simply the sum of the weights of the grains. In contrast, the *wetness* of water is an emergent property because wetness cannot be attributed to individual water molecules. Wetness does not exist at the level of the constituents of the system (the molecules).

In a general sense, the emergent properties of a complex system are related to "robust organization and memory." In other words, complex systems have the property that order or patterns that are stable (or robust) over time emerge from the interactions of their parts. The originally disordered states and behaviors of the parts become synchronized and correlated over time. Note that the emergence of order from disorder describes a dynamic process. Complex systems are therefore dynamic systems, which is also reflected in the term *organization*, which has a double meaning. Organization refers to both the process of organizing something and the result of the process. The organization of a production process involves acquiring raw materials and production factors and combining them in an appropriate way. A firm is an organization in which this process takes place. Importantly, the resulting organization *emerges* in a complex system, suggesting that it is not the result of someone's intentional design.

The definition of complex systems by Prokopenko et al. states that the elements are simple. The simplicity of the element should not be seen as a necessary property, but as a possible one. Thus, a system can be complex even though its elements are simple, but it seems reasonable that the nontrivial interaction of non-simple parts generates complexity at the system level a fortiori. Indeed, the parts of complex systems are often complex systems themselves, implying a *hierarchy of complexity*. The (non-)complexity of the parts is a difference between physical complex systems and biological or social ones. In physics, there is a tendency to ask how complexity can arise from the interaction of simple elements, whereas the parts of biological or social systems are clearly not simple. In economics, agents are sometimes treated as simple, e.g., as so-called *zero-intelligence traders* in models of financial markets, who behave randomly only under minimal constraints such as avoiding bankruptcy. This points to the difference between how systems and their parts really are and how we perceive and model them. Modeling humans as zero-intelligence traders can be a useful *as-if assumption*, which is very common in economics, but in reality humans are clearly not zero-intelligence agents.

The three definitions of complex systems discussed share a similar view, originating in physics, that the dynamical aspects of complexity are most interesting and that complexity can emerge from simplicity. Carlson and Doyle (1999, p. 1412) offer a somewhat different definition of complex systems:

> In engineering and biology, complex systems are almost always intrinsically complicated, and involve a great deal of built in or evolved structure and redundancy in order to make them behave in a reasonably predictable fashion in spite of uncertainties in their environment.

Carlson and Doyle refer to engineered or evolved systems and emphasize their complex structure rather than their dynamics as a key criterion of complexity. They call this type of complexity *highly optimized tolerance* (HOT) because both engineers and evolutionary mechanisms optimize systems for high performance in an uncertain environment. These systems need many highly specialized parts, but also some redundancy of parts to make them robust against expected failures. Modern airplanes, for example, are designed to fly even if one of the engines fails. HOT systems are robust but fragile because they tend to be hypersensitive to perturbations for which the systems were not designed. Most modern technological systems are highly vulnerable to software bugs, for example. For Carlson and Doyle, the *robust-yet-fragile* feature is characteristic of complex systems in biology and engineering.

These different characterizations of complex systems show that there is no simple and consensual definition of complexity. It is therefore very important to be specific about the sense in which the terms complexity or complex system are used. In Sect. 2.7 and in Chap. 3, we will look more closely at different definitions and ways of measuring complexity. You will learn that complexity has so many dimensions that we can speak of different types of complexity, which explains why Carlson and Doyle can define complex systems in a way that seems to contradict the definitions given earlier.

2.6 Complex Adaptive Systems

John Henry Holland (2006, p. 1) defines complex adaptive systems:

> Complex adaptive systems are systems that have a large number of components, often called agents, that interact and adapt or learn.

Holland distinguishes complex adaptive systems (CAS) from complex physical systems (CPS). In complex physical systems, the elements follow fixed physical laws that do not change over time. The elements of CPS do not change either. This is different in complex adaptive systems, where the elements (or agents) change their behavior and potentially their properties in response to interactions with their environment and other agents.

When an agent learns, it can mean that it responds differently to the same external stimulus at different times. The stimulus could be some information or the interaction with an object. For example, a bird might detect and eat a monarch butterfly (Fig. 2.7). The bird soon learns that the insect is not edible. The next time the bird sees a butterfly of this species (or even a similar-looking one), it will leave it alone

Fig. 2.7 Blue jay learning the bad taste of a monarch butterfly. Source: Author

because the bird has learned that the butterfly tastes bitter. Learning implies that a process occurs within the agent that leads to an internal reconfiguration or change in structure. A learning brain creates new synapses between existing neurons. Therefore, it is justified to treat agents of complex adaptive systems as complex systems themselves, whose internal organization affects their behavior. Learning implies that the agent has a *memory*.

Adaptation and learning are related, but not identical. Adaptation is a process that increases the fitness of an agent in a given environment. An adapted agent fits well to its environment. Learning refers to the internal information processing of an agent that can lead to better adaptation. A consequence of adaptation and learning is diversity of behavior and, depending on the time scale and the type of agent, diversity of properties. Adaptation and learning are sources of novelty and change. They thus increase the complexity of systems, because the dynamics of the system are generated not only by changes in the structure of the system, but also by changes in the parts of the system. This kind of change is potentially infinite and leads to a permanent *evolution* of the system. The system and its agents thus have a *history*.

Obviously, the systems of interest to the social sciences in general and economics in particular are complex adaptive systems. A family, for example, is a set of individuals interacting with each other. While the number of family members may be small, it can still be difficult to capture the richness of their relationships and interactions. "Being a family" can be seen as an emergent property that depends not on the properties of the individuals, but on their relationships. It is impossible to define a family in terms of the properties of its members. Family members can be related by consanguinity, which is a straightforward biological criterion. They can also be related by the more difficult social construct of affinity. Affinity is kinship by marriage (or adoption) and affects not only the two (or more) spouses, but also their consanguineous family members, so that two consanguineous families become in-laws. There are many different forms of marriage in different cultures and historical contexts. Marriage is always a social construct and often, but not always, has legal consequences. Family members also learn and adapt over time. This is obvious for children, but adult members also either adapt to each other or separate when they cannot. Families change over time as new members are born or join, and old members die or leave the family. Other social groups, such as religious communities, sports clubs, corporations, unions, political parties, etc., are also complex adaptive systems, often with very large numbers of members. The behavior of these groups depends on their internal structure as well as the diversity of their members and typically changes over time as the groups evolve.

2.7 Complexity Thinking and the Complexity Worldview

Richardson et al. (2001) call complexity science a "gray science for the stuff in between," which is a nice characterization of complexity thinking. As noted above, the complexity sciences have a hard branch and a soft branch with complexity thinking as an intermediate position. The distinction between hard and soft complexity science is both methodological and epistemological.

Methodology refers to the methods and principles of research. It provides a theoretical reflection on the appropriateness of different methods and practices for specific research questions. Hard complexity science argues that quantitative research methods such as mathematical models, statistics, and computer simulations should be used to study questions of complexity. In this respect, hard complexity science is related to neoclassical economics, which also favors quantitative methods. In contrast, soft complexity science considers quantitative methods and mathematical language not rich enough to capture the complexity of social phenomena. Qualitative researchers work with texts rather than numerical data. They use interviews, questionnaires, or participant observation to collect non-numerical data such as written and oral narratives. Qualitative research is often interpretive and searches for meaning, for example, through *thick description*, which takes into account the context and interpretations of the actors involved when studying their behavior.

Epistemology is the theoretical study of *knowledge*, *belief*, and *truth*. It is concerned with what counts as knowledge and what it means to say that we know something. Defining what knowledge is means thinking about the limits of knowledge in terms of what is actually known and what can be known in principle. Related questions are when a belief can count as knowledge, when a belief is justified, meaning that one has good reasons for holding it, and when and how beliefs should be revised in the face of evidence. Truth, which means that a statement corresponds to facts or an observer-independent reality, is seen as a condition for knowledge. Epistemology provides the foundation for the *philosophy of science*, which examines what qualifies as science and the relationship between science, knowledge, and truth. A common conception of science is that of a systematic and formalized way of acquiring knowledge. Science organizes knowledge in the form of theories that make truth claims about the subject under consideration. Hard complexity science tries to develop theories that have a wide range. They make general truth claims and postulate that there are universal laws of complexity that apply to a wide variety of subjects. *General theories* have a high degree of abstraction. They make truth claims about causality that are used for explanation and prediction. In contrast, soft complexity science is more skeptical about the generalizability of empirical findings, which are seen as highly context-dependent and situation-specific.

Appropriate theories that can capture the necessary level of detail are sometimes called ad hoc *theories*, which have a low level of abstraction. Often the goal is not to explain a phenomenon causally, but to *understand* it. *Mid-range theories* lie between general theories and ad hoc theories. They have a limited degree of generalization and take context into account.

There are deep philosophical debates about what can be known and how knowledge can be acquired. Classical science takes a reductionist position, assuming that all phenomena can be described and explained in terms of simpler or more fundamental phenomena. According to this position, a system can be broken down into its parts without loss in order to understand the system, which is called *analysis*. To analyze means to break up or to untie. *Holism* is the opposite of *reductionism*. It holds that systems can only be understood at the level of the whole and are destroyed by the analytical approach.

In principle, all branches of complexity science emphasize the importance of looking at systems and thus have a somewhat holistic perspective. However, they differ in how strong this aspect is, with soft complexity researchers being more holistic than hard complexity researchers. An extreme holism would postulate that the entire universe is one large complex system in which everything is connected to everything else. From this perspective, complex systems are *incompressible* (Richardson et al. 2001), meaning that any representation of a system that is less complex than the system itself implies a loss of some aspects of the system. When we look at systems, we in fact define subsystems of the single complex system by drawing boundaries that seem convenient from the researcher's perspective. The problem is that these boundaries are always arbitrary. Excluded entities can have a major impact on the defined subsystem. We are faced with the dilemma that the radical view of the total interconnectedness of everything may be true, but it is not operational. We are forced to draw boundaries somewhere in order to understand, explain, and predict phenomena, but these boundaries may always be inappropriate.

The concept of irreducibility is similar to that of incompressibility (Jørgensen 2002). In an irreducible system, it is not possible to reduce observations of system behavior to a (natural) law because the system has so many interacting elements. The only way to adequately describe and understand the behavior of the system is to represent the system with models that capture the richness of the interactions.

Complexity thinking can be seen as an epistemology that deals with the dilemma posed by the incompressibility or irreducibility of complex systems. The main idea is that it avoids black-and-white thinking and deals with "stuff in between." Classical Western thinking is characterized by dualities and the desire to distinguish things. In this binary thinking, something either has a certain property or it does not, which is opposed to multi-valued logic. Three-valued logic, for example, adds a third truth value to true and false, which can be called unknown, unknowable, undecidable, irrelevant, or possible. Four-valued logic, also known in Buddhist epistemology, works with the four truth values true, false, both true and false, and neither true nor false. In fuzzy logic, the truth value of something can be between 0 and 1. Complexity thinking does not operate in terms of either-or/black-white, but is interested in the gray. Examples of this *in-between stuff*, most of which will be discussed later in the book, are given in Table 2.1. As we have seen, complex systems have many components rather than few or very many. Similarly, complexity lies between order and chaos. As an epistemological position, this means that complexity thinking avoids subscribing to a seemingly correct paradigm such as soft complexity science or hard complexity science. Incompressibility denies that there can be any one perspective or paradigm that is correct and can adequately describe any subsystem of a larger complex system.

Figure 2.8 shows several ways to illustrate complexity thinking. The bar in (a) is meant to show that pure white and pure black are only the extremes of a broad

Table 2.1 Stuff in between

Polarity/dualism	Stuff in between
Black vs. white	Gray
Small numbers vs. very large numbers	Many
Order vs. chaos	Complexity
True vs. false	Undecidable, true and false, neither true nor false
Reductionism vs. holism	Iterative reasoning
Micro vs. macro	Meso
Stasis vs. motion	Evolution
Equilibrium vs. disequilibrium	Punctuated equilibrium
Knowledge vs. ignorance	Incognizance, unknowability
Rationality vs. irrationality	Bounded rationality, ecological rationality
Market vs. government	Governance
Qualitative vs. quantitative	Mixed methods
General theories vs. ad hoc theories	Mid-range theories

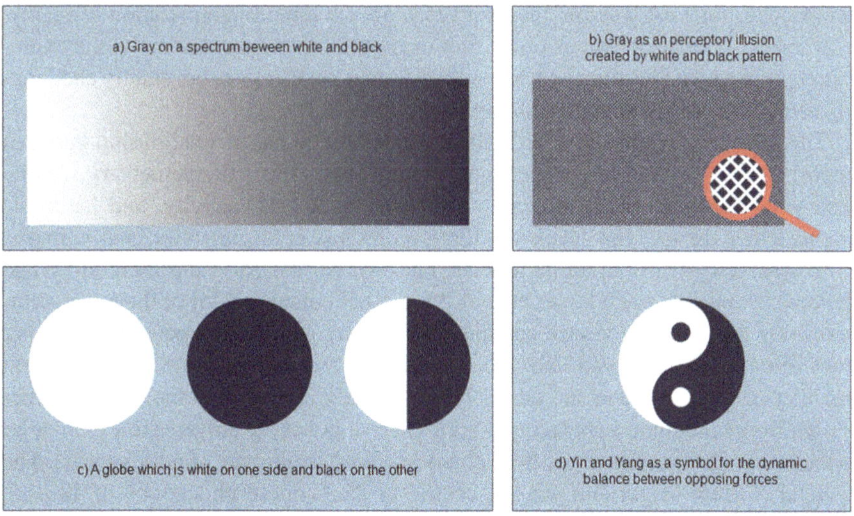

Fig. 2.8 White, black, and gray. Source: Author

spectrum of shades of gray. Most of the bar is gray, and only a small fraction is either white or black, consistent with a worldview that allows for fuzziness and nuance. In the bar, we cannot determine where white or black ends and gray begins. If we were to draw a line between gray and black, it would be arbitrary. It can be helpful to draw boundaries, but we must be aware that they are constructions, not properties of reality. Picture (b) illustrates that the granularity of observation matters. The square appears gray, but when we zoom in, we see that there is no gray at the finer resolution of the object. In fact, the square is made up of black pixels on a white background that only give the impression that the whole square is gray. This image could be seen as a metaphor for *emergence*, because there is no gray at the level of the parts (the pixels), only at the level of the whole (the square). However, it can be helpful to describe the object as gray, even if parts of the system are black or white.

Picture (c) shows a globe that is white on one side and black on the other. That the globe has two different halves can only be perceived if we look at it from the side. If we look at it only from the front or the back, we see only white or black and get a limited knowledge of the true nature of the globe. The globe is neither black nor white, but both black and white. Similar to picture (b), the two halves of the globe teach us not to trust the first appearance of something. There may be—and probably are—different sides to everything that can only be discovered by changing perspective. The philosophy of science called *critical realism* holds that any scientific theory reveals only some aspects of reality, while hiding or distorting others (Geels 2022). The ability to change perspectives is an important aspect of *critical thinking*, which takes nothing for granted. Even what seems obvious should be viewed with skepticism. Complexity thinking argues for multiple perspectives and a pluralistic approach to knowledge generation that makes use of different paradigms. This requires tolerance for seemingly strange approaches and humility about one's own knowledge and methods. Complexity thinking is an exploration of how far different perspectives take us, whether they converge on a common interpretation of reality, or whether some perspectives prove more insightful than others. Ideally, the exploration proceeds in dialectical cycles, with different perspectives constantly challenging each other and eventually leading to a synthesis.

The yin-yang symbol in figure (d) illustrates the dynamic relationship between opposing forces that are nonetheless interrelated and complementary. White represents the *yang* force, which is associated with heat, activity, and hardness, among other things. The black *yin* force represents cold, passivity, and softness. Both represent duality in all its aspects, but together they also represent unity and *dialectical monism*. Each larger area of the symbol contains a dot of the other color, indicating that each force also contains its opposite and has the potential for inner transformation. The curved line also signifies that yin and yang are interdependent and that one gives rise to the other. This is closely related to complexity as order arising from randomness. In fact, yin-yang is a symbol of the universe in which order in the form of polarity emerges from chaos or *wuji* (the ultimate of nothingness). The cyclical concept of yin and yang is central to the Chinese philosophy of *Taoism*, which is based on the *Book of Changes* (*Yi Jing*), one of the oldest classical Chinese texts. In Taoist philosophy, the universe is in constant flux, constantly recreating

Fig. 2.9 Coat of arms of Niels Bohr. Source: GJo (2010), Wikimedia Commons. CC BY-SA 3.0 license (https://creativecommons.org/licenses/by-sa/3.0/deed.en)

itself. The life energy *qi* is constantly changing between its condensed state (order) and its diluted state (unlimited potential), driven by the complementary forces of yin and yang. The physicist Niels Bohr considered complementarity an essential feature of quantum mechanics. According to his *complementarity principle*, nuclear particles have pairs of complementary properties, such as position and momentum, which cannot be observed or measured simultaneously. Therefore, it is never possible to obtain an unambiguous picture of the world, and only many complementary pictures or models together provide a meaningful description. For Bohr, the principle of complementarity was so essential that he chose "contraria sunt complementa" (opposites are complements) as his motto and the yin-yang symbol for his coat of arms (see Fig. 2.9).

The way Morin (1992) discusses how to think about complexity is similar to the Taoist philosophy of a cyclical interplay between polarities. The starting point of his discussion is that the whole and the parts of a complex system must be thought of together in a circular fashion. Neither reductionism, which looks only at the parts, nor holism, which focuses only on the whole, leads to an understanding of complex systems. He defines a system as a composition of *unity out of diversity*, indicating that the whole results from the parts. At the same time, a system is a composition of *internal diversity out of unity*, meaning that the whole exerts an organizing force on

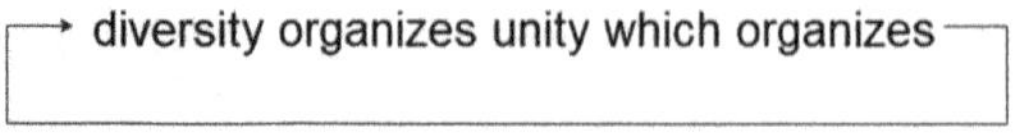

Fig. 2.10 Diversity and unity. Source: Morin (1992), reproduced with kind permission of Elsevier

Fig. 2.11 Recursive thinking about complexity. Source: Morin (1992), reproduced with kind permission of Elsevier

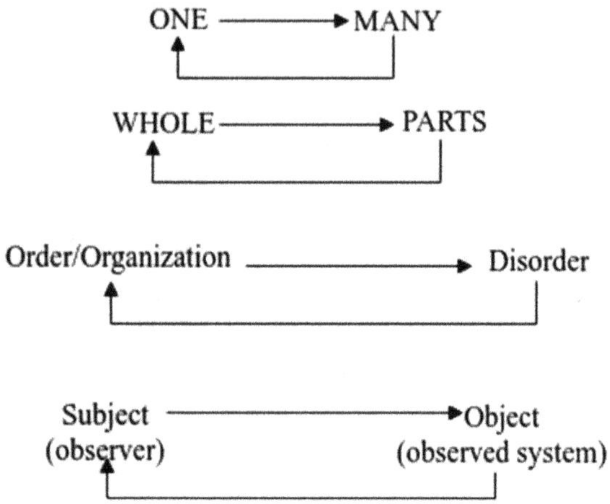

the parts (see Fig. 2.10). A key term is *organization*, which has the double meaning of creating order and of structure as the result of this process. A complex system is dynamic and always contains forces toward dissipation, disintegration, and disorganization. Differentiation creates diversity, which is a disintegrating force. Complex systems have the property of maintaining themselves and thus resisting disintegration despite the creation of diversity. They are in a constant state of reorganization as a result of tension and conflict.

Morin uses the expression *unitas multiplex* for the notion that antagonistic terms are necessarily coupled, which corresponds to Taoist dialectic or dualistic monism. According to this view, complexity cannot be simplified. If we try to simplify it through a reductionist view, the world still remains complex and we gain only a limited understanding. Note that Morin also considers a purely holistic view to be reductionist. A complex system is complex because it combines ideas that are mutually exclusive from a reductionist perspective. Complex systems require recursive thinking, as suggested in Fig. 2.11, because the polarities imply each other.

As mentioned earlier, complexity thinking also recognizes that there is a duality between subject and object that should be treated recursively. On the one hand, a system is a real physical category that imposes itself on the observer's perception. On the other hand, a system is a mental category used by the observer to model, understand, and control reality. Recursive thinking about the subject–object duality implies self-reflection by the observer, who must develop a meta-system of understanding. This meta-system includes the observer and the observed system. It is itself a complex system that leads to a permanent reorganization of the process of knowing. The observer develops self-knowledge and knowledge of knowledge, which implies an awareness of the limits as well as the origins of one's own knowledge. The limits of knowledge include what is fundamentally unknowable, such as the future. Complexity thinking implies acceptance of the ideological component of knowledge. Observers of complex systems are inevitably embedded in culture and context that shape their perception and interpretation of the system. Critical thinking is required to recognize the societal and scientific paradigms that shape how one thinks about the world.

2.8 Complexity Concepts

In characterizing complex adaptive systems, we have already encountered a number of important complexity concepts, such as emergence, adaptation, diversity, and evolution. These and other concepts discussed in this book are critical to understanding complexity, communicating about it, and applying complexity thinking to real-world problems. Concepts are the building blocks of theories.

We have seen that complexity is a multifaceted phenomenon that can occur in different degrees. Rather than looking for a complete list of properties that a system needs to be complex, it is more useful to ask when one system is more complex than another. The degree of complexity depends on the role of different concepts of complexity. For example, a system can be complex without adaptive agents, but adaptive agents are likely to increase the complexity of a system. Similarly, a system with homogeneous agents can exhibit complex behavior, but the degree of complexity of a system increases with the diversity of its parts.

This idea of different degrees of complexity is expressed in Fig. 2.12, taken from Andersson et al. (2014). These authors distinguish between complexity and *complicatedness*, although *dynamic complexity* and *structural complexity* (instead of complicatedness) might be better terms. (Dynamic) complexity is associated with bottom-up *self-organization*, which is a key concept of complexity. This aspect of complexity is concerned with the nontrivial interactions of many agents from which order and structure emerge endogenously. The examples of dynamic complexity (herds, schools, crowds) suggest that the heterogeneity or diversity of the agents plays a minor role. A flock of birds or a school of fish is composed of system elements of the same type (or class). Dynamic complexity can also be understood in a more general sense that includes emergence, evolution, and adaptation in addition to self-organization. This concept of complexity corresponds to the definitions of complex systems given above by Simon, Prokopenko et al., and Ladyman et al. In contrast, structural complexity is associated with top-down organization or intentional design. Technology and organizations (e.g., corporations) are examples of complicated objects with high structural complexity. In this case, diversity is important, but interaction is less relevant because the structure has been imposed on the system and limits the possible or permissible interactions. Structurally complex systems often have *hierarchies* and many different component classes (types of elements), but the number of elements in each class may be small. A computer is a structurally complex system with many different parts organized in a hierarchy of

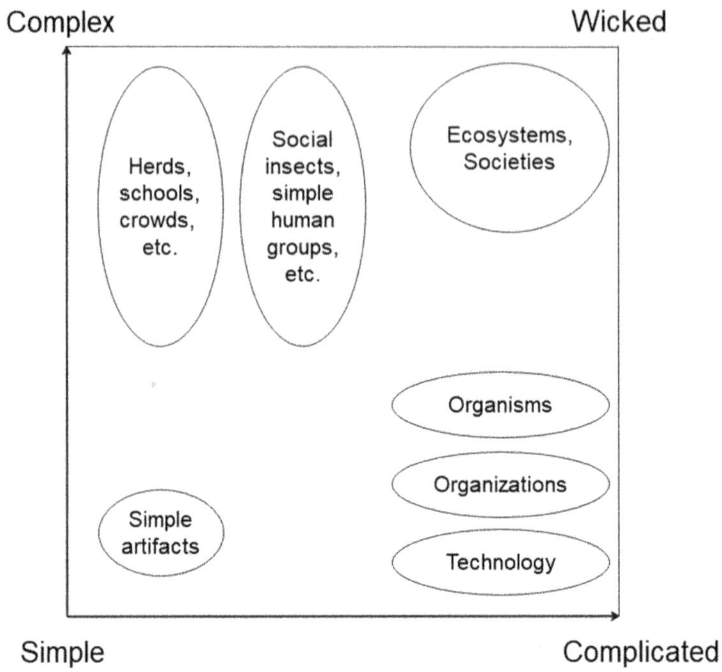

Fig. 2.12 Complex, complicated, and wicked. Source: Andersson et al. (2014), reproduced with kind permission of Elsevier

levels that have specialized functions. Carlson and Doyle's HOT concept corresponds to this kind of complexity. Andersson et al. (2014) define *wicked systems* as systems that are both dynamically complex and structurally complex. The name suggests that they are closely related to the wicked problems discussed in Chap. 1. Wicked systems have a very high degree of complexity. Economies and large human societies are wicked systems.

We want not only to describe the level of complexity of the system, but also to understand and explain the mechanisms involved. The seven concepts in Table 2.2 have already been mentioned and will be explained in detail in Chaps. 6–12. In these chapters, we apply the concepts to economic issues. Complexity economics is the application of complexity concepts to economically relevant problems.

Figure 2.13 helps to understand how some of the complexity concepts are related. The horizontal axis describes both the degree of complexity and time, so the figure suggests an increase in the complexity of systems over time. The horizontal axis indicates levels of observation. The higher the level, the greater the scope, but the coarser the resolution, capturing less detail.

❶ illustrates how initially unrelated entities self-organize by establishing a structure of relationships. Such a complex system can generate emergent properties at a higher level of observation (see ❷). At higher level 2, the system is again an entity among others. The relevant time scale at the higher level is much larger. Over

Table 2.2 Complexity concepts

Concept	Description	Chapter
Nonlinearity and dynamics	Complexity economics is a theory of change. Therefore, interesting economic models must be dynamic. Nonlinear dynamics is the rule; linearity is the exception.	6
Feedback and circular causation	In a complex system, there are no linear chains of causality, but causality is circular. Changes in variables feed back on the variables.	7
Self-organization	Complex systems can create order by themselves without an external controller and intentional design.	8
Emergence and hierarchy	Complex systems are often organized in hierarchies and form systems of systems. Each level of a hierarchy may have different properties, may require its own language for description, and may be subject to its own laws and regularities. The emergence of a higher level has properties that cannot be found at lower levels of the system.	9
Evolution	Evolution is a process of inheritance, variation, and selection by which a system adapts to its environment. Evolution creates novelty and diversity.	10
History	History matters in complex systems. Past events cause future events. Due to feedback path dependence and (inefficient) lock-in on a certain path can be caused by seemingly small and irrelevant events.	11
Adaptation and learning	In complex adaptive systems, agents change their properties and behaviors over time as they adapt and learn. Adaptation adds another layer of complexity to complex systems.	12

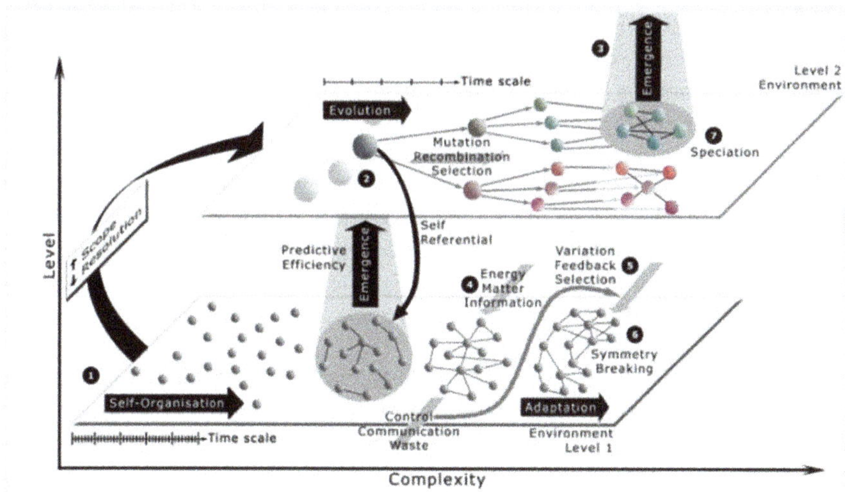

Fig. 2.13 Relationships between complexity concepts. Source: Prokopenko et al. (2009), reproduced with kind permission of John Wiley and Sons

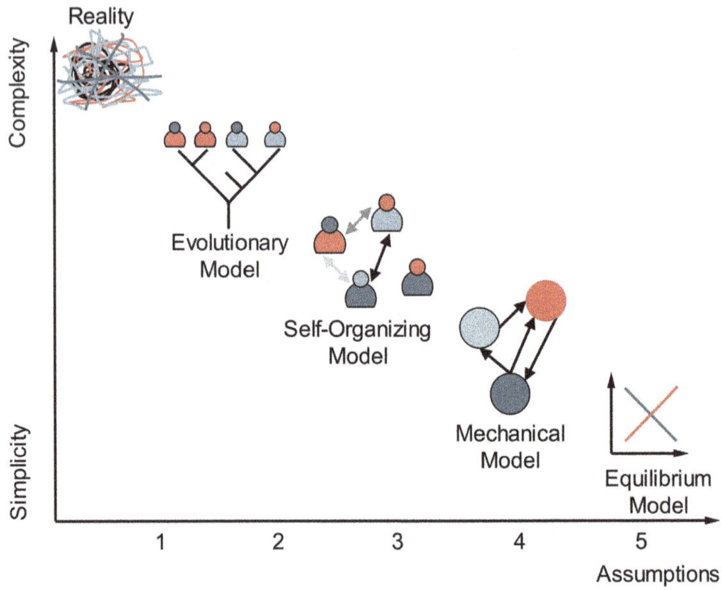

Fig. 2.14 Modeling framework. Source: Author's own figure after Allen et al. (2006)

longer time horizons, evolution with its mechanisms of mutation, recombination, and selection leads to speciation, i.e., the differentiation into new types of entities (see ❼). These species can also form complex systems in which emergence occurs at an even higher level (see ❸). Looking again at level 1, ❹ represents the interaction of a complex system with its environment. The system takes in energy, matter, and information to maintain its structure. The system impacts the environment by emitting waste, communicating with other systems, and exerting control. The environment responds with feedback to the system's output (see ❺). When this feedback contains variation and exerts selection pressure, the system adapts (see ❻). The term *symmetry breaking* means a change in some pattern, e.g., the reconfiguration of the system's structure. It corresponds to level 2 speciation (see ❼). The ability of complex adaptive systems to reconfigure themselves leads to a fundamental openness to the future and unpredictability, which is another interpretation of dynamic complexity.

Figure 2.14 is a useful framework for illustrating how different types of models deal with complexity. Many examples of such models will be shown in later chapters. The ravel in the upper left corner represents reality, which has the maximum degree of complexity. Different types of models reduce complexity by making simplifying assumptions and imposing constraints on the behavior of the system being modeled. Static equilibrium models in the lower right corner can only handle a low level of complexity. Due to strong simplifying assumptions, static models are easy to work with, but have little resemblance to complex reality. To get to the simplest class of models, five assumptions are needed, as indicated by the horizontal axis (see Allen 2000):

1. We must define a boundary between the system at hand and its environment, which is an assumption about the system as such.
2. We need assumptions about the system components, for which some kind of classification is necessary.
3. It is assumed that the system components (agents) are homogenous with regard to one or more of the aspects:
   (a) There is no structure (i.e., direct relationship) between the components.
   (b) The components are all identical.
   (c) The components are diverse, but the diversity is normally distributed around the average.

   The homogeneity assumption implies that the components do not change over time, so their behavior or response to external impulses is fixed.
4. Not only the agents can be described by averages, but also their behavior, which can be derived from average interaction parameters. This assumption eliminates randomness in behavior and implies that the dynamics of the system are deterministic.
5. The system is static and in an equilibrium state. The equations, with which the system is modeled, are simultaneous; i.e., they are all expressed at the same point in time.

In this book, we work backward from the equilibrium models on the right side of Fig. 2.14. We will start with the most simplified neoclassical equilibrium models in Chap. 4 as a reference point. Mainstream economics typically begins its analysis with many strong assumptions that lead to simple and highly stylized models that are inherently far away from complex reality. By gradually relaxing these assumptions, we allow for more complexity and can hope to approximate reality. Complexity researchers are skeptical of the approach of starting with highly unrealistic models and then adding more and more complexity. They argue that we can only make good assumptions and relevant simplifications if we have a deep understanding of the system. We should not reduce the complexity of our models too early, but rather move from left to right in the diagram. In this book, however, we move in the opposite direction for didactic reasons, to better connect complexity economics with neoclassical economics and to show the differences.

Most models in neoclassical economics are static equilibrium models or mechanical dynamic models. Mechanical models have simple trajectories if they are linear, which makes forecasting easy. More sophisticated models, such as dynamic stochastic general equilibrium (DSGE) models, include noise in the form of random shocks, but are still mostly linear or linearized. The first step toward complexity is to allow for nonlinear dynamics and multiple feedbacks, but even models with nonlinear dynamics are still mechanical and assume structural stability. *System dynamics models* belong to this class of models. To model dynamic complexity, we need self-organizing models that avoid the assumptions in step 3; i.e., agent heterogeneity and direct interactions are necessary. This can be done with *agent-based models* and *network models*, which can deal with structure formation and structure change. *Evolutionary models* can represent the highest level of complexity in a formal framework. These models include learning and endogenous differentiation of system components (agents) over time. If we want to get closer to the complexity of reality, we have to abandon formal modeling and move from hard complexity science to soft complexity science. Modeling and hard complexity science thus start with Assumption 1, the precise definition of the system boundary, which is the foundation of any formal modeling. Soft complexity science uses *narrative approaches* and natural language descriptions to approximate the highest levels of real-world complexity. This is what is done in literature and the humanities, such as history and cultural anthropology.

Note that the role of history decreases from left to right in Fig. 2.14. The most complex models are characterized by path dependence, irreversibility, an important role for chance, and context. Because of these factors, model trajectories are often unique in evolutionary models. In this sense, models have a history. Conversely, the role of prediction and control increases from left to right. It is easy to make predictions with (linear) mechanical models because they have fixed structures and fixed behaviors. The structural stability can be used to control the system by appropriate interventions. Mechanical models are universal and have no history. History in the sense of context dependency precludes prediction.

For economists, model types representing different degrees of complexity imply a change in the perception of their own professional role. Traditionally, economists often see themselves as managers or engineers of the economy. The economic literature is replete with analyses of optimal policies and policy recommendations. Moreover, most applied economists would consider forecasting as part of their normal job description. The traditional image of the economy is that of a mechanism or a machine that can be designed, controlled, and predicted. Viewed as a self-organizing system, the economy is more like a garden than a machine. All kinds of plants and flowers grow by themselves. If the economy is perceived as a garden, the economist is like a gardener who arranges, prunes, and fertilizes the plants and fights pests, but ultimately cannot control how the plants flourish. In this role, economists cannot expect to know what the optimal policy would be. They can only learn and experiment about what works and what does not. Interaction with the system is more about creating a fertile environment than direct intervention. At the evolutionary level, the economist can be compared to a naturalist who wants to understand how nature works without intending to intervene. Finally, at the highest level of complexity, the economist would become a mere observer, like a naturalist, marveling at the wonders unfolding.

The change in economic thinking required by complexity economics also concerns our attitude toward the complexity of reality. As noted above, neoclassical economic thinking proceeds from very simple models to more complicated ones. Simplicity is the point of reference. This approach runs the risk of underestimating the complexity of reality. It is important to emphasize that we only reduce complexity in our models and in the way we think about the world. We cannot reduce complexity in the real world, at least not if we cannot design the system. But our ability to design economic systems is extremely limited, and even if we can, the result may still be quite complex. So a central goal of complexity economics is to accept complexity and find ways to deal with it.

Things to Remember

- There is no single definition of complexity. Complex means difficult to understand, predict, and control, but also intertwined. Complexity is often said to lie between order and randomness, or to be DEEP: difficult to describe, explain, engineer, or predict.
- The scientific treatment of complexity can be divided into hard complexity science, soft complexity science, and complexity thinking. Hard complexity science has its origins in physics, works with formal models, and tries to explain "much from little." Soft complexity science does not believe that complex phenomena can be reduced to simple rules. It emphasizes the subjective elements of complexity and favors qualitative and interpretative research methods. Complexity thinking occupies a middle ground between these extremes.
- A system is a unified whole that is composed of parts (or elements) which are connected by relationships. It has a boundary and an environment, with which it interacts, unless it is an isolated system. Systems and their parts have functions.
- A complex system is an ensemble of many elements that interact in non-simple ways, resulting in a robust organization. This definition, which originated in physics, emphasizes the dynamic aspects of complexity. An alternative definition, relevant to engineering and biology, defines complex systems as structurally complicated systems that are robust yet fragile. The complexity of a system is not a binary property (complex vs. non-complex), but a matter of degree. Systems with high dynamic and structural complexity are wicked systems.
- A complex adaptive system (CAS) is a complex system with agents that learn or adapt. All social systems, and especially human systems, are complex adaptive systems. Because the nature and behavior of the agents change over time, CAS are more complex than physical complex systems.
- Complexity thinking entails the particular worldview of dialectical monism, which differs from the worldview of classical science. It requires recursive reasoning, pluralism, and critical thinking. Complexity thinking regards complex systems as incompressible or irreducible; i.e., we cannot represent the systems without losing sight of potentially relevant aspects.
- Complexity thinking does not support thinking in polarities, because it is unlikely that extreme positions are true. From a complexity view, we need multiple perspectives on a complex phenomenon, each of which is

(continued)

incomplete or oversimplified. Extreme assumptions simplify the representation of a problem and highlight certain aspects, but a binary view cannot deal with relevant nuances of complexity or the "stuff in between."

- Taoist philosophy emphasizes the continuous re-creation of the university universe through the complementary forces of yin and yang, which are interdependent and mutually reinforcing. This view is compatible with the view that complexity lies between order and randomness or on the edge of chaos. In this way of thinking, antagonists are always coupled and cannot be understood in isolation. Recursive thinking is required because polarities imply each other.
- Seven important complexity concepts are nonlinearity, feedback, self-organization, emergence, evolution, history, and adaptation. They are closely related to each other and are the building blocks of complexity thinking.
- Modeling reduces the complexity of the representation of reality, not of reality itself. Stronger assumptions lead to simpler models that are easier to predict, but also more distant from complex reality. Mainstream neoclassical economics takes simplicity as the starting point of inquiry. Complications are gradually added to simple models to make them more realistic. From the complexity perspective, this approach is a trap, because it creates an illusion of understanding and control by not getting close enough to the complexity of reality. The complexity view holds that reasonable simplifications of systems can only be made after a detailed study of their complex properties.

References

Allen PM (2000) Knowledge, ignorance, and learning. Emergence 2:78–103. https://doi.org/10.1207/S15327000EM0204_09

Allen PM, Strathern M, Baldwin JS (2006) Evolution, diversity and organisation. In: Garnsey E, McGlade J (eds.). Complexity and co-evolution. Continuity and change in socio-economic systems. Cheltenham: Edward Elgar.

Anderson PW (1972) More is different. Science 177:393–396. https://doi.org/10.1126/science.177.4047.393

Andersson C, Törnberg A, Törnberg P (2014) Societal systems—complex or worse? Futures 63:145–157. https://doi.org/10.1016/j.futures.2014.07.003

Carlson JM, Doyle J (1999) Highly optimized tolerance: a mechanism for power laws in designed systems. Physical Review E 60(2):1412–1427

Castellani B, Gerrits L (2021) 2021 Map of the complexity sciences. https://www.art-sciencefactory.com/complexity-map_feb09.html. Accessed 12 May 2023

Geels FW (2022) Causality and explanation in socio-technical transition research: mobilising epistemological insights from the wider social sciences. Res Policy 51:104537

GJo (2010) Coat of arms of Niels Bohr. https://commons.wikimedia.org/wiki/File:Coat_of_Arms_of_Niels_Bohr.svg. Accessed 17 June 2023

Grassberger P (1991) Randomness, information, and complexity. In: Ramos-Gómez F (ed) Proceedings of the fifth Mexican School on Statistical Physics. World Scientific, 1–162

Greyling L (2017) Vintage car, plants under bonnet. https://pixabay.com/photos/vintage-car-plants-under-bonnet-car-2851455/. Accessed 16 Mar 2023

Holland JH (2006) Studying complex adaptive systems. J Syst Sci Complex 19:1–8. https://doi.org/10.1007/s11424-006-0001-z

Jørgensen SE (2002) Integration of ecosystem theories. A pattern. Springer Science + Business Media, Dordrecht

LACMA. Los Angeles County Museum of Art (2009) Man's waistcoat (image 2 of 4). Image in public domain. https://commons.wikimedia.org/w/index.php?curid=27350916. http://collections.lacma.org/node/214499. Accessed 16 Mar 2023

Ladyman J, Lambert J, Wiesner K (2013) What is a complex system? Eur J Philos Sci 3:33–67. https://doi.org/10.1007/s13194-012-0056-8

Morin E (1992) From the concept of system to the paradigm of complexity. J Soc Evol Syst 15:371–385. https://doi.org/10.1016/1061-7361(92)90024-8

Page SE (2011) Diversity and complexity. Princeton University Press, Princeton

Phelan SE (2001) What is complexity science, really? Emergence 3:120–136. https://doi.org/10.1207/S15327000EM0301_08

Prokopenko M, Boschetti F, Ryan AJ (2009) An information-theoretic primer on complexity, self-organization, and emergence. Complexity 15:11–28. https://doi.org/10.1002/cplx.20249

Richardson K, Cilliers P (2001) Special editors' introduction: what is complexity science? A view from different directions. Emergence 3:5–23. https://doi.org/10.1207/S15327000EM0301_02

Richardson KA, Cilliers P, Lissack M (2001) Complexity science: a "gray" science for the "stuff in between". Emergence 3:6–18. https://doi.org/10.1207/S15327000EM0302_02

Savitsky A (2017) A colony of Pediastrum algae. 1000x. https://commons.wikimedia.org/wiki/File:%D0%9A%D0%BE%D0%BB%D0%BE%D0%BD%D0%B8%D1%8F_%D0%B2%D0%BE%D0%B4%D0%BE%D1%80%D0%BE%D1%81%D0%BB%D0%B5%D0%B9_Pediastrum._1000%D1%85.jpg. Accessed 16 Mar 2023

Simon HA (1962) The architecture of complexity. Proc Am Philos Soc 106:467–482

Measurement of Complexity

3

Contents

3.1 Introduction 72
3.2 Patterns 74
3.3 Complexity and Information 79
  3.3.1 Information 81
  3.3.2 Information Theory 81
  3.3.3 Shannon Entropy 84
3.4 Complexity of Patterns 87
  3.4.1 Entropy and Patterns 87
  3.4.2 Permutation Entropy 90
  3.4.3 Statistical Complexity 94
3.5 Complexity of Systems 97
  3.5.1 Measurement of System Complexity 98
  3.5.2 Structural Complexity 100
  3.5.3 Functional Complexity 103
  3.5.4 Cyclomatic Complexity 105
  3.5.5 Organizational Complexity 107
  3.5.6 Objective and Subjective Complexity 109
References 113

Abstract

This chapter introduces different ways of measuring aspects of complexity. This book is based on the scientific view that measurement enforces precision and links theory to fact. Since complexity is a multidimensional concept, there is no single way to measure it. Many attempts to quantify complexity rely on Shannon entropy from information science, which is explained in detail. How Shannon entropy and other measures can be applied in economics is demonstrated with a number of examples. We can measure the complexity of patterns in data or the complexity of systems. Aspects of system complexity are structural complexity, functional complexity, cyclomatic complexity, and organizational complexity. It

M. Roos, *Principles of Complexity Economics*, Classroom Companion: Economics,
https://doi.org/10.1007/978-3-031-51436-4_3

is also shown how we can distinguish between objective and subjective complexity and how both contribute to the complexity of a system.

Keywords

Entropy · Information · Pattern

Guiding Questions

- What is a pattern?
- How is complexity related to information?
- What is Shannon entropy?
- How can we use information theory to measure the complexity of patterns?
- What is the complexity of a system?
- What is cyclomatic complexity?
- How can we measure organizational complexity?
- Why does complexity have an objective and a subjective dimension?

3.1 Introduction

Having described complexity in the previous chapter, we now discuss how we can measure it. The importance of measurement is well expressed in a famous quote from the physicist Lord Kelvin:

> When you can measure what you are speaking about, and express it in numbers, you know something about it; but when you cannot measure it, when you cannot express it in numbers, your knowledge is of a meagre and unsatisfactory kind: it may be the beginning of knowledge, but you have scarcely, in your thoughts, advanced to the stage of science, whatever the matter may be. (Kelvin 1889, p. 73)

From a soft complexity perspective, the idea of measuring complexity is reductionist, and no quantitative measure can ever capture the full nature of complexity. Every attempt to measure complexity reduces it. Complexity is an autological term, a term that can be applied to itself. In other words, complexity itself is complex. While it may be true that any quantitative measure of complexity is a reduction to one of many possible aspects, measurement is still useful and productive. It prevents loose talk about complexity and forces researchers to be precise. We cannot measure complexity as such, but only certain aspects of complexity. As we will see later, there are many different measures of complexity. Each measure is a definition of a particular aspect or dimension of complexity.

Complexity refers to something, so we can only measure how complex an object is. There are two types of objects of interest. The first kind of objects are systems, such as the economic system as a whole, or particular economic subsystems, such as markets or individual firms. For example, one might ask whether the economy of one country is more complex than the economy of another country, or whether a particular industry has become more complex over time. As discussed in the previous chapter, systems are theoretical constructs. In many cases, we cannot easily identify and delineate social systems. We can define a particular organization as a social system, but in terms of "the economy" it is difficult to say where the system boundary is. Nevertheless, once we have defined a system theoretically, we would like to describe it empirically.

The other object whose complexity we want to measure is data. Economic data is not random; it contains structure or pattern. We can think of economic data as the observable output of economic systems. Analyzing data prevents pure theoretical speculation and is the ultimate justification of theories. Typical data economists deal with are time series of GDP, inflation rate, prices, sales, and so on. Measuring the structure of this data can help us better understand the processes or systems that produced it. Patterns in data are also important for forecasting with econometric methods, which always exploit the structure detected in the data.

There are many different measures of complexity, both for systems and for data. This introductory textbook cannot even attempt to give a comprehensive overview of the multitude of complexity measures. Some measures developed in physics or computer science require quite advanced statistical and mathematical knowledge. What we can do is discuss general approaches to complexity measures. In this chapter, we show some simple examples of complexity measures that can serve as a starting point for more sophisticated methods. Some of them will be discussed in later chapters in combination with the theoretical concepts of complexity. As mentioned above, there are many tools that focus on particular aspects of complexity, so it is necessary to introduce the relevant concepts before it makes sense to ask how we can measure them.

We first consider the complexity of patterns in empirical data before we consider the complexity of systems. The patterns in economic data are the phenomena we want to explain with theories. Models of systems are parts of such theories. At this point, it is useful to distinguish between *data*, *information*, *knowledge*, and *wisdom*, which are often arranged in the so-called DIKW pyramid shown in Fig. 3.1. Like all simplifications, the hierarchical order in the pyramid is useful, but it can also be misleading if interpreted uncritically. The pyramid suggests that there are related concepts at different levels of human understanding. It would be wrong to assume that there is a simple linear progression from bottom to top, since the levels interact in many ways.

Data can be defined as observations of reality, signals perceived by an observer, or symbols such as letters, numbers, words, or images that can be stored and transmitted. Data is raw in the sense that it is unprocessed and has no meaning. *Information* is processed data that is useful and answers questions about describing something, such as "who," "what," "where," or "how many." *Knowledge* can be defined as organized information that answers "why" and "how" questions. We need knowledge to explain what we observe and to use information. *Wisdom* refers to the

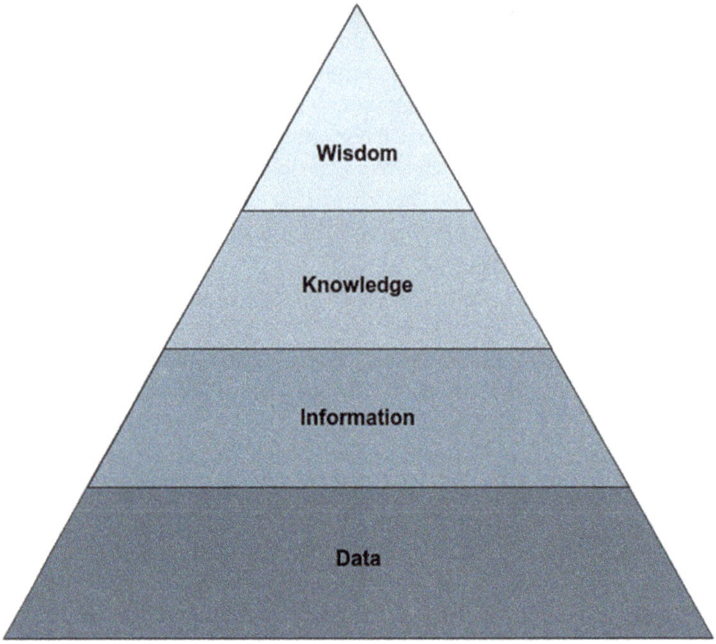

Fig. 3.1 Data, information, knowledge, and wisdom—The DIKW pyramid. Source: Author

human interpretation and meaning of knowledge. In contrast to knowledge, which answers the question "why is it?" wisdom is about "why?" in the sense of "what for?" or "for what purpose?" Wisdom adds normative judgments to knowledge. Quantitative measurement is necessary to move from data to information to knowledge. The level of wisdom, the answer to the question of what it all means, cannot be reached by measuring things.

In Sect. 3.2, we first present examples of patterns in economic data, which are the phenomena from which we begin to create economic knowledge. In Sect. 3.3, we provide a very brief introduction to *information theory*, which provides useful concepts for defining and measuring complexity. We then show in Sect. 3.4 how measures based on information theory can be applied to patterns in data. The chapter concludes with some ideas on how to measure the complexity of systems.

3.2 Patterns

A pattern is a regularity in data, where data is understood as an arrangement of symbols, either in space or in time. When we speak of a regularity, we mean that the pattern is not random, but contains some symmetry or correlation. The existence of a pattern suggests that there is some underlying mechanism or rule other than chance

Fig. 3.2 Pattern in the snow. Source: Wikimedia Commons, by Weiler (2013), public domain

that generated the data. Patterns are thus associated with causality. When we identify something as a pattern, we believe that the pattern was caused by something.

Figure 3.2 shows indentations in the snow that we inevitably identify as a pattern. We interpret some of the indentations as footprints and others as bird wing impressions. It seems natural to interpret the pattern as signs of a fight between a bird and a predator, perhaps a fox or a wolf. When we see this pattern, our brains begin to simulate the possible activities of the animals that might have caused it. Shermer (2011, p. 59) argues that "our brains are belief engines, evolved pattern-recognition machines that connect the dots and create meaning out of the patterns we think we see in nature." The ability to recognize meaningful patterns is an evolutionary advantage because it helps make predictions that promote survival and reproduction. The life of an Ice Age man might have depended on correctly interpreting a pattern like the one in Fig. 3.2. If the predator was a fox, the man might have a chance to take the bird away from the fox and eat it. However, if the predator was a more dangerous animal, such as a wolf, the man might better avoid it. Shermer calls the human tendency to find meaningful patterns everywhere, even in meaningless noise, *patternicity*.

The phenomenon of people sometimes seeing meaningful patterns in randomly generated data is called *apophenia*, or *pareidolia*. A popular example of pareidolia is that people often see faces in inanimate objects, such as the face of a bear on the surface of Mars in Fig. 3.3. While pareidolia can be fun, it can also have behavioral consequences if the person who sees the face of Jesus on a toast interprets it as a divine revelation. Examples of pareidolia in economics and statistics are Gamber's

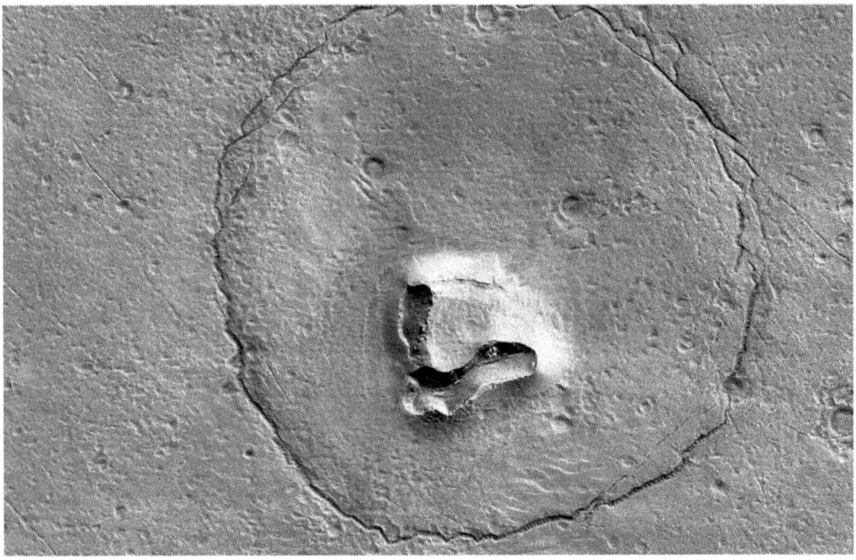

Fig. 3.3 Bear face on Mars. Source: Wikimedia Commons, NASA (2023), public domain

fallacy and the hot-hand fallacy. The *Gamber's fallacy* is the mistaken belief that a particular event of a random process will occur less frequently in the future if it occurred frequently in the past, such as rolling another six on a dice after a series of sixes. The *hot-hand fallacy* is the opposite, namely, an individual's mistaken expectation that a random event is more likely to occur if it has occurred several times in a row in the past. An important goal of science is to determine whether observed patterns are random or not. If a pattern does not appear to be random, then there may be something to explain.

In economics, we do not usually deal with physical objects such as planets or toasts, but with symbolic data such as time series of economic variables. This means that in many cases economics can only observe its object of study indirectly through statistical constructs, such as GDP or the rate of inflation. In other cases, economists can directly observe what they are interested in, such as prices of goods and financial markets. When we rely on statistical constructs to observe economic phenomena—for example, GDP as a measure of a country's aggregate final output—we must keep in mind that the constructs are not theory-free, but are based on a certain body of knowledge. In this sense, we have an interaction between the levels of the DIKW pyramid in Fig. 3.1. What we can observe depends on our prior theoretical knowledge. Furthermore, the patterns we observe in the data may depend on the representation of the data, for example, in terms of spatial and temporal resolution. In other words, in many cases patterns are not just there. Often they are generated by a particular way of looking at the world.

Let's look at a few examples that illustrate what we mean by patterns in economic data. We use visual representations, following the advice of every good econometrics teacher and data scientist to always start with a visual inspection of the data at hand. As a reference, we start with random data in Fig. 3.4, which is called *Gaussian white noise*. The time series of 100 observations consists of independent draws from a normal distribution with a mean of 0 and a variance of 1. The time series looks irregular with no obvious pattern.

The plot of monthly US retail sales in Fig. 3.5 is exactly the opposite of the white noise time series because it is highly ordered and shows strong patterns that are easy

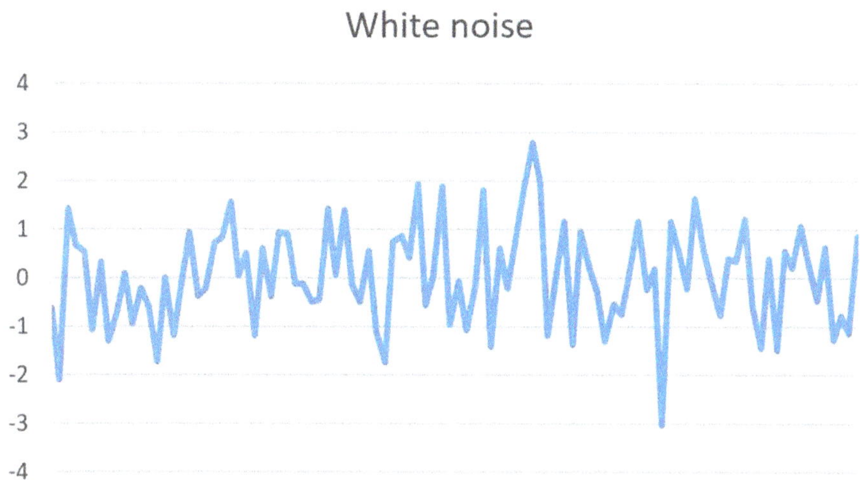

Fig. 3.4 Normally distributed random variable. Source: Author

Fig. 3.5 Monthly US retail sales. Source: Author's own figure with data from U.S. Census Bureau (2023)

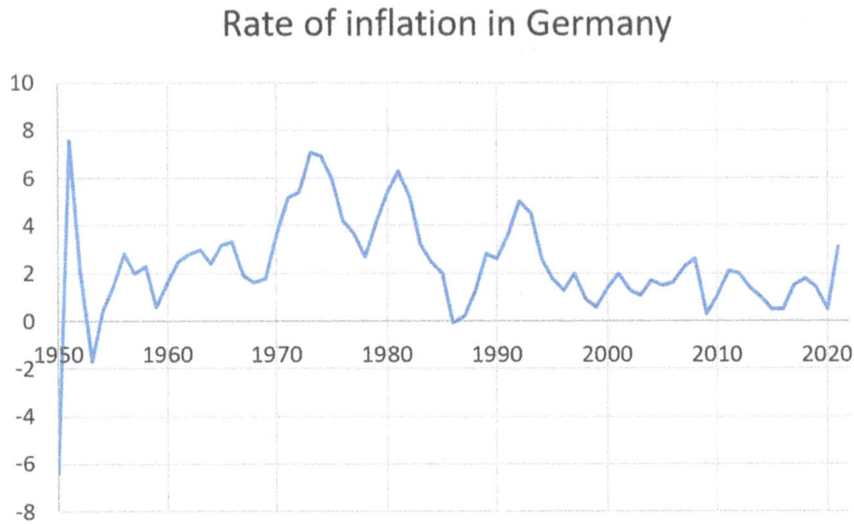

Fig. 3.6 Rate of inflation in Germany. Source: Author's own figure with data from Destatis (2023)

to see. We can see three regularities with the naked eye: (1) there is a clear upward trend that looks linear, (2) there is a strong seasonal pattern with a pronounced spike at the end of each year followed by a similarly pronounced decline, some spikes in the middle of the year, and another decline in the fall, and (3) the amplitude of the seasonal pattern increases over time. In addition, there is an apparent trend break in 2020 that first shifts some observations down and then slightly changes the overall pattern.

Typically, economic data have properties that lie between the randomness of white noise and the strong order in sales figures. Figure 3.6 shows the German inflation rate as measured by the annual percentage change in the consumer price index. The pattern in the inflation data is cyclical, especially in the period between 1970 and 2000. Long periods of rising inflation are followed by periods of falling inflation. Very typical of macroeconomic time series, the inflation rate is highly autocorrelated, meaning that the inflation rate is always close to the previous year's value and usually does not make large jumps (except at the beginning). Somewhat less obvious is the impression that the time series looks different after 2000 than before. In these 20 years, the amplitude of the fluctuations is much smaller than in the earlier period.

Figure 3.7 shows quarterly GDP in Italy, which is another important macroeconomic variable. The most interesting pattern consists of two apparent regimes: a growth regime before 2008 and a stagnation regime after 2008.

An example of the claim that the representation of the data matters for the patterns we can detect is shown in Fig. 3.8. The top panel shows the evolution of the intraday levels of the S&P 500 stock market index between January 1, 2008, and December

Fig. 3.7 Quarterly GDP in Italy. Source: Author's own figure with data from OECD (2023)

31, 2013. Apart from the high autocorrelation, it is not easy to describe the pattern in the data. This is different if we look at the bottom panel, which shows the daily returns derived from the same data. In this time series, we can clearly see several clusters of high volatility.

3.3 Complexity and Information

A useful starting point for a formal treatment of complexity is the concept of information and information theory. For many physicists, information is a dubious concept because it has long been regarded as a subjective entity that defies objective measurement and is difficult to define. Quantum physics radically changed physicists' view of reality and gave a so-called *observer* a central role in determining the state of the quantum system. The state of the system depends on the measurement made, which led to many disputes about how to interpret it. The eminent physicist John Archibald Wheeler formulated five fundamental questions about nature, which he called the *really big questions* (RBQs). The last of these RBQs is "It from bit?" which concerns the relationship between physical things and information. He tentatively answered the questions in the affirmative:

> It from bit. Otherwise put, every it — every particle, every field of force, even the space-time continuum itself — derives its function, its meaning, its very existence entirely — even if in some contexts indirectly — from the apparatus-elicited answers to yes-or-no questions, binary choices, bits. It from bit symbolizes the idea that every item of the physical world has at bottom — a very deep bottom, in most instances — an immaterial source and explanation; that which we call reality arises in the last analysis from the posing of yes-no questions and

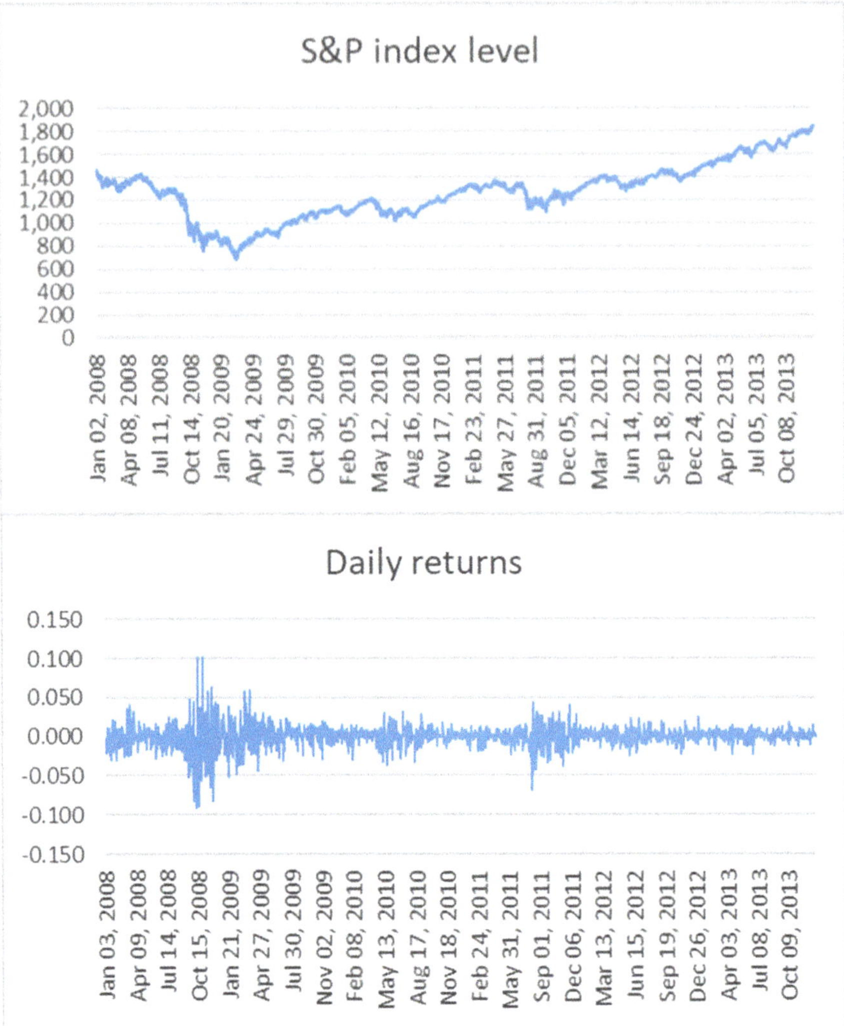

Fig. 3.8 S&P stock market index and daily returns. Source: Author's own figure with data from Yahoo Finance data

> the registering of equipment-evoked responses; in short, that all things physical are information-theoretic in origin and that this is a participatory universe. Wheeler (1989, p. 5)

Complex systems can be characterized by sequences of symbols that describe their states. Thus, they process information and generate information. The complexity of a system is related to the amount of information needed to describe the system and its states.

3.3.1 Information

Information contains the word "form" and has the meaning of giving form to something formless. Synonyms for form are arrangement, configuration, order, organization, pattern, shape, structure, and relationship. We can also understand information as the transfer from one medium to another. The exchange of information—communication between a sender and a receiver—implies that a form is symbolically translated or encoded into a message that can be transmitted through a transmission channel and decoded by the receiver. The symbolic code used to describe the form is irrelevant, as long as both communication partners use the same code.

It is natural for economists to think of information in terms of communication, that is, the exchange of information between two agents. Before a trade can take place between a seller and a buyer, both must at least implicitly exchange information about their valuation of the object to be traded. In a bilateral negotiation, the seller reveals her valuation in the offer and the buyer in the bid. The transmitted form is each agent's relationship to the object, the valuation. The price is the code used for transmission.

More generally, information is anything that an agent can sense or perceive. An agent can be described as an entity that acts on an environment. Another term for agent is IGUS: *information gathering and using system*. So information is a description of the agent's environment. Even if physicists are still struggling with information, it is clear that life is strongly linked to information. Even the simplest living organisms have senses with which they perceive their environment. Organisms need information to find nutrients and sexual partners, or to avoid predators and other dangers. The interaction of organs within an organism depends on information that can be transmitted through nerves or hormones. Information is encoded in DNA, which controls the reproduction of life. To affect the behavior of agents, information must have *meaning* to them. Meaning is generated by the agent that perceives the information. Agents respond to meaningful information, but not to meaningless information. The creation of meaning is a subjective process that is difficult to analyze, but by observing whether or not an agent responds to the information it receives, we can infer whether the information had meaning.

3.3.2 Information Theory

Information theory is a research area at the intersection of probability theory, statistics, information engineering, and computer science. It originated with Claude Shannon's 1948 article "A mathematical theory of communication," in which he proposed a formal framework for defining information and measuring the information content of a message. Shannon was primarily interested in how to achieve lossless transmission of information over electronic channels. His abstract approach proved so useful that there are now many applications beyond the original questions of how to quantify, store, and communicate digital information. Information theory is used in cryptography, neurobiology, linguistics, evolution, and many other fields. Because of this broad applicability in many fields, Stone (2015) compares Shannon's information theory to the great theories of Newton (classical mechanics), Einstein (relativity), and Darwin–Wallace (evolution).

Information theory is an abstract mathematical formalism that does not deal with meaning or knowledge. Semantics is the study of meaning, but Shannon himself considered the semantic aspects of communication irrelevant to the engineering problem he was trying to solve. So while information theory cannot directly help us understand meaning, it is a useful tool for thinking precisely about information and complexity. In line with the idea of complexity thinking, it should be complemented by other approaches that provide additional insights.

We measure information in bits, which is derived from binary digit, that is, a zero or a one. However, it is important to distinguish between binary digits and bits. One bit is the information needed to choose between two equally probable alternatives. The decision tree in Fig. 3.9 is useful for understanding the meaning of a bit. Suppose that you are currently at point **a** and want to travel to point **D**. The tree shows roads that lead from point **a** to various destinations from a bird's-eye view. The road system is such that there are several forks at which a traveler can either turn left or right. The decision to turn left is coded with the digit 0, and the digit 1 stands for the choice of the road to the right.

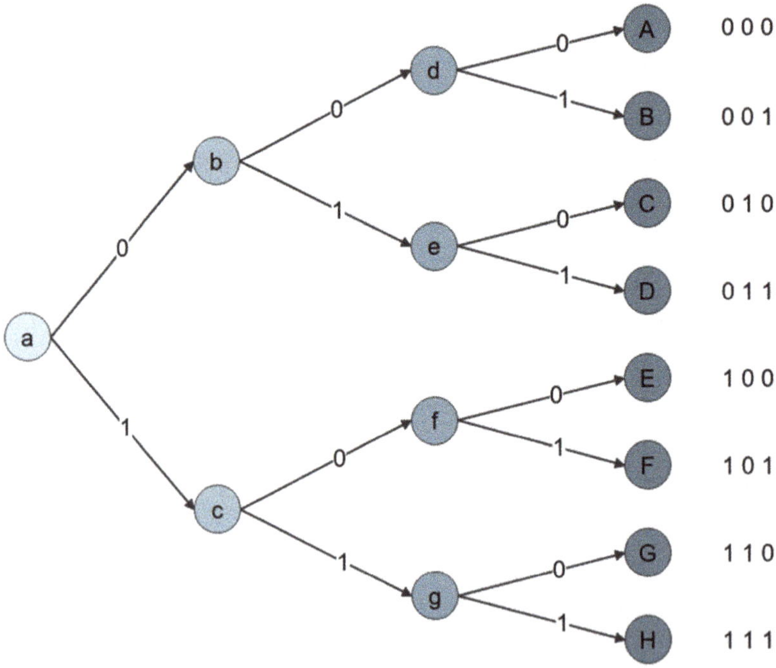

Fig. 3.9 Decision tree. Source: Author

If you do not know how to get from **a** to **D**, each fork represents a choice between two equally probable alternatives. When you ask someone if you should turn left or right at point **a** and get the answer "choose the left road (=0)," you get one bit of information. On your journey, you will then reach point **b**, where you have to choose again between the two alternatives 0 or 1. If you still do not know the complete route, choosing 0 or 1 again has the probability (= 0.5) of being correct. Therefore, the advice to choose 1 provides one more bit of information. It follows that you need three bits of information to find your way from **a** to **D**, if you do not have prior knowledge that allows you to assign a higher probability than 0.5 to any of the choices.

In order to get from **a** to **D**, you must choose "left right right" or "0 1 1" as indicated next to **D**. There are eight possible destinations, which implies three binary choices at the forks: $2 \times 2 \times 2 = 2^3 = 8$. A decision at each fork halves the number of possible destinations that can be reached. So after choosing 0 at **a**, you can only reach the destinations **A**, **B**, **C**, and **D**. In general, if there are n forks (or binary decisions), you have the choice among $m = 2^n$ final destinations. This means that you need $n = log_2 m$ bits of information to make the right choice if all alternatives have a probability of 0.5. In our example, you need 3 bits of information to find the way. The information requirement n can therefore be interpreted as a measure of the difficulty of the choice problem.

Another way to interpret the decision tree in Fig. 3.9 is to think it as a question-and-answer game in which you have to guess a word chosen by an opponent and are only allowed to ask questions that can be answered with "yes" (=1) or "no" (=0). If you can ask $n = 3$ questions, you are able to find out the right word out of a set of eight words. Suppose the set of words is A = snake, B = fish, C = dog, D = cat, E = car, F = airplane, G = radio, H = mixer and that "cat" is the correct word. The problem for you is to ask the right questions that will allow you to quickly reduce the choice set. Asking "Is it an object?" would be a stupid question that provides no information, because all words describe objects. Asking "Is the word mixer?" would not be a good question either, because if the answer is "no," you are left with a set of seven possible words and only two remaining questions. A better first question is "Is it a machine?" because this question splits the word set into two halves of four words each, giving you one bit of information. The next question could be "Does it have legs?" If the answer is "yes," you know that the word must be "dog" or "cat," which can be determined with one further question, e.g., "Is it a dog?" If you are allowed to ask 20 questions, you could in principle find the right answer with 20 bits of information in a set of more than one million words (2^{20} = 1,048,576).

As we have seen, getting an answer to a question (or getting a binary digit 0 or 1) is not equivalent to getting a bit of information. We have emphasized several times that a binary digit only provides a bit of information if the two possible answers have equal probability. If for some reason you already know that the chosen word in the 3 questions game above describes an animal, then getting a "no = 0" to the question "Is it a machine?" does not provide any information, i.e., you get 0 bits of information. Knowing that the answer is that the word does not describe a machine means that the probability that 0 is the correct answer is 1. Knowing that the probability that the answer "no = 0" is correct is 70.7% gives you exactly half a bit of information, as we will argue in the next subsection.

3.3.3 Shannon Entropy

Shannon entropy is a fundamental concept in information theory and an element of several formal measures of various types of complexity, which we will discuss later. Entropy is the average amount of surprise, unpredictability, or uncertainty in a random process, and as such it is a measure of information. Note that there is also the related concept of *thermodynamic entropy*, which is a measure of the number of states a physical system can take, and can be interpreted as the amount of disorder in a physical system. We focus here on the information-theoretic Shannon entropy.

Suppose we consider flipping a coin as an experiment with the possible outcomes head, x_h, and tail, x_t. We can define the random variable

$$X = \begin{cases} 0, & \text{if the outcome is a tail} \\ 1, & \text{if the outcome is a head} \end{cases}$$

So we assign the two outcome values {0,1} to the two possible outcomes $\{x_h, x_t\}$. If we repeat the experiment infinitely many times, we get the *probability distribution* $p(X)$ of X, which is the frequency with which the different outcomes of X occur. The probability distribution of the coin toss experiment can be written as

$$p(X) = \{p(X = x_h), p(X = x_t)\} = \{p(x_h), p(x_t)\},$$

where $p(x_h)$ is the probability of heads and $p(x_t)$ is the probability of tails. If the coin is fair, the two outcomes are equally probable; hence

$$p(X)_{\text{fair}} = \{0.5, 0.5\}.$$

The coin could also be bent so that the outcome x_h is much more likely than x_t, e.g., 90% heads vs. 10% tails. In this case, we call the coin unfair with the probability distribution

$$p(X)_{\text{unfair}} = \{0.9, 0.1\}.$$

We can use this simple experiment to illustrate the concept of *Shannon information* of the outcome of a random process. Shannon information is a measure of surprise. *Surprise* occurs when we observe an unexpected outcome. The more improbable a particular outcome is, the more surprised we are and the more information we receive. We could define the amount of surprise of an outcome x to be $1/p\{x\}$, but for mathematical reasons it is preferable to use to the logarithm (to the base 2) of the inverse of the probability. The Shannon information of a particular outcome is then

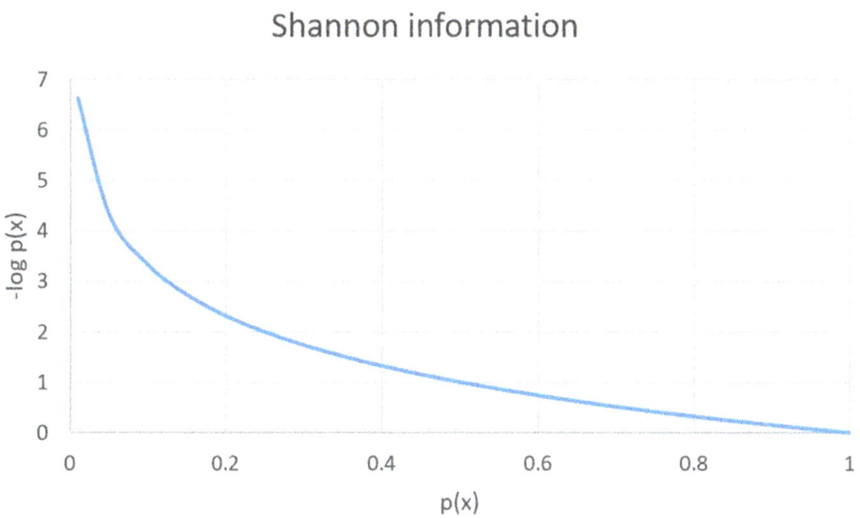

Fig. 3.10 Shannon information as a measure of surprise. Source: Author

$$h(x) = \log_2 \frac{1}{p(x)} \text{ bits} = -\log_2 p(x) \text{ bits}.$$

If the coin in our experiment is fair, a given coin toss will reveal exactly 1 bit of Shannon information, no matter what the outcome is, because $-log_2 0.5 = 1$. However, if the coin is unfair, as in our example above, a toss reveals more or less than 1 bit of information as shown in Fig. 3.10.

If we get a head and $p(x_h) = 0.9$, we get as little information as $h(x_h) = 0.152\ bits$, because heads was the expected outcome. In contrast, the outcome tails surprises us and reveals $h(x_t) = 3.322\ bits$ of information. The definition of Shannon information is the answer to the question from the previous subsection, why we get 0.5 bits of information, when the probability of a correct answer is 0.707: $-log_2 0.707 = 0.5$. To find the probability for any amount of required information, we must compute

$$p(x) = 2^{-h(x)}.$$

Usually, we are not so much interested in the information contained in a particular outcome of a random variable, but in the information content of the entire set of possible values. *Shannon entropy* $H(x)$ measures the expected or average information content of the probability distribution $p(X)$ of a random variable X. It is defined as

$$H(X) = -\sum_{i=1}^{m} p(x_i) \log_2 p(x_i).$$

Shannon entropy is the expected value of the Shannon information of all the outcomes of the random variable

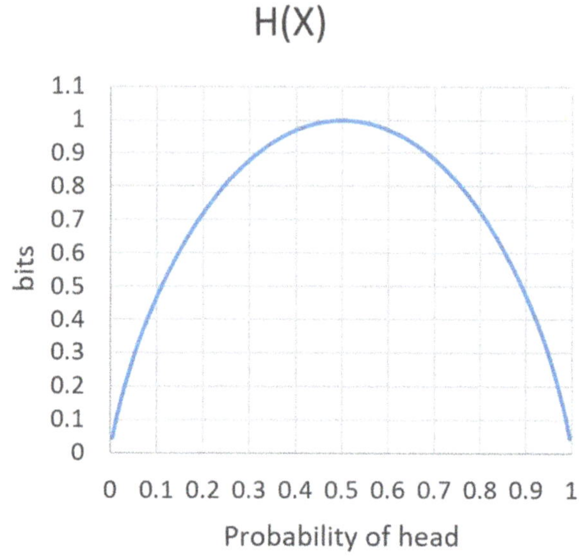

Fig. 3.11 Entropy as a function of coin bias. Source: Author

$$H(X) = E[h(X)] = \sum_{i=1}^{m} p(x_i)h(x_i).$$

We find the expected value by multiplying the Shannon information of each outcome $h(x)$ by the probability of that outcome, $p(x)$, and summing up the products. Since Shannon information is a measure of surprise, Shannon entropy measures the average amount of surprise or uncertainty in a random variable.

A fair coin has an entropy of 1 bit per coin toss, because $H(X) = -(0.5log_2 0.5 + 0.5log_2 0.5) = 1$. The unfair coin with $p(X) = \{0.9{,}01\}$ has an entropy of 0.469 bits per coin flip, because $H(X) = -(0.9log_2 0.9 + 0.1log_2 0.1) = 0.469$. As shown in Fig. 3.11, an unbiased (fair) coin has the highest entropy, while a highly biased coin generates little surprise on average. This result is intuitive, because an unfair coin will produce the expected outcome most of the time, so that on average we learn little from a coin flip.

We need the probability distribution of a random variable to compute the entropy of the variable, because the probability distribution describes our prior expectation of outcomes. Our surprise can only be measured relative to our prior expectation. In practice, the probability distribution is often not given, but must be estimated from empirical frequencies of sample data.

Summing up, Shannon entropy is a useful measure of both uncertainty and information. The two are linked, because uncertainty is reduced by information. We can define information as the difference between entropies before and after a message was sent. If a variable has high entropy, our initial uncertainty is large. This is especially the case, if all possible outcomes are equally probable in which case entropy is maximal. On average, we obtain the most information from the realization of the random variable, when the average uncertainty is largest.

There are many other entropy measures such as Renyi entropy, Tsallis entropy, or Gaussian entropy, of which Shannon entropy is a limit case.

3.4 Complexity of Patterns

We can describe patterns with tools from conventional econometrics, e.g., (auto-) correlation, trends and trend breaks, or moments of distributions. Although these measures are clearly useful, we do not treat them here, but focus information-theoretic measures based on entropy.

3.4.1 Entropy and Patterns

We can use Shannon entropy to describe patterns. Figure 3.12 shows three patterns in a 50x50 grid in two-dimensional space. Each cell $i = 1, \ldots 2500$ in this grid is either black or white. We index the cells row-wise with $i = 1$ for the first cell in the first row, $i = 2$ for the second cell, $i = 51$ for the first cell in the second row, and so on. Pattern a) on the left was generated by a random process with equal probability for each cell to be black or white, i.e., $p(black) = p(white) = 0.5$ for each cell.

Since the cells are numbered consecutively, we can represent the pattern as a sequence of $n = 2500$ random numbers or a *stochastic process*

$$X_{\text{random}} = (X_1, X_2, X_3, \ldots X_{2500}),$$

where $X_1, X_2, \ldots$ are random variables. If we assign the value 1 to the black cells and 0 to the white cells, the realized pattern shown in Fig. 3.12 can be represented as the following sequence of outcomes:

Fig. 3.12 Patterns. Source: Author

$$(x_1, x_2, x_3, \ldots, x_{30}, \ldots)$$
$$= (1,0,0,0,1,1,1,0,0,0,1,0,1,1,1,0,1,0,0,0,0,1,1,1,1,1,0,0,1,0,\ldots.).$$

Cell 1 (top left) is black ($x_1 = 1$), cell 2 (second in the first row) is white ($x_2 = 0$), and so on. The stochastic process that generated pattern a) has a joint probability distribution of X_{random}

$$p(X_{random}) = p(X_1 = x_1, X_2 = x_2, \ldots).$$

Since for each cell the probability that the color is black is 0.5, we can write $p(X_1) = p(X_2) = \ldots p(X_{2500}) = \{p(x_i) = 0, p(x_i) = 1)\} = \{0.5, 0.5\}$. We know that in this case, the entropy of each random variable is 1 bit, i.e.,

$$H(X_1) = H(X_2) = \ldots = H(X_{2500}) = H(X) = -(0.5\, log_2 0.5 + 0.5\, log_2 0.5)$$
$$= 1\ bit.$$

The question now is, what is the entropy of the whole sequence of random variables, X_{random}. If the random variables X_1, X_2, X_3, ... are independent and identically distributed (i.i.d.), which is the case here, then the entropy of the sequence is the sum of the identical entropies

$$H(X_{\text{random}}) = \sum_{i=1}^{n=2500} H(X_i) = nH(X) = n \times 1\ \text{bit} = 2500\ \text{bits}.$$

We can compare the random pattern a) with the complex pattern b) in Fig. 3.12. The complex pattern obviously has more black cells than the random pattern in the center. In general, there are more black clusters of black cells than in pattern a). The probability distribution of the sequence corresponding to the complex pattern is given by

$$p(X_i = 1) = 0.45 + \frac{i}{2500} \times \left(1 - \frac{i}{2500}\right).$$

This means that $p(X_i = 1) < 0.5$ for all $i < 132$ and $i > 2368$. In other words, the first and the last 131 cells are less likely to be black than white, and vice versa for all other cells. Cell 1250 in the middle has the highest probability of being black, $p(X_{1250}) = \{p(X_{1250} = 0), p(X_{1250} = 1)\} = \{0.3, 0.7\}$. The resulting sequence still consists of independent random variables, but they are not identically distributed because the probabilities for each cell are different. As long as the random variables are independent, we can still compute the entropy of the sequence as the sum of the entropies of the random variables, e.g.,

$$H(X_1) = -(0.4504\, log_2 0.4504 + 0.5496\, log_2 0.5496) = 0.9929$$

$$H(X_{1250}) = -(0.3\, log_2 0.3 + 0.7\, log_2 0.7) = 0.8813$$

$$H(X_{2368}) = -(0.5\,log_2 0.5 + 0.5\,log_2 0.5) = 1$$

The entropy of the complex pattern is

$$H(X_{\text{complex}}) = \sum_{i=1}^{n=2500} H(X_i) = 2358.78 < 2500$$

We could also divide the two entropies by the number of variables, $n = 2500$, in order to get the *entropy rate* or the average entropy per variable, which would be 0.9435 and 1, respectively. The complex pattern has less entropy than the completely random pattern, which means that there is less uncertainty ex ante about what the pattern might look like. Since the probabilities of black cells in the center of the grid are greater than 0.5, we can predict that the complex pattern will have more black clusters in the center than the fully random pattern.

The fully ordered pattern c) takes this to the extreme. This pattern is equivalent to the sequence (1, 0, 1, 0, 1, 0, 1, 0, 1, 0, 1, ...). The rule that generates this sequence is

$$x_i = \begin{cases} 1 & \text{if i is odd} \\ 0 & \text{if i is even} \end{cases}$$

This rule is deterministic, so that there is no uncertainty; hence

$$p(X_i) = \{p(x_i = 0), p(x_i = 1)\} = \begin{cases} \{0, 1\} & \text{if i is odd} \\ \{1, 0\} & \text{if i is even} \end{cases}$$

This means that the entropy of each variable is zero, and so is the entropy of the entire sequence

$$H(X_{\text{ordered}}) = 0.$$

So we see that lower entropy implies more order, which makes prediction easier. At the extreme of zero entropy, we have a perfectly ordered pattern that does not require probabilistic statements.

It is important to note that this example of how Shannon entropy can be used to measure the complexity of patterns is a didactic one that serves to illustrate the idea, but has limited practical applicability. One reason for the limited applicability of the example presented is that in practice we do not know the probabilities we need to compute entropy. This does not mean that we cannot use entropy, but that we must first estimate the probabilities. Another weakness of the presented approach is that we did not use knowledge about the spatial arrangement of the data. The conversion of the spatial data into a sequence was arbitrary and only for convenience, but did not play a role in the calculation of the entropy. If the real data of interest is ordered, either spatially or temporally, we should take advantage of this fact, as it is likely to be important in how we define a pattern.

3.4.2 Permutation Entropy

A useful extension of Shannon entropy that can measure the information content of a time series is *permutation entropy*, proposed by Bandt and Pompe (2002). Permutation entropy combines Shannon entropy with symbolic dynamics, which means that the numerical time series is converted into a number of symbolic blocks that capture the order relations between the numerical values. These order relations are called permutations π and describe ordinal patterns in the time series. We can count how often the permutations occur and compute the entropy of the permutations.

Let's look at an example of how this works. Suppose we have the time series of seven values shown in Fig. 3.13:

$$x(t) = \{4, 7, 9, 10, 6, 11, 3\}$$

We now want to create partitions of overlapping vectors from this time series. The simplest case is to form vectors of neighboring values, but we could also use values with a *time delay* greater than 1. We have to choose the length of these vectors, which is called the order n or *embedding dimension*. Bandt and Pompe (2002) recommend using $3 \leq n \leq 7$. Let's use $n = 3$ and collect the vectors of length 3 in a matrix:

$$\begin{bmatrix} 4 & 7 & 9 & 6 \\ 7 & 9 & 10 & 11 \\ 9 & 10 & 6 & 3 \end{bmatrix}$$

The resulting 5 vectors overlap; i.e., the first two vectors share the values 7 and 9, the second and third share 9 and 10, and so forth. The next step is to convert these vectors into permutations that describe the ordinal ranking of the values. In the first vector, we have $4 < 7 < 9$ which could be captured by the permutation $\{1, 2, 3\}$. Similarly, we can preserve the order $10 > 6$, $6 < 11$, $10 < 11$ of the fourth vector with the permutation $\{2, 1, 3\}$. With an order of $n = 3$, we get $3\,! = 1 * 2 * 3 = 6$ possible permutations representing ordinal patterns in the data:

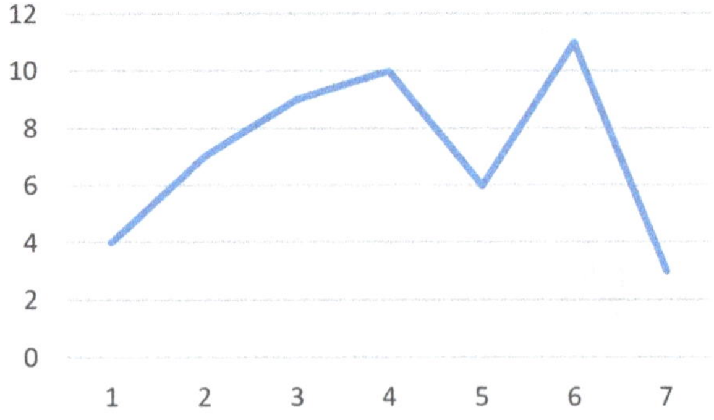

Fig. 3.13 Example time series. Source: Author

$\pi_1 = \{1, 2, 3\}$

$\pi_4 = \{2, 3, 1\}$

$\pi_2 = \{1, 3, 2\}$

$\pi_5 = \{3, 1, 2\}$

$\pi_3 = \{2, 1, 3\}$

$\pi_6 = \{3, 2, 1\}$

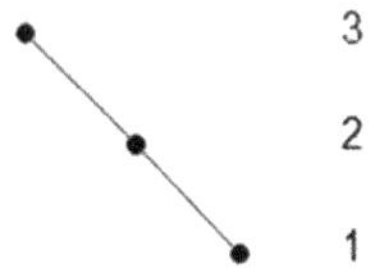

Replacing the original matrix with the corresponding permutations results in the permutation matrix:

$$\begin{bmatrix} 1 & 1 & 2 & 2 & 2 \\ 2 & 2 & 3 & 1 & 3 \\ 3 & 3 & 1 & 3 & 1 \end{bmatrix}$$

We now have to estimate the probability of each permutation, which can be done by using its relative frequency:

$$p(\pi_1) = p(\pi_4) = 2/5$$

$$p(\pi_2) = p(\pi_5) = p(\pi_6) = 0$$

$$p(\pi_3) = 1/5$$

The permutation entropy of order n is defined as

$$PE_n = -\sum_{i=1}^{n!} p_i(\pi_i) \, log\,_2 p_i(\pi_i)$$

To make the measure independent of the number of permutations, we can normalize it by dividing it by the maximum value of PE_n:

$$\bar{PE}_n = \frac{-1}{\log_2 n!} \sum_{i=1}^{n!} p_i(\pi_i) \log_2 p_i(\pi_i)$$

The normalized permutation entropy is always in the interval [0,1]. In our example, we have $PE_3 = 1.5219$ and $\bar{PE}_3 = 0.5887$. As with Shannon entropy, lower values indicate more order and higher values indicate more noise, making the time series less predictable. If every partition of the time series formed a different pattern, we would have five different permutations, resulting in $\bar{PE}_3 = 0.898$. In this case, the time series were very irregular and hard to predict. In contrast, if the time series were generated by a deterministic positive trend, all observations would be represented by permutation π_1, resulting in $\bar{PE}_3 = 0$. A deterministic trend is, of course, perfectly predictable.

So what can we do with permutation entropy? Cánovas et al. (2018) apply permutation entropy to detect structural changes in simulated data and in real data on earthquakes, the gold price, and the NASDAQ stock price index. In their first example, they simulate a time series x_t with 1200 observations, with

$$x_t = \begin{cases} 4x_{t-1}(1 - x_{t-1}) & t \leq 600 \\ \epsilon_t & t > 600 \end{cases}$$

where ϵ_t is a random variable from a uniform distribution on [0,1]. The function used to generate the first half of the time series is the *logistic map* that can generate chaotic dynamics, which is the case here. Permutation entropy is computed for a rolling window with a length of $k = 120$. As Fig. 3.14 shows, permutation entropy increases markedly after $t = 600$, which is when the structural change occurs. As expected, the random part of the time series has a normalized entropy close to 1, while the chaotic part has more structure resulting in the lower entropy of about 0.85.

Henry and Judge (2019) apply permutation entropy of order 4 to the daily stock market nominal returns of the Dow Jones Industrial Average (DJIA) from 1901 to 2016. For this entire period, they calculate a normalized PE of 0.998, which is very close to 1, suggesting a high degree of randomness. This can be interpreted as high efficiency of the US stock market, which processes all available information as predicted by the efficient market hypothesis. However, the picture is somewhat different, when a rolling window with a length of 750 trading days is used

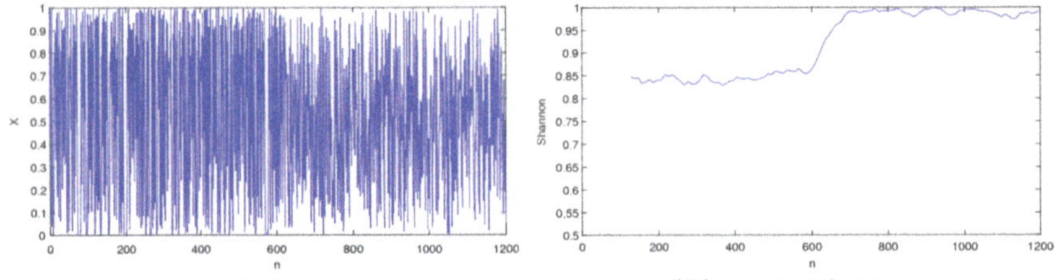

(a) Data series of Example 1.

(b) Shannon permutation entropy.

Fig. 3.14 Permutation entropy to detect a structural change. Source: Cánovas et al. (2018), reproduced with kind permission of Elsevier

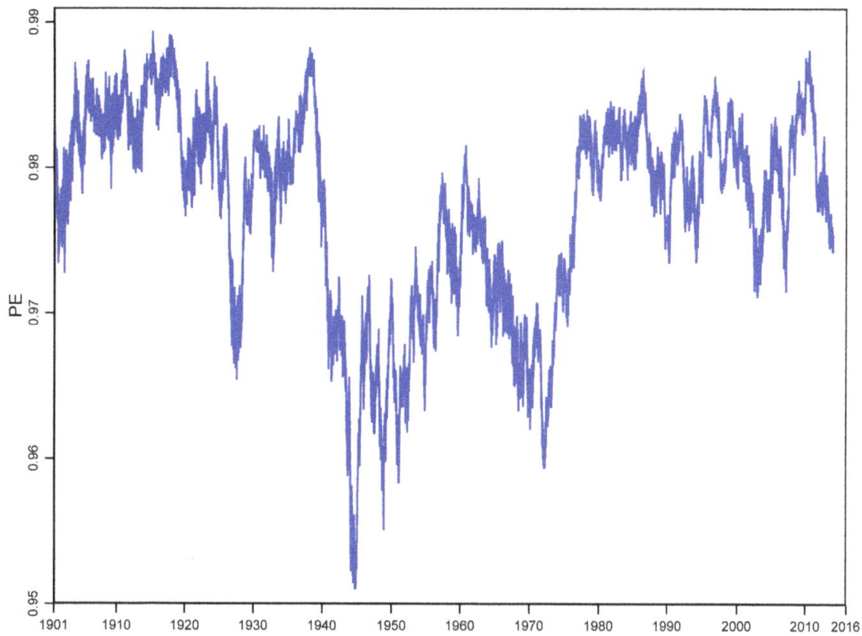

Fig. 3.15 Permutation entropy of daily nominal returns of of the Dow Jones Industrial Average. Source: Henry and Judge (2019). CC BY 3.0 Unported (https://creativecommons.org/licenses/by/3.0/)

in order to compute the evolution of permutation entropy (of order 5) over time (see Fig. 3.15). Two results are noteworthy. The first thing to notice is that $\bar{PE} < 0.99$ when the entropy is computed over 3-year intervals. Thus, in the short run DJIA returns are not fully random, but contain patterns that at least theoretically make them predictable. Second, the average value of $\bar{PE}$ is lower in the period between 1940 and 1975 than at the beginning and end of the entire period, suggesting less efficiency and some structural difference. The complexity measure cannot explain why this apparent structural change occurred. We might think that is related to the Bretton Woods system, but this is only a hypothesis that would have to be explored with other methods. Permutation entropy can help us detect interesting patterns in empirical data that might be worth further analysis.

There are several proposals to correct some of the shortcomings of permutation entropy. Weighted permutation entropy, for example, makes PE more robust to observational noise by giving more weight to the probabilities of permutations that contain large amplitude changes.

3.4.3 Statistical Complexity

As argued earlier, neither perfect order nor pure randomness is complex, but simple. At zero entropy, a pattern is perfectly predictable, and at maximum entropy, a pattern is completely unpredictable. Complex phenomena lie between these extremes, combining order and disorder (see Fig. 3.16).

There are several measures of complexity based on the idea that complexity is highest somewhere between order and disorder. These measures are called *statistical complexity* measures because they aim to capture the statistical or correlational structure of an object. They are often of the form

$$\text{Complexity} = \text{Disorder} \times \text{Order}$$

Thus, a measure of order and a measure of disorder (or randomness) are combined multiplicatively, because complexity is zero if either measure is zero. Disorder is typically measured with some form of entropy. How to measure order is less straightforward. One way has been proposed by López-Ruiz et al. (1995). These authors (LMC) consider physical systems and take a crystal to be perfectly ordered because its atoms are arranged in a perfectly symmetric way, which requires very little information to describe. An ideal gas is completely disordered because its molecules are distributed with equal probability in all accessible states.

From a thermodynamic perspective, the equiprobable distribution of states is an equilibrium. Therefore, they measure order as the deviation from equilibrium or as disequilibrium D, which is counterintuitive for economists. Their complexity measure is hence

$$C_{LMC}(X) = H(X) \times D(X),$$

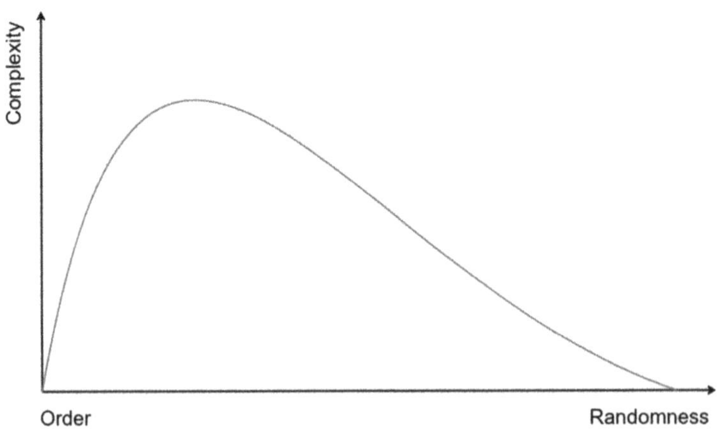

Fig. 3.16 Complexity combines order and randomness. Source: Author

where *H*(*X*) is the Shannon entropy of the random variable *X* and measures disorder. Order D can be measured by the *Kullback–Leibler divergence* or *relative entropy*, which is a type of statistical distance between two probability distributions. For discrete probability distributions *P* and *Q*, it is defined as

$$D_{KL}(P \mid |Q) = \sum_X P(X) \log \left(\frac{P(X)}{Q(X)} \right).$$

A simpler measure of order is the the squared deviation of the actual probability distribution *P*(*X*) from the uniform distribution:

$$D_{SD}(X) = \sum\nolimits_{i=1}^{N} (p_i - 1/N)^2.$$

If there is only one dominant state of the atoms as in a crystal with $p_c = 1$ and the number of possible states N is very large, then $D_{SD} \rightarrow 1$, which would be the maximum value for order. If—as in an ideal gas—all states are equally likely, i.e., $p_i = 1/N$, then $D_{SD} = 0$.

Lamberti et al. (2004) prefer to speak of *non-triviality* instead of statistical complexity. Their measure of statistical complexity or non-triviality is similar to the LMC measure, but corrects some of its shortcomings by measuring disequilibrium (or order) with *Jensen–Shannon divergence* $J[P, U]$ instead of the squared deviation from equiprobability:

$$C_{JS}(X) = \frac{H(P)}{H_{max}} \times \frac{J[P, U]}{J_{max}}.$$

The Jensen–Shannon divergence quantifies the distance of the probability distribution *P*(*X*), which is used to compute the entropy *H*, from the uniform distribution *U* in the following way:

$$J[P, U] = \left(H\left[\frac{P + U}{2} \right] - \frac{H[P]}{2} - \frac{H[U]}{2} \right)$$

J_{max} and H_{max} are normalization constants that are equal to the maximum possible values of *J* and *H*.

Statistical complexity and permutation entropy can be combined in the so-called *complexity-entropy causality plane* (CECP). The spatial representation with statistical complexity on the vertical axis and permutation entropy on the horizontal axis can be used to assess the degree of market (in)efficiency. Permutation entropy quantifies the degree of randomness and thus the potential predictability of a time series. Statistical complexity measures whether some ordinal patterns occur more frequently for a given level of permutation entropy, thus capturing the degree of correlation structure in the time series. The CECP is informative about the efficiency of markets, because we can measure the distance of a point in the plane computed from a financial time series to the vertex with $\bar{PE} = 1$ and $C_{JS} = 0$. A time series with

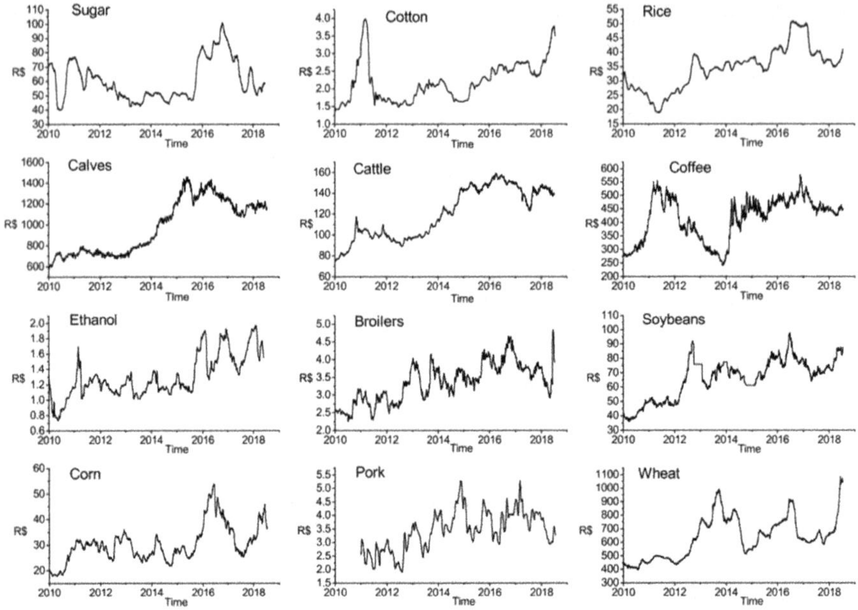

Fig. 3.17 Time series of commodity prices in Brazil. Source: de Araujo et al. (2019). CC BY 4.0 (https://creativecommons.org/licenses/by/4.0/)

these values is completely random with no correlation structure. Zunino et al. (2010) located stock markets of different countries in the CECP and find that the stock markets of developed countries are more efficient (with more random time series of prices) than the stock markets of emerging countries. Similarly, de Araujo et al. (2019) analyzed the prices of Brazilian agricultural commodities shown in Fig. 3.17.

The CECP is shown in Fig. 3.18. The markets for coffee and wheat are close to the right vertex (1,0) and are therefore very efficient. In contrast, the markets for pork, broilers, and cotton are far from the efficiency vertex. The price time series are clearly not random and contain a significant correlation structure with some dominant patterns. The distance from the (1,0) vertex is a natural measure of market inefficiency. When the embedding dimension (order) is set to 5, the Euclidean distance to the (1,0) vertex is 0.132 for coffee and 0.531 for pork. It is also interesting to note that some commodities have similar positions in the CECP, such as cattle and calves, ethanol and sugar, and soybeans and corn, suggesting links between the markets. Since cattle and calves are both part of the beef production chain, their link is obvious. Soybeans and corn are both important animal feeds. Perhaps the most interesting pair is ethanol and sugar, both of which are produced from the same crop (sugar cane). One reason for the similar characteristics of the price series may be that there is a trade-off between using sugar cane to produce either sugar or ethanol. For example, when the world price of oil is high, there is a high demand for ethanol as a substitute for gasoline. In this case, the supply of ethanol should increase and the supply of sugar should decrease. The CECP only shows the patterns in the data; it

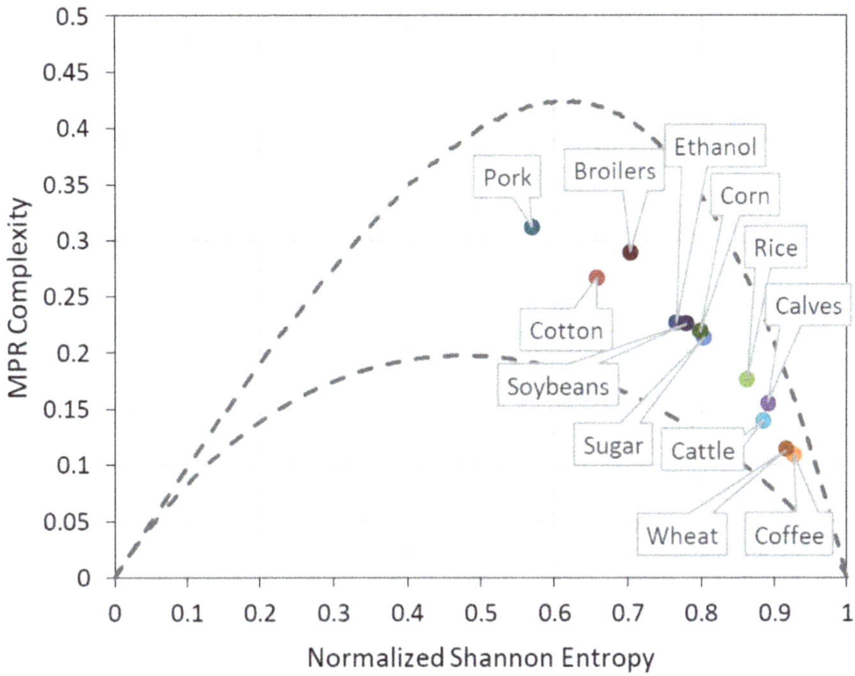

Fig. 3.18 Complexity entropy causality plane for Brazilian commodities. Source: de Araujo et al. (2019). CC BY 4.0 (https://creativecommons.org/licenses/by/4.0/)

does not explain them. It is a useful tool because it reveals patterns that are not apparent in the time series graphs in Fig. 3.17, where the time series of sugar and ethanol, for example, do not look very similar.

3.5 Complexity of Systems

It is not easy to make general statements about the complexity of systems because there are many different types of systems that are difficult to compare. We can distinguish between natural systems, which are created by nature, and artificial systems, which are designed and created by humans. Among natural systems, physical and chemical systems differ from biological systems. Both technical systems, such as cars and airplanes, and social systems, such as corporations and religious communities, are artificial, but of very different kinds. Obviously, a rainforest, a passenger plane, and the program code of a computer game are complex in different ways, which means that the appropriate measures of complexity will vary. Specific approaches to measuring the complexity of systems have been explored in engineering, computer science, biology, and other fields. We cover some basic ideas useful to economists here, while leaving more sophisticated approaches to later chapters.

A good starting point for our discussion is systems engineering, which deals with the design, construction, and management of complex technical systems throughout their life cycles. Examples of complex engineering systems include airplanes, spacecraft, ships, and factories. Systems engineers are interested in complexity because it affects variables such as reliability, cost, production time, and ease of use of the systems. Importantly, systems engineering focuses not only on machines, but also on machine–human systems and systems of systems. While a car is a purely technical system, a car with its driver is a human–machine system whose function depends on both the car and the human driver. Road traffic is an example of a system of systems because it consists of many car–driver systems. Similarly, a container ship is a highly complex system that is part of systems of systems, such as the maritime transportation system and global logistics chains.

Gaspar et al. (2012) distinguish five aspects of system complexity applied to ship design, as shown in Fig. 3.19. Two traditional dimensions are the *structural aspect* and the *behavioral aspect*. The structural aspect refers to the form of the system components and their interrelationships, which together determine the function of the system. The components may be subsystems, such as the propulsion system or the hull of a ship, which are themselves composed of physical objects as components, such as gears and propellers. The behavioral aspect captures how the system performs its function and how it responds to external stimuli. More recent aspects of system complexity are contextual, temporal, and perceptual. The *contextual aspect* refers to the complexity of the system's environment, which is outside the control of the system designer, but should be considered during the design process. In the case of technical systems, the relevant environment includes market variables, regulations, and rules. The *temporal aspect* characterizes changes in the context during the lifetime of the system. The *perceptual aspect* of complexity is related to how the system is interpreted from the perspective of the system stakeholders. Complexity is high when there are many conflicting interpretations of a design decision. For example, a ship designer might consider installing technology to reduce air emissions. While environmental groups would perceive the emission reduction and environmental benefit, ship owners would perceive higher construction costs and ship users would perceive higher maintenance costs. These aspects of the complexity of an engineered system are also relevant to businesses as economic systems that are also designed, at least in part, to serve particular purposes. In the following subsections, we focus mainly on measuring the structural aspects of system complexity.

3.5.1 Measurement of System Complexity

Lloyd (2001) has compiled a list of complexity measures which he organized around three questions:

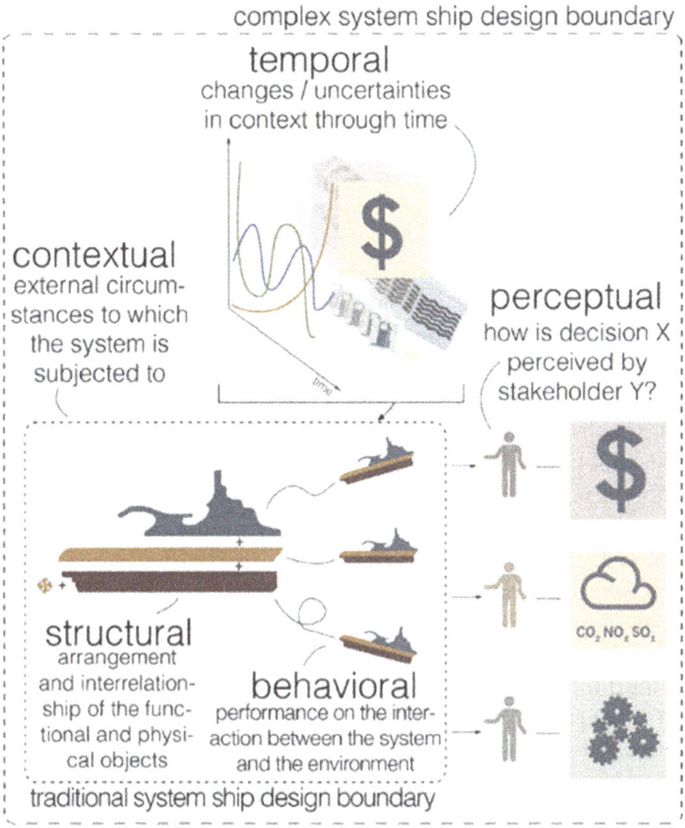

Fig. 3.19 Five aspects of system complexity in ship design. Source: Gaspar et al. 2012, reproduced with kind permission of SNAME

1. How difficult is the object or system to describe?
2. How difficult is it to create?
3. What is its degree of organization?

Kolmogorov complexity (also called *Kolmogorov–Chaitin complexity*, *algorithmic complexity*, or *algorithmic information content*) is a theoretical measure of the difficulty of describing an object. It is given by the length of the shortest computer program that can produce the object as an output. Obviously, this measure depends on the chosen programming language. Therefore, it is defined in terms of a universal description language. To understand the idea of Kolmogorov complexity, we can look the following example strings of 60 characters:

```
1. abababababababababababababababababababababababababababababab
2. ghsixngsjjdsbmnsstqsgahdostzdddgwdccjajkgasmtzzswfpdvquethab
```

The first string can be compressed by decomposing it into the repeated string "ab." A simple description of 17 characters (including spaces) is "write ab 30 times." The second string has no simple pattern that can be used for a simple description and looks random. The shortest pseudocode to describe this string is "write ghsixngsjjdsbmnsstqsgahdostzdddgwdccjajkgasmtzzswfpdvquethab," which consists of 66 characters and is even longer than the string itself. According to Kolmogorov complexity, an object is more complex than another if its shortest algorithmic description is longer. As an information-theoretic measure, its unit is "bits." While we can use examples to illustrate the idea of Kolmogorov complexity, it can be shown that it is not computable for arbitrary input strings. While this measure is theoretically important, it is of limited practical use. For practical purposes, Kolmogorov complexity can be approximated by *Lempel–Ziv complexity* which is based on a compression algorithm that identifies repetitive sequences of a specified maximum length in a string. The Lempel–Ziv complexity is defined as the ratio of the length of the program that executes this algorithm and the length of the original string. It is a tool to quantify the uncertainty in a string or its information content. A string is the more complex and contains more information, the fewer repetitive elements it contains.

Regarding symbolic sequences as objects, there is not much difference between their description and their creation, since a computer program generates these sequences as output. However, we can distinguish *computational complexity* as a measure of the difficulty of creation from *algorithmic complexity* as a measure of the difficulty of description by using different units of measurement. While algorithmic complexity measures the information context in bits, computational complexity and other approaches measure the resources like time, energy, or money needed to actually create the object. If the object is actually created by a computer program, the running time of the program or the amount of memory required are measures of the complexity of the object. Engineered systems such as ships or buildings are more complex if they require more time, material, or human resources.

The most interesting question concerns the degree of organization of a system discussed in the following subsections.

3.5.2 Structural Complexity

Structural complexity depends primarily on the number of components or elements in the system, N. Systems with more components are more complex. They contain more information and are more difficult to describe and build. However, as discussed in Chap. 2, systems have complex behavior because of the interactions between their elements, so we should consider the number of relationships or links between the elements, M. A simple measure of structural complexity is the product of the two:

$$CS = N \times M.$$

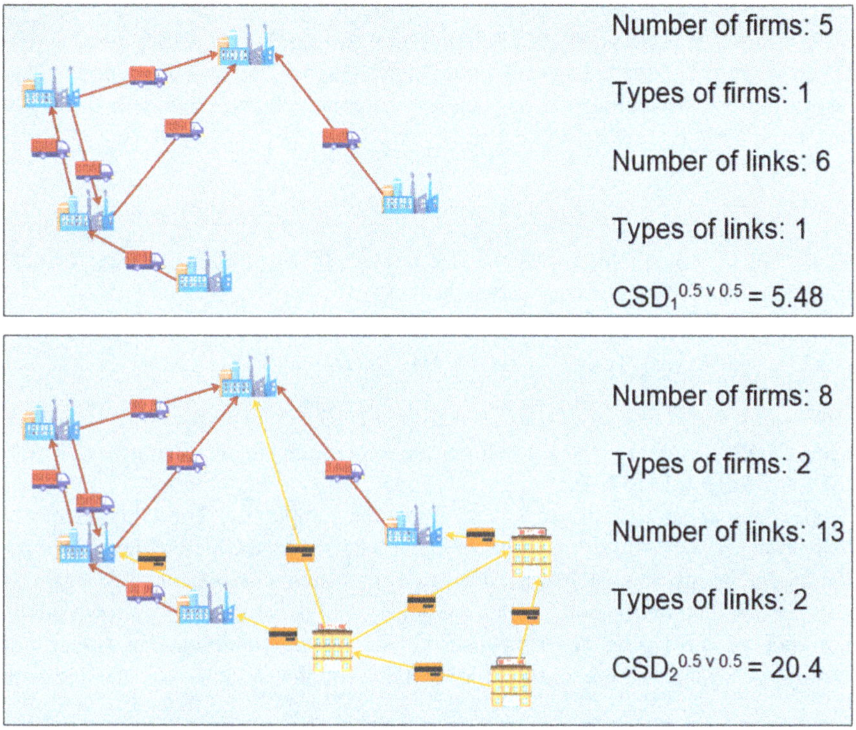

Fig. 3.20 Two economics systems with different structures. Source: Author

But there are other dimensions of structural complexity, such as *diversity* and *hierarchy*. Figure 3.20 shows two economic systems consisting of firms linked by business relationships. The two systems differ in size, i.e., in the number of elements and links, but also in diversity. Unlike the first system, the second system has two types of firms (manufacturing firms and financial firms) and two types of relationships (exchange of goods and credit relationships) represented by the trucks and the credits cards. Intuitively, the second system in the lower part of Fig. 3.20 is more complex than the first system, but this complexity is not only the consequence of the larger number of elements and relationships. Using the measure proposed above, system 1 has a structural complexity of $CS_1 = 5 \times 6 = 30$ and the second of $CS_2 = 8 \times 13 = 104$. Therefore, system 2 would be 3.47 times as complex as system 1. We can use the same logic to define a measure of structural complexity that accounts for diversity by multiplying the number of elements and links by the number of element types D_e and the number of link types D_l:

$$CSD = N \times M \times D_e \times D_l$$

A drawback of this measure is that it grows very fast. We get $CSD_1 = 5 \times 6 \times 1 \times 1 = 30$ for the first system and $CSD_2 = 8 \times 13 \times 2 \times 2 = 416$ for the second. The second system would hence be 13.87 times more complex than the first system, which may not be plausible. Alternatively, we could take the fourth root

$$CSD^{0.25} = (N \times M \times D_e \times D_l)^{0.25}$$

or calculate the complexity measure as the product of two square roots, i.e., treat the structural part and the diversity part separately:

$$CSD^{0.5|0.5} = (N \times M)^{0.5} \times (D_e \times D_l)^{0.5}.$$

We get $CSD_1^{0.25} = 2.34$, $CSD_2^{0.25} = 4.52$ and $CSD_1^{0.5|0.5} = 5.48$, $CSD_2^{0.5|05} = 20.4$. With $CSD^{0.25}$ system 2 is 1.93 times more complex than system 1 and with $CSD^{0.5\,|\,0.5}$ the ratio is 3.72.

Hierarchy is another dimension of structural complexity. The components of many systems are themselves systems. Figure 3.21 shows the hierarchical organization of a company that has two business units as system components. The business units are made up of divisions, which are made up of departments. As shown on the right side of the figure, departments could be further subdivided into teams of employees, which are the most basic elements of the system. We can measure

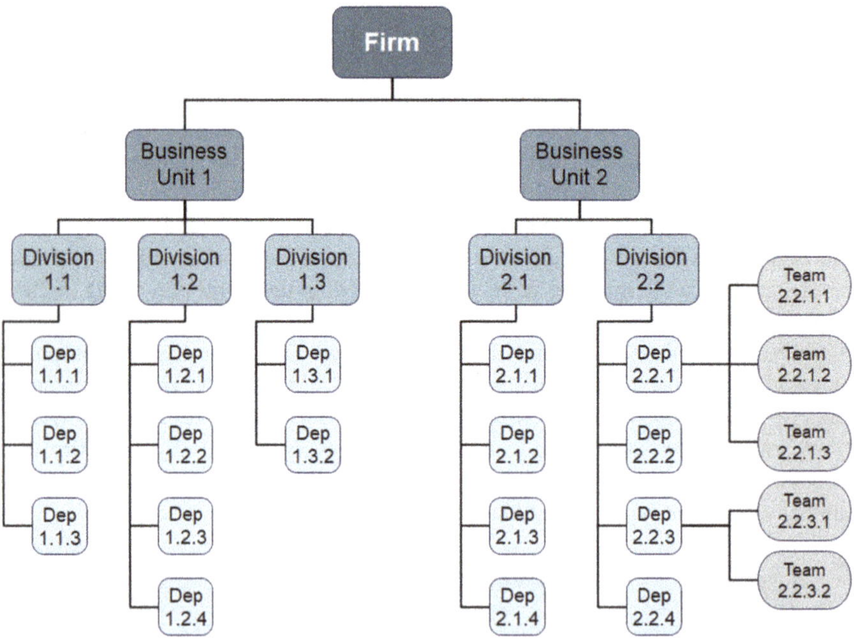

Fig. 3.21 Hierarchical organization of a firm. Source: Author

hierarchy by counting the number of levels of subsystems in a system. In the example in Fig. 3.21, there are five levels: (1) individual, (2) team, (3) department, (4) division, and (5) business unit, so we could use $CH = 5$ as a measure of complexity in the hierarchy dimension.

The measures proposed here are extremely simple and do not have a deep theoretical foundation. Depending on the type of system being considered, e.g., computer software, a ship, or an organism, much more sophisticated measures can be constructed that take into account the particularities of the system. It is unlikely that a sophisticated universal measure of structural complexity can be defined, given the diversity of systems.

3.5.3 Functional Complexity

Functional complexity is of interest in biology with respect to ecosystems and organisms, in computer science with respect to software and in organizational science with respect to the functions of and within an organization. At first glance, it seems easy to define functional complexity: a system is more functionally complex, if it can perform a greater number of different tasks. These functions may have evolved, as in biological and social systems, or may have been designed, as in technical systems. Unfortunately, there are several problems with this seemingly simple definition (see McShea 2000).

The first problem is that it is not easy to determine the number of different functions of a system. For simplicity, let's consider two tools: a hammer and a Swiss Army knife. Spontaneously, most people would say that the Swiss Army knife is more functionally complex than the hammer, because it is designed to perform more functions, such as cutting, opening cans, sawing, driving screws, and so on. The hammer, on the other hand, is only designed for hammering. But we can ask whether hammering nails and hammering rocks are two different functions or just one. Moreover, a hammer can be used for tasks for which it was not designed, e.g., as a weapon, as a piece of sports equipment, as a doorstop, or to make music. On the other hand, there are tasks that a hammer cannot perform, such as driving a screw (although a hammer is sometimes called a Birmingham screwdriver). One way to deal with the problem of function identification is to look at the commonalities between, for example, hammering a nail, hammering a rock, and using the hammer to make music. The hammer is designed to transfer kinetic energy to an object, e.g., to drive a nail into a piece of wood, to break a rock, or to produce a sound. When the hammer is used as a doorstop or a paperweight, we use its gravitational potential energy. A Swiss Army knife may not be ideal for hammering, but in principle we can also use it to transfer kinetic energy to an object, and of course we can also use its gravitational potential energy to weigh something down. In addition, a knife can cut other objects, which a hammer cannot do. In this sense, the Swiss Army knife can perform more different *types* of functions and has a higher functional complexity. For organizations or organisms, it can still be difficult to identify all types of functions.

With respect to organisms, McShea (2000) argues that parts can be used as proxies for functions, implying that organisms with more different parts have greater functional complexity than organisms with fewer different parts. Looking at the parts of a system may in many cases be easier than directly identifying the functions of the system. A part of a system is both highly integrated into the system and to some extent isolated from it. Integration means that the part coordinates its functions with other parts to achieve a system-level function. At the same time, some isolation is necessary to minimize outside interference so that the part can perform its function properly. For example, in a company, production and marketing are different functions that require coordination, but they tend to be largely isolated. The marketing department needs to know the characteristics of the goods produced and may feed back market responses to production to improve the marketability of the products. In general, however, marketing specialists do not participate directly in production, nor do production workers deal with marketing issues. According to McShea, we should not expect a 1:1 relationship between parts and functions of organisms because some parts may have multiple functions or no function at all. However, there should be a strong positive correlation with low variance because parts with no function and parts with many functions should be rare. Parts that had a function in the past but lost it should disappear over time due to selection. Parts with too many functions may become dysfunctional if the different functions compete for limited resources of the parts, e.g., energy.

The same logic can be applied to businesses. Companies with many parts are likely to have more functions than companies with few parts and thus have greater functional complexity. Functional complexity is thus related to division of labor and specialization. The parts of the firm could be either individual employees or subdivisions such as departments. According to this logic, a multinational corporation should be much more functionally complex than a one-person startup.

A one-man startup entrepreneur, such as a computer programmer, must perform many functions, such as programming, acquiring programming work, marketing, obtaining financing, and dealing with taxes. Since the entrepreneur has limited resources in terms of time, energy, and knowledge, he can only perform his main function of programming with low efficiency. Nevertheless, he must invest time and effort in marketing and acquisition; otherwise he will have no work. Hiring an employee allows for a division of labor; e.g., the employee could do all the commercial tasks so that the programmer can focus on programming and advising customers. As a result, the company can take on more programming jobs and generate more revenue. Of course, the commercial functions could be divided even further by hiring more people, such as an accountant, a finance expert, and a marketing expert. However, if there is only one programmer, there may not be enough work for the rest of the team, or there may be some overlap in the functions of the accountant and finance expert, resulting in inefficiency.

In summary, functional complexity can be roughly measured by the number of different parts of the system. It is related to structural complexity, but conceptually different.

3.5.4 Cyclomatic Complexity

The causal structure of a system is also an important determinant of its complexity. *Cyclomatic complexity* is a measure of how complicated the causal structure of a system is. Cyclomatic complexity, proposed by McCabe (1976), is widely used by programmers as a metric for assessing the complexity of software, but it is also useful for describing other systems. The main idea behind this metric is that it becomes very difficult for humans to understand the logic of a computer program when there are many conditionals (if-then-else statements) in the code, because they generate different paths through the program. The more paths there are, the greater the likelihood of errors in the code and the possibility of unexpected behavior.

Cyclomatic complexity can be defined in two ways, either with respect to the control-flow graph of a computer program or with respect to any strongly connected graph. Let's look at the control-flow graph version first. Figure 3.22 shows the control-flow graphs of simple computer programs. There is only one path from the red starting point of the program to the dark blue exit point in graph A. Graph B has a condition where the path is either through the light blue node or through the darker node, so there are two possible paths through the program. The condition has added one path to the first path. Similarly, there are three paths through graph C because there is a second condition that adds another path.

In a single control flow graph, the cyclomatic complexity is equal to the number of binary conditionals plus 1, but it is usually computed as

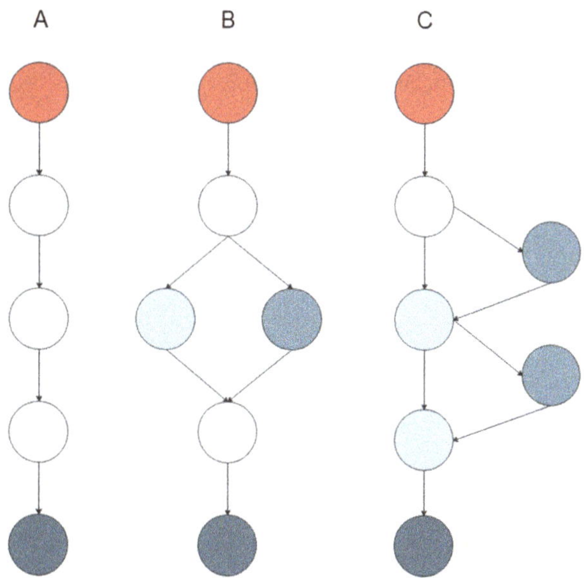

Fig. 3.22 Control-flow graphs of the simple programs. Source: Author

$$CC = M - N + 2P,$$

where M is the number of links, N is the number of nodes, and P is the number of *connected components*. In our examples in Fig. 3.22, each graph A, B, and C consists of one connected component, because all nodes are connected. If A, B, and C belonged to one program, then the graph of that program would consist of three connected components (or unconnected subgraphs). Program A has a cyclomatic complexity $CC = 4 - 5 + 2 = 1$. In program B, we have $CC = 6 - 6 + 2 = 2$, and in program C, we have $CC = 8 - 7 + 2 = 3$.

Alternatively, cyclomatic complexity can be calculated for *strongly connected graphs* as

$$CC = M - N + P.$$

In a strongly connected graph, every node can be reached from every other node. We can convert the graphs in Fig. 3.23 to strongly connected graphs by adding a link between the exit node and the start node, as shown in Fig. 3.23. Instead of paths, cyclomatic complexity in this version measures the number of independent loops or cycles in the graph, which is 1 in graph A and 3 in graph C. When the graphs represent not the control flow of a computer program, but the causal structure of a system, we can interpret each directed link as a causal effect of one node on another in the direction of the arrow. Thus, in graph C, the red node causally affects the white node, and the white node affects the first light blue node and the first dark blue node. In this view, it is obvious that graph C has a more complicated causal structure than graph A, because there are direct and indirect causal effects. The light blue nodes are

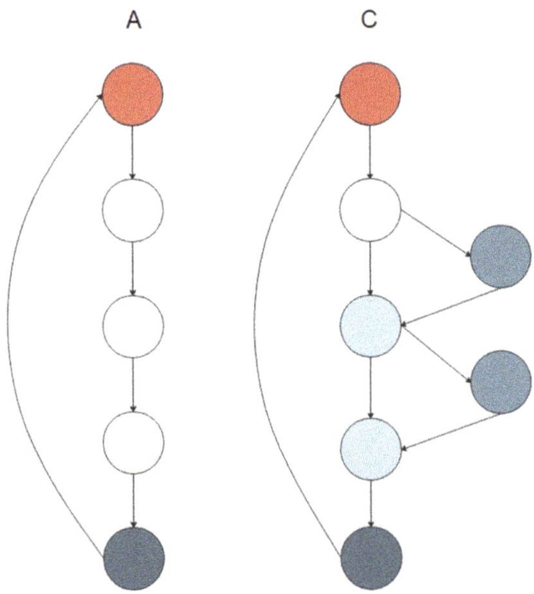

Fig. 3.23 Strongly connected graphs. Source: Author

directly influenced by the neighbor directly above them, but also indirectly influenced by the darker nodes.

3.5.5 Organizational Complexity

Rebout et al. (2021) look at systems from a biological perspective and argue that both biological organisms and social organizations have three important dimensions: diversity, flexibility, and combinability. They argue that a system is more complex if it produces more uncertain outcomes, which depends on its organizational characteristics. Information theory can be used to conceptualize how the uncertainty of the system's output is related to its properties. The organizational complexity of a system can be measured by a composite complexity index

$$K = D + F + C,$$

in which D, F, and C are based on Shannon entropies of diversity, flexibility, and combinability. For each dimension, normalized entropy is computed:

$$h_X = \frac{H_X}{H_{X,\max}} = \frac{-1}{\log_2 S_X} \sum_{i=1}^{S_X} p_{X,i} \log_2 p_{X,i}, \quad X = \{d, f, c\}.$$

It is possible to measure each dimension by several indicators. Therefore, the sub-indexes of complexity D, F, and C are averages of entropies for the n individual indicators:

$$Y = \sum_{j=1}^{n} \frac{1}{n} h_X, \quad Y = \{D, F, C\}$$

For example, *diversity* D might be measured by two variables d_1 and d_2. We hence compute the normalized entropies h_{d_1} and h_{d_2} and resulting in $D = \frac{1}{2} h_{d_1} + \frac{1}{2} h_{d_2}$. Diversity is related to creativity, so more diverse teams in organizations generate more unexpected or uncertain outcomes. We could measure diversity by the shares of employees in a certain age range or by gender.

Flexibility refers to the ability of system elements to change their behavior or state. We could also call it variability or adaptability, which is a property of complex *adaptive* systems. In a company, flexibility could be measured by the degree to which general-purpose technologies or highly specialized technologies are used. A firm that uses highly specialized technologies is less flexible than one that uses more general-purpose technologies. Other measures could be the proportion of employees who are willing to participate in regular training activities, or the proportion of revenues generated in certain markets.

Combinability captures the patterns of interactions between the system elements. A way to measure the patterns of interactions in an organization might be to count how often one member of the organization reaches out to another in order to exchange information. For example, we could count the average number of emails

Table 3.1 Average numbers of emails sent to coworkers per day

	E1	E2	E3	E4
E1		4	1	5
E2	7		1	2
E3	1	3		8
E4	6	4	4	

each employee sends to colleagues in a business day and relate these absolute numbers to the total number of internal emails in order to obtain the probabilities p_{c_i} that we need to calculate Shannon entropy. Table 3.1 gives an example of how this might look like. There are four people in a team, E1, E2, E3, and E4. The numbers in the table are the average numbers of emails the person in each row sends to the people in the columns; e.g., E1 on average sends 4 emails to E2 and 5 to E4. The total number of emails sent in the team is 46, so that the proportion of emails E1 sends to E2 is $p_{1,\,2} = 4/46$. Using these proportions, we get an entropy of $H_c = 3.31$. The maximum entropy in a team of 16 people is $H_{max} = log_2 12 = 3.58$, because people do not send emails to themselves. The maximum entropy, i.e., the level of general interaction, is reached when all members send the same number of messages to each other. Normalizing by this maximum gives $h_c = \frac{3.31}{3.58} = 0.925$.

Let's use the organizational complexity index to compare two hypothetical companies: a startup and an established firm, for which various indicators are shown in Table 3.2. Diversity is measured in the three dimensions gender, age, and nationality. In each case, the share of employees in each of the respective category is shown. The log of the number of categories is the maximum entropy H_{max} for each indicator, e.g., $H_{\max} = \log_2 3$ for the three gender categories male, female, and diverse. The startup is more diverse than the established firm in terms of gender and nationality, but not in terms of the age structure, because its workforce is very young. We measure flexibility only by the share of revenue generated in different markets. If a firm is active in several markets, it is less dependent on specific market conditions and can respond better to risks and opportunities. The startup is active in only one market, while the established firm is more diversified and active in four markets. Accordingly, the startup is not flexible at all, while the incumbent has a high degree of flexibility. No raw data are shown for combinability, since we would need rather large tables of pairwise interactions for realistic numbers of employees. The entropies shown in the table are meant to be the results of an email-counting exercise such as the example in Table 3.1. The assumption behind the entropies is that the email communication is much more evenly distributed among the employees of a small startup than among the employees of a larger company that operates in a variety of markets. The complexity indices for the two firms are

Table 3.2 Organizational complexity of two firms

		Startup		Established firm	
		X	h_X	X	h_X
Diversity: gender shares	Male	0.43	0.863	0.6	0.613
	Female	0.47		0.4	
	Diverse	0.1		0.0	
	H_{max}	$log_2 3$		$log_2 3$	
Diversity: age shares	Young	0.77	0.491	0.28	0.984
	Middle-aged	0.23		0.42	
	Old	0.0		0.3	
	H_{max}	$log_2 3$		$log_2 3$	
Diversity: nationality shares	Domestic	0.54	0.995	0.83	0.658
	Foreign	0.46		0.17	
	H_{max}	$log_2 2$		$log_2 2$	
Flexibility: revenue in markets shares	Market 1	1.0	0	0.39	0.933
	Market 2	0.0		0.31	
	Market 3	0.0		0.18	
	Market 4	0.0		0.12	
	H_{max}	$log_2 4$		$log_2 4$	
Combinability: emails			0.92		0.52

$$K_{\text{startup}} = \frac{1}{3}(h_{d_1} + h_{d_2} + h_{d_3}) + h_f + h_c = \frac{1}{3}(0.863 + 0.491 + 0.995) + 0 + 0.92 = 1.70$$

$$K_{\text{estab}} = \frac{1}{3}(h_{d_1} + h_{d_2} + h_{d_3}) + h_f + h_c = \frac{1}{3}(0.613 + 0.984 + 0.658) + 0.933 + 0.52 = 2.21$$

Perhaps not too surprisingly, the established firm has more overall organizational complexity than the startup, although the startup business has relatively high diversity and high combinability. Note that due to the normalization, $0 \leq K \leq 3$ holds.

3.5.6 Objective and Subjective Complexity

If complex means "difficult to describe, understand, predict, and control," then complexity has both an objective and a subjective component. At least the difficulty of description, but perhaps also the difficulty of control, depends on objective characteristics of the system such as its size, structure, and organization. How difficult it is to understand and to predict the system depends not only on the system, but also on the observer. Understanding is clearly a subjective process that is influenced by the knowledge and cognitive abilities of the observer. As we have

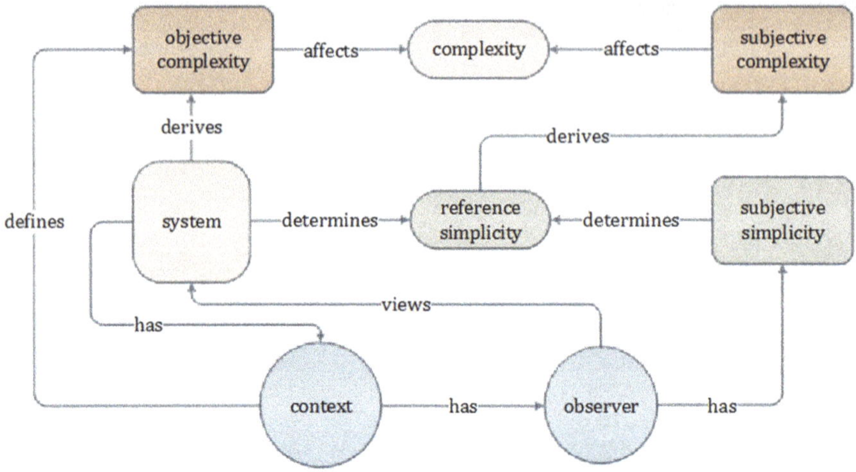

Fig. 3.24 Complexity as a function of objective and subjective complexity. Source: Efatmaneshnik and Ryan (2016), reproduced with kind permission of Wiley and Sons

shown, there are several ways to measure the objective dimension of complexity, but it is not obvious how to deal with the subjective dimension. Efatmaneshnik and Ryan (2016) propose to define subjective complexity as a deviation from a reference simplicity, i.e., an appropriate reference model chosen by the observer (see Fig. 3.24). The observer has an idea of what simple would mean in a given context (*subjective simplicity*). The degree of subjective complexity of a system is then given by the distance $D(S, R)$ between the system of interest S and the simple reference model R. In this concept, the complexity of a system is a function of the objective complexity $\Omega(S)$ and the subjective complexity

$$\mathcal{K}(S) = F[\Omega(S), D(S, R)]$$

The function $F[.]$ is monotonically increasing in both arguments. A simple version is a multiplicative function:

$$\mathcal{K}(S) = \Omega(S) \times D(S, R)$$

To apply this complexity measure to the system in Fig. 3.25, we need a measure of objective complexity, a distance function, and a reference for simplicity. While we could use various measures, we use cyclomatic complexity for the objective dimensions of the two systems. So we have

$$\Omega(S_1) = 16 - 8 + 1 = 9$$

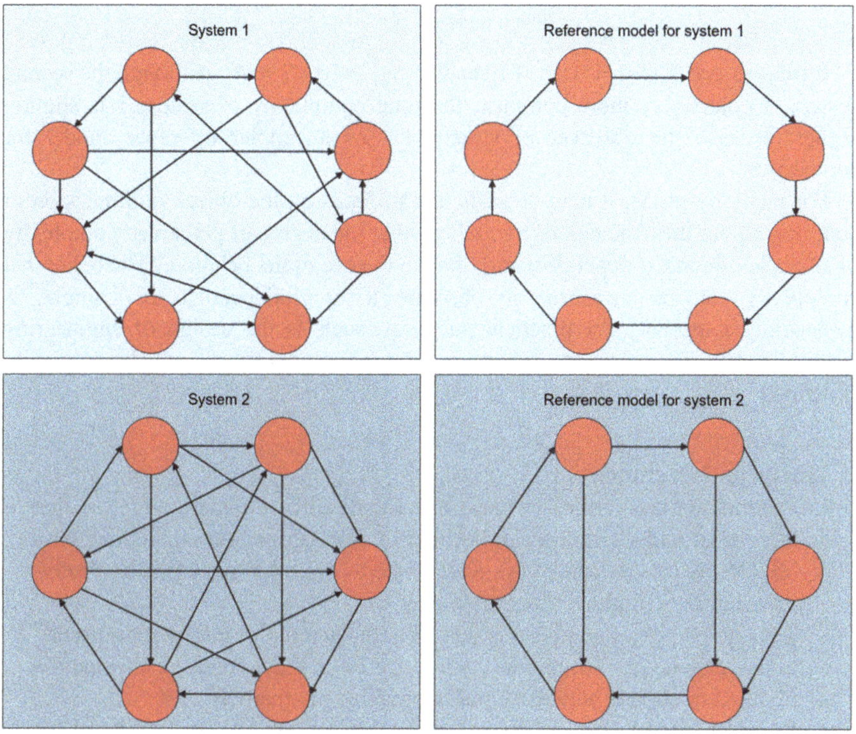

Fig. 3.25 Two systems and reference models for simplicity. Source: Author

$$\Omega(S_2) = 15 - 6 + 1 = 10$$

Objectively, system 2 is more complex than system 1. Again, there are many different ways to measure the distance between the actual system and the reference system. For simplicity, we use the Euclidean distance and stick to cyclomatic complexity as the complexity measure. Let's assume that the observer uses a simple ring as a reference model for system 1 and a slightly more complex model for system 2. The ring as a reference for system 1 is the simplest strongly connected graph and has a cyclomatic complexity of 1. The cyclomatic complexity of the reference model 2 is $CC_2 = 8 - 6 + 1 = 3$. It is important to emphasize that each reference model is a choice of the observer. There is no objective reason for a particular model. For some reason, the observer defines simplicity using the reference model, possibly, because this model is already known and well understood. The Euclidean distances between the systems and the reference models in terms of cyclomatic complexity are

$$D(S_1, R_1) = |9 - 1| = 8$$

$$D(S_2, R_2) = |10 - 3| = 7$$

It follows that $\mathcal{K}(S_1) = 9 \times 8 = 72$ and $\mathcal{K}(S_2) = 10 \times 7 = 70$. Although the second system is objectively more complex, the total complexity of system 1 is slightly higher, because the observer of system 1 uses a simpler reference model for comparison.

For many purposes, it may be sufficient to focus on the objective dimension of complexity, but this framework reminds us that the degree of perceived complexity of an object is context dependent and often in the eye of the beholder. The belief that complexity can be measured in absolute terms, independent of context, is misleading. Especially for practical purposes, such as the design of engineering systems, it is useful to provide an explicit reference model against which complexity is defined.

Things to Remember

- Patterns are regularities in data. The existence of a pattern suggests that there is an underlying causal mechanism. We can measure the complexity of patterns in data and of systems. Systems are often not directly observable, but they produce observable data.
- The complexity of an object is related to the amount of information needed to describe it. In information theory, one bit is the amount of information required to choose between equally probable alternatives.
- Shannon entropy is the average information content of a probability distribution of a random variable. It is a measure of surprise or uncertainty. When a variable has a high entropy, our initial uncertainty is high.
- Permutation entropy is a measure of the lack of regularity in time series. It combines Shannon entropy with symbolic dynamics and requires that numerical time series be transformed into symbolic blocks that capture the order relationships between the observations. Time series are more predictable if permutation entropy is low, because low permutation entropy indicates strong patterns.
- The complexity of systems can be measured by their degree of organization. Structural complexity, which depends on the number and type of entities and their relationships, is one dimension of system complexity. Another dimension is functional complexity, which is related to structural complexity.
- Cyclomatic complexity is a measure of the intricacy of a system's causal structure. When cyclomatic complexity is high, it is difficult to understand the causal logic of a system.
- Diversity, flexibility, and combinability are dimensions of organizational complexity that can be measured by entropy.

(continued)

- Complexity has an objective and a subjective dimension. The objective dimension depends on the observable properties of a system, such as its causal complexity. The difficulty of understanding a system, which is a characteristic of complexity, depends on the knowledge and cognitive abilities of an observer. The subjective aspect can be measured as the deviation from a reference model that the observer considers simple.

References

Bandt C, Pompe B (2002) Permutation entropy: a natural complexity measure for time series. Phys Rev Lett 88:174102. https://doi.org/10.1103/PhysRevLett.88.174102

Cánovas JS, García-Clemente G, Muñoz-Guillermo M (2018) Comparing permutation entropy functions to detect structural changes in time series. Phys A: Statist Mech Appl 507:153–174. https://doi.org/10.1016/j.physa.2018.04.101

de Araujo FHA, Bejan L, Rosso OA, Stosic T (2019) Permutation entropy and statistical complexity analysis of Brazilian agricultural commodities. Entropy 21:1220. https://doi.org/10.3390/e21121220

Destatis (2023). Verbraucherpreisindex und Inflationsrate. In: Statistisches Bundesamt. https://www.destatis.de/DE/Themen/Wirtschaft/Preise/Verbraucherpreisindex/_inhalt.html. Accessed 16 Mar 2023

Efatmaneshnik M, Ryan MJ (2016) A general framework for measuring system complexity. Complexity 21:533–546. https://doi.org/10.1002/cplx.21767

Gaspar HM, Rhodes DH, Ross AM, Ove Erikstad S (2012) Addressing complexity aspects in conceptual ship design: a systems engineering approach. J Ship Prod Des 28:145–159. https://doi.org/10.5957/jspd.2012.28.4.145

Henry M, Judge G (2019) Permutation entropy and information recovery in nonlinear dynamic economic time series. Econometrics 7:10. https://doi.org/10.3390/econometrics7010010

Kelvin L (1889) Electrical units of measurement. In: Thomson W (ed) Popular lectures and addresses, Volume 1: Constitution of matter. Macmillan and Co, London, pp 73–136

Lamberti PW, Martin MT, Plastino A, Rosso OA (2004) Intensive entropic non-triviality measure. Phys A Statist Mech Appl 334:119–131. https://doi.org/10.1016/j.physa.2003.11.005

Lloyd S (2001) Measures of complexity: a nonexhaustive list. IEEE Control Syst Mag 21:7–8. https://doi.org/10.1109/MCS.2001.939938

López-Ruiz R, Mancini HL, Calbet X (1995) A statistical measure of complexity. Phys Lett A 209: 321–326. https://doi.org/10.1016/0375-9601(95)00867-5

McCabe TJ (1976) A complexity measure. IEEE Trans Softw Eng SE-2:308–320. https://doi.org/10.1109/TSE.1976.233837

McShea DW (2000) Functional complexity in organisms: parts as proxies. Biol Philos 15:641–668

NASA, JPL-Caltech, University of Arizona (2023) PIA25709: a bear on mars? https://commons.wikimedia.org/wiki/File:PIA25709-BearFaceOnMars.jpg. Accessed 16 Mar 2023

OECD (2023) Quarterly GDP (indicator). OECD. https://doi.org/10.1787/b86d1fc8-en

Rebout N, Lone J-C, De Marco A et al (2021) Measuring complexity in organisms and organizations. R Soc Open Sci 8:200895. https://doi.org/10.1098/rsos.200895

Shannon CE (1948) A mathematical theory of communication. Bell Syst Tech J 27:379–423. https://doi.org/10.1002/j.1538-7305.1948.tb01338.x

Shermer M (2011) The believing brain: from ghosts and gods to politics and conspiracies—how we construct beliefs and reinforce them as truths. Macmillan

Stone JV (2015) Information theory: a tutorial introduction. Sebtel Press

U.S. Census Bureau (2023) Advance retail sales: retail Trade and Food Services [RSAFSNA]. https://fred.stlouisfed.org/series/RSAFSNA. Accessed 16 Mar 2023

Weiler G, U. S. Fish and Wildlife Service (2013) Predator and prey activity footprints animal traces in the snow. https://commons.wikimedia.org/wiki/File:Predator_and_prey_activity_footprints_animal_traces_in_the_snow.jpg. Accessed 16 Mar 2023

Wheeler JA (1989) Information, physics, quantum: the search for links. In: 3rd international symposium on foundations of quantum mechanics in light. Tokyo, pp 354–368

Zunino L, Zanin M, Tabak BM et al (2010) Complexity-entropy causality plane: a useful approach to quantify the stock market inefficiency. Phys A Statist Mech Appl 389:1891–1901. https://doi.org/10.1016/j.physa.2010.01.007

Complexity Economics

4

Contents

4.1 Introduction 116
4.2 What Is Economics All About? 117
4.3 Neoclassical Economics 119
    4.3.1 A Market Model with Rational Expectations 120
    4.3.2 The Ramsey–Cass–Koopmans Model 124
4.4 Complexity Economics 129
    4.4.1 Complexity Economics and Neoclassical Economics 131
    4.4.2 Complexity Economics and Other Schools of Thought 137
4.5 Methods of Complexity Economics 140
    4.5.1 Nonlinear Dynamics and Chaos 140
    4.5.2 System Dynamics 142
    4.5.3 Agent-Based Modeling 143
    4.5.4 Social Network Analysis 143
    4.5.5 Scenario Analysis 144
References 145

Abstract

This chapter contrasts complexity economics and neoclassical economics. The current economic mainstream is dominated by neoclassical economics. To show that complexity economics is different, it is useful to define neoclassical economics and discuss its main properties. Neoclassical thinking is illustrated with the Muth model of rational expectations and the Ramsey–Cass–Koopmans model of economic growth. The chapter also presents topics where complexity economics has a clear advantage over neoclassical economics and shows the relationships with other economic schools of thought. Complexity economics emphasizes algorithmic thinking, which explains the heavy use of computational methods, which, along with other methods, are briefly introduced at the end of the chapter. The most important computational methods, which are also used in later chapters, are system dynamics and agent-based modeling.

M. Roos, *Principles of Complexity Economics*, Classroom Companion: Economics,
https://doi.org/10.1007/978-3-031-51436-4_4

Keywords

Algorithm · Methods · Neoclassical economics · Nonequilibrium economics · Schools of thought

Guiding Questions

- What is complexity economics?
- What are the main characteristics of neoclassical economics?
- How does complexity economics differ from mainstream neoclassical economics?
- How does complexity economics relate to other non-mainstream schools of thought?
- What is the role of computation in complexity economics?
- What methods are used in complexity economics?

4.1 Introduction

Complexity economics is the application of complexity thinking to economic issues. Complexity thinking implies a particular worldview or *ontology*, that is, a belief about the nature of the world or about how the world *is* and *works*. A core element of the complexity worldview is the observation that the world is characterized by both stability and change. Many phenomena in the natural and social world tend to be stable over considerable periods of time—what considerable means depends on the relevant time scale, which is very different for geological and economic phenomena. Such stable patterns (or patterns of relationships) can be described quite well by deterministic or stochastic mathematical models or "laws." However, patterns of relationships also change over time. Changes can be slow and gradual, or rapid and disruptive.

Gradual change is the result of adaptation and learning by agents in a complex adaptive system. These dynamic processes form the observed patterns or regularities. Gradual change happens all the time and can often go unnoticed because the changes are small. If the gradual change is very slow, we can safely ignore it when describing and analyzing systems within a given time span. The complexity worldview emphasizes that the apparent stability of systems is deceptive. Sometimes, seemingly out of the blue, complex systems undergo disruptive changes that occur rapidly and change the nature of the system.

According to Boulton et al. (2015), the key insight from the complexity worldview is that "the future is a dance between patterns and events":

> Patterns are always under threat of disruption by **events**. These events might be major external shocks such as pandemics, tsunamis, wars, climate change, or migration, or they might be larger-than-average fluctuations – in weather or stock market prices, for example. Or events might be the coming together of several diverse factors – such as a strike by transport workers at the same time as a flu epidemic together with a larger-than-average drop in the stock market – these events together might cause loss of confidence in the economy or the government. Events may also be internal variations from the norm – a higher-than-average birth or death rate, or the death or arrival of a significant leader. And of course what we regard as internal and external depends on how we draw the boundaries around the problem (Boulton et al. 2015, p. 30).

Because of the importance of events and the possibility of regime shifts or radical changes, there is *fundamental uncertainty* about the future. Predictions about the future behavior of a system are based on the assumption that the system has a time-invariant structure. The complexity worldview challenges this assumption and thus posits that there is always more than one possible future.

This worldview is very different from the way neoclassical economics looks at the world. Neoclassical economics is the current mainstream of economic research, teaching, and policy advice. If you have had any economic training, it was most likely neoclassical, even if it was not called that. In many cases, complexity economics reaches different conclusions or addresses different questions than neoclassical economics. To address many of the pressing problems described in Chap. 1, such as climate change, environmental degradation, or societal instability, complexity economics is essential.

In this chapter, we first discuss the question of what economics is in Sect. 4.2. There are different opinions about this, depending on the economic school of thought. Since neoclassical economics is the dominant school of thought, we present a more detailed characterization of it, which serves as a background for the description of complexity economics (Sect. 4.3). Complexity economics shares some features with many other non-mainstream schools of thought, such as evolutionary economics, institutional economics, or post-Keynesian economics, which will be presented in Sect. 4.4. The chapter concludes with a brief overview of some important (formal) methods in complexity economics, such as agent-based modeling and social network analysis. These methods are not part of the mainstream curriculum in economics, but are well established in many other disciplines. The following chapters will show many applications of these methods to economic problems.

4.2 What Is Economics All About?

There has always been a plurality of different schools of thought in economics. It is quite common to distinguish *mainstream economics* from what is often called *heterodox economics*. However, this distinction is flawed because the correct antonym of heterodox is *orthodox*, which comes from the Greek word orthodoxía, meaning right or correct opinion. The terms orthodoxy and heterodoxy were originally used in religion, where orthodoxy refers to the correct beliefs as defined by religious authorities, and heterodoxy refers to opinions that differ from official positions. While in practice there may be an orthodox doctrine in economics as defined by academic authorities, this is not how science should be practiced. It should be a fundamental premise of all scientific inquiry that all scientific truths are always tentative and can always be refuted by better arguments and new evidence. This is in stark contrast to many religions, where religious leaders claim to know eternal truths and churches formulate dogmas that are to be followed but not questioned by church members.

Therefore, mainstream and non-mainstream economics is the preferable pair of words because it does not imply a claim of right vs. wrong. According to the Cambridge Dictionary, mainstream means "considered normal and having or using ideas, beliefs, etc. that are accepted by most people." So mainstream economics is just the kind of economics that most economists practice. There may be good reasons why most economists follow a particular approach, but this cannot mean that the mainstream approach is and should be the only one possible. What is mainstream today will not necessarily be mainstream forever. Moreover, the mainstream has a certain inertia, because young researchers trained in the mainstream learn to accept it as normal and are evaluated according to the mainstream's standards. So the mainstream is partly just tradition. Today, the neoclassical school of thought in the tradition of Leon Walras, Alfred Marshall, Paul Samuelson, Gary Becker, and many others is mainstream, while complexity economics is non-mainstream.

In his popular textbook *Principles of Economics*, N. Gregory Mankiw defines economics as "the study of how society manages its scarce resources." This definition is in the tradition of the famous definition given by Lionel Robbins in his 1932 *Essay on the Nature and Significance of Economic Science*:

> Economics is the science which studies human behavior as a relationship between ends and scarce means which have alternative uses. (Robbins 1932, p. 15)

Robbins introduces this *scarcity definition* of economics as an alternative to what he calls the *materialist definition*, according to which economics is the study of the causes of material welfare. In his search for a general definition of economics, he rejects the material definition because of the difficulty of distinguishing economic activities that increase material welfare from non-economic activities that do not. As an example, he mentions the members of an orchestra who are paid for "work which has not the remotest bearing on material welfare" (Robbins 1932, p. 6).

Gary Becker, who received the Nobel Memorial prize in 1992 "for having extended the domain of microeconomics analysis to a wide range of human behaviour and interaction, including nonmarket behaviour," takes the definition of economics as the science of the rational use of scarce resources even further. In his Nobel lecture, Becker talks about the economic approach:

> The analysis assumes that individuals maximize welfare as they conceive it ... Their behavior is forward-looking, and it is also consistent over time. In particular, they try as best they can to anticipate the uncertain consequences of their actions ... Actions are constrained by income, time, imperfect memory and calculating capacities, and other limited

> resources ... While the economic approach to behavior builds on a theory of individual choice, it is not mainly concerned with individuals... Rational individual choice is combined with assumptions about technologies and other determinants of opportunities, equilibrium in market and nonmarket situations, and laws, norms and traditions to obtain results concerning the behavior of groups. (Becker 1993, p. 386)

Becker applied the economic approach of rational choice—or, as he says "the combined assumptions of maximizing behavior, market equilibrium and stable preferences, used relentlessly and unflinchingly"(Becker 1976, p. 5)—to issues of discrimination, crime, politics, family life, and human behavior in general. He is often accused of economic imperialism. As a consequence, we now have economics of the family, economics of religion, economics of addiction, and other economics of something. This is only possible, because this kind of economics is not defined in terms of a subject matter, but in terms of an approach—as described by Becker. He explicitly says that "the economic approach is a comprehensive one that is applicable to all human behavior"(Becker 1976, p. 8).

Cambridge economist Ha-Joon Chang argues that economics should not be the study of (almost) everything defined in terms of a methodology, but in terms of its subject matter, which is the economy. He defines economics as the study of the economy, "which involves money, work, technology, international trade, taxes and other things that have to do with the ways in which we produce goods and services, distribute the incomes generated in the process and consume the things thus produced" (Chang 2014, p. 27). If economics is defined by its subject matter, then there can and should be many different approaches to economics, each with particular strengths and weaknesses. For instance, neoclassical economics looks at the economy from the perspective of the rational use of scarce resources, while feminist economics has a particular focus on gender-sensitive and inclusive economic inquiry. Complexity economics, as mentioned earlier, looks at the economy from a complexity perspective.

This view on economics calls for pluralism, i.e., the recognition of different approaches and goals of economic inquiry and different perspectives on the economy. True pluralism does not only accept that different approaches exist, but values them with the conviction that each has something valuable to contribute to the understanding of our complex reality. Unfortunately, current mainstream economics is not pluralistic, as evidenced by the use of the neoclassical perspective as the single definition of economics in general.

4.3 Neoclassical Economics

It is helpful to explain the neoclassical approach in some detail in order to make clear how complexity economics differs from mainstream thinking. We will use the model with which John Muth (1961) introduced his idea of *rational expectations* as a microeconomic example and the *Ramsey–Cass–Koopmans model* as a core model in macroeconomics. It is not the aim of this subsection to present an in-depth analysis of these two models, which can be found either in the original papers or in any standard textbook on advanced macroeconomics (e.g., Heijdra 2017, Romer 2019). Rather, the brief presentation of these two models serves to illustrate typical elements in neoclassical models.

4.3.1 A Market Model with Rational Expectations

The iconic image of neoclassical economics is the X-shaped market diagram shown in Figure 4.1. Anyone who has taken at least Econ 101 has seen this diagram, with a linear upward-sloping supply function and a linear downward-sloping demand function representing the neoclassical concept of what is key to a market. The model discussed here gives a twist to the canonical model by assuming that supply is a function of the expected price P^e instead of the actual price P.

To demonstrate what rational expectations are, Muth assumed an isolated market for a nonstorable good that takes time to produce. An example might be a market for an agricultural commodity such as hogs. As is common in neoclassical economics, the market is described by a demand function and a supply function, which are assumed to be linear for simplicity:

$$Q_t^D = d_0 - d_1 P_t, d_1 > 0, \tag{4.1}$$

$$Q_t^S = s_0 + s_1 P_t^e + \varepsilon_t, s_1 > 0. \tag{4.2}$$

The first equation is the demand function, where Q_t^D is the quantity demanded by buyers in period t and P_t is the price in that period. Note that the demand equation describes the total demand of all buyers in the market. While it is assumed that there

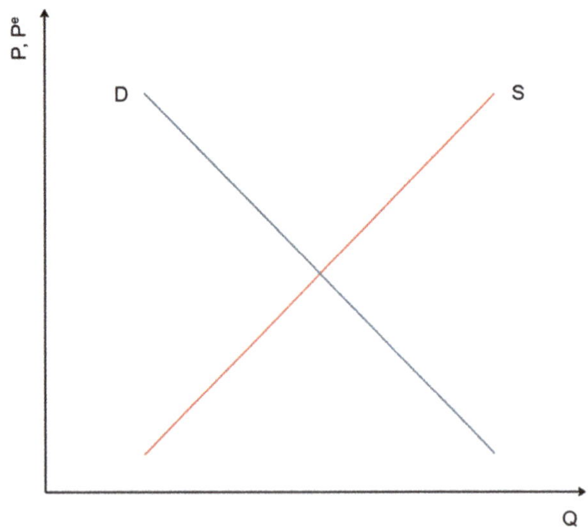

Fig. 4.1 Market diagram. Source: Author

are many individual buyers, they are not modeled. A common assumption is that all buyers are identical, so the market demand function is equal to all individual demand functions scaled up by the number of buyers. Importantly, demand depends on the market price P_t, but not on any other factors, such as personal relationships to particular sellers. There is only one relevant market price.

Equation (4.2) is the supply function with Q_t^S as the quantity supplied in period t and P_t^e as the price that suppliers in the previous period $t - 1$ expect to hold in period t. It is a key assumption of the model that suppliers can only offer their good in the market with a time lag of one period, because production takes time. Thus, they have to decide how much to produce and to offer in the market without knowing the actual market price. This forces them in period $t - 1$ to form a subjective expectation of the market price in period t. Like the demand function, the supply function describes the market supply of a large number of identical suppliers, who are only interested in the market price. The actual quantity supplied to the market depends on random factors such as weather effects or animal diseases represented by the random shock ε_t. The uncertainty is treated as *risk* by assuming that the shocks have a known probability distribution, for example a normal distribution with an expected value of zero and a constant variance σ^2, $\varepsilon_t \sim N(0, \sigma^2)$.

In neoclassical economics, market equilibrium is of central interest. Market equilibrium is defined as the situation in which the quantity demanded is equal to the quantity supplied:

$$Q_t^D = Q_t^S = Q_t. \tag{4.3}$$

The *market equilibrium* is assumed to be the most natural long-run state of the market, i.e., the state to which the market converges and to which it is close most of the time. As in many other models of this type, it is not specified how the market equilibrium is reached. Instead of modeling the equilibration process, the equilibrium is imposed. Without being explicitly mentioned, the idea of a *tâtonnement process* or a *Walrasian auction* is in the background, whereby a hypothetical *Walrasian auctioneer* adjusts the market price up or down until the desired demand equals the desired supply as a function of the price. Importantly, the model does not describe the direct interactions between buyers and sellers. The market is treated as an aggregate entity composed of individual buyers and sellers as elements, but neither the elements nor the relationships between them are modeled. Thus, we do not know who is selling how much to whom. If all sellers and all buyers are identical, one could make the additional assumption that the total quantity traded in the market is evenly distributed among all market participants.

The main purpose of this model is to show how perfectly rational agents would form expectations and how these rational expectations would affect the market. For Muth (1961, p. 316), rational expectations, "since they are informed predictions of future events, are essentially the same as the predictions of the relevant economic theory." More precisely, the "expectations of firms … tend to be distributed, for the same information set, about the prediction of the theory. … The way expectations are formed depends specifically on the structure of the relevant system describing the economy." In this sense, rational expectations are *model-consistent expectations*, as they are also called. They are rational in the sense that information is scarce and valuable and should not be wasted by economic agents. Muth assumes that the economic system generally does not waste information.

Rational expectations require very strong assumptions about the availability of information among the agents. It is assumed that all suppliers know all past prices and quantities, the two market Eqs. (4.1) and (4.2), and the probability distribution of the random shocks. This information is collected in the information set Ω_{t-1} at time $t-1$, when the expectation about the market price is formed:

$$\Omega_{t-1} = \{P_{t-1}, P_{t-2}, \ldots; Q_{t-1}, Q_{t-2}, \ldots; d_0, d_1, s_0, s_1; \varepsilon_t \sim N(0, \sigma^2)\}. \quad (4.4)$$

The key assumption is that the agents in the model know the model; i.e., they have the same information as the economist modeling the market and form their expectations in the same way as the researcher would do it. This is the meaning of model-consistent expectations. The rational expectations assumption postulates that the suppliers' subjective expectations, P_t^e, are equal to the conditional objective expectations given the information set; hence

$$P_t^e = E(P_t | \Omega_{t-1}) \equiv E_{t-1} P_t. \quad (4.5)$$

The model can be solved for the expected market price and the actual market price in the market equilibrium, which is then called the *rational expectations equilibrium.* This is done by first calculating the quantity and the price as functions of the price expected by suppliers assuming that the equilibrium condition (4.3) holds. The actual market price in equilibrium thus depends on the expected price:

$$P_t = \frac{d_0 - s_0 - s_1 P_t^e - \varepsilon_t}{d_1}. \quad (4.6)$$

In the next step, rational expectations of the price in (4.6) are calculated. The resulting rational expectation is

$$P_t^e = E_{t-1} P_t = \frac{d_0 - s_0}{d_1 + s_1} = P^*, \quad (4.7)$$

which is equal to the equilibrium price P^* that would prevail in the absence of stochastic shocks. Thus, suppliers always expect a constant price, which is fully determined by the structural parameters of the demand function and the supply functions. As long as these functions are fixed, rational agents should never expect a different price. However, the actual market price in equilibrium will typically differ from the expected price due to the random shocks:

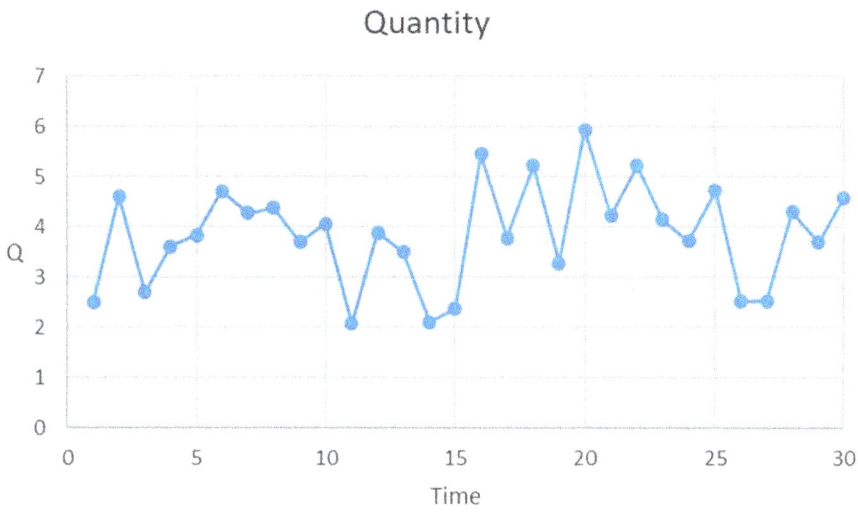

Fig. 4.2 Quantity sold. Source: Author

$$P_t = P^* - \frac{1}{d_1}\varepsilon_t. \tag{4.8}$$

Combining Eqs. (4.1), (4.3), and (4.8), we find that the quantity of the good traded in the market also fluctuates stochastically (see Fig. 4.2). If we choose the parameters $d_0 = 10$, $d_1 = 0.8$, $s_0 = 1$, $s_1 = 0.4$, $\sigma = 1$, then we obtain $P^* = 7.5$ and $Q^* = d_0 - d_1 P^* = 4$. As we see in Fig. 4.2, the actual quantity sold deviates from the quantity related to the rationally expected price due to the stochastic shock, $Q_t = Q^* + \varepsilon_t$.

To sum up, the market model relies on a number of assumptions that are typical[1] of neoclassical models:

(A1) All buyers and all sellers operating in the market are identical.
(A2) The market is described by a market demand function and a market supply function, which are aggregates of individual behavior.
(A3) The relevant variables are the market quantity and the market price.
(A4) Individual behavior and direct interactions between agents are not modeled.
(A5) There is a market equilibrium, which is the typical (or most interesting) state of the market.
(A6) The equilibrium price is reached by an unmodeled *tâtonnement process* or a *Walrasian auctioneer.*
(A7) Uncertainty is treated as risk by adding a random variable with a known probability distribution.

[1] Typical, of course, does not mean that *all* neoclassical models have all these features. There are, for instance, attempts to introduce some heterogeneity of agents.

(A8) Agents have a high degree of rationality and possess the same information as the researcher who models the market.

4.3.2 The Ramsey–Cass–Koopmans Model

The Ramsey–Cass–Koopmans is a macroeconomic growth model. It is based on Ramsey (1928), who proposed a formal model of intertemporal utility maximization. Cass (1965) and Koopmans (1965) independently applied Ramsey's model to macroeconomic growth. The model is conceptually quite simple, but it contains many key ideas that are also part of most of the more sophisticated models in current mainstream macroeconomics. It is therefore ideal for demonstrating the basic ideas of neoclassical macroeconomics.

The model describes an economy with perfectly competitive markets and no externalities. It consists of a large number of identical firms and a large number of identical households. Because firms and households are all identical, they can be treated as a single *representative firm* and a single *representative household*. This representative agent assumption, which is common in many mainstream macroeconomic models, means that firm and household behavior are identical at the microeconomic and the macroeconomic levels. Macroeconomic behavior is derived directly from representative individual behavior, providing so-called *microfoundations* of macroeconomics. Competitive firms produce and sell a single good called output, for which they rent capital and hire labor as factors of production. Households live forever, supply labor, own capital, consume, and save. Their number H is fixed but their size grows at a constant rate n; i.e., they supply more and more labor over time.

In the simplest version, each household member supplies 1 unit of labor at each point in time. The household's decision problem is to choose how much to consume and how much to save over time. This *intertemporal consumption choice* is the key element of the model. The household has an intertemporal utility function:

$$U = \int_{t=0}^{\infty} e^{-\rho t} u(C(t)) \frac{L(t)}{H} dt. \tag{4.9}$$

The household currently lives in the present, $t = 0$, and has perfect foresight; i.e., it knows the entire future up to $t = \infty$. $C(t)$ is the consumption of each household member at time t. The total population in the economy is $L(t)$, such that $L(t)/H$ is the number of members per household. $u(C(t))$ is the so-called *instantaneous utility function* measuring the utility of each household member at a given point in time, depending only on per capita consumption at that time. It is a common practice to assume a *constant-relative-risk-aversion* (CRRA) utility function:

$$u(C(t)) = \frac{C(t)^{1-\theta}}{1-\theta}, \theta > 0. \tag{4.10}$$

The future instantaneous utility of all household members $u(C(t))\frac{L(t)}{H}$ is discounted by the discount factor $e^{-\rho t}$ with the constant discount rate $\rho > 0$. Thus, the consumption in the present moment receives the highest weight, because $e^{-\rho 0} = 1$, while the discount factor becomes very small for the distant future, because $lim_{t \to \infty} e^{-\rho t} = 0$. The discounted instantaneous utilities are integrated (or summed up) over each point in time to infinity.

The perfectly rational representative household is assumed to maximize the intertemporal utility function by the choice of a consumption path *C*(*t*) for each present and future point in time. Of course, the household cannot choose consumption freely, but must obey its *intertemporal budget constraint*:

$$\int_{t=0}^{\infty} e^{-R(t)} C(t) \frac{L(t)}{H} dt \leq \frac{K(0)}{H} + \int_{t=0}^{\infty} e^{-R(t)} W(t) \frac{L(t)}{H} dt. \tag{4.11}$$

This intertemporal budget constraint says that the present value of consumption on the left-hand side must not exceed the present value of total household wealth on the right-hand side of the inequality. $K(0)/H$ is the fraction of the economy's capital stock held by each household at $t = 0$ and $W(t)$ is the real wage per unit of labor, such that $W(t)L(t)/H$ is the real wage earned by the household. The household's lifetime wealth consists of the initial capital stock and the discounted stream of wage earnings. In the discount factor, the discount rate ρ, which is a preference parameter of the household, is replaced by the continuously compounded real interest rate from the present up to time t in the future, $R(t) = \int_{\tau=0}^{t} r(\tau) d\tau$. The reason is that the households' saving at time t, $W(t) - C(t)$ (or borrowing if the expression is negative), earns (or costs) the market interest rate. While the households can hold debt for some time, it is assumed that debt cannot be rolled over forever, which is called the *no-Ponzi-game condition*.

Maximizing the lifetime utility function (5.9) subject to the lifetime budget constraint (4.11) by choosing a consumption path can be done by optimization methods such as the *calculus of variations* or *optimal control*. The optimization results in a first-order condition called the *Euler equation*:

$$\frac{\dot{C}(t)}{C(t)} = \frac{r(t) - \rho}{\theta}. \tag{4.12}$$

The Euler equation, where $\dot{C}(t)$ is the derivative of consumption with respect to time, describes how consumption should optimally change over time as a function of the real interest rate, the discount rate, and the elasticity of substitution between consumptions at any two points in time $1/\theta$, where θ is the coefficient of relative risk aversion in the utility function. If the interest rate that can be earned by saving is equal to the discount rate, $r(t) = \rho$, then it is optimal, not to change consumption. However, if the interest rate is greater than the household's time preference measured by the discount rate, $r(t) > \rho$, then the household should let consumption grow over time, for which current saving must be increased. The Euler equation is the essence of the optimal behavior of forward-looking households in the Ramsey–Cass–Koopmans model.

In order to determine how consumption evolves over time, we need to know the real rate of interest that capital earns. It is assumed that each of the many identical firms has access to the same technology, which is given by the production function

$$Y = F(K, AL), \tag{4.13}$$

where Y is output, K is the stock of physical capital, L is labor, and A is the *effectiveness of labor*, often interpreted as (technological) knowledge. The production function has constant returns to scale and positive but decreasing marginal products, i.e., $F^{'} > 0$, $F^{''} < 0$. The effectiveness of labor grows at a constant rate g, called technological progress. The function $F(.)$ itself is assumed to be constant over time. To simplify the analysis, the production is often expressed in its *intensive form*

$$f(k) = F\left(\frac{K}{AL}, \frac{AL}{AL}\right), \tag{4.14}$$

which is possible due to the assumption of constant returns to scale. $k \equiv K/AL$ is capital per effective labor and $y \equiv Y/AL$ is output per effective labor. Firms maximize profits, but because markets are assumed to be perfectly competitive, they earn zero profit in equilibrium. The necessary condition for a profit maximum is that the factors of production are paid their marginal products

$$r(t) = f'(k(t)), \tag{4.15}$$

$$W(t) = A(t)[f(k(t)) - k(t)f'(k(t))], \tag{4.16}$$

which implies that there is no depreciation of the capital stock, which is a simplifying assumption. The real interest rate thus depends on the capital stock per effective labor $k(t)$. Without depreciation, the change in the total capital stock over time is given by investment, which in a closed economy is assumed to be equal to saving

$$\dot{K}(t) = I(t) = S(t) = Y(t) - C(t). \tag{4.17}$$

This can be written in extensive form, taking into account that $A(t)$ and $L(t)$ grow with constant rates over time:

$$\dot{k}(t) = f(k(t) - c(t) - (n + g)k(t), \tag{4.18}$$

[2]If you are not familiar with differential equations and their analysis in phase diagrams, you can find an introduction in Chap. 6.

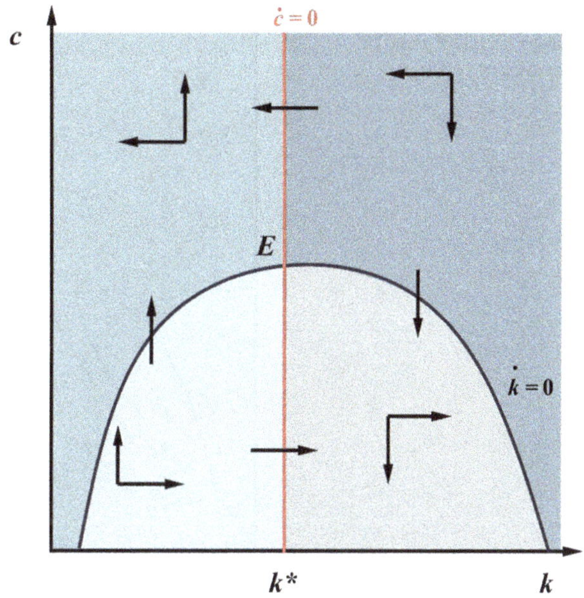

Fig. 4.3 Phase diagram of the Ramsey–Cass–Koopmans model. Source: Author

where consumption is expressed per effective labor, $c(t) = C(t)/A(t)L(t)$. In terms of consumption per effective labor, the Euler Eq. (4.12) is

$$\frac{\dot{c}(t)}{c(t)} = \frac{r(t) - \rho - \theta g}{\theta}. \tag{4.19}$$

The two *differential Eqs.* (4.18) and (4.19) describe the dynamics of the model and are therefore key to analyzing the behavior of the economy. The whole economy can be characterized by two *state variables* $c(t)$ and $k(t)$, their changes $\dot{c}(t)$ and $\dot{k}(t)$, the exogenous parameters n, g, ρ, and θ, and the production technology $f(.)$. All other variables of interest, such as output $Y(t)$ or the wage $W(t)$ can be derived from the state variables. It is a common practice to analyze the model qualitatively using the *phase diagram* in Fig. 4.3, which shows the change in the two variables as functions of the two state variables.[2]

The $\dot{c} = 0$ line shows for which combinations of c and k consumption does not change. This is the case for $f'(k(t)) = r(t) = \rho - \theta g$ (see 4.19). Since the parameters are constant, the real interest rate much be constant which implies a constant value k^*. For $k > k^*$ the interest rate falls, because $f'' < 0$ and hence $r(t) - \rho - \theta g < 0$. This means that consumption falls (rises) to the right (left) of the $\dot{c} = 0$ line as indicated by the vertical arrows pointing down (up). Analogously, the $\dot{k} = 0$ line shows for which combinations of c and k the capital stock per effective labor does not change. Because of the properties of the production function, the $\dot{k} = 0$ has the nonlinear inverted U shape. Applying the same reasoning as before to Eq. (4.18), we can derive the horizontal arrows that show the dynamics of the capital stock above and below the $\dot{k} = 0$ line. For instance, if for a given k consumption is below the $\dot{k} = 0$ line, investment $f(k(t) - c(t)$ is greater than $(n + g)k(t)$, which describes the decrease

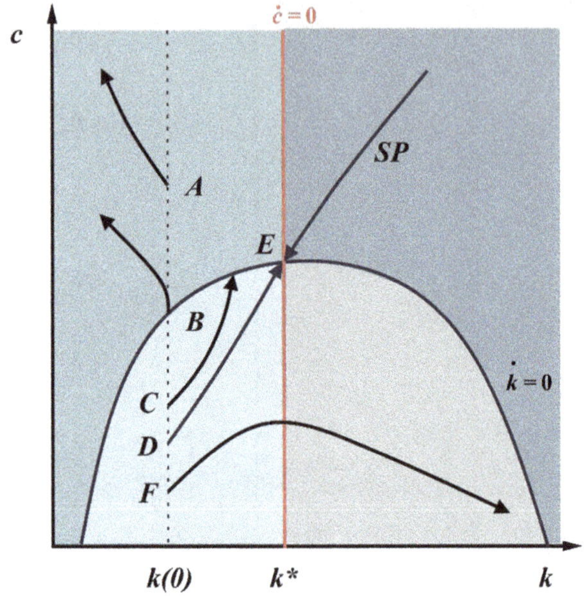

Fig. 4.4 Different trajectories and the saddle path. Source: Author

in capital per effective labor due to the growth of the effective labor force. Thus, for low (high) levels of c the ratio of capital per effective labor grows (shrinks), as indicated by the arrows pointing to the right (left).

The phase diagram shows that there is one point E called the *steady state* of the economy, for which neither c nor k changes, i.e., $\dot{c} = 0$ and $\dot{k} = 0$. This is an equilibrium state of the economy in the sense that the state variables per effective labor are constant over time. It is a dynamic equilibrium in the sense that the levels of the variables C and K grow with the constant exogenous rate $n + g$.

We can use the phase diagram to analyze how the economy evolves over time given an initial capital stock $k(0)$ as shown by various *trajectories* in Fig. 4.4. Let's assume that the economy were at point A with consumption above the $\dot{k} = 0$ line and the $k(0)$ to the left of the $\dot{c} = 0$ line. According to Fig. 4.3, the arrows in this region point up and to the left, such that Eqs. (4.18) and (4.19) imply that consumption grows and capital shrinks. Over time, the economy will approach the c-axis with $k = 0$. However, this implies a collapse of the economy, because without capital, output and consumption must also be zero. Points like B and C will lead to the same long-term results.

A point with a very low initial level of consumption, such as F, will have different dynamics. Initially, both c and k will grow until k reaches the steady-state level k^*. After crossing the $\dot{k} = 0$ line horizontally, k continues to grow, but c must decrease. Thus, the economy accumulates more and more capital with ever decreasing consumption until consumption approaches zero which is also a kind of collapse. Figure 4.4 suggests that there is exactly one level of consumption at point D that fits to the given $k(0)$, such that the economy reaches the steady state at point E. This finding can be generalized to all initial levels of $k(0)$ resulting in a so-called *saddle path* SP leading into E from the southwest and the northeast directions. The saddle path expresses the initial levels of consumption $c(0)$ as a function of $k(0)$ that lead the economy to converge to the steady state.

Like many macroeconomic models, the Ramsey–Cass–Koopmans model has the property of *saddle path stability*, i.e., a single steady-state equilibrium that can only be reached on a single path in the phase diagram. Any point away from the saddle path leads to a collapse of the economy in the long run. The saddle path is a consequence of the intertemporal utility maximization of the representative household (or all households). Only the saddle path is consistent with utility maximization. Therefore, the model implies that the economy is always in the steady state or on the saddle path. If, for example, the economy is at the steady state E and a natural disaster destroys a part of the capital stock, leaving only $k(0)$, the perfectly rational households would immediately adjust their consumption to the level at point F. Since the economy is competitive and there are no externalities, the decentralized market equilibrium in the Ramsey–Cass–Koopmans model is Pareto efficient and maximizes social welfare.

The Ramsey–Cass–Koopmans model shares many of the neoclassical assumptions also made in the previous subsection, such as identical agents, the equilibrium assumption, and the high degree of rationality and information of agents. There are some additional assumptions in the long-run macroeconomic model that deserve special emphasis:

(A9) The macroeconomic (aggregate) behavior of the economy is identical to the microeconomic (individual) behavior, so the economy can be modeled with only two representative agents (one household and one firm).

(A10) The representative household has an infinite planning horizon and optimizes intertemporally.

(A11) The economy is structurally stable. Change is only quantitative, i.e., in terms of the variables Y, A, or K, but the functional forms (e.g., the utility function and the production function) and parameters (e.g., ρ and θ) of the model are forever the same.

4.4 Complexity Economics

The term *complexity economics* was introduced by W. Brian Arthur (1999) in order to describe the "study of the general emergence of structures and the unfolding of patterns in the economy." Complexity economics is the economics of formation and change processes, such as the formation of new markets and industries, the evolution of market structure, innovation and the evolution of technologies, and the development of economies, as opposed to simple economic growth. It is also the study of economic instability in the form of market crashes, economic crises, or the collapse of entire industries.

Another term for complexity economics is *nonequilibrium economics*. Note that nonequilibrium is different from *disequilibrium*. While disequilibrium describes a situation away from equilibrium, which still implies the existence of an equilibrium, nonequilibrium characterizes situations without reference to an equilibrium. Arthur (2015, p. 1) explains it as follows:

> Complexity economics builds on the proposition that the economy is not necessarily in equilibrium: economic agents (firms, consumers, investors) constantly change their actions and strategies in response to the outcome they mutually create. This further changes the outcome, which requires them to adjust afresh. Agents thus live in a world where their beliefs and strategies are constantly being "tested" for survival within an outcome or "ecology" these beliefs and strategies together create... Economics has largely avoided this nonequilibrium view in the past, but if we allow it, we see patterns or phenomena not visible to equilibrium analysis. These emerge probabilistically, last for some time and dissipate, and act at the "meso-level" of the economy (between the micro- and macro-levels). We also see the economy not as something given and existing but forming from a constantly developing set of technological innovations, institutions, and arrangements. Complexity economics thus sees the economy as in motion, perpetually "computing" itself – perpetually constructing itself anew. Where equilibrium economics emphasizes order, determinacy, deduction, and stasis, complexity economics emphasizes contingency, indeterminacy, sense-making, and openness to change.

It is important to understand that complexity economics does not claim that equilibrium is never a useful concept. As Arthur says, patterns can emerge, persist for some time, and then dissipate. At least for some time, such patterns may be quite stable, so that equilibrium analysis may be appropriate. However, these patterns can also disappear, and with them the perceived equilibrium, which may never return. Both organizational and political science know the concept of *punctuated equilibrium*, borrowed from evolutionary biology. Eldredge and Gould (1972) argue that the fossil record of species shows no significant morphological change for very long periods of time, which is called stasis. But suddenly (which can mean within several 10,000 years in biological evolution), new species appear in jumps after periods of stasis. Punctuated equilibrium theory in social theory posits that social systems tend to be stable for long periods of time, undergoing only gradual change due to stabilizing forces such as institutions, cultures, interest groups, habits, etc.. Sometimes, however, radical or revolutionary changes occur with major organizational transformations or policy shifts.

Patterns can change because economic agents constantly adjust their behavior. In particular, economic agents form beliefs and expectations, have intentions, and develop strategies to pursue their goals. People hold beliefs about the economic world and try to make sense of it. These beliefs are contingent and, in principle, can change very suddenly when dramatic events occur that agents did not believe possible. Complexity economics is much closer to biology than to physics, which is the scientific model of neoclassical economics. The objects studied in classical physics, such as gas molecules, always behave in the same way, but living things do not. Formative processes such as cell formation, molecule replication, embryonic development, or the evolution of species are the focus of interest in biology.

It should be clear that the characterization of complexity economics as nonequilibrium economics is perfectly consistent with the definition of complexity economics as the study of the economy as a complex adaptive system.

4.4.1 Complexity Economics and Neoclassical Economics

We can carve out the characteristic features of complexity economics by showing how it differs from the mainstream approach, which is dominated by neoclassical economics. Colander et al. (2004) speak of a holy trinity of assumptions that define neoclassical economics: rationality, selfishness, and equilibrium. However, with the advent of behavioral economics which is now part of mainstream economics, rationality and selfishness can no longer be considered as general assumptions in mainstream economics. Therefore, Arnsperger and Varoufakis (2006) argue that neoclassical economics is defined by the three axioms of (1) methodological individualism, (2) methodological instrumentalism, and (3) methodological equilibration. *Methodological individualism* means that the explanation of socioeconomic phenomena must be derived from behavior at the level of individuals. *Methodological instrumentalism* states that all behavior is understood as a means to maximize preferences. *Methodological equilibration* is the axiomatic imposition of equilibrium as a way to coordinate individual behavior at aggregate levels. The central question is what aggregate behavior would be like in equilibrium, but not whether such equilibrium behavior is likely or how it might materialize. The macroeconomic Ramsey–Cass–Koopmans model presented in the previous subsection is an example of a model with these three axioms. It explains the dynamic behavior of aggregate consumption and aggregate output as a direct result of individual maximization behavior and uses the steady-state equilibrium concept to make predictions.

Especially the equilibrium assumption is key to the neoclassical approach because it is used to move from statements about individual behavior to statements about the behavior of groups in markets or even entire economies. As we will see, complexity economics differs from mainstream economics primarily by not imposing a concept of equilibrium on group behavior. The concept of equilibrium is about mutual consistency of plans or actions, which does not require any change in behavior. Although the precise meaning of equilibrium varies in different branches of economics, it generally implies consistency and no incentive to change behavior. For example, a simple market model, such as the one in Fig. 4.1, consists of a supply schedule and a demand schedule, both of which represent the plans of market agents to supply or demand a given quantity of a good at a given price. Thus, these schedules describe desired behavior, not actual behavior. In the neoclassical model, the aggregate plans are consistent only in equilibrium. It is only at the equilibrium price that the quantity suppliers want to sell and the quantity customers want to buy are identical, so that all plans can be realized. Similarly, the rational expectations hypothesis states that agents do not make systematic forecasting errors. All agents use all available information to form their expectations, including all theoretical and structural information about the economy. Thus, rational expectations imply consistency in three dimensions: first, the expectations of all agents are mutually consistent; i.e., all rational agents take into account how all other agents form their expectations. The resulting *infinite regress* can only be stopped by assuming that all agents form expectations in exactly the same way. Second, rational expectations are model consistent, as argued in the previous section. Third, apart from unpredictable random noise, expectations will be consistent with the actual realization of the variables. Finally, the Nash equilibrium concept in game theory is also about mutual consistency of strategies. In a Nash equilibrium, each player in a game plays the best response to the strategies of the other players, so no one can do better by unilaterally changing his own strategy.

To emphasize again: mainstream economics does not ask under what conditions an equilibrium occurs, or whether a market, an economy, or the behavior in a game is likely to be in equilibrium. Instead, the question is what patterns like market prices and quantities look like, *if* the economy is in equilibrium. In the market model in Sect. 4.3.1, the equilibrium Eq. (4.3) states that $Q_t^D = Q_t^S$ is an assumption, not a result of the model. This assumption is useful, because it allows us to make a prediction about what will happen in the market. Typical statements of neoclassical models are "in equilibrium, the market price will be P^*" or "in equilibrium, aggregate output will grow at the constant rate x." The conventional method of *comparative statics* analyzes how the equilibrium values of the endogenous variables change when there is a change in exogenous variables or model parameters like d_0 or s_0 in the market model. Two types of equilibrium notions are used in the Ramsey–Cass–Koopmans model. The first type of equilibrium is the assumption that in each period, firms operate in a competitive market equilibrium with zero profits forcing them to pay the factors of production their marginal products (see (4.15) and (4.16)). The model assumes that these conditions hold at all times. The second kind of equilibrium is that the economy is on the saddle path or in the steady state, which is a corollary of the assumption of intertemporal utility maximization. The steady state is a pattern with consistency properties. When the economy is in the steady state, neither c nor k, which describe the state of the economy, will change any more, and all behavior is consistent with utility and profit maximization under the assumption of a fixed structure of the economy.

As noted above, Gary Becker defines the economic approach as "the combined assumptions of maximizing behavior, market equilibrium and stable preferences, used relentlessly and unflinchingly." He also claims that the economic approach assumes the existence of markets and the stability of preferences:

> Since economists generally have had little to contribute ... to the understanding of how preferences are formed, preferences are assumed not to change substantially over time, nor to be very different between wealthy and poor persons, or even between persons in different societies and cultures (Becker 1976, p. 5).

Note that these assumptions of the neoclassical approach—maximization, structural stability of preferences, technology, institutions, etc., and equilibrium—entail each other. Only under the assumption of structural stability, a maximization problem is well-defined and solvable. When maximization requires taking into account the behavior of other agents, as in games or models with rational expectations, we also need the equilibrium assumption. As shown in the Ramsey–Cass–Koopmans model, the steady-state equilibrium is an implication of the intertemporal utility maximization.

Complexity economics challenges all three assumptions: it argues that we cannot assume permanent structural stability, which implies that strong maximization is not possible. Consequently, there may be no unique equilibrium, or the economy may be far from any equilibrium state most of the time. As we will see in the following chapters, complexity economics basically rejects all assumptions (A1)–(A12) of the neoclassical models presented in 4.3.1 and 4.3.2. This does not mean that a model in complexity economics can never contain such an assumption. For convenience, a complexity economist might assume that agents are identical or that a market is well described by a demand and a supply function. But this would be the exception rather than the rule. We can think of neoclassical economics as a special case of complexity economics, which is the more general theory. Complexity economics does not just assume that there is an equilibrium, but also asks what might lead to an equilibrium and how it is reached. It also allows for multiple equilibria, which raises the question of which equilibrium is chosen. As a process-oriented approach, complexity economics allows for randomness. Small random events can determine whether one equilibrium or another is reached, which can make a big difference in how a market or an economy evolves.

While equilibrium analysis is concerned with stability, complexity economics is also interested in forces that can destabilize existing patterns and bring about change. Often, these destabilizing forces involve differentiation and heterogeneity of agents. Let's look at some examples.

The simple neoclassical market model assumes that firms and households care only about the price of a good. In practice, however, many firms go to great lengths to **differentiate their products** in order to escape competition and gain market power. It is true that there are models of monopolistic competition in neoclassical economics, such as the Dixit–Stiglitz model. But these models assume that there are different varieties of a product, rather than a permanent process of differentiation by which firms always try to escape competition. Firms can do this by changing the characteristics of their products, but also by offering special customer service and establishing personal relationships with their customers, or by advertising campaigns.

From a complexity perspective, it seems plausible that firms try to **change their customers' preferences** through advertising and often succeed. This is different from neoclassical economics, which assumes that households have fixed preferences (see Becker 1976). The neoclassical approach seeks to explain consumer behavior in terms of changes in the budget constraint, i.e., relative prices and income, rather than in terms of changes in preferences. Since preferences are not easily observable, neoclassical economists, who do not have a theory of preferences, fear that all behavior can be explained by changes in preferences. If customers have fixed and known preferences, the only purpose of advertising is to provide customers with information that they can use rationally. Complexity economics allows for a permanent coevolution of market supply and consumer preferences. Both sides of the market constantly adapt to the behavior of the other side. In order to influence or create preferences, companies even deceive their customers and pretend that their products have properties that they do not have. Preferences change not only because of marketing campaigns by firms. They can also change because of the desire of groups to distinguish themselves from other groups in order to form a group identity. Preferences also change over time, both at the individual level and at the societal level. Most people change their preferences for music, leisure activities, food, clothing, etc., over the course of their lives, so that their tastes are different when they are 15 than when they are 50. At the societal level, tastes and values change over time, too.

Another source of change is *entrepreneurs* who **create new markets** and destroy old ones. They do this by innovating, i.e., by **inventing new products and technologies** and **establishing new business models**. While neoclassical economics focuses on how existing markets work, complexity economics asks how new markets emerge and how existing markets disappear. Entrepreneurial activity transforms not only markets but also existing firms. Some firms thrive and grow, while others stagnate and eventually fail. Innovation within organizations brought about by *intrapreneurs* is another example of structural change that neoclassical economics has little to say about.

Markets do not just consist of firms and households buying and selling goods and services. Each market also has an **institutional framework** that governs how it operates. Neoclassical economics generally abstracts from institutional features, but they are crucial to any market. Institutions are the "rules of the game" and can be formal or informal. *Formal institutions* are laws, contracts, government regulations, and so on. *Informal institutions* are customs, social norms, conventions, etc. Institutions determine whether or not a market can exist, for example a market for human organs, a market for babies, a market for drugs, or a market for real estate. In some cases, such markets may be illegal but still exist. In other cases, social or moral norms may even prevent illegal markets. In legal markets, institutions regulate who can participate in the market, how prices can be set, and what properties the traded goods can have. Labor markets, for instance, are highly regulated in most countries. There are often institutional restrictions on wage setting or institutional entry barriers, e.g., into the labor market for doctors. The institutional framework of markets or the economy is not stable over time, with formal institutions changing faster than informal ones. Moreover, economic agents often deliberately seek to change institutions, for example firms lobbying for laxer labor market rules and trade unions fighting for more worker protection. Thus, economic activity does not only take place within given institutional arrangements, but also aims to change them. The **evolution of institutions** is an important topic in complexity economics, but not so much in neoclassical economics.

Destabilization that drives an economy away from equilibrium can also result from unsustainable **exploitative behavior**. Ponzi games in asset markets are one example for this. They can create asset price bubbles that lead to financial crises.

These Ponzi investors may believe that an asset is overvalued, but if they expect prices to rise and to find another buyer, they may still be willing to invest. Ponzi schemes can mean that professional investors take advantage of the gullibility of naïve investors in a financial market by using better information or more realistic assessments of the fundamental value of an asset. But exploitation can also mean that fraudulent agents actively **deceive** non-professional investors by selling them worthless assets. Overuse of common pool resources is another example of unsustainable behavior that can lead to the collapse of a system. It can be argued that much of the economic success of our current economic system is only possible, because corporations are **destroying ecosystems** and thus overusing natural resources. Degraded or destroyed ecosystems affect our way of life and our economic activities. The fate of the Aral Sea, mentioned in Chap. 1, is an example of overexploitation that has destroyed not only flora and fauna, but also the economic base of thousands of people in the region. Thus, the structure of the local economy has changed as a result of unsustainable behavior.

These examples represent destabilizing forces that cause the change in patterns that is of central interest to complexity economics. They create both off-equilibrium dynamics and changes in the nature of existing equilibria. Many of these forces are seen as externalities or imperfections in neoclassical economics. Complexity economics deals with the imperfect real world instead of the idealized world of neoclassical economics.

Because complexity economics analyzes processes of change rather than equilibrium states, W. Brian Arthur[3] characterizes it as verb-based as opposed to noun-based neoclassical economics. Complexity economics focuses on processes and actions, while neoclassical economics is concerned with entities such as quantities and prices. It is difficult to describe processes with conventional mathematics, which is considered the language of science. The use of geometry, algebra, and calculus makes neoclassical economics similar to classical physics and gives it the appearance of an exact science. Algebraic equations allow us to relate nouns such as quantity and price in the demand Eq. (4.1). The equilibrium condition (4.3) also relates two nouns, but does tell us nothing about the process that produces the equilibrium. Describing processes requires verbs, e.g., markets *form*, industries *evolve*, entrepreneurs *innovate*, consumers *learn*, firms *adapt* to competitive pressures and government regulation, and so on. Since algebra and calculus are not ideal for the analysis of qualitative changes, neoclassical economics focuses on quantitative changes such as the growth of output or the fall of prices, for which the conventional mathematical tools are very useful.

Processes can be described mathematically, but with a different kind of mathematics. We can express processes as *algorithms* and study them *computationally*. An *algorithm* is a finite sequence of instructions in a fixed order for solving a problem. We often use the word algorithm in the context of mathematics and computer science where computational problems are considered. However, any list of well-defined

[3] https://complexity.simplecast.com/episodes/68. Accessed October 26, 2023.

instructions for achieving a specific goal is an algorithm. For example, a recipe for making pancakes is also an algorithm. A pancake recipe could be:

Ingredients: 1.5 cups flour, 3.5 teaspoons baking powder, 0.25 teaspoon salt, 1 tablespoon sugar, 1.25 cups milk, 1 egg, 3 tablespoons melted butter, oil

1. Sift flour, baking soda, salt, and sugar into a bowl.
2. Make a well in the center.
3. Pour milk, egg, and melted butter into the well.
4. Whisk everything to a batter.
5. Heat some oil in a frying pan.
6. When the oil is hot enough, pour a ¼ cup of batter into the pan for each pancake.
7. Flip the pancakes several times until they are golden brown on both sides.

Note that the recipe is based on verbs: sift, make, pour... Each instruction describes a certain procedure that requires a minimum of experience and cooking knowledge on the part of the user. The instructions are therefore not perfectly precise, because they do not mention all the cooking utensils required and imply that the cook knows how to whisk the ingredients or flip the pancakes. Recipes are usually expressed as text, but they can also come in other forms, such as videos or even flowcharts.

An example of a mathematical algorithm is the following simple sorting algorithm for finding the largest number in a list of numbers in random order.[4] A so-called *high-level description* states the algorithm in plain English:

1. If there are no numbers in the set then state that there is no highest number.
2. Assume that the first number in the set is the largest number.
3. For each remaining number in the set: if the number is greater than the current largest number, consider this number to be the largest number.
4. When all numbers have been looked at, consider the current largest number to be the largest number in the set.

This algorithm is similar to a cookbook recipe in that it is also a list of instructions, but it relies heavily on the basic control structures of computer programs: sequence, if-then, and while-do. Notice that the pancake recipe also contains these control structures. The individual procedures are ordered in a sequence, step 6) contains an if-then condition, and step 7) contains a while-do loop.

We can also express the algorithm for finding the largest number in a more formal way, which is closer to the language of computer programs. The following description is called *pseudocode* because it is still plain language, but it follows the structural conventions and standards of programming languages.

[4] See https://en.wikipedia.org/wiki/Algorithm. Accessed October 26, 2023.

```
Algorithm LargestNumber
Input: A list of numbers L
Output: The largest number in the list L
if L.size = 0 return null
largest <- L[0]
for each item in L do
 if item > largest then
 largest <- item
return largest
```

Again note that the algorithm contains verbs such as return, do, and assign, which is expressed by ←. We can conclude that it is possible to apply mathematics to the topics of complexity economics, but this mathematics is different from algebra and calculus. Complexity economics relies on computation or algorithmic mathematics.

Because computation is so important, complexity economics makes heavy use of the computer as a research tool. The use of the computer as a key research tool is another difference from the neoclassical approach. Mainstream economics, of course, also uses computers, especially in applied econometrics. But in mainstream theoretical work, the computer plays a different role than in complexity economics. The ideal mainstream theoretical approach is to write down an algebraic model and solve the equations analytically for as long as possible. Sometimes the resulting equilibrium conditions are nonlinear and cannot be solved algebraically. In this case, neoclassical theorists resort to numerical solutions to characterize the equilibrium. Used in this way, the computer is more of an aid than a central research tool. Neoclassical theorists gain insights through the process of solving their algebraic models themselves, if possible. They suspect that the research process is inappropriate if it takes place inside the black box of the computer. Complexity theorists, on the other hand, accept computation as a powerful way to express and analyze pattern formation processes. The skepticism of neoclassical economists toward the computer and computation as a means of research is somewhat curious, since most of today's research in physics, chemistry, and biology would not be possible without sophisticated research instruments such as particle accelerators, radio telescopes, electron microscopes, or genome sequencers. Insisting on the use of the research tools available to Leon Walras, Alfred Marshall, and Paul Samuelson is like restricting physics to the methods available to Johannes Kepler and Isaac Newton.

4.4.2 Complexity Economics and Other Schools of Thought

As we have seen, complexity economics is primarily about change and the fundamental uncertainty that is a consequence of change. Neoclassical economics is not

[5] https://www.exploring-economics.org/en/orientation/. Accessed October 26, 2023.

concerned with change and uncertainty, but many other non-mainstream schools of thought are, at least with one of the two topics. It is not the purpose of this section to give a complete overview over the various non-mainstream schools of thought in economics. The *Exploring Economics*[5] website is an excellent place to go if you want to explore and compare the different perspectives on economics in detail. Here, we focus mainly on some key differences and similarities between complexity economics and a selection of other non-mainstream approaches. Most economic schools of thought are quite diverse with different branches and sometimes fierce internal debates within the community about the most relevant questions and the appropriate ways to answer them. Therefore, any brief characterization is likely to be oversimplified. One generalization that is probably true is that most non-mainstream schools are less coherent and unified than neoclassical economics. While mainstream economists despise but also fear this sometimes discordant pluralism of opinions and approaches, it can be seen as an inevitable consequence of the complexity of reality.

Change is important in *institutional economics*, *evolutionary economics*, *ecological economics*, and *Austrian economics*. *Institutional economics* is about the evolution of formal and informal institutions that provide the rules of the game for economic activity. There is a traditional branch that is aware of history as well as legal, social, and political processes, which has always been at odds with neoclassical economics. The newer branch of new institutional economics tries to reconcile institutional aspects with the neoclassical approach. The traditional branch is less formal in its methods, preferring qualitative methods such as case studies. New institutional economics is closer to the neoclassical methodology. *Evolutionary economics* focuses on innovation, technological change, and knowledge generation as fundamental drivers of economic change. Like institutional economics, with which it has some overlap, evolutionary economics uses both quantitative and qualitative methods and emphasizes the need to consider economic processes in historical time. *Ecological economics* views the economy as a subsystem of a larger social system, which in turn is embedded in natural systems. A major premise of ecological economics is the existence of *planetary boundaries* that impose limits on economic activity. Approaching or even exceeding these planetary boundaries is not sustainable in the long run and will lead to undesirable changes in the natural ecosystems that affect human life. The main themes of *Austrian economics* are the self-organization of markets and the idea that markets are a discovery process to elicit dispersed knowledge. The economy is seen as far too complex for any centralized management, so that government planning and intervention are seen as futile or even harmful. Only markets can deal with the enormous information problem of coordinating economic resources in an economy with division of labor. Austrian economics rejects the use of formal methods.

Uncertainty is a minor topic in institutional economics, but it is important in evolutionary economics, ecological economics, and Austrian economics. Why uncertainty is relevant in Austrian economics follows from the information problem outlined above. Evolutionary economics emphasizes innovation, which is by definition unpredictable and thus a source of uncertainty. Uncertainty is important in ecological economics, because we do not know exactly where the planetary boundaries are and what will happen if we cross them. There is a strong danger of systemic collapse entailing huge tail risks, which makes it highly problematic to search for optimal sustainability policies, as it is done in neoclassical *environmental economics*. Another school of thought in which fundamental uncertainty is central is *post-Keynesian economics*. In his *General Theory of Employment, Interest and Money*, John Maynard Keynes explains that there are many situations, in which "mathematical expectations," i.e., quantitative outcomes multiplied by quantitative probabilities, are not possible. He proposed that decisions about the distant, fundamentally uncertain future are often driven by *animal spirits*, i.e., a spontaneous optimism and urge to action that has a strong social element. Post-Keynesian economists maintain that concept of fundamental uncertainty is one of the crucial contributions of Keynes's theory, which has been ignored by the so-called *Keynesians,* who are neoclassical economists in the methodological sense.

Behavioral economics is a school of thought that is partly in and partly out of the mainstream. The complexity scientist Herbert Simon, who coined the term *bounded rationality* in the 1950s, is one of the pioneers of behavioral economics (see Simon 1962). He argued that people have cognitive limitations that prevent them from processing information and solving complex problems in a perfectly rational way. He proposed a model of decision-making in which economic agents do not seek the best choices, but make choices that are good enough. Maximization is often not possible because many real-world problems are ill-defined. *Ill-defined problems* have unclear goals, no unambiguously right or wrong answers, and unstated constraints and require a large amount of information that is often not available. In the 1980s, new behavioral economics emerged that is closer to neoclassical economics, because it reintroduces maximization. While behavioral economics in the older tradition is mostly outside the economic mainstream, new behavioral economics has been accepted by the mainstream, because of its willingness to use the method of maximization. One might even say that it has merged with Becker's rational approach when utility functions with other-regarding preferences or hyperbolic discounting are maximized. For Becker, it did not matter what the preferences of the agents were. They might be very strange from an observer's point of view, but as long as agents maximize according to their preferences their approach is rational.

Complexity economics shares many of the mentioned ideas with other schools of thought. It acknowledges the important role of institutions, is interested in the evolution of knowledge and technology, considers the possibility of systemic collapse, and accepts the impossibility of maximizing behavior due to ill-definedness of problems, lack of information, and cognitive limitations. If all these topics are treated in other schools of thought, one might legitimately ask, what is special about complexity economics. We can consider many of the key ideas of the non-mainstream schools of thought as elements of complexity such that there is an inevitable overlap with complexity economics. The special features of complexity economics are twofold. The first is the use of the concept of the economy as a complex adaptive system with its special language and its connections to other complexity fields outside of economics. The complexity perspective can integrate the mentioned schools to some extent and serve as a bridge to other disciplines. The second feature that characterizes complexity economics is the acceptance of computation as a useful method for theoretical research.

4.5 Methods of Complexity Economics

The rise of complexity economics is closely linked to the digital revolution that began in the 1990s with the advent of small, powerful personal computers and the Internet. Of course, computers had been used in economics before, especially in econometrics, but cheap and plentiful computing power made possible simulation models, an alternative research tool to algebra. The history of science is also a history of technological investment. New research tools enable new research approaches. For example, the invention of the telescope was critical to the breakthroughs in astronomy made by Johannes Kepler and Galileo Galilei. Similarly, advances in cell and microbiology depended on the invention of the light microscope. The invention of the electron microscope in the early twentieth century greatly expanded the potential of microscopy. For example, it became possible to identify viruses. More recently, electron microscopes have become an important research tool in materials science, which emerged as a separate field of research in the mid-twentieth century. The computer is the main research tool of (hard) complexity science. It has also opened up new fields of research in many other disciplines, such as computational biology, computational chemistry, computational engineering, computational social science, and others.

Complexity economics makes intensive use of computational methods, but in keeping with the view that dealing with complexity requires multiple approaches, it is also open to other methods. Each method has its strengths and limitations. Ideally, mixed methods should be used frequently, but no one can be an expert in all research methods. Mastering research methods requires intensive training and experience. In practice, most people need to specialize in a few research methods, but it is always recommended to have some basic knowledge of other methods as well. Understanding what other people do is a prerequisite for communicating and collaborating with others.

This subsection provides a brief overview of five methods in complexity science. This overview can neither cover all methods nor explain them in detail. For comprehensive introductions, you should consult specialized textbooks. The overview serves mainly as an introduction to the following chapters, where the presented methods are used to explain complexity concepts.

4.5.1 Nonlinear Dynamics and Chaos

Dynamics is the mathematical subject that deals with systems that evolve over time. Since complexity economics is about economic change, it naturally has a dynamical view of the world. Of course, mainstream economics also studies dynamical phenomena, since economic growth and business cycle fluctuations are inherently dynamical. The mathematical tools for studying of dynamics are *differential equations* and *iterated maps*, which are also called *difference equations*. In many sciences and in economics, systems of linear differential equations or linear difference equations are very popular, because they can be solved analytically. An example of a second-order linear ordinary differential equation (ODE) is

$$\ddot{x} + a\dot{x} + bx = 0, \tag{4.20}$$

with $\ddot{x} = \frac{d^2x}{dt^2}$ and $\dot{x} = \frac{dx}{dt}$. The equation involves a variable x that depends on time, and its first and second derivatives with respect to time, which is why it is of second order. Differential equations treat time as a continuous variable. Difference equations, on the other hand, model time as discrete, i.e., as a sequence of points in time or periods, e.g., $\ldots t-2, t-1, t, t+1, t+2\ldots$. Conventionally, t refers to the current period, $t-i$ to past periods, and $t+i$ to periods in the future. A second-order homogenous linear difference equation is

$$x_{t+2} + ax_{t+1} + bx_t = 0. \tag{4.21}$$

Both (4.20) and (4.21) are linear equations, because all terms appear only in the the first power. There are well-established methods for analyzing and solving linear differential equations of order 1 and 2. Solving such an equation means that we can find a closed form expression that gives us the value of x for any point in time, e.g.,

$$x_t = Am_1^t + Bm_2^t, \tag{4.22}$$

for a homogeneous second-order difference equation, where A, B, m_1, m_2 are constants. Since first-order systems are easier to work with than second-order systems, it can be convenient to transform (4.20) by defining new variables: $x_1 = x$ and $x_2 = \dot{x}$. With these definitions, we can express (4.20) as a system of two first-order differential equations:

$$\dot{x}_1 = x_2 \tag{4.23}$$

$$\dot{x}_2 = -ax_2 - bx_1. \tag{4.24}$$

Unfortunately, while such one- or two-variable linear systems are easy to work with, they adequately describe only a small fraction of real-world phenomena. Most natural and social systems are nonlinear, which is nicely expressed in the quote attributed to the mathematician and nuclear physicist Stanislaw Ulam:

> Using a term like nonlinear science is like referring to the bulk of zoology as the study of non-elephant animals.

Nonlinear systems contain nonlinear terms of the x_i such as products (e.g., x_1x_2), powers (e.g., $(x_1)^3$), or functions (e.g., $\ln(x_1)$or $\cos(x_2)$). Equation (4.18), which describes the evolution of capital per effective labor, is an example of a nonlinear differential equation. In most cases, it is very difficult or impossible to solve nonlinear equations and systems analytically. However, as we have seen, we can analyze them graphically using phase diagrams.

As we will see in Chap. 6, nonlinear dynamics are an important aspect of complex phenomena. Nonlinearity is a direct consequence of interaction between system elements, either in the form of cooperation or competition. Linear systems are simple because they can be decomposed into parts; i.e., the elements can be analyzed in isolation. As we saw in Chap. 2, it is a central property of complex systems that this is not possible. Nonlinear systems have a much richer dynamic behavior than linear systems. Instead of simple equilibria, they typically have attractors of various kinds that describe the long-term behavior of the system. Furthermore, nonlinear systems can have *bifurcations*, i.e., qualitative changes in the dynamics that occur at *bifurcation points*, i.e., special values of system parameters.

Nonlinear dynamical systems can also be characterized by *chaos*, which is aperiodic long-term behavior in a deterministic system that exhibits a sensitive dependence on initial conditions. What this means is explained in Chap. 6. Chaos is fascinating because it looks like randomness, even though there are no random elements in the generating dynamical system. It is also highly relevant to economics because it implies the impossibility of long-term prediction.

In Chap. 6, you will learn why at least a basic knowledge of nonlinear dynamics is necessary in complexity economics. Since this is a rather advanced branch of mathematics, we can only introduce some important concepts without providing in-depth explanations. The textbook *Nonlinear Dynamics and Chaos* by Steven Strogatz (2019) is an excellent introduction for beginners.

4.5.2 System Dynamics

System dynamics is a technique for modeling and simulating nonlinear dynamic systems. In most cases, it is not possible to solve nonlinear systems analytically. While we can learn much about the qualitative behavior of nonlinear systems with few variables using phase diagrams, this method has limitations. Graphical analysis is possible only for low-dimensional systems, but is too complex for systems with many variables. Furthermore, we may be interested in quantitative statements about the behavior of a system, which cannot be obtained from graphical analysis.

System dynamics also uses graphical tools, in particular *causal loop diagrams*, which show the causal relationships between the elements of a system. Causal loop diagrams visualize *feedback loops*, which are critical in system dynamics. The interactions between system elements generate both positive feedback, which amplifies an initial change in a variable, and negative feedback, which dampens initial changes. The interplay of positive and negative feedback produces complex dynamics that are often counterintuitive and difficult to predict without numerical modeling. Thus, computational modeling is another cornerstone of system dynamics. We will use system dynamics in Chap. 7. John Sterman's textbook *Business*

Dynamics: System Thinking and Modeling for a Complex World is a classic in system dynamics (Sterman 2000).

4.5.3 Agent-Based Modeling

Agent-based modeling (ABM) is a computational modeling approach for describing the behavior of individual agents and simulating the aggregate effects resulting from agent interactions. It is an extremely flexible technique that allows us to model virtually any type of behavior and to simulate systems with a high degree of agent heterogeneity. In addition, ABM can address agent learning and adaptation because we can model agent cognitive processes in great detail. With respect to adaptation, which is a key feature of complex adaptive systems, ABM is probably better than any other formal modeling technique. The modeling of behavior, learning, and adaptation is discussed in Chap. 12.

Another strength of ABM is its ability to link different levels of a system in a natural way. Because agents are autonomous, it is not necessary to make equilibrium assumptions to make statements about the aggregate behavior of all agents. When the system in an agent-based model is in an equilibrium state, this is an emergent result of the autonomous actions of the agents. One of the main uses of an agent-based model is to simulate what patterns emerge at the aggregate level from actions at lower levels of the system. This is the main topic of Chap. 9.

While ABM is a very powerful approach, it is also difficult to learn and to apply. Uri Wilensky and William Rand have written the excellent textbook *An Introduction to Agent-Based Modeling: Modeling Natural, Social and Engineered Complex Systems with NetLogo* (Wilensky & Rand 2015). We can also combine ABM and system dynamics, which is more intuitive and easier when aggregate system behavior is the center of interest, but also less flexible.

4.5.4 Social Network Analysis

A *network* is a collection of interconnected entities. In a social network, the entities are social actors, such as people or groups of people. Note that this definition is very similar to the definition of a system as a unified whole composed of parts connected by relationships (see Chap. 2). Thus, social network analysis is another important tool for studying complex systems.

Social network analysis is a set of techniques for describing and exploring patterns in the social relationships formed by individuals and groups. We can visualize the relationships and resulting patterns using graphs. A *graph* is a visual representation of a set of *nodes* (or vertices), which represent social actors, and *edges* (or links), which connect the nodes. The information contained in a graph can also be represented by an *adjacency matrix*, which is a square agent by agent matrix. The entries of the adjacency matrix are ones and zeros that indicate whether or not a relationship exists between two agents. Since an adjacency matrix is a mathematical object, we can use matrix algebra to analyze it. Graph theory, a branch of mathematics, provides many useful tools for analyzing networks.

We do not use social network analysis in this textbook, although it is an important tool. A good introduction is *Social Network Analysis with Applications* by Ian McCulloh et al. (2013).

4.5.5 Scenario Analysis

Scenario analysis (also called scenario planning or scenario thinking) is a method for developing qualitative, long-term scenarios of possible futures. A scenario is a detailed description of the world, often in narrative form. It is important to distinguish between scenarios and forecasts. Economic forecasts are quantitative and predict the most likely future state of the world. They are based on either structural econometric models or time series analysis. Scenario analysis is not concerned with the most likely future, but with a range of possible futures. It is a creative method that usually does not rely on quantitative models, but uses a systemic approach to thinking.

All forecasting methods assume structural stability of the system for which future states are predicted. Fundamental uncertainty, however, implies that the future is open and not predetermined by the past. It is a central tenet of complexity economics that there is continuous structural change, especially over longer time horizons. Therefore, complexity economists should be highly skeptical of long-term predictions, which always assume that the future is somehow similar to the present and the past. Scenario analysis emphasizes that the future may be very different from the present. It is commonly used in strategic planning in business organizations to help executives make investment decisions, develop new products, or increase the resilience of their organizations. It also has a place in scientific research, particularly as a complement to model-based approaches to thinking about the future. You can find a comprehensive treatment of the scenario method in Ulf Pillkahn's *Using Trends and Scenarios as Tools for Strategy Development* (Pillkahn 2008).

Things to Remember

- Complexity economics is the application of complexity thinking to economic issues and implies a specific worldview on the economy. The relationship between change and stability and the resulting fundamental uncertainty are central themes in complexity economics. Complexity economics is about structural change and the formation of economic structures.

(continued)

- Economics is the study of the economy. There are different schools of thought in economics that have different perspectives on the economy. We need different perspectives in order to get a deep understanding of the economy.
- Current mainstream economics is dominated by neoclassical economics, which uses a limited methodology, focuses on the scarcity problem, relies on strong assumptions, and is characterized by equilibrium analysis. Neoclassical economics cannot deal well with structural change and innovation in the economy.
- Complexity economics is more general than neoclassical economics and deals with nonequilibrium phenomena, the question of whether equilibria exist, and how they can be attained. Neoclassical economics can be seen as a special case of complexity economics.
- Complexity economics overlaps with many other non-mainstream schools of thought, such as institutional economics, evolutionary economics, ecological economics, and behavioral economics. They also deal with change and fundamental uncertainty. The defining characteristic of complexity economics is the interpretation of the economy as a complex adaptive system.
- Computation and algorithmic thinking are key elements of economic theory in complexity economics. Computation, which is a modern branch of mathematics, makes it possible to study formation and change processes. Traditional mathematical methods such as algebra and calculus require fixed functional relationships between variables, which are only present in special cases in the economy.
- Nonlinear dynamics, system dynamics, agent-based modeling, social network analysis, and scenario analysis are important research methods in complexity economics.

References

Arnsperger C, Varoufakis Y (2006) What is neoclassical economics? The three axioms responsible for its theoretical oeuvre, practical irrelevance and, thus, discursive power. Panoeconomicus 53: 5–18. https://doi.org/10.2298/PAN0601005A

Arthur WB (1999) Complexity and the economy. Science 284:107–109. https://doi.org/10.1126/science.284.5411.107

Arthur WB (2015) Complexity and the economy. Oxford University Press, Oxford

Becker GS (1976) The economic approach to human behavior. University of Chicago Press, Chicago and London

Becker GS (1993) Nobel lecture: the economic way of looking at behavior. J Polit Econ 101:385–409

Boulton JG, Allen PM, Bowman C (2015) Embracing complexity: strategic perspectives for an age of turbulence. Oxford University Press, Oxford

Cass D (1965) Optimum growth in an aggregative model of capital accumulation. Rev Econ Stud 32:233–240. https://doi.org/10.2307/2295827
Chang H-J (2014) Economics: the user's guide. Bloomsbury Publishing
Colander D, Holt R, Rosser B (2004) The changing face of mainstream economics. Rev Polit Econ 16:485–499. https://doi.org/10.1080/0953825042000256702
Eldredge N, Gould SJ (1972) Punctuated equilibria: an alternative to phyletic gradualism. In: Schopf TJM (ed) Models in paleobiology. Freeman Cooper, pp 82–115
Heijdra BJ (2017) Foundations of modern macroeconomics, 3rd edn. Oxford University Press, Oxford & New York
Koopmans TC (1965) On the concept of optimal economic growth. In: The econometric approach to development planning. Rand-McNally, Chicago
McCulloh I, Armstrong H, Johnson A (2013) Social network analysis with applications. John Wiley & Sons
Muth JF (1961) Rational expectations and the theory of price movements. Econometrica 29:315. https://doi.org/10.2307/1909635
Pillkahn U (2008) Using trends and scenarios as tools for strategy development: shaping the future of your enterprise. John Wiley & Sons
Ramsey FP (1928) A mathematical theory of saving. Econ J 38:543–559. https://doi.org/10.2307/2224098
Robbins LRB (1932) An essay on the nature and significance of economic science. Macmillan & Company
Romer D (2019) Advanced macroeconomics. McGraw-Hill Education
Simon HA (1962) The architecture of complexity. Proc Am Philos Soc 106:467–482
Sterman J (2000) Business dynamics: systems thinking and modeling for a complex world. Irwin/McGraw-Hill, Boston
Strogatz SH (2019) Nonlinear dynamics and chaos: with applications to physics, biology, chemistry, and engineering, 2nd edn. CRC Press, Boca Raton
Wilensky U, Rand W (2015) An introduction to agent-based modeling: modeling natural, social, and engineered complex systems with NetLogo. MIT Press

The Economy as a Complex Adaptive System

5

Contents

5.1 Introduction 148
5.2 Systemic Views on the Economy 149
5.3 Economic Complexity 157
5.3.1 Combination of Specialized Knowledge 158
5.3.2 Measurement of Economic Complexity 160
5.3.3 Empirical Results 167
5.4 The Automobile and Dynamic Complexity 172
5.5 A Conceptual Framework for Socio-technical Transitions 179
5.6 Things to Remember 181
References 182

Abstract

Chapter 5 explains why the economy is a complex adaptive system and presents a number of examples of a systems view of the economy. Systemic thinking is a key element of complexity economics. Unlike natural systems, social systems such as the economy can often be defined in multiple ways, which makes the study of social systems very challenging. The chapter also introduces the concept of economic complexity, which is a useful method for working with high-dimensional economic data. This quantitative approach is complemented by a qualitative account of the history of the automobile as an example of structural economic and societal change caused by technological innovation. Some aspects of this history of the automobile are treated more formally in later chapters, e.g. the technological choice between the internal combustion engine and the electric engine in the early twentieth century. In addition, the chapter introduces the multilevel perspective framework from transition theory as a useful tool for thinking about long-term transformations.

M. Roos, *Principles of Complexity Economics*, Classroom Companion: Economics,
https://doi.org/10.1007/978-3-031-51436-4_5

Keywords

Automobile · Economic complexity · Multilevel perspective · Socio-technical transition

Guiding Questions

- How can we represent the economic system?
- What is the role of knowledge in the economy?
- What is economic complexity?
- Why is the automobile interesting as a case study of the economy as a complex adaptive system?
- What is the multilevel perspective?

5.1 Introduction

We have seen that a defining element of complexity economics is to view the economy as a complex adaptive system. In Chap. 2, we defined complex adaptive systems (CAS) as systems with a large number of components that interact and adapt or learn. So far, we have treated CAS in general and have not applied the concept directly to the economy, although we discussed some examples in the context of how to measure complexity in Chap. 3. This chapter shows how we can think of the economy as CAS. It serves as a bridge between the more general treatment of complexity and complexity economics in the previous chapters and the more specific discussions of complexity concepts in the following chapters. It gives empirical content to the theoretical ideas and motivates why economics can benefit from the complexity approach.

There are many ways to define economic systems. Section 5.2 suggests several approaches to taking a systemic view of the economy. In contrast to many natural and technical systems, in the social world it is often not obvious what exactly belongs to a system and what is outside of it.

Section 5.3 introduces a specific concept of *economic complexity* that can be applied to countries and products. The main idea of this concept is that economic complexity depends on the ability of the economy to use the dispersed specialized knowledge of the large number of agents in the economy. Knowledge is embodied in goods, so that products, production structures, and trade patterns can be used to assess the complexity of the economy. The production of some goods requires very large networks of people and organizations with specialized skills and knowledge, while other goods are less knowledge-intensive and thus require smaller networks. From this perspective, the main economic problem is not the allocation of scarce material resources (as postulated by neoclassical economics), but the generation and combination of specialized knowledge. You will learn which countries have complex economies in this sense and how economic complexity is related to economic growth and income.

The concept of economic complexity is another way of measuring the structural complexity of a system, but it does not explain or describe the processes that created it. Therefore, we use the example of the automobile to show how a product, the industry, and, as a consequence, the economy and society can change over time. Section 5.4 provides a brief history of the automobile to illustrate the transformative power of this remarkable technology. The narrative account of the evolution of the automobile is one way of dealing with dynamic complexity. In later chapters, you will encounter more formal approaches. Narrating change has the advantage of accessibility and richness of detail. Complexity economics—though often formal and quantitative—also needs narrative approaches.

In the last section of the chapter, you will be introduced to the *multilevel perspective* of Frank Geels, which is a theoretical framework to explain the evolution of socio-technical systems. The multilevel perspective is also a non-formal approach, although there have been attempts to implement it in agent-based models. The framework is popular in the applied literature on sustainability transitions.

5.2 Systemic Views on the Economy

In Chap. 2, we saw that systems consist of components and have a boundary around them. In the social sciences, both are constructions by an observer and are not naturally given. A few examples in this section serve to illustrate this point.

Let us start with a version of the circular flow diagram common in mainstream macroeconomics, shown in Fig. 5.1. This simple version of an economy consists of five components: three sectors and two markets. The household sector, the firm sector, and the government sector interact directly, as well as in the labor market and the goods markets. There are two types of interactions between the system elements: flows of physical goods represented by gray arrows and monetary flows represented in orange. All flows of goods through markets have a monetary counterpart, but there are some monetary flows that have no direct equivalent in goods, such as the tax flows and the profit flow.[1] We could also include a financial sector with commercial banks, a central bank and a financial market, but this would not change the general logic of the system. In this diagram, the economy is a closed system with no connections to any outside environment. The conventional way to open it up is to include a "rest of the world" or a second economy, and to include trade in goods, capital flows and possibly labor migration.

The components of systems can be systems themselves, which is certainly the case in the economy. For example, we could zoom in on the business sector and think of it as composed of several industries linked by input–output relationships.

[1] Of course, we could include capital services as a counterpart of the profit flows.

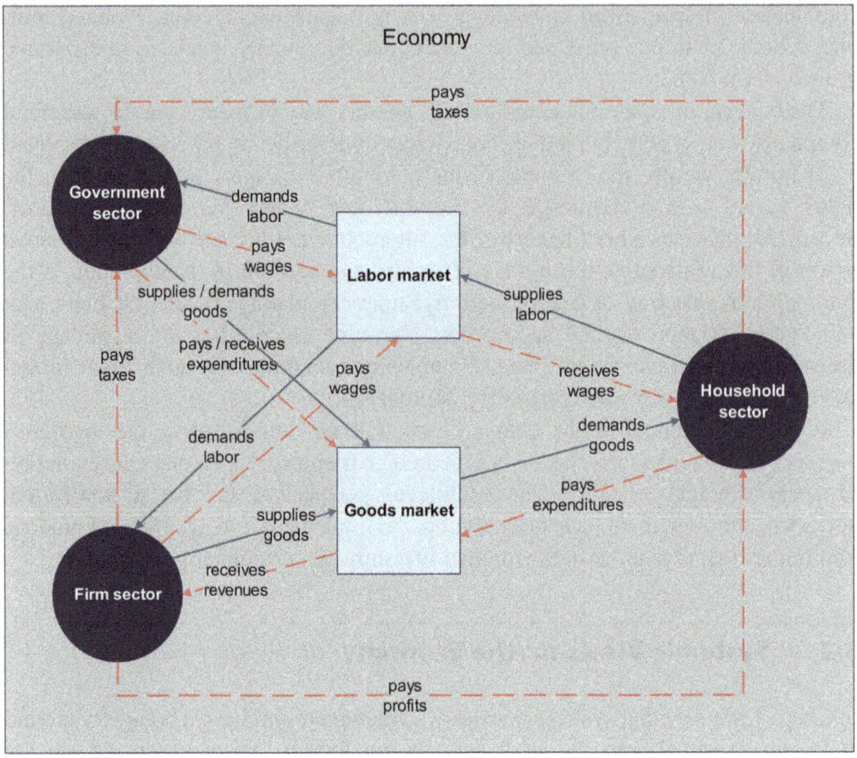

Fig. 5.1 Circular flow diagram in mainstream macroeconomics. Source: Author

Figure 5.2 shows an example of five industries providing intermediate goods and services to each other and to themselves. The flows of intermediate goods and services are represented by arrows whose size is proportional to the monetary value of the transactions. We can see that the service industry provides a lot of services to itself, which is the largest flow in this example. It also sells a large volume of services to trade, restaurants, and hotels. Only a small amount of services is sold to agriculture and mining.

Another way of presenting the same information is shown in Table 5.1, which is called an *input–output table*. The example is a regional input–output table showing sales and purchases in Yucatán, Mexico, in 1993. Reading the table row by row, the numbers represent the sales of each industry to other industries and to final consumers. For example, agriculture and mining sold 243,777,000 Mexican pesos worth of intermediate goods and services to the food and textile industries and 390,375,000 pesos to households. The bold numbers in the upper left partition of the table represent the flows of intermediate goods and services between industries, according to the system in Fig. 5.2.

The lower-left partition contains other expenditures by industries, such as labor and imports, and the upper-right partition contains final demand expenditures by

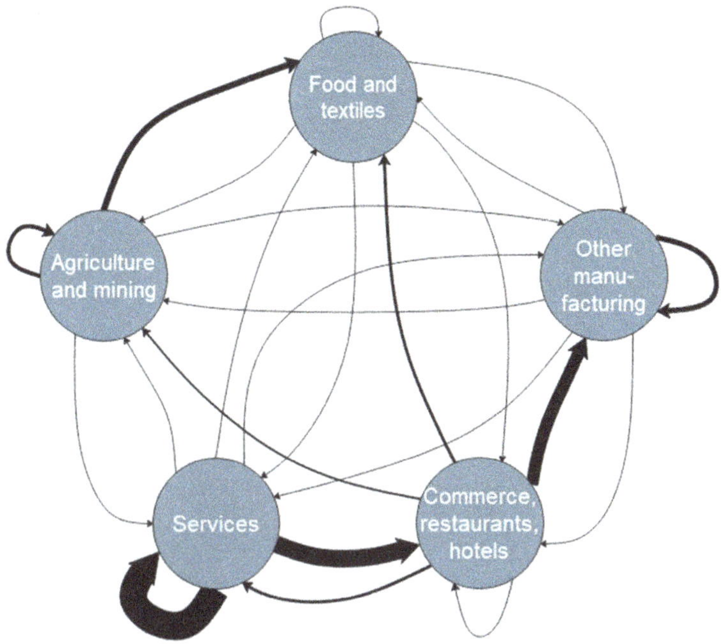

Fig. 5.2 Input–output relationships. Source: Author

households and other purchasers. The economic systems considered so far were very conventional and could be found in many mainstream textbooks. It is important to keep in mind that they are not the only ways to think about the economy as a system. Whenever we define a social system, we include some things and exclude others. In addition, there may be different ways of defining the components and the interactions between them. While this multiplicity of modeling options is not in itself a problem, you should never forget that any model you choose is at best a partial view of reality, never reality itself.

Figure 5.3 illustrates this point. The figure shows a selection of interactions of a household with other households, firms, and other organizations. All of these interactions can be considered economic because they consist of value-creating transactions of goods and services. However, only a small fraction of them are included in the conventional system shown in Fig. 5.1. Mainstream economics focuses mostly on market interactions, which are also represented in Fig. 5.3. The red arrows represent flows of goods and services that households purchase from firms, and the yellow arrows represent labor services that households sell to firms. The figure tells us that households engage in many other activities that are very similar to market activities but are not paid for and therefore not measured in economic accounts. Unpaid care work is an example of a very important activity that is not represented by the system in Fig. 5.1 because it occurs within and between households. Voluntary work in charities, churches, or sports clubs and helping

Table 5.1 Regional input–output table for Yucatán, Mexico (1993)[a]

	Sector purchases					Final demand		
Sector sales	Agriculture and mining	Food and textiles	Other manufacturing	Commerce, hotels, and restaurants	Services	Household consumption	Other final demand	Total output
Agriculture and mining	**175,000**	**243,777**	**42,267**	**0**	**2108**	390,375	379,561	1,233,089
Food and textiles	**47,298**	**33,422**	**156**	**867**	**5063**	509,499	566,641	1,162,947
Other manufacturing	**7742**	**6920**	**210,051**	**3692**	**12,141**	157,201	1,310,810	1,708,557
Commerce, hotels, and restaurants	**71,297**	**128,386**	**451,502**	**60,033**	**114,749**	1,205,139	1,347,968	3,379,074
Services	**48,838**	**26,778**	**59,433**	**621,324**	**1,011,809**	5,497,833	662,960	7,928,975
Salaries	464,264	131,054	270,915	638,641	1,587,520			
Other value added	263,776	286,541	355,101	1,598,486	2,532,475			
Imports	154,875	306,068	319,131	456,030	2,663,109			
Total outlays	1,233,089	1162,947	1,708,557	3,379,074	7,928,975			

Source: Munroe and Biles (2005), reproduced with kind permission of Elsevier
[a] Values in thousands of Mexican pesos

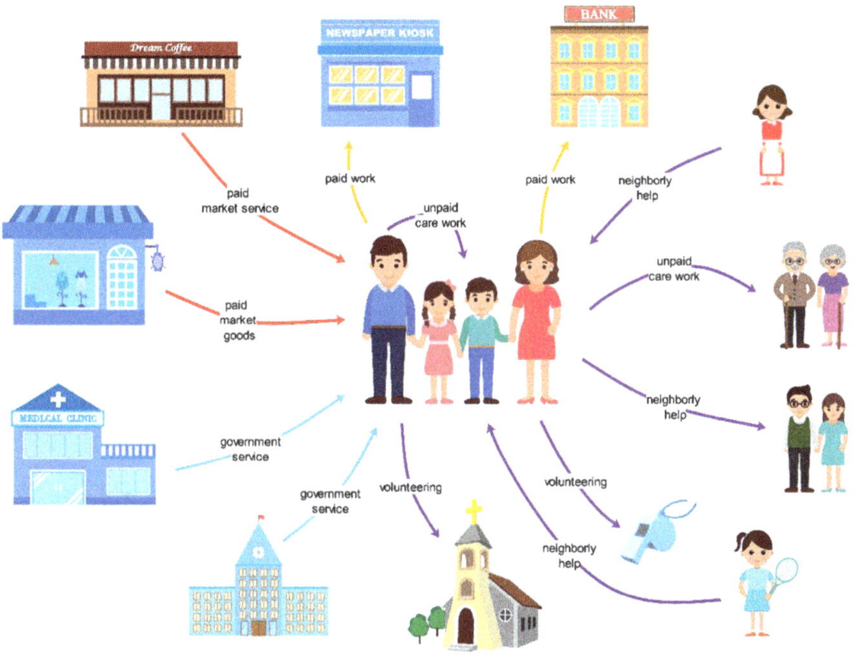

Fig. 5.3 Household interactions. Source: Author

neighbors are other examples. For example, a tennis coach can sell her services, but she can also offer them for free among friends. While the service may be exactly the same, there is a monetary counterflow in the former case, but not in the latter. One might argue—as mainstream economics often does—that only paid market transactions should be defined as economic activities, but what about government services for which there is no direct payment? There is a counter-transaction in the form of taxes, but there is no one-to-one equivalence between the tax paid by an individual household and the services it receives from the government. Moreover, neighborly help is often reciprocal. For example, a family's children may walk the tennis coach's dog while the owner is on vacation. If we define economic activities as all activities that create value for someone, then all the household interactions shown in Fig. 5.3 are economic, whether or not they are traded in a market. Figure 5.3 then represents the economic system of which a given household is a part.

A company is also a system in which employees are elements that form an interconnected structure. As Fig. 5.4 shows, the structures of the connections can look different depending on how we operationalize the system. The top section shows a portion of the organizational chart representing the formal reporting structures. Jones, Williams, Taylor, and Stock are the top executives in the exploration and production division of the large petroleum organization and therefore have a lot of formal authority. In the lower part, we see the actual communication network, i.e. who communicates with whom on a regular basis. The communication graph

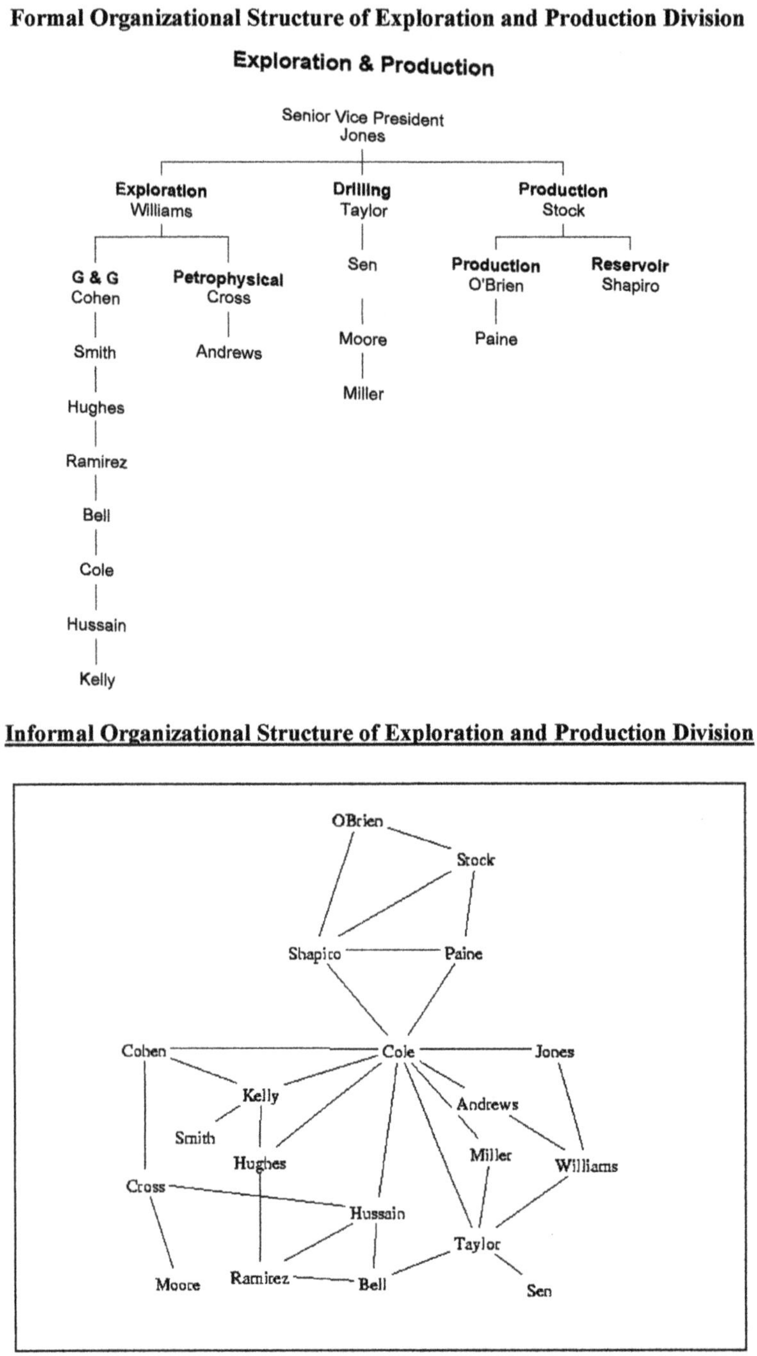

Fig. 5.4 Structures in a firm. Source: Cross et al. (2001), reproduced with kind permission of Elsevier B.V

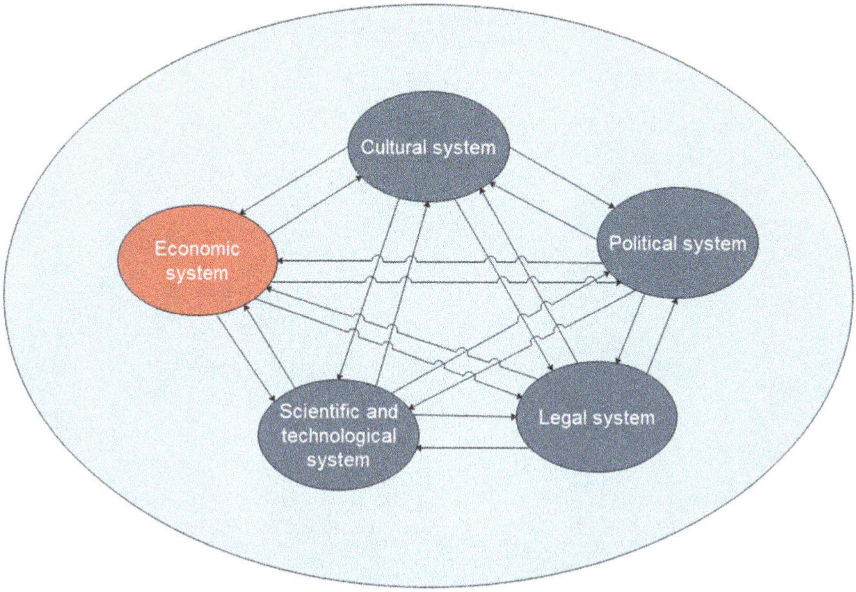

Fig. 5.5 The economy as a part of a societal system of systems. Source: Author

shows that the actual communication pattern is quite different from the formal reporting structure, e.g. Stock and Taylor do not communicate directly with their superior Jones. By far the most important communicator is Cole, who is the only link between the members of the production department (Stock, Shapiro, O'Brian, and Paine) and the rest of the group. We can also see that three people are rather isolated with only one communication contact each: Smith, Moore, and Sen. Although reporting to Taylor, Moore communicates primarily with Cross, who reports to Williams, but not to Taylor. The communication network is critical to the exchange of information and knowledge. If the communication network is dysfunctional, members of the organization cannot work together effectively, resulting in an inefficient use of the organization's human resources.

So far we have considered how to define the components of an economic system, i.e. we have looked at the system. We can also see the economic system as a component of a larger social system of systems, as shown in Fig. 5.5. In this systemic view, the economic system interacts with the cultural system, the political system, the scientific and technological system, and the legal system. In Chap. 2, we defined systems as unified wholes that lose their identity when some components are removed. According to this idea, society cannot function without the economy, but it also needs all the other social subsystems. We also learned that systems have a function or purpose. We could define the function of the economic system as producing goods and activities that are valued by society. The economy cannot do this alone, but needs inputs from the other social subsystems. For example, what is valuable to society is determined by the cultural system. Production requires human

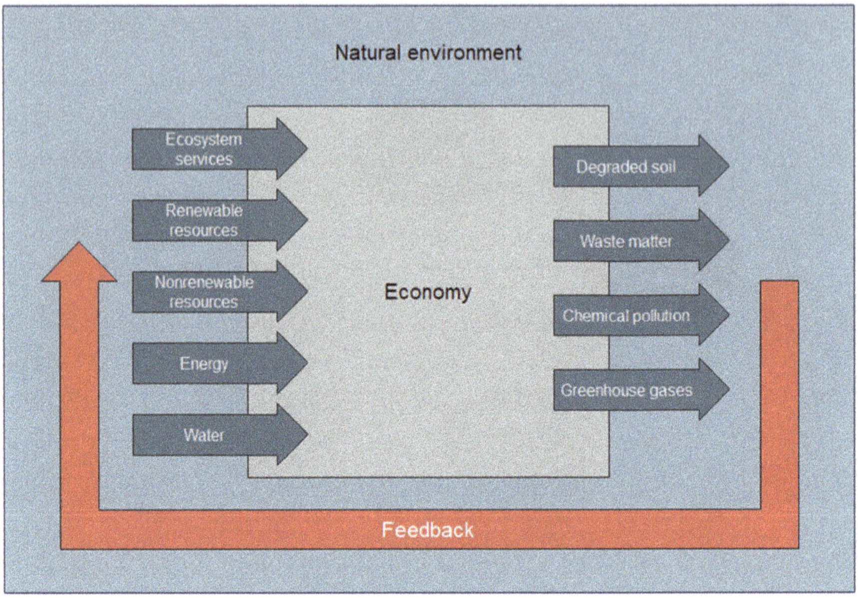

Fig. 5.6 The economic system embedded in the natural environment. Source: Author

capital and technology, which are provided by the scientific and technological system. The political system sets the legal rules by which the economy operates, and the legal system ensures that these rules are applied. At the same time, the output of the economic system is a necessary input for the other systems, since they all require the production and distribution of goods and services. The systems not only have specific functions, but also operate according to their own internal logics. We could argue that the economic system is characterized by the logic of supply and demand in markets, but this can cause problems. First, as discussed above, not all economic activities take place in markets. Second, markets could also be part of other systems, such as the scientific and technological system. An alternative description of the logic of the economic system could be that it is based on voluntary exchange between agents, but one could argue that many people are in principle free not to work, but are in fact forced to offer labor because they would starve otherwise. The possible degree of voluntariness of exchange can be depends on the social system, the solidarity of other people, or the laws established in the other systems, which shows that the economic system cannot be considered independent of the other systems.

Figure 5.6 depicts the economy as an open system embedded in the natural environment, which is another systemic view. All value-creating economic activity depends in some way on inputs from the natural environment. Even pure human services require at least that the human provider be fed, have access to drinking water, and breathe clean air, all of which are provided, even indirectly, by the natural environment. Economic activity in general affects the state of the natural environment through the generation of waste and various forms of pollution. In addition, the extraction of natural resources inevitably degrades natural ecosystems to some extent and can lead to their collapse if the impact is too great. The negative impact of economic activities on the environment leads to feedbacks, such as the depletion of resources or the degradation of the quantity and quality of ecosystem services or water.

The main message of this section is that you should take a system-of-systems view of the economy. The economy is part of larger systems and interacts with other social and natural systems. Treating the economy in isolation neglects important forces that influence economic activities. It may not always be necessary to consider a large number of non-economic systems when we study economic issues, but we should always make a conscious decision whether or not to ignore them. In some cases, it may not be easy to separate the economic system from other social systems, so it may be appropriate to define a techno-economic system, a socio-economic system, or a politico-economic system, considering two of the separate systems in Fig. 5.5 as a unified whole.

The components of economic systems are themselves systems. Similar to the question of whether the economy and the other components of social systems should be separate systems or together form components (such as the techno-economic system), there is no clear way to define the components of the economic system. We can think of the economic system as consisting of sectors, markets, industries, or even individual firms and households. Markets can be seen as systems of interconnected firms and households. Firms and households are systems of individual people. While households are rather small systems, multinational corporations with hundreds of thousands of employees are highly complex systems. To reiterate, the definition of a social system is a choice made by the observer who has a reason to look at the system. The observer's convenience and purpose guide what it should look like.

5.3 Economic Complexity

In Chap. 3, we discussed how to measure the level of complexity of a system. Structural complexity refers to the number and types of elements and the relationships between them. The measures of structural complexity presented were purely descriptive, without any theoretical sophistication. Cyclomatic complexity quantifies the complexity of a system's causal structure by counting the number of independent loops in a strongly connected graph. Organizational complexity is the sum of the diversity, flexibility, and combinability of a system's elements, all measured by versions of Shannon entropy. The idea of organizational complexity is that systems with more diverse, flexible, and combinable elements can produce more uncertain outcomes and are therefore more complex than systems with lower degrees of these properties. These measures are not specific to economic systems, but can be applied to many types of systems.

César Hidalgo and Ricardo Hausmann (2009) propose a method for measuring complexity in economic systems based on economic reasoning. Their concept of *economic complexity* includes the division of labor and specialization, which increase the knowledge in a system, making the system more productive. However, specialization also leads to a dispersion of knowledge, which increases the complexity of the system. The *Economic Complexity Index* (ECI) and *the Product Complexity Index* (PCI) are useful empirical tools for describing patterns in economic systems. In particular, they capture spatial patterns, emphasizing the relevance of the geographic dimension of economic systems. The ECI is particularly interesting because it predicts future economic growth of regions and countries. However, these tools are mainly methods to reduce dimensionality in economic datasets, which are able to detect interesting patterns, but economic complexity is not an elaborated theory that explains the formation of such patterns.

5.3.1 Combination of Specialized Knowledge

One of the key insights of economics, already pointed out by Adam Smith, is that the division of labor greatly increases economic productivity. When a task is divided into subtasks and distributed to multiple agents, each agent can perform the subtask more efficiently than the entire task. Experience, learning, and specialized knowledge are the reasons for higher efficiency. Division of labor is an important cause of increasing returns to scale, i.e. a more than proportional increase in output in response to an increase in inputs. The benefits of division of labor depend on the size of the group of agents working together. In a large group, each agent can acquire highly specialized knowledge and use the specialized knowledge of many others. The productivity-enhancing possibility of specialization is the reason why economists generally favor large markets and international trade.

It is not enough, though, that there are many agents in an economic system for specialization to occur. Within an organization or an economy, there must be appropriate institutions that enable the combination of scattered knowledge and somehow distribute the joint benefits. We can distinguish between *explicit knowledge*, which can be easily acquired by reading a text, for example, and *tacit knowledge*, which is difficult to express or extract and therefore cannot be easily transferred. Acquiring tacit knowledge is a long and costly process that forces capacity-constrained people and organizations to specialize. Most people cannot become a world-leading astrophysicist and a master surgeon in the same lifetime. People need a good education system to acquire specialized knowledge, but they also need confidence that their specialized knowledge will be needed by someone, and that they can rely on others to complement their skills. Highly specialized skills in chemical engineering are not directly useful in meeting a person's needs for food, shelter, and health. A chemical engineer therefore needs food production specialists, construction specialists, and medical specialists. The more specialized a person is, the more he or she must interact with others to benefit from that specialization. Specialization thus correlates with interaction and thus with complexity. This idea is similar to the argument that organizational complexity depends on diversity and combinability, although there the notion of complexity was linked to uncertainty.

The idea behind economic complexity is that the degree of division of knowledge, and thus interactivity, is manifested in the products that are produced in a given place. Modern cars or medical devices are complex products that require an enormous amount of specialized knowledge that can only be generated in large networks of people. Even seemingly simple products such as a toaster embody a great deal of specialized knowledge and skills that no one person possesses.[2] Measuring the complexity of products and the production pattern of a site is therefore an indirect approach to infer the underlying structures that allow specialized knowledge to be generated and combined. Since tacit knowledge is not easily shared, it is tied to geographic space and social networks, so geographic patterns of production are informative about economic knowledge structures.

The geographical concentration of knowledge is demonstrated by Chinazzi et al. (2019), who use a natural language processing method from the machine learning literature to identify the similarity of topics in publications in physics journals. Their approach allows them to construct the research space network in Fig. 5.7, which shows the connections between similar research topics and ten topical categories of the Physics and Astronomy Classification Scheme (PACS), marked by different colors. The map shows, for example, that nuclear physics is strongly connected to the physics of elementary particles and fields, but not to the physics of gases, plasmas, and electrical discharges. The main point is that there is a geographical specialization in physics research. Figure 5.8 shows the four cities where the authors of the research publications are located and shows that each of these cities has a specific expertise in certain topics. While Brussels is strong in nuclear physics, Grenoble is specialized in the category "Condensed matter".

From a complexity perspective, the generation, combination, and productive use of specialized knowledge are key economic problems. The primary function of firms and markets is to manage knowledge and transform it into valuable goods and services. The focus of complexity economics on knowledge is another important difference from neoclassical economics, which conceptualizes firms as organizations that combine physical factors of production such as labor and capital in a cost-minimizing way. The typical neoclassical way of representing a firm is the production function $Y = F(K, AL)$ (see 4.13) together with the assumption of the maximization of the profit function $\Pi = PY - WL - rK$. The aggregation of workers with different knowledge and skills, as well as the aggregation of extremely diverse capital goods such as furniture, computers, and highly specialized laboratory equipment, which embody vast amounts of knowledge, into a single capital stock K, trivializes the problem of knowledge management. If knowledge is location-, network-, and context-specific, the production of goods is not just a matter of

[2]This is nicely demonstrated in Thomas Thwaites's *Toaster Project*, see https://www.thomasthwaites.com/the-toaster-project/ (Accessed 26. October 2023), or the famous essay "I, Pencil" by Leonard E. Read.

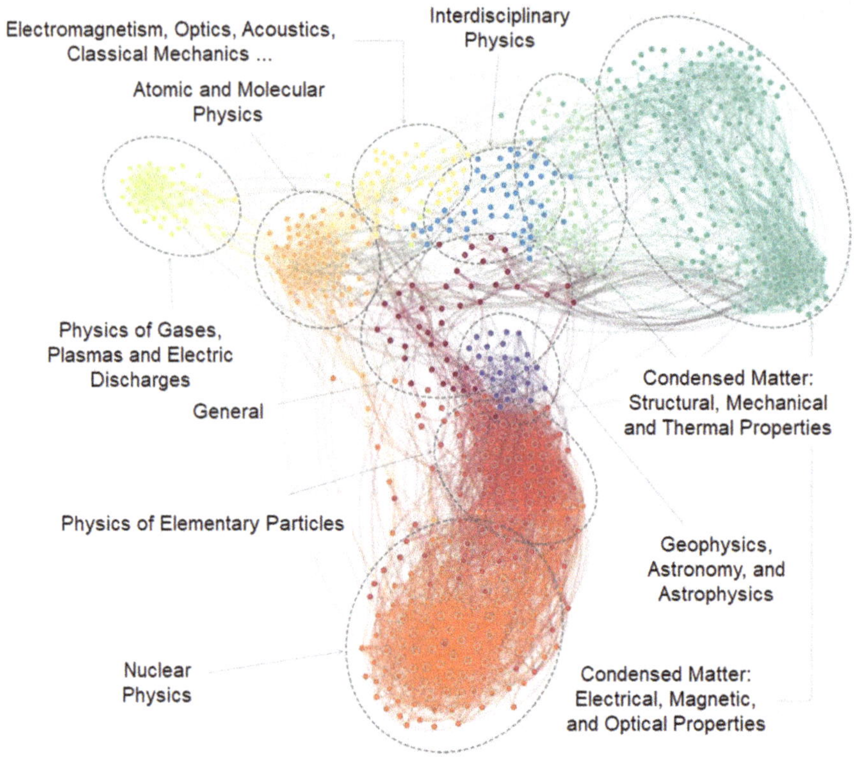

Fig. 5.7 Research space network in physics. Source: Adapted from Chinazzi et al. (2019), licensed under CC-BY 4.0 (https://creativecommons.org/licenses/by/4.0/)

combining quantities of labor and capital in the most cost-effective way. It is a fundamental task of firms to combine the right kind of knowledge in a way that creates value.

5.3.2 Measurement of Economic Complexity

The method of reflections is a way of deriving a quantitative measure of the idea that the ability of a location to use knowledge productively is reflected in its products. Economic complexity is a property of a country in a so-called *bipartite network* connecting two kinds of nodes, in our case countries and products, as shown in Fig. 5.9.

We can define *diversity* $k_{c,\,0}$ as the number of products produced by a country and *ubiquity* $k_{p,\,0}$ as the number of countries that make a product. In the example, the diversity of the Netherlands is 5, because this country produces five products. Argentina has a diversity of 3 and that of Ghana is 1. Frozen fish is the most ubiquitous product, because three countries produce it. X-ray machines and

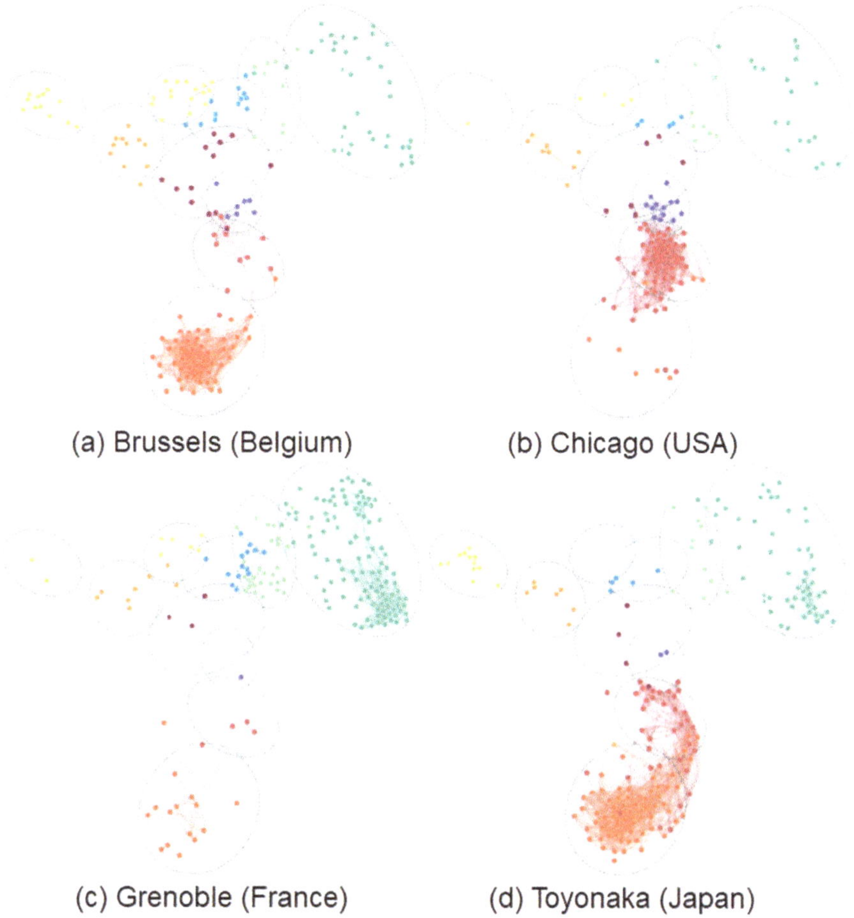

Fig. 5.8 Specialization in the physics research space in four different cities. Source: Chinazzi et al. (2019), licensed under CC-BY 4.0 (https://creativecommons.org/licenses/by/4.0/)

pharmaceuticals are produced only in the Netherlands and therefore have a ubiquity of 1. High diversity is advantageous for a country, because it allows it to be active in many markets. Being able to produce for many markets requires a wide range of capabilities in the country. In contrast, high ubiquity means that a product does not require specialized capabilities and can be produced in many countries. Highly ubiquitous products are of low value to a country, because there is a lot of international competition in these markets. Table 5.2 shows the adjacency matrix M that belongs to the network in Fig. 5.9. The entries M_{cp} of this country-product matrix are 1, if a country is a significant producer of a product and 0 if it is not. The diversity of a country is the respective sum of the rows of all products

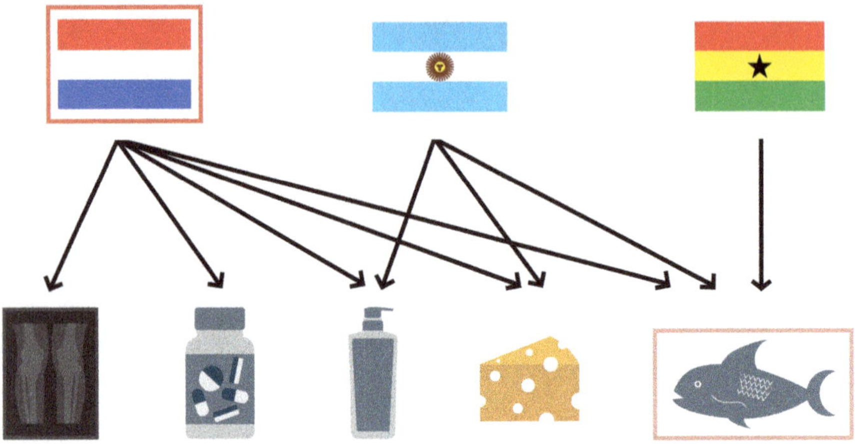

Fig. 5.9 Example of a country-product network. Source: Author's own figure after Hausmann et al. (2011)

Table 5.2 Adjacency matrix of the country-product network

	p1 X-ray machines	p2 Medicaments	p3 Creams & polishes	p4 Cheese	p5 Frozen fish	Diversity $k_{c,\,0} = \sum_p M_{cp}$
c1 Netherlands	1	1	1	1	1	5
c2 Argentina	0	0	1	1	1	3
c3 Ghana	0	0	0	0	1	1
Ubiquity $k_{p,\,0} = \sum_c M_{cp}$	1	1	2	2	3	

$$k_{c,0} = \sum\nolimits_p M_{cp} \tag{5.1}$$

and the ubiquity of a product is the respective column sum over all countries

$$k_{p,0} = \sum\nolimits_c M_{cp}. \tag{5.2}$$

The *method of reflections* calculates the properties of the country-product network in iterations N, $N + 1$, $N + 2$, ... for $N \geq 1$ starting from diversity $k_{c,\,0}$ and ubiquity $k_{p,\,0}$. This is done by the following recursions:

$$k_{c,N} = \frac{1}{k_{c,0}} \sum\nolimits_p M_{cp} \times k_{p,N-1} \tag{5.3}$$

$$k_{p,N} = \frac{1}{k_{p,0}} \sum_c M_{cp} \times k_{c,N-1}. \tag{5.4}$$

These recursions correct the production capabilities of a country by taking into account the characteristics of the products and correct the information about the products by taking into account the production structure of the countries. For the level $N = 1$, the country variable $k_{c,\,1}$ measures the average ubiquity of the products of this country, which tells us how common the products of this country are. In our example, we get

$$k_{c_1,1} = \frac{1}{5}(1 + 1 + 2 + 2 + 3) = \frac{9}{5} = 1.8$$

$$k_{c_2,1} = \frac{1}{3}(2 + 2 + 3) = \frac{7}{3} = 2.33$$

$$k_{c_3,1} = \frac{1}{1}(3) = 3$$

This means that the average ubiquity of the Dutch products is lowest (1.8), while the Argentinean products have an intermediate average ubiquity of 2.33. Ghana produces only Fish, which is a product with high ubiquity, since it is produced in all countries, such that $k_{c_3,1} = 3$.

Similarly, the product variable $k_{p,\,1}$ is the average diversification of the countries producing each product. In other words, we learn how diversified the countries producing that good are. The values of the five example products are:

$$k_{p_1,1} = \frac{1}{1}5 = 5$$

$$k_{p_2,1} = \frac{1}{1}5 = 5$$

$$k_{p_3,1} = \frac{1}{2}(5 + 3) = 4$$

$$k_{p_4,1} = \frac{1}{2}(5 + 3) = 4$$

$$k_{p_5,1} = \frac{1}{3}(5 + 3 + 1) = 3$$

X-ray machines and pharmaceuticals are only produced in the Netherlands, which is the most diversified country, hence $k_{p_1,1} = 5$. All countries produce fish resulting in an average diversification of the fish-producing countries of $k_{p_5,1} = 3$.

The first two steps of the method or recursions already provide interesting insights about locations. We can categorize countries or other locations of production using a graph with diversity $k_{c,\,0}$ on the horizontal axis and the average ubiquity of the countries' products $k_{c,\,1}$ on the vertical axis as in Fig. 5.10. Classifying the two

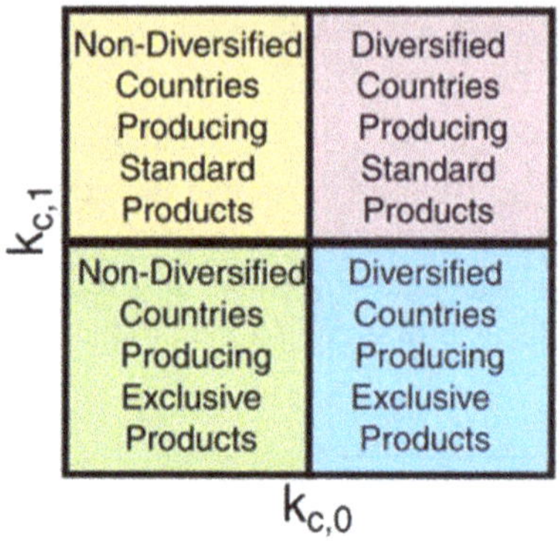

Fig. 5.10 Diversity vs. average ubiquity of countries' products. Source: Hidalgo and Hausmann (2009), reproduced with kind permission of PNAS. PNAS is not responsible for the accuracy of any translations

variables as low and high results in four quadrants: (1) non-diversified countries producing exclusive products ($k_{c,\ 0}$ low, $k_{c,\ 1}$ low), (2) non-diversified countries producing standard products ($k_{c,\ 0}$ low, $k_{c,\ 1}$ high), (3) diversified countries producing exclusive products ($k_{c,\ 0}$ high, $k_{c,\ 1}$ low), and (4) diversified countries producing standard products ($k_{c,\ 0}$ high, $k_{c,\ 1}$ high). Note that standard products are ubiquitous and exclusive products are produced in only a few countries. In our example, the Netherlands is in quadrant (3), Argentina is somewhere near the middle, and Ghana is in quadrant (2). The first recursion already suggests that there seems to be a negative relationship between a country's diversification and the ubiquity of its products. According to the reasoning in the previous subsection, the negative relationship is a consequence of countries' ability to use knowledge. Countries in quadrant (2) have accumulated little knowledge and cannot use it to produce sophisticated exclusive products. They rely on a few standard products that are also made in many other countries. Countries in quadrant (3), on the other hand, have a lot of specialized knowledge allowing them to produce both many different and exclusive goods. Their production structure and thus their underlying knowledge management capabilities are more complex than those of the countries in the other quadrants and especially of those on quadrant (2).

The higher reflections refine the picture. $k_{c,\ 2}$, which requires the average diversification $k_{p,\ 1}$ as a input, measures the average diversification of countries with a similar production portfolio to the country in question. For the Netherlands in our example, this would be $k_{c_1,2} = \frac{1}{k_{c_1,0}}\left(k_{p_1,1} + k_{p_2,1} + k_{p_3,1} + k_{p_4,1} + k_{p_4,1}\right) = \frac{1}{5}(5+5+4+4+3) = 4.2$, and for Ghana, we get, $k_{c_3,2} = \frac{1}{1}3 = 3$. While $k_{c,\ 0}$ is something like the "raw diversification" of a country, $k_{c,\ 2}$ is corrected for the degree of diversification of countries with similar production. Not surprisingly, the degree of raw diversification of the most diversified country c_1 is corrected downward, while the opposite is true for the country with the lowest initial diversification. The second reflection for the products,

Table 5.3 Country-country matrix $M_{cp}M_{c'p}$

	c1'	c2'	c3'
c1	5	3	1
c2	3	3	1
c3	1	1	1

$k_{p,\,2}$, informs us about the average ubiquity of the products made in countries that produce the good in question. The higher levels of reflection with $N \geq 3$ become increasingly more difficult to interpret, but they extract more and more information about the production structure of a country and the sophistication of a product. Note that odd and even iterations have different interpretations. For countries, the even iterations are measures of diversity and the odd iterations measure ubiquity. The reverse is true for the products.

The recursions for the countries converge to a solution of the equation obtained by inserting (5.4) into (5.3). Combining the two equations yields

$$k_{c,N} = \sum_{c'} \tilde{M}_{CC'} k_{c',N-2} \tag{5.5}$$

where

$$\tilde{M}_{cc'} = \sum_{p} \frac{M_{cp} M_{c'p}}{k_{c,0} k_{p,0}}. \tag{5.6}$$

$\tilde{M}_{cc'}$ is a square country-country matrix whose dimension is given by the number of countries. In the original country-product matrix M the countries were represented by the rows c, such that the transpose c' indicates the columns of the country-country matrix. Summing the elements M_{cp} in the country-product matrix and the elements $M_{c'p}$ in the transposed matrix in our three-country examples gives the (unweighted) country-country matrix in Table 5.3.

This matrix tells us how many products the countries c in the rows have in common with the countries c' in the columns. Of course, the diagonal elements show the number of products of each country, e.g. 5 in the country c1 (the Netherlands). The Netherlands and Ghana share one product, $c1c3' = 1$, and Argentina and Ghana also share one product, $c2c3' = 1$. The country-country matrix thus links the countries through their common products. $\tilde{M}_{cc'}$ is a weighted version of the country-county matrix in Table 5.3. We can simplify the notation by writing (5.6) in matrix notation:

$$\tilde{M} = D^{-1} M U^{-1} M', \tag{5.7}$$

where D is the diagonal matrix formed from the vector of country diversity scores and D^{-1} is the inverse of this matrix, M is the country-product matrix, U^{-1} is the inverse of the diagonal matrix constraining the ubiquity scores, and M' is the transpose of M, i.e. the product-country matrix. $\tilde{M}$ is a row-stochastic matrix, which means that its rows sum to one. Thus, it can be interpreted as a Markov transition matrix containing conditional transition probabilities between states. The long-run behavior of the dynamics implied by this matrix is given by its eigenvalues. The first eigenvector is a vector of ones, implying that the system converges to the same asymptotic value, which is uninformative. The *Economic Complexity Index* ECI is therefore defined as the eigenvector E_c associated with the second largest eigenvalue of $\tilde{M}$ normalized by its mean and standard deviation

$$ECI = \frac{E_c - mean(E_c)}{std(E_c)}. \tag{5.8}$$

This index partitions the data in a way that similar countries are placed close together on one dimension and dissimilar countries are placed far apart. In exactly the same way, we can define the *Product Complexity Index* PCI as

$$PCI = \frac{E_p - mean(E_p)}{std(E_p)}, \tag{5.9}$$

where E_p is the eigenvector associated with the second largest eigenvalue of the weighted product-product matrix $\tilde{M}_{pp'}$.

In the three-country-five-products example, we can calculate the ECI as follows. According to (5.7), we start at $\tilde{M} = D^{-1}MU^{-1}M'$:

$$\tilde{M} = \begin{pmatrix} 1/5 & 0 & 0 \\ 0 & 1/3 & 0 \\ 0 & 0 & 1 \end{pmatrix} \begin{pmatrix} 1 & 1 & 1 & 1 & 1 \\ 0 & 0 & 1 & 1 & 1 \\ 0 & 0 & 0 & 0 & 1 \end{pmatrix} \begin{pmatrix} 1 & 0 & 0 & 0 & 0 \\ 0 & 1 & 0 & 0 & 0 \\ 0 & 0 & 1/2 & 0 & 0 \\ 0 & 0 & 0 & 1/2 & 0 \\ 0 & 0 & 0 & 0 & 1/3 \end{pmatrix} \begin{pmatrix} 1 & 0 & 0 \\ 1 & 0 & 0 \\ 1 & 1 & 0 \\ 1 & 1 & 0 \\ 1 & 1 & 1 \end{pmatrix}$$

$$\tilde{M} = \begin{pmatrix} 10/15 & 4/15 & 1/15 \\ 4/9 & 4/9 & 1/9 \\ 1/3 & 1/3 & 1/3 \end{pmatrix}$$

The second largest eigenvalue of $\tilde{M}$ is $\lambda_2 = \frac{\sqrt{10}+10}{45}$ and the associated eigenvector is $E_c' = \begin{pmatrix} \frac{\sqrt{10}}{10} & \frac{2-\sqrt{10}}{6} & -1 \end{pmatrix}$. Normalizing this eigenvector results in $ECI' = \begin{pmatrix} 0.915 & 0.153 & -1.068 \end{pmatrix}$. As expected, the Netherlands have the highest value of of the ECI, Ghana the lowest, and Argentina is in the middle.

The ECI and the PCI have no intuitive interpretation. While the first steps in the method of recursions are easy to grasp, computing the eigenvector associated with the second largest eigenvalue of the weighted country-country or product-product matrix is an abstract way of transforming the data. A good way to think about the ECI (and, by analogy, the PCI) is to understand it as a tool for ordering locations (or products) in a way that maximizes the correlations between countries and products in the country-product matrix M_{cp}. This interpretation supports the impression from the example that countries with a high diversity also produce exclusive goods. We will see in the next subsection that this is indeed the case.

5.3.3 Empirical Results

The method for measuring economic complexity can be applied to a variety of data. While we have discussed the production of countries in the example, this is not the only way to operationalize economic complexity. It is possible to apply the method to geographic units at different scales, such as countries, regions, or even municipalities. Economic complexity can be reflected in the goods produced, but also in the exports of a location or its labor force. Export data are well suited for international comparisons because of their standardized product classifications. In the following sections, we focus on the export data of countries.

It is useful to look first at Fig. 5.11, which corresponds to Fig. 5.10 and plots the diversity of countries, $k_{c,\,0}$, against the average ubiquity of their exported products, $k_{c,\,1}$. This graph confirms the hypothesis of the example that highly diversified countries export goods of low ubiquity, while the exports of less diversified countries are very ubiquitous. The rich industrialized countries such as Germany, the United States, and Italy are the most diversified. The poor countries of the Global South cluster in the upper left quadrant. Note that this pattern contradicts the idea of specialization in the neoclassical theory of international trade. According to the theory of comparative advantage, no country should be diversified. Instead, all countries should have exclusive products and thus should be in the green quadrant (1), which is in fact almost empty.

As argued earlier, the ECI and PCI sort similar countries. Figure 5.12 shows the correlation pattern in the country-product matrix, where countries and exported products are sorted according to the ECI and PCI, respectively. The white areas indicate high correlations. We can see that countries with a high ECI tend to export many goods, but especially those with a high PCI. Countries with a low ECI

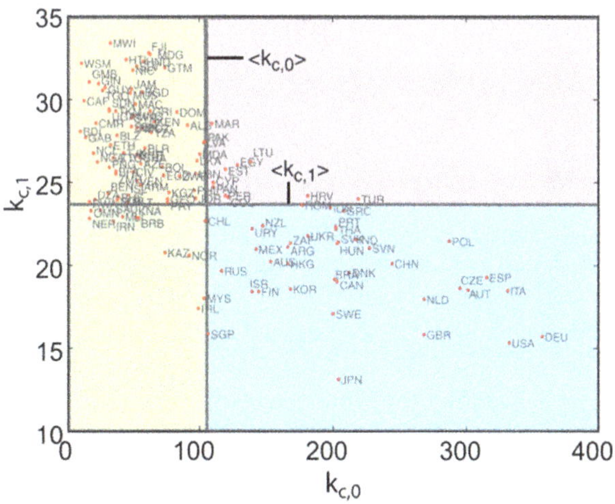

Fig. 5.11 Diversity vs. average ubiquity. Source: Hidalgo and Hausmann (2009), reproduced with kind permission of PNAS. PNAS is not responsible for the accuracy of any translations

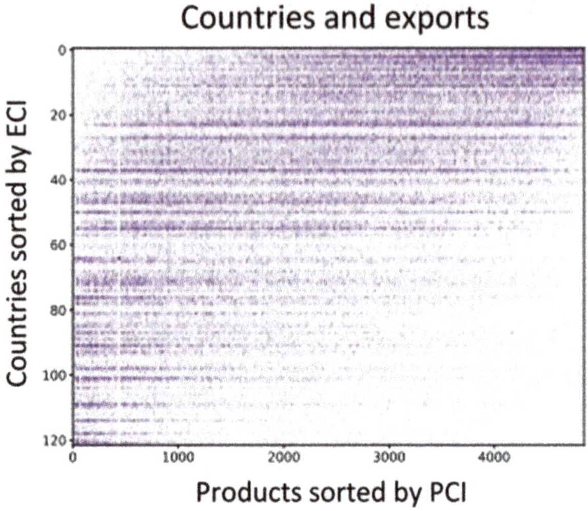

Fig. 5.12 Correlations in country-product matrix. Source: Mealy et al. (2019), licensed under CC-BY 4.0 (https://creativecommons.org/licenses/by/4.0/)

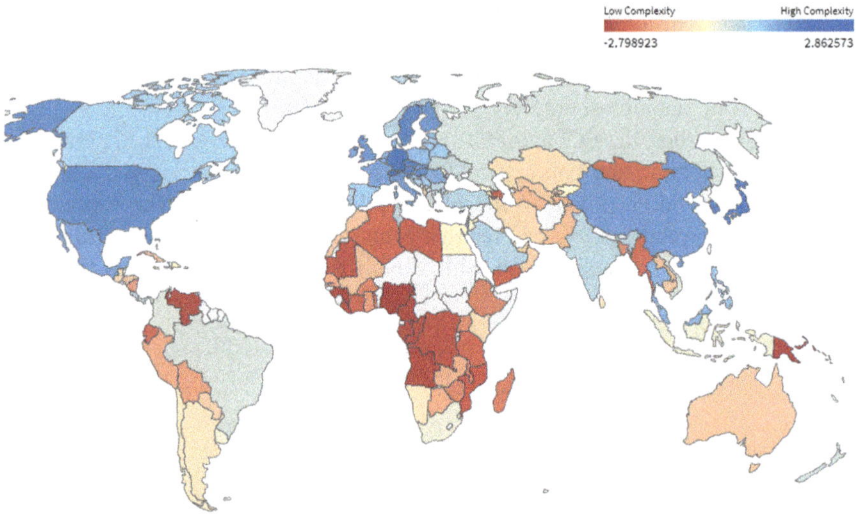

Fig. 5.13 Map of countries according to their ECI in 2019. Source: The Growth Lab at Harvard University (2023). The Atlas of Economic Complexity. http://www.atlas.cid.harvard.edu

specialize in goods with a low PCI, as indicated by the white cloud in the upper left corner.

The map in Fig. 5.13 shows the economic complexity of countries. In 2019, the countries with the highest ECI were Japan (2.49), Switzerland (2.13), Germany (2.07), South Korea (2.05), and Singapore (2.00). Among the 133 countries considered, Nigeria had the lowest ECI (−1.77), followed by Guinea (−1.75), Liberia (−1.70), Papua New Guinea (−1.57), and Cameroon (−1.53). The most and least complex products by PCI are shown in Table 5.4. Chemical products are the most

Table 5.4 Complexity of products

	Product	PCI in 2019
Top 5	Photographic plates and film, exposed and developed, other than motion-picture film	2.75
	Inorganic compounds, liquid/compressed air, amalgams ne	2.41
	Chemical preparations for photographic uses (other than varnishes, glues, adhesives, and similar preparations); unmixed products for photographic uses, put up in measured portions or put up for retail sale in a form ready for use	2.32
	Esters of other inorganic acids of nonmetals (excluding esters of hydrogen halides) and their salts; their halogenated, sulfonated, nitrated, or nitrosated derivatives	2.29
	Of other cermets	2.28
Bottom 5	Peanuts (ground-nuts), not roasted or otherwise cooked, whether or not shelled or broken	−2.53
	Cocoa shells, husks, skins, and other cocoa waste	−2.53
	Niobium (columbium), tantalum, vanadium, or zirconium ores and concentrates	−2.56
	Petroleum oils and oils obtained from bituminous minerals, crude	−2.67
	Tin ores and concentrates	−2.93

Source: The Growth Lab at Harvard University (2023). The Atlas of Economic Complexity. http://www.atlas.cid.harvard.edu

complex, and commodities such as tin ores, petroleum, or peanuts are the least complex.

Figures 5.14 and 5.15 show the export basked in 2019 for the most and least economically complex countries, Japan and Nigeria. Japan has a highly diversified export basked, with ICT as the largest product group, accounting for no more than 12.58% of total export value. In stark contrast, Nigeria relies heavily on crude oil exports, which account for 70.79% of the country's total export value. Japan is also an exporter of cars, machinery, electronics, and chemicals, all of which are highly complex products.

Nigeria's second most important export is petroleum gases. While Nigeria does export some services and goods from the transportation sector, another important sector is agriculture, which also has low product complexity. In this context, the ECI and PCI of the main goods are also a measure of a country's development. Countries with high complexity produce many high-complexity goods, while countries with low economic complexity export few low-complexity goods. The automobile is in the top 10% of the most complex products. Car-exporting countries are mostly rich countries with a high Economic Complexity Index. In 2019, Germany (ECI 2.07, rank 3) was the world's leading car exporter with a share of 19.34% of total exports, followed by Japan (ECI 2.49, rank 1, export share 13.32%) and the USA (ECI 1.57, rank 11, export share 7.35%). Therefore, automobile manufacturing requires a significant amount of technologically advanced knowledge and deep integration of related industries such as steel, machinery, rubber, glass, electronics, etc. To produce

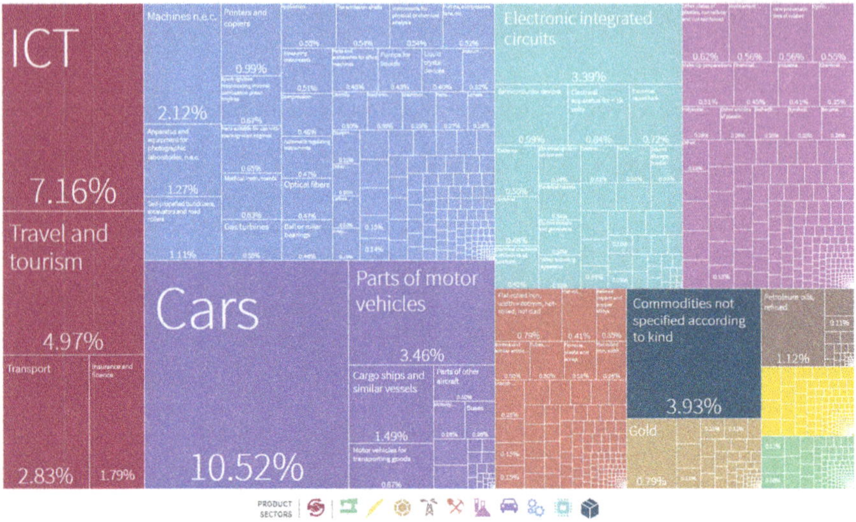

Fig. 5.14 Exports of Japan in 2019. Source: The Growth Lab at Harvard University (2023). The Atlas of Economic Complexity. http://www.atlas.cid.harvard.edu

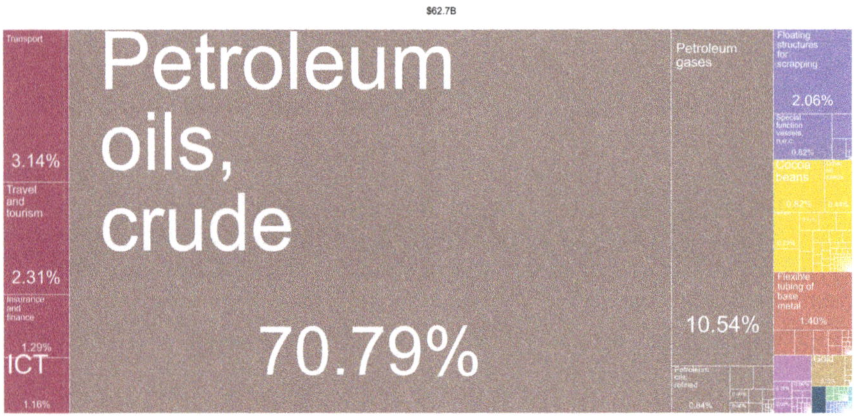

Fig. 5.15 Exports of Nigeria in 2019. Source: The Growth Lab at Harvard University (2023). The Atlas of Economic Complexity. http://www.atlas.cid.harvard.edu

competitive cars, a country needs a strong R&D sector and an education system with high quality education in STEM fields.

Given the ECI ranking of countries, it is not surprising that the ECI is positively correlated with GDP per capita. For countries where natural resource exports account for less than 10% of GDP, the ECI explains 75% of the variance in GDP per capita. More interestingly, the ECI is a predictor of both future income and future economic growth. The relationship with future GDP growth is shown in Table 5.5. The table compares two growth regressions. In column (1), the annualized growth

Table 5.5 Economic complexity and future economic growth

	Annualized growth in GDP pc (by decade) (1978–1988, 1988–1998, 1998–2008)	
Variables	(1)	(2)
Initial Income per capita, log	−0.00017	−0.00638***
	(0.001)	(0.001)
Increase in natural resource exports	0.03980***	0.03682***
• in constant dollars (as a share of initial GDP)	(0.008)	(0.010)
Initial Economic Complexity Index (ECI)		0.04430***
		(0.009)
[ECI] X [Income per capita, log]		−0.00371***
		(0.001)
Constant	0.03036***	0.08251***
	(0.008)	(0.011)
Observations	291	291
R^2	0.285	0.434
Year FE	Yes	Yes

Source: Hausmann et al. (2011)
*** indicates $p < 0.01$

rate of GDP per capita over the three decades between 1978 and 2008 is regressed on the level of GDP per capita at the beginning of each decade and the increase in natural resource exports. This simple regression explains 28.5% of the variance in countries' growth rates, mainly due to natural resource export revenues. Column (2) adds the ECI at the beginning of each of the three decades and an interaction term with income per capita. The R^2 of this model is much higher than that of the first model, with 43.4% of the variance explained. Both the coefficient on the ECI and the interaction term with income are significantly different from zero. Higher economic complexity is associated with higher future growth.

However, this effect diminishes with income, as indicated by the negative coefficient of the interaction term. The positive effect of economic complexity on future growth is robust to the inclusion of control variables that measure the quality of a country's institutions, such as the level of corruption, political stability, or regulatory quality, as well as education variables, such as years of schooling. These simple regressions do not prove causal effects of complexity on growth, but they do support the intuition presented in the previous subsection that the accumulation of knowledge reflected in the structure of production is an important determinant of productivity and economic development.

Interesting support for the claim that tacit knowledge is not easily transferable and therefore geographically concentrated comes from Balland et al. (2020), who analyze the relationship between the complexity of activities and their geographic concentration in the USA. They show that there is a strong positive correlation between the complexity of activities and urban concentration. Highly complex economic activities, such as biotechnology, neurobiology, and semiconductor manufacturing, are disproportionately concentrated in a few large cities. In contrast, less complex activities, such as paper or apparel manufacturing, are less spatially concentrated.

As argued above, the concept of economic complexity is mainly a measurement approach to describe structural properties of economic systems. It suggests mechanisms regarding the causes and consequences of economic complexity, but does not model them. In order to gain a deeper understanding of economic complexity, we need to complement the empirical approach with theoretical modeling.

5.4 The Automobile and Dynamic Complexity

The history of the automobile and the automotive industry in the USA is an excellent case study to demonstrate how the economic system is deeply intertwined with other systems and what is meant by fundamental change (see Heitmann 2018). The following selective narrative account of the history of the automobile in the USA serves to illustrate that conventional economic statistics, such as production figures, sales, or employment, tell only part of the story. In 1924, the USA produced about 3.6 million cars, compared to 8 million in 1950 and 9.2 million in 2021. But these numbers do not tell us anything about the fundamental economic and social changes that have occurred in this century. The production and use of automobiles has had a profound impact on the socio-economic system, but also on the natural Earth system. Today, about 18% of global energy-related greenhouse gas emissions come from road vehicles, i.e. cars, buses, trucks, etc. Thus, cars have been and continue to be a significant driver of climate change.

Given the environmental impact of the automobile, it is interesting to begin the brief historical account from a technological perspective. The invention of the automobile is often dated to the late nineteenth century, e.g. the patent for an automobile granted to the German Karl Benz in 1886. The American George B. Selden had applied for a patent as early as 1879, but the patent was not granted until 1895. These automobiles, and similar ones by other inventors at the same time, were cars with internal combustion engines (ICE) powered by gasoline. However, there had been steam-powered road vehicles with external combustion engines long before that. The Frenchman Nicolas-Joseph Cugnot probably built the world's first automobile—the fardier à vapeur—in 1769, a heavy carriage powered by a steam engine. Other inventors followed, such as the Englishman Richard Trevithick, who built an experimental steam-powered vehicle called the Puffing Devil in 1801. By the mid-1800s, the technology had advanced to the point that France allowed steam vehicles to travel on ordinary roads, while British legislation—the Locomotive Act of 1861—restricted the use of steam automobiles by imposing speed limits and requiring that each vehicle be preceded by a man with a red flag to warn other road users.

In the early twentieth century, steam cars were quite popular in the USA and were more advanced in terms of speed and performance than cars with internal combustion engines. Steam cars were produced until the 1930s, when they began to be supplanted by improved ICE cars, which became much cheaper to produce in the

1920s due to mass production. However, there were experimental attempts to revive steam cars in the 1960s due to the pollution caused by ICE cars. The electric car has a similar history. Early experiments with electric road vehicles date back to the first half of the eighteenth century, particularly in France and the United Kingdom. English inventor Thomas Parker, concerned about the pollution caused by steam engines, built an electric car in 1884. The world's first true electric car was the Flocken Elektrowagen built by German inventor Andreas Flocken in 1888. By the 1910s, electric cars were quite popular in the USA, with a market share of 38% at the turn of the century, second only to steam cars (40%) but ahead of gasoline cars (22%). They were especially popular with affluent women because they were clean, quiet, and required less effort to start than the ICE car, which used a hand crank. The invention of the electric starter for gasoline engines in 1914 eliminated this advantage. In addition, the limited range and inconvenient recharging were disadvantages compared to ICE cars. As a result, electric car technology lay dormant for most of the twentieth century.

Concerns about climate change and technological breakthroughs by Tesla and Japanese and Chinese automakers in the early twenty-first century made electric cars so popular that the future of the automobile may be electric. It is fascinating to imagine how the world might have evolved if technological breakthroughs had made the electric car more competitive than the gasoline car in the 1920s. From a climate change perspective, the world might have lost about 100 years of technological development that is now desperately needed. If the electric car had replaced the gasoline car in the early twentieth century, climate change might be less severe and easier to mitigate today. An important question, therefore, is why the gasoline car was so successful and whether the path it took was inevitable. In retrospect, the actual historical trajectory often seems natural, but from a complexity perspective it is tempting to ask whether and under what circumstances a different trajectory might have been possible.

In the history of the automobile, the American industrialist Henry Ford plays an exceptional role because he introduced low-cost mass production and popularized the gasoline car in the USA. Raised on a farm, he developed an early interest in machines and found employment as a mechanical apprentice in Detroit at the age of 16. Although he had experimented with steam engines as a boy, he found them unsuitable for vehicles, believing them to be too dangerous and too heavy. He was also unconvinced about electric motors. Ford built his first gasoline-powered vehicle, the Ford Quadricycle, in 1896. He continued to improve his models until 1908, when he introduced the famous Model T, a milestone in the history of the automobile. Rather than continuing to improve the car itself, Ford froze the design of the Model T and focused on improving the manufacturing process. The goal was to realize cost advantages that would make it possible to produce a car affordable to the middle and working classes.

At the turn of the century, the automobile was mainly a product for the rich, but Ford dreamed of a car for everyone, for which he saw a huge market. While Ford did not invent the assembly line—it had been in use in the meatpacking industry since the mid-nineteenth century and had been used by the Olds Motor Vehicle Company to mass-produce cars since 1901—he combined it with standardized parts and perfected its use. At Ford's Highland Park plant, the insights of Frederick Taylor's scientific management method were used to increase the efficiency of the assembly process. This was achieved by minimizing wasteful human and machine motion and reducing each human task to its simplest form. Human workers were virtually reduced to elements of the mechanical production process, eliminating the need for creativity or specialized knowledge. The speed of the assembly line was extremely high, requiring concentration and stamina from the workers. Using these methods, Ford was able to increase annual production of the Model T from about 10,000 cars in 1909 to a peak of about 2 million cars in 1923. With a total of 15 million cars sold by the end of production in 1927, the Model T was the best-selling car until 1972, when it was surpassed by the Volkswagen Beetle. The original price of $825 (about $24,900 in 2021) in 1909 fell to $260 (about $4000 in 2021).

Ford made another revolutionary move in 1914 when he doubled the daily wage to $5. This generous wage reduced the unacceptably high turnover rate due to unattractive working conditions on the assembly line. At the same time, Ford envisioned a positive impact on sales of his cars as a result of the increased income of his workers. Today, a manufacturing system of standardized, low-cost goods and high worker wages is called *Fordism*. One wonders if the visionary entrepreneur Henry Ford could have made electric cars so successful if he had found them more attractive than the gasoline car.

General Motors, Ford's great competitor, took a very different approach called *flexible mass production*. General Motors (GM) was founded by William C. Durant, but was heavily influenced by Alfred P. Sloan, who optimized GM's management and created the goal of "a car for every purse and purpose." Unlike Ford, which focused on a single model that was cheap and simple, GM introduced a portfolio of models ranging from low-cost Chevrolet to mid-priced Oldsmobile, Oakland, and Buick to top-of-the-line Cadillac. To keep customers dissatisfied, GM introduced annual model changes with new colors, styles, and even planned obsolescence. To encourage customers to keep buying new models, GM relied heavily on advertising and in 1919 introduced financing plans and its own financing division (GMAC). As a result, by 1929, GM was the second-largest U.S. company with sales of $1504 million, just behind Standard Oil of New Jersey ($1523 million) but well ahead of third-place Ford Motor Company ($1143 million).

The mass production of automobiles since the 1920s has changed American society in many ways. One important aspect is labor. The first cars were built by highly skilled machinists who knew mechanical drawing, physics, and mathematics, could operate machine tools, and could perform assembly operations. Fordism led to a massive deskilling and degradation of labor, resulting in a shift of power from the skilled craftsmen who dominated the shop floor to the capitalists who provided the machinery and reorganized the production process. Aware of the harsh working conditions in his factories, Henry Ford paid high wages and practiced corporate paternalism to improve the living conditions of his African American workers in particular. This paternalism, however, was not evidence of Ford's benevolence, but rather a means of maintaining control. Ford maintained a so-called Service

Department, headed by former boxer and Navy sailor Harry Bennett. The Service Department was an internal security agency composed of football players, boxers, wrestlers, and thugs whose primary mission was to control labor unrest and suppress unionization. Especially in the 1930s, during and after the Great Depression, there were violent clashes with dissatisfied workers who attempted to form unions. These conflicts culminated in the "Battle of the Overpass," in which Harry Bennett's thugs beat two union leaders and which was documented by a newspaper photographer. Photographs of the incident appeared in many national newspapers, influencing public opinion against Ford and ultimately forcing him to sign a contract with the labor union United Auto Workers (UAW).

Another societal change is related to the changing values of American society. Traditionally, Americans valued frugality, practicality, and financial stewardship, which contributed to the success of the down-to-earth Model T. The introduction of car purchases on credit and the stimulation of consumer demand by GM in the 1920s contributed to the development of *consumerism*. The American automobile industry had its golden age in the 1950s, when huge cars with chrome, tailfins, powerful engines, and fancy accessories became popular. Several factors may have contributed to the American passion for opulent automobiles in the 1950s. The car had become part of popular culture in films such as the famous "Rebel Without a Cause" starring James Dean, the road movie genre, rock and roll music, and literature such as Jack Kerouac's "On the Road." Important themes of this car culture are individualism, independence, and autonomy, which contrast with traditional American community values. In addition, the advent of television made it possible to broadcast car commercials. Finally, the U.S. federal government mandated better terms for auto loans, possibly to keep Americans happy during the frightening time of the atomic age and the increasingly harsh conditions of fierce capitalist competition. This is not to say that the automobile and its industry caused this shift in consumer tastes and values, but it certainly interacted with it.

Automobile production in the 1920s may also have had far-reaching economic and political consequences. The automobile boom of the 1920s contributed at least in part to the Great Depression, which began in 1929 and was the most significant economic crisis of the twentieth century. Contemporaries discussed theories of underconsumption and overinvestment as causes of the depression. With the introduction of mass production, productivity rose sharply while wages lagged behind, despite Ford's \$5 a day. High profits went into physical and financial investment, leading to overcapacity and a stock market boom. Underconsumption means that wage earners did not have enough income to buy all the products, leading to cuts in production, layoffs, and reduced investment. While underconsumption theories are controversial in mainstream economic theory, Eichengreen and Mitchener (2004) propose the explanation that a consumer credit boom was a significant factor in the depression, which they link to GM's demonstration that installment credit was a way to sell consumer durables. As a result, by 1927, almost two-thirds of new cars in the United States were purchased on installment credit. Other consumer durables were similarly financed on credit, following the auto industry's example. With the stock market crash in 1929, the credit boom collapsed, leading to a major financial crisis.

The Great Depression severely affected many countries and caused immense economic and emotional damage. It led to the birth of Keynesian macroeconomics, which had a profound impact on both economic theory and economic policy. In the USA, government policy became more interventionist, such as President Franklin D. Roosevelt's New Deal. It is also likely that the Great Depression was a factor in helping Adolf Hitler and the Nazis gain power in Germany, leading to World War II. During the war, the auto industry and other mass-produced industries became the "arsenal of democracy," as President Roosevelt put it. Despite considerable reluctance, the auto industry produced large quantities of tanks, artillery, aircraft parts, ammunition, and military vehicles such as the Jeep for the U.S. government and its allies. War production caused a sharp increase in population in Detroit, home of the Big Three automakers, GM, Ford, and Chrysler. During the war, 400,000 people, including 50,000 blacks, migrated to Detroit, creating both a boom and massive racial conflict.

The migration of African Americans to Detroit continued after the war, and the city's population peaked at more than 1.8 million in the 1950s. In part to avoid the demands of the government-backed UAW, automakers built new factories outside of Detroit. Combined with a white flight movement, in which white residents moved to the suburbs, leaving the black population in the city, Detroit began a long economic decline. The decline of the center of U.S. automobile production was fueled by race riots and the decline of the automobile industry due to increasing international competition from Japanese and European companies and the oil crises of the 1970s. After many years of agony, Chrysler and General Motors filed for bankruptcy in 2009, triggered by the Great Recession that followed the global financial crisis. The city of Detroit, with a population of only 680,000 in 2015, also filed for bankruptcy shortly thereafter. Detroit went from a boom town to a symbol of urban decline, becoming one of the most impoverished and crime-ridden cities in the United States.

Perhaps the most important effect of the automobile has been to change the way of life that is considered normal in modern times. The car made it possible to spatially separate the different spheres of daily life. Car owners could work and shop far from where they lived. Particularly in the United States, this has led to the creation of suburban neighborhoods where people can live but need a car to meet other daily needs (see Fig. 5.16). Of course, the automobile was not the sole cause of the profound changes in living patterns that occurred in the twentieth century, but it was a necessary precondition. Particularly in the United States, the automobile satisfied an existing need for autonomy and mobility. The automobile was a means of connecting cities scattered across the vast country. It also helped to integrate the cities and the countryside. The automobile not only met a need for spatial mobility, but also for social emancipation, especially for African Americans, women, and young people, who gained a measure of independence from racial discrimination, customs, and traditions through the use of automobiles. The automobile met an existing consumer demand, but this demand was leveraged by government and corporate actions of various kinds. The 1928 campaign slogan of future President Herbert Hoover was "A chicken in every pot and a car in every garage," a sign that

Fig. 5.16 Neighborhood in Canton Township, Michigan, USA. Source: Google (2022) Google Earth

by the end of the economically successful 1920s, a car was already part of the image of the good life for the middle class, if not for all classes.

The *Futurama* at the 1939 New York World's Fair, designed by Norman Bel Geddes and sponsored by General Motors, powerfully popularized the idea that the automobile would contribute greatly to societal progress and prosperity. The Futurama was a well-received exhibit and ride that showed how new roads, an automated highway system, and automobiles could improve life 20 years in the future, in 1959–1960. The Futurama promoted the concept of the automobile city, planned and built for the automobile as the dominant mode of transportation (see Fig. 5.17). GM, the sponsor of Futurama, and other corporations were involved in the *General Motors Streetcar Conspiracy*, the alleged goal of which was to dismantle streetcar systems in many U.S. cities and promote the use of automobiles. While it is an open question whether this conspiracy actually played a major role, it is a fact that there was a decline in electric streetcars, leaving many American cities completely dependent on the automobile.

The Futurama exhibit's visions of a national highway system, roads without intersections, villages and suburbs efficiently connected to highways, and cities optimized for automobile traffic were largely realized through public infrastructure investments. Another contributing factor was zoning, a method of urban planning that divides land into zones subject to specific regulations. In the United States, the dominant system is *single-use zoning*, which allows only one type of land use per

Fig. 5.17 An automotive city in the 1939 Futurama diorama. Source: Wikimedia Commons, Garrison (1939), public domain

zone. The commonly defined uses are residential, mixed residential/commercial, commercial, industrial, and space, which includes sports complexes and shopping malls. In his book "Magic Motorways," Futurama designer Bel Geddes expressed many hopes for the realization of his vision:

> *Motoring is one of the most popular recreations there is. It promotes the sense of freedom that comes from greater mobility. It introduces variety, change of scenery, a greater social diffusion, a widening of the horizon. ... An America in which people are free, not in a rhetorical sense, but in the very realistic sense of being freed from congestion, waste and blight – free to move out on good roads to decent abodes of life – free to travel over routes whose very sight and feel give lift to the heart – that is an America whose inner changes may far transcend the alterations on the surface.* Bel Geddes (1940, pp. 293–295)

We now know that modern highways and automobile cities did not reduce congestion or create greater social dispersion, but rather promoted racial and social segregation. But this vision of the 1930s strongly shaped how normal life should be, and created the durable infrastructures that made that life possible. As a result, it is now very difficult to live a different life in the USA, one that does not rely on the private automobile to get to work, retail, recreation, family, or friends. The confluence of people's desire for autonomy, car companies' drive for profit, and government policies to promote prosperity has created a physical, regulatory, and cultural environment in which the car is a virtual necessity. Most people in the USA have no choice but to own a car if they want to live a normal life.

This narrative history suggests that economic developments, such as the introduction of mass production and consumer finance, interacted with social and cultural processes, such as changes in labor relations or racial conflict. It also points to the importance of individual actors, such as Henry Ford, Alfred Sloan, or Norman Bel Geddes, whose vision and entrepreneurship influenced the way we think and act. Historical narratives inspire us to think about how things happened and whether they could have been different. They also remind us of the richness of reality and the multiplicity of events and processes that occur simultaneously. The case study of the automobile serves as an illustration of concepts such as emergence, lock-in, path dependence, (co-)evolution, and other complexity concepts discussed in later chapters.

5.5 A Conceptual Framework for Socio-technical Transitions

A framework that conceptualizes the complex dynamics of socio-technical systems as described in the automotive example is the *multilevel perspective* of Frank Geels (see Geels 2011, 2022). It is widely used to analyze socio-technical transitions that involve deep structural changes. Examples include transitions in transportation, energy, and food systems. The multilevel perspective is designed to take into account changes in technology, policy, markets, consumer practices, infrastructure, cultural meanings, and scientific knowledge. Multiple actors such as corporations, policy makers, consumers, entrepreneurs, and researchers reproduce, maintain, and transform these elements. Together, these actors create complex, long-term processes.

The multilevel perspective (MLP) is an analytical framework that combines concepts from several research fields. From evolutionary economics, it borrows the concepts of trajectories, regimes, niches, speciation, path dependence, and routines. Technology studies add social networks, sense making, and innovation as a social process shaped by broader societal contexts. The notion of rules and institutions providing deep structures for action comes from structuration theory and neo-institutional theory. In line with complexity theory, the MLP views system change as a nonlinear process resulting from the interplay of developments at different levels. The three levels of analysis considered by the MLP and shown in Fig. 5.18 are *niches*, *socio-technical regimes*, and an exogenous *socio-technical landscape*. Niches are the locus of radical innovation, while socio-technical regimes are the locus of established practices and associated rules that stabilize existing systems.

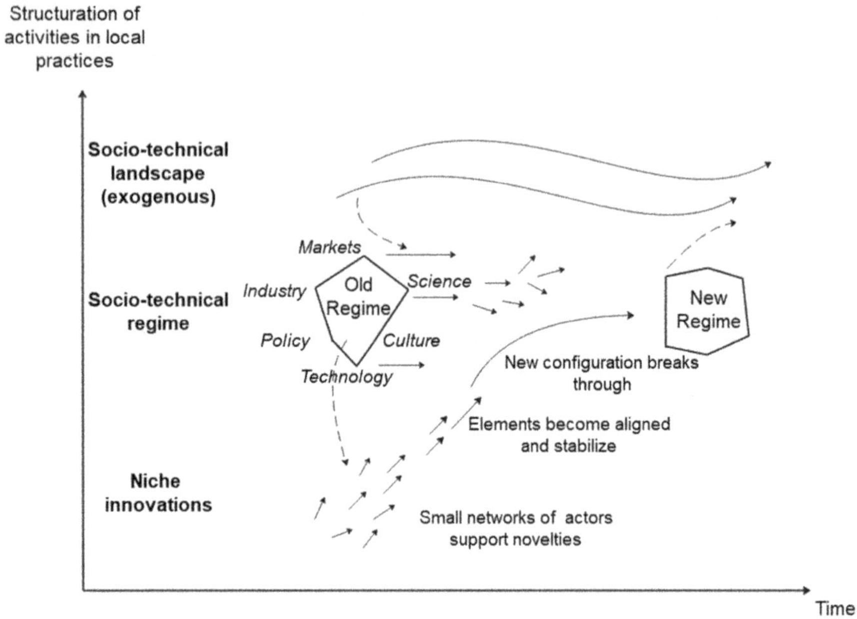

Fig. 5.18 The multilevel perspective framework. Source: Author's own figure after Geels (2011)

The socio-technical regime is a set of rules that coordinate the activities of social groups that reproduce elements of the existing socio-technical system and thereby stabilize it. Examples of regime rules include cognitive routines and shared beliefs, capabilities and competencies, lifestyles and user practices, favorable institutional arrangements and regulations, and legally binding contracts. These rules configure actors, and actors enact, instantiate, and draw upon the rules in concrete actions. The rules create a lock-in that limits the innovations that are possible within the regime. As a result, regimes change only incrementally, with small adjustments along stable trajectories. In contrast, niches are spaces outside the regime where researchers and entrepreneurs work on radical innovations that challenge the existing regime. Systemic change occurs in niches as they grow and generate expectations that are more widely accepted. A window of opportunity, i.e., a favorable historical situation, can enable a niche to overthrow the existing regime and become the new regime. The dynamics of both the regime and the niches are influenced by the socio-technical landscape, which includes demographic trends, political ideologies, and societal values. In the short run, these contextual factors are exogenous to regime and niche actors. In the long run, the landscape level changes slowly, but the MLP does not specify how these changes occur because it is more concerned with the dynamics of regimes and niches.

According to the MLP, socio-technical transitions result from the interaction of processes at the three levels and follow a general pattern. Niche innovations build up internal dynamics, changes at the landscape level create pressure on the regime, and regime destabilization creates windows of opportunity for regime shifts due to radical innovations. In line with complexity theory, the MLP rejects the notion of linear causality from individual drivers to clearly defined effects. Causality is seen as circular or cyclical, with multiple feedbacks in the system, making it impossible to separate causes and effects (see Chap. 7). The MLP has been subject to considerable criticism, but has nevertheless served as a fruitful framework for the study of several historical transitions and also for possible future transitions toward sustainability (see Geels 2019, 2022). Due to various elaborations, it should be interpreted as a cumulative research program rather than a fixed framework or even a model. The following chapters formalize many of the ideas of the multilevel perspective.

5.6 Things to Remember

- There is no single definition of "the" economic system. Instead, there are many ways to represent the economy as a system, either as part of a larger system of systems, or with different definitions of the system elements and their relationships. The systems analyzed by complexity economics are typically more comprehensive than those considered in neoclassical economics.
- The concept of economic complexity is based on the idea that the ability of a country, region, or city to use its knowledge is reflected in its products. More sophisticated products require more complex ways of organizing knowledge. Knowledge tends to be localized because its tacit components are not easily transmitted in writing and in space. The accumulation of tacit knowledge requires direct personal interaction. Complex goods can only be produced by combining different kinds of specialized knowledge.
- The diversity of a country's production portfolio and the ubiquity of a products place of production are basic elements to measure economic complexity. The method of reflections calculates the properties of a country-product network in interactions that specify basic diversity and ubiquity.
- The Economic Complexity Index (ECI) and the Product Complexity Index are measures that rank countries and products in a dimension according to their complexity. The ECI predicts a country's future economic growth. Countries with high ECI scores tend to be rich and diversified and typically produce (and export) products of high complexity.
- The history of the automobile in the USA shows that technology, consumer tastes and values, and government policies interacted in complex ways. Over time, these interactions created a system, in which the automobile became a necessary part of a normal life. The case study of the automobile serves as an illustration of complexity concepts such as emergence, lock-in, path dependence, and (co-) evolution. It also reminds us of the richness of reality and the multiplicity of events and processes that occur simultaneously.
- The multilevel perspective (MLP) is a theoretical framework and a research program for the study of complex socio-technical system transitions. Regimes are a stabilizing force in a socio-technical system, while niches generate

destabilizing radical innovations. The MLP has been applied to many transitions, including shipping, renewable energy, sanitation and clean water, organic food as well as mobility and green cars.

References

Balland P-A, Jara-Figueroa C, Petralia SG et al (2020) Complex economic activities concentrate in large cities. Nat Hum Behav 4:248–254. https://doi.org/10.1038/s41562-019-0803-3

Bel Geddes N (1940) Magic motorways. Random House, New York

Chinazzi M, Gonçalves B, Zhang Q, Vespignani A (2019) Mapping the physics research space: a machine learning approach. EPJ Data Sci 8:1–18. https://doi.org/10.1140/epjds/s13688-019-0210-z

Cross R, Parker A, Prusak L, Borgatti SP (2001) Knowing what we know: supporting knowledge creation and sharing in social networks. Organ Dyn 30:100–120. https://doi.org/10.1016/S0090-2616(01)00046-8

Eichengreen B, Mitchener KJ (2004) The great depression as a credit boom gone wrong. Res Econ Hist 22:183–237

Garrison R (1939) Futurama diorama detail. In: Bel Geddes N (1940) Magic motorways. Random House, New York. https://commons.wikimedia.org/w/index.php?curid=67871017. Accessed 11 Apr 2023

Geels FW (2011) The multi-level perspective on sustainability transitions: Responses to seven criticisms. Environ Innov Soc Trans 1:24–40. https://doi.org/10.1016/j.eist.2011.02.002

Geels FW (2019) Socio-technical transitions to sustainability: a review of criticisms and elaborations of the multi-level perspective. Curr Opin Environ Sustain 39:187–201. https://doi.org/10.1016/j.cosust.2019.06.009

Geels FW (2022) Causality and explanation in socio-technical transitions research: Mobilising epistemological insights from the wider social sciences. Res Policy 51:104537. https://doi.org/10.1016/j.respol.2022.104537

Google (2022) Google Earth. https://earth.google.com/web/search/Canton+Township,+Michigan,+USA/@42.30000516,-83.52189861,212.35100505a,1759.50335069d,35y,0h,0t,0r/data=CokBGl8SWQolMHg4ODNiNTNiZTYxZGQyMjNmOjB4NGNmYzgzMDI2NTc1YTkyMBn5C-KogSdFQCE2OBH92t5UwCoeQ2FudG9uIFRvd25zaGlwLCBNaWNoaWdhbiwgVVNBGAEgASImCiQJxwd4Qz6QNUARxQd4Qz6QNcAZBJX6EeJxQUAhG-SWoooyUcA. Accessed 11 Apr 2023

Hausmann R, Hidalgo C et al (2011) The atlas of economic complexity. Mapping paths to prosperity. Puritan Press, New Hampshire

Heitmann J (2018) The automobile and American life. McFarland & Company, Jefferson

Hidalgo CA, Hausmann R (2009) The building blocks of economic complexity. Proc Natl Acad Sci 106:10570–10575. https://doi.org/10.1073/pnas.0900943106

Mealy P, Farmer JD, Teytelboym A (2019) Interpreting economic complexity. Science. Advances 5:eaau1705. https://doi.org/10.1126/sciadv.aau1705

Munroe DK, Biles JJ (2005) Regional science. Elsevier B.V, Encyclopedia of Social Measurement

The Growth Lab at Harvard University (2023). The Atlas of Economic Complexity. https://atlas.cid.harvard.edu/. Accessed 11 Apr 2023

Nonlinearity

6

Contents

6.1 Introduction 184
6.2 Dynamical Systems 188
    6.2.1 Differential Equations and Difference Equations 188
    6.2.2 Dynamics of One-dimensional Continuous-time Systems 190
    6.2.3 Dynamics of Two-dimensional Continuous-time Systems 194
    6.2.4 Lotka–Volterra Population Models 203
    6.2.5 Bifurcations 208
    6.2.6 Catastrophes 213
    6.2.7 Iterated Maps 215
    6.2.8 Logistic Map and Chaos 217
    6.2.9 Lyapunov Exponent 223
6.3 Business Cycles and Financial Instability 225
    6.3.1 The Goodwin Model of Business Cycles 225
    6.3.2 Great Moderation and Financial Crisis 228
    6.3.3 Minsky's Financial Instability Hypothesis 229
    6.3.4 Keen's Basic Minsky Model 230
    6.3.5 Keen's Minsky Model with Money Creation 232
6.4 Nonlinear Expectation Formation and the Business Cycle 235
    6.4.1 Modified Multiplier–Accelerator Model 237
    6.4.2 Properties of the Model 238
6.5 Nonlinearity in Economics 241
    6.5.1 Applications of Nonlinearity 241
    6.5.2 Empirical Evidence 245
    6.5.3 Nonlinearity and Economic Worldviews 246
References 249

Abstract

Chapter 6 discusses nonlinearity as the first fundamental complexity concept. Many phenomena of interest to complexity science and complexity economics are related to nonlinearity. At the same time, nonlinearity is so pervasive in the natural and social world that it should be considered the normal case. The first

M. Roos, *Principles of Complexity Economics*, Classroom Companion: Economics,
https://doi.org/10.1007/978-3-031-51436-4_6

part of the chapter provides an introduction to the mathematics of nonlinear dynamics, which serves as background for the rest of the book. It is shown that continuous two-dimensional systems can have periodic orbits in addition to fixed points and bifurcations, at which the behavior of the system changes qualitatively. Furthermore, catastrophes and chaos are discussed. In the second part, two exemplary economic models that use this kind of mathematics are presented: a model of financial instability and a model of endogenous business cycles with nonlinear expectation formation. Finally, the role of nonlinearity in economics in general is discussed.

Keywords

Bifurcations · Chaos · Differential equations · Iterated maps · Nonlinear dynamics

Guiding Questions

- What is nonlinearity and why is it important?
- How does nonlinearity relate to complexity?
- How can we mathematically model dynamical systems?
- What is linearization and how can it go wrong?
- What are Lotka–Volterra population models?
- What are bifurcations and catastrophes?
- How can we define chaos?
- Does nonlinearity matter in economics?

6.1 Introduction

The first complexity concept we examine in detail is nonlinearity. As with many other concepts in complexity science, there are different interpretations of what nonlinearity means. One interpretation is that the connection between cause and effect in a complex system is not a simple chain, but a network with feedback loops. This interpretation will be discussed in the next chapter. This chapter deals with the interpretation that the relationships between the variables of a system are nonlinear functions. In particular, we look at *nonlinear dynamics*, which is the change of a system over time described by nonlinear mathematical relationships. Economic textbooks and even research papers often present linear or linearized models. One of the most basic and popular empirical research methods in economics is linear regression. The great advantage of these methods is their simplicity. Linear models can be solved analytically, have unique equilibria, and make unambiguous predictions.

Unfortunately, only a small fraction of the relationships between variables in the real world are linear. Nonlinearity is prevalent in natural systems and even more so in social systems such as the economy. The prevalence of nonlinearity in the social world is unfortunate because nonlinear systems are much more difficult to analyze than linear systems. The reason for the difficulty of nonlinear systems is that they cannot be broken down into parts that can be solved separately and then recombined to learn the behavior of the whole system. In fact, the Greek word analysis (ἀνάλυσις) means "to break down." Strictly speaking, we cannot analyze a nonlinear system if we cannot break it up into parts without losing information. In Chap. 2, we saw that the notion that "the whole is more than the sum of its parts" is a key property of complex systems that results from the interaction of the system elements. Therefore, nonlinearity is also a crucial aspect of complexity.

A very simple mathematical example helps to develop an intuition about the sense in which nonlinear relations are different from the sum of their parts. Suppose a variable z is a quadratic function of two other variables: $z = (x + y)^2$. A common mistake made by high school students is to calculate z as the sum of the squares, but in fact z is equal to the sum of the squares plus the interaction term: $z = x^2 + y^2 + 2xy$. The quadratic function violates the *superposition principle,* according to which $f(x + y) = f(x) + f(y)$. Of course, this example is very simple and only touches on the complications resulting from nonlinearity, but it may serve as a good starting point for further discussion.

Nonlinearity is related to complexity because we find it much easier to think in linear terms. For example, it is well documented that most people have difficulty predicting exponential growth. The behavior of nonlinear systems is often surprising, which is a characteristic of complexity. Two properties of nonlinear relationships often cause problems: the *nonproportionality of cause and effect*, and the *change in direction*. Let us first look at a linear example to see what this means.

Figure 6.1 shows the linear relationship $y = 4 + 0.5x$ with a measurement error. A linear regression line that is fitted to the data describes the data very well. We can see that the point (9, 8.59) lies almost perfectly on the trend line. If the independent variable x changes by a small amount (the cause), e.g. $\Delta x = 0.5$, then the change of the dependent variable y (the effect) will also be small, $\Delta y = 0.4845 * 0.5 = 0.242$. A large cause, e.g. $\Delta x = 10$, will have a large effect, here $\Delta y = 0.4845 * 10 = 4.845$. The linear trend predicts that y will increase from 8.59 to 13.435 in response to a 10 unit increase in x. The actual value at $x = 19$ is $y = 13.05$, so the prediction error is relatively small. We do not have data for $x = 25$, but with a linear relationship between x and y, we can confidently predict that the dependent variable would be close to $y = 16.45$.

The function of the polynomial of degree 7 in Fig. 6.2 has very different properties. It has two local maxima and two local minima, and it changes direction several times. If we try to approximate and predict this function with linear

[1]The following mathematical introduction follows Strogatz (2019) quite closely. More details can be found there.

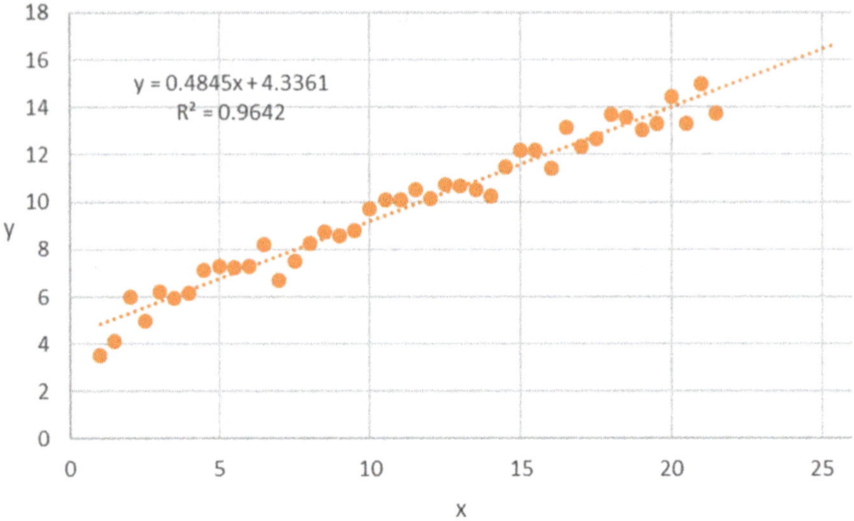

Fig. 6.1 A linear relationship with noise. Source: Author

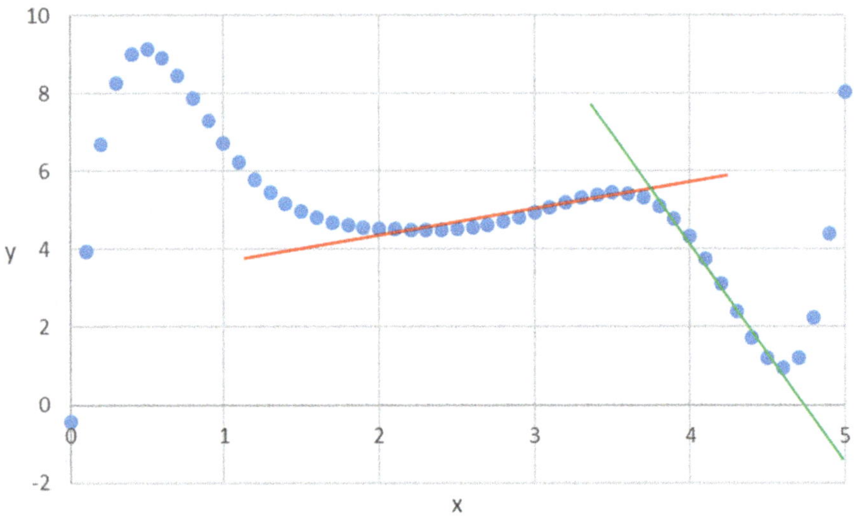

Fig. 6.2 A nonlinear relationship. Source: Author

functions, we will fail dramatically. Suppose we only have data from the interval [2; 3.5] and try to fit a linear regression line. The red regression line would have a positive slope and a very good fit ($R^2 > 0.9$). However, its predictive power outside the interval [2; 3.5] is poor. Similarly fitting a regression line to the data in [3.6; 4.5] yields the negatively sloped green line, which strongly mispredicts the y-values at $x = 5$. Furthermore, the nonlinear function does not have the general property that small changes cause small effects and large changes cause large effects. For example, if x changes from 0 to 0.5, the effect $\Delta y = 9.6$ is large. The large change of $\Delta x = 4.6$ causes only a small effect, $\Delta y = 1.4$.

These examples are very simple, but they illustrate the difficulties that arise from nonlinearity. In Sect. 6.2, we look at *nonlinear dynamical systems*, in which *bifurcations* and *chaos* can occur. Furthermore, these systems can have different kinds of *attractors*, which is a more general concept than the concept of equilibrium. It is not the purpose of this textbook to provide a detailed technical introduction to the large and advanced field of nonlinear dynamics. The interested reader may consult specialized textbooks such as Lorenz (1989), Medio and Lines (2001), or Strogatz (2019).[1] The purpose of Sect. 6.2 is to make you aware that even simple nonlinear models can have complicated and surprising dynamics. Dealing with complexity starts with accepting that even seemingly simple systems can be difficult to understand and to predict, in other words, complex.

After a general discussion of nonlinear dynamics, we present some nonlinear economic models. We begin with a simple version of the *Goodwin model* of business cycle dynamics in Sect. 6.3.1. Next, Sect. 6.3.2 presents a version of the *Minsky model* of financial instability that can generate endogenous financial crises. Section 6.4 contains a model of the business cycle with nonlinear expectation formation, in which bifurcations and chaos occur. These models capture only some aspects of complexity, but they are important, because they tell a very different story about the business cycle and economic crises than the mainstream neoclassical models. In Sect. 4.3, we encountered the neoclassical practice of generating market fluctuations by adding stochastic shocks to linear (or linearized) equilibrium models. The basic idea exemplified in the very simple market model used by Muth in order to introduce the idea of rational expectations is exactly the same approach that mainstream macroeconomists use in their *dynamic stochastic general equilibrium (DSGE) models*. In the midst of the recession caused by the global financial crisis of 2008, Willem Buiter published a philippic denouncing the "unfortunate uselessness of most state of the art academic monetary economics." In particular, he argued that linearizing models trivialize the complex reality. He wrote:

> *So they took these non-linear stochastic dynamic general equilibrium models into the basement and beat them with a rubber hose until they behaved. This was achieved by completely stripping the model of its non-linearities and by achieving the transubstantiation of complex convolutions of random variables and non-linear mappings into well-behaved additive stochastic disturbances. Those of us who have marvelled at the non-linear feedback loops between asset prices in illiquid markets and the funding illiquidity of financial institutions exposed to these asset prices through mark-to-market accounting, margin requirements, calls for additional collateral etc. will appreciate what is lost by this castration of the macroeconomic models. Threshold effects, critical mass, tipping points, non-linear accelerators—they are all out of the window. Those of us who worry about endogenous uncertainty arising from the interactions of boundedly rational market participants cannot but scratch our heads at the insistence of the mainline models that all uncertainty is exogenous and additive. … When you linearise a model, and shock it with additive random disturbances, an unfortunate by-product is that the resulting linearised model behaves either in a very strongly stabilising fashion or in a relentlessly explosive*

manner. There is no 'bounded instability' in such models. The dynamic stochastic general equilibrium (DSGE) crowd saw that the economy had not exploded without bound in the past, and concluded from this that it made sense to rule out, in the linearised model, the explosive solution trajectories. What they were left with was something that, following an exogenous random disturbance, would return to the deterministic steady state pretty smartly. (Buiter 2009)

The models presented in this chapter are alternatives to the mainstream models. They show that the economy is likely to be much less stable than the linearized DSGE models suggest. Section 6.5 concludes the chapter with a general assessment of the importance of nonlinearity in economics.

6.2 Dynamical Systems

In 1976, the biologist and physicist Robert M. May wrote in his article "Simple mathematical models with very complicated dynamics":

Not only in research, but also in the everyday world of politics and economics, we would all be better off if more people realised that simple nonlinear systems do not necessarily possess simple dynamical properties. (May 1976, p. 467)

May notes that in many disciplines it is common to describe a situation, at least to a first rough approximation, by simple first-order difference equations. The usual procedure for studying the dynamical properties of such models is to find constant equilibrium solutions, followed by a linearized stability analysis with respect to small perturbations of the equilibrium state. Such a simplified analysis can lead to very misleading conclusions about the true dynamics of nonlinear systems. He therefore wished that all students learning mathematical models should be exposed to simple nonlinear models in order to acquire a good intuition about complex dynamics. Giving you the opportunity to develop such an intuition with simple examples is exactly the goal of this section.

6.2.1 Differential Equations and Difference Equations

Dynamical systems are used in all of the mathematical sciences and are therefore like a universal language of science. A *dynamical system* is a function (or set of functions) that describes how a state depends on time and thus varies over time.[2] We can distinguish between *continuous-time dynamical systems* and *discrete-time dynamical systems*.

Continuous-time dynamical systems are modeled by *differential equations* that relate time-dependent variables $x(t)$ to their time derivatives, e.g. $\frac{dx(t)}{dt} = \dot{x}(t)$.

[2] Note that here, "system" can refer to a single equation.

Ordinary differential equations (ODE) contain one or more functions of one independent variable (e.g., time) and the derivatives of these functions. In contrast, *partial differential equations* (PDEs) contain functions with multiple variables and their partial derivatives. Differential equations can be linear, if they consist of linear combinations of the derivatives, or nonlinear. The order of a differential equation is given by the number of the time derivatives, i.e. a differential equation is first order, if it only contains the first derivative $\frac{dx(t)}{dt} = \dot{x}(t)$. If it includes the second derivative, $\frac{d^2x(t)}{dt^2} = \ddot{x}(t)$, it is second order, and so on. If the function f that relates the variable x and its derivatives does not depend directly on time, i.e., $\frac{\partial f}{\partial t} = 0$, the system is said to be *autonomous*, otherwise it is *driven*. If the function also depends on other variables, the system is *non-homogeneous* (or inhomogeneous), if it depends only on x it is *homogeneous*. To solve differential equations, we need initial states (or initial conditions), i.e. a value for the variable x at the beginning of the time period considered, $x(0)$ or $x(t_0)$. Solving a differential equation means finding a function of the system's parameters and time that gives the value of $x(t)$ for any t. In many general cases, it is not possible to solve differential equations analytically, such that numerical methods must be used. An example of a non-homogeneous, linear second-order ODE is

$$f(x, \dot{x}, \ddot{x}, r(t), t) = \alpha \frac{d^2x(t)}{dt^2} + \beta \frac{dx(t)}{dt} + \gamma x(t) + \delta r(t) + t = 0. \tag{6.1}$$

The only independent variable in this function is time t, such that is an ordinary differential equation. An example of a nonlinear ODE is

$$\ddot{x} + \frac{g}{L} \sin x = 0, \tag{6.2}$$

which includes the nonlinear term *sin x*.

If we treat time as discrete, we can model dynamical systems with *difference equations* or *iterated maps*. Discrete time means that we index variables by points in time or periods, e.g. $x_t, x_{t+1}, x_{t+2} \ldots$ Conventionally, t stands for the present, $t - i$ represents the past, and $t + i$ represents the future. Discrete time is often convenient in economics, because statistical data for economic variables such as inflation, unemployment, or GDP are only available for longer time periods such as months, quarters, or years. Iterated maps are also attractive, because they are easier to simulate than differential equations. Simulations can easily be done with spreadsheet software. When the iterated maps are linear, linear (matrix) algebra is a powerful tool for analysis. An iterated map is a function f that relates a variable x_t to its own past $(x_{t-1}, x_{t-2} \ldots)$ and/or its own future $(x_{t+1}, x_{t+2} \ldots)$. Similar to differential equations, iterated maps can be linear or nonlinear, depend directly on time and also on other variables. An example of an inhomogeneous linear difference equation of order 2 is

$$f(x_t, x_{t-1}, x_{t-2}, \beta) = \alpha_0 x_t - \alpha_1 x_{t-1} - \alpha_2 x_{t-2} - \beta = 0 \tag{6.3}$$

Often, it is more convenient to write it like this:

$$x_t = a_1 x_{t-1} + a_2 x_{t-2} + b \tag{6.4}$$

6.2.2 Dynamics of One-dimensional Continuous-time Systems

Geometric analysis of dynamical systems often provides more insight than the use of formulas. Of course, geometric analysis cannot easily provide quantitative information, but in many cases we are only interested in the qualitative behavior of the system, for which pictures are very useful. The other powerful tool for analyzing dynamical systems is the computer. We will focus on geometric analysis and start with very simple examples.

Let us look at an autonomous one-dimensional or first-order system, represented by an ordinary differential equation:

$$\dot{x} = f(x) \tag{6.5}$$

Geometric analysis means that we interpret the differential equation as a *vector field*, where vectors indicate the direction of change of the state of the system described by x. To see how this works, consider the linear differential equation

$$\dot{x} = gx \tag{6.6}$$

with $g > 0$. Figure 6.3 shows a phase portrait (or phase diagram) of this differential equation. The horizontal axis is the phase space (or state space), because it shows the possible states of the system. The vertical axis shows the marginal changes of the states over time. The straight line with slope g represents Eq. (6.6).

The origin of the graph is marked with a white circle. This is a so-called *fixed point,* which is a kind of equilibrium. According to (6.6), $\dot{x} = 0$ when $x = 0$, which means that the system does not change its state there. If, for some reason, $x > 0$, the value of x will increase, as indicated by the arrow (or vector) on the x-axis pointing to the right, because $\dot{x} > 0$ in that subset of the state space.

Analogously, the vector pointing to the left means that x decreases for $x < 0$. The vectors in the phase portrait thus inform us about the dynamics of any given value of x. This simple linear differential equation describes exponential growth for all initial values $x_0 > 0$ with a constant growth rate $\frac{\dot{x}}{x} = g$. Exponential growth means that $x(t) = x(0)e^{gt}$. The unique fixed point is *unstable*, because the slightest perturbation $\varepsilon \neq 0$ that takes the system out of the fixed point will trigger perpetual motion taking the system to $+\infty$ or $-\infty$. If the slope of the differential equation were negative, $g < 0$, then the fixed point would be *stable* and the vectors showing the dynamics of the system would point in the opposite directions. Thus, we would have $\dot{x} < 0$ for $x > 0$ and $\dot{x} > 0$ for $x < 0$.

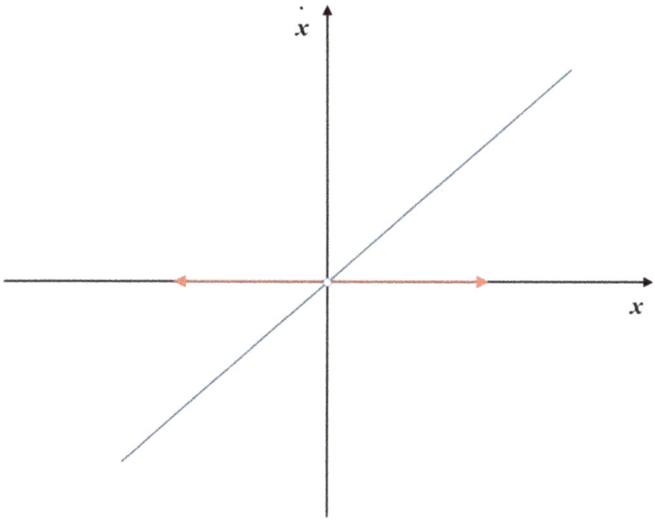

Fig. 6.3 Phase portrait of a linear differential equation. Source: Author

Fig. 6.4 Phase portrait of a nonlinear differential equation. Source: Author

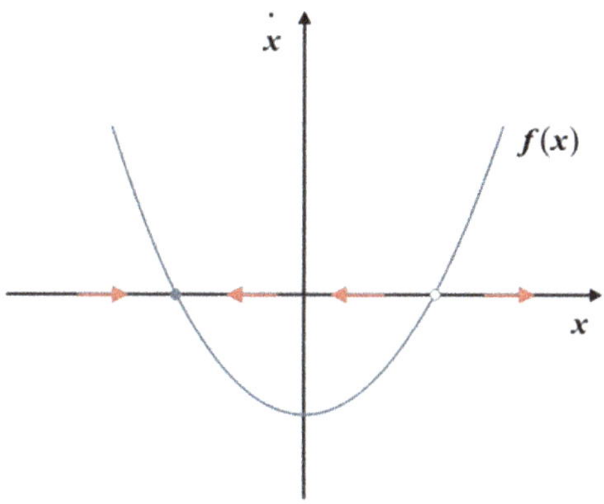

Now let us look at a simple nonlinear differential equation:

$$\dot{x} = x^2 - 1. \tag{6.7}$$

The graph of $f(x) = x^2 - 1$ is shown in Fig. 6.4. This function has two fixed points, for which $\dot{x} = f(x^*) = 0$ holds: $x^* = \pm 1$. As indicated by the full circle in the figure, the left fixed point, $x^* = -1$, is stable, while the other one is unstable (marked by the empty circle). In the interval [-1,1] $f(x) = \dot{x} < 0$, such that x decreases, shown by the vector pointing to the left. For $x < -1$ and $x > 1$, the vector points to the right, because $\dot{x} > 0$. Hence, a small positive perturbation of the fixed point $x^* = 1$ will cause the system to diverge toward infinity, i.e. perpetual growth. The message of this simple example is that nonlinear systems have richer dynamics than linear systems. Unlike linear systems, which have just one stable or unstable fixed point, nonlinear systems can have multiple fixed points. This fact makes it more difficult to predict the long-term behavior of the system. A linear system will either converge to the stable fixed point or diverge toward $\pm\infty$, unless the initial value is equal to the unstable fixed point and there are no perturbations. While it is possible for a system to always be in an unstable fixed point, this is a rather unlikely state, since the slightest disturbance is enough to set the system in motion. In order to predict the long-term states of the linear system, we only need to know the fixed point and the stability of the fixed point, which is given by the sign of g in (6.6).

Predicting the long-term states of the nonlinear system (6.7) requires more information. Now it is important to know the initial value of the system. If the initial value is left of the unstable fixed point, $x(0) < 1$, the state of the system is attracted to the stable fixed point $x^* = -1$, which is therefore called the *attractor* (or *sink*). The unstable fixed point $x^* = 1$ is called a *repeller* (or *source*), because in its neighborhood the system moves away from it. Any initial value $x(0) > 1$ leads to divergence toward ∞. The set of initial values $x(0)$ that lead $x(t)$ to the attractor x^* as $t \to \infty$ is called the *basin of attraction*. In the present case, the basin of attraction of the attractor $x^* = -1$ is the set $[-\infty, 1]$. Note that the stable fixed point is only locally stable. This means that it is only robust against small perturbations. For instance, if the system is initially at $x(0) = -1$ and is then hit by a small shock $\varepsilon = 0.5$, $x(0) + \varepsilon = -0.5$ is still in the basin of attraction, such that x will converge back to -1. However, if the shock is large, e.g. $\varepsilon = 3$, $x(0) + \varepsilon = 2$ is outside the basin of attraction, so x will diverge.

A famous application of a quadratic first-order dynamic system is population growth. Suppose $N(t)$ is the population of an organism at time t. If the population grows at a constant rate r, we get the linear system $\dot{N} = rN$, which corresponds to the system in (6.6) shown in Fig. 6.3. However, the permanent exponential growth implied by this system is highly unrealistic for any biological population. The growth of any biological population will eventually be limited by scarce resources, space, and overcrowding. For simplicity, we can assume that the growth rate decreases linearly with the size of the population

$$\frac{\dot{N}}{N} = r\left(1 - \frac{N}{K}\right). \tag{6.8}$$

The growth rate is large when the population is small, but reaches zero when $N = K$. For $N > K$, the growth rate is even negative, such that the population is shrinking, e.g. due to starvation or stress caused by overcrowding. The parameter K is called the *carrying capacity* of the population's habitat. Rewriting (6.8) leads to the so-called *logistic equation*

$$\dot{N} = rN\left(1 - \frac{N}{K}\right), \tag{6.9}$$

which is a quadratic differential equation similar to (6.7), but with a negative sign on the squared term N^2. The phase portrait is shown in Fig. 6.5.

The logistic equation has an unstable fixed point at $N = 0$ and a stable one at $N = K$. Population growth $\dot{N}$ reaches its maximum exactly halfway between 0 and K at $K/2$. It follows that, if the initial population level is low, the evolution of N over time is S-shaped as shown by the graph in Fig. 6.6. Initially, the graph is convex, because growth increases for $N < K/2$. After the inflection point at $K/2$, the graph becomes concave and asymptotically approaches K.

The logistic equation in (6.9) may be too simplistic for many real biological processes, but it is a good qualitative description of growth processes that are constrained by some limiting factors. It is also used in economics, e.g. to describe

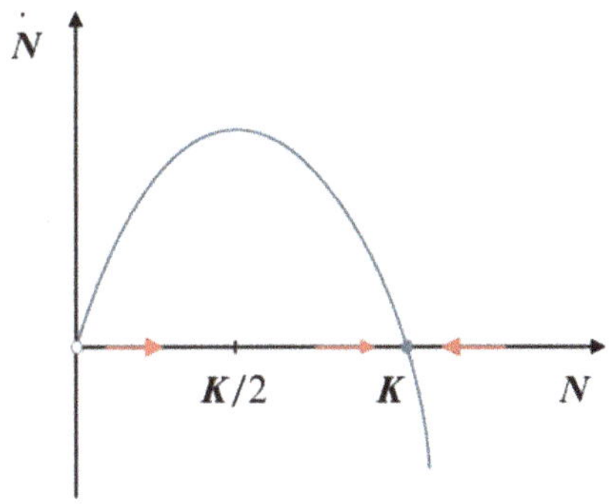

Fig. 6.5 Phase portrait of the logistic equation. Source: Author

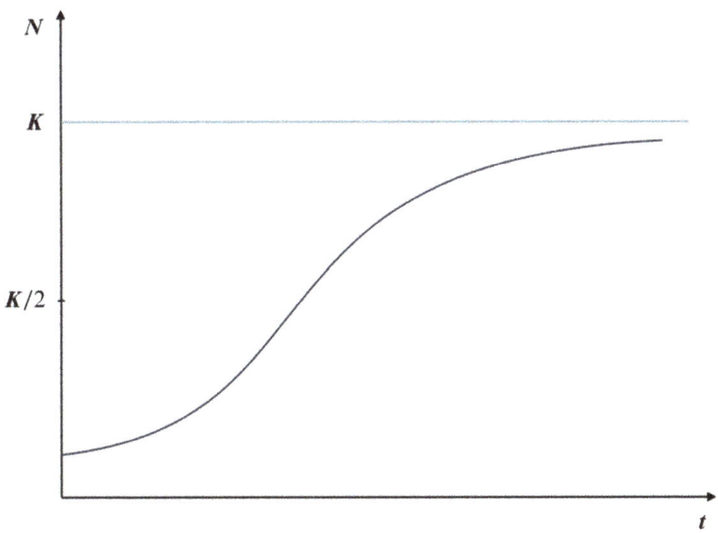

Fig. 6.6 S-shaped dynamics. Source: Author

the market diffusion of new products. It was originally developed in 1838 by Pierre-François Verhulst, who was inspired by the work of Thomas Malthus on population growth. The *Verhulst model* was later rediscovered several times.

6.2.3 Dynamics of Two-dimensional Continuous-time Systems

Interesting economic systems have more than one variable. In fact, they have many more variables, which makes these dynamical systems very difficult to analyze, especially if they are nonlinear. As we will see in this subsection, even two-dimensional dynamical systems can have rich dynamics.

The general form of a two-dimensional system is

$$\dot{x} = f(x, y),$$

$$\dot{y} = g(x, y),$$

where $f(.)$ and $g(.)$ are (potentially nonlinear) functions. As in the one-dimensional case, we can analyze these systems qualitatively using phase portraits, which represent vector fields. Systems with two variables have a two-dimensional state space, such that the phase portrait is also called the *phase plane*. An example is shown in Fig. 6.7.

The state space is spanned by the vertical axis describing the states of y and the horizontal axis for the x-states. The curves with the arrowheads are called *trajectories*. They describe possible paths of $x(t)$ and $y(t)$ through the phase plane. The whole space is filled with trajectories, so we can describe the dynamics of every possible point. To keep the visualization simple, only a few trajectories are shown in Fig. 6.7. Trajectories are typically nonlinear and they can never intersect, because otherwise different future paths would be possible at an intersection point. It can be shown that if the functions $f(.)$ and $g(.)$ are continuously differentiable, there are

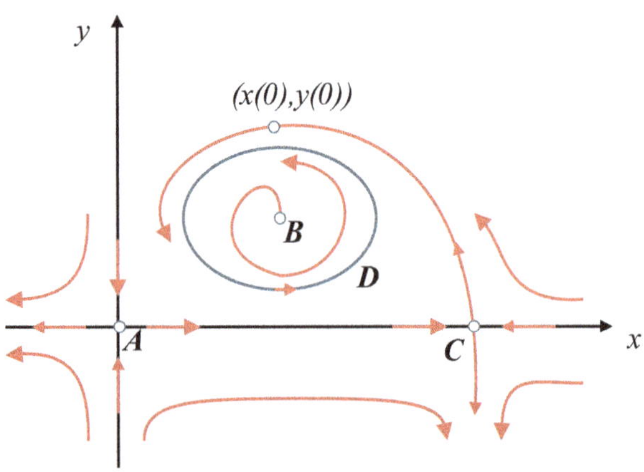

Fig. 6.7 Phase portrait of a two-dimensional system. Source: Author's own figure after Strogatz (2019)

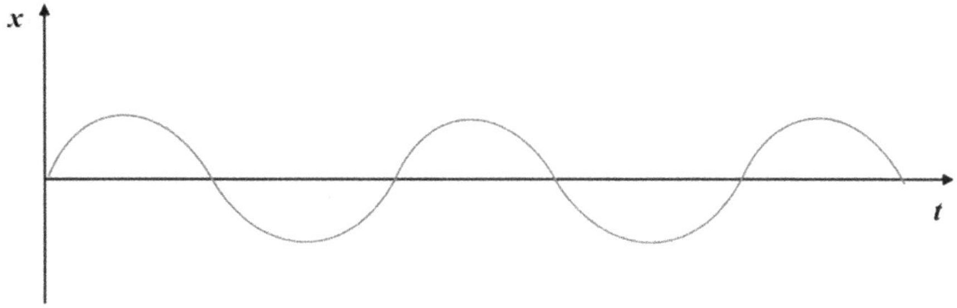

Fig. 6.8 Periodic solution of $x(t)$ on a closed orbit. Source: Author

unique paths $x(t)$ and $y(t)$ for all initial values $x(0)$, $y(0)$. In general, the trajectories cannot be found analytically. We can either try to characterize them geometrically or find them numerically with the help of a computer.

Figure 6.7 shows an example of an initial point $(x(0), y(0))$ on an inward spiraling trajectory, such that from there, $x(t)$ initially moves left and $y(t)$ moves down. Note that this system has several fixed points (or steady states): A, B, and C. The trajectories tell us that they are all unstable. For example, if A is slightly perturbed along the x-axis, the system will either converge to C or diverge to $-\infty$. However, a vertical movement up from A would be corrected, bringing us back to A. Note that a vertical motion upward from B puts the system on an outward spiraling trajectory moving away from B. The trajectory labeled D is interesting, because it is a so-called *closed orbit*. On a closed orbit, each point $(x(t), y(t))$ will be reached again after some time period T such that $(x(t), y(t)) = (x(t + T), y(t + T))$ for all t. A closed orbit is therefore a periodic solution as illustrated for $x(t)$ in Fig. 6.8.

The closed orbit D is particularly interesting here, because it is a *limit cycle*. As can be seen in Fig. 6.7, both the spiral trajectories from the outside (e.g., from point C) and the spirals from the inside (from point B) come closer and closer to D. This means that all solutions starting from these trajectories will eventually converge to the closed orbit and remain there. Therefore, the closed orbit D is stable and represents a long-term behavior of the system that is different from a steady state. Systems with limit cycles exhibit self-sustaining oscillations that do not require external forcing. Limit cycles cannot occur in linear systems, but require nonlinearity. Linear systems can have closed orbits, but they are not isolated like limit cycles. Isolated means that neighboring trajectories spiral either toward or away from the limit cycle. In other words, neighboring trajectories are not closed as they would be with closed orbits of linear systems. Two-dimensional nonlinear dynamical systems can therefore oscillate in their long-run equilibrium instead of converging to a steady state.

The steady states or fixed points of two-dimensional systems can be classified according to their stability and their dynamics. We already know that fixed points can be stable or unstable. A fixed point is stable, if all trajectories in its neighborhood approach it as $t \to \infty$ and stay close to it for all time. The dynamics leading to a fixed point or away from it create characteristic patterns of trajectories, which give the fixed points their names.

A fixed point is a *node*, if all trajectories either lead toward the fixed point (stable node or sink) or away from it (unstable node or source). Figure 6.9 shows a stable node. A node has two so-called *eigendirections*, which are straight-line trajectories described by the eigenvectors $\mathbf{v_1}$ and $\mathbf{v_2}$ of the linear (or linearized) system. One eigendirection is fast and the other is slow. The speed of the eigendirection is determined by the eigenvalue λ associated with the eigenvector. The eigenvalue that is smaller in absolute terms determines the slow eigendirection, to which most trajectories are tangent at the fixed point. A *degenerate node* has only one eigendirection as shown in Fig. 6.10.

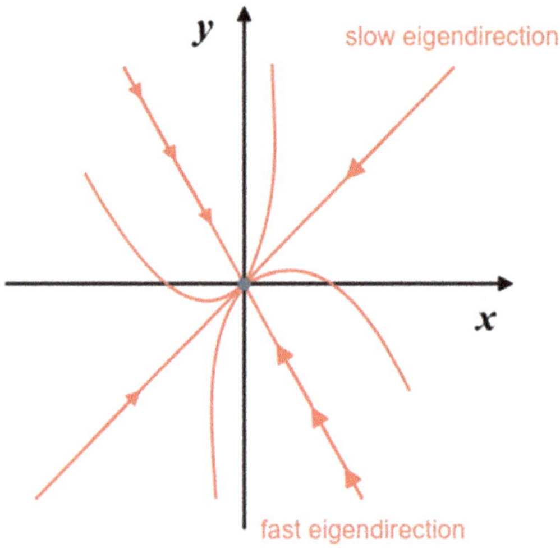

Fig. 6.9 Stable node. Source: Author's own figure after Strogatz (2019)

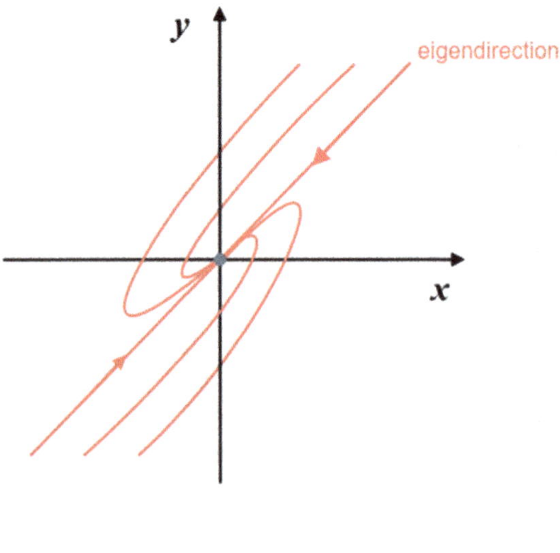

Fig. 6.10 Stable degenerate node. Source: Author's own figure after Strogatz (2019)

If there are two independent eigenvectors with equal eigenvalues, the fixed point is a star node (Fig. 6.11), whose trajectories are straight lines. This means that from any initial value the system moves directly to the fixed point. A special case is when $\lambda = 0$. In this case, every point in the plane is a fixed point and there are no dynamics.

As we saw in the example in Fig. 6.7, the trajectories can also spiral toward or away from a fixed point. Figure 6.12 shows a fixed point that is a stable *spiral*. Spirals occur when the eigenvalues are complex numbers.

In the special case where the eigenvalues are purely imaginary, i.e., they are complex numbers with no real part, the fixed point is a *center* (Fig. 6.13). The trajectories around a center are closed orbits, which implies that a center is *neutrally stable*. This means that the trajectories in the neighborhood of the center are neither attracted to nor repelled from the fixed point.

Fig. 6.11 Star node. Source: Author

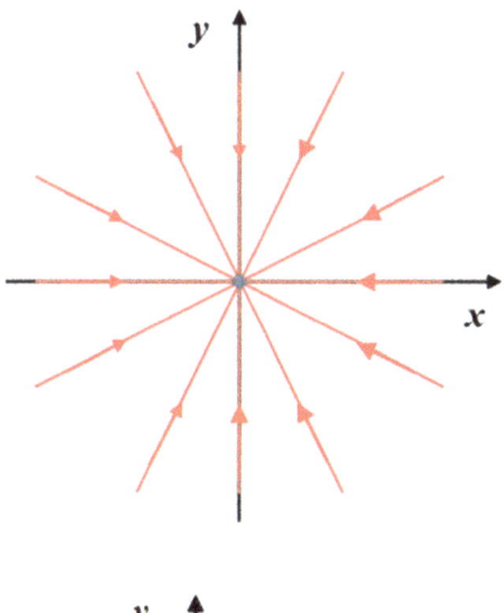

Fig. 6.12 Stable spiral. Source: Author

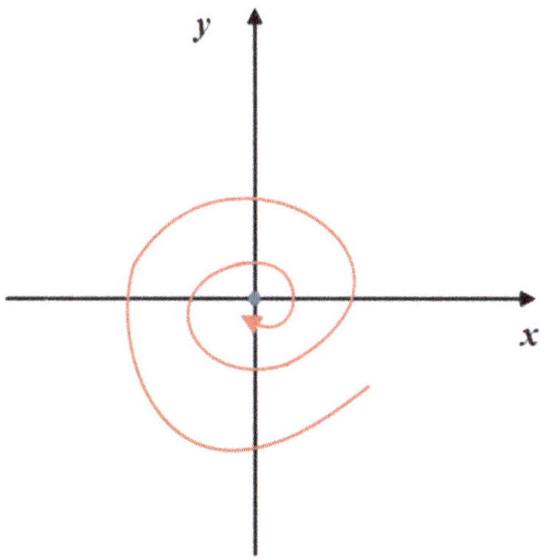

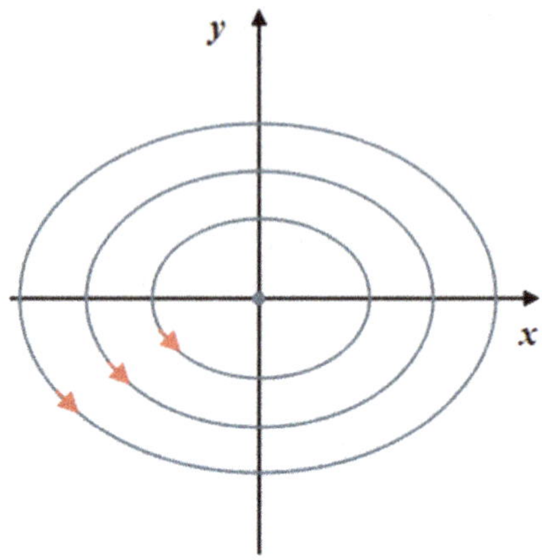

Fig. 6.13 Center. Source: Author

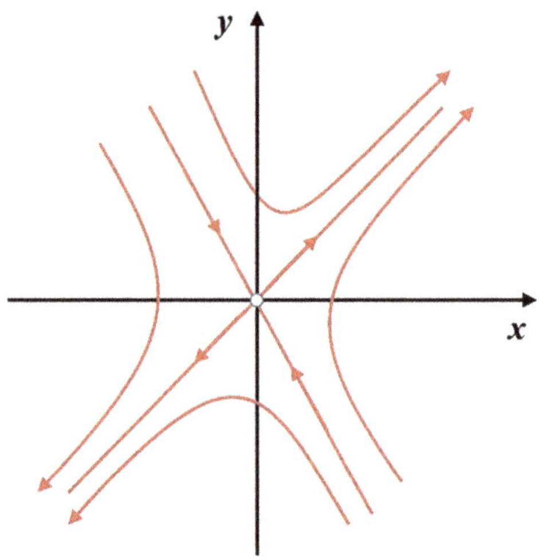

Fig. 6.14 Saddle point. Source: Author

Nodes and spirals can be stable or unstable, and centers are neutrally stable. In all of these cases, we can make unambiguous predictions about the long-run behavior of the system. If a node or spiral is stable, the system will approach the attractor in the long run, and if it is unstable, it will move away from the fixed point. Centers are characterized by periodic oscillations of constant amplitude around the fixed point.

A *saddle point* as shown in Fig. 6.14 is an interesting unstable fixed point, because while most trajectories lead away from it, it has one trajectory that can reach it. This trajectory is called the *stable manifold* (or *saddle path*). Saddle points require two real eigenvalues, of which one is negative and one is positive. The stable manifold is given by the eigenvector with the negative eigenvalue. Many economic models have saddle points as equilibria and are called *saddle path stable* in economics. The Ramsey–Cass–Koopmans model we saw in Chap. 4 has this property.

The phase portraits of the different fixed points depend on the eigenvectors and the eigenvalues. But what does this mean? As mentioned earlier, it is often impossible to find analytical expressions for trajectories in nonlinear systems. Therefore, it is common to *linearize* nonlinear systems at the fixed points and to use the linearized system as an approximation. Often, linearization works well, but sometimes it can be misleading. We will come back to this point, but let us look at the analysis of linear systems.

The linear version of a two-dimensional dynamical system is

$$\dot{x} = ax + by$$

$$\dot{y} = cx + dy$$

with parameters a, b, c, d. It is convenient to write the system more compactly in matrix form

$$\begin{pmatrix} \dot{x} \\ \dot{y} \end{pmatrix} = \begin{pmatrix} a & b \\ c & d \end{pmatrix} \begin{pmatrix} x \\ y \end{pmatrix}$$

or

$$\dot{\mathbf{x}} = A\mathbf{x}, \tag{6.10}$$

where $\mathbf{x}$ denotes a vector. Note that $\mathbf{x}^* = \begin{pmatrix} x \\ y \end{pmatrix} = \begin{pmatrix} 0 \\ 0 \end{pmatrix} = \mathbf{0}$ is always a fixed point in a linear system, because $\dot{\mathbf{x}} = A\mathbf{x}^* = A\mathbf{0} = \mathbf{0}$. In the pictures above, we saw that the dynamics can be determined by vectors that point to or away from the fixed point. Along such a vector $\mathbf{v}$, the system evolves in an exponential motion with growth rate λ according to

$$\mathbf{x}(t) = e^{\lambda t}\mathbf{v}. \tag{6.11}$$

Taking the time derivative of (6.11), substituting into (6.10) and canceling $e^{\lambda t}$ on both sides yields

$$A\mathbf{v} = \lambda\mathbf{v},$$

which is an *eigenequation* (or *eigenvalue equation*). (6.11) is an *eigensolution* of this equation, $\mathbf{v}$ is an *eigenvector* of A, and λ is the corresponding *eigenvalue*. The eigenvalues of a matrix A are given by the *characteristic equation* $det(A - \lambda I) = 0$, where I is the identity matrix. In our linear two-dimensional case, the characteristic equation is

$$det\begin{pmatrix} a-\lambda & b \\ c & d-\lambda \end{pmatrix} = 0.$$

The determinant of a 2x2 matrix is defined as the product of the elements on the main diagonal minus the product of the elements on the antidiagonal, hence

$$(a-\lambda)(d-\lambda)-bc=0,$$

or

$$\lambda^2-(a+d)\lambda+ad-bc=0. \tag{6.12}$$

$a+d=Tr\,A$ is the *trace* and $ad-bc=\det A$ is the determinant of the matrix A. We can thus write the characteristic Eq. (6.12) more compactly as

$$\lambda^2-(Tr\,A)\,\lambda+\det A=0.$$

Since the characteristic equation is quadratic, it generally has two solutions (or *roots*), which are the eigenvalues:

$$\lambda_1=\frac{Tr\,A+\sqrt{(Tr\,A)^2-4\det A}}{2},\lambda_2=\frac{Tr\,A-\sqrt{(Tr\,A)^2-4\det A}}{2}. \tag{6.13}$$

We can find the eigenvector $\mathbf{v}=(v_1,v_2)$ corresponding to the eigenvalue λ by solving the linear system

$$\begin{pmatrix} a-\lambda & b \\ c & d-\lambda \end{pmatrix}\begin{pmatrix} v_1 \\ v_2 \end{pmatrix}=\begin{pmatrix} 0 \\ 0 \end{pmatrix}.$$

If the eigenvalues are distinct, then the corresponding two eigenvectors are linearly independent and span a two-dimensional space. Any initial condition $\mathbf{x}_0$ can then be written as a linear combination of the two eigenvectors:

$$\boldsymbol{x}_0=c_1\mathbf{v}_1+c_2\mathbf{v}_2,$$

where c_1, c_2 are constants. From a given $\boldsymbol{x}_0$, we can determine the constants and find the general solution $\mathbf{x}(t)$ for any point in time:

$$\mathbf{x}(t)=c_1e^{\lambda_1 t}\mathbf{v}_1+c_2e^{\lambda_2 t}\mathbf{v}_2. \tag{6.14}$$

The general solution (6.14) can help us to understand the phase portraits sketched above. Suppose both eigenvalues are real and negative. Then, $e^{\lambda t}\rightarrow 0$ as $t\rightarrow\infty$ such that $\mathbf{x}(t)\rightarrow\mathbf{0}$. Hence, in this case, the fixed point $\begin{pmatrix} 0 \\ 0 \end{pmatrix}$ is a stable node. If both real eigenvalues are positive, $\mathbf{x}(t)\rightarrow\infty$ in the long run, such that we move away from the origin, which is then an unstable node. If one eigenvalue is negative and the other is positive, the eigensolution given by the eigenvector with the negative eigenvalue approaches zero, while the other eigensolution grows exponentially to infinity. This is exactly the behavior that characterizes the saddle point in Fig. 6.13, which means

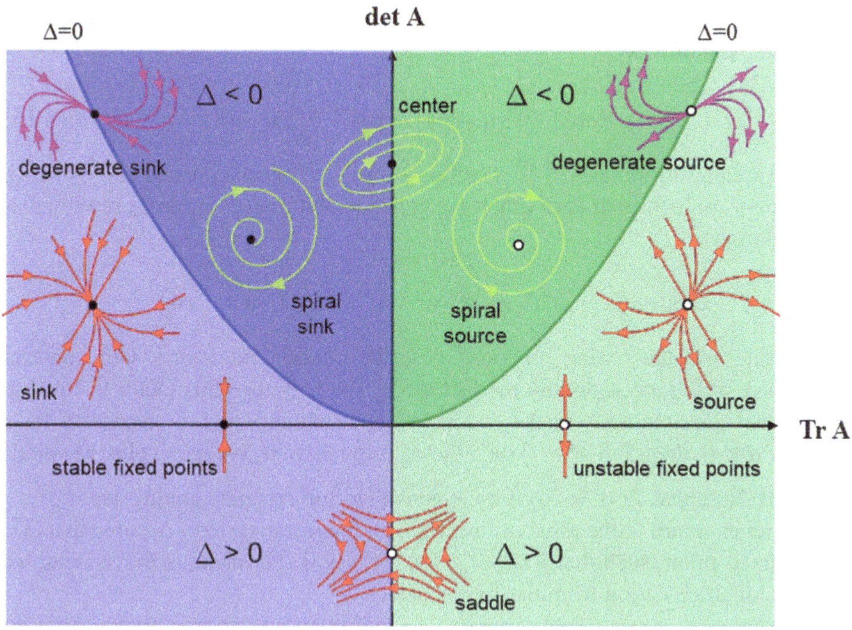

Fig. 6.15 Classification of fixed points. Source: Author's own figure adapted from Maschen (2012)

that a saddle point exists when the characteristic equation has one negative real eigenvalue and one positive real eigenvalue.

The diagram in Fig. 6.15 summarizes the conditions for the different types of phase portraits. The only information we need to classify the phase portraits is the determinant of the matrix A, *det A*, the trace, *Tr A*, and the discriminant of the characteristic equation, $\Delta = (Tr\,A)^2 - 4\det A$. Note that from (6.13), we can derive that $\det A = \lambda_1 \lambda_2$ and $Tr\,A = \lambda_1 + \lambda_2$ holds. The discriminant is important, because it tells us, whether the eigenvalues are real numbers or complex numbers.

If the eigenvalues are real and of opposite signs, then $\det A < 0$ and the fixed points are saddle points. In the borderline case $\det A = 0$, we get a line of non-isolated fixed points, which are either stable (if $Tr\,A < 0$) or unstable (if $Tr\,A > 0$). If $\det A > 0$ holds, the discriminant Δ separates the plane. For real eigenvalues (i.e., $\Delta > 0$), the fixed points are nodes. If the discriminant is negative, the eigenvalues are complex, so we get spirals. There are two other borderline cases: $\Delta = 0$ means that there is only one eigenvalue, resulting in degenerate nodes, and $\mathrm{Tr}A = 0$ implies that the real part eigenvalues is zero, such that we obtain centers instead of spirals.

To understand why spirals and centers occur, we need to look more closely at the general solution (6.14) when the eigenvalues are complex. A complex eigenvalue has a real part α and an imaginary part, $i\beta$, where i is the imaginary unit defined by $i^2 = -1$. The eigenvalues are complex conjugates, $\lambda_1 = \alpha + i\beta$ and $\lambda_2 = \alpha - i\beta$ and so are the associated eigenvectors, $\mathbf{v}_1 = \mathbf{u} + i\mathbf{w}$ and $\mathbf{v}_2 = \mathbf{u} - i\mathbf{w}$. Thus, we can write the general solution as

$$\mathbf{x}(t) = c_1 e^{(\alpha + i\beta)t}(\mathbf{u} + i\mathbf{w}) + c_2 e^{(\alpha - i\beta)t}(\mathbf{u} - i\mathbf{w}). \tag{6.15}$$

Using Euler's formula $e^{(\alpha \pm i\beta)t} = e^{\alpha t}(\cos\beta t \pm i \sin \beta t)$ and constants c_1, c_2 which are complex conjugates of each other, the general solution (6.15) can be rewritten as a real solution

$$\mathbf{x}(t) = e^{\alpha t} \cos \beta t(C_1\mathbf{u} - C_2\mathbf{w}) - e^{\alpha t} \sin \beta t(C_2\mathbf{u} + C_1\mathbf{w}).$$

The sine and the cosine functions describe periodic functions with constant amplitudes, which are scaled by the factor $e^{\alpha t}$. If $\alpha = 0$, then this factor is equal to 1, such that the amplitude of the oscillation is constant, which is necessary for a center. If $\alpha < 0$, then $\lim_{t \to \infty} e^{\alpha t} = 0$ such that $\mathbf{x}(t)$ spirals to $\mathbf{0}$. We get explosive spirals for $\alpha > 0$. Note that $Tr\, A = 2\alpha$, if the eigenvalues are complex conjugates.

Now let us return to the topic of linearizing a nonlinear system. Assume that (x^*, y^*) is a fixed point, such that $f(x^*, y^*) = g(x^*, y^*) = 0$. To linearize the system, we look at a small deviation from the fixed point

$$\tilde{x} = x - x^*$$

$$\tilde{y} = y - y^*$$

Stability analysis means that we ask whether this deviation grows or decays over time, i.e. whether we return to the fixed point or not. So we differentiate the deviations with respect to time and get $\dot{\tilde{x}} = \dot{x}$ and $\dot{\tilde{y}} = \dot{y}$, because x^* and y^* are constants. The difficulty is that

$$\dot{\tilde{x}} = f(x^* + x, y^* + y)$$

$$\dot{\tilde{y}} = g(x^* + x, y^* + y)$$

are nonlinear functions. Linearization means that we approximate the nonlinear function by a linear function, which we can do with a *Taylor series expansion* at the fixed point. The Taylor series of a function $f(x)$ at a point a is a power series of the deviations weighted by the derivatives at that point:

$$f(x) = f(a) + \frac{f'(a)}{1!}(x - a) + \frac{f''(a)}{2!}(x - a)^2 + \frac{f'''(a)}{3!}(x - a)^3 + \ldots.$$

For the linearization, we use only the linear term and ignore the higher-order terms $O = \frac{f''(a)}{2!}(x - a)^2 + \frac{f'''(a)}{3!}(x - a)^3 + \ldots$, because they will be very small if the deviation $(x - a)$ is small. The linearly approximated system is hence

$$\begin{pmatrix} \dot{\tilde{x}} \\ \dot{\tilde{y}} \end{pmatrix} = \begin{pmatrix} \dfrac{\partial f(x^*, y^*)}{\partial x} & \dfrac{\partial f(x^*, y^*)}{\partial y} \\ \dfrac{\partial g(x^*, y^*)}{\partial x} & \dfrac{\partial g(x^*, y^*)}{\partial y} \end{pmatrix} \begin{pmatrix} \tilde{x} \\ \tilde{y} \end{pmatrix} \tag{6.16}$$

or

$$\dot{\tilde{\mathbf{x}}} = A\tilde{\mathbf{x}}.$$

The matrix A containing the first derivatives evaluated at the fixed point is called the *Jacobian matrix*. Note that the derivatives in (6.16) are constant numbers, because they are evaluated at (x^*, y^*). The linearized system can then be treated like the linear system discussed earlier.

The linearized system is only an approximation of the original nonlinear system. The question is whether we make a significant mistake by ignoring the higher-order terms O in the Taylor series expansion. The answer is that it depends. First of all, it should be clear that the exact trajectories of the nonlinear system look different from those of the linearized system. In many cases, the stability of both systems is the same, so we can derive correct qualitative statements about the original system from the linearized one. However, there are some cases where the linearization goes wrong. This happens when at least one eigenvalue is zero or both eigenvalues are purely imaginary. These cases are exactly on the border between stability and instability. Above we called centers neutrally stable. If a trajectory slightly misses its origin after one cycle, we do not get a center, but a stable or unstable spiral.

6.2.4 Lotka–Volterra Population Models

The *Lotka–Volterra models,* based on the work of Alfred Lotka and Vito Volterra in the 1920s, play an important role in the theoretical modeling of population dynamics and are also useful in economics. In Sect. 6.2.1, we saw the Verhulst model of population growth, in which one species interacts with its environment. Alfred Lotka rediscovered the Verhulst model and called the logistic equation the *law of population growth*. The Lotka–Volterra models describe the interaction of two or more species and are therefore at least two-dimensional systems. The species can interact in different ways with one another, for instance as competitors for the same food or as predator and prey.

First, let us look at the *Lotka–Volterra model of competition*. Suppose that both species, e.g. rabbits x and sheep y, compete for the same food, e.g. grass. If only one species lived in the habitat, each would grow to its respective carrying capacity K or L according to the logistic equation. However, when the species share the same habitat, they inhibit each other through conflict and displacement. The Lotka-Volterra equations add negative competition terms py and qx, where p, $q > 0$, to the logistic equation for each species:

$$\dot{x} = rx\left(1 - \frac{x}{K} - py\right)$$
$$\dot{y} = sy\left(1 - \frac{y}{L} - qx\right).$$

In addition to the quadratic terms of the logistic equation, these equations contain the competitive interactions $-rxpy$ and $-syqx$ as another form of nonlinearity. The system has four fixed points (x^*, y^*): $(0, 0)$, $(K, 0)$, $(0, L)$, (x^c, y^c). This means that either no species exists, only one species or both at the inner equilibrium with $x^c = \frac{(1-pL)K}{1-pqLK}$ and $y^c = \frac{(1-qK)L}{1-pqLK}$. A stability analysis can tell us, which fixed point might be reached in the long run.

For simplicity, assume that the parameters are such that

$$\dot{x} = x(3 - x - 2y)$$
$$\dot{y} = y(2 - x - y).$$

These parameters imply that the rabbits x reproduce faster than the sheep y, but are also more negatively affected by the presence of the sheep, perhaps because the sheep are stronger than the rabbits. Linearizing the system yields the Jacobian

$$A = \begin{pmatrix} 3 - 2x - 2y & -2x \\ -y & 2 - x - 2y \end{pmatrix},$$

which we can use to evaluate the types of the four fixed points. Table 6.1 lists the eigenvalues of the fixed points. Using the classification scheme in Fig. 6.15, we conclude that (0,0) is an unstable node, because both eigenvalues are real and positive. In contrast, (3,0) and (0,2) are stable nodes, because both real eigenvalues are negative. The eigenvalues of the fixed point (1,1), where both species coexist are also real, with one positive and one negative. Therefore, (1,1) is a saddle point. Since we do not have any eigenvalues equal to zero or purely imaginary eigenvalues, the linearization does not cause any trouble here.

Combining the information about the fixed point, we can sketch the phase as shown in Fig. 6.16. The stable manifold of the saddle (or saddle path) separates the plane and is therefore called a *separatrix*. On the stable manifold, the system moves toward (1,1), but slightly above or below it, the system will converge toward one of the stable nodes (3,0) or (0,2). The gray shaded area is the basin of attraction of (3,0)

Table 6.1 Eigenvalues of the Jacobian matrix

Fixed point	Eigenvalue λ_1	Eigenvalue λ_2	Type of fixed point
(0,0)	3	2	Unstable node
(3,0)	-3	-1	Stable node
(0,2)	-2	-1	Stable node
(1,1)	$-1+\sqrt{2}$	$-1-\sqrt{2}$	Saddle point

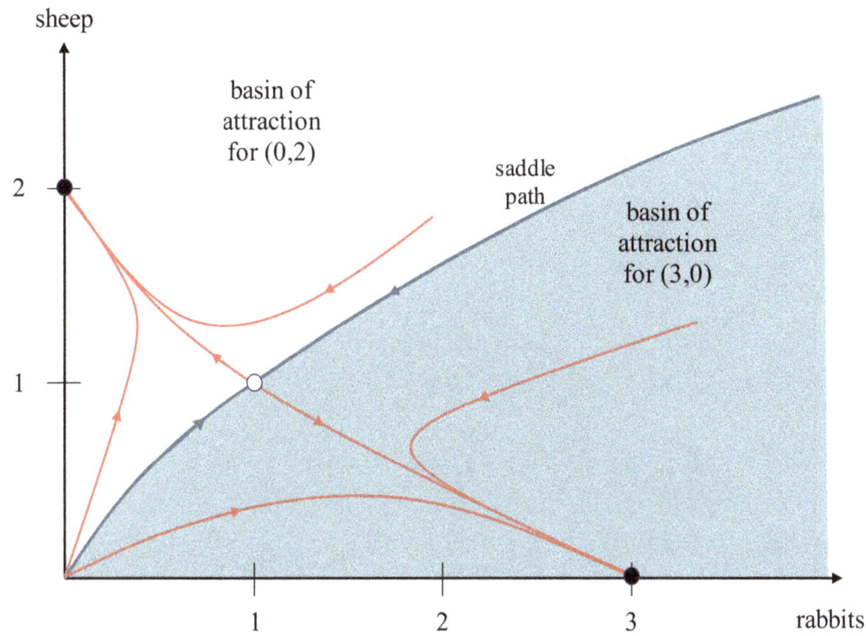

Fig. 6.16 Phase portrait of the competitive model. Source: Author

and the white area above the stable manifold is the basin of attraction for (0,2). We can hence conclude that the most likely outcome is that in the long run, the habitat will be populated in the long run by either sheep or by rabbits alone, although coexistence is possible. Coexistence is not robust to small shocks that drive the system into one of the two basins of attraction of the stable nodes.

Although the model is described as an ecological model, we can easily interpret it as an economic model. Imagine that the model describes the evolution of two industries that produce substitutes that compete in the same market. For example, x could be gasoline cars and y could be electric cars in the early twentieth century (see Fig. 6.17). You may recall from Chap. 5 that in the early 1900s, the market share of electric cars in the USA was larger than the market share of gasoline cars. This would correspond to a point near the origin but above the 45° line. If the stable manifold is concave and thus above the 45-degree line close to the origin, a larger initial market share of electric cars would still be compatible with gasoline cars being the only (or dominant) type of car in the long run. The basin of attraction of (3,0) has some trajectories above the 45-degree line if the stable manifold leaves the origin with a slope greater than 1. But even if the situation at the beginning of the twentieth century is best captured by a point on a trajectory in the white basin of attraction leading to the electric-only fixed point, a perturbation could have driven the system across the separatrix to another trajectory in the gray basin of attraction.

As we learned in Chap. 5, the entrepreneur Henry Ford introduced his popular Model T in 1908 which rapidly increased sales due to its very low cost. We could

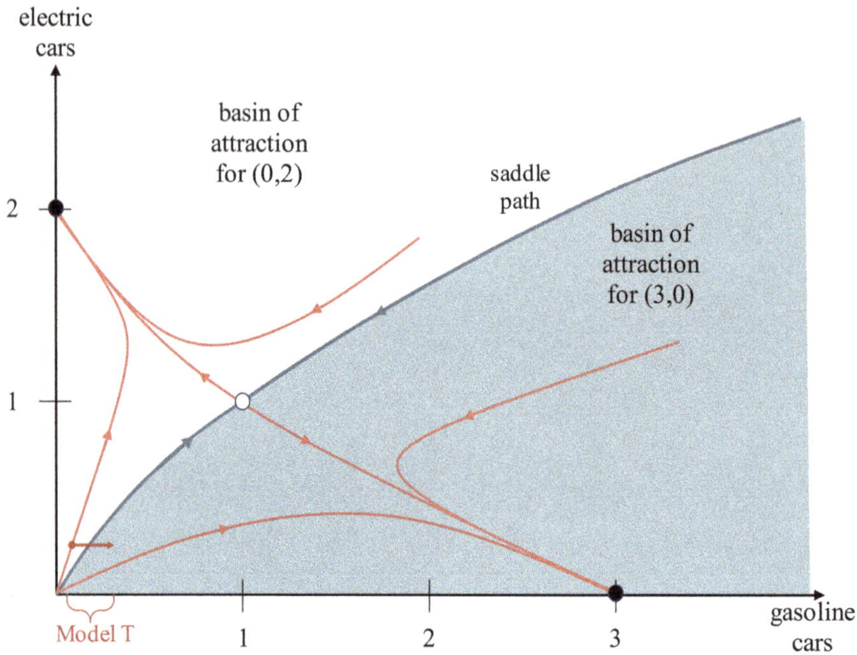

Fig. 6.17 The competition model applied to automobiles. Source: Author

interpret the introduction of the Model T either as a model change or as an exogenous shock leading to a jump from the basin of attraction of electric cars into the basin of attraction of gasoline cars. The message from complexity economics in the second interpretation would be that when trajectories of a dynamical system are close together (as it is the case near the origin in Fig. 6.17), a small exogenous shock (or event) can push the state of the system from one basin of attraction to another and thus have a significant long-term effect. An alternative way to model the introduction of the Model T would be to assume that the growth rate of gasoline car sales inceases due to lower costs, changing the differential equation of $x(t)$ to $\dot{x} = x(3.5 - x - 2y)$. In this case, the saddle point and the stable manifold would shift up and to the left to $(x^c, y^c) = (0.5, 1.5)$. This means that some initial points, which were previously in the white basin of attraction are now in the gray one after the change, without any shock to the state of the system $\mathbf{x}(t)$ itself.

The more familiar Lotka–Volterra model is the *predator–prey model*, where the growth of a prey x (e.g., rabbits) is constrained by a predator y (e.g., foxes) eating the prey. The simplest version of a predator–prey model is as follows:

$$\dot{x} = x(a - by)$$

$$\dot{y} = y(dx - c),$$

where a, b, c, and d are positive constants. In the absence of the predator, the prey population x grows exponentially at rate a. If there is no prey, the predator population y decays at rate c. b captures the predation rate and d is the growth rate of the predator population. The nonlinear interactions occur through $-bxy$ and dxy. It is easy to see that the system has two fixed points: $(0, 0)$ and $(c/d, a/b)$. The Jacobian is

$$A = \begin{pmatrix} a - by & -bx \\ dy & dx - c \end{pmatrix}.$$

The Jacobian tells us that (0,0) is a saddle with the real eigenvalues a and $-c$. The Jacobian matrix for the interior fixed point is

$$A = \begin{pmatrix} 0 & -bc/d \\ da/b & 0 \end{pmatrix}.$$

Since $TrA = 0$, $\det A = ac > 0$ and the discriminant $\Delta = -4ac < 0$, we can conclude that the fixed point $(c/d, a/b)$ is a neutrally stable center. However, we must be careful here, because we cannot rely on the stability analysis of the linearized system in the case of a center. Fortunately, there are other methods to prove that the fixed point is indeed a center. This can be done by using a *Lyapunov function* $F(x, y)$ of the system $\dot{x} = f(x, y), \dot{y} = g(x, y)$ for the fixed point $\mathbf{x}^*$. A Lyapunov function is a continuously differentiable, real-valued function with a minimum at the fixed point, i.e. $F(\mathbf{x}^*) = 0$ and $F(\mathbf{x}) > 0 \; \forall \, \mathbf{x} \neq \mathbf{x}^*$. The function describes the basin of attraction of the fixed point. Its time derivative is

$$\dot{F}(x, y) = \frac{\partial F(x, y)}{\partial x} f(x, y) + \frac{\partial F(x, y)}{\partial y} g(x, y).$$

This derivative describes the dynamics of the system relative to the fixed point. If $\dot{F}(x, y) > 0 \; \forall (x, y)$, then the fixed point is unstable and the state of system is moving away from it. If $\dot{F}(x, y) < 0 \; \forall (x, y)$, the the fixed point is stable, for $\dot{F}(x, y) = 0 \; \forall (x, y)$, the fixed point is neutrally stable (i.e., a center). If $\dot{F}(x, y) = 0 \; \forall (x, y)$, the state of the system in a sense "gets stuck" on its way to the fixed point. Unfortunately, there is no general rule for finding the Lyapunov function, but for the predator–prey model it is known to be

$$F(x, y) = dx - c \ln x + by - a \ln y,$$

whose derivative $\dot{F}(x, y) = 0$ for all (x, y). Hence, the interior fixed point is indeed a center. The motion on the closed orbit is counterclockwise. This can be seen by evaluating the Jacobian for all positive values on the x-axis and on the y-axis. A point on the positive part of the y-axis has a vector pointing straight down to the origin (which is a saddle point) and a point on the positive part of the x-axis has a vector pointing to the right along the axis. Therefore, the vectors in the positive quadrants near the origin will point down and to the right.

We will see the Goodwin model of the business cycle as an economic application of the predator–prey model later in this chapter.

6.2.5 Bifurcations

In complexity economics, nonlinear dynamical systems are interesting not only because of their dynamics, but also because these dynamics can change qualitatively when parameters of the system are varied. Qualitative change can mean that fixed points appear or disappear, or that their stability changes. We call such qualitative changes *bifurcations*, which occur when parameter values reach bifurcation points. Models with bifurcations are one way to model structural economic change that leads to new economic conditions, as discussed in Chaps. 4 and 5. To understand bifurcations, it is sufficient to consider one-dimensional dynamical systems, although they can also occur in higher-dimensional systems. We focus here on the simple one-variable case.

The most basic bifurcation is the *saddle-node bifurcation*, where a parameter variation can create or destroy fixed points. In Fig. 6.4, we saw that the system $\dot{x} = x^2 + r$ has two fixed points for $r = -1$. For any $r < 0$, there are two fixed points at $x^* = \pm\sqrt{-r}$, where the left one is a stable node and the right one is an unstable node. As the parameter r is increased, a bifurcation point is reached at $r = 0$ (see Fig. 6.18). The system $\dot{x} = x^2$ has only one fixed point at the origin instead of two. For $r = 0$, $x^* = 0$ is a saddle point, because it is half-stable: all $x < 0$ approach it and all $x > 0$ move away from it. If $r > 0$, even this fixed point disappears and $x \to \infty$ for all $x(0)$.

Bifurcations are often represented in *bifurcation diagrams* such as the one for the saddle-node bifurcation (or *fold bifurcation,* as it is also called) in Fig. 6.19. A bifurcation diagram plots the state of the system x against the control parameter r that can produce the bifurcation. Because x is the dependent variable, it is on the vertical axis in this diagram. Figure 6.19 shows that there is always an unstable fixed point and a stable fixed point for each $r < 0$, but no fixed points for $r > 0$.

Transcritical bifurcations occur for systems of the form $\dot{x} = rx - x^2 = rx(1 - x)$. Note that the logistic equation is a special case of this function with $x \geq 0$, $r > 0$. The logistic equation has an unstable fixed point at the origin and a stable fixed point $x^* > 0$, as shown in Fig. 6.20 (c). If $r \in \mathbb{R}$, there is a bifurcation point at $r = 0$, where

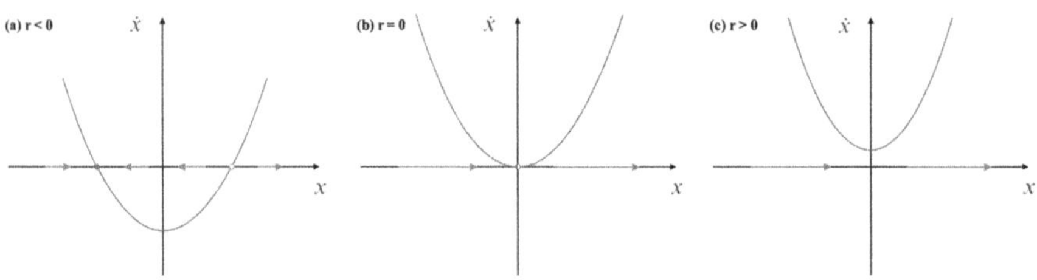

Fig. 6.18 Saddle-node bifurcation. Source: Author

Fig. 6.19 Bifurcation diagram of the saddle-node (or fold) bifurcation. Source: Author

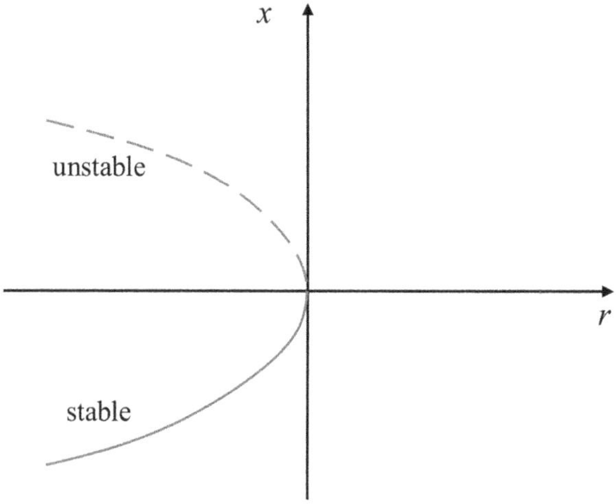

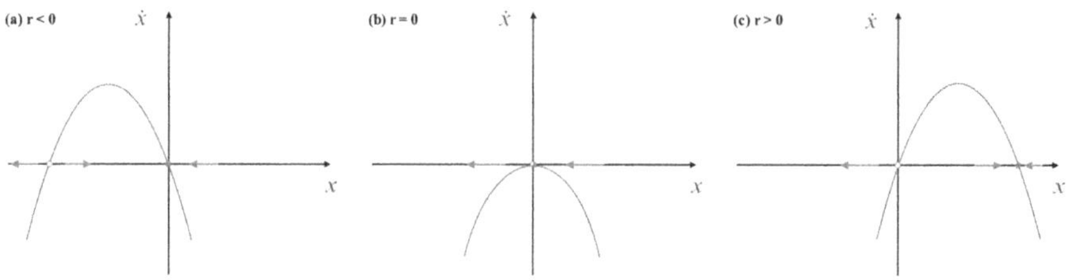

Fig. 6.20 Transcritical bifurcation. Source: Author

Fig. 6.21 Bifurcation diagram of the transcritical bifurcation. Source: Author

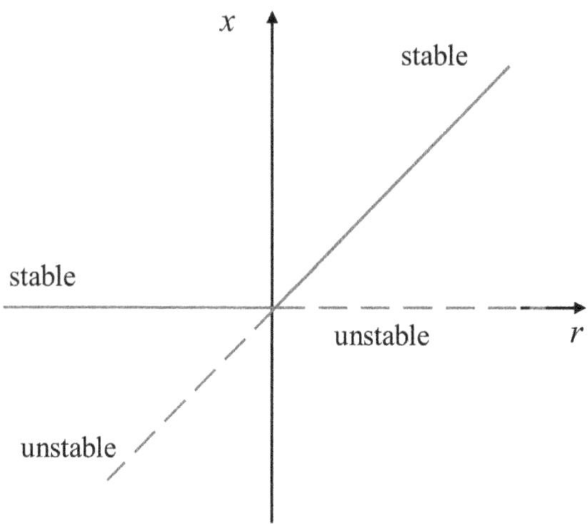

the system has a saddle point at the origin. The origin turns into a stable node for $r < 0$, where the unstable node is $x^* = r$.

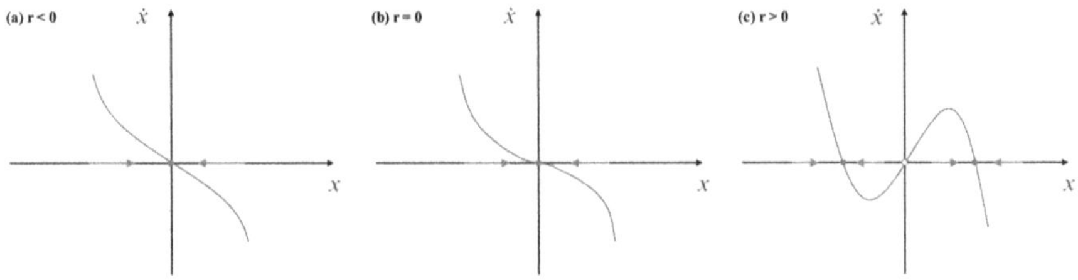

Fig. 6.22 Supercritical pitchfork bifurcation. Source: Author

Fig. 6.23 Bifurcation diagram of the supercritical pitchfork bifurcation. Source: Author

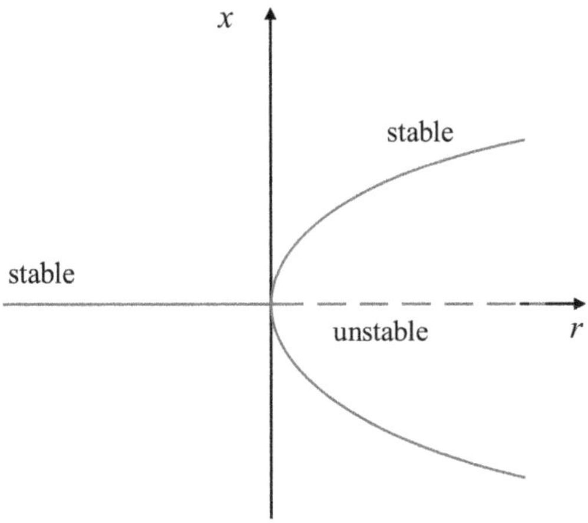

The bifurcation diagram is shown in Fig. 6.21. Note that unlike the saddle-node bifurcation, there are always two fixed points here, but their stability switches at the bifurcation point.

The pitchfork bifurcation occurs in two versions: as a *supercritical pitchfork bifurcation* $\dot{x} = rx - x^3$ and as a *subcritical pitchfork bifurcation* $\dot{x} = rx + x^3$. Let us look first at the supercritical pitchfork bifurcation (Fig. 6.22).

We can see that the system always has fixed point at the origin, which is stable for $r \leq 0$, but becomes unstable for $r > 0$. If the origin is an unstable fixed point, there are two symmetric stable fixed points on either side of the origin at $x^* = \pm\sqrt{r}$. Systems with supercritical pitchfork bifurcations are unpredictable in the sense that two opposite outcomes are possible after a structural change destabilizes the fixed point $x^* = 0$. After the bifurcation point, the state of the system is likely to move from the origin to one of the stable nodes, but it depends on a small random disturbance, which one will be reached. This is different from the transcritical bifurcation, where there is only one stable node (Fig. 6.23).

While the cases $r < 0$ and $r = 0$ seem quite similar, since both have a single stable node at the origin, there is an interesting difference. Notice that $\frac{d\dot{x}}{dx} = r - 3x^2$ with $\lim_{x \to 0} \frac{d\dot{x}}{dx} = r$. Thus, in the neighborhood of the origin, x changes exponentially if $r < 0$. However, as $r \to 0$, the rate of change approaches zero, i.e. changes become extremely slow. In other words, when the system is far away from the bifurcation point, any deviation from the stable fixed point will be quickly corrected, but the closer the system is to the bifurcation point, the slower the correction becomes. This phenomenon is called *critical slowing down*. In the applied literature, the appearance of critical slowing down is interpreted as an early warning signal of a critical transition (i.e., a bifurcation).

In the *subcritical pitchfork bifurcation* $\dot{x} = rx + x^3$ the functions in Fig. 6.22 are mirrored on the horizontal axis, resulting to the bifurcation diagram in Fig. 6.24. The subcritical bifurcation diagram is an inverted version of the supercritical bifurcation diagram. For $r < 0$ the stable fixed point at $x^* = 0$ has a basin of attraction between the two unstable fixed points $x^* = \pm\sqrt{-r}$. Passing the bifurcation point, the origin becomes an unstable fixed point. If $x(0)$ deviates from 0 in this case, it will diverge very fast, so that $+\infty$ or $-\infty$ is reached in finite time, which is called *blow-up*.

No blow-up occurs if the cubic term is counterbalanced by a higher-order term, as in this version of a system with a subcritical pitchfork bifurcation: $\dot{x} = rx + x^3 - x^5$.

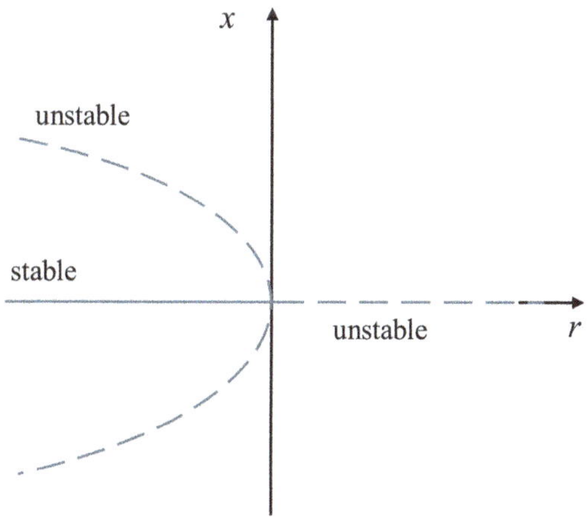

Fig. 6.24 Bifurcation diagram of the subcritical pitchfork bifurcation. Source: Author

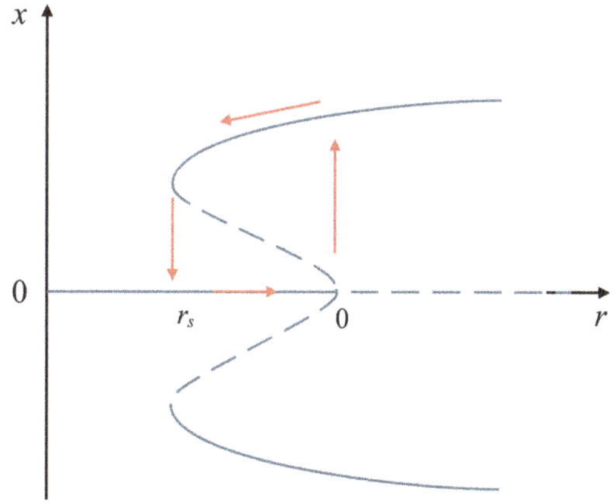

Fig. 6.25 Subcritical bifurcation with jumps and hysteresis. Source: Author

Figure 6.25 shows that the bifurcation has two stable branches for absolute values x beyond a certain threshold. This means that the system does not diverge to $\pm\infty$. Note that this bifurcation diagram has two critical values for r: $r^s < 0$ and $r = 0$. For $r < r^s$ there is only one stable fixed point $x^* = 0$ and for $r > 0$ there are two stable fixed points $0 < |x^*| < \infty$ on the large-amplitude branches of the bifurcation diagram. In the range $r^s < r < 0$, the system has two qualitatively different types of fixed points: $x^* = 0$ and $|x^*| \neq 0$. The unstable fixed point in between is the threshold that separates the basins of attraction. If $x(0)$ is absolutely small, the system converges to 0, otherwise to $|x^*| \neq 0$. This implies that the origin is only locally stable, but not globally. A large shock can drive the system permanently away from $x^* = 0$.

Another interesting property of this system is that *jumps* and *hysteresis* can occur. To see what this means, suppose the system is at x^* for some $r^s < r < 0$. If r increases slowly, nothing happens until $r = 0$ is reached. The fixed point remains locally stable against small deviations. But at $r = 0$ and beyond, $x^* = 0$ becomes unstable such that a small positive perturbation will cause the system to converge to $x^* > 0$, which we call a jump indicated by the upward-pointing arrow in Fig. 6.25. The remarkable feature of the system is that once the system has jumped to the high fixed point, it will stay there, even if r is reduced again. It will only jump back to $x^* = 0$ when r falls to r^s. At least within a certain range, changes in this system are *irreversible* in the sense that variations of the control parameter r around the bifurcation points do not have symmetric consequences. The permanence of qualitative changes in the state of the system is called *hysteresis*. In economics, hysteresis is typically associated with permanently higher unemployment after a recession, e.g. due to loss of skills, demotivation, or stigmatization of the unemployed. Subcritical bifurcations with jumps and hysteresis are also helpful in understanding the concept of *tipping elements* and *tipping points* discussed in the context of climate change and environmental degradation. Climate scientists warn us that once a certain threshold or tipping point of greenhouse gas concentration in the atmosphere (control parameter r) is crossed, the global equilibrium temperature (x^*) can jump to a much higher level due to positive feedback effects such as the melting of ice shields or the thawing of permafrost. Removing CO_2 from the atmosphere by negative emission technologies (called negative CO_2 emissions) will not bring the equilibrium temperature back to its old level.

As mentioned earlier, the simple one-dimensional cases can be generalized to higher-order systems. While in one-dimensional systems bifurcations can only affect fixed points and their stability, closed orbits in two-dimensional systems can also be affected by bifurcations. For instance, in a so-called *supercritical Hopf bifurcation*, a spiral can turn into a center at the bifurcation point.

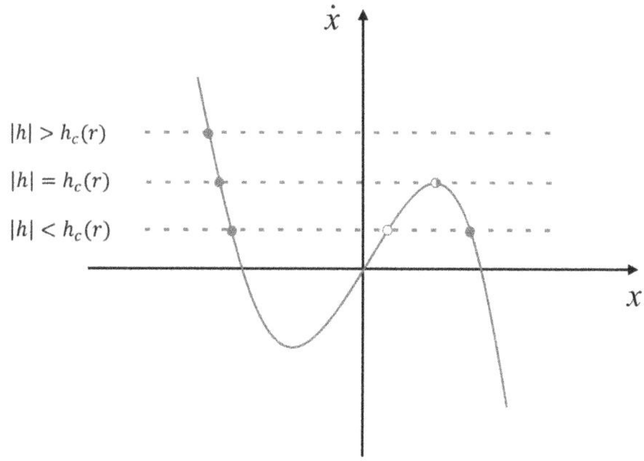

Fig. 6.26 Conditions for fixed points in an imperfect bifurcation. Source: Author

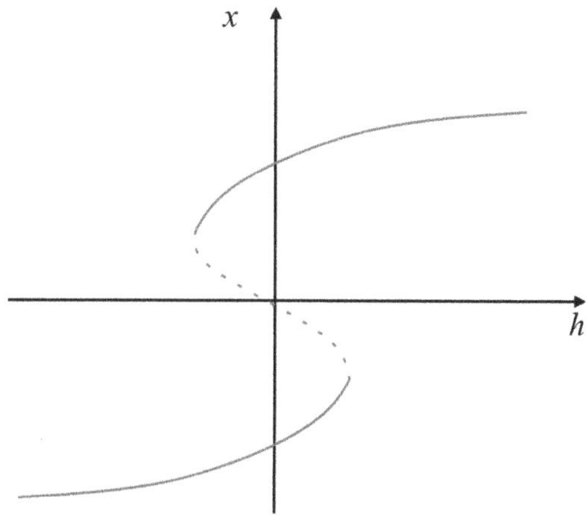

Fig. 6.27 Bifurcation as a function of h for fixed $\boldsymbol{r} > \mathbf{0}$. Source: Author

6.2.6 Catastrophes

Similar jumps and irreversibility as in Fig. 6.25 can occur with *imperfect bifurcations* and *catastrophes*, when a second (*imperfection*) parameter h is introduced, e.g. $\dot{x} = rx - x^3 + h$.

Catastrophe theory deals with systems of this type. To find the fixed points, for which $rx - x^3 = -h$ holds, we draw both sides of this equation in the same diagram as in Fig. 6.26, where we have assumed that $r > 0$. Depending on the value of the imperfection parameter h, there may be one, two, or three fixed points, for a constant $r > 0$. Two fixed points occur, when $|h|$ is tangent to the local minimum or maximum of $rx - x^3$, which is the case for $h_c(r) = \frac{2r}{3}\sqrt{\frac{r}{3}}$. For $|h| > h_c(r)$, the system has one stable fixed point, and for $|h| < h_c(r)$, there are two stable outer fixed points and one unstable fixed point in-between.

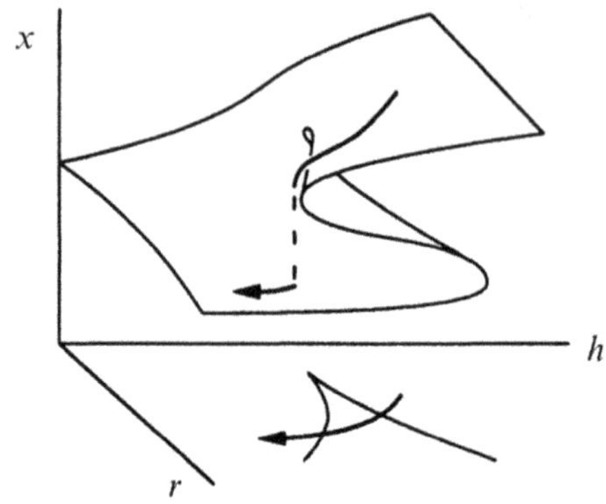

Fig. 6.28 Cusp catastrophe surface. Source: Strogatz (2019), reproduced with kind permission of Taylor & Francis Group LLC

This is shown in the bifurcation diagram in Fig. 6.27. Similar to Fig. 6.25, a jump from the stable fixed point $x^* > 0$ to $x^* < 0$ occurs when the bifurcation point $h = -h_c(r)$ is passed from the right.

So far, we have only considered different values of the imperfection parameter h, with r fixed at a positive value. However, the fixed points of the system depend on both parameters, as shown in the three-dimensional diagram in Fig. 6.28. To understand this *cusp catastrophe surface*, let us focus first on the $h - r$-plane. If r is large enough (more precisely if $r > 0$), we obtain a region defined by the lines $-h_c(r)$ and $+h_c(r)$. As we saw above, the system has three fixed points inside this region and only one fixed point outside. These two lines meet at $r = 0$, resulting in $h_c(0) = 0$. This point is called a *cusp point*. The cusp point occurs, because a supercritical pitchfork bifurcation occurs at $r = 0$ as in Fig. 6.22b. For $r \leq 0$, there can be only one stable fixed point, regardless of the value of h, $rx - x^3$ has no local extrema in this case.

The arrow represents a situation where we start with a high value of h for a given value of r resulting in a single high fixed point of x. Lowering h (for the given r) brings the system first into the region of three fixed points and then in the region of one fixed point again. As argued with reference to Fig. 6.27, lowering h leads to a jump of x, which is called a *catastrophe* in this type of system. The three-dimensional picture in Fig. 6.28 illustrates how a catastrophe occurs. The surface shows all the fixed points of the system as a function of the two parameters. The region in the $h - r$-plane that we discussed earlier is the projection of this surface into the two-dimensional plane. The surface of fixed points of this system is folded, which creates edges of the upper and lower part of the surface. A catastrophe occurs, if, for example, the system starts at a fixed point on the upper part of the surface and then moves toward the upper edge because of a reduction of the parameter h. If the reduction is large enough, the system state is driven over the edge and drops discontinuously to the lower part of the surface. The term catastrophe is meant to capture this discontinuity of the equilibrium state of the system.

6.2.7 Iterated Maps

So far, we have treated time as continuous, but sometimes it is more convenient to work with discrete-time dynamical systems modeled with iterated maps (or difference equations). Especially when we work with computers, treating time as discrete is quite natural. In many economic applications, discrete time is more appropriate than continuous time for describing processes. In general, we do not make shopping decisions at every moment, and firms' decisions to invest or hire are also made in discrete time. Although iterated maps can look very similar to their continuous-time counterparts, their behavior can be very different.

The *logistic map* is a famous example of the rich dynamics of simple one-dimensional discrete-time systems. The logistic map has bifurcations and can generate chaos, which is not possible in continuous-time systems with less than three dimensions. The complex behavior of the logistic map is a warning that we should not naively approximate discrete-time systems with differential equations.

To get an idea of how to work with iterated maps, we start with the linear case again:

$$x_{t+1} = f(x_t) = a + bx_t. \tag{6.17}$$

Similar to the phase portraits we used for the continuous-time systems, we can represent iterated maps graphically as shown in Fig. 6.29. We plot x_{t+1} on the vertical axis against x_t on the horizontal axis and assume that $a > 0$, $0 < b < 1$. The 45-degree line represents the condition $x_{t+1} = x_t$, which is the condition for a fixed point x^* implying no change. The arrows in Fig. 6.29 show a *cobweb* or *cobweb plot* that illustrates how the system evolves over time. If we start with the initial value x_0, the value in the next period x_1 is given by $f(x_0)$, which is above the 45-degree line. Hence, x_1 is greater than x_0 as indicated by the arrow mapping $f(x_0)$ to the 45-degree

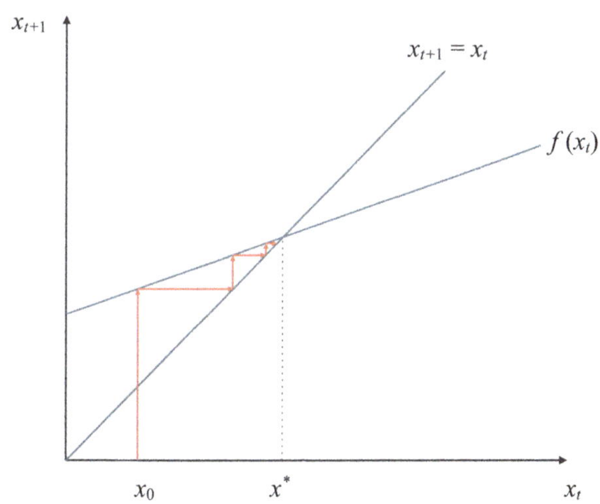

Fig. 6.29 Linear iterated map with stable fixed point. Source: Author

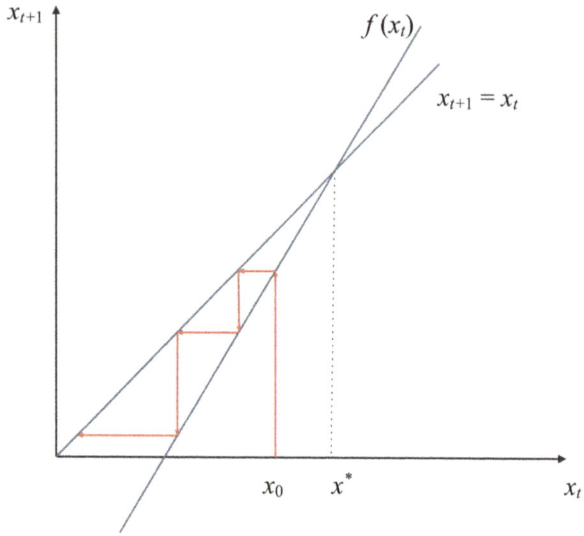

Fig. 6.30 Linear iterated map with unstable fixed point. Source: Author

line to the right of x_0. From there, we move up again to $f(x_1) = x_2$ and so on. We see that the x_t converges over time to $x^* = \frac{a}{1-b}$. While the figure only shows this for an initial value smaller than the value of the fixed point, the same reasoning applies to initial values to the right of x^*, so the fixed point is stable.

If we assume $a < 0$, $b > 1$, then the situation is different (see Fig. 6.30). In this case, the map $f(.)$ is steeper than the 45-degree line and intersects it from below. Analogous to Fig. 6.3, where the graph of the differential equation intersects the x-axis (where $\dot{x} = 0$) from below, we obtain an unstable fixed point. The cobweb plot shows that initial values $x_0 < x^*$ lead to decreasing values of x, while initial values $x_0 > x^*$ would lead to divergence, $x_t \to \infty$ for $t \to \infty$.

In the simple market model presented in Chap. 4 (Eqs. 4.1, 4.2, and 4.3), we assumed that expectations are formed rationally (Eq. 4.5). An alternative assumption about expectation formation, which has some empirical support, is that $P_t^e = P_{t-1}$, i.e. agents expect that the price in the next period t will be equal to the observed price in period $t - 1$. Thus, agents assume that the price does not change, so these expectations are called *static expectations*. With this assumption, the price in market equilibrium evolved according to

$$P_{t+1} = f(P_t) = \frac{d_0 - s_0}{d_1} - \frac{s_1}{d_1} P_t - \frac{1}{d_1} \varepsilon_{t+1}.$$

Ignoring the stochastic shock, the market price would evolve as shown in Fig. 6.31. Starting at $P_0 < P^*$, the price would jump up to $P_1 > P^*$ in the next period, then to $P_2 < P^*$ and so on. Since the quantity demanded is a function of the market price, the quantity in equilibrium in each period has similar dynamics. The cyclical over- and undershooting relative to the steady state is called the *hog cycle* (or *pork cycle*), because it was documented for hog markets as early as the 1920s.

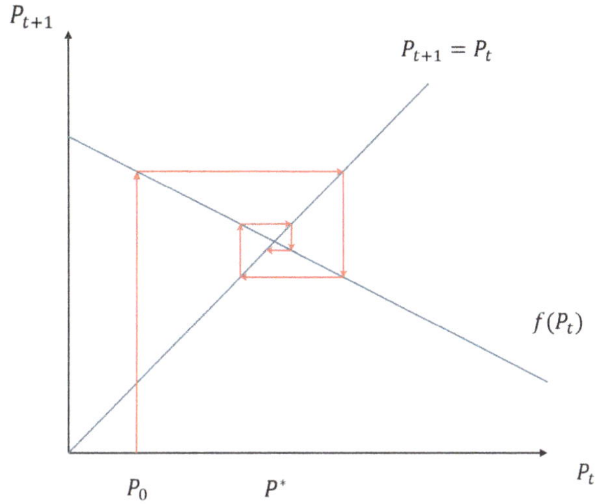

Fig. 6.31 Prices in a hog cycle. Source: Author

Nicholas Kaldor coined the term cobweb theorem in 1934 for this kind of discontinuous dynamics in markets, showing that prices either converge to the fixed point as in Fig. 6.31, or diverge, if the slope of $f(P_t)$ is large in absolute terms, in our case $\frac{s_1}{d_1} > 1$. In general, the fixed point is stable if the elasticity of demand is greater than the elasticity of supply. In the opposite case, it is unstable. When both elasticities are equal, the amplitude of the fluctuations is constant, so that the price constantly alternates between the same high and low value, which is called a *2-cycle*. Hog cycles occur in markets when there is time lag in production and expectations are formed in a backward-looking way. In addition to agricultural markets, they also appear in labor markets, housing markets, and commodity markets.

6.2.8 Logistic Map and Chaos

The discrete-time logistic map looks a lot like the continuous-time logistic Eq. (6.9) we saw earlier:

$$x_{t+1} = rx_t(1 - x_t). \tag{6.18}$$

The variable x_t must be non-negative, which means $0 \leq x_t \leq 1$, and the control parameter is restricted to $0 \leq r \leq 4$. The graph of the logistic map is a parabola with its maximum at $\left(0.5, \frac{r}{4}\right)$, as shown in Fig. 6.32. The logistic map always has the rather uninteresting fixed point $x^* = 0$. For $r < 1$, this is the only fixed point, because the graph of the logistic map is always below the 45-degree line resulting in a cobweb plot similar to the one in Fig. 6.29. Therefore, the origin is stable when it is the only fixed point. For $1 < r \leq 2$, the graph of the logistic map intersects the 45-degree line between 0 and 0.5. It is easy to calculate that this new fixed point is $x^* = \frac{r-1}{r}$.

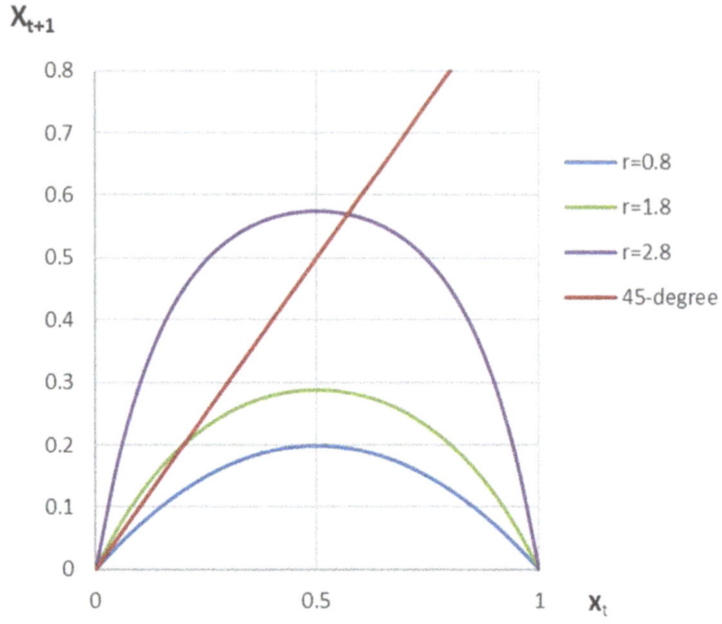

Fig. 6.32 Graph of the logistic map. Source: Author

Drawing the cobweb plots can help us to determine the stability of the inner fixed point and the dynamics of the system. We may guess that for $1 < r < 2$, the fixed point is stable with direct convergence to is similar to the dynamics in Fig. 6.27, because the map intersects the 45-degree line from above with a positive slope. Similar to Fig. 6.31, the map in Fig. 6.32 crosses the 45-degree line from above with a negative slope for $r = 2.8$. Therefore, we might expect oscillations as in the pork cycle.

In fact, the time series graph with the initial value $x_0 = 0.3$ in Fig. 6.33 demonstrates that these conjectures are correct. Since time is discrete, only the dots are meaningful, but for convenience they are connected by lines. For any initial value, the system converges to the fixed point $x^* = \frac{r-1}{r}$, if $1 < r < 3$, either monotonously ($1 < r < 2$) or with oscillations ($2 < r < 3$).

However, the logistic map is not so interesting, because of the different ways in which it approaches the stable fixed point. Instead, it is so fascinating because of the bifurcations that occur for $3 < r < 4$, as shown in the *orbit diagram* in Fig. 6.34.

According to Fig. 6.34, a qualitative change occurs at $r = 3$. Between 3 and 3.44 the diagram looks like a supercritical pitchfork bifurcation, but the two branches do not indicate two different fixed points, but a 2-cycle (or period-2 cycle). From any initial value, the system converges to a state where x alternates between $x^*_{1,2} = \frac{r+1 \pm \sqrt{(r-3)(r+1)}}{2r}$ (see Fig. 6.35), which is similar to the closed orbits we saw in the subsection on two-dimensional continuous-time systems.

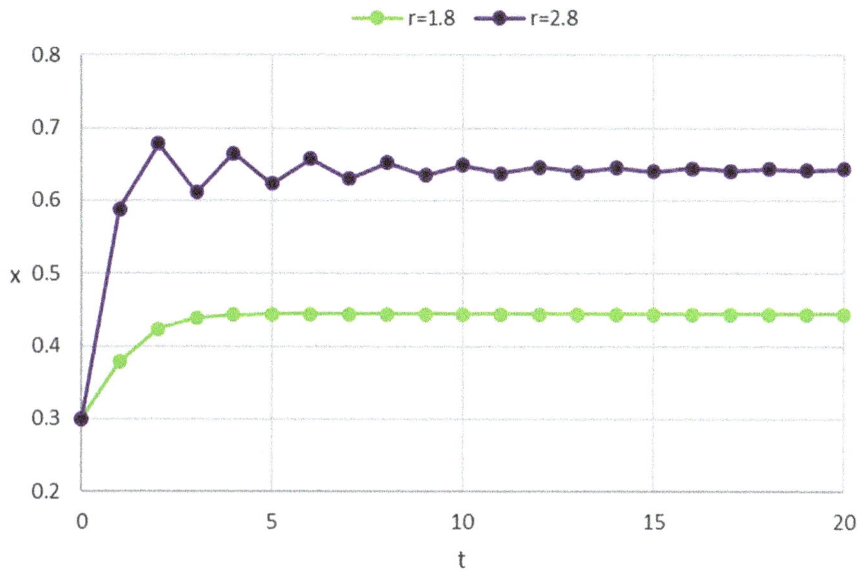

Fig. 6.33 Dynamics of the logistic map for $1 < r < 3$. Source: Author

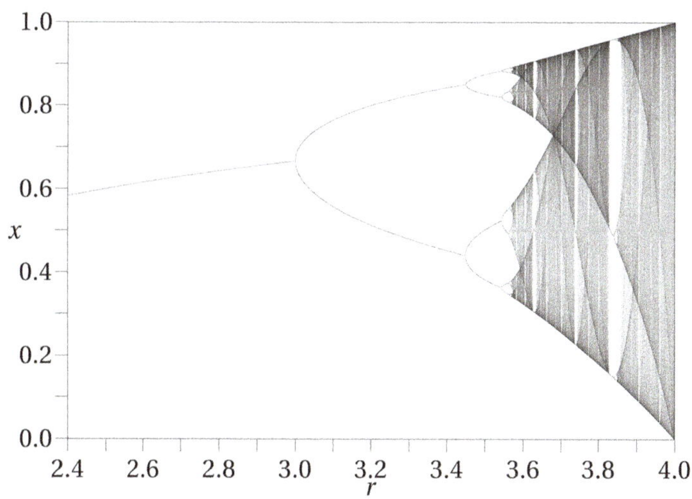

Fig. 6.34 Orbit diagram of the logistic map. Source: Pierce (2011), public domain

A bifurcation where the change of the control parameter converts a stable fixed point into a periodic behavior is called a *flip bifurcation* or *period-doubling bifurcation*. Strictly speaking, the system also has an unstable fixed point, but this fixed point will only be reached if the system starts there. The cobweb of the 2-cycle is shown in Fig. 6.36.

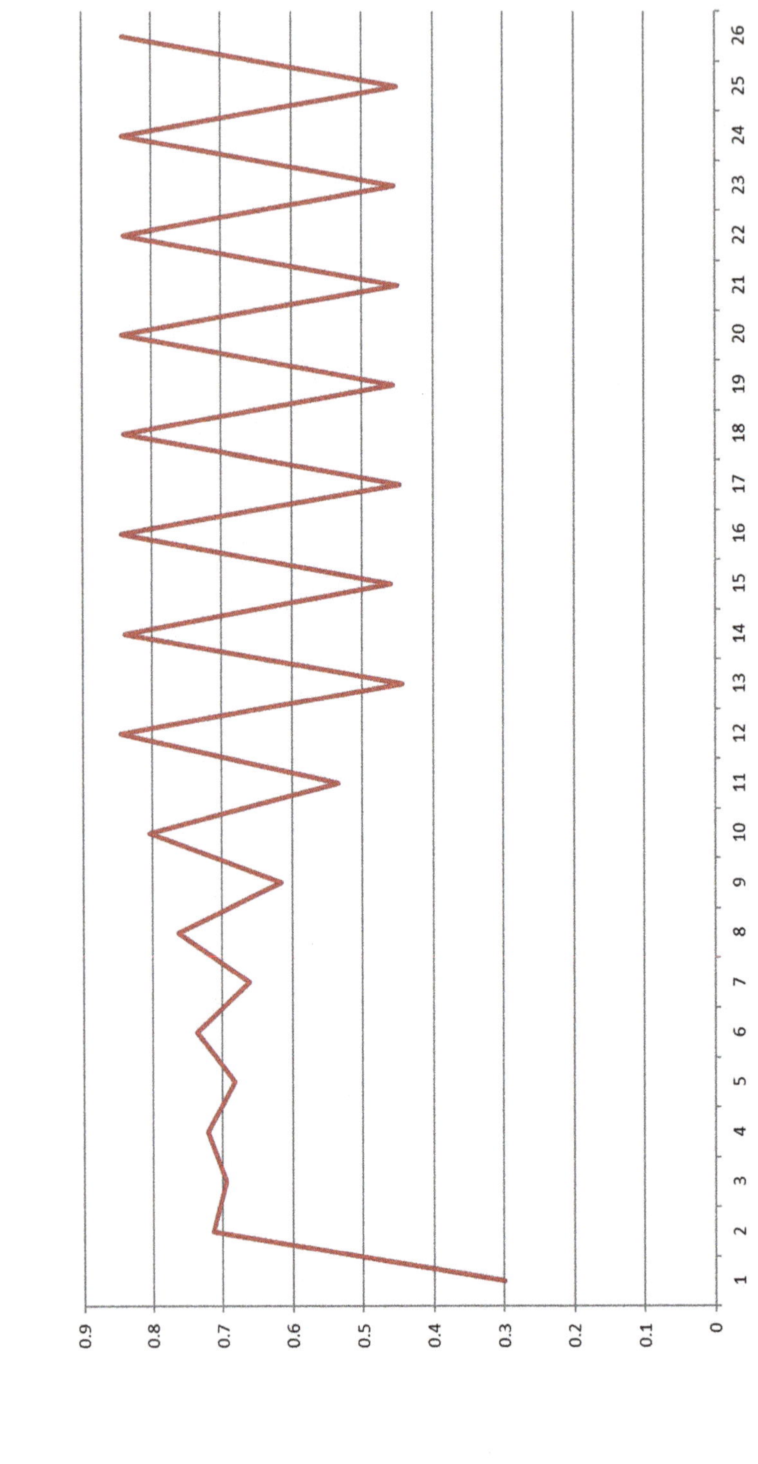

Fig. 6.35 Time series of the logistic map for $\boldsymbol{r} = \mathbf{3.4}$. Source: Author

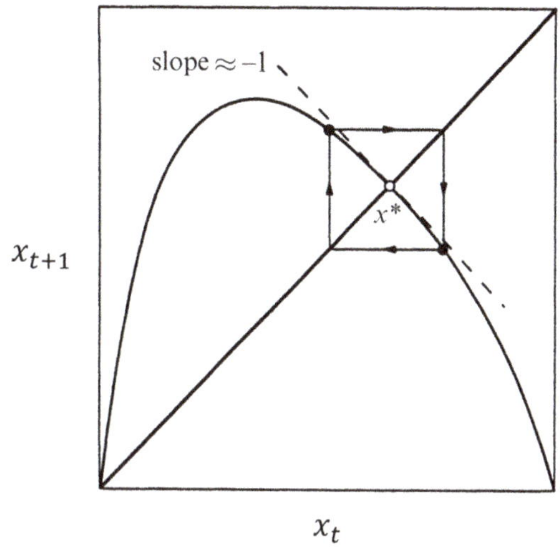

Fig. 6.36 2-cycle in the logistic map. Source: Strogatz (2019), reproduced with kind permission of Taylor & Francis Group LLC

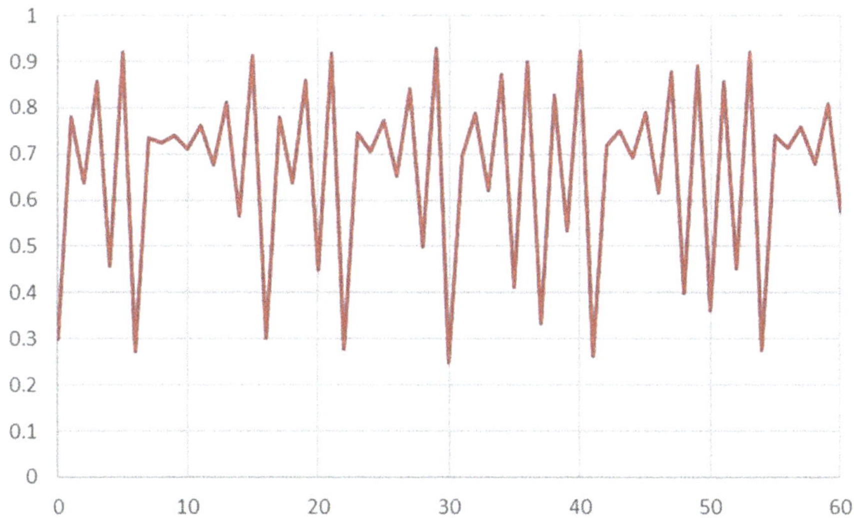

Fig. 6.37 Chaotic behavior for $\boldsymbol{r} = \mathbf{3.71}$. Source: Author

We can see in Fig. 6.34 that there are more period-doublings, leading to 4-cycles, 8-cycles, and so on, i.e. 2^n-cycles in general. The bifurcation value for the 4-cycle (2^2-cycle) starts is $r_2 = 3.449\ldots.$ At $r_3 = 3.54409\ldots$a 2^3-cycle starts and $r_4 = 3.5644\ldots$ is the bifurcation point for a 2^4-cycle.

A very interesting bifurcation occurs at $r_\infty = 3.569946\ldots.$ In Fig. 6.34, it is not easy to see what happens after this point. The answer is that for many values of r (but not for all), *chaos* sets in. Chaos means that the long-term behavior of the system is

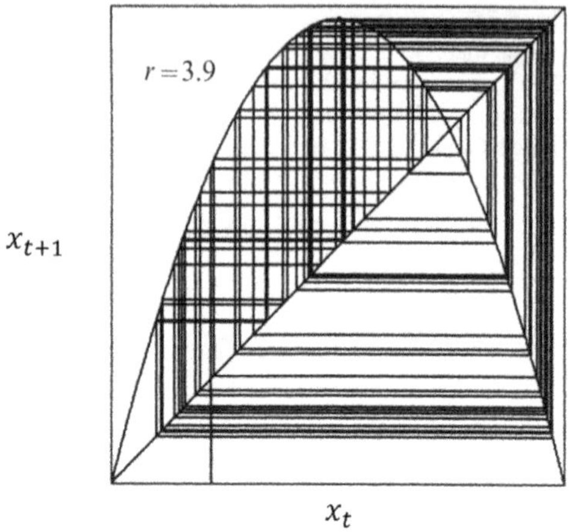

Fig. 6.38 Cobweb diagram of the logistic map for $r = 3.9$. Source: Strogatz (2019), reproduced with kind permission of Taylor & Francis Group LLC

aperiodic, i.e. the system does not converge to a fixed point or a periodic orbit (a 2^n-cycle).

Figure 6.37 shows the time series of x_t for $r = 3.71$. The time series looks random, but it is completely deterministic. There are no repeating patterns, even if we compute the time series for many more iterations. The cobweb diagram in Fig. 6.38 reveals that there is no systematic pattern in the long-term dynamics of the system.

The existence of chaos is important, because it offers a perspective on the economy that is fundamentally different from the mainstream approach. As we saw in Chap. 4 (Fig. 4.2), the conventional equilibrium modeling approach in mainstream economics is to add stochastic shocks to a variable in order to generate real-looking fluctuations. This means that the driver of the dynamics is exogenous and not explained in the model. The alternative of nonlinear modeling, which results in chaotic behavior of a variable, endogenizes the dynamics. The logistic map generates all dynamics by itself; no exogeneous shocks are needed!

The logistic map offers another important lesson to economists. Chaotic variables are unpredictable not only due to the absence of patterns. They are also unpredictable because of their *sensitivity to initial conditions*. Figure 6.39 shows two time series of the logistic map for $r = 3.71$. The two sequences have almost identical initial values: $x_0 = 0.3$ (red time series) and $y_0 = 0.3001$ (blue time series), i.e., y_0 differs from x_0 by 0.033%. In the first ten iteration steps, we can hardly detect any difference in the time series, but over time they look quite different. For example, after 30 steps, we have $x_{30} = 0.2494$ and $y_{30} = 0.6945$, which differ by a factor of 2.78. Small differences at the beginning of the iterations can accumulate in chaotic systems and lead to significant deviations of the system's states over time. If a system is chaotic, even the smallest measurement error in the present will cause dramatic mispredictions in the medium and long term. Sensitivity to initial conditions is also known as the *butterfly effect*. To summarize, chaos can be defined as "aperiodic

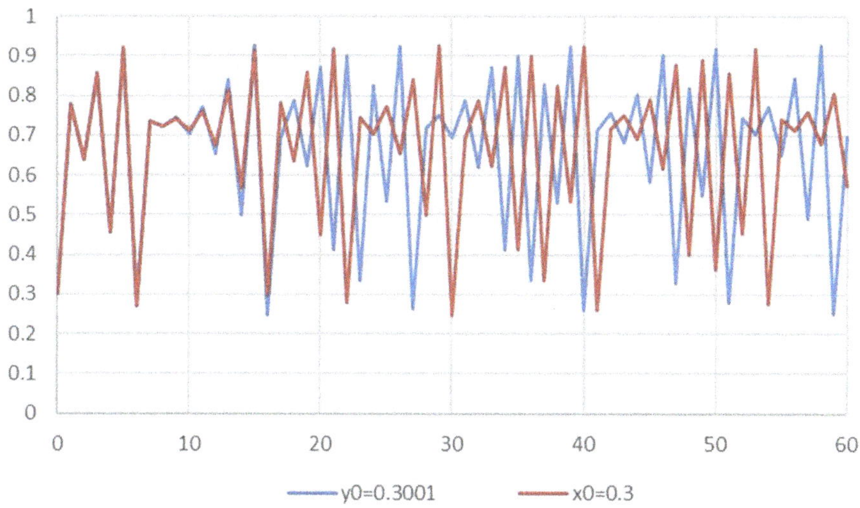

Fig. 6.39 Sensitivity to initial conditions. Source: Author

long-term behavior in a deterministic system that exhibits sensitive dependence on initial conditions" (Strogatz 2019, p. 331).

The logistic map may not be directly relevant to economics, since most interesting economic systems cannot be adequately described by a single variable. Nevertheless, the logistic map has an immense didactic value, since it proves that even very simple one-dimensional systems can have very complex dynamics. Its main lesson for economics should be the awareness that it does not take much to generate complications such as bifurcations, periodic oscillations, chaos, and sensitivity to initial conditions. If even one-variable nonlinear systems can produce these features, things are likely to be much more complex in higher-dimensional nonlinear systems. Continuous-time systems are somewhat tamer than discrete-time systems, but chaos can also occur in continuous-time systems with more than two variables.

6.2.9 Lyapunov Exponent

Sensitive dependence in initial conditions is a property of chaos. In Fig. 6.39, we saw an example of what this means: Very small differences in initial conditions lead to time series that become more and more different over time. While examples are good for a heuristic understanding, research requires more formal criteria. The *Lyapunov exponent* is a formal tool to define the sensitivity to initial conditions and thus to determine whether a system might be chaotic or not.

Let us consider two trajectories in the phase space of a continuous-time dynamical system, as shown in Fig. 6.40. Initially, the trajectories are close together, i.e. the distance at time 0, $||\delta(0)||$, is very small. If the two trajectories diverge, the

Fig. **6.40** Diverging trajectories. Source: Wikipedia Commons, Yapparina (2015), public domain

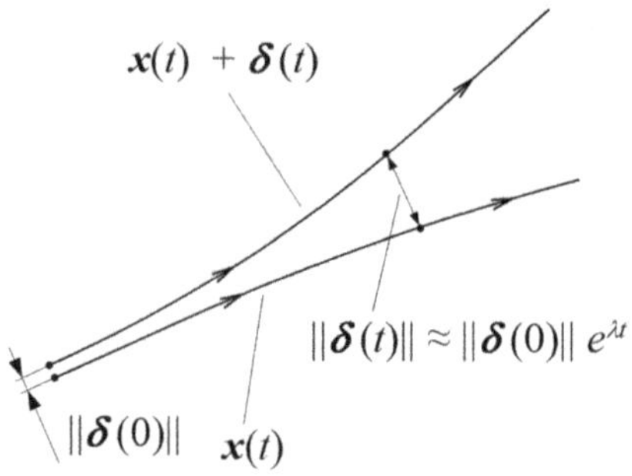

distance $\delta(t)$ between them becomes larger over time. The separation approximately grows exponentially with a given rate

$$\|\delta(t)\| \approx \|\delta(0)\| e^{\lambda t}. \tag{6.19}$$

The separation rate λ is often called the Lyapunov exponent, although this use of the term is imprecise. In a system with n dimensions, two trajectories typically separate not only in one direction, but in all n dimensions, usually at different speeds. Therefore, there is not just one Lyapunov exponent, but a spectrum of n Lyapunov exponents. If the considered time horizon is large, the divergence of two trajectories is governed by the largest of these Lyapunov exponents. Thus, when we speak of *the* Lyapunov exponent λ, we mean the maximum Lyapunov exponent in the entire spectrum. In addition, λ depends in principle on the trajectories and on the initial values. If the trajectories are very close together ($\lim\|\delta(0)\| \to 0$) and the initial values are in the basin of attraction of a given attractor, λ is the same for all $x(0)$. From (6.19), we get $\lambda = \lim_{t\to\infty} \frac{1}{t} \ln\left|\frac{\delta(t)}{\delta(0)}\right|$. It can be shown that in discrete-time systems, the Lyapunov exponent for an orbit starting at x_0 is given by

$$\lambda = \lim_{t\to\infty} \frac{1}{t} \sum_{i=0}^{t-1} \ln|f'(x_i)|. \tag{6.20}$$

The analytical solution of (6.20) can only be found in some cases. Often we have to compute the Lyapunov exponent numerically. If $\lambda < 0$, the distance between two trajectories does not grow with time, but shrinks. This means that the system has a fixed point or a stable periodic orbit, to which two initially close starting values converge. Sensitivity to initial conditions—which is one aspect of chaos—means that the distance between points on two trajectories grows, hence $\lambda > 0$. Note that we focus on the Lyapunov exponent of an attractor, i.e. even with a positive Lyapunov exponent the states of the system remain bounded. The inverse of the Lyapunov exponent, $\frac{1}{\lambda}$, is sometimes called *Lyapunov time*, after which predictability breaks down, because the distance between two trajectories becomes too large. There are empirical methods for estimating the Lyapunov exponent from time series data. These methods can be used to detect nonlinearities in the data and to test, whether the data is random or chaotic.

6.3 Business Cycles and Financial Instability

6.3.1 The Goodwin Model of Business Cycles

One of the central issues in macroeconomics is to explain, why economic activity fluctuates in the short run. There are different definitions of the business cycle, but a useful heuristic definition is that the business cycle consists of a sequence of periods (typically quarters) in which output is above the long-term trend (expansion or boom), followed by periods below the trend (contraction or recession). The estimated long-run trend level of output is often referred to as *potential output,* Y_t^{pot}, and the difference between actual output and potential output is the *output gap*: $\tilde{Y}_t = Y_t - Y_t^{pot}$. Figure 6.41 shows the U.S. output gap in percentage terms from 1949 to 2015. It is obvious that the output gap fluctuates over time, with some deep negative spikes corresponding to the official U.S. recessions, indicated by the shaded areas.

There are two fundamentally different approaches to explaining the phenomenon of the business cycle in the macroeconomic literature. The current mainstream approach assumes a theoretical framework in which output naturally equilibrates to potential output. The observed deviations are assumed to be caused by exogenous shocks to various variables of the macroeconomic system, such as technology shocks to output, preference shocks affecting aggregate demand, or money and price shocks. Formally, the framework typically uses linear or linearized equations with additive stochastic shocks that lead to temporary deviations from the system's stable equilibrium, as we saw it in Chap. 4. In this framework, the fluctuations are mainly "explained" by the occurrence of the shocks that are exogenous to the system.

The alternative approach postulates that the economic system generates fluctuations endogenously, even in the absence of external shocks. These models,

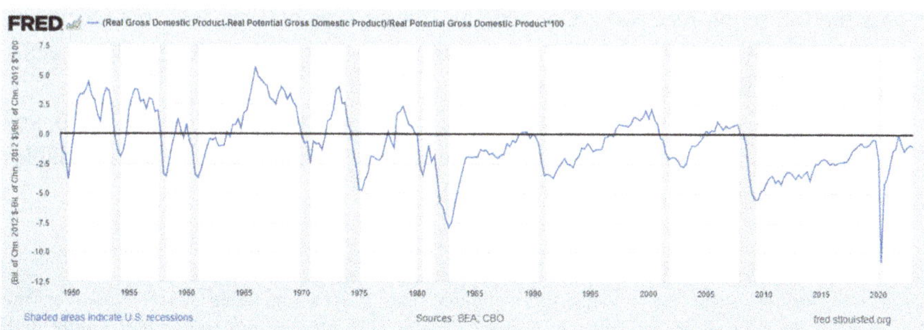

Fig. 6.41 Output gap in the United States. Source: Federal Reserve Bank of St. Louis

which are typically not part of the neoclassical mainstream, assume that the dynamics of the macroeconomic system are driven by nonlinearities.

Goodwin (1967) proposed a model in which changes in output and the macroeconomic income distribution between workers and capitalists generate endogenous business cycles. The Goodwin model is in a Marxian spirit and well-known in the Post-Keynesian community. There is an intense debate in the Post-Keynesian literature as to whether aggregate demand is *wage-led* or *profit-led,* i.e. whether demand rises with an increasing wage share or an increasing profit share. The Goodwin model assumes that demand is profit-led. Formally, the model is identical to the Lotka–Volterra predator–prey model. In the Goodwin model, output is the prey, which, according to the profit squeeze theory, is "eaten up" by the predator's wage share.

In its simplest version (see Stockhammer and Michell 2017), the Goodwin model consists of two differential equations for the change in output y and the macroeconomic wage share w:

$$\dot{y}=y(1-w) \tag{6.21}$$

$$\dot{w}=w(-c+ry) \tag{6.22}$$

The parameters c and r are positive. According to the first equation, output falls when the wage share rises, which corresponds to a fall in the profit share. The so-called profit squeeze theory assumes that investment, which drives the change in output through capital accumulation, is mainly driven by profits. Thus, a lower profit share leads to less investment and a decline in the rate of output growth. The second equation assumes that the wage share rises as output rises. The idea behind this assumption is that workers' bargaining power depends on the level of unemployment which is inversely related to output. When output is high, unemployment is low and workers are strong enough to bargain for rising wages. The opposite effect that high unemployment weakens the labor's bargaining power is sometimes called the reserve army effect.

Note that the nonlinearity of this model is multiplicative. In both equations, the term $y \cdot w$ drives the dynamics. If both variables are high in a boom, the product will be large with a strong positive effect on $\dot{w}$ and the opposite on $\dot{y}$. Thus, a boom breeds the following recession. Conversely, if both variables are low in a recession, wage growth will be very low or even negative and the profit squeeze will be weak, paving the way for an economic recovery.

It is easy to check that the model has two fixed points: $y^* = w^* = 0$ and $y^* = \frac{c}{r}, w^* = 1$. Figure 6.42 shows the phase portrait of the model. If both variables are non-zero, then the *nullclines* of the model are:

[3]Note that, strictly speaking, a wage share greater than 1 does not make sense. However, the dynamics of the model are the same in a more realistic, but also more complicated model with nonlinear transformations of the equations that ensure that the variables remain in the interval [0,1]. See Desai et al. (2006) for details.

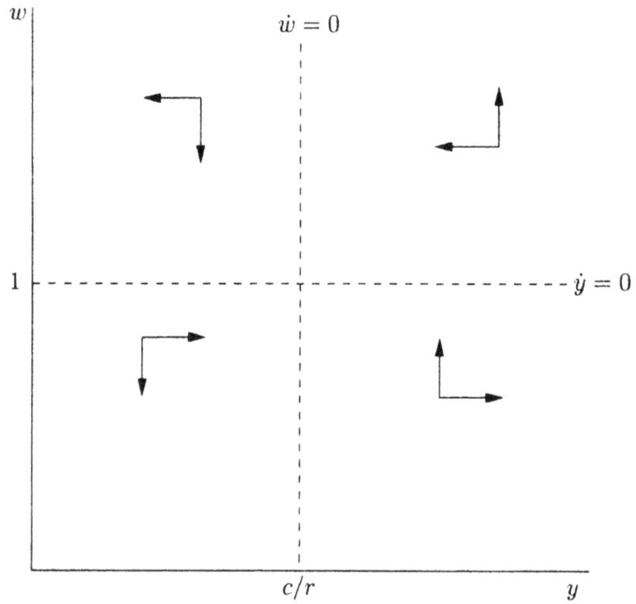

Fig. 6.42 Phase portrait of the Goodwin model. Source: Stockhammer and Michell (2017), reproduced with kind permission of Oxford University Press

$$\dot{y} = 0 \Leftrightarrow w = 1$$

$$\dot{w} = 0 \Leftrightarrow y = \frac{c}{r}$$

If $w > 1$, output will contract,[3] i.e., $\dot{y} < 1$, so that the arrows describing the dynamics of y point to the left above the w-nullcline and to the right below it. Similarly, if $y > \frac{c}{r}$, the wage share will grow, $\dot{w} > 0$, indicated by the upward-pointing arrows to the right of the y-nullcline. The phase diagram thus shows that the dynamics of the model are counterclockwise. We already know that the non-zero fixed point is a center, which means that output and the wage share move on a stable orbit around the fixed point, if the economy is not already at the fixed point.

Figure 6.43 shows the movements of output and the wage share over time (panel (a)) and in the $w - y$-space (panel (b)). In this example, $c = 0, 9$, $r = 0.95$ and the initial values are $y_0 = 0.7$, $w_0 = 0.7$. The economy starts at the end of a recession, where the output minimum of about 0.6 has already been passed, but the wage share is still falling. The wage share continues to fall for a few periods until it reaches its minimum slightly above 0.6, and then starts to grow again. In the expansionary phase, both variables grow until the wage share becomes too large and stifles output growth. This is the upper turning point of the cycle, marking the end of the expansion or boom phase. In the subsequent contraction, the wage share continues to grow for some time until it also reaches a turning point. The model thus predicts a stable

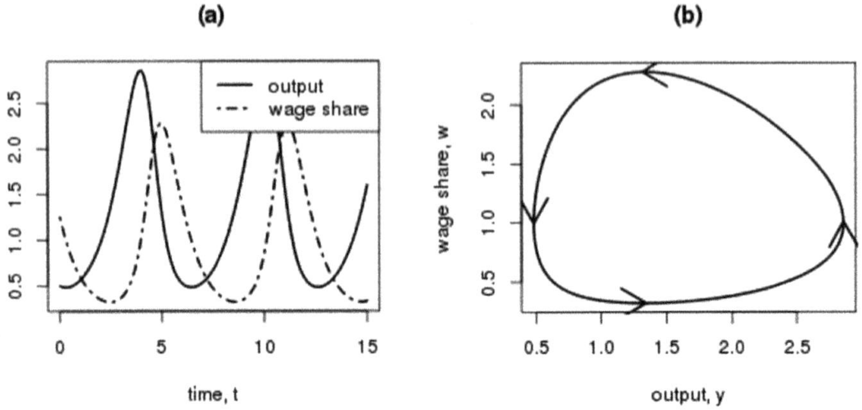

Fig. 6.43 Fluctuations in the Goodwin model. Source: Stockhammer and Michell (2015), reproduced with kind permission of the authors

pattern between the dynamics of output and the wage share, with the wage share lagging the movements in output.

This version of the Goodwin model is, of course, highly stylized and produces regular cycles that look very different from the real fluctuations in output shown in Fig. 6.35. It should be seen as a theoretical model that demonstrates how the interaction of different groups in the economy—in this case, workers and capitalists—leads to permanent cyclical dynamics. The Goodwin model is the basis for Steve Keen's more sophisticated Minsky model, which is presented next.

6.3.2 Great Moderation and Financial Crisis

Nonlinear models can be used to explain the interesting macroeconomic pattern observed in the USA between 1980 and 2010, namely the so-called *Great Moderation* followed by the *Great Recession*. By the early 2000s, mainstream macroeconomists had accepted DSGE models as their main research tool. Just at the time of the financial crisis, Michael Woodford (2009) argued that there was a broad consensus in macroeconomics, especially on the appropriate research methods, and Olivier Blanchard (2009) assessed the state of macroeconomics as good, despite some open questions. Macroeconomists were very confident at that time. According to Robert Lucas (2003), the study of depressions was no longer a macroeconomic priority because the problem of depression prevention had been solved. Similarly, Ben Bernanke argued in 2004 that improved monetary policy was an important reason for the substantial reduction in macroeconomic volatility.

Neoclassical macroeconomists believed that good monetary policy, based on a better understanding of the economy through DSGE modeling, had led to a suppression of the business cycle. However, this may be a misconception. Steve Keen (2013) presents a Post-Keynesian macroeconomic model with several nonlinearities that endogenously generates a period of tranquility followed by a sudden deflationary collapse. Keen's model is a formalization of Hyman Minsky's *Financial Instability Hypothesis* (Minsky 1982), which gained some popularity after the financial crisis. Minsky was a critic of the neoclassical approach, because it cannot generate endogenous instability and crises. For him, economic theory must allow for deep depressions as possible states of capitalist market economies.

6.3.3 Minsky's Financial Instability Hypothesis

The essence of Minsky's Financial Instability Hypothesis is that macroeconomic instability is a consequence of previous stability and vice versa. From this perspective, the Great Moderation and the Great Recession are one phenomenon, not two, with the latter following the former just by chance. The key element in Minsky's story is credit and the attitudes of lenders and borrowers toward it. Figure 6.44 illustrates the main ideas.

The Great Depression of the 1930s motivated Minsky's thinking. The cycle starts with the economy recovering from a previous depression. The economy is doing well again, but both firms and banks are conservative with regard to credit, which corresponds to the top box of the picture. The risk aversion of bankers and firms is high because of the fresh memory of a previous financial crisis. Over time, this memory fades and risk premia are perceived as excessive by both banks and managers. As the economy grows steadily, most investment projects are successful and asset prices rise sharply. The economy enters a phase of speculative borrowing

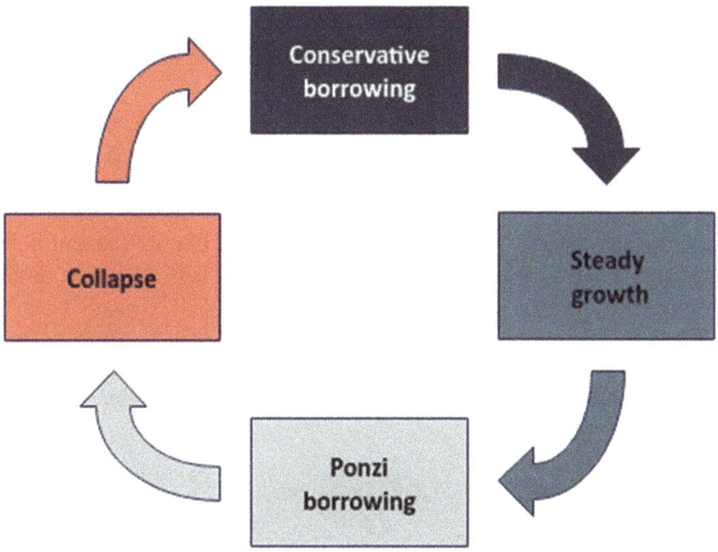

Fig. 6.44 The Minsky cycle of financial instability. Source: Author

with increasing debt financing of investment projects. Due to increased optimism, future cash flows are valued less conservatively than before and credit is extended more generously. The last phase before the crash is the *Ponzi borrowing* phase, which Minsky called the *euphoric economy*. Speculative bubbles develop in asset markets due to the *irrational exuberance* of investors (Shiller 2000). Financial assets or real estate are bought on credit only because of expected increases in asset prices. As in a *Ponzi scheme*, selling an overvalued asset at a profit works as long as speculators can find someone who still believes in rising prices. At some point, the inevitable *Minsky moment* arrives when over-indebted borrowers cannot roll over their debt and have to sell their overvalued assets. This triggers a fall in asset prices, forcing more asset sales and a loss of confidence. The boom collapses.

The system can respond in two ways to the excessive debt that caused the speculative boom and subsequent crash, and to the inadequate cash flow of investors. Either the debt burden can be reduced by high inflation coinciding with low growth and high unemployment. This would be a deep recession as a self-correcting mechanism. Alternatively, if inflation remains low, companies and investors must continue to sell assets, leading to severe asset price deflation, and cut profit margins to increase cash flow. Both of these lead to general price deflation, causing a prolonged depression that, unlike a recession, is not self-correcting.

Steve Keen (2013) proposes a relatively simple formalization of Minsky's story. In a basic version, he incorporates debt into the Goodwin (1967) growth cycle model. The Goodwin model generates growth with endogenous cyclical fluctuations due to the nonlinear (multiplicative) interaction between the wage rate and the level of employment. As employment rises, the wage level will also rise due to the increased bargaining power of workers. This will increase the macroeconomic wage share at the expense of the profit share. The crucial assumption is that, contrary to the standard neoclassical assumption that investment equals private saving, investment is financed by profits. Falling profits thus lead to lower investment and lower output.

6.3.4 Keen's Basic Minsky Model

A Minsky element enters the model by the assumption that investment is financed both by profits Π and by a banking sector that provides new debt to firms $\dot{D}$:

$$I = \Pi + \dot{D} \tag{6.23}$$

Profits are defined as output Y minus total wages wL and interest payments on debt rD:

$$\Pi = Y - wL - rD \tag{6.24}$$

The production structure of the model is very simple. Output is assumed to depend on the capital stock K:

$$Y = \frac{K}{v} \tag{6.25}$$

The level of output determines the level of employment L via labor productivity a:

$$L = \frac{Y}{a} \tag{6.26}$$

The capital stock evolves according to a simple accumulation equation containing investment I and depreciation γK:

$$\dot{K} = I - \gamma K \tag{6.27}$$

The crucial elements of the model are two nonlinear relationships. The first nonlinear relationship is a Phillips curve that translates the employment rate $\lambda = \frac{L}{N}$ into changes of the real wage w:

$$\dot{w} = P_h(\lambda) w, \tag{6.28}$$

where $P_h(\lambda)$ has the function form of a generalized exponential function as in (6.29) and $x = \lambda$:

$$GenExp(x, x_{val}, y_{val}, s, m) = (y_{val} - m) e^{\left(\frac{s}{y_{val} - m}\right)(x - x_{val})} + m \tag{6.29}$$

This nonlinear Phillips curve captures the idea that wages fall only very slowly, when the unemployment is high, but rise sharply when the unemployment rate is low due to the bargaining power of workers.

The second nonlinear relationship is inspired by the Minsky cycle and models investment as a nonlinearly increasing function of the profit rate according to (6.29) with $x = \Pi$. The idea behind this function is that investors extrapolate their experience from the past into the future and invest more and more as profits rise. Fig. 6.45 shows this investment function $I\left(\frac{\Pi}{vY}\right)$.

Finally, it is assumed that both labor productivity a and the population N grow exogenously:

$$\dot{a} = \alpha a \tag{6.30}$$

$$\dot{N} = \beta N \tag{6.31}$$

The model's most interesting variable in our context is the evolution of output over time which can be found using the production function, the investment function, and the capital accumulation function:

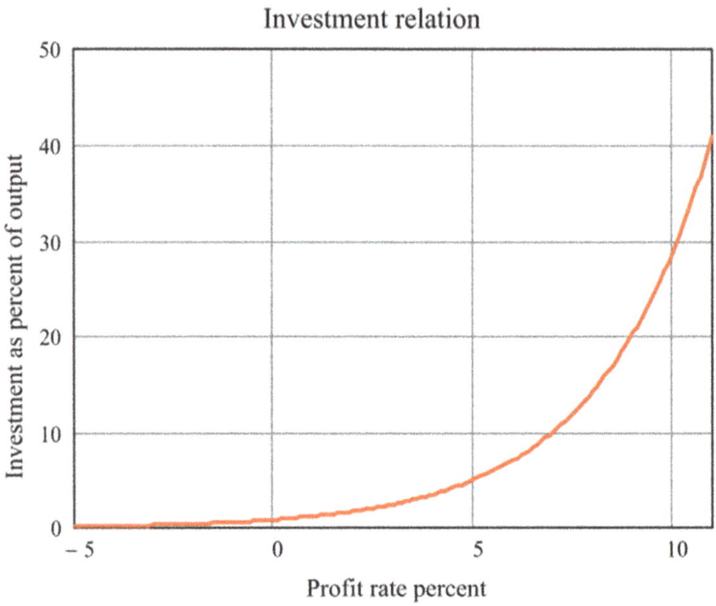

Fig. 6.45 Nonlinear investment function in Keen's Minsky model. Source: Keen (2013), reproduced with kind permission of Elsevier

$$\dot{Y} = \left(\frac{1}{v} I\left(\frac{\Pi}{vY}\right) - \gamma\right) Y \tag{6.32}$$

The model has a stable equilibrium in terms of the employment rate, the profit rate, and the debt-to-output ratio to which it will converge, if the initial conditions are close enough to this equilibrium. However, if the initial conditions are too far away from the equilibrium, the model has unstable cyclical fluctuations, as shown for output in Fig. 6.46.

6.3.5 Keen's Minsky Model with Money Creation

While the basic version of the Minsky model already generates endogenous crises, it is still very simple because it does not include an explicit financial sector. To model a more sophisticated Minsky story that also allows for price dynamics, Keen (2013) presents another version of the model with endogenous money creation by banks.

In the endogenous money version, banks create money by lending to firms, independent of the previously existing base money. Keen uses his dynamic disequilibrium model of money production, which incorporates double-entry bookkeeping of money flows between banks, firms, and households in a so-called *Godley table*. The Godley table keeps track of money flows between five accounts:

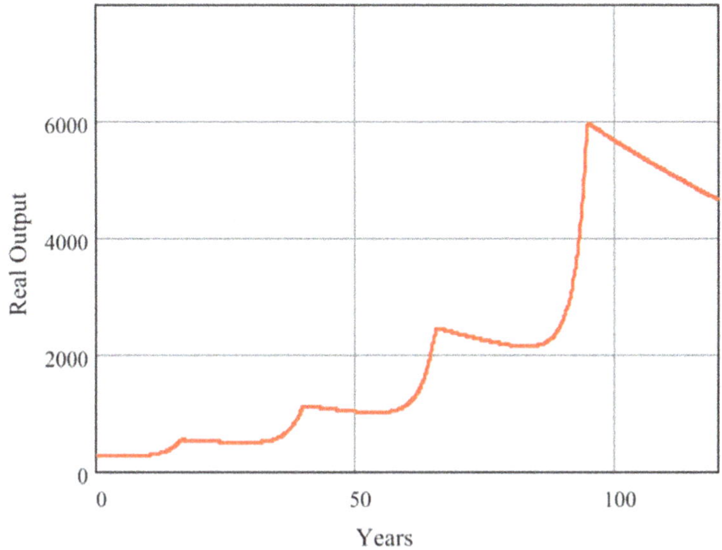

Fig. 6.46 Cyclical breakdown of growth in the basic Minsky model. Source: Keen (2013), reproduced with kind permission of Elsevier

1. A Bank Vault (B_V) representing the banking sector's monetary assets
2. A Bank Transaction Account (B_T) that keeps track of expenditure and interest payments
3. A Firm Loan Ledger (F_L) that records the outstanding debt which the firm sectors owes to the banking sector
4. A Firm Deposit Account (F_D) into which the firm sector deposits borrowed money
5. A Household Deposit Account (H_D) into which wages are paid

The operations recorded in the Godley table are of three different types: money transfers, accounting operations, and money creation. In this still simple model, money creation occurs, when the banking sector finances loans to the firm sector for investment by simply crediting the Firm deposit F_D.

The financial dynamics are described by the following differential equations (see Table 6.2 for the meaning of the equations):

$$\dot{B_V} = \frac{F_L}{\tau_L(\pi_r)} - \frac{B_V}{\tau_V(\pi_r)}$$

$$\dot{B_T} = r_L F_L - r_D(F_D + H_D) - \frac{B_T}{\tau_B}$$

Table 6.2 Flow rates for the entries in the Godley table

Description	Equation
Lending of the existing money stock not in circulation B_V is a function of the rate of profit	$\frac{B_V(t)}{\tau_V(\pi_r(t))}$
The debt F_L is compounded at the rate of loan interest r_L	$r_L \cdot F_L(t)$
Payment of interest on the loan	$r_L \cdot F_L(t)$
Interest on Firm deposits F_D is paid at the deposit rate r_D	$r_D \cdot F_D(t)$
Wage payments depend on the money wage W and the employment level L	$W(t) \cdot L(t)$
Interest on household deposits H_D at the rate r_D	$r_D \cdot H_D(t)$
Bank consumption with a time constant τ_B	$\frac{B_T(t)}{\tau_B}$
Household consumption with a time constant τ_H	$\frac{H_D(t)}{\tau_H}$
The rate of loan repayment is a nonlinear function of the rate of profit	$\frac{F_L(t)}{\tau_L(\pi_r(t))}$
The investment share of output is a nonlinear function of the rate of profit	$Inv(\pi_r(t)) \cdot Y(t)$

Source: Keen (2013), reproduced with kind permission of Elsevier

$$\dot{F_L} = \frac{B_V}{\tau_V(\pi_r)} - \frac{F_L}{\tau_L(\pi_r)} + Y \cdot Inv(\pi_r)$$

$$\dot{F_D} = (r_D F_D - r_L F_L) - WL + \left(\frac{B_V}{\tau_V(\pi_r)} - \frac{F_L}{\tau_L(\pi_r)}\right) + \frac{B_T}{\tau_B} + \frac{H_D}{\tau_H} + Y \cdot Inv(\pi_r)$$

$$\dot{H_D} = r_D H_D + WL - \frac{H_D}{\tau_H}$$

The model now has two parts: a physical production system expressed in real terms and a financial system expressed in monetary terms. The two systems are linked by the price of goods P and the nominal wage W. The model therefore needs two additional equations describing the evolution of the price of goods and the nominal wage. The price of goods is assumed to be a mark-up price, where the price is set as a constant mark-up over the marginal cost of production:

$$\dot{P} = -\frac{1}{\tau_P}\left(P - \frac{1}{1-\sigma}\frac{W}{a}\right) \tag{6.33}$$

The wage-setting equation captures the idea behind the Phillips curve that workers want to be compensated for inflation and have more bargaining power when the employment rate is increasing ($\omega < 1$ is a weighting factor):

$$\dot{W} = W\left(P_h(\lambda) + \omega\frac{\dot{\lambda}}{\lambda} + \frac{\dot{P}}{P}\right) \tag{6.34}$$

The model generates interesting dynamics, as shown in Fig. 6.47. At the beginning of the simulation period, both inflation and unemployment reach high levels

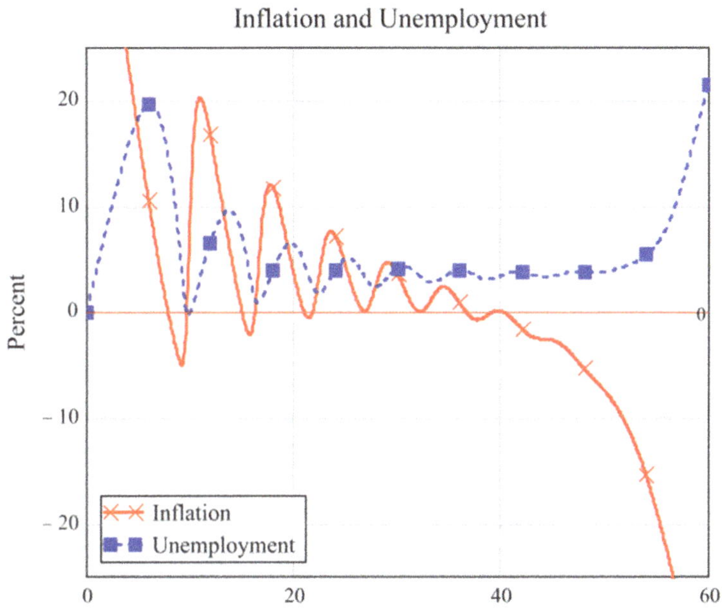

Fig. 6.47 Dynamics of inflation and unemployment in the monetary Minsky model. Source: Keen (2013), reproduced with kind permission of Elsevier

and fluctuate strongly. From period 20 on, the fluctuations become quite small. This can be called a period of moderation. Then, at the end of the period, there is an economic crisis with sharply rising unemployment and accelerating deflation. Steve Keen argues that the behavior of the model is qualitatively similar to the evolution of actual unemployment and inflation in the USA during the Great Moderation, shown in Fig. 6.48.

In line with Minsky's theory, firms become increasingly indebted over the simulation period, as shown in Fig. 6.49. The rather simple and stylized model qualitatively reproduces the patterns observed in the financial crisis that led to the Great Recession. In particular, the fact that the model shows reduced oscillations before a rather sudden economic collapse is an important insight into the possible behavior of nonlinear models.

6.4 Nonlinear Expectation Formation and the Business Cycle

An important lesson of this chapter is that even very simple nonlinear models can have complex dynamics, especially when bifurcations and chaos occur. Westerhoff (2006) proposes a simple macroeconomic model based on Samuelson's multiplier–accelerator model, in which nonlinear expectation formation causes endogenous business cycle dynamics. The model describes a closed economy without a government sector or a financial sector. As in the multiplier–accelerator model, all

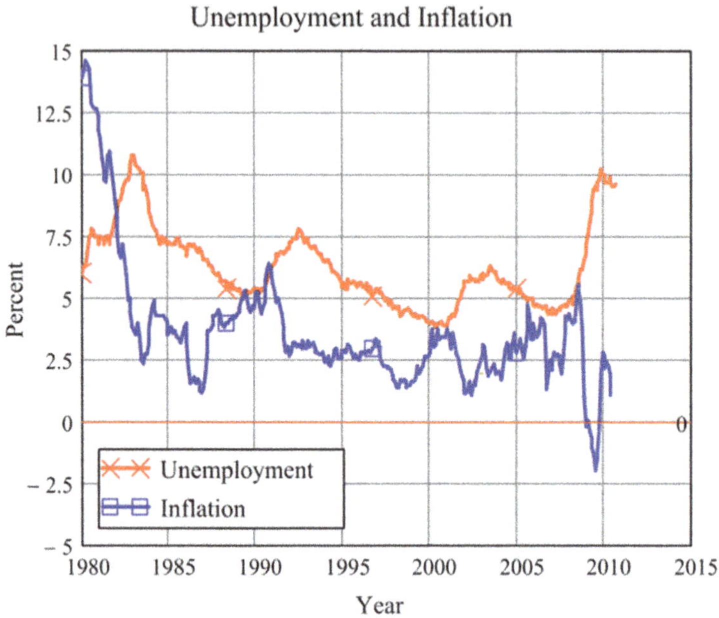

Fig. 6.48 U.S. unemployment and inflation 1980–2010. Source: Keen (2013), reproduced with kind permission of Elsevier

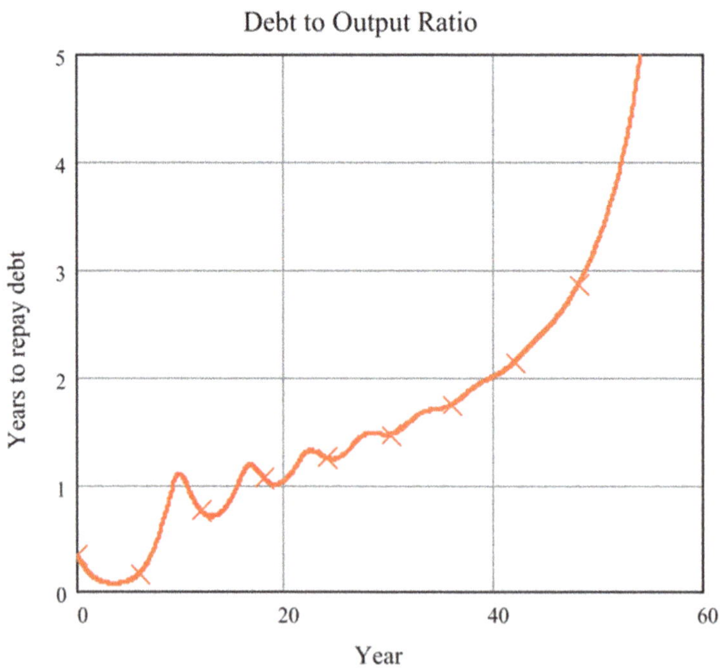

Fig. 6.49 Debt-to-output ratio in the monetary Minsky model. Source: Keen (2013), reproduced with kind permission of Elsevier

dynamics result from the interaction between aggregate output, consumption, and investment.

6.4.1 Modified Multiplier–Accelerator Model

Aggregate consumption in period t is a function of expected income for this period, based on the information up to period $t-1$

$$C_t = aE[Y_t], \tag{6.35}$$

where $0 < a < 1$ is the marginal propensity to consume. The novel feature of this model is the way in which aggregate expectations are modeled:

$$E[Y_t] = W_t E^e[Y_t] + (1 - W_t)E^r[Y_t]. \tag{6.36}$$

Aggregate income expectations are a weighted average (i.e., $0 < W \leq 1$) of two expectation formation rules. *Extrapolative expectations* assume the continuation of a positive or negative trend in income

$$E^e[Y_t] = Y_{t-1} + c(Y_{t-1} - \overline{Y}), \tag{6.37}$$

where $\overline{Y}$ is the long-run equilibrium level of income and c is a positive extrapolation parameter. When income is above (below) its equilibrium level, agents assume that the boom (recession) will continue into the next period. Trend-following behavior is quite common in financial markets as well as in the real economy and is supported by empirical and experimental evidence.

Regressive expectations are the second way to form expectations

$$E^r[Y_t] = Y_{t-1} + d(\overline{Y} - Y_{t-1}), \tag{6.38}$$

where $0 < d < 1$ is a mean-reversion parameter. Regressive expectations follow the opposite logic of extrapolative expectations. When income is away from its equilibrium level, agents expect that it this deviation cannot be permanent and will be corrected by a return to equilibrium.

The weights in (6.36) could be interpreted as the fraction of agents that are trend extrapolators (sometimes called chartists) or mean-reverters (sometimes called fundamentalists). The nonlinearity comes in, because the weights are assumed to vary nonlinearly with the state of the economy

$$W_t = \frac{1}{1 + \left(Y_{t-1} - \overline{Y}\right)^2}.$$

When income is at its equilibrium level, all agents are trend followers, so everyone expects a small deviation to continue in the next period. However, the more output deviates from the equilibrium, the more agents expect it to return such that the share of trend extrapolators declines. If a boom or a recession is extreme, i.e., the deviations from equilibrium are large, almost all agents form regressive expectations, $W_t \to 0$.

Aggregate investment is a function of a trend-following accelerator term and a response to out-of-equilibrium consumption

$$I_t = b(C_t - C_{t-1}) + \left(1 + e\left(C_t - \overline{C}\right)\right) I^a, \tag{6.39}$$

where $e > 0$ indicates how autonomous investment I^a responds to deviations from equilibrium consumption $\overline{C}$. The model is closed by the accounting identity for output, which determines output from the demand side

$$Y_t = C_t + I_t. \tag{6.40}$$

For the analysis of the model, it is convenient to define $x_t \equiv Y_t - \overline{Y}$ and $W_t = h(x_{t-1}) \equiv \frac{1}{1+x_{t-1}^2}$. By using these new variables and substituting (6.35), (6.36), (6.37), (6.38)(6.39) into (6.40), we obtain an autonomous nonlinear second-order difference equation for the deviation of output from its equilibrium

$$\begin{aligned} x_t = &a(1 + b + eI^a)x_{t-1}(1 + h(x_{t-1})(c + d) - d) \\ &- bax_{t-2}(1 + h(x_{t-2})(c + d) - d), \end{aligned} \tag{6.41}$$

which can be written as a two-dimensional first-order nonlinear dynamical system

$$x_t = a(1 + b + eI^a)x_{t-1}(1 + h(x_{t-1})(c + d) - d) - baz_{t-1}(1 + h(z_{t-1})(c + d) - d)$$

$$z_t = x_{t-1}.$$

The nonlinearity arises because of $h(x) \equiv \frac{1}{1+x^2}$ and because x_{t-1} and $h(x_{t-1})$ as well as z_{t-1} and $h(z_{t-1})$ are multiplied.

6.4.2 Properties of the Model

As usual in dynamical systems, we first look for fixed points, for which $x_t = x_{t-1} = x_{t-2} = x^*$ holds. Obviously, $(x^*, z^*) = (0, 0)$ is a solution of the dynamical system (6.41) and a fixed point. Westerhoff calls this fixed point a fundamental steady state, because it corresponds to the steady state of the classical multiplier–accelerator model with $Y_t = \overline{Y} = \frac{1}{1-a} I^a$, $C_t = \overline{C} = a\overline{Y}$ and $I_t = \overline{I} = I^a$. However, substituting x^* into (6.41) leads to a quadratic equation

$$(x^*)^2 = \frac{a(1 + eI^a)(c + 1) - 1}{1 - (1 - d)a(1 + eI^a)},$$

which has two positive solutions and hence two additional non-fundamental steady states, if $\frac{1}{1-c} < a(1 + eI^a) < \frac{1}{1-d}$ holds.

The model is interesting, because it features bifurcations and chaos, as shown in Fig. 6.50. The model is simulated numerically with the parameters $a = 0.5$, $b = 0.5$, $d = 1$, $e = 0$, $I^a = 10$. The extrapolation parameter c is increased in 250 steps from 0 to 20. The two panels in Fig. 6.50 show the results for different initial values. For small values of c, both model runs have a unique fixed point at the fundamental steady state $\overline{Y} = 20$. At c_1 a pitchfork bifurcation occurs where the unique stable fixed point becomes unstable and is replaced by a high (top panel) and a low (bottom panel) stable fixed point. Another bifurcation occurs at $c_2 \approx 7$, but this time, it is not a pitchfork bifurcation, but a *Neimark–Sacker bifurcation*. The Neimark–Sacker bifurcation can be thought of as the analog of the Hopf bifurcation for maps. As mentioned before, a supercritical Hopf bifurcation in a two-dimensional continuous-

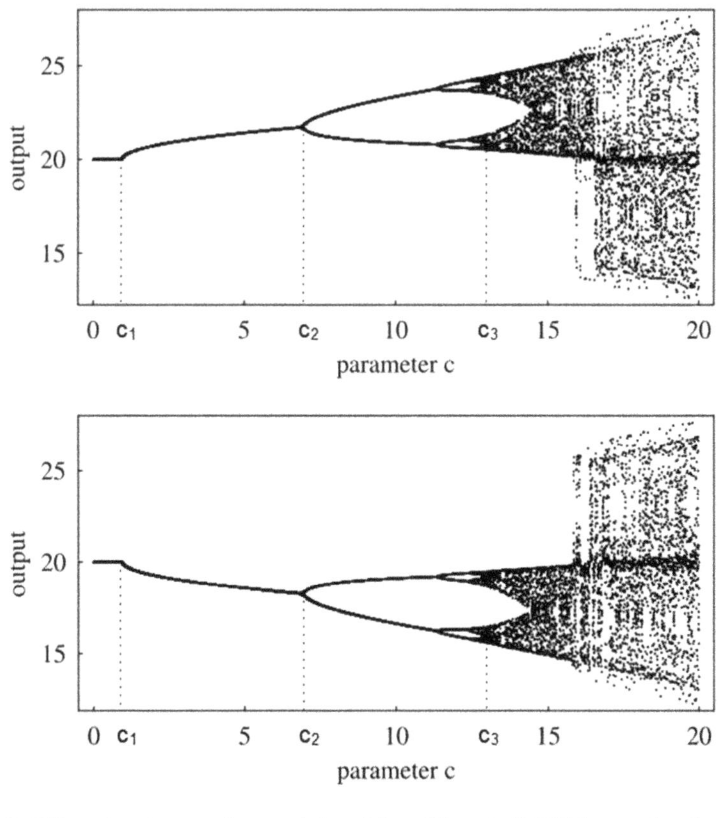

Fig. 6.50 Bifurcation diagram. Source: Adapted from Westerhoff (2006), reproduced with kind permission of Walter de Gruyter and Company

time system means that a spiral fixed point turns into a limit cycle. Something similar happens in the iterated map considered here: the stable fixed point turns into a 2-cycle. Another period-doubling bifurcation sets in at about $c = 12$, before we get chaos at c_3.

Westerhoff shows numerically that the variation of the parameter b also produces Neimark–Sacker bifurcations, but no pitchfork bifurcation. He also shows analytically that there is a stability region given by the conditions (i) $c < \frac{1}{a(1+eI^a)} - 1$ and (ii) $c < \frac{1}{ba} - 1$. If condition (i) is violated, a pitchfork bifurcation occurs. Note that this condition is independent of b. Condition (ii) defines the threshold for Neimark–Sacker bifurcations.

To see what the time series of this model can look like, Westerhoff simulates the model with the parameter set $a = 0.9$, $b = 1.5$, $c = 11$, $d = 0.85$, $e = 0.065$ and $I^a = 10$, resulting in the long-run steady state values $\overline{Y} = 100, \overline{C} = 90$ and $\overline{I} = 10$. Using the stability conditions (i) and (ii) above, we can check that both conditions are violated such that the model does not have a unique stable fixed point. In Fig. 6.51, we can see that the model has chaotic dynamics for this parameter set. The simulation run starts with a high-output regime where output fluctuates irregularly above its fundamental value. Suddenly in period 50, output drops sharply below 100 and then fluctuates for a while in a low-output regime. Thus, a boom with high average output is followed by a recession phase with low average output. The recession is over after about 20 periods, when a new boom begins. This sequence of booms and recessions corresponds to the common notion of a business cycle. It is rather disturbing that there is no obvious pattern in the timing and duration of the booms and recessions. Some phases with high or low output are quite long, while others are short. Moreover, there is no obvious pattern that heralds a shift from one regime to the other. All switches occur out of the blue.

While the pattern of output always fluctuating around a high and a low mean seems unrealistic, the relative magnitudes of the fluctuations of output, consumption, and investment and their covariation are consistent with the stylized facts of the business cycle. Westerhoff shows that the amplitude of consumption fluctuations is smaller than that of output, and that investment is much more volatile than output. Moreover, all three variables vary procyclically, as is the case in the empirical data.

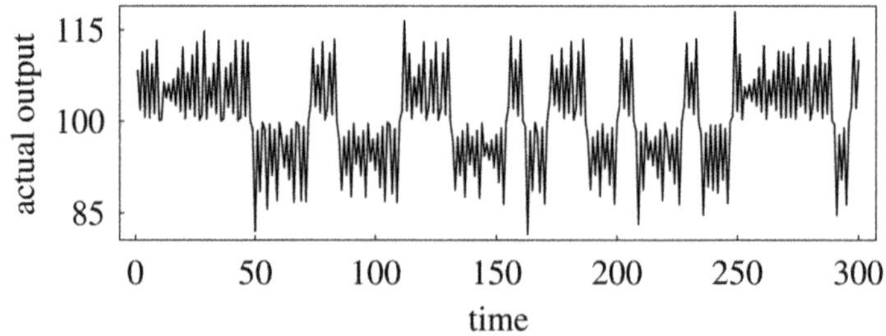

Fig. 6.51 Endogenous business cycle. Source: Westerhoff (2006), reproduced with kind permission of Walter de Gruyter and Company

The driver of the business cycle is the nonlinear way in which expectations are formed. The existence of two regimes results from the extrapolative expectation heuristic, which keeps consumption above or below its fundamental level for a while. The regressive part prevents the model from diverging and keeps the fluctuations within bounds.

6.5 Nonlinearity in Economics

6.5.1 Applications of Nonlinearity

The nonlinear models presented here all deal with the **business cycle**. Nonlinear business cycle modeling has a long tradition in macroeconomics with origins in the 1940s and 1950s and some boom in the 1980s after the advent of chaos theory in the 1970s. Mullineux and Peng (1993) and Orlando and Sportelli (2021) provide surveys of this literature. Perhaps the most important lesson of this literature is the insight that fluctuations in economic variables can be endogenously generated by the system, which is in contrast to the current mainstream view that fluctuations are the result of exogenous stochastic shocks to an otherwise stable system. If we want to understand and explain why business cycles occur, endogenous cycles seem theoretically more appealing than exogenous shocks. Put bluntly, the shocks-view of the business cycle says that fluctuations occur because of unobservable exogenous forces that we cannot explain. Paul Romer (2016) bitingly criticizes this approach as "post-real" and compares it to the *phlogiston theory of combustion* and the *aether theory of light propagation,* which are today considered as scientific misconceptions. Another insight is that shocks can qualitatively change the behavior of the model, if they enter multiplicatively instead of additively, or if they affect parameters that cause bifurcations or catastrophes. Anufriev et al. (2018) highlight the role of expectations in economics, which can be the cause of fluctuations, as the Westerhoff model demonstrates. Expectations drive behavior, but also depend on the state of the economy, creating positive and negative feedback loops that can be the cause of nonlinearities.

Another important macroeconomic issue, for which nonlinearity is relevant, is **growth and development**. *Poverty traps* are the most relevant issue in this context. A country is stuck in a poverty trap, if its per capita income does not converge to the level of richer countries, but remains persistently low. Unless countries (or regions) differ in terms of fundamental characteristics such as time and risk preferences or cultural and institutional factors, neoclassical growth theory predicts that per capita income in all countries (or regions) should converge to the same steady-state level. Neoclassical models such as the Solow–Swan model or the Ramsey–Cass–Koopmans model predict that the growth rate is high far away from the steady state and low close to it implying that poor countries should catch up with the rich ones. Empirical evidence suggests that this does not happen in many countries that are trapped in poverty. Azariadis (1996) reviews a literature that explains poverty traps not by fundamental differences between countries, but by nonlinear capital

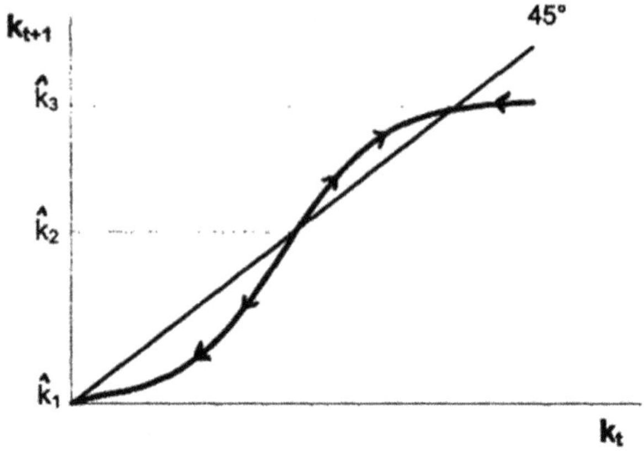

Fig. 6.52 Capital accumulation in a history-driven poverty trap. Source: Azariadis (1996), reproduced with kind permission of Springer Nature

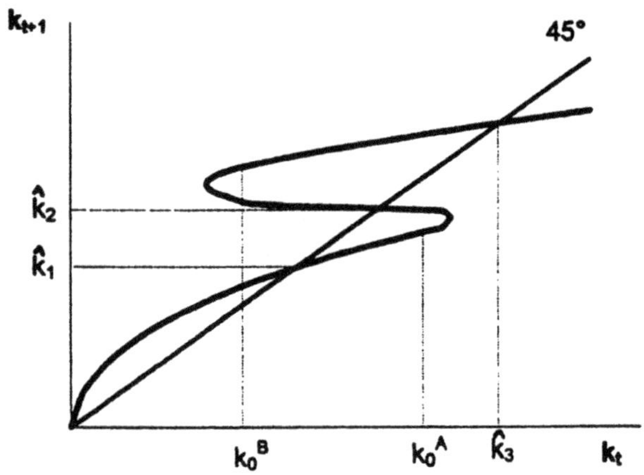

Fig. 6.53 Capital accumulation in an expectations-driven poverty trap. Source: Azariadis (1996), reproduced with kind permission of Springer Nature

accumulation leading to multiple steady states as shown in the nonlinear iterated maps in Figs. 6.52 and 6.53.

Figure 6.52 corresponds to the *historical view* that development differences between countries are due to historical accidents. This means that all countries are structurally identical and therefore subject to the same capital accumulation or growth process, but the initial conditions are different. As we can see, the capital accumulation function has three fixed points: $\widehat{k}_2$, which is unstable, and the stable fixed points $\widehat{k}_1$ and $\widehat{k}_3$. A country with an initial endowment of physical capital, human capital, or technology below $\widehat{k}_2$ will converge to the low steady state $\widehat{k}_1$, while a country starting above this level will reach $\widehat{k}_3$. The role of history is discussed more deeply in Chap. 11.

Figure 6.53, which represents the *expectations view*, tells an alternative story about why poverty traps might exist. Again, countries are assumed to be identical in terms of their structural characteristics, such as preferences, technology, and institutions. In this case, the dynamics are such that even identical initial conditions can lead to convergence to different steady states because of different expectations. A country starting at $k_0{}^B$ could converge to $\widehat{k}_1$ or to $\widehat{k}_3$, depending on whether it is on the low or the high branch of the curved accumulation line. If the high branch is chosen due to optimistic expectations, country B could even overtake country A starting at $k_0{}^A$, if A has pessimistic expectations. The literature suggests a variety of reasons for why history or expectations might lead to poverty traps, e.g. fertility choice, public debt, invention and innovation, or human capital externalities. Note that in many of these stories, externalities and increasing returns to scale in the production function are crucial.

The effects of different types of nonlinearities have also been analyzed in **industrial organization** with respect to **monopoly and oligopoly** (see Puu 2003; Anufriev et al. 2018 for overviews). The Cournot duopoly model taught in introductory microeconomics courses assumes linear demand and cost functions, leading to linear response functions of the two competitors. Together with static expectations, i.e., the assumption that the competitor will produce the same quantity in the next period as in the current period, this linear model has a unique and globally stable steady state (Nash equilibrium). With more than three firms, the Cournot–Nash equilibrium can become unstable. Multiple equilibria and chaotic dynamics can arise if the strong assumptions of the textbook Cournot model are relaxed. Puu (1991), for example, shows that an isoelastic demand function derived from a Cobb–Douglas utility function and differences in the marginal costs of the duopolists make the Cournot equilibrium unstable and generate complex, i.e., periodic or even chaotic, dynamics. Periodic cycles and chaos can also occur when firms only partially know their profit functions. Adaptive rather than static expectations can lead to bifurcations. Even the adaptive behavior of a monopolist who does not have perfect knowledge of the profit function can lead to multiple equilibria and chaotic dynamics (see Puu 2003). When oligopolists not only differ in their marginal costs, but are also heterogeneous in information and rationality, the situation becomes even more complex. Zhang et al. (2007) study a duopoly model with nonlinear cost functions and heterogeneous competitors. They show that if one competitor is boundedly rational and the other is naive, the quantity offered in the market can behave chaotically. Evolutionary models of oligopoly, which are typically nonlinear, describe learning and adaptation and thus the change in behavior over time, adding another layer of complexity. We will discuss this topic in Chap. 12.

A related topic is **technology adoption and diffusion**, which can be analyzed both from the perspective of how firms adopt a new technology and how consumers adopt new products. Lamantia and Radi (2018) model a Cournot duopoly in which firms can choose between two technologies with different marginal costs. The choice is modeled as an evolutionary game in which bifurcations and multiple attractors can occur. Heinrich (2018) uses catastrophe theory to model a market with network externalities, which make it more attractive to adopt a technology or product the more agents have already done so. A constant rate of agents abandoning the technology serves as an imperfection parameter (like the parameter h in Sect. 6.2.6), whose change can cause a cusp catastrophe. A cusp catastrophe can either mean that the market share of adopters of the technology jumps from zero to a positive number, or collapses from a positive equilibrium to zero users. Wijeratne et al. (2009) present a Lotka–Volterra competitive model, as discussed in Sect. 6.2.4, to analyze how two firms compete in the Sri Lankan mobile phone market. A stable equilibrium with two firms in the market is only possible if both firms minimize competition and maximize the effect of promotions. They derive conditions under which a Hopf bifurcation, a transcritical bifurcation, and a pitchfork bifurcation are possible. The canonical model of innovation diffusion in a market was proposed by Frank Bass in 1969. The *Bass model* has been enormously influential in marketing because it includes as parameters both the effect of advertising and the effect of imitation (or word-of-mouth) among customers (see Chap. 7). There are several nonlinear extensions of the original model in which Hopf bifurcations and chaos can occur (Feichtinger 1992; Feichtinger et al. 1995; Kumar et al. 2017; Kumar et al. 2020).

Nonlinear models play an important role in the analysis of **price dynamics** in markets. In Sect. 6.2.7, we considered a simple market model that can incorporate hog cycles and contrasted it with the Muth model with exogenous supply shocks and rational expectations presented in Sect. 4.3.1. Chavas and Holt (1993) model how the nonlinear dynamics of a dairy herd affect milk supply. When milk demand is highly inelastic, milk price dynamics are chaotic, implying unpredictability even in the absence of stochastic shocks. Anufriev et al. (2018) review a fairly large literature on nonlinear price dynamics, with a particular focus on financial and asset markets. A more recent strand of this literature, building on the work of William Brock and Cars Hommes (see Brock and Hommes 1997, 1998; Hommes 2013), examines the role of bounded rationality and behavioral heterogeneity, especially with respect to expectation formation. Similar to Westerhoff's business cycle model in Sect. 6.4, these models assume different rules that agents use to form expectations and switch between rules. Experimental research on expectation formation complements the theoretical models with complex dynamics.

Ho and Saunders (1980), Yang et al. (2009), Barunik and Vosvrda (2009), Diks and Wang (2016), and Wesselbaum (2017) use catastrophe theory in order to model **bank failures, asset market crashes, and financial crises**. The main motivation of this literature is that financial crises and crashes often occur suddenly and sometimes for no apparent exogenous reason. Several papers estimate stochastic cusp catastrophe models and show that they have a good empirical fit.

Finally, nonlinear models with bifurcations and catastrophe theory are relevant for modeling the **critical transitions of natural systems**. Sudden changes during which ecological systems undergo qualitative changes are often called *critical transitions*. Scheffer (2009) provides an excellent overview of how such critical transitions can be modeled as bifurcations and catastrophes. Examples of critical transitions in nature include the collapse of coral reefs and marine ecosystems, the collapse of shallow lakes, the formation of the Sahara desert, or tipping elements in the climate system. Klose et al. (2020) show how we can conceptualize cascades of interacting tipping elements of ecological and climate systems through cusp catastrophes. Some of these phenomena are natural events that occur without human intervention, but many are linked to human activities and have economic consequences. A well-studied example is the collapse of fish populations due to overfishing. Sguotti et al. (2019) and Möllmann et al. (2021) use stochastic cusp catastrophe models to describe the evolution of cod populations in the Atlantic and in the Baltic Seas. Cod stocks collapsed as a consequence of unsustainable fishing and climate change and display hysteresis in the sense that they do not recover even after fishing pressure is reduced (see Chap. 7).

6.5.2 Empirical Evidence

Many of the papers mentioned in this section deal with theoretical models, although some also report empirical support for stochastic cusp catastrophe models in particular. But what can we say about the empirical relevance of chaos and nonlinearity in general? Since the 1990s, researchers have used a variety of statistical techniques to test for the presence of chaos in macroeconomic and financial time series data. The estimation of the Lyapunov exponent discussed in Sect. 6.2.8 is one of these approaches, others are presented in Faggini (2014). Faggini and Parziale (2016) and Faggini et al. (2019) survey the empirical literature asking whether macroeconomic and financial time series are chaotic (and hence deterministic) or stochastic. They conclude that there is little evidence of chaos in macroeconomics, but some evidence of chaos in financial time series. Overall, they interpret the evidence as too controversial to make a strong statement that chaos is relevant. Faggini and Parziale (2016) ask why, in contrast to physics, economics has not been able to prove the existence of chaos despite strong theoretical priors that it might be present in economic data. Their answer is that "data quantity and data quality in economics constitute a significant obstacle in chaotic-economic theory" (p. 62). In particular, macroeconomic time series are very short, consisting of monthly, quarterly, or even annual data, and are very noisy. Moreover, macroeconomic data are aggregated, which can hide chaos in the disaggregated data, and they are subject to frequent measurement changes. That the low frequency of macroeconomic data might be a significant obstacle to detecting chaos is supported by the fact that the evidence for chaos is much stronger in the high-frequency financial data. Another problem may be the inappropriate use of statistical methods. It is quite common in the literature to apply linear filters to the original data, e.g. ARMA time series models, and then to test for correlation in the residuals. The assumption is that after removing linear correlations, the remaining correlations in the residual must be nonlinear. However, it is unclear whether chaotic properties of processes are invariant to linear and nonlinear filters. Finally, there is the problem that approaches from physics may have been applied to economics in a naïve way.[4] Physics has focused on

[4]One could say that this happened for the first time already in the nineteenth century when neoclassical economists simply translated thermodynamic models into economics (see Mirowski 1991).

low-dimensional chaos, i.e., chaos in systems with few variables, but chaos in economics may very well be high-dimensional. The dynamic nonlinear structure of the economy is likely to be much more complex than that of the systems studied in physics. Moreover, the algorithms used to detect chaos have been developed for experimental data from laboratories with a large number of observations and little noise. As mentioned above, we do not have such data in economics. Therefore, better testing methods are needed that can deal with high-dimensional chaos and poor data.

Faggini and Parziale (2016) report that there is much more empirical support for nonlinearity. There is substantial evidence of nonlinearity both in macroeconomic and in financial time series. Thus, even if we cannot be sure whether economic time series are in fact deterministic and only look random due to chaos, we can be quite confident that endogenous cycles, fluctuations, and bifurcations are empirically relevant phenomena in economics. At the same time, the question of whether economic fluctuations are due to endogenous dynamics or exogenous stochastic shocks is ill-posed. It seems likely that both are important for understanding how economic variables evolve. In Chap. 4, we cited Boulton et al. (2015), for whom "the future is a dance between patterns and events." In mathematical modeling language, this can be translated as "the dynamics of a system depend on deterministic nonlinear equations and stochastic shocks." When the shocks affect model parameters, they can cause bifurcations or catastrophes that disrupt an observed pattern, without changing the overall mechanism of the system.

6.5.3 Nonlinearity and Economic Worldviews

Nonlinearity is a fundamental concept in complexity economics, because it is the source of all kinds of "complications" such as multiple equilibria, instability, regime shifts, and chaotic dynamics. From a mainstream perspective, these complications are undesirable, because they make a system difficult or impossible to predict. In his textbook on advanced macroeconomics, Heijdra (2017, pp. 75–76) expresses this view well:

> When a system has multiple equilibria (or stationary points), there may be stable and unstable equilibria. If there is a unique stable equilibrium, we shall choose that equilibrium as the relevant one and can still speak of a stable system. The reason that economists like to focus attention on stable systems is that the alternative is unpalatable: unstable systems are not very useful for understanding the economy. . . . Indeed, even if such a system starts in an equilibrium, a very small shock will permanently displace the system from that equilibrium. Therefore, only by pure coincidence would the system be in an equilibrium. Since economists know a lot more about equilibria than they do about disequilibrium situations, they like to study models that predict that the system converges along an equilibrium adjustment path to a stable equilibrium . . . A very useful piece of methodological advice is contained in the so-called correspondence principle, which was transplanted from physics to economics by Paul Samuelson in his classic Foundations of Economic Analysis published in 1947. In words, the correspondence principle states that we should have confidence in,

> and use, only stable systems. . . . [T]he mathematical conditions that are necessary to have a stable system often enable macroeconomists to sign the steady-state multipliers for changes in government policy or other exogenous variables. . . . We also look in Section 3.5 at a macroeconomic model for which the steady state is not uniquely defined. Instead, the equilibrium at which the economy finally settles depends on the course of history, i.e. the equilibrium is path-dependent. Although this property seems eminently reasonable to historians and other social scientists, it must be stressed that the steady-state equilibrium of most economic models does not depend on the course of history.

This rather long quote is noteworthy because it expresses a very specific attitude of neoclassical economics. In short, the quote says that neoclassical economists prefer theoretical convenience to realism. Neoclassical economists choose their assumptions so that their models have unique stable equilibria because this allows them to make unambiguous theoretical predictions. As shown in this chapter, this requires avoiding most types of nonlinearity. It is clear that this approach leads to mathematically elegant and convenient models that are divorced from reality. The theoretical predictions of these models are unambiguous, but they hold only in the theoretical model world. If the real world is nonlinear, they will fail in most cases.

Rosser (1999) argues that economists have long known that complex dynamics play a role in the economy. He mentions two founding fathers of neoclassical economics, Alfred Marshall and Léon Walras, who clearly separated the "real world" from the world of theory. Walras distinguished between pure and applied economics and considered pure economic theory to be the heart of economics. The study of pure economics is a deductive study of ideal economies, not of reality. If the deductions, for which mathematics must be used, are correct, the model is true, just as geometric deductions are true, even if the real counterparts of circles and ideal triangles are imperfect. In this sense, economic models can never be tested against data, because there is nothing to test except the correct use of mathematics. Once the pure theory of economics is worked out, it can be used in applied economics to detect and improve the shortcomings of the real economy. The main problem with the Walrasian approach is that it implicitly defines what is normal and what is anomalous.

The theoretical world of Walrasian economics, taught in first-year economics courses, sets the anchor for how neoclassical economists think about a problem and how they approach solving it. They start with an abstract and extremely simplified model and ask how much they can explain with it. When they reach the limits of the toy model, they begin to add real-world complications, deviations from the ideal world, or anomalies. Nonlinearity is seen as a complication or anomaly. Complexity economics argues that we should change this perspective. Many of the real-world complications are actually the normal case, and simple situations are anomalous.

The complexity view[5] accepts the complexities of the real world, starts the analysis there, and develops theories that may be simple, but only after careful consideration of the evidence. Complexity economics considers it much more likely

[5] Or Post-Walrasian view, see Colander (2006).

that the world is characterized by nonlinearity, which thus defines the normal case, and views evidence of linearity as a peculiar special case. As a result, complexity economists are not surprised that economic predictions often fail, because they expect very limited predictability a priori.

In this chapter, we have seen very simple, low-dimensional examples of nonlinear systems. While simple nonlinear models are useful for studying many physical phenomena such as the motion of pendulums or the convection of fluids, they are clearly inadequate for economic systems in which many variables interact. Focusing our attention to low-dimensional systems, because we have a well-developed mathematical methodology, is convenient, but not appropriate for the complexity of the economy. Unfortunately, the mathematics of nonlinear systems with many variables is largely terra incognita. Strogatz (2019, p. 11) categorizes the problems of economics and of ecosystems as beyond "The frontier":

> *You'll notice that the framework also contains a region forbiddingly marked "The frontier." It's like in those old maps of the world, where the mapmakers wrote, "Here be dragons" on the unexplored parts of the globe. These topics are not completely unexplored, of course, but it is fair to say the the lie at the limits of current understanding. The problems are very hard, because they are both large and nonlinear.*

It seems that we face a dilemma: we need high-dimensional nonlinear models in economics, but the mathematical tools to analyze them do not exist. All we have are the low-dimensional models used in physics and other sciences, but they are not useful for economics. But the situation is not so bleak. While the low-dimensional models may not capture the full complexity of economic systems, they are of enormous didactic importance in teaching us that linear thinking can easily go wrong. Moreover, not knowing how to analyze systems with many nonlinear differential equations does not mean that we do not have tools for such systems. System dynamics models—the subject of the next chapter—and agent-based models are powerful computational tools

Things to Remember

- In this chapter, we interpreted nonlinearity as the description of relationships between variables by nonlinear functions. In particular, we focused on nonlinear dynamics resulting from nonlinear relationships in dynamical systems where the state of the system depends on time. In contrast to linear systems, prediction in nonlinear systems is difficult or even impossible.
- In nonlinear systems, the superposition principle does not apply which is a formalization of the statement that "the whole is more than the sum of its parts." Nonlinear systems are complex in the sense that it is not easy for an observer to identify causalities and to make predictions.
- Differential equations and difference equations (iterated maps) are common mathematical tools for modeling dynamical systems. There is a well-

(continued)

established body of knowledge how to analyze linear dynamical systems and low-dimensional nonlinear systems. The analysis of high-dimensional nonlinear systems is very hard and largely unexplored.

- It is common practice in science (and economics) to approximate nonlinear functions by linear relationships, which are easier to analyze. The Taylor series approximation is a common tool for linearization. We can often gain valid qualitative insights into the behavior of a dynamical system near a fixed point by linearization. However, linearization can be misleading for large changes and when an attractor has knife-edge stability properties, such as a center.
- Lotka–Volterra models consist of two first-order nonlinear differential equations. They describe the dynamics of two interacting populations. The interaction relationship can be predator–prey or competitive. Originating in biology, Lotka–Volterra models are also popular in economics.
- A bifurcation in a dynamical system is a qualitative change in the system's behavior in response to a small change in a parameter. These qualitative changes are especially related to the number and stability of attractors. A catastrophe is a discontinuous change in a nonlinear dynamical system as a consequence of a small parameter change.
- Chaos is an aperiodic long-term behavior in a deterministic system that exhibits sensitive dependence on initial conditions.
- Nonlinearity is pervasive in the economy. Because of the multiple interactions among social agents, nonlinear relationships are much more likely than linear ones. Nonlinear models have been used in business cycle theory, growth theory, industrial organization, innovation economics, the study of price dynamics, financial economics, and ecological economics. However, mainstream economics prefers to work with linearized models because they are simpler than nonlinear models. Furthermore, nonlinear models often have multiple equilibria, some of which are unstable, making it difficult to predict the behavior of the system. Thus, neoclassical economics often rejects nonlinear models. Complexity economics argues that nonlinearity and its consequences, including multiple equilibria, instability, and unpredictability, should be accepted as the normal case in economic systems.

References

Anufriev M, Radi D, Tramontana F (2018) Some reflections on past and future of nonlinear dynamics in economics and finance. Decisions Econ Finan 41:91–118. https://doi.org/10.1007/s10203-018-0229-9

Azariadis C (1996) The economics of poverty traps part one: complete markets. J Econ Growth 1: 449–486
Barunik J, Vosvrda M (2009) Can a stochastic cusp catastrophe model explain stock market crashes? J Econ Dyn Control 33:1824–1836. https://doi.org/10.1016/j.jedc.2009.04.004
Bass FM (1969) A new product growth for model consumer durables. Manag Sci 15:215–227. https://doi.org/10.1287/mnsc.15.5.215
Bernanke B (2004) Speech by Governor Bernanke on the Great Moderation. YPFS Documents (Series 1). https://www.federalreserve.gov/boarddocs/speeches/2004/20040220/ Accessed 26 Oct 2023
Blanchard O (2009) The state of Macro. Annu Rev Econ 1:209–228. https://doi.org/10.1146/annurev.economics.050708.142952
Boulton JG, Allen PM, Bowman C (2015) Embracing complexity: strategic perspectives for an age of turbulence. Oxford University Press, Oxford
Brock WA, Hommes CH (1997) A rational route to randomness. Econometrica 65:1059–1095. https://doi.org/10.2307/2171879
Brock WA, Hommes CH (1998) Heterogeneous beliefs and routes to chaos in a simple asset pricing model. J Econ Dyn Control 22:1235–1274. https://doi.org/10.1016/S0165-1889(98)00011-6
Buiter W (2009) The unfortunate uselessness of most 'state of the art' academic monetary economics. Voxeu Column 6 Mar 2009, https://voxeu.org/article/macroeconomics-crisis-irrelevance
Chavas J-P, Holt MT (1993) Market instability and nonlinear dynamics. Am J Agric Econ 75:113–120. https://doi.org/10.2307/1242959
Colander D (ed) (2006) Post Walrasian macroeconomics: beyond the dynamic stochastic general equilibrium model. Cambridge University Press, Cambridge
Desai M, Henry B, Mosley A, Pemberton M (2006) A clarification of the Goodwin model of the growth cycle. J Econ Dyn Control 30:2661–2670. https://doi.org/10.1016/j.jedc.2005.08.006
Diks C, Wang J (2016) Can a stochastic cusp catastrophe model explain housing market crashes? J Econ Dyn Control 69:68–88. https://doi.org/10.1016/j.jedc.2016.05.008
Faggini M (2014) Chaotic time series analysis in economics: balance and perspectives. Chaos: an interdisciplinary. J Nonlinear Sci 24:042101. https://doi.org/10.1063/1.4903797
Faggini M, Parziale A (2016) More than 20 years of chaos in economics. Mind Soc 15:53–69. https://doi.org/10.1007/s11299-015-0164-1
Faggini M, Bruno B, Parziale A (2019) Does chaos matter in financial time series analysis? Int J Econ Financ Issues 9:18–24. https://doi.org/10.32479/ijefi.8058
Feichtinger G (1992) Hopf bifurcation in an advertising diffusion model. J Econ Behav Organ 17: 401–411. https://doi.org/10.1016/S0167-2681(95)90016-0
Feichtinger G, Ghezzi L, Piccardi C (1995) Chaotic behavior in an advertising diffusion model. Int J Bifurcat Chaos 05:255–263. https://doi.org/10.1142/S021812749500020X
Goodwin RM (1967) A growth cycle. In: Feinstein CH, Dobb M (eds) Socialism, capitalism and economic growth. Cambridge University Press, Cambridge, pp 54–58
Heijdra BJ (2017) Foundations of modern macroeconomics, 3rd edn. Oxford University Press, Oxford, New York
Heinrich T (2018) A discontinuity model of technological change: catastrophe theory and network structure. Comput Econ 51:407–425. https://doi.org/10.1007/s10614-016-9609-9
Ho T, Saunders A (1980) A catastrophe model of bank failure. J Financ 35:1189–1207. https://doi.org/10.2307/2327093
Hommes C (2013) Behavioral rationality and heterogeneous expectations in complex economic systems. Cambridge University Press, Cambridge
Keen S (2013) A monetary Minsky model of the great moderation and the great recession. J Econ Behav Organ 86:221–235. https://doi.org/10.1016/j.jebo.2011.01.010
Klose AK, Karle V, Winkelmann R, Donges JF (2020) Emergence of cascading dynamics in interacting tipping elements of ecology and climate. R Soc Open Sci 7:200599. https://doi.org/10.1098/rsos.200599

Kumar R, Sharma AK, Agnihotri K (2017) Dynamics of an innovation diffusion model with time delay. East Asian J Appl Math 7:455–481. https://doi.org/10.4208/eajam.201216.230317a

Kumar R, Sharma AK, Agnihotri K (2020) Bifurcation behaviour of a nonlinear innovation diffusion model with external influences. Int J Dyn Syst Differ Equ 10:329. https://doi.org/10.1504/IJDSDE.2020.109107

Lamantia F, Radi D (2018) Evolutionary technology adoption in an oligopoly market with forward-looking firms. Chaos: an Interdisciplinary. J Nonlinear Sci 28:055904. https://doi.org/10.1063/1.5024245

Lorenz H-W (1989) Nonlinear dynamical economics and chaotic motion. Springer-Verlag, Berlin, Heidelberg

Lucas RE Jr (2003) Macroeconomic priorities. Am Econ Rev 93:1–14. https://doi.org/10.1257/000282803321455133

Maschen (2012) Phase plane nodes and stability. https://commons.wikimedia.org/wiki/File:Phase_plane_nodes.svg. Accessed 11 Apr 2023

May RM (1976) Simple mathematical models with very complicated dynamics. Nature 261:459–467. https://doi.org/10.1038/261459a0

Medio A, Lines M (2001) Nonlinear dynamics: a primer. Cambridge University Press, Cambridge

Minsky HP (1982) The financial-instability hypothesis: capitalist processes and the behavior of the economy. In: Financial crises: theory, history, and policy. Cambridge University Press, Cambridge, New York, pp 13–41

Mirowski P (1991) More heat than light: economics as social physics, physics as nature's economics. Cambridge University Press, Cambridge

Möllmann C, Cormon X, Funk S et al (2021) Tipping point realized in cod fishery. Sci Rep 11:14259. https://doi.org/10.1038/s41598-021-93843-z

Mullineux A, Peng W (1993) Nonlinear business cycle modelling. J Econ Surv 7:41–83. https://doi.org/10.1111/j.1467-6419.1993.tb00159.x

Orlando G, Sportelli M (2021) On business cycles and growth. In: Orlando G, Pisarchik AN, Stoop R (eds) Nonlinearities in economics: an interdisciplinary approach to economic dynamics, growth and cycles. Springer International Publishing, Cham, pp 153–168

Pierce J (2011) Logistic bifurcation map high resolution. https://commons.wikimedia.org/wiki/File:Logistic_Bifurcation_map_High_Resolution.png. Accessed 11 Apr 2023

Puu T (1991) Nonlinear economic dynamics. Springer, Berlin, Heidelberg

Puu T (2003) Attractors, bifurcations, & chaos – nonlinear phenomena in economics. Springer, Berlin, Heidelberg

Romer P (2016) The trouble with macroeconomics. In: Commons memorial lecture of the Omicron Delta Epsilon Society. https://paulromer.net/trouble-with-macroeconomics-update/WP-Trouble.pdf. Accessed 4 June 2023

Rosser JB (1999) On the complexities of complex economic dynamics. J Econ Perspect 13:169–192. https://doi.org/10.1257/jep.13.4.169

Scheffer M (2009) Critical transitions in nature and society. Princeton University Press, Princeton

Sguotti C, Otto SA, Frelat R et al (2019) Catastrophic dynamics limit Atlantic cod recovery. Proc R Soc B Biol Sci 286:20182877. https://doi.org/10.1098/rspb.2018.2877

Shiller RJ (2000) Irrational exuberance. Princeton University Press, Princeton

Stockhammer E, Michell J (2015) Pseudo-Goodwin cycles in a Minsky model. Working Paper PKWP1405. Post Keynesian Economics Study Group

Stockhammer E, Michell J (2017) Pseudo-Goodwin cycles in a Minsky model. Camb J Econ 41:105–125. https://doi.org/10.1093/cje/bew008

Strogatz SH (2019) Nonlinear dynamics and chaos: with applications to physics, biology, chemistry, and engineering, 2nd edn. CRC Press, Boca Raton

Verhulst P (1838) Notice sur la loi que la population suit dans son accroissement. Correspondance Mathematique et Physique de l'Observatoire de Bruxelles 4:113–121

Wesselbaum D (2017) Catastrophe theory and the financial crisis. Scot J Polit Econ 64:376–391. https://doi.org/10.1111/sjpe.12133

Westerhoff FH (2006) Nonlinear expectation formation, endogenous business cycles and stylized facts. Stud Nonlinear Dyn Econom 10:4. https://doi.org/10.2202/1558-3708.1324

Wijeratne AW, Yi F, Wei J (2009) Bifurcation analysis in the diffusive Lotka–Volterra system: An application to market economy. Chaos, Solitons Fractals 40:902–911. https://doi.org/10.1016/j.chaos.2007.08.043

Woodford M (2009) Convergence in macroeconomics: elements of the new synthesis. Am Econ J Macroecon 1:267–279

Yang D, Mu D, Yao M (2009) Analysis of financial crisis: a perspective based on catastrophe theory. In: 2009 International Conference on Management and Service Science, pp 1–4

Yapparina (2015) Orbital instability (Lyapunov exponent). https://commons.wikimedia.org/w/index.php?curid=42399467. Accessed 11 Apr 2023

Zhang J, Da Q, Wang Y (2007) Analysis of nonlinear duopoly game with heterogeneous players. Econom Modelling 24:138–148

Feedback, Circular Causality, and System Dynamics

7

Contents

7.1 Introduction ... 254
7.2 Unintended Consequences ... 256
7.3 Causality in the Social Sciences ... 262
7.3.1 Explanation by Reasons, Causes, and Processes ... 262
7.3.2 Types of Causes ... 266
7.3.3 Modeling Causal Mechanisms ... 271
7.3.4 Causality in Economics ... 273
7.4 Feedback and System Dynamics ... 275
7.4.1 Feedback ... 275
7.4.2 Causal Loop Diagrams ... 277
7.4.3 Modes of Dynamic Behavior ... 280
7.4.4 Stock-flow Diagrams ... 289
7.4.5 System Dynamics Models ... 293
7.5 Infection and Diffusion ... 297
7.5.1 The SIR Model ... 297
7.5.2 Sentiment and Narratives ... 301
7.5.3 The Bass Diffusion Model ... 304
7.6 Dynamic Decision-making and Oscillations ... 307
7.6.1 Stock Management Control Problems ... 308
7.6.2 The Beer Distribution Game and the Bullwhip Effect ... 309
7.6.3 System Dynamics Model of the Beer Distribution Game ... 314
7.7 Collapse ... 319
7.7.1 Exploitation of Renewable Common-pool Resources ... 320
7.7.2 Collapse of Civilizations ... 327
7.8 Causal Complexity ... 331
References ... 335

Abstract

Chapter 7 is about feedback, circular causality, and system dynamics modeling. Circular causality due to positive or negative feedback is a major cause of complexity. When the causality between variables is not linear but circular, we

M. Roos, *Principles of Complexity Economics*, Classroom Companion: Economics,
https://doi.org/10.1007/978-3-031-51436-4_7

cannot separate causes and effects, which makes it difficult to predict what will happen in a system. Ignoring feedback can lead to unintended consequences, of which several examples are given. This chapter also provides a broad discussion of causality in the social sciences, which is more difficult than the law-like causality in the natural sciences. System dynamics modeling is an excellent way to analyze the effects of feedback and circular causality. After the thorough discussion of causality, the chapter introduces the basics of system dynamics. As economic applications, the Bass diffusion model based on the SIR model from epidemiology, the beer distribution game, a model of a renewable common-pool resource, and a model of societal collapse are presented.

Keywords

Causality · Causal loop diagram · Stock-flow diagram · Unintended consequences

Guiding Questions

- What is circular or nonlinear causality?
- What does the Law of Unintended Consequences say?
- What is explanation and how can we explain something?
- How can we classify different types of causality?
- What modes of behavior are common in dynamic systems?
- Why are stocks and flows important in system dynamics models?
- Why should economists care about models of contagion?
- What are stock management control problems and why are they so difficult?
- How can economic and societal collapse occur?
- What is causal complexity?

7.1 Introduction

As noted in Chap. 6, nonlinearity is used with two meanings. It can refer to models in which the relationships between variables are nonlinear resulting in nonlinear dynamics. This interpretation of nonlinearity was the subject of Chap. 6. This chapter focuses on the interpretation of nonlinearity that refers to the direction of causality between variables. Everyday thinking, and even much of scientific thinking, assumes *linear causality*, meaning that causality runs in one direction from a cause to an effect. *Circular causality* is another form of causality that is important in systems theory and complexity science. In contrast to linear causality, there is no unidirectional relationship between a cause and an effect, but the variables in a system are causally interrelated and influence each other in multiple directions. Because of feedback, *causal loops* (or *feedback loops*) occur, making it difficult to identify clear causes and effects. In technical terms, *feedback* occurs when the output of a system is also an input. Systems with multiple feedback loops can have complicated and often counterintuitive dynamics, fulfilling our heuristic definition that complex systems are difficult to describe, understand, predict, and control. Ignored feedback loops often lead to *unintended consequences* of actions. A major goal of systems thinking is to identify feedback loops to avoid such unintended consequences.

The method of system dynamics is useful for modeling and analyzing the behavior of systems with multiple feedback loops. System dynamics models are typically represented as diagrams and implemented as computer simulations. In Chap. 6, you learned about the limitations of algebraic modeling with many variables due to analytical intractability, especially in the presence of nonlinear relationships. System dynamics modeling does not require analytical tractability, so it does not need the extreme simplifying assumptions often found in algebraic models. Note that the dynamic models in Chap. 6 and the models that will be presented in this chapter are closely related. In principle, system dynamics models consist of differential equations, but they are presented in a different format and solved numerically. *Causal loop diagrams* are the main tool for developing, representing, and communicating system dynamics models. They are useful for developing an intuition about the effects of circular causality.

We begin the chapter in Sect. 7.2 with some examples of unintended consequences, also known as *side effects*. From a systems perspective, however, there is no reason to distinguish between side effects and main effects. The effects may differ in magnitude, but side effects can be even greater than the main effects. The only reason why some consequences of actions are called side effects is that they were not anticipated in advance. The failure to foresee some effects of one's actions is a result of the complexity and incomplete understanding of the causal relationships in the manipulated system. The observation that human intervention in complex systems often leads to surprising results is often called the *Law of Unintended Consequences*. This law applies to all types of systems that decision-makers try to control: social systems through the use of laws and regulations, natural systems through the use of technology, and economic systems through the use of incentives. Economics has always sought to identify the unintended consequences of private and public actions in the economy and to advise decision-makers how to avoid them. Complexity economics does not depart from this long tradition, but adds new methods to the economist's toolbox. The cartoon in Fig. 7.1 illustrates the idea of ignored circular causality leading to unintended consequences that ultimately harm the decision-maker.

After discussing how we can understand causality in social systems in Sect. 7.3, we continue with a general introduction to system dynamics modeling. Section 7.4 provides a basic understanding of this modeling approach. A more in-depth treatment can be found in Sterman (2000), Bossel (2007), or Bala et al. (2017). In particular, you will learn about *causal loop diagrams*, *stock-flow diagrams*, and *system dynamics models*. We also discuss six fundamental modes of dynamic system behavior. The methodological introduction is the basis for a series of example

Fig. 7.1 The law of unintended consequences. Source: Author

models that demonstrate the potential of system dynamics for complexity economics.

Section 7.5 introduces infection and diffusion models that show how something, such as a virus, an opinion, optimism, or a new product, spreads in a population. The *SIR model* and the *Bass diffusion model* are canonical models of this type. The Beer Distribution Game in Sect. 7.6 is another classic system dynamics model that shows how coordination problems in a supply chain can lead to oscillations. Similar problems arise at the macroeconomic level and explain business cycle fluctuations. Section 7.7 contains models of collapse, a topic often neglected in neoclassical economics, but highly relevant in the context of sustainability. Section 7.8 concludes the chapter with *causal complexity* as another measure of complexity.

7.2 Unintended Consequences

The Law of Unintended Consequences applies to all kinds of human actions, from simple decisions in everyday life to large-scale policies affecting thousands or even millions of people. The management literature (e.g., Senge 1990) refers to *fixes that fail* or *fixes that backfire* as a system archetype (or system pattern) in which an apparent solution to a problem (a fix) has an immediate desired effect that is counteracted in the long run by undesired side effects. Let us look at some examples starting small and then moving to more significant macroscopic cases.

Everyone in the modern world experiences **back pain** from time to time. When your back hurts, it is a natural reaction to avoid activity and rest because any movement is painful. For a long time, even doctors recommended bed rest as a cure for back pain. However, research has shown that bed rest is not an effective treatment and can actually delay recovery (Waddell 1993, Waddell et al. 1997). Instead, patients should stay active and continue their normal activities as much as possible. While rest may provide immediate relief, it has several unintended consequences collectively referred to as disuse syndrome, such as muscle atrophy, loss of bone density, high blood pressure, or joint stiffness. In addition to the physical effects of inactivity, bed rest can have biopsychosocial effects on the patient, such as depression, anxiety, frustration, or anger. In addition to the pain, bed rest makes you feel sick, which delays recovery.

Another problem that many people experience is being overwhelmed with work and having a large **backlog of tasks**. The common approach to this problem is to work harder by speeding up and working overtime. Again, while working harder may seem like an easy solution to the problem, it is often only a short-term fix that makes the problem worse in the long run. Working harder has several unintended effects that increase workload. First, working overtime leads to lower productivity due to fatigue. A task that might be completed quickly when you are fresh and focused may take much longer when your cognitive resources are depleted. Second, working faster increases the likelihood of making mistakes, which typically require additional work to correct. Third, hard-working people attract extra work from others because they appear so productive and resilient. The most counterintuitive solution to the problem of work overload is to slow down and take more breaks.

Other economic examples are known as the **cobra effect**, based on an anecdote from when India was a British colony. The cobra effect refers to misaligned economic incentives that achieve the opposite of what the designers intended. The story of the original cobra effect involves British administrators' concerns about poisonous cobras in Delhi. To reduce the number of cobras, the British offered a bounty for every dead cobra as an incentive to kill the snakes. The anecdote goes that the people of Delhi started breeding cobras to earn an income. When the government learned that most of the cobras being supplied had been bred rather than caught in the wild, the program was terminated, rendering the cobras worthless to the breeders. The breeders released their cobras, which increased the wild cobra population. A similar story, called the Great Hanoi Rat Massacre, is reported from Hanoi in Vietnam under French rule. The cobra effect applies not only to historical curiosities but also to systemic perverse incentives. In many countries, doctors are paid for individual treatments. Combined with universal health insurance, which covers most of the cost of treatment, this payment system can be seen as harmful to health rather than producing optimal health care. When doctors are paid on a fee-for-service basis, they have no financial incentive to encourage patients to take preventive measures. When a sick patient comes in, the physician has an incentive to use all available diagnostic procedures and to prescribe more rather than less treatment. Since patients do not have to pay, they also demand extensive treatment, believing that more treatment is better than less. Such a system leads to systematic overtreatment and significant negative consequences, such as the overuse of antibiotics or X-rays.

Unintended negative consequences of regulation and technology are called **rebound effects**. A *rebound effect* is a behavioral or systemic response to an intervention that diminishes or even overcompensates the intended direct effect on the target variable. Classic examples of rebound effects are well known in resource and environmental economics. For example, more fuel-efficient cars often do not reduce fuel consumption, because car drivers drive more often and longer if their car consumes less gas per mile. Similarly, energy-saving bulbs and LEDs lead to more lighting in private homes and public spaces. According to the *Khazzoom–Brookes postulate*, increased energy efficiency tends to lead to increased energy consumption (similar to what the much older *Jevons paradox says*). Rebound effects typically consist of a direct (or substitution) effect, an indirect (or income) effect, and a system effect due to higher growth. Rebound effects also occur with respect to time, e.g. using faster washing machines more often or commuting longer distances with better connections. As a result, the total time spent on the activity remains constant, even though the activity can be performed more quickly. Finally, there are cases of risk compensation, which means that people take more risks after the implementation of safety policies. This has been reported for more risky driving after the introduction of the seat belt and the airbag or mandatory bicycle helmets.

The **design of systems** is also prone to unintended consequences. Excessive automobile traffic and congestion are major problems in many countries. A standard policy response to congestion is to build more and bigger roads. For a given number of cars, increased road capacity does indeed reduce congestion. However, in the medium and long term, there are many responses by drivers that lead to more traffic and more cars on the road, negating the effects of the newly built road capacity. The additional traffic is referred to as *induced traffic*, which results from more trips per day, longer average trip lengths, expansion of the reachable area, and also reduced attractiveness of alternative modes of transportation when travel time by car is reduced due to new roads. Duranton and Turner (2011) provide evidence for the *Fundamental Law of Road Congestion*, which states that an increase in road capacity leads to a proportional increase in traffic. How to regulate financial institutions is an important economic system design problem. Until the global financial crisis of 2007–2009, there was a strong focus in many countries on microprudential regulation, i.e. regulating what individual banks can and must do. Examples of microprudential measures include restrictions on activities, capital requirements, liquidity requirements, and entry restrictions. All of these measures are designed to make individual banks more stable. Before the financial crisis, it was widely believed that stabilizing all individual banks through microprudential regulation would also stabilize the entire banking system, which turned out to be wrong during the financial crisis. De Haan et al. (2019) show empirically in a cross-country study that some elements of microprudential regulation, in particular activity restrictions and entry restrictions, actually increase systemic risk, which is clearly an unintended consequence. Restricting banks' activities to domestic investment increases the interconnectedness of banks within a country, making their joint failure more likely. Entry restrictions reduce competition, with the possible consequence that more monopolistic banks become more systemically interconnected. The financial crisis has taught regulators that microprudential regulation must be complemented by macroprudential regulation, which directly addresses systemic risk and overall systemic stability.

Perhaps the worst unintended consequences occur when humans intervene in complex natural systems, especially ecosystems. In the fisheries management literature, Moyle et al. (1986) dubbed the unintended consequences of introducing new

Fig. 7.2 Frankie a.k.a The Creature of Doctor Frankenstein in Geneva, Switzerland. Source: Prieur (2018), Wikimedia Commons, public domain

species into an ecosystem the **Frankenstein effect**, to indicate that seemingly small interventions can have monstrous consequences. In the famous novel by Mary Shelley, the scientist Dr. Victor Frankenstein creates a human-like, but ugly and frightening creature that calls itself a monster (Fig 7.2). Hated by Dr. Frankenstein and most other humans, the monster turns against its creator and seeks revenge. A Frankenstein effect occurred after fishery managers introduced the small opossum shrimp into the Flathead River-Lake ecosystem in Northwestern Montana. The shrimp were introduced as food for the kokanee salmon, which were popular with anglers, and also as food for grizzly bears, bald eagles, and other predators. The bears and eagles were important tourist attractions. Fishery managers wanted to increase tourism in the region by having more and larger salmon eating the new shrimp. The result was a collapse of the kokanee salmon population, which caused bears, eagles, and other species such as seagulls, coyotes, mink, and otters to leave the region. Because of the reduced wildlife, park visitation dropped from a high of 46,500 in 1983 to less than 1000 in 1989 (Spencer et al. 1991). The salmon collapse occurred because opossum shrimp are eaten by lake trout, but not by kokanee salmon. Lake trout, in turn, are predators of kokanee. In addition, the opossum shrimp eat zooplankton, which is also a food of the kokanee salmon, creating a food

Fig. 7.3 The food web of the Flathead River-Lake ecosystem. Source: Author

competition (see Fig. 7.3). The addition of just one species altered the complex food web of the ecosystem with dramatic unintended consequences.

The Four Pests Campaign in China from 1958 to 1962 aimed to improve public health by eliminating mosquitoes, rats, flies, and sparrows. Because sparrows eat grain, the government expected to increase grain yields by eliminating them. The population, especially children, were ordered to disturb the birds with noise and kill them in what was called the "Smash Sparrow Campaign." The campaign was successful in killing about 2.1 billion sparrows in 1958. However, it backfired dramatically by contributing to China's Great Famine of 1959–1961, during which at least 16.5 million people died of hunger, with high estimates of 30 million starving (Chen and Wang 2021). The fatal flaw in the campaign was that omnivorous sparrows eat not only grain, but also insect pests such as lepidopterans and locusts. As a result of sparrow extinction, large-scale pest outbreaks destroyed a significant portion of grain production. Chen and Wang (2021) estimate that the slaughter of sparrows caused an annual loss of about 7 million tons of grain, which could have fed about 28 million people. They attribute about one-third of the decline in crop yields to sparrow slaughter.

All of these fixes that backfire have the same formal structure:

1. A decision-maker has a goal, e.g., promoting health, making a region more attractive or ensuring food security.
2. There is a problem in the form of a difference between the actual level and the desired level of a target variable, e.g. actual travel time by car vs. desired travel time or actual grain yield vs. desired grain yield.

3. The decision-makers can influence an instrumental variable that has a direct impact on the target variable, e.g. the number of sparrows eating grain.
4. There are causal relationships between the instrumental variable and other variables that in turn also affect the target variable, e.g. sparrows also eat insect pests that eat grain.
5. The decision-maker is unaware of, ignores, or misinterprets the other causal relationships.
6. The desired level of the target variable is not reached due to the feedback from the other variables influenced by the instrumental variables. Often, the difference between the actual level and the desired level increases.

In particular, ignorance or misinterpretation of other causal relationships (point 5) is closely related to complexity. This point was already discussed by the American sociologist Robert K. Merton, one of the founding fathers of modern sociology. Merton (1936) identifies ignorance and error as two key causes of unintended consequences. Regarding the limits of knowledge, he writes:

> *the social scientist almost invariably finds stochastic (conjectural) associations and not, as in most fields of the physical sciences, functional associations. This is to say, in the study of human behavior, there is found a set of different values of one variable with each value of the other variable(s), or in less formal language, the set of consequences of any repeated act is not constant but there is a range of consequences, any of which may follow the act in any given situation.* (Merton 1936, pp. 898/899)

He also quotes the mathematician Henri Poincaré stating that "small differences in the initial conditions produce very great ones in the final phenomena. . . . Prediction becomes impossible, and we have the fortuitous phenomenon" (Poincaré 1912, p. 2. quoted after Merton 1936, p. 899). Merton also points out that we often have to act on incomplete knowledge, and that limits of time and mental energy constrain the acquisition of more knowledge. There are many forms of error that can enter into purposive action, but Merton points specifically to the fallacy of assuming that "actions which have in the past led to the desired outcome will continue to do so" (Merton 1936, p. 901). This fallacy is an expression of the neglect of what we called *context dependence* in Chap. 2. Errors also occur when actors neglect pertinent aspects of the situation, either because of a "lack of systematic thoroughness in examining the situation" or because of a "pathological obsession where there is a determined refusal or inability to consider certain elements of the problem" (p. 901).

In the remainder of this chapter, you will see how system dynamics can help reduce the ignorance and errors that lead to unintended consequences, although it would be hubris to claim that they can ever be eliminated. But before we get to causal loop diagrams and system dynamics models, the following subsection adds some reflections on causality in the social sciences, echoing the ideas in Merton's quote above.

7.3 Causality in the Social Sciences

7.3.1 Explanation by Reasons, Causes, and Processes

A major goal of scientific research is to explain observed phenomena.[1] Explanation can be defined as the attempt to make understandable why an observed phenomenon occurred by referring to causes, reasons, contexts, and logical relationships. As this definition suggests, explanations can take many forms. Let us start with an example before moving to more general statements.

Explanations are answers to why questions. If someone asks me, "Why are you a professor of economics?" I can answer in several ways. The first answer I might give is: "Because I like the subject and the autonomy of the job, and because Professor X was my favorite comic book hero when I was a kid." This answer provides reasons, which are motives or justifications for a decision or belief. While an interest in economics is likely to be a fairly general reason for being an economics professor, being a fan of Professor X is more specific, but still perfectly legitimate if it was a real motivation for my behavior. An alternative answer might be: "Because I have certain skills and qualities, such as mathematical skills, pedagogical skills, curiosity, and perseverance, that allow me to perform the duties of a professor." This answer mentions causes, which can be defined as something that brings about an effect or makes something happen. We will talk more about causes later. A third answer might sound like this: "Because my life led me there. I studied economics because my best friend did. After graduation, I worked in a company for a short time, which was a terrible experience because my boss was a tyrant. So I decided to go back to university to get a PhD. I admired my PhD supervisor as a role model, and he supported me a lot, even after my PhD, when I was already a postdoc. We wrote some papers together that were well received and helped me get a tenured position." This account describes a process of sequential events and actions that are interrelated. Note that the little story refers to reasons ("because my best friend did it") and causes ("we wrote papers that helped me get a job"). While some aspects of the story have some generality and could apply to other people who are professors (e.g., support from the Ph.D. advisor), others are very specific (e.g., bad work experience as a reason for doing a Ph.D.).

In everyday life, we are often interested in explanations for certain events or states of the world, e.g. "Why was my friend Bob so mean today?", "Why did I not get that job at company X?", "Why does my back hurt?". Researchers also seek **explanations for specific events**, such as the outbreak of World War I or the origin of the COVID-19 pandemic. However, scientific research often seeks **general explanations** that apply not only to specific cases, but to many or even all cases. For instance, Newton's law of universal gravitation applies to all physical objects in

[1] Explanation is not always the goal. In some cases, researchers just want to describe the world or aim to make predictions. Some scholars want to understand (verstehen) and interpret people's reasons and experiences rather than explain them. Finally, researchers may aim to deconstruct dominant worldviews, identify and critique power relations, and raise normative questions.

the universe and can be used to explain why all objects (more precisely point masses) fall to the ground (if they are not flying). Even more, the law of gravitation can also be used to explain the way an object falls to the ground, in particular, the object's velocity at any point in time during a free fall.

We can ask the following general question: "Why are those people, who are economics professors, professors of economics?". When we ask this question, we are not interested in the particular reasons, causes, and biographies of any particular person. Rather, we assume that there are general aspects that all (or most of) professors of economics have in common. There are research papers that perform regression analysis of common factors of professors, such as Graber et al. (2008) who ask "What does it take to get a tenured position [in economics in Germany, Austria and Switzerland]?". These authors examine which factors affect the probability of obtaining a professorship such are age and gender, but also the number and quality of publications in scientific journals. Similarly, Lutter and Schröder (2016) estimate whether factors such as awards, stays abroad, or the prestige of one's doctorate affect the odds of obtaining a tenured position in sociology. Morgan et al. (2022) analyze the role of professors' childhood socioeconomic status. Among other things, they find that "faculty tend to come from highly educated families. Nearly a quarter . . . of faculty report at least one of their parents holds a PhD . . . We estimate that faculty are on average between 12 to 25 times more likely to have a parent with a PhD than the general population. . . . Having a parent with a PhD is universally advantageous for becoming a professor. . . . We find that faculty with PhD parents are far more likely to receive support and encouragement for their academic careers from their parents." The authors of such studies tend to be careful about making strong causal claims, saying rather that a certain factor (e.g., having parents with PhDs) "increases the probability of" something (e.g., being a professor). Nevertheless, the practice of explaining a *dependent variable* by a number of *independent variables* through regression analysis suggests that these independent factors are causes of the dependent variable. Strictly speaking, statistical analyses often show only correlation and have difficulty proving causation. However, the example of the socioeconomic status of current professors when they were children suggests a causality running from childhood experiences in the past to the academic position today, because we typically assume that a cause precedes an effect. Morgan et al. (2022) also suggest a possible *mechanism* for why having parents with a PhD makes it more likely for someone to become a professor: PhD parents are more supportive of academic achievement than other parents.

Similar to the process-oriented answer to the individual questions, the general question of why today's economics professors are in their positions can be answered with reference to processes. These processes must describe social or political processes that affect many people in the same way at a given time. Otherwise, they could not apply to many different people. Such an explanation might describe the typical process of becoming an economics professor (in Germany) in recent years:

1) After high school, people did a BSc and an MSc in an economics program at a university.

2) After graduation, they enrolled in a PhD program or became a research assistant of an economics professor. They wrote a cumulative dissertation consisting of 3–5 papers.
3) After receiving their PhD, they became post-doctoral researcher in a university department or a research institute or obtained a position as assistant professor. In these positions, they conducted mainly quantitative research, which they published in peer-reviewed international economics journals. They also gained experience in teaching and in writing grant proposals for research funding.
4) About 6 years after completing their PhDs, the researchers applied for open professorships (either associate or full) at other universities. If they were invited by the selection committee, they gave a research presentation, held a short lecture, and answered questions from the committee about their experience and plans for the future.
5) If the committee was satisfied with their performance—especially with regard to the quality and quantity of research—they received and accepted an offer from the university.

Note that such a process explains *how* something came to be rather than *why* it is as it is. However, explaining why something is what it is can be closely related to explaining how something became what it is. In our example of economics professors, we might observe that today's professors in Germany are quite different from the professors of 30 years ago. Rosser et al. (2010) describe how economics[2] at European universities underwent a structural change in the 1990s and early 2000s. In the past, economics teaching and research in Europe was often conducted in the national language, such as German, French, or Italian. Each country had its own economic tradition, which was separate from economics in the English-speaking world. Moreover, economists often analyzed the economic, institutional, and political conditions of their own countries and published their results in their native languages, often in books rather than in journals. By the 1990s, this way of doing economics was seen as provincial and old-fashioned. Ph.D. programs similar to those at U.S. universities were introduced in many European countries, and the standards for obtaining a Ph.D. and, a little later, tenure were changed. Whereas in the 1970s and 1980s, it was possible to get tenure as an economics professor at a European university without any publications in international journals, this is impossible today. Thus, an explanation of why economics professors in Germany today are different from their colleagues 30 years ago requires a description and explanation of how qualification and tenure standards have changed in recent decades. Borghans and Cörvers (2009) provide a detailed account of the factors that have contributed to these shifts. The establishment of a European Higher Education Area as part of the European unification process is one of the factors that led to American-style standards for higher education and research in Europe.

[2]Kieser (2004) describes a similar process of "Americanization" in management education in Germany.

Geels (2022) discusses three philosophies of science: *positivism*, *pragmatism*, and *critical realism*. Complexity thinking introduced in Chap. 2 is closest to critical realism, while neoclassical economics is more in the tradition of positivism and pragmatism. The three philosophies of science differ in their views on causality and explanation. Positivism regards causality as *nomothetic*, i.e. as law-like regularities between entities. To explain means to present a deductive, logical, and formal argument based on general theories built on the notion of law-like regularities. Theoretical neoclassical models such as the Ramsey growth model or DSGE models of the business cycle are examples of a positivist approach. Pragmatism is not interested in general laws, but has a practical orientation, adopting a direct cause-and-effect approach. Since the focus is on interventions, pragmatists are mainly interested in finding out which variables need to be changed in order to achieve a desired effect. The explanation follows the logic of regression analysis, in which dependent variables are explained as the effects of independent variables. Much of the current empirical research in neoclassical economics is pragmatic, e.g. the paper by Graber et al. (2008) on the factors that make it more likely to become an economics professor. Critical realism advocates the notion of *generative causality*, in which outcomes are produced by interacting entities, causal mechanisms, and structures. Actors (or agents) are effective causes of what happens in society, and structures define the conditions under which actions occur. Generative causality implies that an explanation provides an account of how outcomes are produced by agents and *causal mechanisms* in structural contexts. In this philosophy of science, causal mechanisms are crucial because they link actors and structural contexts to observed outcomes. Causal mechanisms can be defined as the processes or chains of events that lead to an outcome. Importantly, mechanisms are not general laws that always operate in the same way, but are contingent. Depending on the specific context of a situation, the specific mechanisms that produce an outcome may be different. Thus, we need *middle-range theories* to explain observed phenomena that are neither too general and abstract to ignore context, nor too specific to apply only to a particular case.

To summarize:

- To explain is to make something understandable by giving a reason for or cause for it.
- Explanations can refer to specific events or states of the world, or to general classes of events or states of the world.
- Reasons are justifications or motivations for a decision or a belief. They thus refer to human beings who can make decisions or hold beliefs.
- Causes are factors, events, or actions that bring about an effect or make something happen.
- Reasons and causes explain why something is the way it is.
- Processes and mechanisms explain how something came to be.
- Positivism, pragmatism, and critical realism have different views of causality and explanation. Complexity thinking fits best with critical realism, which adopts the

notion of generative causality and emphasizes causal mechanisms (or processes) for explanation.

7.3.2 Types of Causes

The nature of causality and whether it exists at all are deep philosophical issues. David Hume argued that we cannot observe or prove the existence of causality. The only thing that we can observe is *constant conjunction*. Two events E_1 and E_2 are constantly conjoined if whenever one occurs, the other also occurs. In Fig. 7.4, event E_1 is the movement of bar X to the left and E_2 is the movement of bar Y to the left.

The mechanical arrangement shown in Fig. 7.4 seems simple, but it actually illustrates a number of interesting ideas about causality. First, let us assume that we could only see bar X and bar Y. In this case, we could only observe the two bar moving together in the same direction. Whenever X moves in one direction, Y does the same—*constant conjunction*. Note that this observation alone would not allow us to identify a cause and an effect. We could turn the statement around and say that whenever Y moves in one direction, X does the same. To talk about causality, we need something more: a cause that moves either bar X or bar Y in the first place. For example, there might be a hand that moves bar X to the left, so we would say that moving X to the left is the cause of moving Y to the left. We can make two more observations: First, Y will only move if X moves (unless there is a direct force acting on Y). In other words, the motion of X is necessary for the motion of Y. Second, we do not need any other cause for Y to move—bar Y always moves when we move Y. We say that moving X is *sufficient* to move Y. Now suppose we open the black box that has been hiding the cogs so far. The cogs are the *mechanism* that connects the two bars. Knowing this mechanism, we can explain, why moving bar X leads to a movement of bar Y: Moving rack X to the left, turns cog A counterclockwise. The teeth of cog A transmit the motion to cog B causing it to turn clockwise. Cog B moves cog C, C moves D, and finally the teeth of cog D push against the teeth of bar

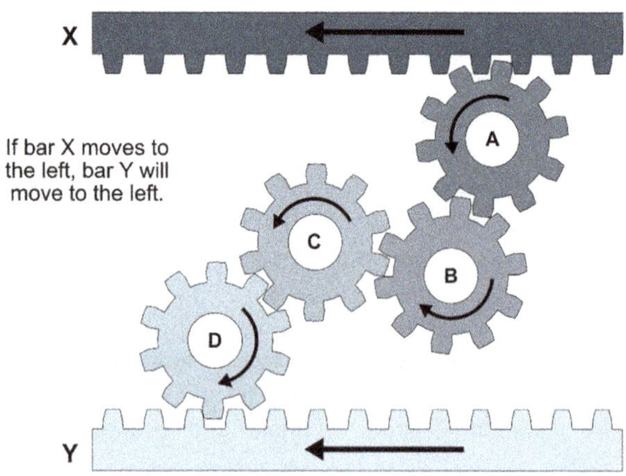

Fig. 7.4 Cause and effect in a system of cogs and racks. Source: Author

Y from the right, causing the rack to move to the left. The gear transmits the initial force applied X to Y. In principle, causation in this system is *deterministic*, i.e. the movement of X is necessary and sufficient for the movement of Y. We say "in principle," because we can imagine situations, in which the causation fails due to some interference of other factors with the system. An *additive interference* occurs when something—say a screw—falls into the gear and gets stuck between two cogs. Then the whole gear is jammed, because something has been added to it that interferes with its normal functioning. Another way in which the mechanism can fail is if one of the cogs falls out of the gear, say C, which would be an example of *subtractive interference*. In this case, the mechanism would function normally up to cog B, but the missing cog C would break the causal chain of transmitting force from X to Y.

Knowing the mechanism behind an observed correlation (or constant conjunction) between two variables is important in order to rule out the possibility that the two are in fact not causally related but have a *common cause*. In particular, if it seems unlikely that two variables are causally related even though they are correlated, we might ask if both of them have a common cause. An example is when the barometer goes down and then a storm comes up. There is a constant conjunction between what the barometer shows and the later weather conditions, but it is—of course—implausible that the barometer causes the weather. Instead, both have a common cause: the drop in atmospheric pressure.

We can use the example of the gear as an analogy to better illustrate what positivism, pragmatism, and critical realism mean. A positivist might try to model the gear with a set of equations describing the motions of the bars and the cogs. This would entail abstracting from specific properties of a particular gear. The model would represent all gears of that type and could be used to make general statements that apply to any gear of that class at any time. A pragmatist is not interested in the cogs, but would only measure the movements of the bars. There may be other bars that move, such as bars U, V, and W. A pragmatist approach would be to define bar Y as the dependent variable and bars U, V, W, and X as the independent variables. The movements of all bars could be measured several times in order to create a data set which could be used for statistical analysis. A regression would find that only X has a significant effect on Y, but not U, V, and W. The statistical relationship between X and Y might not be perfect, if some of the cogs are a little loose, so that Y moves only partially or not at all when X is moved. We could also estimate the average size of the effect telling us how much Y moves to the left, if X is moved to the left by 10 cm. A critical realist might observe the working of the gear over a longer period. She might find out that some of the cogs loosen or wear out, creating slack. As a result, the transmission of the motion becomes weaker over time and may even break down at some point. Thus, the same movement of bar X could cause a different movement of bar Y, depending on the condition of the cogs in the mechanism. While the change in the way the gears work would be a nuisance to the positivist who seeks general theories of the world, the critical realist (and the complexity thinker) accepts that the world is not made up of ideal abstractions, but of

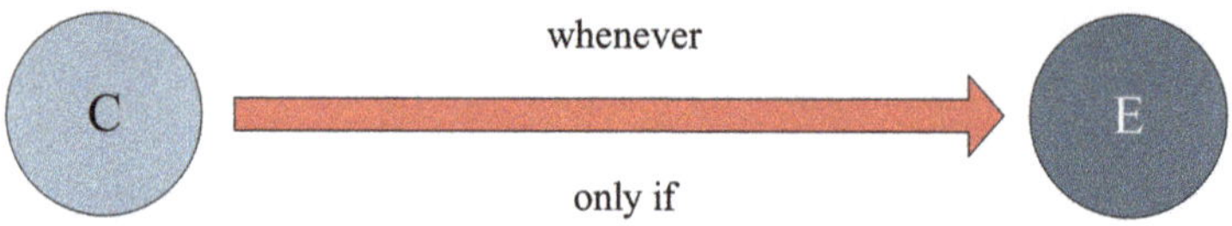

Fig. 7.5 Deterministic causality. Source: Author

Table 7.1 Rabies is a sufficient cause of death

Rabies/Death	No	Yes
No	X	X
Yes		X

Table 7.2 HIV is a necessary cause for AIDS

HIV/AIDS	No	Yes
No	X	
Yes	X	X

real entities that interact and change their behavior over time and in response to changing contextual conditions.

In biological and social systems, it is typically much harder to identify causality than in physical systems. In the (ideal) physical system of the gear, we saw that bar Y always moves if X moves and only moves, if X does so. In other words, the movement of Y was completely determined by the movement of X or the movement of X was both necessary and sufficient for the movement of Y (see Fig. 7.5).

Causes need not always be both necessary and sufficient. Some causes may be sufficient but not necessary for an effect, and others may be necessary but not sufficient. For example, rabies, caused by infection with the rabies virus, is a sufficient cause of death because everyone who contracts the disease will die of rabies due to the inflammation of the brain and meninges. Of course, rabies is not a necessary cause of death because there are many other ways to die. The sufficiency condition therefore excludes the case in Table 7.1 where the cause has no effect.

An infection with HIV is necessary to get AIDS, but not everyone with the HIV virus gets AIDS. Some people have genetic variations that prevent the virus from replicating in the human body. Therefore, we also need additional conditions or causes to get AIDS. As shown in Table 7.2, a necessary cause excludes the case of someone getting AIDS without being infected with HIV, i.e. the effect without that specific cause.

Necessary causes increase the probability of an effect, but do not determine it alone (see Fig. 7.6). This kind of causality is called *probabilistic causality* or *indeterministic causality*. Being infected with HIV makes more likely to die of AIDS. As a matter of fact, the probability of dying of AIDS without being infected with HIV is zero. At the same time, even with an HIV infection, the probability of dying of AIDS is smaller than one, because some people with HIV do not even contract AIDS.

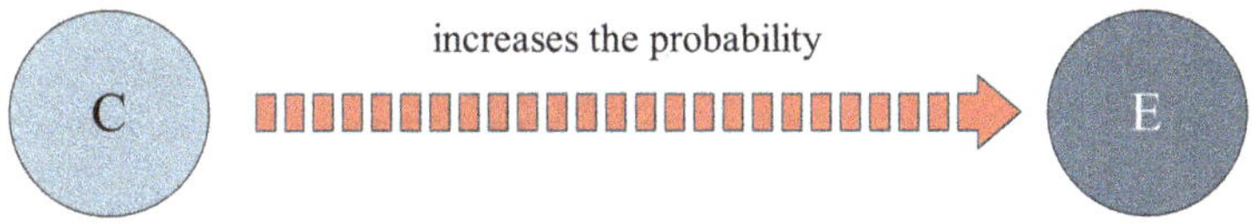

Fig. 7.6 Indeterministic causality. Source: Author

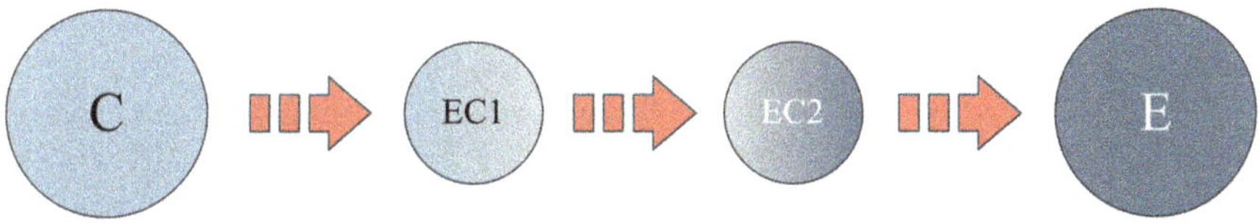

Fig. 7.7 Proximal and distal causes. Source: Author

When an individual person dies after having been in contact with another person infected with a virus, we can trace the causal physical (or physiological) process that led to death. We can trace how the virus was transmitted from one person to another, how it replicated, and what processes it triggered in the body. For example, the HI virus damages the human immune system, causing people with AIDS develop cancer or contract opportunistic infections caused by bacteria, fungi, or other viruses that are normally controlled by an intact immune system. One of these conditions eventually kills the person through its impact on the organism. Causality that describes a physical mechanism, subject to the laws of nature, that links a cause (e.g., contact with an HIV-infected person) to an effect (e.g., death) is called *aleatory causality*.

A causal process (or mechanism) consists of several steps, as shown in Fig. 7.7. In our example, HIV infection is a cause of the effect death, but only a distal or indirect cause, mediated by other relationships. Infection C causes AIDS (EC1), which may then cause Kaposi's sarcoma (a type of cancer). The cancer may be the proximate cause (EC2) of death if it spreads to the lungs and other internal organs. Note that there may be more steps in this causal chain; for example, infection with the human herpes virus that causes Kaposi's sarcoma. There could also be causes that lead to infection C, such as sexual contact with an infected person and transmission of the HIV virus through blood or other body fluids. We could go back even further in the chain and ask why the person had sexual contact with the infected person. In principle, there is no clear first cause, because we can always ask about the cause of a cause. In most situations, however, more proximal (or direct) causes seem more relevant than more distal (or indirect) causes.

If we are not looking at a specific individual, but at a whole population, we can no longer talk about aleatory causality, because there will be many differences between the members of the population. There are different ways to acquire the virus, some people are immune and do not get AIDS, and those with AIDS will get other diseases that cause death in some but not in others. When we analyze the relationship between HIV infection and subsequent death in a population, we can only use the concept of *statistical causality*, which makes statements about statistical regularities. With large data sets of members of a population, we can say which groups are more likely to die after HIV infection, or identify certain behaviors or characteristics of individuals that are correlated with death rates.

When working with statistical causality, we must be aware of the difference between *phenomenal regularities* (or *surface causes*) and *governing regularities* (or *basic causes*). We might find that drug addicts are more likely to die of AIDS than non-addicts. This statistical finding is a phenomenal regularity, because AIDS and the death it causes are not caused directly by drug addiction, but by the practice of sharing needles for injecting drugs, through which contaminated blood can be transmitted. The dominant regularity is this behavior of drug addicts. Finally, we can also define the concept of *fundamental cause* (or *root cause*). It is a solid finding in epidemiological research that there is an inverse relationship between socioeconomic status, health, and life expectancy. On average, people with low socioeconomic status die earlier than people with high socioeconomic status. There are many mechanisms for this relationship, such as more drug use by poor people, unhealthy eating habits, less preventive behavior, less or worse treatment in case of illness, and so on. We could say that all of these immediate causes of death have the same underlying cause: low socioeconomic status.

In the social sciences, including economics, we are typically concerned with statistical causality. To be confident that the statistical regularities we identify are true causal relationships and not spurious or the result of common causes, we can take several approaches. First, we could argue that we have good reasons to believe that some variables are exogenous or predetermined. For example, if we find a correlation between y_t and x_{t-1}, it seems natural to assume that x_{t-1} is the cause of y_t and not vice versa, because we normally assume that a cause precedes an effect in time. Another example could be regulatory and legal changes. If we observe that a new law was passed in a certain year (e.g., introducing a minimum wage) and the wages of certain groups increased, it seems reasonable to assume that the law was the cause of the changes in economic variables. However, arguments are stronger when they are supported by empirical evidence. Therefore, the second way to make a case for true causality is to use some kind of experiment. It is often easier to conduct experiments with physical phenomena than with social phenomena. In our gear example, we can systematically experiment with the bars: we can move bar X a certain amount to the left or right and measure what happens to bar Y. Because we control what happens to bar X, we know that it is the independent variable and that the movements of bar Y depend on it. In social contexts, experiments are also sometimes possible.

To test whether a new drug has the desired effect, medical researchers conduct *randomized control trials*. They randomly divide a large group of people into a treatment group that gets the drug and a control group that gets a placebo instead of the drug. If the groups are large and the group assignment is truly random, then the treatment and control groups should be statistically indistinguishable in terms of their characteristics, i.e. the distributions of age, income, education, prior health status, etc., of the members should be the same. Ideally, the only difference is that the treatment group is exposed to the drug and the control group is not. If we observe a difference in average health status after using the drug, we can conclude that the drug was the cause because it was the only difference. Economists also conduct experiments, either in the laboratory or in the field. For example, we can evaluate the effectiveness of a labor market policy (e.g., special training) by exposing a treatment group to the policy but not a statistically identical control group.

Sometimes there are the so-called *natural experiments*, where the intervention was not intentionally brought about by the researcher, but by some exogenous event (from the researcher's perspective). A classic example of such a natural experiment is the study by Angrist and Krueger (1991), which showed that compulsory schooling laws led to longer school attendance and higher wages. The natural experiment consists in the age variation of individuals in the same school year. Children born in the first quarter of the year reach the legal dropout age earlier than children born in the year. The study finds that students born earlier in the year have lower average educational attainment and subsequently lower wages than students born later in the year, which Angrist and Krueger attribute to the ability to leave school earlier. In many situations of interest to economists, it is not possible to conduct an experiment, and natural experiments have not been identified.

7.3.3 Modeling Causal Mechanisms

Consistent with the previous discussion, the third approach to lending credibility to claimed causality is to model and estimate the causal mechanism. While it may not be possible in the social sciences to pin down aleatory causality as it is in the natural sciences, we often have an idea of the process that typically produces an outcome. Modeling that process and providing empirical support for the steps in the process is a way to rule out the alternative explanations that a correlation between two variables is due to some unobserved common cause or purely random.

A good illustration of this approach can be found in Leahey (2007), who addresses the question of why female faculty members earn less than male academics. Leahey argues that the standard analysis of this question proceeds as shown in Fig. 7.8. In a regression analysis, researcher salary is the independent variable regressed on a dummy variable for gender, a measure of academic productivity such as number of publications, and some other control variables such as age or academic rank. These studies typically find a negative direct correlation between salaries and gender and a positive correlation with productivity, but they do not tell us much about why these correlations exist. Such a regression can tell us whether gender has a direct effect on salaries or whether it works through productivity. If female researchers are less productive than men, then a bivariate correlation between gender and salary may disappear (i.e., the coefficient becomes statistically insignificant) when productivity is included in a multivariate regression. If both gender and productivity are statistically significant in a multivariate regression, we might conclude that gender has an effect on salary that is not due to gender differences in productivity.

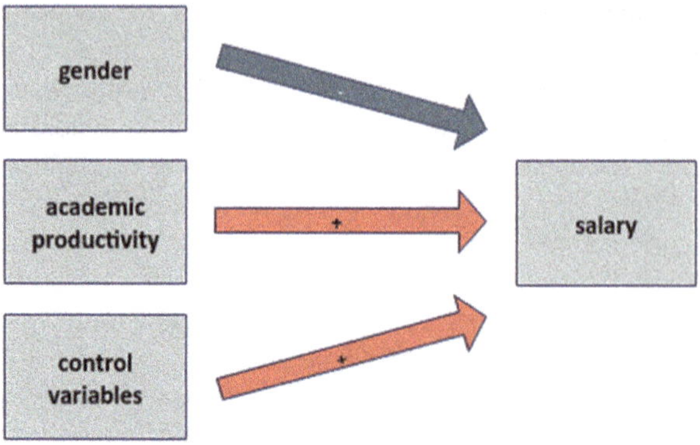

Fig. 7.8 Direct causal effect of gender on academic salaries. Source: Author's own figure after Leahey (2007)

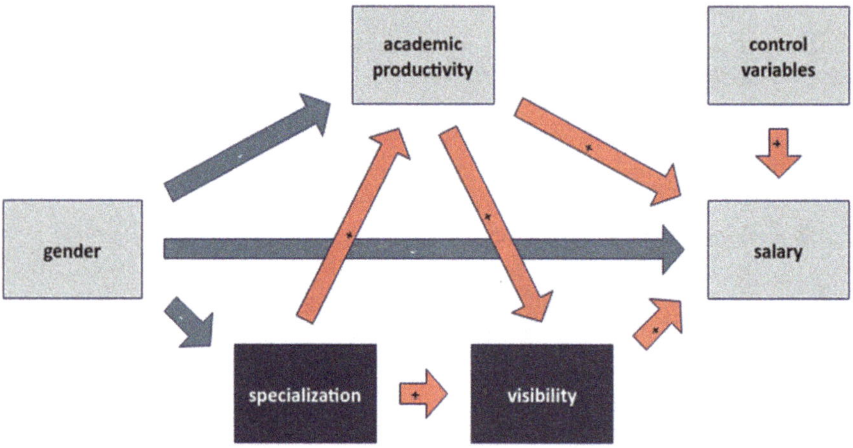

Fig. 7.9 Model of the causal mechanism of the effect of gender on academic salaries. Source: Author's own figure after Leahey (2007)

Leahey (2007) proposes a model of a mechanism through which gender affects academic salaries (see Fig. 7.9). She argues that women specialize less than men because of lower human, social, and cultural capital, and have lower productivity because of structural disadvantages such as family circumstances. Both specialization and productivity are expected to affect visibility in the academic community, which has a positive effect on salary because visibility enhances bargaining power. Importantly, Leahey estimates a simultaneous equation model that accounts for the various hypothesized relationships between the variables, providing a way to test whether the proposed mechanism is supported by the data. Figure 7.10 shows that not all of the hypothesized relationships in the estimated model are significantly different from zero. However, Leahy finds a clear chain from gender through specialization, productivity, and visibility to salary. Moreover, the direct effect found earlier is no longer detectable, suggesting that this chain may indeed explain why women earn less than men in academia.

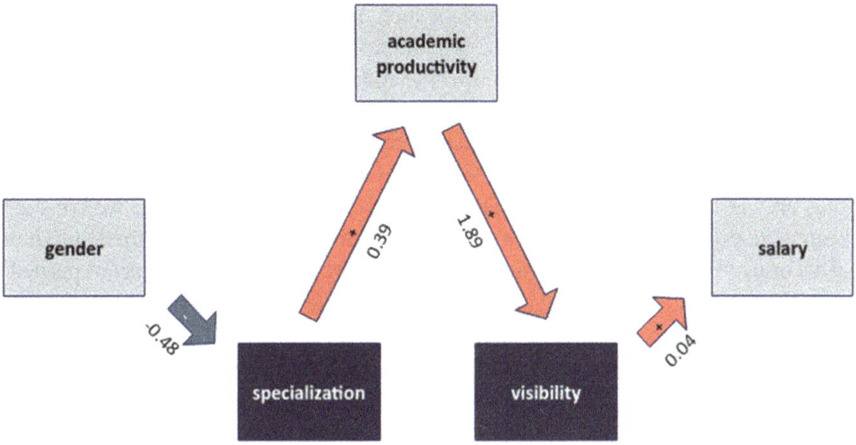

Fig. 7.10 Significant causal chain in the estimated model. Source: Author's own figure after Leahey (2007)

7.3.4 Causality in Economics

Like all scientists, economists are concerned with establishing causality between many different entities, concepts, and events. The types of causal relationships that economists analyze vary considerably, ranging from fairly narrow microeconomic issues to very broad macroeconomic issues. A typical microeconomic question is to identify the causal effects of skills and education on earnings and employment (see Hampf et al. 2017). A representative macroeconomic question concerns the causes of economic growth, which ultimately explains why some countries are very rich and many others are poor. The degree of difficulty in establishing and empirically demonstrating causality varies widely.

It is easy to argue for causality in **accounting identities** and definitions. If we define profits as the difference between revenues and costs, it is straightforward to say that, for given revenues, an increase in costs reduces profits. It must also hold that, for given income, an increase in consumption must cause a decrease in saving, since households, by definition, can either consume or save their income. Finally, given liabilities, a decrease in a firm's assets causes a decrease in the firm's equity.

Exchange is central to economics. Whenever there is a physical or economic exchange, it is also possible to talk about causal relationships. The sale of a good reduces the firm's stock of that good and increases the buyer's stock of that good. Concluding a contract to purchase a good creates an obligation for the seller to deliver the good and for the buyer to pay for it. When both parties fulfill their obligations, the contract results in the transfer of the good from the seller to the buyer and the transfer of money from the buyer to the seller.

Another key issue is **production**. With a given technology, the productive use of inputs causes the creation of physical outputs. The individual production of goods comes close to aleatory causality because it involves physical processes. A baker mixes a certain amount of raw materials such as flour, water, salt, and yeast, and exposes the dough to heat in an oven, which requires energy. The result is bread. At the individual level, there is a fairly specific functional relationship between inputs and outputs, so that we can say that changes in the quantities of inputs cause changes in the quantities of outputs. This technical relationship between inputs and outputs is captured by production functions. Note, however, that straightforward causality holds only at the level of relatively simple individual goods. As soon as we consider complex goods or aggregate output consisting of many goods, e.g. the total output of a firm or even an economy, the functional relationship becomes weaker. In particular, problems arise when output and inputs are defined in very abstract terms, such as "capital," which can include such diverse objects as personal computers, trucks, shovels, factory buildings, and electrolyzers. To aggregate different types of goods, we typically convert physical quantities into monetary quantities by using an economic measure of value. But this process breaks the direct chain of physical causation.

Economic theories almost inevitably involve statements about human and organizational **behavior**. Actions can be the causes of effects, such as a firm's decision to hire or fire workers. The action of hiring increases a firm's employment level and, indirectly, its output (if the new workers are used efficiently). Economic theory also makes claims about the causes of certain behaviors. One causal claim is that agents (want to) buy less of a good when its price increases. In other words, changes in prices cause inverse changes in quantities demanded. A demand function such as $Q^D = f(P)$ with $\frac{\partial f}{\partial P} < 0$ represents such a causal claim about behavior. Strictly speaking, there is a relationship between price and behavioral intention, since demand does not necessarily correspond to actual purchases. Whether an intention translates into actual behavior depends on its feasibility, which may be determined by the level of income or the availability of the demanded quantity of the good. The positivist nature of neoclassical economics is particularly evident in its law-like assumptions about human behavior, which are deductively derived from axiomatic assumptions. Neoclassical consumer choice theory assumes that consumers maximize well-behaved consumer preferences that are complete, reflexive, and transitive, and that exhibit non-saturation and diminishing marginal rates of substitution. Under these assumptions, an individual will always behave in the same way under the same conditions. A change in the relative price of a good will always elicit the same behavioral response (given income and fixed preferences). From a behavioral and complexity point of view, postulating this kind of nomothetic causality is highly questionable. We will discuss this further in Chap. 12.

Finally, economists often make statements about causal relationships between **high-level theoretical concepts**. *High-level concepts*, as opposed to low-level or *primitive concepts*, are defined in abstract or aggregate terms and require significant theoretical underpinnings for their definition. While the potential causal chain between external stimuli and human behavior may be relatively direct, the relationship between higher-level concepts requires more complicated mechanisms. The Phillips curve is an example of a causal relationship between the two higher-level economic concepts of inflation and unemployment. Neither inflation nor unemployment can be observed directly because they are macroeconomic concepts. The theoretical Phillips curve postulates that unemployment and inflation are negatively related in the short run. A causal claim from unemployment to inflation could be made via the following mechanism. When unemployment falls, the bargaining power of workers or unions increases. They can thus negotiate higher nominal wages, which push up firms' labor costs. Firms respond by raising the prices of their products, which raises the general price level. At an even higher level of abstraction, there is a strand of economic research that analyzes the relationship between multidimensional concepts such as economic growth or development and democracy. For instance, Colagrossi et al. (2020) ask: "Does democracy cause growth?". Acemoglu et al. (2019) answer that "democracy does cause growth." There is also research in the opposite direction of causality. Huber et al. (1993) and others analyze "the impact of economic development on democracy." Determining whether there is such a causation and in which direction it runs is incredibly difficult for both practical and theoretical reasons. Practically, data on these issues are very scarce, and we do not have the possibility to run randomized control trials with entire nations. Theoretically, concepts like "economic development" and "democracy" are very broad and can be measured in many (imperfect) ways. Moreover, it is quite unlikely that there are unique, context-independent mechanisms. But with various context-dependent mechanisms, we would expect the empirical results to be inconclusive, which is what we find. Whether we can ever "prove" causality between such high-level concepts in complex systems or whether the most we can expect is to find with plausible empirical support for elements of possible causal mechanisms, is an open question.

7.4 Feedback and System Dynamics

7.4.1 Feedback

Circular causality created by feedback is an important aspect of complexity. In Fig. 7.10, we saw an example of a linear causal chain from gender to specialization, from there to productivity, then to visibility, and in the final step from visibility to salary. This chain contains no feedback and therefore no circular causality. Being female is the first cause of why some academics earn less than others. The proposed mechanism is that women specialize less than men, which makes them less productive in terms of publications. Publication productivity increases visibility in the community, as measured by citations, for example. Visibility, in turn, is the only proximate cause of salary. Note that this story has a clear time dimension: researchers decide early in their careers how much to specialize, and then everything else follows.

Perhaps the world is not as simple as this linear story suggests. In Fig. 7.11, two feedback effects have been added that partially turn the causal chain into a causal loop. The first feedback we can imagine is from salary to productivity. From the

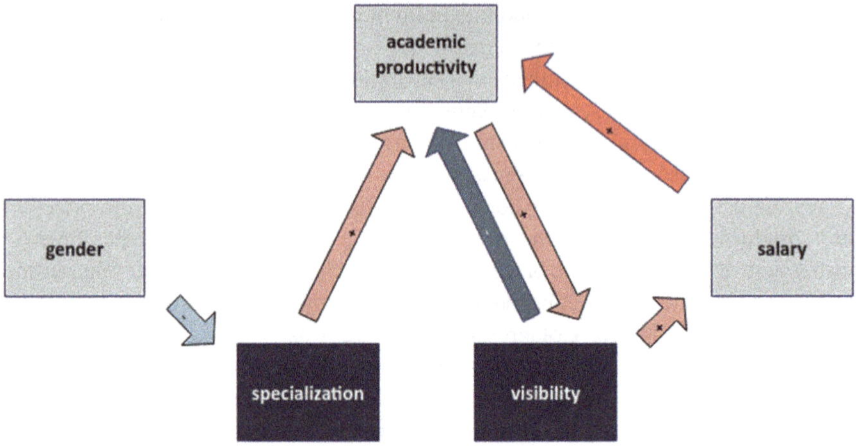

Fig. 7.11 Feedback in the compensation model of academics. Source: Author

perspective of economic incentives, it seems plausible that higher salaries motivate researchers to be more productive. Some universities even financially reward good publications. On the other hand, researchers with low salaries may become demotivated and thus less productive in terms of publications. To compensate for their relatively low university salaries, they might try to earn extra income elsewhere, for example in consulting. This positive feedback from salary to productivity is reinforcing: researchers who are already productive (mostly men) become even more productive because of the financial rewards, while relatively unproductive researchers (mostly women) are demotivated by low salaries and publish even less. The productivity effect of the salary would in turn affect their visibility, leading to further changes in their salaries. Another feedback effect we could imagine is from visibility to productivity. Researchers who are highly visible in the community are often invited as keynote speakers at conferences, for interviews, as experts in public hearings, and so on. All of these activities can distract researchers and consume time, which can affect their publication productivity. Therefore, this feedback is negative, i.e. visibility has an inverse effect on productivity. If salary depends on visibility in the research community, as measured by publication citations, then the negative feedback dampens income dynamics in the opposite direction to the positive incentive effect.

Once the causal mechanism has reached a loop, the story no longer has a beginning and an end, but becomes circular. A causal chain can be interpreted as a finite process that is triggered by something and reaches an endpoint at some point in time. In a circular process, there is not necessarily an end, because effects are also causes that keep the dynamics going. Systems with circular causation have the potential to generate continuous and complex dynamics that can be analyzed using system dynamics models.

In the example in Fig. 7.11, there is a two-way causality between productivity and visibility:

$$productivity \leftrightarrow visibility.$$

Neoclassical economists might say, that such interdependence is nothing special, because even the basic market equilibrium model postulates the simultaneous determination of price P and quantity Q. We have a demand function that depends on price, $Q^D(P)$, a supply function depending on price, $Q^S(P)$, and the equilibrium condition $Q^D(P) = Q^S(P)$, which fixes the equilibrium price. Thus, the quantity depends on the price and the price depends on the quantity:

$$quantity \leftrightarrow price$$

However, there are crucial differences between these two interdependencies. In a market equilibrium model, price and quantity are determined *simultaneously*. We cannot say that the price determines the quantity or vice versa. There is no temporal sequence. The equilibrium condition describes only a state of the world, but not a process. This is different in a system dynamics model which has a time dimension and describes causal processes. Thus, a more precise formulation of the interdependence between productivity and visibility of researchers might be

$$visibility(t + 1) = f(productivity(t))$$

$$productivity(t + 1) = g(visibility(t))$$

In other words, circular causality is not the same as simultaneous determination, because it takes into account the temporal relationships.

7.4.2 Causal Loop Diagrams

The system dynamics approach views *causal loops* as the basic elements of complex systems. The interplay of various loops makes it difficult to predict how a system will behave over time. The basic idea of causal loops is easy to illustrate and to understand.

Figure 7.12 shows a *causal loop diagram* with *positive feedback* that is *self-reinforcing*. Compound interest is an example of a positive feedback loop.[3] If there is a positive interest rate on savings, money in a savings account will generate positive interest income. This is indicated by the top arrow pointing from "Money on account" to "Interest income." The "+" symbolizes that the relationship between savings and interest income is positive: more money in the account leads to more interest income. If the interest income is not withdrawn, but credited to the existing savings account, the amount of money on this account will increase. This is indicated by the lower arrow pointing to the left. The relationship between the interest earned

[3]This figure has been produced with Vensim Professional Version 9.4.0 provided by Ventana Systems Inc. All similar figures were generated by the author with the same software.

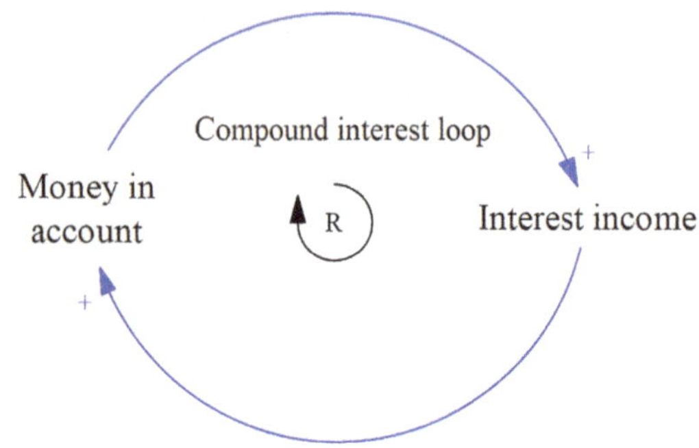

Fig. 7.12 Self-reinforcing loop with positive feedback. Source: Author. Produced with Vensim Professional Version 9.4.0 provided by Ventana Systems Inc.

and the money on the account is also positive (see the "+" at the head of the arrow), because the interest earned adds money to the account. A positive feedback loop consists of at least two positive relationships between two variables, one in each direction.

This loop is self-reinforcing, because a positive amount of money M will generate positive interest income I, which increases the amount of money in the account. With a constant interest rate i, the interest earned and the money in the account will grow over time, which is the compound interest effect:

$$I_t = iM_t$$

$$M_{t+1} = M_t + I_t = M_t + iM_t = M_t(1 + i)$$

$$M_{t+2} = M_{t+1}(1 + i) = M_t(1 + i)(1 + i) = M_t(1 + i)^2$$

$$M_{t+k} = M_t(1 + i)^k \tag{7.1}$$

Money held grows exponentially, approaching infinity in the limit (see Eq. 7.1). Note that we can also reverse this positive feedback loop. Suppose the account is initially overdrawn so that $M_0 < 0$. The account holder is indebted and must pay an interest rate i on the debt, such that the interest income is negative. Assume further that the required interest payments (the negative interest income) can be charged to the account, increasing the existing debt (or making M even more negative). This positive feedback loop is also self-reinforcing, so that with initial debt, the money in the account tends to minus infinity, $\lim_{k \to \infty} M_0(1 + i)^k \to -\infty$. Positive feedback loops can thus lead to infinite growth or to infinite decline.

Figure 7.13 shows the other basic feedback loop: a *balancing loop* with *negative feedback*. Assume that the account holder wants to buy status symbols that show her wealth. Therefore, more money in the account causes the purchase of new status symbols, which is represented by the upper arrow with the "+". To pay for these purchases, the account holder withdraws money from the account, causing the amount of money on the account to decrease. The arrow with the "-"-sign pointing to "money on account" represents this relationship. A negative feedback loop has at least one positive relationship and one negative relationship between two variables.

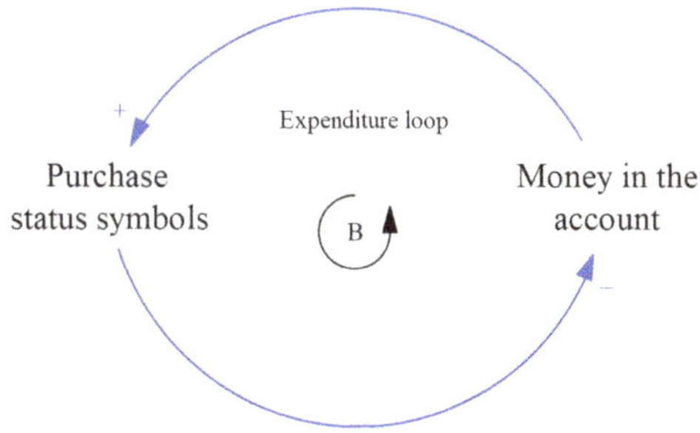

Fig. 7.13 Balancing loop with negative feedback. Source: Author. Produced with Vensim Professional Version 9.4.0 provided by Ventana Systems Inc.

If the account holder always spends a constant fraction s of the money balance on status symbols, the spending S will decrease over time, because the money balance decline as well:

$$S_t = sM_t$$

$$M_{t+1} = M_t(1 - s)$$

$$M_{t+k} = M_t(1 - s)^k \tag{7.2}$$

Equation (7.2) shows that in the long run ($k \rightarrow \infty$), money balances will approach zero, because $0 < s < 1$. We could also reverse this process. If the account holder starts with negative money (debt) on the account, then spending on status symbols should be negative, which could be interpreted as selling owned status symbols. The balancing loop would lead to the sale of status symbols until the debt on the account reaches zero. In the language of the dynamical systems we used in Chap. 6, the system has a stable fixed point at zero money on the account when negative feedback drives the dynamics.

We can combine the two feedback loops into one system, as shown in Fig. 7.14. The account holder now earns interest income, which is credited to the account, but also spends some of the money by purchasing status symbols. The dynamics of the money holdings in the account now depend on both the compound interest loop (self-reinforcing positive feedback) and the expenditure loop (balancing negative feedback). Interest income $I_t = iM_t$ adds money to the account and status symbol purchases $S_t = sM_t$ subtract money, hence

$$M_{t+1} = M_t + iM_t - sM_t$$

$$M_{t+k} = M_t(1 + i - s)^k. \tag{7.3}$$

Equation (7.3) shows that the dynamics of M depend on the relative strengths of the positive and the negative feedback. If the interest rate i (positive feedback) is greater than the spending rate s on status symbols (negative feedback), money

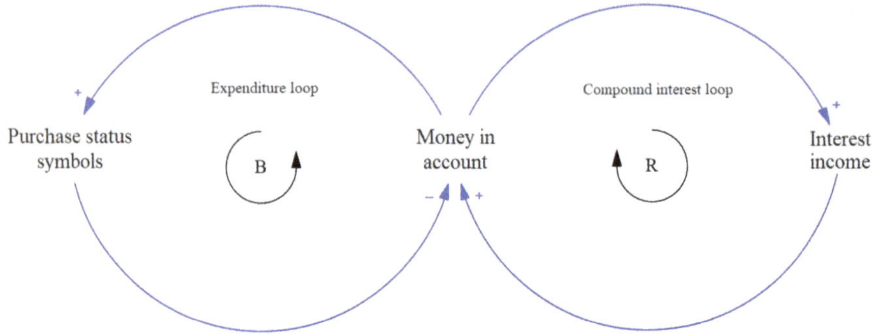

Fig. 7.14 System with a positive and a negative feedback loop. Source: Author. Produced with Vensim Professional Version 9.4.0 provided by Ventana Systems Inc.

holdings will increase. If $i < s$, money holdings will decline, and if the two feedback loops just offset each other, $i = s$, the amount of money in the account is constant. Note that in Eq. (7.3), we have essentially collapsed the positive feedback loop and the negative feedback loop into a single feedback loop that can be either positive or negative depending on the relative magnitudes of the two loops. We can therefore define $I_t - S_t$ as the *net rate of increase*.

The causal loop diagram of this simple system in Fig. 7.13 is sufficient to illustrate the main idea of causal loop diagrams. They typically consist of several interacting positive and negative feedback loops. It is useful to name each loop and to indicate, whether it is balancing (B) or self-reinforcing (R).

7.4.3 Modes of Dynamic Behavior

Simple positive feedback loops generate exponential growth and negative feedback loops equilibrate. Exponential growth and convergence to an equilibrium are common dynamics in (neoclassical) economics. But there are at least four other modes of dynamic behavior that are relevant to economics (see Fig. 7.15).

There is not much to say about **exponential growth**, which is the result of simple positive feedback. Figure 7.16 illustrates the mechanism in a more general way than in the previous example of compound interest. The state of the system is positively affected by the *net increase rate*, which in turn is positively affected by the state of the system. Note that in this terminology, "rate of increase" refers to the absolute rate of change of a quantity, not the percentage rate. In the example in Fig. 7.12, the net increase rate referred to the amount of money earned from interest (minus expenses), not to the constant rate of interest.

Balancing loops with convergence to an equilibrium are a consequence of **goal seeking**, as shown in Fig. 7.17. Goal seeking implies that there is a goal or desired state of the system and that there is some kind of corrective action when there is a discrepancy between the actual state of the system and the desired state. Applied to a

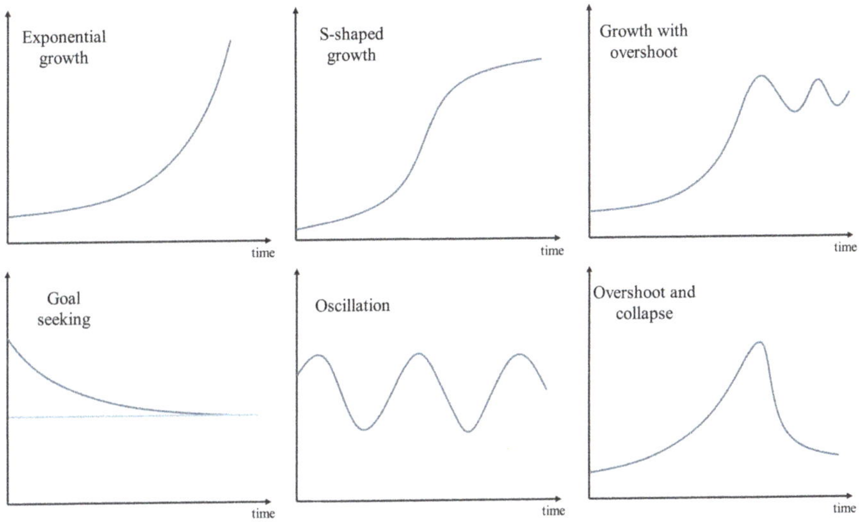

Fig. 7.15 Modes of behavior in dynamical systems. Source: Author

Fig. 7.16 Causal structure generating exponential growth. Source: Author. Produced with Vensim Professional Version 9.4.0 provided by Ventana Systems Inc.

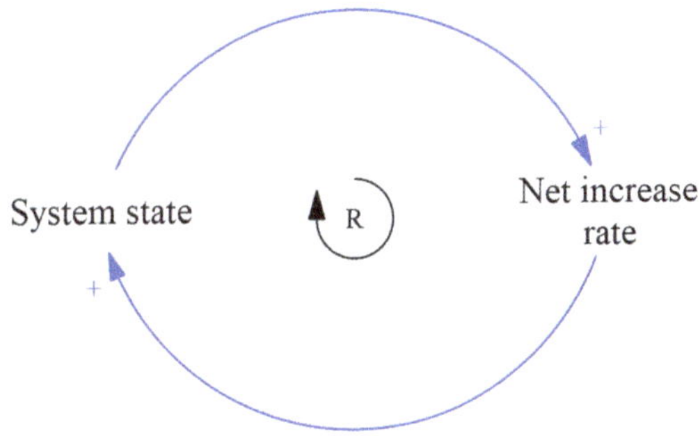

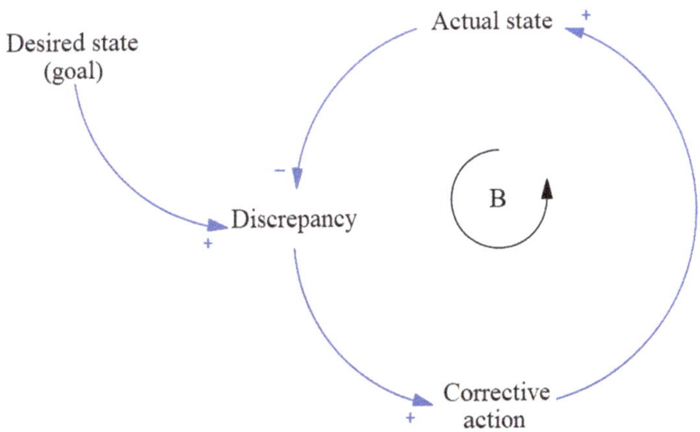

Fig. 7.17 Causal structure leading to an equilibrium. Source: Author. Produced with Vensim Professional Version 9.4.0 provided by Ventana Systems Inc.

Fig. 7.18 Hog prices in the USA. Source: Author's own figure with data from USDA NASS (2023)

market situation, the desired state of the system is the equilibrium of supply and demand. If the actual situation is such that demand is greater than supply, there is a discrepancy, which we call excess demand. An increase in the market price is a corrective action because, in neoclassical theory, it will reduce demand and increase supply, bringing the actual state of the market closer to equilibrium. The discrepancy (excess demand) has a positive effect on the price, which in turn has a positive effect on the quantity traded. The increase in quantity reduces the discrepancy by bringing it closer to the equilibrium quantity, which is the maximum quantity that can be sold. The loop is balanced because the corrective action is a negative feedback that reduces the discrepancy between the actual state and the goal.

In Chap. 6, we saw that oscillations are common in the economy, e.g. in the form of business cycle fluctuations measured by the output gap (see Fig. 6.41) or as price dynamics of the hog cycle (see Fig. 7.18). You already know from our discussion of the hog cycle in Sect. 6.2.7 that time lags are one reason for cyclical price dynamics. When such oscillations are not explosive or dampened, but more or less constant, they are the result of *delays* in a feedback loop, as shown in Fig. 7.19.

The loop in Fig. 7.19 is the same negative feedback loop as in Fig. 7.17, but we have three potential delays in each causal relationship between two variables. The first delay can occur until the system controller (or decision-maker) realizes that there is a discrepancy between the state of the system and the goal. This delay is caused by measurement, reporting, and perception delays. The second delay can occur between the identification of the discrepancy and the corrective action. In a business or government, it takes time for decisions to be made and implemented

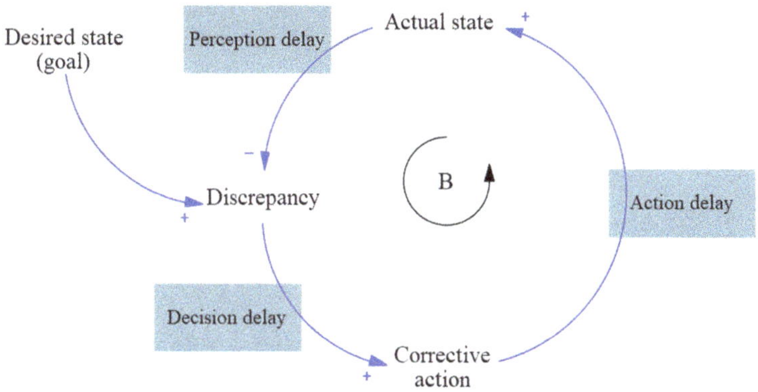

Fig. 7.19 Delays cause oscillations. Source: Author. Produced with Vensim Professional Version 9.4.0 provided by Ventana Systems Inc.

(administrative and decision delays). Finally, it often takes time for the decision to take corrective action to affect the state of the system, which is the action delay. Typical examples of action delays are the lagged response of the economy to changes in interest rates by the central bank or changes in government spending, e.g. on construction. The cause of the oscillation is the overshooting and undershooting of the target due to the lags. Because the negative feedback takes time, the corrective action comes too late and is too strong.

To get the three other modes of dynamic behavior in Fig. 7.15, we must combine positive feedback loops and negative feedback loops. **S-shaped growth** is the result of combining a self-reinforcing loop and a balancing loop as in Fig. 7.14, but with a twist. We have to include a carrying capacity which affects the resource adequacy (see Fig. 7.20).

S-shaped growth is characterized by the change in the percentage growth rate. Initially, the growth rate increases in accordance with the convex shape of the curve that describes the state of the system in the first phase (see Fig. 7.21). However, after some time, the variable describing the state of the system reaches a turning point, after which the curve becomes concave, i.e., the increases become smaller and smaller, approaching zero when the system is close to carrying capacity. To produce S-shaped growth (or logistic growth), the relative strength of positive and negative feedback must change over time. If this were not the case, either the positive or the negative feedback would always dominate, as discussed in the example of compound interest and spending on status symbols in Sect. 7.4.2.

The S-shape implies that positive feedback is stronger when we are far from carrying capacity, but negative feedback takes over as we get closer to carrying capacity. So the growth process is nonlinear. In fact, we already saw this when we discussed the Verhulst model of population growth or the logistic equation in Sect. 6. 2.2 of Chap. 6. For this type of dynamics, it is crucial that the carrying capacity is constant. If it is also increasing, the growth of the system need not be S-shaped. If the carrying capacity decreases, we get a collapse of the system. A constant carrying

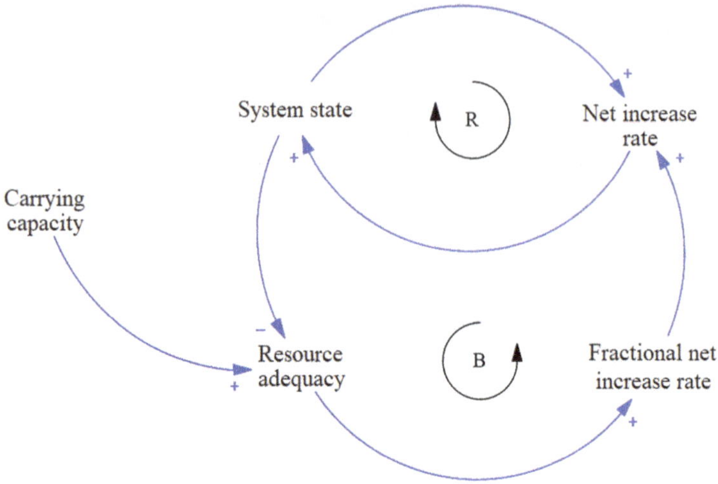

Fig. 7.20 Causal structure that causes S-shaped growth. Source: Author. Produced with Vensim Professional Version 9.4.0 provided by Ventana Systems Inc.

Fig. 7.21 S-shaped growth. Source: Author

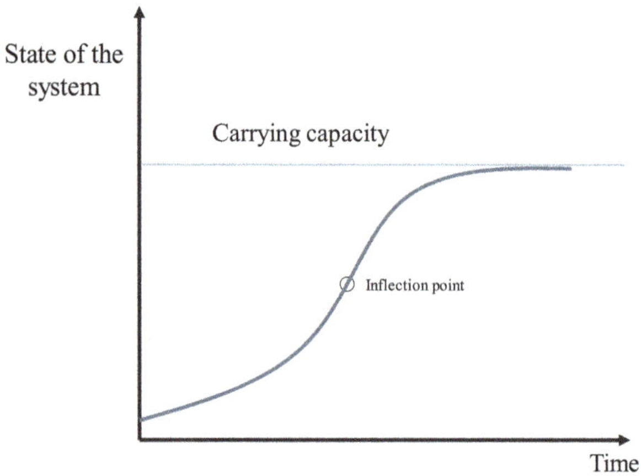

capacity, e.g., the resource endowment of an area or the population and purchasing power of a market, implies that there is less of the resource available to each resource-consuming unit as the system grows. The resource adequacy variable in Fig. 7.20 represents this idea. The system needs resources to grow and sustain itself. When resources are plentiful, the system can grow rapidly. But as the system grows, resources become increasingly scarce, slowing the net rate of growth. When the system has grown so much that it has reached its carrying capacity, the system cannot grow anymore and the net rate of increase is zero.

The tertiary enrollment ratio in several countries is an example of S-shaped growth (Fig. 7.22). In the United States, Norway, and Portugal, the enrollment ratio grew rather modestly from the early 1970s to the mid-1980s, followed by a

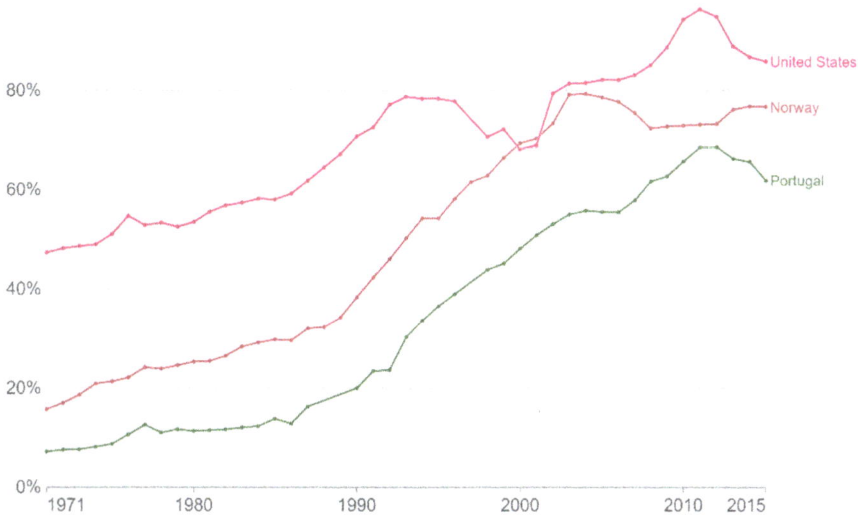

Fig. 7.22 Reaching the carrying capacity. Source: Our World in Data (2023a), based on data published by World Bank Education Statistics (2023). CC BY 4.0 (https://creativecommons.org/licenses/by/4.0/)

period of strong growth. In Norway, the enrollment ratio peaked at 80% in the early 2000s. The ratio declined somewhat, but remained between 75% and 80% until 2015. The dynamics for the USA are somewhat different. After reaching 80%, the enrollment ratio also dropped in the 1990s, but then recovered and even reached 95% in 2012 and stabilized at a high level. Finally, after a long and steady expansion, Portugal reached a maximum of almost 70% in 2011. From 2012 to 2015, the ratio declined, but recovered afterwards. This example shows that S-shaped growth in social systems sometimes does not end with convergence to the carrying capacity, but with oscillations around the carrying capacity or even with a decline (or collapse). A country's carrying capacity for students in higher education depends on the resources of the higher education system and the labor market demand for graduates. If the number of students exceeds the capacity of the education system, the study conditions become unattractive. If the labor market is not ready to employ the graduates, unemployment may occur and wages may fall. The overshoot could then trigger a response from secondary school graduates not to seek tertiary education, so that the enrollment ratio falls below the carrying capacity, and study conditions improve again. Of course, the carrying capacity may change over time as a result of policy decisions.

Growth with overshoot and oscillations occurs when S-shaped growth is combined with delays (Fig. 7.23). The delays in the balancing feedback loop prevent growth from slowing down before carrying capacity is reached. The delay between the state of the system and the resource adequacy implies that the system can overshoot the carrying capacity for some time. The system has some reserves that allow further growth even beyond the carrying capacity, but at some point a

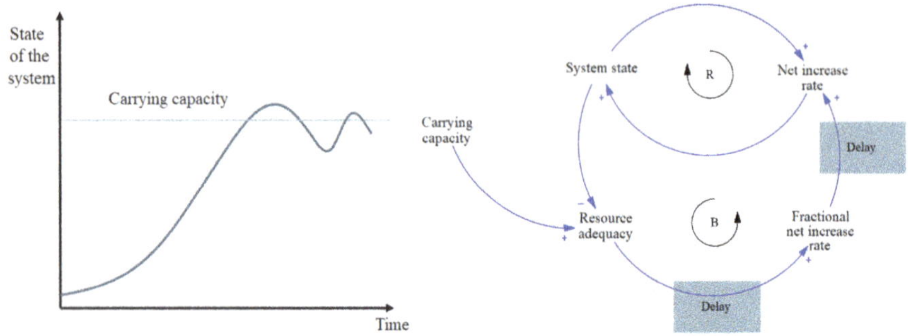

Fig. 7.23 Overshoot and oscillations. Source: Author. Produced with Vensim Professional Version 9.4.0 provided by Ventana Systems Inc.

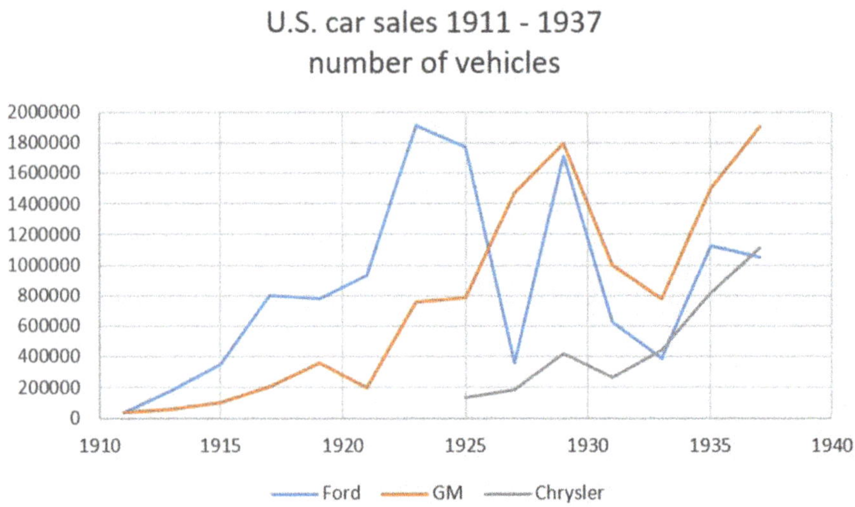

Fig. 7.24 Overshoot of automobile sales in the 1920 and 1930s in the USA. Source: Author's own figure with data from the Report on the Motor Vehicle Industry, Federal Trade Commission, 1939

corrective response will set in that causes the state of the system to fall below capacity. As we saw in the case of oscillations, the delays cause the corrective responses to be too strong.

Overshoot with oscillations describes the auto sales of the Big Three, Ford, General Motors, and Chrysler, in the 1920s and 1930s. In Fig. 7.24, we can see that all three companies experienced exponential sales growth in their early history. You may recall from Chap. 5 that the reason for Ford's success was the introduction of mass production and a dramatic drop in the cost of its Model T. General Motors pioneered consumer financing and flexible mass production with annual model changes. In Chap. 5, overinvestment and underconsumption were mentioned as possible causes of the Great Depression of the 1930s. This theory would fit the

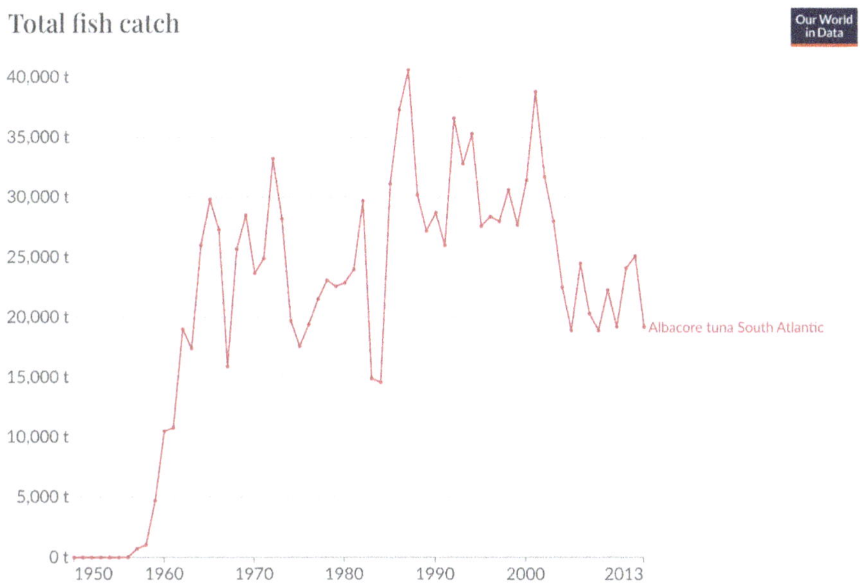

Fig. 7.25 Growth and oscillations in tuna catch. Source: Our World in Data (2018), based on data by RAM Legacy Stock Assessment Database (2018), CC BY 4.0 (https://creativecommons.org/licenses/by/4.0/)

pattern of growth, overshoot, and oscillations. Carrying capacity is the willingness and ability of consumers to buy all the cars produced. In the mid-1920s, consumers did not want to buy the Model T because it was considered old-fashioned. Ford had to respond by introducing new models, which took time and initially led to a decline in sales. GM was able to overshoot its carrying capacity by extending credit to its customers. The stock market and banking crisis of the early 1930s corrected the overshoot, causing GM's sales to plummet. Of course, U.S. automakers' sales did not oscillate around a given market capacity forever. During World War II and in the 1950s and 1960s, the market, and thus the carrying capacity, grew. But at least for the three decades from 1910 to 1940, the overshoot-and-oscillations model is a good description of what happened in this market.

The catch of albacore (longfin tuna) in the South Atlantic is also characterized by growth, overshoot, and oscillation (see Fig. 7.25).

From 1950 to the mid-1960s, the catch grew strongly from 0 t to about 30,000 t. Since then, the catch has fluctuated around 25,000 t per year, but with rather large fluctuations. The carrying capacity in this case is the reproductive capacity of the tuna population. If fishing exceeds the population's ability to reproduce, the population will decline and so will the catch. In 1966, the International Commission for the Conservation of Atlantic Tunas (ICCAT) was established to manage tuna fisheries. Setting catch quotas is one way to prevent permanent overfishing and allow tuna populations to rebuild. Because there is always uncertainty about the current state of the population and how long it will take for the population to rebuild, there are delays

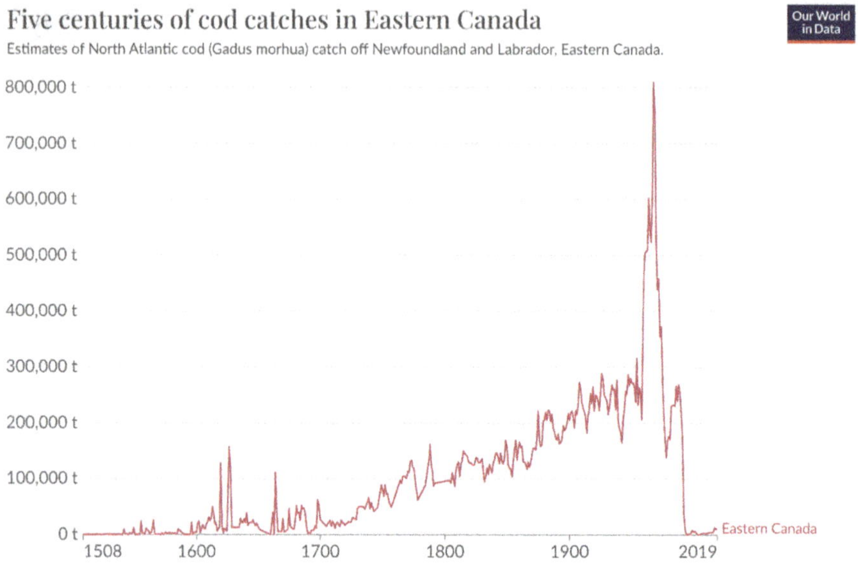

Fig. 7.26 Growth and collapse of Atlantic northwest cod fishery. Source: Our World in Data (2021), based on data by Schijns et al. (2021). CC BY 4.0 (https://creativecommons.org/licenses/by/4.0/)

in the feedback loops that cause oscillations. So far, at least, the South Atlantic albacore fishery appears to be sustainable.

In contrast to the management of the albacore fishery, the management of the cod fishery in the Northwest Atlantic failed dramatically, leading to the collapse of the cod population there in 1992 (Fig. 7.26). The cod fishery had been the economic base of the eastern Canadian coast for about 500 years. In the 1960s, the introduction of new fishing technology, such as large trawlers equipped with radar, sonar, and electronic navigation systems, led to a tripling of the catch. The catch peaked at 810,000 metric tons in 1968, well above sustainable levels (or carrying capacity). The Canadian government attempted to manage the fishery by setting quotas, but the carrying capacity was overestimated to the point that it was permanently damaged by continued overfishing. As a result, the industry completely collapsed in the early 1990s due to the collapse of the cod population.

Figure 7.27 shows the behavior of the system with **overshoot and collapse** and the structure that causes this outcome. The right-hand part of the causal loop diagram contains the positive and negative feedback loops that generate S-shaped growth. What is new is the negative feedback loop on the left, which captures the erosion of carrying capacity due to continued overshoot. As long as the state of the system is above the carrying capacity, the carrying capacity will decrease, keeping the collapse in motion. Only if the corrective decrease in the state of the system is greater than the erosion of the carrying capacity will the collapse come to a halt and the system can stabilize at a low level. If the carrying capacity continues to be eroded faster than the

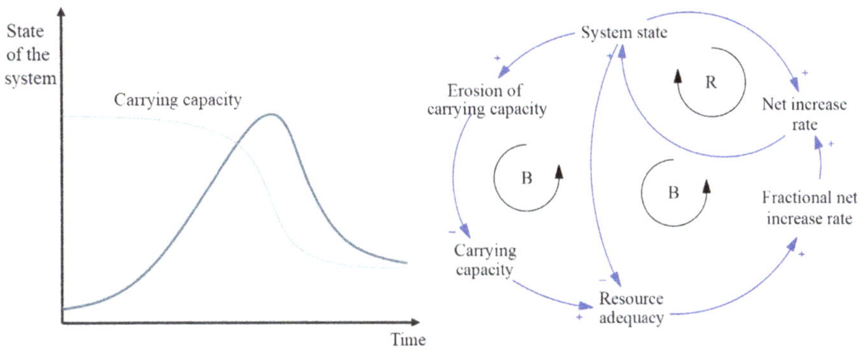

Fig. 7.27 Overshoot and collapse. Source: Author. Produced with Vensim Professional Version 9.4.0 provided by Ventana Systems Inc.

state of the system, a complete collapse, as in the case of the cod fishery, is inevitable.

This subsection has only explained the basic mechanisms of important types of dynamic behavior and provides a number of simple examples of these dynamics. As shown for exponential or logistic growth, these simple models can be represented by simple (nonlinear) differential or difference equations. As argued in Chap. 6, most economic systems are much more complex, involving more variables and feedback loops, than the simple models presented here. We will discuss more complex models of S-shaped growth, oscillation, and collapse later in this chapter.

7.4.4 Stock-flow Diagrams

Causal loop diagrams are very useful for showing the causal relationships between the variables of a system and for identifying feedback loops. They are often a good starting point for analyzing a system. However, they are often not sufficient to capture the dynamics of a system because they do not distinguish between different types of variables. In particular, they do not represent *stocks* and *flows*, which are important concepts in economics and other disciplines. Stocks are built up by *inflows* and depleted by *outflows*. Table 7.3 provides a number of economic examples of stock variables and their associated inflows and outflows. For example, a firm's inventories are increased by the flow of production and decreased by shipments to customers.

In system dynamics, stock variables are conventionally represented by boxes, as in Fig. 7.28. Flow variables are shown as arrows with valves that regulate the flow rates. The inflow arrows point toward the stock, while the outflow arrows point away from the stock. The clouds at the beginning or end of the flow arrows represent *sources* or *sinks*, i.e. resources outside the system boundaries that are not represented in the model. It is a modeling decision whether or not to include the sources or sinks of flows in the model. In an economic model of the labor market, we might include

Table 7.3 Examples of economic stocks and flows

Stock	Inflow	Outflow
Inventory	Production	Shipment
Population	Birth rate	Death rate
Employees	Hire rate	Quit rate
Wealth	Saving	Expenditure
Capital stock	Investment	Depreciation

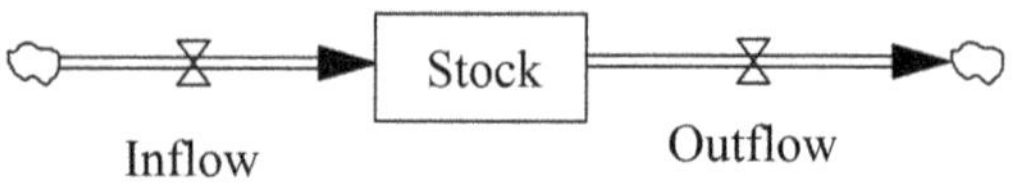

Fig. 7.28 Stock and flows. Source: Author

both the stock of unemployed and the stock of employed, where hiring is a flow from unemployment to employment and leaving is a flow in the opposite direction. Whenever we do not explicitly include sources and sinks in the model, the system is open and has some kind of exchange with its environment.

Stocks play a central role in system dynamics models. First, the state of a system is always determined by one or more stock variables. Therefore, at any point in time, the system can be fully characterized by the level of its stocks. Second, because stocks change only through inflows and outflows, the system acquires inertia and does not change erratically from period to period. Of course, we can model sudden shocks to stocks, such as an exogenous event that destroys part of the stock, which would lead to jumps in the stock variables. But the more important source of dynamics is continuous flows. Third, we have already seen that lags generate oscillations. Delays involve stocks, because stocks cannot be adjusted discretely by decision-makers. Finally, stocks decouple inflows and outflows because different decision processes are involved. The decoupling of flows is relevant because flows generate the dynamics of the model. A stock remains constant if the inflows and outflows are equal, otherwise the stock changes. The change of a system stock (or state) is a disequilibrium situation. Therefore, if there is no direct feedback between inflows and outflows, nothing guarantees that a model is in equilibrium. In fact, whether a system dynamics model ever reaches equilibrium is an emergent property of the system that depends on all the feedback loops involved. A main purpose of system dynamics models is to find out whether a system reaches an equilibrium and whether this equilibrium is stable. The emergence of equilibria (or the failure to reach an equilibrium) is a fundamental difference between system dynamics and neoclassical equilibrium modeling, which *assumes* the existence and attainability of equilibria.

In addition to stocks and flows, system dynamics models also have intermediate or auxiliary variables. They are not necessary to determine the state of the system, which at any point in time is given by the value of the model's stock variables. However, auxiliary variables increase the transparency of the model and help to represent the mechanisms involved in a more precise way. Auxiliary variables can either depend on stocks, on other auxiliary variables, or be exogenously given. They

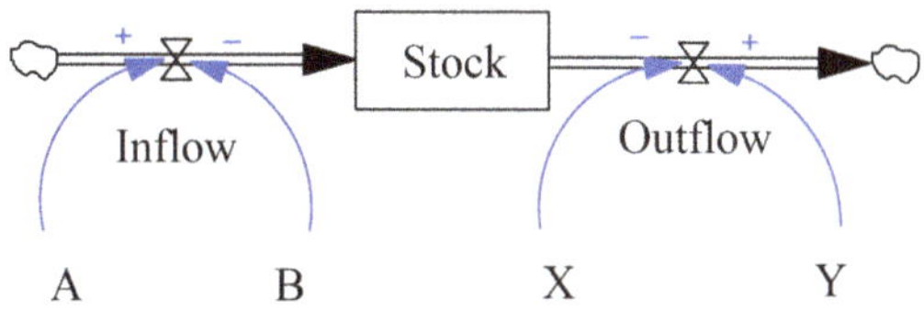

Fig. 7.29 Stock and flows and auxiliary variables. Source: Author. Produced with Vensim Professional Version 9.4.0 provided by Ventana Systems Inc.

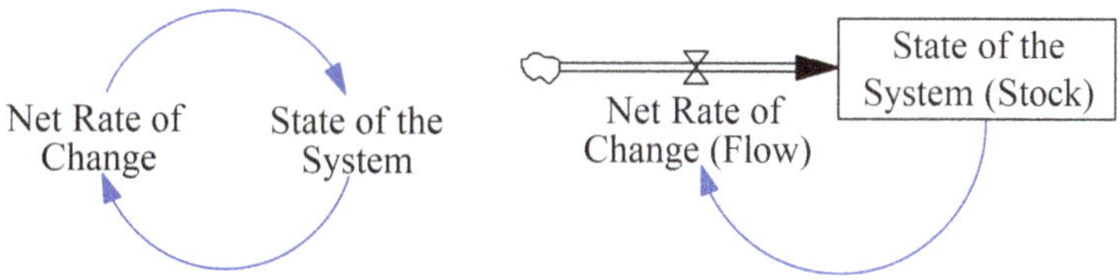

Fig. 7.30 Relation between a causal loop diagram and a stock-flow diagram. Source: Author. Produced with Vensim Professional Version 9.4.0 provided by Ventana Systems Inc.

typically affect the model through their causal effects on the flow variables. Figure 7.29 shows the four auxiliary variables A, B, X, and Y.

Figure 7.30 illustrates that stock-flow diagrams contain more information than causal loop diagrams of the same system. In the left panel, we see a simple causal loop between the two variables "state of the system" and "net rate of change." When the feedback is positive, we get a system with exponential growth, as in Fig. 7.16. The right panel shows the state of the system as a stock and the net rate of change as a flow. In our example of saving, the money in the bank account is clearly a stock, and the net difference between saving and spending (the net rate of change) is a flow that increases or decreases the stock. With a constant interest rate, the interest income earned is the flow that increases the stock of money the owner has in the account.

A simple example is helpful to see how stocks, flows, and auxiliary models are combined in a stock-flow diagram of a dynamic system. Figure 7.31 shows a stock-flow diagram of the well-known Solow–Swan model, which is at the heart of neoclassical growth theory. The Solow–Swan model is very similar to the Ramsey–Cass–Koopmans model discussed in Sect. 4.3.2 of Chap. 4. It is a simpler version of that model, because savings $S_t = sY_t$ are determined by the exogenously given savings rate s, whereas in the Ramsey model they are the result of the intertemporal utility maximization. The Solow–Swan model has three stocks: the capital stock, labor, and technology, shown in blue in the boxes in the diagram. The model assumes that labor and technology grow at exogenously given rates, represented by the flow of population growth and technological progress. Again, it is important to distinguish between the fractional (or percentage) growth rates, which are constant, and the absolute growth rates, i.e., the number of workers added to the labor stock and the amount of new technology, which—of course—are not constant. In contrast to labor and technology, there is also an outflow from the capital stock.

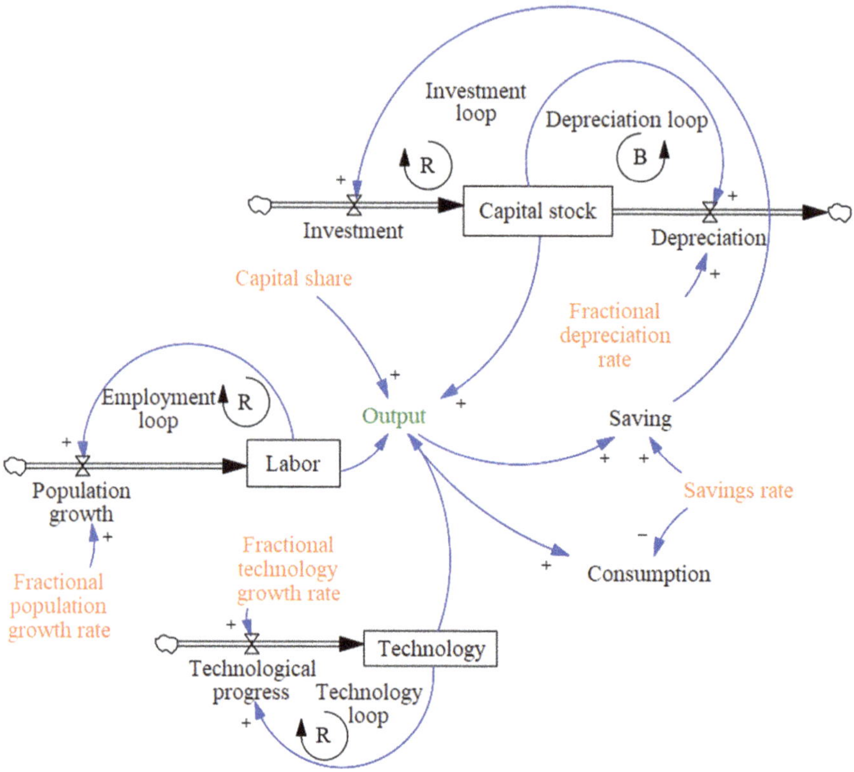

Fig. 7.31 Stock-flow diagram of the neoclassical Solow–Swan growth model. Source: Author. Produced with Vensim Professional Version 9.4.0 provided by Ventana Systems Inc.

Capital is accumulated by the (in)flow of investment and lost by the (out)flow of depreciation. For convenience, the five exogenous parameters of the model are shown in orange. In addition to these constant parameters, the model has three auxiliary variables: output, consumption, and saving. Output is shown in green because it is often the main variable of interest. Nevertheless, output, consumption, and saving are only auxiliary variables that are not needed to fully describe the model. This may seem counterintuitive since we use the model to learn how these variables change over time. They are not necessary in the sense that we can derive them at any point in time if we know the values of the stocks. Using the (Cobb–Douglas) production function, in which the capital share is the only parameter, we can always calculate output for given capital, labor, and technology.

Note that the causal structure of the Solow–Swan model is quite simple. Both labor and technology grow exponentially with positive exogenous fractional growth rates. Consequently, they contribute to the exponential growth of output. The only twist in the model is the evolution of the capital stock, which has an inflow (investment) and an outflow (depreciation) and thus can grow, shrink, or remain constant. Depreciation is fully determined by the exogenous fractional depreciation rate and the current capital stock. Thus, the dynamics of the capital stock and hence of output depend on investment. The key loop that characterizes the system's dynamics is the investment loop: *capital* → *output* → *saving* → *investment* → *capital*.

Due to the diminishing marginal productivity of capital (i.e., *capital share* < 1), the contribution of capital to output decreases as the capital stock grows. Therefore, the investment loop is stronger than the depreciation loop for low levels of the capital stock, such that the capital stock grows, but weaker at high levels of the capital stock. We know from the analytical treatment of the Solow–Swan model that there is a balanced growth path, in which technology grows with the fractional technology growth rate g, labor grows with the fractional population growth rate n, and both the capital stock and output grow permanently with the rate $g + n$. Thus, in the long run, the growth of the level of output is driven by labor and technology, while capital makes not contribution of its own because investment settles at a level that compensates for depreciation and keeps capital growing at the rate of the other two factors. We cannot see this result in the stock-flow diagram, but would have to simulate the model, whose causal structure is shown in the diagram. The Solow–Swan model is not so interesting in terms of its long-terms dynamics (exponential growth), but it is simple enough to show a stock-flow diagram that is easy to understand. You will see more complex structures later.

7.4.5 System Dynamics Models

It is important to understand that there is a difference between stock-flow *diagrams* and system dynamics *models*. Causal loop diagrams and stock-flow diagrams are visual representations of the models, but they are not complete models. The diagrams show the causal structure of a system, which is of invaluable help for talking about and understanding the systems. However, the diagrams do not contain enough information for a complete description of the system and for the analysis of its dynamic behavior. We have already raised this point in the discussion of the Solow–Swan model above. Therefore, we need to specify exactly what the relationships between the variables are. This can be done in algebraic form with equations, which is the conventional representation of the Solow–Swan model. For instance, we assume a Cobb–Douglas production function

$$Y(t) = K(t)^{\alpha}(A(t)L(t))^{1-\alpha}. \tag{7.4}$$

As in Eq. (4.17), the capital stock changes according to

$$\dot{K}(t) = I(t) = S(t) = Y(t) - C(t). \tag{7.5}$$

Thus, at any point in time t, the capital stock $K(t)$ is given by

$$K(t) = \int_{t_0}^{t} (I(s) - D(s))ds + K(t_0), \tag{7.6}$$

where t_0 is the initial point in time and $D(s) = \delta K(s)$ is the level of depreciation for a given fractional depreciation rate δ and the current capital stock. Saving $S(t)$ is determined by

$$S(t) = sY(t), \tag{7.7}$$

for the fractional savings rate s and current output $Y(t)$. This partial representation of the Solow model is sufficient to demonstrate that the model is fully described by a set of (differential and integral) equations, parameter values (e.g., $s = 0.1$), and initial values (e.g., $K(t_0) = 10$).

While algebraic modeling and analysis are very useful for simple system that is not too nonlinear, they quickly become intractable with larger models and significant nonlinearity. In these cases, we must resort to numerical computer simulation models. Computer simulation models require the implementation of the model in some software or computer language. There are many options available, e.g. AnyLogic,[4] Minsky,[5] NetLogo,[6] Powersim,[7] Matlab with Simulink.[8] A popular software for system dynamics models is Vensim from Ventana Systems Inc. Vensim is powerful, easy to use and popular in the system dynamics community. The educational version Vensim[9] PLE (Personal Learning Edition) is freely available for download on PCs at www.vensim.com. Here we show how a (partial) representation of the Solow–Swan model would look like in Vensim.

Vensim integrates stock-flow diagrams with system dynamics models and provides an editor for designing the stock-flow diagram and to defining the mathematical functions behind the causal relationships. There are excellent tutorials[10] and a help function available for Vensim. Details on modeling are also presented in Sterman (2000) and in García (2020). We will focus on some of the basics without going into too much technical detail. Figure 7.32 shows the Vensim workbench with the stock-flow diagram of the Solow–Swan model. By clicking in the function icon and selecting a variable,[11] e.g., `Capital stock`, we open the *equations tool* shown in Fig. 7.33. In this window, there is a field for the name of the variable (see 1) in the upper right corner. The field "variables" (see 2) lists the variables connected in

[4]https://www.anylogic.de/ Accessed 26 October 2023.

[5]https://sourceforge.net/projects/minsky/ Accessed 26 October 2023.

[6]https://ccl.northwestern.edu/netlogo/ Accessed 26 October 2023.

[7]https://powersim.com/ Accessed 26 October 2023.

[8]https://mathworks.com/products/simulink.html Accessed 26 October 2023.

[9]For the models and diagrams in this book, Vensim Professional was used.

[10]See here: https://vensim.com/vensim-video-library/ Accessed 26. October 2023.

[11]We follow the convention of printing variable in computer code or programs in the font `Courier`.

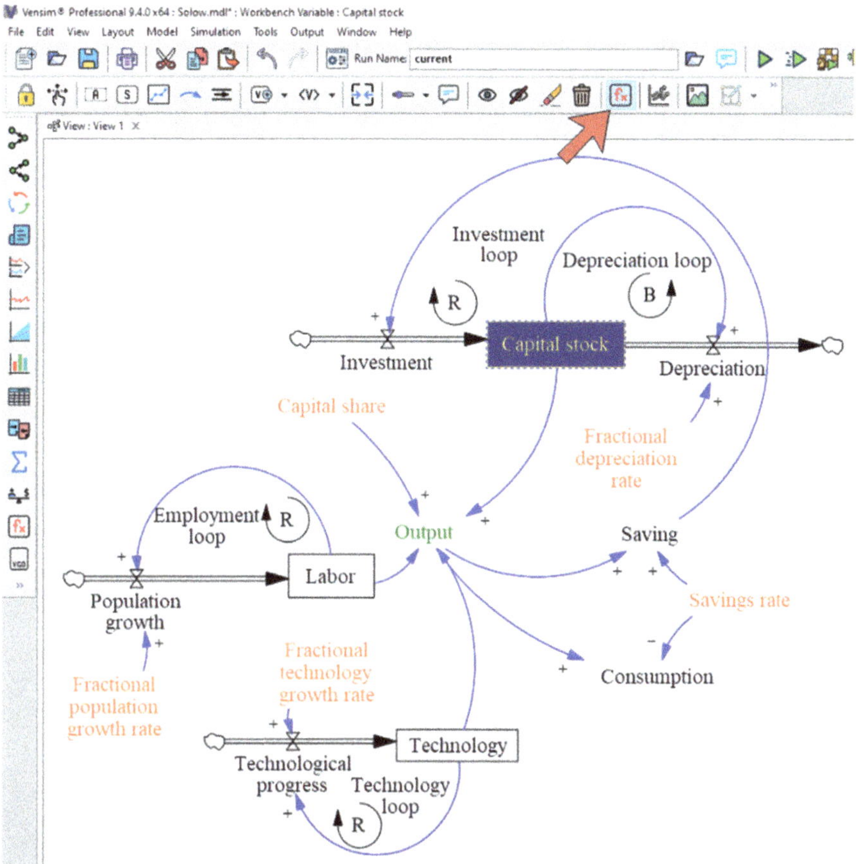

Fig. 7.32 Vensim workbench. Source: Author. Produced with Vensim Professional Version 9.4.0 provided by Ventana Systems Inc.

the stock-flow diagram, here `Capital stock`, `Depreciation` and `Investment`. The field "equations" contains the mathematical definition of the variable, in our case INTEG `(Investment-Depreciation)`, which corresponds to the integral in Eq. (7.6) above. The simulation also needs an initial value (see 4), which in this example is 10.

The equation in the equation tool for `Saving` is `Savings rate*Output`. Figure 7.34 shows the equation tool for the auxiliary variable `Output`:

`Output = Capital stock^Capital share*(Technology*Labor)^(1–Capital share).`

We can use the model to simulate the dynamics we are interested in, such as output $Y(t)$, output per capita $\frac{Y(t)}{L(t)}$ and output per effective labor $\frac{Y(t)}{A(t)L(t)}$. Figure 7.35 shows the graphs of these variables for one setting of parameters and initial values. We see that both `Output` and `Output per capita` grow exponentially—as

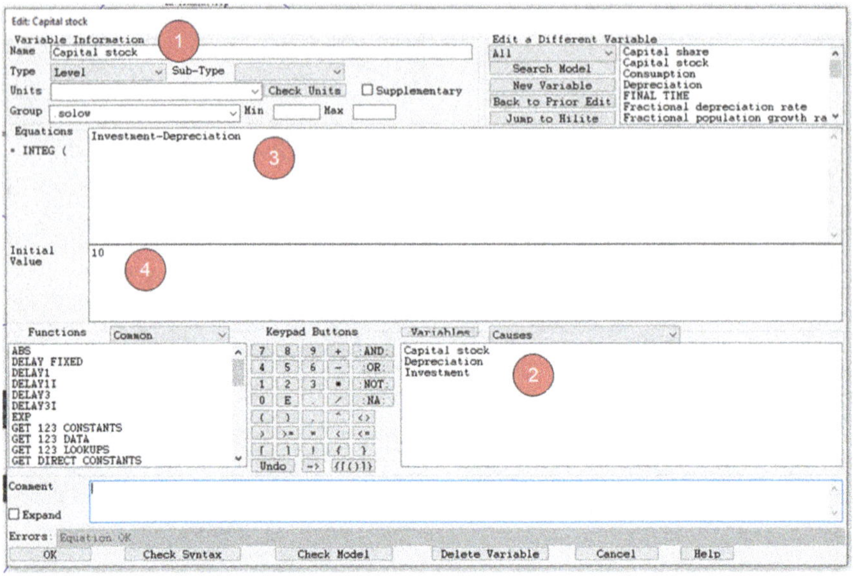

Fig. 7.33 Equations tool for the stock variable `Capital stock`. Source: Author

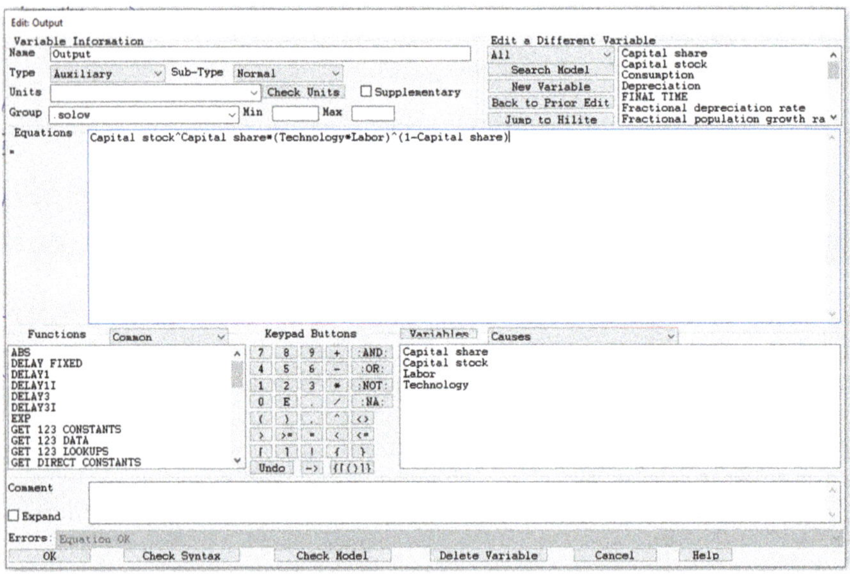

Fig. 7.34 Equations tool for the auxiliary variable `Output`. Source: Author

expected. However, `Output per effective labor` grows only at the beginning until the capital accumulation reaches a steady state. We could, of course, generate many other graphs and also export the simulated data for further statistical

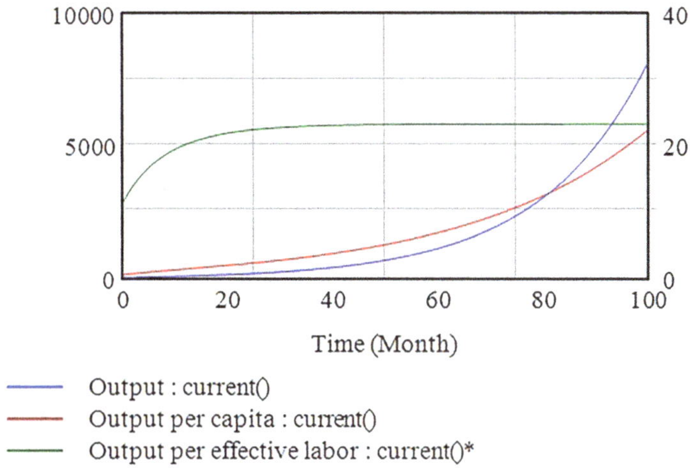

Fig. 7.35 Dynamics of `output` in the Solow model. Source: Author

analysis. Unlike algebraic models, system dynamics models must be explored graphically and statistically, since we do not obtain closed form solutions but numerical output (Fig. 7.35).

7.5 Infection and Diffusion

This section deals with models of infection and diffusion. It may seem odd to talk about epidemiological models in an economics textbook, but as we will see, the infection mechanism is similar to mechanisms of technology adoption and other processes of *social contagion*. Social contagion refers to the spread of behaviors, emotions, or beliefs in a group, which is an important phenomenon in economics.

7.5.1 The SIR Model

We begin our discussion with the *SI model of epidemics* shown in Fig. 7.36. The SI model is probably the simplest model of a contagion process. A population N consists of two groups (or stocks): the susceptible population S, which not infected yet, and the infectious population I, which carries the infectious agent, hence $N = S + I$. These two groups give the model its name.

Initially, we need at least one infected person to start the process. The size of the infectious population positively affects the infection rate, as indicated by the self-reinforcing loop labeled "contagion." The loop has positive feedback because more people are infected when more people are infectious. The infection rate IR is the flow from the susceptible population to the infectious population, or in other words, the number of newly infected people. The infection rate also depends positively on the

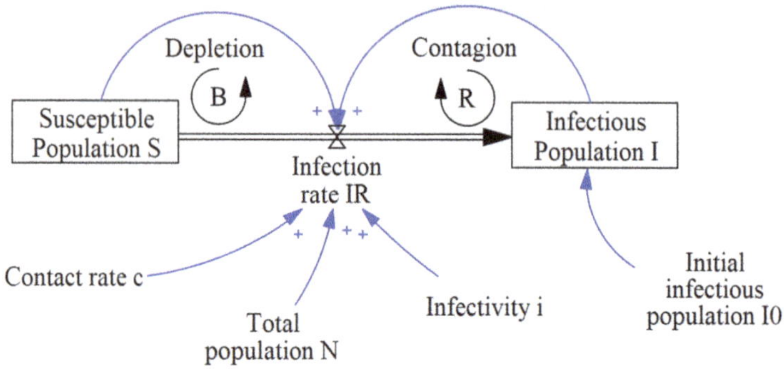

Fig. 7.36 The SI model of epidemics. Source: Author. Produced with Vensim Professional Version 9.4.0 provided by Ventana Systems Inc.

size of the susceptible population. This loop is balancing because the infection rate decreases when the susceptible population decreases. The contact rate c measures how the community interacts. It is given by the number of contacts per person per period of time (e.g., per day). Infectivity i is the probability that a susceptible person will become infected after contact with an infectious person. The model is described by three simple equations:

$$I = INTEG(IR, I_0) \tag{7.8}$$

$$S = INTEG(-IR, N - I_0) \tag{7.9}$$

$$IR = cS\frac{I}{N}i \tag{7.10}$$

The infection rate results from the number of encounters of susceptive people, cS, multiplied by the share of the population that is infected, I/N, multiplied by the probability of infection, i.

The SI model generates an S-shaped curve of the number of infectious people over time (see Fig. 7.37), which is mirrored by the number of susceptible people. Initially, when the number of infectious people is small, only few susceptible people become infected, such that the growth of the infectious people is slow. But this growth accelerates over time with more and more people being infected. When the number of susceptible people as fallen a lot the negative feedback becomes stronger and the curve of infectious people flattens. It must approach the total number of people in the population over time. Figure 7.38 shows that the infection rate has a bell-shaped curve over time with its max occurring when 50% of the population are infectious. As discussed before, the number of infections is small when very few people are infectious (i.e., the positive feedback is weak) and few susceptible people are left (i.e., the negative feedback is strong).

The SI model of epidemics is unrealistic because people generally recover from infection. Some may also die. The SIR model adds to the model the stock of

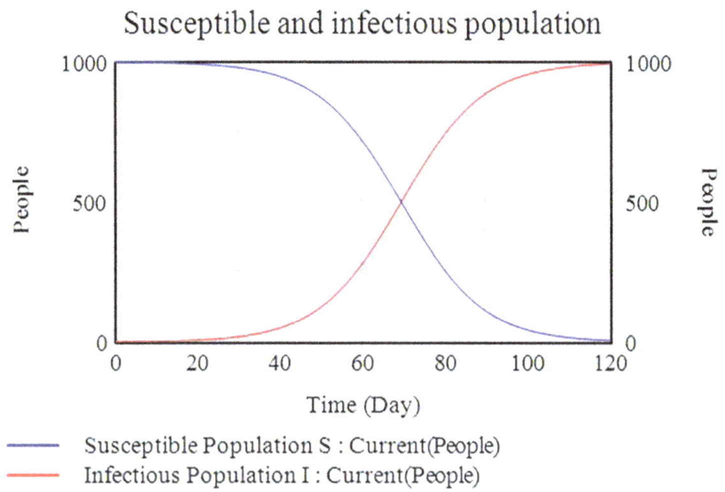

Fig. 7.37 Dynamics of the epidemic. Source: Author

Fig. 7.38 Dynamics of new infections. Source: Author

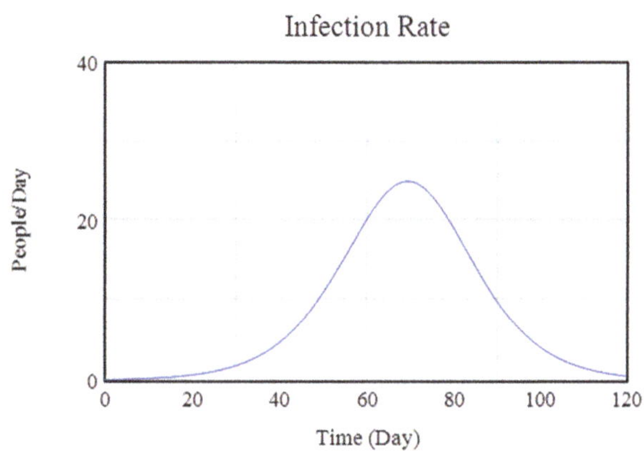

recovered people, R, who are immune to reinfection and no longer infectious. The SIR model is a classic model in epidemiology proposed by Kermack and McKendrick (1927) to model acute infections. Figure 7.39 shows a stock-flow diagram of the SIR model.

The model consists of the same equations as the SI model, i.e. (7.8)–(7.10), but includes two additional equations for the dynamics of the recovered population R and for the recovery rate RR:

$$R = INTEG(RR, R_0) \tag{7.11}$$

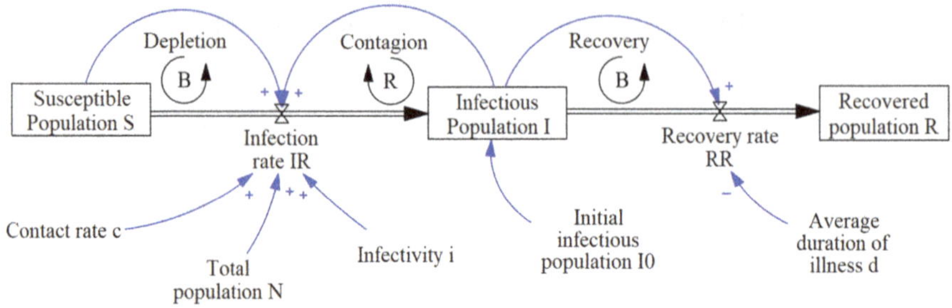

Fig. 7.39 The SIR model of epidemics. Source: Author. Produced with Vensim Professional Version 9.4.0 provided by Ventana Systems Inc.

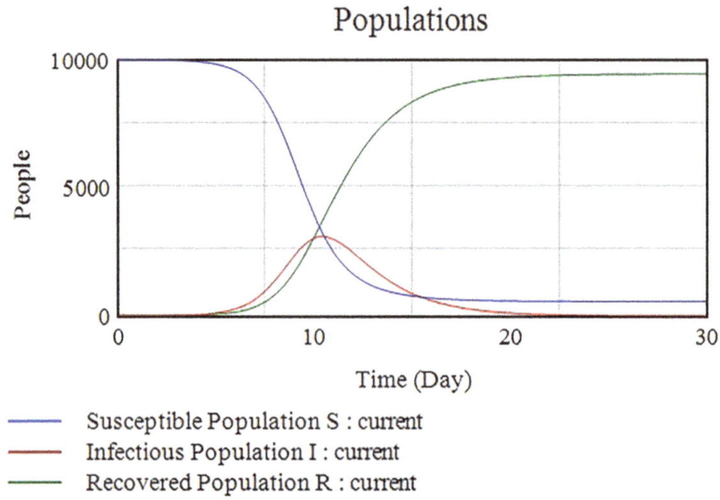

Fig. 7.40 Dynamics of an epidemic in the SIR model. Source: Author

$$RR = \frac{I}{d}, \tag{7.12}$$

where d is the average length of time that people are infectious. Dividing the number of infectious people by d implies that not all people will recover at the same time. $1/d$ decreases exponentially, which means that many people recover quite quickly, but some are infectious for a long time. Recovery adds another balancing loop to the system, working against the spread of the infection. As a result, it can happen that not the entire susceptible population becomes infected as visible in Fig. 7.40. The epidemic may die out due to the recovery before everyone in the population is infected. If the period of the infectiousness is very short, it is even possible that no epidemic will develop because the few people who are initially infected will recover before they can infect others.

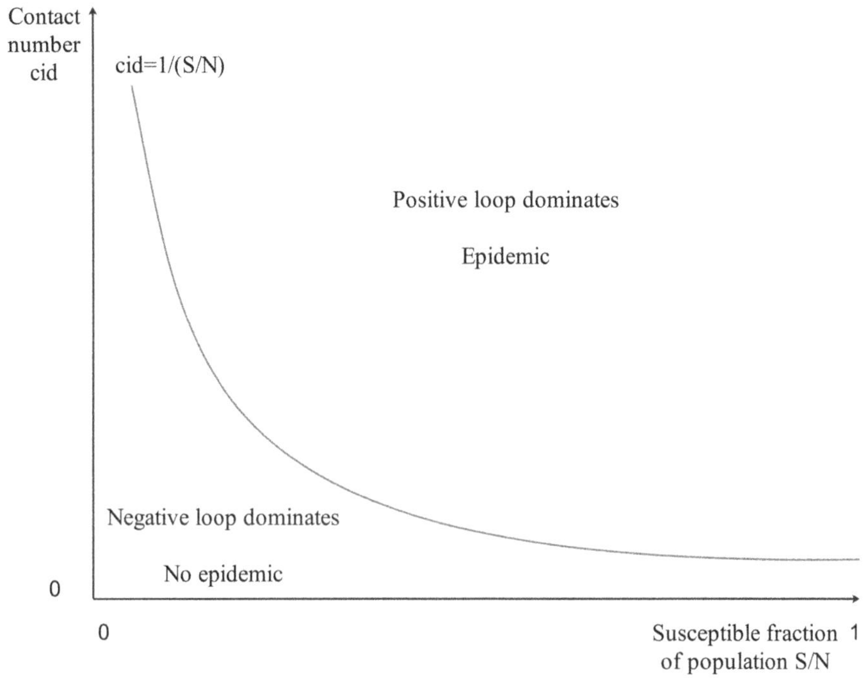

Fig. 7.41 Threshold for the development of an epidemic. Source: Author

There is a threshold for an epidemic to occur. Intuitively, an epidemic requires that the infection rate be greater than the recovery rate: $IR > RR$ or $cS\left(\frac{I}{N}\right)i > \frac{I}{d} \Leftrightarrow cid\left(\frac{S}{N}\right) > 1$. Figure 7.41 illustrates this threshold. To the left of the curve, the infection rate is less than the recovery rate, such that no epidemic occurs. It is easy to see that a smaller contact rate c shifts the curve to the right making it harder for an epidemic to develop. This is the rationale behind quarantines and contact restrictions as measures to control epidemics.

7.5.2 Sentiment and Narratives

Epidemics as such are not of central interest to economists, but the phenomenon of social contagion, which is analogous to contagion with a pathogen, is an important economic issue. As defined above, social contagion refers to the spread of behaviors, emotions, or beliefs in a group. We can imagine that a few individuals exhibit a behavior or experience an emotion for the first time and then "infect" others with it. Others adopt the behavior or belief or experience the emotion as well. We will leave the discussion of the spread of behavior for the next subsection, and focus first on the spread of emotions, beliefs, and the like.

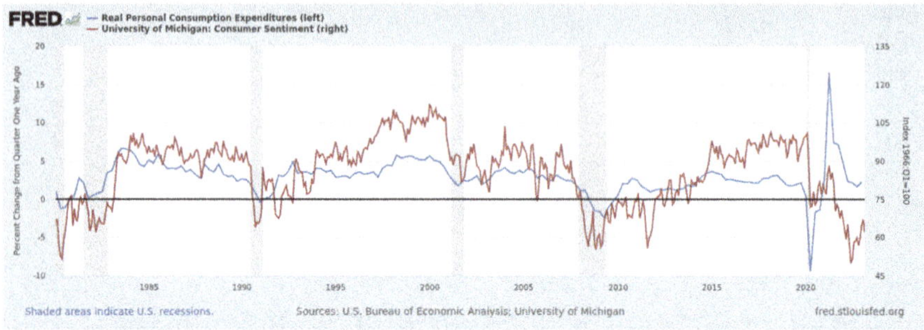

Fig. 7.42 U.S. Consumer sentiment and change in consumption expenditure. Source: Federal Reserve Bank of St. Louis (2023)

In many countries, *consumer confidence* is an important indicator and possibly also a driver of business cycle fluctuations. Measures of consumer confidence were first developed by the economic psychologist George Katona in the 1940s. He created the University of Michigan Consumer Sentiment Index, which has become a leading indicator of the U.S. business cycle. This indicator includes both a measure of consumer expectations and a measure of *consumer sentiment*, which is a construct designed to capture an affective state. Expectations can be seen as the result of a cognitive process, in which agents acquire information and use their knowledge in order to make a prediction about how the future will unfold. In contrast, sentiment refers to a more vague mood or a general optimism or pessimism that an agent may not be able to explain. It is similar to John Maynard Keynes's notion of *animal spirits,* which are instincts or emotions that guide economic behavior, but are not the result of a rational thought process. Consumer sentiment is the result of a social or even societal learning process in which people meet and casually share their attitudes about economic issues. As shown in Fig. 7.42, consumer sentiment is correlated with personal consumption expenditures in the United States, as it is in many other countries. The figure shows that declines in sentiment sometimes precede sharp declines in consumption, e.g. in the recessions in 1990, 2001, and 2008, suggesting that sentiment (or confidence) predicts or even causes consumption drops (see also Roos 2008; Dees and Soares Brinca 2013). Therefore, understanding what drives consumer sentiment could help in understanding business cycles.

On a technical level, it is straightforward to use the SIR model to describe the spread of optimism or pessimism in a population. Suppose that initially most people in a population are neutral about the economic future. They are the susceptible population in the SIR model. For some reason, a small number of people become "infected" with optimism (or pessimism). When these infectious optimists (or pessimists) meet susceptible people, some of them may become infected with optimism as well. If consumer sentiment is an affective state, it may subside over time, similar to recovery from an illness. In this case, the infectious optimists or pessimists no longer influence others and move into the stock of the recovered population in the SIR model.

While it is easy to model a social contagion process like a viral epidemic on a technical level, it may not be so obvious what infectivity or duration of illness means in this context. Robert Shiller (2017, 2019) suggests that the spread of economic narratives can be modeled using the SIR approach and explains why this seems reasonable. Following the Oxford English Dictionary, Shiller (2019, p. xi) defines narrative—which he also calls "thought virus"—as "a story or representation used to give an explanatory or justificatory account of a society, period, etc.". For him,

> *stories are not limited to simple chronologies of human events. A story may also be a song, joke, theory, explanation, or plan that has emotional resonance and that can easily be conveyed in casual conversation. We can think of history as a succession of rare big events in which a story goes viral, often (but not always) with the help of an attractive celebrity (even a minor celebrity or fictional stoc figure) whose attachment to the narrative adds human interest.* (Shiller 2019, p. xi/xii)

The ability to "go viral" or being contagious is a defining element of Shiller's narratives. To do so, they must resonate emotionally with the listener and must have a human interest element. People must find narrative interesting and worth retelling them. But this interest fades over time, even with good stories, so that people "recover" from specific narratives.

Shiller (2017, 2019) argues that the profiteer narrative is helpful in explaining the sharp recession of 1920–1921, for which it is not easy to find more conventional economic causes. Shiller's theory is that the cause of this recession was a consumer boycott against businessmen, who were blamed for keeping prices high after the end of World War I without justification. They were called "profiteers," an unusual word in English, but one that was commonly used in newspapers, books, and public speeches in the early 1920s (see Fig. 7.43). People were angry about the high prices they had accepted during the war, but not after it was over. Profiteer stories about businessmen exploiting consumers and making excessive profits through abnormally high prices proliferated, or "went viral." Shiller compares the frequency

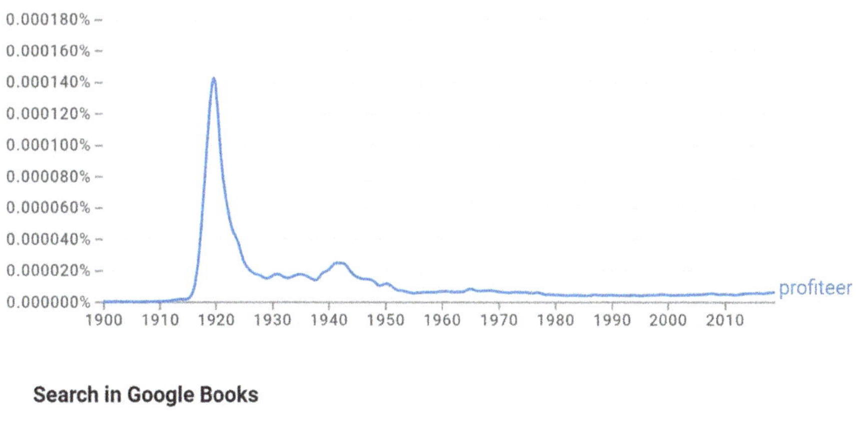

Fig. 7.43 The profiteer narrative during the 1920 recession. Source: Google Books Ngram Viewer

curve of the term "profiteer" in Fig. 7.43 with the curve of the infected population in Fig. 7.40 and explicitly recommends using the SIR model and its variants and extensions to analyze the spread of narratives.

7.5.3 The Bass Diffusion Model

It is not only emotions, beliefs, and narratives that can be socially contagious, but also behaviors. A well-known example of this idea is the adoption of new technologies by consumers. Figure 7.44 shows typical curves of the evolution of the share of households that have adopted a new technology, here color television, microwave ovens, and cell phones since the 1960s in the USA. We can see that the adoption curves are S-shaped. When a technology is very new, only a few pioneers or technology enthusiasts buy the product. Over time, a contagion effect occurs and the adoption rate (comparable to the infection rate) increases, leading to exponential growth. When a significant portion of the population has adopted the new technology, the adoption curve flattens and eventually converges to an equilibrium, often close to 100% of the population.

Frank Bass (1969) developed a model of innovation diffusion that is now the canonical model in the marketing and technology diffusion literature. A key element of this model is that innovations do not simply enter a market on their own (like a virus), but must be marketed by the innovating firm. In other words, a firm that wants

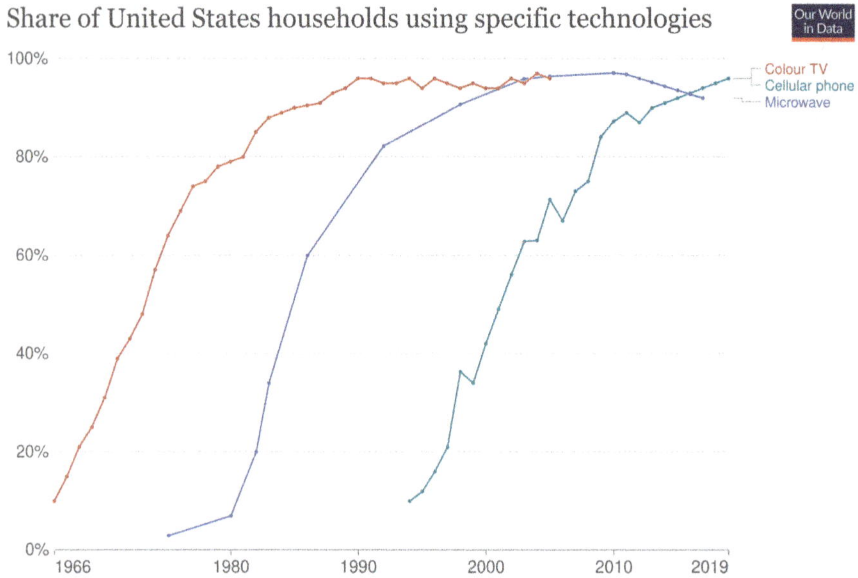

Fig. 7.44 Adoption of three technologies in the USA. Source: Our World in Data (2023b), based on data by Dediu (2017) and Comin and Hobijn (2004). CC BY 4.0 (https://creativecommons.org/licenses/by/4.0/)

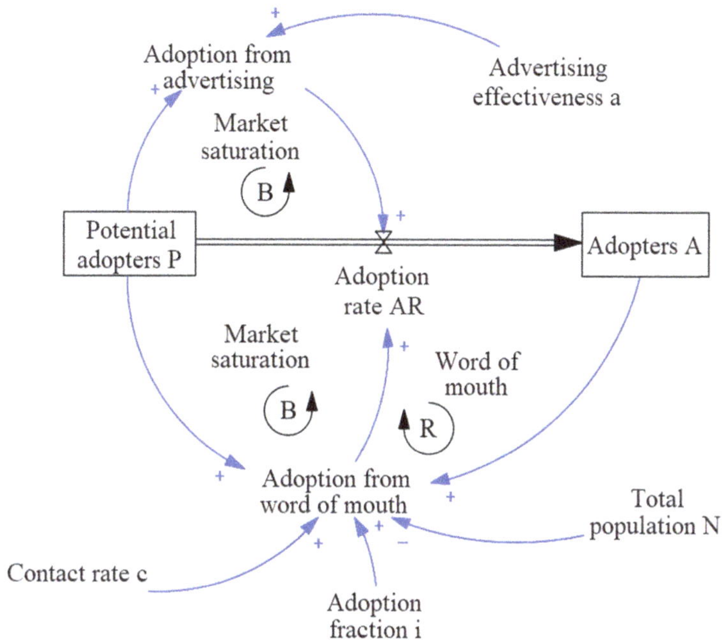

Fig. 7.45 Stock-flow diagram of the Bass diffusion model. Source: Author. Produced with Vensim Professional Version 9.4.0 provided by Ventana Systems Inc.

to sell a new product must persuade consumers to buy it through marketing. Once a certain level of market penetration has been achieved, a social contagion process sets in through word of mouth. Early adopters of the new product will tell others about it, extolling its virtues and persuading others to adopt the product as well. Both advertising adoption and word-of-mouth adoption affect the rate of adoption. Their interplay can produce the observed S-shaped adoption curves.

The stock-flow diagram in Fig. 7.45 has the same structure as the SI model in Fig. 7.36, except that the adoption rate depends on the two endogenous variables, `Adoption from advertising` and `Adoption from word of mouth`. The stock of the susceptible population is now called `Potential adopters` and the actual `Adopters` correspond to the infectious population, which are linked by the flow of the `Adoption rate`. Adoption from advertising is given by the product of the advertising effectiveness a and the number of potential adopters P, hence aP. Adoption through word of mouth is analogous to the infection rate in Eq. (7.10), hence $cP\frac{A}{N}i$.

Therefore, the total adoption rate is given by

$$AR = aP + cP\frac{A}{N}i. \tag{7.13}$$

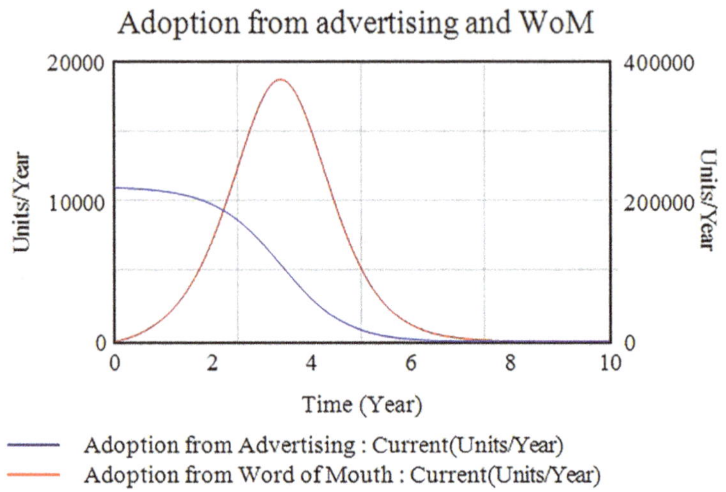

Fig. 7.46 Adoption rates. Source: Author

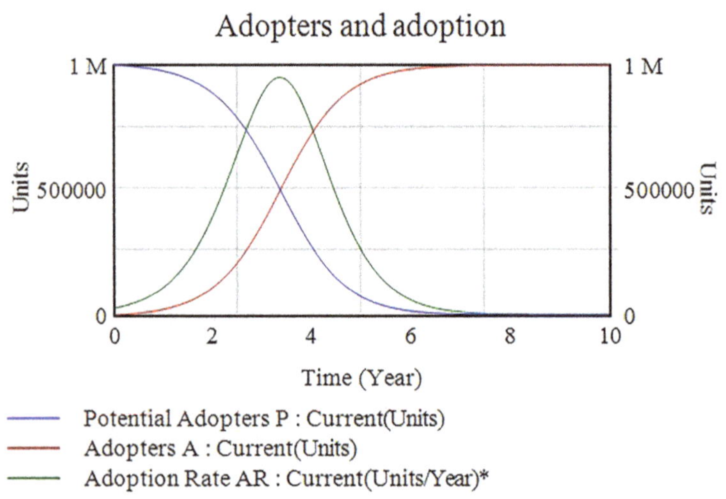

Fig. 7.47 Potential adopters, adopters and the total adoption rate. Source: Author

Adoption from advertising is subject to a balancing loop, because the number of potential adopters decreases. Word-of-mouth adoption is subject to the same balancing loop due to market saturation, but also by the self-reinforcing loop due to ever more adopters. The result is a bell-shaped adoption curve of word-of-mouth adoption, similar to the infection curve and an inverted S-shaped adoption curve from advertising (see Fig. 7.46).

Figure 7.47 confirms that the Bass diffusion model produces an S-shaped curve of adopters like the empirical curves in Fig. 7.44. Since the structure of the model is the same as that of the SI model, it is not surprising that the graphs look like the corresponding graphs in Figs. 7.37 and 7.38.

7.6 Dynamic Decision-making and Oscillations

The infection models deal with relevant empirical problems and are well suited for learning the mechanisms of stock-flow and simple feedback models. However, both in terms of the S-shaped dynamics generated and, even more so, in terms of the structures involved, the models are rather simple. Moreover, the models discussed so far contribute little to our understanding of unintended consequences. In fact, the SIR model and the Bass diffusion model were not very sophisticated in terms of agent behavior, which makes it difficult to talk about unintended consequences of decisions and actions. In the SIR model, it seems more appropriate to speak of *patients* rather than *agents*, since individuals do not decide whether or not to become infected, but rather passively contract the virus. The adoption of new products in the Bass model is also modeled as a rather passive process. Consumers are exposed to advertising and word of mouth, and some of them adopt the product, but the actual decision of consumers to adopt the product or not is not represented.

The topic of this subsection is decision-making in complex dynamic environments. A long tradition of research on *dynamic decision-making* has shown that even highly trained individuals often fail dramatically in such environments. They have only a partial view of the complex situation and do not deal adequately with the feedback they receive. Delays play an important role because they make it difficult to recognize that an event in the system is a feedback to one's own actions. It is often not easy to recognize circular causation, but time delays make it even more difficult to learn that a causal relationship exists.

You already know that feedback loops with goal-seeking behavior and delays cause oscillations, because the response to the discrepancy between the state of the system and the goal is too strong. Such oscillations are well known in supply chain management and operations management as the *bullwhip effect* (Fig. 7.48). The bullwhip effect describes the phenomenon that small changes in consumer demand can cause large swings in production at the other end of the supply chain, which is

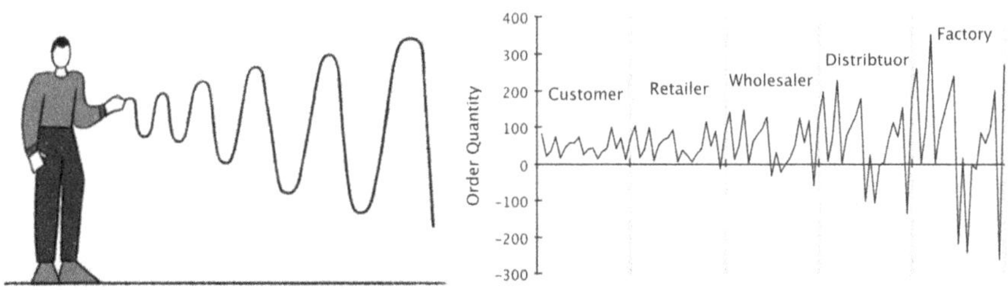

Fig. 7.48 Bullwhip effect. Source: left panel: Author, right panel: Chatfield and Pritchard (2013), reproduced with kind permission of Elsevier

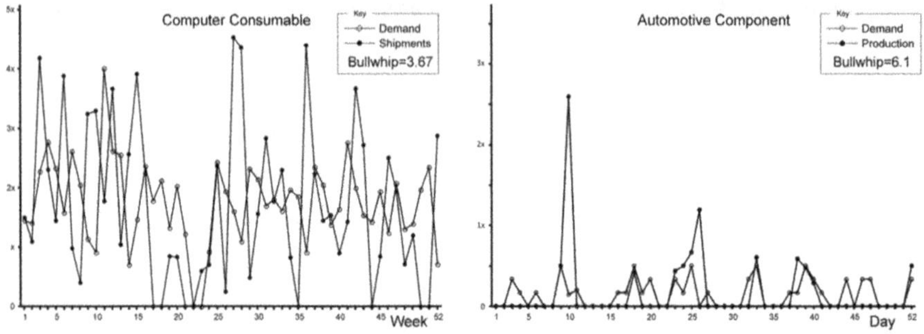

Fig. 7.49 Empirical examples of the bullwhip effect. Source: Wang and Disney (2016). CC BY 4.0 (https://creativecommons.org/licenses/by/4.0/)

also known as *demand amplification* or *variance amplification* (Wang and Disney 2016). Figure 7.49 shows two examples of the bullwhip effect in different industries. The amplitude of production (or shipment) orders is much larger than the amplitude of demand fluctuations.

7.6.1 Stock Management Control Problems

Making decisions in complex, difficult-to-understand situations is also called *dynamic decision-making*, because the environment changes over time either due to external factors or due to actions of the decision-makers. Other agents react to one's own actions, which will change the situation in the future. How other agents, or more generally the system, will react and what this means for one's own future situation is hard to predict at the moment when a decision is made.

Stock management control problems are a common class of dynamic decision-making problems. Stocks can only be controlled by their associated flows, which adds a time dimension to the choice of stock variables. Controlling flows to achieve a desired level of stock is often difficult and can lead to unintended overshooting. An everyday example is what happens when people try to fill a bottle using a funnel. The desired level of inventory is the volume of the bottle, and the control variable is the amount of liquid poured into the funnel that creates an inflow into the bottle. Many people stop pouring liquid into the funnel when the bottle is almost full. But since there is still liquid in the funnel, the result is that the bottle overflows. Controlling the amount of alcohol you drink is a similar problem. Many people stop drinking too late and get drunk because they ignore the alcohol in their stomach, which does not yet affect their feeling of drunkenness. Stopping drinking alcohol when you already feel its effects is like stopping filling a funnel when the bottle is already full.

There are many stock management problems in an economic or business context:

- Managers target inventories of products, intermediate parts, or raw materials by placing purchase orders with suppliers

- Fishery conservation authorities want to maintain fish stocks at a certain level by setting catch quotas
- Forest owners want to maintain a certain size of forest by cutting and planting trees
- The central bank may try to set the money supply through open-market operations
- The government wants to employ a certain number of teachers or other specialists by educating and training them

Maintaining the stock is costly in some way, but situations where the stock is too small to serve its purpose can be even more costly. When the decision problem is complex due to long time lags, long causal chains, multiple feedbacks, nonlinearities, and interdependence with many other agents, decision-makers cannot determine the optimal solution to their problem. They can only hope to make good decisions based on locally rational heuristics, limited information, and imperfect understanding of the whole system.

7.6.2 The Beer Distribution Game and the Bullwhip Effect

System dynamics pioneer Jay Wright Forrester of MIT developed the *Beer Distribution Game* as a teaching tool to illustrate supply chain coordination problems for management students. Since the 1960s, the game has gained a lot of popularity and is now a classic in management education. It can be played as a board game or online.[12] The game is about a simplified supply chain for beer, as shown in Fig. 7.50. The supply chain consists of four sectors or agents: retailers, wholesalers,

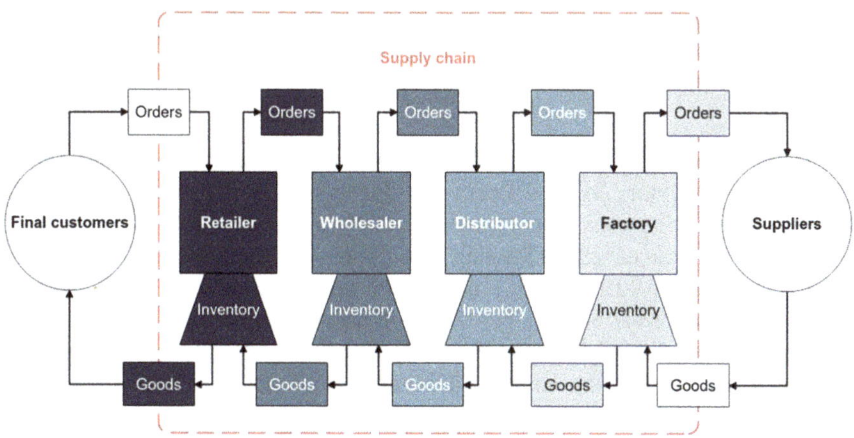

Fig. 7.50 Beer supply chain. Source: Author

[12] For example here: https://mitsloan.mit.edu/teaching-resources-library/mit-sloan-beer-game-online Accessed 26. October 2023.

distributors, and the factory. Outside the chain are final customers, who determine the final demand for beer, and suppliers, who provide the raw materials for beer production. The system has an order flow running from customers to suppliers and a goods flow running in the opposite direction. Obviously, there is feedback from orders to goods, but this feedback is delayed, because it is assumed that production and shipment take time. Thus, at each step in the chain, there is a time delay between the placement of an order and the delivery of the goods.

It is common to play the Beer Game as a board game. A typical arrangement is shown in Fig. 7.51. The game is played by four players representing one of the four sectors of the supply chain. Each player sits at a table representing their respective inventory. At the start of the game, each inventory contains 12 pennies or tokens representing 12 units of beer for sale (e.g., barrels). The game is played in rounds, with one round representing 1 week. The production and delivery time is 2 weeks, which can be realized by two small tables between the inventory tables. Initially there are four barrels of beer at each delivery stage. The initial customer demand is also four barrels per week. There is a fixed sequence of actions and events in each week.

1) All tokens on the production/shipment delay tables are advanced one table to the left, such that each player receives new items to the inventory.
2) Each player takes a card from the table with an incoming order. Retailers learn the demand from customers, wholesalers learn the demand from retailers, and so on. Orders are filled if inventory allows, i.e. the player moves the current number of ordered tokens to the shipping table on the left (or to the end customers). If a player cannot fill an order because there are not enough tokens in inventory, the unfilled orders are recorded as backlog (or backorder) on a record sheet. The total amount to be delivered is the current order plus the accumulated backlog.
3) Order cards are moved from the placed orders table to the income orders table.
4) Each player decides how much to order by writing the ordered amount on a card and placing it on the table "orders placed."

The economic problem arises because both inventory and backlog are costly. Each token in inventory costs $0.5 per week and each token in backlog costs $1 per week. Each player's goal is to minimize the company's total costs over the course of the game. This is achieved by keeping inventories low and avoiding backlogs. A game is usually played over many rounds. In the first round, the final customer demand is four barrels of beer per week. In week 5, there is an unannounced permanent increase in final demand from four to eight barrels. This surprise increase in demand is a shock to the initial equilibrium that all players in the supply chain must deal with.

Sterman (1989) reports the results of 11 beer games played under experimental conditions by undergraduates, MBAs and PhD students, and corporate executives over a 4-year period. The results typically look like Fig. 7.52. In response to increased demand, the retailer places higher orders and depletes inventory because the wholesaler cannot deliver more on short notice. With a short time lag, the

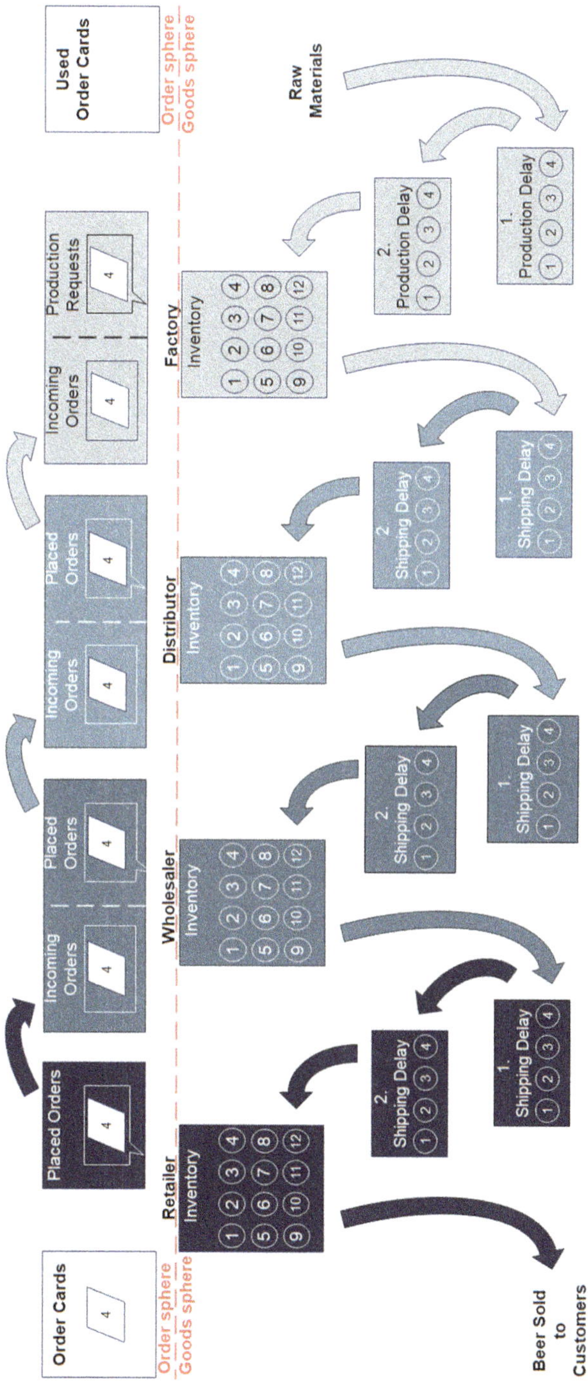

Fig. 7.51 The beer distribution game as a board game. Source: Author

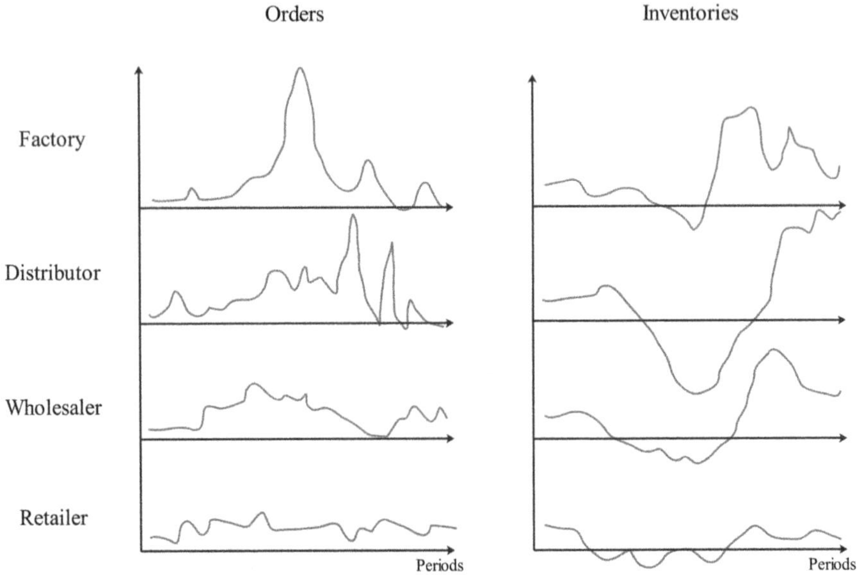

Fig. 7.52 Results from a typical experimental trial of the beer distribution game. Source: Author's own figure after Sterman (1989)

wholesaler's behavior is the same as the retailer's, but with a larger amplitude. The distributor also places higher orders with some time lag and is forced to accumulate a rather large backlog (negative inventory), which induces even higher orders in the second half of the game. Finally, the factory's orders increase in the middle of the game because the distributor's incoming orders continue to increase in the first half of the game. The factory is able to avoid accumulating a large backlog, but its inventory piles up as the distributor's orders fall sharply. Thus, this experiment provides direct evidence of the bullwhip effect under controlled conditions.

The interesting question is why this aggregate pattern emerges. We have already argued that the neglect of feedback and an overshooting response of agents to the dynamics they observe explain the pattern, but it would be nice to understand the agents' behavior in more detail. With the experimental data, we can observe what agents do, i.e., how much they order in each round, but this does not tell us directly why they do so.

According to Sterman (1989), the system behavior of the beer game in his experimental setup is described by a 23rd order nonlinear difference equation. Therefore, human agents have no chance to compute optimal behavior, but must resort to simple decision heuristics. Psychologists and behavioral economists have long argued that the use of simple heuristics is widespread in decision-making (see Kahneman et al. 1982; Gigerenzer and Todd 1999). Sterman argues that the *anchoring and adjustment heuristic* (Tversky and Kahneman 1974) is a natural candidate for agents' behavior in this game. The anchor for the orders placed could be the expected loss rate of tokens in the inventory, $\widehat{L}$. Thus, if an agent expects that she has to deliver four tokens, she will start with four tokens when determining how much to order. This anchor is adjusted if there is discrepancy between the actual stock and the desired stock, ΔS. The stock S is the effective inventory, i.e. the actual inventory minus the backlog of unfilled orders. Potentially, agents could also consider the supply line, which is equal to the sum of orders in mail delay, the backlog of the supplier and the beer in the shipping delay. Agents might also use the discrepancy between the actual supply line and the desired supply line, ΔSL. Reactions to discrepancies between the actual state and the desired state of the system are a key element of goal-seeking behavior. For simplicity, Sterman assumes a linear form of the heuristic according to which agents choose their orders O:

$$O_t = \max\left(0, \widehat{L}_t + \alpha_S \Delta S_t + \alpha_{SL} \Delta SL_t\right). \tag{7.14}$$

Expectations are assumed to be adaptive, $\widehat{L}_t = \theta L_{t-1} + (1-\theta)\widehat{L}_{t-1}, 0 \leq \theta \leq 1$. If S^* and SL^* are the (constant) desired levels of the stock and the supply line, the adjustment terms are $AS_t = \alpha_S(S^* - S_t)$ and $ASL_t = \alpha_{SL}(SL^* - SL_t)$. We can simplify the positive part of the order function by defining $\beta = \alpha_{SL}/\alpha_S$ and $S' = S^* + \beta SL^*$. Adding a stochastic disturbance ε, we obtain

$$O_t = \theta L_{t-1} + (1-\theta)\widehat{L}_{t-1} + \alpha_S(S' - S_t - \beta SL_t) + \varepsilon_t, \tag{7.15}$$

which can be estimated from available experimental data. Sterman (1989) concludes that his estimation results support the hypothesis that the participants in the game use the rule (7.14) to determine their orders, although the individual parameter estimates vary considerably. The mean parameter estimates are $\theta = 0.36$, $\alpha_S = 0.26$, $\beta = 0.34$ *and* $S' = 17$. Furthermore, the desired stock is estimated to be $S^* = 13.9$ and the desired supply line is estimated to be $SL^* = 8.4$.

What can we learn from these estimates about agent behavior and about why we get a bullwhip effect? First of all, agents underestimate the time lag between placing an order and receiving the delivery. The acquisition lag is at least 4 weeks, because it takes 2 weeks until a placed order reaches the supplier and at least another 2 weeks for the ordered quantity to be delivered. Thus, to maintain a constant throughput of 4 units of beer, which is the initial demand, 16 units should be in the supply line, but the estimate of the desired supply line is too low, $SL^* = 8.4$. Second, the agents do not even properly account for the actual supply line. To avoid over-ordering, agents should fully account for the amount of beer in the supply line, i.e. optimally $\beta = 1$ should hold. However, the estimated value is again too low ($\beta = 0.34$). In other words, if an agent has ordered so much in the past such that there is a lot of beer is in the supply line, current orders should be adjusted downward, which agents do not do sufficiently. The resulting over-ordering causes the observed large swings in orders and inventories.

The beer game is a good example of unintended consequences. When asked for their explanations of what happened in Sterman's experiments, the participants typically attributed the oscillations to presumed external fluctuations in final customer demand. Some expressed disbelief when they learned that there was only a one-time shift in final demand and that all fluctuation were endogenous, i.e. a consequence of their own behavior. All agents wanted to stabilize their own orders and inventories in order to minimize their costs, but collectively they created a great deal of instability. They ignored the circular causality of the system and resorted to an *open-loop explanation* (or linear explanation) of what had happened by attributing the origin of the dynamics to unstable external demand.

7.6.3 System Dynamics Model of the Beer Distribution Game

We can build a system dynamics model of the beer game for two purposes. First, we could use the model to check whether the reasoning about the behavior of the agents actually causes effects like those observed in reality or in an experiment. The model is then a test of a hypothesis or theory. The logic is that we are trying to generate an observed pattern by modeling an assumed behavior of agents that we cannot observe directly. We do not know whether agents actually use an anchoring and adaptation heuristic, as Sterman hypothesized. With a model of the system, we can test whether the simulated aggregate pattern resulting from the modeled agent behavior is similar to the empirically observed pattern. If it does, this is no proof that the modeled behavior actually corresponds to the actual behavior of real agents. All we can say is that it is possible to generate the observed pattern with the assumed behavior such that this behavior could be what real agents actually do. Epstein (1999) calls this approach as *generative social science*: a hypothesis about agent behavior is a possible explanation for an observed macroscopic phenomenon if it generates a similar pattern in a simulation. Second, we can use the simulation model as a *flight simulator* or a *virtual laboratory culture dish* to conduct experiments and learn. Without causing real-world damage, we can manipulate the model and observe what happens, which is a good way to learn how the system works. We can systematically change model parameters or behavioral functions to see how they affect the model's output. Decision-makers in business and government can train their intuition and test strategies before putting them into practice.

As with any real-world situation, there are several ways to build a system dynamics model of the beer game. Jolly (2015) builds the model in Fig. 7.53 based on Senge's (1990) description of the beer game. The model is slightly simplified by omitting the distributor.

The model has three types of stocks: inventories, outstanding orders, and backlogs. Inventories are directly linked by flows of beer from the factory to the wholesaler, to the retailer, and to the customers. The order flows and the backlog flows move in the opposite direction. They are not directly connected, since as stocks they only affect each sector separately. The model contains three variables that describe the behavior or real choices by the agents: `Retailer Orders`, `Wholesaler Orders`, and `Brewer Factory Request` printed in red to highlight them. All other variables follow directly from the structural assumptions of the game. To understand how the model works, we need to look at the functions behind

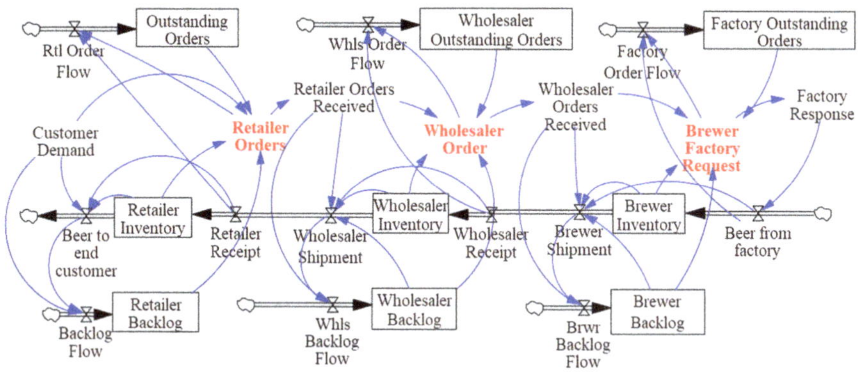

Fig. 7.53 A system dynamics model of the beer game. Source: Jolly (2015), reproduced with kind permission of Rich Jolly

the stock-flow diagram. For the sake of brevity, we will focus only on the wholesaler. The functions of the other agents are analogous.[13] Let us start with the inventory.

$$\begin{aligned}&\text{Wholesaler Inventory}\\&\quad = \text{INTEG (Wholesaler Receipt-Wholesaler Shipment, 12)}\end{aligned} \tag{7.16}$$

$$\text{Wholesaler Receipt} = \text{DELAY FIXED (Brewer Shipment, 2, 4)} \tag{7.17}$$

$$\begin{aligned}\text{Wholesaler Shipment} = \min\ &(\text{Wholesaler Inventory} + \text{WholesalerReceipt},\\&\text{Retailer Orders Received} + \text{Wholesaler Backlog})\end{aligned}$$

Equation (7.16) specifies the current inventory as the accumulated inflow of `Wholesaler Receipt` minus the accumulated outflow of `Wholesaler Shipment`. The initial stock is 12 units. The `Wholesaler Receipt` inflow is equal to the delayed `Brewer Shipment` flow. The second argument of the function DELAY FIXED(., 2,4) in Eq. (7.17) specifies the time lag of 2. The third argument determines the initial output of 4 in the first period. Equation (7.18) says that the wholesaler either ships everything in the `Wholesaler Inventory` plus the current `Wholesaler Receipt` or only the `Retailer Orders Received` + `Wholesaler Backlog`, whichever is smaller. The backlog is determined by the backlog inflow:

$$\text{Wholesaler Backlog} = \text{INTEG (Whls Backlog Flow, 0)} \tag{7.19}$$

[13] The complete Vensim model is available here: http://richjolly.com/stbdownload.html. Accessed 26 October 2023.

$$\text{Whls Backlog Flow} = \text{Retailer Orders Received} - \text{Wholesaler Shipment} \quad (7.20)$$

If `Whls Backlog Flow` is negative, the backlog is set to zero in Eq. (7.19). Note that this is one way to model the dynamics of the backlog. Alternatively the outflow could also be modeled separately. These two equations contain the behavioral assumption that the agent will always reduce the backlog to zero if possible, because a backlog is costly. The outstanding (or placed) orders are modeled analogous to the backlog:

$$\text{Wholesaler Outstanding Orders} = \text{INTEG (Whls Order Flow, } 0) \quad (7.21)$$

$$\text{Whls Order Flow} = \text{Wholesaler Order} - \text{Wholesaler Receipt} \quad (7.22)$$

As noted above, the central assumption concerns how the wholesaler (and all other agents) decide how much to order. In Jolly's model, this is modeled as follows:

$$\begin{aligned}\text{Wholesaler Order}\\ &\text{MAX((Retailer Orders Received} + \text{Wholesaler Backlog}\\ = &- 0.3\text{Wholesaler Inventory}\\ &- 0.08\text{Wholesaler Outstanding Orders} + 4),\ 0)\end{aligned} \quad (7.23)$$

$$\text{Retailer Orders Received} = \text{DELAY FIXED (Retailer Orders, } 2,\ 4) \quad (7.24)$$

Note that Jolly's specification of agent behavior in Eq. (7.23) is slightly different from Sterman's specification in Eqs. (7.14) and (7.15), but not incompatible with Sterman's theory. `Retailer Orders Received + Wholesaler Backlog` could be seen as simple way to form expectations about the expected outflow from the inventory, $\widehat{L}$. The term `−0.3 Wholesaler Inventory` corresponds to $-\alpha_S S_t$ and `−0.08 Wholesaler Outstanding Orders` corresponds to $-\alpha_S \beta SL_t$ in Eq. (7.15). Finally, the value of 4 in (7.23) corresponds with $\alpha_S S'$ in (7.15). Jolly estimated the parameters (−0.3, −0.08, 4) in his behavioral equation using a data set that he constructed from observations of the beer game reported in Senge (1990). Although his approach and the data are slightly different from those used by Sterman, the results are remarkably similar, because $\alpha_S = 0.26 \approx 0.3$, $\alpha_S \beta = 0.26 \times 0,34 = 0.0884 \approx 0.08$ and $\alpha_S S' = 0.26 \times 17 = 4.42 \approx 4$.

We can check how well Jolly's model fulfills the two model purposes. Figure 7.54 contrasts the simulated model output in the upper panel with the observed data below reported in Senge (1990). While the magnitudes of the oscillations are too small in the simulation, the two patterns are qualitatively strikingly similar. Getting the magnitudes right may be a calibration issue, but the logic of the model—in particular, the assumptions about the behavior of the agents—seems to be correct, suggesting that real agents might indeed use a heuristic such as that in Eq. (7.23).

The idea of using the model as a flight simulator can be illustrated with the results in Fig. 7.55. The three panels show the wholesaler's simulated orders, the inventory, and the backlog in the baseline calibration (blue line) with the parameters values as given in Eq. (7.23) and an experiment (red line). In the experiment, we used 0.3 as

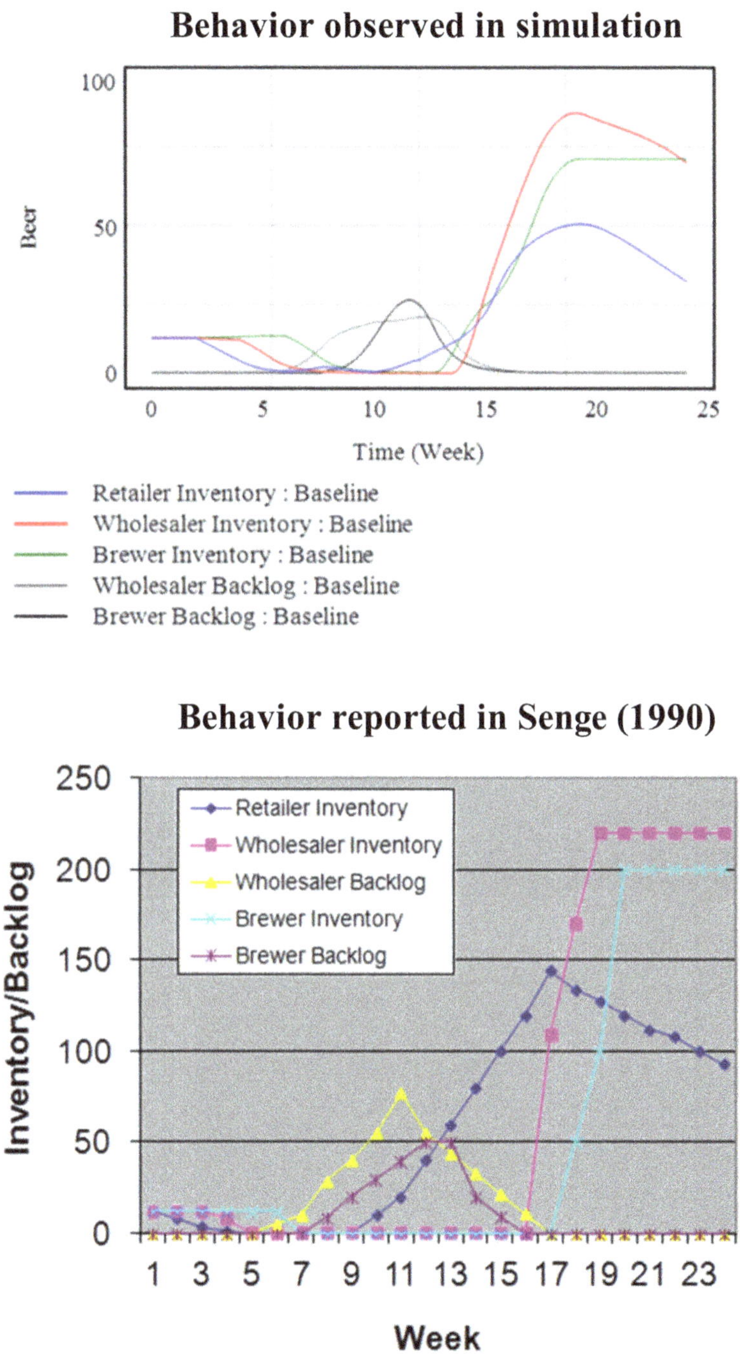

Fig. 7.54 Simulated and observed behavior. Source: Jolly (2015), reproduced with kind permission of Rich Jolly

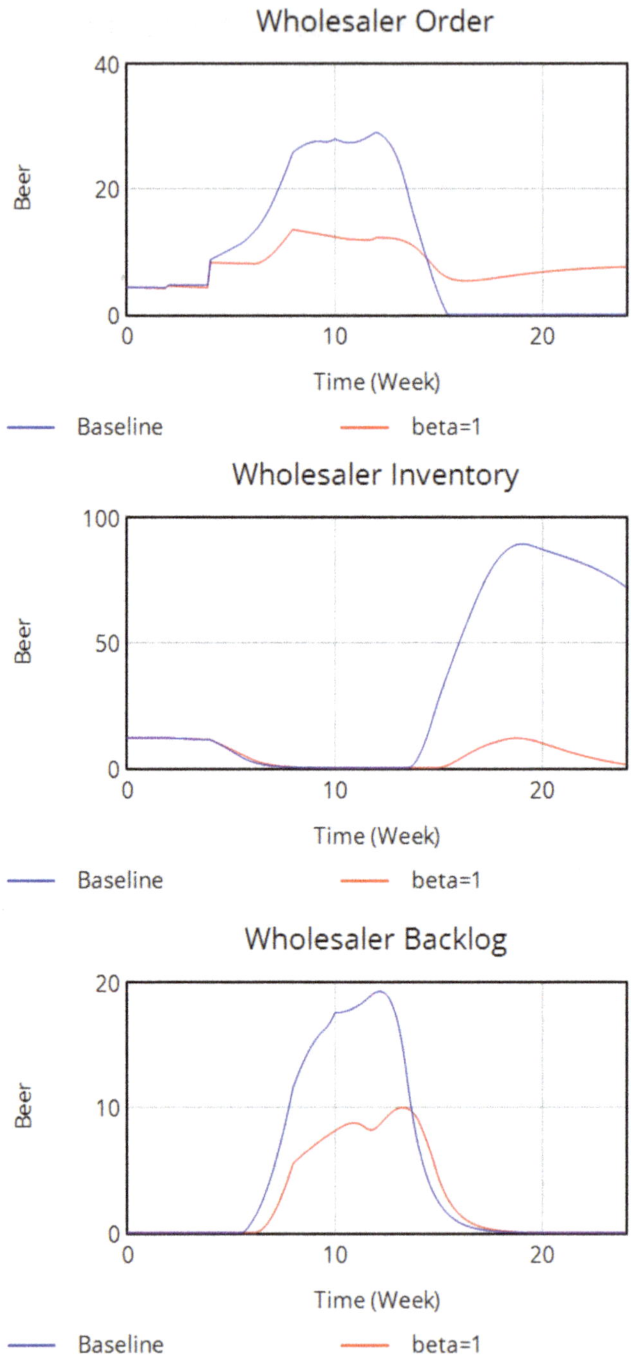

Fig. 7.55 Change in the supply line parameter β. Source: Author

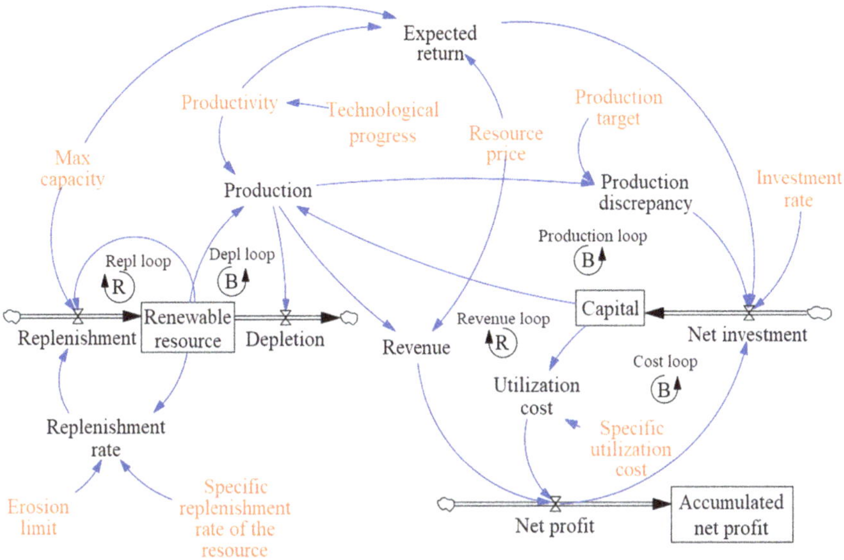

Fig. 7.56 Stock-flow diagram of the exploitation of renewable common-pool resources. Source: Author's own figure adapted from Bossel (2004), used with kind permission of Hartmut Bossel

the adjustment parameter for the `Wholesaler Outstanding Orders` instead of 0.08. This is equivalent to setting $\beta = 1$ in Sterman's specification. Sterman argues that a full consideration of the supply line (or outstanding orders) is the optimal behavior. Figure 7.56 confirms that a full consideration of the supply line ($\beta = 1$) does indeed significantly reduce the fluctuations of the wholesalers variables. This result confirms Sterman's claim that neglecting the supply line leads to overshooting. Furthermore, it teaches the lesson to managers that they should take the supply line into account when calculating their orders.

7.7 Collapse

The most dramatic form of unintended consequences is the collapse of a system. Because of its focus on stable equilibria, collapse is not a central topic in neoclassical economics, but it is a relevant economic phenomenon. Collapse can occur at different levels and in different forms: the bankruptcy of a firm, the collapse of a financial market or system, a deep depression of the economy following a financial or debt crisis, the extinction of a species, the collapse of an ecosystem, and even the fall of a complex human society, i.e. the collapse of civilizations. Since our way of living and doing business is fundamentally unsustainable, the collapse of natural systems and societal collapse in particular should receive much more attention in economics. We therefore focus on these two forms of collapse in this subsection.

7.7.1 Exploitation of Renewable Common-pool Resources

In Fig. 7.27, we saw how the cod fishery off the Atlantic coast of Canada collapsed in the early 1990s after several decades of overfishing. The fishery collapsed because the reproduction of the cod population could not keep up with the fishing rate, resulting in the extinction of cod in the area.

Wild fish populations in the oceans are an example of a *renewable common-pool resource*. Common-pool resources are goods that are publicly available to everyone (or at least to many users), but whose consumption is competitive. It is advisable to distinguish common-pool resources from commons, although this is often not done. *Commons* are resources that are owned or managed by a group. Their use is typically governed by informal norms and social practices created by the community. Garret Hardin (1968) introduced the notion of the *tragedy of the commons* into economic theory, arguing that common-pool resources tend to be overexploited because private benefits are not aligned with social benefits. However, the tragedy of the commons is a misnomer, because the characteristic of commons is that they are managed to prevent overexploitation, which is often successful. Therefore, the phenomenon described by Hardin should better be called the tragedy of the unmanaged commons or the tragedy of common-pool resources. The property of being renewable is important in this context because, if properly managed, permanent or sustainable use of the resource by the group is possible. In addition to fish, there are many other renewable natural resources of great economic importance, especially in poorer countries: game, forests, pastures. However, it would be wrong to think that renewable common-pool resources are only relevant to people in poor countries. Soil and groundwater are also renewable common-pool resources that are essential for food production everywhere.

Figure 7.56 shows the stock-flow diagram of a general model of the exploitation of a renewable common-pool resource. It can be used to model fisheries, but also the grazing of cattle on a pasture or the use of groundwater. The model has three stocks: `Renewable resource`, `Capital`, and `Accumulated net profit`. The latter stock is not really necessary, but interesting from an economic perspective. The `Renewable resource` is increased by the `Replenishment` inflow and decreased by the `Depletion` outflow. The stock of `Capital` is the cumulated `Net investment` flow. Economically, the production loop is central:

$$\text{Capital} \rightarrow \text{Production} \rightarrow \text{Production discrepancy} \rightarrow \text{Net investment} \rightarrow \text{Capital}$$

Capital, e.g. fishing boats, cattle, pumps etc., is used to produce a good, e.g., caught fish, milk, or fresh water, which depends on the renewable resource, e.g. wild fish, grass, or groundwater. The production loop is a balancing loop of a goal-seeking system. If the actual production falls short of the exogenously given production target,[14] there is a production discrepancy:

[14] Exogenous parameters are printed in orange.

$$\text{Production discrepancy} = 1 - \text{Production}/\text{Production target}. \tag{7.25}$$

The corrective action consists in net investment:

$$\text{Net investment} = \text{Production discrepancy} \times \text{Net profit} \times \text{Investment rate} \times \text{Expected return} \tag{7.26}$$

To highlight that net investment is the key choice made by decision-makers in the model, it is printed in red in the diagram. Equation (7.26) contains the behavioral assumptions that investment depends positively on `Net profits` and on the `Expected return`, which is given by

$$\text{Expected return} = \text{Resource price} \times \text{Productivity} \times \text{Max capacity} \tag{7.27}$$

The expected return is optimally based on the maximum capacity of the renewable resource. If there is a production discrepancy, the users of the resource invest into new capital that helps them produce the good from the resource. In principle, negative net investment is also possible if actual production is above the target. In this case, a part of the capital stock would be scrapped. For a given productivity of capital, more goods can be produced from the resource, if more capital is used:

$$\text{Production} = \text{Productivity} \times \text{Renewable resource} \times \text{Capital} \tag{7.28}$$

For instance, fishermen can catch more fish from the local fish population if they have more or larger boats. The revenue loop creates positive feedback. More production leads to higher `Revenue` (at a given price)

$$\text{Revenue} = \text{Resource price} \times \text{Production} \tag{7.29}$$

which has a positive effect on `Net profits`:

$$\text{Net profits} = \text{Revenue} - \text{Utilization cost}. \tag{7.30}$$

Higher profits, in turn, allow agents to invest more, leading to higher capital and higher production. The revenue loop is counteracted by the balancing cost loop, because the utilization of capital is costly:

$$\text{Utilization cost} = \text{Specific utilization cost} \times \text{Capital}. \tag{7.31}$$

With a constant stock of the renewable resource, the three economic loops would lead to an S-shaped growth of production until the production target is reached. Initially, when the capital stock is low, there would be a lot of investment. Over time, the production discrepancy would shrink as the additional capital reduces the desire to invest more. Unfortunately, the production of the good affects the resource by depleting it:

$$\text{Depletion} = \text{Production}. \tag{7.32}$$

There is no feedback from `Depletion` or the stock of the `Renewable resource` to economic activity. In other words, the users of the resource do not consider their effect on the resource. From their perspective, the depletion is an unintended consequence or the result of a governance mechanism. If `Depletion` is greater than `Replenishment`, then the stock of the `Renewable resource` will decline. The replenishment of the resource follows a logistic growth process as in Eq. (6.9) in Chap. 6:

$$\begin{aligned}\text{Replenishment} = {} & \text{Replenishment rate} \times \text{Renewable resource} \\ & \times (1 - \text{Renewable resource}/\text{Max capacity})\end{aligned} \tag{7.33}$$

Without depletion the resource grows up to the maximum capacity of its environment. A key assumption of the model is that the `Replenishment rate` has a discontinuity:

$$\begin{aligned}\text{Replenishment rate} = {} & \text{IF THEN ELSE (Renewable resource} < \text{Erosion} \\ & \text{limit, 0, Specific replenishment rate of the resource)}\end{aligned} \tag{7.34}$$

The permanent collapse of the renewable resource occurs when the stock falls below the threshold given by the `Erosion limit`. The erosion limit is a tipping point of the natural subsystem. The resource can only renew itself if it has a minimum size. Below the limit the replenishment rate is significantly reduced or, as modeled here, even falls to zero. Modeling the collapse with a discontinuity at a threshold is a simplification, because real ecological processes can be quite complicated. However, a discontinuity captures the most important effect that the replenishment is impeded at low levels of the stock. For instance, a fish population cannot reproduce, if the remaining fish are too young. Plants cannot regrow if they are permanently damaged or if the soil is eroded by overgrazing. Excessive use of groundwater can lead to permanent depletion through land subsidence, water salinization, or the interception of the groundwater flow due to reduced water in lakes and streams as a result of falling groundwater levels.

We simulate the model with the following parameter set in the baseline run:

- `Max capacity` = `1,`
- `Productivity` = `1,`
- `Technological progress` = `0,`
- `Resource price` = `1,`
- `Production target` = `0.5,`
- `Investment rate` = `0.1,`
- `Specific utilization cost` = `0.1,`

- `Specific replenishment rate` = `0.1`,
- `Erosion limit` = `0.1`.

The chosen parameter set leads to the typical result that the resource is overexploited, with the depletion always greater than the replenishment (Fig. 7.57). Due to the logistic growth, the replenishment is initially very low. Because of depletion, the stock of the resource decreases (see right panel in Fig. 7.58) causing its growth rate to increase until the maximum growth is reached in year 33. Production also peaks in this year (see left panel in Fig. 7.58). Since the production target is very high at 0.5 and net profits rise initially, there is positive net investment and growth of the capital stock (see Fig. 7.58). The capital stock peaks in year 65, when net profits become negative and in which the erosion limit of 0.1 is reached. Although replenishment drops to zero, depletion continues resulting in an accelerated decline of the resource. In year 82, the stock of the resource is less than 0.01 tons. Once the erosion limit is exceeded, the resource will never recover, because the replenishment rate is always zero.

Figure 7.58 shows that there are two types of collapse in this model. In the baseline model, the `Erosion limit` is equal to 0.1 tons per year. The fall of the replenishment rate to zero below this threshold and the resulting convergence of `Production` and the resource level to zero can be interpreted as the final collapse of the system. However, even without the erosion threshold, the level of production and the stock of the resource fall to very low levels due to overexploitation, as shown in the run "zero erosion" where there is no threshold. In this case, the resource stabilizes in year 126 and then starts to rise again at a very low rate. But even without the ultimate breakdown of the system, we can speak of a collapse of production from 0.044 tons per year to 0.002 tons per year. The dynamics of production in Fig. 7.58

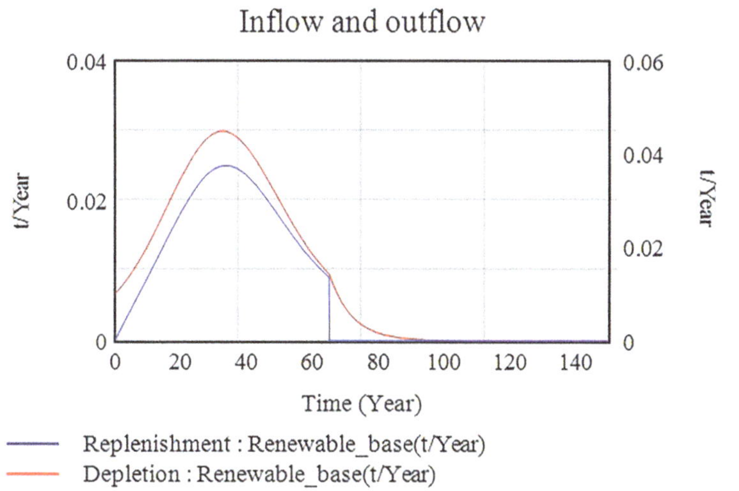

Fig. 7.57 Replenishment and depletion of the renewable resource. Source: Author

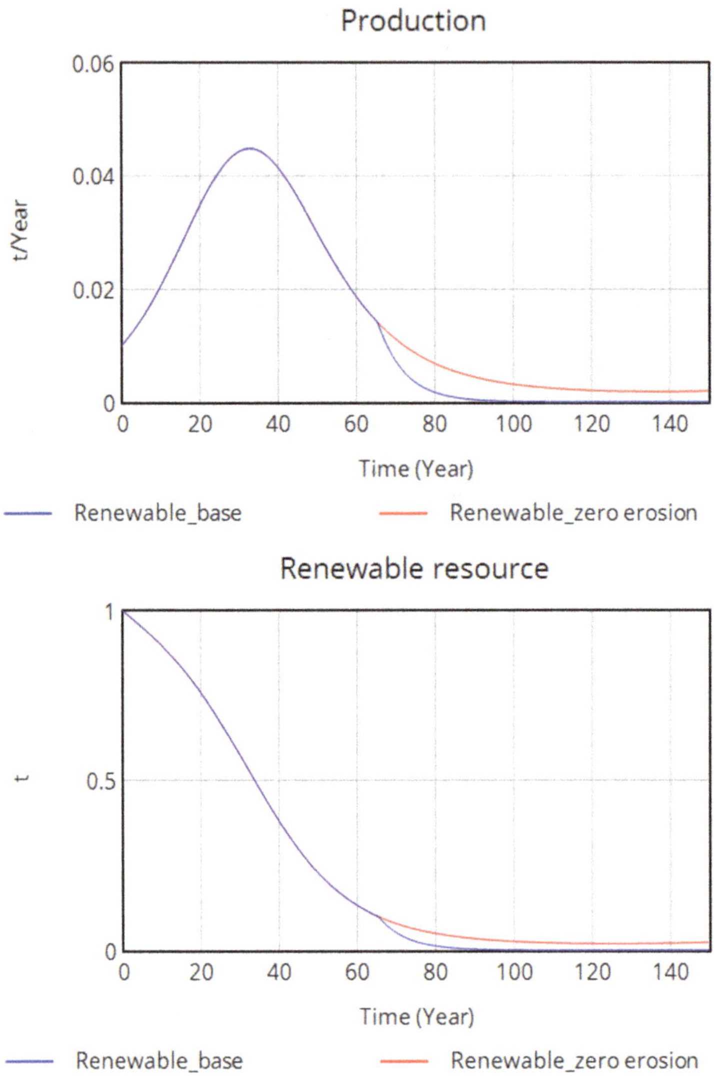

Fig. 7.58 Effect of the erosion limit threshold. Source: Author

look quite similar to the overshoot and collapse pattern shown in Fig. 7.26, but in this model the overshoot occurs right from the start, because the depletion is always greater than the replenishment. In addition, the carrying capacity `Max capacity` is not affected here. We could also model a reduction of the maximum capacity as a result of production; for instance, the destruction of the marine ecosystem by also catching other fish, which are food for the fish considered as the resource (Fig. 7.59).

We can use the model to simulate other scenarios (see Fig. 7.60), for example one with technological progress where `Productivity` is permanently doubled to 2 in year 20. This scenario is similar to the introduction of high-tech trawlers in Canadian cod fishery in the 1960s. In Fig. 7.26, we saw that the catch of cod tripled due to the new trawlers, but plummeted quickly afterwards. The red line in Fig. 7.60 shows the same pattern. More productive capital increases production for a short period of time, but the much higher depletion of the resource causes the erosion limit to be exceeded already in year 26 and a complete elimination of the resource shortly

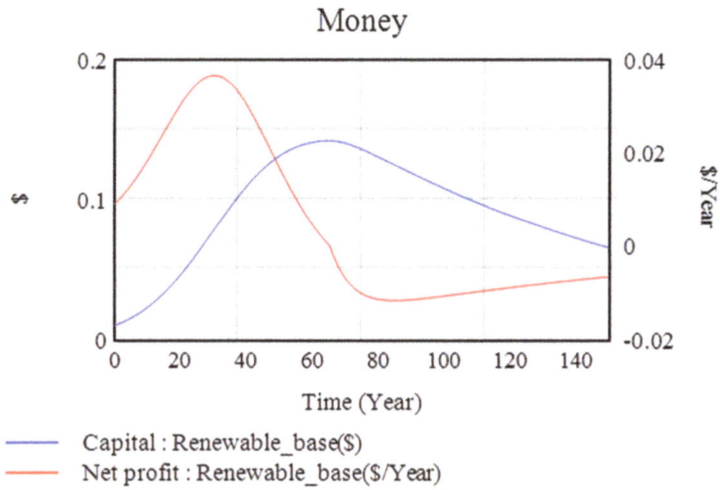

Fig. 7.59 Profits and capital dynamics. Source: Author

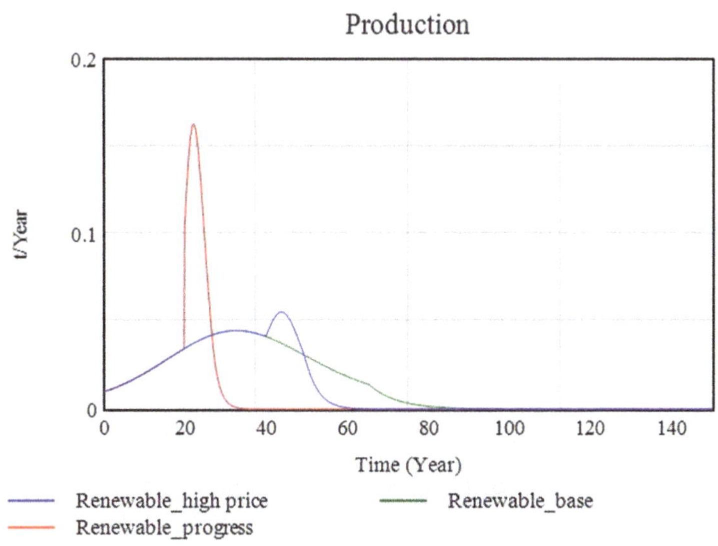

Fig. 7.60 Effect of technological progress and a higher price on production. Source: Author

thereafter. Another scenario is the rise of the `Resource price` by 50% to 1.5 in period 40. In the baseline scenario, production peaks in year 33. We could imagine that the market price rises due to the decrease in supply once customers got used to the good. A permanent increase in the price causes a pattern similar to the productivity increase: production increases sharply for a short time, but then collapses as the resource is quickly exhausted.

The collapse is caused by excessive production targets. In Fig. 7.61, we can see that a much lower `Production target` of 0.05 (medium target) would slow down the collapse, but would not prevent it. A low target of 0.02, on the other hand, leads to a stabilized stock of the resource, because depletion and replenishment can converge in this case. The imposition of exogenous quotas follows this logic, but as discussed earlier, this policy can fail, if the quotas are not strict enough. The alternative way to use a renewable resource sustainably is its endogenous management, which would require a feedback from the stock of the resource to the net investment in capital. A management of the commons would mean that the users respond to the dynamics of the resource in such a way that the investment in capital is coupled to the state of the resource. One way to do this could be to reduce the capital stock when the resource falls below half of the maximum capacity, because that is where the growth rate of the resource is maximized. A further increase of the capital stock with decreasing resource growth leads to exhaustion (Fig. 7.61).

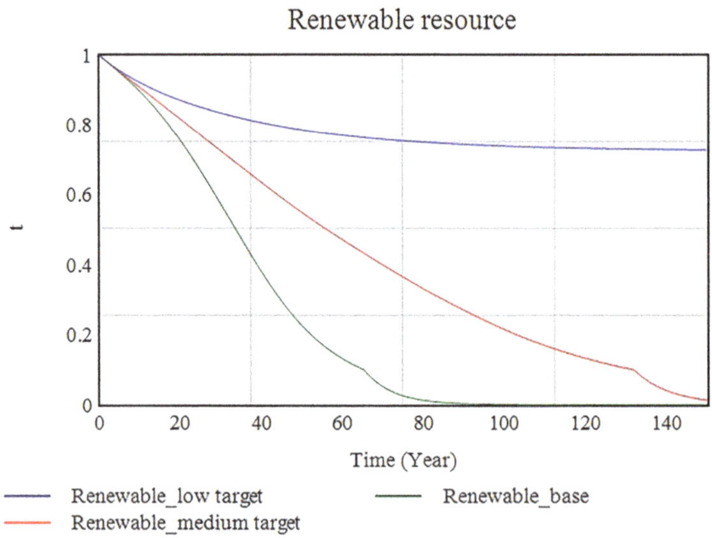

Fig. 7.61 Effect of different production targets on the resource. Source: Author

7.7.2 Collapse of Civilizations

Collapse can happen on a much larger scale, and indeed has happened many times in human history. Many great civilizations such as the Roman Empire or the ancient Maya collapsed. Well-known examples of collapsed smaller societies include Easter Island and the Norse colony in Greenland. The scientific movement of *collapsology* believes that the risk of collapse of our industrial civilization is very high due to resource scarcity, natural disasters, nuclear war, and the overstepping of many planetary boundaries.

Societal collapse is a complicated topic with many dimensions and different manifestations. It is characterized by often dramatic population declines, prolonged economic depression, and loss of social order. Collapsed societies may disappear completely, revert to a simpler state with less societal complexity, or be taken over and absorbed by another society. Population decline can be caused by starvation, disease, violence, or emigration. Economic depression and a decrease in social complexity are a direct result of a lack of people needed to maintain important economic and social functions.

Civilization collapse can have both exogenous and endogenous causes. Changes in climatic conditions, such as prolonged droughts or a drop in average temperature, or natural disasters, such as earthquakes or volcanic eruptions, are common exogenous causes. The more interesting case from a complexity perspective is when collapses occur endogenously, i.e., caused by unsustainable behavior of the civilization itself. Of course, it is also possible that unsustainable behavior undermines a civilization's resilience to exogenous stressors, which are the ultimate triggers of collapse.

There is a large literature in history, archeology, anthropology, geography, and related disciplines about the collapse of civilizations (e.g., Tainter 1988; Diamond 2005) that discusses various explanations for historical collapses. The following system dynamics model illustrates one possible mechanism that can lead to societal collapse. The model has been proposed for the collapse of the Maya population between 600 CE and 800 CE (see Fig. 7.62), but its mechanisms may be more general and applicable to other cases, such as Easter Island, whose population collapsed dramatically around 1500 CE.

One explanation for the collapse of the Maya civilization in the lowlands of Mesoamerica is that the local ecosystem collapsed due to deforestation, resulting in insufficient agricultural yields to sustain the population. García (2020) proposes a simple model for this explanation (see Fig. 7.63). The Maya used a variety of intensive agricultural techniques to produce their food. The model simplifies the agricultural system to just two stock variables: the amount of `Agricultural land` and the `land fertility` land. The amount of food produced is the product of these two stocks:

$$\text{Supply of food} = \text{Agricultural land} \times \text{Land fertility land} \tag{7.35}$$

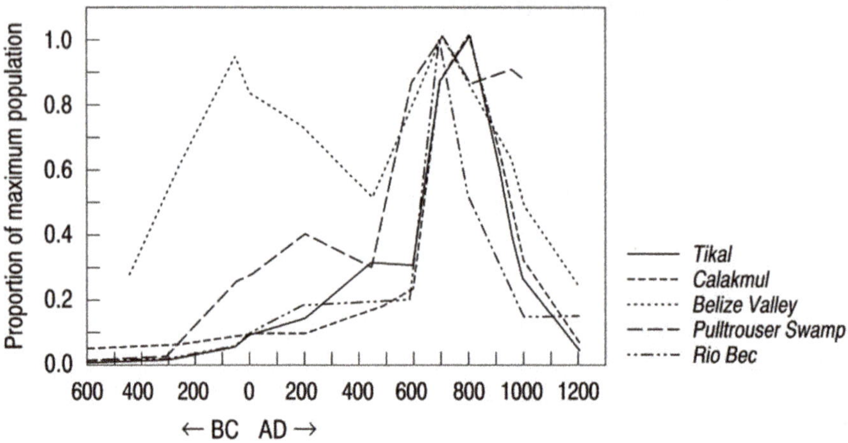

Fig. 7.62 Evolution of the ancient Maya population at different places. Source: Folan et al. (2000), reproduced with kind permission of International Institute for Applied Systems Analysis

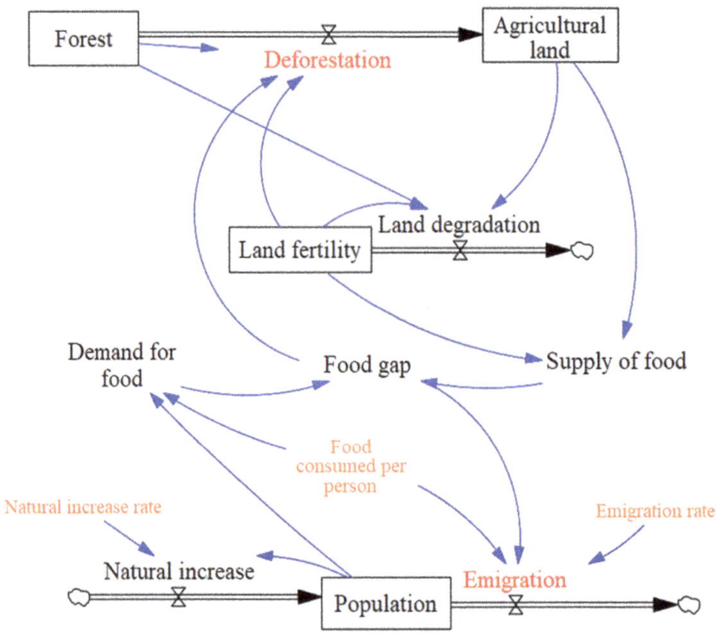

Fig. 7.63 Population decline, deforestation, and ecosystem collapse. Source: Author's on figure adapted from García (2020), used with kind permission of Juan-Martín García

The crucial element of the model is that the fertility of the agricultural land is lost due to land degradation. Fertility decreases by a variable rate that depends on the ratio of `Agricultural land` and `Forest`:

$$\text{Land degradation} = \text{Land fertility} \times \text{MIN}\ \left(1,\ (\text{Agricultural land}/\text{Forest})^{1.9}\right) \tag{7.36}$$

Initially, when the ratio of agricultural land to the size of the forest is small, the rate of land degradation is also small. The model is calibrated so that in the initial year 1000 BCE, there are 8 km^2 of agricultural land and 5000 km^2 of forest in the region. Thus, the initial rate of fertility loss is $(8/5000)^{1.9} = 4.87 * 10^{-6}$. This rate increases exponentially with an exponent of 1.9 which is chosen in order generate the population maximum in the year 800 CE. An increase in the ratio of cleared land to forest makes the local climate warmer and drier and promotes soil erosion.

`Deforestation` is one of the two ways in which the population responds to the `Food gap`, i.e. the discrepancy between the `Demand for food` and the `Supply of food`. The other response is `Emigration`. When a food gap occurs, the population will deforest the amount needed to close the gap at the current fertility of the agricultural land.

$$\text{Deforestation} = \text{MIN}\ (\text{Food gap}/\text{MAX}\ (\text{Land fertility}, 1), \text{Forest} \times 0.04) \tag{7.37}$$

A `Food gap` occurs because the `Supply of food` decreases due to `Land degradation` and because the `Demand for food` = `Food consumed per person` × `Population` increases due to population growth. The `Food consumed per person` is assumed to be constant at 400 kg of food per person and year.

The `Population` is calibrated to grow at a net `Natural increase rate` of 0.17% per year. There is also a normal `Emigration rate` of 0.05, if there is a positive `Food gap` equal to the amount of `Food consumed per person`. The actual `Emigration` depends on the size of the `Food gap`:

$$\text{Emigration} = (\text{Food gap}/\text{Food consumed per person}) \times \text{Emigration rate}. \tag{7.38}$$

Figure 7.64 shows that the simulated population grows exponentially for more than a thousand years and then drops abruptly to zero after peaking in 869. This simulated pattern fits the actual population dynamics in Fig. 7.62 quite well, so the model offers a possible explanation for the collapse.

Figure 7.65 reveals the causes of population decline. In the early centuries, `Land fertility` declines very slowly from an initial value of 5 million kg/(km^2 × year) in the year 1000 BCE. In the year 500 CE, despite 1500 years of land degradation, the fertility is still at 4.136 million kg/(km^2 × year). However, the exponential effect of land degradation gets stronger over time until fertility reaches zero in 888 CE. In response, Mayans accelerate deforestation, which reaches its maximum of 144 km^2/year in 878 CE, compared to 2.12 km^2/year in 800 CE.

Once land fertility has reached a very low level, even massive deforestation will not help. The increasing food gap per capita (see Fig. 7.66) is evidence of the futility of accelerated deforestation. The food gap is always positive in this model, but it takes 1683 years to double from the initial level of 0.68 kg/person to 1.36 kg/person.

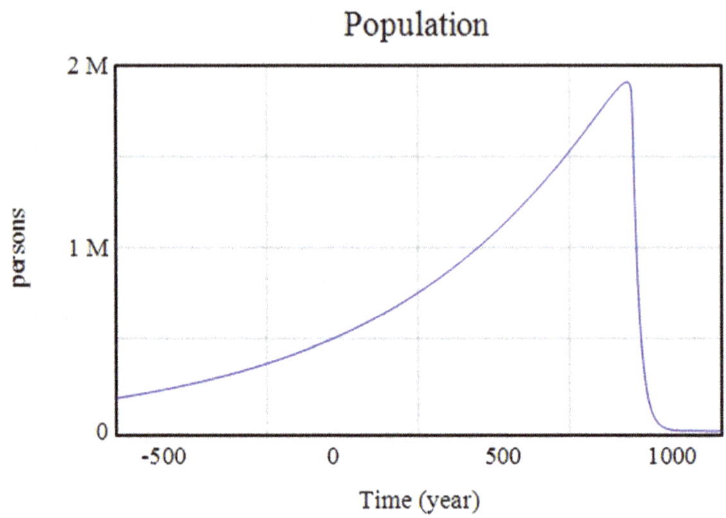

Fig. 7.64 Simulated population dynamics. Source: Author

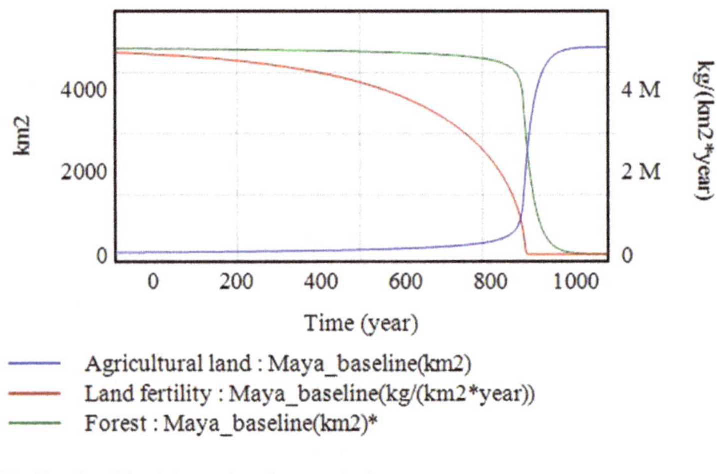

Fig. 7.65 Simulated land dynamics. Source: Author

The next doubling occurs by the year 800, then by 844 and by 864. In 888, the maximum food deficit of 400 kg/person is attained, which means that there is no food left and the maximum emigration rate begins.

Deforestation as a cause of starvation is also a popular explanation for the collapse of the Easter Island civilization. Note, however, that the population of Easter Island had no way to emigrate from their remote island, so the reasons for their depopulation are starvation and mutual killing.

Civilizational collapses like that of the Classic Maya are disturbing. The Maya had a highly developed civilization with great achievements in agriculture, writing,

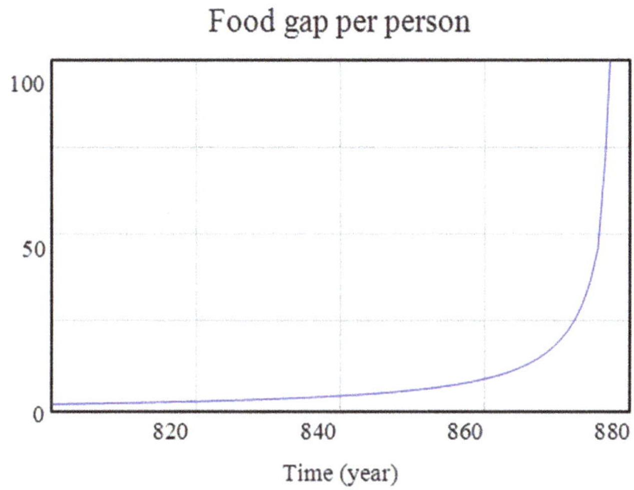

Fig. 7.66 Food deficit over time. Source: Author

art, architecture, mathematics, and astronomy. Tikal, one of their most important cities, had nearly 100,000 inhabitants at its peak and a population density of about 500 inhabitants per km^2. For comparison, London had about 10,000–12,000 inhabitants in the year 800, Paris about 20,000–30,000, and Rome about 50,000. Yet this sophisticated civilization could not avoid collapse. Land degradation as a result of deforestation is probably one factor that caused the collapse, but others such as disease, labor shortages, warfare, and the breakdown of trade relations were probably important as well. Most likely, all of these factors combined to create a level of stress that the Maya civilization, despite its high level of development, could not handle. It would be interesting to know whether the Maya anticipated their collapse, and whether they tried to avoid it by changing their own destructive practices, but were unable to do so quickly enough. Such knowledge would have obvious relevance to our own civilization, whose behavior is just as unsustainable as that of classical Mayan society

7.8 Causal Complexity

Feedback and circular causality make it difficult to understand the behavior of a system. Positive feedback amplifies external impulses, negative feedback dampens them. We have seen in the system dynamics models presented so far that the dynamics of the system variables tend to be highly nonlinear as a result of the interacting feedback loops. Nonlinearity is a key element of complexity. Unintended consequences are often the result of neglected feedback. Decision-makers act as if there is a linear chain from their intervention to a desired outcome, but in fact the causality is circular.

Chapter 3 introduced a number of different ways to measure the complexity of a system, such as structural complexity, cyclomatic complexity, and organizational complexity. *Causal complexity* is another measure of complexity that captures the complexity of a system's causal structures (Naugle et al. 2023). It is defined as a combination of *cyclomatic complexity CC* and *feedback density FD*:

$$CsC = CC \times (1 + FD). \tag{7.39}$$

From Chap. 3, we know that cyclomatic complexity measures the intricacy of a system's causal structure by counting the number of paths in a control-flow graph:

$$CC = M - N + 2P,$$

where M is the number of edges, N is the number of nodes, and P is the number of connected components. Feedback density captures how much of the causal structure is involved in feedback loops:

$$FD = \left(M_{loop} + N_{loop}\right)/(M + N).$$

If the system contains no feedback loops, then $M_{loop} = N_{loop} = 0$ and hence $FD = 0$. If all nodes and edges are part of at least one feedback loop, then $FD = 1$. The feedback density indicates how much of a system's causal structure is circular versus linear. Since feedback loops are a major driver of system behavior and make system understanding and dynamics decision-making difficult, it is reasonable that causal complexity is a positive function of feedback density. The causal complexity metric weights the number of paths through the system (cyclomatic complexity) by the feedback density.

In order to compare different systems or models of systems with respect to their causal complexity, it is advisable to use a standardized representation of the causal structure of the systems. Naugle et al. (2023) suggest using *causal structure diagrams* for this purpose, which are similar to causal loop diagrams, but exclude everything that is not relevant to the causal structure. The causal structure diagram contains all causal relationships between variables, but no exogenous parameters or variables, no specifications of initial conditions, and no summary variables that have no causal effect on other variables.

Figure 7.67 shows a causal structure diagram of the Solow growth model. Compared to the stock-flow diagram of the Solow growth model in Fig. 7.31, the exogenous parameters are omitted as well as consumption, because it has no causal effect on other variables, and saving, because it is equal to investment. The diagram has $M = 11$ edges and $N = 8$ nodes. The two edges from labor and from technology to output are not part of feedback loops, but all nodes are, so $M_{loop} = 9$ and $N_{loop} = 8$. Since all parts of the system are connected, $P = 1$. So we get

$$CC_{Solow} = 11 - 8 + 2 = 5$$

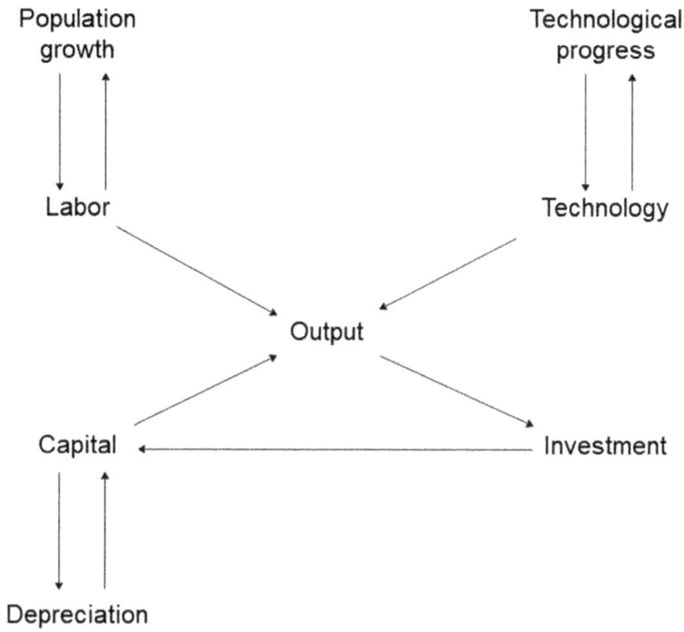

Fig. 7.67 Causal structure diagram of the Solow growth model. Source: Author

$$FD_{Solow} = \frac{9+8}{11+8} = \frac{17}{19} = 0.8947$$

$$CsC_{Solow} = 5(1 + 0.8947) = 9.4737$$

Figure 7.68 is the causal structure diagram corresponding to the stock-flow diagram of the Maya collapse model in Fig. 7.64. Again, the three exogenous parameters in orange are omitted.

The number for this model are:

$$M = 17, N = 11, M_{loop} = 17, N_{loop} = 11,$$

$$CC_{Maya} = 8, FD_{Maya} = 2, CsC_{Maya} = 16.$$

The Maya collapse model has a causal complexity that is 68.89% higher than the causal complexity of the Solow growth model. It has both more paths through the system and a higher feedback density. In fact, every node and every edge of the Maya model are part of at least one feedback loop. Deforestation and land degradation are even part of three feedback loops.

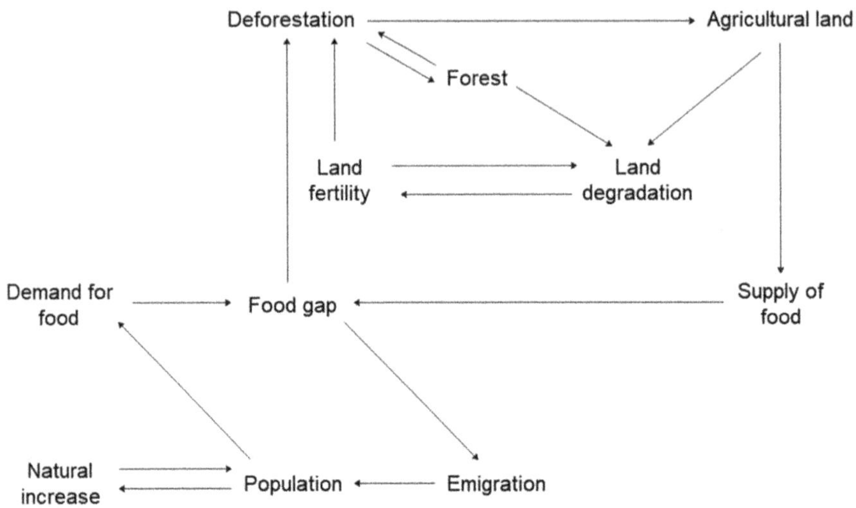

Fig. 7.68 Causal structure diagram of the Maya collapse model. Source: Author

Things to Remember

- Feedback occurs when the output of a system is also an input to the system. Feedback loops create circular causality, where one system variable affects itself through other variables. Circular causality makes it difficult to identify causes and effects and creates a tangled web of causal influences. The behavior of a system with circular causality is difficult to predict. Interventions often lead to unintended consequences that were not anticipated.
- Explanations are answers to why questions that make an observed phenomenon understandable. Reasons and causes explain why things happen. Reasons are motives or justifications for a decision or belief. Causes produce an effect or make something happen. From a complexity perspective, explanation requires describing a mechanism (or process) of how something came to be.
- We can distinguish between deterministic and indeterministic causality. In social systems, we almost always deal with indeterministic or probabilistic causality, where a cause increases the probability of an effect. We can also distinguish between necessary and sufficient causes, and between proximal and distal causes.
- Positive feedback loops are self-reinforcing and lead to exponential growth. Negative feedback loops are balancing and lead to convergence to an equilibrium. Positive and negative feedback loops are the main elements

(continued)

of system dynamics models. Their interaction can produce different types of dynamics.

- In addition to exponential growth and goal-seeking behavior, S-shaped growth, oscillations, growth with overshoot, and overshoot and collapse are dynamic patterns that are relevant to economics. Oscillations are caused by delays. S-shaped growth requires a constant carrying capacity. Collapse occurs when the carrying capacity erodes.
- Stocks describe the state of a system at any point in time. They are changes due to inflows and outflows. Typically, decision-makers can only influence flows, not stocks.
- Complex or dynamic decision-making refers to situations with multiple feedbacks and causal relationships that are only partially known to decision-makers. In addition, delays can impede learning about the causal relationships. From the decision-maker's perspective, the environment is changing in ways that are difficult to understand, making it hard to predict the consequences of one's actions.
- Causal complexity refers to the complexity of the causal structure of a system, which increases with the number of feedback loops in the system. It can be measured by a metric consisting of cyclomatic complexity and feedback density.

References

Acemoglu D, Naidu S, Restrepo P, Robinson JA (2019) Democracy does cause growth. J Polit Econ 127:47–100. https://doi.org/10.1086/700936

Angrist JD, Krueger AB (1991) Does compulsory school attendance affect schooling and earnings? Q J Econ 106:979–1014. https://doi.org/10.2307/2937954

Bala BK, Arshad FM, Noh KM (2017) System dynamics – modelling and simulation. Springer, Singapore

Bass FM (1969) A new product growth for model consumer durables. Manag Sci 15:215–227. https://doi.org/10.1287/mnsc.15.5.215

Borghans L, Cörvers F (2009) The Americanization of European higher education and research. NBER Working paper No. w15217. https://www.nber.org/papers/w15217

Bossel H (2004) Systemzoo 2: Klima, Ökosysteme und Ressourcen. Books on Demand, Norderstedt

Bossel H (2007) Systems and models. Complexity, dynamics, evolution, sustainability. Books on Demand, Norderstedt

Chatfield DC, Pritchard AM (2013) Returns and the bullwhip effect. Transp Res Part E: Logist Transp Rev 49:159–175. https://doi.org/10.1016/j.tre.2012.08.004

Chen H, Wang X (2021) Sparrow slaughter and grain yield reduction during the great famine of China. 23 April 2021. Available at SSRN https://ssrn.com/abstract=3832057 or https://doi.org/10.2139/ssrn.3832057

Colagrossi M, Rossignoli D, Maggioni MA (2020) Does democracy cause growth? A meta-analysis (of 2000 regressions). Eur J Polit Econ 61:101824. https://doi.org/10.1016/j.ejpoleco.2019.101824

Comin DA, Hobijn B (2004) Cross-country technological adoption: making the theories face the facts. J Monet Econ 51(1):39–83. Dataset: http://www.nber.org/data/chat/. Accessed 20 Nov 2023

de Haan J, Jin Z, Chen Z (2019) Micro-prudential regulation and banks' systemic risk. 6 November 2019. De Nederlandsche Bank Working Paper No. 656, 2019, Available at SSRN: httfps://ssrn.com/abstract=3479135 or https://doi.org/10.2139/ssrn.3479135

Dediu H (2017) ASYMCO. http://www.asymco.com/author/asymco/. Accessed 20 Nov 2023

Dees S, Soares Brinca P (2013) Consumer confidence as a predictor of consumption spending: Evidence for the United States and the Euro area. Int Econ 134:1–14. https://doi.org/10.1016/j.inteco.2013.05.001

Diamond J (2005) Collapse: how societies choose to fail or succeed. Penguin Group US

Duranton G, Turner MA (2011) The fundamental law of road congestion: evidence from US cities. Am Econ Rev 101:2616–2652. https://doi.org/10.1257/aer.101.6.2616

Epstein JM (1999) Agent-based computational models and generative social science. Complexity 4: 41–60. https://doi.org/10.1002/(SICI)1099-0526(199905/06)4:5<41::AID-CPLX9>3.0.CO;2-F

Federal Reserve Bank of St. Louis (2023) FRED economic data. https://fred.stlouisfed.org/. Accessed 8 Dec 2023

Federal Trade Commission (1939) Report on motor vehicle industry, Washington

Folan WJ, Faust B, Lutz W, Gunn JD (2000) Social and environmental factors in the classic Maya collapse. In: Lutz W, Prieto L, Sanderson W (eds) IIASA Research Report RR-00-014, pp 2–32

García JM (2020) System dynamics fast guide: A basic tutorial with examples for modeling, analysis and simulate the complexity of business and environmental systems. Independently published, Spain

Geels FW (2022) Causality and explanation in socio-technical transitions research: Mobilising epistemological insights from the wider social sciences. Res Policy 51:104537. https://doi.org/10.1016/j.respol.2022.104537

Gigerenzer G, Todd PM (1999) Fast and frugal heuristics: the adaptive toolbox. In: Simple heuristics that make us smart. Oxford University Press, New York, NY, US, pp 3–34

Graber M, Launov A, Wälde K (2008) Publish or perish? The increasing importance of publications for prospective economics professors in Austria, Germany and Switzerland. Ger Econ Rev 9: 457–472

Hampf F, Wiederhold S, Woessmann L (2017) Skills, earnings, and employment: exploring causality in the estimation of returns to skills. Large-scale Assessments in Education 5:12. https://doi.org/10.1186/s40536-017-0045-7

Hardin G (1968) The tragedy of the commons. Science 162:1243–1248. https://doi.org/10.1126/science.162.3859.1243

Huber E, Rueschemeyer D, Stephens JD (1993) The impact of economic development on democracy. J Econ Perspect 7:71–86. https://doi.org/10.1257/jep.7.3.71

Jolly R (2015) Systems thinking for business: capitalize on structures hidden in plain sight. Systems Solutions Press

Kahneman D, Slovic P, Tversky A (eds) (1982) Judgment under uncertainty: heuristics and biases. Cambridge University Press, Cambridge

Kermack WO, McKendrick AG (1927) A contribution to the mathematical theory of epidemics. Proc R Soc Lond Series A, Contain Pap Math Phys Character 115:700–721. https://doi.org/10.1098/rspa.1927.0118

Kieser A (2004) The Americanization of academic management education in Germany. J Manag Inq 13:90–97. https://doi.org/10.1177/1056492604265301

Leahey E (2007) Not by productivity alone: how visibility and specialization contribute to academic earnings. Am Sociol Rev 72:533–561. https://doi.org/10.1177/000312240707200403

Lutter M, Schröder M (2016) Who becomes a tenured professor, and why? Panel data evidence from German sociology, 1980–2013. Res Policy 45:999–1013. https://doi.org/10.1016/j.respol.2016.01.019

Merton RK (1936) The unanticipated consequences of purposive social action. Am Sociol Rev 1: 894. https://doi.org/10.2307/2084615

Morgan A, LaBerge N, Larremore D et al (2022) Socioeconomic roots of academic faculty. Nat Hum Behav 6:1625–1633

Moyle PB, Li HW, Barton BA (1986) The Frankenstein effect: impact of introduced fishes on native fishes in North America. In: Stroud RH (ed) Fish culture in fisheries management: proceedings of a symposium on the role of fish culture in fisheries management at Lake Ozark, Missouri, March 31–April 3, 1985. American Fisheries Society, Bethesda, Maryland, pp 415–426

Naugle A, Verzi S, Lakkaraju K et al (2023) Feedback density and causal complexity of simulation model structure. J Simul 17:229–239. https://doi.org/10.1080/17477778.2021.1982653

Our World in Data (2018) Fish stocks data explorer. https://ourworldindata.org/explorers/fish-stocks. Accessed 11 Apr 2023

Our World in Data (2021) Five centuries of cod catches in Eastern Canada. https://ourworldindata.org/grapher/long-term-cod-catch. Accessed 16 Mar 2023

Our World in Data (2023a) Gross enrolment ratio in tertiary education, 1971 to 2020. https://ourworldindata.org/grapher/gross-enrollment-ratio-in-tertiary-education. Accessed 19 Nov 2023

Our World in Data (2023b) Share of United States households using specific technologies. https://ourworldindata.org/grapher/technology-adoption-by-households-in-the-united-states. Accessed 11 Apr 2023

Poincaré H (1912) Calcul des probabilités. Éditons J. Gabay, Paris.

Prieur B (2018) Image de Genève (Suisse) en août 2018. https://commons.wikimedia.org/wiki/File:Image_de_Gen%C3%A8ve_(Suisse)_-_2018-08-17_-_en_ao%C3%BBt_2018_-_5.JPG. Accessed 11 Apr 2023

RAM Legacy Stock Assessment Database (2018) Version 4.44-assessment-only. Released 2018-12-22. Retrieved from 10.5281/zenodo.2542919 . https://www.ramlegacy.org/. Accessed 20 Nov 2023

Roos MW (2008) Willingness to consume and ability to consume. J Econ Behav Organ 66:387–402. https://doi.org/10.1016/j.jebo.2006.03.008

Rosser JB, Holt RPF, Colander DC (2010) European economics at a crossroads. Edward Elgar Publishing

Schijns R, Froese R, Hutchings JA, Pauly D (2021) Five centuries of cod catches in Eastern Canada. ICES J Mar Sci 78(8):2675–2683

Senge PM (1990) The fifth discipline: the art and practice of the learning organization. Doubleday/Currency

Shiller RJ (2017) Narrative economics. Am Econ Rev 107:967–1004. https://doi.org/10.1257/aer.107.4.967

Shiller RJ (2019) Narrative economics: how stories go viral and drive major economic events. Princeton University Press, Princeton

Spencer CN, McClelland BR, Stanford JA (1991) Shrimp stocking, salmon collapse, and eagle displacement: cascading interactions in the food web of a large aquatic ecosystem. Bioscience 41:14–21. https://doi.org/10.2307/1311536

Sterman JD (1989) Modeling managerial behavior: misperceptions of feedback in a dynamic decision making experiment. Manag Sci 35:321–339. https://doi.org/10.1287/mnsc.35.3.321

Sterman JD (2000) Business dynamics: systems thinking and modeling for a complex world. Irwin/McGraw-Hill, Boston

Tainter J (1988) The collapse of complex societies. Cambridge University Press, Cambridge

Tversky A, Kahneman D (1974) Judgment under uncertainty: heuristics and biases. Science 185: 1124–1131. https://doi.org/10.1126/science.185.4157.1124

United States Department of Agriculture: National Agricultural Statistics Service (USDA-NASS) (2023) Charts and maps – prices received: hog prices received by month, US. https://www.nass.usda.gov/Charts_and_Maps/Agricultural_Prices/pricehg.php. Accessed 11 Apr 2023

Waddell G (1993) Simple low back pain: rest or active exercise? Ann Rheum Dis 52:317–319. https://doi.org/10.1136/ard.52.5.317

Waddell G, Feder G, Lewis M (1997) Systematic reviews of bed rest and advice to stay active for acute low back pain. Br J Gen Pract 47:647–652

Wang X, Disney SM (2016) The bullwhip effect: Progress, trends and directions. Eur J Oper Res 250:691–701. https://doi.org/10.1016/j.ejor.2015.07.022

World Bank Education Statistics (2023). https://databank.worldbank.org/reports.aspx?source=Education%20Statistics. Accessed 19 Nov 2023

8 Self-organization

Contents

8.1 Introduction ... 341
8.2 Cellular Automata and Agent-Based Models ... 343
8.2.1 Cellular Automata ... 343
8.2.2 Agent-Based Models ... 345
8.3 Self-Organization in the Natural World ... 348
8.3.1 General Characterization ... 348
8.3.2 The Ising Model from Statistical Physics ... 349
8.3.3 A Cellular Automaton of a Chemical Oscillator ... 354
8.3.4 An Agent-Based Model of Flocking Birds ... 356
8.4 Self-Organization in the Human World ... 359
8.4.1 Spatial Patterns ... 360
8.4.2 Temporal Patterns ... 363
8.4.3 Functional Patterns ... 364
8.5 Models of Self-Organization in the Social Sciences ... 368
8.5.1 Simple Contagion ... 368
8.5.2 Social Influence and Complex Contagion ... 372
8.5.3 Segregation and Spatial Organization ... 376
8.5.4 Self-organized Industrial Symbiosis ... 379
8.6 Spontaneous Order ... 384
8.6.1 Hayek on Spontaneous Order ... 384
8.6.2 Hayek's Theory and Complexity Economics ... 388
8.7 The Economy as a Dissipative Structure ... 390
8.7.1 Thermodynamic Equilibrium and Entropy ... 392
8.7.2 Dissipative Structures ... 396
8.7.3 Dissipative Structures in Nature ... 398
8.7.4 The Fourth Law of Thermodynamics ... 401
8.7.5 Relevance for Economics ... 407
References ... 415

M. Roos, *Principles of Complexity Economics*, Classroom Companion: Economics,
https://doi.org/10.1007/978-3-031-51436-4_8

Abstract

This chapter focuses on self-organization, which explains the formation of structure without external control. Self-organization is found in physical, chemical, and biological systems. Examples from these disciplines are used to show that self-organization of agents does not require cognition or purposeful behavior. Self-organization is also found in social systems, but with the complication that it interacts with human-designed organization. Several examples of small-scale self-organization in social systems are presented before discussing large-scale self-organization. Hayek's concept of spontaneous order is introduced and compared with the complexity concept of self-organization. The chapter concludes with a detailed discussion of the concept of dissipative systems and dissipative structure, which originated in chemistry but is highly relevant to economics. In terms of methods, the chapter introduces cellular automata and agent-based models as highly relevant tools for complexity economics.

Keywords

Agent-based models · Cellular automata · Dissipative systems · Energy · Spontaneous order

Guiding Questions

- What is self-organization?
- Why are cellular automata and agent-based models useful tools for studying self-organization?
- What can economists learn from self-organization in nature?
- What are economic examples of self-organized spatial, temporal, and functional patterns?
- How does complex contagion differ from simple contagion, and what is social influence?
- What is the message of Schelling's segregation model?
- What is an industrial symbiosis network and how does it relate to self-organization?
- What does spontaneous order mean?
- Is Hayek's concept of self-organization different from that of complexity economics?
- Why can we interpret the economy as a dissipative structure?
- What is the maximum power principle?
- What are the main lessons from looking at the economy as a dissipative structure?

8.1 Introduction

In Chap. 2, complex systems were defined as systems consisting of many parts that interact in a non-simple way. Non-simple interaction was translated in the previous two chapters as nonlinear interaction with feedback. We have seen that nonlinearity and circular causality can create rich dynamics that make it difficult or even impossible to predict the long-term behavior of a system. But non-simple interaction is only one characteristic of complex systems. Ladyman et al.'s (2013) definition in Chap. 2 also included the element that non-simple interaction leads to robust organization and memory. In complex systems, order emerges from disorder. Complexity is about the emergence of patterns and structure.

The nonlinear models we analyzed in Chaps. 6 and 7 had given structures described by differential equations or causal loop diagrams. They were mechanical in the sense that they are machine-like. A machine is a physical object that does not change its structure. The topic of this chapter is *self-organization*, which is defined as a process by which a system acquires a spatial, temporal, or functional structure without external control or specific intervention. A self-organizing system may import energy, information, or matter from outside, but the structure is not created by an external force or agent. Instead, it is generated by the system itself. The economy as a whole can be seen as a self-organizing system, and some of its elements are self-organizing as well.

The human world, including the economy and other social systems, is the result of both designed order and self-organized order. It is undeniable that humans deliberately create systems. Engineers design machines, buildings, and transportation infrastructures. Entrepreneurs create businesses, and managers organize groups and their actions. Decision-makers make plans, devise strategies, and engage in many other kinds of forward-looking behavior. Yet much social and economic structure is not the product of powerful human creators, but the result of the unintended consequences of many small actions and local interactions. It is a fundamental insight of complexity economics that self-organization interferes with human design and planning. Self-organization is another reason why the economy is unpredictable and uncontrollable. We have already seen that nonlinearity and chaos impede long-term planning and control even in systems with a given structure. The property of complex systems to change their structure and spontaneously generate new patterns is a serious disappointment for those who hope to find optimal long-term policies and ways to shape the economy according to their goals.

Like many other concepts of complexity, self-organization originates from the natural sciences, although similar concepts such as the invisible hand and spontaneous order are central to economics. It is good to learn from the natural sciences, but since the complexity of social systems is much greater than the complexity of most natural systems, we should not apply ideas from physics or biology to economics without careful consideration. The reductionist complexity school, strongly inspired by physics, tends to explain "much from little," i.e. it tries to reduce complicated macro patterns to a few simple rules and simple behavior at the micro level.

Econophysics is the attempt to apply methods from physics to the analysis of economic phenomena, especially the aggregate behavior of financial markets. It is common in this literature to treat economic agents as physical particles that have no intentions or cognition, but simple reaction mechanisms by which they interact with their environment. Even with such zero-intelligence agents, self-organization can occur, which can help explain patterns observed in financial markets. This approach is useful to show what forces might lead to self-organization in markets. However, even if a reductionist model with very simple agents can produce outcomes that we observe in the economy, this does not mean that these models are good explanations, because we know that the behavior of real economic agents is much more complex than the behavior of physical particles. Nevertheless, self-organization models from physics, chemistry, and biology provide valuable insights into how order can emerge from disorder. They point to structural determinants and interaction effects that have consequences beyond goal-directed behavior.

The idea that markets are self-organizing goes back at least to Adam Smith, who used the metaphor of the invisible hand to describe how the outcome of market transactions appears to be ordered even though each market participant is concerned only with his or her private benefit, not with the market or society as a whole. The Austrian School of Economics, with its proponents Carl Menger, Ludwig von Mises, and especially Friedrich August von Hayek, promoted similar ideas. Hayek developed a theory of spontaneous order in which the dispersed knowledge of many market participants is aggregated into market prices. Market prices coordinate the behavior of buyers and sellers, leading to efficient market equilibria. Hayek argued that free market economies always produce better results than centrally planned economies because no central planner can ever have enough information to achieve efficient allocations. The concept of spontaneous order is a case of self-organization, but it has strong normative connotations and is limited to markets. It is therefore less general than the broader complexity concept of self-organization, which originated in the natural sciences.

This chapter is structured as follows. Section 8.2 introduces cellular automata and agent-based models. These formal models are ideal for representing and analyzing self-organizing processes of locally interacting agents with dispersed information. They are used in Sect. 8.3 to show examples of self-organization in physics, chemistry, and biology. These examples are useful for economists because they clearly illustrate four basic features of self-organization: (1) *pattern formation*, (2) *autonomy*, (3) *robustness and resilience*, and (4) *dynamics*. Sect. 8.4 moves on to examples of self-organization in the human world, and particularly in the economy, that involve spatial, temporal, and functional patterns. While this section is intended to provide a non-technical overview of a range of relevant examples, Sect. 8.5 contains a selection of models of human self-organization. These models deal with specific cases in which elements of the economic system organize themselves. The discussion of spontaneous order in Sect. 8.6 and of the economy as a dissipative structure in Sect. 8.7 have a much broader perspective and apply concepts of self-organization to the whole economy rather than to its elements.

8.2 Cellular Automata and Agent-Based Models

Cellular automata (CA) and agent-based models (ABMs) are computational models that can be used to simulate complex dynamics. They are closely related, but CA are simpler than ABMs. While ABMs can have an external environment with which agents can interact, cells in CA—which are like agents—only interact with each other. Furthermore, CA have fixed rules that determine with which other cells a cell can interact with—typically is neighbors—, whereas agents can sometimes move, choose interaction partners, or meet them randomly. Finally, agents are often much more complex in terms of their behavior and possible states than cells. In general, we can think of CA as special cases of ABMs.

8.2.1 Cellular Automata

John von Neumann and Stanislaw Ulam developed the concept of the cellular automaton in the 1940s and 1950s. Von Neumann needed a tractable model for his studies on self-replicating systems, e.g. a robot that builds another robot. Cellular automata were designed to analyze problems of biological organization, self-replication, and the evolution of complexity, making them an important tool in research on artificial life. CA became famous in the 1970s with John Horton Conway's *Game of Life*. Stephen Wolfram is another pioneer who used CA extensively as the main instrument for his *New Kind of Science*, which is the title of his book published in 2002.

A cellular automaton is a discrete computational model. Such a model consists of *cells* which are arranged on a grid, often in two dimensions, but there can also be one-dimensional grids (a line) or higher-dimensional grids. Each cell has one of several possible states, e.g. "on" or "off" or "green," "blue," "red," or "yellow." The states of all cells are updated in discrete time steps from time t to $t + 1$, then to $t + 2$ and so on. The updating of the states follows a fixed rule. The new state of a cell in $t + 1$ depends on its current state and the current states of the other cells in period t.

A cell interacts only with its neighbors. On a 2-dimensional grid, neighbors can be defined as a von Neumann neighborhood or as a Moore neighborhood (see Fig. 8.1.). In a classical *von Neumann neighborhood* (or 4-neighborhood), a cell (in red) has four neighbors (in green) which are the orthogonally adjacent cells. A *Moore neighborhood* comprises all eight adjacent cells, including the four diagonal cells that are omitted in the von Neumann neighborhood. Since each cell only interacts with the cells in its neighborhood, all interaction in a cellular automaton is local.

How a cellular automaton works is best illustrated with the *elementary cellular automaton* popularized by Stephen Wolfram (2002). An elementary cellular automaton has only one dimension. Each cell can have two possible states (0 or 1). The new state of a cell depends on its own current state and on the states of its two immediate neighbors. What happens in the cellular automaton depends on the initial state of all cells and the updating rule.

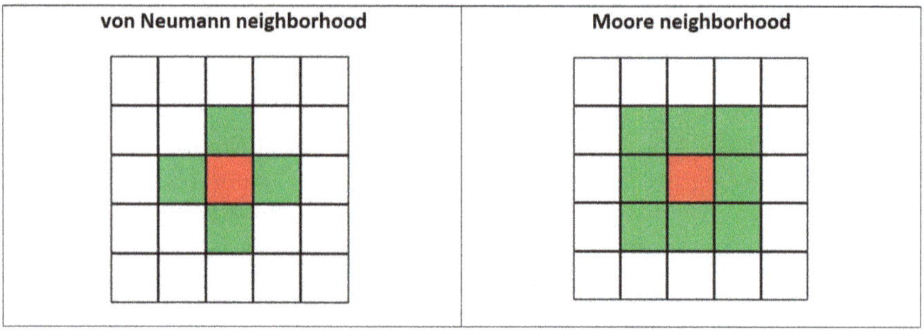

Fig. 8.1 Neighborhoods in a cellular automaton. Source: Author

Table 8.1 Rule 2 in Wolfram code

Pattern in t	111	110	101	100	011	010	001	000
State of center cell in $t + 1$	0	0	0	0	0	0	1	0
Powers of 2	2^7	2^6	2^5	2^4	2^3	2^2	2^1	2^0
In decimals	128	64	32	16	8	4	2	1

Table 8.2 Rule 26 in Wolfram code

Pattern in t	111	110	101	100	011	010	001	000
State of center cell in $t + 1$	0	0	0	1	1	0	1	0
Powers of 2	2^7	2^6	2^5	2^4	2^3	2^2	2^1	2^0
In decimals	128	64	32	16	8	4	2	1

In an elementary cellular automaton, there are $2^3 = 8$ possible configurations for a cell and its neighbors on the left and on the right. For example, 111 means that all three cells are in state 1 and 001 means that the middle cell and its left neighbor are in state 0 and its right neighbor is in state 1. The first row of Table 8.1 shows all possible configurations. The updating rule assigns a state to the center cell in period $t + 1$ for each of these possible configurations in period t. The rule in Table 8.1 states that a center cell will be in state 1 in period $t + 1$ if and only if the configuration in period t was 001. All other configurations lead to the state 0. Stephen Wolfram proposed a numbering system—the *Wolfram code*—for the rules, which works as follows. The possible configurations are listed in descending order as in the first row of Table 8.1. The rule represented by the second row of Table 8.1 is interpreted as a binary number, so $00000010 = 2^1 = 2$. The corresponding decimal number is the number of the rule. Hence, Table 8.1 shows rule 2. Table 8.2 contains rule 26, because $00011010 = 2^4 + 2^3 + 2^1 = 16 + 8 + 2 = 26$.

Let us assume that in period $t = 0$ only one cell is in state 1, shown in black, all other cells are in state 0 (white). Figure 8.2 shows how the cellular automaton with rule 2 behaves over time. Initially, only cell 0 is in state 1. Its neighbors -1 and 1 are in state 0. Rule 2 says that in period 1, only cell -1 will be in state 1 because the configuration for this cell in period 0 is 001. All other cells are in one of the

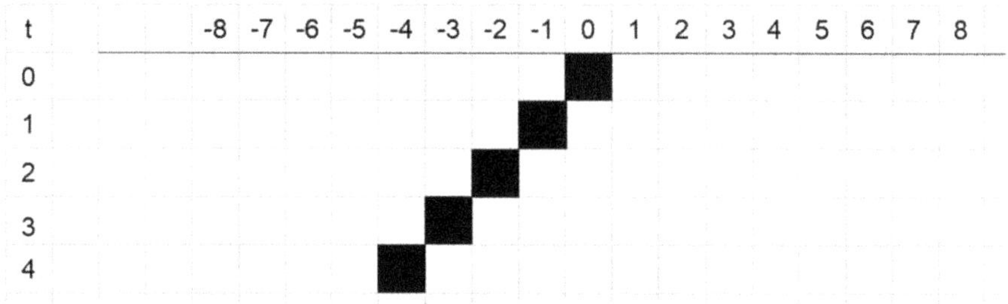

Fig. 8.2 Elementary cellular automaton with rule 2. Source: Author

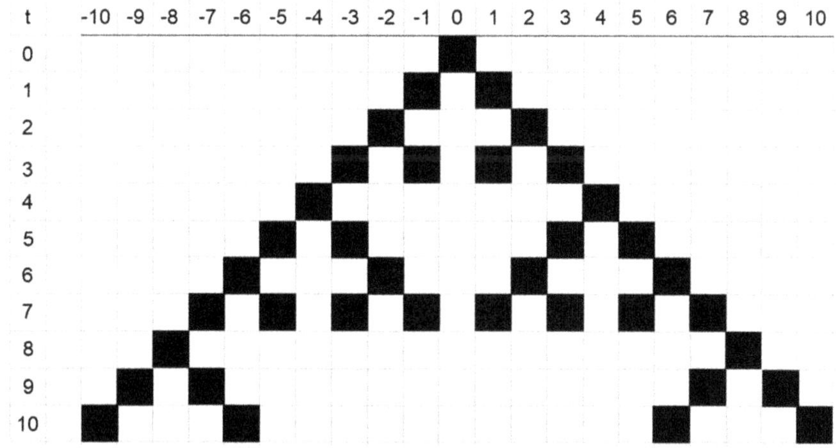

Fig. 8.3 Elementary cellular automaton with rule 26. Source: Author

remaining seven configurations such that they will be in state 0 in period 1. For example, the configuration of cell 0 is 010. By the same logic, only cell −2 is in state 1 in period 2, and so on. Therefore, rule 2 produces a diagonal pattern in Fig. 8.2.

An elementary CA with rule 26 evolves as shown in Fig. 8.3. The resulting pattern is obviously more sophisticated than that of a rule-2 CA.

8.2.2 Agent-Based Models

Agent-based models evolved from cellular automata and have agents instead of cells. Early models were developed in the 1970s and 1980s, but they became more widespread in the 1990s when more powerful computers were readily available.

An agent-based model consists of agents, relationships between the agents, and an environment with which the agents interact (see Fig. 8.4). Agents are uniquely identifiable individuals with a boundary, static and dynamic attributes, and a set of methods that determine the agent's behavior. What an agent represents depends on

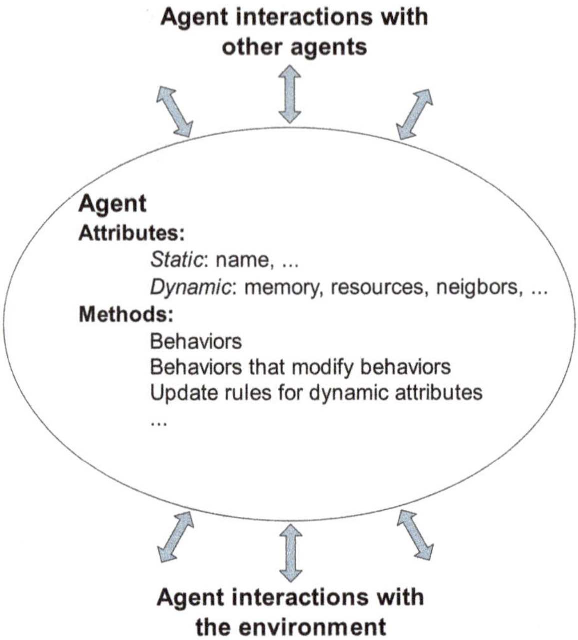

Fig. 8.4 Description of an agent. Source: Macal and North (2010), reproduced with kind permission of Taylor & Francis Group LLC

the purpose of the model. Agents can represent body cells, human individuals, companies, cars, or countries. *Autonomy* is the most important feature of agents. Autonomy means that agents are able to act on their own without external guidance or control. It is a great strength of agent-based models that there is great flexibility in how the behavior of agents can be modeled. The simplest way to model behavior is to provide agents with fixed if-then rules, which makes agents purely reactive to external stimuli. More complex agents have internal goals that they actively pursue, make active decisions, and initiate behavior instead of just reacting to external events. The most complex agents learn and change their behavior, have internal representations of the external world, and make predictions. Technically, agents are *objects* in a computer program that have *methods*. These methods update dynamic attributes such as age, which increases with each time step. Other methods determine or modify the behavior of the agents. Agents can be of different types, for example, households and companies, or factories, wholesalers, retailers, and customers. Types of agents differ in their behavior, but agents of the same type can also be heterogeneous and differ in their attributes. For example, human agents may have different preferences, skills, wealth, information, or social networks.

Agents interact with other agents and with the environment. The distinction between environment and agents is not always clear. In the simplest case, the environment is just a featureless space in which agents move. Interaction with the environment consists only in determining the location of the agents. The environment may also contain objects with which the agents can interact, such as roads or walls that affect the agents' movements, or objects that the agents can collect and

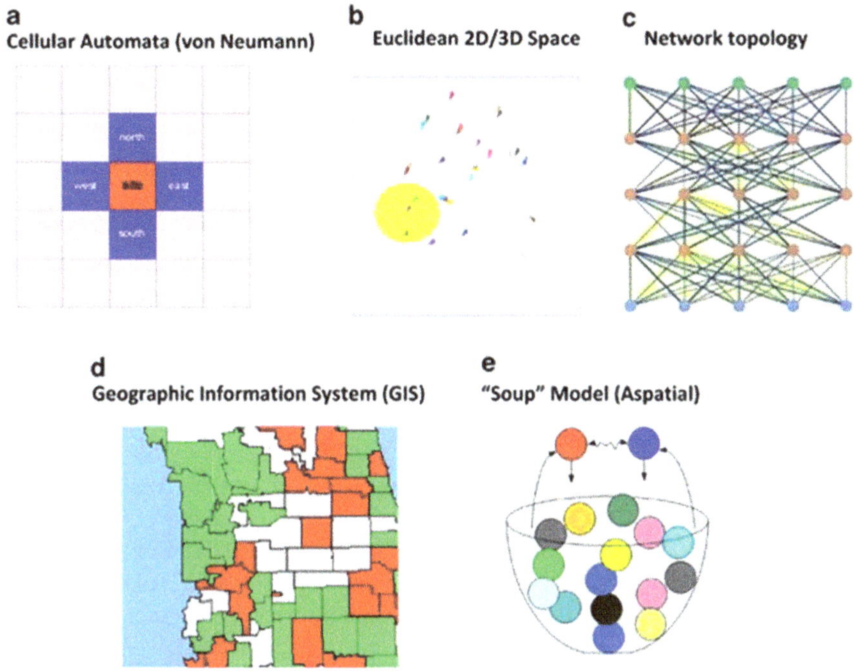

Fig. 8.5 Common interaction topologies in agent-based models. Source: Macal and North (2010), reproduced with kind permission of Taylor & Francis Group LLC

use. Some of these objects may have their own behavior, such as grass that grows or a lake with changing water temperatures and levels. If the environment has behavior, it can be considered a special type of agent, possibly without goals. The environment can also be represented abstractly by global rules or information that affect all agents, which is especially relevant in economic models.

The shape of the environment and the interaction relationships between agents are described by the *topology* of an ABM (see Fig. 8.5). A simple topology could be a continuous featureless 2- or *3-dimensional space* in which agents move either in a directed or random fashion. The Euclidean distance in this space determines which agents can interact with each other. Another popular topology is a 2-dimensional lattice, as in a cellular automata, where agents interact with their neighbors in a Moore or von Neumann neighborhood. Agents can also be connected in networks. Space can be realistically modeled using a geographic information system (GIS). Finally, a model can be aspatial, with random determination of agent interactions.

Agent-based models are very versatile research tools. They play out their strengths when they incorporate the following features that are hard to model with other approaches:

- Heterogeneous agents
- Explicit space

- Local interaction and private information
- Bounded rationality

Not all ABMs have all of these features, but an ABM that does not have at least one of them does not take advantage of the method relative to other modeling approaches. For example, there are heterogeneous agent models in mainstream macroeconomics, but the heterogeneity that can be introduced in general equilibrium models with maximizing agents is very limited if the models are to remain tractable. Bounded rationality of agents is almost a necessity, since fully rational optimization behavior is only possible under strong assumptions in highly simplified settings. Even in relatively simple ABMs with autonomous, heterogeneous agents, it is almost impossible to say what fully rational behavior should be. With ABMs, a skilled modeler can represent virtually any theory or real-world situation. The only limitations are data and time constraints, available computing power, and the usefulness of a highly complex model. The more complex the model, the more difficult it is to understand what is happening in the simulation. The appropriate complexity of an ABM depends critically on the purpose of the model.

As computational simulation models, ABMs are typically run on computers, requiring the writing of computer code. Computer languages such as Java, Python, or Julia are widely used in ABM, but they require advanced programming skills, which can be a hurdle for beginners. The freely available modeling platform NetLogo (https://ccl.northwestern.edu/netlogo/) is a good alternative to programming languages. NetLogo (Wilensky 1999) is easy to learn, has an active user community and extensive documentation and learning materials. The highly recommended textbook by Uri Wilensky and Bill Rand (2015) also uses NetLogo.

8.3 Self-Organization in the Natural World

This subsection provides a general characterization of self-organization, which is then illustrated with models from physics, chemistry, and biology. Cellular automata and a simple agent-based model are used. Self-organization in human systems is more complex than self-organization in natural systems because, in contrast to non-human agents, humans have goals, intentions, high-level cognition, and complex communication. Nevertheless, natural systems are useful for understanding the basic ideas of self-organization.

8.3.1 General Characterization

Self-organization is the emergence of stable patterns through autonomous and self-reinforcing dynamics at the micro level (Anzola et al. 2017). Other definitions exist, but according to Gilbert et al. (2015), most concepts of self-organization share four characteristics: (1) pattern formation, (2) autonomy, (3) robustness and resilience, and (4) dynamics.

In the natural sciences, it is often easier to identify patterns. In Chap. 3, we discussed patterns in economic data, but patterns can be of many kinds. For example, the way members of a group communicate with each other may follow a pattern in terms of who talks to whom, or in terms of the timing of messages. A network of relationships is also a pattern, or the spatial distribution of something. Autonomy has already been mentioned as the ability of agents to act without external direction or control. The same applies to a self-organizing system that forms a pattern by itself or from within. The pattern is the result of the interactions of the parts of the system, not of some external intervention in the system. Meaningful patterns must persist in space and time so that they can be identified. Robustness means that a system and the resulting organization are resistant to change. Resilience often means that the system can recover or repair itself after an external shock. Dynamics means that self-organization is a process, not an outcome. To understand self-organization, we must observe how a system's variables and the relationships between them change over time. Cellular automata and agent-based models are ideal tools for modeling such processes.

Self-organization often requires random fluctuations and feedback. Random fluctuations trigger dynamics that are reinforced by positive feedback. Negative feedback counterbalances the self-reinforcing feedback and prevents the emergence of a perfect order. Together with ongoing random fluctuations, the interplay of positive and negative feedback keeps the process of self-organization in motion. In economics, cooperation and competition can be seen as positive and negative feedback forces, respectively. The random elements in the process of self-organization imply that we can only predict the general pattern, not its specific form.

8.3.2 The Ising Model from Statistical Physics

The Ising model (German pronunciation: [ˈiːzɪŋ]) was developed by the physicist Ernst Ising. It was originally a mathematical model of ferromagnetism, but it can be reinterpreted and applied to other topics, such as the motion of atoms in a gas or the activity of neurons in the brain. It is one of the most studied models in statistical physics. Statistical physics uses methods of probability theory and statistics to analyze physical systems with large numbers of elements, such as solids, liquids, or gases. Methods and models such as the Ising model are also used to study problems in other disciplines such as biology, neuroscience, linguistics, and the social sciences. Applications in social sciences and economics are called *sociophysics* and *econophysics*.

While the original Ising model is a mathematical model, we present here a cellular automaton version. The model is part of the NetLogo model library.[1] The grid (also

[1]Wilensky, U. (2003b). NetLogo Ising model. http://ccl.northwestern.edu/netlogo/models/Ising. Center for Connected Learning and Computer-Based Modeling, Northwestern University, Evanston, IL. Accessed 26 October 2023.

Fig. 8.6 Lattice with random distribution of spins. Source: Author

called a *lattice*) represents a crystalline material consisting of atoms (cells). Each atom has a spin or magnetic moment that can be in one of two states: +1 (up) or −1 (down). Figure 8.6. shows a random spatial distribution of spins +1 in light blue and −1 in dark blue with a share of 50% for each spin. If the spins are aligned, the material is magnetic.

Magnetism can occur by self-organization of the spins depending on the temperature of the system. Each spin can "decide" to flip to its opposite depending on the spins in its von Neumann neighborhood. The behavior of a spin depends on its energy. Spins seek a low energy state, so they have a goal. The energy of a spin in the center of a neighborhood, $E(spin_C)$, is the negative of the sum of the products of its own spin and the four neighboring spins to the north, west, south, and east:

$$E(spin_C) = -(spin_C \times spin_N + spin_C \times spin_W + spin_C \times spin_S + spin_C \times spin_E). \tag{8.1}$$

If all neighboring spins are equal to the center spin, then the energy is minimal, $E(spin_C) = -4$. The maximum, $E(spin_C) = 4$, is reached when the spin is surrounded by four opposite spins. The energy of a spin is thus a measure of the number of opposite neighbors. A spin always flips, if its energy differential *Ediff* is negative after flipping, i.e. if a flip decreases its energy. The energy differential is given by

$$Ediff(spin_C) = 2 \times spin_C * (spin_N + spin_W + spin_S + spin_E). \tag{8.2}$$

Sometimes, however, spins randomly flip to a higher energy state. The probability of a flip to a higher energy state occurs is assumed to be $e^{-EDiff/temperature}$. If $temperature \geq 0$, low temperature makes flips to higher energy states unlikely. With increasing temperature, the probability of such flips increases. High energy gains reduce the likelihood of flipping.

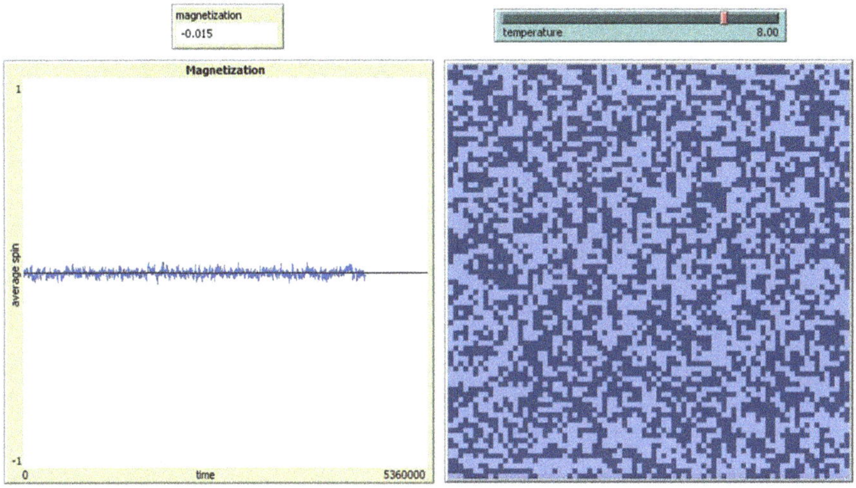

Fig. 8.7 Ising model with high temperature. Source: Author

Figure 8.7 shows the behavior of the system at high temperature (*temperature* = 8.0). The plot on the left shows the evolution of the average spin over time which is equal to the degree of magnetization. The degree of magnetization in the last period of the simulation is -0.015. Throughout the whole simulation, the magnetization fluctuated around zero with small amplitude. This means that the initial distribution of 50% of each spin did not change during the simulation. The spatial distribution of the spins on the lattice in the right panel still looks random or completely mixed. With sufficiently high temperature, i.e. energy in the form of heat coming in, the system remains disordered and does not magnetize.

At low temperatures (e.g., *temperature* = 0.5), spontaneous magnetization occurs, as shown in Fig. 8.8. The time series plot on the left exhibits strong autocorrelation. After a short period with negative average spin, the average spin starts to increase, which means than more and more spins flip to +1. The image of the lattice shows a rather large region all in light blue (spin +1) and a smaller region in dark blue (spin -1). Separation occurs. Note that the lattice is assumed to be a *torus.* This means that the top and bottom edges are adjacent and the left and right edges are adjacent, too. In other words, all cells in the top row are direct neighbors of the cells in the bottom row. This is possible, if the lattice is the surface of a doughnut-like object.

Only after a short while, the system has self-organized into a strong pattern and after another while strong order with all spins being equal to +1 emerges. It should be clear that the outcome could also have been that all spins are -1. We can only predict that with low temperature all spins will be equal, but whether the sign is + or – depends on chance. Thus, we can only predict that some kind of pattern will emerge, but not which one.

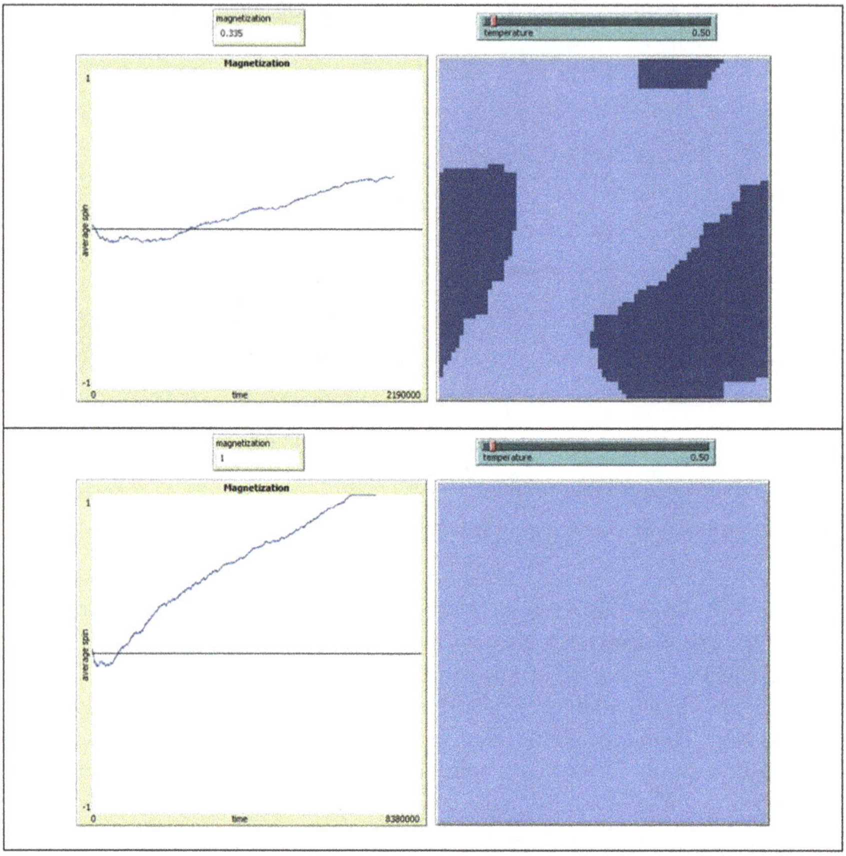

Fig. 8.8 Ising model with low temperature. Source: Author

If the system remains in disorder when temperature is high, but becomes perfectly ordered at low temperature, then there must be a phase transition for intermediate temperatures. In other words, there must be a temperature at which the system changes its behavior. It can be proved that on an infinite lattice this critical temperature is equal to $2/\ln(1+\sqrt{2}) \approx 2.27$. If the grid is finite, but large, the transition occurs near this number. Figure 8.9 shows what happens when *temperature* = 2.27. There are relatively large fluctuations in the average spin, but in the long run, the average spin seems to stabilize near some non-zero value. The corresponding spatial distribution of spins always looks similar to the picture on the right. The majority of spins are of one type, but there are small islands of the opposite spin. These islands are not stable over time, but change their position on the lattice.

When the temperature is slightly above the critical value, e.g., *temperature* = 2.33, the average spin fluctuates in large, persistent swings around zero (see Fig. 8.10). Although on average 50% of each spin are present, they are not randomly distributed

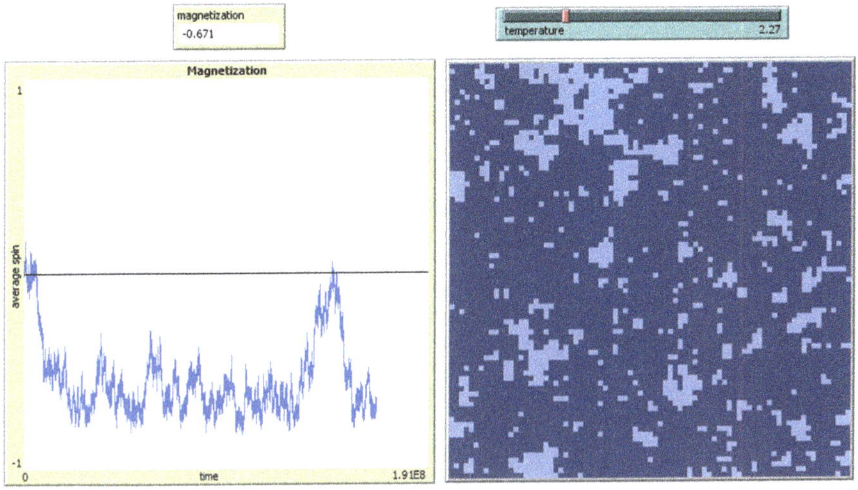

Fig. 8.9 Ising model with intermediate temperature. Source: Author

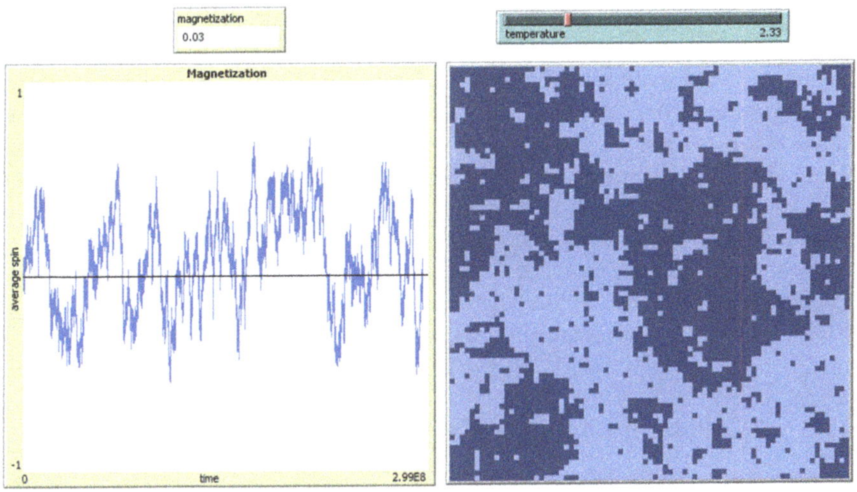

Fig. 8.10 Ising model with temperature above the critical value. Source: Author

on the lattice, but clustered or separated. Thus, there is a local correlation of the spins, which means that they form a pattern.

What does the Ising model teach us about self-organization? First, it illustrates possible meanings of pattern or order as opposed to randomness or disorder. In the figures above, patterns are visible both in the time series of the average spin and in the spatial distribution of the spins on the lattice. We discussed in Chap. 2 that the emergence of patterns, especially complex patterns between randomness and perfect order, is at the heart of complexity. The Ising model shows how such patterns arise

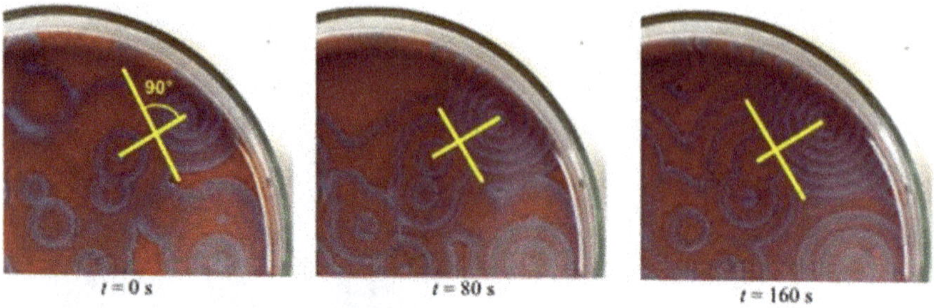

Fig. 8.11 Spirals resulting from a Belousov–Zhabotinsky reaction. Source: Jkrieger (2005), Wikipedia Commons, public domain

from the local interaction of agents whose behavior is determined by a simple rule. Although we have said that the agents "decide" the sign of their spin and that their goal is to minimize their energy, this language is of course metaphorical, since the agents are inanimate entities. Thus, order can arise from rules of interaction that the acting agents do not know or consciously follow. Another insight concerns the role of chance. The complex patterns at intermediate temperatures are maintained by the permanent random switching of some spins to the "undesired" state with higher energy. In the absence of these random disturbances the system converges to the perfectly ordered state even at high temperature.[2] The model features a phase transition from a long-term system state with zero average spin to a system state with positive or negative average spin when the temperature falls below a critical value. Thus, the emergence of order depends on external conditions, but is not caused by them. The external conditions (given by the temperature) provide the precondition for the behavior that generates order.

The *Sznajd model* is a modified version of the Ising model for use in sociophysics. It is often used to model opinion dynamics and political dynamics. We will take a closer look at such models later in this chapter.

8.3.3 A Cellular Automaton of a Chemical Oscillator

In chemistry, the *Belousov–Zhabotinsky reaction* (BZ reaction) discovered by Boris Belousov in 1950 and later described in detail by Anatoli Zhabotinsky in 1964 is an example of a chemical oscillator. A chemical oscillator is a system of multiple chemical reactions that produces temporal oscillations and self-organized spatial structures. BZ reactions involve bromine and an acid. When a BZ reaction occurs in a thin layer of fluid between two glass plates, an amazing pattern of concentric or spiral waves of color change emerge (see Fig. 8.11). The reaction oscillates both in time and space.

---

[2]Except for a few cases where the grid is separated into two stable regions with opposite spins, which is a consequence of the finite size of the grid.

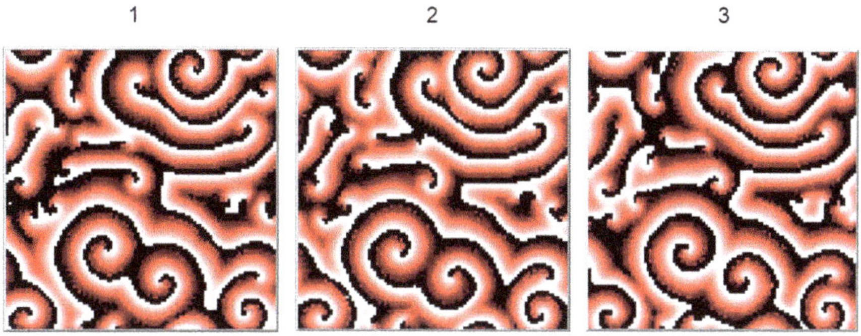

Fig. 8.12 Spirals of a BZ-like reaction in a cellular automaton. Source: Author

When the BZ reaction was discovered, most chemists did not believe that such reactions could occur because they seemed to contradict the *second law of thermodynamics*, which states that an ordered state of a system cannot arise spontaneously from a disordered state. An ordered state has lower entropy than a disordered state, but according to the second law, entropy cannot decrease if an isolated system is left to spontaneous evolution. A spontaneous process, i.e., one without any external input to the system, leads to a thermodynamic equilibrium in which the entropy of the internal energy of the system is highest.

The solution to this apparent puzzle proposed by the Nobel Laureate in Chemistry Ilya Prigogine, is that the BZ reaction is a nonequilibrium reaction far from thermodynamic equilibrium. The second law holds only for closed systems, but the BZ reaction is a *dissipative reaction* in an open system. *Dissipative structures* are characterized by the spontaneous formation of complex and sometimes chaotic structures or patterns. These structures are maintained by a continuous influx of energy and/or matter from outside.

The BZ reaction is interesting because it involves positive and negative feedback mechanisms that generate the dynamics. The reaction is autocatalytic, meaning that it produces a product that is a catalyst for the same or coupled reactions. Obviously, this is a positive feedback mechanism. The complete BZ reaction also involves an inhibiting reaction that replenishes the original input bromide so that the reaction can begin again. This is a negative feedback mechanism.

The NetLogo model library contains a cellular automaton,[3] which is an abstract and very simplified representation of the BZ reaction and produces very similar patterns (see Fig. 8.12). The cells can have two final states: 0 ("healthy") and max-state >0 ("sick"). On the grid, state 0 is shown as black, max-state is shown as white and the possible intermediate states as shades of red. If a cell is in an intermediate state, it is called "infected." Initially, there is a random distribution of

[3]Wilensky, U. (2003a). NetLogo B-Z Reaction model. http://ccl.northwestern.edu/netlogo/models/B-ZReaction. Center for Connected Learning and Computer-Based Modeling, Northwestern University, Evanston, IL. Accessed 26 October 2023.

all states over all cells on the grid. The rules for the behavior of the cells are as follows:

1. A sick cell becomes healthy: IF state = max-state THEN set state 0
2. A healthy cell becomes infected, if enough neighbors in the Moore neighborhood are infected or sick, depending on two parameters k1 and k2
3. An infected cell updates its degree if infectedness by averaging its own state and the states of its neighbors and adding a parameter g

Rule (2) and (3) are positive feedback mechanisms because healthy cells become infected and infected cells increase their degree of infectedness. Rule (1) is the negative feedback mechanism, because when cells reach the end state max-state, the state is reset to "healthy." As we already know from Chap. 7, feedback effects are important because they generate nonlinearities.

The *Brusselator*, proposed by Ilya Prigogine and his group at the Université Libre de Bruxelles, is a mathematical model of autocatalytic reactions such as the BZ reaction. It consists of two nonlinear differential equations that can generate a limit cycle.

8.3.4 An Agent-Based Model of Flocking Birds

Many animals flock in large groups, which sometimes display interesting patterns that often serve a purpose. Fish form schools that confuse predators. The murmurations of starlings also protect them from predators and may serve social purposes. Migratory birds such as geese, ducks, storks, and cranes form V formations by which they can fly more efficiently and save up to 30% of their energy (see Fig. 8.13).

Unlike atoms and molecules, animals have cognition and goals, which makes the organization they achieve more relevant to economists than the order in physical and chemical processes. A V formation of birds or a mumuration of starlings is surely the result of a self-organizing process, because there is no "master bird" telling the others how to fly. It is also unlikely that the birds know that they can save energy by forming a V and therefore do so deliberately. It seems more plausible that the birds follow relatively simple rules for their own behavior, which lead to the emergence of the observed patterns. Macroscopic order is then the result of micro-decisions that are not intended to produce that order. This insight is also relevant to human groups and societies.

The NetLogo model library also includes two agent-based models of bird flocking, one of which generates V formations.[4] In this model, birds are represented by small arrowheads that are initially randomly scattered on the 2-dimensional surface

[4]Wilkerson-Jerde, M., Stonedahl, F. and Wilensky, U. (2009). NetLogo Flocking Vee Formations model. http://ccl.northwestern.edu/netlogo/models/FlockingVeeFormations. Center for Connected

Fig. 8.13 Cranes in a V formation. Source: Hajihusseini (2010), Wikimedia Commons, CC BY 3.0 Unported (https://creativecommons.org/licenses/by/3.0/deed.en)

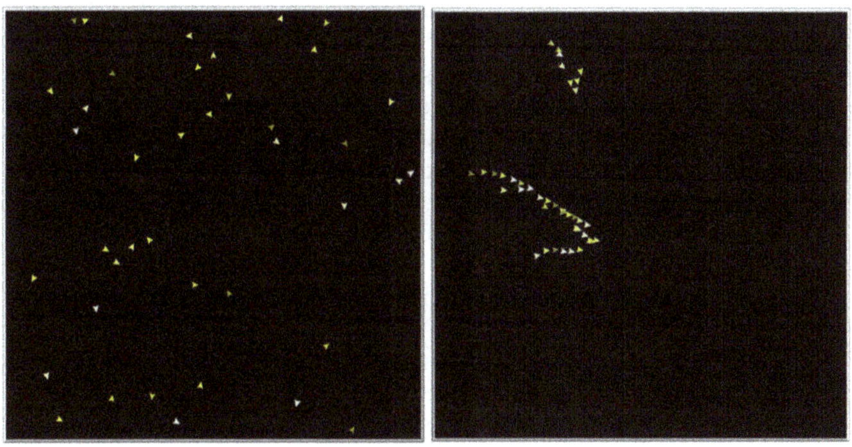

Fig. 8.14 Flocking in an agent-based model. Source: Author

of a torus (see the left panel of Fig. 8.14). The arrowheads indicate the headings of the bird. Each bird-agent can see and fly according the heading, which is initially determined by chance. Agents have a limited range of vision, defined by the

Learning and Computer-Based Modeling, Northwestern University, Evanston, IL. Accessed 26 October 2023

parameters VISION-DISTANCE and VISION-CONE, which are identical for all agents. VISION-DISTANCE defines the radius and VISION-CONE the angle, within which a bird can see another bird. If a bird cannot see another bird, it will continue to fly straight ahead at a speed given by the global parameter[5] BASE-SPEED.

When a bird can see another bird, it adjusts its behavior according to the following rules:

1. If it is too far away from the nearest visible bird, the bird will turn toward the nearest visible bird and speed up to get near it
2. If it is close enough to another bird (determined by the parameter UPDRAFT-DISTANCE), it will randomly move to one side of the bird. It will adjust its heading such that its vision is not obstructed by the other bird (determined by the parameter OBSTRUCTION-CONE)
3. If it gets too close to another bird (determined by the parameter TOO-CLOSE), it will slow down
4. If a bird has an unobstructed view and is sufficiently close, but not too close to another bird, it will set its speed and heading to that of its closest visible neighbor

The rules apply only to local behavior. No bird ever responds to a group of other birds. Each bird simply aligns its behavior to that of its nearest visible neighbor by maintaining an acceptable distance and avoiding an obstructed vision. The alignment occurs through adjustments in speed and flight direction. Over time, these rules lead to the appearance of V formations like those in the right panel of Fig. 8.14. As in the Ising model, we can only predict that a certain pattern—here a V formation—will occur, but we cannot predict how large it will be, whether it will be symmetric or asymmetric, how long it will last or in which direction it will fly. All of these specific characteristics depend on random effects.

The flocking ABM has most of the typical features of ABMs mentioned above:

- The agents are autonomous, because there are behavioral rules for each state of the world. There are two states: either a bird sees at least one other bird, or it does not. If it does not see any, it will fly with the given speed and direction. If it sees another, it will align to it in the way described above
- There is explicit space. This makes sense, because the pattern of interest (a V formation) is a spatial pattern
- Agents interact only locally and have private information. Each bird responds only to its closed visible neighbor, not to the whole population or a group of several individuals. There is no exchange of information. Each agent perceives information by itself (through its own vision) and uses only that information
- Agents are boundedly rational. The exogenous parameters UPDRAFT-DISTANCE and TOO-CLOSE define the acceptable distance to the nearest neighbor.

[5]Global parameters apply to all agents.

Agents try to stay within this range by adjusting their speed by an exogenously given SPEED-CHANGE-FACTOR. There is no goal-maximizing behavior or evaluation of different alternatives

The only missing feature is heterogeneity, since all agents are assumed to be identical. Technically, it would not be difficult to give the agents different parameters or even to define different behaviors for different individuals. However, heterogeneity is not necessary to generate V-formations and is not plausible in this context if all birds are of the same species and have genetically programmed behavior.

The model shows that self-organization can emerge from the interaction of agents with rather limited rationality. It is also a nice introduction to the potential and philosophy of agent-based models. However, while human-agent models share many elements with models of animal behavior from biology, they are often more complicated because very simple behavioral rules may not be adequate for human behavior.

8.4 Self-Organization in the Human World

The examples from physics, chemistry, and biology are helpful to understand the main idea of self-organization, but self-organization in human systems is more complicated and can take many different forms. In this section, we look at some examples of self-organization in the human social world at a qualitative level. Formal models will be discussed in the next section.

Recall the definition of self-organization as a process by which a system acquires spatial, temporal, or functional structure without external control or specific intervention. Thus, the structure is not imposed on the system from the outside, even though the system interacts with its environment. Remember also that self-organization is a property of open systems that exchange energy and/or matter with their environment. The structures in the previous examples were spatial and/or temporal. In economics and other human systems, such structures can also arise, but the self-organization of *functional structure*, which we have not seen so far, may be more relevant.

When we talk about self-organization in economics, we can do so from two different perspectives. First, we can apply the concept to specific subsystems of the economy. This perspective is close to the three examples above and is a microscopic view. Second, we can take a macroscopic view and understand the whole economy as a self-organizing system, which requires much more abstract reasoning. Intuitively, it is obvious that self-organization must be important with respect to human society because there is no one outside the system who could shape or influence the system. If we separate the economic system from the rest of society, then outside interference is possible, but this separation seems arbitrary. The economy as a whole is many orders of magnitude more difficult to describe and understand than, say, the self-organization of a work team. We deal with the microscopic view in this subsection and present the macroscopic concepts of spontaneous order and the economy as a dissipative structure in the next sections.

8.4.1 Spatial Patterns

Spatial patterns are important in economics. Regional and urban economics deals with the distribution of economic activities and factors of production in space, which is highly uneven. *Spatial agglomeration* occurs at different degrees of spatial resolution, i.e., across countries, within a country, or within cities. Cities themselves are spatial agglomerations of economic activity.

Within cities, different types of spatial patterns can be observed. In many cities, the population is sorted by characteristics such as income, education, social class, or ethnicity. Figure 8.15 shows that Detroit is highly segregated by race. You may recall from Chap. 5 that many African Americans migrated to Detroit from the South during World War II. The 1950s and 1960s saw intense racial conflict and white flight to the suburbs. Fifty years later, Detroit remains highly segregated. The black population is almost exclusively concentrated in the city of Detroit, while the population in the outer counties of the Detroit metropolitan area is almost exclusively white. The Hispanic population, which made up about 5% of the population in the 2010 census, is concentrated in southwest Detroit near Mexicantown, which dates back to the 1920s. The residential sorting of an urban population is a typical self-organizing process of interest to social scientists.

Not only do the residential locations of a city's population show spatial patterns, but so do the spatial distributions of a city's functional characteristics. Figure 8.16 shows several maps of Changsha, the capital of Hunan Province in China, a city with a population of about ten million. Maps A and B show that the distributions of

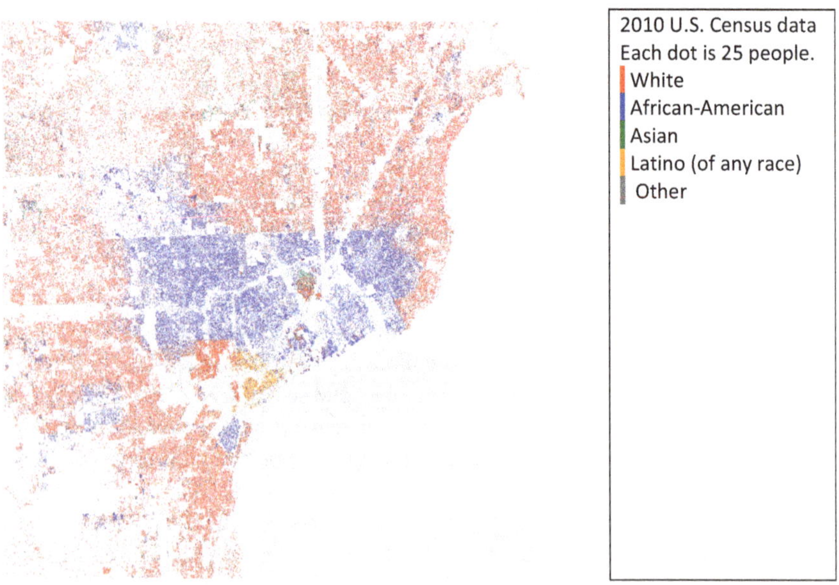

Fig. 8.15 Racial segregation in Detroit. Source: Fischer (2013), Flickr, licensed under CC BY-SA 2.0 (https://creativecommons.org/licenses/by-sa/2.0/)

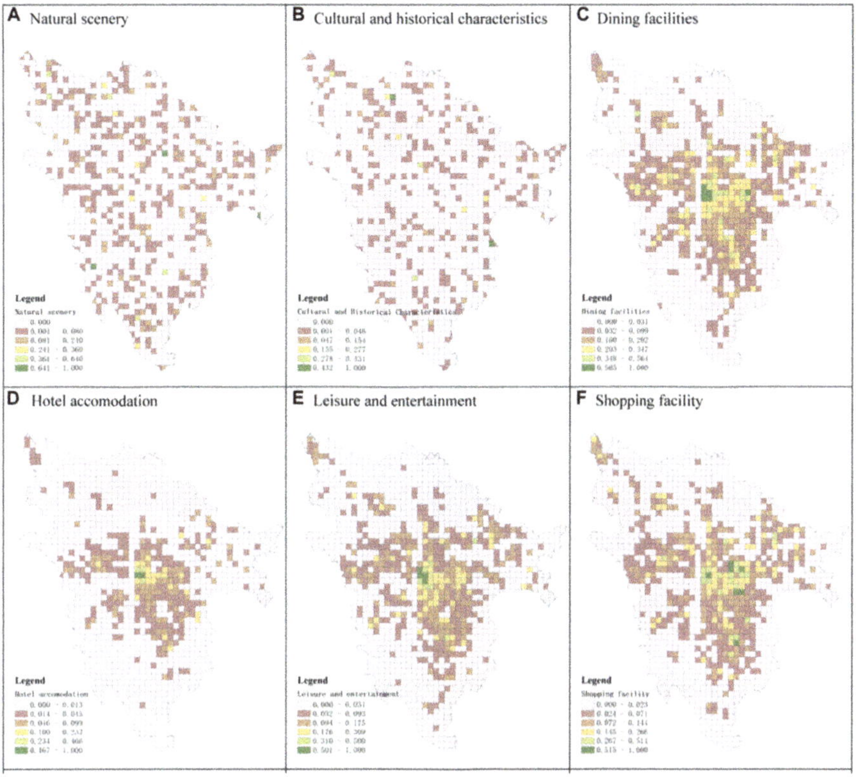

Fig. 8.16 Spatial sorting of city functions in Changsha, China. Source: Xia et al. (2022), licensed under CC-BY 4.0 (https://creativecommons.org/licenses/by/4.0/)

exogenous city characteristics such as natural, cultural, and historical attractions look relatively random. The maps show vitality density data, i.e. the number of mobile phone users in a square of the grid in a given time period, combined with exogenous information about the characteristics of the grid cell. Maps C through F show the vitality densities at locations with commercial facilities such as restaurants, hotels, leisure and entertainment facilities, and shops. They thus represent economic activity, which is the endogenous result of self-organization. A typical core–periphery pattern is visible, with a lot of activity concentrated in a rather small central area, an intermediate level of activity in a region around the center, and a periphery of low activity.

In addition to the spatial dimension, the pattern of economic activity also has a temporal dimension. Figure 8.17 shows the temporal stability of activity during the day based on the standard deviations of the density of cell phone users in a cell. The stability in the core is low, which means that there is a lot of mobility in the core, with many different people spending relatively short periods of time at these facilities and then moving away. In the periphery, on the other hand, the temporal

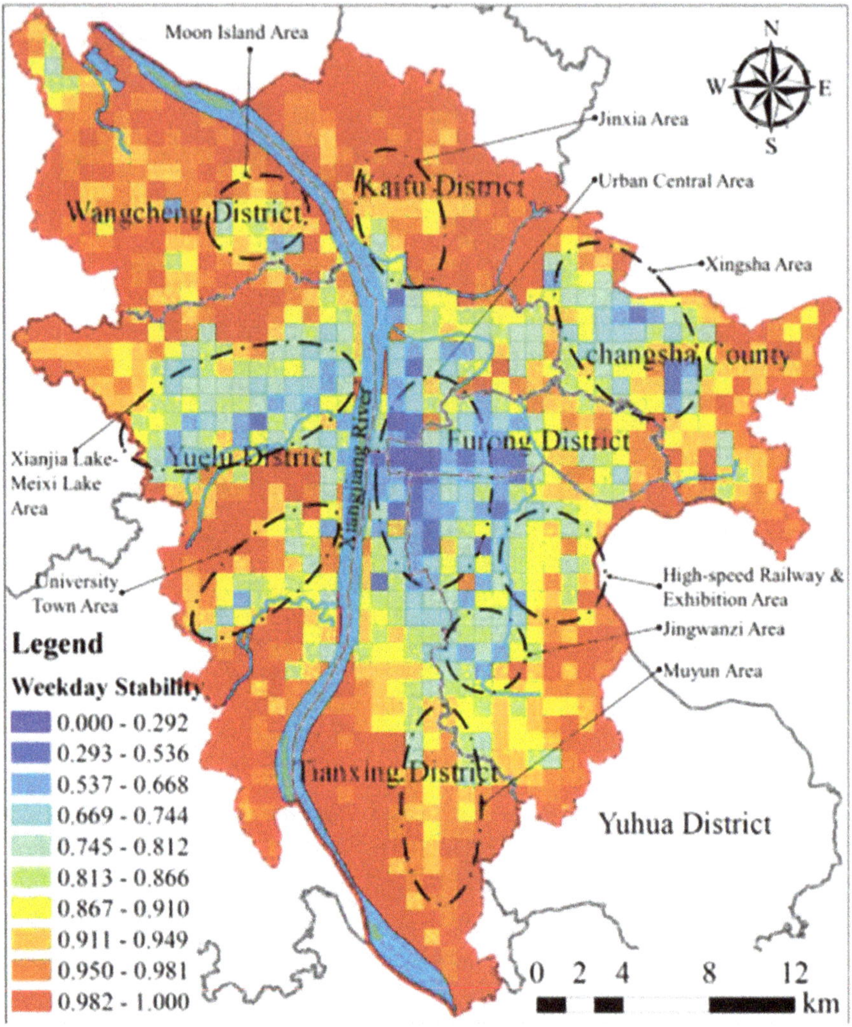

Fig. 8.17 Temporal stability of human activities. Source: Xia et al. (2022), licensed under CC-BY 4.0 (https://creativecommons.org/licenses/by/4.0/)

stability is high because the density of people does not fluctuate as much over time. The results are intuitive: Typically, people spend less time shopping or eating, which often occurs in the core, than working or sleeping, which occurs in the periphery. The spatial agglomeration of economic activity is often the result of a positive feedback process: Firms agglomerate where there are many customers, and customers go where there are many firms. Additional negative feedback loops, e.g., due to competition between firms or rising rents, can maintain the state of system dynamics, with some firms moving away or avoiding the highly agglomerated areas.

8.4.2 Temporal Patterns

The economy is also full of temporal patterns that can be seen in time series such as that for retail sales in Fig. 8.18.

This graph shows a clear seasonal pattern with a large spike in December and a large dip in January. It is obvious that this pattern is caused by Christmas, when many people buy gifts for their family and friends. While the tradition of giving Christmas gifts is very old, cultural practices vary over time and across countries. In some countries, gifts are given in January instead of December. In the USA, there was an active effort by a wealthy New York City elite to change the tradition of giving to the poor to making Christmas a private holiday with gifts for family members, especially children. Japan is not a Christian country, but Christmas became an important event anyway due to American influence after World War II. Traditions and cultural practices are the result of self-organization. They can change over time, but usually do so slowly and are stable for a long time once established.

Another temporal pattern is visible in U.S. home sales (see Fig. 8.19). Most home buyers move in the spring and early summer months. Home sales peak in June and are lowest in January. There may be several reasons for this behavior: the weather is better in the spring and summer, which makes moving more pleasant. During the holiday season in December, people are too busy to move. Finally, families with school-age children wait until the school year begins. The external causes can be reinforced by the expectation that both the supply and prices of houses are higher in the summer. Higher supply gives buyers more choice, and higher prices make selling more attractive. Again, we find a positive feedback loop behind a pattern.

Fig. 8.18 U.S. retail sales. Source: Data from U.S. Census Bureau. advance retail sales (excluding food services), retrieved from FRED Federal Bank of St. Louis

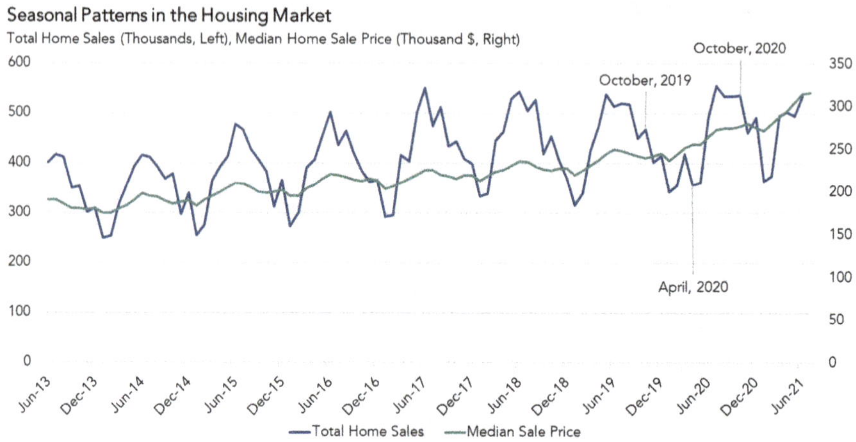

Fig. 8.19 Seasonality in U.S. home sales. Source: Kushi (2021), reproduced with kind permission of Odeta Kushi

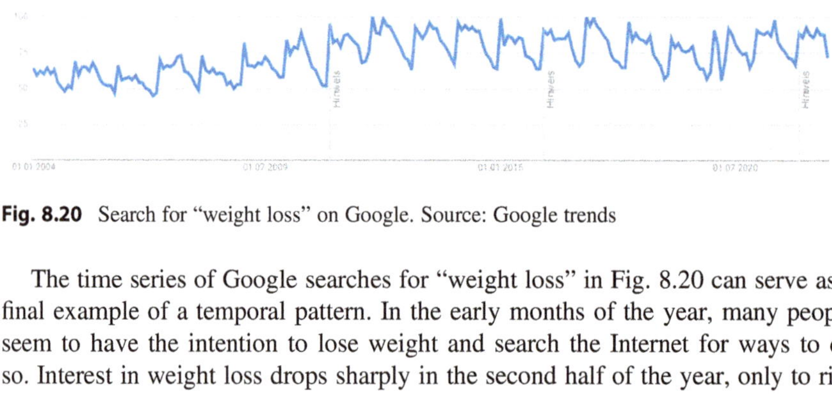

Fig. 8.20 Search for "weight loss" on Google. Source: Google trends

The time series of Google searches for "weight loss" in Fig. 8.20 can serve as a final example of a temporal pattern. In the early months of the year, many people seem to have the intention to lose weight and search the Internet for ways to do so. Interest in weight loss drops sharply in the second half of the year, only to rise again in January. Many people use the turn of the year to take stock of their current lives and make plans for the coming year. Since many people are unhappy about being overweight, they make a resolution to lose weight. The intention may be strengthened by the desire to look good in the summer season and by similar intentions of other people. In particular, interaction among friends, family members, or colleagues can serve as a positive feedback that coordinates the behavior of many people at the same time.

8.4.3 Functional Patterns

Functional patterns are more difficult to visualize than spatial or temporal patterns. A *functional pattern* or *functional structure* is the specialization of the parts of a system based on their function or role in the system. A self-organizing process that generates

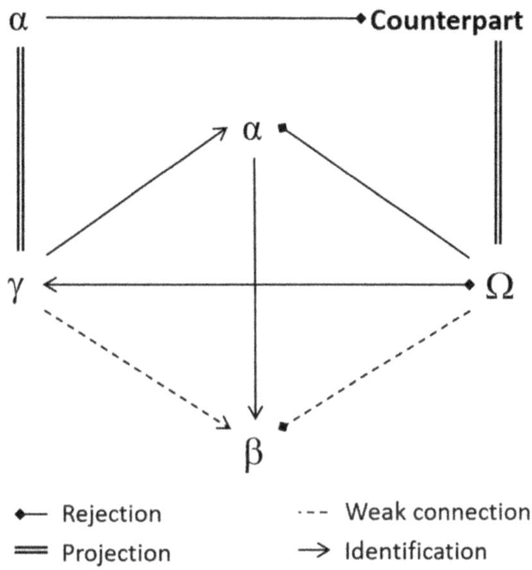

Fig. 8.21 Raoul Schindler's functional psycho-dynamic group position model. Source: Bachmann (2022), licensed under CC-BY 4.0 (https://creativecommons.org/licenses/by/4.0/)

a functional structure hence forms the system, because it assigns functions to the elements of a system and defines the relationships between the elements.

We can illustrate what this means with Raoul Schindler's (1957) functional psycho-dynamic group position model (or rank-dynamic model) from psychotherapy (see Fig. 8.21). The model explains the formation of a social group, which we can interpret as a system. There are many definitions and characterizations of a social group in social psychology, sociology, and other social sciences. Often a *social group* of people is defined as consisting of at least three people who perceive themselves as members of a group. The group members interact, have a common goal, interdependence in relationship, roles or functions that define the structure of the group, and a sense of unity. The minimum number of members in a group is three to distinguish a group from a pair or dyad. In a dyad, any interaction necessarily involves both members, which may not be the case with three members. We speak of a social group only when the members perceive themselves as a group, which may not be the case for a random collection of people at a bus stop or on a bus, which could be called a *mass of people*. However, if the bus breaks down, the people on the bus may begin to define themselves as a group because they share a common fate and may seek a solution to their common problem. Getting the bus running again or finding an alternative way to reach their destination would then be the goal of this group.

Schindler's model describes different functions of group members and their relationships. The functions are also called positions to indicate that group members can leave or change their positions like positions on a playing field. The positions are called Alpha (α), Beta (β), Gamma (γ), and Omega (Ω). Alpha is the position of the group leader who defines the goal of the group and the relationship of the group to another party or counterpart. Therefore, a counterpart is important for group identification. The Alpha has a strong influence on group decisions. Beta is the position of the expert who assists and supports the Alpha: Beta influences the group but does not lead directly. While Alpha is externally focused, Beta is internally focused on the group. The relationship between Alpha and Beta is one of interdependence: Alpha needs Beta's support to lead the group, and Beta needs Alpha to have power. Most members of the group are in the Gamma position, identifying with Alpha and accepting Alpha's leadership. The gammas do the actual work of the group without specific roles. Omega is the opposite position to Alpha, challenging Alpha's definition of the group goal and Alpha's leadership. Therefore, Omega is perceived as a threat by Alpha and Beta and is isolated from the group. When a group forms spontaneously, a process of self-organization sets in through which group members acquire their positions and the group acquires a structure. Because of the antagonism between Alpha and Omega, the resulting structure may be unstable. Furthermore, when some members leave or new members join the group, a new dynamic may emerge that changes the existing structure.

Creamer et al. (2022) attempt to reveal the true social hierarchy within a firm, as opposed to the official one defined by the organizational chart. The organizational chart defines formal power in an organization, but actual power and influence may differ from formal power. Creamer et al. (2022) suggest that a person's real influence in an organization is reflected in communication patterns. Like many other researchers, they use the publicly available email dataset of 158 employees of Enron Corporation, which was involved in a series of accounting scandals and filed for bankruptcy in 2001. Using the 619,449 emails from 1998 to 2002 in the dataset, they construct a CorpRank score using an algorithm that takes into account who communicated with whom, the number of emails sent and received, the average response time, and the sum of responses, among other factors. The average response time to an email is considered an indicator of the importance of the original sender, since more relevant messages are likely to be answered more quickly than less relevant emails. Figure 8.22 highlights the fifteen employees with the highest CorpRank scores in the Enron North American subsidiary. The graph shows that some specialists have a lot of influence that does not correspond to their formal position in the company, while some senior managers (e.g., Mike Swerzbin, rank 26) are relatively unimportant. Unlike the official hierarchy, the informal hierarchy is the result of self-organization.

In the manufacturing industry, it is common to distinguish companies based on their position in the supply chain (see Fig. 8.23). An original equipment manufacturer (OEM) assembles the final product and purchases modules or systems from Tier 1 suppliers. Often, OEMs and Tier 1 suppliers work closely together to design the final product. Tier 1 suppliers typically offer advanced products at a high technological level. They purchase components or semi-finished products from Tier 2 suppliers, which are typically smaller and less technologically advanced. They purchase raw materials or parts from Tier 3 suppliers, whose products, such as wires, screws, plastic parts, or chemicals, may not be specific to the final product. Thus, the degree of specialization increases from lower tiers to higher tiers. From an

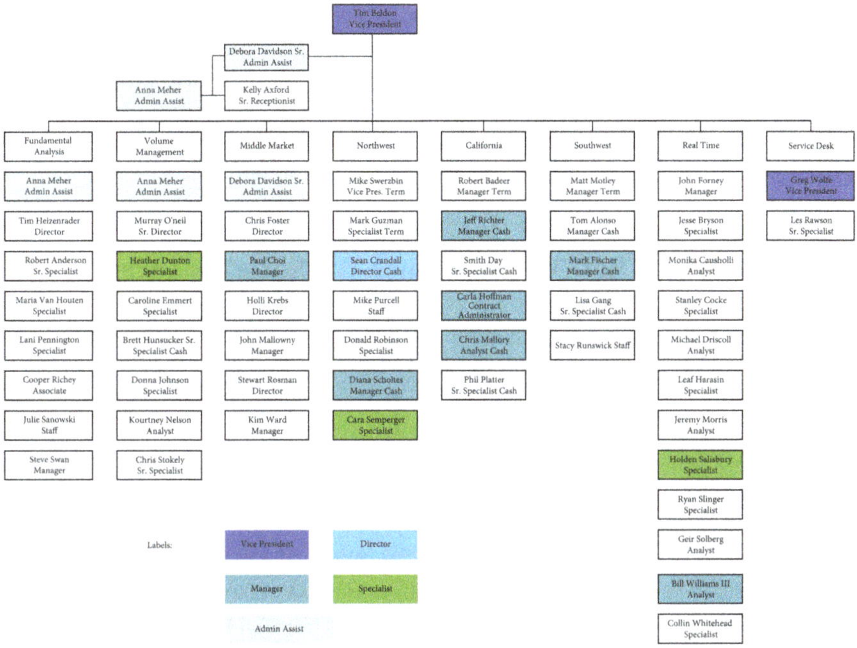

Fig. 8.22 Formal and informal power in a firm. Source: Creamer et al. (2022), licensed under CC-BY 4.0 (https://creativecommons.org/licenses/by/4.0/)

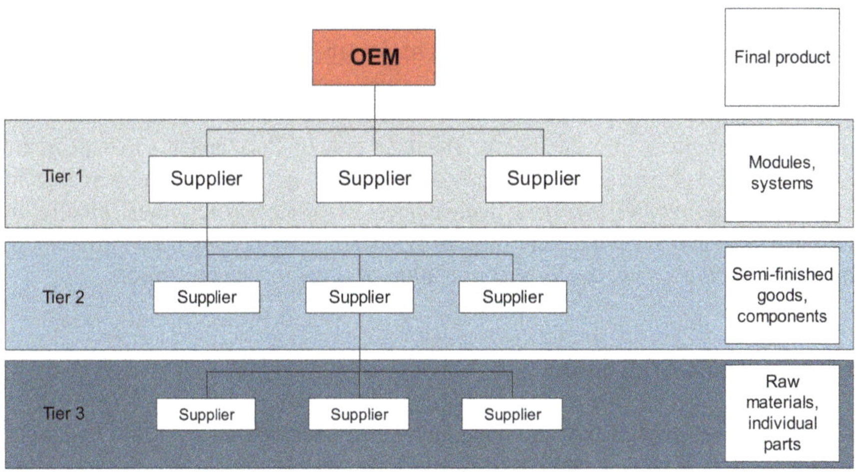

Fig. 8.23 Functional structure in a supply chain. Source: Author

OEM's perspective, the supply chain is pyramidal, meaning that there are always several suppliers at lower levels whose goods are substitutes. Such a structure gives OEMs market power and makes them less vulnerable to supply chain disruptions caused by the failure of individual suppliers. A typical car with an internal combustion engine has about 30,000 parts, requiring considerable specialization among the various suppliers. While OEMs try to influence what and how their suppliers produce at different levels, they do not have perfect control over them due to competition, cooperation, and innovation. Supply chains are at least partially self-organized systems with a high degree of functional structure.

8.5 Models of Self-Organization in the Social Sciences

In contrast to non-human agents, humans have intentions and form beliefs as well as expectations. Furthermore, human behavior is influenced by many internal and external factors and changes over time. These factors make self-organization in the human world highly complex. The models in this subsection are not meant to capture the factors of human self-organization to any realistic degree. Rather, they are didactic examples of how important self-organization mechanisms can be approached with agent-based models.

First, we look at social contagion and social influence, i.e. how opinions, beliefs, or behaviors can spread in a human population. In contrast to the system dynamics models of the previous chapter, agent-based models can explain how groups of people with similar opinions can form in a self-organizing way. Group formation is an important structuring process. Another topic is the formation of spatial patterns, which we present using the *Schelling segregation model*, in which households sort themselves into neighborhoods according to similarity. The models of social influence and spatial segregation are relevant to economics because they show how structures emerge that affect economic behavior and outcomes. However, they do not always explicitly include economic activities such as the production, exchange, and consumption of goods and services. The reason for not including economic activities is simplicity of presentation. The main goal of this chapter is to explain the concept of self-organization as clearly as possible. It is, of course, possible to combine all the models presented with models of economic activities. Finally, to present a clear economic example of self-organization, we consider the formation of *industrial symbiosis*, i.e. the local cooperation of firms to share resources.

8.5.1 Simple Contagion

In Chap. 7, we saw how social contagion can be modeled with system dynamics models such as the SIR model. Models of viral transmission are examples of what Centola (2018) calls *simple contagion*. The defining property of simple contagion is that a single contact with an infected person can be sufficient to become infected and to become a transmitter. This is certainly the case for airborne viruses, but also for simple information. It may also be the case for affective states such as optimism and pessimism.

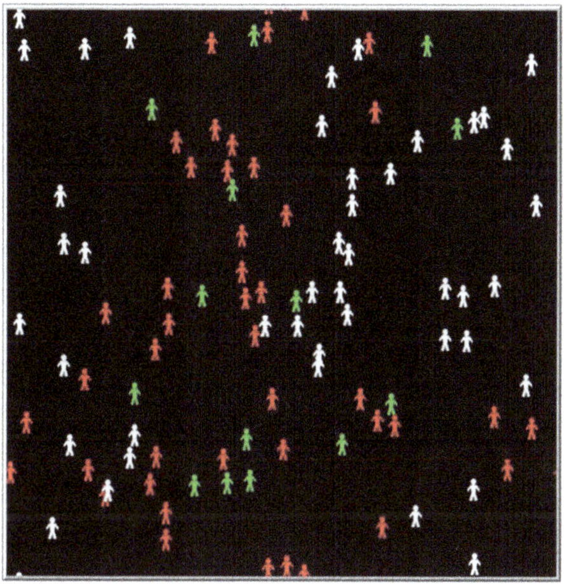

Fig. 8.24 Simple agent-based infection model. Source: Author

Instead of using a system dynamics model, the spread of something like a virus, a piece of information, an opinion, or an affective state can be modeled with agents. We discuss a very simple agent-based epidemiological model of virus transmission that is included in the NetLogo model library (Yang and Wilensky 2011). An important goal of presenting this model is to show how a system dynamics model can be translated into an agent-based model. The "virus" could also be interpreted as a "piece of information" that is passed from one person to another and can be forgotten, analogous to the recovery of an infected person. To model the spread of optimism and pessimism, we would need two "viruses," an "optimism virus" and a "pessimism virus." To keep the exposition short and simple, we focus on just one virus (or affective state) here.

In this model, there are a number N of agents that are either infected with a virus or not. They move randomly on a featureless two-dimensional grid (see Fig. 8.24). Infected agents are shown in red, susceptible agents are shown in white, and recovered agents are shown in green. When a susceptible agent comes close to an infected agent, i.e., they are on adjacent cells of the grid (*patches* in NetLogo language), the susceptible agent becomes infected with an exogenously given probability (`infection-chance`). After a `recovery-time` infected agents recover with an exogenously given probability (`recovery-chance`). Recovered agents are immune to the virus.

The crucial part of the NetLogo code that describes the behavior of the agents, consists of two actions:

```
ask turtles [move]
ask turtles [
      infect
      maybe-recover ]
```

In NetLogo, the default name of an agent is "turtle." The command `ask turtles [ X ]` means that the program will call each agent sequentially in a random order to execute the procedure `X`. Hence, the code above means that the agents will first execute the procedure `move`, and then the procedures `infect` and `maybe-recover`.

A *procedure* is defined by the designer of the model and uses *commands* that are built into NetLogo. In the code, a procedure starts with "to" and finishes with "end." The procedure `move` looks like this:

```
to move
       rt random-float 360
       fd 1
end
```

The command `rt Y` tells the agent to turn Y degrees to the right. Here, Y is given by a randomly chosen real number between 0 and 360 (`random-float 360`). The command `fd Z` tells the agent to move forward by Z units (here $Z = 1$). Thus, the agents in this model first choose a random direction and then move one step forward, generating a random path on the grid.

The procedure `infect` is given by the following code:

```
to infect
      if nearby-uninfected != nobody
      [ ask nearby-uninfected
       [ if random-float 100 < infection-chance
         [ set infected? true ]
       ]
      ]
end
```

The agent first checks if there are any susceptible agents on the patches in the Moore neighborhood (`if nearby-uninfected! = nobody`). If there are none, nothing happens. But if there are susceptible agents, each of them will be called to draw a random number between 0 and 100 (`random-float 100`). If this random number is smaller than the exogenous probability of an infection, then the Boolean variable `infected?` is set to `true`, i.e. the other agent is infected.

The code of the procedure `maybe-recover` is:

```
to maybe-recover
  set infection-length infection-length + 1
  if infection-length > recovery-time
  [
   if random-float 100 < recovery-chance
   [ set infected? false
     set cured? true
    ]
  ]
end
```

First, the duration of the agent's infection is increased by one period (`set infection-length infection-length + 1`). If the agent has been infected long enough (`if infection-length > recovery-time`), then another random number between 0 and 100 is drawn and compared with the exogenous `recovery-chance`. If the inequality is true, then the agent recovers and the Boolean variable for the infection state is set back to `false` and the Boolean variable `cured?` is set back to `true`.

Figure 8.25 shows the output for a run of the model with 100 agents, an infection probability of 30%, and a recovery probability of 60% after 188 time steps (hours). The epidemic is over because every agent has been infected and recovered. The basic reproduction number R0, which represents the number of secondary infections that result from the introduction of an infected person, is 4.04. Note that the graphs in the Populations plot look very similar to the dynamics in the SIR model in Fig. 7.40. The green "Not infected" graph in the ABM is a combination of the susceptible and recovered populations. It reaches its minimum when the number of infected agents is at its maximum.

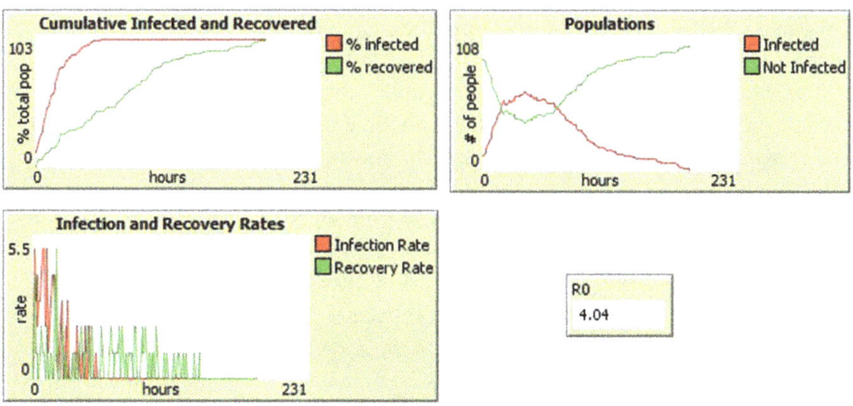

Fig. 8.25 Output of the infection ABM. Source: Author

8.5.2 Social Influence and Complex Contagion

Although it is quite common in the research literature to compare social contagion to viral epidemics, Centola (2018) argues that this comparison is misleading because most social contagions are complex rather than simple. *Complex contagions* require contact with multiple sources of activation, whereas a single contact with one source may be sufficient for simple contagion. The objects of complex contagion are behaviors, knowledge, attitudes, or beliefs. What they have in common is that their adoption involves some kind of cost, risk, or complementarity. In order to adopt the behavior or belief despite the cost, the potential adopter needs *social confirmation* from several other people. There are at least four mechanisms of complex contagion.

First, *strategic complementarity* (or synergy) implies that the value of a behavior increases with the number of others who adopt it. Telephones, email accounts, and social media are examples of this. Being the only person with a phone makes little sense. Second, complex contagion may depend on *credibility*. As more people adopt a behavior or belief, it becomes more credible that it is beneficial or worth the cost of adoption. Examples include new medical treatments, but also rumors, whose credibility increases as more people spread them. Third, some behaviors or views require *legitimacy*, i.e. approval by others. An individual man wearing a skirt risks embarrassment and social sanction, but if many men wear skirts, it is easier for an individual man to do so. Finally, the contagion of emotional excitement is amplified by the number of other excited people. That's why many people prefer to attend sporting events with many others rather than watch them alone on television.

Social confirmation implies that the behavior of one agent depends on the behavior or state of several other agents. Structurally, this is analogous to what happens in the Ising model (see Sect. 8.3.2). In the Ising model, the spin (or state) of a cell (or agent) depends on the spins of its neighbors. The more neighbors with spins opposite to its own, the more likely a cell is to change its spin. The physicists Katarzyna Sznajd-Weron and Józef Sznajd applied a version of the one-dimensional Ising model to the time evolution of opinions in a closed community (Sznajd-Weron and Sznajd 2000), laying the foundation for a large literature in sociophysics based on the *Sznajd model*.

The one-dimensional Sznajd model assumes that there are N agents in a chain. Each agent $i = 1, 2, \ldots, N$ has one of two possible opinions, either $\sigma_i = 1$ or $\sigma_i = -1$. The algorithm, which is repeated in each time step $\Delta t = 1$, is as follows:

1. Pick a single agent at random (uniformly from all N agents); denote it with i
2. If agents i and $i + 1$ share the same opinion at time t, i.e., $\sigma_i(t) = \sigma_{i+1}(t) = \sigma$, they impose it on their respective neighbors: $\sigma_{i-1}(t + 1) = \sigma_{i+2}(t + 1) = \sigma$
3. Otherwise (if $\sigma_i(t) \neq \sigma_{i+1}(t)$), their respective neighbors take opposite states: $\sigma_{i-1}(t + 1) = -\sigma_i(t)$ and $\sigma_{i+2}(t + 1) = -\sigma_{i+1}(t)$

The updating rule contained in rules (2) and (3) is called "united we stand, divided we fall," because two agents with the same opinion can persuade their two

Table 8.3 One run of the 1-dimensional Sznajd model at 5 different points in time

Time	Opinions
0	
4849	
23,308	
45,787	
53,294	

neighbors, but if two agents have different opinions, they will induce their neighbors to oppose their opinions.

Table 8.3 contains the outcome of a NetLogo implementation of the model with 101 agents (Juliao 2014). Blue squares are agents with opinion 1 and red squares are agents with opinion −1. The initial distribution of opinions at $t = 0$ is random. Over time, we first observe a cluster of red agents, but toward the end there is a large cluster of blue agents. Finally, all agents hold opinion 1. The evolution of opinions can be represented by a "magnetization" plot like the one in Fig. 8.26. The degree of "magnetization" corresponds to the average opinion of all agents.

The model has three fixed points or steady states: (1) $S_1 : \sigma_i = \sigma_j = 1 \; \forall \; i \neq j$, (2) $S_2 : \sigma_i = \sigma_j = \; -1 \; \forall \; i \neq j$, (3) $S_3 : \sigma_i = \; -\sigma_{i+1} \; \forall \; i$. Sznajd-Weron and Sznajd (2000) demonstrate that the so-called exit probability of each steady state depends on the initial concentration of an opinion. As Fig. 8.27 shows, the probability of the positive steady state S_1, estimated from 1000 runs of the model, can be described by the power function $p(S_1) = 1.02c_{+1}^{2.12}$, where c_{+1} is the initial concentration of positive opinions. This function implies that the probability of a steady state with only one opinion left (+1 or −1) is about 0.235 when the initial concentration of each opinion is 0.5, such that the probability of ending up in the mixed steady state S_3 (called anti in Fig. 8.27) is 0.53.

Sznajd-Weron et al. (2021) review a literature of more than 100 papers, mostly published in physics journals, that have varied and extended the seminal Sznajd model. One of the first variations was the generalization of the 1-dimensional model to two dimensions by Stauffer et al. (2000). Another generalization is the consideration of more than two opinions or the possibility of continuous opinions.

A crucial difference between the physical Ising model and the sociophysical Sznajd model is that in the latter we can talk about real behavior. There are different updating rules for the Ising model, but they are all different approximations to the laws of nature that determine the spins of the physical particles. In contrast, there are no universal laws that determine how people change their opinions in response to other people's opinions. Therefore, the literature has analyzed the effects of various behavioral rules. One alternative rule to rule (3) in the original model is "if you don't know what to do, do nothing," which states that agents $i - 1$ and $i + 2$ do not change their opinions when the pair of neighbors i and $i + 1$ disagree. Another alternative to rule (3) is "if you don't know what to do, do whatever," i.e. to make a random choice instead of doing nothing. These two rules are confusion rules for the case in which an

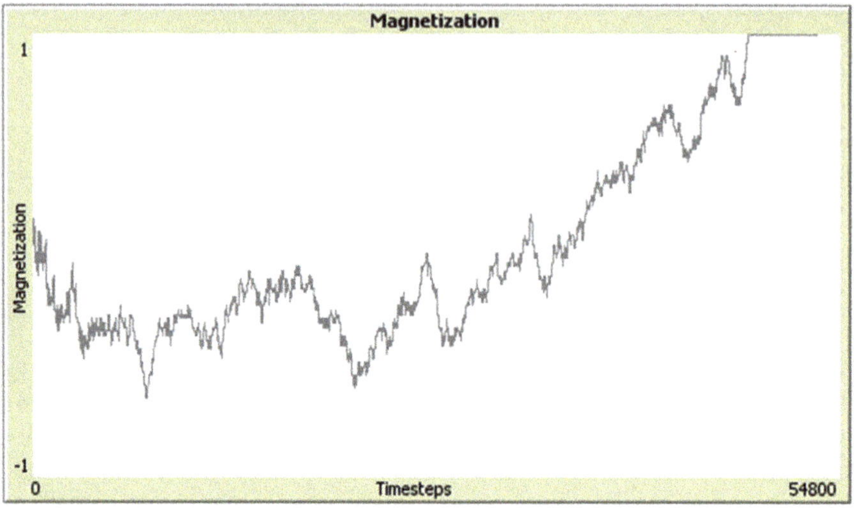

Fig. 8.26 Average opinion in the 1-dimensional Sznajd model. Source: Author

Fig. 8.27 Dependence of the exit probability on the initial concentration of $\sigma_i = +1$. Source: adapted from Sznajd-Weron et al. (2021), reproduced with kind permission of Elsevier

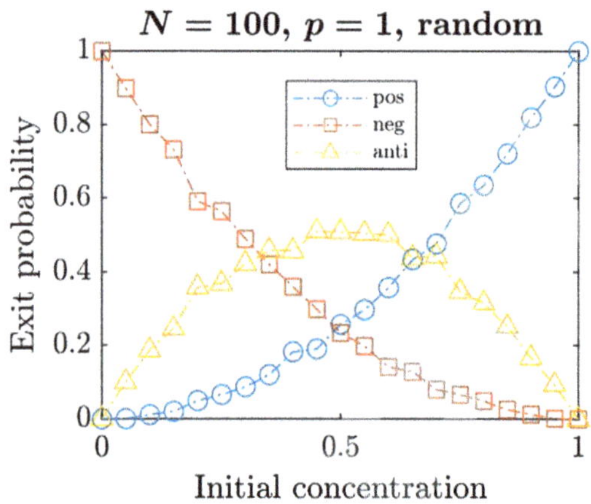

agent cannot obtain social confirmation from the group. The anti-conformity rule is an alternative to rule (2) and says "If agents i and $i + 1$ share the same opinion, choose the opposite opinion." The independence rule describes behavior that is (partially) independent of the behavior of the group in that an agent makes its own choice independent of the behavior of its neighbors with a given probability p. In the majority of papers in this literature, all agents are identical, but there are some papers that introduce heterogeneity. Agents can differ in terms of their behavioral rules, but also in their memory, which affects their behavior, or in their acquired reputation.

The sociophysical literature based on the Sznajd model is interesting, but also somewhat technical. It has received considerable attention here for didactic purposes because the cellular automaton approach is easily accessible. Unfortunately, the sociophysical literature on social opinion dynamics is rather disconnected from a large and older literature in the social sciences that goes back to the 1950s. How people exert social influence on each other is a central topic in sociology and social psychology. Flache et al. (2017) review the literature on agent-based models of social influence, in which *opinions* are understood as a generic concept that can also represent a belief, a behavior, or an attitude. This literature differs from the sociophysical literature in several ways. One technical difference is that the social science literature tends to model opinions as continuous rather than discrete variables. More importantly, this literature is informed by basic psychological theory and empirical evidence about social influence, which is less the case in the sociophysics literature.

The classical approach to social influence, developed in the 1950s and 1960s, assumes that the opinion o of agent i at time $t + 1$ is a weighted average of her previous opinion and the opinions of agents in a reference group at time t:

$$o_{it+1} = o_{it} + \mu \sum_j w_{ij} \left(o_{jt} - o_{it} \right).$$

The parameter $0 < \mu \leq 1$ defines the rate of opinion convergence and smoothes the opinion dynamics. The weights w_{ij} indicate how much influence agent j has on the opinion of agent i. Opinion averaging describes assimilative social influence, i.e. the reduction of opinion differences over time. The typical long-run outcome of these models is perfect opinion consensus as shown in panel A of Fig. 8.28.

However, perfect consensus among all agents is not necessarily the most common finding in the real world, leading Robert Axelrod (1997) to ask: "If people tend to become more alike in their beliefs, attitudes, and behavior when they interact, why do not all such differences eventually disappear?"

Cultural differentiation (Bourdieu 1984) means that distinguishable societal groups emerge with boundaries between them and specific cultures. Panel B of Fig. 8.28 shows the result of a simulation model, in which different groups form with consensus within groups but not between groups. Clustering of opinions and group formation occur when there is a similarity bias, i.e. when social influence depends on

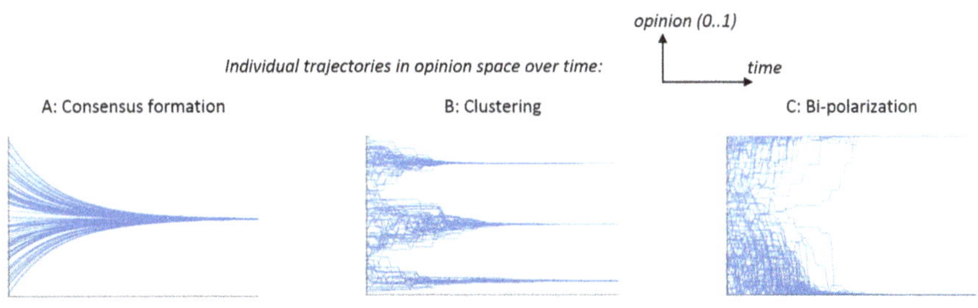

Fig. 8.28 Typical opinion dynamics in agent-based models of social influence. Source: Flache et al. (2017), licensed under CC-BY 4.0 (https://creativecommons.org/licenses/by/4.0/)

agents not being too dissimilar. The following equations describe a mechanism, by which an agent i is influenced by an agent j if their opinions are sufficiently similar:

$$o_{it+1} = o_{it} + f_w(o_{it}, o_{jt})(o_{jt} - o_{it})$$

$$f_w(o_i, o_j) = \begin{cases} \mu & \text{if } |o_i - o_j| \leq \epsilon \\ 0 & \text{otherwise} \end{cases}$$

The weight of j's influence on i, w_{ij}, is now given by a step function. If the distance between the opinions is below a threshold ϵ, then the opinion of i is adjusted toward the opinion of j with the convergence rate μ. If the opinion of j is too different, it will not influence i's opinion.

An issue of high political relevance in many countries is *(bi-)polarization*, i.e. the formation of two groups whose consensus opinions are maximally different from each other (see panel C of Fig. 8.28). The emergence of bipolarization requires a repulsive influence such as rejection, differentiation, or reactance between individuals. One way to implement such a repulsive influence is to use the following weighting function for the adjustment of o_i in response to o_j:

$$f_w(o_i, o_j) = \mu(1 - 2|o_{jt} - o_{it}|).$$

If the difference between the two opinions is small, the weighting function is positive, so o_i converges toward o_j. However, if the disagreement is too large, i.e., $|o_{jt} - o_{it}| > 0.5$, then the opinion of agent i is pushed away from the opinion of j. The two agents become more dissimilar over time. Hence, polarization is the result of negative feedback for small disagreements and positive feedback for large disagreements.

The three updating rules presented here are only examples of many different models in three classes of models. There are many specific mechanisms that are supported by empirical evidence, but empirical research suggests that it may not be possible to specify rules that are independent of contextual factors. For example, individuals appear to be more willing to express opinions in computer-mediated interactions than in face-to-face interactions, which will affect opinion dynamics. Therefore, Flache et al. (2017) call for "mid-range approaches" that do not attempt to explain behavior in general, but are guided by theoretical and empirical arguments about which assumptions are plausible in a given setting.

8.5.3 Segregation and Spatial Organization

The classic model of spatial self-organization is Thomas Schelling's model of segregation (Schelling 1978). As we have seen (see Fig. 8.15), ethnic segregation is common in many cities in the United States and elsewhere. It is easy to explain segregation in terms of intolerance—that is, the unwillingness of agents to live next to neighbors who are different from them in terms of ethnicity, income, education, or

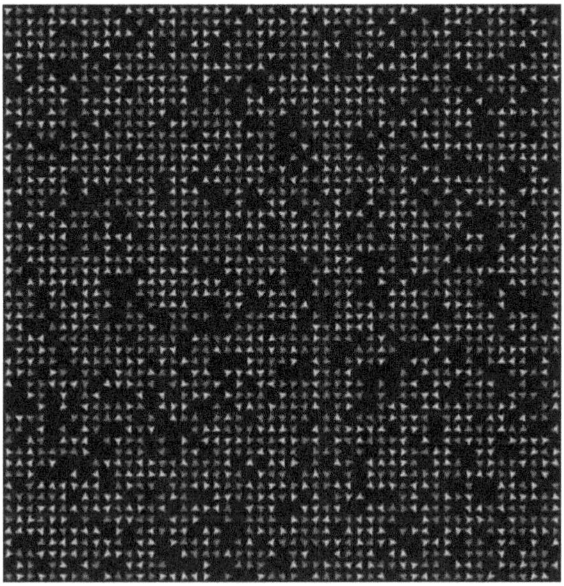

Fig. 8.29 Initial distribution of agents in the Schelling segregation model. Source: Author

other characteristics. Linear thinking would predict that high levels of segregation require high levels of intolerance, but Schelling showed that this intuition is false. Using a simple model of pennies and dimes on a checkerboard, he showed that even low levels of individual intolerance are sufficient to produce pronounced aggregate patterns of segregation. The original Schelling model is a nice example of a non-computerized agent-based model. Today, there are many computational versions of the model, and several models are even included in the NetLogo model library. We present here the simplest version (Wilensky and Rand 2006).

A square torus-shaped lattice consisting of H patches represents a city with each patch representing a house. Each house or patch can be occupied by one agent. There are $N < H$ agents, such that some patches are empty. Agents differ in their color—half are green, half are red—, but are otherwise identical. The color may stand for a discrete characteristic such as ethnicity or religious affiliation. The initial distribution of agents on the lattice is random, as shown in Fig. 8.29.

The core of the NetLogo program (the go procedure, which is executed at each time step) is very simple and consists of one stopping condition and two procedures:

```
to go
  if all? turtles [ happy? ] [ stop ]
  move-unhappy-turtles
  update-turtles
end
```

The program stops if all agents are happy. Otherwise, it runs for another time step. Whether an agent (a turtle) is happy depends on the percentage of similar neighbors in the Moore neighborhood. The happiness of each agent (the Boolean state variable happy?) is determined by the following procedure:

```
to update-turtles
  ask turtles [
     set similar-nearby count (turtles-on neighbors)
        with [color = [color] of myself]
     set total-nearby count (turtles-on neighbors)
     set happy? similar-nearby >= ( %-similar-wanted × total-
        nearby / 100 )
  ]
end
```

First, the agent selected by the ask command counts the number of agents with its own color on the eight neighboring patches and stores it in the variable similar-nearby. Then all neighboring agents are counted (total-nearby). The agent is happy (happy? is true), if the number of similar neighbors is greater than or equal to the number of desired similar neighbors, which is given by %-similar-wanted × total-nearby / 100. The parameter %-similar-wanted is exogenously given and measures the degree of intolerance. If this parameter were equal to 100%, the agent would not tolerate any neighbors of a different color. In the basic version, the degree of intolerance is identical for all agents.

If an agent is unhappy, because there are too few similar neighbors in its current neighborhood, it moves according to the following procedure:

```
to move-unhappy-turtles
  ask turtles with [ not happy? ]
    [ find-new-spot ]
end
```

In the basic version, agents randomly search for new patches, i.e. the procedure find-new-spot says that the agent randomly turns to the right between 0 and 360 degrees and then moves forward between 0 and 10 steps. If the new spot reached in this way is empty, the agent stays there, otherwise it moves again in the same way.

The segregation patterns produced by the Schelling model are clearly visible in Fig. 8.30. Both models start with a random distribution of agents in space, where each agent has about 50% similar neighbors. The pattern on the left results from a degree of intolerance of 30%. Although the agents start with an average of 50% similar neighbors, there are about 17% that do not. These unhappy agents move and cause the dynamics that lead to the resulting segregation after 13 time steps, in which agents have about 72% of similar neighbors. This is the main result of the Schelling model: even if all agents accept to live among a majority of different agents (they

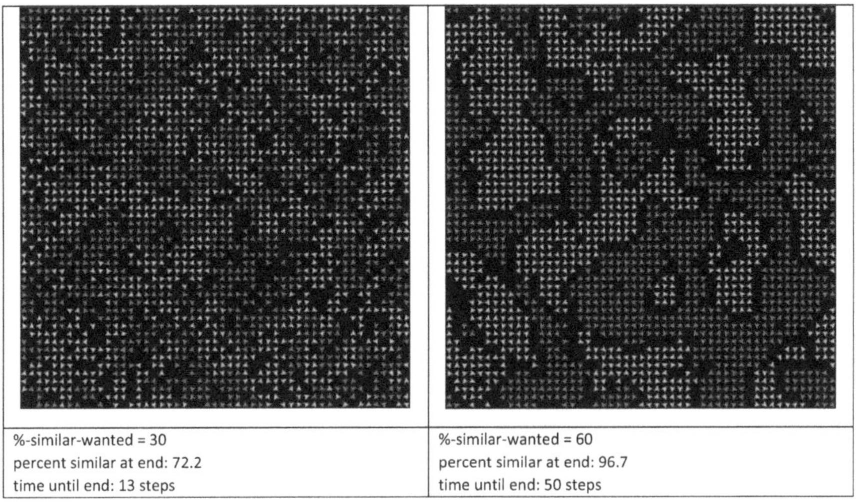

Fig. 8.30 Final distributions of agents in the Schelling segregation model. Source: Author

want only 30% similar neighbors), quite strong segregation with more than 70% similar neighbors can result. To obtain almost perfect segregation with more than 96% similar neighbors, a degree of intolerance of 60% is sufficient (see right panel).

The original Schelling model is, of course, highly stylized and omits many factors relevant to real-world segregation. A rather simple extension is to include more than two types of agents. Another is to include individual degrees of intolerance instead of a common one. We could also assume that agents have a preference not only for similarity but also for diversity. All of these extensions are included in the NetLogo model library (see also Wilensky and Rand 2015). More fundamental modifications have adaptive instead of fixed tolerance levels (Urselmann and Phelps 2018), feature endogenous cultural dissemination as in the previous subsection on opinion dynamics (Gracia-Lázaro et al. 2009), or include economic inequality and a housing market (Bonakdar and Roos 2023).

8.5.4 Self-organized Industrial Symbiosis

Industrial symbiosis is a good example of self-organization of economic activities. *Industrial symbiosis* means that firms in an industrial district collaborate by sharing resources and exchanging materials and energy by-products. They form an *industrial ecosystem* or an *industrial symbiosis network*. In particular, used water, waste heat, or material by-products (often called wastes) from some firms are used as inputs in the production process of other firms. The collaborating firms thus reduce their overall resource and energy demand and form a (partially) circular economy. The prototypical example of an industrial symbiosis is the multi-industry cluster in Kalundborg, Denmark, where the term "industrial symbiosis" was coined in 1989.

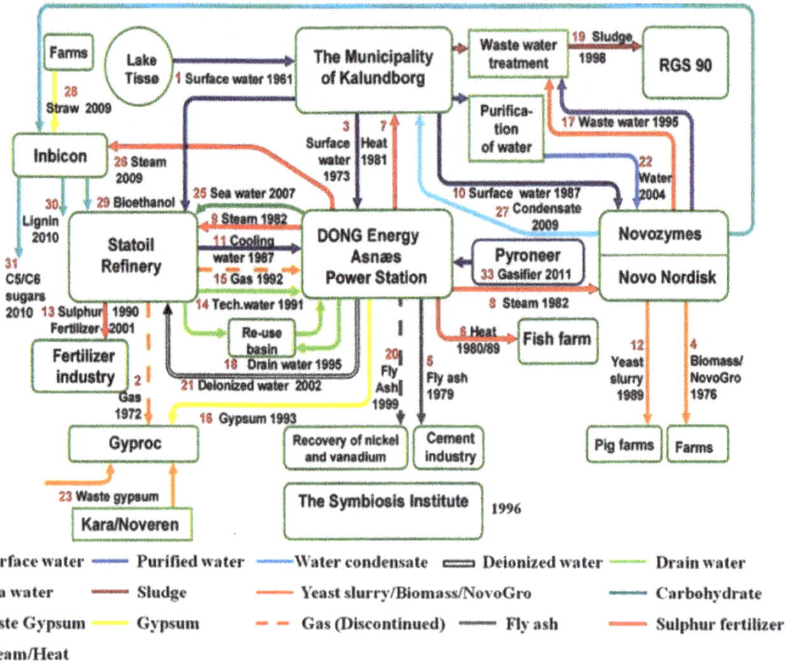

Fig. 8.31 The Kalundborg industrial symbiosis. The numbers from 1 to 33 indicate exchanges of materials and energy and the years shown indicate when the exchanges began. Discontinued exchanges are shown as broken lines. Source: Chertow and Ehrenfeld (2012), reproduced with kind permission of John Wiley and Sons

Figure 8.31 shows the main actors in the Kalundborg symbiosis and the resource and energy flows between them.

Key actors in this ecosystem are the Asnæs power station, the Statoil refinery, the Novo group, the Gyproc plasterboards company, and the municipality of Kalundborg. As shown by the years in the figure, early exchanges between actors began in the 1970s. Different kinds of water flows are especially important, but also material flows such as the waste gypsum flow from the power plant to the wallboard manufacturer Gyproc, or the slurry and biomass sold by the pharmaceutical company Novo Nordisk to farms.

Chertow and Ehrenfeld (2012) propose elements of a mid-range theory of industrial symbiosis. They build on the insight of physicist and ecologist James J. Kay (2001) that industrial ecosystems are self-organizing complex adaptive systems, similar to natural ecosystems, in which structures emerge from local interactions among system elements. One type of symbiotic relationship in biology is called *mutualism*, which means that two otherwise unrelated species exchange materials, energy, or information for mutual benefit. An industrial symbiosis such as the Kalundborg system is an example of economic mutualism. Chertow and Ehrenfeld (2012) propose a three-stage model of how an industrial symbiosis develops.

The first stage is called *sprouting*. Some firms in a region start exchanging resources more or less randomly. This first stage is a pre-stage to a symbiosis. The collaborating firms behave like firms in a normal supply chain described by industrial organization theory or by models of economic agglomeration theories. If the collaborations are successful, they can form the nucleus of an industrial symbiosis. In the second stage (*uncovering*), someone discovers that those collaborations, which are often bi- or trilateral, do not only benefit the parties involved, but also create positive environmental externalities. From this point on, a new cooperative culture with shared beliefs, norms, and values can develop. Stakeholders now want to actively pursue common environmental goals and seek to expand the pairwise collaborations into joint action in a network. The symbiosis becomes intentional and new members join. *Embeddedness and institutionalization* is the final stage, where a previously created institutional entity becomes more active and drives the further development. In the case of Kalundborg, this was the Symbiosis Institute founded in 1996 as part of Kalundborg's industrial development agency. Local actors in a network become embedded through the accumulation of *social capital* and mutual trust, which facilitate further collaboration.

This theory of industrial symbiosis hence incorporates ideas of self-organization that are related to the opinion dynamics and spatial clustering discussed earlier. Opinion dynamics can lead to group formation and shared beliefs and practices. Spatial clustering is observed not only among households, but also among firms (where it is often referred to as *agglomeration*). Both spatial proximity and shared beliefs are necessary for the emergence of industrial symbiosis networks.

Bichraoui et al. (2013) present a simple agent-based model whose purpose is to explore the importance of cooperation and learning for the development of industrial symbiosis. The agents in this model are industrial plants in a region, which form a potential symbiosis network. The agents can establish links with each other, which represent the exchange of materials. Each agent is represented as a set of material inputs and outputs given by random numbers. A key variable is the cooperation norm of a firm, which is either 1 (cooperative) or 0 (non-cooperative). It depends on an exogenously given frequency of cooperation and determines the type of behavior (1 for cooperative, 0 for non-cooperative). Agents perform the following actions per time step (year):

1. Find a partner for the exchange of material: each plant looks for an input (or more, up to a maximum of links set up) among the output of the other plants
2. If the availability of material corresponds to its input, a link between the two entities is created
3. If the cooperation-norm is true and the number of links for the plant is less than the maximum number of links, the behavior variable is 1
4. Eliminate and create a plant: a random plant is picked to die (determined by an exogenous death rate) and a new one is created
5. If learning is turned on and the majority behavior is to cooperate within a radius (determined by a slider), then the plant is set to cooperate (behavior = 1)

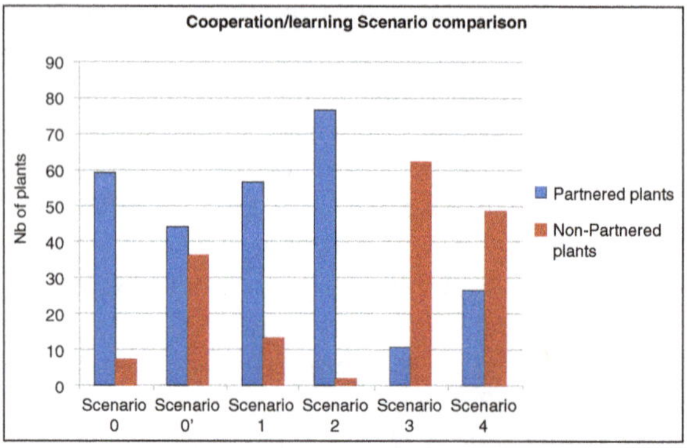

Scenario 0: Cooperation frequency 50%, learning
Scenario 0': Cooperation frequency 50%, no learning
Scenario 1: Cooperation frequency 75%, no learning
Scenario 2: Cooperation frequency 75%, learning
Scenario 3: Cooperation frequency 15%, no learning
Scenario 4: Cooperation frequency 15%, learning

Fig. 8.32 Importance of cooperation frequency and learning for industrial symbiosis. Source: Bichraoui et al. (2013), reproduced with kind permission of Elsevier B.V.

The simple model shows that both the frequency of cooperation and social learning from others promote the number of firms that are partnered, i.e. have links with other firms (see Fig. 8.32). Perhaps not very surprisingly, both the frequency of cooperation and social learning have a positive impact on the number of firms that find a partner. The number of partnered firms is highest in scenario 2 (high cooperation frequency and learning) and lowest in scenario 3 (low cooperation frequency and no learning).

A more interesting, but also significantly more complicated, agent-based model of industrial symbiosis is presented in Ghali et al. (2017). This model does not explicitly consider product flows, but focuses on the social factors (social structure and dynamics, trust, knowledge sharing) that facilitate the exploitation of synergies between plants. The generic decision and interaction processes of all agents are identical, but all agents have their own social attributes, values, and knowledge levels. Agents exchange knowledge, which is the reason for synergies, only with their social contacts. The model is particularly interesting because the agents' behavior is based on Icek Ajzen's (1991) *Theory of Planned Behavior*, a well-known psychological theory that links beliefs (attitudes, subjective norms, and perceived behavioral control) to behavioral intentions and actual behavior. The generalized version of the theory used in the model is shown in Fig. 8.33. The model assumes that knowledge transfer involves the updating of knowledge and social parameters such as trust. The creation of a synergy follows a decision process that first requires the identification of a potential industrial synergy (awareness). A plant becomes aware of potential synergies within its network when its level of knowledge exceeds a certain threshold. A partnership requires that both partners agree to become partners (willingness), which is influenced by trust. Willingness also depends on how many synergies have been created within a particular plant's social contacts, which represents a subjective norm. A plant's attitude toward creating a potential synergy is determined by both willingness and awareness. To

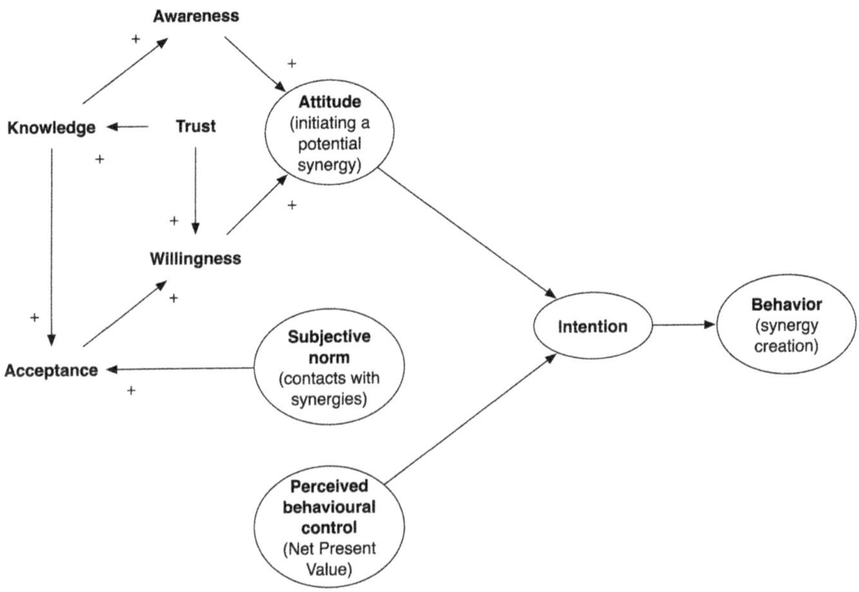

Fig. 8.33 Planned behavior of plant agents in an industrial symbiosis model. Source: Ghali et al. (2017), reproduced with kind permission of Elsevier B.V.

determine whether a potential synergy would be profitable, both potential partners calculate its net present value, which defines the perceived behavioral control of both plants involved. The synergy is created only if both partners deem it profitable. Among other results, Ghali et al. (2017) find that a higher level of social dynamics (i.e., the number of new social connections) significantly promotes the creation of synergies. This implies that industrial parks with a low level of social interactions might not become an industrial symbiosis network through pure self-organization. They might benefit from interventions by contact brokers that increase social connectedness and promote synergy creation.

The literature on industrial symbiosis raises the question of self-organization versus planned organization or organization by design of an external actor. Chertow and Ehrenfeld's theory of industrial symbiosis, but also Ghali et al.'s (2017) model, tells us that self-organization of firms into an industrial symbiosis network can fail. According to Chertow and Ehrenfeld, some actor must develop a bird's eye view of the benefits of collaboration and aim to persuade others to participate. This actor can be one of the participating firms, but it can also be an external agent such as a planning agency. The model of Ghali et al. shows that the amount of synergies that can be realized depends on the social connections between the agents. If there are too few social contacts, self-organization will not occur. In this case, an external promoter that brings agents together could help. However, it would be wrong to assume that industrial symbiosis can be created by design. Policymakers and planners often hope to create eco-industrial parks by attracting specific firms to a district. Chertow (2007) reviewed 15 U.S. industrial development projects and found that few were sustainable. She concludes that top-down planning often fails, and that successful industrial symbiosis networks such as the Kalundborg case are more likely to emerge from bottom-up self-organization (see also Gibbs and Deutz 2007). This does not mean that planners and policy makers cannot support the development of industrial symbiosis in general, but it does mean that one needs to carefully analyze which policy instruments might work under which conditions and at which stage of the process (see Tao et al. 2019). In general, self-organization and organization by design both limit and complement each other.

8.6 Spontaneous Order

Economics knows the concept of *spontaneous order*, which is closely related to the concept of self-organization. Friedrich August Hayek proposed spontaneous order as the result of self-organizing processes in the economy and society. A Nobel laureate, Hayek is the most famous and influential member of the Austrian School of Economics. Modern Austrian School economists rely heavily on Hayek's ideas, which are summarized in this section. Although Hayek's ideas of spontaneous order are compatible with a complexity perspective, there are also significant differences between Austrian economics and complexity economics, which will also be discussed in this section.

8.6.1 Hayek on Spontaneous Order

Hayek (1945) opposed the neoclassical idea that the problem facing society in constructing a rational economic order is an optimization problem whose solution is that "the marginal rates of substitution between any two commodities or factors must be the same in all their different uses" (p. 519). No society can ever solve this problem, because no single mind possesses the necessary data. He rejects the neoclassical assumptions that all relevant information is available, that there is a given system of preferences and that complete knowledge of available means exists. All this information "never exists in concentrated or integrated form, but solely as the dispersed bits of incomplete and frequently contradictory knowledge which all the separate individuals possess" (Hayek 1945, p. 519). The economic problem is hence a *fundamental knowledge problem*:

> *how to secure the best use of resources known to any of the members of society, for ends whose relative importance only these individuals know. Or, to put it briefly, it is a problem of the utilization of knowledge not given to anyone in its totality* (Hayek 1945, p. 520).

Hayek (1976 [1998], p. 107) defines an *economy* as an organization that "consists of a complex of activities by which a given set of means is allocated in accordance with a unitary plan among the competing ends according to their relative importance." Thus, economies such as households, farms, or businesses have agency and make plans. For Hayek, an *organization* is the result of a purposeful act of organizing available means to achieve a goal. We could call it *order by design* or by intention. The national economy should not be called an economy, because it is not an organization in the defined sense, but "a network of many interlaced economies." While there is order in this system of interconnected economies, "the cosmos of the market neither is nor could be governed by . . . a single scale of ends; it serves the multiplicity of separate and incommensurable ends of all its separate members" (Hayek 1976 [1998], p. 108). To distinguish this market order from an economy, Hayek uses the word *catallaxy*, which he derives from the ancient Greek verb *katallatein,* which meant "to exchange" or "to change from enemy into friend." He uses *catallaxy*

> *to describe the order brought about by the mutual adjustments of many economies in a market. A catallaxy is thus the special kind of spontaneous order produced by the market through people acting within the rules of the law of property, tort and contract* (Hayek 1976 [1998], p. 109).

Order is a key concept for Hayek, especially social order. He argues that physics and other natural sciences deal with simple phenomena that can be described by laws often expressed in single mathematical equations. Social phenomena are more complex because of the multitude of factors that influence them. Since we can never hope to find laws in the social sciences, we need the concept of order to discuss complex phenomena. Hayek (1976 [1998], p. 35) defines order as "a state of affairs in which a multiplicity of elements of various kinds are so related to each other that we may learn from our acquaintance with some spatial or temporal part of the whole to form correct expectations concerning the rest, or at least expectations which have a good chance of proving correct." He calls a multitude of people a *society*, if their actions are mutually aligned, which can happen if people know what to expect from others. To satisfy their needs in a society, people need the knowledge of and the cooperation with others. In contrast to tribes, modern societies are so large that much interaction inevitably occurs indirectly with strangers, who are often very different from oneself and pursue different goals. Hayek identifies two kinds of order: *made order* (or organization) and *grown order* (or spontaneous order). Organization is a directed social order designed by someone, whereas spontaneous order is a self-generating or endogenous order. Hayek explicitly relates the idea of endogenous order to self-organization in cybernetics or the physical sciences in general. The central problem of social theory and social policy, according to Hayek, is to answer the question of how a social order emerges from the diverse activities of millions of people.

Because of the knowledge problem, social order must be a spontaneous order. This is true of all kinds of macroscopic order in general, and of the market order or catallaxy in particular. The dispersed knowledge in economic contexts refers not only to abstract scientific and technological knowledge, but also to practical knowledge of specific conditions of space and time. In any profession, even after a long theoretical education, people have to learn a lot of practical knowledge. Businesspeople need a lot of specialized knowledge about their trade, which can only be acquired through experience in the relevant business. Much of the competitive advantage of businesspeople over their competitors depends on the possession and use of such specialized and often transient knowledge.

For Hayek, catallaxy is a wealth-creating game, where a game is defined as "a contest played according to rules and decided by superior skill, strength or good fortune" (Hayek 1976 [1998], p. 115). Wealth is created because all economic agents (or players) contribute to the satisfaction of needs of others, although the players generally do not know the other players or their needs. They can do this by responding to the price signals of markets. Price changes indicate other changes somewhere in the economic system. If the price of a raw material or resource rises, either because it has become scarcer or it is demanded more, because it has become more useful to someone somewhere, it provides a signal. An economic agent does not need to know what has changed in the system. The price signal is enough information to respond in the socially desired way, namely, to demand less of the resource and—if possible—to switch to a cheaper substitute. By demanding less due to a price increase, an agent leaves more of the resource to someone else who can make better use of it. Competitive markets with flexible prices are thus the main mechanism for achieving catallaxy.

Hayek praises the market as the only method by which large-scale cooperation is possible among strangers with different and potentially conflicting goals. The Great Society, i.e., the anonymous modern mass society, is characterized by the absence of a common goal or a clear hierarchy of goals. Even if it were technically possible to organize society by design, it would not be clear which goal should be pursued. In a free market, it is not necessary to have a common goal, because all agents can pursue their own private goals. Through the market, the Great Society is *means-conne*cted not *ends-connected.* This means that market participants do not have to agree on common ends; they can even have opposing goals. Still, they can interact in a market, and the more they differ, the more beneficial the interaction is likely to be for both. Hence, heterogeneity also plays an important role. The possibility that even adversaries can mutually benefit from market interactions is one motivation for Hayek to choose the term catallaxy—the change from enemies to friends. "Catallactics is the science which describes the only overall order that comprehends nearly all mankind" (Hayek 1976 [1998], p. 113).

Hayek compares his concept of spontaneous order in the market, or catallaxy, to the metaphor of the *invisible hand* used by Adam Smith and others, according to which the division of labor and free exchange in markets lead to mutual benefit and social welfare. He finds the argument behind the invisible hand too narrow since division of labor is also practiced in organizations and is therefore not a unique feature of spontaneous order. Moreover, Adam Smith emphasized that the market achieves socially beneficial outcomes—as if by an invisible hand—even though each individual pursues selfish goals. Catallaxy does not in any way imply selfish goals but is silent on the character of each agent's goals. Hayek's point is precisely that spontaneous order in a market economy does not require knowledge of individual goals.

Competition and the chance to make a profit act as a *discovery procedure*, revealing dispersed knowledge. If someone can make a profit by exploiting special circumstances, this is evidence that useful information has been discovered, which also sends a signal to other parties to follow the profitable behavior. Uncovered profit opportunities thus coordinate behavior, which creates order. The profit opportunities are found by trial and error, which inevitably leads to disappointment when expectations about profitable behavior turn out to be wrong. Expectations are adjusted through learning. "The process of adaptation operates, as do the adjustments of any self-organizing system, by what cybernetics has taught us to call negative feedback: responses to the differences between the expected and the actual results of actions so that these differences will be reduced" (Hayek 1976 [1998], p. 125). Hayek describes the goal-seeking behavior that we saw in Chap. 7.

Catallactic spontaneous order is an outcome, but what is the process that generates it? Hayek gives several answers to this question. First, mankind accidentally discovered the price system, which made it possible to develop the civilization we have today. Second, over long periods of history, conventions and other rules that regulate behavior in markets have evolved, along with the morals that induce agents to follow these informal rules. Behaviors become conventions when they prove beneficial and are therefore repeated. Again, Hayek (1979 [1989], p. 163] stresses the role of trial and error: "Man did not adopt new rules of conduct because he was intelligent. He became intelligent by submitting to new rules of conduct." Finally, and this is a crucial element in Hayek's thinking, some rules can be actively chosen to allow further self-organization into a spontaneous order. Hayek insists that these rules must be *abstract rules* that only provide a framework for individual behavior, but never command anyone to perform specific actions. "Rules of just conduct which are end-independent cannot determine what anyone must do . . ., but only what he must not do" (Hayek 1976 [1998], p. 123). He argues that "[s]pecific commands ('interference') in a catallaxy create disorder and can never be just" (p. 128). Interference is seen as an "isolated act of coercion, undertaken for the purpose of achieving a particular result," which will disrupt the overall order, privilege some agents, and disadvantage others. Only abstract rules that allow spontaneous order to emerge are defensible, because they maximize the chances of a randomly chosen person in society. For Hayek, this is the most desirable social order. The government must refrain from applying specific knowledge to particular situations and from correcting undesirable short-term random outcomes by interference. Rather, it should trust that the process of catallaxy will produce the best possible outcome in the long run if left alone. The only abstract rules a legislator can enact are property rights and torts, which give maximum freedom to the players of the catallaxy game. In this way, maximum progress and advancement of civilization can occur because agents are free to experiment with whatever they want. Only when creative minds have the freedom to do unusual things can new things happen. Personal freedom is important, even if most people do not use it. But in order for the few individuals who move society forward with novel ideas to benefit, the greatest freedom must be given to all.

8.6.2 Hayek's Theory and Complexity Economics

Hayek was clearly influenced by complexity thinking. He published an article entitled "The Theory of Complex Phenomena" (Hayek 1964) and referred to precursors of complexity theory such as cybernetics, von Bertalanffy's system theory, information theory, and also to the work of Ilya Prigogine that we will discuss more in the next section (see Hayek 1979 [1998], p. 158/9). His characterization of the economy is very similar to the definitions of complex adaptive systems we saw in Chap. 2:

> *In particular, in order to explain the economic aspects of large social systems, we have to account for the course of a flowing stream, constantly adapting itself as a whole to changes in circumstances of which each participant can know only a small fraction, and not for a hypothetical state of equilibrium determined by a set of ascertainable data.* (Hayek 1979 [1998], p. 159)

A central point of Hayek's thinking is that complexity implies fundamental limits to our knowledge, which takes us back to our heuristic definition of complexity as a state that is difficult to describe, understand, predict, and control. In the categorization used in Chap. 2, Hayek's work would belong to soft complexity science. In his 1974 Nobel Prize speech entitled "The Pretence of Knowledge," Hayek clearly contrasts the social sciences with the physical sciences, because the social sciences have to deal with *essential complexity*, defined as "structures whose characteristic properties can be exhibited only by models made up of relatively large numbers of variables" (Hayek 1989, p. 4). Hayek acknowledges that some branches of physics also deal with complex phenomena arising from a large number of individual elements, but he considers this *unorganized complexity* to be relatively simple. Unorganized complexity means that the character of the resulting patterns depends only on the properties of the individual elements, but not on the manner in which the elements are connected with each other. Unorganized complexity can be analyzed statistically, which is not possible for *organized complexity*, which requires full information about the elements and their connections. Since we can never ascertain this full information in practice, our knowledge will always remain limited and can never reach the precision and completeness of the knowledge in the physical sciences. He criticizes (neoclassical) economists for pretending to have this knowledge and for making numerical predictions which are likely to be wrong due to our imperfect knowledge. Economists, who behave as if they were physicists and as if statistical methods could be used to make predictions, give economics only the appearance of being scientific. For Hayek, such behavior is misleading.

Hayek argues that the best the social sciences can do is to make predictions about patterns. Social science theories predict that we should be able to observe certain patterns in the social system, but not others. Because they exclude certain patterns, they are falsifiable and therefore scientific. The notion of pattern prediction implies a certain superiority of theory over empirics, since we might not be able to see complex patterns in social systems if we did not expect them. This is related to our discussion in Sect. 3.2 of Chap. 3 that many patterns are not just there, but depend on our perspective. Social scientists can never derive precise and testable point predictions about, say, prices or the deviation of wages from the equilibrium wage, because it is impossible to ascertain all the particular facts (or data) relevant to the specific problem. Hayek illustrates the idea of pattern prediction with the analogy of a ball game played by people of roughly equal skill. An observer will never have enough information to predict which team will win, because the outcome depends on the states and actions of each player at each moment of the game. However, if the observer knows the rules of the game, it is possible to identify what kind of game is being played, and what kinds of actions can and cannot be expected. For example, if the observer identifies the game as soccer, one can predict that only the goalkeepers will touch the ball with their hands. Note that we also saw a kind of pattern prediction in the Ising model: we can predict that all spins will be identical if the temperature is low enough, but we cannot say ex ante whether the spins will be $+1$ or -1.

Hayek's thinking shares many concepts with complexity economics as presented in this book. He emphasizes the limits of predicting and controlling complex systems. Economic agents in his theory interact locally on the basis of private information; they are heterogeneous, especially with respect to their goals; they adapt to changing circumstances; and they are necessarily boundedly rational because of their limited knowledge. All of this is very similar to the characterization of agents in agent-based models in Sect. 8.2.2. Hayek also mentions feedback as a mechanism in self-organizing processes, which is consistent with the models we saw earlier.

There are three ways in which Hayekian and Austrian thinking differs from complexity economics. First, Hayek and many Austrian economists are deeply skeptical of the use of mathematics and formal methods in economics. While Hayek has some sympathy for the use of algebraic equations as a tool to clarify theoretical ideas, he does not believe in the usefulness of statistical analysis in economics. Other Austrian economists even reject mathematical theoretical modeling. Complexity economics, based on complexity thinking (as opposed to soft complexity science), considers statistics and formal modeling as useful research tools, provided that the researcher is aware of the limitations of formal methods. Second, Hayek draws a sharp contrast between order and disorder. He equates order with spontaneous order resulting from a catallactic process. As discussed above, Hayek (1976) argues that (government) intervention in a catallaxy creates disorder. Mixtures of specific rules and abstract or planned organization and self-organization do not lead to catallaxy, which he defines exclusively as order. From the perspective of complexity economics, this concept of order is restrictive. In complexity economics, any stable outcome of a self-organization process alone or in combination with planned organization can be defined as a state of order. In complexity economics, order in the sense of symmetry, separation, and correlation is rather synonymous with the more common term "pattern." Finally, Hayek's theory is deeply normative and cannot be separated from his political recommendations. Hayek openly advocates a laissez-faire state that does not interfere with the self-organization of markets, because any interference would destroy the desirable spontaneous order that maximizes the chances of all individuals. Maximizing these opportunities in the long run leads to a specific version of social progress, strongly linked to technological progress and material growth. For him, the problem of economic theory is not only to understand what happens in the economy, but also to prescribe how to achieve his (normative) vision of order. Complexity economics focuses more on analyzing how self-organizing processes work in the economy and what the possible consequences of attempts to control complex systems might be. While value-free research is not possible in the social sciences, complexity economics ideally separates normative and positive statements more than Hayek does.

8.7 The Economy as a Dissipative Structure

Although Hayek was inspired by scientists such as Ludwig von Bertalanffy and Ilya Prigogine, he saw economics as distinct from the physical sciences because of the greater complexity of social systems. He sharply criticized mainstream neoclassical economics for inappropriately applying scientific methods to social systems. While Hayek was probably correct in his criticism that economists should not simply adopt research methods from the natural sciences, he may have been wrong to claim that economics cannot be as scientific as the natural sciences. It is the purpose of this section to explain this claim. In particular, we provide a careful explanation of the scientific concept of a *dissipative structure* and argue that this concept is useful for understanding the economy.

In a detailed historical study, Mirowski (1989) shows that neoclassical economic theory is a flawed emulation of what he calls "proto-energetics," i.e. the theory of classical mechanics of the 1860s, before the rise of modern thermodynamics. The early neoclassical economists William Stanley Jevons, Léon Walras, and Vilfredo Pareto, who pioneered the mathematization of economics, were trained scientists and engineers. Irving Fisher, whom Joseph Schumpeter called "the best economist the United States has ever produced" and whose 1892 Ph.D. dissertation Paul Samuelson called "the best of all Ph.D. dissertations in economics," wrote his dissertation under the supervision of the eminent theoretical physicist Willard Gibbs. Although Fisher was not the first economist to copy the formalism of proto-energetics from physics, he did so in the most sophisticated way and decisively shaped the canonical neoclassical model of consumer choice. Fisher used the physical model of a point mass (particle) moving through a field of force as a metaphor for the functions of a market. He translated "particle" to "individual," "force" to "marginal utility," "work" to "disutility," and "energy" to "utility." He also borrowed the concept of mechanical equilibrium, according to which equilibrium is reached when net energy (energy minus work) is maximized, which he translated into equilibrium when profit (utility minus disutility) is maximized. The transfer of this theory from physics to economics is deeply flawed because the physical theory requires conservation of energy, for which there is no reasonable equivalent in economics. A system in which a quantity like energy is conserved is called a *conservative system.* Conservative systems are isolated systems that do not exchange energy with their environment. In Fisher's formalism, the conservation of energy implies that the sum of total expenditure and the sum of total utility in a closed trading system must be constant, which seems odd. Furthermore, the conservation of energy implies that the system is independent of time. In order to have a unique equilibrium, *false trading* at nonequilibrium prices must be precluded. Technically speaking, conservative systems cannot have any attracting fixed points, but instead have centers. But as we saw in Chap. 6, a center can never be reached if the initial conditions are different from the center. This problem lies behind the assumption of the Walrasian auctioneer, who collects bids and asks to determine the equilibrium prices, before any actual trading takes place. Thus, the physical theory had to be converted into a basically static theory in order to avoid problems with inconsistent dynamics.

Walras, Pareto, and Fisher were confronted with these implausibilities by physicists and mathematicians, but dismissed the critiques and clung to the formalism. Later neoclassical economists, especially Paul Samuelson, aggressively defended the status of economics as a physics-like social science without resolving the fundamental flaws. But the physics of the 1860s, on which neoclassical theory is based did not even contain the concept of *entropy,* which is fundamental to modern thermodynamics and poses a problem for proto-energetics, because it imposes a *direction on time.* In isolated systems, entropy can never decrease. Samuelson, however, tried to discredit critics of neoclassical economics who referred to entropy as cranks or half-baked speculators. Overall, Mirowski (1989, p. 400/401) concludes that neoclassical economics' fixation on mid-nineteenth century physics prevented economists from taking advantage of the scientific breakthroughs in physics in the twentieth century:

> *In the ensuing century, physics has largely repudiated this image of explanation. New forms of explanation have taken their place: stochastic forms, forms allowing for interaction with the observer, forms allowing for emergent novelty arising out of apparent chaos, forms allowing "something for nothing." In such a cultural climate, neoclassical economics must appear atavistic, if not irrelevant.*

With its origins in the physics of the second half of the twentieth century, complexity economics is open to more modern scientific achievements and shares the concerns about the scientific validity of neoclassical economics (see also Sect. 4.4.1 in Chap. 4). It is useful for economists to take a fresh look at the natural sciences, again at physics, but perhaps even more so at biology. In contrast to the

Fig. 8.34 The economy dependent on solar energy, earth energy, and the geobiosphere. Source: Author

neoclassical economists who sought scientific respectability by emulating physics, complexity economists should not simply use physical models metaphorically, but incorporate the scientific theories into their own work. There are at least two important insights from the twentieth century sciences that are relevant to economics. First, the entire history of the Earth, including the history of human civilization, can be understood as self-organizing *dissipative systems far from thermodynamic equilibrium*. Thus, neoclassical economists chose the wrong scientific basis for their theory. Second, we cannot understand economic activity without properly recognizing the role of *energy*. After all, all the energy used by the economic system comes either from the sun or from the earth. Without energy, neither the geobiosphere nor human civilization would exist (see Fig. 8.34).

8.7.1 Thermodynamic Equilibrium and Entropy

Before we can talk about dissipative structures, it is useful to describe *thermodynamic equilibrium* and *entropy*, which are fundamental concepts in thermodynamics. A system is in *thermodynamic equilibrium* if there are no macroscopic flows of matter or of energy within the system. Multiple systems are in thermodynamic equilibrium if there are no macroscopic flows of matter or energy between the systems.

Thermodynamic equilibrium requires that a system be in thermal, mechanical, and chemical equilibrium. *Thermal equilibrium* means that there is no flow of thermal energy, which implies that there are no temperature differences. *Mechanical equilibrium* means that no work is being done in the system implying that there is constant pressure everywhere. *Chemical equilibrium* means that the concentrations of reactants and products in a chemical reaction are constant, such that no change in the properties of the system can be observed. In thermodynamic equilibrium, there is no macroscopic change. This means that microscopic exchange can occur at the particle level, but in a perfectly balanced way.

This characterization of thermodynamic equilibrium is rather crude and can be qualified in many ways. A basic qualification is whether thermodynamic equilibrium refers to an ideal state in an isolated system or to approximate equilibrium states in real systems. An *isolated system* does not interact with other systems. In particular, it does not exchange matter and energy with other systems. In practice, true isolated systems do not exist, with the possible exception of the universe as a whole. For all other systems, the concept of an isolated system is a theoretical hypothesis that can often be a useful approximation of real-world situations when interactions with the environment are small and/or slow. A *closed system* allows the exchange of energy (heat or work) with the environment or another system, but not of matter. Finally, an *open system* exchanges both energy and matter with its surroundings.

The energy U contained in a thermodynamic system is called the *internal energy*. In an isolated system, the internal energy is constant. In a closed system, the internal energy changes due to heat transfer, Q, and the work done by the system on its surroundings, W, hence

$$\Delta U = Q - W.$$

This is *the first law of thermodynamics*, which states that energy can be transformed but must be conserved. Heat is the state of energy associated with the random motion of molecules. Without heat, there is no motion. Heat is necessary for energy transformation, but because the motion of molecules associated with heat is disorganized, some of the heat energy is unusable. In an open system, where the transfer of matter is possible, the internal energy also changes due to the internal energy of the transferred matter, hence $\Delta U = Q - W + \Delta U_{matter}$. The first law of thermodynamics for a closed system can also be expressed for infinitesimal changes as $dU = \delta Q - \delta W$, where d denotes an exact differential (or total or full differential) and δ is an inexact differential whose integral is path dependent. If the work is done by change of volume V at constant pressure P, we can write $\delta W = PdV$. According to the second law of thermodynamics, the change in heat is related to the change in entropy S for a given temperature T. For a reversible process, the *second law of thermodynamics* states that

$$dS = \frac{\delta Q}{T}.$$

Therefore, we can state the *fundamental thermodynamic relation* for a closed system in thermal equilibrium as $dU = TdS - PdV$, which combines the four important thermodynamic quantities absolute temperature T, entropy S, pressure P, and volume V.

In Chap. 3, Shannon entropy H was introduced as a measure of the information content of a probability distribution:

$$H = -\sum_i p_i \log_2 p_i.$$

In statistical thermodynamics, entropy S is defined in a very similar way using the *Gibbs entropy* formula:

$$S = -k_B \sum_i p_i \ln p_i.$$

Here, k_B is the *Boltzmann constant* and p_i refers to the probability of *microstate i* of the system. A thermodynamic system consists of individual particles, each of which can be in a particular state. In the Ising model we saw in Sect. 8.2.2, the states of the particles were their spins (+ or −). A microstate of a system is one specific configuration of all possible Ω configurations of individual states. For example, if there are four particles that can have two states (+ or −), there are $\Omega = 2^4 = 16$ possible microstates: {(+,+,+,+), (+,+,+,−), (+,+,−,+), (+,−,+,+), (−,+,+,+), (+,+,−,−), (+,−,+,−), (−,+,−,+), (−,−,+,+), (+,−,−,+), (−,+,+,−), (−,−,−,+), (−,−,+,−), (−,+,−,−), (+,−,−,−), (−,−,−,−)}. Each microstate has an energy E_i. A macrostate, which has macroscopic properties such as temperature, pressure, volume, and density, can be achieved with different microstates. The system's internal energy is the average of energies over all microstates: $U = \sum_{i=1}^{\Omega} p_i E_i$. Work W and heat Q are macroscopic properties of a thermodynamic system that result from the underlying microstates. Work is the transfer of energy associated with an ordered, macroscopic action of the system. In this case, the distribution of individual energy states does not change, but the energy levels do: $\delta W = \sum_i p_i dE_i$. Heat, on the other hand, is associated with disordered, microscopic action of the system. This means that the distributions change while the values of the energy levels do not change: $\delta Q = \sum_i E_i dp_i$.

We have already seen that Shannon entropy is maximized when all states are equally likely, i.e. when the distribution is completely random. Shannon entropy is thus a measure of the uncertainty of a system. Thermodynamic entropy has similar interpretations, which is not surprising given the analogous definitions of Shannon entropy H and Gibbs entropy S. Thermodynamic entropy is often interpreted as a measure of disorder in the system, although there is much debate about the meaning of disorder. Another interpretation of thermodynamic entropy is that it measures the lack of knowledge or uncertainty about the microstates of a system. It is intuitive that the more microstates there are, the greater the uncertainty about the microstates of the system. We can illustrate this using the Boltzmann version of entropy and the Ising model.

Ludwig Boltzmann defined the entropy of the macrostate of an ideal gas as a function of the number of microstates of the gas,[6] Ω. The microstates of a gas are given by the positions and the momenta of the individual gas molecules. The formula for *Boltzmann entropy* is

$$S = k_B \ln \Omega.$$

Let us assume that all molecules have the same momentum. Then the microstates depend only on the position of the molecules in space. If all molecules are clustered in a few positions, then there are few microstates. However, if the molecules are all scattered in space, there are many possible arrangements of the molecules, i.e. microstates. Boltzmann's formula assumes that for each macrostate, all related microstates are equally probable. The probability of each microstate is then the inverse of the number of microstates, $1/\Omega$. The number of microstates can be determined by counting all possible permutations of the possible states of the molecules, $\Omega = \frac{N!}{\prod_i N_i!}$, where N is the total number of molecules, i denotes the possible conditions (e.g., the position), and N_i is the number of molecules in condition i.

The Ising model can serve as an example of how Boltzmann entropy is related to the state of the system. In the Ising model, there are only two possible conditions of the atoms: +1 and − 1. Let us assume that we have a lattice with $N = 16$ atoms. If $N_+ = N_- = 8$, we get $\Omega = \frac{16!}{8!8!} = 12{,}870$ possible microstates of how the positive and the negative spins can be arranged on the lattice. If there are 12 positive spins and 4 negative spins, we get $\Omega = \frac{16!}{12!4!} = 1{,}820$ and with 15 positive spins, there are 16 possibilities to locate the one negative spin, $\Omega = \frac{16!}{15!1!} = 16$. Hence, the Boltzmann entropy in the Ising model is largest when the frequency of positive and negative spins is 50%. In this case, there is no magnetization and at high temperature, the spins are randomly scattered over the lattice (see Fig. 8.7).[7] Entropy is low at low temperature, when spontaneous magnetization occurs and a temporally stable ratio $\frac{N_+}{N_-} \neq 1$ has been attained. An increase in temperature means that heat energy is added to the system, which requires an increase in entropy according to the second law of thermodynamics.

[6] Boltzmann used W instead of Ω. We use Ω in order to avoid confusion with work W.

[7] Strictly speaking, Boltzmann entropy is not the right entropy measure here, because the probability of the microstates is not the same. Close to the critical temperature, there is spatial correlation of the spins (See Figure 8.10), which means the individual probabilities are not independent of each other. The spatial pattern is a kind of order. Therefore, Boltzmann entropy overestimates the real entropy at intermediate temperatures. Since the spatial correlation vanishes at high temperature, the error is smaller there.

Erwin Schrödinger wrote the Boltzmann equation as $S = k_B \ln D$ and interpreted D as the quantitative measure of the atomic disorder caused by heat motion and random mixing of particles. If we define $Or = 1/D$ as order, we obtain

$$-S = k_B \ln 1/D = k_B \ln Or.$$

Negative entropy is thus a measure of order. Finally, we can define *negentropy* *NE* as

$$NE = S_{eq} - S,$$

where S_{eq} is the maximum entropy possible in thermodynamic equilibrium. Negentropy is the higher, the further away the system is from equilibrium. It can be interpreted as a measure of information about the system, because a system in thermodynamic equilibrium with $S = S_{eq}$ cannot be distinguished from its environment. Therefore, we call $I = NE$ *thermodynamic information*. The *negentropy principle of information*, derived by Léon Brillouin, states that the production of one bit of information requires energy of at least $k_B \ln 2$ *joule* $\approx 10^{-23}$ *joule* per degree Kelvin. There is thus a direct relationship between energy and information (see Tribus and McIrvine 1971). Shannon entropy and thermodynamic entropy are essentially the same concept, although Shannon entropy is more general and is applicable to all kinds of uncertainties and systems.

8.7.2 Dissipative Structures

The concept of dissipative structures, proposed by the physical chemist and 1977 Nobel Laureate in Chemistry, Ilya Prigogine, is important in giving a precise scientific meaning to self-organization. While it was originally used to describe and explain physical phenomena such as lasers, turbulent flows, convection or cyclones, and chemical phenomena such as the Belousov–Zhabotinsky reaction, it has also become popular in the study of living organisms and ecosystems in biology. It is a small step from dissipative structures in biology to economic dissipative structures, as we will see.

In contrast to conservative systems, *dissipative systems* are thermodynamically open systems that exchange energy and matter with their environment. They are self-organizing in the sense that they produce internal order (organization) by dissipating energy, i.e. by producing entropy in their environment. The resulting order, which is a temporary steady state far away from thermodynamic equilibrium, is called a *dissipative structure*. A dissipative structure is a dynamic equilibrium, in which the state of the system is kept constant over time by balancing inflows and outflows. Dynamic equilibrium is a familiar concept in economics. For instance, the capital stock in a steady state (which is a dynamic equilibrium) is constant if investment (the inflow) is equal to depreciation (the outflow) (see Figs. 7.28 and 7.31 in Chap. 7).

The important elements of dissipative structures are that they occur in open systems and that they maintain their order by degrading energy. Let us see what that means.

To understand why dissipative structures are important, we need to consider thermodynamic equilibrium and the concept of irreversibility. *Irreversibility* means that a process proceeds in one direction only and cannot be reversed. An isolated thermodynamic system approaches thermodynamic equilibrium, which is an irreversible process. A formulation of the second law of thermodynamics is that the entropy of an isolated system must increase until it is maximized at thermodynamic equilibrium. Thus, in an isolated system, order decreases with time. This property of entropy gives time a direction, we speak of *entropy as the arrow of time*. As mentioned earlier, perhaps the only isolated system is the universe.[8] The second law of thermodynamics therefore suggests that the entropy of the entire universe will increase until the universe reaches a thermodynamic equilibrium in which macroscopic processes come to a halt. This state is often referred to as the *heat death* of the universe. Although in practice there are no isolated systems, we can use this concept to describe some real-world phenomena. Imagine a container filled with water and a dye. Suppose that initially all the dye is on one side and all the water is on the other side of the container, possibly because there was a barrier in the middle that was removed. Over time, the dye and water will mix until the concentration of the dye in the water is the same everywhere. Then the mixed liquid will have the same pale color everywhere. During the mixing process, the dye is concentrated in some parts of the container, creating patterns of darker and lighter colors. Irreversibility means that in practice we never observe the opposite process. Although in principle the dye and water molecules could separate due to their random motion, this is highly unlikely for large numbers of molecules. In this sense, the second law of thermodynamics is a statistical law that says it is extremely unlikely that there is spontaneous order in large numbers of particles such as the 6×10^{23} atoms in one mole of a gas. Since we observe all kinds of order everywhere in the universe, we need a theory that explains the motions away from thermodynamic equilibrium, which is the theory of dissipative structures.

In open systems, we can divide the change of a system's entropy over time, dS, into an internal part, d_iS, and an external part, d_eS, (Nicolis and Prigogine 1977), hence

$$dS = d_iS + d_eS.$$

The external part refers to the entropy flow due to the exchange of energy or matter between the system and its environment. The internal part is the entropy production within the system. According to the second law of thermodynamics, the internal entropy of the system cannot decrease, because of the irreversible processes inside the system, such as diffusion, heat production, and chemical reactions, hence

[8] Physicists are not sure about this, but there are no other isolated systems in the strict sense.

$$d_iS \geq 0.$$

In an isolated system, $d_eS = 0$ and hence $dS = d_iS \geq 0$. An open system can exchange entropy with its environment. If there is a sufficiently large inflow of external negative entropy, $dS_e = -dS_i < 0$, the system can maintain its order, $dS = 0$. If the decrease in the external contribution is greater than the internal entropy production, $dS_e < -dS_i < 0$, then the total entropy of the system decreases, which is equivalent to an increase in the order of the system. An inflow of negative entropy is an inflow of negentropy. We can also say that dissipative systems import order or information from outside. We can conclude that all systems must be dissipative structures and therefore open or at least not isolated. Otherwise they would lose their order and move out of the steady state toward the thermodynamic equilibrium according to the second law of thermodynamics. In order to produce or maintain their organized structure, they require low-entropy energy inputs. However, this implies that dissipative structures reduce the order of their environment.

We said above that dissipative structures degrade energy in the process of creating order. Degradation implies that there must be different qualities of energy. One way to define the quality of energy is whether it is able to do work. Thermal energy (heat) generally has a lower quality than other forms like electricity or mechanical motion, because low-temperature waste heat cannot be recovered to do work. According to the second law of thermodynamics, a change in entropy corresponds to a change in heat. Therefore, the exchange of entropy between an open system and its environment occurs through heat. The energy that has the potential to do work is called *exergy* (or *available energy* or *potential energy* or *useful energy*). The exergy of a system is defined relative to the system's environment and requires an energy differential between the system and the environment. This differential can arise due to differences in temperature, chemical composition, or electrical potential. If the system is in equilibrium with its environment in the sense that there no differentials, then exergy is zero. Thus, exergy is related to material and energy flows between the system and the environment and corresponds to the portion of an energy flow that can be made to do useful work. Due to the creation of entropy and the generation of low-temperature waste heat, exergy is destroyed in energy conversion processes—in contrast to energy, which is conserved. Thus, degradation of energy means loss of exergy. Maintaining order in a dissipative structure requires a permanent supply of exergy.

8.7.3 Dissipative Structures in Nature

So far, the discussion of dissipative structures and self-organization has been rather abstract and focused on the physical aspects. Dissipative structures are central to nature. In fact, all forms of life are dissipative structures. The basic unit of life is a *cell* that has a metabolism. *Metabolism* is the set of all chemical reactions that take place within a cell. A cell's metabolism extracts energy from the environment and converts it into energy that can be used to synthesize organic material, especially proteins, and to sustain the cell's vital processes. A cell is a dissipative structure that creates internal order at the expense of increasing disorder in the environment. When the supply of external inputs ceases, a cell cannot maintain its metabolism and dies. A cell can also die due to the ingestion of *toxins*, i.e. chemical substances that damage the cell's biomass or interfere with its metabolism.

Figure 8.35 illustrates cellular respiration as a form of metabolism. A cell is a dissipative system with a membrane as its boundary. Through the membrane, the cell takes in nutrients (especially glucose $C_6H_{12}O_6$), minerals (especially nitrogen and phosphorus), and oxygen O_2. The main outputs of the cell are carbon dioxide CO_2 and water H_2O. Cell respiration releases energy in the form of heat given off to the environment and chemical energy (see Fig. 8.36), mainly in the form of adenosine triphosphate (ATP), which is used for internal energy transfer.

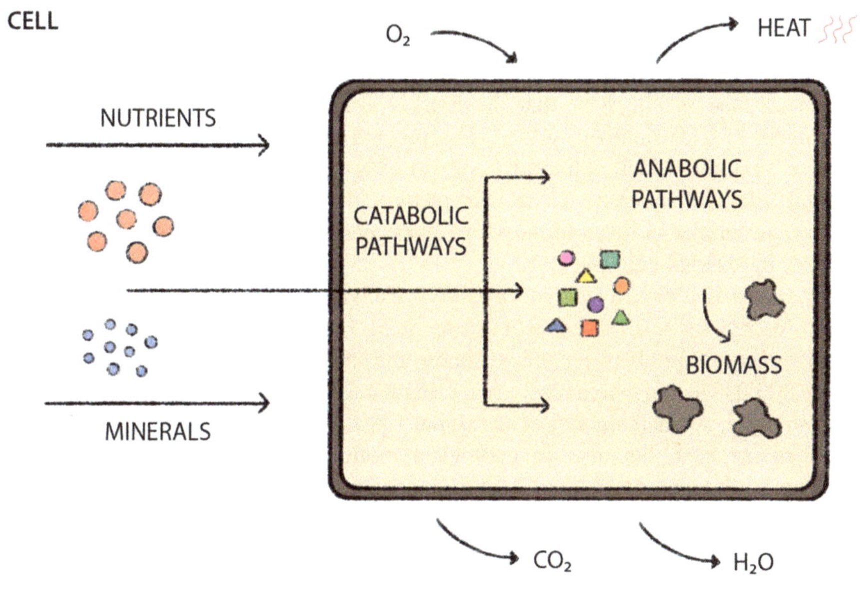

Fig. 8.35 Cell respiration. Source: Author

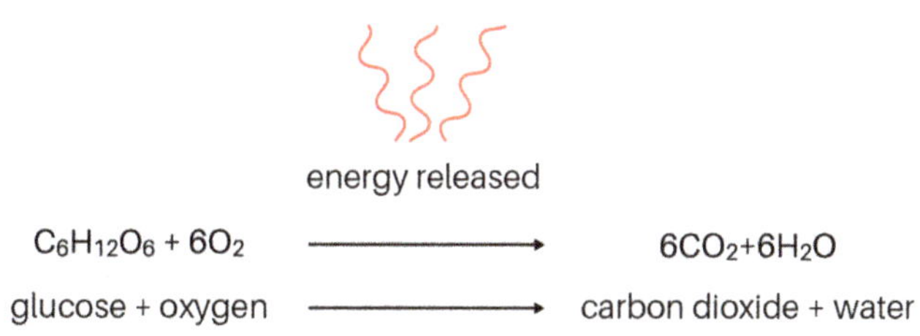

Fig. 8.36 Release of energy during cellular respiration. Source: Author

Metabolism consists of two sets of pathways called catabolism and anabolism. *Catabolism* is the set of pathways that break down large input molecules into smaller units and release energy. *Anabolism* is the set of pathways that build biomass, specifically in the form of the 20 amino acids that are the building blocks of proteins. Amino acids are composed of nitrogen N, carbon C, oxygen O, and hydrogen H and are the basic structures—or the alphabet—of life. Catabolic processes increase entropy because they destroy the structure of complex macromolecules by breaking them down into smaller parts. Conversely, anabolic processes decrease entropy by creating order in the form of highly complex macromolecules such as proteins.

It is a very important insight that natural processes in the *biosphere* (the biological world) are cyclical, as shown in Fig. 8.37. The process of cellular respiration works in *heterotrophic* organisms, i.e. organisms that cannot produce their own food, but require organic matter as food. All animals, fungi, and some bacteria are heterotrophs. They are also called *consumers* in the food chain. The food for heterotrophic organisms comes from *autotrophic* organisms that produce organic matter through photosynthesis. Plants, algae, and many bacteria are autotrophs. They are called *primary producers*.

We can see in Fig. 8.37 that the Earth's joint metabolism of producers and consumers is a dissipative system. The process requires external energy in the form of sunlight, which autotrophs convert into organic matter. They thus create internal order and increase external entropy through heat production. Consumers use the organic matter in respiration, which also generates heat and contributes to an increase in external entropy.

The Earth is a closed system, because it exchanges energy with space, but not matter (except for small inputs from meteorites). Figure 8.38 shows the accounting of daily energy flows between the biosphere and space and within the biosphere (see Odum 2007). The biosphere receives approximately 4000 kcal/m^2 of energy per day from sunlight. A small amount of additional 1 kcal is provided by the hot interior of the Earth as heat, but also as geological motion. In addition to the resulting 4001 kcal, producers receive 0.1 kcal from consumers, e.g. from pollinating insects or the transport of mineral by animals. Producers convert the total of 4001.1 kcal of energy into 1 g/m^2 of organic matter per day, which contains about 4 kcal of organic potential energy. 3997.1 kcal/m^2 per day are dissipated as heat. The 4 kcal contained in the organic matter are converted by the consumers into 0.1 kcal flowing back to

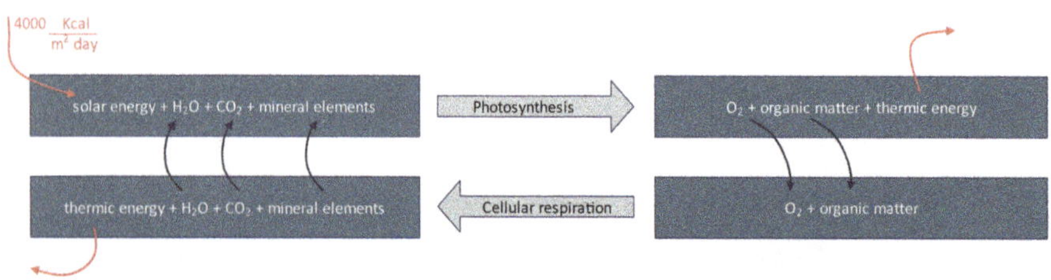

Fig. 8.37 Cyclical Earth metabolism of photosynthesis and cellular respiration. Source: Author

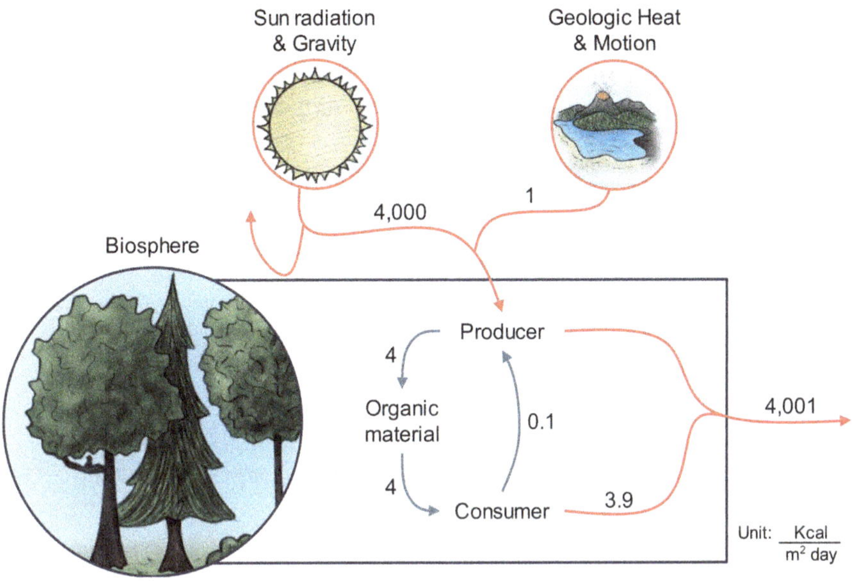

Fig. 8.38 Daily energy flow of the Earth metabolism in the biosphere. Source: Author

the producers and 3.9 kcal of heat. Thus, a total of 4001 kcal/m^2 of heat energy is radiated back into space.

From an economic perspective, the ecological term consumer may be misleading, because the consumers of the organic matter provided by the producers perform work that can be classified as storing work and processing work. *Storing work* involves the production of biomass (see Fig. 8.37). *Processing work* is useful from the perspective of the system's function. Some of this work consists of actions that control other activities in the system through feedback loops. Useful work requires potential or available energy (= exergy). In physical terms, *power* is the work per unit of time, $P = dW/dt$ or the flow of exergy.

8.7.4 The Fourth Law of Thermodynamics

Following Alfred Lotka and others (e.g., Boltzmann and Schrödinger), Howard T. Odum formulated the *maximum power principle* for thermodynamics in open systems (Odum and Pinkerton 1955), which has also been proposed as the *fourth law of thermodynamics*. The maximum power principle can be expressed as follows:

> *During self-organization, system designs develop and prevail that maximize power intake, energy transformation, and those uses that reinforce production and efficiency.* (Odum 1995, p. 311)

The maximum power principle can be interpreted as an attempt to formalize the process of evolution in ecosystems. In this view, evolution is a struggle for useful energy or exergy. Those systems that organize themselves to maximize power will prevail. Another formulation of the maximum power principle is:

> *Systems which maximize their flow of energy survive in competition. In other words, rather than merely accepting the fact that more energy per unit of time is transformed in a process which operates at maximum power, this principle says that systems organize and structure themselves naturally to maximize power. Systems regulate themselves according to the maximum power principle. Over time, the systems which maximize power are selected for whereas those that do not are selected against and eventually eliminated. ... Odum argues ... that the free market mechanisms of the economy effectively do the same thing for human systems and that our economic evolution to date is a product of that selection process.* (Gilliland 1978, pp. 101–102)

Note that both versions of the fourth law of thermodynamics relate evolutionary success to power, i.e. the inflow or capture of exergy. Jørgensen (2002, p. 339) suggests an alternative formulation of the fourth law:

> *If a system is moved away from thermodynamic equilibrium by the application of a flow of exergy, it will utilize all avenues available to build up as much dissipative structure (store as much exergy) as possible, to reduce the effects of the applied gradient.*

While this version of the fourth law is very similar to the maximum power principle, it differs in that the goal of evolution is exergy storage rather than exergy capture. In other words, evolution is a struggle for exergy and results in the maximization of stored exergy rather than power.

The maximum power principle postulates the maximization of *energy transformation*, which implies different qualities of energy or an *energy hierarchy*. Odum (2007, p. 65) defines an organization as a *hierarchy* when "many units of one kind combine to support another kind of unit that feeds back control." As an example, he uses an army as an organization, in which many privates support the actions of fewer sergeants, whose control actions feed back to the soldiers (see Fig. 8.39).

Odum conceptualized the energy hierarchy very much like a hierarchical human organization. In fact, he even claims that human organizations are special cases of energy hierarchies. He proposes the universal hierarchical self-organization of energy systems as a fifth law of energy stating that "all the energy transformations known can be connected in a series network according to the quantitity of one kind of energy required for the next" (Odum 2007, p. 65).

Figure 8.40 shows the transformation of solar energy into electrical light through a series of intermediate steps. The figure shows the steps and the available power after each step. To obtain 1 kcal/unit of time of electrical light, 14 kcal/[time] of electrical power is required, which is generated in a power plant. For this, the power plant needs coal with a power of 50 kcal/[time], which comes from 800 kcal/[time] of wood fossilized by geological processes. The plants needed 2.4 10^6 kcal/[time] of sunlight in order to produce the wood. Odum argues that one unit of power at one step or scale cannot be directly compared with one unit of power at another scale,

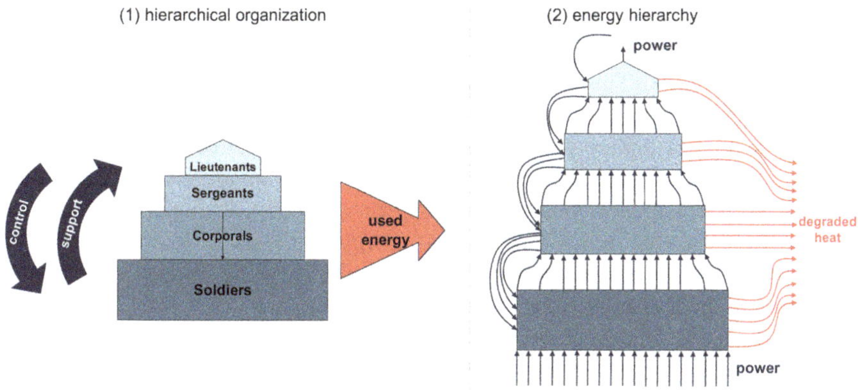

Fig. 8.39 An army as an example for a hierarchical organization and an energy hierarchy. Source: Author

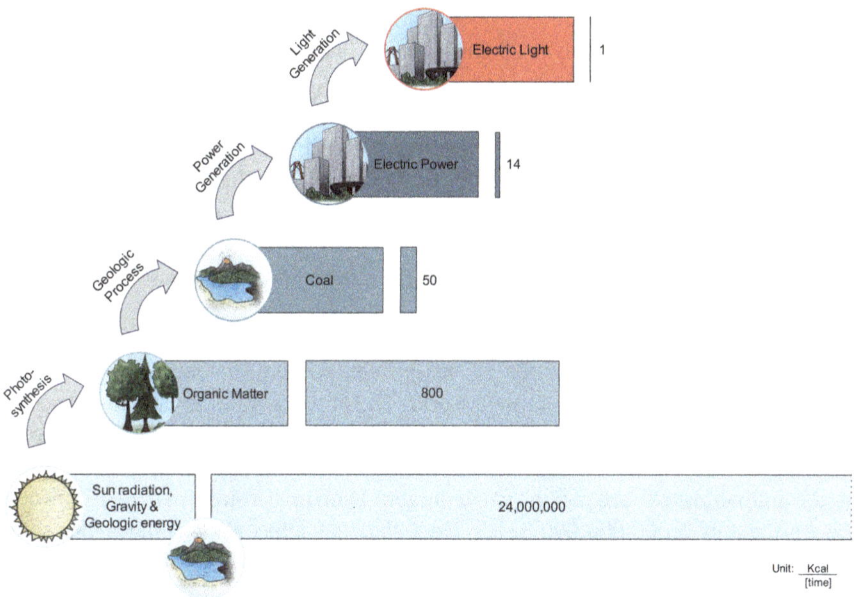

Fig. 8.40 Energy transformation from sunlight to electric light. Source: Author

because power at higher levels of the hierarchy is more valuable than power at lower levels. In general, it is not possible to easily substitute one form of energy for another. For instance, plants cannot substitute fossil fuel for photosynthesis and humans cannot substitute sunlight for food. High-quality energy, such as electricity or human services, is more concentrated and more flexible than the same amount of low-quality energy contained in coal. More flexible means that it can be applied in a wider range of uses. In addition, higher levels control lower levels through reinforcing feedback. This reinforcing feedback makes it possible to amplify the capture of lower-level energy.

To make energy and power comparable at different scales of the energy hierarchy, Odum defined *emergy* and *empower*. *Emergy* is the available energy of one kind that has been previously consumed directly or indirectly, to make a product or service. It is measured in the same units as energy (e.g., kcal or joules J), but with the prefix em- (e.g., emkcal). Emergy is embodied energy. Since solar energy is at the bottom of the hierarchy, it makes sense to use it as a numeraire and to express all kinds of energy at higher scales in solar emkcal (sekcal) or solar emjoules (sej). *Empower* is emergy flow per unit of time. 1 kcal of solar energy is equal to 1 sekcal. We define *solar transformity* as

$$\text{Solar transformity} = \text{Solar empower}/\text{Power}$$

or

$$\begin{aligned}\text{Solar transformity} &= (\text{Solar emergy}/\text{Time})/(\text{Energy}/\text{Time}) \\ &= \text{Solar emergy}/\text{Energy}.\end{aligned}$$

In the example in Fig. 8.40, plants need 2.4 10^6 kcal/[time] solar energy = 2.4 10^6 sekcal to produce power from wood of 800 kcal/[time]. Therefore, the solar transformity of wood is 2,400,000 sekcal / 800 kcal = 3000 sekcal/kcal. The solar transformity of coal is 2,400,000 sekcal / 60 kcal = 40,000 sekcal/kcal and the solar transformity of electric light amounts to 2.4 10^6 sekcal/kcal. In the example, it has cost 2.4 10^6 sekcal to produce 1 kcal of electric light.

Table 8.4 gives some estimates of the solar transformities of different kinds of energy flows. The first four kinds of energy after sunlight belong to physical and geological processes in the inanimate world. The emergy flows in the biosphere are much larger than the emergy flows in the geosphere. Protein foods have solar transformities between 1000,000 seJ/J and 4,000,000 seJ/J. The solar transformities in the human world are again much larger. Human services can have a solar transformity of 5,000,000,000 seJ/J. Note that the table also includes the solar transformity of information, which can reach up to 10^{13} seJ/J.

There are several ways to relate information to energy. We already learned earlier that the generation of 1 bit of information requires 10^{-23} *joule* per degree Kelvin. So we can estimate the information content of an information carrier and multiply it by the energy per bit. Alternatively, we can calculate the emergy of an information carrier such as a book. For example, suppose it takes an author 2 years to write a book. An average person needs 2500 kcal or 10,465,000 J per day, which amounts to 7,639,450,000 J in 730 days. To obtain the emergy of the book, we need an estimate of the author's transformity. Odum (1988) estimates the solar transformity of a person with post-college education to be 343 × 10^6 seJ/J. Let us assume an experienced author with a transformity of 500 × 10^6 seJ/J. Hence, the emergy of the

Table 8.4 Typical solar transformities

Item	Solar emjoules per joule (sej/J)
Sunlight	1
Wind kinetic energy	623
Unconsolidated organic matter	4420
Geopotential energy in rivers	23,564
Mechanical energy, waves, tides	17,000—29,000
Consolidated fuels	18,000–58,000
Food, greens, grains, staples	24,000—200,000
Protein foods	1000,000—4,000,000
Human services	80,000—5,000,000,000
Information	10,000—10,000,000,000,000

Source: data taken from Odum (1995)

manuscript (or the first copy) is $7.6 \times 10^9\ J \times 500 \times 10^6\ seJ/J = 3.8 \times 10^{18} seJ$. If the manuscript is printed as a book, we need to know the energy of a book. Just taking the energy content of 1 g of paper as 4 kcal and assuming that the book weighs 500 g, one copy of a printed book has an energy of 8.4×10^6 J and 1000 copies add up to 8.4×10^9 J. Dividing the emergy of the manuscript by the energy of 1000 copies of the book gives a transformity of 4.5×10^8 seJ/J for each copy of the book.

Information plays a crucial role in self-organization, because it conserves already attained structure and transfers it in time. Information can be stored the system itself, e.g. in the proteins and in the DNA of an organism. It can also be extracted from the system and stored as a plan of the system's structure on a carrier such as a book or a hard disk. Information transfer, which is an energy flow, allows energy from lower levels in the hierarchy to be controlled and amplified.

The relationship between information and energy, or more precisely exergy, becomes even clearer in the Jørgensen's formulation of the fourth law of thermodynamics. Recall that he considers evolution as a struggle for exergy rather than power. Another version of this fourth law of thermodynamics or the *thermodynamic law of ecology* is:

> *If a system receives a throughflow of exergy, the system will utilize this exergy to move away from thermodynamic equilibrium. If there are offered more than one pathway to move away from thermodynamic equilibrium, the one yielding the most stored exergy (i.e. with the most ordered structure or the longest distance to thermodynamic equilibrium in the prevailing conditions) will be selected.* (Jørgensen 2002, p. 148)

We stated earlier that distance from thermodynamic equilibrium is thermodynamic information or negentropy. A self-organizing system uses exergy in energy, mass, or information conversion processes and to build structure. Structure is therefore stored exergy and stored information. This stored exergy allows the structure to do work. Jørgensen (2007) argues that the structural complexity of ecosystems should increase as a consequence of the thermodynamic law of ecology, similar to the

Table 8.5 Evolution of exergy density and exergy flow rate over time

Emergence of	10^6 years ago	Exergy density (kJ/g)	Exergy flow rate (W/kg)
Primitive cells	3800	91	0.097
Jellyfish	700	1702	92
Primitive fish	450	6171	247
Amphibians	270	12,866	514
Dinosaurs	150	16,830	841
Birds	100	18,326	9164
Mammals	50–35	39,775	19,887
Early primates	30	39,981	19,991
Homo habilis	2.0	40,261	35,525
Homo sapiens	0.1	40,635	43,460

Source: data taken from Jørgensen (2007)

consequences of Moore's law in computing. He states that "a self-organizing system as an ecosystem or an organism should develop toward higher and higher complexity and the growth rate of complexity is proportional to the already achieved self-organization" (Jørgensen 2007, p. 491). As evidence for the thermodynamic law of ecology, he calculates the eco-exergy density (in kJ/g) and the eco-exergy flow rate (in W/kg) for living organisms throughout the Earth's history (see Table 8.5). From primitive cells to amphibians, dinosaurs, birds mammals, and primates, organisms became more complex with growing exergy density and exergy flow rates. Plotted against time, one could see that the increase in the exergy flow rate was even faster than exponential. Thus, the acceleration mentioned in Chap. 1 is not a recent phenomenon but seems to be a feature of evolution and thermodynamics.

Because of self-organization an *ecosystem*—i.e., a community of organisms in a physical environment—has different properties at early and late stages of development (see Table 8.6). Initially, the system is poorly organized, has high entropy and little information, but is growing rapidly. Once the system has matured, it contains a lot of information, has well organized patterns, and hence has low entropy. Growth is controlled by well-developed feedback mechanisms so that the system reaches a steady state. Very importantly, in a mature ecosystem there is a lot of *symbiosis*—i.e., long-term biological interaction between different organisms—accompanied by narrow specialization of many organisms in niches. As a result, a mature biological ecosystem has nearly closed mineral nutrient cycles. The system thus exchanges little matter with its environment. Overall, mature ecosystems are quite resistant to external perturbations.

A remarkable feature of mature ecosystems is that they have nearly closed cycles of inorganic matter. The matter contains the ordered structure and information that the system develops. The cycling of matter allows the system to reorder the structure using the energy input from the sun. Without cycling, the structure would remain static and without energy input, it would decay due to the second law of thermodynamics. In order to understand the cycling property of ecosystems, we must look at the entire ecological network of organisms and the interactions between them.

Table 8.6 Development of ecosystems over time

Properties	Early stage	Mature stage
Community energetics		
Production/respiration	$\neq 1$	Close to 1
Production/biomass	High	Low
Yield	High	Low
Entropy	High	Low
Exergy	Low	High
Community structure and individual properties		
Total biomass	Small	Large
Inorganic nutrients	Extrabiotic	Intrabiotic
Diversity	Low	High
Patterns	Poorly organized	Well organized
Niche specialization	Broad	Narrow
Size of organisms	Small	Large
Life cycle	Simple	Complex
Life span	Short	Long
Nutrient cycling		
Mineral cycles	Open	Closed
Nutrient exchange rate	Rapid	Slow
Homeostasis and overall properties		
Internal symbiosis	Underdeveloped	Developed
Stability (Resistance to shocks)	Poor	Good
Information	Low	High
Growth form	Rapid growth	Feedback controlled growth
Feedback control	Poor	Good

Source: adapted from Jørgensen (2002)

8.7.5 Relevance for Economics

You may wonder why an economist should know all this difficult stuff about physics and biology. The answer is simple: because the economy is tightly coupled to the geobiosphere (i.e., the natural environment) through flows of energy and matter. Figure 8.41 shows the economy as part of an energy hierarchy, sandwiched between the natural environment and human society. The primary source of energy is sunlight, represented by the circle outside the system boundaries. In the symbolic language developed by Howard Odum to describe energy systems, the symbol ⬡ represents a stock of a resource or an asset. ⏚ represents a heat sink that absorbs dissipated energy. In this illustration, the economy consists of three sectors: agriculture, mineral extraction, and manufacturing. The primary sectors depend on energy flows from the environment, while manufacturing receives its energy from the primary sectors, e.g. in the form of mined fossil fuels or agricultural produce. Note that each energy transformation is accompanied by an energy loss due to dissipated heat. This is inevitable, because increasing order in the system requires the export of entropy. The economy provides energy in the form of goods and services to the human society, i.e. to people. People, in turn, transform their energy into information. Both information (or knowledge) and people (as labor) feed back into the economy, where they control the economic activity.

The important message of Fig. 8.41 is that all economic activities, and all human activities in general, require inputs from the natural environment and ultimately rely on the (fossil) energy stocks and solar radiation. As such the economy must be subject to the laws of thermodynamics, particularly the conservation of energy and of matter. This is an important insight, because conventional circular flow diagrams, such as in Fig. 5.1 in Chap. 5, focus only on the circular flow of goods, factors of production, and money between producers and consumers (see Fig. 8.42).

However, every product contains emergy, structure and hence thermodynamic information. We have seen that thermodynamic information (or negentropy) is defined as the entropy distance from thermodynamic equilibrium. It is embedded in every material object produced by humans and in humans themselves. Therefore, Ayres (1994) proposes to think of the economy as a processor of (thermodynamic) information (see Fig. 8.43). We can distinguish three types of information: (1) thermodynamic information associated with the chemical composition of materials, (2) morphological information associated with shape, form, and structure, as well as control information needed to guide motion or make decisions, and (3) symbolic information associated with control processes and knowledge. Control information

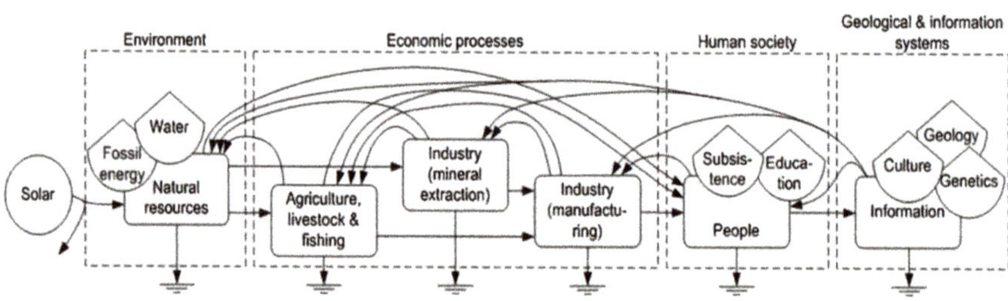

Fig. 8.41 The economy as part of an energy hierarchy. Source: Giannetti et al. (2019), reproduced with kind permission of Elsevier B.V

Fig. 8.42 Circular economic flow on mainstream economics. Source: Author

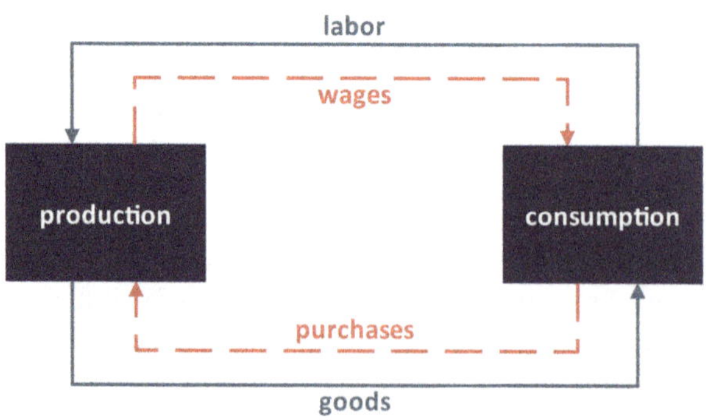

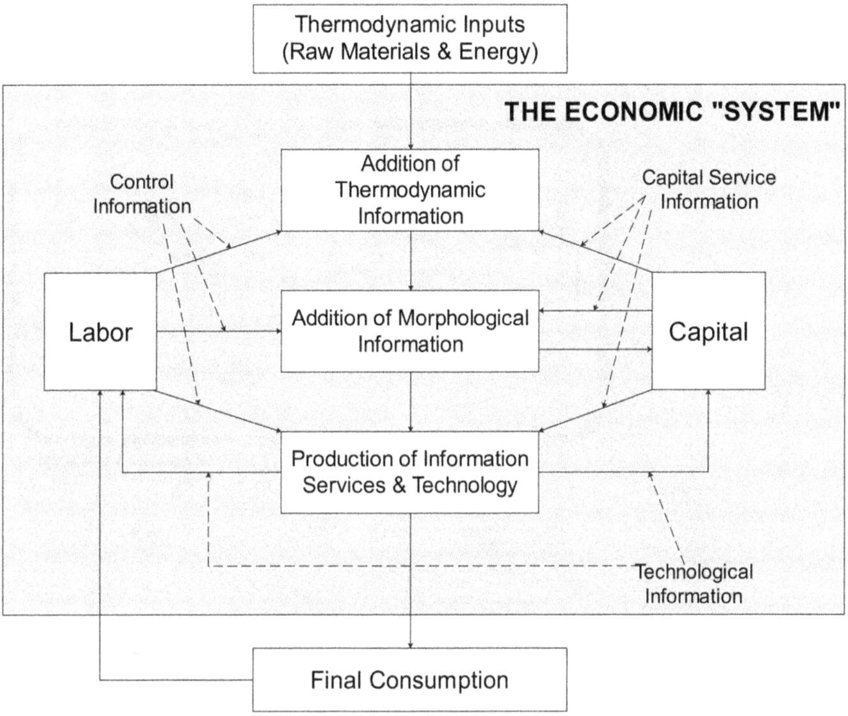

Fig. 8.43 The economy as an information-transformation system. Sources: Ayres (1994), reproduced with kind permission of Springer

is embodied in human brains, while symbolic information can be stored and processed using information technology. According to Fig. 8.43, economic activity consists of three stages, each of which adds information and value to the raw materials as primary inputs. In the first stage, the raw materials are extracted, refined, purified and finally chemically recombined into finished materials with desired properties. In the second stage, the finished materials are transformed into products by shaping and forming them. In the third stage, the products are used to provide services to consumers.

The biophysical perspective on the economy emphasizes that flows of money and goods are not possible without resources taken from the geobiosphere (i.e., environmental systems). Brown and Ulgiati (2011) estimate the total emergy flow supporting the economy in 2008 and compare it to the monetary value of the Gross World Product (GWP) of \$60.6 trillion (see Fig. 8.44).

The environmental systems received a total emergy flow (or empower) of 15.2×10^{24} seJ from solar energy, tidal energy, and geothermal energy (renewable inputs), which they passed on to the economic producers. In addition, the economy received an emergy flow of 88.8×10^{24} seJ from non-renewable fossil fuels and minerals (especially coal, petroleum, natural gas, nuclear energy, calcium carbonate,

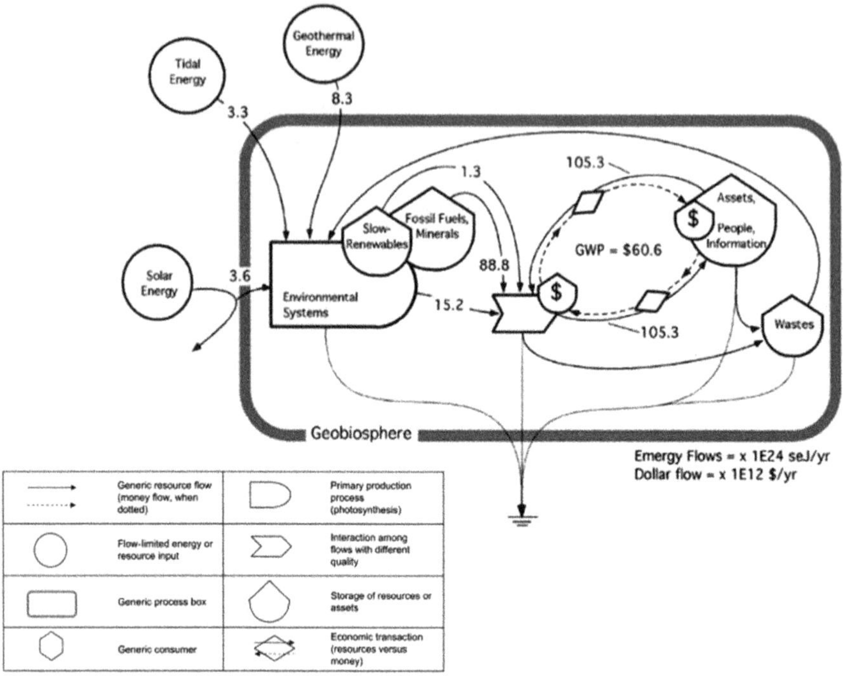

Fig. 8.44 Emergy flows in the global economy in 2008. Source: adapted from Brown and Ulgiati (2011)

phosphate, and selected metals) and to a small extent from slowly renewable inputs (i.e., soils, forest biomass, peat, and fisheries). Note that the non-renewable inputs account for 84% of the total 105.3 seJ of emergy that the global economy received and used in 2008. Brown and Ulgiati (2011) also show that the amount of emergy from renewables was constant throughout the twentieth century, but the amount of emergy from non-renewables increased steadily along with the GWP. They and other authors (e.g., Odum 2007) argue that the very high economic production cannot be maintained without the high emergy influx from non-renewable sources, which cannot be replaced by renewables. The current amount of emergy from renewables is overestimated, because many renewables, such as biofuels, currently need fossil fuels to be produced.

The point that even agricultural produce in modern industrial agriculture requires significant amounts of non-renewable inputs is captured in Howard Odum's statement that "the industrial man eats potatoes partly made of oil." Odum (2007) presents a calculation of the various emergy inputs required to produce corn on 1 hectare of land in Illinois in the 1980s. The required inputs to produce 1.9×10^{10} calories of corn per year are shown in Fig. 8.45, expressed in units of 10^{13} solar emcalories per year. The emergy of the renewable inputs of sunlight, wind, and rain amounts to 11 units. Nature adds another 1.5 units in the form of soil and nutrients.

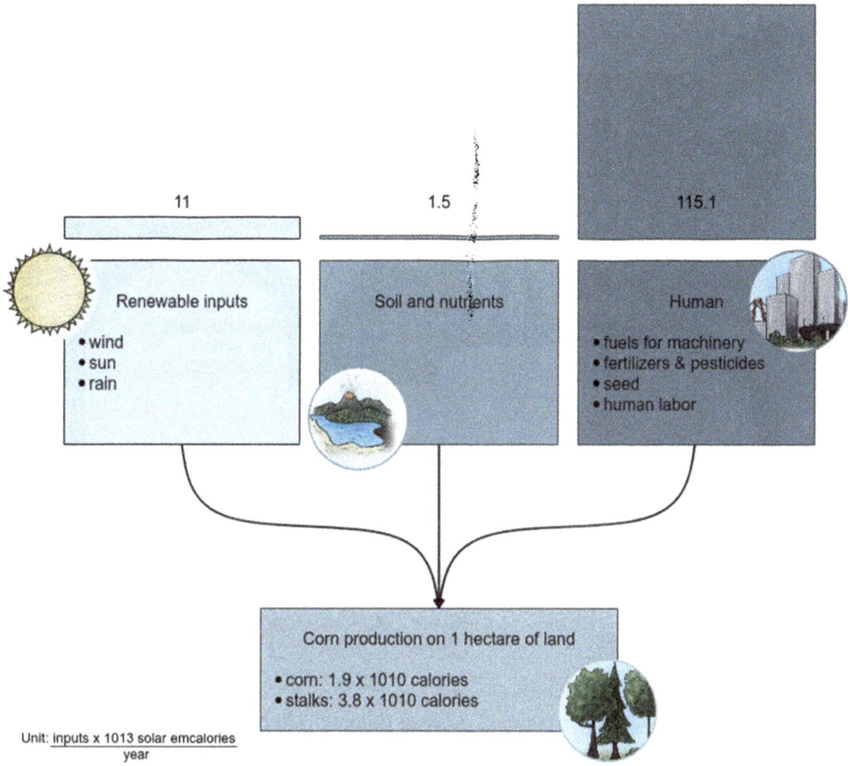

Fig. 8.45 Emergy of inputs in intensive industrial corn production in the USA. Source: Author

Humans add 8 units of fuel for agricultural machinery, 39.6 units of fertilizers (N, P, and K), 1.9 units of pesticides, 3.6 units of seeds, and 62 units of human labor services. The sum of the emergy supplied by humans is 115.1 units. Thus, nature provides 9.8% of the emergy, while humans supply 90.2% of the total of 127 x 10^{13} solar emcalories.

Note that after services (48.9%), fertilizers (31%), in particular phosphorus (19.6%), are the most important input. This example demonstrates the usefulness of the emergy concept, because it provides a natural accounting unit for very different kinds of goods and services. Emergy is also applicable to natural inputs such as wind, rain, and sunlight, for which there is no monetary market price that economists normally use as an accounting unit.

The emergy flow diagram in Fig. 8.44 contains another important element: wastes from production and consumption. Part of their emergy flows back to the environmental system and a part is dissipated as waste heat. This observation is another very important lesson. We saw earlier that biological ecosystems at a mature stage have almost closed cycles of matter. Our current economic system does not conserve matter, making it more similar to biological ecosystems at an early stage of development. Figure 8.46 shows the material flows of non-metallic minerals, metal ores,

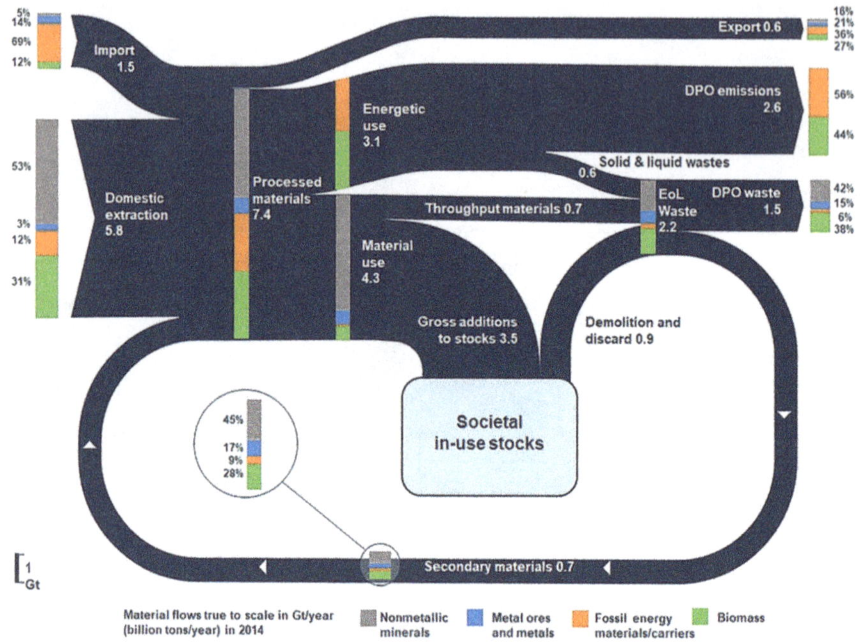

Fig. 8.46 Material flow diagram for the European Union in 2014 (Gt per year). Source: Mayer et al. (2019), licensed under CC-BY 4.0 (https://creativecommons.org/licenses/by/4.0/)

fossil fuel carriers, and biomass in the European Union. In 2014, the EU economy processed 8 Gt of materials, of which only 7.5% (0.6 Gt) came from recycling, but 72.5% (5.8 Gt) originated from domestic extraction. Of the 4.2 Gt materials for material use, 3.5 Gt (83.3%) resulted in new societal stocks, i.e. built structure. 4 Gt of matter were dissipated into the environment—2.5 Gt as emissions to the air from energetic use and 1.5 Gt as solid and liquid wastes from production, energy generation, and from the disposal of old societal stocks. Hence, in 2014, each newly built Gt of societal stock was accompanied by 4/3.5 Gt = 1.14 Gt of waste matter. The waste materials still contain exergy that affects the environment. Ayres (1998) points out that the chemical potential of these wastes can disrupt the delicately balanced bio-geochemical cycles and cause damage. Even small amounts of some chemicals can be toxic to organisms and disrupt life processes. Mature natural ecosystems have reached an inherently stable steady state after millions of years of evolutionary selection. They are not adapted to many inorganic substances, such as heavy metals and new complex chemical products that are dissipated as waste from production and consumption.

In summary, the biophysical view of the economy as a dissipative structure intimately coupled to the geobiosphere provides at least four important insights. First, it teaches us that all economic processes require material inputs and energy. We cannot imagine a completely dematerialized economy. Economic information is embodied in structures that require matter and energy for their production and maintenance. Without a permanent supply of energy from outside, the existing structures will decay over time due to the second law of thermodynamics. Second, most energy today comes from non-renewable sources. The strong economic growth since the industrial revolution has depended on the use of concentrated energy in the form of fossil fuels. Some researchers argue that it is unlikely that we can sustain similar levels of economic production and growth, or even the existing societal complexity, without fossil fuels. There is plenty of renewable energy, especially in the form of sunlight, but its quality in terms of the energy hierarchy is low. Third, there are fundamental differences between natural ecosystems and the current economic system. Natural ecosystems have been optimized by evolutionary forces over hundreds of millions of years and have reached a mature stage. They have nearly closed material cycles and have many corrective feedback mechanisms that keep them in a steady state, or homeostasis. In contrast, our current economic system is very young and in an early stage of development. It has a high throughput of energy and materials, low circularity, and generates uncontrolled cancerous growth. Fourth, the economic system increases entropy in natural systems, which threatens the functioning of natural systems and ultimately the foundations of human life.

Things to Remember

- Self-organization is a process by which an initially disordered system acquires spatial, temporal, or functional structure without external control or specific intervention. Order emerges from disorder through local interactions between parts of the system. Self-organization is often triggered by random events that are amplified by positive feedback. The resulting order is typically quite robust to external perturbations. There are four basic characteristics of self-organization: (1) pattern formation, (2) autonomy, (3) robustness and resilience, and (4) dynamics.
- Self-organization is a key complexity concept, because it explains the endogenous formation of order and structure from non-trivial bottom-up interactions. It is closely associated with dynamic complexity.
- Cellular automata and agent-based models are computational tools that can be used to study the effects of local interactions of autonomous agents. Agent-based models are more flexible than cellular automata. They consist of agents, relationships between the agents, and an environment. Typical features of agent-based models that are difficult to deal with in other models are agent heterogeneity, explicit space, local interaction, private information, and bounded rationality.
- Models from physics, chemistry, and biology show that self-organization can occur with agents following very simple rules. The Ising model from statistical physics illustrates how order can emerge from randomness and that emergent patterns can be random. The chemical oscillator called the

(continued)

Belousov–Zhabotinsky reaction is a dissipative reaction in an open system. It shows that self-organization is caused by positive and negative feedback and is therefore typically a nonlinear process. Swarm models from biology emphasize the importance of local interaction and bounded rationality.

- Spatial patterns in the economy refer to the distribution of economic agents and activities in space. Temporal patterns are visible as seasonal fluctuations in time series. They result from the synchronized activities of many agents in the economy. Functional patterns are more difficult to identify. They refer to the differentiation of functions, roles, or statuses of economic agents.
- Opinions, beliefs, and behaviors spread in a population through the social influence of some agents on others. Unlike the spread of a virus or simple information, opinion dynamics are complex contagion processes that require multiple social confirmations. The Sznajd model is an application of the Ising model to opinion dynamics. Opinion clustering and bipolarization are important topics in the social science literature on opinion dynamics and social influence.
- The Schelling segregation model is a canonical model that demonstrates how stark macroscopic patterns (in space) can arise from rather moderate microscopic motives and interactions. It proves that strong segregation according to agent characteristics can be the result of rather mild degrees of intolerance.
- Industrial symbiosis illustrates the self-organization of firms in a local economic ecosystem. Firms share resources for their mutual benefit and the benefit of the environment. Planning attempts to create eco-industrial parks often fail. However, policy interventions can promote the formation of industrial symbioses once a promising core has developed from the bottom up. Industrial symbiosis refers to the complicated relationship between self-organization and planned organization.
- The Austrian economist Friedrich August Hayek distinguished between made order and grown order. Spontaneous or grown order is the result of self-organization in society and the economy. He argues that spontaneous order must be more efficient than government-created economic order because of the problem of dispersed knowledge in the economy. No central planner can ever use as much knowledge as decentralized decision-makers can. Based on this premise, he makes the normative claim that government should only create abstract rules for individual behavior, but should not directly intervene in the economy. Thus, Hayek's theory of economic self-organization is deeply normative, whereas the complexity perspective focuses more on describing and understanding different self-organization processes.

(continued)

- The chemist Ilya Prigogine developed the concept of dissipative systems (or structures) that are far from thermodynamic equilibrium. Dissipative systems are thermodynamically open systems that exchange energy and potentially matter with their environment. They are self-organizing in the sense that they produce internal order by dissipating energy, i.e. producing entropy in their environment. This concept is relevant to economics because economic activity requires energy and materials from nature to build all kinds of structures. It also points to the problem that a high throughput of energy and matter in the economy is not sustainable, so that permanent real economic growth in terms of material output is unlikely to be possible.
- The maximum power principle says that those systems survive competition and selection that maximize power intake, energy transformation, and those uses that increase production and efficiency. It is also called the fourth law of thermodynamics. Because of this principle, self-organizing systems move away from thermodynamic equilibrium and store exergy in ordered structure.
- The theory of dissipative structures teaches four lessons about the economy: (1) All economic processes require material inputs and energy. (2) Most of the energy used in today's economy comes from fossil fuels, which provide energy of higher quality than sunlight and other renewables. (3) The current economic system is like an ecosystem in an early stage of development with high throughput of energy and materials, low circularity, and uncontrolled cancerous growth. (4) The economic system increases entropy in natural systems, which threatens the functioning of natural systems and ultimately the foundations of human life.

References

Ajzen I (1991) The theory of planned behavior. Organ Behav Hum Decis Process 50:179–211. https://doi.org/10.1016/0749-5978(91)90020-T

Anzola D, Barbrook-Johnson P, Cano JI (2017) Self-organization and social science. Comput Math Org Theory 23:221–257. https://doi.org/10.1007/s10588-016-9224-2

Axelrod R (1997) The dissemination of culture: a model with local convergence and global polarization. J Confl Resolut 41:203–226. https://doi.org/10.1177/0022002797041002001

Ayres RU (1994) Information, entropy, and progress: a new evolutionary paradigm, 1st edn. American Institute of Physics Melville, New York

Ayres RU (1998) Eco-thermodynamics: economics and the second law. Ecol Econ 26:189–209. https://doi.org/10.1016/S0921-8009(97)00101-8

Bachmann T (2022) Functional group positions and contact behavior in problem-solving groups. Gr Interak Organ Z Angew Organ 53:131–144. https://doi.org/10.1007/s11612-021-00613-6

Bichraoui N, Guillaume B, Halog A (2013) Agent-based modelling simulation for the development of an industrial symbiosis - preliminary results. Procedia Environ Sci 17:195–204. https://doi.org/10.1016/j.proenv.2013.02.029

Bonakdar SB, Roos M (2023) Dissimilarity effects on house prices: what is the value of similar neighbours? J Econ Interac Coord 18:59–86. https://doi.org/10.1007/s11403-022-00370-9
Bourdieu P (1984) Distinction: a social critique of the judgement of taste. Harvard University Press, Cambridge
Brown MT, Ulgiati S (2011) Understanding the global economic crisis: a biophysical perspective. Ecol Model 223:4–13. https://doi.org/10.1016/j.ecolmodel.2011.05.019
Centola D (2018) How behavior spreads: the science of complex contagions. Princeton University Press, Princeton
Chertow MR (2007) "Uncovering" industrial symbiosis. J Ind Ecol 11:11–30. https://doi.org/10.1162/jiec.2007.1110
Chertow MR, Ehrenfeld J (2012) Organizing self-organizing systems. J Ind Ecol 16:13–27. https://doi.org/10.1111/j.1530-9290.2011.00450.x
Creamer GG, Stolfo SJ, Creamer M et al (2022) Discovering organizational hierarchy through a corporate ranking algorithm: the Enron case. Complexity 2022:e8154476. https://doi.org/10.1155/2022/8154476
Fischer E (2013) Racial distribution map (2010 Census) of Metro Detroit. https://commons.wikimedia.org/wiki/File:FischerDetroit2010Census.png and https://www.flickr.com/photos/walkingsf/5560480146/sizes/o/in/set-72157626354149574/. Accessed 15 May 2023
Flache A, Mäs M, Feliciani T et al (2017) Models of social influence: towards the next frontiers. J Artif Soc Soc Simul 20:2. https://doi.org/10.18564/jasss.3521
Ghali MR, Frayret J-M, Ahabchane C (2017) Agent-based model of self-organized industrial symbiosis. J Clean Prod 161:452–465. https://doi.org/10.1016/j.jclepro.2017.05.128
Giannetti BF, Marcilio MDFDFB, Coscieme L et al (2019) Howard Odum's "self-organization, transformity and information": three decades of empirical evidence. Ecol Model 407:108717. https://doi.org/10.1016/j.ecolmodel.2019.06.005
Gibbs D, Deutz P (2007) Reflections on implementing industrial ecology through eco-industrial park development. J Clean Prod 15:1683–1695. https://doi.org/10.1016/j.jclepro.2007.02.003
Gilbert N, Anzola D, Johnson P et al (2015) Self-organizing dynamical systems. In: Wright JD (ed) International encyclopedia of the social & behavioral sciences, 2nd edn. Elsevier, Oxford, pp 529–534
Gilliland M (1978) Energy analysis: a new public policy tool. Westview Press, Boulder
Gracia-Lázaro C, Lafuerza LF, Floría LM, Moreno Y (2009) Residential segregation and cultural dissemination: an Axelrod-Schelling model. Phys Rev E 80:046123. https://doi.org/10.1103/PhysRevE.80.046123
Hajihusseini H (2010) Eurasian Cranes migrating to Meyghan Salt Lake, Markazi Province of Iran. https://commons.wikimedia.org/w/index.php?curid=31237576. Accessed 11 Apr 2023
Hayek FA (1945) The use of knowledge in society. Am Econ Rev 35:519–530
Hayek FA (1964) The theory of complex phenomena. In: Bunge M (ed) Critical approaches to science and philosophy. Routledge, New York
Hayek FA (1989) The pretence of knowledge. Am Econ Rev 79:3–7
Hayek FA (1998) Law, legislation and liberty: a new statement of the liberal principles of justice and political economy. Routledge, London
Jkrieger at German Wikipedia (2005) Belousov-Zhabotinsky_reaction. https://commons.wikimedia.org/wiki/File:Bzr_raum.jpg. Accessed 11 Apr 2023
Jørgensen SE (2002) Integration of ecosystem theories: a pattern. Springer, Dordrecht
Jørgensen SE (2007) Evolution and exergy. Ecol Model 203:490–494. https://doi.org/10.1016/j.ecolmodel.2006.12.035
Juliao C (2014) Sznajd Model. https://www.modelingcommons.org/browse/one_model/4156#model_tabs_browse_procedures. Accessed 15 May 2023
Kay JJ (2001) On complexity theory, exergy, and industrial ecology: some implications for construction ecology. In: Kibert CJ, Sendzimir J, Guy GB (eds) Construction ecology: nature as a basis for green buildings. Routledge, London

Kushi O (2021) Will housing market seasonality return to normal? In: First American. https://blog.firstam.com/economics/will-housing-market-seasonality-return-to-normal. Accessed 11 Apr 2023

Ladyman J, Lambert J, Wiesner K (2013) What is a complex system? Eur J Philos Sci 3:33–67. https://doi.org/10.1007/s13194-012-0056-8

Macal CM, North MJ (2010) Tutorial on agent-based modelling and simulation. J Simul 4:151–162. https://doi.org/10.1057/jos.2010.3

Mayer A, Haas W, Wiedenhofer D et al (2019) Measuring progress towards a circular economy: a monitoring framework for economy-wide material loop closing in the EU28. J Ind Ecol 23:62–76. https://doi.org/10.1111/jiec.12809

Mirowski P (1989) More heat than light: economics as social physics. In: Physics as nature's economics. Cambridge University Press, Cambridge

Nicolis G, Prigogine I (1977) Self-organization in nonequilibrium systems: from dissipative structures to order through fluctuations. John Wiley & Sons, New York

Odum HT (1988) Self-organization, transformity, and information. Science 242:1132–1139. https://doi.org/10.1126/science.242.4882.1132

Odum HT (1995) Self-organization and maximum empower. In: Hall CAS (ed) Maximum power: the ideas and applications of H.T. Odum. University Press of Colorado, Colorado

Odum HT (2007) Environment, power, and society for the twenty-first century: the hierarchy of energy. Columbia University Press, New York

Odum HT, Pinkerton RC (1955) Time's speed regulator: the optimum efficiency for maximum power output in physical and biological systems. Am Sci 43:331–343

Schelling TC (1978) Micromotives and macrobehavior. W. W. Norton & Company, New York

Schindler R (1957) Grundprinzipien der Psychodynamik in der Gruppe. Psyche 11:308–314

Stauffer D, Sousa AO, De Oliveira SM (2000) Generalization to square lattice of Sznajd sociophysics model. Int J Mod Phys C 11:1239–1245. https://doi.org/10.1142/S012918310000105X

Sznajd-Weron K, Sznajd J (2000) Opinion evolution in closed community. Int J Mod Phys C 11: 1157–1165. https://doi.org/10.1142/S0129183100000936

Sznajd-Weron K, Sznajd J, Weron T (2021) A review on the Sznajd model — 20 years after. Phys A Statist Mech Appl 565:125537. https://doi.org/10.1016/j.physa.2020.125537

Tao Y, Evans S, Wen Z, Ma M (2019) The influence of policy on industrial symbiosis from the Firm's perspective: a framework. J Clean Prod 213:1172–1187. https://doi.org/10.1016/j.jclepro.2018.12.176

Tribus M, McIrvine EC (1971) Energy and information. Sci Am 225:179–190

Urselmans L, Phelps S (2018) A Schelling model with adaptive tolerance. PLoS One 13:e0193950. https://doi.org/10.1371/journal.pone.0193950

Wilensky U (1999) NetLogo. http://ccl.northwestern.edu/netlogo/. Center for Connected Learning and Computer-Based Modeling, Northwestern University, Evanston

Wilensky U (2003a) NetLogo B-Z Reaction model. https://ccl.northwestern.edu/netlogo/models/B-ZReaction. Accessed 26 October 2023

Wilensky U (2003b) NetLogo Ising model. https://ccl.northwestern.edu/netlogo/models/Ising. Accessed 26 October 2023

Wilensky U, Rand W (2006) NetLogo Segregation Simple model. https://ccl.northwestern.edu/netlogo/models/SegregationSimple. Accessed 26 October 2023

Wilensky U, Rand W (2015) An introduction to agent-based modeling: modeling natural, social, and engineered complex systems with NetLogo. MIT Press, Cambridge

Wilkerson-Jerde M, Stonedahl F, Wilensky U (2009) NetLogo Flocking Vee Formations model. https://ccl.northwestern.edu/netlogo/models/FlockingVeeFormations. Accessed 26 October 2023

Wolfram S (2002) A new kind of science. Wolfram Media

Xia X, Zhang Y, Zhang Y, Rao T (2022) The spatial pattern and influence mechanism of urban vitality: a case study of Changsha, China. Front Environ Sci 10:942577. https://doi.org/10.3389/fenvs.2022.942577

Yang C, Wilensky U (2011) NetLogo epiDEM basic model. https://ccl.northwestern.edu/netlogo/models/epiDEMBasic. Accessed 26 October 2023

Emergence, Levels, and Hierarchy 9

Contents

9.1 Introduction 420
9.2 Levels and Hierarchies 424
9.2.1 Hierarchies in the Social World 428
9.2.2 Levels in the Economy 429
9.2.3 Fallacy of Composition and Representative Agents 435
9.3 Emergence 441
9.3.1 Weak Emergence 443
9.3.2 Strong Emergence 448
9.4 Macrofoundations of Microeconomics 450
9.4.1 Downward Causation 451
9.4.2 The Emergence Paradigm in Sociology 452
9.4.3 Multiple Equilibria and Indeterminacy 456
9.5 Institutions in Economics 457
9.5.1 New Institutional Economics 458
9.5.2 Traditional Institutional Economics 459
9.5.3 A Model of the Emergence of Norms 463
9.6 Emergent Macroeconomics 468
9.6.1 The Flaws of Neoclassical Macroeconomics 469
9.6.2 The Generative View to Macroeconomics 471
9.6.3 Stylized Facts 473
9.6.4 An Agent-Based Business Cycle Model 475
9.6.5 Other Agent-Based Macro Models 485
References 490

Abstract

This chapter deals with the difficult topic of emergence. Complexity science is sometimes called the science of emergence, meaning that a system can have properties that are not found in its parts. The concepts of simple emergence, weak emergence, and strong emergence are introduced. While self-organization describes the formation of structure at one level of the system, emergence always

M. Roos, *Principles of Complexity Economics*, Classroom Companion: Economics,
https://doi.org/10.1007/978-3-031-51436-4_9

requires at least two levels. Complex systems are often organized on multiple levels that form a hierarchy. Economics knows the micro level of agents and the macro level of the system, but it can be useful to think of additional levels such as a meso level. From a complexity perspective, the common practice in economics of working with representative agents, which eliminates the difference between levels, is a major fallacy of composition. The common practice of providing microfoundations to macroeconomics is contrasted with the idea of providing macrofoundations to microeconomics, which is related to the concept of downward causation. Institutions are an important instance of an emergent phenomenon with the capacity of downward causation. How institutions can emerge is shown with a formal model. As an alternative to mainstream macroeconomics, the chapter introduces emergent or agent-based macroeconomics.

Keywords

Fallacy of composition · Institutions · Macroeconomics · Macrofoundations · Representative agents

Guiding Questions

- In what sense is "more different"?
- How can we define levels and hierarchies in economics?
- Why is it not enough to consider only a microeconomic level and a macroeconomic level?
- Why does neoclassical economics commit a fallacy of composition?
- What does the Mantel–Sonnenschein–Debreu theorem say and why is it important?
- What is the difference between simple and complex emergence?
- What is weak emergence and what is strong emergence?
- What does irreducibility mean?
- Why do we need macrofoundations of microeconomics?
- Why is it important to consider institutions in economics?
- What is emergent macroeconomics?

9.1 Introduction

Complexity science is sometimes called the science of emergence, but emergence is a difficult concept. Roughly speaking, it means that a system or entity has properties that its parts do not have, consistent with the idea that the whole is more than the sum of its parts. While this characterization is intuitive, it is not precise. Historically, emergence has often been associated with mystery, which is why Herbert Simon emphasized that his description of complex systems as wholes that are more than the sum of their parts was not meant in an ultimate metaphysical sense. One of the origins of the concept of emergence is the *mind-body problem* that has puzzled philosophers for many centuries. The question concerns the relationship between consciousness in the human mind and the physical body. René Descartes was a famous proponent of the *dualist view* that mind and matter are different things. In his Cartesian dualism, the mind is independent of the body and can exist outside the body. The *monist view*, on the other hand, denies that there are two distinct kinds of entities or substances. *Material monism* (or *physicalism*) says that everything is physical, and that no other substance exists. Thus, mental phenomena can be fully explained by, or reduced to, physical processes. The view that every phenomenon in the world, including mental states, can be completely reduced to physical states is called *reductionism*. Some forms of *emergentism* argue that this is not possible, and that *emergent properties* cannot be reduced to or deduced from other more fundamental properties. The philosophical debate has many ramifications that cannot be discussed here, but it provides important concepts and insights that are relevant to emergence in the social world and especially in economics. We focus on emergence in the context of complexity science, starting again with the natural sciences and then moving on to the social sciences.

In the mid-twentieth century, there was a widespread belief that elementary particle physics was the most fundamental science, providing the fundamental laws of nature for everything else. Accordingly, solid-state physics would be a kind of applied particle physics, and chemistry would be applied solid-state physics. Nobel laureate Philip W. Anderson, whose field was solid state physics (or what is now called condensed matter physics), rejected this view and famously argued that "more is different" (Anderson 1972). Anderson did not deny that biological or chemical processes are subject to the fundamental laws of elementary particle physics, so that reductionism is a valid approach. However, he argued that the *reductionist hypothesis* does not imply the *constructionist hypothesis*, according to which it is possible to start from the most fundamental physical laws and reconstruct the universe. He proposed the hierarchy of sciences shown in Table 9.1 and argued forcefully that "science X is not 'just applied Y' . . . [, because at] each state entirely new laws, concepts, and generalizations are necessary, requiring inspiration and creativity to just as great a degree as in the previous one. Psychology is not applied

Table 9.1 Anderson's hierarchy of sciences

Science X	Science Y
Solid state or many-body physics	Elementary particle physics
Chemistry	Many-body physics
Molecular biology	Chemistry
Cell biology	Molecular biology
. . .	. . .
Psychology	Physiology
Social sciences	Psychology

biology, nor is biology applied chemistry" (Anderson 1972, p. 393). The reasons for the failure of the constructionist approach are scale and complexity. Scale refers to the number of entities, and complexity refers to the organization of these entities, i.e. structural complexity.

The idea that "more is different" implies that emergent properties are not just upscaled properties of system elements. We therefore distinguish emergent properties from *resultant properties*, which are aggregations of individual properties. For example, the total income of a group of people is a resultant property, but not an emergent one. The same is true of the total consumption expenditure of all households. For GDP it is less clear, whether it is resultant or emergent, but we will discuss this later in this chapter.

Emergence is related to self-organization because emergent properties are not just multiples of individual properties but result from the possibly different properties of individual entities and the interactions between those entities. Self-organization generates the structural complexity necessary for emergence to occur. As shown in Fig. 9.1, emergence also requires a concept of different levels, e.g. a micro level and a macro level. Self-organization occurs at one level and emergence occurs at a higher level of the system. To understand emergence, therefore, we need a concept of levels or *hierarchy*. As we will see, it is often easier to define levels in the natural world than in the social world. For example, in the human body, it is natural to think of cells as lower-level entities than organs, which are composed of cells. In economics, we distinguish between the microeconomic level of individual agents and the macroeconomic level of the whole economy, which is often defined at the national

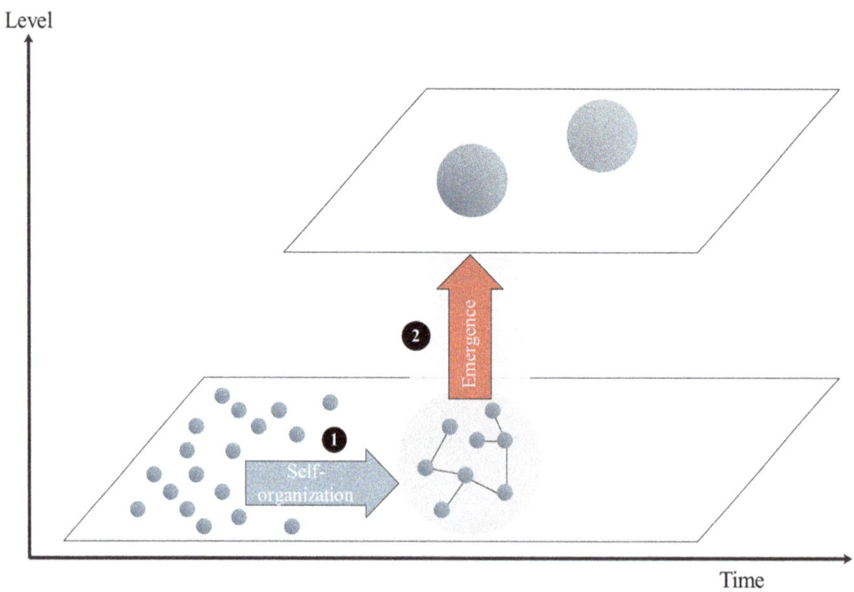

Fig. 9.1 Relationship between self-organization and emergence. Source: Author's own figure adapted from Prokopenko et al. (2009)

level of a country. But both the micro and macro levels are not as naturally defined as the cell and organ levels in an organism.

How the relationship between the microeconomic level and the macroeconomic level is treated is a crucial difference between complexity economics and neoclassical economics. Current mainstream neoclassical economics analyzes the macroeconomy from a microeconomic perspective. In the 1970s, the *rational expectations revolution* or *microfoundations revolution* took place, which rejected Keynesian macroeconomics as incompatible with neoclassical microeconomic theory. The leaders of this revolution—the New Classical economists Robert Lucas, Thomas Sargent, Ed Prescott, and others—called for an approach in which all macroeconomic phenomena are derived from the optimal decisions of microeconomic agents with rational expectations. Macroeconomics should not be different from microeconomics in terms of methodology as it had been until the 1970s. Instead, there should be a unification of microeconomics and macroeconomics, i.e. just one economic theory. In the words of Peter Howitt (1987, p. 273):

> *The lack of clear connection between macroeconomics and microeconomics has long been a source of discontent among economists. Arrow (1967) called it a ' major scandal' that neoclassical price theory cannot account for such macroeconomic phenomena as unemployment. Lucas and Sargent (1979) argued that Keynesian macroeconomics is 'fundamentally flawed' by its lack of a firm microfoundation. Countless students and practitioners alike have complained of the schizophrenic nature of a discipline whose two major branches project such radically different views of the world. ... [T]here is the reductionist methodological predisposition that economists of almost all persuasions share to some degree, according to which no explanation of economic phenomena is truly satisfactory if it does not reduce the phenomena to a question of individual actions by basic decision-making units.*

By the mid-1980s, the microfoundations project had been very successful. The Keynesian economist James Tobin observed that a "counter-revolution has swept the profession" (Tobin 1986, p. 350):

> *it is scarcely an exaggeration to say that no paper that does not employ the 'microfoundations' methodology can get published in a major professional journal, that no research proposal that is suspect of violating its precepts can survive peer review, that no newly minted Ph.D. who can't show that his hypothesized behavioral relations are properly derived can get a good academic job.*

Whereas neoclassical economics is *reductionist* or *anti-emergentist*, complexity economics argues that there *is* a difference between the macroeconomy and the microeconomy due to emergence. Thus, there may be good reasons for different research methodologies in macroeconomics and microeconomics, just as physicists use classical mechanics rather than quantum mechanics to describe the behavior of objects larger than atoms.

In Sect. 9.2, the concept of hierarchy and levels is further explored because it is necessary for the discussion of emergence. We also discuss important differences between physical systems and social systems that make it much more difficult to define a hierarchy of phenomena in the social world. Nevertheless, we argue that it is useful to distinguish at least a microeconomic and a macroeconomic level, and that the macroeconomy has properties that are not present at the microeconomic level. This section also criticizes mainstream neoclassical economics for committing the fallacy of composition and not properly accounting for the differences between levels.

Section 9.3 introduces several concepts of emergence that have been proposed in the philosophy, complexity, and the social sciences literature, in particular, *weak emergence* and *strong emergence*. Weak emergence is sometimes associated with simulation, which can be illustrated by Steven Wolfram's approach and John Conway's *Game of Life*. Strong emergence is a more contested concept that grants the macroscopic level some autonomy over the microscopic level, which raises important questions about causality.

In Sect. 9.4, the idea of providing macrofoundations to microeconomics is introduced. This idea is related to the concept of downward causation, which means that emergent higher levels can causally influence lower levels. In contrast to neoclassical economics, which believes that the behavior of individuals can be understood in isolation, complexity economics argues that individual behavior never occurs isolated from social context. The emergent social context influences how people think and what they do. Institutions are an example of such social context. How economics deals with institutions as emergent social phenomena that exert downward causation is explained in Sect. 9.5.

Section 9.6 is devoted to emergent macroeconomics, bottom-up macroeconomics, or agent-based macroeconomics. The advent of computer technology has provided powerful tools for conducting microfounded macroeconomic analysis in a more plausible way than neoclassical economics. According to the generative view of social science, emergent macroscopic phenomena should be "grown" from empirically well-supported microspecifications. Since the early 2000s, there has been a great deal of research on agent-based macro models, and these models now have the potential to replace the currently dominant but heavily criticized DSGE models.

9.2 Levels and Hierarchies

Emergentists posit a layered model of the world. They see the world as organized in a hierarchy of levels that are interrelated. Lower levels are more fundamental but also simpler than higher levels. The degree of complexity, especially structural and functional complexity, increases with the levels. Evolution leads to increasing complexity by adding more levels to the hierarchy. Table 9.2 suggests 12 different levels of the world system and the time of their appearance.

This hierarchy, taken from Fromm (2004), resembles Anderson's (1972) list of sciences, with physics being the most fundamental, followed by chemistry, biology, anthropology, and the social sciences. A notable fact in this list is that the time scale at which new levels appear is logarithmic, meaning that more complex levels appear

Table 9.2 Historical evolution of levels

Level	Domain	Event/Entities	Time scale
0	Physical	Big Bang First fundamental particles, atoms, molecules, galaxies, and solar systems	– 10,000,000,000 years
1	Chemical	Formation and solidification of planets, first life, cells without nucleus (procaryotes), oxygen increases	−1000,000,000 years
2	Biological	Cells with nucleus (eucaryotes), multicelluar organisms, plants colonize land, first vertebrates, dinosaurs	−100,000,000 years
3	Biological	Extinction of dinosaurs Mammals	−100,000,000 years
4	Biological	Primates, hominid families	−10,000,000 years
5	Anthropological	*Homo sapiens*	−1000,000 years
6	Anthropological	Extinction of ice age animals, *Homo sapiens sapiens*, tribes	−100,000 years
7	Social	Civilization: Language, settlements, households	−10,000 years
8	Religious	Civilization: Writing, religions, societies, cultures, first nations, sciences	−1000 years
9	Political	Communication: Printing, firms, national companies, first computers	−100 years
10	Economic	Communication: Computing, international companies, first networks of computers	−10 years
11	Digital	Internet	1 year
12	Artificial	Artificial intelligence	10 years

Source: Fromm 2004

faster than simpler ones. Thus, the evolution of complexity seems to be accelerating. Apparently, simpler structures are harder for evolution to achieve than more complex structures, suggesting that positive feedback plays an important role.

Boulding (1956) characterized different levels of theoretical systems in terms of their complexity and arranged them in a *system of systems*. This system of systems forms a *hierarchy of systems* in which the higher levels contain the lower levels and are more complex than the lower levels. At each level, new characteristics appear that make the system more difficult to analyze, understand, and predict. Table 9.3 summarizes this hierarchy of complexity.

We have used the terms hierarchy and levels without defining them. In everyday language, a *hierarchy* is a system in which people or things are arranged according to their importance. Importance can be derived from the agent's power or ability to control other agents. Lane (2006) distinguishes four different types of hierarchies, some of which overlap and some of which contradict each other. *Order hierarchy* refers to an ordering according to the values of a variable of interest shared by the elements of the system. Thus, we could define a hierarchy of firms or cities according to their size. In systems of firms and systems of cities, we typically find *power-law*

Table 9.3 Boulding's hierarchy of complexity

Level	Type	Characteristics	Examples	Scientific discipline/ approach
1	Framework	Static structure	Arrangement of atoms in a crystal, anatomy of the gene, mapping of the earth	All disciplines, verbal or pictorial description
2	Clockwork	Simple dynamic systems with predetermined, necessary motions	Steam engine, planetary system	Classical natural science with equilibrium system of (differential, difference) equations, neoclassical economics
3	Cybernetic system	Control mechanism or cybernetic system, transmission and interpretation of information are part of the system	Thermostat that maintains a preset temperature by responding to difference between actual temperature and desired values	Engineering, physiology, social science using models with feedback
4	Cell	Open system or self-maintaining structure, throughput of material and energy crucial	Living cells like amoeba	Cell biology with theories of metabolism
5	Plant	Division of labor among cells to form a cell-society with differentiated and mutually dependent parts; genotype vs. phenotype	Trees and flowers with roots, leaves, seeds, etc.	Botany, plant physiology
6	Animal	Increased mobility, teleological behavior and self-awareness; organization of information intake into a knowledge structure of image	Higher animals, especially those with a highly developed brain, e.g. birds	Zoology, neurology, cognitive science
7	Human	Self-consciousness and self-reflexibility; language and symbolism; speech; awareness of history	Individual human as a system	Physiology, cognitive science, psychology
8	Social organization	Social system as a set of roles tied together with channels of	Family, social group, firm, market, nation	Social sciences, e.g. history, sociology,

(continued)

Table 9.3 (continued)

Level	Type	Characteristics	Examples	Scientific discipline/ approach
		communication; content and meaning of messages, values		complexity economics, political science
9	Transcendental	Inescapable unknowables	God	

distributions of size. In such hierarchies, the levels are called *ranks*, where the largest entity has rank 1, the second largest has rank 2, and so on. *Inclusion hierarchy* means that there is a recursive organization of entities, with higher-level entities completely containing lower-level entities. In other words, lower-level entities add up perfectly to higher-level entities, and higher-level entities are only composed of them, nothing else. For example, the human body contains organs, which contain cells, which contain organelles, and so on. In the administrative hierarchy of a state, the nation may contain states, which contain counties or districts, which are further subdivided into municipalities. A *control hierarchy* comes closest to the everyday definition above because it refers to a control system in which orders flow down the hierarchy and information and requests flow up the hierarchy. Examples include a church, an army, or a corporation. Finally, a *level hierarchy* refers to the existence of ontologically distinct levels at which different level-specific entities interact at particular spatiotemporal scales. Higher-level entities may be composed of lower-level entities and have more extended spatiotemporal scales. When higher-level entities are composed of lower-level entities, they are structurally more complex and may perform more complex functions. An economic example of a level hierarchy is: employee—department—establishment—company—corporate group. Note that a level can also be interpreted as a subsystem of a larger system (or system of systems).

The different concepts are not mutually exclusive, so the same system could be seen as an order hierarchy, a control hierarchy, or a level hierarchy, for example. We can describe a system of cities as an order hierarchy by sorting the cities by population. Often (though not always) the size of a city correlates with its political and administrative importance in a country, so the control hierarchy of the city system would be similar to its order hierarchy. Larger cities are more economically complex than smaller ones and perform special functions in a country. Typically, a country's largest cities are its trade hubs, financial centers, and innovation engines. Using complexity and functions as a criterion implies a level hierarchy.

Which concept of hierarchy we use and how we define levels is often a matter of analytical convenience and the specific questions at hand. Especially in the social world, there are often many ways to define hierarchies and levels.

9.2.1 Hierarchies in the Social World

Anderson's hierarchy of sciences ends with "the social sciences" (Table 9.1), which corresponds to Boulding's hierarchy of complexity, in which human social organization is at the top (apart from the transcendental). Whereas the organization of the natural sciences corresponds to the ontological levels of their subjects, there is no clear hierarchy of the social sciences. The organization of the social sciences is functional: economics (production and exchange), political science (power), sociology (social organization), anthropology (culture), geography (place). We can construct level hierarchies in each of these disciplines, but it is questionable whether these are adequate descriptions of the world, because social systems are tightly interwoven. For this reason, intellectuals such as sociologist Bruno Latour and historian Carlo Ginzburg reject the notion of a hierarchical ordering of the social world because it oversimplifies complex social reality (Lane 2006). The very fact that there are several social sciences is evidence of the high complexity of human social organization. Although necessary in principle, it may be impossible for us to achieve a complete understanding of the human social world in its entirety.

There are important differences between physical entities and humans that complicate the unambiguous identification of hierarchies in social reality. We have already discussed this point in Chap. 2 with respect to the identification of social systems. The first complication is that spatial location is not a necessary criterion for belonging to a human social system. One can be a citizen of a city or country without being there. Companies need a registered business address, but it is possible that no one works there and that the employees of a company are scattered all over the world. On the other hand, when we talk about a physical, chemical, or biological system, it is clearly identified in space, so that its levels have the same spatial location. As a consequence of spatiality, physical entities are only part of multiple systems if these systems form a hierarchy. At any given time, a particular carbon atom can belong to only one system of subsystems, e.g. the body of a particular person with its organs and cells. Humans can be part of several systems that do not form a hierarchy, such as a family, a church, a company, and a club. Because humans are members of multiple non-hierarchical systems, human systems are causally related not only vertically but also horizontally.

For example, an employee's work performance may suffer when a family member becomes ill. In principle, the employee's family and company are separate systems, connected only because the employee is a member of both. But through this connection, the two systems can influence each other. We could even think of other, more indirect connections. For example, a child may have problems at school because her mother has problems at work. The company where the mother works and the daughter's school are not even connected by the same person, but there can still be an influence because the mother and daughter interact at home. Furthermore, people have intentionality and can partly choose the systems they belong to. People can change their jobs and their membership in a club. They can even leave or be excluded from systems they were born into, such as their home country or family. Intentionality also affects hierarchies. This is evident in control hierarchies, where people at the top of the hierarchy have the intention to influence the behavior of people at lower levels. Control hierarchies are also often created intentionally, rather than being the emergent result of a self-organizing process. The legal system of a country can be interpreted as a hierarchy with intentional vertical influences both bottom up and top down. The citizens of a country either elect lawmakers or even decide directly on laws in referenda, which is an intentional bottom-up process. Once a law is in force, it regulates the behavior of individuals top down, also intentionally. Human behavior is thus, at least in part, the result of deliberately chosen collective rules, which is very different from the physical world, where entities do not choose their rules of interaction.

In summary, hierarchies in social systems are entangled in many ways. There are many cross-cutting interactions both vertically, i.e., between levels, and horizontally, i.e. within the same level. Talking about the same level can be a bit misleading when different hierarchies are involved, because strictly speaking a level belongs to a hierarchy. The vertical interaction between levels of a hierarchy is at the heart of emergence, which we discuss later in this chapter. The discussion here warns us not to believe in naturally given hierarchies in social systems.

9.2.2 Levels in the Economy

Notwithstanding the difficulties with hierarchies in the social world, it is common to distinguish at least two levels in the economy: a microeconomic level and a macroeconomic level. The microeconomic level is the level of action. In economic theory, households and firms are the (inter-)acting agents, although both are *collectives* made up of individuals. The macroeconomic level, which is the level of the system, is usually defined as all economic activities and phenomena in a country. Thus, the economic system is considered to be the *national economy*.

Both the definition of economic agents and the definition of the system level in mainstream economics can be questioned and are the result of convention and convenience rather than economic argument. As noted above, firms and households are collectives, not individuals. It is therefore not obvious why they should be the most fundamental units of economic analysis rather than individual persons. When a household consists of several people, there is a problem of aggregating individual preferences into household preferences. Moreover, a household choice is a collective decision, which is conceptually different from an individual choice. For example, the purchase of a family car may be the result of family bargaining and thus a compromise that depends on the preferences and power of the family members. Everyday experience suggests that in many cases no individual family member would choose the family car. We can imagine a situation where a family buys a silver station wagon, although each member would prefer a completely different vehicle, e.g. father -> yellow bicycle instead of car, mother -> white SUV, daughter -> green mini hatchback, son -> red coupe. Furthermore, the "family preference" and hence the choice may not be stable over time, if the composition of the household changes, e.g., a new member is born or a member leaves the family, or if the influence of individual members on the negotiation process changes, e.g. children grow older. Therefore, the "same" household may make completely different choices at two points in time, even though both income and prices are unchanged. Similarly, a firm is a collective that may consist of hundreds of thousands of very heterogeneous individuals. It is common in mainstream theory to assume that the goal of a firm is to maximize profits, but the employees and stakeholders of a firm may have additional goals such as job security, power, job satisfaction, prestige, revenue growth, market share growth, personal income maximization, and many more, all of which are likely to affect the behavior of the firm.

Defining the national economy as the macro level of an economic system has historical and practical reasons, but it is also questionable. The only true macroeconomy is the world economy. National economies are interrelated in many ways, such as through trade and factor flows. An argument for the national economy as the appropriate macro level is that the legislation that sets the rules for the economy and economic policy is determined by national political actors. But in many cases this is no longer true. For example, monetary policy in many EU countries is conducted by a supranational institution, the European Central Bank. Similarly, much economic regulation in the EU takes place at the union level rather than at the national level. Even countries that are not members of an economic union are subject to supranational regulation, such as international trade agreements. Another issue concerns multinational corporations, which often operate in more than a hundred countries and are therefore subject to different regulations, policies, market conditions, and so on. Considering only a fraction of their activities in one country can be misleading. In some cases, large multinationals may be headquartered in a low-tax country, but most of their main activities take place elsewhere. To avoid such complications, many mainstream macroeconomic models assume closed (national) economies, which is a fiction except for very few countries such as North Korea.

But despite these problems, let us assume that we can define a microeconomic level, such as the level of households and firms, and a macroeconomic level, such as the national economy. A key question is how these levels relate to each other. Fig. 9.2 suggests one way of thinking about the micro–macro relationship.

A reductionist perspective, which is the dominant one in current mainstream economics, postulates that macroeconomic entities are caused by the actions of microeconomic agents, as indicated by the red upward-pointing arrows labeled β_1 and β_2. This view is probably correct, although it is incomplete, as we will argue later. By definition, microeconomic agents are the only entities in an economic system that can perform actions. Therefore, anything that can be observed at higher levels is somehow caused by what happens at lower levels.

So what are macroeconomic entities? An *entity* is something that exists in some way, concretely or abstractly. Macroeconomic entities are not directly observable, which means that their existence can be difficult or impossible to prove. They are often theoretical concepts for which statistical constructs have been developed to make them observable. It is important to distinguish between the observable measure and the macroeconomic unit, because in many cases the measure is an imperfect

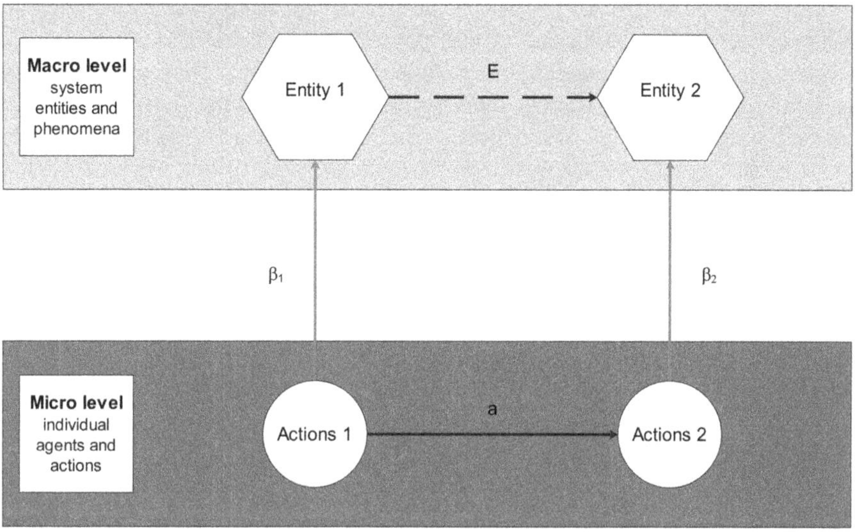

Fig. 9.2 Macro and micro level in the economy. Source: Author

Table 9.4 Macroeconomic entities

Class	Label	Examples	Characteristics
I	Basic quantitative concepts	Output, inflation, unemployment, economic growth	Measurable by statistical constructs, uncontested
II	Empirical regularities	Phillips curve, Beveridge curve, Okun's law	Statistical correlations between basic concepts
III	Theory-dependent concepts	Asset market bubble, output gap, NAIRU, aggregate capital, systemic risk	Often not directly measurable, depend on specific models, contested
IV	Properties of the macroeconomy	Complexity, openness to trade, innovativeness, polarization, cohesion, segregation, rule-of-law	Measurable empirical properties, often not part of theories, parameters
V	Qualitative concepts	Monetary order, financial architecture, type of capitalism	Comprehensive descriptions of institutional organization, not easily measurable
VI	Abstract high-level concepts	Inequality, freedom, knowledge, poverty, development, social welfare, well-being	Difficult to measure, often different approximations, uncontested in principle

representation of the unit. Table 9.4 lists a number of macroeconomic units and classifies them into six different classes. The main criteria for the classification are the degree of measurability and their role in macroeconomic theories.

There is no fundamental dispute about the basic concepts in Class I, in the sense that there is such a thing as the aggregate output of an economy or a change in the price level. These are measured by statistical constructs such as GDP and the rate of change of the GDP deflator or the consumer price index. These measures may be imperfect, but they are still widely accepted and available. The Phillips curve—i.e., a negative relationship between the rate of inflation and the rate of unemployment—is an example of a class II empirical regularity. They are often found in empirical data, although they may not be invariant over time. Class III theory-dependent concepts are not generally accepted. In the *Cambridge Capital Controversy*, neoclassical and Post-Keynesian economists fiercely debated whether it made sense to aggregate various capital goods into a variable called "aggregate physical capital." If one denies it, as the Post-Keynesians of Cambridge, UK, did, then the neoclassical production function used in the growth model proposed by Robert Solow of Cambridge, USA, does not make sense. Such debates occur even within neoclassical economics, for example on the question of whether or not asset market bubbles exist. An asset price bubble is defined by the deviation of the observable asset price from the unobservable fundamental price. The empirical properties of the economy in Class IV are often used in empirical studies as explanatory factors of, for example, economic growth, but they are less often considered as phenomena to be explained. We saw in Chap. 5 how the complexity of an economy can be measured and that the Economic Complexity Index has explanatory power for GDP growth (Table 5.5). Class V includes entities whose existence is undisputed, but which are difficult to measure with single quantitative indicators. A country or region certainly has a monetary regime that defines what counts as money and how money can be created. The monetary order includes the rules that govern banking and the interaction between private banks and the central bank. Finally, abstract concepts such as inequality or social welfare are important in our thinking about economies, but there is often controversy about what they actually mean and how they might be operationalized. Most economists probably accept social welfare as an important goal of economic activity and economic policy, but there are intense philosophical, ideological, and statistical debates about how to define and measure it.

Macroeconomic theory aims to explain macroeconomic patterns, which are changes in macroeconomic entities over time or relationships between different entities. In Fig. 9.2, "Entity 1" and "Entity 2" could be understood as the same entity (e.g., output, unemployment, or inequality) but at different points in time. A reductionist approach explains such a change from the bottom up: microeconomic actions (e.g., production decisions by firms) at time 1 lead to the measured value of the macroeconomic entity (e.g., aggregate output). If we observe that the macroeconomic unit has changed over time, it must be because the microeconomic actions have changed in the meantime. We can also explain an empirical regularity such as the Phillips curve in this way: price-setting and employment decisions at time 1 produce a combination of the inflation rate and the unemployment rate. Different decisions at time 2 lead to a different combination of inflation and unemployment, so that we get two points in the inflation-unemployment space that could be described by a Phillips curve. The entities could also be different, e.g. "Entity 1" = economic complexity and "Entity 2" = economic growth. We might assume or know from empirical evidence that there is a relationship between the entities, such as the positive impact of economic complexity on economic growth documented in

Table 5.5. Again, we can look for the micro factors and actions that cause the macro entities. An explanation for the relationship E between the entities is thus given by the relationship at the micro level. This logic, that all macroeconomic entities and the relationships between them are derived from microeconomic actions (as shown in Fig. 9.2), is what is meant by the *microfoundations of macroeconomics*. Neoclassical macroeconomics derives everything that happens at the macroeconomic level from deep or *fundamental parameters* at the microeconomic level, such as household preferences and firms' production technology. These deep parameters are assumed to be invariant (in particular, unaffected by macroeconomic events) and determine the microeconomic actions that generate macroeconomic observations.

However, this is not the only way of doing macroeconomic theorizing. There are approaches that relate macroeconomic entities directly to each other without explicit microfoundations. In particular, Keynesian and Post-Keynesian macroeconomics directly specify functional relationships between macroeconomic variables. The Keynesian consumption function or the Keynesian investment function in the IS-LM model still taught in many undergraduate macroeconomics courses are examples of this approach. Keynesian models were the mainstream approach in research in the 1950s and 1960s, but were vehemently attacked in the New Classical revolution of the 1970s. Post-Keynesian theory has never been mainstream. Prominent Post-Keynesian thinkers such as Piero Sraffa, Nicholas Kaldor, Luigi Pasinetti, and Wynn Godley, or more recently Steve Keen and Mark Setterfield, were and are highly skeptical about the need for explicit microfoundations (see King 2012; Lavoie 2022). This is not to say that Post-Keynesian economists are not interested in microeconomics or do not have theories of microeconomic behavior. However, many Post-Keynesians argue that it is reasonable to construct purely macroeconomic models that do not formally incorporate the microeconomic level. Instead, stable relationships between macroeconomic units can be derived from accounting identities and definitions, robust empirical observations, and structural theorizing, so that useful macroeconomic models can be developed to enable forecasting and policy analysis. This approach is similar to pragmatic approaches in physics that choose the appropriate level of analysis for the problem at hand. For example, the *ideal gas law* $pV = nRT$, which relates pressure p, volume V, temperature T, the amount of the substance n in a gas, and the ideal gas constant R, is a macroscopic law. It works well without recourse to the microscopic level of the gas molecules. In fact, pressure, volume, and temperature are state variables of the system that refer only to the macroscopic level. A microscopic particle does not have a temperature in the same sense as a macroscopic object or a gas, but it does have a kinetic energy and a velocity at which it moves.

While the distinction between micro and macro levels is standard in economics, several schools of thought, such as institutional, social, and evolutionary economics, argue that there is also a *meso level* in between (van Staveren 2020). According to this line of thinking, macroeconomic phenomena cannot be directly linked to individual agents, but are mediated through a meso level that has an ontological status. Having an ontological status means that the meso level has genuine entities that are not just aggregates of individuals.

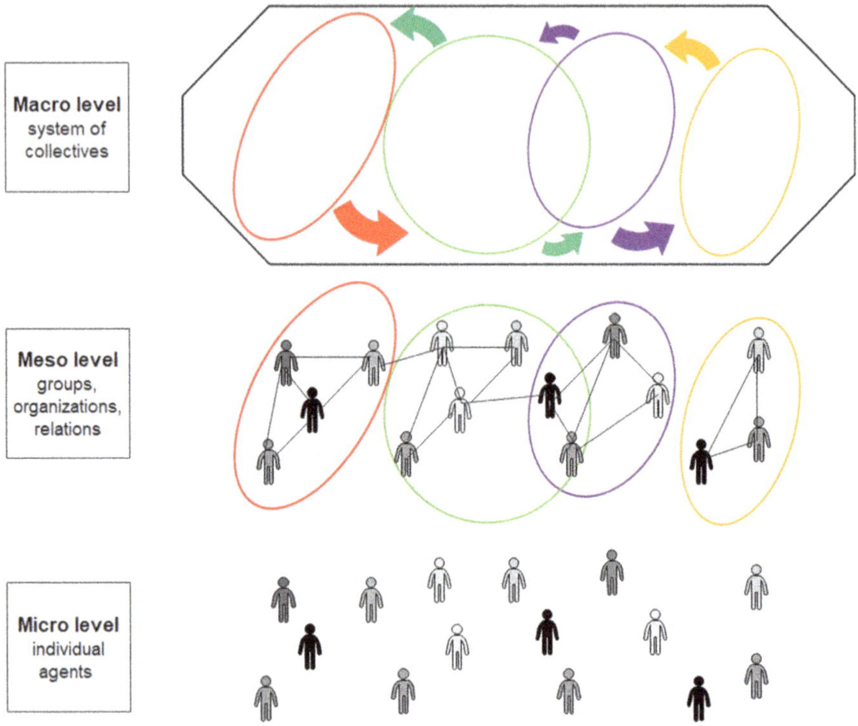

Fig. 9.3 Micro–meso–macro. Source: Author

Figure 9.3 illustrates how the meso level differs from the micro and macro levels. Microeconomics treats agents as isolated individuals who maximize their private objective functions regardless of the social context. The different shades of gray suggest that agents are heterogeneous. Mesoeconomics, on the other hand, recognizes that individuals are related to others, as shown by the connecting lines between agents. Through these *social ties* (as links are called in sociology), individuals form social groups, represented by the colored ellipses in the figure. Social groups have a sense of identity, shared social norms, and often a common goal or purpose. *Organizations* are social groups that have some formal structure, such as corporations, governments, associations, political parties, etc. Membership in a social group binds individuals together, but groups can also emerge from social ties and the resulting interactions in self-organizing processes. The ties within a group are called *bonding ties*, while the ties that connect groups are called *bridging ties*. In the example in Fig. 9.3, the red group and the green group are connected by a bridging tie between two individuals. The purple group and the orange group are not connected because there are no bridging ties between them. The green group and the purple group partially overlap because two individuals belong to both groups. Belonging to multiple groups is the normal case for individuals. For example, an individual may be an employee of a firm, but also a member of a trade union or a member of a political party. The macroeconomic level is the system level at which social groups, but not individuals, interact. Even groups that are not linked by bridging ties between some of their members can interact collectively. For example, two investment banks can trade with each other in a financial market without any personal relationships between their employees.

The meso level is also the level of *rules* or *institutions* that enable, guide, facilitate, or constrain individual behavior in a social context. Institutions can be formal, such as laws, regulations, legal codes, contracts, or informal, such as customs, traditions, social or moral norms, conventions. Institutions can be understood as "rules of the game" (North 1991), or more precisely as "systems of established and prevailing social rules that structure social interactions" (Hodgson 2006, p. 2). Some individual behavior is only possible because of the rights granted to an individual. You can only get a mortgage on a house if you have a property right in the house. Individual behavior can be facilitated when institutions reduce the need for constant, time-consuming individual decisions by searching for and weighing alternative options. Following a social norm by doing what other people do thus reduces the complexity of individual behavior. If the institution is reasonable, it is welfare enhancing because it reduces the cost of individual decision-making. On the other hand, institutions can also reduce social welfare if they are out of touch with current realities and unduly constrain individual behavior. For example, the tradition that the eldest son learns the same trade as his father may have made sense in times when education was provided by the father and knowledge and material assets were best preserved within the family. Today, however, there are formal vocational training institutions and most assets are tradable in markets. Under these conditions, the tradition of following in one's father's footsteps is an outdated constraint.

9.2.3 Fallacy of Composition and Representative Agents

The relationship between different economic levels is a long-standing topic in economics. According to Wray (2006, p.1), "one of the most important concepts to be taught in economic is the notion of the fallacy of composition: what might be true for individuals is probably not true for society as a whole." Indeed, the *fallacy of composition* is discussed in many introductory textbooks. Finocchiaro (2016) discusses the susceptibility of economic reasoning to the fallacy of composition and provides a more precise definition: "By fallacy of composition I mean an argument of composition that commits a fallacy. An argument of composition is one which concludes that a whole or group has a certain property because the parts of the whole or members of the group have that property. ... A fallacy is a common type of argument that appears to be correct but is actually incorrect" (Finocchiaro 2016, p. 17). It is a common theme in economics textbooks that lay economic thinking is often subject to the fallacy of composition.

Economists like to think of their discipline as the art of avoiding the fallacy of composition. In this view, the study of economics reveals flaws in economic arguments that seem convincing to laypeople. A classic example is the *paradox of thrift* (or the *paradox of saving*): it sounds intuitively plausible that aggregate saving in an economy will increase if all households save more. But if all households become more thrifty, aggregate consumption, and hence aggregate demand, may fall, reducing aggregate income. With lower aggregate income, total saving may fall even though each household is trying to save more.

There are many other examples where individually beneficial behavior can lead to suboptimal collective outcomes, which is the standard prediction of the *prisoner's dilemma*. An individual firm may be able to increase sales and profits by lowering wages, because it gains a competitive advantage over other firms with higher costs. But a collective wage cut could reduce aggregate income and aggregate demand so that all firms can sell less and profits fall. For an individual bank, it may be very profitable to be highly leveraged, but if all banks are highly leveraged, there is high systemic risk in the financial sector, which can lead to a financial crisis. In a stock market crash, it is individually rational to sell stocks, but the collective fire sales fuel the crash even more. Similarly, in a banking crisis, it makes sense for individual customers to withdraw their savings from their accounts, but if all account holders do so, they cause a bank run and drive the bank into illiquidity.

But it is not only laymen who fall into the fallacy of composition, but also economists themselves. This is the case when they use representative agents. A *representative agent* is a fictional decision-maker who is "typical" of a group of decision-makers. Economists use representative agents in their mathematical models to deal with the problem of how to aggregate a large number of agents. The idea is that we can describe behavior at an aggregate level, such as aggregate consumption, by the decision problem of a single agent, such as a household. We encountered this in Chap. 4 in the discussion of the Ramsey–Cass–Koopmans model. The Ramsey–Cass–Koopmans model assumes that the dynamics of aggregate consumption expenditure follows directly from the decisions of a household, which is representative of all households in the economy. Representative agents are ubiquitous in all types of microeconomic and macroeconomic models.

Microeconomics textbooks often present consumer choice theory before introducing market demand. They derive individual consumer demand curves from utility maximization with preferences that satisfy basic rationality requirements such as completeness, transitivity, and non-saturation. Some introductory textbooks implicitly suggest that the properties of individual demand curves carry over to market demand curves. For example, Samuelson and Nordhaus (2010, p. 91) state:

> *The demand curve for the entire market is obtained by summing up the quantities demanded by all the consumers. Each consumer has a demand curve along which the quantity demanded can be plotted against the price; it generally slopes downward and to the right. If all consumers were exactly alike in their demand and if there were 1 million consumers, we could think of the market demand as a millionfold enlargement of each consumer's demand curve. In fact, of course, people differ in their tastes. Some have high incomes, some low.*

They do not discuss what such market demand functions might look like, but present an example of two linear individual demand functions that are easy to add. Pindyck and Rubinfeld (2018) do the same. Their Chap. 3 presents the theory of individual consumer choice, which they use as a starting point for deriving market demand in Chap. 4. They write:

> *So far, we have discussed the demand curve for an individual consumer. Now we turn to the market demand curve. ... In this section, we show how market demand curves can be derived as the sum of individual demand curves of all consumers in a particular market.* (Pindyck and Rubinfeld 2018, p. 144)

Again, an example of the addition of three linear demand curves is presented. Although these textbooks do not explicitly claim that the market demand function always looks similar to the previously derived individual demand functions, the inexperienced student might conclude this from the presentations. There is no warning that this is not true. In his more advanced textbook, Varian (1992) also discusses the aggregation of individual demand functions into a market demand function. He notes that the aggregate demand function inherits the property of continuity if all the individual demand functions are continuous, and asks whether other properties are also inherited:

> *Is there an aggregate version of Slutsky's equation or of the Strong Axiom of Revealed Preference? Unfortunately, the answer to these questions is no. In fact, the aggregate demand function will generally have no interesting properties other than homogeneity and continuity. Thus, consumer theory in general imposes no constraints on aggregate behavior* (Varian 1992, p. 153).

Varian's statement is devastating for neoclassical consumer theory, because it cannot guarantee under general conditions that the market demand functions obey the *law of demand* according to which there is an inverse relationship between the market price and the quantity demanded. The law of demand is fundamental to neoclassical theory, because it is a precondition for a unique market equilibrium. Figure 9.4 shows a market demand function that violates the law of demand and has seven intersections with the supply curve such that there are seven market equilibria, some of which may be stable while other are likely to be unstable. With multiple equilibria, the model is unable to make unambiguous predictions about the market price and the quantity sold in the market.

Only under very special conditions aggregate market behavior will look as if it were generated by a representative consumer behaving according to the neoclassical consumer theory. As shown by Gorman (1961), a representative consumer can be constructed only if all individual consumers i have an indirect utility function of the following type:

$$v_i(p, m_i) = a_i(p) + b(p)m_i, \tag{9.1}$$

where p is the market price of the good and m_i is the income of the consumer. Note that the utility function is additively separable and that the part related to income,

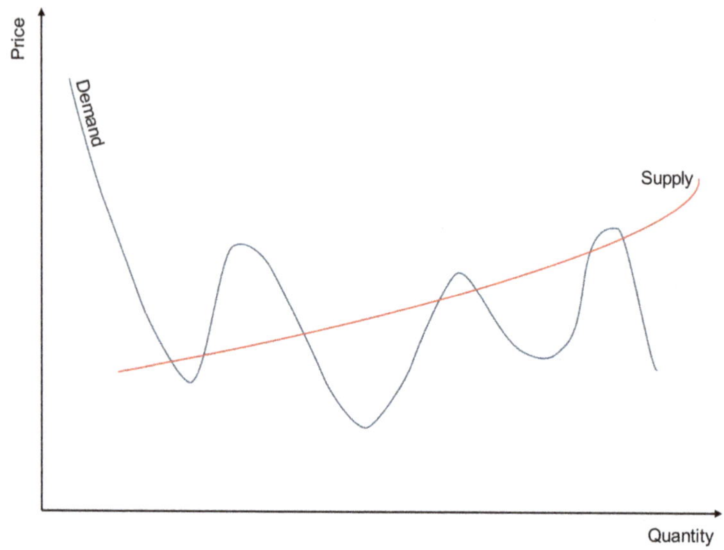

Fig. 9.4 Market with a demand function that violates the law of demand. Source: Author

$b(p)m_i$, is identical for all consumers. With this utility function, the individual demand function has the form:

$$x_i(p, m_i) = \alpha_i(p) + \beta(p)m_i. \tag{9.2}$$

A special case of the Gorman utility function is when the utility function is *homothetic*, i.e. $v_i(p, m_i) = b(p)m_i$. The Cobb–Douglas function with identical exponents for all consumers is of this type. The important property of the Gorman utility function is that it generates linear Engel curves with identical slopes. The *Engel curve* relates the quantity of a good demanded to an individual's income. Engel curves are used to characterize goods as *normal goods or inferior goods.* A good is said to be normal, if the Engel curve is upward sloping, i.e. if a consumer demands more of the good as income increases. In contrast, a good is called inferior if the demand for it decreases with rising income (e.g., junk food).

Let us see what happens when the consumers' demand functions are not of the Gorman type. Suppose there are two consumers 1 and 2 with the following demand functions for a good:

$$x_1 = \frac{\beta}{p}\left(\alpha_1 + m_1^\gamma\right), \tag{9.3}$$

$$x_2 = \frac{\beta}{p}\left(\alpha_2 - m_2^\gamma\right), \tag{9.4}$$

with $\alpha_1 > 0, \alpha_2 > 0, \beta > 0, \gamma > 0$. The good is a normal good for consumer 1, but an inferior good for consumer 2. If we sum up the two demand functions, we obtain the aggregate demand function:

$$X = \frac{\beta(\alpha_1 + \alpha_2)}{p} + \frac{\beta}{p}\left(m_1^\gamma - m_2^\gamma\right). \tag{9.5}$$

The problem with this demand function is that it does not describe an unambiguous relationship between aggregate demand $X = x_1 + x_2$ and aggregate income $M = m_1 + m_2$. If both consumers have identical incomes $m_1 = m_2$, then the aggregate demand function is independent of aggregate income. If we double the income of each consumer, aggregate demand will remain constant because the increase in the demand by consumer 1 is exactly offset by the decrease in the demand by consumer 2. But now suppose we double aggregate income by tripling the income of one consumer while holding the income of the other consumer fixed. If we triple the income of consumer 1, aggregate demand will increase. However, if we triple the income of consumer 2, aggregate demand will fall. In what sense can a representative consumer represent this? The answer is that it cannot. Unless the Engel curves of different consumers are linear with identical slopes, relative income changes will always affect aggregate demand, even if aggregate income remains constant.

The problem that we cannot assume that the market demand function has the same properties as the individual demand functions unless we assume a special and unrealistic type of utility function extends to the issue of the uniqueness and stability of a general equilibrium in many markets. The *Sonnenschein–Mantel–Debreu theorem*[1] states that the *excess demand functions* (the difference between the quantity demanded and the quantity supplied) of many utility-maximizing agents inherit only the properties of continuity and homogeneity of degree zero from the individual excess demand functions and satisfy Walras's law. This implies that it is not guaranteed that the excess demand functions are downward-sloping. But without this property, there is no reason to assume that there is a unique and stable general equilibrium.

These results imply that individually rational behavior does not automatically translate into aggregate behavior that can be characterized by a representative agent with the same rationality. But the reverse case can also be true, namely that market outcomes are very consistent with the predictions of rational behavior even though we know that individual agents are at best boundedly rational and have limited information. Discussing a variety of experimental results, Smith (1982, 1989, 1994) argues that the aggregate outcome of market interactions can approximate optimal predictions even though the experimental participants have little understanding of the optimization problem. Smith identifies institutions as the reason for this result, in particular the rules of the experimental markets. For example, continuous double

[1] Sonnenschein (1972, 1973), Mantel (1974), Debreu (1974)

auctions tend to produce more efficient outcomes than posted-offer markets because they provide useful information to agents.

There are other cases that demonstrate that microeconomic and macroeconomic properties are not identical. Caballero (1992) shows that asymmetric employment responses of individual firms to good and bad business cycle shocks do not necessarily carry over to the aggregate unless all firms start with identical conditions and are affected by the same shocks. If there is sufficient heterogeneity among firms, the cross-sectional distribution can offset the asymmetric behavior of firms so that the aggregate employment response is symmetric. Similarly, Caplin and Spulber (1987) show that price stickiness due to menu costs at the firm level does not carry over to the aggregate level if there is a distribution of firms with different price adjustment thresholds.

Finally, Jackson and Yariv (2019) prove that representative agents can only be constructed from very specific individual utility functions. Their definition of a representative agent is that the utility function of the representative agent is a weighted average of the n individual utility functions of the same type:

$$V\left(\sum_{i=1}^{n} \lambda_i x_i; \overline{a}\right) = \sum_{i=1}^{n} \lambda_i V(x_i; a_i),$$

where $V(.)$ is the utility function, x_i is the private allocation (e.g., consumption) of agent i, a_i is an individual characteristic (e.g., risk-aversion parameter, discount factor, wealth endowment), and λ_i is a weight (e.g., corresponding to the relative fractions of different groups in the population). For private allocations, the utility function must be linear in the allocation x and additively separable in the type parameter a, hence

$$V(x, a) = cx + h(a), \tag{9.6}$$

where c is a real-valued constant and $h(.)$ is a function with $h(\overline{a}) = \sum_i \lambda_i h(a_i)$. Importantly, utility functions common in macroeconomics such as strictly concave utility functions, CRRA or CARA utility functions of exponentially-discounted utilities do not have this form. The general impossibility of constructing representative agents with the same utility functions as the individual agents is a big disappointment for macroeconomic DSGE modeling. One of the supposed advantages of DSGE models over pure aggregate models is that the utility function of the representative household is a natural and correct welfare criterion (Blanchard 2009). Many papers in the DSGE literature conduct welfare analyses of fiscal and monetary policies or determine optimal welfare-maximizing policies. However, if the utility function of the fictitious representative agent differs from the utility functions of the individual agents, it is not clear in which respect it can be interpreted as a welfare measure.

At the heart of the problems with representative agents is the *aggregation problem* (Hartley 1997). When microeconomic entities are different, it is generally not possible to aggregate them in a consistent way. Consistency means that the analysis of the aggregate does not lead to different results than the analysis at the disaggregated level. We have seen several examples where it is not possible if the agents are heterogeneous. The representative agent cannot be interpreted as an average (or "typical") agent of different agents, because

> *well-behaved individuals need not produce well-behaved representative agents; ... the reaction of a representative agents to change need not reflect how the individuals would respond to change ... [and] the preferences of a representative agent over choices may be diametrically opposed to those of society as a whole* (Kirman 1992, p. 134).

In general, consistent aggregation is only possible, if all agents are identical in terms of their characteristics, including wealth and income. The assumption of perfectly identical agents is, of course, highly unrealistic. Therefore, Kirman (1992, p. 119) argues

> *that the 'representative' agent deserves a decent burial, as an approach to economic analysis that is not only primitive, but fundamentally erroneous.*

9.3 Emergence

So far, our discussion of the difficulties of linking the macroeconomic and microeconomic levels has been largely unrelated to emergence. Chorafakis (2020) calls aggregation the nemesis of emergence, so emergence seems to be related to non-aggregation. As we saw in the previous section, aggregation is generally not possible when entities are heterogeneous and when relationships between variables (e.g., demand and income) are nonlinear. We might therefore expect that heterogeneity and nonlinearity are also important for emergence. Wimsatt (1986) lists four criteria for aggregation to be possible. First, the parts of the system must be *intersubstitutable* without affecting the properties of the system. Second, the properties of the system do not change qualitatively when parts are added or removed. Third, the parts can be decomposed or reaggregated. Fourth, the interactions between the parts are not cooperative or inhibitory, or in other words, there is no positive or negative feedback between the parts. The first three criteria imply homogeneity of the parts, and the last criterion is about linearity of interaction. For most social systems, the criteria for aggregation are not met. The problem of aggregation and emergence are also related because they both describe the existence of different properties at different levels of a system. However, emergence is a more powerful concept. Intuitively, emergence describes a process by which something new appears at a higher level that cannot be found at the lower level of the system. This "something new" can be a property or a pattern, where the pattern is the result of (self-)organization of the elements of the system. In a social context, "something new" can also mean "unintended," i.e. a systemic outcome that was not planned by the individual decision-makers whose actions together produced the aggregate result.

The literature distinguishes between different types of emergence, which will be explained in the following subsections. A rather uninteresting type of emergence is simple or nominal emergence. *Nominal emergence* means that a system as a whole has macro properties that its micro-elements do not have. This type of emergence is quite common and applies to any machine or composite object. For example, an airplane can fly, but its parts alone cannot. A gas has pressure, but its molecules do not. Water is a liquid, but hydrogen and oxygen atoms are not. The average income of a group is also a nominally emergent property, because it makes little sense to talk about the average income of an individual. Nominal emergence does not deserve special attention here, because the properties of the aggregate are determined by the parts in a straightforward and therefore predictable way. Machines are designed to have certain functions and properties. The macroscopic properties of a gas can be derived from its microscopic parts by the laws of statistical mechanics. In general, we can relate nominally emergent properties to lower-level properties by some law-like relationship.

Similarly, Halley and Winkler (2008) distinguish between *simple emergence*, which corresponds to nominal emergence, and *complex emergence*. The dividing line between the two concepts is self-organization as shown in Fig. 9.5. Complex emergence occurs only in complex systems that exhibit self-organization. Consistent with our discussion in Chap. 8, they define self-organization as "a dissipative nonequilibrium order at macroscopic levels, due to collective, nonlinear interactions

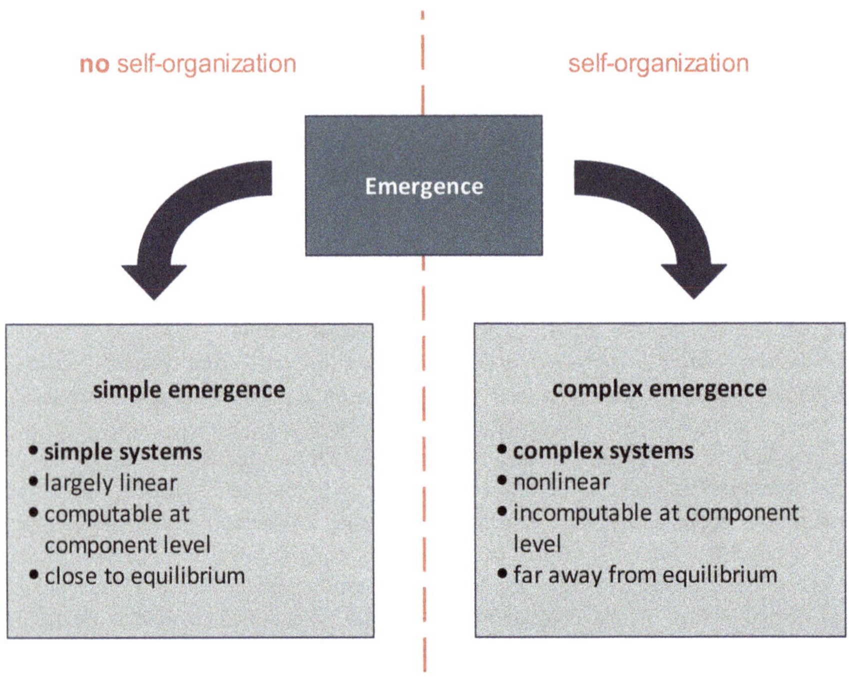

Fig. 9.5 Self-organization and emergence. Source: Author

between multiple microscopic components. This order is influenced by interplays between intrinsic and extrinsic factors, and decays upon removal of the energy source" (Halley and Winkler 2008, p. 11).

The more interesting complex types of emergence are characterized by novelty, unpredictability, and irreducibility. It is common to distinguish synchronic and diachronic emergence as well as weak and strong emergence. *Synchronic emergence* refers to the coexistence of something novel at a higher level with objects of properties at a lower level at the same time (from Actions 1 to Entity 1 in Fig. 9.2). *Diachronic emergence* describes the emergence of novel phenomena across time, i.e. something new appears in history that was not there before (from Actions 1 to Entity 2 in Fig. 9.2). Weak and strong emergence have in common that the novel phenomenon is unpredictable in the sense that we cannot relate macro-level properties to the micro-level in a law-like fashion. The difference between weak and strong emergence is the notion of irreducibility. A weakly emergent phenomenon can in principle (but not in practice) be reduced to the micro-level properties, but a strongly emergent phenomenon is irreducible in principle.

9.3.1 Weak Emergence

One version of weak emergence has been proposed by the philosopher Mark Bedau (1997, 2002). It is closely related to Herbert Simon's characterization of complex systems in which "given the properties of the parts and the laws of their interaction, it is not a trivial matter infer the properties of the whole" (Simon 1996, p. 184). The key feature of this kind of emergence is practical unpredictability. This means that the system's aggregate properties and behavior are fully determined by its constituents and their interactions. The micro rules determine everything that happens in the system and there is only a bottom-up causality. Thus, in principle, we can reduce the system to its parts and could also predict its behavior from micro phenomena. However, we cannot do this in practice, because of the large number of micro-element interactions that are nonlinear and context dependent. Based on this insight, Bedau proposed the following definition for weak emergence:

> A macrostate P of system S with microdynamic D is weakly emergent if and only if P can be derived from D and S's external conditions but only by simulation.

The microdynamic is given by the properties of the elements and their interaction rules. The external conditions are only the initial conditions of the micro-elements, if the system is deterministic. If the system is stochastic, then the stochastic shocks also belong to the external conditions. Bedau's definition postulates, that it is possible to derive a weakly emergent macrostate of a system, because the causal mechanism is fully known. However, due to its complexity, there is only one way to do this, which is simulation. *Simulation* means that the system must iteratively go through each time step so that the microdynamics are fully executed. There is no "short-cut" to this procedure such as a mathematical formula that we could use in order to derive a future state without having computed the intermediate steps. To illustrate what this means, consider the second-order difference equation

$$x(n) = ax(n-1) + bx(n-2). \tag{9.7}$$

If we have two initial conditions $x(0)$ and $x(1)$, we can compute $x(2)$. Using $x(2)$ and $x(1)$, we can compute $x(3)$ and so on. This iterative computation would be a simulation of the system. However, for difference equations of this type, there is a shortcut, because we know that the general solution is

$$x(n) = C_1\lambda_1^n + C_2\lambda_2^n, \tag{9.8}$$

where $C_{1,\,2}$ are constants and $\lambda_{1,\,2}$ are the roots of the characteristic equation. For systems with weak emergence, we cannot find an algebraic solution from which we can directly compute the values of $x(n)$ for any n.

A classic example of a system with weak emergence is John Conway's *Game of Life* (or simply *Life*). Life is a two-dimensional cellular automaton that was designed to generate unpredictable life-like patterns. Its rules are very simple. The system consists of an (infinite) two-dimensional grid of square cells, which can be either dead or alive, indicated by color (e.g., white for dead and green for alive). The initial configuration of dead and alive cells on the grid is random. The system's microdynamics are determined by the rules in Table 9.5, according to which each cell interacts with its neighbors in the Moore neighborhood.

Hence, the future state of a cell depends on the current state of its neighbors, more precisely on the number a of neighbors, which are currently alive. A cell is "born," if it has exactly three living neighbors. A living cell remains alive if it has two or three living neighbors. A cell dies if it has less than two or more than three living neighbors.

These very simple rules of interaction create unpredictable patterns and dynamics. Some of the resulting patterns resemble higher order entities, so we can speak of emergence. A random initial configuration in period 0 is shown in Fig. 9.6. We have no way of predicting what the configuration will look like in future periods other than by running a simulation. Figure 9.7 shows what the configuration looks like in period 83. The overall pattern no longer looks random. A few "objects" have

Table 9.5 Interactions rules in the Game of Life

Cell born	Cell dies	Cell stays alive	Cell dies

a = 3	a < 2	1 < a < 4	a > 3

Fig. 9.6 Random initial configuration in the Game of Life. Source: Author

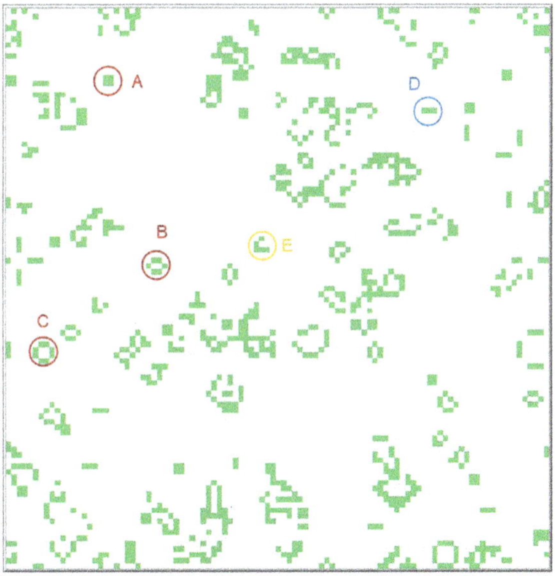

Fig. 9.7 Configuration in period 83. Source: Author

emerged, marked by the labeled circles. Of course, these objects are simply special configurations of living cells in a neighborhood, but to the human observer they appear to have new properties. The objects and their locations on the grid are the macrostate of the system.

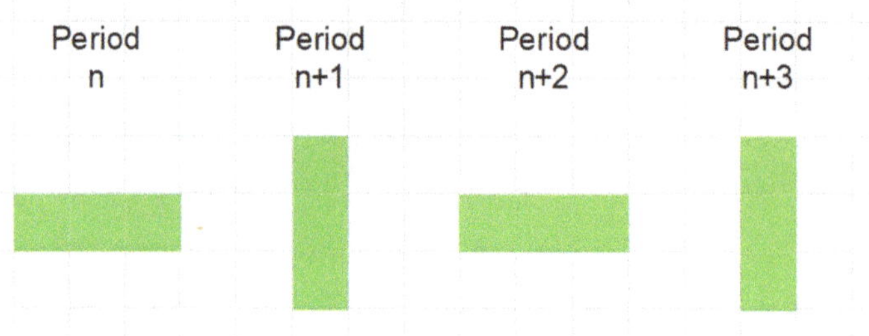

Fig. 9.8 A blinker. Source: Author

The objects in the red circles are called "still lifes" because they do not change from one period to the next. Object A is called a "block," B is a "beehive," and C is a "pond." Each of the four living cells in a block and the other still lifes has three living neighbors, so the objects reproduce themselves. Object D is a "blinker," which is a two-period oscillator. A blinker is a configuration of three living cells arranged horizontally in one period and vertically in the next period (Fig. 9.8). We can interpret a blinker as an entity with a new behavior (oscillation), although the rules of the Game of Life do not define such an entity or any behavior. The only entities defined by the system design are cells, which have no behavior but only a state that depends on the states of other cells.

The Game of Life thus generates patterns of cells in the state "alive," which we can interpret as new objects that have properties that the individual cells do not have, e.g. being a still life, being an oscillator, or being able to "move" over the grid. These new objects are weakly emergent. From an initial random configuration, we can only deduce whether and where these objects emerge by going through the game step by step.

A particularly interesting object is marked with an E in the orange circle. It is the so-called glider, which belongs to the object category of "spaceships." Spaceships can "move" over the grid. Figure 9.9 shows how a glider evolves over time.[2] From period n to period $n + 1$, the glider moves down one row, because a new cell is born in the bottom row, while the cell in the top row with only one neighbor dies. From period $n + 1$ to $n + 2$, two cells die and one is born, creating the original shape, but reversed. From $n + 2$ to $n + 3$, the glider moves one column to the right, because the single cell on the left dies and a new one is born on right of the three vertical cells. In period $n + 4$ the original shape is restored, but shifted one row down and one column to the right. If a glider does not "collide" with other objects, it can move forever on an infinite grid.

Weak emergence is related to what Steven Wolfram (2002) calls *computational irreducibility*, which says that some computations in complex systems cannot be reduced by mathematical shortcuts. He writes:

[2]Note that this glider is a mirror image of the glider in Fig. 9.7. The glider in Fig. 9.7 moves down and to the left.

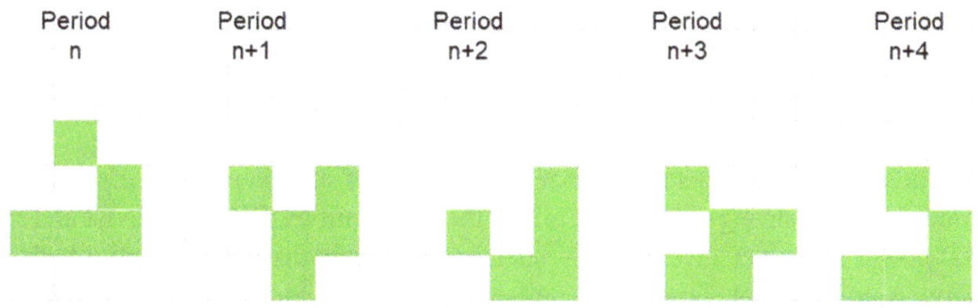

Fig. 9.9 A glider. Source: Author

> *So what this means is that systems one uses to make predictions cannot be expected to do computations that are any more sophisticated than the computations that occur in all sorts of systems whose behavior we might try to predict. And from this it follows that for many systems no systematic prediction can be done, so that there is no general way to shortcut their process of evolution, and as a result their behavior must be considered computationally irreducible.* (Wolfram 2002, p. 741)

Wolfram came to this conclusion from his study of the one-dimensional cellular automata presented in Chap. 8. He argues that if it is possible to work with traditional mathematical formulas, the system must show great computational reducibility. This is the case if the behavior in the system is either uniform or repetitive and thus implies symmetries. He considers such systems to be simple. Computational irreducibility is the reason why Wolfram sees the need for a "new kind of science" that must be computational:

> *So what does this mean for science? In the past it has normally been assumed that there is no ultimate limit on what science can be expected to do. And certainly the progress of science in recent centuries has been so impressive that it has become common to think that eventually it should yield an easy theory—perhaps a mathematical formula—for almost anything. But the discovery of computational irreducibility now implies that this can fundamentally never happen, and that in fact there can be no easy theory for almost any behavior that seems to us complex. . . . Any accurate model for a system that exhibits computational irreducibility must at some level inevitably involve computations that are as sophisticated as those in the system itself. . . . Given these models the only way to find out what they do will usually be just to run them. But the point is that if the structure of the models is simple enough, and fits in well enough with what can be implemented efficiently on a practical computer, then it will often still be perfectly possible to find out many consequences of the model.* (Wolfram 2002, pp. 748–750).

Since the economy is a complex (adaptive) system with at least weak emergence and computational irreducibility, we should not expect reductionist mathematical models to produce valid (theoretical) predictions. Agent-based computational models are therefore the better alternative. We will see examples of how they can be used in macroeconomics later in this chapter.

9.3.2 Strong Emergence

Strong emergence means that the prediction of higher-level properties is not only impossible in practice due to the complex interactions of the parts, but also impossible in principle. The macro level is then *irreducible* to the micro level.

Not all philosophers of science accept the notion of strong emergence. A common argument against strong emergence is that the only entities that really exist and have causal power are lower-level entities, such as neurons in the brain or individuals in a society. Anything that happens at higher levels, such as the feeling of pain in a person's mind or the formation of a church by a group of people, must be caused by the lower-level entities. However, strong emergence does not require that higher-level objects be given ontological status and that there be no upward causation from lower-level entities. One concept of weak causality from lower to higher levels is supervenience. *Supervenience* (from Latin "super" = "above, additional" and "venire" = "to come") means that something comes in addition to something else. It implies a concept of weak causality, such that higher-level phenomena are caused by lower-level ones, but not perfectly. The definition of supervenience is:

▶ A set of properties or facts X supervenes on a set of facts or properties Y if and only if (iff) a difference in Y is necessary for any difference in X to be possible.

The causal relationship between the levels described by supervenience is imperfect, because a change at a higher level cannot occur without a change at a lower level, but the reverse is possible. Supervenience does not imply irreducibility and thus strong emergence. It is merely a concept that accepts causal influence from lower levels to higher levels. Strong emergence requires that the higher level is somehow autonomous from the lower level, even though it supervenes (or depends) on it. Sawyer (2005) argues that irreducibility, and thus autonomy of the higher level from the lower, results from the combination of multiple realizability and wild disjunction.

Multiple realizability means that the same higher-level state or property can be implemented or realized by different lower-level states. For example, the feeling of pain can be realized by a variety of different neurobiological terms and concepts. Similarly, there are many ways in which "being a church," "being a family," "being an organization," or "being a company" as higher-level properties can be realized by individual beliefs, dispositions, and behaviors. *Wild disjunction* means that the descriptions of different lower-level states are unrelated to one another. If we want to describe what a company is in terms of the beliefs, dispositions, and behaviors of the individuals associated with it, we are probably forced to use wildly disjunctive microeconomic or psychological descriptions. It is probably even more difficult to describe what capitalism is using economic terms and concepts that refer to individual firms or even psychological terms and concepts that refer to individual people. Figure 9.10 illustrates multiple realizability and wild disjunction. The higher-level state Y can be realized by the lower-level states x_1 or x_2 or x_3 and so on, all of which require very different descriptions. The important point is that the lower-level

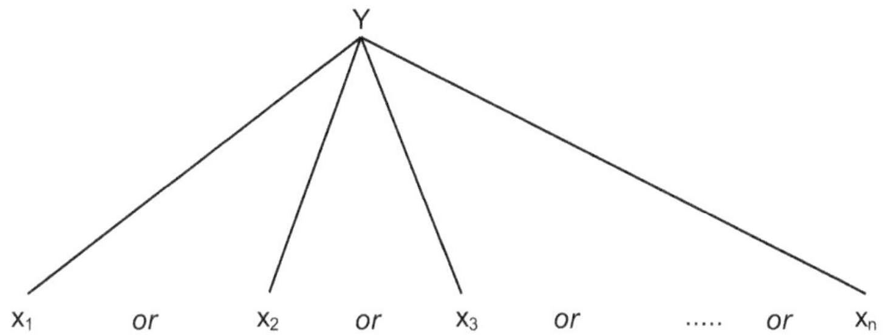

Fig. 9.10 Multiple realizability and wild disjunction. Source: Author

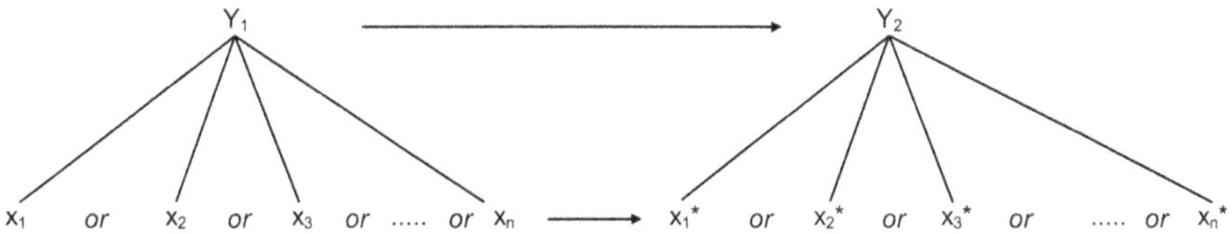

Fig. 9.11 A macro law. Source: Author

supervenience bases are not related to each other in a law-like fashion, and thus cannot be translated into each other. If this is the case, Y is not reducible to micro-level explanations of the different realizations of X, i.e. $x_1, x_2, \ldots x_n$.

Irreducibility can justify the existence of aggregate scientific laws in sociology or economics, which is an argument against *methodological individualism* according to which all social phenomena must be explained in terms of the motivations and actions of individuals. Figure 9.11 illustrates why this is the case. Suppose there is a regular relationship between Y_1 and Y_2 that we can call a social or macro law. Sawyer (2002, p. 550) gives a sociological example of such a law "if a group has the property of being a church, then its degree of solidarity will be higher than groups that do not have this property." Such a social law is meant to be general, i.e. to hold for all groups that are churches, regardless of its specific realization in any given society or culture.

With multiple realizability and wild disjunction, a church can be realized in many ways:

$$Y_1 \leftrightarrow x_1 \text{ or } x_2 \text{ or } x_3 \text{ or} \ldots \text{or } x_n.$$

The relation between the macro property and the micro level ($\leftrightarrow$) is called a *bridge law*, which contains properties and concepts of both the macro and the micro levels. It is an identity relation such as "a church is a group of people that believe in the resurrection of Jesus Christ" or "a church is a group of people who practice religious rites." Similarly, we can define solidarity as the "willingness of the members of a group to give material support to other group members in need" or as "the bond of unity between individuals against a common enemy." The problem with methodological individualism, or the reduction of aggregate laws to the individual level, is that the macro law $Y_1 \rightarrow Y_2$ would require a micro law such as:

$$x_1 \; or \; x_2 \; or \; x_3 \; or \ldots \rightarrow x_1^* \; or \; x_2^* \; or \; x_3^* \ldots$$

A scientific law should have the form "whenever a, then b," but a micro law in Fig. 9.10 would read "whenever x_1 *or* x_2 *or* x_3 *or*..., then x_1^* *or* x_2^* *or* x_3^*...". The relationship between disjunctive alternative events or properties to one another is more like an enumeration than a law.

An economic example might be the macro "law" that "capitalism fosters economic growth," which seems empirically well grounded. But there are many ways to define capitalism or instantiate capitalism. There are different *varieties of capitalism,* with different institutions, different roles for the state, or different industrial relations. And there are many explanations for the sources of economic growth, such as technological progress through research and development, creative destruction by entrepreneurs, the accumulation of human capital, certain kinds of ethics, or the incentives created by an interest-based financial system. Both capitalism and economic growth may be strongly emergent macro phenomena, whose relationship cannot be explained by law-like relationships between micro phenomena.

9.4 Macrofoundations of Microeconomics

Neoclassical macroeconomists insist on the microfoundations of macroeconomics because they consider microeconomics to be more fundamental than macroeconomics. Since individuals are the only entities that can act, and there is a well-developed theory of individual behavior, microeconomics should be the terra firma from which all economic theories should start. However, as we have seen, we cannot easily aggregate individual behavior. Moreover, it is questionable whether neoclassical microeconomic theory can really provide a firm foundation for economic theorizing, and whether we actually know more about microeconomics than about macroeconomics (see Hartley 1997). First, empirically estimated models of the behavior of individual producers and consumers may be misspecified. The aggregation of economic variables and the relationships between these aggregated variables could reduce specification errors. As a result, the estimated aggregate relationships might be more robust than individual ones due to the aggregation gain. Second, 50 years of research in behavioral economics has shown that real people rarely behave as predicted by neoclassical rational choice theory. Behavioral economics has not (and may never) produce a single alternative model of human behavior. Instead, there are many different models with different applications, most of which "repair" some shortcoming of the neoclassical models. The *heuristics approach* of Gerd Gigerenzer and colleagues (e.g., Gigerenzer and Gaissmaier 2011) departs more from neoclassical rational choice theory, but has not developed a systematic theory of when individuals behave in a particular way. Third, and most importantly in the context of emergence, we cannot understand individual behavior in isolation. In fact, apart from artificial economic experiments in the laboratory, human behavior rarely occurs in isolation and independent of a social context. The social context is emergent and refers to a level above the level of the individual. The same individual may behave very differently at work, in the family, or in a sports club. For example, a woman may be a leader at work, a cooperative parent at home, and a γ-type group member (see Fig. 8.21 in Sect. 8.4.2) on the soccer team. Her level of cooperativeness is then not only an intrinsic personal trait, but is also determined by her role in the social context. Thus, several authors have argued that there is a need for *macrofoundations of microeconomics* (e.g., Colander 1993; Hahn 2003). The idea of macrofoundations is closely related to the notion of downward causation, which has been intensively discussed in philosophy of science and sociology. Economics has been concerned with the emergence of institutions that exert downward causation on individuals.

9.4.1 Downward Causation

In a microfoundations paradigm, the only causal relationship between the micro and macro levels is bottom up, as in Fig. 9.2. If bottom-up causation were indeed the only type of causality in multilevel systems, macro-level phenomena, or *social structure* as it is called in sociology, would simply be epiphenomena. An *epiphenomenon* is an emergent, higher-level result that has no causal effect on other phenomena, either macro or micro. *Downward causation*, on the other hand, runs top down from the macro to the micro level, as indicated by arrow 1 in Fig. 9.12.

Variations of Fig. 9.12 are often called *Coleman's bathtub* or *Coleman's boat* after the American sociologist James Coleman, whose "Foundations of Social

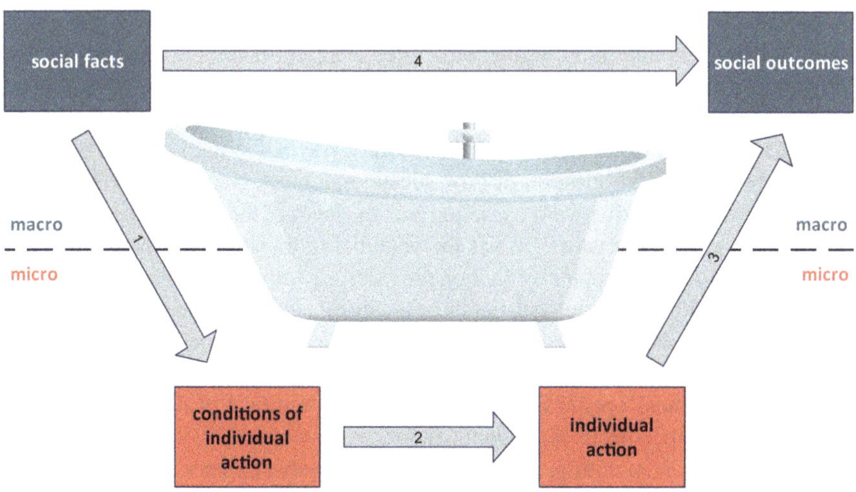

Fig. 9.12 Macro–micro–macro scheme. Source: Author

Theory" dealt with the question of how to relate the micro level and the macro level of a social system. In this scheme, the macro–macro relationship 4 may or may not be one of true causation. If it is interpreted as a real causation, it is called *autonomous causation*, which says that "[s]ocial properties are real and have causal powers that are autonomous from the causal powers of their composing individuals" (Sawyer 2003, p. 206). If one rejects autonomous causation, because one grants ontological status only to the micro level (as many sociologists and philosophers of mind do), then the true causal chain from social facts to social outcomes runs through the micro level via the downward causation 1 (macro–micro), the micro–micro link 2, and the upward causation 3 (micro–macro). Downward causation means that social facts determine the conditions for individual action and cause individuals to behave in a certain way.

9.4.2 The Emergence Paradigm in Sociology

Sawyer (2005) describes how sociology has theorized about the relationship between different levels of society during the twentieth century and identifies three paradigms. In the 1950s and 1960s, the *structure paradigm* dominated, emphasizing abstract, impersonal collective entities, and top-down causation. This paradigm considers only two levels: the macro level of social structure and the micro level of the individual. Within this paradigm, structural determinism sees the social structure as fundamental and the individual as socioculturally determined. In contrast, for methodological individualism, individuals are foundational and determine social structure through their actions, beliefs, and intentions. The *interaction paradigm*, which emerged in the 1960s as an alternative to the structure paradigm, focused on the link between individuals and social structure. It added interaction as a third level of ontological status to the analysis and claimed that this level, with its laws of interaction between individuals, was fundamental. However, this paradigm did not explain how stable structures emerge from the interactions of individuals, i.e., it had no theory of social emergence, nor did it consider how social structure constrains individual action. The *emergence paradigm* developed in the 1990s in the context of what Sawyer calls the third wave of systems theory based on complexity theory. The question of how social emergence occurs and how higher-level emergents exert downward causation is at the heart of the emergence paradigm.

While the emergence paradigm has the potential to transform sociology, it is not yet fully developed. Complexity theory provides an important foundation for the emergence paradigm in sociology, but there are three aspects that require attention to make complexity theory applicable to social systems. First, social systems have no clearly defined boundary, which makes them radically more open than natural systems. This radical openness makes reductionist approaches difficult and calls for more holistic perspectives. Second, the interconnections in social systems are more complex than in natural systems. Interaction between people involves symbolic communication and the transfer of meaning and interpretation, which is different from the transfer of information in natural systems. Third, agents in social

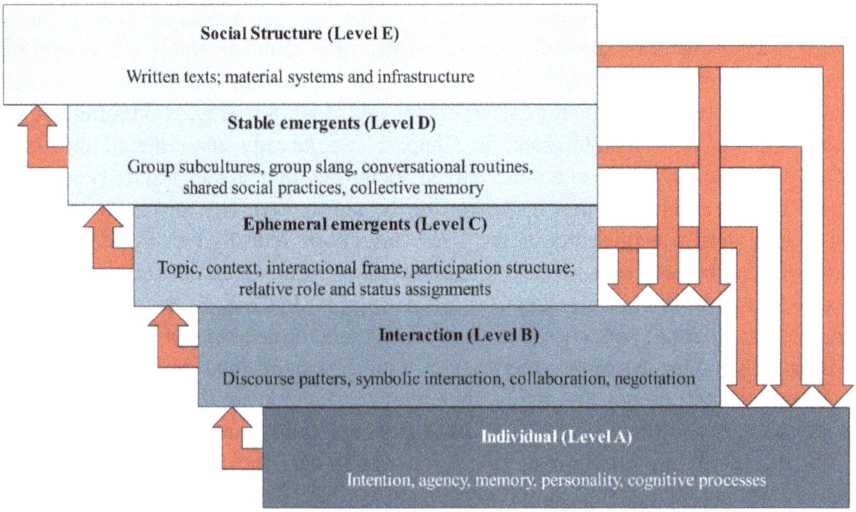

Fig. 9.13 Levels of social analysis in the emergence paradigm. Source: Author's own figure adapted from Sawyer (2005)

systems are aware that they are part of systems and form representations of the systems and emergent macropatterns. They also have intentions to influence the system, which is not the case for components of natural systems.

The emergence paradigm adds two meso-levels to the three levels considered in the interaction paradigm (see Fig. 9.13): the level of ephemeral emergents (Level C) and the level of stable emergents (Level D). Level C includes interactional frames, which are interpretive schemas that individuals use to perceive, understand, organize, and communicate about reality. Interactional frames emerge from collective action in a conversation and at the same time enable further collective action. Each action can change the emergent frame, making it a dynamic structure. In group interactions, roles and status assignments emerge that also affect how individuals interact. *Ephemeral emergents* are not stable over time and occur only within single encounters. In contrast, *stable emergents* persist across multiple encounters and represent the collective history of a group. The duration of their stability can range from weeks to generations. The distinction between ephemeral emergents and stable emergents is similar to Émile Durkheim's distinction between social currents (or social facts) and crystallized currents. Similarly, Georg Simmel (1950, p. 10) noted that "as [interactions] crystallize, the attain their own existence and their own laws, and may even confront or oppose spontaneous interaction itself." Many of the mechanisms of emergence are still unknown, but agent-based models can be used to simulate processes of emergence.

The level of social structure (level E) consists not only of *crystallized social facts,* but also of *materialized social facts*. The materialized aspects of society include texts (e.g., legal codes, project plans, organizational charts, procedural and operations manuals), production technologies, architecture, networks of communication and transportation, and other infrastructures. Because they are physical objects, these materialized aspects of society are even more stable than the stable emergents of level D. Their emergence differs from the social emergence of the other levels in that they are the outcome of historical processes and does not require ongoing social interaction for their maintenance. In Chap. 5, we already encountered the road infrastructure in the USA as a materialized social fact that shapes the daily lives of Americans. We also saw that the vision of the automotive city and a nation-wide highway system was presented at the 1939 New York World's Fair Futurama. The Futurama can be seen as evidence of a stable emergent in which the automobile was discussed as an important element of societal progress. In Chap. 5, we also discussed that the car-oriented infrastructure in the USA exerts a downward causation on individual behavior, because Americans rely on the car for their daily activities.

Sawyer (2005) argues that many phenomena at level E are the purview of other social sciences. Political science studies documents and records to understand why political systems are configured. Education researchers look at textbooks, school architecture, school location, or school records to understand the educational system. Economists are interested in studying technologies, factory locations, or trade agreements that are materialized facts of the economic system. If the pervasive mechanisms of emergence and downward causation are the same in different social systems, then sociology is the most general social science and provides important insights for other (applied) social sciences such as economics and political science.

As the arrows in Fig. 9.13 suggest, there can be downward causation from higher levels to level A of individuals or to level B of interactions between individuals. That is, ephemeral emergents, stable emergents, or the social structure affect either the behavior of individuals or the interaction between them. An example of downward causation from level D to level A is provided by Axtell (2000), who analyzes the effect of agent interaction topologies on the retirement behavior of individuals. In the agent-based model, agents decide when to retire. The population consists of rationals, who retire at the earliest age allowed by law, imitators, who play a coordination game in their social networks, and agents behaving in a random fashion. The imitators retire when the fraction of retired agents in their network exceeds a threshold. Axtell shows that after a change in the legal retirement age, the transition time and dynamics from the old norm of the actual retirement age to the new norm are very different depending on the type of social networks of the imitators. For a given fraction of rational agents, the transition is much lower in a lattice network than in a random graph network. The existing network type can be interpreted as a stable emergent in the population. Since different network types lead to different outcomes, but decisions in the model are made by individuals, there must be downward causation. A similar result is obtained by Macy and Skvoretz (1998), who study how trust and cooperation evolve among strangers in an agent-based model. Agents play prisoner's dilemma games with exit options either with their neighbors or with strangers. The authors vary both the number of neighbors an agent interacts with and the probability of interacting with a stranger. The model shows that the rate of cooperation with strangers is higher when the size of neighborhoods is smaller, because smaller neighborhoods facilitate the emergence of a convention of trusting strangers.

We can also demonstrate downward causation through the effect of different systems of collective decision-making on the group decision with a simple model. This would be an example of downward causation from level D to level B. Suppose there is a group of ten people, say ten professors in a university department. Each member of the group has a preference for a decision that the group must make collectively. Let us assume that the group's decision can be measured by a real number in the interval $[-1, 1]$. In practice, many decisions involve discrete variables rather than continuous ones, but let us consider the continuous case as an approximation. For example, suppose the group has to decide who to hire for a vacant position in the department. The relevant characteristic might be how mainstream the candidates are, where 1 indicates " fully mainstream" and -1 indicates "fully non-mainstream." Table 9.6 gives an example of the preferences of different professors for the mainstreamness of candidates. Professor I would prefer the most mainstream candidate, while Professor J has the strongest non-mainstream preference.

We also assume that group members differ in their power to succeed in group debates. Being successful means getting support for one's proposal, which may depend on rhetorical skills, status in the group, or personality. The third column shows an absolute measure of power, which can range from 0 to 1. In absolute terms, Professor F is the most powerful, while Professor E has the least power. Relative power is obtained by normalizing the sum of the power values to 1, which can be interpreted as the weight of each person's preference in a group debate.

Table 9.7 illustrates that different collective decision mechanisms lead to different results. "Anonymous voting" is simply the average of individual preferences, which

Table 9.6 Preference and power of group members

Professor	Preference	Power	Relative power in department	Section	Relative power in section
A	0.7	0.3	0.075	I	0.333
B	0.6	0.4	0.1	I	0.444
C	0.8	0.2	0.05	I	0.222
D	−0.2	0.4	0.1	II	0.333
E	−0.4	0.1	0.025	II	0.083
F	−0.1	0.7	0.175	II	0.583
G	0.8	0.5	0.125	III	0.263
H	−0.2	0.3	0.075	III	0.157
I	0.9	0.6	0.15	III	0.315
J	−0.9	0.5	0.125	III	0.263

Table 9.7 Outcomes of different collective decision-making schemes

Anonymous voting	Group debate	Section voting	Section speaker debate
0.2	0.2125	0.2485	0.1644

could be realized if all individual preferences were collected and averaged without regard to individual power. "Group debate" could be the result of an open discussion in the whole group, where each individual's preference is weighted by their relative power in the whole group (department). We could imagine more powerful individuals speaking longer or more often, or otherwise being able to persuade others of their own preferences. The outcome of the group debate is then a weighted average of the individual preferences. Another mechanism could be to first have a section debate and then a section vote. For example, the department could be organized into a macroeconomics section (Section I), a microeconomics section (Section II), and an applied economics section (Section III). Each section determines the preferred candidate by debate, i.e. as a group average with weights according to the relative power of the members in the section. The "section vote" is then the unweighted result of the three section preferences. Finally, each section might have a speaker who is the most powerful professor in the section. The departmental decision could be the result of a "section speaker debate" in which each section's preference is weighted by its speaker's relative power in the group of speakers. We can interpret these mechanisms as stable emergent properties of the group that are consciously or unconsciously accepted by group members. Since they affect the outcome of the members' interaction at level B, there is downward causation.

9.4.3 Multiple Equilibria and Indeterminacy

Colander (1993)—and similarly Axtell (2007)—provide a theoretical macroeconomic argument for why macrofoundations of microeconomics are important. The argument is that it is likely that there is no unique macroeconomic general equilibrium. We have already seen that this is a consequence of the Mantel–Sonnenschein–Debreu theorem. Multiple equilibria arise in nonlinear models (as discussed in Sect. 6.6.1) and from interdependencies between agents' actions that lead to coordination problems. Without a selection criterion among multiple equilibria, there is indeterminacy in the model because all equilibria are possible and equally likely. Multiple equilibria whose selection depends on the coordination of agents are called *sunspot equilibria*, because an exogenous random variable unrelated to economic fundamentals (like a sunspot) can serve as a coordinating device if it is used by all agents. If all agents believe that prices will rise in the future due to a bad crop caused by a sunspot, prices may indeed rise due to increased demand in the present. This belief is self-fulfilling, even if there is no real connection between the sunspot and the crop. This idea is similar to the expectation-based poverty trap described in Sect. 6.6.1 (see Fig. 6.53), where a country can get stuck in a bad equilibrium if investors are pessimistic about the country's prospects.

Expectation-driven equilibria could lead to more volatility in output than we actually observe. Walrasian macroeconomists who ignore the Mantel–Sonnenschein–Debreu theorem might argue that the observed relative stability of aggregate output is evidence against multiple equilibria. The claim might be that multiple equilibria and indeterminacy are a theoretical possibility but practically irrelevant. Colander counters this view by arguing that microeconomic decisions are not independent of the macro context in which they are made. The macro context imposes institutional constraints on individual decision-makers. Conventions and institutional constraints on individual behavior stabilize aggregate output because they coordinate the behavior of many individual agents. They are the macrofoundations of microeconomic behavior. Conventions and institutional constraints are stable emergents, but they can change over time. If the macro constraints change, instability and indeterminacy may result. Therefore, a study of the macrofoundations is necessary to understand the microeconomic choices and to predict what equilibrium might be collectively chosen.

In this view, the collective "choice" of a macroeconomic equilibrium is not a conscious one, because individuals face a Hayekian information problem. In contrast to the Muthian notion of rational expectations, boundedly rational individuals have neither the necessary information nor the cognitive capacity to determine a rational expectations equilibrium:

> *[Herbert] Simon argues that deciding over an entire range of possible choices exceeds the processing capacity of economic decision making units. Because it does, the decision making process has meaning only with a macro context. There is not one-to-one mapping between aggregate results and individual decisions. Put another way, the aggregate economic acquires a life of its own. ... In the macrofoundations-of-micro perspective one cannot escape process, one cannot meaningfully relate noncontextual individual choice theory with macro analysis until one has first determined the relevant macro context within which decision is made.* (Colander 1993, p. 452)

The macrofoundations approach requires, as a first step, determining the institutional structure of the economy in which individual decisions are made. This can be done deductively, empirically, or by simulation. Simulation has been proposed by Axel Leijonhufvud (1993). The simulation approach is consistent with Sawyer's proposal to explore the emergence of social facts through agent-based simulation models and with the notion of downward causation. In the words of Colander:

> *In Leijonhufvud's approach, the macrofoundations of micro would be determined by simulation. Micro decisions would be analyzed contingent on the simulation-determined institutional structure.* (Colander 1993, p. 453)

9.5 Institutions in Economics

Economics has long been interested in institutions. *Traditional Institutional Economics* dates back to the early twentieth century and was (and is) critical of context-free neoclassical analysis. Important members of this school of thought were Thorstein Veblen, Wesley Mitchell, and John R. Commons. In the second half of the twentieth century, *New Institutional Economics* (NIE) was established by economists such as Ronald Coase, Douglass North, Elinor Ostrom, and Oliver Williamson, all of whom were awarded the Nobel Memorial Prize.

9.5.1 New Institutional Economics

New institutional economics is closer to neoclassical mainstream economics and emphasizes the role of information, property rights, and transaction costs for economic activity. In this branch of institutional economics, an important function of institutions is to reduce transaction costs. North (1991, p. 97) gave a well-known definition of institutions:

> *Institutions are the humanly devised constraints that structure political, economic and social interaction. They consist of both informal constraints (sanctions, taboos, customs, traditions, and codes of conduct), and formal rules (constitutions, laws, property rights).*

In line with NIE thinking, he states that

> *transaction costs are a critical determinant of economic performance. Institutions and the effectiveness of enforcement (together with the technology employed) determine the cost of transacting. Effective institutions raise the benefits of cooperative solutions or the costs of defection, to use game theoretic terms. In transaction cost terms, institutions reduce transaction and production costs per exchange so that the potential gains from trade are realizeable.* North (1991, p. 98).

Oliver Williamson (2000) presents a figure similar to the one in Fig. 9.14 in which he places NIE at levels 2 and 3. The figure clearly shows that there is both upward and

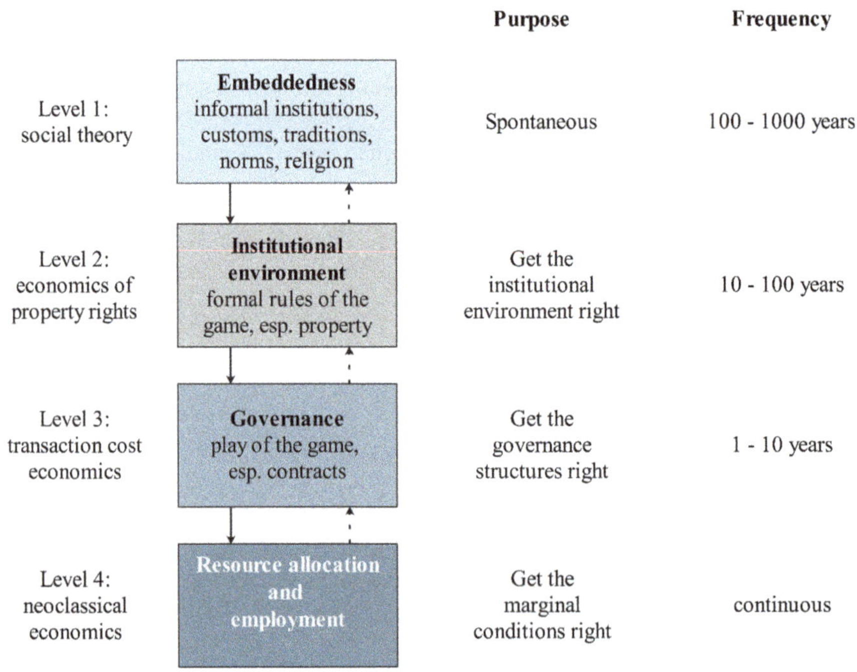

Fig. 9.14 Economics of institutions. Source: Author's own figure based on Williamson (2000)

downward causation between the levels represented by the arrows. Unlike the previous level diagrams we have seen in this chapter, Williamson characterizes the levels by activities and time scales.

Level 1 is the highest level and refers to informal institutions that change very slowly. Mark Granovetter's (1985) concept of embeddedness, according to which most behavior is tightly embedded in networks of interpersonal relationships, belongs to level 1, which could also be called the level of culture. While Williamson acknowledges an impact of this level on economic activity, he confesses ignorance about the mechanism by which informal institutions emerge and delegates this issue to social theory or sociology. For most economic issues, level 1 can be treated as exogenous because informal institutions can take centuries to change. The second level is called the institutional environment, which is created both by evolutionary processes and by design. It is the level of formal rules, such as constitutions, laws, and especially property rights, which are a precondition for the existence of markets and private entrepreneurship. Except for rare, sweeping reforms, the formal rules of the game change only slowly, over decades. The most important level for NIE is level 3, the level of governance. The formal rules of the game provide the general ex ante framework for economic transactions, but in practice contracts are always incomplete. Enforcing such contracts in the courts is costly, so economic parties often seek to manage contracts and resolve disputes directly through private ordering. The refinement, administration, and renewal of contracts through appropriate governance structures occur over a period of 1 year to a decade. Finally, level 4 includes the continuous economic activity of production, employment, and trade, which is the domain of standard neoclassical analysis.

9.5.2 Traditional Institutional Economics

Geoffrey Hodgson (2006), who is a more traditional institutional economist, criticizes North for not being clear enough about the difference between formal institutions and informal constraints. He defines "*institutions* as systems of established and prevalent social rules that structure social interactions" (Hodgson 2006, p. 2). By this definition language, money, law, social norms, systems of weights and measures, table manners, and corporations (and other organizations) are all examples of institutions. Hodgson's more general definition differs from the narrower definition of North in at least two respects. For North, institutions are "humanly devised," whereas Hodgson's definition is much closer to the sociological concept of social facts that can emerge from interaction without having been devised. "Generally, institutions enable ordered thought, expectation, and action by imposing form and consistency on human activities. They depend upon the thoughts and activities of individuals but are not reducible to them" (Hodgson 2006, p. 2). Furthermore, for Hodgson institutions both enable and constrain behavior. The rules of language, for example, enable us to communicate. Institutions can also change the purposes, aspirations, or preferences of agents and are thus downward causal.

In addition to institutions, Hodgson also defines conventions and rules. A *convention* is a particular instance of an institutional rule. For instance, all countries have traffic rules, but whether one drives on the left or the right is a convention. The definition of *rule* is:

> *The term rule is broadly understood as socially transmitted and customary normative injunction or immanently normative disposition, that in circumstance X do Y* (Hodgson 2006, p. 3)

In other words, a rule makes behavior more likely, but does not determine it. Rules can be codified—like legal rules—or not codified—like norms of behavior and social conventions. When a rule is codified, a violation of the rule can be explicitly identified. Norms and social conventions can be tacit or explicit knowledge in a community. Hodgson argues that formal rules rely on informal rules because codified rules are rarely complete. He therefore suggests that instead of speaking of formal and informal institutions, we should speak of legal and non-legal, and explicit and implicit rules or institutions. It is important to emphasize that institutions in this sense are understood as enduring systems of embedded and established social rules, not individual rules. In this broad sense, institutions also include the informal basis of all structured and enduring behavior.

Institutions have effects because their rules are embedded in shared habits of thought and behavior. *Habits* are propensities or dispositions to behave in a certain way, triggered by a particular context or stimulus. Through habits, institutions acquire durability, power, and authority, and become customary. A law that is ignored is not a rule. New laws, therefore, usually need to be enforced in such a way that new behavior becomes customary and acquires normative status. More generally, there must be incentives, disincentives, or sanctions for enforcing rules, which may originate outside or inside a group. For contracts or other legal norms, there is external enforcement by courts and other legal or governmental institutions. When a group enforces its own rules, there is self-organization. A group may punish or even ostracize members who violate the group's code of honor. But group members may also have a self-interest in following the group's rules, for example, by using the group's language or slang because they want to be understood. The use of language is an example of a coordination game. The words used to describe objects and activities and their pronunciation are arbitrary. As the existence of many languages proves, an object can be named in many ways. To enable communication, a group must coordinate to use the same words and to pronounce them in (roughly) the same way. This can be achieved through *social norms*, i.e. shared expectations about generally accepted behavior.

Table 9.8 is an example of a coordination game between two players who must decide which language to use. If they both speak the same language, they can communicate and receive a positive payoff, otherwise communication is impossible and they receive a payoff of zero. The game has two Nash equilibria in pure strategies: both speak English or both speak Urdu. In a Nash equilibrium, each player plays a best response to the other player's strategy, which implies that no

Table 9.8 Coordination game

		Player 2	
		Speak English	Speak Urdu
Player 1	Speak English	10 10	0 0
	Speak Urdu	0 0	10 10

player can do better by unilaterally changing his own strategy. Thus, if player 1 knows or expects that player 2 will speak Urdu, she will optimally do the same. This knowledge or expectation can be derived from the social norm of the country: in Pakistan, the norm is to speak Urdu, and in the United Kingdom, the norm is to speak English.

For the philosopher John Searle (1995, 2005) language is the most fundamental institution, because all other institutions depend in some way on communication and language. But language does not presuppose other institutions. Searle also proposes a connection between the subjective realities of agents and objective social reality. Groups adopt a *we-intention* or a *collective intentionality*, which means that they have a common goal. Each member expects that the others share this goal and will behave accordingly. For example, if 22 people have the we-intention to play soccer, they constitute the game through the collective intention. Twenty-two people running around and kicking a ball individually without the collective intention to play soccer do not constitute a soccer game. In this sense, a we-intention is more than the sum of *I-intentions* (or individual intentions). It is through collective intentionality that a group creates a social reality or an institution. This can be expressed by the proposition: "X counts as Y in C." X can be a statement, an object, a person, or an event. Y is a *status function* that is attributed to X by the group and C is the context in which the group acts. A common economic example is the institution of money. A certain piece of paper issued by a government authority (object X) counts as a medium of exchange (status function Y) in a country (context C), because the economic agents in that country accept it, i.e. have the we-intention to use the piece of paper for payments. Another example is functions in a company. A certain person X is the boss (status function Y) in a company (context C), because everyone who works in the company accepts this. According to Searle

> *Status functions are the glue that holds human societies together. Think not only of money, property, government, and marriage, but also of football games, national elections, cocktail parties, universities, corporations, friendships, tenure, summer vacations, legal actions, newspapers, and industrial strikes. . . . [P]residential elections, baseball games, and 20 dollar bills look different, but the underlying mechanism that produces them is the same: the assignment of status functions with their accompanying deontologies according to constitutive rules.* (Searle 1995, p. 9)

Searle also explains why institutions are enabling: because they create a special kind of power, which he calls *deontic power*. This power is capable of creating rights and authorizations as well as duties and obligations. Deontic powers are associated with status functions. If a person has the status of a priest, he can baptize and wed other people. Thus, a person can only become a Christian by being baptized by a priest. A baptism by a person who speaks the same words and performs the same rite as a priest is not valid, if the person is not recognized as a priest. The same is true for the power of attorney in a corporation. A person can only act and sign on behalf of a corporation if procuration has been given, i.e. a status function has been assigned. Searle expresses this as "We accept (S has power (S does A)." The logic is that a person S has the power to do some things, because the power is derived from the respective status function Y and this person has been given this status function, i.e. S = X and "X counts as Y in C."

Searle (1995, p. 17) regards

> *the invention of the limited liability corporation, like the invention of double-entry book-keeping, universities, museums, and money, as one of the truly great advances in human civilization. But the greatest advance of all is the invention of status functions, of which these are but instances. It is not at all necessary that there should exist status functions. Non-human animals do not appear to have them. But without them, human civilization, as we think of it, would be impossible.*

In Hodgson's concept of institutions as socially embedded systems of rules, organizations such as firms are also institutions. But they are special kinds of institutions that have three additional characteristics. First, they have criteria for distinguishing members from non-members, and thus for establishing organizational boundaries. Second, organizations have principles of sovereignty about who is in charge. Finally, organizations have chains of command that delineate responsibilities and functions. Organizations need structures that provide rules of communication, responsibility, membership, or sovereignty in order to function. These structures emerge in the way described by Searle (1995, p. 17):

> *So, what amounts to the corporation when we set it up? It is not that there is an X that counts as the corporation, but, rather, that there is a group of people involved in legal relationships, thus so and so counts as the president of the corporation, so and so counts as a stockholder in the corporation, etc., but there is nothing that need count as the corporation itself, because one of the points of setting up the corporation was to create a set of power relationships without having to have the accompanying liabilities that typically go with those power relationships when they are assigned to actual human individuals. … The corporation is, so to speak, created out of nothing. The president is president of the corporation, but he is not identical with the corporation.*

Institutions can be very durable because of positive feedback. Once established, institutions provide incentives and constraints on individual behavior. When agents behave in accordance with these incentives and constraints, they develop the habit of doing so. In addition, agents' preferences and expectations are shaped by institutions. Through these effects of downward causation, institutions create

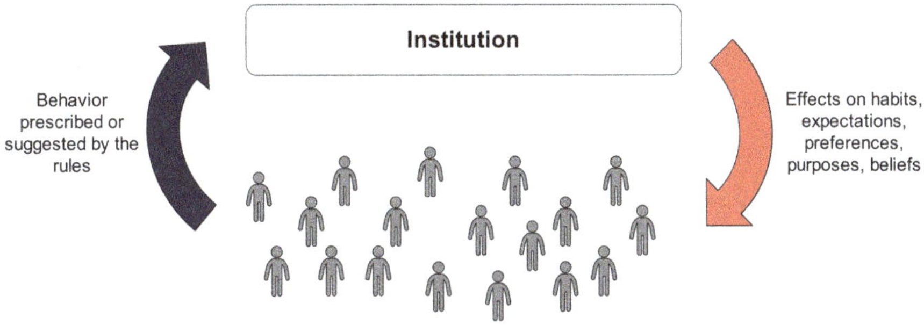

Fig. 9.15 Upward and downward causation. Source: Author

behavior that reinforces and perpetuates them through upward causation. This two-way causation between institutions and agents' actions is illustrated in Fig. 9.15.

In Sect. 9.2.2, we discussed the problem that, in general, we cannot aggregate individual behavior in a way that guarantees a particular aggregate behavior. According to the Mantel–Sonnenschein–Debreu theorem and similar results, we cannot infer that the law of demand holds (i.e., there is a downward-sloping market demand function) from the aggregation of individual utility-maximizing behavior. However, the fact that agents must obey budget constraints alone may be sufficient to generate the law of demand without any reference to utility maximization (see Gode and Sunder 1993; Grandmont 1992; Hildenbrand 1994). If this result is more general, then we do not even need macrofoundations of microeconomics in the sense that we first determine how macro structures affect individual behavior and then derive macro outcomes from individual actions. Instead, it may be sufficient to look at the institutional structure to explain aggregate outcomes, for example in markets.

9.5.3 A Model of the Emergence of Norms

The agent-based model of political scientist Robert Axelrod (1986) explores the emergence of social norms. It is a theoretical model that follows the *KISS principle*: keep it simple, stupid. This means that the assumptions about the agents are quite simple and the complexity of the model lies in its results. Such models are ideal for theoretical exploration because they allow robust statements to be made about what happens in the model. If the model is too complex, it can be very difficult or even impossible to find out and explain how the results came about.

Robert Axelrod became known for his work on the evolution of cooperation. His interest is primarily, but not exclusively, in cooperation in international politics, which was triggered by the conflict between East and West during the Cold War. The prisoner's dilemma is central to his research. Table 9.9 contains exemplary payoffs for a 2-player prisoner's dilemma. If both players cooperate, each receives a payoff of 3. However, in a one-shot game, cooperation is not a Nash equilibrium because each player can do better by defecting. A defecting player receives a payoff of

Table 9.9 The prisoner's dilemma

		Player 2	
		Cooperate	Defect
Player 1	Cooperate	3 3	5 0
	Defect	0 5	1 1

5, while the cooperating player receives 0. The unique Nash equilibrium in pure strategies is defection by both players, giving each a payoff of 1.

The 2-player prisoner's dilemma is interesting because it is an abstraction of many real-world situations in which there is an incentive for unilateral defection, even though cooperation would maximize joint welfare. Disarmament between two countries is an example from international politics. Both countries do better by cooperating and keeping their armies small, but each country gains a strategic advantage by defecting and building an army that is stronger than its opponent's. Advertising is an example from economics. Advertising is costly, so each of two competitors in a market has an interest in keeping advertising expenditures low, but each can gain an advantage by advertising more than the other. The same logic applies to pricing in a duopoly, where both firms would benefit from keeping prices high, but have an incentive to undercut the competitor in order to increase market share. The details of the situation, and especially the (expected) payoffs, differ in all these and similar cases, of course, but the basic structure of the problem is the same and is well illustrated by the example in Table 9.9.

Game theory predicts that rational and selfish players will choose defection in the prisoner's dilemma, but in reality we observe a lot of cooperation. The classical prisoner's dilemma is a one-shot game, i.e. it is played only once. In real life, one-shot situations do exist, but repeated interaction among the same agents is common. Folk theorems in game theory predict that cooperation can be achieved in a repeated prisoner's dilemma if the time horizon is infinite and the players discount the future little or not at all. However, in repeated games with a known finite time horizon, cooperation is typically not a Nash equilibrium because both players have an incentive to defect in the last round. But if this is the case, then there is no incentive to cooperate in the penultimate round, and so on. The mechanism by which cooperation can be achieved in repeated games is punishment: a cooperating player can punish a defector by a *grim trigger strategy*, i.e. by never cooperating again after a defection. Game theory makes very strong assumptions about the rationality and behavior of agents and ignores the social context. An important feature of real life is that agents adapt their strategies over time.

Robert Axelrod studied the iterated prisoner's dilemma empirically in this famous tournament (Axelrod 1980a, 1980b). Axelrod asked a number of game theorists from economics, sociology, political science, and mathematics to submit strategies for the iterated prisoner's dilemma. The strategies were paired and played against each other in a computerized round-robin tournament. The strategy that achieved the highest score was the simplest of all submitted strategies: tit for tat. *Tit for tat* is a reciprocal strategy that starts with cooperation in the first round and then does what the opponent did in the previous round. Thus, cooperation is responded with cooperation and defection is responded with defection. While reciprocal behavior can achieve cooperation in repeated 2-player games, it does not work well in n-player games. Many social dilemmas in reality are situations in which many agents interact instead of just two, for example all kinds of *tragedy of the commons* problems.

Axelrod (1986) argues that much of the coordinated and cooperative behavior observed in many social contexts is achieved through norms. He proposes a theory of norms that explains, how norms emerge, how norms are maintained, and how one norm displaces another. He develops his theory using an agent-based model of an iterated n-player prisoner's dilemma using a procedure inspired by a *genetic algorithm* that allows for the evolution of new strategies. A genetic algorithm is an artificial intelligence technique that mimics the exchange and recombination of genetic information between two agents. We discuss genetic algorithms in detail in Chap. 10. Axelrod's theory of cooperative behavior governed by norms assumes that punishment is necessary to enforce the cooperative behavior demanded by the norm. He defines that a "norm exists in a social setting to the extent that individuals usually act in a certain way and are often punished when seen not be acting in this way" (Axelrod 1986, p. 1097). The norms game (see Fig. 9.16) is a version of the prisoner's dilemma game. A defecting player receives a temptation payoff $T = 3$ and all others are harmed with a payoff $H = -1$. If a player does not defect, nobody gets anything. This payoff structure is similar to the normal prisoner's dilemma, but the norms game has a twist. A defection by player i can be observed by other players with a probability S. A player j who has observed a defection can choose to punish the defecting player i. A punishment is costly to both the punished and the punishing player. The defector i receives a punishment payoff $P = -9$ and the punisher's payoff is the enforcement cost $E = -2$. This two-stage game hence requires strategies in two dimensions. A player's boldness is the first dimension. If the boldness of player i is greater than the probability of being detected, $B_i > S$, then player i will defect. The second dimension of the strategy is vengefulness V_i, which is the probability that player i will punish another player after observing the defection.

Axelrod runs simulations with 20 players in a generation. A simulation runs for 100 generations. Each player in the initial generation has two random values from the set {0,1,2,...7} for the two strategy dimensions. Each player gets four opportunities to defect. For each of these four opportunities, the payoff from defecting or not defecting plus the punishment after detection and punishment are recorded. Furthermore, the payoffs resulting from the defections of others and from one's own punishment are added. The sum of all these payoffs is the total score of each player in a generation. Depending on the total score, players reproduce before being eliminated from the game. Players with average performance will have one offspring. Unsuccessful players who are one standard deviation below the

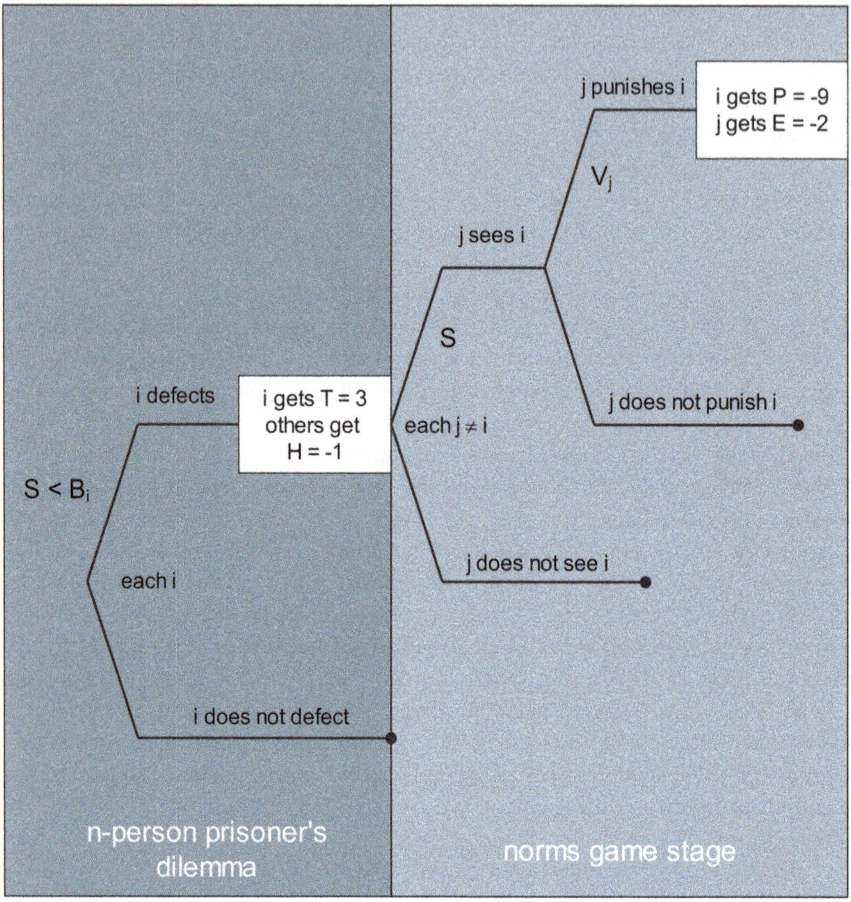

Fig. 9.16 Norms game. Source: Author's own figure based on Axelrod (1986)

population average have no offspring, and very successful players who are one standard deviation above the average have two offspring. The total number of offspring is set to 20 to keep the population constant. Normally the offspring are identical to the parent, but with a 1% chance there is a mutation that changes the strategy of the offspring. Thus, players with successful strategies will reproduce more than those with less successful strategies. In addition, new strategies can arise by chance.

The simulation of 100 generations is repeated five times. Figure 9.17 summarizes the outcomes and the dynamics of the simulations. The outcome is the average boldness and vengefulness of the final generation of a simulation run. The results are quite mixed. In one run, the average boldness was very low ($B < 1$) and vengefulness was high ($5 < V < 6$). Hence, a norm of not defecting emerged in this run, as all agents had a relatively high willingness to punish defectors. In two other runs,

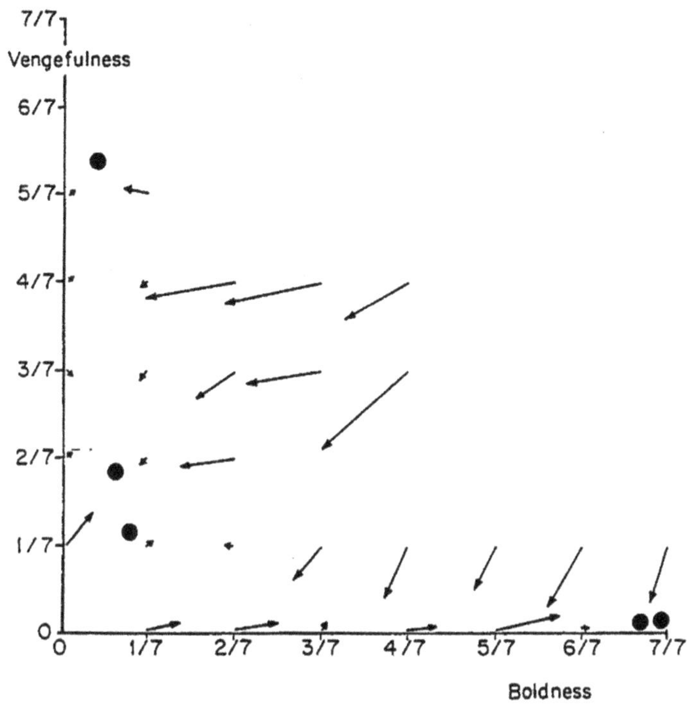

Fig. 9.17 Outcomes of the norms game. Source: Axelrod (1986), reproduced with kind permission of Cambridge University Press

boldness was also low ($B < 1$), and so was vengefulness ($V < 2$). The two remaining runs produced very high boldness (B~7) and extremely low vengefulness (V~0). In other words, in these runs, defection was pervasive in the final generation, and no one was willing to punish this behavior.

The arrows show the dynamics derived from all 500 generations in the five runs. They show how boldness and vengefulness changed from one generation to the next. The dynamics suggest a pattern in which the emergence of a non-defection norm is unlikely in the long run. When both strategy values are intermediate, boldness falls because defection is costly due to punishment. But as boldness decreases, vengefulness tends to decrease as well, because punishment is costly to punishers. As a result, boldness increases while vengefulness remains low.

Since punishing defectors alone is not sufficient to guarantee the emergence of a stable norm of non-defection, Axelrod introduces another stage to the game (see Fig. 9.18) and calls the resulting game the metanorms game. The new stage adds the possibility of punishing players who observe a defection but do not punish it. Thus, not enforcing a norm is now punished, which is called a metanorm.

The introduction of the metanorm stage changes the results of the simulation dramatically, as Fig. 9.19 shows. In all runs, a very strong norm of not defecting emerges along with a strong norm of punishing defectors. The dynamics show that

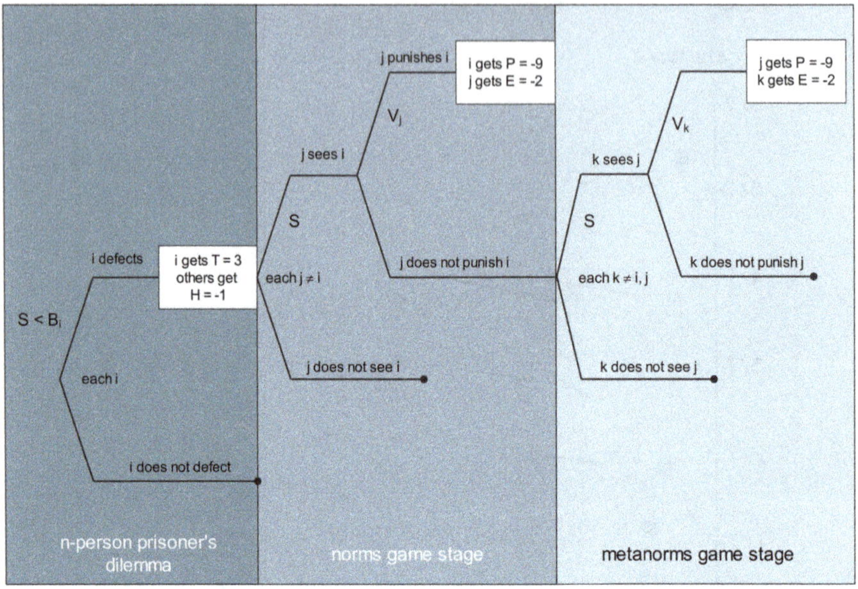

Fig. 9.18 Metanorms game. Source: Author's own figure based on Axelrod (1986)

punishing nondefectors strongly increases vengefulness and keeps it high. High vengefulness, in turn, reduces boldness. Axelrod calls this system *self-policing* because there is no external enforcement of norms. This result is achieved if the initial average level of vengefulness is sufficiently high. If the first generations do not punish enough, the non-defection norm can still collapse.

A norm is an institution as defined by Hodgson, as explained in the previous section. Axelrod's model shows that punishment by the group, both of defectors and of non-punishers, is one mechanism by which such a norm can emerge and lead to continued cooperation. He also discusses other mechanisms such as dominance, internalization, deterrence, social proof, membership, law, and reputation.

Axelrod's approach of using agent-based models to study the emergence of cooperation and norms was groundbreaking, triggering much further research. Bianchi and Squazzoni (2015) review 20 years of ABM research in sociology, in which cooperation plays a prominent role. Elsenbroich and Gilbert (2014) discuss how various sociological and psychological theories of norms can be, and have been, implemented in agent-based models.

9.6 Emergent Macroeconomics

It should be evident by now that emergence is central to macroeconomics. Indeed, one can argue that the main task of economics is to explain how higher-level entities and properties emerge in the economy, while the explanation of individual behavior

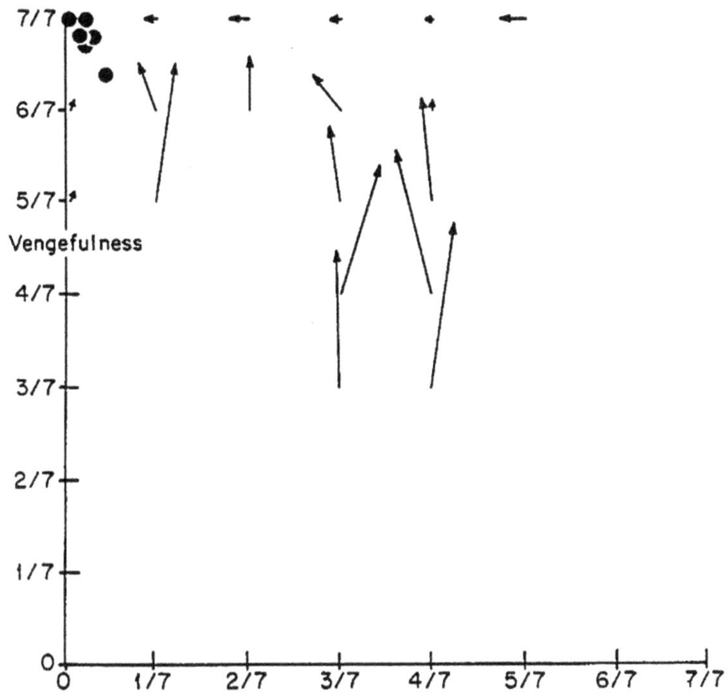

Fig. 9.19 Outcomes of the metanorms game. Source: Axelrod (1986), reproduced with kind permission of Cambridge University Press

can be left to psychology and sociology. In this subsection, *emergent macroeconomics* is proposed as an alternative to the neoclassical DSGE approach. We first summarize the main shortcomings of the DSGE approach before explaining the *generative view of macroeconomics* (or emergent macroeconomics). This is followed by a brief discussion of the notion of *stylized facts*, which is helpful for understanding the model presented at the end of the subsection.

9.6.1 The Flaws of Neoclassical Macroeconomics

In Sect. 9.2, you learned that neoclassical macroeconomics is deeply flawed. It has at least three major problems. First, mainstream DSGE models have highly unrealistic microfoundations. Even mainstream macroeconomists like Olivier Blanchard admit this fact:

> *There are many reasons to dislike current DSGE models. First, they are based on unappealing assumptions. Not just simplifying assumptions, as any model must be, but assumptions profoundly at odds with what we know about consumers and firms.* (Blanchard 2018, p. 45)

In particular, agents are not perfectly rational, they are often not forward-looking, they have little information about the economy, and they are not all identical. David Colander calls the current mainstream *Walrasian macroeconomics*, which assumes that agents have high-level information processing capabilities and operate in information-rich environments. He calls for an alternative research program, which he calls *Post Walrasian macroeconomics*. This research program assumes that agents have low-level information processing capabilities and operate in information-poor environments (Colander 2006, p. 2).

The second problem is aggregation. Without making very unrealistic assumptions, we cannot guarantee that there is a unique and stable general equilibrium, nor that the representative agent resembles the individual agents in any way. Even the fundamental law of demand cannot be derived from individual optimization behavior unless we restrict the analysis to a few specific utility functions.

Finally, neoclassical macroeconomics does not explain many interesting and relevant phenomena in a plausible way. Solow (2005) laments that there is a short-run branch and a long-run branch of macroeconomics that treat the business cycle and endogenous growth separately, even though they are likely to influence each other. The global financial crisis of 2007–2009 was a major blow to mainstream theory, demonstrating that it cannot realistically incorporate the financial sector and generate large endogenous crises. A related problem is the difficulty of the theory to explain and deal with money. There have been attempts to improve DSGE models after the financial crisis, but Dosi and Roventini (2019, p. 19) do not consider them successful:

> *Summing up, we suggest that the recent developments in DSGE camp are just patches added to torn clothes. But how many patches can one add before trashing it? Lindé and Wouters (2016), after having expanded the benchmark DSGE model to account for the zero-lower bound, non-Gaussian shocks, and the financial accelerator, conclude that such extensions "do not suffice to address some of the major policy challenges associated with the use of non-standard monetary policy and macroprudential policies." More radically, we do think that the emperor is naked: DSGE models are simply post-real (Romer 2016) and additional patches are a waste of intellectual (and economic) resource that pushes macroeconomics deeper and deeper in to a "Fantasyland" (Caballero* 2010).

Moreover, the DSGE approach cannot deal with structural change or generate qualitative novelty. This is a serious omission, because 100 years ago the economy was not only much smaller in terms of GDP, but also very different.

Perhaps its greatest theoretical shortcoming is that neoclassical macroeconomics cannot explain how millions of heterogeneous agents coordinate in a decentralized way so that the economy is in an ordered state most of the time (but not always). Neoclassical economics simply assumes the existence of market equilibria and general equilibrium across markets and sectors. Even more, it assumes that the economy is always at or close to this equilibrium, without showing whether and how an equilibrium could be reached. Yet equilibria are emergent outcomes of decentralized interactions and as such are worth explaining. The Cambridge economist Frank Hahn, who has made major contributions to general equilibrium theory, came to this conclusion more than 30 years ago:

> *Thus we have seen economists abandoning attempts to understand the central question of our subject, namely: how do decentralized choices interaction and perhaps get coordinated in favor of a theory according to which an economy it to understood as the outcome of the maximization of a representative agent's utility over an infinite future? Apart from purely theoretical objections it is clear that this sort of thing heralds the decadence of endeavor just as clearly as Trajan's column heralded the decadence of Rome. It is the last twitch and gasp of a dying method. It rescues rational choice by ignoring every one of the questions pressing for attention.* (Hahn 1991, p. 47–48)

9.6.2 The Generative View to Macroeconomics

There are several names for an alternative macroeconomics in line with complexity thinking: *emergent macroeconomics* (Delli Gatti et al. 2008), *bottom-up adaptive macroeconomics* (Delli Gatti et al. 2011), *agent-based macroeconomics* (Dosi and Roventini 2019), *agent-based computational economics* (Tesfatsion 2006), or *multi-agent system macro* (Axtell 2006). They all share the same conviction, namely that the economy should be viewed as a complex adaptive system and that agent-based models are the appropriate tool for its analysis.

This new kind of macroeconomics belongs to a more general new research program for the social sciences that Epstein (1999, 2006) calls *generative social science*. The general idea of generative social science is that:

> *explaining the emergence of macroscopic societal regularities, such as norms or price equilibria, requires that one answer the following question: How could the decentralized local interactions of heterogeneous autonomous agents generate the given regularity?* (Epstein 1999, p. 41).

The generativist's experiment that answers this generativist question is as follows:

> Situate an initial population of autonomous heterogeneous agents in a relevant spatial environment; allow them to interact according to simple local rules, and thereby generate—or "grow"—the macroscopic regularity from the bottom up (Epstein 1999, p. 42).

If one is able to "grow" a macroscopic regularity from a given microspecification, one has found a potential explanation for the relevant real-world pattern. If this is not possible, then the microspecification can be ruled out as an explanation. By growing a macroscopic pattern, the researcher proposes a mechanism that links the micro and macro levels, which is necessary for a convincing explanation. There may be several microspecifications from which a macroscopic pattern can be grown. In this case, it is an empirical matter to identify the most appropriate one. Empirical input validation is a major difference between generative social science and neoclassical macroeconomics. Neoclassical economics allows and even requires axiomatic assumptions about individuals and their behavior, even when they are in clear contradiction to empirical observations. Generative social science, on the other hand, favors realistic micro assumptions. If two models fit an observed macroscopic pattern equally well, the one with the more realistic micro assumptions is preferred. Whether the micro assumptions are empirically valid can be determined by psychological or organizational research, laboratory experiments, or microeconomic empirical evidence. Information from surveys and observation of business practices can also be used to validate behavioral assumptions. Thus, emergent macroeconomics is closely linked to behavioral and organizational research.

Emergent macroeconomics eschews macro assumptions as much as possible. Directly assuming macro structures or properties may sometimes be a convenient modeling shortcut, but in principle it is preferable to generate them from micro assumptions. Highly implausible macro assumptions such as the existence of aggregate technology shocks, common knowledge of the true structure of the economy by all agents, or a centralized market clearing process (unless there is actually a market maker in the market) are to be avoided.

Probably the most general and important emergent regularity in the social world is order. Under normal conditions, the social world is usually characterized by a high degree of order in many dimensions. Given that coordinating behavior in complex systems is not easy, as we saw in the beer game in Chap. 7, the general existence of social order is surprising. In market economies, most markets clear, producing neither shortages nor surpluses. In recent decades, the economies of many countries have grown steadily year after year. Armed conflicts between states are the exception rather than the rule. Conflict and violence between the citizens of a country are contained. In general, the daily lives of many people are fairly stable and predictable. Even recessions or major political events often do not fundamentally disrupt this order. Economic and political systems are often quite resilient, able to withstand even rather large shocks. However, order and stability are sometimes disrupted in unexpected ways and by seemingly small events. For example, the global financial crisis of 2007–2008 was triggered by events in the subprime segment of the U.-S. housing market, which is a relatively small part of the overall market in the USA and, of course, the world. The financial crisis disrupted financial markets and led to unconventional monetary policy for more than a decade. In political science, the concept of *punctuated equilibrium* refers to the observation that social systems often exhibit considerable stability and only gradual change over long periods of time, as well as sudden and radical change. More on punctuated equilibrium is said in Chap. 11.

Despite pervasive order, there are always islands of disorder in social systems. All societies are plagued by crime, poverty, unemployment, inequality, and other problems. But rather than being separate phenomena, social order and disorder may be the results of similar processes. For example, economic growth and inequality are likely the results of the same economic processes with positive feedback (or increasing returns to scale). Both social order and disorder should be seen as unintended emergent consequences of many decentralized actions that are either coordinated or uncoordinated. The assumption of macroscopic equilibria may be convenient for analysis, but it leaves one of the key properties unexplained. To understand how order emerges and disappears, we need to grow systems from the bottom up.

9.6.3 Stylized Facts

The goal of emergent macroeconomics is to explain macroscopic regularities or macro patterns. Because we cannot easily observe the economy, economics makes extensive use of stylized facts. *Stylized facts* are broad tendencies in the data that ignore individual details. They are attempts to generalize empirical findings by identifying common patterns underlying a variety of specific facts. The term stylized facts was coined by Nicholas Kaldor (1961) in the context of developing macroeconomic theory on the basis of limited and imprecise macroeconomic data. Kaldor argued for the freedom of the theorist to generate theoretical models from broad tendencies without regard to measurement problems or troublesome individual cases. Kaldor proposed six stylized facts about economic growth:

1. Aggregate output and productivity of labor grow at a steady trend rate
2. Capital per worker increases over time
3. The profit rate on capital is constant over time
4. The capital-output ratio is constant over long periods
5. The wage share and the profit (capital) share of national income are constant
6. There are appreciable differences in the rate of growth of labor productivity and of total output in different societies, the range of variation . . . being of the order of 2–5%

Kaldor argued that "[n]one of these 'facts' can be plausibly 'explained' by the theoretical constructions of neo-classical theory" (p. 179) and used them as the starting point for his alternative explanatory model. The negative relationship between the unemployment rate and the inflation rate (the Phillips curve), the inverse relationship between the vacancy rate and the unemployment rate (the Beveridge curve), and the negative relationship between output growth and the change in the unemployment rate (Okun's law) can also be regarded as stylized macroeconomic facts. Unlike facts in the natural sciences, stylized facts about the social world are not stable and can change over time.

Hirschman (2016) defines stylized facts as simple empirical regularities in search of theoretical, causal explanations. He emphasizes that stylized facts are both descriptive and normative. They are descriptive, because they make claims about the kinds of things that exist in the world. These factual claims can take various forms, e.g., associations, correlations, rates of incidence or trends, but they are not understood as explanations or theories. At the same time, however, they cannot be atheoretical, because they involve some minimal interpretation of how to read the data. They are "lightly theorized descriptions—theories of what is and what is worth noticing" (Hirschman 2016, p. 608). Their normativity derives from their claims that the identified regularities are more important than other possible characterizations of the evidence. Stylized facts represent the researcher's interpretation of what is a pattern and what is noise or irrelevant detail. Because the collective capacity of researchers to pay attention to problems and deal with them is limited, stylized facts that point to the most notable aspects of a phenomenon are helpful in using scarce resources efficiently. To form the basis of a field of research, there must be consensus about the stylized facts. Yet consensus is not guaranteed. Instead of accepting proposed stylized facts, researchers might criticize them for failing to capture the most important aspects, reject them as false, or ignore them. Stylized facts thus represent competing or contested claims about the most relevant aspects of reality that merit the development of theories.

A good example for a contested stylized fact is scaling. *Scaling* means that there is a *power-law relation* between two variables X and Y:

$$Y = kX^{\alpha} \tag{9.9}$$

In this power law, α is the power-law exponent and k is some constant. With a power law, the relative change in one variable X results in a proportional relative change in the other variable Y, i.e. Y scales as X^{α}. This scaling is independent of the initial values of both variables. For example, the area of a square scales with the square of the length of the sides (i.e., $\alpha = 2$). If the length is doubled, the area quadruples: $\frac{\Delta Y}{Y} = \alpha \frac{\Delta X}{X} = 2 \times 2 = 4$. For complexity researchers, it is a stylized fact that many variables follow a power-law probability distribution like the Pareto distribution. If a random variable X is Pareto distributed, then its survival function (or tail cumulative distribution function) is given by

$$\Pr(X > x) = \left(\frac{x_m}{x}\right)^{\alpha} \textit{for } x \geq x_m, \tag{9.10}$$

where $\alpha > 0$ and x_m is the minimum possible value of X. Gabaix (2009) documents that there are many empirical power laws in economics and finance regarding income and wealth, the size of cities and firms, stock market returns, trading volume, international trade, and executive compensation. A special case of the Pareto distribution is the *Zipf distribution* with $\alpha = 1$. Axtell (2001) reports that firm size in the United States is distributed according to a Zipf distribution, and Rubini et al. (2012) report the same for European countries (see Fig. 9.20).

Note that the axes in Fig. 9.20 are both in log-scales. Power laws produce linear graphs in log-log coordinate systems where the absolute slope of the graph is equal to α. According to *Zipf's law*, a Zipf distribution describes the relationship between the size of variable and the rank, i.e. the rank-size distribution. In other words, in Fig. 9.20, we could also order firms according to their size and assign rank 1 to the largest firm, rank 2 to the second largest, and so on. Plotting the log of the rank against the log of the size would also produce a straight line. Zipf's law has been shown to hold for city sizes worldwide.

While complexity researchers are fascinated by the ubiquity of power laws in the natural and social world and argue that they must be crucial elements of scientific

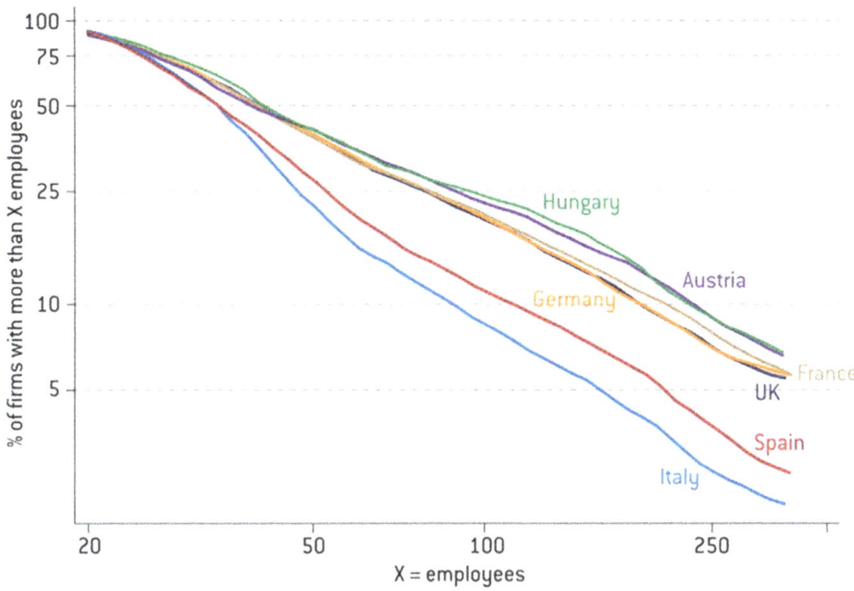

Fig. 9.20 Firm size distribution in different European countries. Source: Rubini et al. (2012), republished under Breughel's republishing policy (https://www.bruegel.org/publications)

theories, neoclassical economists tend to ignore them. This is not surprising, since stylized facts about power laws typically involve heterogeneity, e.g., in the size of firms, for which theories using representative agents are not well suited. As with other stylized facts, the validity of Zipf's law for firm size has been questioned by some researchers due to estimation problems (e.g., Bottazzi et al. 2015). Bee et al. (2017) argue that the firm size distribution of French firms converges to Zipf's law for multi-product firms, while the log-normal distribution is a better fit for small single-product firms.

9.6.4 An Agent-Based Business Cycle Model

Dosi et al. (2006) present a relatively simple agent-based model of endogenous business cycles that illustrates many features of emergent macroeconomics quite well. The model is designed to explain a number of accepted macroeconomic stylized facts about the business cycle dating back to the 1930s and 1940s:

SF1 Investment is considerably more volatile than output
SF2 Consumption is less volatile than output
SF3 Investment, consumption, and change in inventories tend to be procyclical and coincident variables

SF4 Aggregate employment and unemployment rates tend to be lagging variables. The former is procyclical, whereas the latter is anticyclical

These stylized facts can be operationalized with standard deviations and cross-correlations of macroeconomic time series. Stock and Watson (1999) provide these figures for the U.S. economy. The use of these statistics is also common to check the outcome validity of mainstream RBC and DSGE models (see Heijdra 2017, p. 731).

The main point of Dosi et al. (2006) is to show that their agent-based model can reproduce the stylized facts in a similar way to algebraic neoclassical models, while being more realistic and able to explain additional stylized facts. Following the logic of generative social science, models with more realistic assumptions are preferable to less realistic models. Furthermore, it is more difficult to reproduce a larger number of stylized facts in a model. Thus, a model has more explanatory power if it can accommodate more (and qualitatively different) stylized facts.

Dosi et al. claim that their model is more realistic, because it incorporates assumptions consistent with the following microeconomic stylized facts:

SF5 Investment is lumpy

SF6 Investment is influenced by firms' financial structure

SF7 Firms are the main locus where technological accumulation takes place. Technological learning—as well as its directions and rates—is carried out by firms in ways which are strongly shaped by: (a) firm-specific abilities; (b) richness of perceived unexploited opportunities. As a consequence, technological learning and accumulation tends to be mostly local: technical advances typically occur in a neighborhood of currently-mastered technologies

SF8 Innovations take time to diffuse, because firms need time to master new technologies and to develop new skills

SF9 Most innovations are industry-specific

The paper cites much evidence from the industrial dynamics and technological change literature to support these stylized facts, which guide the authors' choice of modeling firms' investment and innovation behavior. Most importantly, the lumpiness of investment is modeled by target-and-trigger behavior, which is interpreted as the result of a routinized investment rule of prudent, risk-averse firms that are boundedly rational and cannot fully anticipate the uncertain future. Moreover, SF7 and SF9 are taken as evidence against economy-wide aggregate technology shocks. Instead, firms innovate more or less successfully, which is represented by firm-specific stochastic changes in the productivity of new capital goods. In this way, the model combines business cycle fluctuations and economic growth, which have a common source in the development of more productive capital goods by individual firms.

The additional stylized facts that the model is also supposed to match refer to micro-level statistical regularities that are revealed by the evolution of firm productivity, firm size, and firm growth over time:

SF10 Productivity dispersion among firms is considerably large
SF11 Inter-firm productivity differentials are quite persistent over time
SF12 Firm size distributions tend to be considerably right skewed, with upper-tails made of few large firms. These patterns vary significantly across different sectors
SF13 Firm growth-rate distributions are not Gaussian and can be well proxied by fat-tailed, tent-shaped densities.

All of these stylized facts SF10—SF13 refer to the heterogeneity of firms. Note that SF12 about the firm size distribution is a typical stylized fact of complexity scholars, as discussed in the previous subsection. Dosi et al. do not make the strong claim that the firm size distribution follows Zipf's law, but only claim that it is right skewed, which is compatible with a Pareto distribution, but also with a log-normal distribution. The important point is that they take into account properties of the data that are ignored by neoclassical macroeconomists. The observed heterogeneity of firms can be treated in an agent-based model, but not in a model with a representative firm. The heterogeneity of agents can be an emergent property of systems. Dosi et al. do not assume that firms are heterogeneous at the outset, but allow for heterogeneity to emerge during the simulation.

The model economy consists of L workers/consumers and two types of firms: F_1 producers of a homogeneous consumption good and F_2 producers of heterogeneous machine-tools (or capital goods). The consumption-good producers need the machines from the capital-good producers. The producers of capital goods perform R&D and improve the productivity of their machines. Workers sell one unit of labor to firms in both sectors and consume all of the income they receive.

The event schedule for each time period $t = 1, 2, \ldots$ in the simulation is as follows:

1. Consumption-good producers decide on production based on their expected demand and invest in new capital goods if necessary to achieve the desired production. Investment is financed first by own liquid assets and then, if necessary, with debt, because internal financing is assumed to be cheaper than external financing.
2. In the capital good market, the market shares of capital-good producers are updated according to the competitiveness of each capital-good producing firm.
3. The consumption good is produced and the unemployment rate as well as the monetary wage is determined. The total demand for the consumption good is allocated to individual firms according to their price competitiveness.
4. Firms with negative liquid assets and/or a non-positive market share exit the market and are replaced by new firms that are random copies of existing firms. Capital-good firms perform R&D with stochastic success.

[3]Dosi et al. also consider other kinds of expectation formation such as adaptive expectations, accelerative expectations and micro-macro expectations. The overall results depend little on the way in which expectations are formed.

Let us start the presentation of the details of the model with the **consumption-good sector**. In each period t, the starting point for each firm j in this sector is the expected demand for its good, which is assumed to be myopic, i.e. firms expect only what they sold in the previous period[3]:

$$D_j^e(t) = D_j(t-1). \tag{9.11}$$

This way of forming expectations rests on the assumption that firms are boundedly rational and use simple rules to deal with pervasive market uncertainty. The difference between inventories remaining from the previous period $N_j(t-1)$ and the expected demand yields the desired level of production Q_j^d:

$$Q_j^d(t) = D_j^e(t) - N_j(t-1). \tag{9.12}$$

Firms need labor and capital to produce output. Production technology is such that output is linearly related to the capital stock. Therefore, the desired capital stock is

$$K_j^d = \frac{Q_j^e}{u^d}, \tag{9.13}$$

where u^d is the desired level of capacity utilization, which is a parameter. Firms invest in new capital for two reasons: either to expand the capital stock or to replace old capital. Expansion investment EI takes place when the desired capital stock is greater than or equal to a trigger level of capital, $K_j^{trig} = K_j(t)(1+\alpha)$:

$$EI_j(t) = K_j^{trig} - K_j(t) \text{ } if \text{ } K_j^d(t) \geq K_j^{trig}(t). \tag{9.14}$$

This model of expansion investment captures the stylized fact SF5 (lumpy investment), because investment only occurs when the target capital stock exceeds a trigger that is sufficiently above the current level of the capital stock. The capital stock consists of machines of different generations (or vintages). Each machine has a production capacity of one unit of output. Machines of different vintages differ in terms of their labor productivity coefficient $A_{i,\tau}$, where i denotes the firm that has produced the machine and τ denotes the generation. At time t, each firm j owns the set $\Xi_j(t)$ of machines of all vintages. The capital stock is the sum of all machines owned by the firm:

$$K_j(t) = \sum_{A_{i,\tau}} g_j(A_{i,\tau}, t), \tag{9.15}$$

where $g_j(A_{i,\tau}, t)$ is the absolute frequency of machine $A_{i,\tau}$ at time t. The labor productivity coefficient determines how much labor is required to operate a machine, i.e. one machine requires $1/A_{i,\tau}$ units of labor. Therefore, the unit labor cost of each machine at the nominal wage w is

$$c(A_{i,\tau},t)=\frac{w(t)}{A_{i,\tau}}. \tag{9.16}$$

A firm scraps an old machine, if the average market price for a new machine, $p^*(t)$, is less than or equal to the unit labor cost disadvantage, i.e. if $p^*(t) \leq b[c(A_{i,\tau}, t) - c^*(t)]$, where $c^*(t)$ is the average unit labor cost of new machines and $b > 0$ is a parameter. Replacement investment, $RI_j(t)$, is equal to the sum of all scrapped machines. Firms must finance both production and investment before selling their output. First, they use their stock of liquid assets from the previous period, $NW(t-1)$. If its internal funds are not sufficient, a firm borrows up to a maximum debt/sales ratio Ω_{max} at an interest rate r. If both internal funds and maximum debt are not sufficient to finance production, production is rationed and no investment is undertaken. If there is sufficient financing for production, but not to finance both expansion investment and replacement investment, firms will finance expansion investment first.

The average productivity π_j over all machines is the sum of the labor productivities weighted by the share of the respective machines in the capital stock:

$$\pi_j(t)=\sum_{A_{i,\tau}} A_{i,\tau}\frac{g_j(A_{i,\tau},t)}{K_j(t)}. \tag{9.17}$$

The average productivity of the capital stock determines the unit cost of production:

$$c_j(t)=\frac{w(t)}{\pi_j(t)}. \tag{9.18}$$

Markets are not perfectly competitive, such that each firm can set a price as a mark-up $\mu > 0$ over the unit cost of production:

$$p_j(t)=(1+\mu)c_j(t). \tag{9.19}$$

Due to differences in the size and composition of their capital stock, firms differ in their production costs and hence also in terms of the price they charge for their output. In contrast to neoclassical models, this heterogeneity is not assumed away and there is no market price that is identical for all firms and consumers.

The average productivity determines a firm's labor demand L^D for the actual production level Q:

$$L_j^D(t)=\frac{Q_j(t)}{\pi_j(t)} \tag{9.20}$$

Actual production can differ from desired production because firms may not be able to finance the desired level. Profits Π are the difference between sales revenue and labor costs and interest payments on debt:

$$\Pi_j(t) = p_j(t)S_j(t) - c_j(t)Q_j(t) - rDebt_j(t). \tag{9.21}$$

The change in liquid assets is equal to the difference between profits and internal investment costs.

The **sector that produces capital goods** is modeled analogously to the consumption-good sector. The main difference is that machinery producers need only labor for production, but no capital. Each machine producer $i = 1, 2, \ldots, F_2$ sells its latest generation of products described by the labor productivity coefficient $A_{i,\tau}$. It is assumed that the unit cost of production depends on the labor productivity coefficient of the produced vintage:

$$c_i(t) = \frac{w(t)}{A_{i,\tau}}. \tag{9.22}$$

The price of machines is also a mark-up over unit cost:

$$p_i(t) = (1 + \mu)c_i(t). \tag{9.23}$$

Labor demand of a machine producer depends on the actual production level and labor productivity:

$$L_i^D(t) = \frac{Q_i(t)}{A_{i,\tau}}. \tag{9.24}$$

The financing conditions in the capital sector are the same as in the consumption-good sector. Firms prefer internal financing before resorting to debt. Thus, profits and net liquid asset hence evolve analogously as for the consumption-good firms.

Every machine-producing firm tries to improve its product through technological change. The outcome of innovation efforts is uncertain, which means that a new machine may be better or worse than the current vintage in terms of labor productivity:

$$A_{i,new} = A_{i,t}(1 + \epsilon) \tag{9.25}$$

with $\epsilon \sim U(\imath_1, \imath_2)$ and $\imath_1 < 0 < \imath_2$. A firm sells the new machines only if $A_{i,\,new} > A_{i,\,\tau}$. In this case, the index τ is increased by one.

So far, we have described the behavior of the individual firms in the two sectors. The next step is to describe how the two **markets** for the consumption good and for the capital goods function. Dosi et al. take a modeling shortcut here. They do not model how individual buyers and sellers meet in the markets, but describe a mechanism that allocates total demand to individual firms according to their competitiveness. The competitiveness of consumption-good producers is

$$E_j(t) = -\omega_1 p_j(t) - \omega_2 l_j(t), \tag{9.26}$$

where $\omega_{1,\,2}$ are non-negative parameters and l_j is the level of demand that firm j was unable to satisfy in the previous period. This equation describes a negative aggregate consumer response to price increases and to the unavailability of the good. The average competitiveness of the sector is the sum of each firm's competitiveness, weighted with the firm's past market share

$$\overline{E}^j(t) = \sum_{j=1}^{F_1} E_j(t) f_j(t-1). \tag{9.27}$$

Market shares evolve according to replicator dynamics, by which the past market share is adjusted up or down depending on whether a firm is more or less competitive than the sector average:

$$f_j(t) = f_j(t-1)\left(1 + \chi_1 \frac{E_j(t) - \overline{E}^j(t)}{\overline{E}^j(t)}\right), \chi_1 \geq 0. \tag{9.28}$$

Each firm receives a fraction of aggregate demand expenditure that is equal to its market share:

$$D_j(t) = C(t) f_j(t). \tag{9.29}$$

The mechanism that allocates total investment expenditure I to the producers of capital goods is the same. The only difference with the consumption-good sector is that the competitiveness of capital-good producers depends on the productivity of the machines they offer:

$$E_i(t) = -\omega_3 p_i(t) + \omega_4 A_{i,\tau}, \omega_{3,4} \geq 0. \tag{9.30}$$

Finally, the **labor market** needs to be modeled. The labor supply grows at a constant rate η in each period. Total labor demand is the sum of labor demands in the two sectors. Aggregate employment is the minimum of labor demand and labor supply:

$$Emp(t) = \min\left(L^D(t), L(t)\right). \tag{9.31}$$

This means that unemployment can occur when labor supply is greater than labor demand. Hence, the labor market is not automatically cleared by the wage rate. The wage is determined by institutional and market factors, namely the inflation of the consumer price index cpi, the growth of average productivity $\overline{A},$ and the change in the unemployment rate U:

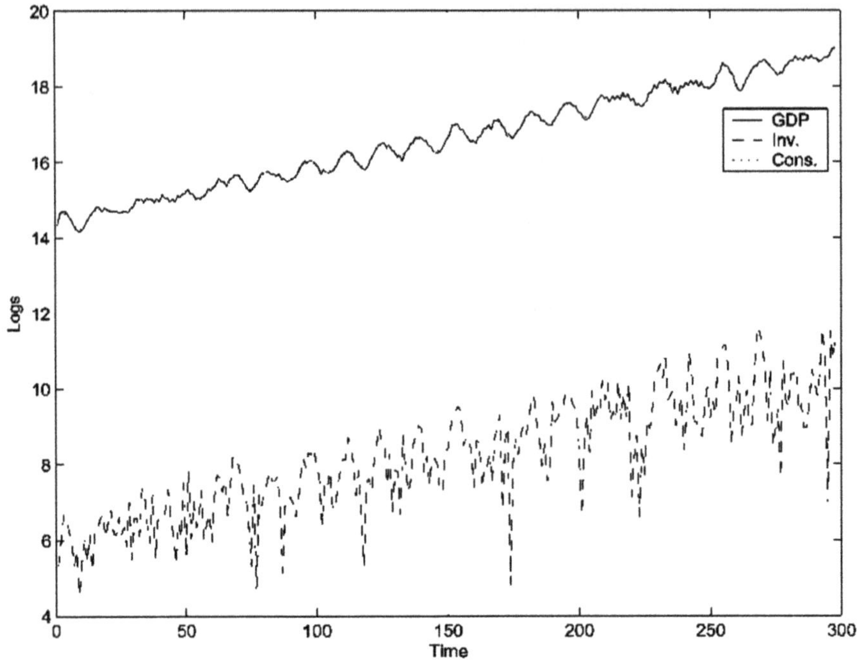

Fig. 9.21 Output, investment, and consumption. Source: Dosi et al. (2006), reproduced with kind permission of Springer Nature

$$w(t) = w(t-1) + \left(1 + \psi_1 \frac{cpi(t) - cpi(t-1)}{cpi(t-1)} + \psi_2 \frac{\overline{A}(t) - \overline{A}(t-1)}{\overline{A}(t-1)} + \psi_3 \frac{U(t) - U(t-1)}{U(t-1)}\right). \tag{9.32}$$

The parameters $\psi_{1,\,2,\,3}$ characterize the labor market institutions like the degree of price indexation or the degree of unionization.

The model is simulated over 300 periods. To obtain robust results that do not depend on the stochasticity of a single run, it is common to perform multiple runs and average the results over these runs. The only stochastic element in this model is the firm-specific outcome of the R&D effort.

In Fig. 9.21, we can see that aggregate output, consumption, and investment all grow over time and exhibit regular fluctuations.[4] Thus, the model provides a unified framework for both economic growth and the business cycle. The model captures the stylized facts SF1 and SF2 because consumption is less volatile than output and investment is much more volatile. Under myopic expectations, the standard

[4]In fact, the time series of consumption is hard to see, because it is almost identical to the time series of GDP. This is due to the fact that consumer spend all of their income in each period.

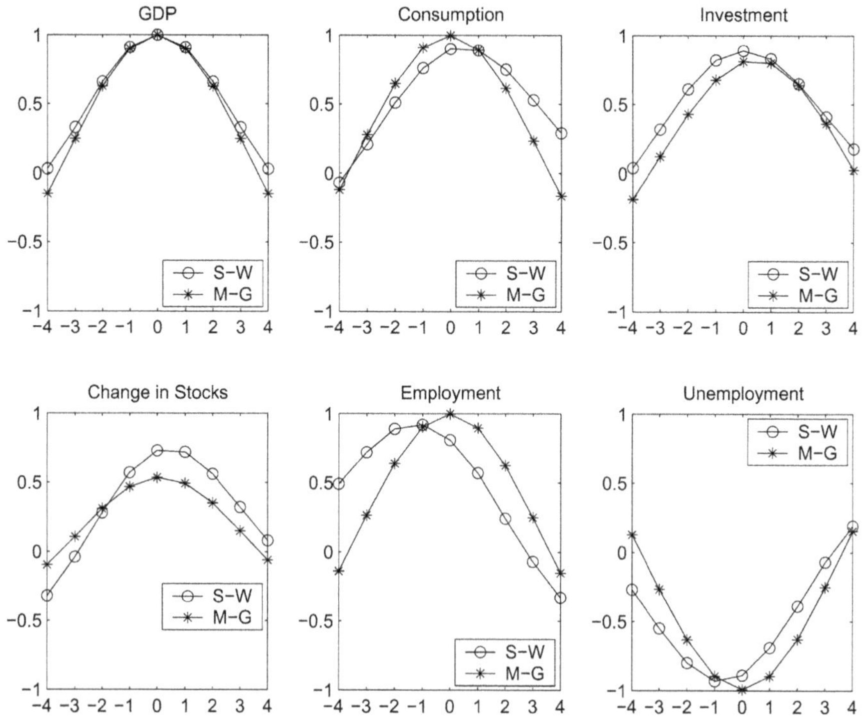

Fig. 9.22 Cross-correlation patterns. Source: Dosi et al. (2006), reproduced with kind permission of Springer Nature. S-W is empirical data from Stock and Watson (1999), M-G refers to model-generated data

deviation of consumption is about 0.86 of the standard deviation of output, while the relative standard deviation of investment is 3.15.

Figure 9.22 shows the cross-correlations between the macro variables and output (GDP) at different leads and lags, both for the empirical data reported in Stock and Watson (1999) (indicated by circles) and for the model-generated data (indicated by asterisks). The upper left panel shows the autocorrelation of output at different lags ($-1, -2, \ldots$) and leads ($1, 2, \ldots$). The contemporaneous correlation of output with itself at lag 0 is, of course, equal to 1. The model is able to match the empirical autocorrelation structure of output quite well. The second panel in the top row shows that consumption is a procyclical and coincident variable with respect to output. The highest correlation of consumption with output occurs at lag 0, so the variable is coincident. It is procyclical because all cross-correlations are positive. The model data are similar to the empirical data, although the cross-correlations at lags $0, -1$, and -2 are slightly higher than those reported by Stock and Watson (1999) and lower for some lags. The cross-correlation patterns for investment and inventories

[5] They refer to the working paper, however.

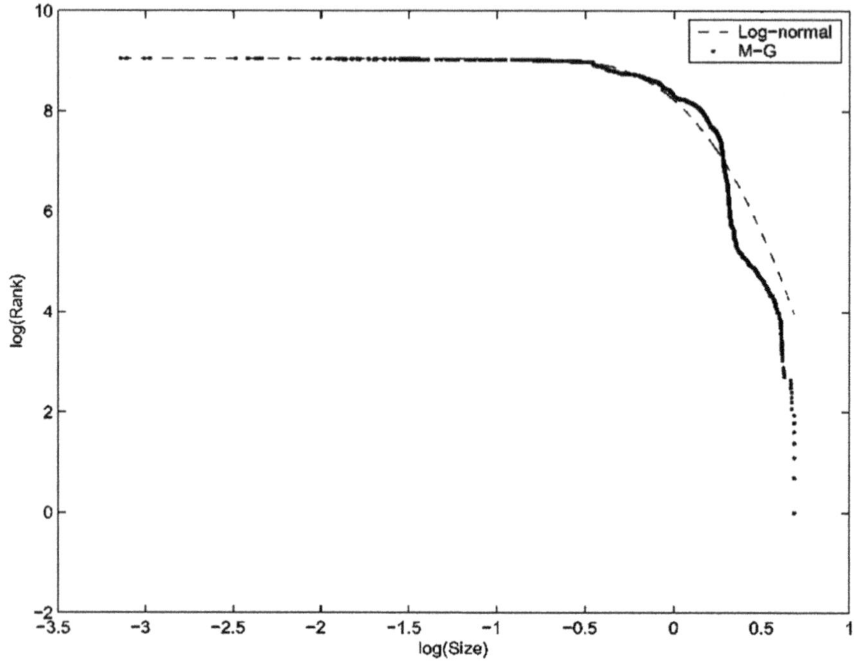

Fig. 9.23 Rank-size distribution of consumption-good firms measured by sales. Source: Dosi et al. (2006), reproduced with kind permission of Springer Nature

are also realistic. Overall, therefore, the model is able to reproduce the stylized facts of SF3. The model performs somewhat less well with respect to SF4 because, in contrast to the empirical data, employment and unemployment are not lagged but coincident variables in the model. Nevertheless, the magnitude of the cross-correlations is realistic.

Dosi et al. report that the model also supports the stylized facts SF10 and SF11 regarding productivity dispersion and the persistence of productivity differentials over time without presenting data in the paper.[5]

Stylized fact SF12 is matched by the model as visible in Fig. 9.23, which shows the rank-size distribution of the consumption-good producers in terms of their sales. The figure shows that there are very few large firms, but many medium and small firms, such that the distribution is right skewed, as found in empirical data.

Finally, Fig. 9.24 supports stylized fact SF13 according to which the distribution of the growth rates of firms can be approximated by a tent-shaped density function. In particular, the property that the distribution has fat tails is obvious. This means that large growth events—both positive and negative one—occur quite frequently.

This emergent macroeconomic model is quite simple and contains a number of strategic assumptions to avoid too much complexity. In particular, market processes are simplified in a way that is plausible, though not completely decentralized. A fully decentralized model would also represent how individual transactions between

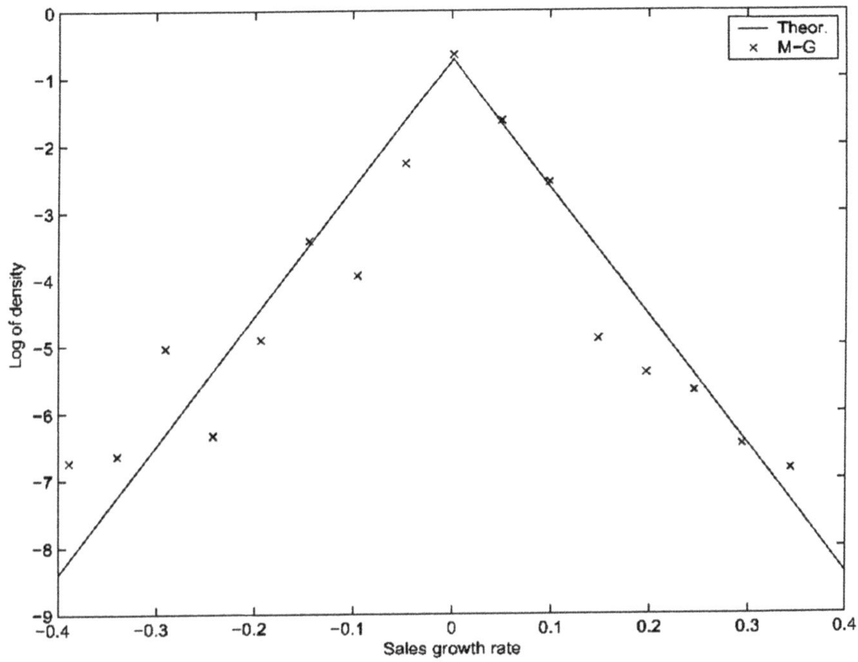

Fig. 9.24 Firm growth-rate distribution. Source: Dosi et al. (2006), reproduced with kind permission of Springer Nature

buyers and sellers occur in markets. The model has many realistic features, such as the bounded rationality of heterogeneous agents. Despite its simplicity, it is capable of reproducing both standard macroeconomic stylized facts and stylized facts about distributions that are important from a complexity perspective. These aggregate patterns arise from assumptions about the behavior of firms and from the institutional structure of the model, which is given by the way markets operate. The fact that firms can exit and enter markets is an institutional factor, as is the fact that market shares evolve over time as a function of firms' competitiveness. The most explicit institutional structure relates to the way in which the wage rate is determined.

9.6.5 Other Agent-Based Macro Models

The model of Dosi et al. (2006) was one of the first agent-based macro models. Since then, the literature on emergent macroeconomics has grown rapidly and made significant progress. Dawid and Delli Gatti (2018) provide a good survey of the

[6] It is also a pun on the originators names, because "gatti" is the Italian word for "cats."

models that have been developed. They group the models into seven families called AGH, CATS, EUBI, EUGE, JAMEL, KS, and LAGOM.

The AGH framework was developed by Ashraf, Gershman, and Howitt (Ashraf et al. 2016, 2017). It emphasizes the role of financial factors in business cycle fluctuations and abstracts from the accumulation of physical capital. It has been extended and used to analyze monetary and macroprudential policies.

The CATS model family was developed by Domenico Delli Gatti, Mauro Gallegati, and their coauthors in Ancona and Milan. CATS stands for *Complex Adaptive Trivial Systems*[6] and captures the idea that complex system behavior can emerge from simple (or almost trivial) individual behavioral heuristics. As in the AGH framework, financial factors are important, but the models typically also include capital goods and a capital sector. This family of models is quite large and includes models of financial accelerators, early warning indicators of financial crises, and the effects of monetary policy.

EUBI, which stands for Eurace@Unibi, and EUGE have the same origin, namely the EURACE project funded by the European Commission 2006–2009, carried out by a consortium of seven universities in France, Germany, Italy, the United Kingdom, and Turkey. The aim of the project was to develop an agent-based modeling platform for the simulation and analysis of macroeconomics and economic policies. After the funding period, Herbert Dawid and his coauthors continued at the University of Bielefeld (Unibi) and Silvano Cincotti, who was the EURACE project coordinator, and his coauthors continued at the University of Genoa (EUGE). While EUGE was developed to focus on the interaction between the macroeconomy and the financial sector (and later also for the analysis of energy and climate policy), EUBI focuses more on capital accumulation, embodied technological progress, and skill dynamics. As EURACE was a European project, both EUBI and EUGE cover several regions or countries.

JAMEL is an acronym for Java Agent-based MacroEconomic Laboratory. These models were developed in France by Isabelle Salle and Pascal Seppecher (see Seppecher and Salle 2015). JAMEL incorporates consumer sentiment and opinion dynamics as discussed in Chap. 8.

The KS (Keynes meeting Schumpeter) family is another large group of models. It was developed in Pisa by Giovanni Dosi, Giorgio Fagiolo, Andrea Roventini and coauthors and builds on the model of Dosi et al. (2006) presented in the previous subsection. "Keynes meeting Schumpeter" indicates that these models combine macroeconomic aspects and features from evolutionary economics. Embodied technological progress represented by different vintages of capital goods is an example of these features.

Finally, LAGOM (which is a Swedish word for "just the right amount" or "in balance") was developed by Carlo Jaeger and coauthors (e.g., Mandel et al. 2010) for policy analysis.

A model that does not belong to these families is the model of Matthias Lengnick (2013). It is of particular interest because of its simplicity. Lengnick calls it a

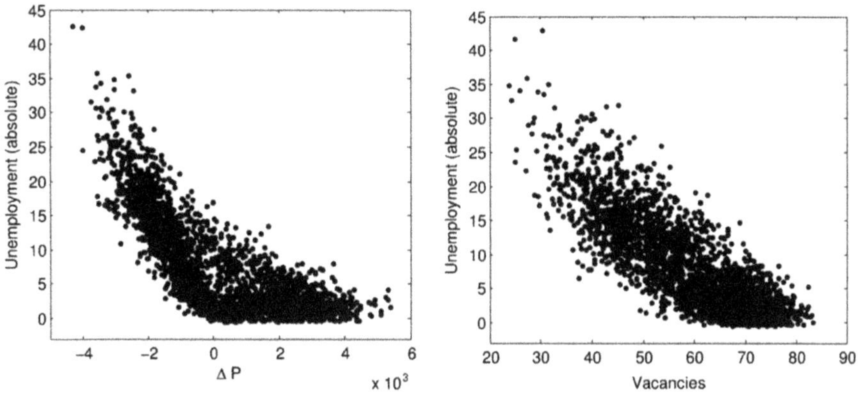

Fig. 9.25 Phillips curve and Beveridge curve as emergent outcomes. Source: Lengnick (2013), reproduced with kind permission of Elsevier B.V

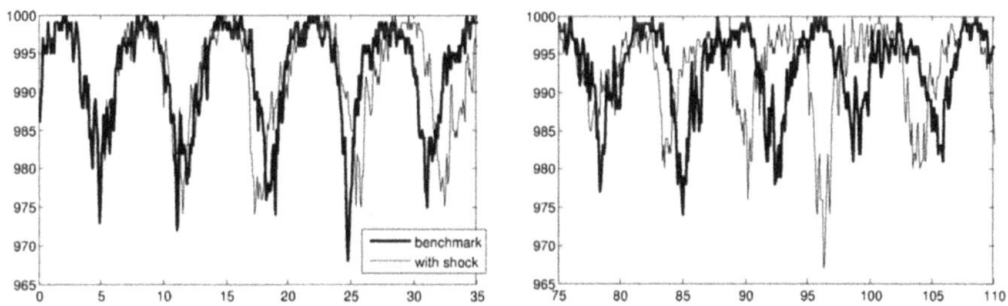

Fig. 9.26 Butterfly effect. Source: Lengnick (2013), reproduced with kind permission of Elsevier B.V.

"minimal model" of a macroeconomy consisting only of households and firms. In contrast to Dosi et al. (2006), Lengnick explicitly models the interaction between households and firms, which are connected in networks. Thus, there is no market allocation mechanism, but all market transactions are decentralized. Thus, the coordination of decentralized actions is central to the model, with household and firm actions occurring at different frequencies over time. In addition to business cycle fluctuations, the model generates a Phillips curve and a Beveridge curve as emergent outcomes (see Fig. 9.25).

Another interesting property of the model is that it displays *sensitivity to initial conditions,* or a *butterfly effect* (see Chap. 6). Lengnick introduces a very small shock into the model by reducing the demand of a single household by 5% in a single day. He then simulates the dynamics of aggregate output with and without the shock (benchmark). Figure 9.26 demonstrates that, in the long run, the small shock has a huge impact on the dynamics of the business cycle. For the first 10 model years, we can see little difference between the two time series. However, after about 85 model years, the phase of the business cycle has shifted, such that the benchmark economy experiences a boom in year 96 while the shocked economy is in a deep recession (see right panel).

The very recent publication by Poledna et al. (2023) proves that agent-based macro models have reached a high degree of maturity and are no longer purely theoretical models. Poledna et al. present an agent-based macro model for the Austrian economy that is very detailed and fits a wide variety of micro and macro data from national accounts, sector accounts, input–output tables, government statistics, census data, and business demography data. The model includes financial and non-financial corporations, households, and a general government. The business sector is composed of 64 industries. Sectors interact with the rest of the world through imports and exports. The model is a 1:1 representation of the Austrian economy, i.e. each agent in the model represents one of the 8.8 million inhabitants of one of the more than half a million registered firms. The calibrated model is used to perform out-of-sample forecasts of macroeconomic aggregates such as GDP, inflation, household consumption, or investment over time horizons ranging from 1 quarter to 12 quarters. The forecasting performance is compared with time series forecasts using VAR(1) and VECM models and, in particular, with an Austrian version of the DSGE model by Smets and Wouters (2007). The Smets and Wouters model is widely cited and is considered a sophisticated standard model in the DSGE literature. The ABM has an out-of-sample forecasting performance similar to time series models and the DSGE model, but it is much more detailed and allows for highly disaggregated analyses. Poledna et al. see their model as a first simple prototype that can demonstrate the potential of agent-based macroeconomic models. With sufficient data, such "big data ABMs" could revolutionize macroeconomic forecasting and policy analysis.

Axtell and Farmer (2022) share a similar vision. They envision that with sufficient funding, economic modeling could evolve in much the same way as computational modeling of weather and climate. Like weather models that use real-time data, agent-based economic models could become *mirror worlds* or *digital twins* of the real world:

> *Sometime within the next few decades it should become possible to produce high fidelity, digital models of economies in which every household, every consumer, every firm, every worker, and every policy-maker are represented in some way. It is our belief that technologies like ABM will play an important role in such developments* (Axtell and Farmer 2022, p. 47).

Things to Remember

- Generally speaking, emergence means that a system has properties that the parts of the system do not possess. Emergence requires a concept of different levels of a system. Higher levels are not just aggregations of lower-level entities, but are qualitatively different, requiring different

(continued)

terminologies for their description and different approaches for their analysis.

- Unlike natural systems, it is not easy to define levels in social systems. The reason is that social systems are not clearly identified in space and do not have clear boundaries. Hierarchies in social systems are tangled in many ways, with many vertical and horizontal cross-cutting interactions.
- In economics, we typically distinguish between the micro level of individual agents and the macro level of system entities and properties. However, neither the definition of the micro level nor the macro level is natural. Firms and households are not individual agents, but social collectives. The macro level, defined according to national borders, is also problematic, because the borders of states are not necessarily identical with the boundaries of economic systems. Furthermore, it can be argued that the gap between individuals and the economic system as a whole is too large, so that at least a meso level is needed in between. It is at the meso level that groups and organizations interact, which is fundamental to the emergence of macro properties.
- A fallacy of composition is a false argument that a whole or group has a certain property because the parts of the whole or the members of the group have that property. Economists often point to economic fallacies of composition committed by laypeople. However, neoclassical macroeconomic thinking itself is subject to various fallacies of composition. Under general conditions, we cannot assume that microeconomic behavior is the same as macroeconomic behavior. The construct of the representative agent is valid only under very restrictive assumptions, in particular that all agents are identical, which is counterfactual.
- The Mantel–Sonnenschein–Debreu theorem states that aggregate excess demand functions inherit only Walras' law, continuity and homogeneity of degree zero from individual excess demand functions. This implies that the existence of a unique and stable general equilibrium cannot be assumed, even if all individuals behave individually rationally. Thus, the pervasive assumption of a unique and stable (general) equilibrium in mainstream economics is unwarranted.
- Simple or nominal emergence means that a system as a whole has macro properties that its micro-elements do not possess. Complex emergence is characterized by novelty, unpredictability, and irreducibility. Complex emergence occurs only in complex systems characterized by self-organization.
- Weak emergence means that emergent macroproperties can only be derived by simulation. They are practically irreducible to microproperties. Weak emergence is often found in complex systems. A related concept is

(continued)

computational irreducibility. It implies that the study of complex systems should be computational rather than algebraic.

- Strong emergence means that macroproperties irreducible to microproperties in principle. This can be the case due to multiple realizability and wild disjunction. With strong emergence, the macro level has autonomy from the micro level. Strong emergence is a contested concept in philosophy of science.
- Human behavior is dependent on social context. Roles, norms, conventions, and expectations of others influence how people behave. It therefore makes little sense to analyze the behavior of individuals in isolation from their social context, as neoclassical microeconomics does. Social context, or social structure, is an emergent property that exerts downward causation on individuals. Since complex economies are likely to have multiple equilibria, economists need criteria for determining how individuals coordinate toward an equilibrium. Institutions are coordination devices. The macrofoundations of microeconomics are provided by the consideration of institutions in economic analysis.
- Institutions emerge and they constrain and enable individual behavior. Institutions are systems of established and prevailing social rules that structure social interactions. Organizations like firms are special kinds of institutions. Money, property rights, laws, and social norms are institutions too.
- Emergent macroeconomics is an alternative to the neoclassical DSGE approach in macroeconomics. Emergent macroeconomics uses agent-based models to grow the economy from the bottom up. It attempts to reproduce stylized facts at the macro level from assumptions about micro agents and their interactions that are realistic and supported by empirical evidence. Agent-based macroeconomic models have been refined over the past 15 years. They can now explain many macro and micro stylized facts and have a forecasting performance that is comparable to established methods in mainstream macroeconomics.

References

Anderson PW (1972) More is different: broken symmetry and the nature of the hierarchical structure of science. Science 177:393–396. https://doi.org/10.1126/science.177.4047.393

Ashraf Q, Gershman B, Howitt P (2016) How inflation affects macroeconomic performance: an agent-based computational investigation. Macroecon Dyn 20:558–581. https://doi.org/10.1017/S1365100514000303

Ashraf Q, Gershman B, Howitt P (2017) Banks, market organization, and macroeconomic performance: an agent-based computational analysis. J Econ Behav Organ 135:143–180. https://doi.org/10.1016/j.jebo.2016.12.023

Axelrod R (1980a) Effective choice in the prisoner's dilemma. J Confl Resolut 24:3–25. https://doi.org/10.1177/002200278002400101

Axelrod R (1980b) More effective choice in the prisoner's dilemma. J Confl Resolut 24:379–403. https://doi.org/10.1177/002200278002400301

Axelrod R (1986) An evolutionary approach to norms. Am Polit Sci Rev 80:1095–1111. https://doi.org/10.2307/1960858

Axtell R (2000) Effects of interaction topology and activation regime in several multi-agent systems. In: Moss S, Davidsson P (eds) Multi-agent-based simulation. Springer, Berlin, pp 33–48

Axtell RL (2001) Zipf distribution of U.S. firm sizes. Science 293:1818–1820. https://doi.org/10.1126/science.1062081

Axtell RL (2006) Multi-agent systems macro: a prospectus. In: Colander D (ed) Post Walrasian macroeconomics, 1st edn. Cambridge University Press, pp 203–220

Axtell RL (2007) What economic agents do: how cognition and interaction lead to emergence and complexity. Rev Austrian Econ 20:105–122. https://doi.org/10.1007/s11138-007-0021-5

Axtell RL, Farmer JD (2022) Agent-based modeling in economics and finance: past, present, and future. J Econ Lit:1–101. https://doi.org/10.1257/jel.20221319

Bedau MA (1997). Weak emergence. Philos Perspect 11:375–399

Bedau MA (2002) Downward causation and the autonomy of weak emergence. Principia 6(1):5–50

Bee M, Riccaboni M, Schiavo S (2017) Where Gibrat meets Zipf: scale and scope of French firms. Phys A Statist Mech Appl 481:265–275. https://doi.org/10.1016/j.physa.2017.04.012

Bianchi F, Squazzoni F (2015) Agent-based models in sociology. WIREs Comput Stat 7:284–306. https://doi.org/10.1002/wics.1356

Blanchard O (2009) The state of macro. Ann Rev Econ 1:209–228. https://doi.org/10.1146/annurev.economics.050708.142952

Blanchard O (2018) On the future of macroeconomic models. Oxf Rev Econ Policy 34:43–54. https://doi.org/10.1093/oxrep/grx045

Bottazzi G, Pirino D, Tamagni F (2015) Zipf law and the firm size distribution: a critical discussion of popular estimators. J Evol Econ 25:585–610. https://doi.org/10.1007/s00191-015-0395-7

Boulding KE (1956) General systems theory—the skeleton of science. Manag Sci 2:197–208. https://doi.org/10.1287/mnsc.2.3.197

Caballero RJ (1992) A fallacy of composition. Am Econ Rev 82:1279–1292

Caballero RJ (2010) Macroeconomics after the crisis: time to deal with the pretense-of-knowledge syndrome. J Econ Perspect 24:85–102. https://doi.org/10.1257/jep.24.4.85

Caplin AS, Spulber DF (1987) Menu costs and the neutrality of money. Q J Econ 102:703–725. https://doi.org/10.2307/1884277

Chorafakis G (2020) Emergence versus neoclassical reductions in economics. J Econ Methodol 27: 240–262. https://doi.org/10.1080/1350178X.2020.1727549

Colander DC (1993) The macrofoundations of micro. East Econ J 19:447–457

Colander D (ed) (2006) Post Walrasian macroeconomics: beyond the dynamic stochastic general equilibrium model. Cambridge University Press, Cambridge

Dawid H, Delli Gatti D (2018) Chapter 2 - Agent-based macroeconomics. In: Hommes C, LeBaron B (eds) Handbook of computational economics. Elsevier, pp 63–156

Debreu G (1974) Excess demand functions. J Math Econ 1:15–21. https://doi.org/10.1016/0304-4068(74)90032-9

Delli Gatti D, Gaffeo E, Gallegati M et al (2008) Emergent macroeconomics: an agent-based approach to business fluctuations. Springer Science & Business Media

Delli Gatti D, Desiderio S, Gaffeo E et al (2011) Macroeconomics from the bottom-up. Springer Science & Business Media, Milano

Dosi G, Roventini A (2019) More is different ... and complex! The case for agent-based macroeconomics. J Evol Econ 29:1–37. https://doi.org/10.1007/s00191-019-00609-y

Dosi G, Fagiolo G, Roventini A (2006) An evolutionary model of endogenous business cycles. Comput Econ 27:3–34. https://doi.org/10.1007/s10614-005-9014-2

Elsenbroich C, Gilbert N (2014) Modelling norms. Springer, Dordrecht

Epstein JM (1999) Agent-based computational models and generative social science. Complexity 4: 41–60. https://doi.org/10.1002/(SICI)1099-0526(199905/06)4:5<41::AID-CPLX9>3.0.CO;2-F

Epstein JM (2006) Generative social science: studies in agent-based computational modeling. Princeton University Press, Princeton

Finocchiaro MA (2016) Economic reasoning and fallacy of composition, part I: the problem. Eris 1: 17–38

Fromm J (2004) The emergence of complexity. Kassel University Press, Kassel

Gabaix X (2009) Power laws in economics and finance. Ann Rev Econ 1:255–294. https://doi.org/10.1146/annurev.economics.050708.142940

Gigerenzer G, Gaissmaier W (2011) Heuristic decision making. Annu Rev Psychol 62:451–482. https://doi.org/10.1146/annurev-psych-120709-145346

Gode DK, Sunder S (1993) Allocative efficiency of markets with zero-intelligence traders: market as a partial substitute for individual rationality. J Polit Econ 101:119. https://doi.org/10.1086/261868

Gorman WM (1961) On a class of preference fields. Metroeconomica 13:53–56. https://doi.org/10.1111/j.1467-999X.1961.tb00819.x

Grandmont J-M (1992) Transformations of the commodity space, behavioral heterogeneity, and the aggregation problem. J Econ Theory 57:1–35. https://doi.org/10.1016/S0022-0531(05)80038-9

Granovetter M (1985) Economic action and social structure: the problem of embeddedness. Am J Sociol 91:481–510. https://doi.org/10.1086/228311

Hahn F (1991) The next hundred years. Econ J 101:47–50. https://doi.org/10.2307/2233836

Hahn F (2003) Macro foundations of micro-economics. Economic Theory 21:227–232

Halley JD, Winkler DA (2008) Classification of emergence and its relation to self-organization. Complexity 13(5):10–15

Hartley JE (1997) The representative agent in macroeconomics. Routledge, London

Heijdra BJ (2017) Foundations of modern macroeconomics, 3rd edn. Oxford University Press, Oxford

Hildenbrand W (1994) Market demand: theory and empirical evidence. Princeton University Press, Princeton

Hirschman D (2016) Stylized facts in the social sciences. Sociol Sci 3:604–626. https://doi.org/10.15195/v3.a26

Hodgson GM (2006) What are institutions? J Econ Issues 40:1–25. https://doi.org/10.1080/00213624.2006.11506879

Howitt P (1987) Macroeconomics: relations with microeconomics. In: Eatwell J, Milgate M, Newman P (eds) The new Palgrave: a dictionary of economics. The Macmillan Press Ltd, London, pp 273–276

Jackson MO, Yariv L (2019) The non-existence of representative agents. CEPR Discussion Paper DP13397

Kaldor N (1961) Capital accumulation and economic growth. In: Lutz FA, Hague DC (eds) The theory of capital: proceedings of a conference held by the International Economic Association. Palgrave Macmillan, London, pp 177–222

King JE (2012) The microfoundations delusion: metaphor and dogma in the history of macroeconomics. Edward Elgar Publishing, Cheltenham

Kirman AP (1992) Whom or what does the representative individual represent? J Econ Perspect 6: 117–136. https://doi.org/10.1257/jep.6.2.117

Lane D (2006) Hierarchy, complexity, society. In: Pumain D (ed) Hierarchy in natural and social sciences. Springer, Dordrecht, pp 81–119

Lavoie M (2022) Post-Keynesian economics: new foundations, 2nd edn. Edward Elgar Publishing, Cheltenham

Leijonhufvud A (1993) Towards a not-too-rational macroeconomics. South Econ J 60:1–13. https://doi.org/10.2307/1059926

Lengnick M (2013) Agent-based macroeconomics: a baseline model. J Econ Behav Organ 86:102–120. https://doi.org/10.1016/j.jebo.2012.12.021

Macy MW, Skvoretz J (1998) The evolution of trust and cooperation between strangers: a computational model. Am Sociol Rev 63:638–660. https://doi.org/10.2307/2657332

Mandel A, Jaeger C, Fürst S, et al (2010) Agent-based dynamics in disaggregated growth models. halshs-00542442

Mantel RR (1974) On the characterization of aggregate excess demand. J Econ Theory 7:348–353. https://doi.org/10.1016/0022-0531(74)90100-8

North DC (1991) Institutions. J Econ Perspect 5:97–112. https://doi.org/10.1257/jep.5.1.97

Pindyck RS, Rubinfeld DL (2018) Microeconomics, 9th edn. Pearson Education Limited, Harlow

Poledna S, Miess MG, Hommes C, Rabitsch K (2023) Economic forecasting with an agent-based model. Eur Econ Rev 151:104306. https://doi.org/10.1016/j.euroecorev.2022.104306

Prokopenko M, Boschetti F, Ryan AJ (2009) An information-theoretic primer on complexity, self-organization, and emergence. Complexity 15:11–28. https://doi.org/10.1002/cplx.20249

Rubini L, Desmet K, Piguillem F, Crespo A (eds) (2012) Breaking down the barriers to firm growth in Europe: the fourth EFIGE policy report. Bruegel, Brussels

Samuelson PA, Nordhaus WD (2010) Economics, 19th edn. McGraw-Hill/Irwin, New York

Sawyer RK (2002) Nonreductive individualism: part I—supervenience and wild disjunction. Philos Soc Sci 32:537–559. https://doi.org/10.1177/004839302237836

Sawyer RK (2003) Nonreductive individualism part II—social causation. Philos Soc Sci 33:203–224. https://doi.org/10.1177/0048393103033002003

Sawyer RK (2005) Social emergence: societies as complex systems. Cambridge University Press, Cambridge

Searle JR (1995) The construction of social reality. The Free Press, New York

Searle JR (2005) What is an institution? J Inst Econ 1:1–22. https://doi.org/10.1017/S1744137405000020

Seppecher P, Salle I (2015) Deleveraging crises and deep recessions: a behavioural approach. Appl Econ 47:3771–3790. https://doi.org/10.1080/00036846.2015.1021456

Simmel G (1950) The sociology of Georg Simmel. The Free Press, New York

Simon HA (1996) The sciences of the artificial. The MIT Press, Cambridge, MA

Smets F, Wouters R (2007) Shocks and frictions in US business cycles: a Bayesian DSGE approach. Am Econ Rev 97:586–606. https://doi.org/10.1257/aer.97.3.586

Smith VL (1982) Markets as economizers of information: experimental examination of the "Hayek hypothesis". Econ Inq 20:165–179. https://doi.org/10.1111/j.1465-7295.1982.tb01149.x

Smith VL (1989) Theory, experiment and economics. J Econ Perspect 3:151–169. https://doi.org/10.1257/jep.3.1.151

Smith VL (1994) Economics in the laboratory. J Econ Perspect 8:113–131. https://doi.org/10.1257/jep.8.1.113

Solow RM (2005) Reflections on growth theory. In: Aghion P, Durlauf SN (eds) Handbook of economic growth. Elsevier, pp 3–10

Sonnenschein H (1972) Market excess demand functions. Econometrica 40:549–563. https://doi.org/10.2307/1913184

Sonnenschein H (1973) Do Walras' identity and continuity characterize the class of community excess demand functions? J Econ Theory 6:345–354. https://doi.org/10.1016/0022-0531(73)90066-5

Stock JH, Watson MW (1999) Chapter 1 Business cycle fluctuations in us macroeconomic time series. Handbook of Macroeconomics Vol 1, Part A, Elsevier: 3–64

Tesfatsion L (2006) Chapter 16 Agent-based computational economics: a constructive approach to economic theory. In: Tesfatsion L, Judd KL (eds) Handbook of computational economics. Elsevier, pp 831–880

Tobin J (1986) The future of Keynesian economics. East Econ J 12:347–356 van Staveren I (2020) The meso level in economics. In: Dolfsma W, Hands DW, McMaster R (eds) History, methodology and identity for a 21st century social economics. Routledge, London, pp 124–136

Varian HR (1992) Microeconomic analysis, 3rd edn. W.W. Norton & Company, New York

Williamson OE (2000) The new institutional economics: taking stock, looking ahead. J Econ Lit 38: 595–613. https://doi.org/10.1257/jel.38.3.595

Wimsatt WC (1986) Forms of aggregativity. In: Donagan A, Perovich AN, Wedin MV (eds) Human nature and natural knowledge: essays presented to Marjorie Grene on the occasion of her seventy-fifth birthday. Springer, Dordrecht, pp 259–291

Wolfram S (2002) A new kind of science. Wolfram Media

Wray LR (2006) Teaching the fallacy of composition: the federal budget deficit. cFEPS Policy Notes 2006/1

Economic Evolution, Novelty, and Diversity 10

Contents

10.1 Introduction 497
10.2 Novelty 500
10.2.1 Some Theoretical Considerations on Novelty 500
10.2.2 A Short History of Technical Inventions 502
10.3 Evolution as Process and Theory 507
10.3.1 Theory of Evolution 508
10.3.2 Genetic Algorithms 512
10.3.3 Fitness Landscape 517
10.3.4 Virtual Creatures 521
10.3.5 Cultural Evolution 524
10.4 Coevolution of Behaviors and Social Institutions 529
10.5 The Economy as an Evolutionary System 534
10.5.1 Evolution as Computation 537
10.5.2 Economic Evolution 539
10.5.3 Evolutionary Economics and Complexity Economics 542
10.6 Evolution of Knowledge 543
10.6.1 Knowledge of an Individual Person 544
10.6.2 Knowledge of an Organization 547
10.7 Evolution of Social Technologies 549
10.7.1 Cladistic Classification 549
10.7.2 Evolutionary Systems Modeling 551
10.8 Diversity 558
10.8.1 Kinds of Diversity 558
10.8.2 Framework for Analyzing Diversity 563
10.8.3 Diversity, Complexity, and Coping with External Stress 567
References 576

Abstract

This chapter takes a long-term view of economic evolution. Evolutionary theory is another important part of complexity economics. It is particularly helpful in explaining the emergence of innovation and new knowledge or novelty. After

M. Roos, *Principles of Complexity Economics*, Classroom Companion: Economics,
https://doi.org/10.1007/978-3-031-51436-4_10

some theoretical thoughts on novelty, a brief history of technological inventions is given to show that fundamental novelty is rare and that many inventions are recombinations and improvements of existing ideas. This chapter presents an explanation of evolution in biology and then moves on to the more general computational view of evolution, of which both biological and economic evolution are instances. It argues why the economy is not like an evolutionary system, but is in fact an evolutionary system. For complexity economics, genetic or evolutionary algorithms are a useful technical tool, along with cultural algorithms, cladistics, and evolutionary systems modeling, all of which are explained. This chapter also discusses the relationship of complexity economics to its sister discipline, evolutionary economics. The chapter concludes with some thoughts on diversity and resilience in systems. Diversity is both a condition and a result of evolution; in other words, diversity breeds diversity.

Keywords

Computation · Genetic algorithm · Innovation · Inventions · Resilience

Guiding Questions

- Why is evolution important to economics?
- How can something novel emerge?
- What are examples of combinatorial evolution in technology?
- What are the main principles of evolution?
- How does a genetic algorithm work?
- What is a fitness landscape?
- What is the difference between genetic evolution and cultural evolution?
- Why is the economy an evolutionary system?
- What does the computational view of evolution say?
- What is a kene?
- What is a cladogram and how can it be used in economics?
- What is the role of synergy in evolution?
- How does diversity relate to evolution and complexity?
- What are the different dimensions of diversity and how can we measure them?
- What is the difference between robustness and resilience?
- What is the relationship between robustness, complexity, and evolvability?

10.1 Introduction

Complex adaptive systems have the ability to adapt to their environments over time. They can both shape their environments and adapt to changing environmental conditions. We have already seen that complexity is related to heterogeneity or diversity. In Chap. 3, we defined the structural complexity of a system in terms of the number and diversity of its components. Similarly, we defined functional complexity as depending on the number and diversity of functions that the parts can perform within the system. The theory of evolution can help us understand how complex systems change and how the diversity of their parts develops. Through evolution, entities change over time, i.e., new entities (or species) evolve from existing ones, and some entities disappear. Speciation is the hallmark of evolutionary modeling. The model types we have seen so far (especially algebraic models and system dynamics models, but also many agent-based models) describe the behavior and interactions of existing entities, but not the appearance of new ones. Evolutionary theory is a theory that applies not only to biological evolution, but also to other complex adaptive systems. Evolutionary economics has long used the insights of evolutionary theory. It is a sister of complexity economics. The two schools of economic thought are closely related, but differ slightly in their methods and focus.

Complexity science views change in terms of self-organization and emergence. You learned in Chap. 9 that emergence refers to the appearance of new system properties. Diachronic emergence describes the appearance of novel phenomena over time, which is closely related to evolution. Figure 10.1, which is a cutout from Fig. 2.13 in Chap. 2, illustrates the relationship between evolution and emergence.

Selection, recombination, and mutation are the central mechanisms of evolution. They lead to speciation, the process by which a new species emerges that is different from other species and has novel characteristics. Between 6.5 million and 9.3 million years ago, humans began to diverge from apes, developing habitual bipedalism, improved manipulation and, later, cognition. Humans (homo) and chimpanzees (pan) had a previously unknown last common ancestor that had evolved from other hominid and hominoid species (see Fig. 10.2). While gorillas and chimpanzees practice knuckle-walking, humans evolved the novel trait of bipedalism, which "may have allowed humans to escape the great ape 'specialization trap'-an adaptive feedback loop between diet, specialized arboreal locomotion, cognition, and life history" (Almécija et al. 2021, p. 1). Upright walking on only two legs freed the hands from locomotion and allowed for the creation and use of tools. Tool use creates a positive feedback that increases brain size and cognition, which allows for culture and ultimately civilization.

Again, the evolution of new species with novel properties is not just a topic in biology, it is also central to economics. Economic systems, especially capitalist ones, constantly generate new firms, new products, new technologies, and new markets. Economic growth, development, and progress are therefore not only quantitative but also qualitative phenomena. Where neoclassical economics treats growth from the quantitative side of **more** production and **more** consumption, complexity economics

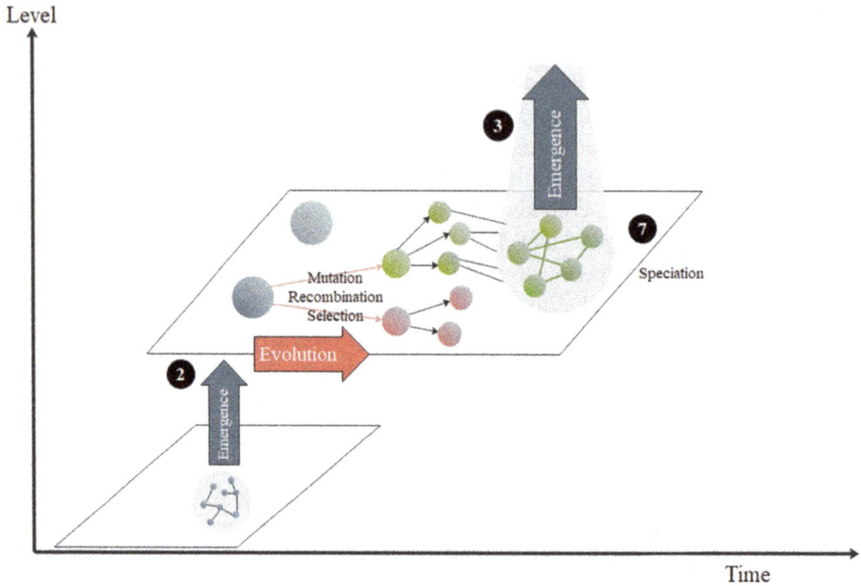

Fig. 10.1 Relation between evolution and emergence. Source: Author's own figure based on Prokopenko et al. (2009)

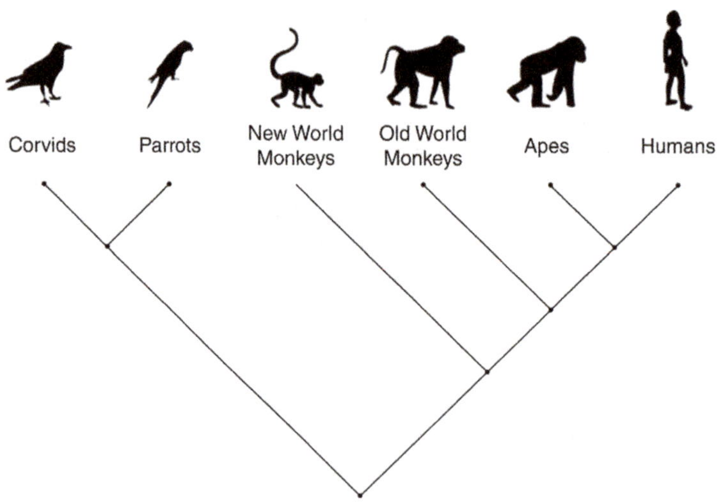

Fig. 10.2 The evolutionary history of birds, monkeys, apes, and humans. Source: Miller et al. (2019). CC BY 4.0 (https://creativecommons.org/licenses/by/4.0/)

focuses on the evolution of **different** goods and **different** economic practices. After all, we are not only richer than people were 100 years ago, we also live differently.

In Sect. 10.2 of this chapter, we first discuss novelty, which links emergence and evolution and is important in any theory of qualitative economic change. We ask how novelty is possible and recount a brief history of technological inventions that illustrates the cumulative and recombinant nature of technology.

Section 10.3 provides a succinct overview of evolution as a process and a theory. Since complexity economics is largely computational, we also present a basic version of a genetic algorithm from computer science that captures the main mechanisms of evolution. Evolution can be understood as a search algorithm in a fitness landscape, an important concept also introduced in this section. The evolution of artificial creatures is an interesting application of genetic algorithms that further illuminates how evolution works. The section concludes with a brief discussion of cultural evolution, which we need to understand human behavior.

An agent-based model of cultural evolution in which behaviors and institutions coevolve is presented in Sect. 10.4. The model explains how institutions help maintain altruistic behavior that benefits a group but is an evolutionary disadvantage to the individual. A key element of this model is intergroup conflict, which is a selection mechanism at the group level. Groups that have evolved institutions that maintain group-beneficial altruistic behavior have a fitness advantage in conflicts with non-altruistic groups.

Section 10.5 introduces the economy as an evolutionary system. The goal of this section is to convince you that evolutionary theory is useful for understanding the economy, and that evolution is not only a biological process, but also an economic one. In other words, applying the mechanisms of evolution to the economy is not just metaphorical: the economy is an evolutionary system. The computational view of evolution treats biological and economic evolution as special cases of the same class of evolutionary search algorithms. We also briefly discuss evolutionary economics and its relation to complexity economics.

The following sections discuss the evolution of various aspects of the economy. The evolution of knowledge in Sect. 10.6 is the most general aspect and is central to evolutionary economics. The creation of new knowledge, the organization of knowledge, and its use are fundamental to all economic activities. The evolution of knowledge can be analyzed using the concept of a *kene*, which is defined as a basic unit of knowledge similar to a *gene*. Section 10.7 focuses on the evolution of social technology, which is a particular form of knowledge. As in biology, we can use cladistics to classify technologies according to their evolutionary history. An evolutionary model replicates the evolution of manufacturing systems in the automobile industry.

Section 10.8 concludes the chapter with a discussion of the implications of diversity. Diversity is both a result of and a precondition for evolution. It is also an important element in the performance of firms, regions, and countries, and it matters for the resilience of economic systems.

10.2 Novelty

Novelty has preoccupied thinkers at least since the time of the ancient Greek philosophers (see North 2013). Parmenides, who lived around 500 BCE, had the idea that all things must have been formed from pre-existing things, which was later called *ex nihilo nihil fit* (Latin for "nothing comes from nothing"). Ancient creation myths postulated the existence of an eternal formless matter called *chaos* in Greek mythology. The Greek primordial deities Erebus (the male personification of darkness) and Nyx (the female personification of night) were born out of chaos. The Greek philosophers were skeptical about the possibility of novelty, believing either in *recurrence*, i.e., the cyclical reappearance of existing things over time, or in the *recombination* of existing elements, which allows for unlimited novelty, if the new combinations are accepted as truly novel. In sharp contrast to this view, Christian theology postulated that matter was not eternal, but was created by God in a divine act, which is called *creatio ex nihilo* (Latin for "creation out of nothing"). The Christian notion of *creatio ex nihilo* influenced Western thought for many centuries. It implied a cyclical notion of novelty similar to the Greek concept of recurrence. According to this view, there can be nothing truly novel, but only a rediscovery of the original novelty created by God, which is expressed in the dictum *non nova, sed nove* (Latin "not new, but anew").[1] Interestingly, the word "innovate" comes from the Latin "innovare," which means "to renew" or "to reform." The old English meaning of innovation was "to change into something new." Even Francis Bacon, the father of empiricism and of the scientific method, was influenced by this Christian idea of novelty:

> *Bacon rather pridefully takes biblical scripture as his model, comparing instauration to the work of reform, and he defends scientific investigation as a mimetic recapitulation of the Creation itself. Science, by this account, uncovers the original novelty packed into nature by its first creator, much as the church was supposed to do within its sphere of influence. . . . Return to origins did involve a new beginning, for science as for religion before it, insofar as it enabled the recapture of the original novelty of the first things.* (North 2013, pp. 48/49).

Bacon's view of science is that of a new beginning: the scientist himself must return to the origin and form his own view from observation and experimentation instead of relying on old books. Even today, it is very hard to escape from these old ideas, as the following paragraphs will show.

10.2.1 Some Theoretical Considerations on Novelty

Ulrich Witt (2009) reflects on novelty from the perspective of evolutionary economics. He defines novelty as

[1] Return is an important Christian concept: God was reborn in Christ, and Christ was resurrected from the dead.

> *something that was unknown before a particular point in time and that, hence, was discovered or created at that point in time* (Witt 2009, p. 312).

Novelty is relative to existing propositional or procedural knowledge on facts, rules, or theories. It thus depends on a subject that is a carrier of knowledge. We can distinguish between universal (or absolute or objective) novelty and domain-specific (or relative or subjective) novelty. *Universal novelty* means that something appears for the very first time, while *domain-specific novelty* is new only in some domain (e.g., a country or for a person), but could have been known already earlier in another domain.

Another distinction is between discovery and invention. A *discovery* refers to something that pre-existed but was unknown before. Humans discover things in nature, such as continents, stars, new species of plants and animals, caves, minerals, and so on. Discovering something may involve, but does not require, a creative act. For example, someone can discover a cave in the mountains just by walking around, while the discovery of a new star may require the construction of a telescope. Sometimes discoveries result from a mixture of purposeful creative experimentation and serendipity. Famous examples are the accidental discoveries of penicillin by Alexander Fleming or X-rays by Wilhelm Röntgen. Both Fleming and Röntgen conducted experiments with some purpose, but their groundbreaking discoveries were not planned.

An *invention* is the creation of a new thought that materializes in the form of a new artifact, process, or practice. Inventions are rarely purely accidental, because inventors often have the intention of solving a problem. This means that they often pre-select existing ideas or elements that they believe will be helpful for their purpose. But chance often plays an important role in invention as well. In the early eighteenth century, Johann Friedrich Böttger, a German alchemist, was searching for the philosopher's stone, a mythical substance that could turn other metals into gold. He was imprisoned by the monarch of Saxony, Augustus the Strong, who ordered him to produce gold. Böttger's alchemical experiments were unsuccessful in producing gold, but led to the European invention of (hard paste or white) porcelain. The English inventor and apothecary John Walker invented the friction match in 1826. While trying to find a way to easily start a fire, the successful mixture of chemicals that he used to make the first matches was a serendipitous discovery.

Witt (2009) argues that the creation of new ideas or cognitive concepts involves two operations. The first operation, which is generative, (re)combines existing elements into something new. The second operation is interpretative and integrates the new combination into an existing or emerging concept. In other words, the interpretative operation gives meaning to the invention. While it is possible to automate the generative operation mechanically or electronically, e.g., by computer algorithms, the interpretative operation takes place in the human mind. The possible, but not necessary, third operation is evaluative and assesses the utility of a new idea or its advantage over already known ones. The evaluative operation can also be performed in a technical way using some evaluation criterion.

Recombining existing ideas or elements is an inductive process. If the result is novel, it cannot be predicted ex ante, that is, derived from premises. In this sense, novelty is weakly emergent and diachronic, because induction takes time. Once something new has emerged, it may also take time for its meaning to be understood.

The emergence of novelty is a potentially never-ending process as newly created concepts are reused and recombined. This is expressed in Fig. 10.1, where a new entity emerges from the recombination of existing entities and may be subject to evolutionary recombination at a higher level. The process is *autocatalytic*, i.e. it generates the inputs for its own continuation. However, if the interpretative operation is seen as a necessary element of novelty, then cognitive and communicative constraints may limit the growth of knowledge because the interpretative operations become increasingly difficult. There may be limits to scientific growth if it becomes impossible to integrate all newly created concepts (see Csermely 1999).

Witt (2009) suggests that there may be different *degrees of novelty*. From an ex post perspective, i.e., after something new has been discovered or invented, we can classify a discovery or invention as either fundamental or follow-up, with the former having a higher degree of novelty than the latter. A *fundamental novelty* implies some discontinuity with previous thinking and practice, whereas a *follow-up novelty* is a gradualist improvement and therefore less novel. From an ex ante perspective, however, it is hardly possible to assess the degree of novelty. According to Witt, the only assessment we can make ex ante is whether the degree of novelty is minimal, maximal, or in between the two extremes. No further cardinal or ordinal measurement is possible.

> *The ex ante degree of novelty is minimal (but not necessarily zero) if the generative operation is known and the interpretative operation is trivial in the sense that the meaning of all its possible outcomes is known beforehand. The degree of novelty is maximal where the generative operation is not known and no constraint can be imposed on the outcome of the interpretative operation* (Witt 2009, p. 317).

As an example of minimal novelty, Witt suggests a lottery in which six balls, numbered from 1 to 49, are randomly drawn from an urn. In this case, we know the generative operation, and the interpretative operation is trivial because the only possible outcomes are combinations of six different integers between 1 and 49. There is still some novelty involved, because we cannot know ex ante when which combination will be generated. Obviously, minimal novelty and its associated uncertainty are amenable to probabilistic reasoning, while novelty that is not minimal is not. Novelty that is greater than minimal is too unstructured to infer degrees of probability.

10.2.2 A Short History of Technical Inventions

The theoretical considerations from the previous subsection become more vivid when we look at some examples of important technical inventions. Encyclopedias and textbooks often attribute groundbreaking inventions to famous inventors, such as the invention of the printing press by Johannes Gutenberg in the mid-fifteenth century, the invention of the steam engine by James Watt in the late eighteenth century, or the invention of the automobile by Carl Benz in 1886. There is no denying that these inventors made significant contributions, but in all of these examples, the novelty of these inventions was domain-specific rather than universal.

Johannes Gutenberg's printing press was a recombination of existing technologies. He combined movable type, paper, ink, and the wine press. Printing with movable metal type was known in China as early as the twelfth century. The first books with movable metal type were printed in Korea in the thirteenth century. The oldest surviving book printed with movable metal type is the Korean Jikij of 1377. Printing and papermaking were also known in the Muslim world during the Golden Age of Islam from the eighth to the fourteenth century. The screw press for pressing grapes or paper, which Gutenberg used to mechanize printing, was introduced by the Romans in the first century AD. Ink is a very old invention, known in ancient Egypt and China. It was widely used in Europe at the time of Gutenberg, but he improved it by using oil instead of water to make it adhere better to metal type. So Gutenberg did not invent printing as such, but he invented a machine and a process that made printing much easier and faster, making mass production of printed products like books possible. This led to the so-called *printing revolution*, i.e. the widespread use of the printing press in Europe and the resulting spread of knowledge and ideas.

The Scottish inventor James Watt is often credited with inventing the steam engine, but what he really did was to improve on earlier designs such as that of Thomas Newcomen. In 1712, Newcomen constructed the *atmospheric engine* or *Newcomen fire engine*, which created a partial vacuum by condensing steam in a cylinder. The resulting pressure differential between the cylinder with partial vacuum and the outside atmosphere drove the piston into the upright-standing cylinder, producing a power stroke that could be used to pump water from a mine. The principle that Newcomen used and put into practice was described in a 1690 publication by the Frenchman Denis Papin. Papin built prototypes of his machine, but they were not used in practice. Even earlier, the Spaniard Jerónimo de Ayanz y Beaumont designed and built a steam-powered water pump for mines, for which he received a Spanish patent in 1606. A steam turbine was invented by the Ottoman polymath Taqi ad-Din (or al-Din). In 1551, he described a steam-generating machine that could move a wheel at the end of an axle that rotated a spit. Ad-Taqi's invention is often considered the first steam-powered engine with practical use. The *aeolipile,* or *Hero's engine,* was a water-filled container with steam jets that could spin around an axle, when the water was heated from below (see Fig. 10.3). The Greek mathematician and engineer Hero (or Heron) of Alexandria published a description of this machine in the first century CE. The aeolipile was a curiosity with no practical use. But even Hero was not the first to describe the principle of using steam to move objects. The aeolipile was described by the Roman architect and engineer Vitrivius around 30–20 BCE. It is likely that the aeolipile was known already earlier, since

Fig. 10.3 The aeolipile as an early steam engine. Source: Wikimedia Commons, public domain, by Woodcroft (1876)

both Hero and Vitrivius cite the Greek inventor and mathematician Ctesibius, who lived in Alexandria from 285–222 BCE and is known as the "father of pneumatics."

A similar story can be told about the automobile. Its "official" inventor was the German Carl Benz, who was granted a patent for the Benz-Patent-Motorwagen in 1886 (see Fig. 10.4). In the second half of the nineteenth century, there was fierce competition between inventors in different countries and also between different technologies for the first practical self-propelled road vehicle. Wheeled vehicles are a very old technology with evidence dating back to the middle of the fourth millennium BCE. Vehicles with wheels were used in Europe and Mesopotamia as early as 3500 BCE. For millennia, these vehicles had to be drawn either by humans or by animals such as camels, donkeys, horses, or oxen.

The development of the automobile, i.e., a self-propelled vehicle, depended on the availability of a suitable engine that was small and light enough to be transportable. In the nineteenth century, steam engines were available, as well as electric motors and the first internal combustion engines. Both electric motors and steam engines had a head start on the internal combustion engine. The first electric car was built by the Scottish inventor Robert Anderson in the 1830s. Steam-powered cars were even older. The British inventor and engineer Richard Trevithick built working steam-powered road vehicles such as the *Puffing Devil* in 1801 and the

Fig. 10.4 Benz Patent-Motorwagen. Source: Mendoza (2016), Wikimedia Commons, public domain

London Steam Carriage in 1803 (see Fig. 10.5). In 1770, the French inventor Nicolas-Joseph Cugnot built the *fardier á vapeur* ("steam dray"), which was a heavy wagon with a steam engine designed to carry cannons or other heavy military equipment (see Fig. 10.6).

The idea of a steam-powered vehicle can be attributed to the Flemish Jesuit Ferdinand Verbiest, who was a missionary in China and designed a steam-propelled toy vehicle for the Kangxi Emperor in 1672. A much earlier idea for a self-propelled car came from Leonardo da Vinci, who described an automobile in his Codex Atlanticus (1478–1519). Leonardo's design, which he did not build, was to be driven by springs like a clockwork mechanism (see Fig. 10.7). The history of the automobile shows that the idea of a self-propelled car was far from new in the nineteenth century.

So what can we learn from this brief history of inventions? One lesson is to distinguish between the final breakthrough that makes an invention practical and the initial idea. Gutenberg, Watt, Benz, and many other inventors were not the first to come up with a great new idea. Their achievement was to recombine and refine existing ideas, many of which were hundreds or even thousands of years old. Taking an idea and making it practical requires a lot of engineering or problem-solving.

Fig. 10.5 London Steam Carriage by Trevithick and Vivian from 1803. Source: Felton (1803), Wikipedia Commons, public domain

Fig. 10.6 Cugnot's fardier á vapeur. Source: F. A. Brockhaus (1769), Wikimedia Commons, public domain

Many practical obstacles must be overcome before a good idea actually works well in everyday life.

Another lesson is that the time must be ripe for an invention to be successful. Trevithick's London Steam Carriage, for instance, could drive with a speed of up to 9 miles per hour, which was about the same speed of the first Benz Patent-Motorwagen. While the Benz car could carry two people, the Steam Carriage had a capacity of seven or eight passengers. Trevithick and his cousin Andrew Vivian obtained a patent for the steam coach, but could not find investors or buyers for the expensive new technology. By the end of the nineteenth century, however,

Fig. 10.7 Replica of Leonardo da Vinci's automobile. Source: Crochet (2011), Wikipedia Commons. CC BY 3.0 unported (https://creativecommons.org/licenses/by-sa/3.0/deed.de)

automobile production was taking off in France, Germany, the United States, and other countries. Similarly, Taqi ad-Din's steam-powered, self-rotating spit was apparently ahead of its time.

Finally, technology evolves through the recombination of existing building blocks, which W. Brian Arthur (2009) calls *combinatorial evolution*. Early technologies formed from primitive components themselves become components or building blocks of more advanced technologies. A wine press combined with movable type creates the printing press, and a cart combined with a steam engine makes the steam car. Yet some combinations are dead ends like the steam car, while others are so fundamental and universally useful that they can be recombined in many ways (e.g., wheels, gears, electricity).

10.3 Evolution as Process and Theory

Evolution is generally understood as the process by which populations of living organisms change over time in response to changes in their environment. Modern evolutionary theory, which postulates that species evolve and new species appear, as opposed to the older view of constant biological types, was developed by Charles Darwin and, in parallel, Alfred Russel Wallace in the mid-nineteenth century. Darwin's 1859 book, "On the Origin of Species by Means of Natural Selection, or the Preservation of Favored Races in the Struggle for Life," introduced a scientific theory of evolution that is considered the foundation of evolutionary biology. This section serves as a brief introduction to the principles of (biological) evolution, which is the basis for the application of evolutionary thinking to economics in the next section.

10.3.1 Theory of Evolution

Modern evolutionary theory in biology is a synthesis of various concepts such as Darwinian natural selection, Mendelian genetics, and population genetics. The main ideas of evolutionary theory are as follows. Living beings inherit characteristics encoded in their genes from their parents. Offspring are not identical copies of their parents, so there is variation in a population of a species. *Variation* is the result of genetic recombination during reproduction and mutation. Evolution occurs when natural selection and genetic drift cause certain characteristics to become more or less frequent in a population.

Genetic information is arranged on chromosomes, which are made up of deoxyribonucleic acid (DNA). DNA is composed of two chains of polynucleotides that form a double helix. Each strand of the double helix contains the nucleobases cytosine (C), guanine (G), adenine (A), and thymine (T). Two pairs of nucleobases can bind: adenine with thymine and cytosine with guanine. The sequence of these base pairs is a script that encodes biological information necessary for the development, growth, function, and reproduction of organisms (Fig. 10.8).

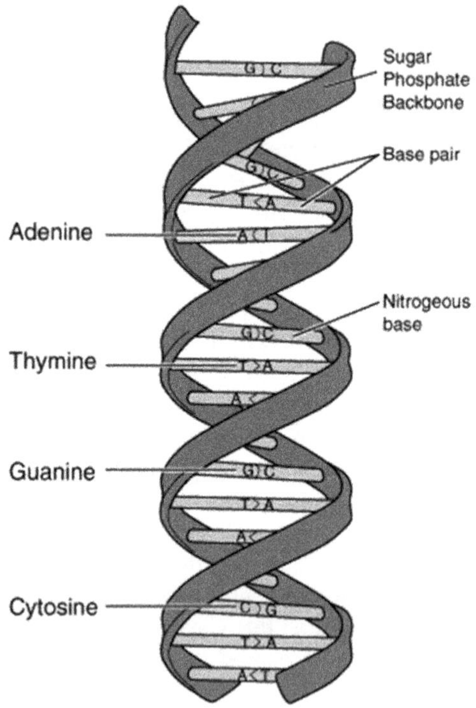

Fig. 10.8 DNA double helix. Source: Wikimedia Commons, public domain, https://commons.wikimedia.org/wiki/File:DNA-structure-and-bases.png

A molecular *gene* is a segment of a chromosome. In Mendelian genetics, a gene is a basic unit of heredity. All the genes that can be stored on one or more chromosomes are called the *genome* of an organism. The location of a gene on a chromosome is called a locus. A locus can have alternative DNA sequences called *alleles*. In other words, members of a population can have slightly different gene sequences due to different alleles. An organism's *phenotype*, or observable characteristics or traits, results from its *genotype*, or genetic code. Because the genotype can consist of different alleles, the phenotype of an organism can vary. For example, people can be blond or black-haired, or brown- or blue-eyed, depending on their alleles.

In sexual reproduction, the set of chromosomes from one parent is randomly combined with the set of chromosomes from the other parent so that the offspring receives half of each parent's genetic material. Thus, sexual reproduction is a recombination of genetic information. This process of genetic recombination is called *chromosomal cross-over* and creates variation in the genetic information.

Mutation, which is another source of variation, is the cause of novelty. The sequence of base pairs in the genome can change spontaneously due to random replication errors or due to external causes such as chemicals or radiation. Figure 10.9 shows five different types of chromosomal mutations. Mutations can be passed on to offspring (germline mutations) or not (somatic mutations). In addition, mutations can have different effects on the fitness of the organism. Harmful mutations decrease the fitness of the organism, beneficial mutations have a favorable effect, and neutral mutations have no effect on fitness.

Genetic drift means that the frequency of an existing allele in a population changes randomly. Whether a particular allele is passed on to offspring depends on chance. Due to genetic drift, an allele can completely disappear from a population by pure chance, which reduces genetic variation.

Natural selection is a complement to genetic drift, which leads to the evolution of new traits in a population over time. As mentioned earlier, mutations can be harmful, neutral, or beneficial to the fitness of an organism. *Fitness* can be defined as the ability of an individual to have more offspring, and thus produce copies of its own genotype, in a given environment. It is therefore a measure of *adaptedness* to environmental conditions, i.e. the degree to which an individual can survive and reproduce in an environment. If a mutation produces traits that are helpful in a particular environment, the individual has a better chance of surviving and reproducing in that environment. Conversely, harmful mutations make survival and reproduction less likely. For example, the ability to digest a certain food that no one else can digest is an advantage that increases fitness. A very conspicuous skin or fur color, on the other hand, may be a disadvantage because it may attract the attention of predators. Evolution by natural selection requires that the traits created by mutation can be passed on to offspring (see Fig. 10.10). In contrast to genetic drift, natural selection can create new traits.

Variation by itself tends to produce more and different genotypes, increasing entropy or disorder. A set of all different genotypes shows no order. Order is created by selection, which eliminates some genotypes and copies others. Thus, selection

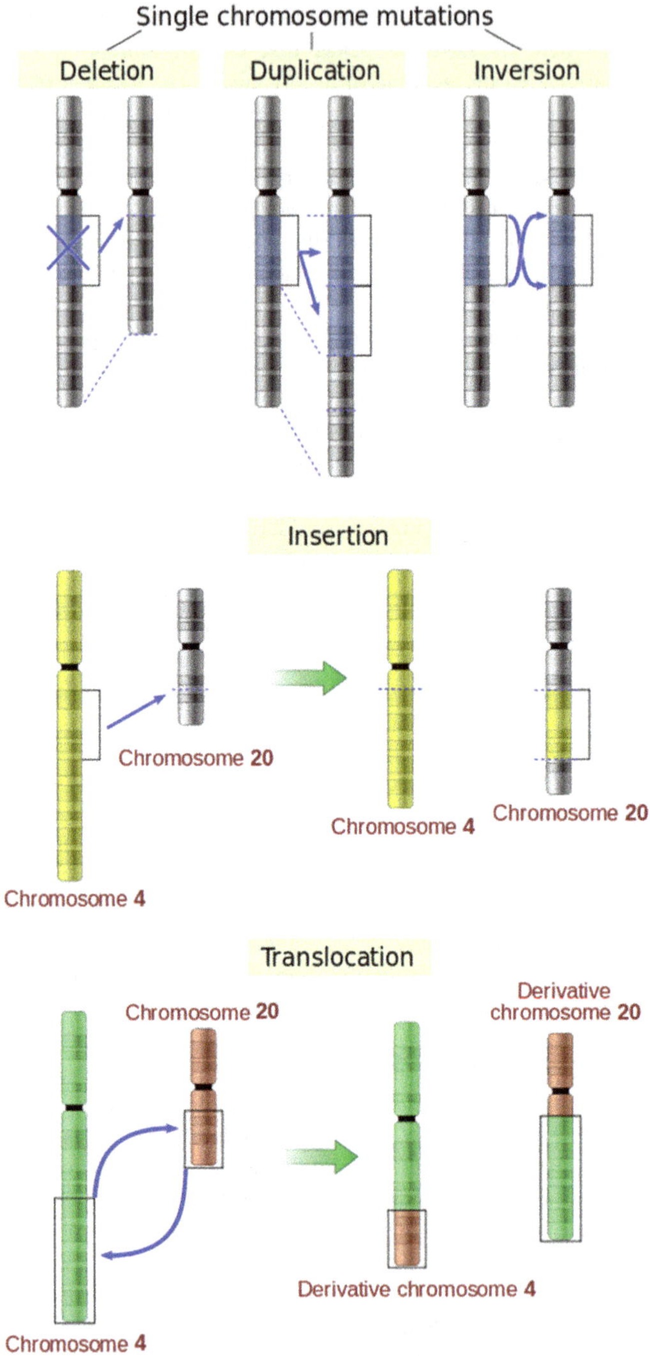

Fig. 10.9 Types of chromosomal mutations. Source: Mrabet (2009), Wikimedia Commons, public domain

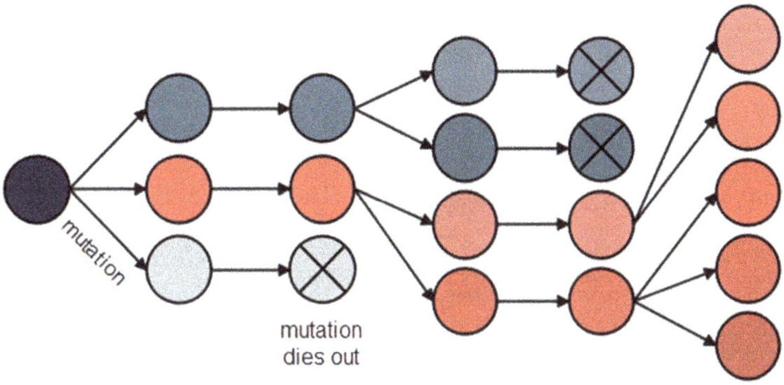

Fig. 10.10 Mutation and natural selection. Source: Author

reduces entropy. Selection is a constraint on variation. Fitness can be interpreted as a property of an organism (or system) that determines the probability of being selected, and thus being able to survive and reproduce. Note that fitness has the two dimensions of stability, i.e., difficulty of destruction, which implies survival, and productivity, or ease of production. If a genotype has high fitness (greater than one), its number will increase. If fitness is low (less than one), the number of instances with that genotype will decrease and eventually reach zero. Evolution creates complexity between order and randomness when neither variation nor selection dominates.

In population genetics, fitness is interpreted not only as a property of individuals, but also of the entire population of the same individuals with a particular genotype or phenotype. It can be defined as the probability of having offspring. The *relative fitness* f_i of a genotype i in a population determines, how the share of individuals with that genotype $s_i = n_i/N$, where n is the absolute number and N is the size of the total population, changes over time:

$$s_i(t) = \frac{f_i}{\overline{f}} s_i(t-1),$$

where $\overline{f}$ is the average relative fitness in the population. This means that the share of a genotype will grow (shrink) in a population, if its relative fitness is greater (smaller) than the average. For the change in a genotype's relative frequency, we can write:

$$\Delta s_i = s_i(t) - s_i(t-1) = \frac{f_i - \overline{f}}{\overline{f}} s_i(t-1).$$

Assume that genotype i is a new mutation and the rest of the population has genotype j. The change in the mutant genotype's share is then given by

$$\Delta s_i = \frac{f_i - \overline{f}}{\overline{f}} s_i(t-1) = \frac{f_i - f_j}{\overline{f}} s_i(t-1)[1 - s_i(t-1)],$$

because $\overline{f} = s_i f_i + s_j f_j = s_i f_i + (1 - s_i) f_j$. Thus, the mutant genotype's share will grow in the population, if it has a greater relative fitness than the existing genotype, $f_i > f_j$. Suppose $f_i = (1 + \alpha) f_j$ with $0 < \alpha \ll 1$. Then, we get

$$\Delta s_i = \frac{\alpha}{1 + \alpha s_i} s_i(1 - s_i) \approx \alpha s_i(1 - s_i).$$

This means that the relative share of the mutation grows approximately logistically when the advantage over the existing genotype is small.

10.3.2 Genetic Algorithms

Genetic algorithms, developed by the computer scientist and complexity researcher John Holland in the 1960s and 70s (Holland 1975, 1992), emulate the process of biological evolution. In the context of complexity economics, they are interesting for several reasons. They can help to better understand how evolution works, since they are a formalization of the evolutionary principles of recombination, mutation, and selection. They are also useful for solving practical problems, especially search and optimization problems in engineering, logistics, management, and economics. Another application is evolutionary art, where algorithms are used to generate music, images, or objects that are aesthetically appealing to humans. Genetic algorithms are also used as research tools to study phenomena generated by complex adaptive systems. They can also be used to implement the emergence of novelty in agent-based models. Axelrod's model of the emergence of norms in Chap. 9 contains a genetic algorithm.

Genetic algorithms are *metaheuristics*, i.e. algorithms designed to provide sufficiently good approximate solutions to optimization problems, especially in cases where there is incomplete or imperfect information or where computational capacity is limited. Unlike optimization algorithms, they consist of a sequence of abstract steps that can be applied to general sets of problems. Optimization algorithms are more specific and require more detailed information about the problem. Genetic algorithms are instances of evolutionary algorithms, which are nature-inspired algorithms. There are many variants of genetic algorithms that differ in their specific implementation (see Fig. 10.11). However, they all share the four basic operations: encoding, selection, cross-over, and mutation. We will focus on the basic classical genetic algorithm with binary coding, roulette wheel selection, single-point cross-over, and bit-flipping mutation.

Figure 10.12 shows pseudocode for the classical genetic algorithm. The basic idea is to have a population of possible solutions to a problem, which can be thought of as chromosomes. Chromosomes have different alleles. According to a goal, it is evaluated how well a chromosome with a certain allele solves the problem, i.e. its

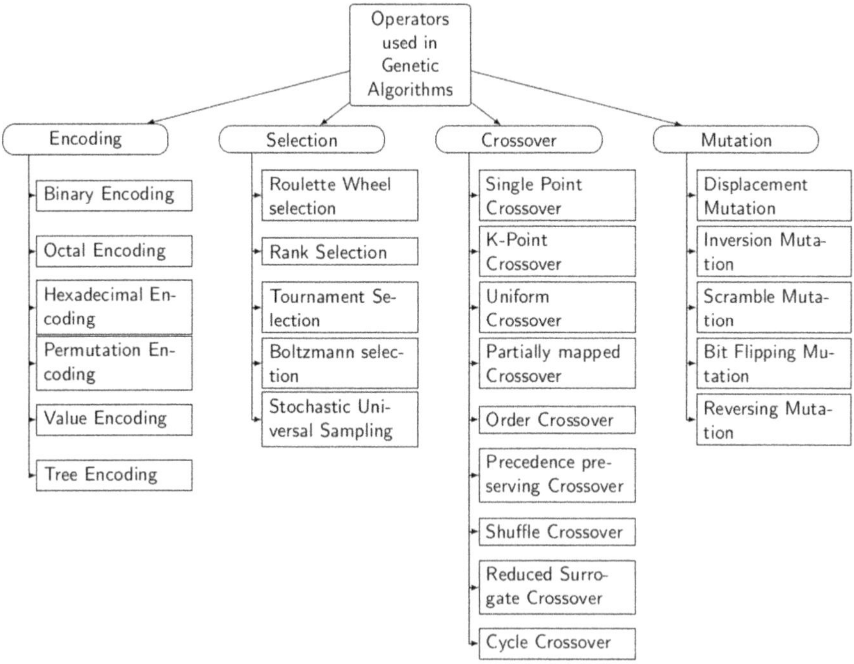

Fig. 10.11 Variants of genetic algorithms. Source: Katoch et al. (2021), reproduced with kind permission of Springer Nature

fitness is evaluated. Then an evolutionary process of selection, cross-over, and mutation is used to find the best solution.

Step 1 consists in converting potential solutions to a problem into a particular form according to an **encoding** scheme. With binary encoding, each chromosome consists of a string of bits, 0s and 1s, of a given length. The following string could be interpreted as a chromosome with ten genes:

1	0	0	1	1	0	0	1	1	1

Step 2 is to determine an **initial set** of n chromosomes (potential solutions). This is the first generation of the population. Often, the first generation is determined randomly in order to spread the potential solutions as evenly as possible in the search space.

In **step 3**, the **fitness** of each chromosome is evaluated. Fitness can be utility, profit, payoff, or a similar measure, depending on the nature of the problem.

Step 4 is the **selection** step, in which those chromosomes are selected that will breed the next generation. With the simple roulette wheel mechanism, each chromosome gets a probability of being selected according to its relative fitness, i.e. the individual fitness value relative to the sum of all fitness values. Therefore, more

Input:
Population Size, n
Maximum number of iterations, MAX
Output:
Global best solution, Y_{bt}

---

begin
Generate initial population of n chromosomes Y_i $(i = 1, 2, \ldots, n)$
Set iteration counter $t = 0$
Compute the fitness value of each chromosomes
while $(t < MAX)$
Select a pair of chromosomes from initial population based on fitness
Apply crossover operation on selected pair with crossover probability
Apply mutation on the offspring with mutation probability
Replace old population with newly generated population
Increment the current iteration t by 1.
end while
return the best solution, Y_{bt}
end

Fig. 10.12 Pseudocode of the classical genetic algorithm. Source: Katoch et al. (2021), reproduced with kind permission of Springer Nature

successful chromosomes (i.e., better solutions) have a higher chance of being selected for reproduction.

In **step 5,** pairs selected chromosomes for the recombination of their respective genomes. With single-point **cross-over**, a fragment before or after a cross-over point is swapped between two chromosomes. In the following example, the last four elements of two paired chromosomes are swapped:

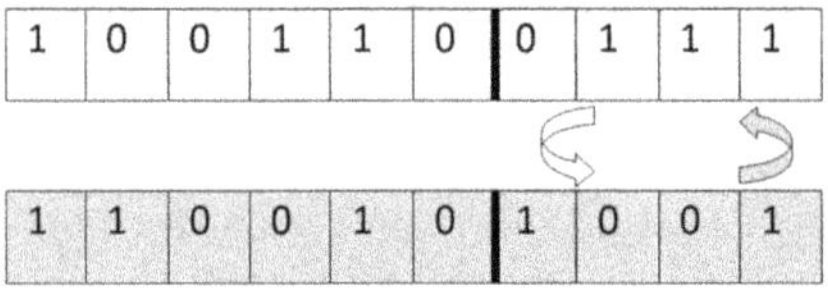

The cross-over results in two new chromosomes:

1	0	0	1	1	0	1	0	0	1

1	1	0	0	1	0	0	1	1	1

Step 6 performs **mutations** on some of the offspring chromosomes. Some genes of some chromosomes are chosen with a low probability according to some random mechanism. The bit-flipping mutation replaces the value of chosen gene with its opposite:

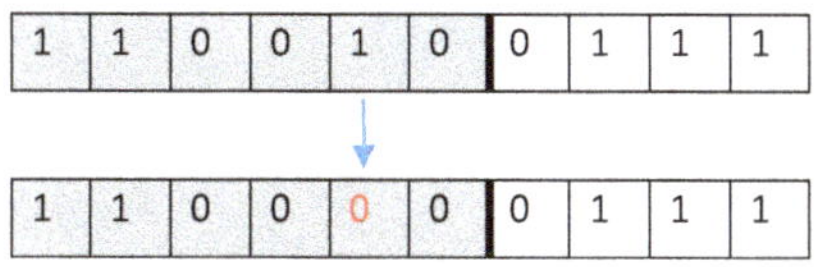

Other mutation methods shift or invert segments within a chromosome. In addition to cross-over, mutation is another source of randomness in a genetic algorithm. Mutation maintains diversity in the population, but should not occur too often because it somewhat counteracts the other operations.

The algorithm runs either until a good solution has been found or until a prespecified number of generations have been reached.

We can demonstrate the application of the genetic algorithm with the knapsack problem. The *knapsack problem* is a standard problem in combinatorial optimization and was studied by the mathematician Tobias Dantzig already in 1897. The story of the problem is that a knapsack has to be packed with items that have a value and a weight. The objective is to pack the most valuable items without overloading the knapsack, which can carry a maximum weight. The knapsack problem can be formulated as a decision problem ("Can a total value of at least V be achieved without exceeding the maximum weight W?") or as an optimization problem (see below). The decision problem is in the computational complexity class of *NP-complete* problems, which are considered as computationally hard problems. This means that although it is possible to verify a solution quickly (i.e., in polynomial time), there is no known way to find a solution quickly (i.e., in polynomial time). The standard case is the 0–1 knapsack problem where the items are non-divisible, i.e. an item can either be packed into the knapsack, $x_i = 1$, or not, $x_i = 0$. Formally, the optimization problem is given by

$$\max_{x_i} \sum_{i=1}^{n} v_i x_i \ s.t. \sum_{i=1}^{n} w_i x_i \leq W \ and \ x_i \in \{0, 1\},$$

where W is maximum weight that the knapsack can carry.

Figure 10.13 shows an example with five items with value v and weight w and a knapsack with a weight limit of 4 kg. We can solve this problem by checking the total value and the total of each combination of items. For example, including the book and the apple would yield a value of 170 and a weight of 680 g, while including the laptop computer and the smartphone would yield a value of 830 and a weight of 2680 g. By checking all the combinations, we find that the best feasible solution consists of the laptop, the smartphone, and the water bottle ($v = 1010$, $w = 3980g$). Since a decision (in or out) is binary and we have five items, the total number of item

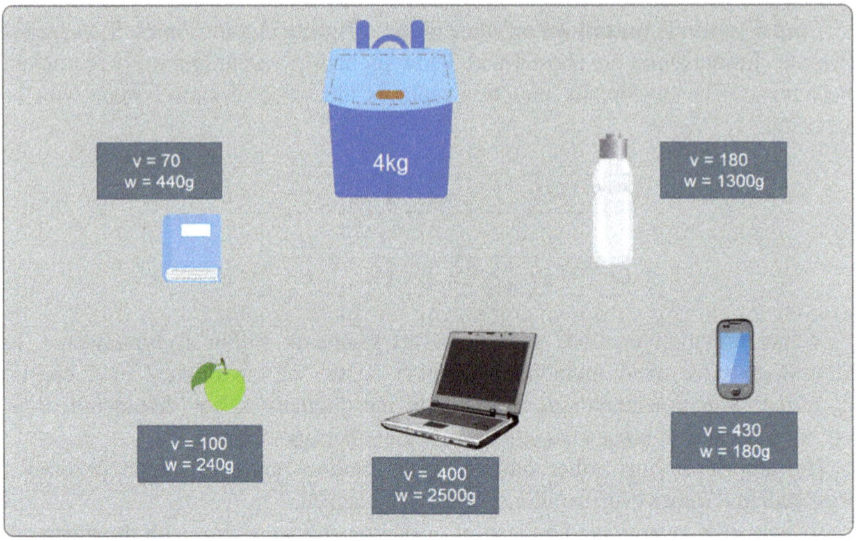

Fig. 10.13 The knapsack problem. Source: Author

combinations is $2^5 = 32$. With this small number of items, it is quite easy to solve the problem by hand, but with 10 items, we already have $2^{10} = 1{,}024$ combinations. With 20 items, the number of combinations is equal to 1,048,576. Since the number of combinations grows exponentially, it will take even a computer a long time to check all the combinations one by one. Such an approach is called *brute-force search* in computer science. The exponential growth of the number of possible solutions and the resulting time and computational effort is called *combinatorial explosion*. At some point, combinatorial explosion makes *brute-force* search either practically impossible or very expensive. The genetic algorithm is an alternative to brute-force search that can find good solutions to many search and optimization problems. Let us see how this works.

Encoding possible solutions as binary strings is easy in this case. Figure 10.14 shows two strings (or chromosomes) for possible solutions. We need to specify the order of the items and assign 1 or 0 to each item, if it is selected or not, respectively. So the chromosome (1 0 1 0 1) in the example means that we choose the book, the laptop, and the bottle, but not the apple and the smartphone. For the first generation, we need to define a set of chromosomes, e.g. (1 0 1 0 1), (1 0 1 1 0), (1 1 1 1 1), (0 0 1 0 0), and (0 1 1 0 0).

The next step is to determine the fitness of each chromosome, which is given by the sum of the values in this example. However, we must satisfy the feasibility constraint given by $W = 4000g$. Since the solution of chromosome (1 0 1 0 1) is not possible, because $w = 4240g > 4000g$, we assign a value of 0 to this chromosome (see Fig. 10.14). The second chromosome in the example is feasible, so $v((1\ 0\ 1\ 1\ 0)) = 900$.

					V	W
1	0	1	0	1	0	4240g
1	0	1	1	0	900	3120g

Fig. 10.14 Two chromosomes for the knapsack problem. Source: Author

With the roulette wheel mechanism, the selection probability assigned to each chromosome of first generation is $p_i = v_i/V$, with the total value of all five combinations being equal to $V = 1{,}800$. Therefore, the probability assigned to the second chromosome is $p((1\ 0\ 1\ 1\ 0)) = \frac{900}{1{,}800} = 0.5$ and the chromosome with only the laptop receives $p((0\ 0\ 1\ 0\ 0)) = \frac{400}{1{,}800} = 0.222$.

Assuming that these two chromosomes ((1 0 1 1 0) and (0 0 1 0 0)) are selected and paired and that the cross-over occurs at the last two genes, we obtain two new chromosomes: (1 0 1 0 0) and (0 0 1 1 0), both of which are feasible. The values are $v((1\ 0\ 1\ 0\ 0) = 470$ and $v((0\ 0\ 1\ 1\ 0)) = 830$. The fitness of both is better than the parent (0 0 1 0 0), but (slightly) worse than that of the parent (1 0 1 1 0). By random mutation, it could happen that (0 0 1 1 0) becomes (0 0 1 1 1), which would already be the optimal solution. In the same way, some other pairs of chromosomes with be selected and recombined. Since infeasible combinations are assigned a value of zero, they are never selected and thus become irrelevant. The chromosomes that are already close to the optimal solution have a higher selection probability and will hence be selected more often. Given enough time, the genetic algorithm will generally find a good solution.

10.3.3 Fitness Landscape

Why does the genetic algorithm find good solutions to hard computational problems? Understanding how the genetic algorithm works also provides insight into how evolution works. In fact, we can interpret evolution as a computational mechanism that adaptively optimizes the fitness of organisms. In fact, the genetic algorithm is a formalization of the main principles of evolutionary theory. The *fitness landscape* introduced by Wright (1932) is a helpful concept for understanding how evolution (and the genetic algorithm) works.

A typical fitness landscape, as shown in Fig. 10.15, is a three-dimensional visualization of the fitness of genotypes as a function of two genes. The two horizontal axes span genotype space, and the vertical axis assigns a fitness level to

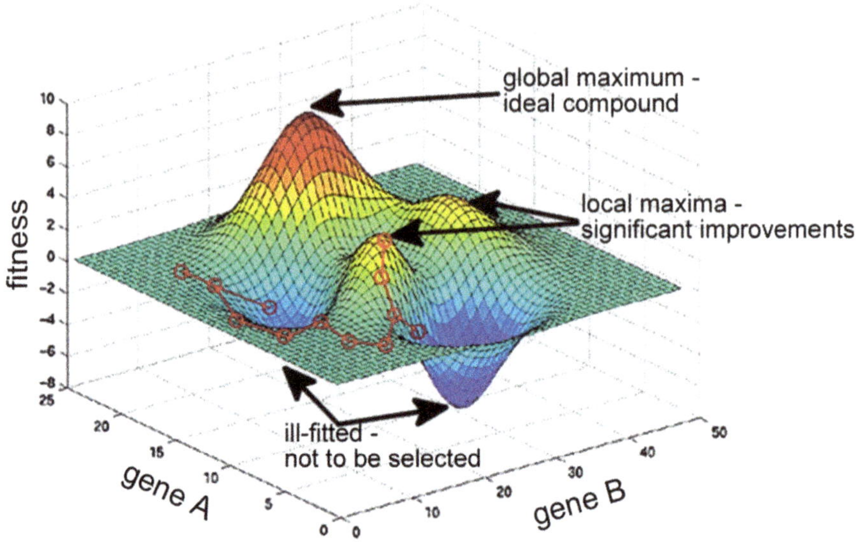

Fig. 10.15 An example of a fitness landscape. Source: Rodrigues et al. (2021), licensed under CC-BY 4.0 (https://creativecommons.org/licenses/by/4.0/)

each gene combination. In the example, the fitness function has a global maximum (with a red peak), two local maxima (yellow), and a global minimum (the blue trough). Such graphs look like landscapes with mountains, hills, and valleys, hence the name. When there are several local maxima and minima, we speak of a *rugged landscape*. The graphs also include a population of genotypes, shown as red circles. The higher up in the landscape a genotype is, the better it functions, which means it is more likely to survive and reproduce. Thus, parents on hills have a higher probability of producing offspring that will be on the same hill if both parents are close to each other. Evolution explains why populations tend to climb the highest hill in the fitness landscape over time.

We can illustrate this with a very simple model. Assume that a genotype Γ_i consists of two genes, $\gamma_1 \in \{0, 1, 2, 3, \ldots\}$ and $\gamma_2 \in \{0, 1, 2, 3, \ldots.\}$. The fitness $F \in \{0, 1, 2, 3, 4, 5\}$ of a genotype Γ_i depends on the combination of the alleles, i.e. the specific values of the two genes, $F_i = F(\gamma_{1i}, \gamma_{2i})$. The selection probability for reproduction depends on fitness, $p(F_i)$, for instance $p(5) = 0.9$, $p(4) = 0.75$, $p(3) = 0.65$, $p(2) = 0.5$, $p(1) = 0.3$ *and* $p(0) = 0$. Let us assume for simplicity that two matched parents produce two offspring by swapping the second gene.[2] After reproduction, mutation can occur both to parents and to offspring in each of the

[2] A complete model would also need assumptions about the sequence of the selection, the matching process, and whether and when an old genotype disappears. For the point to be made here, this information is not necessary.

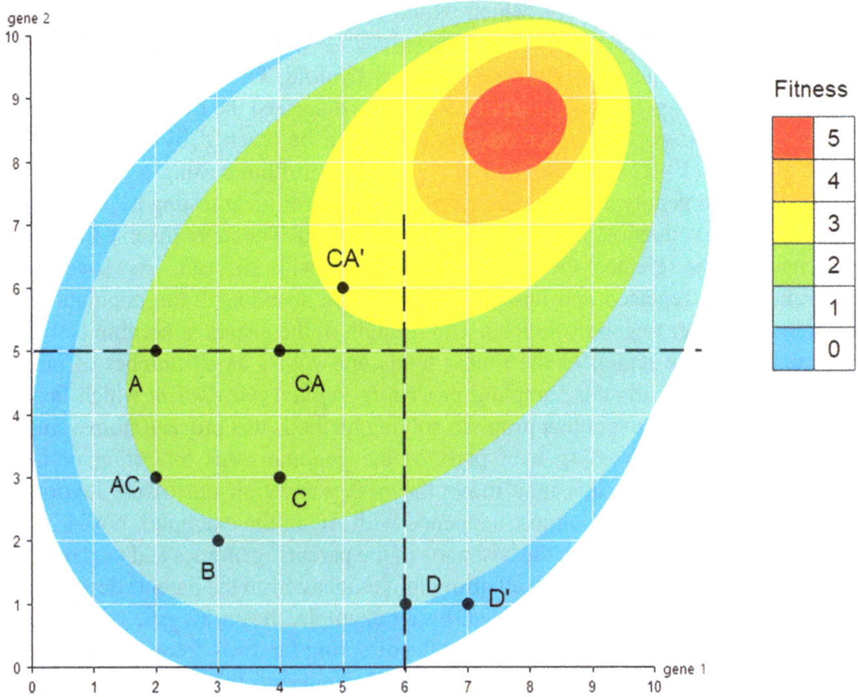

Fig. 10.16 A 2-dimensional contour plot of a fitness landscape with one peak. Source: Author

two genes by a random change of the allele. Assume that we have for first-generation genotypes *A*, *B*, *C* and *D* with $\Gamma_A = (2, 5)$, $\Gamma_B = (3, 2)$, $\Gamma_C = (4, 3)$ and $\Gamma_D = (6, 1)$.

Figure 10.16 contains a contour plot of a fitness landscape with one peak in the northeast. The four first-generation genotypes are located in the southwest. *A* and *C* sit in the green area with fitness level 2 and *B* and *D* are further downhill with fitness level 1. Assume that *A* and *C* are selected and paired. With a cross-over of the second gene, γ_2, their offspring are *AC* and *CA*. While both new genotypes are still in the green region, *AC* inherited the weaker gene combination, locating it at the edge of the lower fitness level, whereas *CA* received the better combination moving it closer to the peak. The fitness landscape shows the importance of mutation. Without mutation, the population cannot leave the rectangle defined by $\gamma_1 = 6$ and $\gamma_2 = 5$ represented by the dashed lines. Hence, the population cannot maximize its fitness in this setting by cross-over alone. There are two mutant genotypes in the landscape, CA' and D'. The mutation was clearly beneficial for CA' increasing the fitness level to 3. In contrast, D' experienced a harmful mutation, which decreased its fitness level to 0, such that D' will not be selected for reproduction and will eventually disappear from the population. The model is, of course, a strong simplification. By swapping the entire second gene, new generations cannot be anywhere between the parents, which restricts the space that can be reached by recombination. Alternatively, we could assume that the cross-over results in linear combinations of the first genes and the second genes, respectively, which would locate the offspring on a connecting line between the parents.

The main message of this simple model is twofold. First, it demonstrates the importance of first-generation diversity. The more dispersed the first generation is in the fitness landscape, the larger the space that can be reached by recombination alone. Holland (1992) describes this as a genetic algorithm casting a net over the landscape. Each genotype can be interpreted as an experiment testing a solution for survival and reproduction. Some fail and some succeed. The more diverse the set of experiments, the greater the chance that some will succeed. As successful experiments are repeated and unsuccessful ones are abandoned, the population as a whole gets closer to good solutions. The strength of the genetic algorithm is that it can sample a large region of the fitness landscape with a small number of initial solutions. Holland calls this sampling procedure *implicit parallelism* which favors the genetic algorithm over other problem-solving methods that proceed from a single starting point only. Crossing over parts of the genome leads to testing of new regions. In some cases, this may move the next generation out of the favorable region of the parents (as it almost happened with *AC* in the example), but in other cases the offspring will inherit the best parts of the parents' genomes and thus reach a better fitness region. How far the offspring moves away from the parents depends on how much of the genome is resampled. In our example, the entire gene is swapped, which is a fairly large change that moves the offspring far away from the parents. If only a smaller part of the gene is crossed over (Holland calls this a compact *building block*), the offspring will stay in the vicinity of the parents. This reduces the risk of losing a good solution, but also the chance of finding a better one.

The second message is that mutation prevents the population from getting stuck at a local maximum. Mutation itself does not improve the evolution to a better solution. As we saw in the example, it can lead to improvements as well as deteriorations. But without mutations, the population cannot leave the space spanned by the genomes of the first generation. If this space contains regions of poor fitness, the space will become smaller over time as genotypes with poor fitness die out. The example in Fig. 10.16 contains only one global maximum, but the fitness landscape in Fig. 10.15 contains two local maxima in addition to the global maximum. Without mutation, the population might simply climb an intermediate hill (a local maximum) and stay there. Mutation can be interpreted as exploring new and different solutions in other regions. The genetic algorithm thus contains an element of exploitation (cross-over), which gradually improves solutions, and an element of exploration (mutation), which tests new solutions. Obviously, there is a trade-off between these two elements. Mutation keeps the search process in motion, but inhibits gradual adaptation to the highest fitness levels. Therefore, mutation is necessary, but should not be excessive.

Variation in the genome and mutation are also important when the fitness landscape changes. Changes in the fitness landscape can occur due to changes in the environmental conditions of the population, for example due to other species or changes in climatic conditions. When this happens, traits that maximized fitness under the old conditions are no longer optimal, so the population must adapt to the new conditions. Re-adaptation is facilitated by genetic diversity and mutation. Changing fitness landscapes, and thus continuous adaptation and evolution, are the normal case in nature.

10.3.4 Virtual Creatures

As mentioned above, genetic algorithms can be used to solve practical problems and to learn more about evolution. There is an interesting literature on virtual creatures created with genetic algorithms based on the seminal work of Karl Sims (1994a, b), which has both practical value and illustrates how evolution works. Since 2013, there is even a Virtual Creatures Competition (Kriegman 2019).

Karl Sims is a digital media artist and visual effects software developer. Sims (1994a) describes the problem of software developers in the field of computer graphics and animation that there is a trade-off between the complexity of realistic virtual entities and the designer's control over the creation process. Interesting, complex creatures with physically plausible behavior are difficult to design. Therefore, Sims tested whether interesting creatures with physically plausible behavior could evolve from a genetic algorithm without direct designer control. The building blocks for the creatures are cubes of various shapes that can be connected by several types of realistic joints, and sensors that can detect stimuli from the environment. In addition to the body, the algorithm also developed a brain structure or control system that controls the behavior of the creatures. The bodies and the control system evolved together. The randomly designed first generation of genotypes of the creatures were placed in a realistically simulated 3D physical environment that had the properties of either water or land. The behavior that the creatures were to develop was locomotion, either as swimming in the water environment or as "walking" or jumping on land. Another behavior was to follow or avoid light relative to a simulated light source. The fitness function of the genetic algorithm rewarded speed for swimming and walking and height above the ground for jumping.

Figure 10.17 shows some of the creatures that evolved in the simulation (aquatic creatures in the left panel, land creatures in the right panel).[3] Many of the creatures have developed quite realistic motion patterns that resemble those of real animals, such as the turtle-like creature A, the water snake B, or creature C that moves like a manta ray. Land creature D moves like an inchworm. Creature E was originally a water creature that developed a sidewinding ability on land. The locomotion of creature F is quite unusual, but effective: it moves in a rowing style.

An important finding of this experiment is that a population of interbreeding creatures often converges to homogeneity. However, separate evolutionary runs can produce very different creatures with different locomotion strategies. Since the genetic algorithm can be seen as an optimization procedure, it is not surprising

[3] A video showing how the creature move can be found here: https://archive.org/details/sims_evolved_virtual_creatures_1994. Accessed 26 October 2023.

Fig. 10.17 Creatures evolved for swimming and walking. Source: Sims (1994a), reproduced with kind permission of ACM (Association for Computing Machinery)

that after enough runs only one type of creature remains. This type of creature has reached a local or even the global fitness level in the constant fitness landscape. To evolve multiple species and thus maintain diversity, niches may be required, such as different types of resources on which different species can specialize.

To find out whether it is possible to generate virtual creatures of higher complexity, Sims (1994b) describes a system with competition and coevolution among creatures. Competition between different creatures changes the fitness landscape, forcing the creatures to evolve in a sustained manner rather than adapting once to a static environment. The competition is designed so that two creatures try to gain control over a cube placed in the middle between them. The cube symbolizes a resource whose control determines a creature's fitness. In his simulations, he found a strong coevolutionary pattern in which no species has a permanent advantage over the other, and each species is constantly challenged to readapt to the new fitness landscape. The coevolving species alternate in their relative fitness: sometimes one species has a higher relative fitness, sometimes the other.

Virtual creatures and evolutionary computing can and have been used to design physical robots with desired characteristics. This is done in the field of evolutionary robotics, which aims to create general algorithms for robot generation (Doncieux et al. 2015).

In terms of complexity economics, the more relevant aspect of virtual creatures in virtual ecosystems is that they are tools for learning more about evolution. Importantly, as Pennock (2007) argues, what happens in virtual worlds with virtual creatures is not just *like* evolution, it *is* evolution. The processes in the virtual worlds are real evolutionary processes, not just simulations of real evolution, because the very mechanisms described by evolutionary theory are at work. Evolutionary theory does not require that inheritance, selection, and variation (i.e., recombination and mutation) of genetic information occur in organic material. Ultimately, evolution is a theory about information. Genes are units of information that organisms use to perform functions. Information can be represented, stored, and transmitted in many ways. There is no reason why representing information as strings of nucleobases is "more real" than representing it as ones and zeros in a computer code or any other method. The main difference between biological evolution and virtual evolution is how the information is processed, i.e. what kind of phenotype is generated, and how the fitness of a genotype is determined, i.e. what the mechanism behind the fitness function is. But these differences are not essential for evolution.

Lehman et al. (2020) present a collection of anecdotes about researchers in evolutionary computation and artificial life who have been surprised by the creativity of their evolutionary algorithms to find novel and unexpected solutions. These authors define *creativity* as the invention of something that is both original in the sense of novel and effective in the sense of functional. They write:

> *these stories of digital evolution "outsmarting" the researchers who study it provide more than an exercise in humility; they also provide insight and constructive knowledge for practitioners, because they show the pervasiveness of such obstacles and how, when necessary, they can be overcome. Furthermore, these cases demonstrate that robust digital models of evolution do not blindly reflect the desires and biases of their creators, but instead they have depth sufficient to yield unexpected results and new insights. Additionally, these cases may be of interest to researchers in evolutionary biology as well as animal and plant breeding, because of their compelling parallels to the creativity of biological evolution.* (Lehman et al. 2020, p. 276)

The collection of surprises can be divided into four categories: misspecified fitness functions, unintended debugging, exceeding the experimenter's expectations, and convergence with biology. Specifically for engineering purposes, algorithm designers choose fitness functions with the intention that the algorithm will find an optimal solution. This can often fail because evolution finds loopholes that satisfy the letter of the law, but not the spirit. An example of such a surprise is that some of Sims' (1994a) land creatures evolved the behavior of somersaulting or growing very tall and then simply falling down instead of walking. The fitness function Sims used to evolve walking rewarded speed, which could be very high because of the large potential energy expended in falling. Similarly, in an attempt to evolve jumping, the virtual creatures simply grew very tall without moving, because the fitness function rewarded maximum elevation of the creature's center of gravity.

An example of an unexpected but valid solution is an algorithm that was asked to find ways for a six-legged robot to walk with some of its legs broken (Cully et al. 2015). The researchers expected that the algorithm could not find a solution for the case where all six legs were broken, but the algorithm did. The solution found was for the robot to flip over and walk on its elbows.

Interesting results have been obtained in virtual ecosystems such as Tierra or Avida, which resemble biological evolution. For example, such artificial life systems can evolve parasitism and ongoing coevolutionary dynamics to counteract it, i.e. an evolutionary arms race. Virtual evolution can produce cases where the discovery of a niche opens opportunities for others through predation, symbiosis, or scavenging in addition to parasitism. It has also been found that the evolution of complex behavior can involve temporary setbacks, where mutations lead to a temporary decrease in average fitness. There is also the phenomenon of evolutionary computer programs becoming larger and larger, full of useless junk code. This may be an evolutionary strategy against the disruptive effects of mutation and recombination. If a genotype contains a lot of neutral code, there is less chance that mutations or cross-overs will damage critical code. Such a result can be interpreted as a separate evolutionary agenda from that of the programmer. The algorithm designer wants to find the fittest genotype, but the evolutionary program seeks protection against perturbations by recombination and mutation. Finally, it has been observed that evolutionary processes can hide genetic code that is costly to the individual because it promotes cooperative or altruistic behavior. One might expect that algorithms that maximize individual fitness would eliminate such genes, but this does not always happen. Instead, cooperative genes may overlap with crucial metabolic genes that are necessary for the organism to function. In this case, mutations cannot easily eliminate the cooperative behavior without destroying the critical metabolic functions.

The experience that researchers can be "outsmarted" by their own evolutionary algorithms is an important lesson for mechanism designers in economics. Mechanism design, for which Leonid Hurwicz, Eric Maskin, and Roger Myerson received the 2007 Nobel Memorial Prize, is also called reverse game theory. It aims to find economic mechanisms or incentives that induce rational agents in strategic settings to behave in ways that achieve the designer's goals. This idea can be applied to the design of markets, regulatory regimes, or corporate management strategies. If the environment for which a mechanism is designed is an evolutionary one, we should expect that the designers of the mechanism will also be outwitted by the incentivized agents. It is then the rule rather than the exception that apparently well-designed rules and incentives fail to produce the desired behavior in the long run.

10.3.5 Cultural Evolution

If evolutionary theory is not tied to biology, but rather describes processes involving heredity, variation, and natural selection, then it can be applied to human culture. Biologist Peter Richerson and anthropologist Robert Boyd (2005) argue that we need both genetic and cultural evolution to understand human behavior. They define culture as "information capable of affecting individuals' behavior that they acquire from other members of their species through teaching, imitation, and other forms of social transmission" (Richerson and Boyd 2005, p. 5). Cultural information can be described as ideas, knowledge, beliefs, values, skills, and attitudes. It is mostly stored in the human brain, though not necessarily consciously, but also in artifacts such as books. The transfer of this information occurs from brain to brain through learning. Richerson and Boyd emphasize that biological and cultural evolution interact. How we learn and what we learn have physiological and psychological elements that are part of human biology and thus subject to genetic evolution. But cultural evolution also has some autonomy from biological evolution.

An example of how cultural evolution overrides biological evolution is the human willingness to eat bitter-tasting plants. Normally, bitter taste is a signal that a plant is inedible or even poisonous. However, humans have discovered that some bitter plant components have medicinal value. Through cultural evolution, the belief in the medicinal value of some plants spread through human populations, causing humans to overcome their biological aversion to bitter taste. While some separations of cultural evolution from biological evolution are beneficial, others may be more detrimental from a biological perspective. For example, it is a common observation that as countries become richer, birth rates decline. At the individual level, some careers that require high levels of education and considerable time resources may be difficult to reconcile with having (more) children. Thus, individuals who are culturally very successful in a society may have fewer offspring than others who are less successful by cultural standards.

Cultural evolution is important because it is much faster than genetic evolution. *Homo sapiens* emerged about 300,000 years ago and developed the behavioral and cognitive traits that distinguish *Homo sapiens* from other human and primate species 160,000–70,000 years ago. Since then, human evolution has accelerated dramatically, leading to our current civilization, while our closest animal relatives still live as our common ancestors did millions of years ago. Human evolution is exceptional because of its cultural components.

Richerson and Boyd (2005) propose a model of cultural evolution that can be summarized as shown in Fig. 10.18. They call the diverse elements of cultural information (values, beliefs...) that are transmitted through social learning *cultural variants*. Cultural variants are loosely analogous to genes, but should not be interpreted as gene-like particles. The model assumes that parents transmit their own cultural variant more or less unbiased to their children through explicit and implicit teaching. This process is similar to the inheritance of genes. However, as children grow older, they also learn from other adults by observing and imitating their behavior or by explicit teaching. This type of transmission is biased if people are more likely to adopt some cultural variants than others, which can be seen as a form of cultural selection. Some cultural variants may be more likely to be adopted than others because they are easier to learn, seem more attractive, or because the people being imitated are frequent, socially successful, or prestigious.

Richerson and Boyd argue that natural selection applies to culturally transmitted variation in the same way that it applies to genetic variation. The necessary conditions for natural selection are that genetic or cultural variants affect people's behavior and that they compete. Cultural variants compete for the cognitive and time resources of learners and for the control of behavior. People may know different cultural variants, but learning cultural variants by imitation occurs only if knowledge of cultural variants translates into observable behavior. For example, parents may be

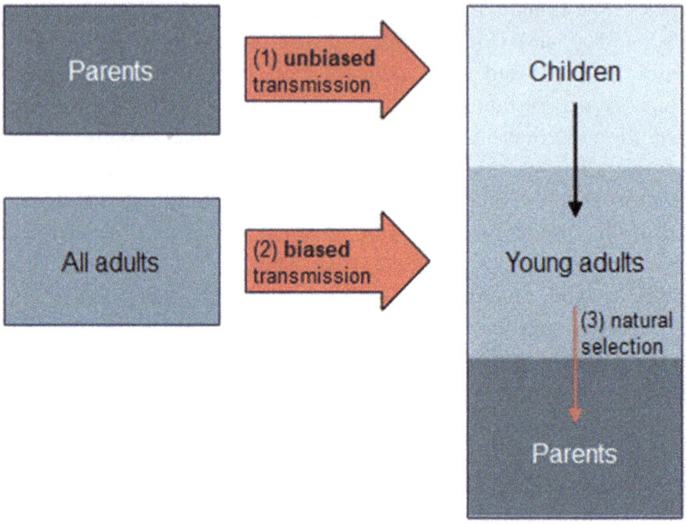

Fig. 10.18 A model of cultural evolution. Source: Author's own figure after Richerson and Boyd (2005)

able to speak several languages, but their children will only learn the language or languages actually spoken at home. Natural selection on cultural variants occurs because of the differential success and hence reproduction of variants in their respective social and institutional environments. As a result of natural selection, the relative proportions of different cultural variants in a population change.

An example based on the research of sociologist Sonya Salamon illustrates how this model of cultural evolution works. Salamon (1984, 1985) studied farmers in Illinois and found that ethnic background influenced both attitudes toward family and the purpose of farming and practices related to land transfer. Richerson and Boyd simplify Salamon's research in an illustrative model that assumes there are only two ethnic backgrounds of farmers in a community: farmers of German origin and Yankee farmers from other parts of the United States. They live close together and have access to the same soil, but they exhibit different cultural variants. German farmers have "yeoman" values, meaning they value family life, see farming as a way of life, and want to pass their land and farm on to one of their sons or daughters in the hope that they will continue farming. As a result, they rarely sell or buy land and almost never rent. Yankee farmers, on the other hand, have "entrepreneurial" values, i.e. they view their farms as businesses. They buy or rent land according to economic conditions and specialize in the most profitable use of the land. They do not actively encourage their children to enter farming and place a high value on education.

According to the model, German farmers pass on yeoman values to their children and Yankee farmers transmit entrepreneurial values. Biased cultural transmission occurs when entrepreneurial values are more attractive to young adults, including those from German families. This may be the case because the entrepreneurial style of farming produces higher incomes and requires less labor. However, yeoman farmers are more likely to stay in the community and continue farming, while entrepreneurial people are more likely to give up farming and move away. Yeoman values also lead to higher birth rates than entrepreneurial values. These are natural selection mechanisms. As a result of this natural selection, the yeoman cultural variant may persist or even grow in the community despite the biased transmission in favor of the entrepreneurial cultural variant. This model prediction is consistent with evidence presented by Salamon (1984) that Germans owned about 20% of the land in some communities in 1890, but about 60% in 1978.

Guiso et al. (2006) report similar results. They use the World Values Survey to compare levels of generalized trust among U.S. citizens whose ancestors immigrated to the United States from different countries. Ancestral country is interpreted as a proxy for culture, and trust is a *prior belief*. The reference group is people with ancestors from Great Britain. Guiso et al. find that Americans with Scandinavian ancestry report significantly higher levels of trust (20.7% higher) than British Americans. People with ancestry from Germany, Switzerland, Austria, or the Netherlands report slightly lower trust (−6.5%). Immigrants from Italy, Spain, Portugal, and Greece report significantly lower levels of trust (−25%), but still higher than those from Africa (−38.5%) or India (−40.8%). The level of trust among these U.S. immigrants is similar to the average level of trust in the countries of origin today, even though it is not the respondents themselves but their ancestors who came from those countries. The correlation between the respondents' trust and the average trust in the countries of origin is 0.6. Guiso et al. (2006, p. 32) interpret this result as "consistent with the idea that priors have a cultural component, which is transported to the New World and continues to affect individual beliefs even in the new environment and several generations later." They show that trust is positively related to the likelihood of becoming an entrepreneur and provide other evidence that culture affects economic outcomes.

Because cultural evolution is much faster than genetic evolution, computer scientists have developed *cultural algorithms* that implement the principles of cultural evolution (Reynolds 2018; Maheri et al. 2021). Cultural algorithms combine the micro-evolutionary perspective of the transmission of traits between individuals through genetic evolution with the macro-evolutionary perspective of the formation and transmission of generalized beliefs (or cultural variants) based on individual experiences through cultural evolution. Consistent with the concept of downward causation, generalized beliefs can constrain individual behavior. Cultural algorithms have two spaces in which learning, optimization, and transmission of information can occur: the population space and the belief space (see Fig. 10.19). Therefore, they adopt a dual inheritance perspective based on *dual inheritance theory*, which combines genetic and cultural evolution. As postulated by Richerson and Boyd (2005), genetic evolution and cultural evolution interact. Genetic variation can lead to cultural variation, which can influence genetic selection, and vice versa.

The difference between a genetic algorithm and a cultural algorithm is that the cultural algorithm takes into account the knowledge that individuals in the

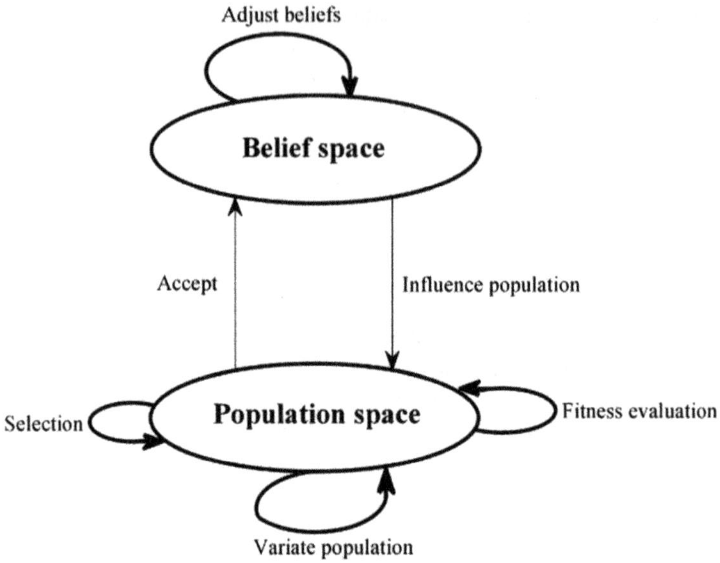

Fig. 10.19 Schematic representation of a cultural algorithm. Source: Maheri et al. (2021), reproduced with kind permission of Elsevier B.V

population acquire. This knowledge has problem-specific components that can be categorized as situational knowledge, normative knowledge, domain knowledge, topographical knowledge, and history (or temporal) knowledge. Knowledge is stored in a network in the belief space. Not all knowledge of all individuals is stored, but only the knowledge of selected individuals, determined by the acceptance function based on some criterion. The update function adjusts the existing knowledge network by the knowledge of the selected agents. The influence function assigns knowledge sources from the belief space to all individuals. This happens randomly. Agents acquire knowledge directly and through the knowledge of their neighbors. Then, each agent can decide which knowledge source (the directly acquired knowledge source or a function of the neighbors' knowledge) will influence its behavior. There can be different mechanisms to distribute knowledge, such as random selection, weighted majority voting, or auctioning. The transfer of knowledge between the population space and the belief space via the acceptance function, the update function, and the influence function is called the communication protocol. In the population space, the fitness of each agent is determined by a fitness function and a new generation is generated. As in other evolutionary or genetic algorithms, individual solutions (or traits) are genetically encoded in the population space.

Cultural algorithms are powerful problem-solvers because they separate the knowledge accumulated by a population from the individuals in the population. This principle is called *population thinking*, which views evolution as occurring in a population but not at the level of the individual. Learning can occur in parallel in the population space and the belief space. The belief space is a collective repository of information that can vary from generation to generation and contains good solutions found by some individuals. Since the knowledge stored in the cultural repository is larger than the knowledge of individuals and extends beyond their lifetimes, the cultural system as a whole can deal with problems at scales much larger than those that individuals can tackle.

Maheri et al. (2021) survey a large literature that has applied cultural algorithms to solve practical problems. Cultural algorithms have been used extensively in civil engineering, mechanical engineering, chemical engineering, electrical engineering, and computer science. Some other applications are reported from anthropology, economics, archeology, biology, and physics.

10.4 Coevolution of Behaviors and Social Institutions

As we have seen, we cannot understand human evolution only in biological terms, but must also consider cultural evolution. Culture includes knowledge, values, and attitudes, as well as practices and institutions. Chapter 9 showed how Robert Axelrod used a genetic algorithm to model the emergence of cooperation norms as an example of an institution. However, Axelrod's model is not really a model of cultural evolution as discussed in the previous section. Axelrod wanted to explain how the norm of not defecting in a prisoner's dilemma (an informal institution) can emerge within a group as a result of punishment. In contrast to models based on the dual inheritance of (genetic) personal traits and cultural knowledge and practices, Axelrod's model considers only the individual traits of boldness and vengefulness that affect individual behavior. The only cultural aspect, the practice of punishing defectors or non-punishers, is built into the game but does not evolve. Only the genetic evolution of the relevant personal traits determines the results of the model.

Bowles et al. (2003) propose an agent-based model in which behaviors and institutions coevolve. Altruistic and non-altruistic behaviors evolve genetically, and the social institutions of within-group resource sharing and group segmentation are transmitted culturally. The purpose of the model is to explain why altruistic behavior can persist in a population even though it is costly to the individual and thus reduces individual fitness. The explanation is that altruism benefits the group, which can be an evolutionary advantage when there is competition between groups. Bowles et al. suggest that their model can be applied to the first 50,000 or 100,000 years of modern human existence, before the invention of agriculture and human sedentariness.

As in Axelrod's model, the prisoner's dilemma is used in order to describe altruistic and non-altruistic behavior. Table 10.1 contains the payoffs resulting from the interaction between altruists A and non-altruists N. Altruist behave in a such way that there is a benefit b to other individuals, with whom they interact. For the altruist, this behavior creates a cost c. It is assumed that $b > c$ holds, such that the joint payoff of two altruists is higher than the sum of the payoffs of a pair consisting of an altruist and a non-altruist or two non-altruists, i.e. $2(b - c) > b - c > 0$. When

Table 10.1 The altruism game

	Altruists	Non-altruists
Altruists	b–c b–c	b −c
Non-altruists	−c b	0 0

non-altruists interact with altruists, they receive higher payoffs and hence higher fitness. Therefore, selection within a group works against altruists. Bowles et al. assume that the share of altruists p in a group j evolves according to a replicator dynamic equation in the absence of group institutions:

$$\Delta p_j = p_j(1 - p_j)(\pi^A - \pi^N) = p_j(1 - p_j)(-c),$$

where π^A is the altruists' payoff and π^N the payoff of non-altruists. Since$(\pi^A - \pi^N) = -c < 0$ holds, the share of altruists will converge to zero over time.

Two institutions can work against the negative selection against the altruists. The first institution is within-group resource sharing. Kaplan et al. (1985) and others have documented that food sharing is practiced by the Aché, an indigenous hunter-gatherer people in Paraguay. Male Aché hunters are not allowed to eat from their own prey. Wild game is distributed equally among all families of the group. The Aché also share other foods such as palm starch, honey, fruit, and insect larvae, but less equally than meat. Prehistoric hunter-gatherers may have had similar practices. In the model, the resource sharing institution can be represented by a linear tax $t \in [0, 1)$, which is collected from the group members' payoffs, with the proceeds being distributed equally to all members of the group. The effect of such a redistribution scheme is to reduce the difference between A and N payoffs:

$$\pi^A - \pi^N = -(1 - t_j)c.$$

The second institution is a convention that leads to the segmentation of the group. Without the segmenting institutions, all members of a group interact randomly, such that the probability of meeting an A or an N depends on the respective proportions of those types in the group. The segmenting institution makes it more likely that altruists will interact with other altruists, perhaps because they try to avoid non-altruists, or because altruists live close together and thus meet more often. Instead of being equal to the share of altruists in group j, p_j, the probability of an altruist interacting with another altruist is given by

$$s_j + (1 - s_j)p_j \geq p_j.$$

Hence, $0 \leq s_j \leq 1$ can be defined as the degree of segmentation in group j. If $s_j = 1$, the group is perfectly segmented, because an altruist would never interact with a non-altruist within the same group. The effect of segmentation on the expected payoff difference is

$$\pi^A - \pi^N = s_j b - c.$$

The combined effect of the two institutions on the replication of altruists in the group is given by

$$\Delta p_j = p_j(1 - p_j)(1 - t_j)(s_j b - c).$$

Depending on the degree of segmentation, the change in the share of altruists Δp_j can be positive, negative, or zero. Redistribution alone cannot undo the advantage of non-altruists, unless there is perfect redistribution with $t = 1$.

The agent-based model developed by Bowles et al. (2003) introduces intergroup conflict and endogenizes the evolution of group institutions, thus extending the mathematical model above. The total population consists of $n = 400$ individuals divided into 20 groups with an average group size of 20 individuals. The group size is approximately constant and varies only by random migration between the groups with a migration rate of 0.2 per generation. Furthermore, conflicts between groups, which occur with a probability of $k = 0.25$ per generation, also change the group size. With a mutation probability of $e = 0.0005$, an offspring in the next generation is of the opposite type of its single parent, i.e. an A switches to N or vice versa. Initially, all individuals are of type N.

Each individual receives a baseline payoff of 10 units of the resource that is independent of pair interactions. The benefit of altruistic behavior is $b = 2$ and the cost is $c = 1$. Each individual produces offspring in the next generation proportional to its share of the group's total material payoff. Thus, in a group of only 20 N individuals, each N individual will produce one N offspring individual, such that the group will permanently reproduce itself in the absence of mutation and conflict. Without institutions, the expected payoff difference between non-altruists and altruists is approximately equal to $\pi^N - \pi^A = c = 1$, such that non-altruists receive about 10% more payoff and thus produce 10% more offspring than altruists.

If there is a conflict between two groups, the group with the higher total payoff net of institutional costs wins, and all members of the losing group die. The winning group occupies the site of the losing group and replicates itself. Importantly, the new occupants of the site adopt the institutions of the group from which they descended. The institutions s and t of each group vary stochastically in each period. The chance of mutation for each institution is equal to 0.1. When the value of the institution changes, it either increases or decreases by 0.1 with equal probability.

Figure 10.20 summarizes the sequence of events in each simulation period:

1. Each member of a group is randomly paired with another member with a matching probability given by the distribution of types p_j and the degree of segmentation s_j. The pairs play the altruism game and receive the payoffs according to the types and the resource sharing tax t_j.
2. Each member produces offspring of its own type with a probability given by its share of the total group payoff.

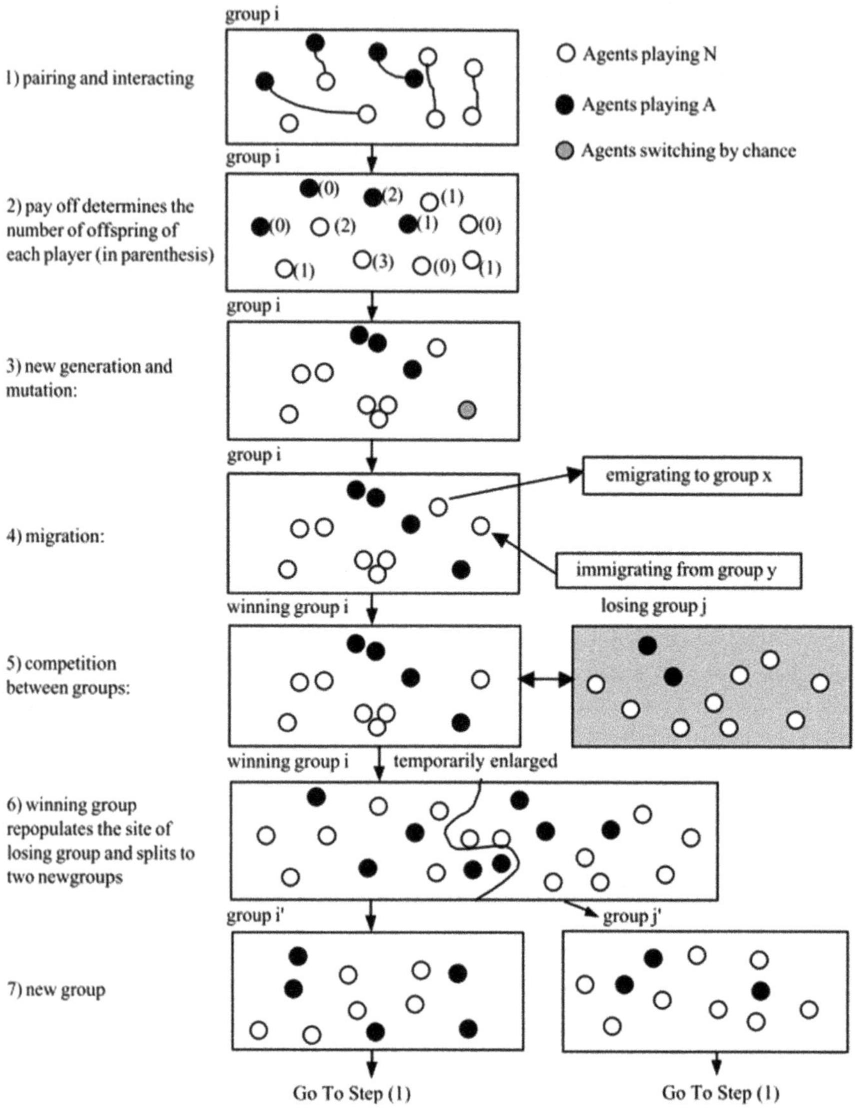

Fig. 10.20 Schematic representation of individual- and group-selection in the ABM. Source: Bowles et al. (2003), reproduced with kind permission of Elsevier B.V

3. After the replication is complete, old members die and a type-switching mutation occurs among the new members with probability e.
4. With probability m, each member of a group migrates to a group randomly selected from the other groups.
5. Each group is selected with probability k to engage in conflict with another group. Conflicting groups are randomly paired. In a pair, the group with the highest total

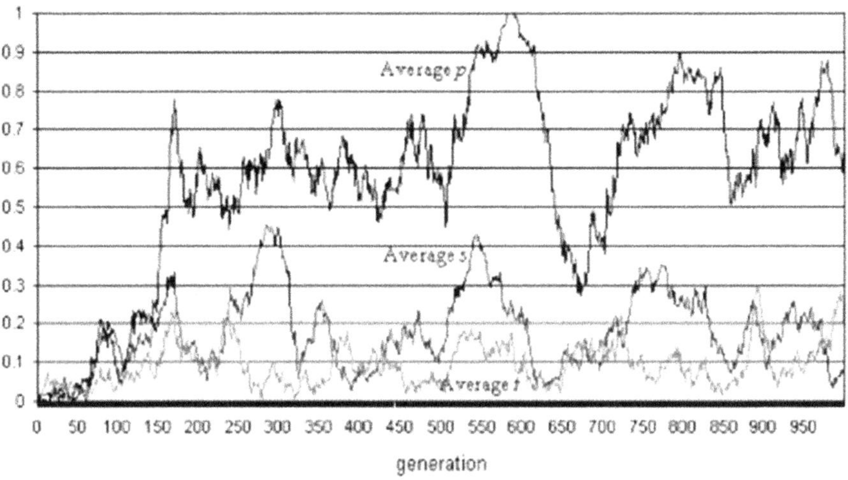

Fig. 10.21 Dynamic interaction between individual traits and group institutions. Source: Bowles et al. (2003), reproduced with kind permission of Elsevier B.V

payoff (net of the costs of sharing and segmentation) wins. The cost of maintaining the institutions is assumed to be $0.5(s^2 + t^2)$.

6. Replicas of the members of the winning group replace the members of the losing group. The temporarily enlarged winning group randomly splits into two new groups, both of which adopt the institutions of the winning group.

Figure 10.21 shows a 1000 period history of a single run starting with no altruists, $p(0) = 0$, and no institutions, $s(0) = 0$, $t(0) = 0$. Between periods 50 and 100, there a significant random increase in average segmentation, which immediately leads to an increase in the average fraction of altruists. Further increases in s and t cause a significant increase in p starting in period 150. As expected, the institutions increase the fitness of altruists relative to non-altruists within groups and increase their overall proportion in the population. When the share of altruists is high, i.e., $p > 0.5$, institutions become less valuable, because the chances of interacting with non-altruists decrease. Since institutions are costly, they can become a burden in intergroup conflict. When p is high, groups with high levels of s and/or t are more likely to lose against groups with weaker institutions, causing the average levels of the institutional variables to fall. This effect is clearly visible in Fig. 10.21 around period 550 and after period 750. Weaker institutions, in turn, disfavor the replication of altruists. Thus, there is a clear coevolution of type-dependent behavior and social institutions.

Bowles et al. provide simulation evidence that the proportion of altruists in the total population depends negatively on group size and migration rate, but positively on the frequency of intergroup conflict (see Fig. 10.22). In all cases, each of the two institutions alone increases the proportion of altruists, and both institutions together strongly favor altruists. Without institutions, large shares of altruists are only

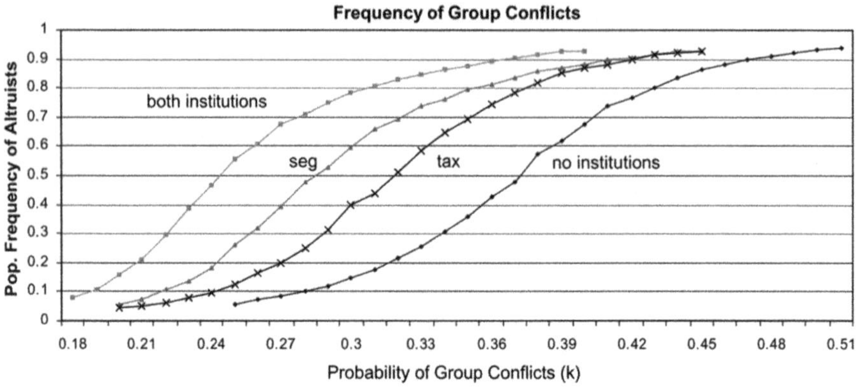

Fig. 10.22 Dynamic interaction between individual traits and group institutions. Source: Bowles et al. (2003), reproduced with kind permission of Elsevier B.V

possible with strong group-selection pressure from a high frequency of intergroup conflict. Group-level selection (as opposed to individual-level selection) supports the coevolution of group-beneficial individual behavior (altruism) and supporting institutions, despite the costs that institutions impose on the group.

10.5 The Economy as an Evolutionary System

As early as 1898, Thorstein Veblen asked: "Why is economics not an evolutionary science?". Referring to the modern sciences of anthropology, ethnology, psychology, and biology, he claimed that "economics is helplessly behind the times, and unable to handle its subject-matter in a way to entitle it to standing as a modern science" (Veblen 1898, p. 373). Veblen regarded an evolutionary science as a "close-knit body of theory" about a process or an unfolding sequence. Such a theory must take into account that an evolutionary process of development is based on cumulative causation, i.e., that new steps of development follow from past achievements. He criticized the economists of his time for not having such a theory and for holding a spiritual belief in natural laws to which economic agents are subject. He also challenged the field for focusing on capital accumulation as an engine of development while neglecting human agents as the real drivers. The economic mainstream believed in the "hedonistic man" (his word for the utility-maximizing homo economicus), whom he did not see as the "prime mover." For Veblen, the notion of man as an isolated and unaltered entity responding mechanistically to external stimuli is fundamentally flawed. He gives an almost lyrical description of this conception:

> *In all the received formulations of economic theory, whether at the hands of English economists or those of the Continent, the human material with which the inquiry is concerned is conceived in hedonistic terms; that is to say, in terms of a passive and*

> *substantially inert and immutably given human nature.... The hedonistic conception of man is that of a lightning calculator of pleasures and pains, who oscillates like a homogeneous globule of desire of happiness under the impulse of stimuli that shift him about the area, but leave him intact. He has neither antecedent nor consequent. He is an isolated, definitive human datum, in stable equilibrium except for the buffets of the impinging forces that displace him in one direction or another. Self-poised in elemental space, he spins symmetrically about his own spiritual axis until the parallelogram of forces bears down upon him, whereupon he follows the line of the resultant.* (Veblen 1898, pp. 389/390)

As an alternative, Veblen suggests viewing the economic agent as

> *product... of his hereditary traits and his past experience, cumulatively wrought out under a given body of traditions, conventionalities, and material circumstances; and they afford the point of departure for the next step in the process. The economic life history of the individual is a cumulative process of adaptation of means to ends that cumulatively change as the process goes on, both the agent and his environment being at any point the outcome of the past process.* (Veblen 1898, pp. 390/391).

Veblen goes on to claim that "all economic change is a change in the economic community," which is an early expression of evolutionary *population thinking*, i.e. Darwin's idea that species do not consist of unchanging types, but are populations of organisms with a variable pool of inherited information. This cumulative change in populations affects how people think about the world and how they behave. For Veblen, evolutionary economics must be a theory of cultural growth driven by economic interest, through which economic institutions emerge. It should be obvious that Veblen's characterization of evolutionary economics is very similar to the theory of cultural evolution and dual inheritance theory described above. Thus, Veblen can be seen as a father of evolutionary economics, but his thinking was not taken up by his contemporaries, who embarked on the neoclassical path instead.

Another pioneer of evolutionary economics was Joseph Schumpeter, who became famous for his book *The Theory of Economic Development,* published in German in 1911 at the age of 28 (Schumpeter 1911). Schumpeter rejected the neoclassical focus on market equilibria and conceived of capitalist economies in a permanent state of disequilibrium. He understood "development" as evolution. Capitalist economies are dynamic and evolve all the time. *Entrepreneurs* are key drivers of this evolution, because they innovate by creating new combinations of existing ideas. But entrepreneurs are not just inventors who come up with a new product or a new technology. Inventing something new is not enough from an economic perspective. To be economically successful, the entrepreneur must also market the new product, which requires economic *innovation*, i.e. changing existing economic structures. The innovator must be able to attract resources, set up production and in many cases establish a new market that did not exist before. In his later book *Capitalism, Socialism and Democracy* (Schumpeter 1943, 2003, pp. 82/83), he describes capitalism as an "evolutionary process":

> *Capitalism, then, is by nature a form or method of economic change and not only never is but never can be stationary. And this evolutionary character of the capitalist process is not*

> *merely due to the fact that economic life goes on in a social and natural environment which changes and by its change alters the data of economic action; this fact is important and these changes (wars, revolutions and so on) often condition industrial change, but they are not its prime movers. Nor is this evolutionary character due to a quasi automatic increase in population and capital or to the vagaries of monetary systems of which exactly the same thing holds true. The fundamental impulse that sets and keeps the capitalist engine in motion comes from the new consumers' goods, the new methods of production or transportation, the new markets, the new forms of industrial organization that capitalist enterprise creates.*

His famous term for the disruptive nature of this organic process through innovation is *creative destruction*:

> *The opening up of new markets, foreign or domestic, and the organizational development from the craft shop and factory to such concerns as U.S. Steel illustrate the same process of industrial mutation—if I may use that biological term—that incessantly revolutionizes the economic structure from within, incessantly destroying the old one, incessantly creating a new one. This process of Creative Destruction is the essential fact about capitalism. It is what capitalism consists in and what every capitalist concern has got to live in.* (Schumpeter 2003, p. 83)

He refers to this process of creative destruction as a "perennial gale" as opposed to a "perennial lull," which is the perspective of neoclassical mainstream economics.

Although Veblen and Schumpeter were outstanding visionary economists, evolutionary thinking remained marginalized throughout most of the twentieth century. The seminal book[4] "*An Evolutionary Theory of Economic Change*" published by Richard Nelson and Sidney Winter in 1982, marks the true birth of modern evolutionary economics. Nelson and Winter's explicit aim was to propose an alternative theoretical framework to neoclassical economics (which they call orthodox economic theory) that does not rely on equilibrium analysis and maximizing agents. They propose an evolutionary theory that is not a 1:1 transfer of concepts from biology to economics, but the appropriate development of an economic evolutionary theory. They reject maximizing behavior as an explanation for the decision rules of firms, because firms often do not have a single-valued global objective function, no well-defined choice set, and generally do not make maximizing choices. Instead, they argue that firms' regular and predictable patterns are *routines*. Firms have established procedures for performing necessary operations such as producing things, ordering materials, hiring and firing employees, advertising, or obtaining financing. These routines are analogues to genes in biological evolutionary theory. They are inherited over time and change due to unpredictable events such as the "results of tumultuous meetings or confrontation with complex problems under crisis conditions" (Nelson and Winter 1982, p. 15). Deliberate search activities also alter routines, but with random success. Importantly, routines are subject to economic selection, because some routines work better than others under prevailing market and industry conditions. Firms with better routines make profits and grow, while

[4]It had more than 50,000 citations in Google Scholar as of January 2023.

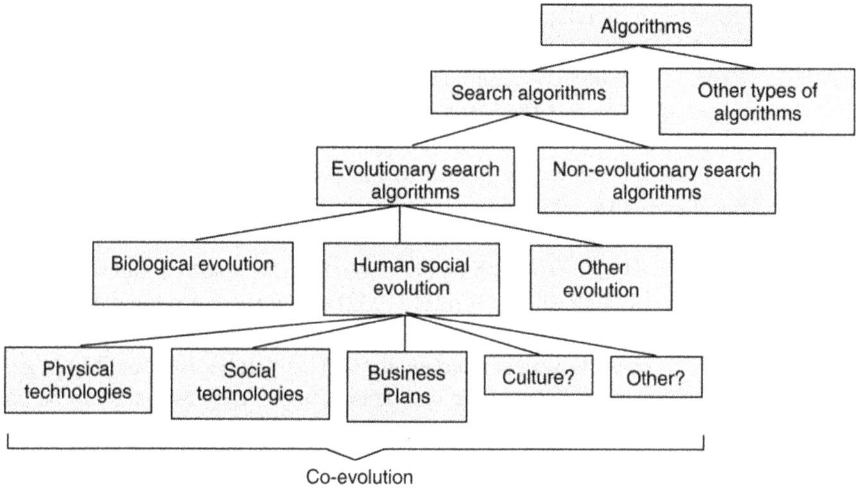

Fig. 10.23 Evolution as an algorithm. Source: Beinhocker (2011), reproduced with kind permission of Cambridge University Press

those with inferior routines shrink and eventually disappear from the market. This kind of selection is often called *retention* in evolutionary economics. Nelson and Winter propose to model economic evolution as stochastic Markov processes, in which the conditions of a firm or an industry in each time period are given by the conditions in the previous period from which they evolve according to some probability distribution. While Nelson and Winter applied their theory to some models on industry dynamics, economic growth, innovation, and technological progress, their main goal was to develop an evolutionary theoretical framework capable of dealing with the deficiencies of neoclassical economics. It inspired a large body of subsequent research that has developed models on the evolution of economic behavior, goods, technologies, and institutions (see Hodgson 2019, Hodgson and Lamberg 2018).

10.5.1 Evolution as Computation

Beinhocker (2006, 2011) offers a perspective on evolution that is consistent with the complexity approach, because he links evolution to information theory, computation, and self-organization. This perspective sees evolution as a form of computation or as a specific form of algorithm (see Fig. 10.23).

Note the difference between the computational view of evolution and the way how we introduced the genetic algorithm above. In Sect. 10.2.3, we introduced genetic algorithms as an emulation of biological evolution. In the computational view of evolution, both biological evolution and human social evolution are specific classes of algorithms, such that algorithm is the more general concept. In Chap. 4, we defined an algorithm as a finite sequence of instructions in a fixed order for solving a problem. Similarly, Beinhocker (2011, p. 399) defines an algorithm as "a process that takes some set of inputs, manipulates those inputs in a sequence of steps according to a set of rules, and then produces a set of outputs." A *substrate-neutral* algorithm can run in a variety of environments and operate on a variety of input types, i.e. it is not defined by or bound to the particular substrate on which it operates. This means that an evolutionary algorithm can run on the substrate of DNA, but also on a computer.

As shown in Fig. 10.23, evolution can be thought of as a search algorithm in a combinatorial space of possibilities. Wright (1932) estimated that a typical genome may have 1000 genetic loci, and that 10 different types of alleles are possible at each locus, giving 10^{1000} possible genetic combinations. This number is incredibly large; the estimated number of particles in the visible universe is only estimated to be on the order of 10^{80}. Biological evolution searches this large possibility space for maxima in the dynamic fitness landscape.

Beinhocker calls the combinatorial space of possibilities the *design space*. A design has a purpose and solves a problem. In biology, fit designs enable organisms to survive and reproduce. Human designs meet some human needs. Some designs are more fit for purpose or solve problems better than other designs. Evolutionary algorithms search for fit designs according to fitness functions that are generated by the respective environments. Fit designs proliferate, while unfit designs disappear. Importantly, designs of things must be distinguished from the thing itself. A design consists of information that can be encoded in a *schema*. Examples of schemas are the strings of nucleobases, equations, blueprints, diagrams, and manuals that can be stored in DNA, human brains, computers, or books. The physical rendering of a design is called an *interactor*, because it is the physical rendering of the design that interacts with the environment and is evaluated by the fitness function. Interactors consist of energy and matter. The rendering is done by someone or something that reads the schema and builds the interactor and is called the *reader/builder*. The reader/builder could be a female womb in which an organism grows, or a carpenter who builds a chair from a blueprint. The reader/builder can have knowledge, so the schema only needs to be sufficient, but not complete. Consider the recipe for pancakes in Chap. 4, which requires the cook to know when the oil in the pan is hot enough to begin frying. Since the rendering occurs in the physical word, only those designs that do not violate the laws of physics and that are feasible with existing technology and the knowledge of the reader/builder can actually be built. The number of feasible designs is hence smaller than the number of all designs, and the number of designs actually built is again much smaller.

Evolutionary algorithms work well, if the fitness function is *rough-correlated*, meaning that small variations of high-fitness designs tend to have high fitness, while small variations of low-fitness designs are likely to have low fitness. We have already seen that genetic algorithms tend to keep the number of large variations due to stochastic effects (mutations) low.

The evolution as computation view is related to complexity theory, because evolutionary algorithms create order from disorder and complexity from simplicity.

Often, designs are modular, i.e. simple designs are modules of more complex ones. This means that the number of possible designs depends not only on the number of basic designs, but also on the number of modules that can also be combined into even larger modules. The existence of modules implies order. In Chap. 8, you learned that mature ecosystems tend to have low entropy, high exergy, high diversity, and large organisms. We also saw that the exergy density of organism has increased tremendously throughout Earth's history. Evolution tends to fill environmental niches, which means that more and more regions of the design space are opened up by the recombination of modules into new systems. Since niches require specialization, more and more new functions are needed, leading to increasing overall complexity. Evolution uses free energy in order to reduce the entropy of a system. Free energy is used to find fit designs and to recombine them into new modules, which in turn are recombined. From an information-theoretic perspective, the recombination of existing information creates new information, which reduces information entropy (see Chap. 3). In Chap. 8, we discussed that Shannon (information) entropy and thermodynamic (physical) entropy are essentially the same concept and that there is a direct relationship between energy and information. Hence, we can also say that evolutionary algorithms reduce physical entropy by ordering matter and energy, whenever a reader/builder renders a design. This discussion shows that evolution is closely related to self-organization and Prigogine's concept of dissipative structures. Beinhocker (2011, pp. 415/416) notes:

> *[F]rom the point of view of information theory and computation, it is almost impossible to talk about evolution without referring to self-organization, and vice versa. Evolution needs self-organization to bootstrap the process of evolutionary search and order creation, while self-organization leads to conditions where the logic of differentiation, selection and retention can take hold.*

10.5.2 Economic Evolution

As suggested in Fig. 10.23, human social evolution in general and economic evolution in particular are special cases of computational evolution, on a par with biological evolution. From the evolution-as-computation view, the economy is an evolutionary system, and there is no need to transfer concepts from biology to economics by analogy. Beinhocker (2006, 2011) shows how the computational perspective can be applied to the economy. He proposes that the evolutionary algorithm searches three economically relevant design spaces: physical technologies, social technologies, and business plans. Firms are viewed as interactors, and entrepreneurs and employees as readers/builders. Technologies and business plans are seen as schemata that can be expressed as bit strings and are therefore amenable to computation.

Physical technologies (PTs) are defined as "methods and designs for transforming matter, energy and information from one state into another in pursuit of a goal or goals" (Beinhocker 2011, p. 407). Researchers, engineers, and technicians read PT schemata such as technical manuals, blueprints, chemical formulas, etc., and build physical artifacts such as machines or buildings. Those artifacts are interactors in the physical environment, more or less fit for their respective purposes. *Social technologies* (STs) are "methods and designs for organizing people in pursuit of a goal or goals" (Beinhocker 2011, p. 408). All kinds of strategies and social rules are social technologies. STs are not only institutions in the sense of "rules of the game," but also strategies of how to play the game.

Beinhocker uses the example of soccer to illustrate the difference between an institution and social technologies. The rules of soccer are the institution, but the STs of a soccer team could also include the cultural norms of the team, the job description of the goalkeeper, and the tactics of the game. Schemas encoding STs could be soccer tactics manuals, strategy charts, or the experience of the team captain. The soccer coach or team captain as reader/builder renders these designs to the soccer team as interactor. Physical and social technologies coevolve, as exemplified by the Industrial Revolution. The steam engine as a physical technology led to the organizational form of the factory, which is a social technology. On the other hand, the joint-stock company as a social technology made it possible to develop and build physical technologies. Some PT and ST inventions had meta-effects on the evolutionary process itself, because they improved the speed and effectiveness of the evolutionary search process. Examples of such meta-inventions are the printing press, the telephone, and the computer as PTs, and organized markets, money, and double-entry bookkeeping as STs.

Physical and social technologies play a role in all types of social systems. In the economic system, businesses combine PTs, STs, and business plans in order to pursue economic goals. "A business is a person, or an organized group of people, who transform(s) matter, energy and information from one state into another with the goal of making a profit" (Beinhocker 2011, p. 409). Note that according to this definition, a business is not identical to a firm, which might consist of several businesses. A business plan is a schema that encodes the design of a business.

Economic evolution is a coevolutionary search process in the three design spaces of PTs, STs, and business plans. The renderings of PTs and STs are combined into business plans, which are rendered into businesses. The activities of businesses in turn change the respective fitness functions, necessitating a new search for new PTs, STs, and business plan designs.

An important difference between biological evolution and economic evolution consists in the role of the reader/builder's intentionality. The creation of novelty in biological systems is driven by random variation through genetic recombination and mutation. The mechanisms of biological evolutionary search do not involve intentionality, but the economic search for better physical and social technologies and better business plans does. Inventors, engineers, managers, and other human designers do not simply experiment randomly to find better solutions to their goals, but use all kinds of existing knowledge from which they derive hypotheses where and what to search. In other words, they perform informed search. But given the vastness of possible design combinations, the complexity of the interactors and the environments, and the imperfect knowledge of the fitness function, purely rational deduction is impossible. Beinhocker calls the process of combining deductive insights with tinkering experimentation as *deductive tinkering*. Human designers often try to improve on existing solutions that are already working well. They make informed guesses about how to proceed, learn from the feedback, and try to understand why some solutions work well and others do not. Nevertheless, serendipitous discoveries are inevitable. Importantly, intentional and informed search behavior does not mean that the whole search process is not evolutionary. Evolution as computation requires that there be variation in designs, not that the origin of that variation be completely random. The key point is that it is impossible for any human designer to find the optimal solution by deduction and that it is selection through competitive pressure that separates better from worse solutions.

The idealized process of economic evolution works like this. An entrepreneur, perhaps an inventor, has discovered a new physical technology, such as the first working automobile with an internal combustion engine. To make it available to many other people, he must find social technologies to organize the large-scale production of the automobile. He therefore needs people to produce the cars and to deliver them to interested users. In a market economy, production and supply are typically organized through markets, so the entrepreneur must pay for materials, capital, and workers. A business plan is needed to ensure that there is sufficient funding for production and possibly profit. The combination of physical technology, which is embodied in the product, social technology, which organizes the production process, and the business plan, which makes production possible and profitable, is tested in markets. The entrepreneur must succeed in the financial markets to obtain financing for the investment, in the labor markets to attract skilled workers, and in the product market where a sufficient number of customers must be willing to buy the product at a price that at least covers the cost of production. In all these markets, the entrepreneur normally faces competition: other entrepreneurs promise higher financial returns to financial investors, other firms offer potentially better jobs to workers, and in the product market, other firms offer alternative solutions to customers' needs and wants. At any point in time, the combination of physical technology, social technology, and business plan that an entrepreneur (or, more generally, a business) has chosen may be more or less successful. Successful means that the business can survive and potentially grow, i.e. produce more output, attract more workers, sell more units of the product, and make more profit. Successful design combinations can be copied by other businesses and thus proliferate. If the business cannot raise enough capital, attract enough skilled workers, or sell enough output to recoup production costs and provide a living for the entrepreneur, the business will fail and the chosen design combination will disappear.

What is a successful design combination at one time is unlikely to remain successful over time. Other businesses are experimenting with new design combinations. They offer new products, more attractive financial investments, more efficient ways of organizing production, and/or better jobs for workers. This means that the fitness landscape changes over time. If a company does not improve its design combination, it will become less fit in the changing fitness landscape. It will lose funding, workers, and/or sales in the product market. Evidence suggests that it is not easy for existing firms to adapt to changing environmental conditions. Daepp et al. (2015) estimate that the typical half-life of publicly traded firms in the United States between 1950 and 2009 was about 10 years, meaning that half of the firms in a cohort die within 10 years. They show that the frequency distribution of firm lifespans is roughly exponential, with a hazard rate of about 0.099 per year, or a nearly 10 percent chance of dying in the next year. While some firms can live very long (sometimes hundreds of years), the average lifespan of a firm is on the order of a few decades. Since the 1960s, the average lifespan has fallen from around 30 years to less than 20 years in the 2000s, which could be interpreted as evidence of increased competitive pressure.

The literature on the relationship between firm age and firm performance discusses both liabilities of newness and liabilities of aging (Coad 2018). *Liability of newness* refers to the observation that new firms are more likely to fail because they lack experience, routines, reputation, social capital, knowledge, etc., and are therefore at a disadvantage relative to established firms. However, the *liability of senescence* refers to the observation that accumulated rules, routines, and structures in organizations tend to ossify over time and lead to structural rigidity that negatively affects firm performance. *Liability of obsolescence* means that firms become less able to adapt to environmental changes. If these liabilities exist, then there will be a tendency for firms to be most successful at an intermediate age. When they are no longer young, they have efficient and productive routines that allow them to be competitive in their markets. At the same time, these routines are still flexible and not yet rigid, allowing the firm to remain adaptive and innovative. While some firms can avoid ossification, most will become obsolete, so that economic evolution occurs more at the industry level through entry and exit than at the firm level through constant renewal.

10.5.3 Evolutionary Economics and Complexity Economics

Evolutionary economics and complexity economics are "sister sciences" (Dopfer 2011), because they both deal with questions of structure and change and apply the concept of evolution to the economy. Both of them are alternatives to neoclassical mainstream economics, sharing the conviction that equilibrium thinking is highly restrictive and that boundedly rational agents cannot find global optima by maximization behavior in a complex and ever-changing environment. Since the two approaches are closely related, it is natural to ask how they differ.

The answer is that complexity economics starts from the premise that the economy is a complex adaptive system and uses the concepts developed in the complexity sciences to understand the economy. Adaptation and evolution are only a part of these concepts. As we have seen in previous chapters, nonlinearity, feedback, self-organization, and emergence are also important. This is not to say that these concepts play no role in evolutionary economics. On the contrary, many evolutionary economists accept the idea of the economy as a complex adaptive system. But the notion of complex adaptive systems and the related concepts of complexity are central to complexity economics, not to evolutionary economics. They define the theoretical core of complexity economics. However, according to Hodgson and Lamberg (2018), evolutionary economics does not have a unifying theoretical and methodological core. Their bibliometric analysis shows that Nelson and Winter (1982) sparked a lot of interest in evolutionary economics, but also that no strong cluster has emerged around their approach. The field of evolutionary economics never took root in economics departments, but flourished in business schools, innovation studies departments, sociology departments, science policy departments, and other multidisciplinary institutes. Evolutionary economics has been strongly focused on the study of innovation and technological change and has produced many theoretical and policy-relevant insights. However, Hodgson and Lamberg argue that the field is too fragmented and specialized and has not developed an "over-arching theory, a common conceptual vocabulary, and common research questions promising answers that demonstrate the superiority of the approach" (Hodgson and Lamberg 2018, p. 179). Similarly, Witt (2008) concludes that there is little agreement among evolutionary economists about what is specific to evolutionary economics.

Another difference is that complexity economics relies more on information theory and computation than evolutionary economics. Computational methods such as agent-based modeling are also used in evolutionary economics, but there are also strong clusters that do not work computationally or are even skeptical of it. Witt (2008) notes a pragmatic openness to different methodological approaches in evolutionary economics, including qualitative historical narratives, but also evolutionary game theory. In general, complexity economics is closer to physics and its (modern) methods, while evolutionary economics is more inspired by biology (see Dopfer 2011).

In summary, there is no need to overemphasize the differences between the two fields. The main differences can be found in the origins of the fields, i.e. systems theory, information theory and physics in the case of complexity economics, and (evolutionary) biology in the case of evolutionary economics. Many questions, worldviews, and approaches are similar, so there may be considerable convergence in the future.

10.6 Evolution of Knowledge

How new knowledge is generated is a key issue in evolutionary and complexity economics. Indeed, it can be argued that economic activity is not so much about the production and distribution of goods as it is about the acquisition and use of knowledge. The use of resources to produce goods and services is important, of course, but ultimately the knowledge available in an economy determines what is and can be done. Technical knowledge determines what can be produced, institutions as socially coordinating knowledge structure social life, organizational knowledge in firms guides business activity, and behavioral and cognitive knowledge enables individuals to act.

Knowledge has two important properties that are relevant in an economic context. First, the knowledge of different agents is diverse. There are no two agents with identical knowledge, and no single agent can have all the knowledge possessed by the entire population. Knowledge diversity is the source of competitive advantage, enables mutually beneficial cooperation, and is the source of novelty. Second, knowledge is structured. We can think of knowledge as an organized system or network of information embodied in a person or an organization. In this view, knowledge is not just a collection of isolated facts or pieces of information, but a meaningful arrangement of information. Information is organized by different types of theories. When agents learn, they integrate new information into the existing knowledge system. It is difficult to learn things that are unrelated to what the learner already knows.

This section demonstrates how knowledge can be modeled. We start with the knowledge of an individual person and then discuss the knowledge of an organization such as a company. The model is stylized, i.e. it aims at capturing important features, but obviously ignores many details. It is loosely related to the SKIN (simulating knowledge dynamics in innovation networks) model (Gilbert et al. 2001, 2007), which is an agent-based model framework that has been used to simulate the evolution of knowledge in firms and industries. In contrast to the SKIN framework, we do not discuss complete models of knowledge evolution, but focus on the representation of knowledge.

10.6.1 Knowledge of an Individual Person

A *unit of knowledge* is a triple $k = \{C, A, E\}$, where C is a capability, A is an ability, and E is a level of expertise, all of which expressed as integers from a given interval. *Capabilities* refer to the domain of knowledge, e.g. a scientific field like biology or a hobby like gardening. The *ability* refers to a particular application in the field, such as identifying birds or pruning a cherry tree. The *expertise level* indicates how well the agent holding the knowledge is able to perform the ability. The complete knowledge base of an agent is called a *kene*, which is analogous to a gene. A kene K is a collection of knowledge triples, e.g.

$$K = \left\{ \begin{Bmatrix} C \\ A \\ E \end{Bmatrix}, \begin{Bmatrix} C \\ A \\ E \end{Bmatrix}, \begin{Bmatrix} C \\ A \\ E \end{Bmatrix}, \begin{Bmatrix} C \\ A \\ E \end{Bmatrix} \right\} = \left\{ \begin{Bmatrix} 2 \\ 1 \\ 4 \end{Bmatrix}, \begin{Bmatrix} 2 \\ 3 \\ 2 \end{Bmatrix}, \begin{Bmatrix} 4 \\ 2 \\ 6 \end{Bmatrix}, \begin{Bmatrix} 5 \\ 3 \\ 1 \end{Bmatrix} \right\}$$
$$= \{k_1, k_2, k_3, k_4\}.$$

In this example, the individual has capabilities in the domains 2 (e.g., biology), 4 (e.g., gardening), and 5 (e.g., physics). In domain 2, the agent has the abilities 1 and 3 with the expertise levels 4 and 2, respectively. It is helpful to represent the kene in a knowledge map, as shown in Fig. 10.24. In this C-A-space, the numbers (and shades of green) indicate the expertise level. We can define E_{ij} as the expertise level of capability C_i and ability A_j.

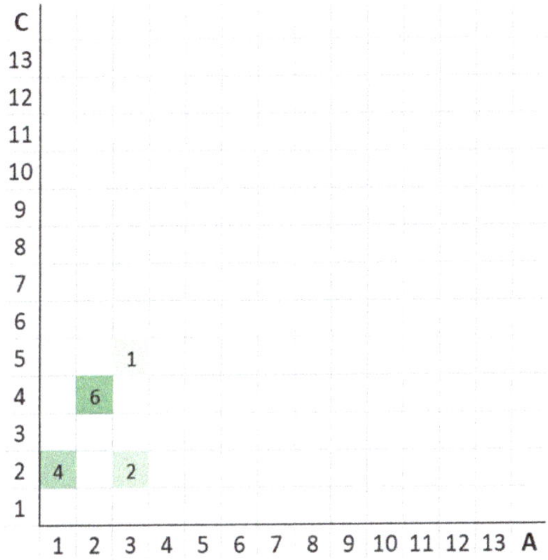

Fig. 10.24 Knowledge map of an individual. Source: Author

This knowledge map does not meet the criterion that knowledge is structured. The individual knowledge units are not connected, such that the map is patchy. Furthermore, it is restrictive to assume that the space is bounded from the left and from below. It seems more realistic that knowledge is open in all directions. Therefore, Fig. 10.25 shows a more realistic knowledge map.

Except for {4, 5,1} and {−3, 3, 1}, all units of knowledge in this map are connected. The individual has a core of knowledge with high levels of expertise near the origin. Furthermore, the horizontal extension of the knowledge is greater than the vertical one. It may be useful to interpret the two dimensions of the space. For example, the abilities with positive values could be practical abilities and manual abilities, and those with negative values could be theoretical or cognitive ones. Positive-valued capabilities could be interpreted as social knowledge and those with negative values as knowledge about the technology. The four quadrants then represent the dominant knowledge of different types of individuals, e.g. QI social worker, QII craftsman, QIII engineer, QIV psychologist.

A model of knowledge requires not only a representation of knowledge, but also a theory of how knowledge is acquired, i.e. a theory of learning. We can distinguish between the improvement of existing knowledge and the acquisition of new knowledge. An individual can reach a higher level of expertise by frequently using existing knowledge, which is *learning by doing*. Conversely, expertise decreases through forgetting when knowledge is not used. For example, fluency in a language requires that the individual actually speak the language. If a person only learns a language in class, but never practices it afterwards, the level of expertise will decrease again. Acquisition of new knowledge can be intentional or unintentional. You can learn a new language by taking a language course (i.e., intentionally) or by picking up a few words and phrases while on vacation in a foreign country (i.e., without active intention). In general, learning success depends on motivation and intention. This

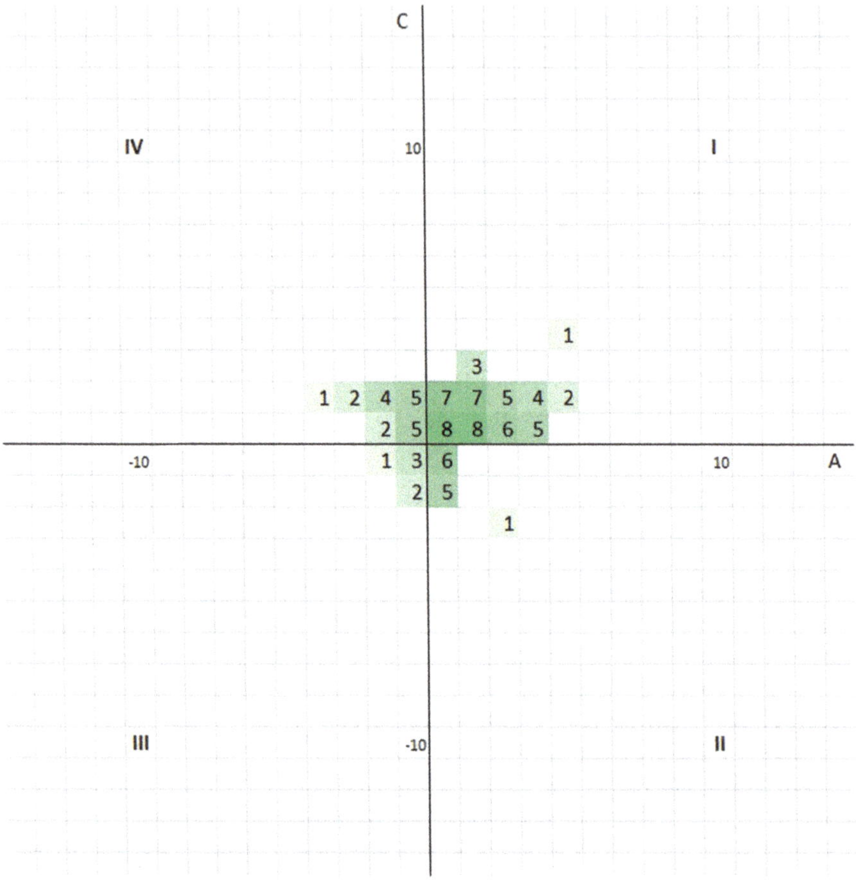

Fig. 10.25 More realistic knowledge map of an individual. Source: Author

means that the probability of learning new capabilities or abilities is higher when an individual has the intention to learn something new. In addition, it is easier to learn something that is related to something you already know than to learn something that is unrelated to your existing knowledge. Learning is cumulative, i.e. it is easier to understand and remember knowledge that can be integrated with existing knowledge. Finally, we can assume that it is easier to learn new abilities for a given capability (i.e., in a given domain) than it is to learn new capabilities. If you already know the basics of French, it is easier to learn advanced French grammar or French proverbs than it is to learn the computer language Python or calculus.

To model this kind of learning in an agent-based model, we need to formalize the statements. Let us say that learning occurs when the level of expertise E_{ij} of a given type of knowledge $[C_i, A_j]$ increases by one, formally $\ell(C_i, A_j) = E_{ij} + 1$. Let $\mathcal{CA}_{ij}$ be the set of the four adjacent types of knowledge, i.e.,

$\mathcal{CA}_{ij} = \{[C_{i-1}, A_j], [C_{i+1}, A_j], [C_i, A_{j-1}], [C_i, A_{j+1}]\}$, and $\overline{\mathcal{CA}_{ij}}$ be the set of all other types of knowledge. Analogously, $\mathcal{E}_{ij}$ is the set of expertise levels of the adjacent types of knowledge, $\mathcal{E}_{ij} = \{E_{i-1j}, E_{i+1j}, E_{ij-1}, E_{ij+1}\}$. We can model learning stochastically and define the probability of learning a certain type of knowledge as $p_{ij} = prob(\ell(C_i, A_j))$. Using this formalism, we can specify the description of the learning process. For example, we can make assumptions about how learning is related to the existing level of expertise of that type of knowledge, i.e. express p_{ij} as a function of E_{ij}, $p_{ij} = f(E_{ij})$. It seems plausible to assume that the slope of this function is positive and smallest close to $E_{ij} = 0$, which means that learning is hard when there is no prior knowledge about something and gets easier with higher levels of expertise. But learning also depends positively on the levels of expertise in related fields, i.e. $p_{ij} = f(E_{ij}, \mathcal{E}_{ij})$. Assuming that the transfer of knowledge between abilities is easier than between capabilities, this implies that $\frac{\partial f}{\partial E_{i\pm 1j}} < \frac{\partial f}{\partial E_{ij\pm 1}}$ *for* $E_{i\pm 1j} = E_{ij\pm 1}$.

But learning depends not only on the available expertise, but also on the set of the individual's characteristics I and on the set of context conditions $\mathcal{K}$, i.e. $p_{ij} = f(E_{ij}, \mathcal{E}_{ij}, I, \mathcal{K})$. The set of the individual's characteristics may include general intelligence, aptitude for certain types of knowledge, motivation, effort expended, and so on. Context conditions for individual learning refer to, among other things, the availability and quality of teaching materials and teachers among others. Depending on the specific situation to be modeled, different assumptions can be made about $p_{ij} = f(E_{ij}, \mathcal{E}_{ij}, I, \mathcal{K})$ and its derivatives.

10.6.2 Knowledge of an Organization

Consistent with the work of Nelson and Winter (1982), an organization has tacit knowledge that is embedded in its routines. This knowledge is a type of cultural knowledge that lies beyond the knowledge of individuals. We abstract from this type of knowledge here and focus on the knowledge of the organization's members, the aggregation of which can be viewed as the knowledge of the organization. In the example in Fig. 10.26, the organization consists of three individuals, indicated by the different colors. The knowledge of a group or organization is larger and more diverse than the knowledge of any individual, because it is extremely unlikely that any two individuals will have identical kenes.

An organization can acquire knowledge in two different ways: new people joining the organization bring in new knowledge from outside, and insiders can learn. Since the first case is straightforward, let us focus on the second. Individuals in a group can learn by themselves, but they can also learn collaboratively. Collaborative learning can mean that one individual learns something from another, or that both learn something together that is new to both. Collaborative learning requires that the individuals have kenes that overlap or are close together, as is the case for the blue and green kenes in Fig. 10.26. The brownish kene of the third individual in quadrant III is very different from the others, making it difficult for them to communicate and learn from each other. In this example, the blue kene might belong

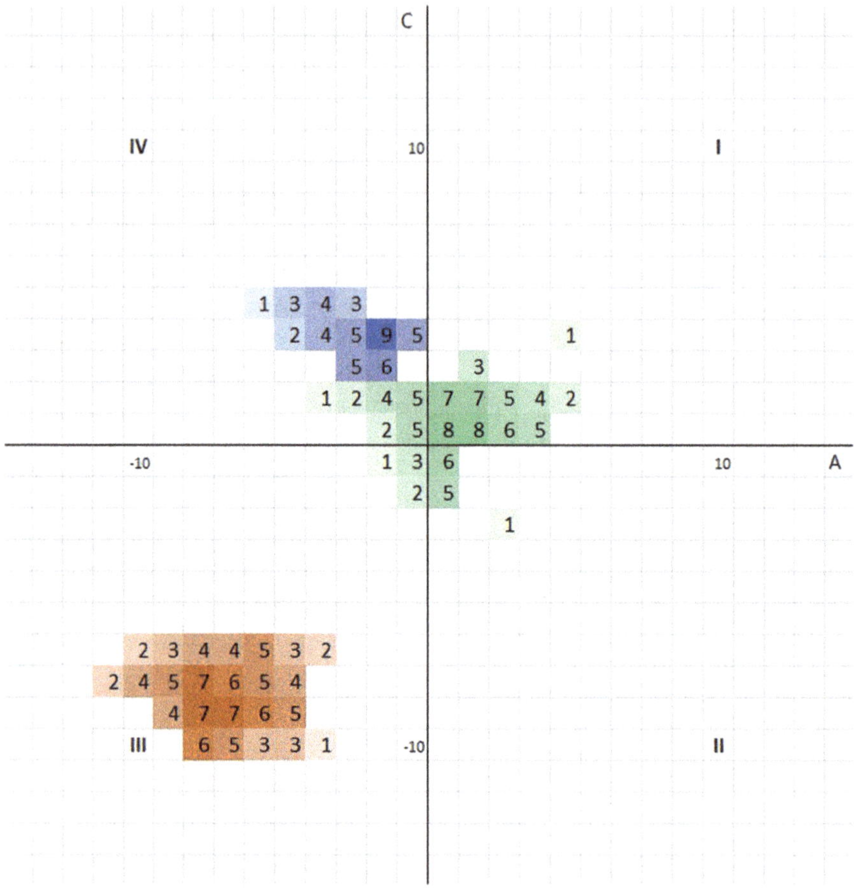

Fig. 10.26 Knowledge map of an organization. Source: Author

to an organizational psychologist and the brown kene to a mechanical engineer. While it is not impossible for the two to learn from each other, it will require considerable effort from both of them because they do not share any kind of knowledge (which, of course, is unrealistic).

In contrast, collaborative learning between the blue psychologist and the green individual, e.g. a manager, is easy, because they have two adjacent units of knowledge: {2,–3,2} and {2,–2,4} in the green kene and {3,–3,5} and {3,–2,6} in the blue kene. The manager may be able to gain more expertise $\ell(2,-3)$ by observing the psychologist or by communication between the two. Futhermore, by collaborating, the two may find it easier to gain expertise in $[C,A]=[3,-1]$ together than individually. Together they have three adjacent types of knowledge, whereas the blue individual has two and the green individual only one. Therefore, complementary but not too different knowledge facilitates joint knowledge production.

A complete model of organizational learning would require specifying exactly how individuals interact and exchange information, which is not done here. The proposed representation of organizational knowledge can be used to describe how firms innovate. An innovation such as a new product, a new service, or a new process is the result of a combination of different units of knowledge. In general, any output of a firm can be understood as a combination of units of knowledge. It is an innovation in the market if there is no alternative with a similar combination of knowledge. More precisely, it is the design of a product or process that is the combination of knowledge, not the actual implementation. Formally, we could express this as

$$D^j = \{k_i, k_j, \ldots, k_n\},$$

where D^j is the design for a product j and k_i, k_j... are units of knowledge. The actual product is a function of this design, but also of other factors Ω such as the materials used, the quality of the machinery used, or the manual skills of the workers:

$$P^j = f(D^j, \Omega).$$

The properties of the product, $p_1^j, p_2^j, p_3^j, \ldots$, e.g. usefulness for a certain purpose, quality, beauty, ... are emergent properties, which do not follow directly from any element in D^j or Ω.

10.7 Evolution of Social Technologies

This section introduces two techniques useful for modeling evolution in economics: cladistics and evolutionary systems modeling. Both are applied to the evolution of manufacturing systems in the automotive industry. The organization of manufacturing is an example of social technologies that firms combine with physical technologies and business plans.

10.7.1 Cladistic Classification

Cladistics is a classification method that is common in biology, but can also be used in economics. Cladistic classifications of species or entities are based on how recently they share a common ancestor. They thus trace the evolutionary history of entities, resulting in tree-like representations, so-called *cladograms*. The trees have *clades* or branches (clade is derived from ancient Greek κλάδος, kládos = branch), which represent groups of entities with common ancestors. Since cladistic classifications are derived from history, they are in principle unique and unambiguous as long as the historical process is known.

Classifications are useful for organizing and communicating concepts. They also help formulate hypotheses about relationships and discover new research questions.

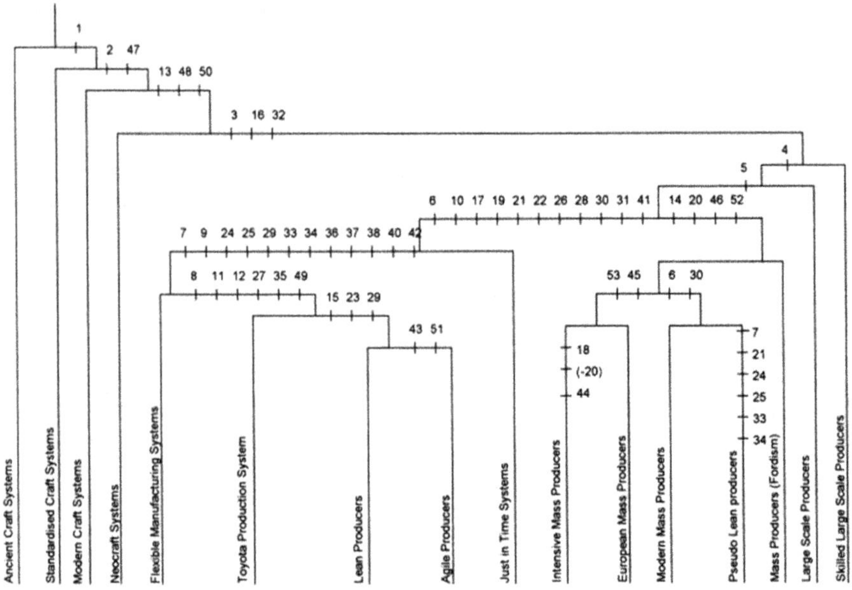

Fig. 10.27 Cladogram of manufacturing systems in the automotive industry. Source: McCarthy et al. (2000), reproduced with kind permission of Elsevier B.V.

In economics and business, they can inform decision-makers about strategic choices and changes.

Figure 10.27 is a cladogram of manufacturing systems in the automotive industry proposed by McCarthy et al. (2000) based on data taken from historical and other studies of the automotive industry. The cladogram contains 16 groups (or *taxa*) of manufacturing systems:

1. Ancient craft systems
2. Standardized craft systems
3. Modern craft systems
4. Neocraft systems
5. Flexible manufacturing systems
6. Toyota production systems
7. Lean production
8. Agile production
9. Just in time systems
10. Intensive mass producers
11. European mass producers
12. Modern mass producers
13. Pseudo lean producers
14. Mass producers (Fordism)

15. Large-scale producers
16. Skilled large-scale producers.

These taxa are the result of the taxonomy (i.e., the classification) and are named by McCarthy et al. (2000) to describe the most important characteristics of the respective manufacturing systems. The characteristics (or cladistic characters), which are indicated by the numbers in the cladogram, are presented in Table 10.2.

The cladogram shows that all manufacturing systems in the automotive industry evolved from what are called "ancient craft systems." The first automobiles in the 1890s were made by skilled craftsmen as unique copies. Character "1," which indicates the system property "standardization of parts," separates ancient craft systems from other systems such as standardized craft systems or modern craft systems. Modern craft systems are distinguished from standardized craft systems by characters "2" (production time standards) and "47" (division of labor). Standardized craft systems are the ancestors of modern craft systems. By adding "13" (large-volume production), "48" (employees are system tools), and "50" (product focus) to modern craft systems, we obtain neocraft systems. The cladogram also shows that large-scale production is the ancestor of two sister groups, both of which share "5" (automation), but differ in a variety of characters. The first sister group consists of flexible manufacturing systems, Toyota production system, lean production, agile production, and just-in-time production and roughly corresponds to the evolution of the automotive industry in Japan. The second sister group includes intensive mass production, European mass production, modern mass production, pseudo lean production, and mass production (Fordism), all of which correspond to the USA and the European way of automotive manufacturing.

McCarthy et al. (2000) suggest that their classification could inform strategic management. Managers could learn where their organization is in the evolutionary process and what is needed to advance to another stage. For instance, to move from lean production to agile production, "43" (agile automation for different products) and "51" (parallel processing in equipment) would have to be introduced. A cladogram can therefore be interpreted as a firm's past and future history, telling managers, where the organization has come from, where it is, and where it might go.

10.7.2 Evolutionary Systems Modeling

A cladistic classification of manufacturing systems is a useful descriptive tool, but it neither explains nor predicts the evolution of systems. It simply captures the actual historical path taken, which could have been different. Since evolution is an effective search algorithm, it is likely to end up in the same region of the fitness landscape if the landscape does not change. However, there may be many different ways to get to the highest mountain. This means that the actual historical evolution may be just one of many that could have happened. Evolution is a mixture of determinism and chance.

Table 10.2 Automotive cladistic characters

1	Standardization of parts	28	100% inspection sampling
2	Assembly time standards	29	U-shaped layout
3	Assembly line layout	30	Preventive maintenance
4	Reduction of craft skill	31	Individual error correction
5	Automation (machine paced shops)	32	Sequential dependency of workers
6	Pull production system	33	Line balancing
7	Reduction of lot size	34	Team policy (team motivation, pay, and autonomy)
8	Pull procurement planning	35	Toyota verification of assembly line (TVAL)
9	Operator-based machine maintenance	36	Groups vs. teams
10	Quality circles	37	Job enrichment
11	Employee innovation prizes	38	Manufacturing cell
12	Job rotation	39	Concurrent engineering
13	Large-volume production	40	ABC costing
14	Suppliers selected primarily by price	41	Excess capacity
15	Exchange of workers with suppliers	42	Flexible automation for different products
16	Socialization training (master/apprentice learning)	43	Agile automation for different products
17	Proactive training programs	44	Insourcing
18	Product range reduction	45	Immigrant workforce
19	Automation	46	Dedicated automation
20	Multiple subcontracting	47	Division of labor
21	Quality systems (procedures, tools, ISO 9000)	48	Employees are systems tools and simply operate machines
22	Quality philosophy (culture, way of working, TQM)	49	Employees are system developers
23	Open book policy with suppliers, sharing of cost data and profits	50	Product focus
24	Flexible, multifunctional workforce	51	Parallel processing (in equipment)
25	Set-up time reduction	52	Dependence on written rules
26	Kaizen change management	53	Further intensification of labor; employees are considered part of the machine and will be replaced by a machine if possible
27	TQM sourcing; suppliers selected on the basis of quality		

Source: adapted from McCarthy et al. (2000)

Baldwin et al. (2005a) propose an approach to modeling evolutionary systems inspired by Prigogine's Brusselator model of self-organization (see Chap. 8). The key idea is that nonlinear nonequilibrium systems can create and destroy structure through self-organization. However, self-organization works with given types of entities, whereas evolution relies on diversity and change of system components. Individuals explore the fitness landscape and some succeed, others do not. Evolution is a sequence of experiments by individual system elements. Positive feedback reinforces successful experiments and suppresses unsuccessful ones.

In a series of papers, Baldwin et al. apply these ideas to the evolution of manufacturing systems in order to explore different evolutionary trajectories and to gain a better understanding of organizational processes. They explicitly refer to the cladogram presented in the previous subsection with its 53 characters that are labeled as business practices or character-states CS (we could also call them social technologies). The model assumes that the 53 character-states already exist, similar to Beinhocker's concept of the design space in which all kinds of (social) technologies are located. A firm adopts a set of practices from the population of all N character-states. $P(k) \geq 0$ is the performance of practice k within the firm, with higher values indicating better performance and higher importance in the organization. The total performance of the firm is the sum of all individual performances

$$Total\ performance = \sum_k P(k).$$

The key assumption of the model is that the practices interact with each other. A positive interaction of a practice h is called *synergy* and a negative interaction is called a *conflict*. The *net synergy* of practice h in the presence of the other applied practices is given by[5]

$$Synergy(h) = \sum_k (Pair(h,k) \times P(k)).$$

$Pair(h, k)$ is an element of a matrix containing the positive, neutral, or negative pair interactions between all 53 character-states. The pair matrix was constructed from data collected in a survey among experts in manufacturing firms in the UK automotive industry. The performance P of each practice h evolves according to the following differential equation:

$$\begin{aligned} \frac{dP(h)}{dt} &= (bP(h) \times (1 + .01P(h))) \times (1 + .2Synergy(h)) \\ &\times \left(1 - \frac{Total\ performance}{N}\right) - mP(h), \end{aligned}$$

where b and m are parameters that describe the natural growth or decline of each practice. *Total performance* acts as a crowding factor that hinders the growth of the practices. The important point is that the performance of a practice increases when $Synergy(h) > 0$ and deceases otherwise. Thus, whether a practice is successful, and

[5] In Allen et al. (2007) the product of $Pair \times P$ is normalized by the term $1 + dist(h,k)$, but it is unclear, how the distance $dist(h,k)$ is defined and why it is necessary.

hence gets amplified, depends on its positive or negative synergies with practices that already exist in a firm.

Baldwin et al. (2005b) use this model in order to simulate the evolution of automotive manufacturing practices. The system starts from the standardized craft system with character-state 1 (standardized part), whose initial performance is set to 2, and all character-states are introduced in a random sequence after every 500 time steps. The simulation is run for 100,499 time steps, such that 200 character-states can be introduced. Already existing characteristics can be reintroduced at a performance level of 2, which can be an improvement or a deterioration depending on the simulated performance at the time of the reintroduction.

Table 10.3 shows the sequence of introduction of selected character-states in a run and whether they were successful (CS I) or not (CS F). In this run, character-state 13 was introduced first at time 500. It was successful until time 25,000, when it failed and was eliminated. It was reintroduced at time 28,500 and remained active until 30,500, and so on. Some practices like state 5 are introduced and never fail. Others, like character-state 4, try to "invade" several times (e.g., 7000, 14,500, or 63,000), but fail to establish themselves and disappear in the same period. Character-state 14 invades successfully in period 1000, but then gets kicked out in period 5000 and cannot reinvade despite several attempts (periods 20,000, 22,000, 87,500).

This simulation run demonstrates that the performance of a practice depends on the mix of all the practices in place in a system at any given time. The same practice may be successful at some times and not at others. Some practices, e.g., character-state 48, may be beneficial for long periods of time (e.g., from 3000 to 19,500), but then become obsolete forever. Evolutionary change can be interpreted as a succession of instabilities of previously stable sets of interacting entities.

Figure 10.28 shows the performance of the 53 character-states in the final period of the example run according to Table 10.2. In this final state, 19 practices are missing: 4, 7, 13, 14, 15, 20, 23, 28, 31, 32, 35, 40, 41, 45, 46, 47, 48, 52, and 53. Baldwin et al. argue that the final configuration is similar to the "agile production" manufacturing system, although some practices are missing. They show that four other runs with different random sequences generate quite similar final configurations, even though some practices (e.g., 11, 12, or 29) are missing in some runs. This finding supports the claim that evolution has a certain degree of determinism and reaches similar final states on different paths if the fitness landscape is invariant. In this model, the fitness landscape is represented by the pair matrix.

Baldwin et al. (2003) present a different set of experiments. They start with the manufacturing system of modern mass production and simulate how the configuration of practices changes over time as additional character-states are introduced, either individually or in bundles. This exercise addresses the question of what would happen if the management of a modern mass producer wanted to change its production system by introducing practices from other systems.

Before Baldwin et al. conduct their experiments, they first simulate a stable configuration of modern mass production (see Fig. 10.29). The initial configuration of practices consists of the 17 modern mass producers in the cladogram in Fig. 10.27. Each practice is assigned an initial performance of 5 units (see the panel for $T = 50$

Table 10.3 Time sequence of innovations and failures

Time	C S I	C S F	Time	C S I	C S F	Time	C S I	C S F	Time	C S I	C S F
0	1		25,500	42		50,500	52	52	75,500	17	
500	13		26,000	24		51,000	17		76,000	9	
1000	14		26,500	49		51,500	17		76,500	4	4
1500	5		27,000	44		52,000	16		77,000	49	
2000	23		27,500	10		52,500	18		77,500	9	
2500	27		28,000	47	47	53,000	2		78,000	27	
3000	48		28,500	13		53,500	2		78,500	50	
3500	30		29,000	26		54,000	33		79,000	52	52
4000	21		29,500	49		54,500	45	45	79,500	39	
4500	32		30,000	28		55,000	36		80,000	48	48
5000	35	14	30,500	17	13. 28	55,500	52	52	80,500	21	
5500	17	32	31,000			56,000	39	36	81,000	25	
6000	38		31,500	39		56,500	31		81,500	10	
6500	16		32,000	6		57,000	3	31	82,000	32	
7000	4	4	32,500	40		57,500	3		82,500	19	32
7500	16		33,000	43		58,000	20	20	83,000	12	
8000	28		33,500	10		58,500	18		83,500	29	
8500	8	28	34,000	49	40	59,000	16		84,000	16	35
9000	32		34,500	31		59,500	16		84,500	18	
9500	1		35,000	13		60,000	23		85,000	6	
10,000	31	32	35,500	50		60,500	48	48	85,500	42	
10,500	50		36,000	12		61,000	25	23	86,000	50	
11,000	4	4	36,500	1		61,500	43		86,500	18	
11,500	51		37,000	52	52	62,000	26		87,000	48	48
12,000	29		37,500	23	13. 31	62,500	32		87,500	14	14
12,500	21	29	38,000	20	20	63,000	4	4	88,000	29	
13,000	30		38,500	8		63,500	29	32	88,500	8	
13,500	37		39,000	1	23	64,000	29		89,000	41	
14,000	26		39,500	44		64,500	48	48	89,500	30	
14,500	4	4	40,000	6		65,000	49		90,000	36	
15,000	28		40,500	49		65,500	8		90,500	7	
15,500	38	28	41,000	28		66,000	30		91,000	31	
16,000	21		41,500	18	28	66,500	38		92,500	32	7. 31
16,500	6		42,000	46	46	67,000	28		92,000	39	
17,000	28		42,500	28		67,500	1	28	92,500	17	32
17,500	1	28	43,000	6	28	68,000	52	52	93,000	5	
18,000	12		43,500	21		68,500	42		93,500	1	
18,500	39		44,000	27		69,000	51		94,000	22	
19,000	7		44,500	42		69,500	35		94,500	9	
19,500	4	4. 48	45,000	11		70,000	41		95,000	39	
20,000	14	7. 14	45,500	22		70,500	44	41	95,500	20	20

(continued)

Table 10.3 (continued)

Time	C S I	C S F	Time	C S I	C S F	Time	C S I	C S F	Time	C S I	C S F
20,500	20	20	46,000	21		71,000	6		96,000	7	
21,000	20	20	46,500	27		71,500	48	48	96,500	34	
21,500	39		47,000	22		72,000	19	29	97,000	24	7
22,000	14	14	47,500	43		72,500	38		97,500	3	
22,500	44		48,000	39		73,000	34		98,000	44	
23,000	13		48,500	28		73,500	19		98,500	19	
23,500	1		49,000	21	28	74,000	16		99,000	46	46
24,000	47		49,500	45	45	74,500	42		99,500	9	
24,500	1		50,000	52	52	75,000	48	48	100,000	41	41
25,000	50	13									

Source: Baldwin et al. (2005b), reproduced with kind permission of Taylor & Francis Group LLC

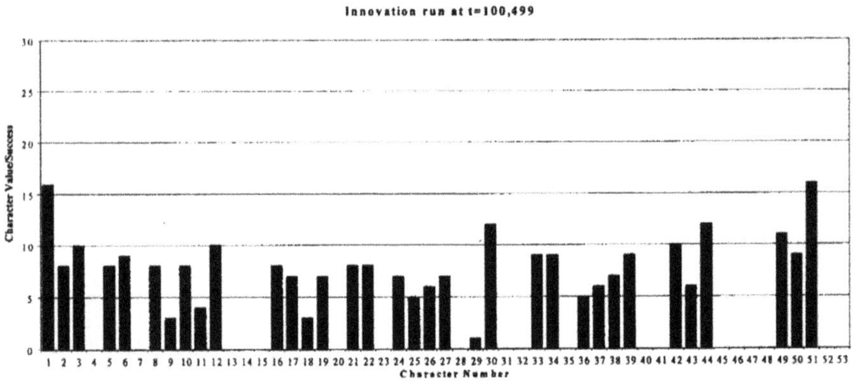

Fig. 10.28 End configuration. Source: Baldwin et al. (2005b), reproduced with kind permission of Taylor & Francis Group LLC

in the upper left corner of Fig. 10.29). Over time, the performance of some practices increases significantly (e.g., characteristics 1, 13, 30, and 46), while others decrease and eventually disappear (characteristics 4, 14, 47, and 48). Baldwin et al. conclude that the simulation is useful because it roughly reproduces a particular manufacturing system from the empirical cladogram.

One of the experiments looks at the introduction of quality policies into the stable modern mass producer system. This is done by using the final configuration from Fig. 10.29 (T = 12,000) for the new simulations. Baldwin et al. first introduce practice 21 (quality systems) individually with a starting performance of 5. They find that the introduction of quality systems had a negative effect on characteristic

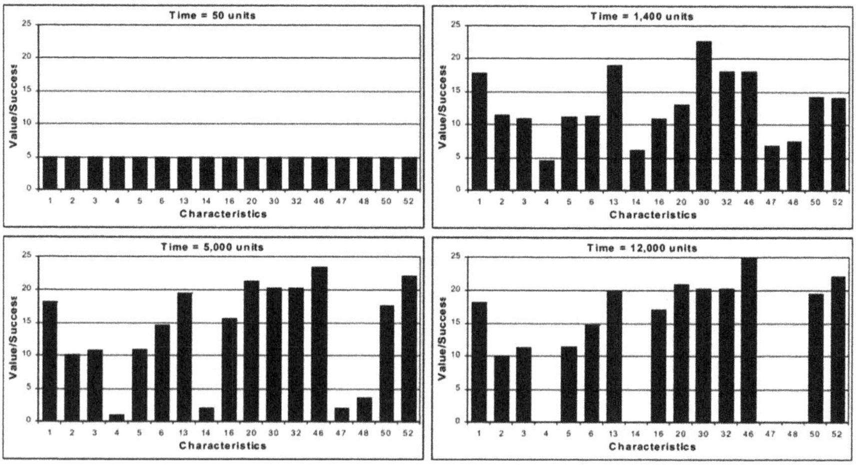

Fig. 10.29 Stabilization of modern mass production. Source: Baldwin et al. (2003), reproduced with kind permission of Taylor & Francis Group LLC

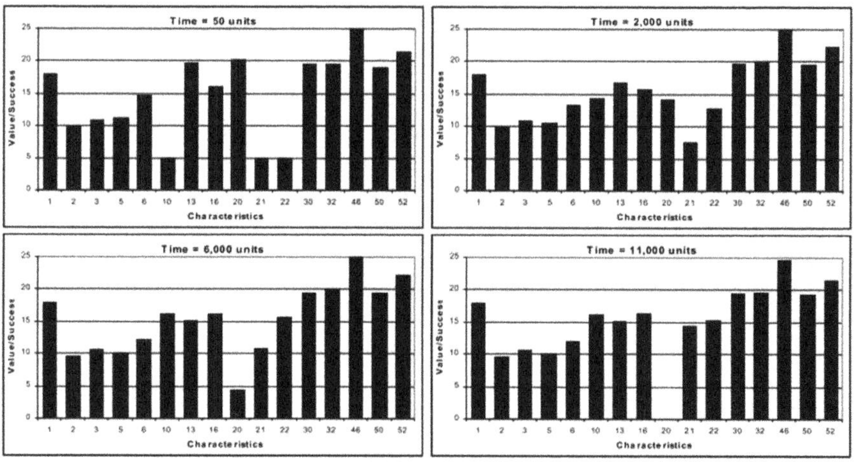

Fig. 10.30 Introduction of quality policies into modern mass production. Source: Baldwin et al. (2003), reproduced with kind permission of Taylor & Francis Group LLC

20 (multiple subcontracting), which became unstable and failed. In another experiment, several practices related to quality (quality circles 10, quality systems 21, and quality philosophy 22) were introduced as a package.

As shown in Fig. 10.30, all three practices are successful and become established over time. Again, the quality policies eliminate CS 20 (multiple subcontracting), not immediately, but over time. They also reduce the performance of CS13 (large-volume production), but without causing it to fail. The evolutionary model thus shows that the introduction of new practices into an established manufacturing system can have disruptive consequences in the sense that established, high-performing practices are incompatible with the new practices and must therefore disappear from the system. Changing an evolved system can require a major transformation, not only to establish new practices, but also to unwind old practices that become dysfunctional in the new configuration.

10.8 Diversity

Chapter 2 introduced dynamic complexity and structural complexity. Pure dynamic complexity results from the self-organization of similar or even identical individuals. In contrast, structural complexity, which is the result of design or optimization, is characterized by a diversity of system elements. The theory of highly optimized tolerance defines complex systems as hierarchical, highly structured, and composed of many different parts. You may recall from Chap. 2 that the theory of highly optimized tolerance applies to engineered systems, but also to systems that have been optimized by evolution. Thus, complexity (structural or functional) and evolution are related to diversity.

There is a twofold relationship between diversity and evolution. On the one hand, evolution needs diversity because it recombines existing information. In Sect. 10.3.3, we saw that greater diversity in the initial gene pool allows evolution to search a larger space in the fitness landscape by recombination, even without mutation. Limited diversity constrains the range of possible innovations that explore the fitness landscape. On the other hand, evolution generates diversity through recombination and mutation, or variation. Functional differentiation and specialization in ecosystems are typical outcomes of evolutionary processes (see Sect. 8.7.4 in Chap. 8). Evolution tends to fill niches in ecosystems, and each species that occupies a niche opens up new niches for other species, so there is a positive feedback mechanism.

10.8.1 Kinds of Diversity

Heterogeneity and diversity are often used interchangeably. In economics, heterogeneity is the more common term, but in evolutionary contexts, diversity is more appropriate. Assessing diversity requires that we can discern a difference between objects and classify them according to some criterion. Classification produces classes of objects or types.

In many cases, there is no unique way to classify objects, and the criterion chosen by the classifying observer is somewhat subjective and arbitrary. For example, consider the collection of objects in Fig. 10.31. How would you sort them into classes? The most obvious criterion might be living things (or animals) and non-living objects (or geometric shapes), which would give us two classes. Other classification criteria might be size or color, which would apply to both animals and geometric shapes. But does it make sense to put an orange fish, an orange cat, an

Fig. 10.31 Diversity. Source: Author

orange triangle, and an orange circle in the same group? We can also create subgroups and use the number of vertices to distinguish the geometric shapes. The number of vertices is a discrete variable that is easy to identify: we have circles with no vertices, triangles with three vertices, tetragons, and a pentagon. But what about the stars? There are two stars with five vertices, but should they be grouped with the pentagon? And what about the ring? It has no vertex, but should it be in the same class as the circles? Size is a continuous variable, but how do we operationalize it? Should we measure area, height, or greatest extent? We could discretize size into large, medium, and small, but then we need thresholds. Similar problems arise with color. We could use broad color classes like blue, green, yellow, and orange, but is the four-pointed star green or blue? Should we use hues and group only those objects that have exactly the same hue? To make things even more complicated, we could also combine different criteria, such as size, color, and shape, and distinguish between small blue squares, small yellow squares, and large blue squares. Obviously, the more criteria we use to define a class, the fewer objects it will contain. If we apply too many criteria, we end up with an idiosyncratic class for each object, making classification pointless. On the other hand, some combination of criteria is useful, e.g. living or non-living and number of vertices for the inanimate objects.

How we define classes or types depends on the purpose of the classification. Similar to what was said about stylized facts in Chap. 9, classification relies on theoretical concepts. Epstein (2019) reports findings from villages in the Soviet Union in the 1930s, where some villagers still lived traditional lives and were illiterate, while others had been forced to work on collective farms and had been exposed to schooling. The traditional villagers were unable to perform classification tasks that required simple abstract concepts, while those exposed to modern life

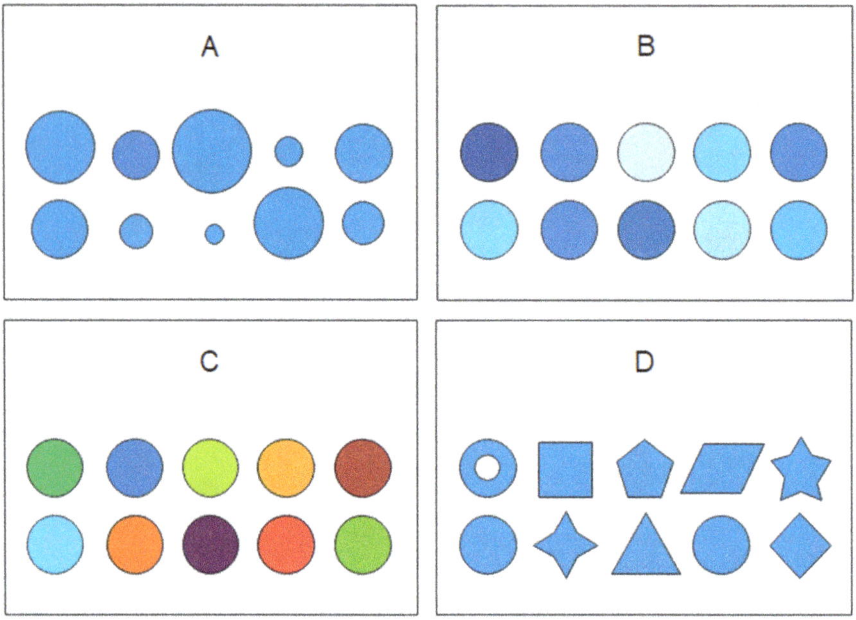

Fig. 10.32 Variety and disparity. Source: Author

could do so easily. For example, one task involved describing skeins of wool in a range of colors. The "modern" villagers spontaneously formed color groups even when they did not know the name of a particular color. The "premodern" villagers, however, refused to form groups, arguing that no two skeins were alike. They gave various descriptions such as "cotton in bloom," " decayed teeth," or "a lot of water." Traditional villagers also had difficulty identifying an object that did not belong to a group, such as a child and three adults, or a hammer, saw, hatchet, and log. One response to the suggestion that a boy was different from the adults was that "the boy must stay with the others" or that he could help them while they worked. Similarly, one villager did not accept that a log did not belong in a group of tools because the tools were useless without the log. Premodern villagers were not accustomed to using abstract concepts to make classifications. In the same way, scientific classifications in biology, economics, or any other field require the existence of some theoretical concepts.

Like complexity, diversity has multiple dimensions. Page (2010) distinguishes between diversity within a type, diversity across types, and diversity in community composition. Diversity within a type refers to a measurable attribute of a type, such as the size of the circles or the darkness of the shades of blue in panels A and B of Fig. 10.32. Measures of variation, such as variance or standard deviation, capture this type of diversity. Variance is defined as

$$\sigma^2 = \sum_{i=1}^{m} \frac{(x_i - \bar{x})^2}{m},$$

where $\bar{x}$ is the arithmetic mean of all m observations of the attribute x. The variance, and thus the within-type diversity is large when many observations are far away from the mean.

Diversity across types refers to the distribution across types, such as the different colors in panel C of Fig. 10.32. In this example, we could identify five different types (green, blue, red, orange, and violet). The *generalized entropy function* can be used to measure diversity across types:

$$H_N^\alpha(p_1, p_2, \dots p_N) = \left(\sum_{i=1}^{N} p_i^\alpha\right)^{\frac{1}{1-\alpha}},$$

where p_i is the proportion of type i in the population and N is the number of types. The generalized entropy function includes a number of special cases: (i) for $\alpha = 0$, we simply get the number of types, $H_N^p = N$, (ii) $\alpha = 2$ gives the diversity index $H_N^a = \left(\sum_{i=1}^{N} p_i^2\right)^{-1}$, which is the inverse of the Herfindahl–Hirschman index used in economics to measure the concentration in an industry, and (iii) $\alpha \to 1$ gives the Shannon information entropy discussed in Chap. 3.

The entropy measures do not take into account how different the types are. To capture the extent of the differences, we need a distance measure. Weitzman (1992) proposed a diversity measure based on the distance between types, $d(i,j) > 0$. *Weitzman diversity* of a set of types, $W(S)$, can be computed recursively by the following algorithm:

1. Start with the empty set S and set $W(S) = 0$.
2. Add a randomly chosen type i to S.
3. Choose a type j, which is closest to a member of S according to $d(.,.)$.
   (a) Increase $W(S)$ by the distance from j to S.
   (b) Add type j to S.
4. If there are types that do not belong to S yet, go to step (3), else stop.

Weitzman uses the perfect taxonomy of a perfectly complete genealogical tree represented in a cladogram to measure the distance between the types (or species). Two species i and j have a distance of 1, i.e., $d(i,j) = 1$, if they both descend directly from one common ancestor. In the cladogram in Fig. 10.33, this is the case for types A and B, C and D, and for E and F. To find the common ancestor of types C and E or F, one must go up two levels in the tree, such that their distance is 2. The distance between A and C is 3, $d(A, C) = 3$, because their common ancestor is on level 3.

Applying the algorithm, we find that the Weitzman diversity of these six types is equal to 8, $W(\{A, B, C, D, E, F\}) = 8$. If we randomly start with type C, the nearest

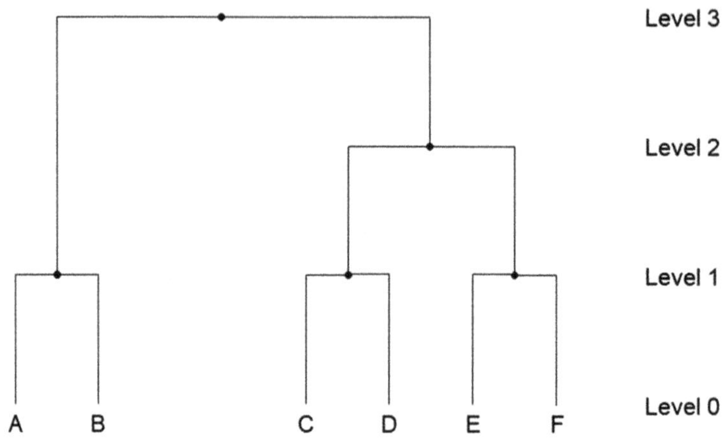

Fig. 10.33 Three levels in a cladogram. Source: Author

neighbor is D, with a distance of 1, so $W(\{C, D\}) = 1$. The next chosen type closest to S is E or F, both with a distance of 2, hence $W(\{C, D, E\}) = 1 + 2 = 3$. Continuing with F, A, and B we add 1, 3, and 1 summing up to 8 in total.

In principle, we could also compute the Weitzman diversity for the populations C and D in Fig. 10.32, even though we do not have a cladistic distance between the types. We could define the distance between the colors in panel C according to the color spectrum violet, blue, cyan, green, yellow, orange, and red and assume a distance of 1 between each color. Then, we get $W(\{violet, blue, green, orange, red\}) = 6$, because cyan and yellow are missing such that $d(blue, green) = d(green, orange) = 2$. The distance between the types in panel D could be given by the difference in the number of vertices, e.g. $d(circle, triangle) = 3$.

Diversity of community composition complements diversity within and between types by the way the types are related to each other. Not only can types be different, but so can the relationships between them, as shown in an example of three families in Fig. 10.34. In this example, there are three kinds of relationships: a partnership relationship (←*PP*→), a parent–child relationship (←*PC*→), and a sibling relationship (←*S*→). The three families are composed of the same proportion of males and females (three each), such that their diversity across types is identical if sex is used as a criterion for types.

The relationships define the roles of the individuals in their families. Note that types can be seen as inherent to the individuals and independent of context, whereas the roles are not and depend on the relationships. In family A, a man and a woman are partners, and both are parents of a second woman, who also has a male partner. The woman, but not the man, is the parent of two other individuals who are siblings. Hence, the siblings are the children, the couple in the middle are their parents (with the husband being the stepfather), and the couple at the top are the grandparents of the maternal children. Family C has exactly the same number of types and of the different relationships (four parent-child, two partnerships, one sibling relationship),

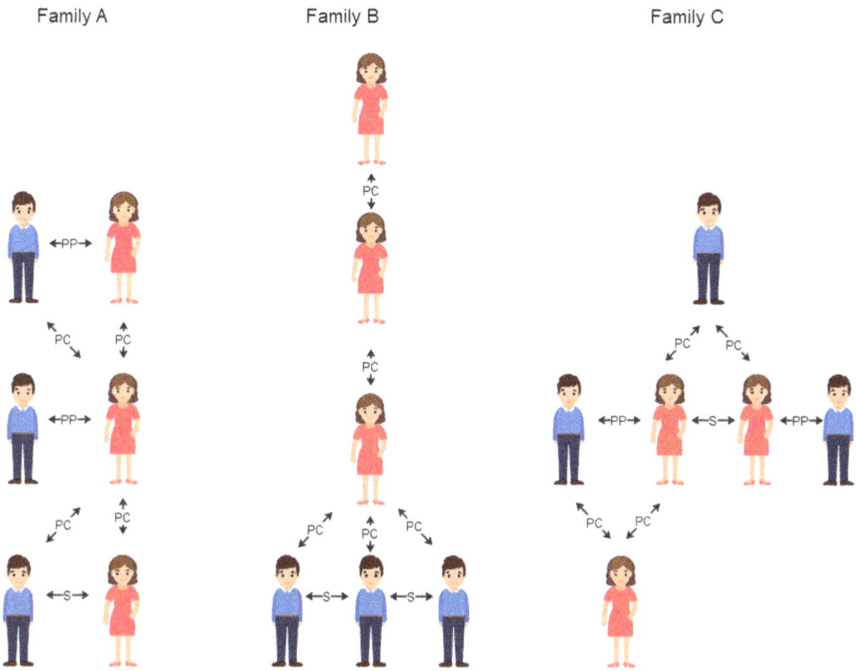

Fig. 10.34 Three families with different compositions. Source: Author

but the composition is different. In this family, two adult sisters live together with their father, their respective partners and the daughter of the first sister and her husband. Family B consists of a single woman with three sons, the woman's mother, and her grandmother, who is the boys' great-grandmother. It is not straightforward to measure the diversity of community composition and to say, which family is more diverse. What one could do is to apply an entropy measure to the between-type relationships for a given diversity of types.

10.8.2 Framework for Analyzing Diversity

Diversity is an important issue in many disciplines and contexts, including ecology, science and technology studies, business and economics. It can foster creativity and innovation, increase the problem-solving ability of teams, support learning, promote equity and equality, and help manage uncertainty and diversify risk. As another benefit of diversity, Page (2010) presents the *diversity prediction theorem*, which states that when a set of N individuals make predictions about the value of an outcome, the collective error is equal to the average individual error minus the prediction variance. Formally:

$$(v - \bar{s})^2 = \sum_{i=1}^{N} (v - s_i)^2 - \sum_{i=1}^{N} (s_i - \bar{s})^2,$$

where v is the true value of the outcome, s_i is the prediction of person i, and $\bar{s}$ is the collective prediction in the form of the arithmetic mean of all individual predictions. Note that the collective error is smaller (c.p), if the prediction variance—in other words the within-group diversity—is larger.

But diversity can also have downsides. Risk diversification can lead to foregone profits, team diversity can increase transaction costs, and product diversity increases costs because the benefits of specialization, standardization, and economies of scale are not realized. Stirling (2007) proposes a general framework for assessing the costs and benefits of diversity in a variety of contexts. The framework is a heuristic rather than an index, because the importance of different dimensions of diversity and the overall importance of diversity can be highly context-specific, making it meaningless to define a single index.

Stirling (2007) defines three dimensions of diversity across types: variety, balance, and disparity. *Variety* is the number of categories or types. *Balance* is a function of the pattern of distribution of elements across categories and describes how much of each type we have. It is therefore related to entropy. *Disparity* is the manner and degree to which types differ from each other, which is a statement about the distance between types.

The measure of diversity D proposed by Stirling called *balance/disparity-weighted variety* is defined as

$$D = \sum_{ij(i \neq j)} d_{ij} \times p_i \times p_j,$$

where d_{ij} is the distance between two types i and j and $p_{i,\,j}$ are the proportions of the elements belonging to a type. Balance is captured by the proportions and the distance measures disparity. D is similar to *Rao's quadratic entropy index* (Rao 1982), which is well-known in biology. Unlike Rao's quadratic entropy, which sums over all elements, the summation in D runs only across the half-matrix of $(N^2 - N)/2$ - non-identical pairs of N elements (i.e., $i \neq j$). The distance function could be the Euclidean distance in a type space, but other distances could be used as well. The type space could look like the knowledge space in Fig. 10.26. To generalize the measure, Stirling introduces two parameters $\alpha \in \{0, 1\}$ and $\beta \in \{0, 1\}$:

$$\Delta = \sum_{ij(i \neq j)} (d_{ij})^{\alpha} (p_i \times p_j)^{\beta}.$$

The four different permutations of the values of α and β yield four variants of the diversity measure, which focus on different diversity dimensions. $\{\alpha, \beta\} = \{0, 0\}$ focuses only on variety, because only the $(N^2 - N)/2$ non-identical pairs of types are summed up. $\{\alpha, \beta\} = \{0, 1\}$ introduces balance, $\{\alpha, \beta\} = \{1, 0\}$ adds disparity to variance, and $\{\alpha, \beta\} = \{1, 1\}$ includes all three dimensions.

Systems are not only characterized by diversity, but have other properties, too. Diversity can be valuable by itself or because it has desirable effects on the system. For example, in economic systems, diversity can help to hedge ignorance, foster innovation, mitigate lock-in effects, or increase fairness, but it may also compromise other aspects of system performance. A system S can be assigned a value $V\{S\}$, which depends on the perspective taken by a system observer. The value of the system can be expressed as the aggregate value of the system elements' performance $V\{E\}$ and the value of diversity $V\{P\}$, which depends on the portfolio-level properties and cannot be reduced to the individual elements, $V\{S\} = V\{E\} + V\{P\}$. The aggregate value of the system elements i can be expressed as a weighted sum:

$$V\{E\} = \sum_i \sum_c w_c \times s_{ic} \times p_i,$$

where w_c is the weight given to a criterion c, s_{ic} is the performance value of element i under criterion c, and p_i is the proportion of the element. The portfolio value including diversity can be expressed as

$$V\{P\} = \delta \Delta' = \delta \sum_{ij(i \neq j)} (d_{ij})^\alpha (p_i \times p_j)^\beta \iota_{ij}.$$

There are two modifications of the diversity measure. The first is a weighting parameter, δ, which scales the importance of the portfolio properties for the total system value. Since it is possible for diversity to have a negative overall, δ could be negative, although it is normally assumed to be positive. The second modification ι_{ij} reflects portfolio interactions that are captured by small positive or negative deviations from unity, $\iota_{ij} = 1 \pm \partial\iota$, $\partial\iota \ll 1$. If $\iota_{ij} = 1$ for two elements in the portfolio, they do not interact. $\iota_{ij} > 1$ captures a synergy, $\iota_{ij} < 1$ a tension between two types.

The framework can be used to explore different perspectives and assumptions regarding the individual performance of elements, system interactions, and diversity on the overall value of the system. Since parameters such as w_c and δ are typically subjective, the framework is not intended to derive an unconditionally optimal solution, for which objective parameters are necessary. Rather, the different weights can be varied to see how different scaling of performance and diversity would contribute to the overall value. For each chosen parameter, the proportions of the elements, p_i, are chosen such that $V\{S\}$ is maximized.

Figure 10.35 illustrates a hypothetical example of how an area of land might be composed of different habitat types A, B, C, and D, all of which have different economic and ecological values. The economic value may depend on the value and yield of the agricultural production, but also on the attractiveness to tourists. Ecological values can depend on the suitability of habitats for endangered species

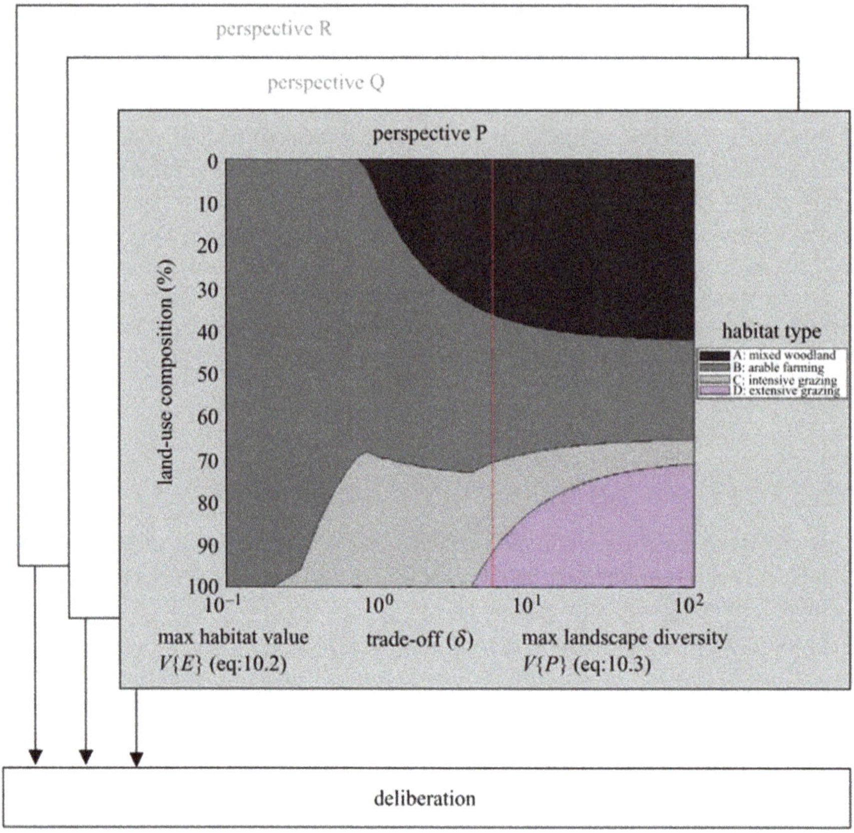

Fig. 10.35 Relationship between habitat diversity and other aspects of landscape value. Source: Stirling (2007), reproduced with kind permission of The Royal Society (U.K.)

and the internal biodiversity of the habitats themselves. The diagram has δ on the horizontal axis and the proportions of the four habitat types on the vertical axis. If a low value of δ is chosen, the value-maximizing land-use composition consists of arable farming (B) alone or together with intensive grazing (C). Mixed woodland (A) enters at $\delta \approx 1$. Extensive grazing (D) is added to the mix rather late. The vertical red line shows the value of δ where $V\{E\} = V\{P\}$. The boxes "perspective R" and "perspective Q" suggest that the picture could also look different, if different weights or criteria were chosen for measuring performance, or if α and β were different. Above all, the framework is a tool to make different perspectives transparent and to be able to communicate about the consequences of normative parameter choices.

10.8.3 Diversity, Complexity, and Coping with External Stress

In many fields, e.g. biology, regional economics, management science, psychology, it is an important question how a system responds to stressors. Stressors are environmental conditions, external stimuli or events that cause stress to a system. They can be temporary shocks or permanent pressures on the system. A system is stressed when its normal functioning is disrupted. Open self-organizing and self-regulating systems achieve a state of *homeostasis*, which is a dynamic equilibrium (or steady state) in which the system maintains its functions. Originating in biology, where homeostasis means the optimal functioning of a living organism, the term can also be applied to social systems such as businesses and other organizations. Stress is the state of a system that deviates from homeostasis because external perturbations disrupt the regulatory processes. In biology, it is debated whether diversity can help systems cope with stressors. In the social sciences, including economics and management, much research aims to identify the determinants of organizational or systemic resilience, of which diversity is one (see Reinmoeller and van Baardwijk 2005; Martin-Breen and Anderies 2011; Duchek et al. 2020). As the terminology is sometimes ambiguous, it is helpful to define the terms stability, robustness, and resilience, which are sometimes used synonymously.

Stability (also called *engineering resilience*) means that a system returns to its old equilibrium after a disturbance. This meaning is consistent with the meaning of stability in dynamical systems discussed in Chap. 6. In applied contexts, stability can also refer to the rate at which a system returns to equilibrium. *Robustness* refers to the ability of a system to withstand external perturbations without undergoing major structural changes. Thus, the system continues to function in its current form. If the stress becomes too great, the system breaks down and ceases to function. *Resilience* (or *ecological resilience*) is the ability of a system to persist and continue functioning by adapting to the perturbation. Resilience implies a structural transformation with a movement to a different equilibrium, sometimes one that is better performing than the original one.

The model in Fig. 10.36 illustrates how a system (e.g., a business) is affected by external stressors and how it copes with them. Under normal operating conditions, the system produces some kind of performance that depends on its operating capacity. For example, a firm produces output and generates profits with its factors of production and available knowledge. The output generates resources, such as retained profits, which can be used to maintain and expand operating capacity. This feedback loop is goal-seeking because a deviation of actual performance from the target (the performance gap) leads to an adjustment of the resources devoted to operating capacity. External stressors create external stress that reduces performance. For example, cyberattacks can disrupt a company's normal operations if telecommunications systems or online sales platforms are not functioning due to an attack.

A system can respond to external stress in at least two ways. First, it can try to compensate for the stress. In the example of the cyberattack, a company might try to communicate with customers and suppliers by mail instead of electronic channels. If

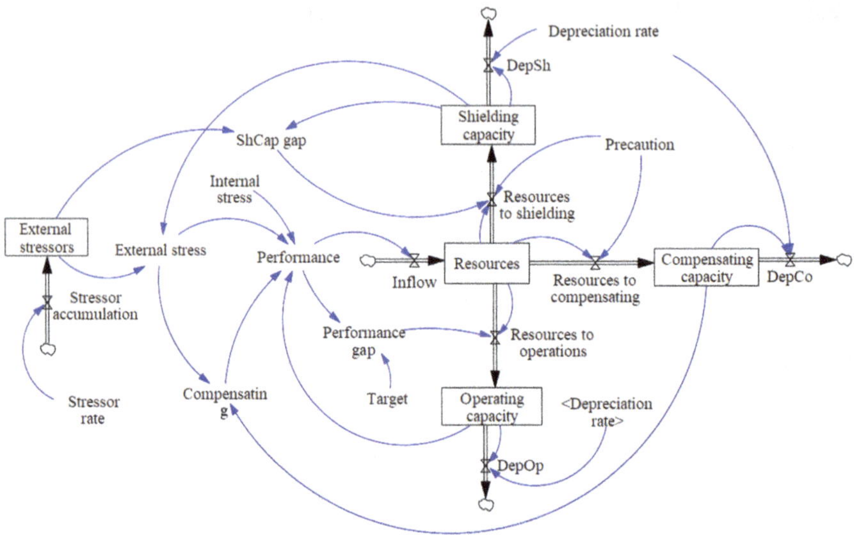

Fig. 10.36 System responses to external stressors. Source: Author

its own computer servers are affected, it could try to rent external server capacity. Whether and how much stress can be compensated for depends on the system's compensating capacity, which must be built up by dedicating resources to it. Second, a system may attempt to shield itself from the stressors by devoting resources to creating shielding capacity. IT security personnel and systems would create such shielding capacity against the stressors caused by cyberattacks. Adequate shielding capacity can reduce or even prevent external stressors. Shielding is a precautionary measure that attempts to deal with stress ex ante by avoiding it, whereas compensation deals with stress ex post, by reducing the impact of realized stress. Shielding capacity is built when there is a gap (ShCap gap) between the existing shielding capacity and the stock of external stressors. Ideally, the shielding capacity is large enough to neutralize all stressors so that no stress occurs. However, building such capacity requires anticipating potential future stressors and investing resources ex ante. The extent to which this is done depends on the degree of precaution of the system controller. The same is true of the compensating capacity that must be in place when the stress occurs. If stress occurs but there is no compensating capacity, the system has no way to relieve the stress in the short term.

Figure 10.36 also shows that there is a trade-off in the use of resources. Resources can be invested either in operational capacity, which directly increases performance, or in the capacity to cope with stress. The capacity to handle stress, either by shielding or compensating, determines the robustness or resilience of the system. If the stress permanently reduces the system's performance because the system cannot cope with the stress, the system's resources will be so depleted that the system cannot even maintain its operating capacity in the long run. In this case, the system breaks down and stops working.

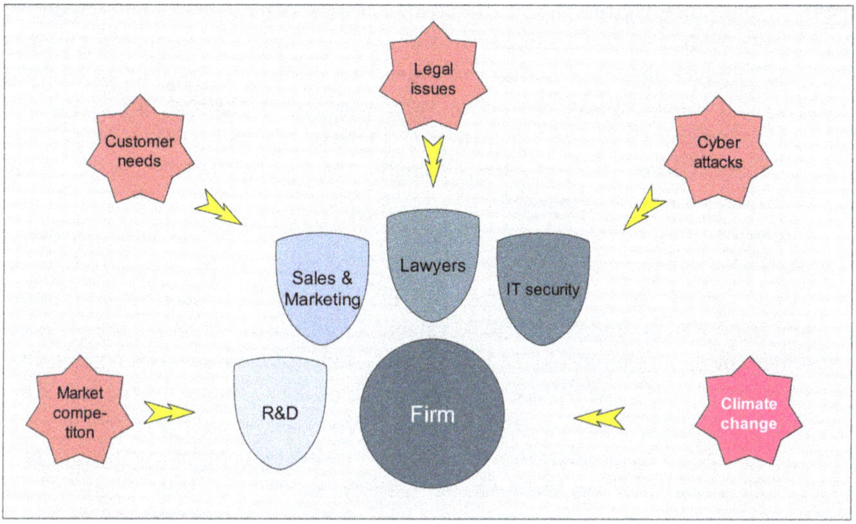

Fig. 10.37 Law of requisite variety. Source: Author

The model does not show how diversity contributes to robustness and resilience. Diversity comes in, because external stressors are diverse. According to W. Ross Ashby's *law of requisite variety* (Ashby 1956), the number of a system's responses should be equal to the number of disturbances that have distinct effects on performance. If a system has at least as many responses available as the number of disturbances to which it is exposed, the system has control over the environment or *autonomy*. If the number of available responses is too small, the system will experience stress that can ultimately cause its breakdown. Ashby's law of requisite variety is illustrated in Fig. 10.37.

In this example, the system, which is a firm, is exposed to five different types of disturbances or stressors: market competition, customer needs, legal issues, cyberattacks, and climate change. Market competition can cause stress because competitors come up with better or cheaper products. The company's appropriate response is innovation, which is carried out in the R&D department. Changing customer needs can lead to a decrease in sales, which is also a stress for the company. The task of the sales and marketing department is to identify changing customer needs and convince customers that the company's products meet their needs. The company has lawyers to deal with legal issues and an IT security department to fend off cyberattacks. What this system lacks is an adequate response to the stressor of climate change. Climate change could damage production facilities due to extreme weather conditions or lead to stranded assets. It could also affect the company's supply and product markets in countries that are severely affected by climate change. The challenge for this company is therefore to develop an appropriate response to climate change, or in other words, to adapt. This example illustrates the difference between robustness and resilience. A robust company does not have an adequate response to protect itself from the effects of climate change, but it can compensate for the effects, at least for a while, for example by rebuilding production facilities that have been destroyed by storms or floods. A resilient company will develop the necessary shielding capacity against climate change. Of course, this adaptation requires a transformation of the firm, e.g. in terms of its business model, the geographical scope of its operations, the nature of its capital, etc. The company must be flexible enough to evolve.

Another way of understanding the difference between robustness and resilience is to consider the *highly optimized tolerance* (HOT) framework proposed by Carlson and Doyle (1999, 2002). This approach emphasizes that there are important differences between complex physical systems, in which self-organization plays an important role, and engineered and evolved systems, which are characterized by structural complexity. The difference between (dynamic) complexity and structural complexity (or complicatedness) was already expressed in Sect. 2.8 of Chap. 2. Structural complexity is characterized by a diversity of component classes in a system and hierarchical organization. As Carlson and Doyle (2002) explain, this structural complexity does not necessarily increase the functionality of a system, but rather its robustness. They give the example of automobiles, of which old and new types have the same functionality but different levels of complexity. There may be old and new types both capable of carrying the same number of passengers at the same speed over the same distance. But new types are safer, more robust, and require less maintenance because they are equipped with sophisticated control systems for airbags, ride control, anti-lock brakes, anti-skid control, cruise control, satellite navigation, emergency notification, cabin temperature control, and automatic radio tuning. All of these systems are designed to make the car more resistant to accidents, but they add significant structural complexity. HOT systems achieve robustness through redundancy of parts to cope with component failure, feedback control, and configurations with safety margins. They are either designed to be robust by engineers or have evolved robustness through natural selection. The key point is that they can be very fragile to rare or unanticipated external conditions, design or manufacturing flaws, or an unintended, non-trivial rearrangement of the interconnection of internal parts. Modern cars with lots of IT can fail because of software problems in a line of code. Most organisms can cope well with organic substances in their environment, but they are highly sensitive to small amounts of heavy metals or other toxins that are not naturally present in their habitat. HOT systems are robust because they have been optimized to be so, either by engineers or by evolution. But they are not resilient because they cannot adapt themselves to novel external or internal stressors.

Bar-Yam (2004) and others have reinterpreted the law of requisite variety as a *law of requisite complexity*, which states that a system must be at least as complex as the environment it is trying to control. One way to understand this is to compare the complexity of the information in the environment to the ability of the system to process and interpret that information. To respond appropriately to disturbances, a system must be able to detect them and understand how they affect the system. For example, an organization without IT security specialists may observe that its IT systems are not functioning properly, but it may not be able to identify the problems as a result of a cyberattack. Similarly, a company that does not conduct market research may observe that sales are declining, but may not know why. If a system's information processing capability is too low, it will not be able to correctly interpret complex environmental information and choose the right responses.

In biology, complexity is commonly defined as functional separation and functional integration. This definition can also be applied to organizations. *Functional separation* means that some system elements or subsystems specialize in certain functions. Specialized elements can perform functions better than non-specialized (generalist) elements. Thus, greater functional separation (or specialization) is a prerequisite for higher system performance and information processing capability. However, functional separation alone is not sufficient for efficient functioning and high complexity. The different functions must also be integrated, i.e. they must be coordinated to work well together. How much coordination is needed depends on the task the system is responding to and how many elements are needed to perform that task.

Functional integration, i.e., the coordination of multiple system elements that are required to perform a specific task together, typically requires different levels or a hierarchy of control in an organization. It is the job of managers and administrators to control and coordinate the work of specialists. Coordination involves evaluating information processed by specialists, combining and integrating diverse information to make sense of the complex environment, choosing among different options for action, and sequencing actions. If an organization is to survive and thrive in a complex environment, it needs high functional complexity with extensive functional separation, but also high functional integration.

The *law of requisite hierarchy* states that "the weaker in average are the regulatory abilities and the larger the uncertainties, the more hierarchy is needed in the organization of regulation and control to attain the same result of regulation, if possible at all" (Aulin-Ahmavaara 1979, p. 262). This statement means that if a single regulator (i.e., a specialized functional unit) cannot deal with a disturbance alone, but several regulators can, a hierarchy is needed. Limited regulatory capacity and high uncertainty are consequences of environmental complexity, such that greater environmental complexity requires more hierarchy.

Autopoiesis is the ability of a (living) system to reproduce itself. It is another concept from biology that has found its way into cybernetics and general systems theory and has been applied to social organizations. A functioning firm also reproduces itself by hiring workers, purchasing inputs, generating revenues, and reinvesting profits. A firm also maintains and restructures its internal organization, which is measured in terms of information and complexity. According to Gershenson (2015), autopoiesis in a general sense can be understood as the relationship between the complexity of a system and the complexity of its environment. If a system's autopoiesis is greater than one, it has greater complexity than its environment, which gives the system autonomy from the environment. If the autopoiesis is less than one, the complexity of the environment is greater than the complexity of the system, which means that the environment dominates the dynamics of the system. In other words, the system is controlled by external forces.

Tainter (1995) and Heylighen (1999) suggest that complexity in biological and social systems tends to grow over time as a result of (co-)evolution. For Tainter, complexity is a result (or a means) of problem-solving, where a problem is defined as a discrepancy between a desired state and the actual state of a system. Since ever new problems arise, partly as a result of the unintended consequences of previous attempts to solve problems, complexity increases. Similarly, Heylighen argues that some systems and their environments coevolve. As a system increases its complexity in order to match or exceed the complexity of its environment, the environment, consisting of other systems, tends to adapt and increase its complexity as well. This self-reinforcing interaction (or positive feedback loop) of complex adaptive systems is called the *red queen hypothesis*,[6] which states that systems (or species) must constantly adapt and evolve just to survive due to coevolutionary pressure from competing species. Positive feedback can also explain the acceleration of complexity evolution discussed in Chap. 1 and shown in Table 8.4.

In contrast to Heylighen, who considers selection for simplicity (or decomplexification) rather unlikely, Tainter argues that social systems can collapse, leading to decomplexification, if their complexity becomes too great. He suggests that there are diminishing returns to complexity in problem-solving, as the simplest solutions are implemented first. At some point, the net benefits of complexity may diminish because complexity is costly in terms of energy, time, labor, money, or other resources. If the resources are not sufficient to sustain ever-increasing complexity, system collapse is inevitable, resulting in a decrease in complexity. Similarly, Saunders and Ho (1976) argue that evolution tends to increase the complexity rather than the fitness or organization of systems. However, changes in organization are important for the adaptability or evolvability of a system.

A similar theme is present in the literature on the robustness and long-term success of firms. There are many examples of large and once very successful firms failing because they are unable to adapt to new circumstances. Miller (1990) calls the phenomenon that very successful firms often decline and fail the *Icarus paradox*, after Icarus from Greek mythology. Icarus was able to fly with artificial wings made of wax. Being able to fly made him so giddy that he flew too high and the sun melted the wax on his wings, causing him to fall into the sea and drown. Miller argues that the very factors that lead to the initial success of firms, such as focused strategies, confident leadership, and galvanized corporate cultures, can eventually cause decline because they inhibit adaptation. The problem with failing firms is not so much that they are too complex, but that their organization is too rigid to adapt. Such firms have often developed a high degree of structural and functional complexity, with many specialized departments, which allows them to cope with known external stressors and to be highly efficient in normal operations. They are therefore highly resilient to

[6]The term alludes to the Red Queen in Lewis Carroll's *Through the Looking-Glass,* who explains to Alice that in Looking-Glass land she has to run all the time to keep in the same place.

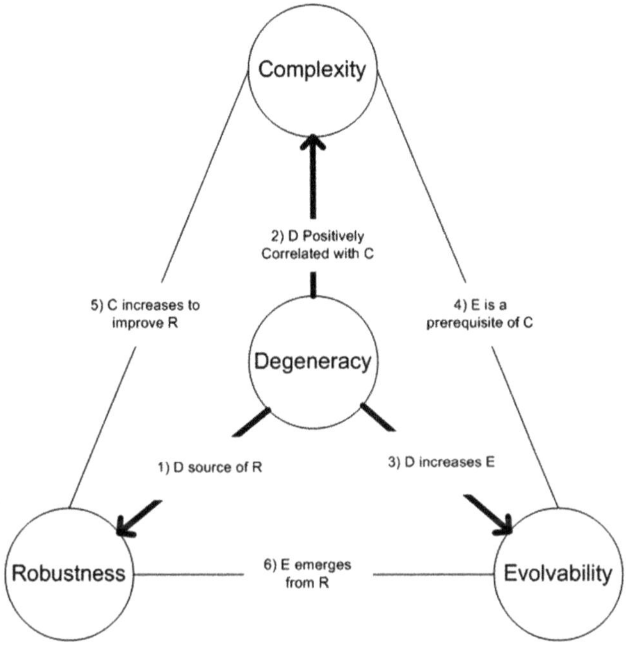

Fig. 10.38 Degeneracy as a link between complexity, robustness, and evolvability. Source: Whitacre (2010), licensed under CC-BY 2.0 (https://creativecommons.org/licenses/by/2.0/)

the conditions that existed when they became successful. Their success results from efficient use of resources and effective exploitation of market potential. The literature on organizational ambidexterity emphasizes that firms must be able to both exploit current opportunities and explore future ones. To survive, firms must identify future risks and opportunities, which implies that not all resources can be used to deal with current risks and opportunities. But identifying future risks and opportunities is not enough. Dealing with them requires the organization to evolve, which involves structural, functional, and behavioral changes.

Whitacre (2010) suggests that in biology, the apparent conflict between robustness and evolvability is resolved by degeneracy (see Fig. 10.38). *Degeneracy* means that structurally dissimilar components of a system can perform similar functions. In other words, a function can be realized in multiple ways, using different agents and different pathways. Degeneracy gives a system both redundancy and excess capacity. Components can perform certain functions under some conditions, but different functions under other conditions. Degeneracy is ubiquitous in biological systems. Whitacre and Bender (2010) argue that degeneracy plays an important role in evolution because it reconciles robustness and evolvability.

Figure 10.39 is an illustration of degeneracy and its benefits in an organizational context. The square grids represent two-dimensional knowledge spaces, such as the capabilities and abilities discussed in Sect. 10.6. In the square on the left, there are twelve specialists, represented by circles, each occupying a particular location in the

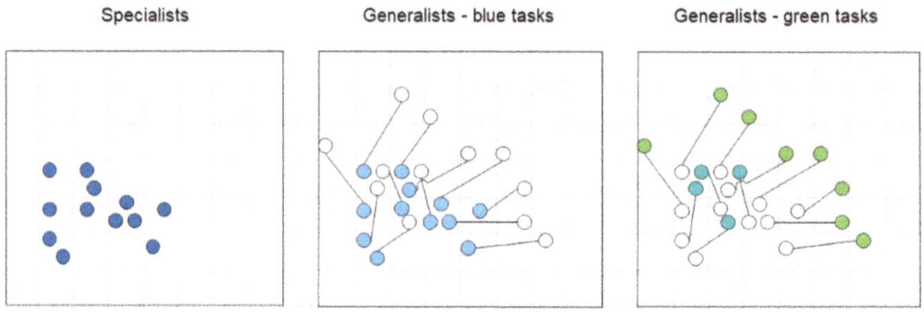

Fig. 10.39 Transformation in the knowledge space due to degeneracy. Source: Author

knowledge space. Some spaces are occupied by multiple agents, so there is a degree of redundancy in the system. If one of these specialists is unavailable, a substitute is available. The specialists are highly productive in their work, which is indicated by the dark color. There is no degeneracy in the system on the left, in contrast to the system represented by the square in the middle and on the right. Here, each agent can occupy two locations, represented by two circles connected by a line. These agents are generalists, not specialists, because they can perform different tasks. They are less productive than the specialists, indicated by the lighter shade of blue. In the middle panel, the generalists are active in the same places as the specialists on the left. Therefore, the system in the middle and the system on the left can perform the same functions, but with different performance.

The system on the left, on the other hand, is rigid. It cannot perform different functions because all its components are highly specialized. The system consisting of generalists can change its behavior when all or some of the generalist components switch to their other tasks in the knowledge space, as shown in the square on the right. The system has retained some tasks, shown in turquoise, but has replaced most of the old tasks with new ones further up and to the right in the knowledge space. Note that the retained tasks are now performed by different agents than before. Thus, a system with degeneracy can change its internal configuration without changing its components. It is more flexible than a system composed of highly specialized components, and therefore more adaptable.

Things to Remember

- Evolution describes the appearance of new entities in a system, for example new species in biology or new firms, products, and markets in an economy. In contrast to self-organization, evolution can explain structural change in a system in terms of its elements, not in terms of the relationships between them.
- Novelty is something that was unknown before a particular point in time and is therefore discovered or created at that point in time. Novelty may be universal or domain-specific. New ideas result from the recombination of existing thoughts.
- Technological inventions are also the result of recombining existing technology and knowledge. The history of inventions shows that it can take a long time from the initial idea to the final breakthrough that makes the invention practically

useful. Inventions typically require the solution of many practical problems or engineering tasks. But even working inventions may not become economically successful if market conditions are not favorable.

- The principles of evolution are inheritance, selection, and variation. Variation occurs through recombination and mutation. Fitness is the ability to survive and to reproduce. It is a measure of adaptedness to environmental conditions. Species that are well adapted thrive and reproduce, and those with low fitness sooner or later disappear.
- Genetic algorithms are metaheuristics designed to provide sufficiently good approximate solutions to optimization problems. They are computer algorithms inspired by natural evolution that are well-suited to search problems.
- A fitness landscape graphically represents fitness as a function of (two) genes. It can have local and global maxima determined by ecological conditions. When ecological conditions change, the fitness landscape can change as well. Genetic algorithms search the fitness landscape for maxima.
- Digital evolution can find surprising solutions to problems that outsmart the designers of the evolutionary algorithms. This observation suggests that evolutionary systems may be hard to control by mechanism design.
- Cultural evolution describes the transmission, selection, and variation of culture, understood as information capable of influencing the behavior of individuals that they acquire from other members of their species through teaching, imitation, and other forms of social transmission. Human cultural evolution interacts with, but is much faster than, genetic evolution. It has allowed humans to develop civilization and to evolve in a very different way from other primates. Cultural evolution can explain why altruism, which benefits the group but is a disadvantage to the individual, has evolved in human groups along with social institutions.
- More than 120 years ago, Thorstein Velben proposed that economics should be an evolutionary science. Joseph Schumpeter also saw the capitalist economy as an evolutionary system in which entrepreneurs create constant novelty through creative destruction. Evolutionary economics gained some popularity starting in the 1980s with the seminal work of Nelson and Winter. It is a sister discipline of complexity economics. The computational view of evolution regards both biological and economic evolution as special cases of evolutionary search algorithms. Economic evolution selects businesses that are combinations of physical technologies, social technologies, and business plans.
- A kene is a way of formally representing human knowledge. It is a collection of knowledge triples, where each triple is a knowledge unit consisting of a capability, an ability, and a level of expertise. Kenes can be recombined like genes by evolutionary algorithms. They can also be represented in knowledge maps.
- A cladogram is a classification scheme in the form of a tree-like representation of entities derived from their evolutionary history. It shows which entities share common ancestors. Cladograms have been used to classify technologies in economics. They can be used as benchmarks for evolutionary simulation models.
- Diversity is both a prerequisite and a result of evolution. We can distinguish between diversity within types, diversity across types, and diversity in

community composition. Diversity across types has the dimensions of variety, balance, and disparity. In economic systems, diversity has many benefits, such as risk diversification, smaller prediction errors, higher creativity, or hedging ignorance, but it can also be costly in terms of lower system performance due to less specialization. Diversity is also related to robustness and resilience. A system needs sufficient variety or complexity to cope with external stressors. Engineered and evolved systems often have highly optimized tolerance, making them very robust to expected or frequent disturbances, but fragile to rare and unexpected changes. Resilience requires that a system be able to adapt to changing external circumstances.

References

Allen PM, Strathern M, Baldwin JS (2007) Complexity and the limits to learning. J Evol Econ 17: 401–431. https://doi.org/10.1007/s00191-006-0051-3

Almécija S, Hammond AS, Thompson NE et al (2021) Fossil apes and human evolution. Science 372:eabb4363. https://doi.org/10.1126/science.abb4363

Arthur WB (2009) The nature of technology: what it is and how it evolves. Penguin

Ashby WR (1956) An introduction to cybernetics, 1st edn. Chapman & Hall Ltd, London

Aulin-Ahmavaara AY (1979) The law of requisite hierarchy. Kybernetes 8:259–266. https://doi.org/10.1108/eb005528

Baldwin JS, Allen PM, Winder B, Ridgway K (2003) Simulating the cladistic evolution of manufacturing. Innovations 5:144–156. https://doi.org/10.5172/impp.2003.5.2-3.144

Baldwin JS, Allen PM, Ridgway K, Winder B (2005a) Evolutionary systems: modelling organisational innovation. Innovations 7:389–401. https://doi.org/10.5172/impp.2005.7.4.389

Baldwin JS, Allen PM, Winder B, Ridgway K (2005b) Modelling manufacturing evolution: thoughts on sustainable industrial development. J Clean Prod 13:887–902. https://doi.org/10.1016/j.jclepro.2004.04.009

Bar-Yam Y (2004) Multiscale variety in complex systems. Complexity 9:37–45. https://doi.org/10.1002/cplx.20014

Beinhocker ED (2006) The origin of wealth: evolution, complexity, and the radical remaking of economics. Harvard Business Press, Boston

Beinhocker ED (2011) Evolution as computation: integrating self-organization with generalized Darwinism. J Inst Econ 7:393–423. https://doi.org/10.1017/S1744137411000257

Bowles S, Choi J-K, Hopfensitz A (2003) The co-evolution of individual behaviors and social institutions. J Theor Biol 223:135–147. https://doi.org/10.1016/S0022-5193(03)00060-2

Brockhaus FA (1769) Cugnots Dampfwagen, Paris 1769. K Dampfkessel, CC Dampfzylinder; stündlich 4 km. https://commons.wikimedia.org/w/index.php?curid=3170175. Accessed 15 May 2023

Carlson JM, Doyle J (1999) Highly optimized tolerance: a mechanism for power laws in designed systems. Phys Rev E 60:1412–1427. https://doi.org/10.1103/PhysRevE.60.1412

Carlson JM, Doyle J (2002) Complexity and robustness. Proc Natl Acad Sci 99:2538–2545. https://doi.org/10.1073/pnas.012582499

Coad A (2018) Firm age: a survey. J Evol Econ 28:13–43. https://doi.org/10.1007/s00191-016-0486-0

Crochet.david (2011) Musée de léonard de Vinci au clos lucé à amboise. https://commons.wikimedia.org/wiki/File:Amboise_clos_luc%C3%A9_inventinos_de_vinci_automobile.jpg?uselang=de. Accessed 15 May 2023

Csermely P (1999) Limits of scientific growth. Science 284:1621–1621. https://doi.org/10.1126/science.284.5420.1621f

Cully A, Clune J, Tarapore D, Mouret J-B (2015) Robots that can adapt like animals. Nature 521: 503–507. https://doi.org/10.1038/nature14422

Daepp MIG, Hamilton MJ, West GB, Bettencourt LMA (2015) The mortality of companies. J R Soc Interface 12:20150120. https://doi.org/10.1098/rsif.2015.0120

Doncieux S, Bredeche N, Mouret J-B, Eiben AE (2015) Evolutionary robotics: what, why, and where to. Front Robot AI 2:4. https://doi.org/10.3389/frobt.2015.00004

Dopfer K (2011) Evolution and complexity in economics revisited. Papers on Economics and Evolution No. 1102. urn:nbn:de:gbv:27–20110630–113058-2

Duchek S, Raetze S, Scheuch I (2020) The role of diversity in organizational resilience: a theoretical framework. Bus Res 13:387–423. https://doi.org/10.1007/s40685-019-0084-8

Epstein D (2019) Range: how generalists triumph in a specialized world. Riverhead Books, New York

Felton W (1803) London steam carriage, road locomotive by Trevithick and Vivian, demonstrated in London in 1803. https://commons.wikimedia.org/wiki/File:Trevithicks_Dampfwagen.jpg. Accessed 15 May 2023

Gershenson C (2015) Requisite variety, autopoiesis, and self-organization. Kybernetes 44:866–873. https://doi.org/10.1108/K-01-2015-0001

Gilbert N, Pyka A, Ahrweiler P (2001) Innovation networks - a simulation approach. J Artif Soc Soc Simul 4:1–8

Gilbert N, Ahrweiler P, Pyka A (2007) Learning in innovation networks: some simulation experiments. Phys A Statist Mech Appl 378:100–109. https://doi.org/10.1016/j.physa.2006.11.050

Guiso L, Sapienza P, Zingales L (2006) Does culture affect economic outcomes? J Econ Perspect 20:23–48. https://doi.org/10.1257/jep.20.2.23

Heylighen F (1999) The growth of structural and functional complexity during evolution. In: Heylighen F, Aerts D (eds.) The evolution of complexity. Kluwer Academic Publishers.

Hodgson GM (2019) Evolutionary economics: its nature and future. Cambridge University Press, Cambridge

Hodgson GM, Lamberg J-A (2018) The past and future of evolutionary economics: some reflections based on new bibliometric evidence. Evol Inst Econ Rev 15:167–187. https://doi.org/10.1007/s40844-016-0044-3

Holland J (1975) Adaptation in natural and artificial systems. University of Michigan Press, Ann Arbor

Holland JH (1992) Genetic algorithms. Sci Am 267:66–73

Kaplan H, Hill K, Cadeliña RV et al (1985) Food sharing among ache foragers: tests of explanatory hypotheses [and comments and reply]. Curr Anthropol 26:223–246. https://doi.org/10.1086/203251

Katoch S, Chauhan SS, Kumar V (2021) A review on genetic algorithm: past, present, and future. Multimed Tools Appl 80:8091–8126. https://doi.org/10.1007/s11042-020-10139-6

Kriegman S (2019) Why virtual creatures matter. Nat Mach Intell 1:492–492. https://doi.org/10.1038/s42256-019-0102-8

Lehman J, Clune J, Misevic D et al (2020) The surprising creativity of digital evolution: a collection of anecdotes from the evolutionary computation and artificial life research communities. Artif Life 26:274–306. https://doi.org/10.1162/artl_a_00319

Maheri A, Jalili S, Hosseinzadeh Y et al (2021) A comprehensive survey on cultural algorithms. Swarm Evol Comput 62:100846. https://doi.org/10.1016/j.swevo.2021.100846

Martin-Breen P, Anderies JM (2011) Resilience: a literature review. Institute of Development Studies Background Paper, Brighton. https://opendocs.ids.ac.uk/opendocs/handle/20.500.12413/3692

McCarthy I, Ridgway K, Leseure M, Fieller N (2000) Organisational diversity, evolution and cladistic classifications. Omega 28:77–95. https://doi.org/10.1016/S0305-0483(99)00030-4

Mendoza A de (2016) 1885 Benz. https://commons.wikimedia.org/wiki/File:1885Benz.jpg. Accessed 15 May 2023

Miller D (1990) The Icarus paradox: how exceptional companies bring about their own downfall. HarperCollins, New York

Miller R, Boeckle M, Jelbert SA et al (2019) Self-control in crows, parrots and nonhuman primates. WIREs Cogn Sci 10:e1504. https://doi.org/10.1002/wcs.1504

Mrabet Y (2009) Types of chromosomal mutations. https://commons.wikimedia.org/w/index.php?curid=8466919. Accessed 15 May 2023

Nelson RR, Winter SG (1982) An evolutionary theory of economic change. The Belknap Press of Harvard University, Cambridge, MA.

North M (2013) Novelty: a history of the new. University of Chicago Press, Chicago

Page SE (2010) Diversity and complexity. Princeton University Press, Princeton

Pennock RT (2007) Models, simulations, instantiations, and evidence: the case of digital evolution. J Exp Theor Artif Intell 19:29–42. https://doi.org/10.1080/09528130601116113

Prokopenko M, Boschetti F, Ryan AJ (2009) An information-theoretic primer on complexity, self-organization, and emergence. Complexity 15:11–28. https://doi.org/10.1002/cplx.20249

Rao CR (1982) Diversity and dissimilarity coefficients: a unified approach. Theor Popul Biol 21: 24–43. https://doi.org/10.1016/0040-5809(82)90004-1

Reinmoeller P, van Baardwijk N (2005) The link between diversity and resilience. MIT Sloan Manag Rev (July 1)

Reynolds RG (2018) Culture on the edge of chaos: cultural algorithms and the foundations of social intelligence. Springer

Richerson PJ, Boyd R (2005) Not by genes alone: how culture transformed human evolution. University of Chicago Press, Chicago

Rodrigues JF, Florea L, de Oliveira MCF et al (2021) Big data and machine learning for materials science. Discov Mater 1:12. https://doi.org/10.1007/s43939-021-00012-0

Salamon S (1984) Ethnic origin as explanation for local land ownership patterns. In: Schwarzweller HK (ed) Research in rural sociology and development: a research annual focus on agriculture. Jai Press Inc, Greenwich

Salamon S (1985) Ethnic communities and the structure of agriculture. Rural Sociol 50:323–340

Saunders PT, Ho MW (1976) On the increase in complexity in evolution. J Theor Biol 63:375–384. https://doi.org/10.1016/0022-5193(76)90040-0

Schumpeter JA (1911) Theorie der wirtschaftlichen Entwicklung: Eine Untersuchung über Unternehmergewinn, Kapital, Kredit, Zins und den Konjunkturzyklus. Duncker und Humblot, Leipzig

Schumpeter JA (2003) Capitalism, socialism and democracy. Routledge, London

Sims K (1994a) Evolving 3D morphology and behavior by competition. Artif Life 1:353–372. https://doi.org/10.1162/artl.1994.1.4.353

Sims K (1994b) Evolving virtual creatures. In: Proceedings of the 21st annual conference on computer graphics and interactive techniques. Association for computing machinery, New York, pp 15–22

Stirling A (2007) A general framework for analysing diversity in science, technology and society. J R Soc Interface 4:707–719. https://doi.org/10.1098/rsif.2007.0213

Tainter JA (1995) Sustainability of complex societies. Futures 27:397–407. https://doi.org/10.1016/0016-3287(95)00016-P

Veblen T (1898) Why is economics not an evolutionary science? Q J Econ 12:373–397. https://doi.org/10.2307/1882952

Weitzman ML (1992) On diversity. Q J Econ 107:363–405. https://doi.org/10.2307/2118476

Whitacre JM (2010) Degeneracy: a link between evolvability, robustness and complexity in biological systems. Theor Biol Med Model 7:6. https://doi.org/10.1186/1742-4682-7-6

Whitacre J, Bender A (2010) Degeneracy: a design principle for achieving robustness and evolvability. J Theor Biol 263:143–153. https://doi.org/10.1016/j.jtbi.2009.11.008

Witt U (2008) What is specific about evolutionary economics? J Evol Econ 18:547–575. https://doi.org/10.1007/s00191-008-0107-7

Witt U (2009) Propositions about novelty. J Econ Behav Organ 70:311–320. https://doi.org/10.1016/j.jebo.2009.01.008

Woodcroft (1876) Aeolipile illustration. https://commons.wikimedia.org/wiki/File:Aeolipile_illustration.png. Accessed 15 May 2023

Wright S (1932) The roles of mutation, inbreeding, crossbreeding, and selection in evolution. In: Proceedings of the sixth international congress of genetics, vol 1, pp 356–366

History and Path Dependence

11

Contents

11.1 Introduction 582
11.2 Historical and Ahistorical Economics 585
11.2.1 Economic Thinking vs. Historical Thinking 585
11.2.2 The Arrow of Time 591
11.2.3 Historical Economics 594
11.3 Path Dependence 596
11.3.1 Negative Definition of Path Dependence and Ergodicity 597
11.3.2 Positive Definition of Path Dependence 600
11.3.3 Reasons for Path Dependence 601
11.4 Lock-in 610
11.4.1 Some Examples of Lock-in 611
11.4.2 Responses to the Liebowitz–Margolis Critique 614
11.4.3 Types and Causes of Systemic Lock-in 616
11.5 Path Formation and Path Change 619
11.5.1 Critical Junctures 619
11.5.2 A Framework for Path Formation 621
11.5.3 Punctuated Equilibrium and Path Changes 622
11.6 The History of the Automobile in the Twentieth Century 627
11.6.1 Was the Gasoline-Fueled ICE a Good Choice? 627
11.6.2 Decisive Factors for the Choice of the ICE 629
11.6.3 Positive Feedback and Path Stabilization 632
11.7 Modeling Future Transitions of the Automobile 633
11.7.1 Model 634
11.7.2 Application to Sustainable Road Transport 636
References 641

Abstract

This chapter differs from the previous chapters in that it deals with the more qualitative approach of economic history. Complexity economists are convinced that history matters, which means that the economy does not always converge to the same equilibrium regardless of initial conditions. The chapter argues that

M. Roos, *Principles of Complexity Economics*, Classroom Companion: Economics,
https://doi.org/10.1007/978-3-031-51436-4_11

historians have a very different way of thinking about the world than economists. Historical economics, which is related to complexity economics, applies this way of thinking to economics. The evolution of the economy is often path dependent, so that small events can lead the economy to one of several equilibria. If this is true, attention to historical detail is important in explaining economic phenomena observed in the present. The chapter also introduces the concepts of lock-in, critical junctures, and punctuated equilibrium. It is argued that inefficient lock-in is more common than neoclassical economists would like to believe. These concepts are illustrated with a narrative account of the history of the automobile. Finally, the chapter shows how some of these concepts can be formally modeled.

Keywords

Critical juncture · Lock-in · Punctuated equilibrium · QWERTY · Transition

Guiding Questions

- *What does it mean to say that history matters in economics?*
- *How do the approaches of neoclassical economics and history differ?*
- *What is teleological thinking and what is genealogical thinking?*
- *What is the arrow of time?*
- *How can we define path dependence?*
- *What are reasons for path dependence?*
- *Is lock-in to an inefficient path likely or not?*
- *What causes lock-in?*
- *What are critical junctures and what is a punctuated equilibrium?*
- *How do paths form and change?*
- *What were critical factors in the history of the automobile in the early twentieth century?*
- *How can we formally model transitions from one path to another?*

11.1 Introduction

History matters in complexity economics. Nonlinearity, positive feedback, self-organization, diachronic emergence and evolution all imply that a particular past created a particular present. If the past had been different, the present state of a complex system would be different today. This is what we mean when we say that history matters.

Everyday intuition and experience readily accept that history matters. We experience our lives as a sequence of small or large events and decisions that have consequences. A familiar example might be the breakup of a friendship after an argument. Two friends might argue about what to do on a Friday night. They may both have had a bad day, so the argument becomes unfair and insults are exchanged. Both might say things that should not be said and that cannot be taken back. The next day, each friend feels hurt and ashamed. Since no one takes the initiative to apologize, the friendship ends. There may have been many arguments before, none of which was a big problem, but this one fight escalated and caused the friendship to break up. The important point is that a single, clearly identifiable event can be attributed as the cause of later events. If one of the friends had cancelled the meeting because of the bad day, the argument would not have happened and the friendship would have continued. The idea that single events—even small ones—matter and can have big effects is expressed in the popular nursery rhyme *For Want of a Nail*:

> *For want of a nail the shoe was lost.*
> *For want of a shoe the horse was lost.*
> *For want of a horse the rider was lost.*
> *For want of a rider the message was lost.*
> *For want of a message the battle was lost.*
> *For want of a battle the kingdom was lost.*
> *And all for the want of a horseshoe nail.*

These examples may sound trivial, because the attribution of causality to individual events seems obvious. However, it is worth illustrating how we use to think in everyday life in order to show the contrast with neoclassical economics, which is ahistorical. *Ahistorical* means that history in the sense of a succession of past events does not play a role in neoclassical mainstream economics. Dynamic models in economics rely on a concept of *time*, but this time is abstract or theoretical and not linked to history. Paul David (2001, p. 38) notes a neoclassical *déformation professionelle* with respect to history:

> *For many economists, their own sunk costs in mastering that discipline have produced a facility for reasoning that suppresses natural, human intuitions about historical causation. They thus have a 'learned incapacity' (in Thorstein Veblen's apt phrase) to see how historical events could exert a causal influence upon subsequent outcomes that would be economically important.*

In many papers, Paul David has argued for *historical economics*, i.e., an economics that takes history seriously, which has provoked resistance from some mainstream economists (e.g., Liebowitz and Margolis 1995). Whether or not history matters in economics makes a big difference in terms of methodology, economic explanations, predictions, and policy recommendations. This issue is therefore another fundamental difference between neoclassical economics and other schools of thought. As argued above, complexity economics is highly compatible with David's view of historical economics. Key concepts such as path dependence, lock-in, irreversibility, and contingency fit very naturally into a complexity view of the economy. Another recurring theme in historical economics is that sequencing and timing matter. The

Fig. 11.1 Two valleys separated by a mountain. Source: Author

same event can have different effects at different times because the structure of the economy can be different. From a neoclassical perspective, the influence of timing is troubling because it implies that the effects of economic policy can vary over time. Recent empirical work on the multipliers of fiscal policy confirms such a view (Gechert and Rannenberg 2018). Even more unsettling for neoclassical economists is the view that the historical evolution of the economy may follow different paths rather than always converging to the same equilibrium, and that we cannot predict the path, its end state, or its welfare properties. In the historical view, a path may well be inefficient and is more likely to be the result of historical accidents than the outcome of maximizing a welfare function.

Section 11.2 explains the difference between historical and ahistorical approaches to economics in more detail and introduces the concept of the arrow of time. We also discuss the difference between economics in time and economics in historical time.

The claim that history matters can be translated into the statement that there is path dependence in the economy. Section 11.3 defines and formalizes path dependence, for which the concept of ergodicity is helpful. Intuitively, path dependence is like choosing between two valleys separated by a mountain, as shown in Fig. 11.1. The path we have been traveling along branches out in front of us. We can choose either the path in the left valley or the path in the right valley without knowing where they will lead us. Shortly after choosing one path, we can still change to the other path by climbing the hill between the valleys (we assume that we cannot or do not want to go back). But the mountain gets higher and higher the further we go, so it becomes more and more difficult to change the valley by climbing over the mountain. So we can get stuck in the valley we have chosen. W. Brian Arthur (1994) popularized the idea of path dependence in the economy, especially with regard to technology.

In Sect. 11.4, we look at and discuss some examples of lock-in, such as the familiar QWERTY layout of computer keyboards. Lock-in is often associated with inefficiency and market failure, which is difficult for some economists to accept. We summarize the main arguments for and against inefficient lock-in and present a number of types and causes of lock-in.

Section 11.5 presents a process view of path formation and path change. There is a rich literature in political science on the dynamics of path dependence. We introduce the concepts of critical junctures and punctuated equilibrium from that literature and show why they are useful in economics.

The history of the automobile in the twentieth century, already the subject of Chap. 5, is discussed in more detail in Sect. 11.6. At the beginning of the twentieth century, the internal combustion engine became the dominant technology and displaced available alternatives, so that a certain path was chosen and lock-in occurred. This example is ideal for discussing the issue of inefficient lock-in, the role of historical accidents and contingency, and the mechanisms that stabilize a path.

While Sect. 11.6 follows the narrative style of historical economics, Section 11.7 presents a computer simulation model based on transition theory that simulates a possible future change in paths away from the gasoline-fueled internal combustion engine toward more sustainable modes of road transportation.

11.2 Historical and Ahistorical Economics

Traditionally, the academic discipline of history counts as a humanity, while economics considers itself a (social) science. Both the goals and the methods of the humanities and the sciences are different. The call for historical economics thus suggests a major reorientation of the field.

11.2.1 Economic Thinking vs. Historical Thinking

Economics is also called economics science. Like the natural sciences, economics seeks to establish economic laws that have general validity and applicability. Although there may be conditions, under which the laws apply, a proposition must be sufficiently general to qualify as a law. In economics, this means that, in the extreme, economic laws should apply in all countries and at all times. Economics textbooks are full of economic laws, e.g. the law of demand, the law of supply and demand, the law of one price, Okun's law, Say's law, the law of diminishing returns, or Gossen's laws. Analogous to the fundamental theorems of thermodynamics or the fundamental theorems in mathematics, economics knows the fundamental theorems of welfare economics or the fundamental theorems of asset pricing. There are other

[1] See https://mises.org/wire/ten-fundamental-laws-economics Accessed 02 November 2023.

famous propositions that are called theorems instead of laws, e.g. the Coase theorem, the Modigliani–Miller theorem, the Stolper–Samuelson theorem, or the Heckscher–Ohlin theorem. In mathematics, *theorems* are statements that can be proved deductively by logical arguments from axioms and previously proved theorems. Some economists, such as the Austrian economist Antony Mueller argue that there are fundamental economic laws that cannot be changed and that should be obeyed by reasonable policy makers. The tenth law in his list of ten fundamental economic laws[1] is:

> *10. All genuine laws of economics are logical laws*
> *Economic laws are synthetic a priori reasoning. One cannot falsify such laws empirically because they are true in themselves. As such, the fundamental economic laws do not require empirical verification. Reference to empirical facts serve merely as illustrative examples, they are not statements of principles. One can ignore and violate the fundamental laws of economics but one cannot change them. Those societies fare best where people and government recognize and respect these fundamental economic laws and use them to their advantage.*

Other economists, such as Nobel laureate Lawrence Klein, are a bit more cautious. Klein states:

> *There <u>are</u> laws of economics. The degree of uncertainty shown by the noise component is not always appreciated by the outsider. . . . It is not easy to establish laws of economics, and it is especially dangerous to draw strong conclusions or base important decisions of apparent correlations, especially in simple bivariate relationships that are discerned in small samples or other sources of limited evidence. Many of these apparent laws break down on embarassing* occasions. (Klein 1983, p. 44/45)

As an econometrician and empirical macroeconomist, Klein has empirical laws rather than logical laws in mind. Following Alfred Marshall, he considers economic laws to be "*tendencies* rather than as precise causal statements" (p. 24). He also agrees with Marshall's distinction between inexact laws, e.g., in meteorology, seismology, and economics, and exact ones, as in astronomy. Despite these differences, most mainstream economists probably agree that there are some law-like relationships in the economy that can be formulated in economic models and estimated with econometric methods. The typical theory-driven training of neoclassical economists often begins with theoretical concepts and "core truths of economics" (see Samuelson and Nordhaus 2010, Preface and Chap. 1) or "principles of economics" (Mankiw 2016).

Historians work in a very different way. Historical reasoning always begins with reading sources and acquiring knowledge about historical facts and events. The concept of *events* is central to history:

> *by analyzing causes and consequences we better understand historical events such as the granting of city rights by a count in the Middle Ages or opening of the checkpoints in the Berlin Wall by the East German authorities in November 1989. Reasoning about these events contributes to the development of historical understanding and the appropriation of*

> *knowledge that can be used to interpret new information about the past, both inside and outside of school.* (van Boxtel and van Drie 2018, p. 149).

Historical reasoning can be defined as a process in which central facts (about events and structures) and concepts are arranged to build an interpretative historical case, which then requires analysis, synthesis, hypothesis generation, and interpretation (van Boxtel and van Drie 2018, p. 151). The outcome of historical reasoning is history:

> *As historians pore through documents and assess their status, they simultaneously begin to build theories and models about the past they are investigating. Once they have exhausted the archive of sources, they impose a theory of events on the evidence, attempting to craft an explanation that sticks as close as possible to a preponderance of that evidence. Because holes can exist in the evidence trails, historians need to fill in those holes. The result is an account that explains the past—a 'history' of the events. Typically, histories are written in narrative form using all the rhetorical strategies common to that genre.* (VanSledright 2004, p. 231).

If history is an account that explains past events, it is important to define what an event is. An *event* can be defined as something that happens or as a noteworthy or important happening.[2] Of course, whether something is noteworthy or important is a subjective interpretation that requires theorizing similar to what was said about stylized facts in Chap. 9. There are philosophical subtleties in the precise definition of events (Schneider 2023), but a general property is that they are usually understood to be particular happenings, occurrences, or changes that cannot be repeated at different times. In other words, events occur at a particular place and time and are not universal classes of occurrences. This is why history never repeats itself, as many historians would argue.

Andrews and Burke (2007) have developed an approach to teaching history that describes the shared foundations of the discipline and which they call the *five C's of historical thinking*: change over time, context, causality, contingency, and complexity. It is obvious that history is about change over time, but it also deals with continuity in some aspects of life. *Context* refers to the embeddedness of historical sources in the values, attitudes, and beliefs of their time, which were often quite different from the way we think. A historical text is a product of its time and is influenced by relevant events or conditions that motivated the author to write it. *Causation* is a crucial element of historical arguments to explain past changes. Van Lunteren (2019) reports that since the cultural turn in the humanities and social sciences, many historians have eschewed causal explanations, arguing that historians should focus on *verstehen* (understanding) rather than *erklären* (explaining). Nevertheless, van Lunteren argues that causal explanation is possible and reasonable. He emphasizes that historical causality does not imply inevitability, but rather simply requires "forging meaningful connections between prior and later events" (van

---

[2] https://www.merriam-webster.com/dictionary/event Accessed 02 November 2023.

Table 11.1 Differences between economics and history

Neoclassical economics	History
Equilibrium	Change
Teleological thinking	Genealogical thinking
Continuous locomotion	Individual events
Determinacy	Contingency
Stylized facts	Historical details

Lunteren 2019, p. 323). Because historians cannot experimentally prove causality, van Boxtel and van Drie (2018, p. 150) state that "criteria that are used to assess the quality of historical explanation include coherence, complexity of the explanation, clarity of argumentation, and the extent to which the explanation draws on historical facts." *Contingency* means that any historical outcome depends on a number of prior conditions, which in turn depend on even more antecedent conditions, and so on. For Andrews and Burke (2007), "the core insight of contingency is that the world is a magnificently interconnected place. Change a single prior condition, and any historical outcome could have turned out differently." Contingency implies that individuals and their actions shape the course of human events. History might have been different, if Karl Marx had immigrated to the USA instead of France, where he met Friedrich Engels. Adolf Hitler survived some 40 actual or planned assassination attempts. World War II might not have happened if one of the six attempts to kill him before the outbreak of the war had succeeded. For Andrews and Burke, *complexity* has a moral, an epistemological, and a causal dimension, resulting in a messy world that we cannot know directly.

It should be clear by now that (neoclassical) economics and history differ in the way they think about the world. Table 11.1 summarizes some key differences. In neoclassical economics, equilibrium is the normal state of the world, which is the absence of change. History, on the other hand, focuses on change in the sense of a permanent disequilibrium. Of course, neoclassical economics also considers deviations from equilibrium due to shocks or changes in the equilibrium, but equilibrium is always the point of reference. Similarly, history also knows continuity, but change is the focus of interest.

David (1993, 1994, 2001) characterizes mainstream economic thinking as teleological, whereas historical reasoning is genealogical. *Teleological reasoning* (from Greek τέλος, telos = "end" or "goal" and λόγος, logos = "explanation" or "reason") explains something in terms of its end, goal, or purpose. The idea that the economy is attracted to a general equilibrium is teleological. So is the use of Nash equilibria in game theory. In Chap. 4, we discussed the Ramsey–Cass–Koopmans model of economic growth, which has a saddle path leading to a steady state with positive levels of capital and consumption. For a given initial level of the capital stock, the steady state is reached only if the representative consumer chooses the right level of consumption on the saddle path. The model predicts that the representative consumer will do this such that the economy converges to the steady state. The rationale for this prediction is the assumption of utility maximization by the consumer. The saddle path is the path that maximizes utility and satisfies the transversality condition. A similar reasoning applies to the general neoclassical presumption that the outcomes of market competition are efficient due to the maximizing behavior of market participants. Teleological reasoning is also called *functionalist thinking*, which explains the existence of something in terms of the function it serves. For instance, New Institutional Economics explains the existence of certain institutions by their property of reducing transaction costs. The argument is: rational agents have invented a certain institution in order to reduce transaction costs. The institution is therefore a rational or efficient solution to an economic problem.

Genealogical reasoning (from Greek γενεαλογία, genealogía = "the making of a pedigree") explains current events or states of the world as consequences of earlier states or events. The result is a supposedly causal sequence of events from the starting point to the present. Of course, one can ask what the appropriate starting point should be. This kind of reasoning is subject to an infinite regress, because any chosen starting point of an explanation must be the consequence of even earlier events. The choice of where to start a genealogical explanation is a matter of analytical convenience. Explanations that ignore the genealogy of events are often synchronic, that is, they explain a present state of the world in terms of other contemporaneous states. This is simply a shortcut, because it basically sets the starting point of the explanation at the present. But all present states have a history and a process by which they came to be. Synchronic explanations may be convenient, but they are incomplete.

Relatedly, it is natural for economists to think of change as "continuous locomotion" (David 2001) that can be expressed in differential equations like those of the Ramsey–Cass–Koopmans model. For many, mathematics, and especially calculus, is the language of science or even "the language God talks" as the physicist Richard Feynman quipped (Strogatz 2019). Continuous locomotion in economics is thus a sign of economics' ambitions to be a science and its orientation toward physics. History reasons in terms of discrete and clearly identifiable events. Teleological reasoning and economic laws imply a deterministic worldview, in which certain dynamics, such as convergence to a unique equilibrium, are necessary. Contingency, in contrast, allows that the course of history could have been different and that the future is open. Because we know only one past, we perceive it as a necessary and linear evolution, but contingency says that there were many points at which history could have taken a different course as shown in Fig. 11.2. The green branches indicate counterfactual histories that we do not know. History can be thought of as a branching process similar to speciation in biological evolution, except that there is only one branch of the cladogram. Alternate or *counterfactual history* hypothetically explores what might have happened if history had taken a different turn at the so-called *points of divergence* or historical turning points. There are collections of counterfactual histories told by historians, who ask, for instance, what might have happened, if the Spanish Armada had conquered England in 1588, if Napoleon had

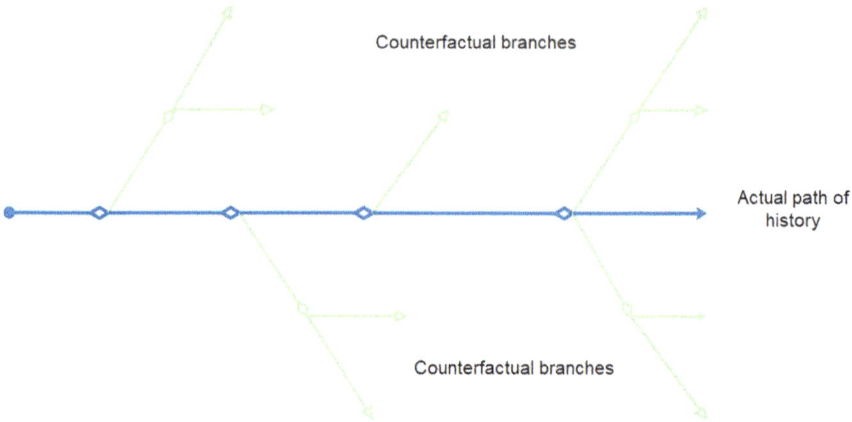

Fig. 11.2 Branching. Source: Author

invaded North America, if Lenin had not reached St. Petersburg in 1917, or if D Day had failed in 1944 (Cowley 1999, 2001).

Finally, economists try to eliminate all irrelevant details in the evidence in order to obtain stylized facts and to identify the relevant mechanisms or laws. For historians, details matter. Lane (2006) describes how the (micro-)historian Carlo Ginzburg thinks about complexity and hierarchy, in contrast to scientists like John Holland or Phil Anderson. Ginzburg's method is called the *conjectural paradigm*, which means that signs or clues from individual cases are interpreted using experience in order to discover "coherence, the hidden unity, of people making history" (Lane 2006, p. 33). The assumption is that there is coherence in history, but that it is not directly observable:

> *We can characterize and understand complexity, from this point of view, only after a thorough exploration of all the details, however irrelevant they might appear a priori, about all the entities at all ontological levels of an individual complex system.* (Lane 2006, p. 33)

Ginzburg compares this approach to that of an ancestral hunter, who

> *learned to reconstruct the shapes and movements of his invisible prey from tracks on the ground, broken branches, excrement, tufts of hair, entangled feathers, stagnating odors. He learned to sniff out, record, interpret, and classify such infinitesimal traces as trails of spittle.* (Ginzburg 1989, p. 102)

The key point is that we cannot know which details are relevant and which are irrelevant until we have considered all available details.

11.2.2 The Arrow of Time

The physicist Arthur Eddington coined the term *arrow of time* to describe the concept that time has a direction and is therefore asymmetric. Time moves in one direction, from the past to the present to the future, and does not move backward. The second law of thermodynamics, which states that entropy does not decrease in isolated systems, defines the *thermodynamic arrow of time*. Many laws of physics are T-symmetric, i.e. they also hold when time is reversed. However, this is not the case for many macroscopic phenomena. If we see two pictures of a glass before and after it has fallen to the ground, we immediately know which one was taken earlier in time. Because of entropy, a broken glass on the ground will never reassemble by itself and move up from the ground. Similarly, we can often easily tell whether a video of natural processes is running forward or backward, such as a sugar cube dissolving in a cup of tea, or the growth and decay of a flower. Entropy gives time a direction.

In general, neoclassical economic models are T-symmetric. Of course, dynamical models have a time structure that cannot be reversed, i.e. in these models $t - 1$ precedes t, which is followed by $t + 1$. But this is not what we mean by saying that the models are T-symmetric. They are symmetric in time in the sense that there is nothing in these models that prevents economic processes from running in two directions. In real business cycle models and DSGE models, all shocks can be positive and negative, including technology shocks. In an RBC model, positive and negative technology shocks give rise to symmetric adjustment dynamics of an RBC model, represented by impulse-response functions. In the steady state of the Ramsey–Cass–Koopmans model that was presented in Chap. 4, growth can be both positive and negative. It is counterfactual that the growth rates of population and the effectiveness of labor are negative ($n < 0$, $g < 0$), but technically the model works as long as the economic variables remain positive.

Is there something similar to the thermodynamic arrow of time in social systems and especially in the economy? First, we have to note that the economy is subject to the laws of physics, as discussed in Chap. 8, so we should expect the thermodynamic arrow of time to hold for the economy as well. However, we also saw in Chap. 8 that the economy is an open system far from thermodynamic equilibrium. Self-organizing systems away from thermodynamic equilibrium reduce their internal entropy when free energy is available. These systems build dissipative structures by exchanging matter and especially energy with the environment. A dissipative structure is thus the result of a balance between the tendency to increase entropy and the countervailing energy that keeps the structure away from thermodynamic equilibrium. Figure 11.3 illustrates this idea. The low entropy of the balls in the top panel can be maintained only as long as there is a force pushing against the orange board that keeps the balls in their triangular arrangement. If the energy holding the board in

[3]They replace "ecosystems" in the original text by "economic systems" and "rules."

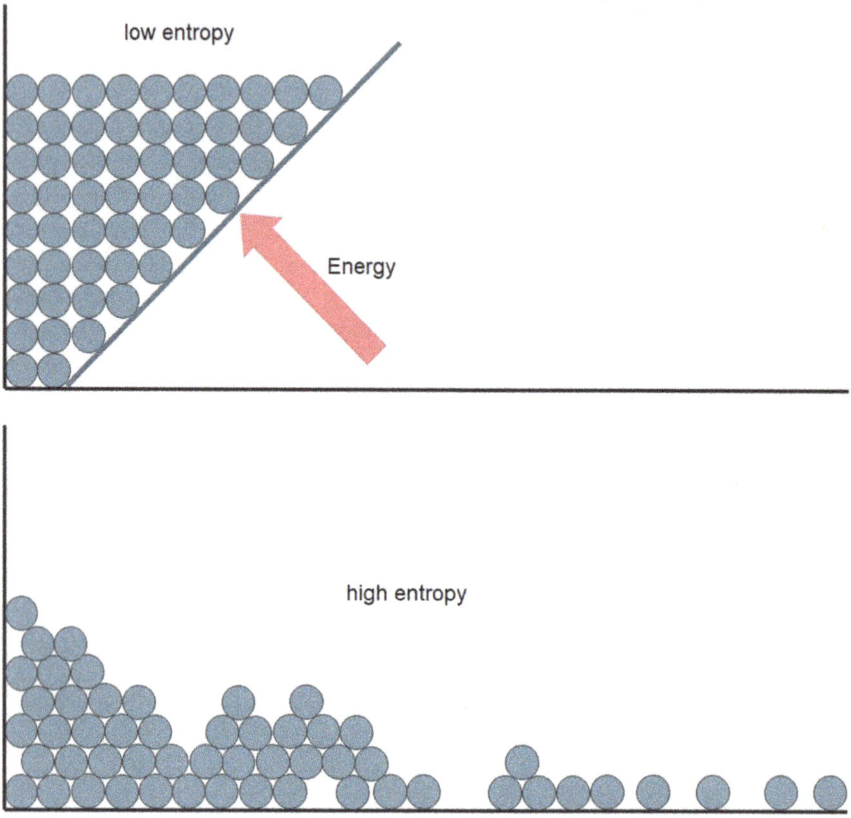

Fig. 11.3 Dissipative structure requiring energy. Source: Author

place is removed, the balls will fall and spread out on the floor, increasing the entropy.

Therefore, we can interpret the accumulation of dissipative structure as an economic arrow of time. But what does this mean? Many economists subscribe to the notion of economic progress, which is associated with economic growth and development. Over time, the possibilities of production and consumption have expanded. There have been technological advances and increasing globalization, allowing for more trade and international division of labor. The expansion of markets and economic and political freedom is also associated with growth and development. Could all these phenomena be related to thermodynamics and the theory of dissipative structures?

Raine et al. (2006) offer such an interpretation. They argue that it is a well-established result in modern evolutionary economics that the evolution of economic systems is a process of increasing structural complexity due to the production of new knowledge. Modifying[3] Schneider and Kay's (1994) reformulation of the relationship between the entropy law and the evolution of complex systems, they argue that

> *as **economic systems** grow and develop, they should increase their total dissipation, develop more complex structures with more energy flow, increase their cycling activity, develop greater diversity and generate more hierarchic levels, all to abet energy degradation. **Rules** which survive in economic systems are those that funnel energy into their own production and reproduction and contribute to autocatalytic processes which increase the total dissipation of the system . . . We believe that our thermodynamic paradigm makes it possible for the study of **economic systems** to be developed from a descriptive science into a predictive science founded on the most basic principles of physics.* (Raine et al. 2006, p. 356)

Dissipative systems need energy or energy gradients for system maintenance and structural development. Unlike simple physical and chemical systems, biological and economic systems can alter their local environments to exploit energy gradients. Socio-economic systems seek and use new knowledge to find new ways to transform energy. This quest for energy transformation through new knowledge can be seen as the ultimate engine of economic growth and development. As a result, economic systems expand their structural complexity (structure of interactions), their cyclical activity (habits, routines, competences, and institutions), and their hierarchical depth (organization and modular composition). Technological structures provide the physical basis for the transformation of energy. Organizational rules achieve the coordination of specialized system elements. Through these structures, economic systems can harness the materials and energy they need to sustain themselves, otherwise the systems would decay due to the law of entropy. Economic growth results from the coevolution of knowledge and the physical capital needed to transform energy, leading to greater complexity. More complex structures are favored by evolution because they can utilize free energy better than simpler structures. Therefore, Raine et al. (2006) argue that economic systems do not reach growth limits as easily as ecological systems because they constantly create new knowledge.

In short, we can speak of an economic arrow of time that consists in the ever-increasing complexity of the economy in various dimensions. This increase in complexity requires a growing inflow of free energy, but at the same time makes it possible to exploit new sources of energy. It follows from the second law of thermodynamics, however, that complexity will stagnate or decrease again if the influx of energy into the economy stops. The model of the collapse of Mayan society presented in Chap. 7 showed this. Note that the increase in complexity does not necessarily mean that there is an increase in overall well-being or economic efficiency. As discussed in Chap. 10, evolution seems to maximize complexity, but not necessarily fitness. Therefore, the view presented here does not support the notion of a Panglossian world, i.e., that the present world is the best of all conceivable worlds, reflecting an overall maximum of utility and/or profit.

11.2.3 Historical Economics

The Post-Keynesian Cambridge economist Joan Robinson criticized neoclassical economics for many reasons, but also for how it treats time (see Turk 2010 for an overview). She contrasted the *logical time* of abstract economic models, which is simply a measure of duration, with the *historical time* of human experience and the vagaries of economic activities. Robinson criticized the use of physical models in economics that have no arrow of time such that temporal changes are reversible. Moreover, abstract physical models place economics outside of human experience and historical context. Context is important, because it determines how people make sense of their world, what they expect, and thus how they behave.

Historical economics that responds to the Robinson critique should therefore be *economics in time*, but also *in historical time*. "In time" means that economic models should have an arrow of time with a clear differentiation between the past, the present, and the future and the irreversibility of time. This is achieved by introducing path dependence into economic models, which will be discussed in the following section.

Economics "in historical time" refers to the consideration of the historical context, which includes worldviews, values, roles, interpretations, norms, institutions, motives, interests, and behaviors. To illustrate what this means, two quotations are helpful. The credo of Alfred Krupp, the German steel manufacturer and inventor in the mid-nineteenth century, was: "The purpose of work should be for the common good, then work brings blessings, then work is prayer." Chinese entrepreneur Jack Ma, who founded the technology company Alibaba, once said: "My job is making money, helping other people make money. I am spending money, trying to make sure more people get rich, because you cannot spent a lot of money, right? So my job is spending money, helping others." How can we interpret these two statements from two very different businessmen in two different countries in two different centuries? And how did the values and attitudes expressed in these quotes influence the behavior of the two men and their companies? Part of the necessary context is that Alfred Krupp's company was the largest of arms manufacturer of the era, earning Krupp the nickname Cannon King. He had close ties to the King of Prussia, but refused the title of nobility when it was offered to him. He introduced health insurance, social services, and built housing for his workers, but he tightly controlled his workers and demanded an oath of loyalty and obedience. Jack Ma, on the other hand, is not only the founder of Alibaba, but also of the philanthropic Jack Ma Foundation, which earned him a place on Forbes' list of Asia's 2019 Heroes of Philanthropy. Nevertheless, he is a proponent of the Chinese 996-hour workweek: 9 am to 9 pm, 6 days a week. In 2020, he disappeared from public view after criticizing the Chinese government. True historical analysis requires reading many more statements by these people, comparing them with what other people have said about them, finding out on what occasion the two businessmen made their statements and why, what they did, and so on. As explained above, a historian's approach is hermeneutic or interpretive, with the goal of making sense of what relevant people in history said or did in the context of their time. While "economics in time" is possible with path dependency models, it is hard to imagine how "economics in historical time" could be done with formal models. Narrative approaches and detailed case studies with thick descriptions may be the only way to address this part of Robinson's critique.

The tension between path-dependent economic change and evolution and ideosyncratic events in historical context is also expressed by Boulton et al. (2015) when they say that "the future is a dance between patterns and events" (p. 29). Patterns of relationships, as they call them, created by institutions, routines, norms, and so on, generate paths that can be studied to some extent scientifically and analytically. System dynamics models, for example, make use of such patterns of relationships. As long as these patterns are relatively stable, they can be used for prediction. However,

> *patterns are always under threat of disruption by events. The events might be major external shocks such as pandemics, tsunamis, wars, climate change, or migration, or they might be larger-than-average fluctuations—in weather or stock market prices, for example... Events may also be internal variations from the norm—a higher-than-average birth or death rate, or the death or arrival of a significant leader.* (Boulton et al. 2015, p. 30)

But events are not just additive shocks to paths that produce temporary deviations, as is assumed in many neoclassical models. Events can also invade patterns:

> *Wherever they come from, these events and variations may cause the current patterns to shift, to 'tip' into something new. This may be a smooth and relatively fast transition, such as that caused by the introduction of the internet or of text messaging. Or it may lead to collapse and subsequent chaos as was the result of the plague in Europe in the fourteenth century, the crisis caused by the South Sea Bubble in 1720, or the complex ongoing situations in the Middle East that have followed the Arab Spring of 2011. Or change may be a slow process, whereby societies become increasingly dominated by the few—be they individuals or firms or nations—where diversity is lost and power is concentrated.* (Boulton et al. 2015, p. 30/31)

Thus, events create instability that leads to an emergent future. Understanding how events change existing patterns requires attention to the particularity of detail that cannot be captured by abstract mathematics and a focus on averages.

To some extent, the world is mechanical and predictable, but there is always an element of chaos and unpredictability, too. Boulton et al. (2015, p. 32) conclude:

> *This dance between detail and structure, between science and history, between form and individualism, is at the heart of the contribution of evolutionary complex systems thinking.*

Hence, historical economics needs complexity thinking as discussed in Chap. 2. There, we characterized complexity thinking as "gray science for the stuff in between," in an intermediate position between hard (complexity) science and soft (complexity) science. The appropriate methodology of historical economics is a mix of quantitative and qualitative approaches, which will be presented in the remainder of this chapter.

11.3 Path Dependence

Path dependence is one translation of what it means that history matters. If a dynamical process is path dependent, then its evolution depends on the initial conditions and the sequence of states reached, i.e. its own history. We can use both deterministic models and stochastic models to make this characterization more formal.

In Chap. 6, you learned that deterministic nonlinear models can have multiple attractors or equilibria. An example of a model with four fixed points is the Lotka–Volterra competition model, shown again in Fig. 11.4. To repeat, this model has four fixed points (0,0), (3,0), (0,2), and (1,1). Since the origin is an unstable node, the system will be there if it starts there and is not disturbed. However, if the origin is the starting point of the dynamics and a perturbation occurs, the system will end up at one of the other three fixed points. Which one the system reaches depends on the path "chosen" by the perturbation. If the perturbation leads to a point on a path in the white basin of attraction (e.g., path 1), then the system will reach the fixed point (0,2) in the long run. A point on path 3 in the gray basin will lead to the fixed point (0,3), and a point on the saddle path (path 2) will cause convergence to the interior fixed point (1,1). Thus, the long-run outcome of this system is path dependent. Different starting points or histories determine the state to which the system converges. A model with path-independent processes would have only one globally stable equilibrium, which is reached no matter where the system starts and which points in the phase diagram are visited.

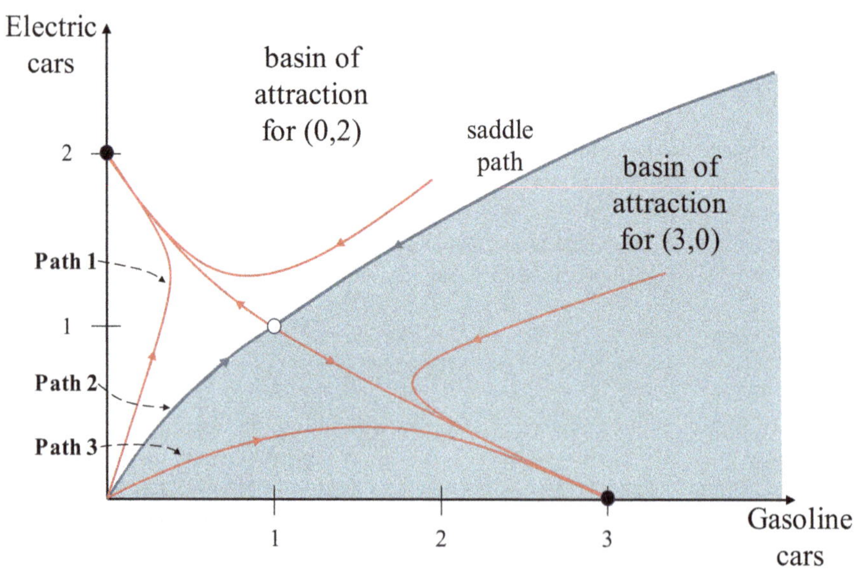

Fig. 11.4 Path dependence in a deterministic model with multiple attractors. Source: Author

David (2001) provides two formal definitions of path dependence for stochastic processes: a negative one describing what path dependence is not and a positive one in terms of the probabilistic properties of a path-dependent process. We discuss both in the following subsections, as well as reasons for and examples of path-dependent processes in economics.

11.3.1 Negative Definition of Path Dependence and Ergodicity

The negative definition is:

▶ *Processes that are non-ergodic, and thus unable to shake free of their history, are said to yield path-dependent outcomes.*

To understand this definition, we need to know what ergodicity means. The concept was introduced by Ludwig Boltzmann into statistical mechanics in the 1880s in order to rigorously define what it means for gas molecules to mix well in thermodynamic equilibrium. A stochastic process is ergodic if the system eventually visits all parts of the state space with a stationary limiting probability distribution. A path-dependent process does not visit all possible states in the limit.

A simple *Markov chain* model can be used to illustrate this property. Markov chains are quite popular in economics, for example to model labor market dynamics. In a Markov chain with a discrete state space, there are a finite number of states that the system can take. The defining characteristic of a Markov chain is the Markov property that the transition probability from one state to another between two periods (in discrete time) is independent of time. This means that a Markov process has no memory. All we need to know to predict the future state in the next period is the current state. Future and past states are independent, so the past (or history) of the process is irrelevant.

Let us look at a simple example of a Markov chain of a stock market.[4] The stock market can be in three states: (1) bull market, (2) bear market, and (3) stagnant market. The transition matrix P contains the transition probability from one state to another:

$$P = \begin{bmatrix} 0.9 & 0.075 & 0.025 \\ 0.15 & 0.8 & 0.05 \\ 0.25 & 0.25 & 0.5 \end{bmatrix}.$$

We read the transition matrix as follows: entry p_{ij} is the probability of moving from the state in row i to the state in column j. Thus, $p_{11} = 0.9$ is the probability that the stock market will remain in state 1 (bull market) if it is currently there. $p_{23} = 0.05$ is the probability that the stock market will move from state 2 (bear) to state

[4]The example is taken from https://en.wikipedia.org/wiki/Examples_of_Markov_chains Accessed 02 November 2023.

3 (stagnant) and so on. Assume that in period n the system is in state 2, which can be represented by the vector

$$x^{(n)} = [0\ 1\ 0].$$

We can find the stochastic distribution of states in the following period $n + 1$ by multiplying the initial vector by the transition matrix

$$x^{(n+1)} = x^{(n)} P = [0.15\ 0.8\ 0.05],$$

which simply yields the second row of the transition matrix. To find $x^{(n\ +\ 3)}$, we must perform this operation three times

$$x^{(n+3)} = x^{(n+2)} P = x^{(n+1)} PP = x^{(n)} PPP = x^{(n)} P^3,$$

which gives $x^{(n\ +\ 3)} = [0.3575\ 0.56825\ 0.07425]$ if we start in state 2. Thus, after three periods, the stock market is bearish with a probability of 0.56825. The long-run distribution is found by taking the N-th power of the transition matrix to the limit:

$$\lim_{N \to \infty} P^N = \begin{bmatrix} 0.625 & 0.3125 & 0.0625 \\ 0.625 & 0.3125 & 0.0625 \\ 0.625 & 0.3125 & 0.0625 \end{bmatrix}.$$

We observe that there is a stationary limiting distribution of the three states. All states will be visited in the long run with the probabilities shown. Note that these probabilities are identical, no matter whether we start in state 1, 2, or 3. Therefore, this process shakes free of its history. A Markov chain is ergodic if it is possible to get from any state to any other state with positive probability.

Let us look at a counterexample of a Markov chain that is not ergodic. Consider the following transition matrix of a Markov process with five states:

$$P = \begin{bmatrix} 1 & 0 & 0 & 0 & 0 \\ 0.7 & 0 & 0.3 & 0 & 0 \\ 0 & 0.7 & 0 & 0.3 & 0 \\ 0 & 0 & 0.7 & 0 & 0.3 \\ 0 & 0 & 0 & 0 & 1 \end{bmatrix}.$$

This Markov chain has two special states, state 1 and state 5. These states are called *absorbing states*, because once they are reached, the system will stay there, $p_{ii} = 1$. States 2, 3, and 4 are called *transient states*, because we can reach states 1 and 5 from them, but not vice versa. A state i is a transient state if there exists a state j that can be reached from i, but state i cannot be reached from state j. A state that is not transient is a *recurrent state*. The limiting distribution of this Markov chain is given by:

$$\lim_{N \to \infty} P^N = \begin{bmatrix} 1 & 0 & 0 & 0 & 0 \\ 0.953448 & 0 & 0 & 0 & 0.0465517 \\ 0.844828 & 0 & 0 & 0 & 0.155172 \\ 0.591379 & 0 & 0 & 0 & 0.408621 \\ 0 & 0 & 0 & 0 & 1 \end{bmatrix}.$$

This Markov chain is not ergodic, because not all states are recurrent. As we saw earlier, states 2, 3, and 4 are transient and will not be reached again, if the system is absorbed in either state 1 or state 5. Ultimately, the system will end up in one of the two absorbing states, if it starts in one of the transient states. Obviously, the dynamics of this system depend on the initial conditions and also on the random transitions. Starting in state 4, the system eventually reaches state 1 with a probability of 0.59 and state 5 with a probability of 0.41.

You may have encountered ergodicity in the context of time series analysis. An economic time series is a single realization of a stochastic process. Therefore, we cannot infer the moments of the stochastic process in a cross-section. For statistical inference on time series, we must assume that the process is ergodic. In a time series context, this means that the sample moments of a finite time series converge to the constant moments of the population as time goes to infinity. The process is *mean ergodic* if

$$\lim_{T \to \infty} E\left[\left(\frac{1}{T}\sum_{t=1}^{T} x_t - \mu\right)^2\right] = 0$$

and *variance ergodic* if

$$\lim_{T \to \infty} E\left[\left(\frac{1}{T}\sum_{t=1}^{T} (x_t - \mu)^2 - \sigma^2\right)^2\right] = 0,$$

where μ and σ^2 are the mean and the variance of the population. To be ergodic, a process must be stationary, i.e. its unconditional joint probability distribution must not change as the process is shifted in time. This implies that the mean and variance of the time series must not change over time. Many macroeconomic time series (e.g., GDP, prices) have a unit root, so they are not stationary because of an increasing variance, which implies that they are not ergodic. Unit roots plague macroeconomic analysis both for econometric reasons and because they imply the persistence of shocks and path dependence, which is not consistent with mainstream macroeconomic theory.

A *random walk* is a stochastic process with a unit root and is therefore non-ergodic. A one-dimensional random walk can be written as

$$y_t = y_{t-1} + \epsilon_t,$$

where the disturbance ϵ_t is a random variable assumed to be identically and independently distributed (i.i.d.), often with an expected value of 0 and a variance of 1. For a Gaussian random walk, the disturbance is assumed to be normally distributed. It is easy to see that a random walk can be expressed as a sum of past disturbances:

$$y_{t-1} = y_{t-2} + \epsilon_{t-1}$$
$$y_{t-2} = y_{t-3} + \epsilon_{t-2}$$
$$\dots$$
$$y_1 = y_0 + \epsilon_1$$

Hence

$$y_t = y_{t-2} + \epsilon_t + \epsilon_{t-1} = y_{t-3} + \epsilon_t + \epsilon_{t-1} + \epsilon_{t-2} = \dots = y_0 + \sum_{\tau=1}^{t} \epsilon_\tau .$$

A random walk is a nice illustration of what path dependence means. The current value of a variable following a random walk, y_t, can be expressed as the sum of its initial value, y_0, and the sum of all stochastic disturbances that have occurred in the meantime. The process has memory in the sense that each disturbance has a permanent effect. If one disturbance had been different, the current value of y_t would be different. Moreover, the past of the process is not indicative for the future. If the expected value of the disturbance is 0, the best prediction for y_{t+1} is equal to y_t. Since each random disturbance can be interpreted as an historical event, a random walk comes close to the notion of history being a sequence of events.

11.3.2 Positive Definition of Path Dependence

David (2001) also defines path dependence positively:

▶ *A path-dependent stochastic process is one whose asymptotic distribution evolves as a consequence (function of) the process' own history.*

This positive definition is broader than the negative definition, because it allows for stochastic processes that have multiple asymptotic distributions. In other words, the asymptotic distribution is not fixed, but emerges along a path. How can we imagine this?

The *Pólya urn model* is a statistical model in which the probability of an event depends on past realizations of the event. Imagine an urn filled with a blue and b orange balls, say ten of each initially ($a = b = 10$). The Pólya process works as follows: At each time step, one ball is randomly drawn from the urn. We observe its color and put it back into the urn together with another ball of the same color. This mechanism makes the probability of a color being drawn path dependent. The more balls of a color are drawn early in a trial, the more likely it becomes that the same color will be drawn later. The proportion of blue balls at draw n, and thus the probability of drawing a blue ball then, is given by

$$P_n(blue) = \frac{a + \sum_{i=1}^{n} X_i}{a + b + n},$$

where $X_i = 1$ if the *ith* ball is blue and 0 otherwise. If we start with $a = b = 10$ and we have drawn 2 blue balls, the probability of a blue ball in round 10 is $P_{10}(blue) = \frac{12}{30} = 0.4$. However, if the number of blue draws was 8, then $P_{10}(blue) = \frac{18}{30} = 0.6$. Figure 11.5 shows how the number of blue and orange balls and the proportion (probability) of blue balls evolve in one trials over 500 periods. Initially, orange balls are only slightly more frequent, but over time the difference between orange and blue balls increases. Therefore, the proportion of blue balls decreases and stabilizes at about 42% after 500 periods.

As shown in Fig. 11.6, the proportion of blue balls stabilizes over time, but at different levels. After 500 periods, the ratio of blue balls to orange balls in these five trials can be 65:35, 60:40, 45:55, or 33:67. In some cases, e.g., Trial 1 (light blue) and Trial 2 (orange), the proportion of blue balls immediately increases or decreases. On other cases, e.g., Trial 3, the proportion increases first, but falls again in the long run. Randomness matters especially in the early periods and determines the long-run path.

In the long run (e.g., after 5000 periods), the distribution of blue and orange balls can vary significantly. The empirical distribution of balls over many different trials can be well approximated by a beta density function. Thus, the Pólya urn model has many different asymptotic distributions of blue and orange balls depending on the history. In particular, early draws are important because they strongly influence the direction of the process. The Pólya urn model formalizes the claim that the sequence of events can matter.

The Pólya urn model is an abstract statistical model that has path dependence, but it does not explain it. It generates path dependence, because each draw makes future draws of the same color more likely due to the replacement rule. This is a positive feedback mechanism that amplifies individual (random) events. Causes of such positive feedback in the economy are presented in the next subsection.

11.3.3 Reasons for Path Dependence

There are at least six categories of reasons for positive feedback creating path dependence:

[5] In the literature, "increasing returns" is often used as a synonym for positive feedback in the context of path dependence. This use of the term is imprecise. It is more accurate to think of increasing returns to scale as one of several reasons for positive feedback.

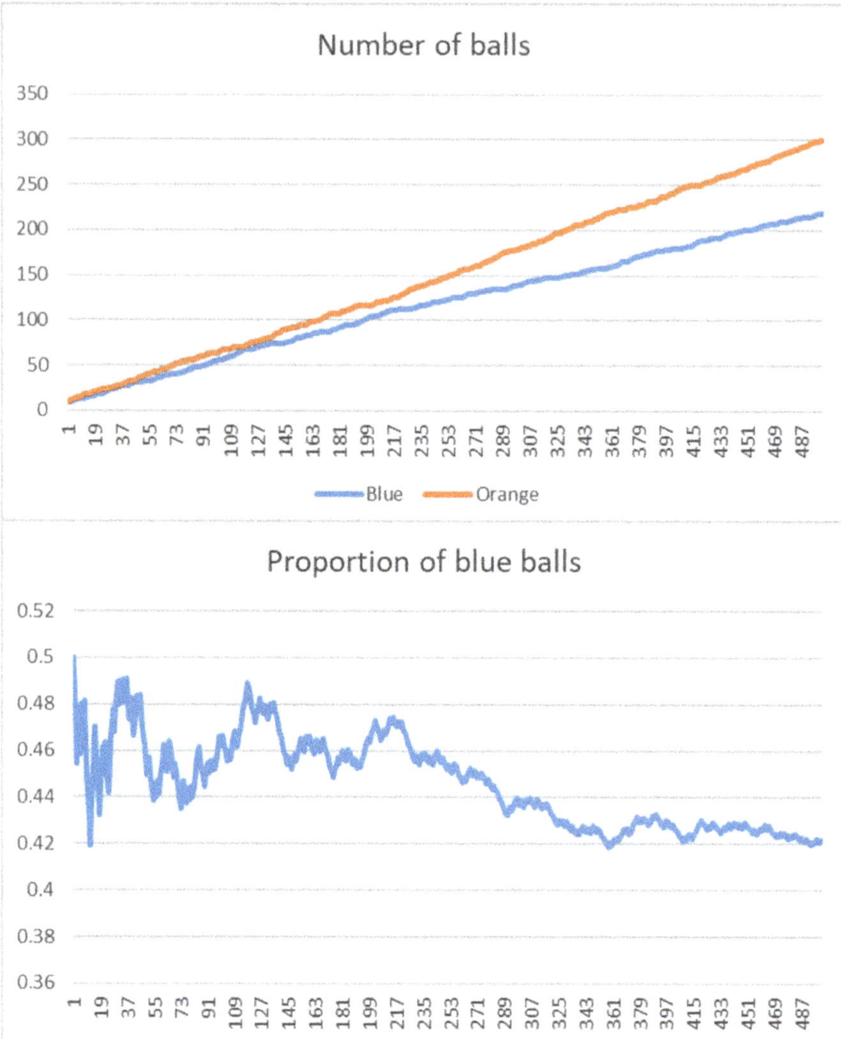

Fig. 11.5 Path of a Pólya urn model. Source: Author

1. Increasing returns to scale
2. Learning effects
3. Positive externalities
4. Complementarities
5. Expectations
6. Institutions

Let us look at these reasons and at some economic examples.

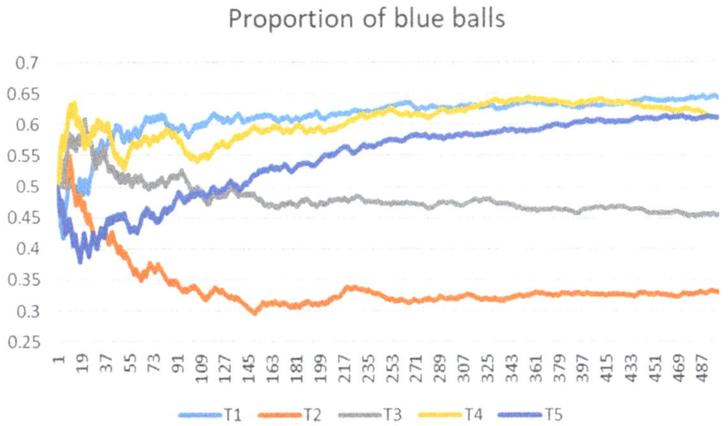

Fig. 11.6 Five paths of blue balls in the Pólya urn model. Source: Author

Increasing returns to scale[5] occur when there are large setup or fixed costs in production, developing a technology, or establishing an organization. The fixed costs can be spread over more units of output as production increases, resulting in decreasing average costs. When fixed costs are high, economic agents have a strong incentive to specialize in one activity rather than incur the fixed costs multiple times. This is easy to see with a simple example. Suppose that total costs TC depend on fixed costs f and variable costs with constant marginal costs μ:

$$TC(y) = f + \mu y.$$

Suppose that a firm can choose between producing the quantity y of a good in one factory and producing the same quantity split up between two factories $y = x_1 + x_2$. For comparison, we assume that the firm must incur the same fixed costs twice in order to produce x_1 and x_2 and that the marginal costs are the same. It is obvious then that the total costs and hence the average costs of producing x_1 and x_2 are higher than those of producing y:

$$TC(x_1, x_2) = 2f + \mu(x_1 + x_2) = 2f + \mu y.$$

Figure 11.7 shows the average costs as a function of the total quantity produced for $f = 20$ and $\mu = 2$. Especially for small production quantities, there is a large cost advantage to specializing in one good instead of two.

Fixed costs are high in industries that require large investments in physical capital, such as steel, automobiles, chemicals, or mining. They are also large when R&D is important, as in the pharmaceutical industry or software development. The positive feedback mechanism that leads to path dependence is obvious: once the setup investment has been made, it is beneficial for a firm to produce more of the same product because each additional unit lowers the average cost, which increases profits at a given price.

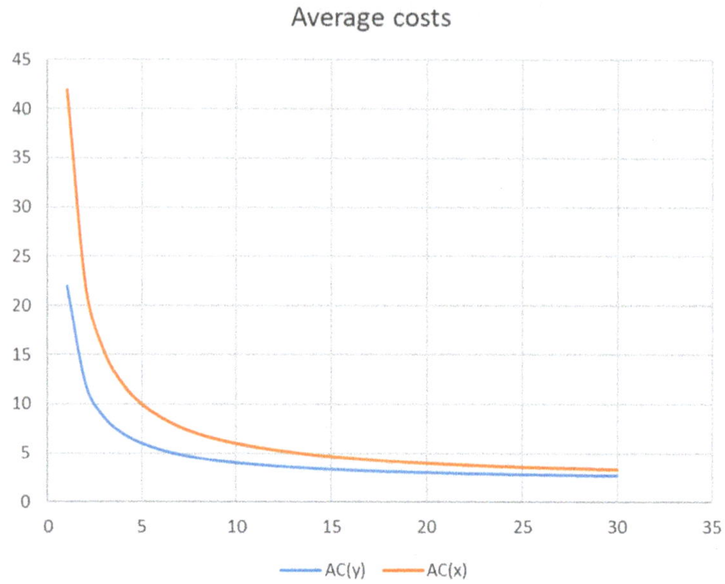

Fig. 11.7 Average costs of producing y in one factory or x in two factories. Source: Author

Learning effects or experience effects describe the empirical finding that a task requires less time when it is performed more often. Individuals also learn how to use equipment more efficiently and how to organize their work better. The engineer Theodore Paul Wright documented learning effects in aircraft production in 1936 (Wright 1936), so learning or experience effects are often called *Wright's law*. Wright's law can be expressed as a power function:

$$C_n = C_1 n^{\log_2 PR},$$

where C_n is the cost of producing the *nth* unit, C_1 is the cost of the first unit, n is the total number of units, and PR is the progress ratio. If we double the number of units, we get

$$C_{2n} = C_1 (2n)^{\log_2 PR} = C_n \times PR.$$

Thus, the progress ratio measures the fraction to which costs will fall as cumulative production doubles. $LR = 1 - PR$ is called the learning rate.

Wright (1936) found a learning rate of 20% in aircraft production. Experience effects of about 15% to 20% have also been found in other industries such as shipbuilding, machinery, or automobile production. For example, Abernathy and Wayne (1974) report a rate of progress of 85% for Ford's Model T production between 1909 and 1923. A well-known recent example is the decline in the cost of solar panels in the photovoltaic industry, as shown in Fig. 11.8. Since the 1970s, an

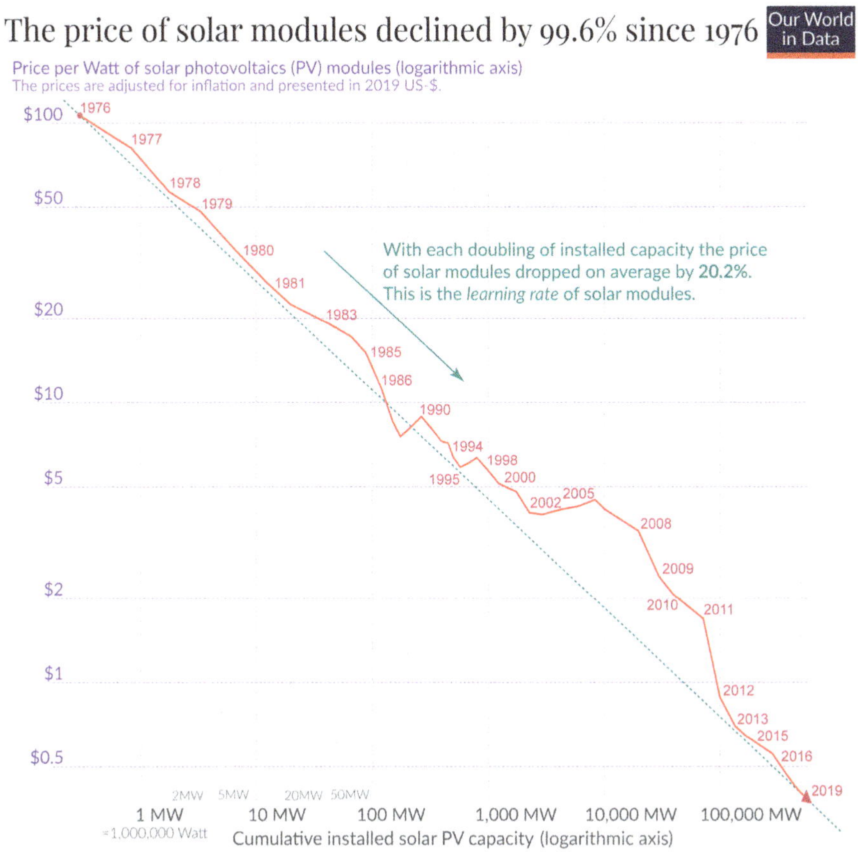

Fig. 11.8 Experience curve in the photovoltaic industry. Source: Roser (2020). CC B 4.0 (https://creativecommons.org/licenses/by/4.0/)

average learning rate of 20% has been observed. Experience effects also lead to cost degression, creating a similar incentive as increasing returns to scale.

There are several types of *positive externalities* that generate positive feedback effects. One type is *network externalities*. A network externality occurs when a potential user of a network makes the network more attractive to others by joining. The benefit to each user increases with the number of other users. *Metcalfe's law* states that the utility of a telecommunications network (e.g., telephone, fax, e-mail) is approximately equal to the square of the number of users, or more precisely $U = n(n - 1)$. Each of the n members can reach $n - 1$ other members in such a network. If you are the only person, who owns a phone, the phone is useless. Similarly, messaging platforms like WhatsApp or social networks like Facebook become more attractive the more people use them and can thus be contacted. The utility of social networks increases even more with the number of users than the utility of telecommunications networks, because social networks can have valuable subgroups. *Reed's law* states that the utility of a social network is $U = 2^n - n - 1$, which already exceeds $n(n - 1)$ for 4 users. A final example of network externalities are dating apps or platforms, whose attractiveness also depends on the number of users, similar to telecommunications networks. It is easy to see how network externalities lead to path dependence. Assume that there are two incompatible telecommunications networks, such that cross-network communication is not possible. If both initially have 10 existing users, a new potential user is indifferent between the two and can randomly choose, e.g. network 1. The next user, however, has a choice between a network with utility $U_1 = 11 \times 10 = 110$ and one with utility $U_2 = 10 \times 9 = 90$. If network 1 is chosen again, its utility increases to $U_1 = 12 \times 11 = 132$, and so on. Thus, network 2 becomes relatively less and less attractive and is likely to be abandoned over time. The crucial point is that the initial situation was perfectly symmetric; network 2 could also have been the survivor if early users had happened to make different choices. In industries with strong network externalities, firms have a strong incentive to grow their user base faster than their competitors in order to stay in the market.

Another important type of externalities that cause path dependence are *agglomeration economies*. In regional economics or the so-called new economic geography[6] (see Schmutzler 1999, Fujita et al. 1999), *agglomeration* refers to the spatial clustering of economic activities such as production, consumption, or R&D. Spatial concentrations of population are also called urban agglomerations. The existence of cities is an agglomeration phenomenon. But industries in a country are also locally concentrated, for example the U.S. automotive industry is highly agglomerated in the Midwestern states. Many cities have a banking district and an entertainment district. *Marshallian spillovers* describe intra-industry or specialization externalities due to labor market pooling, specialized input sharing, or knowledge spillovers. For instance, a supplier in the auto industry will benefit from locating near other automotive suppliers, because there is a local labor market for specialized workers. When similar firms are located close to each other, it is also easier for them to cooperate in innovation networks and to share knowledge. *Jacobian* (or Jacobs) *externalities* refer to diversification or urbanization externalities. Here complementarities between different skills or knowledge are beneficial. It is hypothesized that cities are particularly creative places because diverse people exchange ideas there, leading to novelty through the recombination of distinct knowledge. Finally, the new economic geography describes an agglomeration mechanism that works through price effects due to transportation costs. If there are fixed costs of production, firms have an incentive to concentrate production in one place because of increasing returns to scale. If there are transportation or other spatial transaction costs, prices are assumed to be lower in the region of production than elsewhere. This creates an incentive for mobile workers to move to that region. But then, more firms also have an incentive to locate there because the local demand for

[6] It should rather be called "new geographical economics," but Paul Krugman (1991) labeled it new economic geography, infuriating many geographers for selling old wine in new bottles.

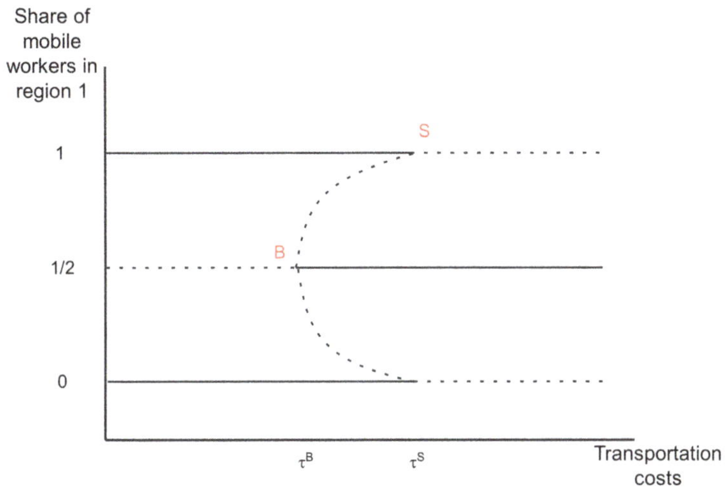

Fig. 11.9 Bifurcation diagram in the core–periphery model. Source: Author's own figure based on Fujita et al. (1999)

goods is greater. Thus, the decision of mobile workers to locate in a region creates a market externality for mobile firms and vice versa. In other words, firms want to be where there are many consumers/workers, and consumers/workers prefer to live near firms, creating a positive feedback loop.

New economic geography models assume a featureless space with ex ante identical regions and an equal distribution of mobile workers and firms across the (two) regions. A historical accident can cause a firm to relocate from one region to the other, setting the agglomeration economies in motion. The "tomahawk" bifurcation diagram in Fig. 11.9 shows the equilibrium locations of mobile workers and firms depending on the level of transportation costs between the two regions. When transportation costs are high, only the equal spatial distribution of mobile factors can be an equilibrium. However, once transportation costs fall below a critical level τ^B (e.g., due to infrastructure improvements), a break point B is reached, where the symmetric equilibrium becomes unstable. For low transportation costs, only a full agglomeration of all mobile factors in one of the two regions will result in a spatial equilibrium such that a core–periphery pattern emerges. Which region becomes the agglomerated core and which becomes the vacated periphery depends on history.

Complementarities (or synergies) also cause positive feedback. In the evolutionary model in Sect. 10.7.2 of Chap. 10, the performance and hence evolution of a manufacturing practice depended on its net synergy with all other established manufacturing practices. For example, practices associated with Fordist mass production, such as supplier selection by price, dedicated automation, or dependence on written rules, are complementary but do not create synergies with practices used in agile production, such as agile automation, exchange of workers with suppliers, and employees as system developers. The model presented in Chap. 10 showed that the success or failure of a newly introduced practice depends on the timing and use of other synergetic practices. It may be impossible to introduce a new practice at one point in time because of a lack of complementary practices, but later attempts may be successful if synergy-creating practices have been adopted in the meantime. If the adoption of one practice influences the later chances of successfully adopting another practice due to synergy, we have a path-dependent process. Note that this is again an argument based on sequencing and timing.

Another form of complementarity is called *technical interrelatedness*. The hardware and software of computers and other technical devices are technically interrelated. Not every software is available for every operating system, and not every operating system runs on every computer. For example, the popular Microsoft Office software is not available for the Linux operating system. Technical interrelatedness plays a role in the connection between computers and peripherals such as hard drives, monitors, printers, keyboards, headphones, and so on. A monitor is only useful if it can be connected to a standard computer and vice versa. So it makes sense to standardize the connections, as happened with the Universal Serial Bus (USB). Originally there were a variety of different connectors, but today USB is the standard for many devices.

There are also important complementarities between certain goods and infrastructure. For example, cars need roads, repair shops, and parking space. If they run on gasoline, they also need a network of gas stations, which in turn requires a complex supply chain to provide the gasoline. Electric cars need charging stations, which require an adequate electricity system. Duranton and Turner (2011) present evidence from the USA supporting the *fundamental law of highway congestion*, according to which new lane kilometers on roads increase vehicle kilometers traveled one-for-one. Thus, building new roads increases traffic, but more traffic creates political pressure to build new roads to reduce congestion. Traffic induced by new roads and road construction due to high traffic form a positive feedback loop. More cars lead to more roads, which lead to more cars.

Path dependence can also arise through *expectation formation* in pure coordination games, where there is no technical complementarity, but where agents benefit from doing the same thing. Pure coordination games were discussed in Sect. 9.5.2 using the example of language choice. When people from different countries meet, they must choose a language in which to communicate. Suppose a German and an Italian meet for the first time. Neither speaks the native language of the other, but both speak English and French fluently. Choosing the same language is a pure coordination game; one language is as good as the other for the partners, because no one has an advantage by speaking one language better than the other. What matters is that they agree on the same language. Experience shows that two people often stick to the language they used when they first met. This is often the case even in multilingual couples. The language chosen at the first meeting may depend on the context. If the German and the Italian meet at an international scientific conference where the working language is English, it is natural that they both speak English. But if they meet while on vacation in France, they might be more likely to choose French. In both cases, they might not know that they both speak the alternative language. The next time they meet, they both know that the other speaks the language they used before (either English or French). Therefore, it is natural for them to use the same language again, because they can rightly expect their partner to understand them. It is possible that they discover that they can communicate in a different language only after a long time, and then it may feel very uncomfortable for them to use the other language.

A similar argument was introduced into economics by Thomas Schelling (1960). Schelling argued that people use *focal points* that have some kind of prominence or salience to coordinate without communication in a pure coordination game. One of his examples, which became quite famous, is the question of where and when you would expect to meet another person in New York City if you did not have the opportunity to communicate. The most common answer given by a group of Schelling's students was "noon at Grand Central Terminal." This is not inherently better than alternatives such as Central Park or the Empire State Building, but it seems to have salience for the respondents. Again context is likely to determine what is salient to the agents in a given situation. If the expectation is correct, it is self-fulfilling, so it may be used again in the future. David (1994) generalizes this idea and argues that the emergence of conventions in the sense of mutually consistent expectations creates path dependence. The best response to mutually consistent expectations is a *Nash equilibrium* in game theory. A Nash equilibrium is self-stabilizing, because no player has an incentive to change expectations or behavior.

Relatedly, David (1994) argues that *institutions* create path-generating feedback. He argues that in addition to coordinating expectations, institutions "assign individuals to well-defined roles in which their anticipated range of actions turns out to be consistent (as a Nash equilibrium) with the actions of other individuals" (p. 210). Role typing occurs in firms when firms define job profiles and hire people who fit those profiles. These people have skills, attitudes, and values that are consistent with those of the organization and behave (more or less) in ways that are expected by the organization. Membership in organizations, or institutionalized activities in general, "is made conditional on a tolerable degree of conformity with the behaviours delineated by a well-specified role" (p. 211). But organizations not only select their members who conform to their values. They also shape the values and behaviors of their existing members through many forms of incentives and sanctions. Learning role types and role expectations requires time and investment on the part of individuals and is thus a form of investment in durable capital. Unlike physical capital, this institutional capital does not wear out with repeated use, but rather becomes more refined and deeply rooted. Indeed, unlearning established roles is difficult and requires considerable effort. This makes it difficult to transform existing institutions and change course.

The large number of examples and the variety of feedback mechanisms suggest that path dependence is not an oddity in the economy, but rather the normal case. We should expect to see it in the evolution of technology, institutions, markets, firms, politics, consumption patterns, and so on.

11.4 Lock-in

Path dependence is related to the concept of lock-in, but they are not identical. Lock-in is often used in the sense of being trapped on an inefficient or technologically inferior path. Path dependence alone does not tell us whether a particular path is socially or economically desirable or not. For analytical clarity, it is desirable to distinguish between the description of a phenomenon (path dependence) and its normative evaluation (inefficient lock-in).

It is important to raise this point because the aforementioned paper by Liebowitz and Margolis (1995), which has received considerable attention, conflates path dependence and inefficient lock-in and attempts to downplay the economic relevance of path dependence by arguing that competitive markets rarely make inefficient choices. Their argument has two main parts. Their first argument is that rational agents should not be expected to make choices that are inferior in the long run if this is foreseeable ex ante. Choosing an option that is inefficient in the long run, even if it may be a good choice in the short run, is an avoidable error. They find it theoretically implausible that rational agents make avoidable errors. Thus, if there is a case in which we find ex post that another option would have been better, Liebowitz and Margolis would argue that the error was probably unavoidable due to imperfect knowledge of the future. Rational agents may have imperfect knowledge of the future due to fundamental uncertainty, but they should be expected to act optimally on the knowledge available at the time of the decision. The second part of the argument introduces the concept of remediability. An inferior choice is *remediable* if there are feasible alternatives and the benefits of switching to such an alternative exceed the costs of switching. If the costs of switching are higher than the benefits of the alternatives, then switching does not make sense, even though one might wish that an alternative had been chosen in the first place. However, if switching costs are lower than the benefits, then rational market participants will make the investment to improve the market outcome. Failure to do so would be a truly inefficient market failure, which Liebowitz and Margolis (1995) argue is theoretically unlikely and empirically rare.

So what does the Liebowitz–Margolis critique mean for path dependence and lock-in? With respect to path dependence, the answer should be clear. It is hard to deny that there are many situations in which different paths are possible, and that individual choice may play a role in which path is chosen. Even Liebowitz and Margolis accept this, so path dependence itself is not directly the target of criticism. What is disputed is the relevance of inefficient lock-in, which is difficult to assess empirically because of the lack of a counterfactual. In this section, we look at some examples of potential inefficient lock-in, discuss some theoretical responses to the Liebowitz–Margolis critique, and present some types of lock-in.

11.4.1 Some Examples of Lock-in

The classic example of an inefficient lock-in is the QWERTY layout of letters on a typewriter or computer keyboard (David 1985). In 1936, August Dvorak and his brother-in-law William Dealey patented an alternative layout—the Dvorak Simplified Keyboard (DSK) or Dvorak layout—that was intended to provide faster and more ergonomic typing. Despite many attempts by Dvorak and others, the DSK did not replace the QWERTY layout as the standard keyboard. David (1985) tells a story about why the QWERTY layout became dominant, and why it was not replaced by the supposedly better alternative, the DSK. The story begins with the invention of a mechanical writing machine—or Type Writer—with upstroke type bars by Christopher Latham Sholes in 1867. This machine had the drawback that the print point was covered by the paper carriage, so the writer could not directly see what he or she was writing. The upstroke bars often collided and jammed when pressed in rapid succession by a fast typist. Since the print point was not visible, this was often not noticed for some time, with the result that a sequence of the same letter was printed because of the jammed bars. The QWERTY layout was found to be a solution to this problem, as it reduced the frequency of type bar collisions. Beginning in 1873, the Sholes QWERTY typewriter was manufactured and marketed by the gun manufacturer E. Remington and Sons. By the 1880s, the success of the Sholes-Remington QWERTY typewriter was not guaranteed, as both alternative keyboard layouts and alternative typing mechanisms had been developed in the 1870s. Down-stroke and front-stroke machines had visible printing dots, and, in 1872, Thomas Edison received a patent for an electric printing wheel device that did not have the problem of clashing type bars. Nevertheless, the Shole-Remington QWERTY had a small lead over its competitors in the 1880s and 1890s, when typewriters became popular in the business world. In the late 1880s, touch typing, using all ten fingers on the keyboard, was developed and adapted to QWERTY from the beginning. Typists began to learn touch typing, which was faster than the four-finger hunt-and-peck method. As more people were able to touch type on QWERTY, it became advantageous for employers to purchase QWERTY Remingtons, which in turn created an incentive to learn QWERTY touch typing. While the technical (or hardware) costs of switching to alternative machines and keyboard layouts decreased, the software costs of changing typists' skills increased. Switching from QWERTY touch typing to another layout would have been costly for the growing number of professional typists. Thus, the quasi-irreversible investment in specific touch typing skills caused the lock-in to QWERTY. It seems safe to conclude that this story describes a path-dependent process.

Whether lock-in is inefficient or not depends on the superiority of alternative keyboard layouts such as the DSK. Liebowitz and Margolis (1990) claim that the evidence for the higher efficiency of DSK mentioned by David (1985) is weak, but other studies (West 1994; Okadome 2007) confirm at least small advantages of DSK. Since today's computer software allows switching to Dvorak even on a QWERTY keyboard, there is virtually no additional cost to learning Dvorak instead of QWERTY touch typing. Therefore, even small efficiency gains from using Dvorak could have a positive overall effect. But overall, the QWERTY-Dvorak controversy may not be important enough for endless debates about inefficient lock-in. It serves as a nice example to introduce the topic, but other examples may be more relevant. Even David (1985, p. 332) saw it this way in the opening section of his seminal paper: "Standing alone, my story will be simply illustrative and does not establish how much the world works this way. This is an open empirical issue and I would be presumptuous to claim to have settled it."

Nuclear reactors are a more compelling case of lock-in to an inferior technology. Robin Cowan (1990) argues that although it is not possible to prove it conclusively, there is strong evidence that the currently dominant light water reactor technology is not the best technology, neither economically nor technically. Alternative technologies such as heavy water reactors and gas graphite reactors are available and could have cost advantages, but light water technology has become dominant and entrenched due to dynamically increasing returns in the form of learning by doing and learning about payoffs. Cowan documents that when nuclear technology was very new in the 1950s, there was a lot of uncertainty and debate about the best type of reactor for civilian power generation. At a conference in 1955, some 100 different types of reactors were deemed not obviously impractical, but three years later the number of types being seriously considered had fallen to 12. Practical research and implementation efforts were conducted primarily in four countries: the United States, Canada, France, and the United Kingdom. France and the United Kingdom focused independently on gas graphite reactors, and Canada worked on heavy water reactors. The USA was the key player in determining market dynamics. Initially, research was conducted on several types of reactors. Cowan argues that three factors drove the choice of the light water path: (1) the role of the U.S. Navy, (2) geopolitical considerations in the USA after the development of the Soviet atomic bomb, and (3) U.S. government subsidies.

At the end of World War II, the U.S. Navy wanted small reactors to power submarines that could be ready for deployment quickly. Captain Hyman Rickover, who was in charge of the Navy's nuclear propulsion program, played a crucial role. Despite limited knowledge of the relative merits of the various technological options, he committed himself to the light water reactor and did everything he could to get these reactors built quickly, which was done by Westinghouse and, at Rickover's initiative, General Electric. The choice of light water was driven mainly by military requirements, not by economic considerations to produce cheap electricity for civilian use. After World War II, the United States believed it would have a monopoly on nuclear technology for twenty years. With the explosion of the first Soviet atomic bomb in 1949 and the first British bomb in 1953, it became clear that this belief was mistaken. As both countries developed civilian nuclear power capabilities, the U.S. government feared that the Soviet Union, in particular, would provide cheap energy technology to developing nations, thereby drawing them into its political camp. To counter this perceived geopolitical threat, it became a priority in the USA to invest in civilian nuclear reactors. This was done using light water technology because light water reactors were the most advanced due to the efforts of the Navy. To develop the market and expand its international influence, the

U.S. government paid large subsidies to export and establish light water technology in Europe. These government efforts and the already well-developed U.S. market led France and the United Kingdom to abandon their own R&D efforts on gas graphite technology and adopt light water reactors. The key point is that the light water reactor was developed to meet military requirements, not to maximize the safety and cost efficiency criteria important for civilian use. Due to strong learning effects and other positive feedbacks, the small development advantage of light water technology was sufficient to capture most of the civilian market.

Two even more significant examples of inefficient and societally harmful lock-in—not only of single technologies, but of whole systems—are discussed in the sustainability literature: agri-food system lock-in and carbon lock-in. These issues are very broad and have many dimensions, such that a full discussion is not possible here. We therefore only sketch some of the issues and emphasize that these cases are rather convincing examples of socially inferior path dependence.

An agri-food system is defined as a "web of actors, processes, and interactions involved in growing, processing, distributing, consuming, and disposing of foods, from the provision of inputs and farmer training, to product packaging and marketing, to waste recycling" (IPES 2015, p. 3). De Schutter (2017) reports that current agri-food systems cause many serious problems and are unsustainable in several ways. First, although the current high levels of agricultural production allow for a high caloric intake for many people, the nutritional transition to a Western diet, which contains large amounts of fat, sugar, and salt, has serious health implications. Middle-income countries such as Mexico, Brazil, and South Africa suffer from malnutrition, overweight, and obesity. Second, industrial agriculture in the global North, combined with protectionist policies and export subsidies, has led to rural poverty in developing countries due to competitive pressures on local farmers. Third, large international corporations have great power in global food chains, exacerbating poverty especially in the least developed countries. Finally, the current industrial agri-food system generates a variety of negative environmental impacts. Monocultures and the intensive use of pesticides, herbicides, and fungicides lead to an enormous loss of biodiversity. Mechanized farming and overuse of synthetic fertilizers degrade soils and lead to loss of soil fertility. Nitrogen- and phosphate-based fertilizers pollute fresh water and cause eutrophication of the oceans. There are planetary boundaries for both land degradation and for nitrogen and phosphorus fluxes in the biosphere and oceans, and the latter are clearly being exceeded. In addition, current agriculture is a significant producer of greenhouse gas emissions that cause climate change. There are many proposals for superior agri-food systems, but the transition is blocked by multiple technical, political, social, and institutional lock-in effects (see Magrini et al. 2018; Magrini et al. 2019; Conti et al. 2021; Black et al. 2022).

Gregory Unruh (2000) coined the term *carbon lock-in* to describe that

> *industrial economies have become locked into fossil fuel-based technological systems through a path-dependent process driven by technological and institutional increasing returns to scale. This condition … arises through a combination of systematic forces that*

> *perpetuate fossil-fuel based infrastructures in spite of their known environmental externalities and the apparent existence of cost-neutral, or even cost-effective, remedies.* (Unruh 2000, p. 817)

Seto et al. (2016) state:

> *Carbon lock-in generally constrains technological, economic, political, and social efforts to reduce carbon emissions. Given the predicted magnitude and timeline of its worst impacts, an effective response to climate change will require large-scale and relatively rapid disruption to existing systems. Carbon lock-in poses significant challenges to making such changes on the necessary timetable, especially when the changes needed require undoing quite entrenched and reinforced patterns and institutions in multiple technological, economic, political, and social systems.* (Seto et al. 2016, p. 427)

The causes and mechanisms of these system lock-ins are much more complex than the QWERTY narrative. Understanding agri-food system lock-in and carbon lock-in therefore requires a thorough analysis of the facts and historical processes. However, at least with respect to carbon lock-in, it seems clear that the current fossil system is not only inefficient, but unsustainable and likely to lead to climate catastrophe. Given that unchecked global warming is likely to make large parts of the Earth uninhabitable, the total switching costs to a non-fossil economy cannot be greater than the potentially extremely high costs of a climate catastrophe (see Weitzman 2009).

11.4.2 Responses to the Liebowitz–Margolis Critique

The Liebowitz–Margolis critique is an attempt to defend the worldview that the outcomes of competitive markets are either efficient or subject only to unavoidable inefficiency. The critique is primarily concerned with the case where a technology or practice is widely used even though a superior alternative is available that is not adopted despite a net gain from switching. Liebowitz and Margolis associate this situation with irrational behavior. Why would rational agents forgo an opportunity for higher profits and utility?

In the QWERTY example, it is easiest to see how a market correction of an inefficient path dependence might work. If the DSK does indeed significantly increase the speed of typists and thus reduces the cost of typing, an employer may invest in Dvorak typewriters and (re)train typists at its own expense. After a while, this investment will pay for itself and give the company a competitive advantage over other companies still using QWERTY machines. When the competitors realize the source of the cost advantage, they will follow suit and adopt Dvorak as well. At the end of this process, private profit-seeking will have corrected the error of the QWERTY path.

Note that this argument hinges on at least two conditions. First, employers must know, or at least strongly believe, that switching to Dvorak would actually increase productivity enough to make the investment worthwhile. But since the scientific evidence on the superiority of DSK over QWERTY is still inconclusive after many years of research, it may be impossible for an employer to answer this question. Assuming that there are some companies that take the risk, implement DSK, and actually reduce typing costs, there is no guarantee that other companies will observe this benefit and correctly attribute it to the implementation of DSK, as there can be many reasons for cost advantages.

In the QWERTY example, there is a discussion about the superiority of DSK in two dimensions. First, DSK may be more efficient, allowing faster typing. Another advantage discussed might be that DSK is more ergonomic than QWERTY. Even if DSK does not speed up typing, it could be beneficial to typists by preventing repetitive strain injuries. If we assume that DSK has no speed advantage but is preferable from an ergonomic perspective, the case is more complicated. Employers would have no direct economic benefit from adopting DSK and bearing the investment costs. They might expect their typists to become less productive in the long run due to hand injuries, but they might not see this as their problem and simply hire new typists instead of preventing the problem. It could be argued that the typists themselves have an incentive to learn DSK instead of QWERTY in order to prevent their own health problems. But first, this does not help if employers do not provide DSK typewriters, and second, there are many health problems that people could prevent themselves without doing so (e.g., by exercising more, eating healthier, using social media less, etc.). From an employer's perspective, we could see typing-related health problems as a negative externality. If they are not forced to internalize it, they will not do so because they do not have to bear the social costs (at least not directly).

To reiterate, the QWERTY case may not deserve too much attention by itself, because the potential inefficiencies and drawbacks may actually be small. But its simplicity allows us to discuss broader issues in a way that is easy to grasp and apply to other cases. Leaving the QWERTY example, there are several possible responses to the Liebowitz–Margolis critique.

First, efficiency differences are difficult to prove because of the counterfactual problem. There may be strong arguments for inefficient lock-in, but actually proving it will generally be impossible. Uncertainty can be an obstacle to path-switching investments. In general, path switching is rare, even when it is possible and beneficial. David (2007) criticizes the approach of comparing the welfare of two different situations together with the assumption that the better one is chosen as an ahistorical static framework. He argues that the more realistic description of agents' behavior is *path-constrained amelioration*:

> *Seen in truly historical perspective, a great deal of human ingenuity, especially the sort that is said to be 'mothered by necessity' if not by opportunity, is devoted to trying to cope with the consequences of past mistakes whose economic costs are threatening to become 'serious'; to assuring, somehow, that the more pernicious effects will be moderated, if not abated altogether. Of necessity (because we live without perfect foresight), much of this effort is remedial. It is undertaken ex post, by contriving technological 'fixes' and 'patches,' by commandeering temporary task forces to handle emergencies that established organizational structures and routines are discovered to be handling badly, by sustained efforts at*

> *'reforming' (not reinventing) long-standing institutions; and, yes, by concerted educational campaigns to 'un-train' people who have through historical circumstance learned habits of mind, or unthinking reactions that are proving in one way or another to be personally and socially dysfunctional.* (David 2007, p. 106)

Path-constrained amelioration is well compatible with Joseph Tainter's notion of increasing complexity through problem-solving (see Sect. 10.8.3 in Chap. 10). The unforeseen and unintended consequences of actions cause problems that are fixed as they become apparent. Due to uncertainty and limited foresight, they are not prevented in advance. Amelioration and problem fixing are adaptive behaviors characteristic of complex adaptive systems.

Second, while efficiency is of primary interest to neoclassical economists, it need not be the only criterion by which to judge lock-in. Different paths are likely to have different distributive consequences between providers of technological alternatives, but also between firms and consumers. As argued above, the current global agri-food system systematically disadvantages small farmers, especially in poor countries. Such an assessment may be another reason to consider a locked-in situation as undesirable, even if it were efficient. In the presence of negative externalities, such as environmental damage, health problems, and climate change, market outcomes are not welfare-maximizing, which is standard wisdom in mainstream economics.

Third, there is the issue of timing. It may not be possible to switch to superior paths because of time lags and the long lifespans of some capital goods. The normal operating life of a nuclear reactor is 40 years, but the U.S. Office of Nuclear Energy argues that American reactors could be used for up to 80 years (Office of Nuclear Energy 2022). Planning and construction of a new nuclear power plant typically takes about 12 years.

Finally, if complementarities between the activities and technologies of different agents are a major reason for path dependence, then no agent can easily break out of a lock-in on its own. A coordination problem arises that may be difficult to solve if the interests of the agents involved differ. Switching to a different path may be beneficial for some agents, but not for all. Even if there is a net gain, it may not help because it is often difficult to convince and compensate the loser of a reform.

11.4.3 Types and Causes of Systemic Lock-in

We encountered the problem of systemic lock-in above with the examples of the agri-food system and the fossil fuel-based energy system. The transportation system or the health care system are other examples of socio-technical systems. System lock-in is related to the discussion of system evolvability in Chap. 10. A system that has limited evolvability is locked in. One difference with the evolutionary literature is that "lock-in" suggests that something should be done about it. A locked-in system should be reformed to increase welfare, but reform is difficult for a variety of reasons. Seto et al. (2016) present three types of carbon lock-in: (1) infrastructural and technological, (2) institutional, and (3) behavioral. Buschmann and Oels (2019) add discursive lock-in as a fourth type. While these types of lock-in are discussed in the context of carbon lock-in, they are more generally applicable to other systemic lock-ins.

Technology and infrastructure are the foundations of socio-technical systems. The energy system needs technologies to produce energy, such as nuclear reactors, coal-fired power plants, or gas-steam power plants. Power plants also need supply and distribution infrastructure, such as gas pipelines, coal docks in ports, high-voltage transmission lines, transformer stations, and so on. Seto et al. (2016) explain that technological and economic forces lead to inertia, especially due to long lead times, large investments, sunk costs, and long amortization periods. In addition, externalities are a pervasive problem, especially when technology choices are made by private actors. As discussed in the case of light water reactors, early random choices can be significant if reinforced by learning effects and economies of scale.

Institutional lock-in differs from technological lock-in in that it is often not an unintended by-product of some kind of increasing returns, but the actively sought outcome of institutional design. Powerful economic, social, and political actors create institutions as instruments of distribution and power. They either want to reinforce a status quo path that favors their interests, or they try to establish a new path that is more favorable to them. Interest groups coordinate their actions to structure institutional rules, norms, and constraints to promote their goals. Pierson (2000) argues that path dependence is even more likely in politics than in economics because of some characteristics of the political system. He argues that transparency is lacking, learning is difficult, and political time horizons are short, all of which lead to a status quo bias of political institutions. Political arrangements are particularly difficult to change because they are generally designed to be difficult to overturn. Political actors want to avoid having their decisions reversed by their successors. In addition, political actors want to make credible commitments in order to gain credibility. Supermajority or unanimity rules are devices that are desirable obstacles to institutional change.

Behavioral lock-in occurs at the individual and group levels. At the individual level, people learn and form habits. Each person develops routines to manage daily life efficiently. Contrary to the assumption of neoclassical economics, not every action is based on a conscious decision with rational consideration of costs and benefits. Since our mental capacity is limited, we develop many habits that automate our behavior to some degree. For example, we usually do not actively decide whether to brush our teeth in the morning. We just do it because our parents taught us to. Similarly, there are many products that we routinely buy in the supermarket, such as toothpaste or cereals. We may try new products from time to time, but it is common to stick with a particular brand unless we have a strong reason to switch. Habitual behavior is largely unconscious. According to Wood et al. (2002), approximately 43% of daily behaviors are habitual. Established habits are difficult to change because they are hardwired into our brain structures. Habits can be changed by establishing new routines, which are sets of behaviors that are repeated frequently and intentionally. If we are persistent enough, a routine becomes a habit and no longer requires mental effort. Forming a new habit can take considerable time. Lally et al. (2010) conducted a study in which automaticity occurred between 18 and 254 days, with an average of 66 days after the start of a new routine. Lock-in occurs at the group level because groups develop behavioral social norms and shared lifestyles. A certain way of living is perceived as normal in a peer group. What we eat, how we dress, what we do in our leisure time, and so on are largely determined by what is consistent with the social norms of our reference group and what other people expect of us. Violating such norms can be very costly for individuals, who risk being ostracized and losing their social identity (Akerlof 2002, 2007). Lifestyles and shared social practices coevolve with technologies, infrastructures, and institutions. U.S. car culture (see Chap. 5) is a good example of the coevolution of car technology, road infrastructure, and a particular lifestyle. In most of the United States, people rely on their cars for most aspects of their lives. But even in other countries where alternatives to driving, such as public transportation or bicycling, are more readily available, the habit of driving is a major behavioral lock-in that makes system change difficult.

In the tradition of the French philosopher Michel Foucault, a *discourse* is a way of thinking and communicating that constructs our perception and experience of the (social) world. This definition is based on the assumption that language does not simply describe reality as it is, but constitutes it. "A discourse assigns meaning, defines power relations and creates subjects and objects through practices. A discourse is always in competition with other discourses and is struggling for its reproduction (by practices) and for dominance in a field" (Buschmann and Oels 2019, p. 2). The struggle for dominance is also called the struggle for discursive hegemony, which is achieved when discourse structuration and discourse institutionalization have occurred. Discourse structuration means that one discourse dominates the process of collective sense-making in a group or political domain. Discourse institutionalization is achieved when a discourse is institutionalized in a set of institutional arrangements. For example, the way GDP is defined and measured by statistical agencies institutionalizes how we think and talk about economic growth, since GDP is the conventional measure of aggregate economic activity. Discursive lock-in occurs when a particular group has achieved discursive hegemony, so that a particular worldview dominates. This worldview suggests how different ways of doing things are to be evaluated and how certain actions are to be accepted as reasonable, while others are to be rejected as absurd. We might say that there is a general discursive lock-in that regards economic growth as desirable or even obligatory. In political debates, positions that regard no-growth or even de-growth economies as desirable are often ridiculed as utopian or naive. Discursive lock-in is important because it stabilizes established power relations, social and political practices, and makes it difficult to even discuss alternative paths.

[7] This subsection relies heavily on the materials provided by Collier and Munck.

11.5 Path Formation and Path Change

The previous sections explained what path dependence means and why a system can become locked in on a particular, possibly suboptimal, path. In this section, we discuss how we can describe the formation of a path in an analytical framework. While paths can become stable and resistant to change over time, sometimes path changes occur. When an established path is broken and a shift to a new path occurs, we often speak of revolutions, reforms, or disruptions, which are relatively rare events. In political science, the theory of critical junctures and the concept of punctuated equilibrium are widely used. They are also useful for thinking about change in the economy, especially if institutions are seen as an important element of the economic system.

11.5.1 Critical Junctures

"A critical juncture is (1) an episode of institutional innovation, (2) occurring in divergent ways, and (3) generating contrasting and enduring legacies" (Collier and Munck 2018).[7] Critical junctures are large and discontinuous changes that occur rapidly. They are historical turning points (or branching points) that decisively shape the evolution of an entity. The idea of critical junctures was introduced by Lipset and Rokkan (1967) to explain party systems in Western Europe over four centuries. They argue that four critical junctures (the Reformation and Counter-Reformation in the sixteenth and seventeenth centuries, national revolutions in the eighteenth and nineteenth centuries, the Industrial Revolution, and the Russian Revolution in 1917) left a cumulative legacy that consolidated in the 1920s into distinct types of persistent European party systems. Critical junctures are closely related to social cleavages: social cleavages can lead to critical junctures, which in turn can deepen the cleavages. The legacy of a critical juncture is a stabilized institutional path.

Extending Lipset and Rokkan's (1967) three-step template of cleavage, critical juncture, and legacy, Collier and Collier (1991) propose a five-step template for analyzing hypothesized causal links in a historical process (see Fig. 11.10). Antecedent conditions include many different features of the economy, society, politics, and the state that can lead to social cleavage. The cleavage is a shock to the system that leads to conflict and crisis. The critical juncture triggered by the shock is an

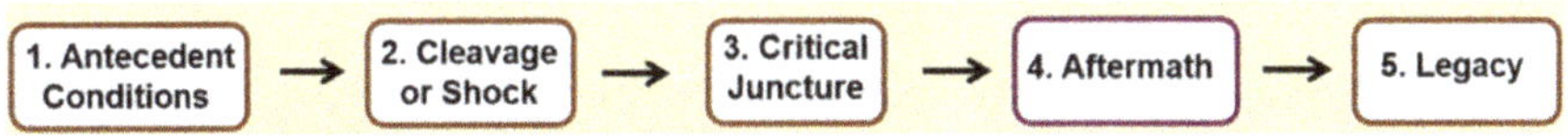

Fig. 11.10 Five-step analytical framework for critical junctions. Source: Collier and Munck (2018), licensed under CC BY-SA 4.0 (https://creativecommons.org/licenses/by-sa/4.0/)

important episode of institutional formation. The aftermath of the critical juncture describes the steps through which the legacy emerges and takes shape. Finally, the legacy is the phase of enduring and stable institutions. To show that a critical juncture occurred in a historical episode, differentiation is necessary. This means that the researcher should demonstrate in a cross-case analysis that the aftermath and legacy can be different after the same critical juncture with comparable antecedent conditions and cleavage. A cross-case analysis is an attempt to deal with the problem of the unobservable counterfactual.

Joel Rast's (2009) study of urban development strategies in Chicago and Milwaukee after World War II is a vivid example of the critical juncture approach. At the end of World War II, both cities were in a similar situation: they were suffering from an industrial crisis, a flight of the white middle class to the suburbs, and the decline of the inner city. In addition, the mayors of both cities had adopted a caretaker approach to governance, focusing on good basic services and sound fiscal policies, but little active urban development in the 1930s and 1940s. Federal and state urban renewal legislation in the late 1940s provided cities with incentives and resources for large-scale redevelopment, particularly through housing policies and public–private partnerships. Rast sees urban renewal legislation as a critical juncture for the two cities, which took two very different paths. While Chicago chose to redevelop its downtown, Milwaukee focused on industrial development to create jobs and expand the city's tax base. These choices led to very different trajectories in the decades that followed, despite similar starting points. Two aspects stand out. First, Chicago's path was characterized by a strong positive feedback mechanism and was therefore very robust. Chicago's downtown redevelopment activated a network or regime of developers, business leaders, and building trades unions that developed mutual trust and a common sense of purpose that gave the regime the power to pursue the ambitious program over time. In contrast, Milwaukee's redevelopment depended on ad hoc coalitions that often fought each other over divergent interests. The second interesting aspect is the role of chance and timing that can be observed in the Milwaukee case. As in Chicago, a group of businessmen pushed for downtown redevelopment in the 1940s. But Milwaukee voters elected socialist Frank P. Zeidler as mayor in 1948, who favored industrial development over downtown "glamour projects." He was succeeded in 1960 by Democrat Henry Maier. Despite his personal preference for downtown redevelopment, Maier continued Zeidler's industrial development program because it had already produced some increasing returns and thus had an advantage over the alternative of downtown redevelopment, which was plagued by competing civic groups with their own divergent agendas. Rast argues that the Milwaukee case is an example of the importance of single events and timing:

> *Had the Democrat Henry Maier been elected mayor In 1948 rather than in 1960, there is very reason to believe that Milwaukee's postwar development path would have resembled Chicago's much more than it did. Most likely, Maier would have pursued an approach similar to Daley's, working closely with downtown business leaders and orienting the city's urban renewal program around downtown development. The impact of a Socialist mayor on*

[8] Acemoglu and Robinson (2012) use the term "critical juncture," but not Acemoglu et al. (2001).

development policy, had it come late rather than early in the postwar period, would likely have represented a temporary disruption of a long-term redevelopment program focused largely on downtown. (Rast 2009, p. 416).

Another example of alternative paths after a critical juncture is the paper by Acemoglu et al. (2001), although it does not explicitly refer to the critical juncture framework. The authors ask the question, why there are large differences in per capita income across countries today. Their answer is that different institutional paths are the explanation. Some countries have better institutions that secure property rights and encourage investment in physical and human capital than others. Acemoglu and Robinson (2012) call growth-promoting institutions *inclusive institutions*, because they bestow equal rights and entitlements to many groups and individuals allowing them to be productive. In contrast, *exclusive* (or extractive) *institutions* privilege only certain groups and exclude many others from political and economic life, hindering economic growth and development. For Acemoglu et al. (2001), the arrival of European colonialists was a critical juncture[8] in Africa, Asia, the Americas, and Australia. The argument is that the mortality of Europeans due to climate and diseases was the key factor. In regions with high mortality rates, Europeans established exclusive institutions to exploit the region's resources without settling there. In regions with low mortality, however, Europeans settled and established better institutions similar to those in their home countries. When the European colonies became independent countries, they inherited either the good or the bad institutions, which is a crucial determinant of their past and current economic performance. Acemoglu et al. (2001) present econometric evidence to support their story.

11.5.2 A Framework for Path Formation

A truly historical perspective focuses on processes and aims to explain how a state of the world came to be. Our discussion of paths and lock-in has focused mainly on the reasons for path dependence and the properties of given paths, not on the actual formation of paths in time.

Sydow et al. (2009) propose a theoretical framework that explains how a path is established (see Fig. 11.11). The framework was originally proposed to conceptualize how path dependence arises in organizations, but it is also applicable to other path-dependent processes because Sydow et al. derive it from the general literature on path dependence. They divide a path formation process into three phases: Phase I (preformation phase), Phase II (formation phase), and Phase III (lock-in phase).

In the preformation phase, decision-makers have many options for action. These actions may relate to the choice of a technology, a firm's product, an organizational structure, a policy strategy, and others. At this stage, the consequences of an action choice are highly uncertain and cannot be reliably predicted. A choice that triggers self-reinforcing dynamics, often unintended, can be seen as a critical juncture.

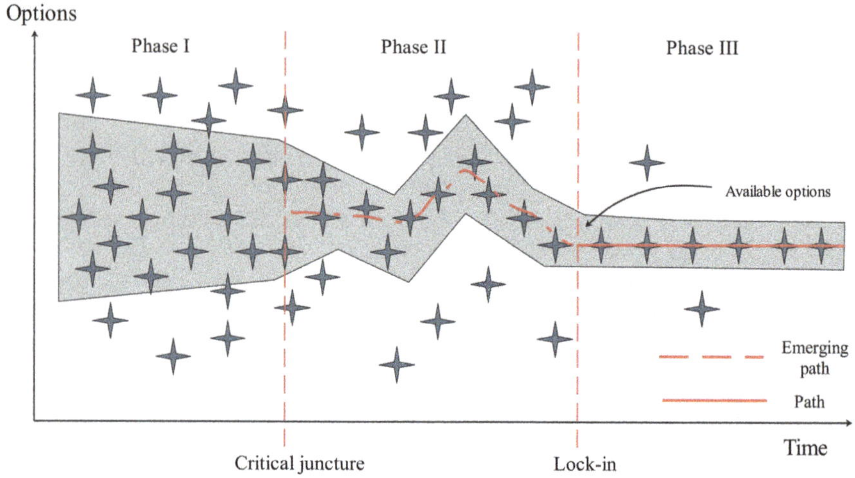

Fig. 11.11 Phases of path formation. Source: Author's own figure based on Sydow et al. (2009)

In the formation phase, positive feedback dynamics create a dominant pattern of action that makes other options less and less feasible. The narrowing scope of action makes the chosen path increasingly difficult to reverse, although it is still possible to do so.

The range of available options has become so narrow in the lock-in phase that the dominant action pattern becomes fixed and flexibility is lost. The action pattern reproduces itself, even when there are indications that it is inefficient. A single path has formed.

11.5.3 Punctuated Equilibrium and Path Changes

Although the concept of path dependence is accepted in political science, especially after the influential paper of Pierson (2000), some scholars consider it too static or deterministic, if the end stage of a path formation process is one single path. As mentioned above, history is always characterized by both stability and change. Stephen Krasner (1984) transferred the concept of punctuated equilibrium from evolutionary biology to political science.

In biology, the concept of punctuated equilibrium was introduced as an alternative to phyletic gradualism, a theory that postulates that evolution occurs gradually, with small incremental changes such that branches of species diverge slowly (see Fig. 11.12). In contrast, punctuated equilibrium postulates that, according to the fossil record, there are long periods of little evolutionary change (stasis), with more sudden leaps or splits of species into new ones.

This idea of episodes of dramatic change after periods of equilibrium (or stasis) corresponds to revolutions, major political reforms, or path breaking, the rare shift to a new path. From an evolutionary perspective, new paths emerge not just once, but

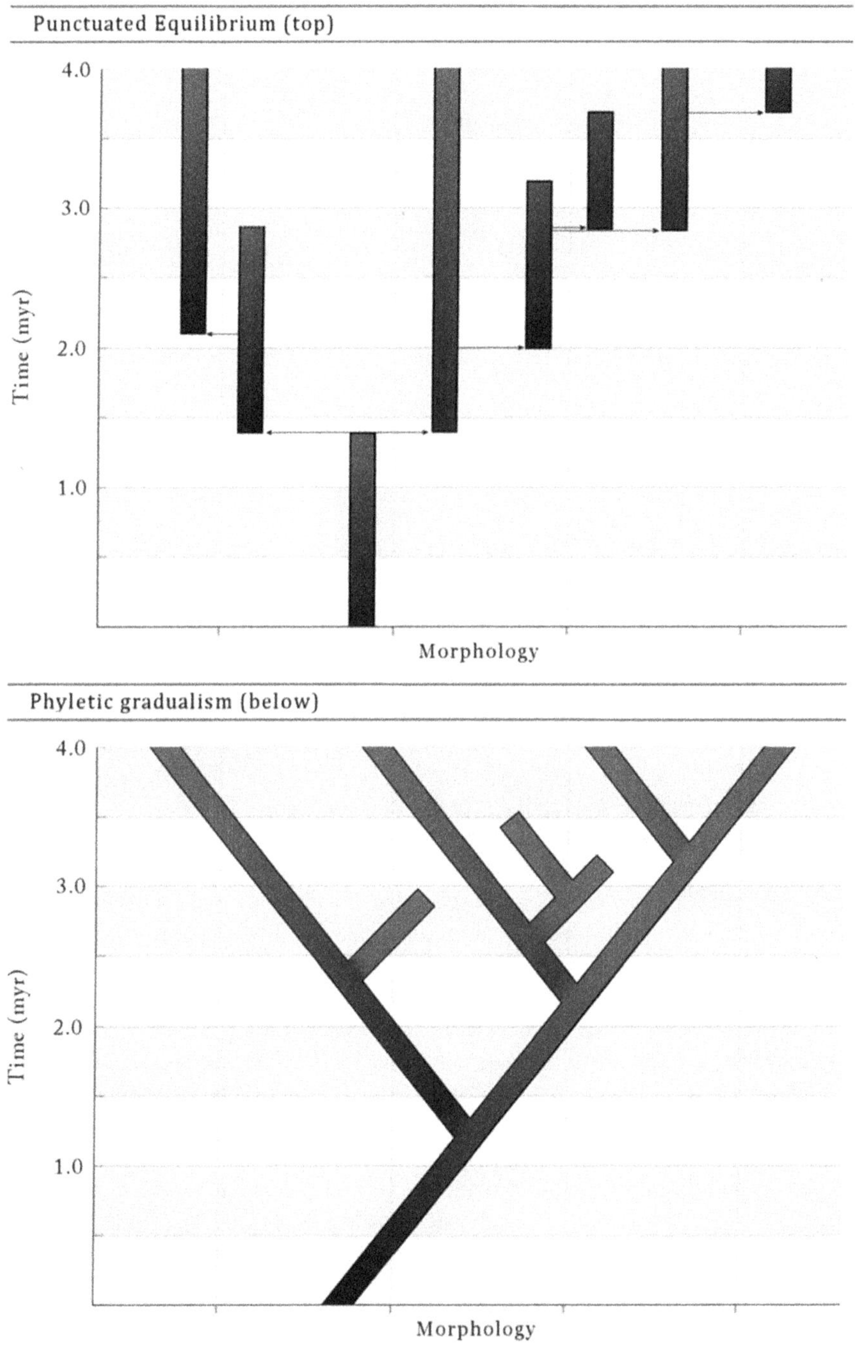

Fig. 11.12 Punctuated equilibrium. Source: Wikimedia Commons, by Chavez (2018), CC BY-SA 4.0 (https://creativecommons.org/licenses/by-sa/4.0/deed.en)

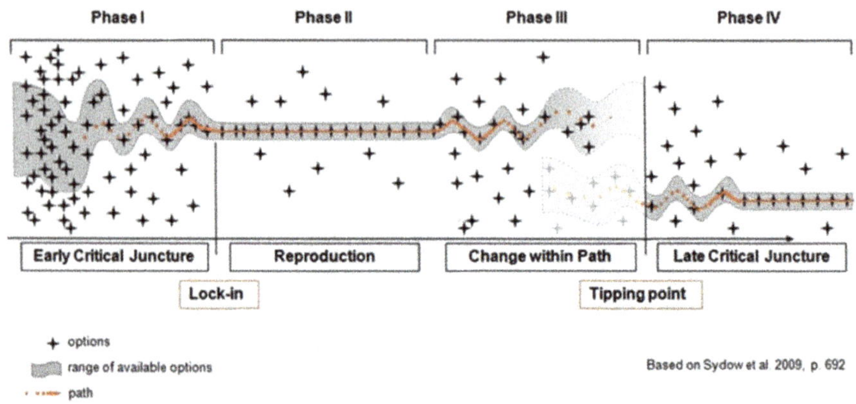

Fig. 11.13 Path formation and path switching. Source: Selbmann (2015), licensed under CC-BY 4.0 (https://creativecommons.org/licenses/by/4.0/deed.en)

again and again. Therefore, we need to explain not only how a path is formed, but also how it is broken. Selbmann (2015) proposes an extended analytical framework that also allows for switching from one path to another. Her framework distinguishes four phases instead of three (see Fig. 11.13).

Phase I is called *early critical juncture*. From multiple available options, one is chosen by a more or less contingent event at a critical point in time. Once a particular path is initiated, positive feedback occurs so the path stabilizes and lock-in occurs (Phase II). This phase is called *reproduction*. In politics, but also in organizations, power asymmetries widen and discursive hegemony is achieved, i.e. discourse communities share and reproduce similar worldviews. Selbmann also emphasizes that the timing and sequence of events matter. Small events that happen early can have large effects, because the option space is still wide, but large events that happen later may have little effect because a robust path with strong positive feedback has been established.

The first two phases in Selbmann's framework correspond to the three phases in Sydow et al. (2009) shown in Fig. 11.11. Selbmann's phases III and IV are new and explain change despite path dependence. Phase III is called *changes within path*. In this phase, the mechanisms that reproduce the path are weakened by new exogenous and/or endogenous factors. Thus, the action space becomes wider again, but is still linked to an existing path. These changes within a path can lead to a tipping point, at which the equilibrium or path is broken and phase IV, called *late critical juncture* is entered. A late critical juncture establishes a new path. Figure 11.13 only describes the different state of path formation and path change. The previous subsections explained the mechanisms behind path formation, but the mechanisms that lead to changes within paths and of paths in phases III and IV deserve some discussion. Following Streeck and Thelen (2005), Selbmann (2015) explains some mechanisms based on the historical institutionalism literature for policy paths.

Changes within a path are a necessary, but not sufficient condition for a change of path. For a change of path to be possible, the mechanisms and institutions that stabilize the existing path must be weakened. Such weakening is often the result of gradual or "creeping incremental endogenous changes." There are five mechanisms that lead to the creeping destabilization of a path: (1) institutional layering, (2) institutional conversion, (3) institutional displacement, (4) institutional drift, and (5) institutional exhaustion.

Institutional layering occurs, when new (political) coalitions add new structures or rules to existing institutional systems. The new coalitions are not powerful enough to replace the existing institutional arrangement due to lack of support or the inability to mobilize, but the small additions to the institutional framework can erode the self-reinforcing mechanism that reproduces the path. The new elements set in motion new dynamics and crowd out elements of the old system. *Institutional conversion* refers to a redirection of existing institutions to new purposes by new actor constellations. This can happen when new actors interpret existing rules in their own interests or circumvent or subvert rules that are in conflict with their interests. *Institutional displacement* occurs when subordinate institutions gain importance and salience relative to dominant institutions. Taken-for-granted organizational forms and practices are challenged, and existing incoherence becomes apparent. *Institutional drift* is a result of "non-decisions" or the failure to update institutions when faced with exogenous pressures. As external conditions vary, institutions must adapt to be maintained. They will decay, if they are not recalibrated in response to changes in the political and economic environment. Finally, *institutional exhaustion* means that institutions gradually break down or erode over time because of self-consumption, decreasing returns or overextension. Note that institutional exhaustion is similar to Tainter's concept of decreasing returns to complexity mentioned in Chap. 10. Over time, institutions can grow so large that they require more resources than are available to maintain them. They may also become more complex due to a growing number of exceptions to institutionalized rules and special provisions that deprive them of their legitimacy and/or their practicability.

Three main groups of actors can initiate and drive the change processes described above. The first group are marginal groups or former losers of change. They do not benefit from the current institutional arrangement and have little to lose from deviant behavior and non-compliance. Entrepreneurs and skilled actors form the second group. They actively mediate different interests and reform proposals and are able to motivate other actors to engage in transformation processes. These actors are also called *change agents*. Third, new political coalitions can emerge with actors from different social networks who negotiate change.

A late critical juncture is associated with a long-lasting and fundamental change in institutions, policies, or practices. They can occur through endogenous changes within a path alone, when the cumulative impact of these incremental changes becomes so large that a tipping point is reached. Smaller or larger exogenous events can be catalysts for late critical junctures. If the self-reinforcing mechanisms of a given path are strong, even large exogenous shocks or events may not lead to a change in path. For example, a robust political system can withstand economic depressions or natural disasters without disruption. But a political system already weakened by internal conflict and the erosion of its stabilizing institutions could collapse in response to an external shock, such as insurgency or the legal takeover of power by radical actors.

Since the literature on punctuated equilibrium, critical junctures, and path switching is mainly a literature in political science, which is focused on the evolution of institutions and policies, one might ask why it should be relevant to economists. The economic literature on path dependence, which was strongly shaped by Arthur (1989, 1994), is more interested in the evolution of technology. This interest in technology is consistent with mainstream and non-mainstream theories of economic growth and development in which technology plays an important role. However, it is straightforward and useful to combine the ideas from political science (e.g., punctuated equilibrium) with those on innovation in economics in research on the political economy of technological change, as Joel Mokyr (1990, 1992, 1994, 2000) has done. In a frictionless neoclassical world, it is natural to assume that useful technological inventions are adopted quickly because of their potential to increase social welfare. The extremely rapid adoption of the smartphone since the introduction of the iPhone in 2007 might serve as an example. However, history is full of counterexamples that show that innovations did not succeed, at least not initially. As discussed in the brief history of inventions in Chap. 10, the time was not ripe for Trevithick's London Steam Carriage at the beginning of the nineteenth century. When steam-powered vehicles finally became commonplace on English roads in the mid-nineteenth century, they were slowed down by *Red Flag Acts* (or locomotive acts), which stipulated that all road locomotives, including automobiles, were not allowed to travel faster than 4 mph in the country and 2 mph in town. In addition, a man carrying a red flag had to walk in front of road vehicles, ostensibly to warn other road users, but in fact to enforce the speed limit and make the new vehicles less attractive.

Mokyr (1998) argues that resistance to new technologies is a widespread historical phenomenon. The introduction of a radically new technology is often the subject of intense debate and public discourse. Subgroups of society, such as workers, capital owners, landlords, etc., fear that a new technology will threaten their interests, often for very rational reasons. They have accumulated specific assets adapted to the existing technology, such as formal skills, tacit knowledge, reputation, specialized equipment, ownership of certain natural resources, barriers to entry that secure monopoly positions, and community-based nonpecuniary assets. Thus, they try to prevent a new technology from entering the markets.

> *The central principle of the political economy of technological change is that resistance almost always takes place through non-market mechanisms, although non-competitive market behavior, such as denying innovators access to credit, has also been a widely-employed strategy. One method was through legal means: the technological status quo used government power through licencing, safety regulations, tariffs and manipulation of education and research facilities to nip innovations in the bud. An alternative was to use extralegal means: strikes and demonstrations, as well as illegal 'Luddite' tactics such as*

> *arson, and other forms of personal violence have been highly effective means to combat innovation*. (Mokyr 1992, p. 329/330)

Mokyr views technology and institutions (both formal and informal) as two coevolving systems. From this perspective, it is possible to explain technological progress despite initial institutional resistance. New technologies and the entrepreneurs, interest groups, and new coalitions associated with them can weaken existing institutions and allow changes within the existing path, as explained above. Mokyr (1998) argues that it is difficult to construct simple economic models with these features, but that a combination of political economy and historical studies provides insights into the dynamics of technology and institutions. The following sections show how this can be done.

11.6 The History of the Automobile in the Twentieth Century

The history of the automobile in the early twentieth century is a rich example of path formation, inefficient lock-in, and the role of historical accidents. We can use it to show the importance of key events and individuals, the timing of actions, and institutional factors. As discussed in Chap. 5, at the beginning of the twentieth century, there were three technological options: steam cars with a 40% market share in the United States, electric cars with a 38% market share, and gasoline cars with a 22% market share. This state of affairs can be seen as a preformation phase of a path formation, in which the race was still open. Today we know that the gasoline-powered car won the race, although its market share was significantly lower than that of the other types. Therefore, it was not necessarily obvious that this type of automobile would eventually dominate.

We can ask a number of questions that a close examination of the historical facts can illuminate. Was the choice of the gasoline-fueled internal combustion engine (ICE) a good choice? What led to that choice? Did individual people and events play an important role? What positive feedback stabilized the path? What can we say about a counterfactual history?

11.6.1 Was the Gasoline-Fueled ICE a Good Choice?

The answer to this question depends, of course, on the criterion of "goodness." As economists, we would like to have a measure of net benefit or net social welfare that takes into account all costs and benefits, and use this measure to compare different alternatives. A full quantitative cost–benefit analysis is probably not feasible, mainly because we cannot reliably quantify the counterfactual if the electric car or the steamer had been chosen. Nevertheless, it is possible to argue that the gasoline car was probably not a good choice because of its impact on human health and climate change.

The internal combustion of gasoline and diesel is incomplete and produces the harmful exhaust gases carbon monoxide (CO), hydrocarbons (C_XH_Y), and nitrogen oxides (NO_X), as well as particulate matter (especially soot). Nitrogen oxides also react with the hydrocarbon ethane in the presence of sunlight to form ground-level ozone. Exhaust from gasoline engines is a major contributor to air pollution and smog. Anenberg et al. (2019) estimate that in 2015 alone, approximately 242,000 deaths worldwide were attributable to particulate matter and ozone from tailpipe emissions in G20 countries. Inhalation of nitrogen oxides increases the risk of lung cancer and can cause or aggravate respiratory diseases such as bronchitis and heart disease. It is safe to conclude that local emissions from gasoline cars in cities have caused millions of air pollution-related deaths and continue to cause more.

Lead pollution from gasoline-powered vehicles may be an even bigger problem than air pollution. In the early days of the internal combustion engine, engine knock was a serious problem. Engine knock, caused by the uncontrolled ignition of the air–fuel mixture, is a nuisance to passengers, but it can also reduce engine performance and even lead to engine destruction. To prevent engine knock, tetraethyl lead was added to gasoline between 1923 and 1996 in the USA and even until 2021 in Algeria (Ritchie 2022). Lead is highly toxic and can cause severe brain damage. The World Health Organization (2022) estimates that about one million people worldwide died from lead exposure in 2019. Although lead was banned as an anti-knock agent in gasoline in many countries in the 1990s, it remains a problem because it is a non-biodegradable heavy metal that persists in soil or organisms. McFarland et al. (2022) found that in 2015, about half of the American population (more than 170 million people) had clinically worrisome levels of lead in their blood as children. The risks of this lead exposure are lower IQ and long-term health impairments such as reduced brain size, greater likelihood of mental illness, and increased cardiovascular disease. The authors estimate that the cumulative IQ of affected Americans today has dropped by 824 million points, an average of three points per person.

Electric cars would have avoided these problems. They produce no local exhaust and do not require lead as an anti-knock agent. Lead was and is used in batteries, but it does not dissipate from batteries the way it does from exhaust. Steam cars do not knock either. They do produce exhaust, but Burton (1976) argued that modern steam engines could achieve similar efficiencies to gasoline engines, but with much lower pollutant emissions.

In terms of its contribution to climate change, the gas ICE also has an unfavorable record. Carbon dioxide emissions from the combustion of gasoline and diesel in ICEs are a significant determinant of global warming. Ironically, there are high hopes today that the electric car will replace the gasoline car, even though the gasoline car lost the race after 1914 (Sulzberger 2004). The contribution of steam engines to climate change depends on the fuel used to generate the heat. In principle, many fuels are possible, such as kerosene, diesel, coal, but also wood or other biomass. All forms of biomass are carbon neutral because they emit only as much carbon as was taken out during the growth process.

It should be noted, however, that ICEs can also be fueled with ethanol, i.e. alcohol, which is also carbon neutral. As early as 1905, there was a debate in the USA about the benefits of using ethanol instead of gasoline to fuel automobiles (McCarthy 2001). Ironically, ethanol would also have solved the problem of engine knock. In addition to electric and steam cars, another possible path with less climate impact would have been internal combustion with alcohol. Therefore, from an environmental and public health perspective, perhaps the worst of the four available options became the actual path.

11.6.2 Decisive Factors for the Choice of the ICE

From the perspective of contemporary observers at the turn of the twentieth century, none of the three technologies was clearly superior (Amatucci 2015). Steam vehicles were the most technologically mature. In 1906, a Stanley steam car—the Stanley Rocket Steamer—set a land speed record of 127 mph (204 km/h) at Daytona Beach. Steamers had a wide range of power that was easy to control, they were quiet, free of vibration, and easy to start. Their disadvantages were a short delay in starting, visible exhaust, and limited range due to the need to refill water. Electric vehicles were also quiet, free of vibration, easy to control, and easy to start. Another advantage was their cleanliness due to the lack of exhaust, which, along with the ease of starting, made them popular with women. The disadvantages of electric cars were basically the same as today: they were heavy due to the batteries, had a limited range and few charging stations, and took a long time to recharge. The main strength of gasoline-powered vehicles was their long range and the wide availability of gasoline. Disadvantages were dangerous physical starting with a hand crank that could take 5 minutes and often caused injury, smoky exhaust, and gear shifting.

In the early years, gasoline and electric cars were seen as somewhat complementary, and an early market segmentation emerged. Electric cars were not suitable for touring outside of towns due to their limited range. In addition, American roads between cities were very poor and mostly unpaved. Gasoline-powered cars were powerful enough to drive on rough terrain, but electric cars were not. Electric cars were seen as the ideal town cars and were especially popular with wealthy women who did not like the heavy cranking of gasoline cars. Several events and circumstances eventually ended the era of early electric vehicles (Sulzberger 2004). The first blow was Henry Ford's mass production of the gasoline-powered Model T beginning in 1907. Ford's dream was to democratize the automobile, which had been the vehicle of the rich. The smoky, noisy, and dangerous vehicle was a nuisance to many non-drivers, but the solution to this problem was not stricter health and environmental regulations, but the cheap car affordable to less well-off people. The publicly visible division of the U.S. population into a few who could afford a car and many who could not was a problem for Americans' self-image as a fairly egalitarian society (McCarthy 2001). The Model T was simple, functional, robust, easy to repair, and affordable for ordinary families. From his earliest years, Ford was fascinated by the internal combustion engine and did not believe in the electric or steam car. The second blow to the electric car came with the invention of the electric self-starter in 1911 by electrical engineer Charles F. Kettering, who later became vice president of General Motors Research Corporation. Electric ignition eliminated one of the major disadvantages of the gasoline car and opened up a large market for electrical component suppliers, who gradually switched from supplying electric car manufacturers to ICE manufacturers. Two other systemic circumstances contributed to the demise of the electric car. First, efforts to expand the battery charging infrastructure failed. Although some electric utilities knew that they could increase efficiency and profits through load leveling by charging the batteries of electric cars during off-peak hours, i.e., at night, many utilities remained passive. According to Sulzberger (2004), utilities criticized automakers for not producing cheaper electric cars, and automakers criticized utilities for not expanding the charging infrastructure. So there was a coordination problem that could not be solved. Second, some states, such as New York, began taxing vehicles by weight in the 1920s to pay for road wear and tear. The heavier weight of electric cars thus became an additional disadvantage.

Why the gasoline car eventually dominated the steam car is less obvious. Technically, the steam car had a slight advantage in the early years. The Stanley Motor Carriage Company, founded in 1902 by twins Francis E. Stanley and Freeland O. Stanley, produced fairly sophisticated vehicles. One drawback of the early Stanley steamers was that they did not have condensers to recycle water for reuse in the steam engine. As a result, a Stanley steamer used about a gallon of water per mile and had to be refilled every 30 to 50 miles. An anecdote links this technical feature to a historical accident (Arthur 1984): the outbreak of hoof-and-mouth disease in North America in 1914. To prevent the spread of the disease, horse troughs were removed from public places, which posed a problem for steam cars because they relied on horse troughs—in addition to ponds and streams—to refill their water tanks. It took the Stanley brothers three years, until 1917, to develop a condenser and boiler system that extended the range of the steam car. While Arthur (1984) sees the removal of horse troughs as the "horseshoe nail" that sealed the fate of the steam car, others (e.g. Strohl 2020) do not deny that hoof-and-mouth disease had an impact, but doubt that it was decisive. Another problem with steam cars was that many people feared the risk of boiler explosions, although no such incidents were reported after 1890. Finally, some states, such as New York (again), required special licenses for all steam engines, whether they were used industrially, in a locomotive, or in an automobile.

The most important reason for the decline of the steam car is probably found in the personalities of the entrepreneurs involved. McLaughlin (1954) reports that the Stanley brothers were skilled inventors on a par with Henry Ford or Thomas Edison with a wide range of interests and abilities. At young age, for example, they had taught themselves to carve violins. Despite lacking college education, they were able to perfect a photographic dry plate and to invent and patent various types of X-ray apparatus. According to McLaughlin (1954, p. 40) the "Stanley brothers entered the business of making automobiles as an experiment to see whether they could make a car which would out-perform all the cars they had seen at an automobile fair in Boston in 1899." In contrast to Henry Ford, the Stanley brothers were great inventors, but less skilled businessmen. They tried to keep their business small and did little to improve their production, financing, or sales methods. Because they continued to rely on old-fashioned craftsmanship, their company was hampered by the limited availability of skilled workers, while Ford's standardized mass production made it possible to hire all kinds of unskilled workers. As a result, the Stanley Company and other steam car manufacturers could not compete with the low costs and the high production volumes of the Detroit-based gasoline car manufacturers, which adopted modern production techniques. McLaughlin (1954, p. 46) concludes:

> *It cannot be argued with any confidence that the final adoption of the internal combustion engine as the standard engine for use in private automobiles was solely or even principally the result of its inherent superiority as a form of motive power. More likely it was the result of the fact that those automotive engineers who decided to adopt the internal combustion engine decided also to introduce at the same time a series of radical innovations in production engineering and in distribution. In this case at least the relative success of the rival innovations depended as much upon the managerial abilities of the entrepreneurs responsible as upon the technical merits of the alternative forms of power.*

Having argued why the internal combustion engine outrivaled the steam engine and the electric engine, the question remains why the chosen fuel was gasoline instead of ethanol. Originally, gasoline was a useless by-product to kerosene, which was used as lamp oil and was the predominant commercial product from petroleum. Since there was little use for it, it was quite cheap. McCarthy (2001) describes how engineers and experts in the United States were skeptical about using gasoline to fuel automobiles. Although the Swedish chemist Svante Arrhenius predicted the relationship between carbon dioxide emissions and global warming as early as 1896, this issue was not a major concern at the time (although the Popular Mechanics Magazine published an article on the subject in March 1912). The experts were concerned about the limited supply of the non-renewable resource petroleum and the monopoly of John D. Rockefeller's Standard Oil. Alcohol (ethanol) was seen as a renewable, clean, safe, and less odorous substitute for gasoline: "By 1906, alcohol had become the preferred alternative to gasoline. There were pros and cons to both fuels, but there was no great debate or controversy among the experts about the best alternative" (McCarthy 2001, p. 51).

The main obstacle to the use of alcohol was its price relative to gasoline. Production costs were twice as high, and a sin tax intended to discourage drinking raised the price to $2.50 per gallon, about ten times the price of a gallon of gasoline. Although denatured ethyl alcohol for automobiles was allowed to be sold tax-free beginning in 1907, the price remained twice that of gasoline because it had to be made undrinkable. In addition, farmers and alcohol producers—mainly whiskey distillers—made no effort to increase production to reduce costs. Distribution was another problem, because unlike gasoline, for which Standard Oil provided a distribution network, fuel alcohol was not widely available. Finally, because of its lower caloric content, more alcohol than gasoline is needed to produce the same amount of power. The technical problems associated with this issue could have been overcome with appropriate R&D and investment, but by 1907 the automobile industry was already heavily committed to gasoline, so only a substantial price difference between the two fuels would have induced automakers to make the investment.

A later opportunity to switch to ethanol was its potential to solve the problem of engine knock. Ethanol has many of the same anti-knock properties as lead. But this opportunity was not taken because General Motors engineer Thomas Midgley Jr., commissioned by his boss Charles Kettering, invented a new fuel called Ethyl, gasoline blended with tetraethyl lead to prevent knocking. Ethyl was a huge success and cemented the dominance of gasoline. Again, individuals played a crucial role. Midgley was a mechanical engineer by training, but he was a skilled inventor who acquired the chemical skills necessary to find the right chemical anti-knock agent by testing 33,000 different compounds. A sad fact is that both Midgley and Kettering knew that lead was highly toxic and that ethanol would be an alternative (Johnson 2023). As a result of his experiments, Midgley himself suffered from lead poisoning. Moreover, once the mass production of tetraethyl lead began, many workers became ill and some even committed suicide due to lead-induced insanity. Because lead causes hallucinations of swarming insects, the ethyl plant was soon called the "house of butterflies" or the "loony gas building." Johnson (2023) argues that Kettering and Midgley decided to use lead anyway because they could patent Ethyl but not alcohol. Thus, the profit motive of GM dominated known health concerns.

To sum up, the years between 1905 and 1915 were an early critical juncture in the history of the automobile. Several options were available for powering automobiles, none of them clearly superior from a technical point of view. Several individuals with their values, attitudes, and skills were decisive: Henry Ford, Charles Kettering, the Stanley brothers, Thomas Midgley. Coincidental events such as hoof-and-mouth disease may have played a role, as did external conditions such as the poor state of American roads and biased legislation—taxes on ethanol and vehicle weight, licensing requirements for steam engines. There was also a failure of coordination, as electric utilities and automobile manufacturers could not coordinate, nor could farmers and alcohol producers to counter the Standard Oil monopoly. The critical juncture probably occurred with the start of Ford's mass production of gasoline ICE cars in 1907, with the lock-in caused by Kettering's invention of the electric starter in 1911.

11.6.3 Positive Feedback and Path Stabilization

Briggs et al. (2015) discuss how the path of the U.S. automobile industry stabilized and reproduced itself after what they call automotive modal lock-in (AML). The path refers not only to the technology of the gasoline ICE, but to the whole system built on this technology, which they call a *socio-technological regime*, a *techno-institutional complex,* or a *large socio-economic regime* (LSER). They distinguish three different phases in the history of the industry: 1900–1920, 1920–1970, and 1970 to the present.

Their first phase from 1900 to 1920 corresponds to what Selbmann (2015) calls Phase I (early critical juncture). This period is characterized primarily by market forces and the actions of consumers and producers. By 1920, the ICE cars had virtually displaced the electric cars and steamers.

The second phase (1920–1970), which corresponds to Selbmann's Phase II ("reproduction"), involves broader socio-economic linkages and, in particular, greater state involvement. In the 1920s, road infrastructure was still inadequate and an obstacle to further market expansion. Automobile manufacturers were beginning to feel the effects of competition and diminishing returns. As described in Chap. 5, manufacturers developed marketing, advertising, and financing to keep the market growing. The government financed the expansion of the road network, influencing living and travel patterns as well as consumer attitudes. Finally, a system of fuel providers and maintenance and support services developed. The automobile became the dominant mode of transportation, and an LSER developed with strong and dense linkages between consumers, automobile manufacturers, automobile suppliers, service providers, and the government.

In Selbmann's framework, the last phase since 1970 could be interpreted as Phase III ("change within the path"). In the 1970s, the USA and many other countries were hit by the oil crises, and dependence on imported oil became apparent. Further market growth was unlikely due to saturation and foreign competition. In addition, the private and societal costs—especially in terms of health and environmental problems, but also in terms of existing infrastructure—became more obvious. On the one hand, consumer, environmental and climate protection movements began to call for change. On the other hand, the auto and oil lobbies lobbied to protect their markets and prevent change. Whether and how we enter the final phase of the Late Critical Juncture remains to be seen.

11.7 Modeling Future Transitions of the Automobile

In light of the current political goal of halting climate change, as negotiated among nations in the 2015 Paris Agreement, it is necessary to phase out the use of fossil fuel ICE automobiles. While changes in the trajectory of the gasoline ICE automobile may already be occurring, we may not yet have entered Selbmann's Phase IV of the Late Critical Juncture. A Late Critical Juncture establishes a new path. Although thinking about the future is similar to thinking about counterfactual history, historical reasoning has a limit when it comes to the future. Modeling can help structure our thinking about the future and develop possible scenarios of what might happen.

In this section, we present an agent-based model by Köhler et al. (2009) that generates scenarios about the possible future paths of the automobile. The model is based on the multilevel perspective framework of transition theory (Geels 2005) introduced in Chap. 5. Similar to the discussion in this chapter, transition theory emphasizes the interdependence of institutions and infrastructures that make up societal systems and subsystems. These interlocking economic, social, cultural, infrastructural, and regulatory subsystems are associated with a range of social groups. Cognitive, normative, and regulatory institutions stabilize and reinforce the system. The concept of a regime, which can be understood as a particular set of practices, rules, and shared assumptions that govern the system and its actors, represents these institutions. Because a regime resists innovation and change and tends to focus on optimizing existing practices, it represents lock-in. Transition theory analyzes how lock-in can be broken through regime transformation or regime change.

11.7.1 Model

The model was part of the MATISSE project funded by the European Union from 2005 to 2007. The approach is described in Haxeltine et al. (2008) and Bergman et al. (2008).

The model is a combination of an agent-based model and a system dynamics model and aims at representing transitions in socio-technical systems. Here, we present only the conceptual framework. Details and equations can be found in Bergman et al. (2008). There are a small number of complex aggregate agents of the following types: the *regime* is the strongest agent that dominates the system. It is a subsystem consisting of actors, e.g. firms, lobby groups, institutions, and infrastructures. The regime can be understood as a particular set of practices, rules, and shared assumptions that dominate the whole system. It is oriented toward system optimization rather than innovation. Therefore, the regime has established a path that it seeks to reproduce. *Niches* are actors and technologies outside the regime. They focus on innovation, but have little power. *Empowered niche agents (ENAs)* are niches that have become strong enough to threaten the dominance of the regime and to become the regime themselves. Each agent occupies a specific location in the practices space, as shown in Fig. 11.14.

The agents are aggregate agents, i.e. clusters of more elementary agents that are not explicitly modeled. Each agent has a metabolism described by an internal system dynamics model, as shown in Fig. 11.15. The metabolism collects, allocates, and spends resources. The amount of resources available depends on the external support of microagents that are consumers/citizens and other external or landscape factors.

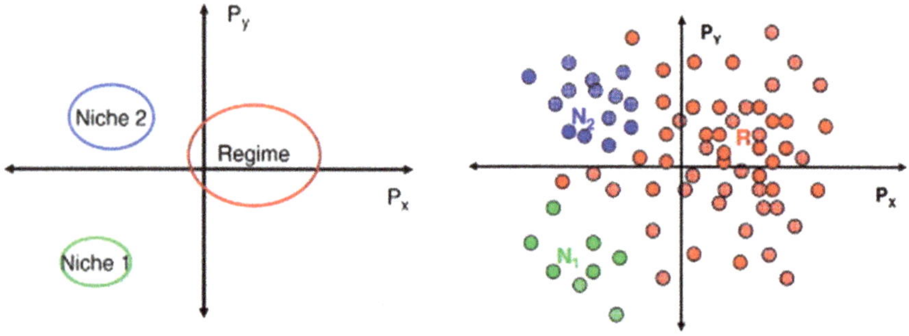

Fig. 11.14 Agents and supporters in a two-dimensional practices space. Source: Köhler et al. (2009), reproduced with kind permission of Elsevier B.V

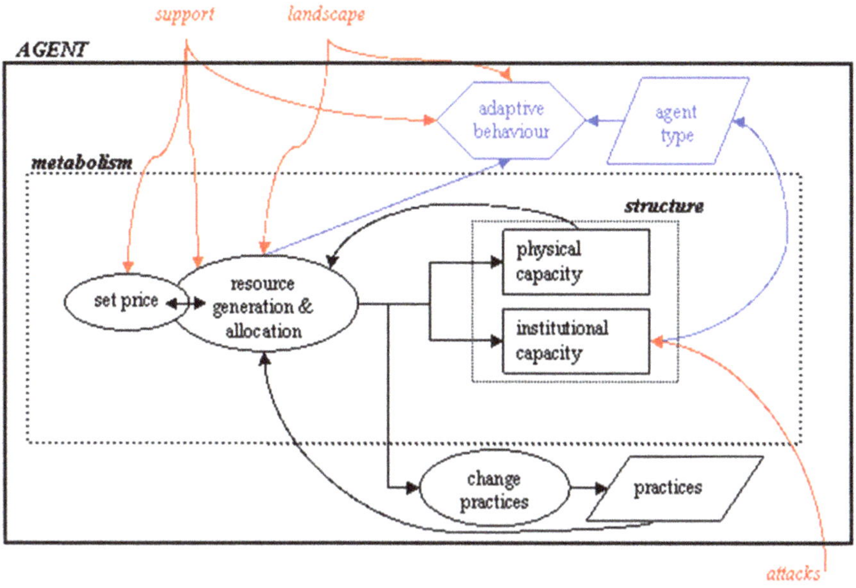

Fig. 11.15 Agent metabolism. Source: Bergman et al. (2008), licensed under CC-BY 4.0 (https://creativecommons.org/licenses/by/4.0/)

The only behavior of supporters (consumers/citizens) is to support (e.g., vote for) an agent according to their preferences and to move in the practices space corresponding to their preferences (see Fig. 11.15). An agent with many supporters can generate a large amount of resources. Resources are spent either on physical capital, which increases the ability to generate resources, or on institutional capacity, which determines its strength, i.e. its ability to influence other agents, the landscape, and supporters. The landscape represents exogenous factors and sends signals to the agents to which they respond. Attacks by other agents reduce institutional capacity.

Agents possess several behaviors, called mechanisms, which determine their dynamics and interactions with other agents. Adaptation is the movement in the practices space to attract followers. Niche formation occurs in parts of the practices space where there are supporters but no agents. Absorption of a niche can occur through the regime. Niche clustering means that several niches merge to form a new, stronger niche. Transformation means that an agent changes its type to another. When a niche gains enough strength through its institutional capacity, it transforms into an empowered niche. Similarly, an empowered niche can transform into a new regime. Downward transformations occur when an agent loses strength.

Two types of transitions can occur in the model. The first is *regime change*, which means that the incumbent regime loses support so that its strength falls below a critical threshold and the regime becomes an ENA. At the same time, an ENA gains support and strength and transforms into the new regime. The second type of transition is *regime evolution*, in which the regime changes its practices through adaptation and/or absorption of niches, thus moving to a new position in the practices space.

The model does not explicitly refer to the path dependence literature in economics or political science, but it is obviously related to it. The model is designed to simulate both historical paths (or pathways as the authors call them) that actually occurred. This serves mainly as a verification procedure to show that the model behaves in a reasonable way. The main purpose of the model is to simulate possible future transition paths to a more sustainable world. Note that such a transition can be seen as a path change, even if it is not called one.

11.7.2 Application to Sustainable Road Transport

The socio-technological regime that has evolved from the lock-in on the gasoline-fuel internal combustion engine in road transport is unsustainable in terms of climate change, public health, and environmental impacts. However, the automotive industry is also an important source of material wealth and automobility generates utility through its flexibility. Thus, society faces the problem of how to retain the social and economic benefits associated with the automobile while reducing its negative environmental, economic, and social impacts. In other words, a path change or transition seems necessary, which will probably require both technological and institutional changes (e.g., electric and fuel cell vehicles, customized mobility, teleworking, zoning policies). The model simulates such a transition and analyzes what conditions might be necessary for a path change to take place.

Agents are characterized by their location in the practices space and receive support from consumers/citizens who have preferences for these practices. As shown in Fig. 11.14, supporters are also located in the practices space. For simplicity, the example in the previous subsection presented a two-dimensional practice space. The model in Köhler et al. (2009) contains six practices that reflect sustainability and the main decision dimensions of passenger transport choice: CO_2 emissions of vehicles (gCO_2/km), transport costs (€/year), ICT use, the structure of the built environment (mixed-use zones that influence mobility decisions), and the split between private and public transport (person-km/year). Most of the practices can be measured quantitatively with available data, while ICT use and built environment structure are described with qualitative indicators. Each agent starts with a specific combination of these practices.

The model has eight agents: the regime and seven niches. The regime is characterized by the use of ICE technology fueled by gasoline or diesel and higher personal mobility as well as transportation demand. Niche 1 is similar to the regime, but the main technology is hybrid cars instead of ICE cars. Niche 2 is biofuel cars, and Niche 3 is fuel cell cars that run on hydrogen. The remaining niches do not just replace the technology of private vehicles but focus on changes in ownership patterns (from car ownership to car sharing) and behavioral changes. Niche 4 focuses on the use of public transportation. Niche 5 is called "slow modes" and favors walking and bicycling, resulting in low demand for transportation. Niche 6 represents the practices of car sharing and mobility as a service. Finally, niche 7 also represents low transport demand due to the use of ICT for homeworking.

At the beginning of the simulation there are three groups of supporters, which correspond to the observed population groups in the UK with data from 2000 to 2003. Mainstream car drivers are a rather heterogeneous group with a high transport demand, which is mainly met by using their own conventional ICE vehicle. Green car drivers are more homogeneous. They also have high personal mobility but use biofuels or hybrid cars. The third group consists of non-drivers who rely on public transportation and slow modes of mobility.

The logic of the analysis is to define exogenous landscape signals and simulate how the system responds to them. The landscape signals capture expected societal and policy changes between 2000 and 2050. They can affect the positions of the supporters in the practices space or change model parameters. Five landscape and policy signals are used here:

1. The influence of climate change on values pushes supporters' preferences toward lower CO_2 emissions.
2. Consumers accept higher external costs due to a rise in oil prices for the same quality of transport.
3. An ICT wave starts in 2007, which increases ICT use amongst supporters.
4. Public transport investment increases.
5. Planning of the built environment increases public mobility and lowers transport demand over time.

Figure 11.16 shows how the landscape signals are implemented. (1) and (2), represented by the yellow and orange lines, are step functions that start to increase in the 2010s. The assumption behind this shape is that as climate change progresses, society responds to specific events such as storms, floods, and droughts. The other signals increase linearly, with different slopes indicating different implementation speeds.

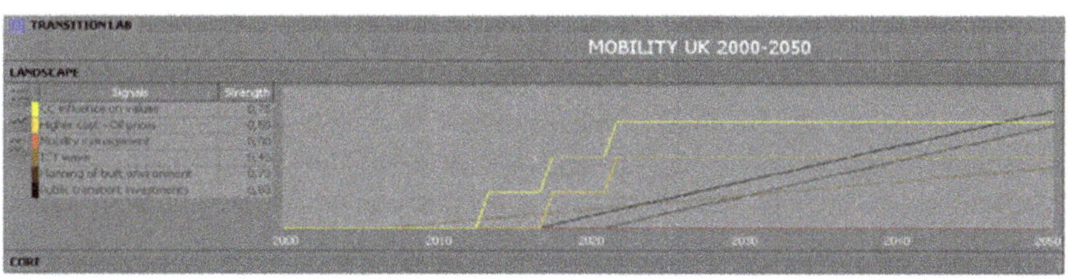

Fig. 11.16 Landscape signals. Source: Köhler et al. (2009), reproduced with kind permission of Elsevier B.V

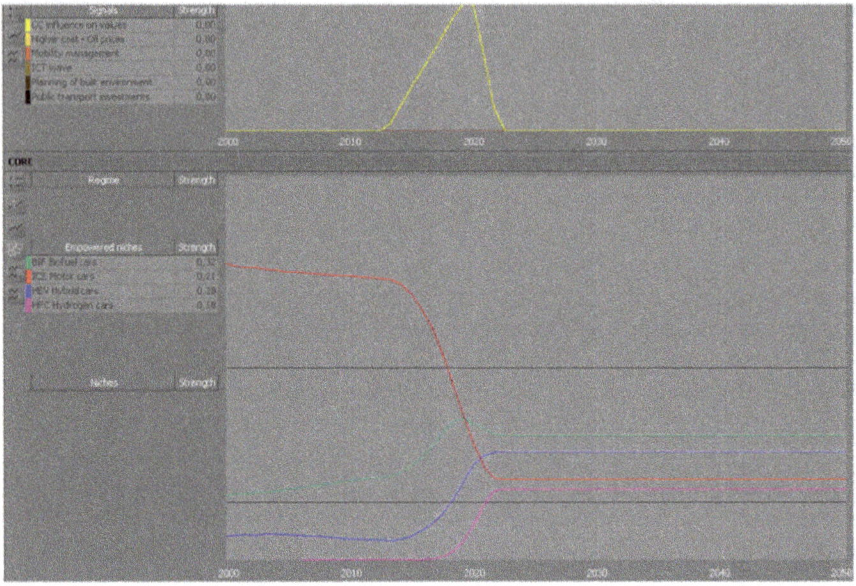

Fig. 11.17 Baseline case with only one landscape signal. Source: Köhler et al. (2009), reproduced with kind permission of Elsevier B.V

Before simulating their transition scenarios, the authors run a baseline case with only the four car-based agents and a single landscape signal (see Fig. 11.17). This signal is a temporary effect of climate change on the value of supporters between 2013 and 2022. This single, temporary signal is strong enough to transform the ICE regime into an empowered niche (red line). However, it is not sufficient to transform any of the three empowered niches into a new regime. Köhler et al. conclude that temporary concerns about climate change alone do not bring about a transition or a change of path. In the new situation, there are four empowered niches of comparable strength, any one of which could become a new regime. In the language of Sydow et al., the new situation corresponds to a new preformation phase with multiple options for a new path. The main message of Köhler et al. is that political signals seem to be necessary for the transition to a new and more sustainable regime.

The main result of the paper is shown in Fig. 11.18, which contains several runs of the model with all eight agents and the full set of landscape signals. The ICE regime declines, becomes a niche, and virtually disappears by the 2040s. Biofuel cars (green line) are the (second) strongest niche for a long time, but fail to become a new regime. They are followed by hybrid cars (blue line) and later by hydrogen cars (magenta line). The only non-car niche that becomes an empowered niche is public transport, but it remains weaker than the other two empowered niches. Niches with more radical lifestyle changes, such as slow modes or car sharing, never gain significant strength. As in the baseline case, no new regime emerges, but in 2050 hydrogen cars are closed to transformation into the regime. A variant of the model

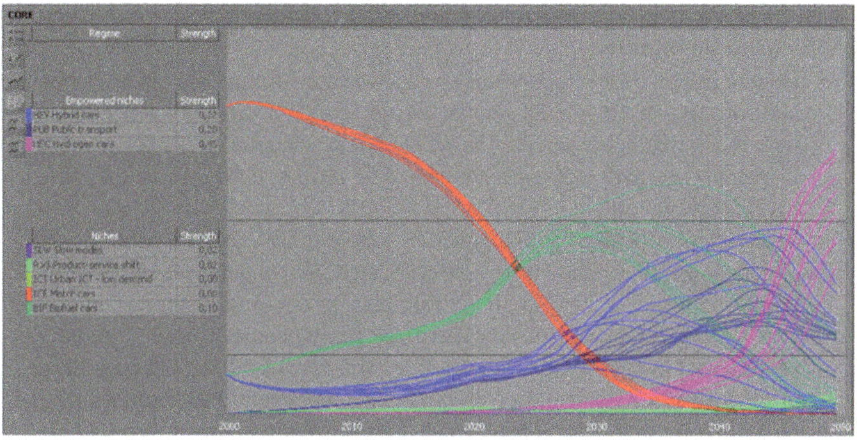

Fig. 11.18 Transition scenario with all landscape signals. Source: Köhler et al. (2009), reproduced with kind permission of Elsevier B.V

includes learning curves that reduce the cost of a technology as it becomes more widespread. In this variant, hydrogen cars become the new regime by 2050.

The model shows that technological transitions are more likely than lifestyle transitions, which require sustained environmental pressure on society and behavioral change on the part of consumers. The authors draw three policy conclusions:

> *Firstly, a large-scale shift in the preferences—and therefore choices—of consumers and also strong and lasting policy action is a prerequisite for a transition to a sustainable mobility system. A corollary of this is that this shift must be maintained for a long time (20–30 years), or indeed permanently, for the radically different technologies to be able to develop to the point where they can outcompete the initially cheaper and preferred current and near-to-market technologies. …*
>
> *Secondly, what may seem to be the most successful alternative in the next 10 years may not be the best option in the long run. It is necessary to continue to support radical alternative technological niches, even while biofuels and hybrids begin to take off and challenge the ICE regime. …*
>
> *Thirdly, radical institutional and behavioural change will probably be harder to achieve than technological change. The challenge for policy makers is to inspire and connect to grassroots support for social change in order to effectively introduce potentially unpopular changes (e.g., fuel tax increases, parking restrictions); and to demonstrate the wider benefits of such changes (e.g., reduced air pollution, more reliable public transport) to garner this support.* (Köhler et al. 2009, p. 2994)

The model demonstrates how computational methods can be used to formalize the notions of path dependence, path changes, and the claim that history matters.

Things to Remember

- History matters when individual events determine future outcomes. Important concepts of a historical perspective on economics are path dependence, lock-in, contingency, and the role of historical accidents. If history matters, we cannot assume that the economy will always converge to the same equilibrium state.
- Economists seek to establish general economic laws that are abstract and widely applicable. These laws are formulated in mathematical models with "continuous motion" of economic variables. In contrast, historians emphasize the importance of historical detail and contingency. History is seen as a sequence of events. While they try to establish causal links between these events in narrative form, they do not believe in general historical laws.
- Historical reasoning is genealogical, i.e., it explains current states of the world as consequences of earlier events. Neoclassical economic reasoning is teleological or functionalist, i.e. economic phenomena are explained in terms of their functions or the goals of economic agents.
- Time has a direction that cannot be reversed. Like many physical models, economic models are often symmetric in time and can be run forward and backward in time. Real economies are dissipative structures subject to the second law of thermodynamics. Entropy increases unless there is a permanent inflow of exergy. Since this has been the case in the past, the complexity of economic systems has increased.
- Deterministic processes are path dependent if they have multiple attractors and their dynamics depend on initial conditions. Stochastic processes are path dependent, if they are non-ergodic. Their asymptotic distribution evolves as a function of the process' own history.
- Path dependence is caused by positive feedback. Positive feedback in the economy can result from increasing returns to scale, learning effects, positive externalities, technical and organizational complementarities, mutually consistent expectations, and institutions.
- While path dependence does not necessarily result in an avoidable inefficient lock-in, there are examples of inefficient and societally harmful lock-in. Market forces do not necessarily lead to efficient outcomes, even when uncertainty about the future is low. The highly toxic gasoline additive lead was commercialized with full knowledge of its harmful effects on human health and despite the availability of a less harmful alternative.
- Lock-in means that a system is hard to change or to reform. We can distinguish between infrastructural and technological lock-in, institutional lock-in, behavioral lock-in, and discursive lock-in. All of them are important in explaining why it is so difficult to transform socio-technical systems.
- In political science, critical junctures are historical turning points at which large and discontinuous changes occur rapidly. Punctuated equilibrium is a

(continued)

concept that describes periods of stability occasionally interrupted by critical junctures. Political scientists apply these concepts mainly to the evolution of institutions. They are also important in economics, especially because of the coevolution of technology and institutions. Rather than being smooth and continuous, the history of technological change should be thought of as one of punctuated equilibrium.

- Paths form at early critical junctures, when one of several available options is chosen and lock-in occurs. Through self-reinforcing mechanisms, such as the formation of institutions, the path stabilizes and reproduces itself. As new actors appear and institutions change, the stabilizing mechanisms weaken, allowing changes within a path. When the stabilizing mechanisms have been weakened to a great extent, external or internal events can cause a change in paths at a late critical juncture.
- Between 1905 and 1915, the U.S. automobile industry locked into a path of gasoline-powered internal combustion engines. Factors such as key entrepreneurs (e.g., Henry Ford), external conditions (e.g., the poor state of American roads), biased legislation, and coordination failures played an important role.
- Path formation and change are often described narratively in historical case studies. This approach is informative because it can reveal relevant historical details and events. Formal modeling informed by qualitative case studies is also possible. We can use agent-based models (possibly combined with system dynamics models) to analyze how established paths are transformed and new paths are reached.

References

Abernathy WJ, Wayne K (1974) Limits of the learning curve. Harv Bus Rev 52:109–119

Acemoglu D, Robinson JA (2012) Why nations fail: the origins of power, prosperity and poverty. Profile Books Ltd, London

Acemoglu D, Johnson S, Robinson JA (2001) The colonial origins of comparative development: an empirical investigation. Am Econ Rev 91:1369–1401. https://doi.org/10.1257/aer.91.5.1369

Akerlof GA (2002) Behavioral macroeconomics and macroeconomic behavior. Am Econ Rev 92: 411–433. https://doi.org/10.1257/00028280260136192

Akerlof GA (2007) The missing motivation in macroeconomics. Am Econ Rev 97:5–36

Amatucci M (2015) The world that chose the machine: an evolutionary view of the technological race in the history of the automobile. Int J Automot Technol Manag 15:43–62. https://doi.org/10.1504/IJATM.2015.067091

Andrews T, Burke F (2007) What does it mean to think historically? In: Perspectives on history: the newsmagazine of the American Historical Association. https://www.historians.org/research-and-publications/perspectives-on-history/january-2007/what-does-it-mean-to-think-historically. Accessed 26 May 2023

Anenberg SC, Miller J, Henze DK et al (2019) The global burden of transportation tailpipe emissions on air pollution-related mortality in 2010 and 2015. Environ Res Lett 14:094012. https://doi.org/10.1088/1748-9326/ab35fc

Arthur WB (1984) Competing technologies and economic prediction. IIASA Options 2:10–13

Arthur WB (1989) Competing technologies, increasing returns, and lock-in by historical events. Econ J 99:116–131. https://doi.org/10.2307/2234208

Arthur WB (1994) Increasing returns and path dependence in the economy. University of Michigan Press, Ann Arbor

Bergman N, Haxeltine A, Whitmarsh L et al (2008) Modelling socio-technical transition patterns and pathways. J Artif Soc Soc Simul 11:1–7

Black J, Courtney P, Maye D et al (2022) Constrained sustainability and resilience of agricultural practices from multiple lock-in factors and possible pathways to tackle them: an assessment of three European farming systems. In: Meuwissen M, Feindt PH, Garrido A et al (eds) Resilient and sustainable farming systems in Europe. Cambridge University Press, Cambridge, pp 88–111

Boulton JG, Allen PM, Bowman C (2015) Embracing complexity: strategic perspectives for an age of turbulence. Oxford University Press, Oxford

Briggs M, Webb J, Wilson C (2015) Automotive modal lock-in: the role of path dependence and large socio-economic regimes in market failure. Econ Anal Policy 45:58–68. https://doi.org/10.1016/j.eap.2015.01.005

Burton RL (1976) Recent advances in vehicular steam engine efficiency. SAE Technical Paper 760340. https://doi.org/10.4271/760340

Buschmann P, Oels A (2019) The overlooked role of discourse in breaking carbon lock-in: the case of the German energy transition. WIREs Climate Change 10:e574. https://doi.org/10.1002/wcc.574

Chavez M, (2018) Punctuated equilibrium. https://commons.wikimedia.org/wiki/File:PunctuatedEquilibrium.png. Accessed 8 Dec 2023

Collier RB, Collier D (1991) Shaping the political arena: critical junctures, the labor movement, and regime dynamics in Latin America. Princeton University Press, Princeton

Collier D, Munck GL (2018) Research on critical junctures: template, examples, best practices. In: Critical junctures project. http://www.critical-juncture.net/. Accessed 12 Mar 2023

Conti C, Zanello G, Hall A (2021) Why are agri-food systems resistant to new directions of change? A systematic review. Glob Food Secur 31:100576. https://doi.org/10.1016/j.gfs.2021.100576

Cowan R (1990) Nuclear power reactors: a study in technological lock-in. J Econ Hist 50:541–567. https://doi.org/10.1017/S0022050700037153

Cowley R (ed) (1999) What if? The world's most foremost military historians imagine what might have been. Berkeley Books, New York

Cowley R (ed) (2001) What if? II: eminent historians imagine what might have been. Penguin Publishing Group, New York

David PA (1985) Clio and the economics of QWERTY. Am Econ Rev 75:332–337

David PA (1993) Historical economics in the Longrun: some implications of path-dependence. In: Snooks G (ed) Historical analysis in economics. Routledge, London, pp 29–40

David PA (1994) Why are institutions the 'carriers of history'?: path dependence and the evolution of conventions, organizations and institutions. Struct Chang Econ Dyn 5:205–220. https://doi.org/10.1016/0954-349X(94)90002-7

David PA (2001) Path dependence, its critics, and the quest for "historical economics". In: Garrouste P, Ioannides S (eds) Evolution and path dependence in economic ideas. Edward Elgar Publishing, Cheltenham & Northampton, MA, pp 15–40

David PA (2007) Path dependence: a foundational concept for historical social science. Cliometrica 1:91–114. https://doi.org/10.1007/s11698-006-0005-x

De Schutter O (2017) The political economy of food systems reform. Eur Rev Agric Econ 44:705–731. https://doi.org/10.1093/erae/jbx009

Duranton G, Turner MA (2011) The fundamental law of road congestion: evidence from US cities. Am Econ Rev 101:2616–2652. https://doi.org/10.1257/aer.101.6.2616
Fujita M, Krugman P, Venables AJ (1999) The spatial economy: cities, regions, and international trade. MIT Press, Cambridge and London
Gechert S, Rannenberg A (2018) Which Fiscal Multipliers Are Regime-Dependent? A Meta-Regression Analysis. J Econ Surv 32:1160–1182. https://doi.org/10.1111/joes.12241
Geels FW (2005) Technological transitions and system innovations: a co-evolutionary and socio-technical analysis. Edward Elgar Publishing, Cheltenham/Northampton
Ginzburg C (1989) Clues: roots of an evidential paradigm. In: Myths, and the historical method. Johns Hopkins University Press, Baltimore, pp 96–125
Haxeltine A, Whitmarsh L, Bergman N et al (2008) A conceptual framework for transition modelling. Int J Innov Sustain Dev 3:93–114
IPES Food (2015) The new science of sustainable food systems: overcoming barriers to food systems reform. https://www.ipes-food.org/_img/upload/files/NewScienceofSusFood.pdf Accessed 8 June 2023
Johnson S (2023) The brilliant inventor who made two of history's biggest mistakes. N Y Times Mag. 15 March 2023
Klein LR (1983) Some Laws of economics. Bull Am Acad Arts Sci 36:23–45. https://doi.org/10.2307/3823680
Köhler J, Whitmarsh L, Nykvist B et al (2009) A transitions model for sustainable mobility. Ecol Econ 68:2985–2995. https://doi.org/10.1016/j.ecolecon.2009.06.027
Krasner SD (1984) Approaches to the state: alternative conceptions and historical dynamics. Comp Polit 16:223–246. https://doi.org/10.2307/421608
Krugman P (1991) Increasing returns and economic geography. J Polit Econ 99:483–499. https://doi.org/10.1086/261763
Lally P, van Jaarsveld CHM, Potts HWW, Wardle J (2010) How are habits formed: modelling habit formation in the real world. Eur J Soc Psychol 40:998–1009. https://doi.org/10.1002/ejsp.674
Lane D (2006) Hierarchy, complexity, society. In: Pumain D (ed) Hierarchy in natural and social sciences. Springer, Dordrecht, pp 81–119
Liebowitz SJ, Margolis SE (1990) The fable of the keys. J Law Econ 33:1–25. https://doi.org/10.1086/467198
Liebowitz SJ, Margolis SE (1995) Path dependence, lock-in, and history. J Law Econ Org 11:205–226. https://doi.org/10.1093/oxfordjournals.jleo.a036867
Lipset SM, Rokkan S (1967) Cleavage structures, party systems and voter alignments. In: Party systems and voter alignments: cross-national perspectives. Free Press, New York, pp 3–64
Magrini M-B, Anton M, Chardigny J-M et al (2018) Pulses for sustainability: breaking agriculture and food sectors out of lock-in. Front Sustain Food Syst 2:64. https://doi.org/10.3389/fsufs.2018.00064
Magrini M-B, Béfort N, Nieddu M (2019) Chapter 24 - Technological lock-in and pathways for crop diversification in the bio-economy. In: Lemaire G, Carvalho PCDF, Kronberg S, Recous S (eds) Agroecosystem diversity. Academic Press, pp 375–388
Mankiw NG (2016) Principles of economics, 8th edn. Cengage Learning, Boston
McCarthy T (2001) The coming wonder?: foresight and early concerns about the automobile. Environ Hist 6:46–74. https://doi.org/10.2307/3985231
McFarland MJ, Hauer ME, Reuben A (2022) Half of US population exposed to adverse lead levels in early childhood. Proc Natl Acad Sci 119:e2118631119. https://doi.org/10.1073/pnas.2118631119
McLaughlin CC (1954) The Stanley steamer: a study in unsuccessful innovation. Explor Econ Hist 7:37–47
Mokyr J (1990) Punctuated equilibria and technological progress. Am Econ Rev 80:350–354
Mokyr J (1992) Technological inertia in economic history. J Econ Hist 52:325–338. https://doi.org/10.1017/S0022050700010767

Mokyr J (1994) Cardwell's law and the political economy of technological progress. Res Policy 23: 561–574. https://doi.org/10.1016/0048-7333(94)01006-4
Mokyr J (1998) The political economy of technological change: resistance and innovation in economic history. In: Berg M, Bruland K (eds) Technological revolutions in Europe. Historical perspectives. Edward Elgar Publishing Ltd, Cheltenham, pp 39–64
Mokyr J (2000) Knowledge, technology, and economic growth during the industrial revolution. In: van Ark B, Kuipers SK, Kuper GH (eds) Productivity, technology and economic growth. Springer US, Boston, MA, pp 253–292
Office of Nuclear Energy (2022) What's the lifespan for a nuclear reactor? Much longer than you might think. In: Energy.gov. https://www.energy.gov/ne/articles/whats-lifespan-nuclear-reactor-much-longer-you-might-think. Accessed 26 May 2023
Okadome T (2007) A performance evaluation on DSK and Qwerty keyboards. Int J Comput Process Lang 20:15–35. https://doi.org/10.1142/S0219427907001573
Pierson P (2000) Increasing returns, path dependence, and the study of politics. Am Polit Sci Rev 94:251–267. https://doi.org/10.2307/2586011
Raine A, Foster J, Potts J (2006) The new entropy law and the economic process. Ecol Complex 3: 354–360. https://doi.org/10.1016/j.ecocom.2007.02.009
Rast J (2009) Critical junctures, long-term processes: urban redevelopment in Chicago and Milwaukee, 1945–1980. Soc Sci Hist 33:393–426. https://doi.org/10.1017/S0145553200011068
Ritchie H (2022) How the world eliminated lead from gasoline. In: Our world in data. https://ourworldindata.org/leaded-gasoline-phase-out. Accessed 26 May 2023
Roser M (2020) Why did renewables become so cheap so fast? https://ourworldindata.org/cheap-renewables-growth. Accessed 16 May 2023
Samuelson PA, Nordhaus WD (2010) Economics, 19th edn. McGraw-Hill Irwin, Boston
Schelling TC (1960) The strategy of conflict. Oxford University Press, Oxford
Schmutzler A (1999) The new economic geography. J Econ Surv 13:355–379. https://doi.org/10.1111/1467-6419.00087
Schneider S (2023) Events. In: Internet encyclopedia of philosophy. https://iep.utm.edu/events/. Accessed 26 May 2023
Schneider ED, Kay JJ (1994) Life as a manifestation of the second law of thermodynamics. Math Comput Model 19:25–48. https://doi.org/10.1016/0895-7177(94)90188-0
Selbmann K (2015) Explanation of genesis, continuity and change of policy: analytical framework. Innov Ener Policies 4:1000115
Seto KC, Davis SJ, Mitchell RB et al (2016) Carbon lock-in: types, causes, and policy implications. Annu Rev Environ Resour 41:425–452. https://doi.org/10.1146/annurev-environ-110615-085934
Streeck W, Thelen KA (eds) (2005) Beyond continuity: institutional change in advanced political economies. Oxford University Press, Oxford
Strogatz S (2019) The language of calculus. Science Friday. https://www.sciencefriday.com/articles/the-language-of-calculus/. Accessed 26 May 2023
Strohl D (2020) Did an outbreak of hoof-and-mouth disease lead to the demise of Stanley and steam cars in general? In: Hemmings. https://www.hemmings.com/stories/2020/12/18/did-an-outbreak-of-hoof-and-mouth-disease-lead-to-the-demise-of-stanley-and-steam-cars-in-general. Accessed 26 May 2023
Sulzberger C (2004) Early road warrior, part 2 - competing electric and gasoline vehicles. IEEE Power Ener Mag 2:83–88. https://doi.org/10.1109/MPAE.2004.1338129
Sydow J, Schreyögg G, Koch J (2009) Organizational path dependence: opening the Black box. Acad Manag Rev 34:689–709. https://doi.org/10.5465/amr.34.4.zok689
Turk MH (2010) The arrow of time in economics: from Robinson's critique to the new historical economics. Eur J Hist Econ Thought 17:471–492. https://doi.org/10.1080/09672560903204981
Unruh GC (2000) Understanding carbon lock-in. Energy Policy 28:817–830. https://doi.org/10.1016/S0301-4215(00)00070-7

van Boxtel C, van Drie J (2018) Historical reasoning: conceptualizations and educational applications. In: Metzger SA, Harris LM (eds) The Wiley International handbook of history teaching and learning. John Wiley & Sons, Ltd, Hoboken, pp 149–176

van Lunteren F (2019) Historical explanation and causality. Isis 110:321–324. https://doi.org/10.1086/703333

VanSledright BA (2004) What does it mean to think historically . . . and how do you teach it? Soc Educ 68:230–234

Weitzman ML (2009) On modeling and interpreting the economics of catastrophic climate change. Rev Econ Stat 91:1–19. https://doi.org/10.1162/rest.91.1.1

West LJ (1994) Keyboard efficiencies revisited: direct measures of speed on the Dvorak and standard keyboards. Delta Pi Epsilon J 36:49–62

Wood W, Quinn JM, Kashy DA (2002) Habits in everyday life: thought, emotion, and action. J Pers Soc Psychol 83:1281–1297. https://doi.org/10.1037/0022-3514.83.6.1281

World Health Organization (2022) Lead poisoning. In: World Health Organization: newsroom. https://www.who.int/news-room/fact-sheets/detail/lead-poisoning-and-health. Accessed 26 May 2023

Wright TP (1936) Factors affecting the cost of airplanes. J Aeronaut Sci 3:122–128. https://doi.org/10.2514/8.155

Adaptation, Learning, and Behavior

12

Contents

12.1 Introduction ... 648
12.2 Modes of Behavior and Learning ... 652
  12.2.1 Modes of Behavior ... 653
  12.2.2 A Conceptual Model of Consumer Behavior ... 655
  12.2.3 Types of Learning ... 659
12.3 Rational Behavior and Maximization ... 660
  12.3.1 What Makes Decisions Difficult ... 660
  12.3.2 Computational Complexity ... 663
  12.3.3 As-if and Approximation ... 666
  12.3.4 Example of Intertemporal Utility Maximization ... 668
12.4 Behavior and Learning of Boundedly Rational Individuals ... 670
  12.4.1 Heuristics and Biases ... 673
  12.4.2 Fast and Frugal Heuristics ... 676
  12.4.3 Learning ... 681
12.5 Cultural Adaptation and Imitation ... 685
12.6 Collaborative Problem-solving and Social Learning ... 690
  12.6.1 Collaborative Problem-Solving ... 691
  12.6.2 Social Learning ... 694
12.7 Sense-making and Narratives ... 698
References ... 705

Abstract

This chapter identifies adaptation as the last major complexity concept. Unlike complex systems in physics and chemistry, the economy is a complex adaptive system, meaning that its parts—the economic agents—change their characteristics and behavior over time. Because of this property, complex adaptive systems are more difficult to analyze than complex systems. To understand adaptation, it is necessary to discuss the behavior and learning of agents, i.e. to adopt a microeconomic perspective. Based on insights from computational theory, the chapter argues that maximization is possible only for simple economic

M. Roos, *Principles of Complexity Economics*, Classroom Companion: Economics,
https://doi.org/10.1007/978-3-031-51436-4_12

problems, which are rare. Most economic problems that are interesting are NP-hard and therefore intractable. Complexity economics rejects the standard rational choice approach of neoclassical economics in favor of the theoretically and empirically more plausible bounded rationality approach. In this respect, complexity economics overlaps with some branches of behavioral economics. An agent-based model of collective problem-solving and social learning is presented to emphasize that behavior has not only an individual but also a social aspect. Moreover, the chapter briefly discusses the link between complexity economics and the recently emerged narrative economics, which highlights the importance of sense-making for economic agents.

Keywords

Bounded rationality · Heuristics · Maximization · Narratives · Satisficing

Guiding Questions

- *How are adaptation, learning, and behavior related?*
- *What are four important modes of behavior and how do they differ?*
- *How can we categorize learning?*
- *What makes decisions difficult?*
- *Why is computational complexity a useful concept for decision-making?*
- *What is an NP-hard problem?*
- *What are as-if assumptions and how do they relate to decision-making?*
- *How can we define satisficing?*
- *What is the message of the "heuristics and biases" research program?*
- *What is the message of the "fast and frugal heuristics" research program?*
- *Why can simple heuristics outperform more sophisticated approaches?*
- *What modes of learning are relevant in economics?*
- *Are humans adapted to the cognitive niche or the cultural niche?*
- *What makes collective decision-making difficult?*
- *What is social learning?*
- *How do narratives relate to learning and behavior?*

12.1 Introduction

Adaptation is the final key concept of complexity that we will discuss. In Chap. 2, we distinguished between complex systems and complex adaptive systems. In the latter, agents adapt or learn; in the former, they do not. Complex systems are physical systems whose components are atoms, molecules, or particles. They are informative for economics because they show that complex phenomena of self-organization and emergence can occur without active behavior by agents. The components of physical and chemical systems obey the laws of nature, but do not exhibit behavior. This statement raises the question of what we mean by behavior. We can define behavior as the actions and reactions of a system to internal and external stimuli, which would also apply to inanimate systems. In everyday language, there is nothing wrong with saying, "The car is behaving strangely today." In biology and psychology, however, the term behavior is reserved for animals and humans, although there is a blurred line between some actions and reactions of animals and those of plants.

In economics, we are interested in human behavior, which is often equated with decision-making. However, not all behavior involves conscious choice. Habitual behavior, which accounts for about 43% of daily behavior (Wood et al. 2002), has little to do with what we mean by decision-making. On the contrary, its main purpose is to conserve the limited mental energy we need for deliberate cognitive processes.

Complex adaptive systems have an additional layer of complexity compared to complex systems because agents can change their properties and behavior over time. The resulting change in the nature of the system is directly related to ongoing off-equilibrium dynamics, novelty, evolution, and historicity, at least in the sense that time has an arrow. These concepts have been the subject of the previous chapters. In this chapter, we look at the way adaptation occurs in human systems, especially economic systems. We take a micro perspective. In human systems, we can also speak of group behavior or organizational behavior. But since groups and organizations are themselves systems, their aggregate behavior is an emergent result of the behavior of their members. We focus on individuals as the ultimate agents of behavior.

Adaptation is a process that increases the fitness of an agent in a given environment. An adapted agent is well adapted to its environment. A famous example of adaptation in biology is Darwin's finches, a group of about 18 bird species that evolved from a single species on the isolated Galápagos Islands. The birds differ primarily in the shape and size of their beaks (see Fig. 12.1). Beaks are a physical characteristic of birds, but because they serve a specific purpose, they are also related to behavior. Each species has adapted to an ecological niche with a different food source. For example, the large ground finch (No. 1 in Fig. 12.1) has specialized in cracking nuts with its large, short beak. The Green Warbler (No. 4) has a long, slender bill and is adapted to eating small insects and spiders.

Physical characteristics are not very relevant to economics, but the adaptation of agents' behavior to their economic, social, technological, and institutional environment is. While this environment is mostly exogenous to the individual, it is endogenous from a population perspective. In fact, humans adapt to their natural environment by shaping the socio-technical environment. Adaptation is not just a matter of the distant human past, when *Homo sapiens* discovered and adapted to different habitats after migrating out of Africa. Even today, migrants have to adapt to new living conditions when they cross national borders or migrate from rural areas to urban agglomerations. It will be an important issue in the future as well, because humans are changing the Earth's climate and ecosystems. Humans have always changed the ecosystems they have inhabited, for example by wiping out about 85%

Fig. 12.1 Galápagos finches with different beaks. Source: Gould (1882), Wikimedia Commons, public domain

of Australia's megafauna shortly after arriving there about 45,000 years ago, or by converting forests and swamps into farmland. Today, however, humans are using modern technology to change the Earth's conditions on a global scale and at an enormous rate. If human societies cannot stop the destruction of ecosystems and climate change, they will have to adapt to the changes they have caused.

Some human behaviors are innate or hardwired, such as infant crying and maternal bonding. These instincts are genetically transmitted, so adaptation of instinctive behavior is a very slow process, taking many generations and often thousands of years. However, most human behavior is learned in some way, allowing for much faster adaptation. Humans can even learn to overcome instincts or innate aversions. For example, most animals and children have an aversion to bitter tastes because the bitterness of plants in most cases indicates that they are toxic. But adult humans enjoy the bitter taste of coffee, beer, asparagus, olives, etc., and accept the bitterness of medicines. Adult humans who are well adapted to modern life have also learned to suppress their fight-or-flight instinct in stressful situations. For example, if a student feels challenged by the professor's questions in an oral exam, it is neither socially acceptable to attack the professor nor to run away. The adaptation of human behavior occurs largely through several types of learning. In general, human learning is the acquisition of new understanding, knowledge, skills, and behaviors. Values, attitudes, and preferences are also learned. In general, learning can be individual or social, active or passive.

Adapting to changing conditions may also require unlearning or forgetting some beliefs and behaviors. At the individual level, unlearning behaviors that have become habitual can be very difficult. At the social level, changing existing social norms that guide the behavior of groups can also take a long time, such as changing the social meaning of masculinity and codes of honor. There is an evolutionary logic that learned individual and social behaviors change slowly because they should be preserved if they increase fitness. However, if the environment is changing rapidly and rapid adaptation is required, the robustness of the learned behavior may be an obstacle, raising again the issue of adaptability (or evolvability) versus robustness discussed in Chap. 10.

In Sect. 12.2, we set the stage for the rest of the chapter by presenting a schema with four different types of human behavior, of which reasoning and rational decision-making is only one. We also provide a rough classification of learning types. The main purpose of this section is to organize the following exposition, in which the scheme is explained in more detail.

Rational decision-making and maximization are the standard assumptions about behavior in neoclassical economics. Both from the perspective of behavioral economics and complexity economics, maximizing or optimizing behavior is very challenging in most real-world situations, and thus a rare special case of human behavior. In Sect. 12.3, we discuss some findings from computational complexity and behavioral economics that support this claim. In the face of complexity and uncertainty, maximization is impossible. Moreover, it is questionable whether we can assume that real people behave as if they were maximizing objective functions, since approximations to maximizing behavior can be as complex as maximization itself.

Section 12.4 is devoted to individual behavior and learning. Heuristics or rules of thumb are an important alternative to optimization behavior. We also discuss the concept of bounded rationality proposed by complexity pioneer and behavioral economist Herbert Simon. There are two major views of heuristics in the psychology and behavioral economics literature. The first view, called heuristics and biases, holds that heuristics often lead to systematic deviations from rational behavior. The second view, fast and frugal heuristics, argues that heuristics often have ecological rationality and can perform better than seemingly more rational behavior. Views on learning also differ. For many neoclassical economists, Bayesian learning is the rational approach they use in their models, but empirical evidence shows that individuals have difficulty applying Bayesian learning. The creation of mental models through experience, which are cognitive representations of the world, is an alternative approach to learning.

Section 12.5 deals with cultural adaptation and imitation. Humans differ from other animals in their ability to learn from others and to accumulate cultural knowledge that far exceeds individual understanding. Imitation without a deep understanding of why the imitated behavior is appropriate is an important element of cultural adaptation.

Of course, humans not only imitate others, but also actively collaborate with others to solve problems. Collaborative problem-solving, the subject of Sect. 12.6, is seen as a critical twenty-first century skill in a world of increasing complexity. Solving complex problems requires the knowledge and skills of many people. However, collaboration is not only a cognitive challenge, but also a social one. Social learning is both a prerequisite and a result of collaborative problem-solving. An agent-based model shows how social learning in a group can lead to a mental model of the problem that is partially shared by the members of the group.

The chapter concludes with a discussion of narratives in Sect. 12.7 Narratives are sense-making stories that motivate behavior. As of 2017, narrative economics is a burgeoning field interested in learning how people interpret their world and how narratives proliferate in a population as a means of coping with underlying economic uncertainty. The sharing of narratives can be seen as a form of social learning.

12.2 Modes of Behavior and Learning

Humans are very special animals. We have larger brains than most other animals and superior cognitive capacities. Furthermore, human language and the symbolic representation of both concrete things and abstract ideas are unique. Abstract thinking and reasoning about cause-and-effect relationships allow inferences to be made even in novel situations. In contrast to other animals, which have evolved *dedicated intelligence*, domain-specific learning, and behavior adapted to specific environments, humans have evolved *improvisational intelligence*, i.e. highly flexible cognitive capacities that allow us to acquire locally adaptive behavior in a wide range of environments (see Boyd et al. 2011). These capacities have allowed us to adapt to the *cognitive niche* (Pinker 2010), which is, of course, very broad.

Given the undeniable cognitive power of humans, it seems very natural to many economists to assume that human behavior is generally rational. Despite many years of research in behavioral economics demonstrating manifold problems with rational behavior, the perfect decision-maker is still the standard model in mainstream economics. Yet humans have a much broader repertoire of modes of behaviors. The psychologist Daniel Kahneman, who received the Nobel Memorial Prize in Economics Sciences in 2002, distinguishes two models of thinking in this book “Thinking, fast and slow” (Kahneman 2011). *System 1*, which is the older part of our evolution and which we share with other animals, is fast, automatic, emotional, stereotypical, and unconscious. We use it frequently and easily for most of our tasks. *System 2* is slow, effortful, logical, and calculating. It corresponds to the rational decision-making of homo economicus. Because it requires effort to use, it must be consciously activated, and because it is quickly exhausted, we rarely do so.

Although Kahneman’s approach adds a mode of thinking to rational decision-making, it is still incomplete, because it focuses on the individual alone. As we will see later in this chapter, Kahneman ignores the very important cultural or social dimension of our thinking and behavior. Boyd et al. (2011) argue that humans are adapted to the *cultural niche* rather than the cognitive niche.

12.2.1 Modes of Behavior

Based on insights from behavioral and complexity economics, we can identify four distinct modes of human behavior: (1) habitual behavior, (2) reasoning, (3) imitation, and (4) collaborative problem-solving. These four modes of behavior differ along two dimensions (stakes/costs and problem complexity), so they can be arranged in a two-by-two matrix as shown in Table 12.1.

Kahneman's distinction between automatic thinking with System 1 and deliberate thinking with System 2 can serve as a dimension of modes of thinking and resulting behavior. Kahneman (2011) argues that using System 2 requires a great deal of effort, whereas System 1 is used automatically with little effort. Therefore, we must choose to reason and actively override the spontaneous processes and outcomes of System 1. To do this, we usually need a reason, which is provided by high benefits. When a problem is important in the sense that we have much to gain or lose, we are more motivated to reason than when the problem is of little importance to us. Thus, when benefits are low, we rely on low-cost automatic behavior, and when benefits are high, we are willing to incur the higher costs of deliberate behavior.

The second dimension of behavior is whether we tackle a problem individually or socially, i.e. with the help of others. From an anthropological and evolutionary perspective, Boyd et al. (2011, p. 10918) "argue that humans may be smarter than other creatures, but none of us is nearly smart enough to acquire all of the information necessary to survive in any single habitat." From the very different perspective of educational science, Hung (2013) states:

> *Most real world problems are complex. As opposed to … simple, linear, well-structured problems that have one single straightforward solution, complex problem solving … involves more sophisticated cognitive processing in order to properly and effectively address the intricacy and uncertainty inherent in these problems. Even more so, problems in professional workplaces today are so complex that they exceed the cognitive capacity of any individual and therefore require a team of members who possess different but complementary expertise in order to solve the problem … For example, designing the structure of a nuclear power plant entails a team of ~ 200 civil engineers. A multi-million dollar new business investment plan necessitates a team of business managers and analysts in the decision-making process. Problems with this degree of complexity exist in many professions. The success of solving these large scale complex problems not only relies on individual team members' expertise, but more importantly, the collective problem solving ability of the team.* (Hung 2013, p. 366)

Table 12.1 Four modes of human behavior

Determinants			Benefits	
			Low	High
		Type of Behavior	**Automatic**	**Deliberate**
Complexity of the problem	Low	**Individual**	Habitual behavior	Reasoning
	High	**Social**	Imitation	Collaborative problem-solving

It seems safe to conclude, then, that both survival in our pre-modern history and success in our modern world require problem-solving abilities well beyond the cognitive capacity of any individual. Individually, we can solve only fairly simple problems. For more complex problems, we need social support. You may recall from Chap. 3 that we can understand complexity as a function of objective and subjective complexity. The objective complexity of a system and the challenges of understanding, predicting, and controlling it depend on the size and structure of the system. We have seen that this can be measured by the cyclometric complexity or causal complexity of the system. Subjective complexity depends on the distance of a system from what an observer considers simple, which in turn depends on the observer's education and cognitive abilities. The degree of complexity, in both its objective and subjective dimensions, determines whether we solve problems individually or socially.

Table 12.1 assigns each behavior type to a combination of high or low complexity and high or low benefit. When the complexity of a problem is low and the benefits to the agent are low, we expect habitual behavior. Because habits are hardwired into the structure of the brain, habitual behavior is effortless and automatic. It makes sense to develop habits for low-benefit activities in order to save mental energy for important behaviors. However, this does not mean that some people do not develop habits for high-benefit behaviors. For example, many people have developed bad eating habits that are likely to cause disease in the long run. The problem is that once a habit is established, changing it may involve high costs that may not be incurred even though the benefits are high. Therefore, it is the net benefit rather than the gross benefit that is relevant. In the remainder of this chapter, we will not discuss habits much because they are not conducive to adaptation. As discussed in the previous chapter, they can lead to behavioral lock-in, which prevents adaptation to new environmental conditions.

Reasoning is a sensible behavior when the payoff is sufficiently high and the complexity low enough to find a good solution individually. Reasoning should not be limited to maximization or deductive reasoning. Rather, it is used here in a broad sense to include any instance in which an individual actively thinks about a problem in order to solve it. Such reasoning need not be logically correct or analytical. It can also be associative and based on heuristics or rules of thumb. In fact, formal reasoning, including the proper use of logic, is a skill that requires considerable training, often at the university level. Even academically educated people often have difficulty reasoning logically, especially, but not only, in areas in which they have not been trained. Different types of individual reasoning are the subject of Sects. 12.3 and 12.4.

Imitating others is often a good idea when a situation is difficult for an individual to understand and the costs associated with understanding are high relative to the benefits. The English saying "When in Rome, do as the Romans do" suggests imitating more knowledgeable people. For a short-term visitor to a foreign place, imitating the locals and following their behavior is a low-cost strategy that avoids inappropriate behavior. The relevant property of imitation is that the imitator does not seek or need to understand why the imitated person behaves as observed. Just following their example is enough to be successful. As we will see later, it is possible that the behavioral role models themselves do not know why they behave in a certain way because they also copy what others do. Much of the cultural adaptation discussed in Sect. 12.5 relies on imitation.

Collective or collaborative problem-solving is even more costly than individual reasoning because all the transaction, coordination, and communication costs of group interaction must be added to the cost of individual reasoning. Therefore, many people avoid working collaboratively unless there are clear advantages to doing so. These benefits are greater the more complex a problem is and the greater the net benefits of solving it. Section 12.6 takes a closer look at collaborative problem-solving and social learning.

The ideas summarized in Table 12.1 should be interpreted as a heuristic framework that provides a useful classification of basic modes of human behavior, rather than as an elaborate theory. It does not claim that net benefits and complexity are the only determinants of these modes, or that there are not cases in which a box in the matrix is filled with another mode of behavior.

12.2.2 A Conceptual Model of Consumer Behavior

Wander Jager (2000) has developed a meta-model of consumer behavior that is very similar to the framework presented above. Jager also distinguishes four modes of behavior, which he calls repetition, deliberation, imitation, and social comparison. For each of these modes, he uses appropriate psychological theories. In his model, the two dimensions that determine the choice of the appropriate mode are uncertainty and the level of need satisfaction. The main motivation for developing his model was to investigate why consumers often behave in environmentally unsustainable ways. The model is embedded in a larger macro framework and integrates many psychological insights, especially from environmental psychology. The purpose of Jager's meta-model is to serve as a theoretical foundation for an agent-based simulation model in which the artificial consumers are called *consumats* (a portmanteau of consumer and automat). We present here a conceptual model of consumer choice that is inspired by the consumat approach in Jager (2000), but differs from it to make it more compatible with the discussion in the previous subsection. We omit many details and functional forms in order to focus on the main ideas.

Let us assume that goods are characterized by their properties, from which consumers derive their utility or which have value for consumers. This is an old idea already proposed by Lancaster (1966). Some goods are simple with only a few characteristics, e.g. toothpaste (taste, capacity to clean the teeth), and others can be highly complex, like a house with many characteristics (e.g., size, location, design, age, insulation, technical equipment, ...). Note that complexity depends on the number of properties that are potentially valuable to the consumer, not on the technical complexity of the good. Let $n_i \in N$ be the number of properties of good i and $\Pi_i = \{\pi_{i1}, \pi_{i2}, \ldots, \pi_{in_i}\}$ be the set properties of good i. Each property j has a value for the consumer, $v(\pi_{ij}) \geq 0$, such that the total value of the good is the sum of the values of the properties, $V_i = \sum_{n_i} v(\pi_{ij})$. Value is a subjective concept that the consumer assigns to the good. It is expressed in monetary terms and corresponds to the willingness to pay, i.e. the consumer will buy the good only if the value is at least equal to the price.

Complexity arises for the consumers, because it may be difficult for them to determine the value of a good, both ex ante and ex post. Some properties are not observable before the purchase, e.g. the taste of toothpaste. For other goods, consumers may find it difficult to assess their value even after the purchase. For instance, many properties of high-tech goods such as computers or automobiles might have a clear value from the perspective of an expert, but not from the perspective of a layperson. As argued above, complexity has an objective and a subjective aspect. The complexity of good i from the perspective of consumer c is assumed to be a function of the good's properties and the consumer's knowledge k about the good, $C_{ci}(\Pi_i, k_{ci})$. We assume that it takes mental effort e for the consumer c to determine the values of the properties, whose amount depends on the complexity of the product: $v_c(\pi_{ij}) = f(C_{ij}, e_{cij})$. In some cases, knowledge about the good is easily acquired after the purchase, e.g. the taste of toothpaste. In other cases, however, even after the purchase, the consumer may not learn much about certain properties, e.g. the health effects of a food's ingredients. In the first case, complexity is reduced by newly acquired knowledge, but in the second case, a purchase does not by itself reduce the product's complexity. We assume that it takes positive effort to assign a value to a property. If the consumer exerts no effort to determine the value of a property, the value is zero, i.e. $v_c(\pi_{ij}) = 0$ when $e_{cij} = 0$. The total effort expended by the consumer on the good is $E_{ci} = \sum_{n_i} e_{cij}$.

Now let us think about how we could formalize the benefits and costs of the consumer choice problem. We assume that the benefit B for consumer c is a function of the difference between the assigned value and the price of the good p, $B_{ci}(V_{ci} - p_i)$, expressed in utility terms (assuming we could measure it). The costs relate to the cognitive process associated with the problem, so they are also measured in utility terms. They include the mental effort to assign value, the mental cost of deliberation d including the metacognition devoted to the problem, and possibly the cost of collaborating with others t, $C_{ci}(E_{ci}, d_{ci}, t_c)$. The effect of collaborating in a team is that less own effort is required to determine the value of the good, since the effort and knowledge of others can be utilized. The net benefit of a good for the consumer is then $NB_{ci} = B_{ci} - C_{ci}$.

We can now formalize, how a consumer chooses a mode of behavior M. Suppose a consumer has critical thresholds for the complexity and net benefit of a good: $\tilde{C}_{ci}$ and $\tilde{NB}_{ci}$. The mode of behavior is then given by:

$$M=\begin{cases} H & \text{if } C_{ci}<\tilde{C}_{ci} \text{ and } NB_{ci}<\tilde{NB}_{ci} \\ R & \text{if } C_{ci}<\tilde{C}_{ci} \text{ and } NB_{ci}\geq\tilde{NB}_{ci} \\ I & \text{if } C_{ci}\geq\tilde{C}_{ci} \text{ and } NB_{ci}<\tilde{NB}_{ci} \\ CDM & \text{if } C_{ci}\geq\tilde{C}_{ci} \text{ and } NB_{ci}\geq\tilde{NB}_{ci} \end{cases},$$

where *H* stands for habit, *R* for reasoning, *I* for imitation, and *CDM* for collaborative decision-making. First, note that the net benefit depends on the price of the good. If the price of a good is high, the net benefit can only be high if the good obtains a high value, which requires high effort. But high mental effort also increases the mental cost. Therefore, high effort pays off only if the good is not too complex, since value is also a function of complexity. If the good is complex, then high net benefits can be obtained by using the expertise of others. While collaborating with others causes a (team) collaboration cost *t*, it makes it possible to reduce one's own mental effort in determining value. Let us look at some examples.

Toothpaste has low complexity because it has only few properties that can be easily inspected. It also has a low price. Let us assume that it has only two relevant properties: taste and cleaning power, which may be subjective. A low-cost *habitual behavior* could be as follows:

1. Buy a brand of toothpaste at random.
2. Invest (little) effort to check its properties and assign a value.
3. If the assigned value is above the price, such that the benefit *B* is positive, buy it again. Otherwise, go back to 1.

This procedure requires little effort only the first time the toothpaste is purchased. The net benefit will be positive in all future periods once a toothpaste is found that provides a positive benefit B. This is an example of Herbert Simon's *satisficing behavior*, which does not seek the best possible solution, but a sufficiently good one.

Computer software is an example of a product that encourages *reasoning*. Many commercial software products have basic functionality, such as performing calculations, writing and editing text, or editing images. Often there are different packages that offer additional features on top of the basic functionality, such as advanced features, cloud services, more memory, special user support, or discounts on updates. The software user must decide which of these additional features to purchase. This problem is similar to the knapsack problem presented in Chap. 10. The consumer wants to solve the maximization problem

$$\max_{\pi_j} \sum_{j=1}^{n_i} v_j\pi_j \ s.t. \sum_{j=1}^{n_i} p_j\pi_j \leq p_i^{max} \ and \ \pi_j \in \{0,1\},$$

where π_j is a software feature from the set of all available n_i features for software *i*, v_j is the value of the feature, p_j is the (additional) price of the feature, and p_i^{max} is the maximum price the consumer is willing to pay for the software. Note that there are two kinds of costs associated with solving this problem: first, the consumer must expend effort to determine v_j for each feature. Second, there is the deliberation cost d_i of solving the optimization problem. Both costs increase as the number of features n_i increases. As we saw in Chap. 10, the possible combinations of features, and thus the deliberation cost, increase exponentially, such that we can only expect a sufficiently high net benefit for a small n_i.

Trendy "superfoods" can serve as an example of the *imitation* mode. On social media, people claim that some foods, such as certain berries or chia seeds, have special health benefits. Whether these claims are true or not is difficult to determine for the average consumer and even for many experts, so the complexity is high. On the other hand, the low potential value severely limits the possible net benefits. Since the price of these goods is typically relatively low, a single good reason may be enough to generate a positive benefit, such as the positive feeling of doing something good for one's health. And since other people may know more about the food than the consumer, their claims may be true. The only necessary cost is that of choosing a trustworthy person to imitate. If the consumer makes no attempt to verify the claimed health benefits, the effort and deliberation costs are zero. The imitation algorithm is:

1. Choose a person to imitate.
2. Make the same choice as this person.

How can we imagine *collaborative problem-solving* in the context of consumption? A consumer may seek advice or recommendations from others and choose among the recommended options. It is very common for consumers to consult advisors for complex, high-value goods and services, such as financial investments, insurance products, health services, housing, or vacations. Suppose a consumer wants to take a three-week vacation. Relevant attributes could be: destination country, ocean vs. mountain, city trip, activities, hotel, vacation home, meals, transportation, travel insurance, service, and many more. For each of these categories of properties, there are many instances, so the number of possible combinations of properties is huge. On the other hand, a vacation can be quite expensive and the expected benefit should be high, since many people consider the vacation trip as an important event in the year. Despite the many online booking options available today, travel agencies still exist to provide advice and prepackaged travel packages. This type of collaborative problem-solving is described by the following algorithm

1. Select a small number of experts.
2. Inform each of them of your goals and key decision criteria.
3. Ask each expert to suggest a small number of options.
4. Evaluate each option and select the best one (analogous to individual reasoning).

Of course, there is no guarantee that this procedure will find the overall best solution, especially when the number of possible solutions is large. While the values that the experts assign to the features may not perfectly match the values that the consumer would assign, this error can be overcompensated by large reductions in effort and deliberation costs. The expert's pre-selection reduces the dimensionality of the consumer's reasoning problem, since only bundles of properties need to be compared, rather than creating the bundles in the first place.

12.2.3 Types of Learning

Learning refers to the internal reconfiguration or change in structure of an agent's brain. A learning brain creates new synapses between existing neurons. Learning refers to an agent's internal processing of information that can lead to better adaptation. Human learning can occur in a variety of ways. Rather than delve deeply into the psychology of learning, which is a broad and diverse field, we will simply contrast three dimensions of learning that can serve as a heuristic framework.

The first dimension is intentional versus unintentional learning. Learning can happen quite automatically without an active intention to learn. This type of learning is called *operant conditioning* in psychology. Spontaneous behavior creates reinforcements or punishments that increase or decrease the behavior in the future. For example, a child may accidentally touch a hot stove and be "punished" with burnt fingers. The child learns that the stove is hot and touching it causes pain. Next time, the child will stay away from the hot stove. Another example is how adults respond to infants' smiles. When adults smile back at infants, infants have a positive experience that reinforces smiling. However, when adults do not smile back, the infant becomes frustrated and smiling behavior may become extinct (Hulsebus 1974). Of course, people often actively intend to learn something, either through their own experimentation or study, or by asking others or observing what they do. A related distinction is whether the learner is aware of the learning process or not, i.e. whether the learning is conscious or unconscious.

The second dimension might be called practical versus theoretical. Practical learning can occur through observation and trial-and-error experimentation. The learner observes cause-and-effect relationships and memorizes (consciously or unconsciously) some if-then rules. For example, young children learn that objects always fall to the ground when they are dropped. Another example is that thunderstorms are announced by rapidly rising cumulus clouds, darkening of the sky, and increasing wind. After observing the dynamics of a thunderstorm, we can derive a rule that says if we observe these warning signs, then we should expect a thunderstorm. Such a rule need not correspond to the actual causal relationship between two events. It may also reflect a stable correlation due to more complicated causal mechanisms. For example, we might observe that there is a correlation between geese migrating south or north and the length of the day or the daily temperature. But, of course, the geese do not cause the change in temperature or day length. Theoretical learning means that we try to understand the causal mechanisms behind observed phenomena. It aims at general, abstract rules.

Third, one can learn either by oneself or from or with others. Individual learning occurs, but in many cases other people are involved in the learning process. Learning from others can occur without any active instruction from them. We may simply observe what others are doing and imitate their behavior, or infer why they are behaving in the observed way. Active teaching occurs in many situations, such as relationships between parents and children, masters and apprentices, teachers and students, or even among peers.

Because of its importance for adaptation, it is useful to introduce the anthropological concept of enculturation, which is similar to the concept of socialization in sociology. *Enculturation* is the process by which culture is transmitted. Culture includes values, norms, worldviews, and practices. Through enculturation, an individual becomes a member of a group and adapts to the existing culture. The enculturation process includes informal and unintentional as well as intentional aspects on the part of the learner and on the part of the adults, other parents, and peers who form the cultural community. Many values and norms are transmitted from parents to children through everyday practice without explicit teaching. But parents, schools, or religious communities also formally teach children or new members what is considered right or wrong, acceptable or unacceptable. Depending on age and cultural environment, individuals may or may not be consciously and intentionally enculturated. While children may be more passive in the process, adolescents or adults may actively intend to become a member of a particular group and thus very consciously adopt its culture.

12.3 Rational Behavior and Maximization

In Chap. 4, we saw that many economists, such as Gary Becker, equate the economic approach to the study of human behavior with rational choice in the sense of maximizing behavior under constraints. Rational choice theory has also been adopted by other social sciences, such as political science and sociology, and is a central element of decision theory, especially but not only in its normative branch, which deals with optimal decision-making. From a complexity perspective, rational choice theory is highly implausible as a description of what real people do, and in general should not form the behavioral basis of reliable economic models. This section explains why.

12.3.1 What Makes Decisions Difficult

Our intuitive definition of complexity of a system or situation is that it is difficult to describe, understand, predict, or control. The VUCA concept discussed in Chap. 1 provides reasons for these difficulties from the perspective of a decision-maker (e.g., in the military or in business). Making a (good) decision is hard when the world is changing (volatility), when the future is highly uncertain (uncertainty), when the decision affects a complex system (complexity), or when relevant information is missing or conflicting (ambiguity).

Change implies that we cannot be sure that an apparent causal relationship, or at least an empirical correlation that was robust in the past, will continue to hold in the future. In financial risk management, *correlation breakdown* is the term used to describe the phenomenon that the correlation between asset prices changes dramatically during major market events (see Loretan and English 2000). Risk management strategies that use stable correlations between assets in a financial portfolio to diversify risk can suddenly fail when they are most needed, such as in a financial crisis. If a system does not respond to an intervention in the same way as it did in the past, we cannot use experience to guide our decisions. Change can also make decisions difficult if it happens faster than we are able to learn new things and unlearn old routines that can be deeply internalized. Decision-making itself can be subject to routines that guide how we gather and interpret new information, how we use experience, and how we apply decision criteria.

Uncertainty is a key concept in decision theory. A classic distinction is between certainty, risk, and uncertainty. *Certainty* refers to a situation, in which the consequences of actions are known. *Risk* means that we know what outcomes are possible and that we also know the probabilities of those outcomes. A typical example of risk is rolling a six-dice. We know the possible outcomes (1, 2, 3, 4, 5 and 6) and the probability of each number (1/6 if the die is fair). Frank Knight (1921) distinguished risk from uncertainty (therefore often called *Knightian uncertainty*), which refers to situations where we cannot measure the uncertainty, i.e. assign probabilities. While this distinction is widely accepted, there are also distinctions that are somewhat less common. For situations where the possible outcomes are known but the probability distribution is not, experimental economics uses the term *ambiguity*. This concept goes back to Keynes (1921) and is formalized with the so-called Ellsberg urn (Ellsberg 1961).

An *Ellsberg urn* contains balls of different colors (e.g., red and black) whose mixture is not known. So when we draw a ball from the urn, we know that it will be red or black, but we have no way of assigning an ex ante probability to each color. Two other terms are *fundamental uncertainty* and *radical uncertainty*. They are not clearly defined, but both refer to a radically unknown and unknowable future. A pragmatic approach is to not distinguish between radical and fundamental uncertainty, and to use both terms for situations, where we know neither the possible outcomes nor the probabilities. Applied to the case of the urn, under radical uncertainty we do not even know what is in the urn. There may be red and black balls in it, but there may also be some with of other colors. Possibly, the urn contains some other objects as well, e.g. dice or sweets or spiders. As Keynes (1937, p. 214) said: "We simply do not know."

Bradley and Drechsler (2014) propose a different classification. They distinguish between ethical, option, and state space uncertainty, which are distinct from state uncertainty. They define *state uncertainty* as the empirical uncertainty that is measured by a probability function over the states of a world. *Ethical uncertainty* means that a decision-maker cannot assign precise utilities to consequences. In other words, the decision-maker may know what can happen, but cannot say which outcomes are desirable. *Option uncertainty* means that the precise consequences of an action in different states of the world are unknown. *State space uncertainty* arises when an agent does not know how to construct an exhaustive state space, i.e. which states of the world are possible. Bradley and Drechsler further argue that these types of uncertainty are characterized by the three dimensions nature, object, and severity of uncertainty. *Nature of uncertainty* refers to whether a judgment is being made about what could be the case (modal uncertainty), what is the case (empirical uncertainty), and what should be the case (normative uncertainty). *Object of uncertainty* refers to whether a judgment is made about the actual world (factual uncertainty) or about non-actual worlds (counterfactual uncertainty). *Severity of uncertainty* refers to the difficulty of making a judgement. Severity can be classified as

1. Ignorance: The decision-maker has no relevant information for the judgement.
2. Severe uncertainty: There is only enough information to make partial or imprecise judgment.
3. Mild uncertainty: There is sufficient information to make a precise judgment.
4. Certainty: The value of the judgment is given or known.

Yet another distinction is made by Herbert Simon (2000). He distinguishes between uncertainty about the future environment, about the reactions of other actors, and about the changes in one's own tastes and values.

Decision-relevant system complexity refers to the behavior of a system rather than its structure, although the two are related. When structural complexity is high, it is difficult to understand and predict how the system will behave. We have seen in previous chapters that cyclomatic complexity and causal complexity are useful measures of how difficult it is to understand the behavior of a system. Note, however, that both of these measures, strictly speaking, apply to models of systems, not to the systems themselves, which in many cases cannot be observed directly. A decision-maker always relies on a mental representation or model of the world, which may vary in its ability to capture the decision-relevant factors of the real world. Another aspect of complexity relevant to decisions is computational complexity, which is discussed in the following subsection.

In light of the above discussion, ambiguity can be seen as a special case of uncertainty. We can either define it as a situation in which possible outcomes are known, but not probabilities, or—and this is more in line with the VUCA interpretation—as empirical uncertainty about the description of the actual state of the world. In either case, it is an example of severe uncertainty, where the available information about the world and the problem is insufficient to make an accurate judgment.

Most of these complications make it difficult or even impossible to formulate a well-defined optimization problem that can be solved as in rational choice theory. Situations of risk can be formalized using expected utility theory, which models the choice among risky prospects (or lotteries) by rational agents. A risky choice option consists of a number of possible outcomes or payoffs x_k and their probabilities p_k. Each outcome is evaluated with a utility function $u(.)$. We can then define the *expected utility of a risky prospect* as

$$EU(p) = \sum_k u(x_k)p_k.$$

A rational agent should choose the lottery with the highest expected utility from a set of several lotteries. Apart from the fact that extensive research in behavioral and experimental economics since the 1970s has demonstrated that expected utility theory does not describe well what real people do (see, e.g., Starmer 2004), it is only applicable under very specific assumptions. In particular, situations under Knightian or radical uncertainty cannot be analyzed with expected utility theory, if neither the set of x_k nor the corresponding probabilities p_k are known.

12.3.2 Computational Complexity

Rational choice may also be impossible for reasons other than those presented in the previous subsection. Even well-defined decision problems under certainty may be too computationally complex to solve. Bossaerts and Murawski (2017) argue that most models of human decision-making and metacognition are intractable from a computational point of view. Computational complexity theory (CCT) provides a theoretical framework to describe exactly what it means for a decision to be difficult.[1]

Bossaerts and Murawski begin their discussion with the everyday example of shopping in a supermarket. Rational choice theory assumes that a decision-maker chooses a basket of goods whose utility is maximized subject to the feasibility condition of the budget constraint. Since we cannot buy fractions of the goods on offer, this is a discrete choice problem similar to the now familiar 0–1 knapsack problem. The consumer must decide whether to put a good i into the basket ($x_1 = 1$) or not ($x_i = 0$). Each good has a utility v_i and a price p_i and the consumer has a maximum budget W that can be spent. The optimization problem is then

$$\max_{x_i} \sum_{i=1}^{n} v_i x_i \; s.t. \sum_{i=1}^{n} p_i x_i \leq W \; and \; x_i \in \{0, 1\},$$

which is the basic 0–1 knapsack problem.[2] The knapsack problem is a combinatorial problem because it involves comparing different combinations of items in the basket (or knapsack). If the supermarket in the example had only 100 different items, the number of possible combinations would be approximately equal to 10^{30} (in fact it is equal to $2^{100} \approx 1.267 \cdot 10^{30}$). Checking all these combinations for the highest total utility and their feasibility given the budget constraint would be intractable for the

[1] The following discussion is based on Bossearts and Murawski (2017).

[2] There are also other versions of the knapsack problem, such as the bounded knapsack problem, where multiple units of x up to an upper bound can be chosen, or the unbounded knapsack problem, where there is no upper bound. The 0–1 problem is the simplest and most fundamental case.

world's fastest supercomputer, which would quickly run out of memory. Even if that supercomputer had enough memory, the computation would take millions of years. With 1000 available goods in the supermarket, the number of possible combinations would be about 10^{301}. Remember that the total number of atoms in the universe is estimated to be approximately 10^{80}. Since an average supermarket has about 40,000 different goods in stock, the number of possible combinations is effectively infinite, which makes it clear that solving this problem is infeasible for even the best supercomputer, let alone the average consumer.

Computational complexity theory classifies computational problems according to their inherent difficulty. *Computational complexity* is defined as the worst-case growth of the computational resources required to solve a computational problem as a function of the size of the input. Computing time, which depends on the number of computations, and memory are the most commonly studied resources. The size of the input is the number and length of variables given to the computational algorithm. In the supermarket example, the number of items in stock was the size of the input. CCT knows four classes of problems in terms of time complexity, i.e. the increase in time needed to solve the problem as a function of the size of the input. The classes are called P, NP, NP-complete, and NP-hard.

Class P contains all problems that a sequential computer can solve with in an amount of time that grows as a polynomial function of the size of the input. For example, if the time complexity is described by a quadratic function, the time quadruples if we double the size of the input, e.g. from 5 variables to 10: $\frac{10^2}{5^2} = \left(\frac{2n}{n}\right)^2 = 2^2 = 4$. For problems in this class, there exist algorithms, which are called *efficient* and whose running time has an upper bound given by a polynomial function of the input size. Class P problems such as sorting arrays or non-integer linear programming are tractable, i.e. they can usually be solved in reasonable time.

Class NP comprises all problems for which there is no known polynomial-time algorithm to find a solution. However, given solutions to problems in this class can be verified in polynomial time. We therefore distinguish between the *optimization problem* of finding a solution and the *decision problem* of whether a given solution satisfies a given value. While the decision problem of NP problems is tractable, the optimization problem is often intractable, because the required resources exceed the available ones. Most practical computational problems belong to class NP. The class of *NP-complete problems* contains the hardest problems in class NP. The knapsack decision problem as well as thousands of other practically relevant problems is NP-complete.

The problems contained in the *class NP-hard* are at least as hard as the hardest problems in class NP, but are not necessarily contained in class NP. If an NP-hard problem is not contained in class NP, then its decision problem cannot be solved in polynomial time. The 0–1 knapsack optimization problem is NP-hard, as are many models of cognition based on computational problems. The required solution time of NP-hard problems often grows exponentially with the input size. For example, if the number of variables in the knapsack problem doubles from 5 to 10, the time required increases by a factor of $\frac{2^{10}}{2^5} = 2^5 = 32$. Doubling from 10 inputs to 20 inputs increases

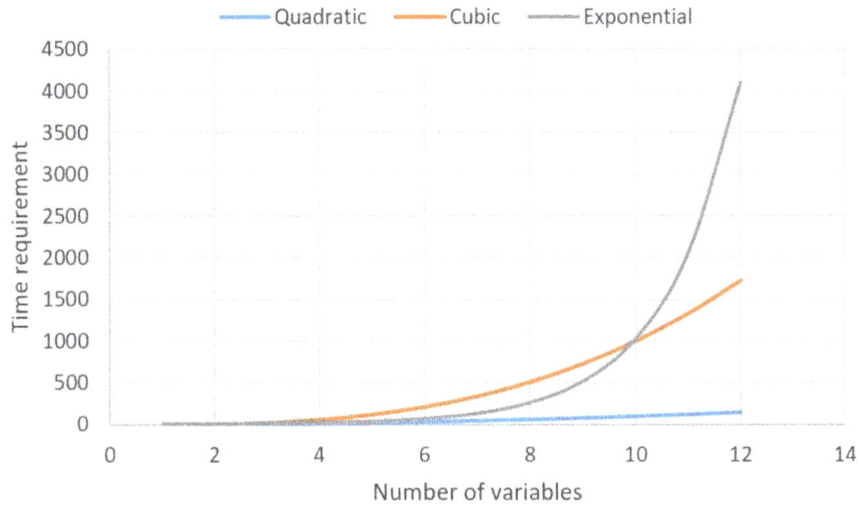

Fig. 12.2 Polynomial and exponential time requirements. Source: Author

Table 12.2 Examples of runtime

Runtime	$n = 10$	$n = 20$	$n = 40$	$n = 80$	$n = 100$
n	$0.5\ \mu s$	$1\ \mu s$	$2\ \mu s$	$4\ \mu s$	$5\ \mu s$
n^2	$5\ \mu s$	$0.02\ ms$	$0.08\ ms$	$0.32\ ms$	$0.5\ ms$
2^n	$51.2\ \mu s$	$52.43\ ms$	$15.27\ h$	$1.9 \cdot 10^9\ years$	$2 \cdot 10^{15}\ years$

the time requirement by the factor $2^{10} = 1{,}024$. Figure 12.2 shows how the time requirement grows from 1 to 12 input variables for a quadratic, a cubic, and an exponential case.

Figure 12.2 visualizes what exponential growth really means and how quickly the time requirement of these problems increases. To get an even better idea of the difference between polynomial and exponential time requirements, Table 12.2 shows examples of linearly, quadratically, and exponentially growing runtime for different numbers of inputs. Note that an algorithm with exponential runtime would need $1.9 \cdot 10^9$ years to solve a problem with 80 variables, which is about the age of the Earth. A problem with 83 variables would take $15 \cdot 10^9$ years, which is about 1 billion years more than the age of the universe.

CCT shows that many problems described by neoclassical rational choice theory are computationally intractable. These problems include utility maximization problems and Bayesian belief updating problems. This does not mean that all such problems are intractable, since human cognitive resources may be sufficient to solve such problems with few variables. But as we have seen, even for computers, running time grows very fast for NP-hard problems of moderate size.

The results of the CCT are relevant for human decision-making, as shown by Murawski and Bossaerts (2016), who conducted an experiment on how human subjects solve the knapsack problem, which they view as a representation of problems in budgeting, time management, production, logistics, combinatorial auctions, and portfolio optimization. Since technological innovation is combinatorial (see Chap. 10), the knapsack problem is also relevant to innovation and intellectual discovery. The experiment shows that human performance declines with the computational complexity of the problem. "Consistent with the very nature of the knapsack problem, only a minority of participants found the solution—often quickly—but the ones who did appeared not to realise" (Murawski and Bossaerts 2016, p. 1). Interestingly, participants were found to exert significantly more effort beyond the point where the marginal gain was positive and economic performance—the experiment was incentivized with monetary payoffs—increased with difficulty. Murawski and Bossaerts argue that the participants' behavior contradicts rational choice theory because they extended their effort beyond the point where the marginal gain of effort became zero.

12.3.3 As-if and Approximation

A standard argument in neoclassical economics is that the maximization problems of rational choice theory are not meant to describe what real agents actually do. Rational choice models are seen as as-if models that predict the outcome of agents' behavior, but not the behavior itself. This as-if argument goes back to Milton Friedman's (in)famous 1953 essay "The methodology of positive economics," in which he compares economic decision-makers to expert billiard players.

> *It seems not at all unreasonable that excellent predictions would be yielded by the hypothesis that the billiard player made his shots* ***as if*** *he knew the complicated mathematical formulas that would give the optimum directions of travel, could estimate accurately by eye the angles, etc., describing the location of the balls, could make lightning calculations from the formulas, and could then make the balls travel in the direction indicated by the formulas. Our confidence in this hypothesis is not based on the belief that billiard players, even expert ones, can or do go through the process described; it derives rather from the belief that, unless in some way or other they were capable of reaching essentially the same result, they would not in fact be expert billiard players.*
>
> *It is only a short step from these examples to the economic hypothesis that under a wide range of circumstances individual firms behave* ***as if*** *they were seeking rationally to maximize their expected returns (generally if misleadingly called 'profits') and had full knowledge of the data needed to succeed in this attempt;* ***as if****, that is, they knew the relevant cost and demand functions, calculated marginal cost and marginal revenue from all actions open to them, and pushed each line of action to the point at which the relevant marginal cost and marginal revenue were equal. Now, of course, businessmen do not actually and literally solve the system of simultaneous equations in terms of which the mathematical economist finds it convenient to express this hypothesis, any more than leaves or billiard players explicitly go through complicated mathematical calculations or falling bodies decide to create a vacuum.* (Friedman 1953, p. 21/22).

Friedman argues that it does not matter if the assumptions are unrealistic, as long as the theory makes good predictions. For him, the quality of the predictions is the most important criterion for judging a theory. He goes further to say:

> *Truly important and significant hypotheses will be found to have 'assumptions' that are wildly inaccurate descriptive representations of reality, and, in general, the more significant the theory, the more unrealistic the assumptions (in this sense).* (Friedman 1953, p. 14)

Thus, whether economic agents actually behave rationally and maximize objective functions is irrelevant if rational choice models predict market outcomes well. Philosopher of science Daniel Hausman (2021) criticizes this view because it immunizes economic theory against criticism and falsification, which is unscientific. He writes:

> *All that matters is whether the predictions concerning market phenomena turn out to be correct. And since anomalous market outcomes could be due to any number of uncontrolled causal factors, while experiments are difficult to carry out, it turns out that economists need not worry about ever encountering evidence that would strongly disconfirm fundamental theory. Detailed models may be confirmed or disconfirmed, but fundamental theory is safe. In this way one can understand how Friedman's methodology, which appears to justify the eclectic and pragmatic view that economists should use any model that appears to 'work' regardless of how absurd or unreasonable its assumptions might appear, has been deployed in service of a rigid theoretical orthodoxy. . . .*
>
> *[Friedman's methodological views] are still enormously influential, and they still serve as a way of avoiding awkward questions concerning simplifications, idealizations, and abstraction in economics rather than responding to them.*

Friedman argues that economic agents do not literally maximize expected returns, but that the result of their behavior is such as if they did so. He defends this "maximization of returns hypothesis" with two arguments. The first is "natural selection" in markets. He claims that firms that do not at least come close to maximizing returns would lose resources and would not stay in business for long. This argument obviously does not apply to consumers, because there is no mechanism that drives consumers who do not maximize utility out of the market. But even for firms, this argument is unconvincing for several reasons. First, it has long been observed that there are significant and quite persistent differences in profits between firms even within the same industry (e.g., Geroski and Jacquemin 1988). If market selection leads to profit maximization, profit differentials should disappear and profits should converge to the same high level. Second, as Beinhocker (2006, p. 408ff) argues, survival in markets requires sufficient profits, but not necessarily maximum profits. The point is that firms have multiple stakeholders, and they are fit in a market if they meet a multidimensional fitness function that satisfies many stakeholders better than other firms. Third, Friedman is not precise about the time dimension of his argument. He seems to suggest that profits must always be maximized, but as we argued in Chap. 10, firms face a trade-off between short-term efficiency (or profit maximization) and long-term endurance and adaptability. The Icarus paradox describes the empirically well-documented fact that firms that generate high returns in the short run often fail in the long run due to insufficient adaptation to changing market conditions. Finally, an arbitrage argument is sometimes used to defend profit maximization. Firms that do not maximize profits could be taken over by other firms or investors who exploit the unexploited profit opportunities. However, not every firm is traded in a market, and often acquiring firms fail to increase profitability because of problems with different corporate cultures, different firm routines, and different stocks of tacit knowledge.

Friedman's second argument is that the "behavior of businessmen in some way or other approximate[s] behavior consistent with the maximization of returns" (Friedman 1953, p. 22). In this view, a maximization model is a parsimonious description of an unknown approximation procedure. Bossaerts and Murawski (2017) argue that it is implausible from a computational point of view that agents can find *efficient approximation algorithms* that do not provide exact solutions to a problem, but are guaranteed to closely approximate exact solutions. The PCP theorem (probabilistically checkable proofs) is one of the most important theorems in computational complexity theory. A version of it states that approximating solutions to many optimization problems is as hard as computing exact solutions. Approximation by inexact algorithms may be possible, but then it is unknown how close such an algorithm approximates the solution.

12.3.4 Example of Intertemporal Utility Maximization

The problem of intertemporal utility maximization is an example of a mathematically hard problem. The assumption that consumers maximize an intertemporal utility function subject to an intertemporal budget constraint is central to all mainstream macroeconomic models. We discussed a simplified version of the problem as part of the Ramsey–Cass–Koopmans model in Chap. 4. This model was simplified, because it did not involve income uncertainty, which is a crucial feature of real-world intertemporal problems.

Allen and Carroll (2001, p. 255) argue that

> *under realistic descriptions of utility and uncertainty, the optimal consumption/saving decision is so difficult that only recently have economists managed to find solutions, using numerical methods that require previously infeasible amounts of computation.*

However, they show that the exact solution can be closely approximated by a simple buffer-stock saving rule that also describes well what real consumers do. The research question of their paper is whether consumers are able to learn, through trial and error, the optimal values of the two parameters of the model that give the best approximation to the exact solution.

They represent the utility maximization problem as follows. The goal of the consumer is to maximize expected lifetime utility by choice of a consumption path

$$\max_{\{C_s\}_t^\infty} E_t\left[\sum_{s=t}^{\infty} \beta^{s-t} u(C_s)\right]$$

subject to a budget constraint in all periods that allows saving at an interest rate of zero

$$X_{s+1} = X_s - C_s + Y_{s+1} \forall s$$

and a "cash-on-hand constraint" that prevents credit financed consumption

$$C_s \le X_s \forall s.$$

In this problem, X_s is the total resources available for consumption in a period, β is the discount factor, which is assumed to be equal to 0.95, $u(.)$ is the instantaneous utility function, which is assumed to be of the CRRA type, i.e. $u(C) = C^{1-\rho}/(1-\rho)$ with $\rho = 3$, and Y_s is the income in period s. Income is assumed to be stochastic with a distribution that roughly matches the empirically observed dynamics in the USA. There are three possible realizations of income, $Y_s \in \{0.7, 1, 1.3\}$ with probabilities $(0.2, 0.6, 0.2)$.

Since "finding the exactly correct nonlinear consumption policy rule (as economists have done) is an extraordinarily difficult mathematical problem" (Allen and Carroll 2001, p. 256), consumers cannot be expected to achieve this. However, it can be shown that a simple heuristic of buffer-stock saving can approximate the optimal solution very closely. The goodness of the approximation can be measured by the *sacrifice value*, which is the maximum amount of his initial wealth $X_t = 1$ that a perfectly rational consumer would be willing to spend in order to avoid having to switch from the optimal rule to the approximation. A numerical simulation yields a very low sacrifice value of 0.003 for the best approximation. The buffer-stock saving rule is defined as follows:

$$C^\theta(X) = \begin{cases} 1+\gamma\left(X-\overline{X}\right) & \text{if } 1+\gamma\left(X-\overline{X}\right) \le X \\ X & \text{if } 1+\gamma\left(X-\overline{X}\right) > X \end{cases}.$$

The heuristic is very intuitive: the consumer has a target level $\overline{X}$ of liquid assets for consumption, which is used to smooth consumption in the face of a stochastic income. If the actual level of liquid assets X (the buffer stock) falls below the target level, the consumer consumes less in order to increase the buffer stock. If the buffer stock is above the target, the consumer can consume more and the buffer stock falls. The linear rule above with $\gamma > 0$ implements this logic for the problem at hand. Recall that expected income is equal to 1. Hence, if $X = \overline{X}$, then consumption equals income, $C^\theta(X) = 1$. If $X > \overline{X}$, then $C^\theta(X) = 1 + \gamma\left(X - \overline{X}\right) > 1 = Y$. If $X < \overline{X}$, then $C^\theta(X) = 1 + \gamma\left(X - \overline{X}\right) < 1 = Y$. The condition in the rule ensures that consumption satisfies the "cash-on-hand constraint" $C \le X$.

The linear consumption rule has two parameters: $\theta = \left\{\gamma, \overline{X}\right\}$, i.e. the adjustment parameter γ and the target for the buffer stock. The minimum sacrifice value is reached for the optimal parameters $\theta^* = \{0.233, 1.243\}$. Allen and Carroll perform a simulation experiment, in which 1000 artificial consumers perform a grid search over 20 possible values for $\gamma \in [0, 1]$ and 20 values for $\overline{X} \in [1, 3]$, yielding a total of 400 possible rules. The best of the possible rules in this set is $\theta = \{0.25, 1.2\}$ with a sacrifice value of 0.007. In the simulation, each consumer considers each of the 400 possible rules for n periods and m times and estimates the value of the lifetime utility function of each rule. In order to obtain an estimate of the value of lifetime utility, a consumer must apply each rule for multiple periods (n). Furthermore, to minimize noise, each estimation must be repeated m times to obtain a consistent estimate. Therefore, the minimum time required to test all 400 rules for n = 10 periods and only one trial (m = 1) is 4000 periods. Allen and Carroll show, that for n = 10 and m = 1, the mean sacrifice value of the best rules chosen by consumers is 0.289, which is a poor approximation of the optimal solution. In this case, only 7% of the 1000 consumers find a rule with a sacrifice value less than 0.05. For a mean sacrifice value of 0.045 and a success rate of 0.68 (percentage of consumers finding a good rule), about one million periods are necessary. A success rate of about 85% with a mean sacrifice value of 0.028 requires about four million search periods.

The parameters of the problem (the discount factor and the income process) are chosen so that a period corresponds to 1 year. An individual search process by consumers that leads to a reasonable approximation of the optimal consumption choice by a large fraction of consumers would thus take millions of years. Allen and Carroll admit that their grid search algorithm is not very efficient, but even if consumers used a highly efficient hill-climbing algorithm, the minimum number of periods required to find a good approximation is not less than 10,000 periods (i.e., years). The conclusion from this simulation experiment is that consumers would take a very long time to find the parameters of the buffer-stock saving rule through individual learning that generate a good approximation of the exact optimal solution to the intertemporal utility maximization problem.

12.4 Behavior and Learning of Boundedly Rational Individuals

Methodological individualism, one of the pillars of neoclassical economics (see Chap. 4), explains all socioeconomic phenomena in terms of the decisions and actions of individuals. Examples of economic decisions made by individuals include what to buy, how to make an investment (e.g., in education or housing), how much and where to work, how much to save and how much to borrow, how to choose a portfolio of assets, or how to manage risk (e.g., by buying insurance). As consumers or suppliers of labor, individuals are often one side of a market. In neoclassical logic, therefore, we must understand the decisions and behavior of individuals if we are to explain market dynamics. In some cases, individuals need to form expectations about market or aggregate variables, such as the rate of inflation, interest rates, or the rate of unemployment. In these situations, the expectation is an input to the actual decision problem, such as a decision to save, borrow, or invest.

Computational complexity casts doubt on whether we should assume that all such behavior of individuals can be described as solutions to maximization problems. There is no doubt, however, that individuals make such decisions, but the question is how they do it if they do not maximize. Not maximizing does not mean that individuals are not thinking about a problem or that their behavior is irrational. Individuals may still try to find a good solution to a problem, even if actual maximization of an objective function is not possible. Given the informational and cognitive limitations that people face in making complex decisions, they can still be *boundedly rational*, as Herbert Simon has suggested. Simon contrasts the *substantive rationality* of a decision, which evaluates its outcome, with its *procedural rationality* (see Simon et al. 1992).

In a world characterized by complexity, uncertainty, and limited cognitive capacity, it makes little sense to consider as rational only those decisions that produce the best possible outcomes that an omniscient decision-maker could achieve. Procedural rationality is concerned with the effectiveness of the procedures by which an agent with limited information and information processing capacity chooses actions. The process of reaching a decision requires searching for information (what information, where and how to search, how much information), evaluating and processing that information, and deciding on a decision rule or procedure. Procedural rationality means that agents think about the steps in this process and have good reasons for what they do. It includes meta-decision-making (or cognitive control), i.e. thinking about the nature of the problem and the appropriate way to deal with it. Issues of meta-decision-making are the resources available to the decision-maker (e.g., time, knowledge, and access to information), the difficulty of the problem, and its relevance to the decision-maker. Since decision-making is costly in terms of cognitive effort, time, and possibly money, there should be a positive relationship between the effort invested in a problem and its relevance. Problems that are more relevant to the decision-maker deserve more resources than less important problems. Note, however, that finding the optimal effort is also often an intractable NP-hard problem. If agents wanted to determine optimal effort, they would need to know exactly how hard the problem is, but assessing the difficulty typically requires solving the problem. This means that the optimal allocation of resources to deal with the problem is even harder than solving the problem itself, since the latter is part of the resource allocation problem. We can conclude that meta-decision-making is also unlikely to be a maximization process, but how real people do it is an open research question (see Bossaerts and Murawski 2017).

The relevance of a problem to the decision-maker is expressed in the aspiration level. If optimization is not possible, the agent may seek a solution that is "good enough," i.e. that meets a given aspiration level or acceptability threshold. Simon calls this behavior *satisficing* (a combination of *satisfy* and *suffice*). Table 12.3 illustrates a satisficing algorithm. A decision-maker searches for options to solve a problem, such as products that satisfy a particular need. The table implies that each

Table 12.3 Satisficing

	Option 1	Option 2	Option 3	Option 4	**Option 5**	...	Option n
Value	6	1	9	3	**11**	...	
Is ≥ 10?	No	No	No	No	**Yes**	...	
Search	Next option	Next option	Next option	Next option	**Stop**		

available option can be assigned a numerical value. Furthermore, the decision-maker wants to reach a value of 10, which is the aspiration level. This algorithm is a sequential search in which the agent checks the value of one option after another. If the value of an option is not satisfactory, the next option is checked until the first option that meets the aspiration level is found. Once a sufficiently good option is found (Option 5 in this example), the search stops and no more options are checked, even if there are still many options available. It is possible that some of the additional options are better than the chosen one, but this does not matter from a satisficing perspective. The choice of the level of demand is critical to the outcome of satisficing algorithms. Selten (1998) proposes a theory in which agents adjust their aspiration levels when they find that they are unattainable.

Over many centuries, logic has been developed as a way to reason and solve problems. Since not all problems are deterministic and often not all information is available, statistics has been developed since the seventeenth century as an additional way to think rationally. Gigerenzer (2021) calls rules for decision-making based on logic and statistics logical rationality, which is the foundation of modern science. Parallel to the development of modern science based on *logical rationality*, there was also a tradition of using heuristics to solve problems. A *heuristic* (from Greek εὑρίσκω (heurískō) = "I find, discover") is a practical method or approach based on intuition or experience that allows one to find a solution to a problem with limited time and information. Heuristics can be thought of as mental shortcuts that provide sufficiently good, but not necessarily optimal, solutions. Philosophers and mathematicians such as René Descartes, Joachim Jungius, Leonhard Euler, and George Pólya developed and used heuristics to solve otherwise intractable problems or to supplement logic.

Herbert Simon saw heuristics as a problem-solving method associated with bounded rationality. In psychology, economics, and decision sciences in general, heuristics became a very active area of research. In the 1970s and 1980s, the heuristics and biases approach pioneered by Amos Tversky and Daniel Kahneman dominated the literature. This view has been challenged since the 1990s by the ecological rationality approach of Gerd Gigerenzer, which builds on the insights of Herbert Simon and Reinhard Selten.

---

[3]Since the Nobel Prize is not awarded posthumously, only Kahneman received it, along with experimental economist Vernon L. Smith.

12.4.1 Heuristics and Biases

In the 1960s, the two psychologists Amos Tversky and Daniel Kahneman began a long-running collaboration on human decision-making that ended with the untimely death of Tversky in 1996 and was rewarded with the 2002 Nobel Memorial Prize in Economics for Kahneman.[3] The Nobel Memorial Prize indicates that this work was enormously influential in economics and contributed to the establishment of behavioral economics. The mathematician Leonard J. Savage developed *subjective expected utility theory* (Savage 1954), which combined the work of Frank Ramsey and John von Neumann on rational decision-making under uncertainty with Bayesian probability theory. Savage's theory is a normative theory of decision-making based on three pillars: a set of choice axioms, the maximization of subjective expected utility, and Bayesian updating of probabilities. Gigerenzer (2021) calls the concept of rationality that rests on Savage's theory and which corresponds to the standard model of decision-making in neoclassical economics *axiomatic rationality*.

In many experiments, Tversky and Kahneman showed that real people often do not behave according to axiomatic rationality. Instead, people often use heuristics to make judgments or decisions. In their seminal paper, Tversky and Kahneman (1974) present three heuristics that people use when making probability judgments under uncertainty, and introduce the notion that the use of these heuristics can lead to serious and systematic errors (or biases). Axiomatic rationality (especially Bayes' rule) serves as a benchmark against which the errors are assessed. Bias is the systematic deviation from the judgment under axiomatic rationality caused by the use of heuristics.

The *representativeness heuristic* is used in order to assess the probability that an object A belongs to a class B or that an event A originated from a process B. Representativeness means that people use the degree to which A resembles B as an estimate of the probability. If A and B are similar, then the probability that A belongs to or originates from B is judged to be high. Tversky and Kahneman illustrate judgment by representativeness with an example of an individual described as follows:

> *Steve is very shy and withdrawn, invariably helpful, but with little interest in people. A meek and tidy soul, he has a need for order and structure, and a passion for detail.*

Representativeness is used when people are asked to rate the likelihood that Steve is in a particular occupation from a list of possibilities, e.g. farmer, salesman, pilot, librarian, or doctor. Representativeness compares the description of Steve to the stereotype of the occupation. According to Tversky and Kahneman, this method can lead to serious errors because it neglects several factors that should influence judgments of probability. One such factor is the prior probability of outcomes, which is neglected by the representativeness heuristic. The description of Steve may resemble the stereotype of a librarian, so the assumed probability that he is a librarian is high. However, the base frequency of farmers is much higher than that of librarians (in other words, there are many more farmers than librarians in the population). Therefore, a priori, it is much more likely that Steve is a farmer. Axiomatic rationality requires that people use Bayes' rule to estimate the probability, taking into account the prior probabilities. Experimental evidence confirms that people do in fact violate Bayes' rule, ignoring the effects of sample size, regression to the mean, the properties of chance, and the principles of predictability.

The second heuristic discussed by Tversky and Kahneman (1974) is the *availability heuristic*. It is used when people are asked to estimate the frequency of a class or the probability of an event, such as the risk of heart attack in middle-aged people. The availability heuristic estimates probability by the ease with which instances of the class or occurrences of the event can be recalled. For example, someone who can recall several cases of heart attack among his or her acquaintances is likely to estimate a higher probability than someone who does not know anyone who has had a heart attack. Possible biases related to the availability heuristic are biases due to the retrievability of instances, biases due to the effectiveness of a search set, imaginability biases, or illusory correlation biases.

The *anchoring-and-adjustment heuristic* is a third heuristic that can lead to bias. The heuristic is used to estimate numerical quantities, such as the population of a country, the height of a mountain, or the answer to a computational problem. According to the heuristic, people make such estimates by starting with an initial value (or anchor), which may be a given cue or the result of a partial calculation, and adjusting from there. Anchoring means that the adjustment is typically insufficient, so that the estimate is biased toward the anchor. Insufficient adjustment was demonstrated in an experiment in which subjects were asked to estimate the percentage of African countries that are members of the United Nations. Before making their estimate, subjects were given a number between 0 and 100, determined by a spinning wheel of fortune. They were asked whether the percentage to be estimated was less or greater than the given number and then to adjust from the anchor to their point estimate. The median estimate of the groups given 10 as an anchor was 25%, and those given 65 estimated the percentage to be 45%. Even payoffs for accuracy did not reduce this bias. Another example is estimating a product of numbers within 5 seconds. One group estimated the product written as

$$8 \times 7 \times 6 \times 5 \times 4 \times 3 \times 2 \times 1$$

and another group estimated the result of

$$1 \times 2 \times 3 \times 4 \times 5 \times 6 \times 7 \times 8.$$

The median estimate of the first group was 2250, while the second group estimated the product to be 512. The correct answer in both cases is 40,320. The bias seems to occur because subjects quickly perform the first one or two multiplications in each sequence and imperfectly adjust the results upward.

The heuristics and biases research program discovered a list of other judgment heuristics, such as the affect heuristic, the effort heuristic, the familiarity heuristic, or the simulation heuristic. The program influenced research in psychology, but especially in economics, which discovered many ways in which decision-making deviates from the axiomatic rationality of homo economicus. Some common biases include action bias—the tendency to take action even when inaction might be more effective; confirmation bias—the tendency to seek out and interpret information that confirms one's preconceptions; or salience bias—the tendency to focus on salient or emotionally striking facts and ignore less salient ones.

Some prominent biases that are particularly relevant to economic behavior are the endowment effect, hyperbolic discounting, mental accounting, and the money illusion. The *endowment effect* describes the observation that people's willingness to accept, i.e., what they are willing to give up to obtain an object, is higher than their willingness to pay, i.e., what they would be willing to pay to obtain the same object. *Hyperbolic discounting* is an empirically supported alternative to exponential discounting in intertemporal choice theory. It means that people have a very high preference for immediate consumption over future consumption. It leads to inconsistent choices over time because the same deferral of consumption, say by a week, is discounted much more heavily when the reference point is the present than when it is in the distant future. Dynamic or time inconsistency means that individuals make choices today that their future selves would prefer not to have made, even though the information is the same in the present and in the future. *Mental accounting* describes the phenomenon that people seem to have different mental accounts for different sources of income and wealth, as well as for different categories of expenditures. The propensity to spend from these different accounts varies. For example, \$100 received as a gift may be spent entirely, but \$100 received as a bonus from an employer and credited to a different mental account may be spent at a much lower percentage. Such a practice violates the economic assumption that money should be fungible, i.e. income from different sources should be perfectly interchangeable. *Money illusion* is a cognitive bias in which agents confuse the nominal and real value of money. People subject to the money illusion prefer a 5% increase in nominal wages despite 5% inflation to a 1% increase with no inflation.

After initial resistance to these and other "anomalies" of economic behavior (Thaler 1991), economics had to accept that the documented behaviors were robust and difficult to reconcile with models based on axiomatic rationality. The field of (new) behavioral economics emerged in the 1980s and 1990s. In contrast to the earlier work of Herbert Simon and Reinhard Selten, which is sometimes called old behavioral economics, the new field is concerned with how to reconcile the anomalies with the neoclassical approach and how to correct the "irrational" behavior. Werner Güth called the new behavioral economics a neoclassical repair shop (e.g., Güth 2002, p. 21):

> *There are so-called new equilibrium ideas. I refer to this as a neoclassical repair shop. The starting point is that orthodox theory—meaning that you apply the common laws of rationality to material incentives and derive a solution—is strongly rejected in many instances, for instance in the case of the ultimatum game. And then, what those people will do is to somewhat repair the game-theoretic representation; they have richer utility functions, but they would never question rationality.*

The main point of the neoclassical repair shop is to continue modeling behavior as maximization, but with modified utility functions, alternative discounting models, dual-self models, or other extensions of the conventional modeling framework. In many cases, behavioral economic models are still as-if models and do not aim at more descriptive theories. The second main research goal is to find out how people can be "nudged" toward (more) rational behavior by benevolent policy makers. Nudge theory and nudging have been popularized in economics by Thaler and Sunstein (2008). For them, nudging means changing the *choice architecture*, i.e. the conditions under which irrational agents make their choices, so that their choices become more rational and more in line with their own self-interest. Again, axiomatic rationality prescribes how rational agents should behave. Deviations from it are irrational and can (and should) be corrected by nudging.

12.4.2 Fast and Frugal Heuristics

Psychologist Gerd Gigerenzer and his collaborators in the ABC Group (Adaptive Behavior and Cognition) at the Max Planck Institute for Human Development have developed a very different view of heuristics and rationality (see Gigerenzer et al. 1999). For them, fast and frugal heuristics are tools in the mind's adaptive toolbox that often exhibit ecological rationality. Decision-makers select one of the heuristics in their toolbox that seems appropriate for the problem at hand by intuitively assessing its ecological rationality.

Gigerenzer (2021) argues that Savage's axiomatic rationality is only a useful concept for small worlds, as Savage himself asserts. Savage (1954) defined a *small world* as a set S of mutually exclusive and exhaustive future states of the world and a set C of mutually exclusive and exhaustive consequences of actions given a particular state. Savage mentions playing chess and planning a picnic as examples outside of small worlds, such that his axiomatic rationality does not apply. Playing chess is not a small world, because the number of all possible states S is too large to be exhaustively determined. Finding the optimal sequence of moves among the approximately 10^{120} possible sequences is a computationally intractable (or NP-hard) problem. Planning a picnic is different, because it is an ill-defined problem. The set of states S is not only large, but also unknown due to uncertainty. The same is true for the set of consequences C.

Following Savage, Gigerenzer postulates that axiomatic rationality is limited to small worlds. But if axiomatic rationality is not applicable to large worlds with intractable or ill-defined problems, then there is no point in using it as a normative reference model for such problems, as is done in the heuristics and biases research program and in behavioral economics. Why should optimization be considered the only rational behavior for problems that even supercomputers cannot solve due to intractability or uncertainty? Asking this question shifts the focus from the cognitive limitations of the decision-maker to the nature of the problem. A more meaningful concept of rationality should consider not only the individual, but also the nature of the problem and the environment in which the problem is situated. It makes no sense to use axiomatic rationality as a measure of rationality without considering whether its proposed solutions are feasible in principle. In line with the discussion of

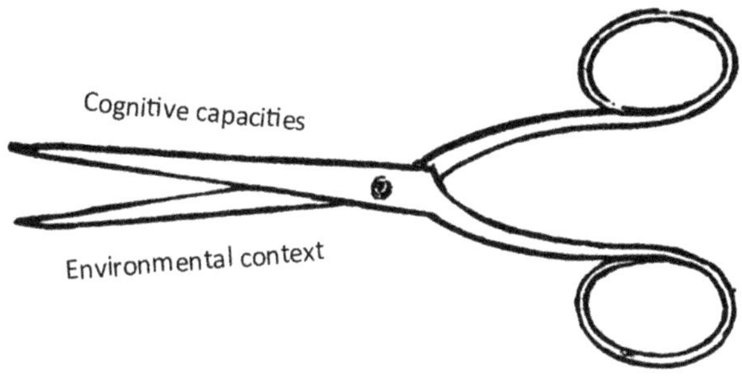

Fig. 12.3 Simon's scissors. Source: Author

computational complexity, Gigerenzer assumes that small worlds are the exception rather than the rule.

Gigerenzer (2008) refers to Herbert Simon's metaphor of the two blades of a pair of scissors (see Fig. 12.3). To understand behavior and to assess its rationality, one must look at both the mind and the environment and at how they interact and fit together.

> *Studying only one blade will not reveal why scissors cut so well. Similarly, studying only the mind can mislead researchers into confusing adaptive heuristics with cognitive deficits . . . The link between mind and environments is the topic if the study of ecological rationality: In which environment does a given heuristic perform well and where will it fail?* (Gigerenzer 2008, p. 22)

Ecological rationality is an alternative conception to logical or axiomatic rationality. It focuses on the fit between cognitive strategies and the structure of the environment. "A heuristic is ecologically rational to the degree that it is adapted to the structure of the environment" (Gigerenzer 2021, p. 3548). Thus, the use of heuristics is not always rational, but in those cases where a heuristic is adapted to the environment in which it is used, it is often better than other problem-solving approaches.

The quality of a problem-solving method can be judged by three criteria: 1) ease and speed of use, 2) information requirements, and 3) accuracy. The ABC research program identified a number of fast and frugal heuristics that are easy to use and need little information about the problem. Table 12.4 lists ten fast and frugal heuristics for different types of problems. We already encountered satisficing in Table 12.3.

"Take the best" is an example of a one-reason heuristic. Table 12.5 illustrates what this means. Suppose there are n cues about a problem that consists of choosing between two alternatives (Option 1 and Option 2). For example, a student might want to choose between two classes and predict the expected grade. The available cues could be class size, average grades given by the professor in the past, time of the seminar, number of required readings, and frequency of office hours. The cues need to be ranked by their validity, that is, their predictive power, which can be measured by how often the inference was correct when a cue was crucial. Let us assume that the average grade has the highest validity, followed by class size and the number of papers to read. The values of the first two cues are identical for the two seminars, but

Table 12.4 Ten fast and frugal heuristics in the adaptive toolbox

Heuristic	Definition
Recognition heuristic	If one of two alternatives is recognized, infer that it has the higher value in the criterion.
Fluency heuristic	If one alternative is recognized faster than another, infer that it has the higher value on the criterion.
Take the best	Infer which of two alternatives has the higher value by (a) searching through cues in order of validity, (b) stopping the search as soon as a cue discriminates, (c) choosing the alternative this cue favors.
Tallying	To estimate a criterion, do not estimate weights but simply count the number of favoring cues.
Satisficing	Search through alternatives, and choose the first one that exceeds your aspiration level.
1/N, equality heuristic	Allocate resources equally to each of N alternatives.
Tit-for-tat	Cooperate first, keep a memory of size 1, and then imitate your partner's last behavior.
Default heuristic	If there is a default, do nothing about it.
Imitate the majority	Look at a majority of people in your peer group, and imitate their behavior.
Imitate the successful	Look for the most successful person and imitate his or her behavior.

Source: adapted from Gigerenzer (2008)

Table 12.5 Take-the-best heuristic

	Value cue 1	Value cue 2	Value cue 3	. . .	Value cue n
Option 1	2	20	−6		
Option 2	2	20	−3		
Difference?	No	No	Yes		
Action	Next cue	Next cue	Choose 2	Stop	

they differ for the third cue. The student assumes that more papers to read makes it more difficult to get a good grade, so she measures the value of this cue as the negative of number of papers. Since the required reading in Seminar 1 is 6 papers versus 3 papers in Seminar 2, Option 2 appears easier and therefore better than Option 1. The student chooses option 2 because the third cue is the first one that allows her to distinguish between the two options. Thus, the take-the-best heuristic relies on one reason for the decision. All other cues with lower validity are ignored. The take-the-best heuristic is an example of a *lexicographic rule* that applies a strict relevance hierarchy of criteria.

Gigerenzer (2021) cites a number of studies showing that the take-the-best heuristic has predictive performance that is as good as or better than that of more complex models such as multiple regression or sophisticated machine learning algorithms, even though it ignores valid information. The finding that a heuristic

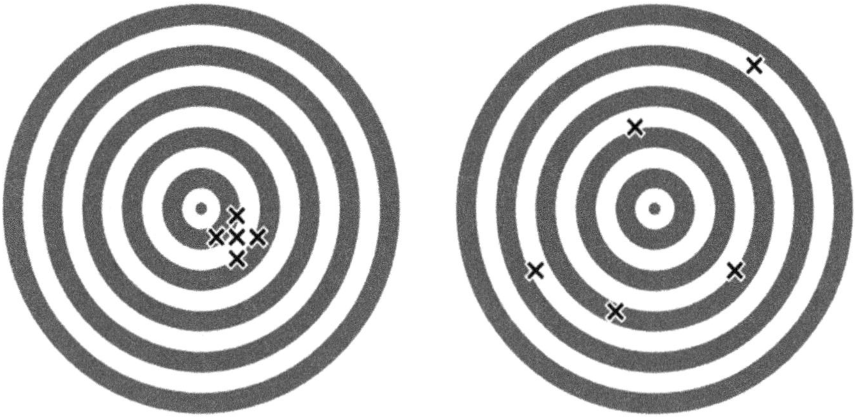

Fig. 12.4 Bias versus variance of predictions. Source: Gigerenzer (2021), CC BY 4.0 (https://creativecommons.org/licenses/by/4.0/)

H makes a more accurate prediction than an alternative method M, even though it uses only a subset of the information M, is called the *less-is-more effect.*

One explanation for the less-is-more effect is the *bias–variance dilemma* of prediction under uncertainty illustrated in Fig. 12.4. Suppose the problem is to estimate the true value μ of a variable in a population based on M random samples. Each sample produces an estimate x_m, and the mean of all the estimates is $\overline{x}$. In Fig. 12.4, the bull's eye in the center represents the true value μ and each cross stands for an estimate x_m from a sample m. Uncertainty in this problem is minimal, because the population is stable and the samples are random. In such a case, the prediction error Δ can be decomposed into its three sources:

$$\Delta = (\overline{x} - \mu)^2 + \frac{1}{m}\sum_m (x_m - \overline{x})^2 + \varepsilon.$$

The first term depends on the bias, $\overline{x} - \mu$, which is the average deviation of the mean of the sample estimates from the true value. The second term is the variance of the estimates, i.e. the mean squared deviation of the sample estimates from their mean. Finally, ε is unsystematic noise with zero mean and uncorrelated with bias. The two dartboards in Fig. 12.4 illustrate bias and variance.

The estimates on the left board are all close together, meaning they have low variance. However, they systematically deviate from the true value, because they are all below and to the right of the center. Therefore, there is a bias in these estimates. The opposite is true for the dartboard on the right. There is no bias, because the estimates are scattered in all directions around the target, but the variance is considerable. The prediction error can be small despite the bias if the bias is moderate and the variance is small (left dartboard). Conversely, the prediction error can be large even with zero bias if the variance of the estimates is large (right dartboard).

Fast and frugal heuristics, such as the take-the-best heuristic, can be more accurate than complex methods because they can have less variance. Due to many free parameters, methods such as multiple regression can have a good in-sample fit because the model is flexible enough to fit the observed data. However, despite a good in-sample fit, the out-of-sample prediction error can be high, which is called *overfitting*. The problem of overfitting can occur because, in situations of uncertainty, data consist of a predictable structural component (signal) and random noise. Ideally, we would like to filter out the noise and identify the structure with high precision. The fit of a flexible model with many parameters may be too good in the sense that it fits not only the structure but also some of the noise, which is not informative. If we have multiple samples, then the prediction of such a model will be partly based on noise, resulting in a prediction error. Since the noise should be uncorrelated across multiple samples from the same population, the variance of the estimates is high because different noise is combined with the same structure. The result is an unbiased estimate with high variance, as in the right dartboard in Fig. 12.4. In contrast, frugal heuristics are more robust to noise because they ignore some of the data. They also do not have adjustable parameters. Heuristics are not overly sensitive to the peculiarities of different samples, which reduces the variance of their estimates.

The ABC research program refers to the human mind as an adaptive toolbox that provides several simple but accurate heuristics for making decisions under uncertainty. "Adaptive" can refer to several aspects of the toolbox. First, the decision-maker can adapt to the situation at hand by more or less consciously choosing the appropriate heuristic that is ecologically rational. Choosing the right heuristic is a matter of individual learning. Second, heuristics consist of building blocks that can be used to construct new heuristics or to adapt them to new situations. For example, tit-for-tat can be adapted to tit-for-two-tats, i.e., retaliation only occurs after two defections, to prevent cooperation from breaking down after an accidental defection. Third, heuristics are adapted to evolved capabilities and environmental conditions. They can be simple because they rely on evolved cognitive capacities such as recognition memory, recall memory, imitation, or reciprocal altruism.

Kaaronen et al. (2023) present a variety of heuristics or rules of thumb used in different traditional cultures in the areas of agriculture, foraging, social learning, moral decision-making, and technological development. All are well adapted to their respective environments. For example, many cultures use biological laws or bioindicators to guide the use of natural resources. Often, simple if-then rules are used: if event x occurs, then do y. The event x may be the arrival of migratory birds or fish, or the flowering of a particular plant. The signal x does not have to be causally related to the consequence y. Stable correlations or patterns are sufficient to make good decisions, for example in resource management. Kaaronen et al. report on a traditional Javanese seasonal calendar in which the beginning of the rainy season is indicated by the bud of the Gadung yam. The onset of the dry season can be inferred from the budding of the cotton tree or the sound of the coconut bug.

Knowing the timing of the rainy and dry seasons is crucial for the timing of sowing or harvesting. An example from foraging is the rule of Finnish mushroom hunters to avoid all white mushrooms. Although there are many edible white mushrooms in Finland, there is also the white *Amanita virosa*, known as the "destroying angel," which is one of the most poisonous mushrooms in the world. Eating just the cap can kill an adult human. The "avoid all white mushrooms" heuristic is clearly inefficient, but it prevents deadly mistakes. Two rules of thumb for social learning are "copy the most successful individual" and "learn from elders." Success can be inferred from first-order cues such as generosity, self-confidence, or cultural titles. Old age is a first-order cue to experience and accumulated knowledge.

These examples can be used to explain that ecological rationality depends on the fit of the heuristic to a particular environment, which may break down if the environment changes. Kaaronen et al. (2023) discuss how climate change and biodiversity loss invalidate many bioindicators. Migration can also cause problems, for example when mushroom foragers use heuristics adapted to their place of origin in a new environment where they do not work. "Learn from the elders" makes sense in a stable environment with slow technological progress, but in the rapidly changing modern world it might be reversed to "learn from the young." Finally, sensible heuristics can be exploited by profit-seekers. In their 2015 book "Phishing for Phools," Nobel laureates George Akerlof and Robert Shiller argue that profit-seeking firms manipulate and deceive customers, exploiting their cognitive biases (Akerlof and Shiller 2015). One example of such manipulation is the common practice in advertising of having celebrities endorse a product. This practice exploits the copy-the-successful heuristic, but destroys its ecological rationality because the celebrity's success is typically unrelated to the advertised product.

12.4.3 Learning

Learning is a way for individuals to adapt to their environment. Nobel laureate and experimental economist Reinhard Selten distinguishes between reinforcement learning and belief learning[4] (Selten 1991). *Reinforcement learning* means that success and failure influence the choice probabilities. Over time, agents learn to do more often, what was successful in the past and to avoid actions that led to failure. Importantly, reinforcement learning does not require an understanding of the situation. Agents do not need to know why certain actions led to success or failure. All they need to do is to observe the correlation between actions and outcomes.

Belief learning is different because it involves reasoning about the situation. Selten (1991) discusses two very different forms of belief learning: Bayesian updating and the development of cognitive maps or mental models. Bayesian updating fits well with the concept of axiomatic rationality and is widely accepted

[4]Selten calls reinforcement learning rote learning. He also considers imitation to be a form of learning, but we will ignore imitation here.

in economics as a plausible way to model learning, despite empirical evidence against its use by real people. Many economists recognize that it is not plausible to assume that economic agents simply know how to form rational expectations or play equilibrium strategies in games. A learning literature that asks whether optimal behavior can be learned often assumes Bayesian learning, e.g. Bray and Savin (1986) and Feldman (1987) for rational expectations and Jordan (1991) for Nash equilibria in games. Cognitive maps are representations of the mental models that agents use when reasoning about causality in systems. There have been efforts in psychology and political science to elicit individuals' mental maps of the economy, but so far the interest of economists has been limited.

Bayesian updating or Bayesian inference is a statistical model based on Bayes' theorem or *Bayes' rule*. The key idea is that a posterior probability is estimated using a prior probability and a likelihood function that takes into account observed evidence. Since evidence is used to update a prior probability into a posterior probability, Bayes' rule is a normative learning rule. Bayes' rule can be expressed as

$$P(A|B) = P(A)\frac{P(B|A)}{P(B)},$$

where A and B are two events, $P(A)$ and $P(B)$ are the unconditional probabilities of A and B, $P(A|B)$ is the conditional probability of A given that B is true and $P(B|A)$ is the conditional probability of B given that A is true. $P(A|B)$ is the posterior probability of A given B, $P(A)$ is the prior probability of A and $P(B|A)$ is the likelihood of A given a fixed B. In a context of statistical inference, we could replace A with H for a hypothesis to be tested by data, and B with E for empirical evidence collected or observed after the prior probability $P(H)$ on the hypothesis was formed. In this interpretation, Bayesian inference or updating is done by the rule:

$$P(H|E) = P(H)\frac{P(E|H)}{P(E)}.$$

Bayesian learning hence works like this: first, a hypothesis is formed and given a prior probability $P(H)$. Then, data are collected or observed. Applying Bayes' rule is a rational way to update the probability of the hypothesis given the evidence. The probability of the hypothesis after observing evidence, $P(H|E)$, is the result of the learning process.

There is an enormous amount of empirical evidence, mostly from experiments in psychology and experimental economics, that people violate Bayesian updating in various ways (Selten 1991; Benjamin 2019). There is also evidence that trained professionals for whom correct statistical reasoning is important, such as health professionals, often fail to apply Bayesian reasoning correctly (e.g., Whiting et al. 2015). On the other hand, people can be trained and learn to improve their Bayesian reasoning (see Brase and Hill 2015). Nevertheless, it cannot serve as a general model of how most people learn from new information.

The concept of mental models offers a very different perspective on learning. *Mental models* refer to individuals' subjective and internalized representations of the external reality that surrounds them (see Jones et al. 2011). These models are constructed based on an individual's unique life experiences, perceptions, and understanding of the world. They serve as a tool for reasoning and decision-making and can influence an individual's behavior. In addition, mental models play an important role in filtering and storing new information. Although mental models serve as a means for individuals to represent and interact with the world, their accuracy is inherently limited and subjective to each individual. This is because mental models are incomplete representations of reality and are context dependent, making them potentially inconsistent across situations. Mental models are highly dynamic in nature, as they must adapt to ever-changing circumstances and evolve through learning over time. Research on naive theory, or layman's reasoning, attempts to determine how laypeople think about the world and how they assign causal relationships between concepts. Cognitive maps, similar to the causal loop diagrams presented in Chap. 7, can be used to visualize people's mental models.

Leiser and Drori (2005) conducted a questionnaire study among psychology students, high school students, grocery store owners, and teachers in Israel on their understanding of inflation. The participants were given nine economic concepts, e.g., price, COL index, inflation, supply/demand, and were asked to link those that they thought were related. This exercise resulted in the cognitive maps shown in Fig. 12.5. Confirming the hypothesis that mental models depend on personal life experiences, the cognitive maps differ between the groups. For teachers, inflation is closely related to wages, which are their main source of income. Both inflation and taxes reduce their income. Teachers see a relationship between supply/demand and prices, but there is no direct relationship between prices and inflation. Shopkeepers see a close link between inflation and the interest rate, which is important to them because rising interest rates reduce customers' purchasing power and thus shopkeepers' income. In contrast to teachers, wages are not very relevant for shopkeepers. Students have a rather fragmented understanding of inflation and the other economic concepts. They cannot relate the interest rate to any other concept. Since they do not earn wages, wages are peripheral to their maps. Interestingly, students organize the concepts in two circles, creating feedback loops. Students interpret taxes and budget as macroeconomic variables, while teachers and shopkeepers think about them from their own microeconomic perspective.

Mental models are typically functional rather than complete or accurate representations of reality. They are constructed with a specific purpose or use in mind. They provide a simplified representation of reality that allows people to interact with the world around them. Due to cognitive limitations, it is not possible or desirable to represent every detail of reality. Instead, mental models are influenced by an individual's goals, motives, background knowledge, and existing knowledge structures. According to Sterman's (1994) study of mental models, people tend to take an event-based, open-loop view of causality. They often ignore feedback processes, fail to recognize time lags between actions and responses, and overlook nonlinearities that may affect the strength of different feedback loops as a system

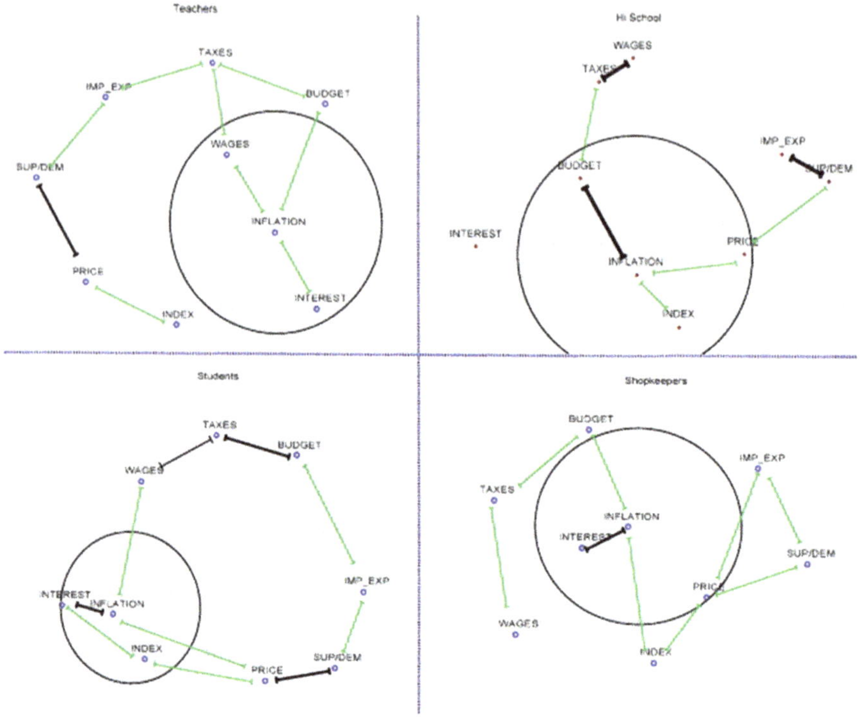

Fig. 12.5 Laypersons' cognitive maps of inflation. Source: Leiser and Drori (2005), reproduced with kind permission of Elsevier B.V

evolves. Leiser and Krill (2017) discuss a number of studies showing that lay thinking and lay mental models are very different from how economists think about the economy. Thus, without formal education, it is very difficult to acquire an adequate understanding of economic systems. Even with formal education, it seems difficult for people to internalize economic principles. Walstad and Allgood (1999) present evidence that even college seniors who have taken an economics course have limited knowledge of basic economics.

Learning can be understood as the active construction and modification of an individual's mental models from available information. Selten (1991) refers to causal diagrams as representations of mental models and uses the example of advertising to explain the learning process. A causal diagram depicts the links that connect a decision variable, such as advertising, to a target variable, such as profits. Two causal chains in a diagram might be:

1. Advertising increases sales and sales increase profits.
2. Advertising increases cost and cost decreases profits.

Individuals engage in qualitative reasoning based on such causal chains. One chain may provide a rationale for increasing advertising, while another may argue for reducing it. Conflicting chains are resolved by assessing the relative importance of the causal links. For example, if the causal link between advertising and cost is considered to be the least important, the second chain can be ignored and a decision to increase advertising can be based on the first chain. However, this only determines the direction of change, not the amount of change, which must be determined in some other way. Belief learning affects judgments of importance, as experience may reveal that the impact of advertising on costs is more critical than its impact on sales. The process of belief learning can be modeled in a manner similar to that of reinforcement learning.

In economic experiments, it is common to let subjects play a few rounds without pay so that they can learn the rules of the experiment. Sometimes the research question is whether subjects can learn theoretically predicted behavior through repetition. In other cases, such learning is intended to increase the external validity of an experiment, because it is argued that people are familiar with the problems in their everyday lives that the experiment is intended to represent. In such cases, the observed behavior at the end of the experiment is often different from the behavior at the beginning and is considered more representative of behavior outside the laboratory. From the vantage point of behavioral economics, Loewenstein (1999) and Camerer and Loewenstein (2004) criticize this learning in highly repetitive experimental settings as unrealistic. First, they argue that there are many real-world situations that occur only a few times in a person's lifetime, so learning by repetition should not be expected. Examples include marriage, educational choices, saving for retirement, or the purchase of large durable goods such as houses or cars. Agents cannot gain enough experience and receive enough feedback to learn better behavior in these cases. Second, even when decisions are made more frequently, real-world environments are not as stable as experimental settings in the laboratory. Changing environmental conditions interfere with learning through repetition and trial and error. Finally, humans are not very good at transferring learning across settings. Loewenstein (1999) cited examples in which subjects failed to transfer learning from one experimental setting to another, or even learned the wrong lessons.

12.5 Cultural Adaptation and Imitation

Modern *Homo sapiens* evolved in Africa about 70,000 years ago. Between 50,000 and 60,000 years ago, humans, who were tropical hunter-gatherers, left Africa and quickly spread all over the globe except Antarctica. Emigrants from Africa reached the latitude of Moscow by 40,000 years ago and the Arctic Ocean by 30,000 years ago. By 5000 years ago, they had basically inhabited all possible terrestrial habitats, which were extremely diverse. In terms of food, natural resources, and climate, habitats such as tropical rainforests, northern steppes, the Australian outback, and the Artic have nothing in common. No other mammal or bird species has managed to adapt to such a wide range of living conditions.

An interesting question is how humans were able to achieve this amazing adaptation to all kinds of natural niches. As discussed above, Boyd et al. (2011) contrast two competing hypotheses. The first hypothesis postulates that humans are so adaptive because of their improvisational intelligence and their ability to learn from each other. The ability to use cause-and-effect reasoning allows them to make inferences about local environmental contingencies that are represented in mental models of the world. Superior cognitive capacities allow humans to invent tools and weapons to solve problems posed by the environment. According to Pinker (2010, p. 8994)

> *These cognitive stratagems are devised on the fly in endless combinations suitable to the local ecology. They arise by mental design and are deployed, tested, and fine-tuned by feedback in the lifetime of individuals.*

The cognitive niche hypothesis thus emphasizes individual problem-solving capacities that are augmented by learning from other individuals. Once an individual has found a good solution to a problem, others can learn it at a cost that is less than the cost of solving the problem themselves.

Boyd et al. (2011) challenge this view and favor the alternative cultural niche hypothesis. In line with our discussion of the limits of human reasoning and problem-solving, they argue that cultural learning is key to understanding how humans have been able to adapt to the extremely wide range of environments. As an example, they discuss the traditional living conditions of the Central Inuit in the Arctic, for example on King William Island in northern Canada, beyond the Arctic Circle. In winter, average monthly temperatures there range from −25 °C to −35 °C. Because of the lack of trees, there is no wood for fires or to make tools or shelters. In a fairly detailed account, Boyd et al. (2011) describe the sophisticated clothing, tools, weapons, kayaks, and snow houses that the Inuit invented with the limited resources available. They also describe hunting methods and the knowledge needed to assess weather conditions, travel on ice, manage dogs, or find food. The key argument is that no one person could ever develop all this knowledge and solve all the problems of survival in extremely harsh conditions.

To support their claim that individual ingenuity is not enough to survive in hostile environments, Boyd et al. present two kinds of evidence. The first is what they call “the lost European explorer experiment,” in which European explorers became stranded and struggled in an unfamiliar habitat where an indigenous population flourished. These explorers often suffered and died unless they received help from the indigenous people. A prominent example is the expedition of British Arctic explorer Sir John Franklin and his crew to the northern coast of North America in 1845–1846. After their ships became trapped in the ice at King William Island in the winter of 1846, the crew abandoned the ships and attempted to escape on foot. Ultimately, all members of the expedition died in the territory where the Central Inuit had lived for nearly a thousand years. One could go even further and argue that most North Americans and Europeans who are adapted to living in urban environments will have trouble surviving alone in much less hostile conditions, such as the

Canadian or Scandinavian wilderness. A modern example is Christopher McCandless, aka Alexander Supertramp, who starved to death in the Alaskan wilderness in 1992 at the age of 24. Although McCandless was an academic high achiever with a bachelor's degree in history and anthropology from Emory University and was prepared to live off the land in Alaska, he survived only 113 days in the Alaskan spring and summer. His story is told in Jon Krakauer's book *Into the Wild* and a movie based on the book.

The second type of evidence is the loss of useful technologies in small, isolated populations. For example, Pacific islanders appear to have lost knowledge of canoes, pottery, and bows and arrows. By 1850, the Polar Inuit of northwest Greenland could not make kayaks, leisters, or bows and arrows, and had limited hunting skills, even though other Inuit populations possessed this knowledge. The Polar Inuit appear to have lost their skills during an epidemic in the 1820s that killed older members of the community who possessed the relevant knowledge. The remaining population was unable to reinvent the technologies on its own.

Both the cognitive niche hypothesis and the cultural niche hypothesis emphasize the importance of learning from others, but there are crucial differences in how this learning is conceived. The cognitive niche hypothesis posits that some individuals discover solutions to problems and understand why these solutions are better than alternatives. They then share these insights with others, including the understanding of why the solutions work, thus saving the individuals being taught the cost of investigation. In contrast, the cultural niche hypothesis emphasizes learning and adaptation at the population level rather than at the individual level. This means that cultural evolution, which occurs over generations, accumulates and recombines knowledge in different forms, creating cultural knowledge beyond the understanding of the individuals who use it. Some individuals may have deeper insights into causal mechanisms and why cultural solutions to problems work and may also pass them on, but this causal understanding is not necessary for the process to work. As Boyd et al. (2011, p. 10923) explicitly state:

> *Often individuals will have no idea why certain elements are included in a design, nor any notion of whether alternative designs would be better. We expect cultural learners to first acquire the local practices and occasionally experiment or modify them. At times this will mean that cultural learning will overrule their direct experience, evolved motivations, or reliably developing intuitions.*

How to make a bow is an example of complex technological knowledge that can be transferred culturally without a deep understanding of individual bow makers. The optimal design of a bow depends on the environment in which it will be used. It may depend on the kind of wood or other material available, the prey being hunted, or the way the hunter uses the bow, for example, while riding a horse or sneaking up on prey. The size and proportions of the archer are also important, such as the length of the arms. Consequently, bows vary in many dimensions that are relevant to their performance, such as length, width, cross-section, taper, and degree of recurve. Boyd et al. (2011) argue that it is much harder to design a useful bow from scratch than it is to tinker with an existing design and improve it by making small modifications. They discuss the example of a learner who observes that his uncle's bow shoots farther than his own. The learner observes that the uncle's bow is thicker, but less tapered, and uses a different plait for attaching the sinew. The learner may copy all three features to improve his own bow, even though only the plaiting was causal for the difference in performance. If there is a reliable statistical relationship between plaiting and power, the form of plaiting will adapt to increase power. Understanding the causal relationship is beneficial because it allows for the elimination of extraneous characteristics, such as the color of a bow. However, an exact understanding of causation is not necessary as long as the correlation remains reliable. Including irrelevant features, such as thickness or color, will only introduce noise. By assembling different components of technology from different successful individuals, imitators can generate new and more efficient tools and techniques over generations without the need for improvisational insights. Kaaronen et al. (2023) describe how traditional bowyers used rules of thumb based on body measures to fit the bow to the user. For example, the width of the grip should be four fingers for a powerful bow and three fingers for a light hunting bow. The quality of the bow could be judged by auditory cues, such as the sound the bow makes when it is snapped. Such rules of thumb, especially when they use body measures such as arm length, are easy to apply, easy to remember, and easy to teach from master to apprentice. They can also be passed on in the form of stories or proverbs, which is often the case in oral cultures with little or no written literature.

There is evidence that people who use culturally transmitted heuristics do not understand why they use certain heuristics or follow social norms. Kaaronen et al. (2023) report that some Finnish mushroom foragers can describe rules of thumb without being able to explain why they are used. Boyd et al. (2011) mention food taboos for pregnant and lactating women in the Fiji Islands. Women learn that they are not allowed to eat certain fish during pregnancy and lactation. The rationale behind the taboos is to prevent fish poisoning, as many marine species in the region contain toxins that are dangerous to pregnant women and nursing infants. When asked about the taboos, women offer various causal explanations, but typically do not relate them to disease prevention.

Selective learning from others is an important aspect of cultural learning. It makes sense to imitate or accept lessons from individuals who are successful in their environment and therefore appear to possess relevant knowledge. Learning from successful individuals is common in traditional societies, where the models might be successful hunters or craftsmen, and in the modern world, where children and teenagers imitate successful soccer players, singers, or social media influencers. Cultural evolution has created a strong tendency to learn from others rather than individually from environmental cues, which of course happens. Imitating what others do, even if it goes against one's intuitions, can lead to the accumulation of cultural knowledge that goes beyond individual understanding. An example is the practice of seasoning food with chili peppers, which makes sense because the peppers contain capsaicin, which eliminates food-borne pathogens. Capsaicin is a chemical defense of the pepper that causes a burning sensation in the mouth and prevents the plant from being eaten by mammals. Humans can learn to overcome their aversion to the pain, which they do not get used to, but learn to reinterpret as excitement.

Imitating the behavior of others seems to be a powerful human ability. Whiten et al. (2009) describe experiments with children and chimpanzees on imitation and the mechanisms of cultural learning. Both human children and chimpanzees are able to imitate fairly complex behavioral sequences with high fidelity. Chimpanzee communities can thus socially learn specific foraging techniques and develop a degree of culture. There appear to be two differences between humans and chimpanzees. Human children show a strong tendency to over-imitate. When an adult showed young children of 3 or 5 years of age how to open a box with a complicated mechanism, the children copied obviously causally irrelevant actions, such as tapping the side of the box with a feather. The children did so even when asked to identify "stupid and unnecessary" actions, and even when instructed to avoid irrelevant actions. In contrast, chimpanzees are more selective in copying actions and avoid unnecessary actions. Over-copying has also been observed in human adults and seems to increase with age in children. The human learning strategy is to copy everything first and then correct the behavior later, i.e. to weed out irrelevant aspects. According to Whiten et al. (2009, p. 2425),

> *we are such a thorough-going cultural species that it pays children, as a kind of default strategy, to copy willy-nilly much of the behavioral repertoire they see enacted before them. Children have the longest childhoods of any primate, much of which is spent in play, practice and exploration, so there is plenty of opportunity to weed out wrongly assimilated aspects of the actions observed.*

Another difference between humans and chimpanzees is that the latter can learn fairly complex tasks through sophisticated copying, but quickly develop routines. This means that newly learned behaviors quickly become crystallized and thus resistant to cumulative or other changes. Humans, on the other hand, can combine multiple learned behaviors, allowing for cumulative cultural learning.

Over-imitation raises the possibility of maladaptation as irrelevant or even unreasonable behaviors and beliefs spread through a population. Superstition and all kinds of belief in supernatural powers, pseudoscience, and conspiracy theories can result from uncritical imitation of others. While the superstitious belief that a black cat crossing one's path is a bad omen is harmless, the idea of drinking bleach to cure COVID-19 or cancer can be deadly. The English saying "starve a fever, feed a cold," which dates back to the Middle Ages and recommends fasting when you have a fever, is contradicted by modern medical knowledge. A fever indicates that the immune system is fighting an infection, which requires energy, so a general recommendation to reduce caloric intake is incorrect and potentially harmful.

12.6 Collaborative Problem-solving and Social Learning

Based on the insights of the previous chapters, it seems safe to say that the complexity of the human world has been increasing at an accelerated rate since at least the middle of the twentieth century. In many dimensions, the complexity of the modern world poses insurmountable challenges to the problem-solving capacity of individuals, which already reaches its limits when confronted with problems of moderate complexity. Cultural adaptation, which occurs over generations, is too slow to keep up with the rapid pace of technological, economic, political, social, and environmental change. Therefore, it is not surprising that collaborative problem-solving (CPS) is seen as a key twenty-first century skill that is "critical to efficiency, effectiveness, and innovation in the modern global economy" (Graesser et al. 2018, p. 59). CPS can be seen as an adaptation to increasing complexity.

CPS is a critical skill needed not only in the home, but also in the workplace and in the community. The complexity of today's problems requires teams to combine collective performance with the unique expertise of team members. Effective participation in CPS requires both cognitive and social skills. Cognitively, team members must be able to define the problem, recognize each member's knowledge and skills, identify areas where knowledge or skills are lacking, collaborate on possible solutions, and track progress toward the group's goals. From a social perspective, the success of a team depends on its members' ability to establish a common understanding, to cooperate and complement each other's actions, and to coordinate their efforts to develop and evaluate solutions.

CPS introduces a new level of complex problem-solving by adding the element of collective cognition (see Hung 2013). When problem-solving shifts from an individual to a team, the team's performance is not simply the sum of its members' individual performances. Instead, the complexity of CPS requires a reconceptualization of complex problem-solving in line with general systems theory and complexity theory, which suggest that the whole is greater than the sum of its parts. CPS involves not only the individual cognition of team members, but also an emergent cognitive process that results from the team working together as a whole. This emergent team cognition accounts for a significant portion of the cognitive constructs and processes involved in team-based complex problem-solving. CPS encompasses both well-coordinated collective processing (emergent team cognition) and distributed cognitive processing (individual cognition configured toward a common goal). Thus, the complexity of CPS is due not only to the scale of the problem at hand, but also to the intricate cognitive, psychological, social, and behavioral interactions among individual team members during the problem-solving process.

Team-based problem-solving typically involves highly complex and ill-structured problems. Ill-structured problems are inherently complex and multidimensional, involving multiple domains of knowledge, varying levels of expertise, and complicated variables. In addition, these problems tend to be exacerbated by their lack of transparency, multiple interpretations, and interdisciplinary nature. To effectively solve such challenges, problem-solving teams must exhibit cognitive and collective adaptability to cope with unanticipated obstacles or changes. Therefore, to effectively solve complex and ill-structured problems, team members must collectively and systematically reason through the problem space as a cognitive system and devise the most feasible (typically not optimal) solution. In the context of complexity theory, interrelationships and interdependencies are critical to making a system work, rather than simply viewing it as a collection of individual parts. In CPS, team members are configured into a cognitive system with functional and interconnected relationships to collectively perform a variety of cognitive functions to solve a specific problem. Each team member's tasks are dependent on, or influenced by, the timely completion and quality of the work of other team members. If one team member fails to complete his or her tasks on time or produces poor-quality work, it can not only affect his or her own work, but also set off a chain reaction that affects the work of the entire team.

Hung (2013) notes that complex, ill-structured problems are inherently dynamic and uncertain during the problem-solving process. Therefore, adaptation is crucial for a team to navigate through the dynamic complexity in team-based problem-solving. To cope with changes and unexpected obstacles, the CPS team must adapt to the situation. Coordination and reconfiguration play an important role in facilitating the adaptation process. However, habituation can prevent team members from moving efficiently and effectively from the existing configuration to the new one, and even cause resistance to reconfiguration. Therefore, team members need to make a behavioral and psychological commitment to the change, which requires more effort. The effectiveness of the CPS team's adaptation process indicates whether the team is merely capable of solving routine problems or whether it is a high-functioning and adaptive cognitive system that can learn and grow.

Collective problem-solving overlaps with social learning. On the one hand, CPS requires a shared understanding of the problem and its context, so that learning about the problem together is a prerequisite for CPS. On the other hand, social learning is also an outcome when a team collaborates to solve a problem. Team members refine their own perceptions and acquire new knowledge from their collaborators. Social learning in this sense is closely related to the development of shared mental models.

12.6.1 Collaborative Problem-Solving

Graesser et al. (2018) expect the complexity of socio-technological systems in industry, military, and academia to increase further in the twenty-first century. Collaborative cognition and problem-solving are also becoming more important due to the societal involvement of multiple stakeholders. Distributed knowledge must be integrated to solve problems of complexity. Moreover, the diverse views of the stakeholders involved make the problems wicked.

According to Graesser et al. (2018), CPS is characterized by three features: (1) the problem to be solved by the group is novel (as opposed to a routine task), (2) objective accountability, meaning that the quality of the solution is visible to team members, and (3) interdependence, i.e., no single individual can solve the problem alone, but provides resources from different areas of expertise and diverse perspectives. These characteristics distinguish CPS from collaborative work, collaborative learning, and collaborative decision-making.

The need to solve novel problems distinguishes CPS from collaborative work, in which groups implement established solutions to routine tasks. While the main challenge of collaborative work is to coordinate the tasks of team members according to a known script, no such script or plan exists when a problem has not been encountered before. CPS must therefore start with a description of the problem, an idea of a goal state in which the problem is solved, and a plan of how to reach that goal. These tasks involve multiple social challenges, as different and potentially conflicting views of team members must be reconciled. Objective accountability distinguishes CPS from collaborative learning, which focuses on individual learning with the help of others rather than on solving a problem. The extent of individual learning is not visible during the collaborative learning process—it becomes observable through test scores on the acquired knowledge of the subject—but the progress in solving the problem can be evaluated during the process. Team members can also observe the quality of the solutions found to the problem. Interdependency implies a differentiation of roles among team members working on different aspects of the problem. This is in contrast to collaborative decision-making, where all team members are given identical questions, items to evaluate, or decisions to make, and typically have access to the same information.

Potential advantages of solving problems collectively include:

- A division of labor can enhance quality
- Diverse kinds of knowledge, perspectives, and experiences are available
- The ideas of team members stimulate other team members, allowing new ideas might to emerge from the interaction and
- Multiple members improve evaluation of the products of collaboration

However, working collaboratively is also challenging and involves a number of difficulties, such as

- Inefficient communication (e.g., team members wasting time with irrelevant discussion)
- Social loafing (e.g., a team member fails to deliver)
- Diffusion of responsibility (e.g., team members assume that other team members will complete tasks) and
- Disruption of productive discussion, idea generation, and evaluation due to conflict, disagreement, and false information

Given the presence of both advantages and disadvantages of CPS, we cannot expect that collaboration is always better than working alone in terms of learning, judgment, and decision-making, which is supported by the available empirical evidence. Some studies point to the problem of *social contagion of memory*, which describes the phenomenon that in groups, inaccurate contributions by members go undetected and become encoded by group members and used in subsequent tasks. Graesser et al. (2018) call for more research on collaborative problem-solving, a rather new topic in the psychological literature.

An important early source of evidence on CPS is the 2015 assessment of the Program for International Student Assessment (PISA) conducted by the OECD. More than 500,000 15-year-old students from 52 countries participated in the PISA CPS 2015 assessment. The results of the assessment, reported in OECD (2017), document that deficits in CPS are a global problem. The collaboration competencies were categorized into four levels. The highest level 4 demands that students perform tasks that require complex forms of collaboration on very difficult problems to solve, such as overcoming social barriers in team behavior, resolving or avoiding team conflicts, and taking the initiative to lead the team. The lowest levels, 0 and 1, require only the lowest form of complexity in collaboration and problem-solving. Across OECD member countries, about 8% of students scored at Level 4, 28% scored at Level 3, 35% scored at Level 2, and the remaining 28% scored no higher than Level 1.

Employers in the USA lament that schools and colleges are not preparing students with the skills needed in modern work environments, especially with regard to teamwork, communication, and interpersonal skills (Graesser et al. 2018). Currently, teachers are not prepared to teach collaborative problem-solving and it is not part of standard curricula. Therefore, improving teaching in this direction is an adaptation to changing economic conditions. In addition to problem-solving skills, the training of social skills is crucial.

Teamwork is a social process that involves communication, the exchange of ideas, and a shared understanding of the problem and its components. The team must negotiate and agree on how the different parts of the problem are connected, what tasks need to be performed, and what solutions are possible. This is in contrast to individual problem-solving, where these elements are typically managed internally without the need for external input. In addition to managing the problem itself, there is a need to manage the relationships between team members and the effects of their actions. Collaborators must be aware of the importance of these social factors and be equipped with the necessary social skills. Compared to individual problem-solving, CPS requires additional levels of psychological processing related to social cognition.

Team members work together to develop a shared understanding of the problem and common goals using a variety of inputs. They then formulate a course of action that takes into account the roles, duties, limitations, and assignments of each team member. This process is typically an evolving and interactive one in which team members and the team as a whole gain an understanding of the components of the problem by interpreting information from multiple sources and responding to changing circumstances. Through collaboration, a shared mental model emerges.

12.6.2 Social Learning

Social learning is a term that is used with different meanings in various literatures. One interpretation of social learning is that individuals learn in a social context. They learn from others through imitation or active instruction.

Another meaning, which is the subject of this subsection, is learning at the group level rather than at the individual level. Reed et al. (2010) define this type of social learning as "a change in understanding that goes beyond the individual to become situated within wider social units or communities of practice through social interactions between actors within social networks." The result of this kind of social learning is a shared belief system of the respective social group. The term *belief system* is used here in a broad sense that includes *mental models* as well as normative, evaluative, affective, and motivational elements (Abelson 1979). As we have seen, mental models are cognitive representations of the external world that people use to interact with the world and to make decisions. People use them to understand and explain what they observe in the world and to anticipate the future. However, people do not only form representations about how the world works, they also hold beliefs about how the world ought to be. Belief systems include representations of alternative worlds in addition to the mental models of the existing world that can motivate people to take action to change the existing world (Abelson 1979). The evaluative and prescriptive part of the belief system is the *value system*.

The notion of shared belief systems is similar to Denzau and North's (1994) concept of shared mental models as a basis for communication and cultural learning. Ideologies and institutions can be viewed as categories of shared mental models. Denzau and North assert that shared mental models provide a framework and a common language that facilitate communication, and that over time the mental models of individuals within a group tend to converge through communication. Without communication, individual learning would cause the mental models of different individuals to diverge as each person adapts his or her mental model to his or her own private experiences. Therefore, communication and the development of ideologies and institutions are interdependent processes that coevolve over time.

Sayama et al. (2011) present an agent-based model that allows studying the effects of mental model formation on the effectiveness of group discussion. The model focuses on the cognitive dimension of collective problem-solving, in particular social learning in the sense that each individual contributes some idiosyncratic knowledge to the knowledge of the group. Some social aspects are also represented, such as responding to others' suggestions, but the model does not address the previously mentioned problems of collective problem-solving, such as social loafing, diffusion of responsibility, or conflict.

A group tries to find an optimal solution to a complex multidimensional problem represented by a multimodal utility function. The true utility function is unknown, but each agent constructs an individual utility function from opinions about the problem. Each dimension of the true utility function is an aspect of the problem. A particular value in a dimension is called a choice, and a plan is a set of choices for all aspects of the problem. An opinion is a pair of a plan and a proposed utility value associated with that plan. Each agent starts with a memory of p opinions about the problem, randomly sampled from the true utility function and subject to some noise. The initial opinions represent each agent's initial understanding of the problem. If there were no noise, the original opinions would correctly represent the true utility function. The larger the noise component, the less the original opinions are related to the true utility function. Opinions are updated as a result of group discussion. Agents store the opinions expressed by others in their memory and thus dynamically create a mental model (i.e., an individual utility function) of the problem, which gradually becomes a shared mental model as more and more input from team members is added to the original opinions.

The group discusses a group plan to be implemented at the end, i.e. they try to solve the problem collectively. A schematic overview of the group discussion process is shown in Fig. 12.6. Each round of group discussion consists of five steps. First, each agent individually tries to improve the utility of its individual plan by performing a hill search within a small local space. The result is updated plans for each individual. Second, a speaker is randomly selected from all group members with equal probability. Third, the selected speaker chooses an aspect of the problem and proposes to replace the current choice in the group plan with her own choice and makes an estimate of the resulting change in utility. The new proposed

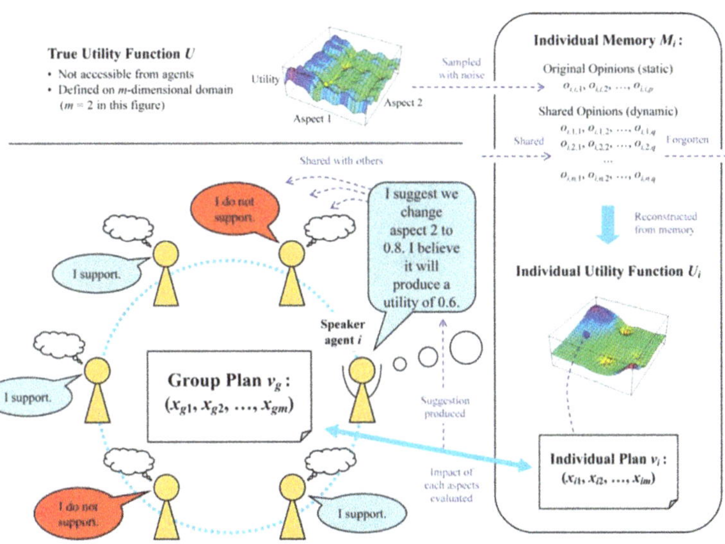

A schematic illustration of our agent-based model. A group consisting of n agents iteratively attempts to revise the group plan (lower left) to increase its utility. There is a true utility function (upper left), which is not directly accessible from the agents. They have a limited amount of information about the true utility function in the form of their original opinions sampled from it. Each agent has a memory that can store p opinions of its own and up to q opinions expressed by each of other agents (upper right). Agents reconstruct models of the utility function (individual utility function; right) from those memorized opinions, based on which they try to improve the utility of their own individual plans (lower right). In each iterative step, a randomly selected speaker considers which aspect of its individual plan has the most significant impact if incorporated into the group plan, and then makes a suggestion (the revised group plan and its expected utility; center). The suggestion is shared with other agents and they respond to it based on their respective individual utility functions. This cycle repeats for a fixed number of iterations.

Fig. 12.6 Overview over the collective problem-solving agent-based model. Source: Sayama et al. (2011), reproduced with kind permission of John Wiley and Sons

plan and estimated utility form an opinion that is presented to the group. Fourth, all other group members evaluate the proposed new plan using their own individual utility functions. If a listener concludes that the proposal will increase utility, he is convinced, expresses his support, and changes his individual plan accordingly (individual acceptance). If the own evaluation does not result in an estimated increase in utility, the listener will not change the own plan. However, with some positive probability, support may be expressed anyway to give the proposal a chance (social acceptance). This probability depends on the "temperature" of the agent's cognition, which measures the tolerance toward low-utility proposals. This temperature decreases hyperbolically over time. This means that initially group members are open to different ideas, allowing for the exploration of different options. Over time, they become more conservative and risk-averse, and their exploratory behavior diminishes. Finally, the group determines whether to incorporate the speaker's proposal into the group plan by counting the number of supportive responses from group members. If the support is above a threshold, the group plan is updated. The acceptance threshold increases linearly with time, so that group-level acceptance becomes more difficult over time.

Figure 12.7 shows some results of the model. We see a 2-dimensional problem space, i.e. a problem with only two aspects, in the perception of two agents. The first two squares in the top row represent the individual utility functions before the group discussion, i.e. the original opinions. The colors indicate the level of utility

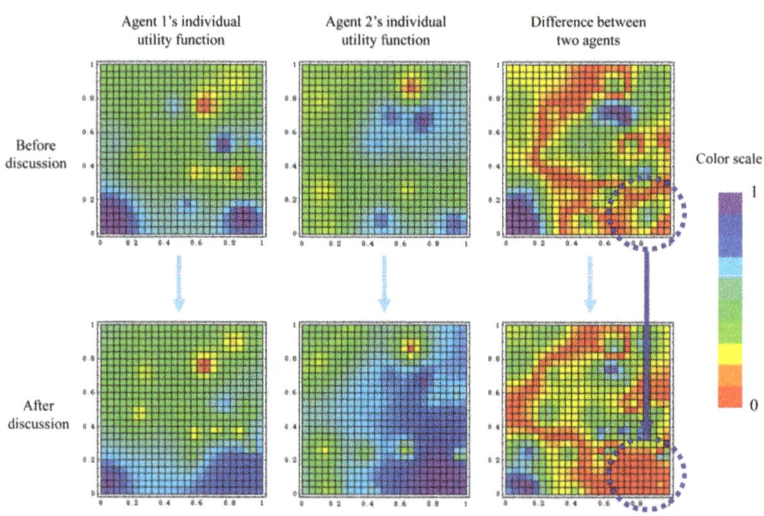

An example of individual utility functions of two agents and the formation of shared mental models in a limited area of the problem space. Through discussion, two agents come to agree upon a range of plans in which they initially differed. They have converged on a local maximum near the bottom left of the problem space and developed a shared utility function in the nearby area, which indicates their information exchanges took place mostly around that area. The rest of the problem space largely remains nonconvergent, leaving a great amount of disagreements between the two utility functions. Parameters: $n = 2$, $q = 40$, $t_e = 100$.

Fig. 12.7 Formation of a (partially) shared mental model through group discussion. Source: Sayama et al. (2011), reproduced with kind permission of John Wiley and Sons

associated with the respective plans regarding the choices in the two dimensions of the problem. We observe that the two agents agree on some opinions, but not on others. The third square in each row represents the differences between the utility functions. Purple and blue indicate high values, and orange and red indicate low values. Note that there is a big disagreement about the lower left corner of the problem space, where low values are chosen on both dimensions of the problem. Agent 1 believes that choosing low values would yield high utility (purple), but Agent 2 expects only moderate utility (green). Accordingly, the disagreement is large (purple in the third square). In the lower right corner of the room, there is a moderate initial consensus. Agent 1 also expects high utility in this region, while Agent 2 expects slightly lower utility. As the dotted circle in the third grid shows, the difference in the assigned utility levels is moderate (green). The bottom row of the grid shows the two individual mental models and the shared mental model after the group discussion. There was considerable convergence in the lower right corner, but not in the lower left corner or in other areas of the individual utility functions. This means that a partially shared mental model emerged in the course of the group discussion.

The model of Sayama et al. (2011) shows some mechanisms at work in group discussions related to collective problem-solving. During these discussions, social learning occurs because initially heterogeneous mental models partially converge due to information exchange and individual and collective evaluation of the elicited private information. A key finding of this model is that there is rapid convergence to a shared mental model only in a limited region of the problem space. Once the discussion reaches a region where individual plans are similar, it gets stuck there. The shared model is refined in the identified region, but not in others, because no new information about the other regions is revealed. The discussion becomes more and more closed. This result is independent of the size of the agents' memory, since it is positive.

The model thus shows that unstructured discussion is not sufficient to produce a mental model of the problem that is shared by all members of the group. This finding supports the earlier claim that social learning has both a cognitive and a social dimension. Leadership may be an aspect of the social dimension of social learning and CPS. A member of the group who assumes or is given the role of leader could structure the discussion and prevent the group from repeating similar questions and stagnating the discussion. The leader could ask members for their opinions on certain aspects that they would not bring up on their own. The leader might also try to activate more passive members. The key to exploring the full problem space is to maintain a diversity of opinions and to draw attention to areas of conflicting views. Another social aspect is to reduce the impact of time on the discussion. It is normal and necessary for the discussant to become less open during the learning process, but if this happens too early, there will be path dependence because the initial contributions will have too strong an influence on the emerging shared mental model.

12.7 Sense-making and Narratives

According to W. Brian Arthur (2021), agents who respond to ill-defined situations by "making sense" or recognizing some aspects of them and choosing their action strategies or predictions based on these interpretations are at the heart of complexity economics. He points to modern psychology that shows how agents use narrative, imagination, and computation to make sense of ill-defined circumstances. Chater and Loewenstein (2016) suggest that there is a drive for sense-making, similar to drives such as hunger, thirst, and sex. They present an economic model in which individuals have two goals that drive their behavior. The first goal, which they call valence, is to construe one's life in a positive way. Sense-making is the second goal, i.e. construing one's life in such a way that it makes sense. Both goals involve events that occur only in an individual's mind. Chater and Loewenstein argue that the human brain has autonomous sense-making capabilities that are involuntary and serve only to simplify information as much as possible. In a sense, one could interpret sense-making as an adaptation of information about the world to the (simple and limited) mental model of the individual. After discussing the psychological underpinnings of sense-making, they present their model, which can be applied to the study of curiosity, boredom, flow, confirmation bias, information avoidance, consumer choice, aesthetic preference, concern about others' beliefs, conspiracy theory and religion, the role of the "good life" in decision-making, and the importance of narrative.

Robert Shiller initiated what could become a narrative turn in economics. In his presidential address to the American Economic Association (Shiller 2017), he sparked a general interest in narratives and narrative economics, which he elaborates on in Shiller (2019). Shiller argues that narratives are important because they help explain economic phenomena such as recessions or bubbles in financial markets. A narrative turn, which occurred in the 1980s and 1990s in other social sciences such as political science, psychology, and sociology, means that researchers become interested in subjective human understanding and sense-making, but also in social discourse. In economics, a narrative turn would constitute a paradigm shift because it reflects a broader shift away from a focus on individual rationality and toward a recognition of the importance of social and cultural factors in shaping economic behavior. It also emphasizes the importance of subjectivity and the need for ambiguous interpretations, which does not fit well with the practice of neoclassical economics, which assumes that rational individuals know the objective environment in which they act as it is.

Narratives can be seen as a means of social learning that creates shared belief systems and group identity. We can define a *collective economic narrative* as a sense-making story about some economically relevant topic that is shared by members of a group, emerges and proliferates in social interaction, and suggests action (Roos and Reccius 2024). Sense-making requires that the story be connected to the *belief systems* of the people involved. In contrast to personal narratives, which are parts of the belief system of a single person, social narratives involve the belief systems of at least one teller and one listener of the story. The teller may want to share his/her view of the world with the listener. Whether this can succeed depends on the degree of overlap between the belief systems of the two agents. If the belief systems are too different, a narrative may make perfect sense to the teller, but not at all to the listener. An example might be a neoclassical economist and a complexity economist talking about economic growth and progress. The complexity economist is likely to have a quite different belief system about the origins, consequences, and valuations of economic growth than the neoclassical economist.

For a story to qualify as a collective narrative, it must be understandable to the members of a group and should be told by and within the group. For a group to understand a story, its members must share a belief system to some degree. A shared belief system becomes a defining characteristic of the group. If the mental models or value systems of the group members are very different, they cannot form a shared meaningful narrative. A shared belief system not only serves as a prerequisite for a shared sense-making narrative, but can also be shaped by narratives. By exchanging personal narratives, group members can identify the areas where their belief systems converge and diverge. Building a group identity may require group members to modify their belief systems to better align with those of their peers. Narratives are told by groups, but they also influence group identity and composition and how the group views the world, creating a circular causality. Thus, we can say that groups, their shared belief systems, and the narratives they tell coevolve.

Collective narratives are not the product of an individual, but emerge from repeated interactions among members of a group or groups. The process of collective sense-making occurs through interactive communication among individuals who share similar belief systems. The storyteller cannot know exactly which parts of the story will resonate with listeners because it is impossible to observe the complete belief system of others. In addition, the originator of a story does not know how and to whom the story will be retold. If the initial listeners like the story, they will share it with others, and it will spread through the group. The parts of the story that resonate with the listeners are retold, and the less compelling parts are dropped or modified. As different versions of a story circulate in the group, the group can try to integrate them into a consensus version that captures the essence of the different versions. Ultimately, a group narrative emerges that no one person imagined and no one could have predicted.

Narratives emerge not only from within-group interactions, but also from intergroup interactions. One group's narrative may be challenged by another group with a different belief system. When groups compete in some arena, they may have an incentive to differentiate their narratives rather than align them. The evolution of a group narrative depends in complex ways on the participants, as well as the rules and practices of intergroup discourse.

In economics, narratives are significant because they provide guidance to economic agents, suggesting actions they can take. Social scientists study narratives not for their intrinsic interest, but because they serve a function in groups or social systems. Narratives are particularly important in enabling groups to act in the face of uncertainty about the future (Beckert and Bronk 2018). They serve to coordinate group action by aligning members' expectations and evaluations of outcomes.

However, narratives alone are not sufficient; they must be integrated with group members' shared belief systems to simulate and evaluate the consequences of action.

Suggesting what to do in an uncertain world is another interpretation of sense-making, along with explaining observed phenomena. In situations of uncertainty, people often have a desire to act, even when the knowledge base for rational decision-making is limited. This impulse to act is sometimes called *action bias*. Narratives can play a role in creating or destroying consumer and investor confidence, which is part of Keynes's concept of *animal spirits*. Akerlof and Shiller (2010) argue that stories can shape people's behavior and that they contributed to the housing bubble in the US prior to the 2008 financial crisis. Similarly, Reinhart and Rogoff (2009) argue that before every financial crisis, financial analysts tell stories about why "this time is different," leading investors to continue buying assets despite conventional standards indicating an overvaluation of assets.

Shiller (2017) provides examples to support his idea of economic narratives that can have a significant impact on macroeconomics. One such example is the Great Depression narrative that emerged between 2007 and 2009 in the USA. To demonstrate the prevalence of this narrative, he cites the spike in the frequency of the phrase "Great Depression" in news articles, newspapers, and books during this period. He also refers to Google Trends search data to argue that people were not particularly interested in the specific historical details of the events of the 1930s, as search terms related to those details were not highly searched.

However, what Shiller describes is not a single narrative of the Great Depression, but a public discourse about the Great Depression (see Roos and Reccius 2024). More specifically, the discourse surrounding the Great Depression in 2007–2009 was not about the historical event itself, but rather about the perceived similarities between the current situation and that of 1929–1934, and what this means for the present. Given the economic relevance of the crisis at that time, it is reasonable to assume that people were trying to make sense of the events that were unfolding. Shiller tells a stylized story that highlights the apparent similarities between the two time periods and suggests that people were trying to learn from history to make sense of the current situation, which is an example of sense-making. However, the story does not provide explicit recommendations for action, which is a key aspect of our definition of narratives. Discourse refers to the existence of multiple competing narratives about a particular issue, each of which is shared by different groups and proposes different interpretations and actions. At least three different narratives of the Great Depression emerged in this discourse, which can be described as follows:

1. *Fiscal stimulus is needed to prevent another Great Depression*
2. *Monetary policy makers have learned the lessons from the Great Depression*
3. *The elites have forgotten the lessons from the Great Depression*

The first narrative is mentioned by Shiller himself: "In 2007–2009 presidents and prime ministers invoked parallels to the Great Depression to justify their requests to apply stimulus" (Shiller 2017, p. 996). This can be formulated as a three-event narrative: (i) the passive fiscal policy in the 1930s prolonged the Depression, which

(ii) led to the development of Keynesian theory advocating for expansionary fiscal policy in a liquidity trap, and consequently, (iii) strong fiscal intervention can avoid a long and deep depression following the 2007–2009 crisis. This narrative proposes a clear course of action. The key element of this narrative consists in the sense-making connections between the events.

The second narrative concerns a different group, central bankers, but is related to the first. During the financial crisis, the public became aware early on that Ben Bernanke, the chairman of the Federal Reserve Bank, had studied the mistakes made in monetary policy in the 1930s. As a result, a narrative emerged that was similar to the one about fiscal policy, but with the added element of personalization. The narrative went something like this: "In the 1930s, the central bank exacerbated the recession by keeping interest rates high. Ben Bernanke recognized this mistake by studying the history of the Great Depression. As head of the Fed, Bernanke knows how to avoid repeating past mistakes." This narrative was told by both policy observers and Bernanke himself in public speeches. It served to exonerate the Fed, and especially its chairman, from the accusation that it had contributed to the crisis through misguided policies. The suggested course of action is to look for other culprits.

The third narrative stands in stark contrast to the second and highlights the failure of elites to learn from the Great Depression, leading to the financial crisis. The narrative is highly critical of neoclassical mainstream economists and neoliberal policymakers for deregulating financial markets. It goes something like this: "After the Bretton Woods system was negotiated in 1944, financial crises were rare. Over time, however, the lessons of the interwar period were forgotten, and both economists and politicians pushed for financial liberalization. This led to a high risk of financial turbulence and culminated in the global financial crisis." This narrative is shared by economists critical of the mainstream of their profession, such as Nouriel Roubini or Paul Krugman, as well as political activists such as Naomi Klein. The proposed course of action is political reform, either in the form of Obama's new liberalism or radical anti-capitalist measures. It also suggests a reform of neoclassical economics.

Narratives are not just a subject of economic study, as Robert Shiller has suggested. Rather, they also play a role in the way economists work, as Deirdre McCloskey's work demonstrates. McCloskey (1983) does not use the term "narrative" when discussing the use of rhetoric in economics, but narratives or stories can be seen as rhetorical devices. She argues that many economists do not adhere to the official methodology of modernism in their actual practice. Instead of using the so-called scientific method to uncover the truth, economists try to persuade others of their ideas. Falsification, which is a crucial aspect of the *scientific method*, is limited in economics. Therefore, economists cannot achieve certainty by proving what is right or wrong, but can only weigh reasons to arrive at conclusions that are more or less likely or plausible. This process of weighing arguments is the essence of rhetoric, as opposed to the common understanding of rhetoric as the use of verbal tricks or dishonest sophistry. McCloskey (1983) defines rhetoric as exploring thought through disciplined conversation. The most important rhetorical device in economics is *metaphor*, which involves describing something by comparing it to something else that is considered similar. Economics is metaphorical because it uses models that purport to resemble reality to describe the economy. By making unrealistic, simplifying assumptions, economists create a kind of fiction with their models. Stories are needed to connect the abstract models to reality.

McCloskey (1983, 1985) suggests that economics would benefit in several ways if economists acknowledged the inevitability of rhetoric in their field. First, it would remind economists that their metaphors are not reflections of reality, but rather a form of *fiction*. While fiction can be useful for learning by enabling mental simulations, policy recommendations based on models with unrealistic assumptions can be harmful to society. Second, accepting the communicative nature of academic discourse and teaching and recognizing the value of well-chosen rhetoric could improve the quality of scientific debates. Finally, by replacing problematic modernist methodology with improved rhetorical and literary thinking, economics could improve its "foreign relations" with other disciplines. McCloskey suggests that such a methodological shift would move economics away from the natural sciences and toward the social sciences and humanities, which may be a more appropriate domain for the discipline.

Narrative economics can be seen as a natural part of complexity economics because narratives are one of the many emergent phenomena that arise from the interactions of agents in a complex system and can play a role in shaping the overall behavior of the system. Narratives are closely related to agents' belief systems and their desire to make sense of their complex environment. As we saw in Chap. 2, complexity always has an objective side and a subjective side. The ambiguity and subjectivity of narratives and the meaning they create complement the more objective analysis of complexity with formal models that we discussed in the previous chapters. But we need this plurality of approaches and perspectives in holistic complexity thinking.

Things to Remember

- Agents in complex adaptive systems change their behavior over time due to adaptation or learning. These models thus have an additional layer of complexity compared to (physical) complex systems in which agents always behave in the same way. Adaptation and learning are key determinants of novelty, evolution, and historicity.
- Rational decision-making in the sense of individual maximization behavior is only a small part of the human behavioral repertoire. It is a subcategory of reasoning, which also includes the use of heuristics. Other modes of behavior are habitual behavior, imitation, and collaborative problem-solving. The modes differ along the dimensions of automatic/deliberate and individual/social.

(continued)

- Learning refers to an individual's internal processing of information and results in a reconfiguration of knowledge and brain structure. Learning can be intentional or unintentional, practical or theoretical, and can occur individually or with or from others. Enculturation is the process by which an individual learns to become a member of a group with a particular culture.
- Decisions are difficult due to changes in the environment, uncertainty, system complexity, and lack of relevant information about the decision problem. Most of these complications make it difficult or even impossible to formulate a well-defined optimization problem that can be solved as in rational choice theory.
- Computational complexity theory classifies computational problems according to their inherent difficulty. Computational complexity is defined as the worst-case growth of computational resources (e.g., time) required to solve a computational problem as a function of the size of the input. Computational complexity can be used to evaluate the difficulty of optimization problems.
- NP-hard problems are the most difficult computational problems. There are no known algorithms that can solve these problems in polynomial time. Many NP-hard problems are characterized by exponential growth in the required resources, making them intractable very quickly. Only small NP-hard problems can be solved with available resources, especially on reasonable time scales.
- Economists often defend utility and profit maximization as as-if assumptions. They do not claim that economic agents actually solve difficult optimization problems, only that they behave as if they did. Even if they do something else, their behavior can reasonably be described in terms of optimization. However, computational complexity theory has shown that approximations are often as hard as the actual maximization problem itself. It is therefore unclear why the actual behavior of agents should be close to the maximization behavior.
- Satisficing means that an agent does not try to find the best solution to a problem, but only a sufficiently good one that satisfies a level of aspiration. Satisficing is a heuristic behavior that Herbert Simon described as boundedly rational, given people's limited cognitive and informational resources.
- The heuristics and biases research program initiated by Amos Tversky and Daniel Kahneman argues that people use heuristics to make judgments and decisions that often systematically deviate from rational decision-making. It aims to be descriptively realistic while maintaining the normative ideal of rational choice theory. Behavioral economics, strongly influenced by this

(continued)

research program, often looks for ways to correct the biased behavior of individuals.

- The fast and frugal heuristics research program, championed by Gerd Gigerenzer and colleagues, argues that many heuristics have ecological rationality and are well adapted to the environments in which they evolved. These heuristics often outperform more sophisticated approaches when used in the right circumstances. This research program rejects rational choice as a normative ideal because it is not feasible in many situations.
- The prediction error of a prediction method can be decomposed into bias, variance of the estimates, and noise. Noise is unavoidable, but bias and variance are method dependent. There is a bias–variance dilemma. Econometric methods are often unbiased, but may have large variance because they also adjust for noise in the sample. Simple heuristics are often biased, but are more robust to noise and can therefore have lower variance. The prediction error of a heuristic with moderate bias but low variance may be less than the prediction error of an unbiased statistical method with large variance.
- Reinforcement learning is a simple form of learning. Success is rewarded and failure is punished, which influences future behavior. Belief learning refers to the understanding of a situation. Bayesian updating is a common form of rational adjustment of probabilities in light of new evidence. Mental modeling refers to the cognitive representation of causal relationships among variables. People construct mental models of their world based on their life experiences.
- Adaptation to the cognitive niche means that human intelligence, in particular the ability to identify cause-and-effect relationships and to engage in metaphorical abstraction, is a key factor in the adaptation of humans to different habitats. In contrast, the cultural niche hypothesis suggests that much of the knowledge necessary for survival is beyond the comprehension of individuals and is created through cultural evolution. In support of this view, there is evidence that humans often use ecologically rational heuristics without a deep understanding of why they work.
- Collaborative problem-solving involves creating collective cognition, that is, combining and integrating the diverse distributed knowledge of team members. Collective cognition requires that team members share a mental model of the problem. Effective collective problem-solving requires social skills to deal with inefficient communication, social loafing, diffusion of responsibility, and conflict. Only a minority of students worldwide have good collective problem-solving skills.
- Social learning is a change in understanding that occurs in groups through social interaction. Shared belief systems and mental models are the result of

(continued)

social learning. Shared belief systems facilitate coordinated action by group members in pursuit of common goals.

- Narratives are sense-making stories that suggest action. Collective narratives are shared by groups, create group identities, and help create shared mental models or belief systems. By suggesting actions, they enable groups to act in the face of uncertainty when there is no rational basis for forming expectations.

References

Abelson RP (1979) Differences between belief and knowledge systems. Cogn Sci 3:355–366

Akerlof GA, Shiller RJ (2010) Animal spirits. How human psychology drives the economy, and why it matters for global capitalism. Princeton University Press, Princeton

Akerlof GA, Shiller RJ (2015) Phishing for phools. Princeton University Press, Princeton

Allen TW, Carroll CD (2001) Individual learning about consumption. Macroecon Dyn 5:255–271

Arthur WB (2021) Foundations of complexity economics. Nat Rev Phys 3:136–145. https://doi.org/10.1038/s42254-020-00273-3

Beckert J, Bronk R (2018) Uncertain futures. Imaginaries, narratives, and calculation in the economy. Oxford University Press, Oxford

Beinhocker ED (2006) The origin of wealth: evolution, complexity, and the radical remaking of economics. Harvard Business Press

Benjamin DJ (2019) Errors in probabilistic reasoning and judgment biases. In: Handbook of behavioral economics: applications and foundations, vol 1. Elsevier, Amsterdam, pp 69–186. https://doi.org/10.1016/bs.hesbe.2018.11.002

Bossaerts P, Murawski C (2017) Computational complexity and human decision-making. Trends Cogn Sci 21:917–929. https://doi.org/10.1016/j.tics.2017.09.005

Boyd R, Richerson PJ, Henrich J (2011) The cultural niche: why social learning is essential for human adaptation. Proc Natl Acad Sci 108:10918–10925. https://doi.org/10.1073/pnas.1100290108

Bradley R, Drechsler M (2014) Types of uncertainty. Erkenntnis 79:1225–1248. https://doi.org/10.1007/s10670-013-9518-4

Brase GL, Hill WT (2015) Good fences make for good neighbors but bad science: a review of what improves Bayesian reasoning and why. Front Psychol 6:340. https://doi.org/10.3389/fpsyg.2015.00340

Bray MM, Savin NE (1986) Rational expectations equilibria, learning, and model specification. Econometrica 54:1129–1160. https://doi.org/10.2307/1912325

Camerer CF, Loewenstein G (2004) Behavioral economics: past, present, future. In: Camerer CF, Loewenstein G, Rabin M (eds) Advances in behavioral economics, pp 3–51

Chater N, Loewenstein G (2016) The under-appreciated drive for sense-making. J Econ Behav Organ 126:137–154. https://doi.org/10.1016/j.jebo.2015.10.016

Denzau AT, North DC (1994) Mental models: ideologies and institutions. Kyklos 47:3–31

Ellsberg D (1961) Risk, ambiguity, and the Savage axioms. Q J Econ 75:643–669

Feldman M (1987) An example of convergence to rational expectations with heterogeneous beliefs. Int Econ Rev 28:635–650. https://doi.org/10.2307/2526571

Friedman M (1953) The methodology of positive economics. In: Essays in positive economics. University of Chicago Press, Chicago, pp 3–43

Geroski PA, Jacquemin A (1988) The persistence of profits: a European comparison. Econ J 98: 375–389
Gigerenzer G (2008) Why heuristics work. Perspect Psychol Sci 3:20–29. https://doi.org/10.1111/j.1745-6916.2008.00058.x
Gigerenzer G (2021) Axiomatic rationality and ecological rationality. Synthese 198:3547–3564. https://doi.org/10.1007/s11229-019-02296-5
Gigerenzer G, Todd PM, the ABC Research Group (1999) Simple heuristics that make us smart. Oxford University Press, Oxford
Gould J (1882) Illustration of Darwin's finches or Galapagos finches. https://commons.wikimedia.org/wiki/File:Darwin%27s_finches_by_Gould.jpg. Accessed 16 May 2023
Graesser AC, Fiore SM, Greiff S et al (2018) Advancing the science of collaborative problem solving. Psychol Sci Public Interest 19:59–92. https://doi.org/10.1177/1529100618808244
Güth W (2002) Chapter 3: interview. In: Andersson FN, Holm H (eds) Experimental economics: financial markets, auctions, and decision making: interviews and contributions from the 20th Arne Ryde symposium. Springer Science & Business Media
Hausman DM (2021) Philosophy of economics. In: Zalta EN (ed) The Stanford encyclopedia of philosophy, winter 2021. Metaphysics Research Lab, Stanford University. https://plato.stanford.edu/archives/win2021/entries/economics
Hulsebus RC (1974) Operant conditioning of infant behavior: a review. In: Reese HW (ed) Advances in child development and behavior. JAI, pp 111–158
Hung W (2013) Team-based complex problem solving: a collective cognition perspective. Educ Technol Res Dev 61:365–384. https://doi.org/10.1007/s11423-013-9296-3
Jager W (2000) Modelling consumer behaviour. Universal Press
Jones NA, Ross H, Lynam T et al (2011) Mental models: an interdisciplinary synthesis of theory and methods. Ecol Soc 16:46. http://www.ecologyandsociety.org/vol16/iss1/art46/
Jordan JS (1991) Bayesian learning in normal form games. Game Econ Behav 3:60–81. https://doi.org/10.1016/0899-8256(91)90005-Y
Kaaronen RO, Manninen MA, Eronen JT (2023) Rules of thumb, from Holocene to Anthropocene. Anthropocene Rev 10:685. https://doi.org/10.1177/20530196221149105
Kahneman D (2011) Thinking, fast and slow. Farrar, Straus and Giroux, New York
Keynes JM (1921) A treatise on probability. Macmillan, London
Keynes JM (1937) The general theory of employment. Q J Econ 51:209–223
Knight F (1921) Risk, uncertainty and profit. Houghton Mifflin, Boston
Lancaster KJ (1966) A new approach to consumer theory. J Polit Econ 74:132–157
Leiser D, Drori S (2005) Naïve understanding of inflation. J Socio-Econ 34:179–198. https://doi.org/10.1016/j.socec.2004.09.006
Leiser D, Krill Z (2017) How laypeople understand the economy. In: Ranyard R (ed) Economic psychology, pp 139–154
Loewenstein G (1999) Experimental economics from the vantage-point of behavioural economics. Econ J 109:25–34
Loretan M, English WB (2000) Evaluating correlation breakdowns during periods of market volatility. International Finance Discussion Papers No. 658, SSRN 231857
McCloskey DN (1983) The rhetoric of economics. J Econ Lit 21:481–517
McCloskey DN (1985) The rhetoric of economics. University of Wisconsin Press, Madison
Murawski C, Bossaerts P (2016) How humans solve complex problems: the case of the knapsack problem. Sci Rep 6:34851. https://doi.org/10.1038/srep34851
OECD (2017) PISA 2015 results (Volume V). Collaborative problem solving. PISA, OECD Publishing, Paris
Pinker S (2010) The cognitive niche: coevolution of intelligence, sociality, and language. Proc Natl Acad Sci 107:8993–8999. https://doi.org/10.1073/pnas.0914630107
Reed MS, Evely AC, Cundill G et al (2010) What is social learning? Ecol Soc 15:r1. http://www.ecologyandsociety.org/vol15/iss4/resp1/

Reinhart CM, Rogoff KS (2009) This time is different. Eight centuries of financial folly. Princeton University Press, Princeton
Roos M, Reccius M (2024) Narratives in economics. J Econ Surv 38(2):303–341. https://doi.org/10.1111/joes.12576
Savage LJ (1954) Foundations of statistics. John Wiley & Sons
Sayama H, Farrell DL, Dionne SD (2011) The effects of mental model formation on group decision making: an agent-based simulation. Complexity 16:49–57. https://doi.org/10.1002/cplx.20329
Selten R (1991) Evolution, learning, and economic behavior. Game Econ Behav 3:3–24
Selten R (1998) Aspiration adaptation theory. J Math Psychol 42:191–214
Shiller RJ (2017) Narrative economics. Am Econ Rev 107:967–1004. https://doi.org/10.1257/aer.107.4.967
Shiller RJ (2019) Narrative economics: how stories go viral and drive major economic events. Princeton University Press, Princeton
Simon HA (2000) Bounded rationality in social science: today and tomorrow. Mind & Society 1:25–39. https://doi.org/10.1007/BF02512227
Simon H, Egidi M, Viale R, Marris R (1992) Economics, bounded rationality and the cognitive revolution. Edward Elgar, Cheltenham
Starmer C (2004) Developments in nonexpected-utility theory: the hunt for a descriptive theory of choice under risk. In: Camerer CF, Loewenstein G, Rabin M (eds) Advances in behavioral economics. Princeton University Press, Princeton
Sterman JD (1994) Learning in and about complex systems. Syst Dyn Rev 10:291–330. https://doi.org/10.1002/sdr.4260100214
Thaler RH (1991) The winner's curse: paradoxes and anomalies of economic life. The Free Press, New York
Thaler RH, Sunstein CR (2008) Nudge: improving decisions about health, wealth, and happiness. Yale University Press
Tversky A, Kahneman D (1974) Judgment under uncertainty: heuristics and biases: biases in judgments reveal some heuristics of thinking under uncertainty. Science 185(4157):1124–1131
Walstad W, Allgood S (1999) What do college seniors know about economics? Am Econ Rev 89:350–354
Whiten A, McGuigan N, Marshall-Pescini S, Hopper LM (2009) Emulation, imitation, over-imitation and the scope of culture for child and chimpanzee. Philos Trans R Soc Lond B Biol Sci 364:2417–2428. https://doi.org/10.1098/rstb.2009.0069
Whiting PF, Davenport C, Jameson C et al (2015) How well do health professionals interpret diagnostic information? A systematic review. BMJ Open 5:e008155. https://doi.org/10.1136/bmjopen-2015-008155
Wood W, Quinn JM, Kashy DA (2002) Habits in everyday life: thought, emotion, and action. J Pers Soc Psychol 83:1281–1297. https://doi.org/10.1037/0022-3514.83.6.1281

Conclusion: What Does it all Mean? 13

Too large a proportion of recent "mathematical" economics are mere concoctions, as imprecise as the initial assumptions they rest on, which allow the author to lose sight of the complexities and interdependencies of the real world in a maze of pretentious and unhelpful symbols.
John Maynard Keynes (2018, p. 266)
Stop trying to control. Let go of fixed plans and concepts, and the world will govern itself.
Laozi

Contents

13.1 Introduction 710
13.2 Ten Lessons for Complexity Thinking 710
13.3 Why Does it Matter? 716
13.4 The Complex Economy and Complexity Economics 723
References 728

Abstract

This chapter concludes the book by summarizing the top ten lessons for complexity thinking. The relevance of complexity thinking is demonstrated by comparing the neoclassical and complexity approaches to the analysis of climate change. Some thoughts on how complexity economics might contribute to a new economic order and policy follow.

Keywords

Complexity thinking · Climate economics · Eudaimonic economy · Lessons

M. Roos, *Principles of Complexity Economics*, Classroom Companion: Economics,
https://doi.org/10.1007/978-3-031-51436-4_13

13.1 Introduction

The main goal of this textbook is to offer a new perspective on economics by explaining the principles of complexity thinking. Complexity thinking lies between hard and soft complexity science. It is a way of looking at the complex world, informed by rigorous models, without forgetting that all models are ultimately reductionist, limited in their applicability, and ignore potentially important aspects.

Throughout this book, many computational and some analytical models have been presented, but the focus has not been on teaching how to model and how to analyze those models in a systematic way. Instead, the models have always been used to convey an insight and to develop an intuition for an underlying concept or principle. The models are applications of the more fundamental theory of complexity. Therefore, what you should take away from this book is not the details of the various models, but the specific way of thinking and a thorough understanding of the most important complexity concepts. These complexity concepts are nonlinearity, feedback, self-organization, emergence, evolution, history, and adaptation. They are necessary to understand what it means that the economy is a complex adaptive system.

But how do you apply these complexity concepts to your thinking? How can you develop a robust complexity mindset and how can it help you address economic problems? This concluding chapter summarizes ten concise lessons that will help you develop a complexity mindset. They are the essence of the previous chapters. Applying these lessons to economic problems often makes a big difference in the analysis, conclusions, and potential policy recommendations compared to mainstream neoclassical thinking. Climate change, one of the most pressing problems of our time, serves as an example of this difference.

Despite its relevance to the challenges of the twenty-first century, complexity economics is still at an early stage of development. We conclude with some remarks on the current state of the field and the task for the future.

13.2 Ten Lessons for Complexity Thinking

The following ten lessons are easy to remember and take you a long way toward a complexity mindset. They summarize the most important take-aways from this textbook.

1. **Know the limits.**

Complexity imposes limits on our knowledge. It is the very nature of complexity that we have only limited understanding of complex phenomena. Of course, all sciences know that the world is complex. The traditional approach of modern science is reductionist, i.e. to model and analyze only parts of systems such that our limited mind can cope with the resulting degree of complexity. However, the reductionist approach does not reduce the complexity of the system itself, but only of its representation in a model. Therefore, understanding how a model of reality works does not imply that we understand the real system. This does not mean that modeling is not useful. Models help us to understand some aspects of the complex reality. Complexity thinking requires that we do not confuse the models with reality and that we be very careful about transferring insights from a model to the real world.

This general limit to our understanding applies to all systems, complex or not. Two other limits are more specific to complex systems: limits to prediction and limits to control. Due to nonlinear dynamics, structural change, novelty, and fundamental uncertainty, the predictability of complex adaptive systems is inherently limited. While short-term prediction may be possible, the stable structure required for longer prediction horizons is often not present. Limits to the control of complex adaptive systems arise from self-organization, evolution, and adaptation. Again, this is not to say that all control is impossible, but complex adaptive systems tend to adapt to the regulatory environment that is imposed on them, which may counteract the intentions of the controller.

The limits of prediction and control are particularly relevant to economics, where there is both a public demand and an intrinsic desire of economists to predict the course of the economy and to recommend optimal policies. Most likely, economists will never achieve what engineers can do in their fields. Knowing one's limits is an expression of wise humility.

2. **Embrace in-betweenness, pluralism, and dialectic thinking.**

Complex systems are incompressible or irreducible, i.e. they cannot be reduced to simpler systems without losing some of their aspects. Of course, we do reduce complex systems by modeling some of their aspects, but not others, which means that there are always multiple ways to do this. Integrating various reductionist models of a complex system into a meta-model is a challenge, because the approaches chosen may be incompatible.

Reducing irreducible systems has implications for the truth status of the reductionist model. The statistician George Box (1979) coined the aphorism "All models are wrong, but some are useful." The models are wrong in the sense that they do not represent the whole truth about reality. The ecologist and philosopher of science Richard Levins (1966) also reflected on the relationship between simplified models with artificial or unrealistic assumptions and reality and formulated that "our truth is the intersection of independent lies." Thus, where different independent models agree, there seems to be some truth. Single models or approaches cannot claim to be true, but together false models allow us to approach the truth. What we need to approach the truth is a plurality of models and methods, or, in other words, pluralism.

Each approach or perspective can make valid statements, even if these statements appear to contradict each other. In Chap. 2, we used the metaphor of a globe that is white on one side and black on the other to illustrate the importance of different perspectives. It is both true and false to say "the globe is white" and "the globe is black. Depending on the position of the observer, the globe appears to be black or white, but in reality it is both. The other example was the gray square made up of black and white pixels. When you zoom in, there is no gray, only black and white. But from a distance, the eye of the observer cannot identify the individual pixels, but blends them into a uniform gray area. So is it wrong to say that the square is gray? From a short distance, yes; from a long distance, no. Complexity is characterized by in-betweenness or ambiguity. Complexity lies between order and chaos, between the few and the very many, between stasis and motion, between robustness and fragility. It is between polarities that constitute a spectrum of possibilities. There is a tension and a cyclical interplay between the polarities that requires a dialectical view. A stable equilibrium can be punctuated and destabilized by the same forces that led to its creation. Individuals can be individually stupid but collectively smart, or individually rational but collectively irrational.

For economics, this aspect of complexity thinking implies a greater openness to different questions, ontological assumptions, and methodological approaches than those currently embraced by the mainstream. There is no one right way to do economics.

3. **Think systemically.**

A system consists of interconnected parts within a boundary that separates the system from an environment. The system and its parts have functions that define why the system is a unified whole. Systemic thinking has both a holistic and a reductionist aspect. The holistic aspect focuses on the function and characteristics of the system as a whole that result from the parts and their interactions. The reductionist aspect seeks to understand the characteristics, workings, and functions of the parts. The whole and its parts define each other. There cannot be a whole without parts, and a part can only be a part of a whole. Neither makes sense without the other.

Thinking systemically requires a definition of the boundary of the system and its parts, as well as an understanding of how the parts interact with each other. It is also necessary to consider how a system interacts with other systems or its environment. In practice, there are no isolated systems, especially in the social world. Social systems are open and exchange energy, matter, and information with their environment.

Neoclassical economics tends to treat the economy as an isolated system, but complexity economics recognizes that the economy is embedded in and deeply intertwined with other systems, such as society and the natural environment. We do not always need to model integrated socio-economic or natural-ecological systems, but we need to consider the exchanges across the boundary of the economy with the other systems.

4. **Accept nonlinearity as the normal case.**

Just as most animals are not elephants, most systems in the natural and social world are not linear. Modeling systems as linear is convenient because it guarantees tractability and predictability. But it is also dangerous, because nonlinear systems have very different properties, so a linear approximation can lead to wrong conclusions.

Nonlinear dynamical systems can have multiple equilibria or other types of attractors. Their behavior can be chaotic and change qualitatively with small changes in parameters at bifurcations. All of these characteristics make it difficult to impossible to predict the behavior of nonlinear dynamical models. The ability of nonlinear systems to generate cyclical dynamics or permanent acyclic fluctuations provides a different perspective on the business cycle than the conventional approach of augmenting linear systems with additive stochastic shocks. From the perspective of complexity economics, macroeconomic fluctuations are an endogenous outcome of the system, not a consequence of unobservable exogenous shocks.

Human intuition is very poor with respect to nonlinear dynamical systems. So it is understandable that we intuitively prefer linear models, but science should counterbalance our innate linearity bias. Complexity science assumes by default that the system to be modeled is nonlinear and expects a justification for a linear approach. This mindset differs from approaches that start with simple linear cases and consider nonlinear extensions as special cases. Linearity is the special case; the normal case is nonlinearity.

5. **Watch out for feedback.**

Feedback is closely related to nonlinearity. Linear causality leads to simple cause-and-effect chains, whereas feedback creates loops and circular causality. Ignoring feedback results in surprise by side effects and unintended consequences. You should always wonder where and how the empire will strike back.

Linear or linearized dynamical models in economics tend to grow exponentially or converge to a unique stable equilibrium. In a nonlinear world, other modes of system behavior are possible, such as oscillations or S-shaped growth or system collapse. Nonlinear systems can also switch between different regimes with qualitatively different properties. Complexity thinking makes one sensitive to such possibilities.

Positive feedback is a destabilizing force in the sense that it can cause a variable to grow or shrink, while negative feedback stabilizes a system at an equilibrium. In an evolutionary setting, however, positive feedback can lead to the dominance of one path or one type of agent. In economics, positive feedback is often translated with "increasing returns," which play an important role in theories of endogenous growth and spatial agglomeration of economic activity.

Understanding the feedback structure of a system provides insight into its stability and evolutionary path. Real systems often have a complicated feedback structure with multiple positive and negative feedback loops, whose relative strength can change over time. Changes in the feedback structure can have dramatic long-term effects. A system can be transformed by changing the strength of positive and negative feedback loops.

6. **Expect self-organization.**

Many people tend to see a will or a designer behind observed order, but order can arise through self-organization without a central controller of the system. In the economy, there is a lot of design and planned control; for example, in firms or by policy makers such as governments and central banks. The important lesson of complexity economics is that self-organization can interfere with designed order and counteract attempts to control a system.

This has two implications. On the one hand, we should ask ourselves what kind of self-organization might emerge that could undermine our attempts to design a certain order in an economic system. For example, regulating a particular financial market in order to stabilize the financial system might lead to the emergence of a new alternative market that is not subject to the regulation. On the other hand, in some cases, self-organization might be an alternative to planned organization. This idea underlies the notion that markets can solve many problems better than government planners. But this is not always true and depends on the circumstances under which self-organization occurs.

From a physical point of view, self-organization requires some form of energy. Dissipative systems create structure through self-organization only when they exchange matter and/or energy with their environment. Viewing the economy as a dissipative system highlights the importance of energy for economic activity. As Keen et al. (2019, p. 41) put it: "capital without energy is a sculpture" and "labour without energy is a corpse."

7. **Be aware that scale matters.**

It is a fallacy of composition to assume that what is true at the level of the parts is also true at the level of the system. Emergence teaches us that systems are organized hierarchically and that each level in the hierarchy has its own behavior and rules. We therefore need an appropriate language for each level and its phenomena. Systems can have properties that are not found in their parts. These system properties emerge from the interactions of the parts.

To a complexity economist, it is fundamentally wrong to model a high-level entity in the same way as the individuals that make up the entity. A firm does not behave like an individual manager, market demand is different from individual demand, and aggregate consumption differs from the consumption on an individual household. These differences are qualitative, not just given by a scaling factor. The modeling trick of representative agents violates the fundamental complexity concept of emergence. The neoclassical dream of a unified economic theory that applies equally to all levels of a system is unscientific. Physicists, the idols of economists, have no trouble using different theories for the subatomic scale, the molecular scale, and the astronomical scale.

8. **Consider the economy as an evolutionary process.**

Novelty, which is a fundamental driver of economic change, is the result of purposeful recombination of existing knowledge as well as discoveries by chance. The computational view of evolution considers both biological evolution and economic evolution as instances of (evolutionary) search algorithms. From this perspective, there is no need to apply concepts from evolutionary biology to economics. Biological evolution and economic evolution can differ in details as long as both are understood as search algorithms based on inheritance, selection, and variation. Evolutionary processes tend to maximize fitness, which is the ability to survive and reproduce in a given environment. In the economy, this does not necessarily imply the maximization of profits or utility. Evolution produces diversity, but it also relies on diversity to find good solutions in the fitness landscape.

In human societies, genetic evolution is still at work, but at very slow pace. Cultural evolution is much faster, leading to the accumulation of cultural knowledge that far exceeds individual knowledge. Cultural evolution, which works through imitation and selective learning from others, results in practices and institutions that are well adapted to specific environments.

The finding that evolutionary computer algorithms can outsmart their designers is an important result, because it suggests that there are limits to our ability to design rules to achieve an intended outcome. Evolution also teaches us that there is a trade-off between a system's robustness, performance, and adaptability. In addition, evolution tends to increase complexity over time.

9. **Pay attention to detail and context.**

When there is positive feedback in a system, small decisions and single historical events can matter. They can create a stable dynamic path with a particular evolution that could have been different. Such paths can be inefficient, and an economy can be locked into an undesirable path. Complexity economics is sensitive to history and tends to explain phenomena as the result of past events rather than current circumstances or system functioning.

When history matters, it is unlikely that one can formulate very general economic laws that apply everywhere and at all times. There may be law-like relationships that have some limited validity in particular cases and in a particular context, but they may break down if the context changes. This also means that economic policies do not always have the same effects everywhere.

The complexity perspective on economics turns the conventional approach to economics upside down. Neoclassical economists are often quick to produce stylized facts and abstractions of real-world situations. It is seen as a great strength to start with an abstract, a highly simplified model that focuses on a simple mechanism. While this approach can be useful for building theory, it is not a good way to arrive at reliable policy recommendations. Models that are useful in practice must include all relevant details, which requires a detailed analysis of the facts before a simplified model can be created. Complexity thinking involves paying attention to detailed descriptions of the messy world before generating an oversimplified representation.

10. **Have a realistic view on human behavior.**

Humans and human behavior are also complex. Without a doubt, people often use their intelligence to solve problems and to pursue their goals. But habits, social norms, imitation, emotions, and irrationality are also important in many cases. It is hard to say whether any of these modes of behavior are representative.

Because of its systems perspective, complexity economics emphasizes the social dimension of behavior. Almost always, people are not isolated individual decision-makers. They are typically members of various groups with particular cultures and shared belief systems. Individual behavior is both enabled and constrained by institutions and often depends on the behavior of others. And human adaptation and learning are largely social or cultural phenomena.

Regarding the concept of rationality, complexity economics challenges the notion that infeasible maximization should serve as the normative ideal of rational behavior. Humans do not have the cognitive capacity to solve more than the simplest maximization problems. Computational complexity theory shows that most economically relevant optimization problems are intractable. More importantly, most practically relevant economic problems are ill-defined due to changing circumstances, fundamental uncertainty, complex causal relationships, and missing or ambiguous information. The use of well-adapted heuristics can be ecologically rational. We cannot judge the rationality of behavior by looking only at the individual. Herbert Simon's metaphor of pair of scissors reminds us that rationality should not be defined as an absolute concept, but must be seen relative to the respective environment.

13.3 Why Does it Matter?

In many cases, complexity thinking will lead to different conclusions than neoclassical economics. This can be illustrated by one of the greatest challenges of our time: climate change. In 2018, William Nordhaus was awarded the Nobel Memorial Prize in Economic Sciences "for integrating climate change into long-run macroeconomic analysis." Nordhaus applied conventional neoclassical analysis to the interaction between aggregate economic production and climate change by augmenting the Ramsey–Cass–Koopmans model with a climate model. His DICE (dynamic integrated climate-economy) model was the prototype for many neoclassical integrated assessment models that are used to analyze climate change from an economic perspective. While the first versions of DICE were published in the early 1990s (Nordhaus 1993), Nordhaus continues to update and use the model (see Nordhaus 2019; Barrage and Nordhaus 2023). For comprehensive discussion of neoclassical climate economics, see Roos and Hoffart (2020). We do not discuss the model in detail here, but present what complexity thinking tells us about climate change and how this differs from neoclassical thinking. We do this by applying the 10 lessons presented above.

1. **Know the limits.**

The climate system and the economy are complex systems that are difficult to predict and control. There is great uncertainty about the future course of climate change and its impact on the economy. At the same time, there is evidence that unmitigated climate change could have catastrophic consequences for life on Earth and the sustainability of human civilization. While the risk of such catastrophic outcomes may be low, the stakes are extremely high.

Given the impossibility of reliably predicting the dynamics of climate change, complexity economics dares not recommend any kind of optimal policy that suggests the existence of an optimal climate path. While it is true that there are benefits and costs to mitigating climate change, we have no way of estimating them with sufficient precision to determine their optimal relationship.

But this is what William Nordhaus does:

> *The DICE model is primarily designed for policy optimization, although it can also be run as an evaluation model for given policies. In both settings, the approach is to maximize an economic objective function (the goal implicit in the problem). For the DICE model, the objective function refers to the economic well-being (or utility) associated with a path of consumption.* (Barrage and Nordhaus 2023, p.3)

Rather than trying to find optimal policies, complexity thinking recommends a precautionary approach that focuses on avoiding worst-case outcomes.

2. **Embrace in-betweenness, pluralism, and dialectic thinking.**

Neoclassical climate economics has been much criticized, both by economists (e.g., Ward 2019; Roos and Hoffart 2020; Keen 2021; Stern et al. 2022) and non-economists (e.g., Rising et al. 2022). A key criticism is that Nordhaus considers a temperature increase of about 3 °C to be optimal in the sense that it balances the costs and benefits of mitigation in terms of GDP. However, scientific projections suggest that global food production could be cut by half if the global average temperature rises by 3 °C (Lynas 2020).

A complexity perspective accepts that the same issue should be approached from different angles and that efforts should be made to integrate diverse and even conflicting findings in order to achieve a comprehensive understanding of the complex world. Pluralism requires a serious response to criticism from other perspectives. Nordhaus, however, has kept his modeling framework essentially unchanged for 30 years, merely fine-tuning the model without addressing any of the serious criticisms. Hood (2020) quotes climate economist Gernot Wagner as saying in an interview that it would have helped climate policy if Nordhaus had won the Nobel 20 years earlier, but that the 2018 award was a step backward in many ways.

3. **Think systemically.**

For a complexity economist, it is natural to consider the economy as part of a larger socio-economic system, or even as part of a socio-environmental system. Moreover, the "environment" consists of many interacting subsystems, such as the climate system, the biosphere, the cryosphere, and the marine system. Thus, there are complex interdependencies between climate change, biodiversity loss, land degradation, ocean acidification, glacial melting, freshwater loss, etc. The economy must exchange matter and energy with natural systems. Decreasing entropy in society and the economy must lead to higher entropy in the environment, which can undermine the functioning of natural systems.

While Nordhaus is to be commended for communicating with climate scientists in the 1970s and 1980s and linking the economy to the climate system, the way neoclassical climate economics defines the systems is simplistic. The DICE model ignores many relevant systemic effects:

> *It is important to note that the studies which form the basis of this estimate generally omit potentially significant climate change impact channels, such as biodiversity loss, ocean acidification, extreme events, social unrest, etc.* (Barrage and Nordhaus 2023, p. 8/9)

It is therefore not surprising that the DICE model predicts rather moderate GDP losses due to climate change, even for high temperature increases:

> *damages are estimated to be around 3.12% of output at a 3°C global warming over pre-industrial temperatures and 12.5% of output with 6 °C warming.* (Barrage and Nordhaus 2023, p. 9)

Lynas (2020) tries to assess what a temperature increase of 6 °C above the normal temperature of the Holocene could mean for life on Earth in a short period of time. A similar increase occurred at the end of the Permian 251 million years ago, resulting in the extinction of about 90% of all species. If mechanisms similar to those at the end of the Permian were to occur in our world, the projected damage could be very different:

> *Superimpose what palaeoclimatic science tells us about conditions at the Permian–Triassic boundary onto Earth today and we can try to visualise at least some of the scenes. Imagine all the world's forests burning simultaneously, from the Arctic to the equator. Night fails to fall, as the world is lit by flames. When the smoke clears away, all that is left of the world's once-teeming tropical forests and snow-covered boreal woodlands is a layer of soot and charcoal spread thickly on the bare ground. Imagine all the resulting dead and dying plant remains being washed into the oceans by monsoons of biblical intensity. The layers of wood and debris combine with the carcasses of animals to form floating mats that wash up with the dead tides along the world's shorelines. The heat is so extreme that only a few animals can survive, hidden in burrows from the fierce daytime sun, or cowering in cooler nooks and*

> *crannies along rocky watercourses. Ecosystems and food webs cease to exist in any functional sense. In the daily battle for survival, the big winners are those that feast on the dead—detritivores, bacteria and fungi.* (Lynas 2020, p. 260/261)

Even if we do not reach such apocalyptic conditions, climate change is likely to cause much social unrest, conflict, and international migration from regions that become uninhabitable for humans. These effects may dominate the narrow economic effects represented in the DICE model. Neoclassical climate economics does not think systemically enough.

4. **Accept nonlinearity as the normal case.**

Nonlinear dynamical systems can have bifurcations. Chap. 6 discussed the subcritical bifurcation with jumps and hysteresis, which captures well the concept of tipping points in climate science. If the temperature rises above a critical temperature such that the Greenland ice shield begins to melt, the system jumps to a different state and will not return to the old equilibrium state even if the temperature falls below the critical temperature again. The same is true for coral reefs. If they have died because the temperature in the oceans has risen too much, they will not return in human time scales, even if the temperature drops again. The climate system and ecosystems are characterized by irreversibility. Once a tipping point is passed, the systems change their state permanently, meaning that we cannot simply scale them up or down.

Nordhaus (2019) apparently does not take irreversibilities into account. He analyzes two scenarios that he sees as alternatives to the 2-degree target of the 2015 Paris Agreement. He suggests that the 2-degree target could be interpreted to mean that the global temperature does not rise more than 2 °C on average over a 100-year or 200-year time horizon. In the 200-year scenario, the temperature path is close to his optimal path, and the temperature would rise by about 3.2 °C by 2100. By the middle of the twenty-second century, the temperature would have to fall below 2 °C. Nordhaus' proposal is a serious misunderstanding of the 2 °C goal. Climate scientists want to limit the temperature increase to avoid tipping points that could lead to runaway global warming. In other words, once a tipping point has been reached, the global temperature could remain high or even increase, even if anthropogenic greenhouse gas emissions are subsequently reduced or become negative.

5. **Watch out for feedback.**

Nonlinearity and feedback are closely related. Climate scientists warn of tipping points such as the melting of the Arctic and Antarctic ice shields, the thawing of permafrost, the dieback of the Amazon rainforest, the shifting of the Monsoon, or a change in the Atlantic thermohaline circulation. Each of these events has a positive feedback effect on temperature rise. Ice shields reflect sunlight back into space, which has a cooling effect. If the white area on the Earth's surface is reduced, the cooling effect that counteracts global warming is diminished. Rainforests are huge carbon sinks. If they die as a result of climate change, the Earth's ability to remove carbon dioxide from the atmosphere will be reduced, and worse, additional carbon dioxide stored in the trees will be released. As a cascade of tipping elements sets in, the positive feedback is amplified to the point where global warming accelerates and we completely lose control of the climate.

As argued above, the DICE model does not include such climate feedbacks. It also ignores other important feedbacks. For example, both population growth and technological progress are exogenous in the DICE model. The consequences of climate change may negatively affect both. In addition, climate change may affect social norms and values, which are important for public policy. Increased resource scarcity, climate damage, and international migration could increase aggression and conflict. Psychological research suggests that climate change has both direct and indirect effects on aggression and violence (Miles-Novelo and Anderson 2019). Aggression and violence, in turn, can affect productivity, technological progress, and politics. On the other hand, crises can also lead to greater solidarity among affected people.

6. **Expect self-organization.**

Xu et al. (2020) show that for millennia, the majority of the human population has lived in areas with a fairly narrow temperature band of 11 °C to 15 °C mean annual temperature. Current crop and livestock production is also concentrated within this temperature band. Climate change will shift the geographic location of this temperature more in the next 50 years than it has shifted in the last 6000 years. Depending on the degree of global warming, 1 to 3 billion people are projected to be affected by the shift in the climate band to which we are adapted. It seems unlikely that this large proportion of the world's population, most of whom live in poor countries, will be able to adapt so quickly to climatic conditions that are much harsher than those favored by human populations over the past 6000 years. It is much more likely that many of these people will migrate to areas with better climatic conditions, which can be seen as an instance of self-organization.

Migration and other forms of adaptation to climate change are changing societal structure, production conditions, and trade patterns. It is impossible to predict what the world will look like in 50 or 100 years, but it is implausible to assume that the structure of the economy remains unchanged, as DICE does by assuming a fixed model structure.

7. **Be aware that scale matters.**

Climate change involves highly complex distributional issues. While most of the greenhouse gas emissions that cause climate change originate in the industrialized countries of the Global North, most of the direct climate damages are inflicted on people in the poor Global South. Climate change mitigation could hamper these countries' transition to economic development unless a rapid solution is found to how these countries can produce cheap non-fossil energy. Complexity economics emphasizes that living and production conditions are highly heterogeneous across countries and across individuals within countries. People also differ in their preferences and needs within countries and even more so between countries.

These problems are hidden behind the representative agent whose welfare function is maximized in the DICE model. Even the aggregation of individual utility functions into a global welfare function is heroic. Should we really assume that the welfare of climate refugees in Bangladesh can be represented by the same utility function as the welfare of a rich North American citizen? Probably not. It also seems plausible that the intertemporal elasticity of substitution of a drought-starved child in the Horn of Africa is different from that of a middle-class child in Europe.

Even if a welfare function could be found that is representative of all people in all countries, it is doubtful that actual market behavior comes close to maximizing such a welfare function, as Nordhaus claims. In theory, decentralized markets only achieve the same optimal outcome as a benevolent social planner if they are perfectly competitive, free of externalities, and if all agents are rational maximizers. Neither of these assumptions is true in reality.

8. **Consider the economy as an evolutionary process.**

The evolutionary side of complexity economics is interested in culture and technology. The use of fossil fuels and the emission of greenhouse gases are not just a particular aspect of certain production technologies. They are deeply embedded in our culture and way of life. Fossil energy has long been abundant and cheap, so we have developed a carbon culture in which many aspects of our daily lives depend on coal, oil, and natural gas. Fossil fuels are needed to produce food, chemicals, and pharmaceuticals; for heating, transportation, and production capital; and to generate electricity for our appliances and consumer electronics. Decarbonizing the economy to mitigate climate change is both a technological challenge, as new forms of energy production and substitutes for fossil fuels as production inputs must be developed, and a cultural challenge, as energy may become more expensive or available in less convenient forms, affecting our daily habits. Complexity economics asks how technological and cultural decarbonization processes might evolve and what could be done to facilitate technological and cultural adaptation. An important aspect is the speed of such processes, because cultural evolution takes time, but climate change is proceeding very rapidly.

Neoclassical climate economics focuses almost exclusively on carbon pricing as the main instrument of decarbonization. It applies the Pigouvian logic of the internalizing external effects, which aligns private decisions with social welfare. While this approach is not inherently wrong, it overlooks two important aspects. First, it is of little help to call for a carbon tax at a certain level that would achieve the desired decarbonization, if we do not know how to implement it politically. Public policy is influenced by the prevailing culture, such that significant policy changes may require some cultural shift. Second, a carbon tax provides an incentive to develop new technologies and to change behavior, but it does not address the question of how to achieve systemic change. What needs to change is not a set of individual production technologies, but an entire socio-technical regime including institutions. Understanding how this can happen requires an evolutionary perspective.

9. **Pay attention to detail and context.**

Like many other neoclassical models, the DICE model is highly abstract and an extremely simplified representation of the real world. Nordhaus is aware of this and adheres to the common neoclassical belief that simplification is a virtue. He writes:

> *Many simplifications are also buried in the functional forms of models. For example, the DICE model relies on the Cobb-Douglas function to represent the production process. This is likely to overestimate substitution in some areas and underestimate it in others. Additionally, it may suggest a degree of smoothness in substitution that is not present when there are only a small number of processes, in which case an activity analysis framework would be preferable. … We must put these concerns about oversimplification in the context of the questions that are being asked. The purpose of models is not to be an exact replica of real-world processes. Aside from the impossibility of achieving that goal, greater detail would actually be less valuable for many purposes. Instead, models are used for insights into key questions.* (Barrage and Nordhaus 2023, p. 20)

Other simplifications that he mentions, and whose treatment he considers beyond the scope of the DICE model, are the inefficient real-world tax structure, externalities, and other market failures such as monopolies and regulation in the energy sector, economies of scale, and informational inefficiencies. He also introduces a generic "backstop technology" into the DICE model that can replace all fossil fuels, without explicitly explaining how it works.

Indeed, abstraction and simplification can be very powerful tools for gaining theoretical insights. There is no reason per se to reject stylized theoretical models, but the DICE model is more than a theoretical exercise. As noted above, it is designed for policy optimization, i.e. it has a normative purpose. From a complexity perspective, it is presumptuous to make very explicit statements about optimal policy for one of society's greatest challenges based on a stylized theoretical model. Many of the problems with the DICE model have already been mentioned. Another problem related to the lack of detail is that there is only one aggregate consumption good in the model. If Nordhaus's estimate that a 3 °C temperature increase would lead to a loss of about 3% of output is correct, one could argue that this is far from catastrophic. However, if most of this output loss occurs in agriculture (agriculture accounts for about 4% of global GDP), humanity will be in serious trouble.

10. **Have a realistic view on human behavior.**

As a neoclassical model, DICE models assume individually rational behavior in terms of utility and profit maximization. Barrage and Nordhaus (2023, p. 3) claim that the use of optimization can be interpreted "as a means of simulating the behavior of a system of competitive markets." Apart from the fact that many markets in the world economy are imperfectly competitive, intertemporal utility maximization is an unrealistic model of behavior (see Chap. 12). It is therefore questionable to what extent the model describes the behavior of the real-world economy.

Behavioral assumptions are particularly important for the response of agents to carbon pricing as the main neoclassical instrument for combating climate change. Consumption patterns are determined not only by cost–benefit considerations, but also by habits, social norms, traditions, and institutions. As a result, the elasticity of demand for many goods and services to a carbon price may be very low, at least in the short run. It is also likely to vary considerably with household income and wealth. While it may be significant for poor households, it is likely to be very small or even zero for (very) rich households. However, due to their lifestyle and investment patterns, the richest households have a much larger carbon footprint than middle class or poor households. Moreover, the investment behavior of both firms and households is lumpy. A household is unlikely to insulate its home and invest in a new heating system immediately after a carbon tax on natural gas is introduced. The household may pay higher gas bills for a few years until the old central heating system breaks down. Legislation and other types of direct regulation are likely to have a much more immediate effect.

Another important aspect is that the neoclassical model assumes that agents simply accept a carbon tax. In reality, however, there is a lot of political resistance to this instrument. For many people, the causal link between carbon pricing and climate change mitigation is not obvious. A realistic view of human behavior should therefore include the possibility that agents will either try to avoid carbon pricing if they can, or lobby against it, both of which greatly reduce the effectiveness of the instrument.

13.4 The Complex Economy and Complexity Economics

Throughout this book, we have argued that the economy is a complex adaptive system and that complexity economics is the right way to think about it. Thinking about the economy has several dimensions: we want to understand how the economy is and how it works, we want to think about how it should be, and, building on our normative views, we want to think about how policies, regulations, and formal institutions should be designed to influence the economy to achieve our goals.

Note that there is a circularity here. The economy does not just exist, but is influenced or even created by human actions. Thus, economic theories and models are not just tools for understanding the economy and informing economic policy. Economic theories and ideas actively shape the economic system, rather than merely describing and explaining it. The idea that economic theories at least partly create the economic world is called the *performativity thesis* (Callon 1998; MacKenzie et al. 2007). The performativity of economic theory has important implications for how we think about the role of economics in society. Rather than being neutral or objective tools, economic theories are seen as active agents that can shape economic reality by influencing the actions and decisions of individuals and organizations, as well as the policies and regulations that govern economic activity.

A good example of understanding performativity is gross domestic product (GDP). We cannot directly observe aggregate output or economic growth. Without a measure for these theoretical concepts, they do not really exist. Without a standardized statistical concept, we cannot compare the economic size of two countries or the evolution of a country's economic performance over time. As a result, macroeconomic policy would be impossible. The way we construct such a statistical measure shapes our perception of a country's wealth and performance. The conventional wisdom is that GDP growth is good, but there are numerous criticisms of GDP as a measure of well-being (see Stiglitz et al. 2010). An alternative to GDP—the Genuine Progress Indicator (GPI)—starts with personal consumption expenditures and corrects for income inequality and environmental costs, among other things. Unlike GDP, which has risen in all developed countries and many others since the 1970s, the per capita GPI has stagnated globally since then. Thus, whether we believe that well-being has increased or stagnated depends on the concept by which we agree to measure it.

Beinhocker (2020) compares the existing economic system, which is strongly shaped by neoclassical theory, with a possible economic system based on complexity economics. Following the historian Yuval Harari (2015), he describes the economy—similar to other social structures—as an imagined order. This means that the economy does not exist as a real thing, but is made up of ideas and concepts. He argues that concepts such as economic value, money, markets, growth, GDP, wages, or the idea of a job are not part of the physical world or governed by physical laws. Rather, they are human concepts that have been imagined throughout our history, so that the economy is a product of our imagination. The set of ideas that make up the economic system can be divided into four categories: (1) moral philosophy, (2) behavioral theory, (3) economic theory, and (4) economic and political ideology. Moral philosophy provides the normative basis for human behavior and the purpose and design of the economy. Behavioral theory provides models of how economic agents act and the determinants of their behavior. Economic theory explains economic phenomena and answers economically relevant questions. It is based on moral philosophy, which influences what kinds of questions are considered relevant, and on behavioral theory. The normative views of what the economy should be and how to achieve that goal are elements of economic and political ideology, which guides political action. Ideology makes use of economic theory and moral philosophy.

According to Beinhocker, *market capitalism*, as our current economic system is called, is a coherent imagined order consisting of *maximizing utilitarianism* as the relevant moral philosophy, *homo economic*us as the dominant behavioral theory, *neoclassical economic*s as the mainstream economic approach of the past century, and *neoliberalism* as the resulting ideology. All elements fit together neatly (see Fig. 13.1). Utilitarianism sees the pursuit of pleasure and the avoidance of pain as key features of human nature. Moral behavior maximizes the most pleasure for the most people and minimizes the most pain. All actions must be judged by their

Fig. 13.1 The current imagined order. Source: Author

success in maximizing pleasure and minimizing pain. Unlike the consequences of actions, intentions do not matter from this moral perspective. Homo economicus is a translation of maximizing utilitarianism into a theory of human behavior. Maximizing pleasure as a normative goal is interpreted as a behavioral assumption: people actually maximize their utility (or pleasure) in a fully rational and selfish way. Neoclassical economics ingeniously combines utilitarianism and the model of homo economicus. It shows in the first theorem of welfare economics, that under certain conditions such as the assumption of perfect competition, the results of the assumed individual behavior are actually morally desirable. Individuals maximize their private utility and competitive markets lead to the maximization of social efficiency. In other words, what is best for the individual is also good from a social perspective.

From there, it is straightforward to arrive at the policy conclusions and to the economic and political ideology of neoliberalism. If individuals know best what is in their interest, and if competitive markets maximize efficiency, then leave markets alone unless there are barriers to competition or externalities. Economists such as Friedrich Hayek, Milton Friedman, and James Buchanan advised conservative politicians such as Margaret Thatcher in Britain, Ronald Reagan in the United States or Augusto Pinochet in Chile to pursue free-market policies, deregulation, and privatization.

Market capitalism has created enormous wealth and incredible technological progress. But capitalism is also blamed for many societal problems, such as environmental destruction and climate change, inequality, social isolation, and unhealthy lifestyles. Based on its moral foundations that emphasize individualism, it is strong in promoting individual freedom and self-fulfillment, but weak in maintaining and fostering social cohesion. Its approach to solving social problems by incentivizing individual behavior appears to have its limits.

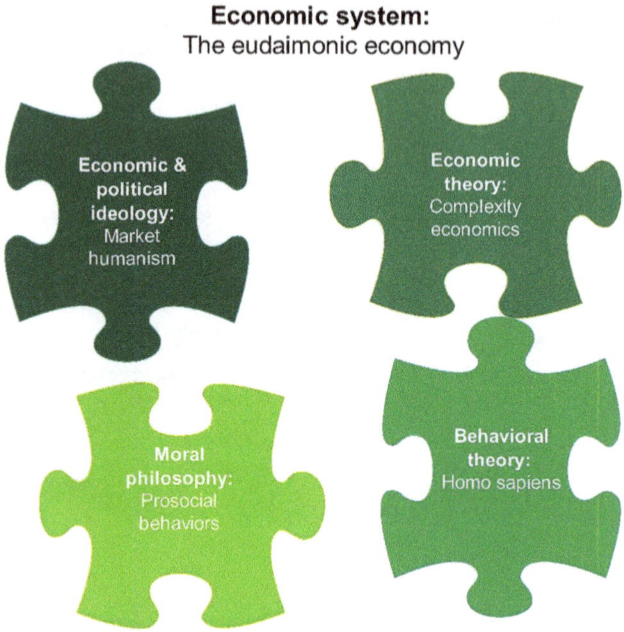

Fig. 13.2 A possible new imagined order. Source: Author

Beinhocker (2020) proposes an alternative economic system of the eudaimonic economy with complexity economics at its core. The unconnected pieces of the jigsaw puzzle in Fig. 13.2 symbolize that this possible new imagined order does not yet have the same coherence as market capitalism. It is the task of future complexity research to refine the individual pieces and to put them together. Beinhocker only sketches some ideas about the elements of the alternative order. The eudaimonic economy alludes to Aristotle's concept of *eudaimonia* which can be translated as "being in tune with a good spirit," "happiness," or "well-being" and which was the highest human good in the ancient Greek tradition. Its main goal is to maximize human and non-human flourishing and to create prosperity by solving human problems, which is done cooperatively.

In this book, we have covered complexity economics extensively, and we have also touched on an alternative behavioral theory. The behavioral theory that fits well with complexity economics differs from the homo economicus model in two ways. First, *Homo sapiens* is boundedly rational, unlike homo economicus, who has unlimited computational power. Second, and perhaps more importantly, *Homo sapiens* is a deeply social creature. Humans need other humans to survive and thrive. Their identity, values, preferences, knowledge, and behaviors depend on the groups or communities to which they belong. The most basic community is the family, which unlike a household is not just a community of purpose that benefits from the division of labor of its members as Gary Becker would see it. A family is also an emotional and value community that cultivates empathy and altruism. To emphasize this aspect of the human nature, *Homo sapiens* has also been called homo socialis, homo cooperans, and homo reciprocans. Since it cannot be denied that humans do not always cooperate and also behave selfishly in many circumstances, Lindenberg (1990) proposes the model of *homo socio-economicus* as a general model of humans in the social sciences.

There are several approaches in moral philosophy that can provide the foundation for eudaimonic economics. Aristotle's *virtue ethics* is closely related to the concept of eudaimonia. Virtues are morally good dispositions to think, feel, and act, which are character traits to be cultivated. While virtue ethics was displaced in Western philosophical thought by utilitarianism and deontological ethics, i.e., ethics based on rules, duties, and obligations, it experienced a modern revival in the second half of the twentieth century with works by Elizabeth Anscombe, Alasdair MacIntyre, Martha Nussbaum, Amartya Sen, and Michael Sandel. The economist Arjo Klamer (2017) uses virtue ethics for his concept of a value-based economy. A related philosophy is *communitarianism*, which opposes extreme individualism and emphasizes that people's social identities and personalities are largely defined by community relations and interactions. Relevant writers in this philosophical school include Alasdair MacIntye, Michael Sandel, and Charles Taylor. Sociologist Amitai Etzioni combines communitarianism with his work on socioeconomics, which is an attempt to integrate economic and sociological thinking. Another philosophical approach that is compatible with complexity theory is *pragmatism*. Although pragmatism is not primarily a moral philosophy, it can be used to derive normative positions that can inform policy making (see Ansell and Geyer 2017). Pragmatism emphasizes the limits of knowledge, embraces pluralism, and a pragmatic theory of truth that relates truth claims to their practical uses and successes.

Probably the most work remains to be done in terms of an economic and political ideology consistent with complexity economics. For Beinhocker, *market humanism* places the solution of human problems at the center of economic activity. Those activities that solve human problems are socially desirable and are the social duty of the economy. Thus, prosperity should not be defined in terms of material wealth, but in terms of the availability and quality of solutions to human problems. An important lesson of complexity economics for economic policy is to move away from trying to find optimal solutions to complex or wicked problems, and to promote social learning, experimentation, adaptation, and adaptability. The focus of policy making and analysis should shift from desired outcomes to the process of improving conditions. Finally, it is clear that attention should shift from the individual to groups and networks and the interactions between individuals. Poverty, for example, should not be seen as the result of individual choices, but in the context of the individual's living conditions. Rather than relying solely on direct economic policy instruments such as taxes and subsidies, economic policy should pay attention to the formation and reconfiguration of networks and institutions and seek to influence social norms.

Complexity economics offers no simple answers to complex problems, not at this stage of its development, and probably not in the future. The most important lesson it can teach us is that real complexity does not disappear when we construct simpler representations of the complex world. We therefore need breadth and versatility of thinking, as well as a wide range of different perspectives, to deal with complexity. We also need critical thinking and a good sense of what is plausible and what is not. This textbook will hopefully help you develop these skills.

Complexity Lessons to Remember

1. Know the limits
2. Embrace in-betweenness, pluralism, and dialectic thinking
3. Think systemically
4. Accept nonlinearity as the normal case
5. Watch out for feedback
6. Expect self-organization
7. Be aware that scale matters
8. Consider the economy as an evolutionary process
9. Pay attention to detail and context
10. Have a realistic view on human behavior

References

Ansell C, Geyer R (2017) 'Pragmatic complexity' a new foundation for moving beyond 'evidence-based policy making'? Policy Studies 38:149–167. https://doi.org/10.1080/01442872.2016.1219033

Barrage L, Nordhaus WD (2023) Policies, projections, and the social cost of carbon: results from the DICE-2023 model. NBER Working Paper 31112.

Beinhocker ED (2020) Can complexity economics save the world? In: Arthur WB, Beinhocker ED, Stanger A (eds) Complexity economics. Dialogues of the applied complexity network. Proceedings of the Santa Fe Institute's 2019 Fall Symposium. Santa Fe Institute Press, Santa Fe

Box GEP (1979) Robustness in the strategy of scientific model building. In: Launer RL, Wilkinson GN (eds) Robustness in Statistics. Academic Press, pp 201–236

Callon M (1998) Introduction: the embeddedness of economic markets in economics. In: Callon M (ed) The laws of the markets. Blackwell, Oxford

Harari Y (2015) Sapiens: a brief history of humankind. HarperCollins, New York

Hood M (2020) Climate economics Nobel may do more harm than good. https://phys.org/news/2020-07-climate-economics-nobel-good.html. Accessed 24 Apr 2023

Keen S (2021) The appallingly bad neoclassical economics of climate change. Globalizations 18: 1149–1177. https://doi.org/10.1080/14747731.2020.1807856

Keen S, Ayres RU, Standish R (2019) A note on the role of energy in production. Ecol Econ 157: 40–46

Keynes JM (2018) The general theory of employment, interest, and money. Palgrave Macmillan, Cham

Klamer A (2017) Doing the right thing – A value based economy. Ubiquity Press, London

Levins R (1966) The strategy of model building in population biology. Am Sci 54:421–431

Lindenberg S (1990) Homo socio-oeconomicus: the emergence of a general model of man in the social sciences. J InstTheor Econ 146:727–748

Lynas M (2020) Our Final Warning: Six Degrees of Climate Emergency. HarperCollins Publishers. Kindle-Version

MacKenzie D, Muniesa F, Siu L (2007) Introduction. In: MacKenzie D, Muniesa F, Siu L (eds) Do economists make markets? On the performativity of economics. Princeton University Press, Princeton

Miles-Novelo A, Anderson CA (2019) Climate change and psychology: effects of rapid global warming on violence and aggression. Curr Clim Change Rep 5:36–46. https://doi.org/10.1007/s40641-019-00121-2

Nordhaus WD (1993) Rolling the 'DICE': an optimal transition path for controlling greenhouse gases. Resour Energy Econ 15:27–50

Nordhaus W (2019) Climate change: The ultimate challenge for economics. Am Econ Rev 109: 1991–2014. https://doi.org/10.1257/aer.109.6.1991

Rising J, Tedesco M, Piontek F, Stainforth DA (2022) The missing risks of climate change. Nature 610:643–651. https://doi.org/10.1038/s41586-022-05243-6

Roos M, Hoffart F (2020) Climate economics. A call for more pluralism and responsibility. Springer Nature, Cham

Stern N, Stiglitz J, Taylor C (2022) The economics of immense risk, urgent action and radical change: towards new approaches to the economics of climate change. J Econ Methodol 29:181–216. https://doi.org/10.1080/1350178X.2022.2040740

Stiglitz JE, Sen A, Fitoussi J-P (2010) Mis-measuring our lives. Why GDP doesn't add up. The New Press, New York

Ward B (2019) A Nobel Prize for the creator of an economic model that underestimates the risks of climate change. https://www.lse.ac.uk/granthaminstitute/news/a-nobel-prize-for-the-creator-of-an-economic-model-that-underestimates-the-risks-of-climate-change/. Accessed 24 April 2023

Xu C, Kohler TA, Lenton TM et al (2020) Future of the human climate niche. Proc Natl Acad Sci 117:11350–11355. https://doi.org/10.1073/pnas.1910114117

Index

A

Abilities, 3, 4, 10, 23, 25, 30, 58, 64, 67, 75, 107, 109, 113, 143, 148, 160, 164, 181, 271, 287, 303, 349, 425, 476, 497, 509, 521, 544–547, 563, 567, 570, 571, 573, 575, 630, 631, 635, 651, 653, 654, 662, 686, 689, 690, 704, 713, 715, 720
Acidification, 15, 718
Action bias, 675, 700
Adaptation, 28, 33, 54, 61, 63, 68, 116, 143, 243, 314, 387, 521, 535, 542, 570, 572, 635, 636, 647–705, 710, 711, 716, 720, 721, 727
Adaptedness, 509, 575
Adjacency matrix, 144, 161, 162
Aeolipile, 503, 504
Agent-based modeling, 33, 43, 117, 143, 145, 486, 543
Agglomeration
  spatial, 360, 362, 381, 606, 713
Agglomeration economies, 360, 362, 606, 607, 713
Aggregation problem, 440, 470
Ahistorical, 583–595, 615
Algorithm
  cultural, 527–529
  efficient approximation, 668
  genetic, 465, 499, 512–517, 520, 521, 528, 529, 537, 538, 575
Allele, 509, 512, 518, 519, 538
Ambidexterity
  organizational, 573
Ambiguity, 23–25, 30, 32, 46, 660–662, 702, 712
Amplification
  demand, 308
  variance, 308
Anabolism, 400
Analysis, 4, 23, 25, 27, 32, 42, 49, 56, 65, 66, 79, 93, 117–119, 126, 130, 133, 135, 142–145, 179, 185, 188–190, 199, 202, 204, 207, 238, 244, 247, 249, 263, 265, 267, 271, 293, 294, 297, 342, 389, 424, 429, 433, 440, 441, 452, 453, 457, 459, 470–472, 486, 488, 490, 536, 543, 587, 594, 599, 614, 620, 627, 637, 702, 710, 715, 716, 722, 727
Animal spirits, 139, 700
Anti-emergentist, 423
Apophenia, 75
Artificial intelligence (AI), 11, 14, 28, 43, 425, 465
As
  if, 388, 666–668, 676, 703
As-if
  assumption, 52, 703
Attractor, 142, 187, 192, 198, 224, 244, 249, 596, 640, 713
Autocatalytic, 355, 356, 502, 593
Autonomy, 175, 176, 179, 262, 342, 346, 348, 349, 413, 424, 448, 490, 525, 552, 569, 571
Autopoiesis, 571
Autotrophic, 400

B

Balance, 279, 486, 564, 565, 576, 591, 713, 717
Basin of attraction, 192, 204–207, 211, 224, 596
Bass diffusion model, 256, 304–307
Bass model, 244, 307
Bayesian updating, 673, 682, 704
Bayes' rule, 674, 682
Beer distribution game, 309–319

M. Roos, *Principles of Complexity Economics*, Classroom Companion: Economics,
https://doi.org/10.1007/978-3-031-51436-4

Belief
prior, 527
Belousov-Zhabotinsky reaction (BZ reaction), 354, 355, 396, 414
Bias-variance dilemma, 679, 704
Bifurcation
diagram, 208–212, 214, 607
flip, 219
fold, 208, 209
imperfect, 213
Neimark-Sacker, 240
period-doubling, 219, 240
point, 208, 210–212, 214, 221
saddle-node, 208–210
subcritical pitchfork, 210–211
supercritical Hopf, 212, 240
supercritical pitchfork, 210, 214, 218
transcritical, 208–210, 244
Biodiversity
loss of, 19, 613
Biosphere, 400, 401, 404, 613, 718
Bit, 79, 82–86, 88, 100, 112, 384, 396, 404, 429, 512, 513, 515, 539, 586
Boltzmann constant, 394
Boundary, 15, 33, 43, 44, 46–48, 56, 58, 65–67, 73, 117, 138, 139, 149, 289, 327, 345, 375, 399, 407, 452, 462, 489, 613, 712, 718
Bounded rationality, 43, 57, 244, 348, 413, 414, 485, 651, 672
Bridge law, 449
Brusselator, 356, 552
Brute-force search, 516
Budget constraint
intertemporal, 125, 668
Building block, 61, 68, 400, 507, 680
Bullwhip effect, 307–314
Butterfly effect, 222, 487

C

Calculus of variations, 125
Cambridge capital controversy, 432
Capability, 3, 29, 161, 163, 164, 180, 470, 544–547, 571, 573, 612, 680, 698
Capital
Cambridge controversy, 432
social, 381, 542
Capitalism
market, 6, 8, 34, 724–726
varieties of, 450
Carrying capacity, 192, 203, 283–285, 287, 288, 324, 335
Catabolism, 400
Catallaxy, 385–387, 389
Catastrophe
cusp, 214, 244, 245
Catastrophe theory, 213, 244
Causality
aleatory, 269, 271, 273
circular, 253–335, 341, 699, 713
deterministic, 268, 334
generative, 265, 266
indeterministic, 268, 269, 334
linear, 181, 254, 713
probabilistic, 268, 334
statistical, 270
Causal loop, 254, 277
Causal loop diagram, 142, 255, 262, 277–280, 288, 289, 291, 293, 332, 341, 683
Causal mechanism, 112, 265, 266, 271–273, 275, 276, 443, 659
Causal structure diagram, 332–334
Causation
autonomous, 452
Cause
basic, 270
common, 51, 267, 270, 271
first, 269, 275
fundamental, 270
surface, 270
Cellular automaton
elementar, 343–345
Center, 12, 88, 89, 136, 143, 176, 197, 198, 201–203, 207, 212, 227, 249, 344, 350, 361, 391, 427, 523, 679, 727
Certainty, 25, 661–663, 701
Change
agent, 625
of direction, 190, 685
economic theory of, 32
evolutionary theory of economic, 536
within path, 624
regime, 635
Chaos, 28, 33, 40, 42, 57, 58, 68, 140–142, 187, 215, 217–224, 237, 239–241, 243–246, 249, 341, 391, 500, 595, 712
Characteristic equation, 199–201, 444
Choice architecture, 676
Chromosome, 508, 509, 512–517
Clades, 549
Cladistics, 499, 549–552, 562
Cladogram, 550, 551, 553, 556, 561, 562, 575, 589
Class NP, 664
Class NP-hard, 664

Class P, 664
Climate
  crisis, 15
Climate change, 3, 15, 19, 22, 27, 28, 34, 117, 172, 173, 212, 245, 569, 570, 595, 613, 614, 616, 628, 633, 636–638, 650, 681, 710, 716–721, 723, 725
Closed orbit, 195, 197, 207, 212, 218
Cobweb, 215–219, 222
Coleman's bathtub, 451
Coleman's boat, 451
Collapse, 5, 6, 8, 15, 17, 19, 22, 34, 128, 129, 135, 139, 157, 229, 230, 235, 244, 245, 256, 259, 283, 285, 288, 289, 319–331, 333–335, 468, 572, 593, 595, 626, 713
Collapsology, 327
Collective, 429, 430, 436, 442, 452, 453, 455, 457, 461, 474, 489, 529, 559, 563, 564, 618, 653, 655, 690, 691, 694, 695, 697, 699, 704, 705
Collective intentionality, 461
Combinability, 107–109, 112, 157, 159
Combinatorial explosion, 516
Commons
  tragedy of the, 320, 465
Communitarianism, 727
Complementarity
  strategic, 372
Complex
  techno-institutional, 632
Complexity
  algorithmic, 100
  causal, 113, 256, 331–335, 662
  computational, 100, 515, 651, 663–666, 668, 671, 677, 703, 716
  cyclomatic, 105–107, 110–112, 157, 332, 335, 662
  dynamic, 61, 64, 65, 149, 172–179, 413, 558, 570, 691
  essential, 388
  Kolmogorov, 99, 100
  Lempel-Ziv, 100
  organized, 388
  sciences, 4, 33, 42–44, 55–57, 66, 67, 140, 184, 254, 388, 389, 420, 421, 497, 595, 710, 713
  statistical, 94–97
  structural, 61, 67, 100–104, 112, 157, 332, 422, 497, 558, 570, 592, 593, 662
  talking, 44
  thinking, 43, 44, 55–61, 67, 82, 116, 144, 265, 266, 388, 389, 595, 702, 710–717
  unorganized, 388
  worldview, 33, 34, 42, 55–61, 116, 117
Complexity-entropy causality plane (CECP), 95–97
Complexity science
  hard, 43, 44, 55, 57, 66, 67, 140, 595, 710
  soft, 43, 44, 55, 57, 66, 67, 388, 389, 595, 710
Complexity theory, 4, 33, 179, 181, 388, 452, 538, 691, 727
Complexus, 40
Complicatedness, 570
Components
  connected, 106, 332
Concept
  high-level, 274, 275
  primitive, 274
Conditoning
  operant, 659
Confirmation
  social, 372, 374, 414
Conflict, 6, 7, 25, 28, 30, 60, 175, 176, 179, 203, 360, 463, 472, 499, 531, 533, 534, 553, 573, 619, 625, 692–694, 704, 719, 720
Constant conjunction, 266, 267
Constructionist hypothesis, 421
Consumat, 655
Consumer confidence, 302
Consumer sentiment, 302, 486
Consumption
  intertemporal, 124
Contagion
  complex, 372–376, 414
  simple, 368–372
  social, 297, 301, 303, 305, 368, 372
Context, 5, 20, 28, 30, 31, 43, 44, 46, 54–56, 61, 66, 98, 100, 110, 112, 135, 148, 159, 169, 179, 212, 232, 241, 256, 262, 265, 270, 275, 303, 308, 320, 359, 386, 421, 424, 434, 435, 441, 443, 450–452, 457, 460, 461, 464, 465, 473, 490, 512, 544, 547, 558, 562–564, 567, 573, 587, 594, 595, 599, 602, 608, 609, 617, 658, 682, 683, 691, 694, 715–716, 722, 727
Context dependence, 23, 261
Contingency, 130, 583, 585, 587–589, 640, 686
Control problem
  optimal, 309
  stock management, 308–309
Correlation breakdown, 661
Creatio ex nihilo, 500
Creative destruction, 536, 575

Critical juncture
late, 624, 625, 633, 641
Critical slowing down, 211
Critical transition, 244
Crossover
chromosomal, 509, 510
Cultural evolution, 499, 524–529, 535, 575, 687, 688, 704, 715, 721
Cultural selection, 525
Cusp point, 214
Cynefin framework, 23

D
Data, 8, 9, 11, 17–19, 40, 55, 73–80, 86, 90, 92, 112, 166, 185, 225, 241, 245, 246, 275, 296, 313, 349, 432, 473, 483, 484, 488, 550, 553, 636, 637, 680, 700
Decision making
dynamic, 307–319
Deductive tinkering, 541
Degeneracy, 573, 574
Delay, 90, 256, 257, 282, 283, 285, 286, 307, 310, 313, 335
Demand
profit-led aggregate, 226
wage-led aggregate, 226
Deontic power, 462
Design space, 538–540, 553
DICE model, 716–722
Difference equation, 141, 188–190, 215, 238, 249, 289, 312, 444
Differential equation
ordinary (ODE), 141, 189, 190
partial (PDE), 189
Differentiation
cultural, 375
Digital twin, 11, 12, 488
Discounting
hyperbolic, 139, 675
Discourse
public, 626, 700
Discovery, 14, 138, 387, 447, 501, 502, 524, 666
Discovery procedure, 387
Disequilibrium, 94, 130, 246, 290, 535, 588
Disorder, 11, 40, 41, 51, 84, 94, 341, 342, 352, 353, 387, 389, 394, 399, 413, 472, 509, 538
Disparity, 560, 564, 565, 576
Dissipative
reaction, 355, 414
structure, 355, 359, 390–415, 591, 640
Dissipative system far from thermodynamic equilibrium, 396, 397, 415
Divergence
points of, 589
Diversity
across types, 560–562, 564, 575, 576
of community composition, 562, 563, 576
prediction theorem, 563
Weitzman, 561, 562
within a type, 560
Dual inheritance theory, 535
Dualism
Cartesian, 421
Dualist view, 421
Dynamical system
continuous-time, 188, 190–203, 223
discrete-time, 188, 215
nonlinear, 32, 33, 42, 65, 140–142, 184, 187, 195, 238, 244, 249, 711, 713, 719
Dynamical systems theory, 42
Dynamics
chaotic, 49, 140–142, 240, 243, 246
nonlinear, 32, 33, 42, 65, 140–142, 145, 184, 187, 244, 711

E
Economic complexity index (ECI), 158, 166–171, 181, 432
Economic development
theory of, 535
Economics
agent-based computational, 471
Austrian, 138, 342, 384, 488
behavioral, 131, 139, 145, 450, 648, 651, 653, 663, 675, 676, 685, 703
complexity, 4, 5, 32–33, 62, 63, 65–67, 115–145, 148, 149, 159–166, 181, 206, 208, 246–249, 255, 341, 384, 388–391, 423, 424, 427, 497, 499, 512, 522, 542–543, 575, 582, 583, 651, 653, 702, 712–717, 720, 721, 723–728
ecological, 138, 139, 249
environmental, 257
evolutionary, 138, 145, 179, 433, 486, 497, 499, 500, 535, 537, 542–543, 575, 592
heterodox, 117
historical, 583, 585–595
in historical time, 138, 584, 594
institutional, 117, 138, 145, 457–459, 589
mainstream, 34, 65, 117–119, 131, 132, 137, 139, 140, 145, 151, 153, 175, 222,

249, 408, 429, 430, 458, 489, 536, 542, 588, 616, 626, 652, 724
neoclassical, 5, 31, 32, 55, 65, 117, 119–139, 145, 148, 159, 181, 247, 265, 274, 280, 390, 391, 423, 424, 470, 471, 497, 536, 537, 583, 588, 591, 617, 640, 651, 666, 670, 673, 701, 712, 724, 725
new institutional, 138, 457–459, 589
non-equilibrium, 4, 32
old behavioral, 675
orthodox, 117, 536
post-Keynesian, 117, 139
in time, 584, 594
traditional institutional, 457, 459–463
Economy
eudaimonic, 726, 727
euphoric, 229
national, 385, 429, 430
Econophysics, 342, 349
Ecosystem
industrial, 380
Edges, 55, 56, 68, 74, 76, 143, 214, 332, 333, 351, 386, 388, 519
Effectiveness of labor, 126, 271, 591
Efficient, 92, 96, 129, 342, 414, 440, 541, 542, 571–573, 589, 614–616, 640, 664, 668, 670, 688
Eigendirection, 196
Eigenequation, 199
Eigensolution, 199, 200
Eigenvalues, 166, 196–204, 207
Eigenvectors, 166, 196–200, 202
Ellsberg urn, 661
Embeddedness, 381, 459, 587
Emergence
complex, 442, 489
diachronic, 443, 497, 582
nominal, 442, 489
simple, 442
strong, 424, 443, 448–450, 490
synchronic, 443
weak, 424, 443–447, 489
Emergentism, 421
Emergents
ephemeral, 453, 454
stable, 453, 454, 456, 457
Emergy, 404, 405, 408–411
Empower, 404, 409
Enculturation, 660, 703
Endowment effect, 675
Energy
available, 398, 401, 404
internal, 355, 393, 399
potential, 103, 398, 400, 523
useful, 398
Energy hierarchy, 402, 403, 407, 408, 413
Energy transformation, 393, 401–403, 407, 415, 593
Engel curve, 438, 439
Engine
atmospheric, 503
Hero's, 503
Entities, 44, 46, 48, 49, 56, 62, 64, 79, 81, 112, 121, 135, 143, 265, 268, 273, 354, 381, 420–422, 425, 427–433, 440, 441, 444, 446, 448, 450, 452, 468, 488, 489, 497, 502, 521, 534, 549, 553, 554, 574, 575, 590, 619, 714
Entrepreneurs, 104, 134, 135, 174, 179, 180, 205, 341, 450, 527, 535, 539, 541, 575, 594, 625, 627, 630, 631, 641
Entropy
as the arrow of time, 397
Boltzmann, 395
Gibbs, 394
permutation, 90–93, 95, 112
rate, 89
Shannon, 84–87, 89, 90, 92, 95, 107, 108, 112, 157, 394, 396
thermodynamic, 84, 392–397
Environments, 10, 44, 81, 149, 203, 290, 342, 459, 507, 591, 649, 711
Epiphenomenon, 451
Epistemology, 55, 56
Equilibrium
chemical, 392, 393
market, 119, 121–123, 129, 132, 277, 342, 437, 470, 535
mechanical, 391
Nash, 132, 243, 460, 463, 464, 588, 609
punctuated, 57, 130, 472, 585, 619, 622–627, 640, 641
rational expectations, 122
sunspot, 456
thermodynamic, 355, 392–398, 402, 405, 408, 415, 591, 597
Ergodicity, 584, 597–600
Eudaimonia, 726, 727
Euler equation, 125, 126
Eutrophication, 16, 613
Events, 5, 40, 76, 116, 179, 206, 262, 346, 425, 531, 582, 658, 715
Evolution
combinatorial, 507
cultural, 499, 524–529, 535, 575, 687, 688, 704, 715, 721

Evolution (*cont.*)
directed, 14
regime, 636
theory of, 497, 507–512
Excess demand function, 439, 489
Exergy, 398, 401, 402, 405–407, 412, 415, 539, 640
Ex nihilo nihil fit, 500
Expectations
extrapolative, 237, 241
model-consistent, 122, 132
rational, 119–124, 133, 187, 244, 423, 457, 682
regressive, 237, 238
static, 216, 243
Expectations view, 243
Expected utility theory
subjective, 673
Experiments
natural, 271
Expertise level, 544, 547
Explanation
linear, 314
open-loop, 314
Externalities
network, 605, 606

F

Fallacy
of composition, 424, 435–441, 489, 714
Gamber's, 75–76
hot-hand, 76
Fardier á vapeur, 172, 505, 506
Feedback
density, 332, 333, 335
negative, 142, 241, 278–280, 282, 283, 288, 298, 331, 334, 349, 355, 356, 362, 376, 387, 414, 441, 713
positive, 142, 212, 276–280, 283, 297, 298, 321, 331, 334, 349, 355, 356, 363, 364, 376, 413, 425, 462, 472, 497, 553, 558, 572, 582, 601, 603, 605, 607, 608, 613, 620, 622, 624, 627, 632–633, 640, 713, 715, 720
Feedback loop, 142, 184, 241, 254, 255, 277–280, 282, 283, 285, 288–290, 307, 331–335, 362, 363, 401, 497, 567, 572, 607, 608, 683, 713
Financial instability hypothesis, 229–230
Fitness
relative, 511–513, 522
Fitness landscape, 499, 517–522, 538, 541, 551, 553, 554, 558, 575, 715
Fixed point
stable, 192, 208, 210–215, 218, 219, 239, 240, 279
unstable, 192, 193, 198, 208, 210–213, 215, 216, 219
Fixes that fail, 256
Flexibility, 30, 107–109, 112, 157, 346, 622, 636
Flows, 105, 106, 149–151, 230, 233, 234, 289–291, 297, 305, 308, 310, 314, 315, 320, 322, 335, 380, 382, 392, 396–398, 400–402, 404–412, 427, 430, 698
Focal point, 609
Forms, 15, 40, 81, 116, 153, 194, 254, 349, 428, 499, 587, 652, 714
Functional separation, 571
Functions, 14, 45, 79, 120, 155, 184, 267, 361, 427, 497, 584, 651, 712

G

Game of life, 343, 424, 444–446
Genealogical reasoning, 589
Generalized entropy function, 561
Genes, 13, 426, 499, 508, 509, 515, 517–520, 523–525, 536, 575
Genetic drift, 508, 509
Genomes, 12–14, 137, 509, 514, 520, 538
Genotypes, 426, 509, 511, 512, 517–521, 523, 524
Genuine progress indicator (GPI), 724
Goal seeking, 280, 307, 313, 335, 387, 567
Godley table, 233, 234
Good
inferior, 438, 439
normal, 438, 439
Goodwin model, 187, 208, 225–228, 230
Graph
strongly connected, 105, 106, 111, 157
Great moderation, 228–229, 235
Great recession, 176, 228, 229, 235
Grim trigger strategy, 464
Group
social, 54, 364, 365, 426, 434, 435, 694
Growth
exponential, 185, 190, 192, 200, 207, 224, 278, 280, 281, 286, 289, 291–293, 295, 304, 329, 334, 335, 516, 664, 665, 703, 713
with overshoot, 285, 287, 335
S-shaped, 283–285, 288, 289, 321, 335, 713

H

Habits, 130, 270, 460, 462, 593, 616–618, 654, 657, 716, 721, 723

Heterogeneous agents, 347, 348, 389, 434, 441, 470, 471, 485
Heterotrophic, 400
Heuristic
anchoring-and-adjustment, 674
approach, 450, 672
availability, 674
representativeness, 674
Hierarchy
of complexity, 52, 425–428
control, 427
inclusion, 427
level, 427
order, 425, 427
of systems, 425
High-level description, 136
Highly optimized tolerance (HOT), 53, 62, 558, 570, 576
Historical view, 242, 584
History
counterfactual, 589, 627, 633
Hog cycle, 216, 217, 244, 282
Holism, 56, 57, 59
Homeostasis, 407, 413, 567
Homo economicus, 534, 652, 675, 724–726
Homo socio-economicus, 727
Homothetic, 438
Hysteresis, 211, 212, 245, 719

I
I-intention, 461
Imperfection, 135, 213, 214, 244
In-betweenness, 711–712, 717–718
Incompressible, 43, 56, 67, 711
Individual intentionality, 461
Inference
additive, 267
subtractive, 267
Infinite regress, 132, 589
Inflows, 289, 290, 292, 308, 315, 320, 335, 396, 398, 402, 593, 640
Information
negentropy principle of, 396
Shannon, 84–86, 561
thermodynamic, 396, 408
Information theory, 43, 74, 79, 81–84, 107, 112, 388, 537, 539, 543
Innovations, 4, 10, 20, 24, 30, 129, 130, 134, 138, 145, 179–182, 243, 244, 249, 304, 368, 427, 476, 480, 500, 535–537, 543, 544, 549, 552, 555, 558, 563, 565, 569, 606, 619, 626, 631, 634, 666, 690
Input–output table, 150, 152, 488
Institutional conversion, 625
Institutional displacement, 625
Institutional drift, 625
Institutional economics, 117, 138, 145, 458
Institutional exhaustion, 625
Institutionalization, 381, 618
Institutional layering, 625
Institutions
formal, 134, 138, 459, 460
informal, 134, 138, 459, 460, 529
Intelligence
dedicated, 652
improvisational, 652, 686
Intensive form, 126
Interactions, 11, 49, 76, 118, 149, 185, 335, 341, 422, 497, 593, 655, 712
Interactors, 538–540
Interrelatedness
technical, 608
Intersubstitutable, 441
Intertemporal
consumption choice, 124
Intrapreneurs, 134
Inventions, 140, 172, 173, 243, 462, 499, 501–507, 523, 529, 540, 574, 575, 611, 626, 630, 632
Invisible hand, 341, 342, 386
Irreducibility
computational, 446, 447, 489
Irreducible, 56, 67, 443, 447, 448, 489, 711
Irreversibilities, 66, 213, 397, 583, 594, 719
Irreversible
quasi-, 611
Iterated map, 141, 189, 215–217, 240, 242, 249

J
Jacobian externalities, 606
Jacobian matrix, 203, 204, 207
Jevons paradox, 258

K
Kenes, 499, 544, 547, 548, 575
Keynesian, 139, 176, 423, 433, 701
Khazzoom-Brookes postulate, 258
KISS principle, 463
Knapsack problem, 515–517, 657, 663, 664, 666
Knowledge
unit of, 463, 499, 544, 545, 548, 549

L

Laissez-faire state, 390
Landscape
  fitness, 499, 517–522, 538, 541, 551, 553, 554, 558, 575, 634, 715
  socio-technical, 179, 180
Lattice, 347, 350–354, 377, 395, 454
Law
  of demand, 437, 438, 463, 470, 585
  economic, 585, 586, 640, 715
  first of thermodynamics, 393
  fundamental of highway congestion, 608
  ideal gas, 50, 433
  Metcalfe's, 605
  of population growth, 203
  of requisite complexity, 570
  of requisite hierarchy, 571
  of requisite variety, 569, 570
  second of thermodynamics, 355, 393, 395, 397, 398, 406, 413, 591, 593, 640
  thermodynamic of ecology, 405, 406
  of unintended consequences, 255, 256
  Wright's, 604
  Zipf's, 474, 475, 477
Learning
  by doing, 545
  reinforcement, 681, 685, 704
Less-is-more effect, 679
Level
  meso, 130, 433–435, 453, 489
Liability
  of newness, 542
  of obsolescence, 542
  of senescence, 542
Limit cycle, 195, 240
Limits to Growth, 14
Linearization, 199, 202–204, 249
Lock-in, 63, 179–181, 565, 583, 585, 610–618, 621, 622, 624, 627, 632, 634, 636, 640, 641, 654
Logistic equation, 192, 193, 203, 204, 208, 217, 283
Logistic map, 92, 215, 217–223
London Steam Carriage, 505, 506, 626
Loop
  balancing, 278–280, 283, 300, 306, 320
  self-reinforcing, 278–280, 283, 306, 334
Lotka-Volterra model, 203, 206, 249
  of competition, 203, 596
Lyapunov exponent, 223–225, 245
Lyapunov function, 207
Lyapunov time, 224

M

Macroeconomics
  agent-based, 424, 471, 488, 490
  bottom-up adaptive, 471
  emergent, 424, 468–488
  multi-agent system, 471
  Post Walrasian, 471
  Walrasian, 456, 470
Macrofoundations
  of microeconomics, 424, 450–457, 463, 490
Market humanism, 727
Markov chain, 597–599
Marshallian spillovers, 606
Materialist definition
  of economics, 118
Meaning, 2, 23, 24, 32, 40, 43, 51, 52, 55, 56, 59, 60, 73–75, 78, 79, 81, 82, 117, 122, 131, 179, 233, 254, 353, 355, 367, 394, 396, 424, 427, 452, 457, 500–502, 526, 538, 542, 564, 567, 618, 651, 675, 679, 691, 694, 702, 719
Memory, 51, 52, 54, 100, 118, 230, 341, 374, 597, 600, 657, 664, 678, 680, 692, 695, 697
Mental accounting, 675
Mental model, 681–684, 691, 693–699, 704, 705
Meso level, 130, 433–435, 453, 489
Mess, 25–27, 34
Metabolism, 45, 398–401, 426, 634, 635
Metaheuristic, 512, 575
Metcalfe's law, 605
Method of reflections, 160, 162, 181
Methodological equilibration, 131
Methodological individualism, 131, 449, 450, 452, 670
Methodological instrumentalism, 131
Methodology, 55, 119, 138, 145, 248, 423, 583, 595, 666, 667, 701, 702
Microfoundations
  of macroeconomics, 124, 433, 450
Microstate, 394, 395
Minsky model, 187, 228, 230–233, 235, 236
Minsky moment, 230
Mirror world, 488
Model
  agent-based, 4, 66, 143, 149, 248, 342–349, 356–359, 368, 369, 375, 377, 381, 382, 389, 413, 424, 447, 453, 454, 457, 463, 465, 468, 471, 475–485, 488, 490, 497, 499, 512, 529, 531, 544, 546, 633, 634, 641, 652, 655, 694, 695

Bass, 244, 256, 304, 307
CATS, 486
DICE, 716–722
evolutionary, 4, 66, 243, 497, 499, 557
Goodwin, 187, 208, 225–228, 230
heterogeneous, 348, 697
Lotka-Volterra, 203–208, 226, 244, 249, 596
Minsky, 187, 228, 230–236, 294
network, 4, 33, 66
Pólya urn, 600–603
predator-prey, 203, 206–208, 226, 249
Ramsey-Cass-Koopmans, 119, 124–129, 131–133, 198, 242, 291, 436, 588, 589, 591, 668, 716
Schelling segregation, 368, 376–379, 414
SIR, 256, 297–302, 304, 307, 371
system dynamics, 4, 65, 248, 255, 256, 262, 276, 277, 290, 293–297, 314–319, 327, 331, 335, 368, 369, 595, 634, 641
Sznajd, 354, 372–374, 414
Verhulst, 194, 203, 283
Monism
dialectical, 58, 67
material, 421
Multi-level perspective (MLP), 149, 179–182, 633
Multiple realizability, 448, 449
Mutation, 64, 466, 497, 508–513, 515, 517–521, 523, 524, 531, 532, 536, 538, 540, 558, 575
Mutualism, 380

N
Narrative
collective economic, 698
economic, 700
Narrative turn, 698
Negentropy, 396, 398, 405, 408
Neoliberalism, 724, 725
Network
bipartite, 160
industrial symbiosis, 379, 381, 383, 384
Network models, 4, 33, 66
Niche
cognitive, 652, 686, 687, 704
cultural, 652, 686, 687, 704
empowered, 635, 638
Nitrogen cycle, 15
Node
degenerate, 196, 201
Nomothetic, 265, 274
Non nova, set nove, 500
Nonproportionality of cause and effect, 185
Non-triviality, 95
No-Ponzi game condition, 125
Norms
social, 134, 434, 435, 459–461, 463, 490, 618, 688, 720, 723, 727
Novelty
degrees of, 502
domain-specific, 501, 503
follow-up, 502
fundamental, 502
universal, 501, 503
NP-complete, 515, 664
Nullcline, 226, 227

O
Observer, 24, 25, 45, 46, 48, 60, 66, 73, 79, 109–113, 139, 149, 157, 249, 389, 391, 445, 558, 565, 629, 654, 701, 711, 712
Ontology, 116
Optimal control, 125
Orbit, 184, 195, 197, 207, 212, 218, 219, 222, 224, 227
Order
by design, 385
grown, 385, 414
imagined, 724–726
made, 385, 414
Organization, 6, 42, 73, 130, 148, 243, 332, 341, 422, 497, 582, 649, 711
Oscillation, 195, 198, 202, 218, 222, 235, 256, 282, 283, 285–290, 307–319, 335, 354, 446, 713
Outflow, 289–292, 315, 316, 320, 335, 396
Output
gap, 225, 282, 431
potential, 225
Overfitting, 680
Overshoot, 283, 285–289, 308, 312, 319, 324, 335

P
Paradigm
conjectural, 590
emergence, 452–456
interaction, 452, 453
structure, 452
Paradox of thrift, 435–436
Parallelism
implicit, 520

Parameters
  deep, 433
Pareidolia, 75
Path-constrained amelioration, 615, 616
Path dependence, 63, 66, 179, 181, 581–641
Path formation, 585, 619–627, 641
Pattern
  formation, 40, 42, 137, 158, 342, 348, 358, 368, 413
  functional, 342, 364–368, 414
Patternicity, 75
Pattern prediction, 389
Performativity thesis, 723
Phase diagram, 126–129, 142, 190, 227, 596
Phase plane, 194
Phase transition, 33, 50, 352
Phenotype, 426, 509, 511, 523
Philosophy of science, 55, 58, 265, 451, 490
Physicalism, 421
Planetary boundaries, 15, 138, 327, 613
Pluralism, 10, 33, 34, 44, 67, 119, 138, 711–712, 717–718, 727, 728
Polarization, 376, 431
Pólya urn model, 600–603
Ponzi game, 134
Poverty trap, 241–243, 456
Power law distribution, 425, 427
Power law relation, 474
Pragmatism, 265, 267, 727
Prediction
  pattern, 117, 389
Prisoner's dilemma, 454, 463–465, 529
Problem
  of aggregation, 441
  decision, 124, 139, 309, 436, 515, 663, 664, 670
  fundamental knowledge, 384
  ill-defined, 139, 676, 698, 716
  Knapsack, 515, 517, 657, 663, 664, 666
  mind-body, 421
  n-body, 49
  NP-complete, 515, 664
  one-body, 49
  optimization, 31, 348, 439, 512, 515, 575, 662–664, 668, 703, 716
  three-body, 49
Product complexity index, 166, 181
Properties
  emergent, 52, 54, 62, 421, 422, 442, 456, 477, 490, 549
  resultant, 422
Pseudocode, 100, 136, 512, 514
Puffing devil, 172, 504

Q
Quadratic entropy index, 564

R
Randomized control trial, 270, 275
Randomness, 40, 41, 58, 65–67, 78, 92, 94, 95, 133, 142, 353, 354, 413, 511, 515, 601
Random walk, 599, 600
Rank, 169, 181, 271, 365, 366, 427, 474, 484
Rationality
  axiomatic, 131, 274, 471, 673–677, 682
  bounded, 43, 57, 244, 348, 413, 414, 485, 648, 651, 672
  logical, 672
  procedural, 671
  substantive, 671
Reader/builder, 538–540
Reason, 2, 7, 9, 11, 15, 19, 24, 27, 32, 48, 55, 65, 83, 89, 96, 111, 118, 125, 157, 190, 228, 243, 255, 262–266, 275, 330, 341, 363, 422, 430, 447, 489, 523, 588, 597, 615, 621, 630, 653, 663, 671, 701
Rebound effect, 257, 258
Recombination, 30, 64, 465, 496, 497, 500, 502, 503, 507–509, 512, 514, 519, 520, 523, 524, 539, 540, 558, 574, 606, 715
Recurrence, 500
Red flag act, 626
Red queen hypothesis, 572
Reductionism, 56, 59, 421
Reductionist hypothesis, 421
Regime
  large socio-economic, 632
  socio-technical, 179, 180, 722
  socio-technological, 632, 636
Regularity
  governing, 270
  phenomenal, 270
Relationship, 23–25, 27, 31, 40, 44, 45, 52, 54, 55, 58, 62, 65, 67, 79, 81, 98, 100, 101, 104, 112, 118, 121, 133, 142, 144, 145, 157, 184, 231, 248, 254, 267, 269, 273, 282, 289, 345, 347, 365, 414, 422, 430, 433, 435, 441, 449, 450, 474, 497, 539, 562, 586, 652, 659, 671, 683, 691, 704, 716
Remediable, 610
Repeller, 192
Representative
  agent, 124, 129, 435–441, 470, 475, 489, 714, 721
  firm, 124

household, 124, 125, 129
Reproduction, 75, 81, 320, 508, 509, 514, 518, 519, 593, 618, 624, 633
Resilience
ecological, 567
engineering, 567
Resource
renewable common-pool, 320–326
Retention, 537, 539
Revolution
microfoundations, 423
printing, 503
rational expectations, 119–124, 133, 187, 244, 423, 457, 682
Risk, 13, 18, 32, 66, 108, 121, 123–125, 139, 229, 241, 258, 327, 372, 436, 520, 564, 573, 615, 628, 630, 661, 674, 701, 717
Robustness, 342, 348, 349, 413, 567–570, 572, 576, 651, 712, 715
Rough-correlated, 538
Routine, 179, 180, 536, 537, 542, 547, 593, 595, 617, 618, 661, 668, 689, 691, 692
Rule
abstract, 387, 414, 659
lexicographic, 678

S
Sacrifice value, 669, 670
Saddle path, 128, 129, 132, 204, 588, 596
Saddle path stability, 129
Saddle point, 198, 200, 201, 204, 206–208
Satisficing, 657, 671, 672, 677, 678, 703
Scaling, 52, 474, 565, 714
Scarcity definition
of economics, 118
Scenario analysis, 144, 145
Schelling model, 377–379
Schema, 453, 538, 540, 651
Science
new kind of, 343, 447
Selection
cultural, 525
natural, 507–509, 511, 524–527, 570
Self-organization, 33, 61, 63, 138, 339–415, 422, 441, 442, 460, 497, 537, 539, 552, 558, 570, 574, 648, 710, 711, 714, 720, 728
Self-policing, 468
Sense-making, 130, 179, 618, 652, 698–702, 705
Sensitivity to initial conditions, 222–224
Separatrix, 204, 205
Side effects, 25, 28, 255, 256, 713
SI model of epidemics, 297, 298
Simplicity
subjective, 110
Simulacrum, 12
Simulations, 11, 12, 33, 55, 140, 189, 235, 240, 255, 294, 295, 314, 316, 348, 351, 375, 424, 443, 444, 457, 465–467, 477, 486, 489, 521–523, 531, 533, 554, 556, 575, 585, 637, 655, 669, 670, 675, 702
Singularity
technological, 28, 34
Sink, 192, 196, 289, 290, 407, 720
SIR model, 256, 297–302, 304, 307, 368, 371
Small world, 676, 677
Social facts
crystallized, 453
materialized, 453, 454
Social science
generative, 314, 471, 472, 476
Social ties, 434
Society, 5, 12, 14, 22, 27, 28, 62, 118, 132, 149, 155, 174, 175, 265, 303, 319, 327, 331, 342, 356, 359, 384–388, 407, 408, 414, 425, 426, 435, 441, 448, 449, 452–454, 461, 472, 473, 525, 566, 586, 593, 595, 619, 626, 629, 636, 637, 639, 650, 688, 702, 712, 715, 718, 722, 723
Sociophysics, 349, 354, 372, 375
Solar transformity, 404, 405
Sonnenschein-Mantel-Debreu theorem, 439, 456, 463, 489
Spiral, 195, 197, 198, 201–203, 212, 240, 354
Spontaneous
order, 342, 359, 384–390
Sprouting, 381
Stability, 6, 65, 66, 116, 129, 132, 133, 144, 171, 188, 192, 195, 202–204, 207, 208, 212, 218, 229, 240, 249, 258, 361, 362, 407, 439, 453, 456, 472, 511, 567, 622, 641
Stable
neutrally, 197, 198, 203, 207
saddle-path, 198
Stable manifold, 198, 204–206
Stacey matrix, 25, 26
State
absorbing, 598, 599
recurrent, 598, 599
transient, 598, 599
State variable, 127, 128, 378, 433

Status function, 461, 462
Steady state, 128, 129, 131–133, 188, 195, 216, 239–243, 247, 296, 373, 396, 398, 406, 412, 413, 567, 588, 591
Stock, 15, 78, 117, 153, 231, 273, 364, 436, 540, 588, 664
Stock-flow diagram, 255, 289–295, 305, 315, 319, 320, 332
Stress, 30, 195, 331, 387, 567–576
Stressor, 30, 327, 567–570, 572, 576
Structure
  functional, 341, 359, 364, 365, 367, 368, 413
  social, 382, 451–454, 490, 724
Stuff in between, 56, 57, 68
Stylized facts, 240, 469, 473–478, 482, 484, 485, 490, 559, 587, 588
Substrate-neutral, 538
Superposition principle, 185, 249
Supervenience, 448, 449
Surprise, 23, 84–86, 112, 248, 310, 523, 713
Symbiosis
  industrial, 368, 379–384, 414
Symmetry breaking, 64
Synergy, 372, 382, 383, 553, 565, 607, 608
System
  autonomous, 189, 190
  belief, 694, 698–700, 702, 704, 705, 716
  closed, 44, 149, 355, 393, 400
  complex, 4, 42, 48, 50–54, 56, 57, 59–64, 67, 80, 98, 116, 142, 143, 157, 184, 185, 255, 275, 341, 390, 421, 442, 446, 486, 489, 558, 582, 590, 592, 595, 647–649, 660, 702, 711, 717
  complex adaptive, 32, 33, 42, 53–55, 61, 63, 64, 67, 131, 139, 143, 145, 147–182, 380, 388, 471, 497, 542, 572, 616, 647–649, 702, 710, 711, 723
  conservative, 391, 396
  dissipative, 392, 396, 398–400, 415, 593, 714
  driven, 189, 205, 226, 540
  homogenous, 65
  information gathering and using, 81
  isolated, 44, 67, 355, 391, 393, 397, 398, 591, 712
  of systems, 63, 98, 155, 157, 425, 427
  value, 565, 694, 699
System 1, 101, 102, 111, 112, 652, 653
System 2, 101, 102, 111, 652, 653
System dynamics, 4, 33, 65, 142–143, 145, 248, 253–335, 362, 368, 369, 595, 634, 641
System dynamics models, 4, 248, 255, 256, 262, 276, 277, 290, 293–297, 314–319, 327, 331, 335, 369, 595, 641
System open, 44, 156, 355, 359, 393, 396–398, 414, 415, 426, 591
Systems theory
  complex, 42
  general, 42, 690
Systems thinking, 30–32, 34, 255, 595

T

Tame problem, 26, 34
Tâtonnement process, 123
Taylor series expansion, 202, 203
Technology
  physical, 540, 541, 575
  soical, 499, 539–541, 549–558, 575
Teleological reasoning, 588, 589
Tendency, 52, 75, 473, 542, 586, 591, 675, 688, 689
Theorem
  PCP, 668
  Sonnenschein-Mantel-Debreu, 439
Theory
  ad-hoc, 56, 57
  general, 25, 55–57, 133, 139, 265, 267
  middle-range, 265
Thermodynamic arrow of time, 591
Thermodynamics
  first law of, 393
  fourth law of, 401–407
  second law of, 355, 393, 395, 397, 398, 406, 413, 591, 593, 640
Thinking
  complexity, 43, 44, 55–61, 67, 82, 116, 145, 265, 266, 388, 389, 595, 702, 710–717
  convergent, 31
  creative, 30–32
  critical, 30–34, 58, 61, 67, 728
  dialectic, 711–712, 717, 728
  divergent, 31
  functionalist, 589
  historical, 585–590
  population, 529, 535
Ties
  bonding, 434
  bridging, 434, 435
  social, 434
Time
  arrow of, 397, 584, 591–594
  delay, 90, 307, 310
  historical, 138, 584, 594

logical, 593
Tipping
element, 212, 244, 720
point, 187, 212, 624, 625, 719
Tit for tat, 465, 678, 680
Topology, 347, 454
Torus, 351, 357, 377
Tragedy of the commons, 320, 465
Trajectory, 65, 66, 128, 173, 179, 180, 188, 194–199, 203, 205, 206, 223, 224, 553, 620, 633
Transition
phase, 33, 50, 352
Transition theory, 585, 633
Truth, 20, 33, 55, 56, 118, 586, 701, 711, 727
21st century skills, 5, 29–32, 34, 652, 690
2-cycle, –, 217, 219, 221, 240

U
Ubiquity, 160–165, 167, 181, 436, 474, 573
Uncertainty
degree of, 586
ethical, 661
fundamental, 42, 117, 139, 144, 145, 610, 661
Knightian, 661, 663
nature of, 662
object of, 662
option, 661
radical, 661, 663
severity of, 662
state, 661
Uncovering, 381
Unintended consequences, 255–262, 307, 313, 319, 322, 334, 341, 572, 616, 713
Unitas multiplex, 60
Unknowns
known, 3
unknown, 3
Utilitarianism, 724, 725, 727
Utility
expected, 662, 663, 673
Utility function
constant-relative-risk-aversion, 124, 440, 669
instantaneous, 124, 125, 669

V
Variation, 63, 64, 117, 125, 208, 212, 240, 268, 271, 373, 451, 473, 508, 509, 511, 520, 523–525, 527, 538, 540, 541, 558, 560, 575, 595, 715
Variety
balance-weighted, 564
disparity-weighted, 564
Vector field, 194
Verhulst model, 194, 203, 283
Virtual creatures, 521–524
Virtue ethics, 727
Volatility, 23–25, 79, 228, 456, 660
VUCA, 5, 23–25, 29, 30, 32, 34, 600, 662

W
Walrasian
auction, 121
auctioneer, 121, 123, 391
We-intention, 461
White noise
Gaussian, 77, 78
Wicked problem, 5, 25–27, 30, 31, 34, 62, 727
Wild disjunction, 448, 449, 490
Wisdom, 73, 74, 616, 724
Wolfram code, 344
Wright's law, 604

Z
Zero-intelligence
agent, 52, 342
Zipf distribution, 474
Zipf's law, 474, 475, 477

GPSR Compliance
The European Union's (EU) General Product Safety Regulation (GPSR) is a set of rules that requires consumer products to be safe and our obligations to ensure this.

If you have any concerns about our products, you can contact us on

ProductSafety@springernature.com

In case Publisher is established outside the EU, the EU authorized representative is:

Springer Nature Customer Service Center GmbH
Europaplatz 3
69115 Heidelberg, Germany

www.ingramcontent.com/pod-product-compliance
Lightning Source LLC
Chambersburg PA
CBHW060722100926
51093CB00034B/294
9783031514357